THE OXFORD HANDBOOK OF

COMPARATIVE FOREIGN RELATIONS LAW

THE OXFORD HANDBOOK OF

COMPARATIVE FOREIGN RELATIONS LAW

Edited by

CURTIS A. BRADLEY

OXFORD UNIVERSITY PRESS

OXFORD
UNIVERSITY PRESS

Oxford University Press is a department of the University of Oxford. It furthers the University's objective of excellence in research, scholarship, and education by publishing worldwide. Oxford is a registered trade mark of Oxford University Press in the UK and certain other countries.

Published in the United States of America by Oxford University Press
198 Madison Avenue, New York, NY 10016, United States of America.

Library of Congress Cataloging-in-Publication Data
Names: Bradley, Curtis A., editor.
Title: The Oxford handbook of comparative foreign relations law/edited by Curtis A. Bradley.
Description: New York: Oxford University Press, 2020. | Includes bibliographical references and index.
Identifiers: LCCN 2018043341 | ISBN 9780190653330 ((hardback): alk. paper)
Subjects: LCSH: International law. | International relations.
Classification: LCC KZ3410 .O923 2020 | DDC 342/.0412—dc23
LC record available at https://lccn.loc.gov/2018043341

1 3 5 7 9 8 6 4 2

Printed by Sheridan Books, Inc., United States of America

To my wife, Kathy

Preface

This book ambitiously seeks to lay the groundwork for a new field of study and teaching known as "comparative foreign relations law." Comparative foreign relations law compares and contrasts how nations, and also supranational entities such as the European Union, structure their decisions about matters such as entering into and exiting from international agreements, engaging with international institutions, and using military force, as well as how they incorporate treaties and customary international law into their domestic legal systems. The legal materials that make up a nation's foreign relations law can include, among other things, constitutional law, statutory law, administrative law, and judicial precedent. It can also include norms, customs, or conventions relating to governmental conduct that do not necessarily have legal status. Although the collection of legal materials relating to foreign relations law has long been the subject of study in the United States, it has only recently become an area of scholarly focus in other countries.

The book consists of forty-six chapters, written by leading authors from around the world. Some of the chapters are empirically focused, others are theoretical, and still others contain in-depth case studies. In addition to being an invaluable resource for scholars working in this area, the book should be of interest to a wide range of lawyers, judges, and law students. Foreign relations law issues are addressed regularly by lawyers working in foreign ministries, and globalization has meant that domestic judges, too, increasingly are confronted by them. In addition, private lawyers who work on matters that extend beyond their home countries often are required to navigate issues of foreign relations law. An increasing number of law school courses in comparative foreign relations law are also now being developed, making this volume an important reference for students as well.

My own work seeking to define and study comparative foreign relations law began about six years ago. I had been teaching and writing about U.S. foreign relations law since the mid-1990s, and I was becoming increasingly interested in how other nations handled comparable issues. With respect to the domestic regulation of the use of military force, for example, many commentators in the United States have concluded that the War Powers Resolution enacted by Congress in 1973 has not worked well in terms of preserving a meaningful role for the legislative branch. I wondered whether other nations had managed to do better in this regard.

My curiosity was heightened in 2013 when the Obama administration was contemplating using military force against Syria in response to its use of chemical weapons. President Barack Obama had been planning to act without seeking congressional approval but then at the last minute changed his mind. In explaining his decision to seek congressional support, one of the developments that he cited was the decision of the British prime minister—despite the history in Britain of an executive prerogative to use force—to accept a vote in Parliament against the use of force. In his public statement explaining his decision to go to Congress, Obama referred to "what we saw happen in the United Kingdom this week when the Parliament of our closest ally failed to pass a resolution with a similar goal, even as the Prime Minister supported taking action."[1]

I subsequently planned a conference on comparative foreign relations law to be held in Geneva, as part of the summer program that Duke Law School operated there. That conference, which took place in July 2015, primarily featured scholars from the United States and Europe.[2] Seeking to broaden the project to other regions of the world, I applied for funding and was fortunate enough to receive a fellowship from the Carnegie Foundation. The fellowship allowed me to organize conferences on the topic in Tokyo in 2016 and South Africa in 2017.[3] I also held a conference in the Netherlands in the summer of 2018, as part of Duke Law School's new summer program there.[4] These conferences provided opportunities to engage with scholars and government officials from Asia, Africa, and Latin America. I also organized and edited a symposium of short essays relating to comparative foreign relations law in the online publication *AJIL Unbound*.[5]

Over the course of the project, it has become apparent that many countries, especially constitutional democracies, are struggling with similar foreign relations law questions. These questions include: How can legislatures stay involved in foreign affairs decision-making despite having less access to information and less ability to act quickly than the executive? How can nations preserve domestic constitutional values and structures in the face of globalization and transnational governance? Should courts police allocations of foreign affairs authority or instead leave it to political actors to work this out among themselves? How can courts and other actors reconcile tensions between comity toward other nations and giving effect to fundamental norms of international law?

This book is divided into seven parts. Part I considers general issues about how to define and study comparative foreign relations law as a field. Part II addresses the domestic processes that nations use for concluding international agreements. Part III

[1] *Statement by the President on Syria* (Aug. 31, 2013), *available at* https://obamawhitehouse.archives.gov/the-press-office/2013/08/31/statement-president-syria.

[2] Duke-Geneva Conference on Comparative Foreign Relations Law, *available at* https://law.duke.edu/news/duke-university-geneva-conference-comparative-foreign-relations-law/.

[3] Duke-Japan Conference on Comparative Foreign Relations Law, *available at* https://law.duke.edu/news/duke-japan2016/; Duke-Pretoria Conference on Comparative Foreign Relations Law, *available at* https://law.duke.edu/news/duke-south-africa-conference/.

[4] Comparative Foreign Relations Law: Methodology, Common Themes, and the Future of the Field, *available at* https://law.duke.edu/internat/leiden/academic-conference/.

[5] *See* Curtis A. Bradley, *Introduction to Symposium on Comparative Foreign Relations Law*, 111 AJIL Unbound 314 (2018).

focuses on the impact of federalism on the conduct of foreign affairs. Part IV explores how nations engage with, and disengage from, international institutions. Part V compares how nations apply international law within their domestic legal systems. Part VI considers how nations apply rules of sovereign and foreign official immunity and also more generally how they take account of norms of international comity. Part VII concludes by addressing how nations structure decisions to use military force. For each part, chapters that are conceptual or empirical come first, followed by chapters that focus on particular countries or on the European Union. Authors have been encouraged to engage with each other so that the volume reflects a conversation and not merely discrete contributions. The international conferences mentioned above helped to facilitate such dialogue.

This book is only the first stage of developing a field of comparative foreign relations law. Although the book has a number of general empirical chapters, there is much that we still do not know about foreign relations laws and practices around the world. Moreover, as the chapters in Part I of this book show, there are reasonable disagreements about how best to define the field of study, and about what tools we should use to analyze it. These conceptual and methodological issues would benefit from additional consideration in the coming years. Furthermore, the actual teaching of comparative foreign relations law is still in its early stages, even in the United States, and the field will inevitably become more sophisticated as new teaching materials are developed. My own thinking about comparative foreign relations law has already benefited from teaching short courses on the topic in Geneva and The Hague, in partnership with Joris Larik from Leiden University.

I owe special thanks to Duke Law School's former dean, David Levi, who supported this project in countless ways and repeatedly encouraged me to continue with it. I am also thankful to the Carnegie Foundation for funding my fellowship proposal. In addition, I am indebted to my colleague Larry Helfer, who participated in the project from the beginning and frequently offered me valuable advice. Last but not least, I thank my wife, Kathryn Bradley, who not only gave me her typically wonderful and unwavering spousal support, but also acted as an unofficial rapporteur at the conferences that led up to this book.

Curtis A. Bradley
Durham, North Carolina
December 2018

Note to Readers

Contents

PART III FEDERALISM AND FOREIGN AFFAIRS

PART IV ENGAGING WITH, AND DISENGAGING FROM, INTERNATIONAL INSTITUTIONS

PART V DOMESTIC APPLICATION OF INTERNATIONAL LAW

PART VI IMMUNITY, COMITY, AND RELATED ISSUES

PART VII THE USE OF MILITARY FORCE

Notes on the Contributors

Ernest Yaw Ako is a barrister and solicitor of the Supreme Court of Ghana and a Lecturer in Public International Law at the Faculty of Law, University of Cape Coast, Ghana. He holds degrees from the University of Ghana, the Kwame Nkrumah University of Science and Technology, and the University of Pretoria. He is a doctoral researcher and Academic Associate at the Centre for Human Rights, Faculty of Law, University of Pretoria, and his principal research interests are in public international law and international human rights law with a particular focus on Ghana and Africa. Mr. Ako is a member of the International Law Association, South African Branch, and an associate editor of the *South African Journal on Human Rights*.

Anamika Asthana is an Assistant Professor of Political Science at Jesus and Mary College, University of Delhi, India. She is also a Ph.D. candidate at the School of International Studies, Jawaharlal Nehru University, New Delhi. Her research interests include nuclear politics, foreign policy, and political philosophy.

Andrea Bianchi is Full Professor of International Law at the Graduate Institute since 2002. His research interests range from international law theory to treaty interpretation, jurisdictional immunities, and counterterrorism. He has recently authored International Law Theories: An Inquiry into Different Ways of Thinking (2016).

Eirik Bjorge is a Professor of Law at Bristol University. In addition to having published numerous articles in leading journals, he is the author of The Evolutionary Interpretation of Treaties (2014), and Domestic Application of the ECHR: Courts as Faithful Trustees (2015). He has edited, and translated from the French, Bernard Stirn's Towards a European Public Law (2017), and is currently, with Sir Franklin Berman KMCG QC, revising and rewriting the chapters on the law of treaties in Oppenheim's International Law. He has co-edited two collections of essays, A Farewell to Fragmentation: Convergence and Reassertion in International Law (2015), and Landmark Cases in Public International Law (2018).

Curtis A. Bradley is the William Van Alstyne Professor of Law at Duke Law School, where he is a co-director of the Law School's Center for International and Comparative Law. His scholarly expertise spans the areas of international law in the U.S. legal system, the constitutional law of foreign affairs, and federal jurisdiction. In 2004, he served as Counselor on International Law in the Legal Adviser's Office of the U.S. State

Department. From 2012–2018, he served as a Reporter for the American Law Institute's Restatement (Fourth) of the Foreign Relations Law of the United States. He is currently a co-editor-in-chief of the *American Journal of International Law*, and he also serves on the U.S. State Department's Advisory Committee on International Law. He has written numerous articles concerning international law, U.S. foreign relations law, and constitutional law, and he is the author of Foreign Relations Law: Cases and Materials (6th ed. 2017) (with Jack Goldsmith), and International Law in the U.S. Legal System (2d ed. 2015). In 2016, he received a Carnegie Fellowship to support his work on comparative foreign relations law.

Congyan Cai is a Professor of International Law at Xiamen University School of Law, China. His teaching and academic fields cover international legal theory, Chinese international law and policy, and international investment law. He has published many articles in journals such as the *American Journal of International Law*, the *European Journal of International Law*, and the *Journal of International Economic Law*. His latest publication is The Rise of China and International Law (forthcoming 2019). He previously was a Fulbright Scholar and Global Research Fellow at NYU School of Law (2011), a Visiting Professor at Columbia University School of Law (2014), and a Senior Fellow at Humboldt University School of Law (2016).

Amichai Cohen is a Professor of International law at the Ono Academic College, Faculty of Law, Israel, and a Senior Fellow at the Israel Democracy Institute, where is he the director of the program on National Security and Democracy. He was a Visiting Professor at Columbia Law School (2014) and the American University–Washington College of Law (2009–2010). He holds an LL.B. from the Hebrew University in Jerusalem, and an LL.M. and J.S.D from the Yale Law School. His research focuses on international humanitarian law, Israeli national security law, and the application of international law in Israeli law. He is the co-author of Israel's National Security Law: Political Dynamics and Historical Development (2012). Professor Cohen would like to thank Lee Tel-Ari for her excellent research assistance.

Charles-Emmanuel Côté is Full Professor at the Faculty of Law of Laval University, in Canada, where he teaches public international law, international economic law, and constitutional law. He is co-director of the Faculty's Centre for International and Transnational Law (CDIT) and is a lawyer called to the Bar of Quebec. He previously held a position of constitutional and institutional policy adviser at the Government of Quebec. Professor Côté also worked at the *Centre de droit de la consommation* of the University of Louvain in Belgium, on legislative assistance programs of the European Commission in Central and Eastern Europe and former USSR countries. His book on the participation of private persons to the settlement of international economic disputes received a prize from the International Chamber of Commerce. His current research focuses on the international legal aspects of federalism, state responsibility in international investment law, and freedom of movement for professionals.

Paul Craig is the Professor of English Law at St. John's College, at the University of Oxford. His research interests are constitutional law, administrative law, comparative public law, and EU law. He has written extensively across these areas. His most recent book is UK, EU AND GLOBAL ADMINISTRATIVE LAW, FOUNDATIONS AND CHALLENGES (2015). He is also the U.K. alternate member on the Venice Commission on Law and Democracy.

Marise Cremona is Professor Emeritus at the European University Institute, Florence. She was Professor of European Law, and a co-director of the Academy of European Law, at the European University Institute from 2006–2017. Between November 2009 and June 2012 she was Head of the Department of Law at the EUI and between June 2012 and August 2013 she was President *ad interim* of the EUI. She is a member of the editorial board of the *Common Market Law Review*. Her research interests are in the external relations law of the European Union, in particular the constitutional basis for EU external relations law and the legal and institutional dimensions of EU foreign policy.

William S. Dodge is Martin Luther King, Jr. Professor of Law at the University of California, Davis, School of Law. He served as Counselor on International Law to the Legal Adviser at the U.S. Department of State from 2011 to 2012 and as Co-Reporter for the American Law Institute's RESTATEMENT (FOURTH) OF FOREIGN RELATIONS LAW from 2012–2018. Professor Dodge is co-author of the casebook TRANSNATIONAL BUSINESS PROBLEMS (5th ed. 2014) and co-editor of INTERNATIONAL LAW IN THE U.S. SUPREME COURT: CONTINUITY AND CHANGE (2011). He has more than fifty other publications in books and law reviews. Professor Dodge received his B.A. in History, summa cum laude, from Yale University in 1986 and his J.D. from Yale Law School in 1991. After law school, he served as a law clerk for Judge William A. Norris of the U.S. Court of Appeals for the Ninth Circuit and for Justice Harry A. Blackmun of the U.S. Supreme Court.

Carlos Espósito is Professor of Public International Law at the University *Autónoma* of Madrid (UAM). He has been a former Counselor and Deputy Legal Adviser at the International Law Department of the Spanish Ministry of Foreign Affairs and Cooperation (2001–2004). Professor Espósito was Vice President of the European Society of International Law (2011–2014) and is a co-editor of the ESIL Book Series. He has been a member of the board of editors of the *REDI* (*Spanish Journal of International Law*). He has published extensively on general international law, including numerous articles in journals and reviews, and seven books as author or editor. Professor Espósito studied law at the University of Buenos Aires, and earned his doctorate degree from the University *Autónoma* of Madrid in 1995.

Shaheed Fatima Q.C. is a barrister at Blackstone Chambers, London. She specializes in international law, public law, and commercial law. Her practice extends beyond English courts and includes the European Court of Human Rights, UN treaty bodies, arbitral tribunals, and the EU courts. In January 2017, *The Lawyer* magazine named her one of its "Hot 100" leading lawyers; in December 2013 she was listed in *Chambers UK*'s Top Junior Bar 100; in October 2013 she was awarded Junior of the Year in Human Rights and Public Law (by Chambers Bar Awards; having been shortlisted in the same category in 2011); and in 2007 she was awarded the Human Rights Lawyer of the Year Award (by *Liberty and Justice*). Prior to being appointed Queen's Counsel in 2016, Ms. Fatima was a member of the Attorney General's Public International Law "A" Panel (2014–2016) and the Attorney General's "A" Panel (2011–2016), having previously been on the "B" Panel (2009–2011). She is the lead author of PROTECTING CHILDREN IN ARMED CONFLICT (2018); working on the second edition of her book, INTERNATIONAL LAW AND FOREIGN AFFAIRS IN ENGLISH COURTS (forthcoming 2019); and a founding editor of the transatlantic national security blog, "Just Security." She has taught law at Pembroke College/University of Oxford, Harvard Law School, NYU School of Law, and the Graduate Institute in Geneva. She is a trustee of the British Institute of International and Comparative Law; an Advocacy Trainer for Gray's Inn; and a member of their Scholarships Committee.

Mathias Forteau is Professor of Public International Law at the University of Paris Ouest and has been Adjunct Professor at the NYU School of Law from 2015 to 2018. He is a former member of the International Law Commission (ILC) of the United Nations (2012–2016) and former Secretary-General of the French Society for International Law (Société française pour le droit international) (2008–2012). He is the co-director of the *French Yearbook of International Law* (*Annuaire français de droit international).* He was also a member of the International Advisory Panel for the RESTATEMENT (FOURTH) OF THE FOREIGN RELATIONS LAW OF THE UNITED STATES prepared by the American Law Institute. In the last twenty years, he has served as counsel or advocate for states in a number of international cases, in particular before the International Court of Justice and the International Tribunal of the Law of the Sea. At the University of Paris Ouest he directs a seminar on the relationship and articulation between international law and domestic laws. He would like to thank Morgane Champeaux (University of Paris Nanterre, LLM Student, 2016–2017) for her research assistance.

Jean Galbraith is a Professor at the University of Pennsylvania Law School. She is a scholar of U.S. foreign relations law and public international law. Her research focuses on the allocation of foreign affairs powers among U.S. governmental actors and, at the international level, on the structure and development of international legal regimes. She has published in leading general interest law journals and international law journals. She received her B.A. summa cum laude from Harvard University and her J.D. from the University of California, Berkeley, School of Law. After graduating law school, she served as a law clerk at the D.C. Circuit (for Judge Tatel) and the Supreme Court of the United States (for Justice Stevens). She has also served as an Associate Legal Officer at the International Criminal Tribunal for the former Yugoslavia (working for Judge Meron).

Tom Ginsburg is the Leo Spitz Professor of International Law at the University of Chicago, where he also holds an appointment in the Political Science Department. He holds B.A., J.D., and Ph.D. degrees from the University of California at Berkeley. He currently co-directs the Comparative Constitutions Project, an NSF-funded data set cataloging the world's constitutions since 1789. His latest book is How to Save a Constitutional Democracy (with Aziz Huq). He is a member of the American Academy of Arts and Sciences. Before entering law teaching, he served as a legal adviser at the Iran-U.S. Claims Tribunal, The Hague, Netherlands, and he has consulted with numerous international development agencies and governments on legal and constitutional reform. He currently serves as a senior adviser on Constitution Building to International IDEA.

Monica Hakimi is a Professor of Law at the University of Michigan Law School. Her research focuses on how international law operates and adapts to contemporary challenges, particularly in the areas of human and national security. Professor Hakimi is currently a contributing editor of EJIL Talk!, the blog that is affiliated with the *European Journal of International Law*; on the board of editors of the *American Journal of International Law* and the *Texas National Security Review*; a member of the executive council of the American Society of International Law; and on the advisory board of the Institute of International Peace and Security Law at the University of Cologne, Germany. Between 2003 and 2006, she was an attorney-adviser in the Office of the Legal Adviser at the U.S. Department of State.

Oona A. Hathaway is the Gerard C. and Bernice Latrobe Smith Professor of International Law at Yale Law School, Professor of International Law and Area Studies at the Yale University MacMillan Center, and Professor of the Yale University Department of Political Science. She is a Vice President of the American Society of International Law and member of the Advisory Committee on International Law for the Legal Adviser at the United States Department of State. In 2014–2015, she took leave to serve as Special Counsel to the General Counsel at the U.S. Department of Defense, where she was awarded the Office of the Secretary of Defense Award for Excellence. She is the Director of the Yale Cyber Leadership Forum and was a principal investigator on a Hewlett Foundation grant to study cyber conflict. She has published more than twenty-five law review articles and The Internationalists: How a Radical Plan to Outlaw War Remade the World (with Scott Shapiro, 2017).

Laurence R. Helfer is the Harry R. Chadwick, Sr. Professor of Law and co-director of the Center for International and Comparative Law at Duke University in Durham, North Carolina. He is also a Permanent Visiting Professor at iCourts: The Center of Excellence for International Courts at the University of Copenhagen, which awarded him an honorary doctorate in 2014. Professor Helfer's research interests include international human rights, treaty design, international adjudication, and the interdisciplinary analysis of international law and institutions. He has co-authored four books and published more than seventy journal articles on these and other topics. He is a co-editor-in-chief of the *American Journal of International Law.*

Jan-Henrik Hinselmann is a Research and Teaching Fellow at the Institute of Public International Law and European Law of the Georg-August-University Göttingen. He teaches German constitutional law and, in particular, German foreign relations law. Hinselmann is also a former editor-in-chief of the *Goettingen Journal of International Law* (*GoJIL*), and he has published in the areas of public international law and European law.

Duncan B. Hollis is a Professor of Law at Temple University Law School and a nonresident scholar at the Carnegie Endowment for International Peace. Professor Hollis's scholarship focuses on treaties, interpretation, and cyberspace. He is editor of the Oxford Guide to Treaties (2012), which was awarded the 2013 ASIL Certificate of Merit for High Technical Craftsmanship and Utility to Practicing Lawyers, as well as National Treaty Law and Practice (2005), which offered a comparative perspective on how nineteen nation states engage with treaties in their domestic systems. Professor Hollis's articles have covered a range of subjects implicating U.S. foreign relations law as well as others that examined the role of interpretation in international law and the challenges of regulating global cybersecurity. Professor Hollis is an elected member of the American Law Institute, where he served as an adviser on its project to draft a Restatement (Fourth) of the Foreign Relations Law of the United States. He is also an elected member of the Organization of American States' Inter-American Juridical Committee and currently serves as its Rapporteur for Binding and Non-Binding Agreements.

Happymon Jacob is an Associate Professor of Disarmament Studies at the School of International Studies, Jawaharlal Nehru University, New Delhi. He is a columnist with *The Hindu*, and hosts a weekly show on national security at *The Wire.in*. He has been a participant in several India-Pakistan track-two dialogues, and directs the Chaophraya India-Pakistan Dialogue (India Chapter). He is a former Visiting Professor at the Fondation Maison des Sciences de l'Homme Paris and a Senior Global Challenges Fellow at the Central European University in Budapest. Professor Jacob is the author of Line on Fire: Ceasefire Violations and Indo-Pak Escalation Dynamics (2019), and of THE Line of Control: Traveling with the Indian and Pakistani Armies (2018). Website: happymonjacob.com.

Stefan Kadelbach is Professor of Public International Law, co-director of the Institute of Public Law, and a member of the "Cluster of Excellence 'Normative Orders'" at Goethe University, Frankfurt am Main (Germany). His working fields are German and comparative constitutional law, public international law, and constitutional EU law, with an emphasis on foreign relations law, federalism, multilevel governance, human rights, and general international law. Professor Kadelbach has published various books and articles on these fields and functioned as a rapporteur on the implementation of international human rights by domestic courts for the International Law Association's International Human Rights Law Committee.

Karen Knop is a Professor at the Faculty of Law, University of Toronto, where she has also served as editor of the *University of Toronto Law Journal* (2007–2012) and associate dean for research (2016–2018). Her scholarship is broadly concerned with the challenges of gender and cultural differences to core concepts in public international law, including sovereignty, self-determination, nationality, and the relationship between international and domestic law. In recent work, she develops alternative approaches to these topics by turning to private international law and foreign relations law. Professor Knop's book Diversity and Self-Determination in International Law (2002) was awarded a Certificate of Merit by the American Society of International Law. She is the editor of Gender and Human Rights (2004) and a co-editor of *Re-Thinking Federalism: Citizens, Markets and Governments in a Changing World* (1995) (with Sylvia Ostry, Richard Simeon, and Katherine Swinton). In 2017, she and Professor Robert Wai received a Social Sciences and Humanities Research Council of Canada grant to support their research project "A Missing Field: Foreign Relations Law of Canada," of which her chapter in this *Handbook* is a part.

Joris Larik is Assistant Professor at Leiden University, where he focuses on the external relations of the European Union, comparative and multilevel constitutional law, and global governance reform. For his research on the global legal ramifications of "Brexit," he received a Fulbright-Schuman Fellowship in 2017 at the Johns Hopkins University Paul H. Nitze School of Advanced International Studies in Washington, D.C., and in 2018 a Leiden Global Interactions Breed Grant. Dr. Larik's work has been acknowledged with several awards, including NATO's Manfred Wörner Essay Award (2008), the Outstanding Paper Award from the Center for German and European Studies at Georgetown University (2012), and the Mauro Cappelletti Prize for the Best Thesis in Comparative Law (2014) from the European University Institute. He is the author of Foreign Policy Objectives in European Constitutional Law (2016), co-author of ASEAN's External Agreements: Law, Practice and the Quest for Collective Action (2015), and co-editor of Just Security in an Undergoverned World (2018). He has published numerous journals, including *Common Market Law Review, European Foreign Affairs Review, European Law Review, Global Policy, Netherlands International Law Review, Survival, University of Pennsylvania Journal of International Law,* and *Yearbook of European Law.*

Jaemin Lee is currently Professor of Law at School of Law, Seoul National University in Seoul, Korea. He obtained his LL.B., LL.M., and Ph.D. from Seoul National University; LL.M. from Georgetown University Law Center; and J.D. from Boston College Law School. His major areas of teaching and research are public international law and international economic law. He has published articles and books (including book chapters) on various topics of public international law, international trade law, and international investment law. From 1992 until 2001, he served as a foreign service officer in the Korean Ministry of Foreign Affairs. Between 2001 and 2004, he practiced law with Willkie Farr & Gallagher LLP (Washington, D.C., office) as an associate attorney of the firm's international trade group. He has been appointed by the government of Korea to serve in the dispute settlement proceedings of the Korea-US FTA, Korea-EU FTA and Korea-Chile FTA. At various occasions and fora, he has represented the Korean government in international litigation. He can be reached at 82-2-880-7572 (office) or via e-mail at jaemin@snu.ac.kr.

Jenny S. Martinez is the Dean and the Richard E. Lang Professor at Stanford Law School. Her research focuses on international courts and tribunals, international human rights, national security, constitutional law, and the laws of war. Prior to joining the Stanford faculty in 2003, she was an associate legal officer at the UN International Criminal Tribunal for the Former Yugoslavia. She also clerked for Justice Stephen Breyer at the U.S. Supreme Court and Judge Guido Calabresi on the U.S. Court of Appeals for the Second Circuit. She received her J.D. from Harvard Law School and her B.A. from Yale University.

Hiromichi Matsuda is Assistant Professor of Law at International Christian University, Tokyo, Japan, where he teaches and writes in the areas of Japanese constitutional law, human rights law, international law, and comparative foreign relations law. He received his J.D., *cum laude* from the University of Tokyo School of Law in 2011 and served there as a research associate in the year 2011–2012 and 2013–2015, and as a lecturer in the year 2015–2016. He received his LL.M., Harlan Fiske Stone Scholar from Columbia Law School in 2013, where he focused on "Human and Constitutional Rights" and "Constitution and Foreign Affairs," and served as an editor of *Columbia Human Rights Law Review*. He is currently focusing on the domestic effects of international norms in various constitutional legal systems worldwide, including the U.S., European, Japanese, and Chinese legal systems. The contribution to this book was supported by Nomura Foundation and JSPS KAKENHI Grant Number 17K18103.

Campbell McLachlan is Professor of International Law at Victoria University of Wellington. He holds a Ph.D. from the University of London and the Diploma *cum laude* of The Hague Academy International Law. He is author of FOREIGN RELATIONS LAW (2014)—the first modern study of this field in relation to the United Kingdom and the Commonwealth. He is a specialist editor of DICEY, MORRIS & COLLINS ON THE CONFLICT OF LAWS (15th ed. 2012) and co-author of INTERNATIONAL INVESTMENT ARBITRATION: SUBSTANTIVE PRINCIPLES (2nd ed. 2017). He is joint editor-in-chief of *ICSID Review-Foreign Investment Law Journal*. He served as President of the Australian & New Zealand Society of International Law from 2006 to 2009. He was awarded the New Zealand Law Foundation International Research Fellowship in 2011 and has been a Visiting Fellow at All Souls College Oxford, the Lauterpacht Research Centre in Cambridge, and at New York University. In 2018 he took up a Senior Research

Fellowship within the research project "KFG International Rule of Law: Rise or Decline?" in Berlin. In 2015, he was elected to the *Institut de Droit International* and serves as Rapporteur of its Eighteenth Commission on "The Equality of Parties before International Investment Tribunals." In 2016, he was elected to the Arthur Goodhart Visiting Professorship in Legal Science in the University of Cambridge for the year 2020–2021. He served as an international adviser to the American Law Institute's Restatement (Fourth) of Foreign Relations Law project. He is also a practicing barrister and arbitrator (NZ, call 1984, QC 2007).

Mario Mendez is a Reader in Law at Queen Mary University of London (QMUL) and is a former co-director of the Centre for European and International Legal Affairs (CEILA). His research and teaching are in the fields of EU, UK, and Comparative Constitutional Law. He is the author of The Legal Effects of EU Agreements: Maximalist Treaty Enforcement and Judicial Avoidance Techniques (2013), and co-author of Referendums and the European Union: A Comparative Inquiry (2014).

Cameron Miles is a barrister practicing from 3 Verulam Buildings in London. He is a public international lawyer with a particular focus on state responsibility, state immunity, the law and practice of international courts and tribunals, and international investment law. He holds an LL.M. and Ph.D. from the University of Cambridge and has published peer-reviewed articles in the leading journals, including the *British Yearbook of International Law*, the *American Journal of International Law*, the *Heidelberg Journal of International Law*, and the *Journal of International Dispute Settlement*. He is the author of Provisional Measures before International Courts and Tribunals (2017) and the co-editor of Landmark Cases in Public International Law (2017).

Tadaatsu Mori is currently Minister at the Embassy of Japan in the Republic of Belarus. Prior to that assignment, he was Director of the Treaties Division in Japan's Ministry of Foreign Affairs (2015–2017). He has been a career diplomat since 1991 and has expertise in international law, trade affairs, Japan-U.S. economic relations, and Russian affairs. He served at the Embassy of Japan in Washington, D.C., as a counselor for economic affairs (2006–2008). He also served at the Embassy of Japan in Moscow three times throughout his diplomatic career, most recently as Political Minister (2012–2015). He was a CNAPS Visiting Fellow at the Brookings Institution in 2010, Professor at Kobe University's Graduate School of International Cooperation Studies in 2011–2012, and Director of APEC Division in 2012. Mr. Mori conducted regional studies as a special student at the Russian Research Center, Harvard University (1993–94), and also studied at Moscow State Institute for International Relations (MGIMO) (1994–1995).

Tadashi Mori is a Professor at the Graduate Schools for Law and Politics at the University of Tokyo, where he has taught since 2010. He received his LL.B. and LL.

M. from the University of Tokyo in 1992 and 1994, respectively, and his LL.M. from Georgetown University Law Center in 1996. He was a Graduate Visiting Student/Academic Visitor at the University of Oxford from 2003 to 2005. He received his Ph.D. (Law) from the University of Tokyo in 2008. Professor Mori was a Research Assistant at the University of Tokyo from 1997 to 2000, and taught at Tokyo Metropolitan University from 2000 to 2010. His publications include ORIGINS OF THE RIGHT OF SELF-DEFENCE IN INTERNATIONAL LAW: FROM THE CAROLINE INCIDENT TO THE UNITED NATIONS CHARTER (2018). He is thankful to his research assistants, Akari Oba and Yosuke Mochizuki. His work was supported by JSPS KAKENHI Grant Number JP26380057.

Richard Frimpong Oppong is an Associate Professor at the Faculty of Law, Thompson Rivers University in British Columbia, Canada, and a Fellow of the Ghana Academy of Arts and Sciences. He holds degrees from the University of Ghana, University of Cambridge, Harvard Law School, and the University of British Columbia. In 2012, he held the post of Director of Studies (Private International Law) at The Hague Academy of International Law. He was a member of the Working Group of The Hague Conference on Private International Law that developed *The Hague Principles on Choice of Law in International Commercial Contracts, 2015*. His principal research interests are in private international law, regional economic integration, and international dispute settlement, with a special focus on Africa. He has published widely on these subjects, including three books, one co-edited book, and forty-two articles, book chapters, and book reviews. Two of his publications have won international awards, namely, the 2013 American Society of International Law prize in Private International Law and the 2014 James Crawford Prize of the Journal of International Dispute Settlement.

Andreas L. Paulus holds the Chair of Public and International Law at the Georg-August-University Göttingen. Professor Paulus teaches public law, international law, European law, and legal philosophy. Since March 2010, he has served as justice of the First Senate of the German Federal Constitutional Court (*Bundesverfassungsgericht*). Paulus also served as counsel and adviser of the Federal Republic of Germany before the International Court of Justice in the LaGrand (*Germany v. United States*) and Certain Property (*Liechtenstein v. Germany*) cases. His publications cover international legal theory, the United Nations, and international adjudication, as well as international criminal law and human rights. Judge Paulus is co-editor of the third edition of the Simma commentary on the UN Charter (2012).

Anne Peters is Director at the Max Planck Institute for Comparative Public Law and International Law Heidelberg (Germany), and a professor at the universities of Heidelberg, Freie Universität Berlin, and Basel (Switzerland), and a William W. Cook Global Law Professor at the University of Michigan. She has been a member (substitute) of the European Commission for Democracy through Law (Venice Commission) in respect of Germany (2011–2014), and served as the President of the European Society of International Law (2010–2012). Born in Berlin in 1964, Professor Peters studied at the universities of Würzburg, Lausanne, Freiburg, and Harvard, and held the chair of public international law at the university of Basel from 2001 to 2013. Her current research interests relate to public international law, including its history, global animal law, global governance and global constitutionalism, and the status of humans in international law. Her books (authored and co-edited) include Global Constitutionalism from European and East Asian perspectives (2018); Beyond Human Rights (2016); The Freedom of Peaceful Assembly in Europe (2016); Immunities in the Age of Global Constitutionalism (2015); Animal Law: Reform or Revolution? (2015); Transparency in International Law (2013); Oxford Handbook of the History of International Law (2012), which won the American Society of International Law Certificate of Merit; Conflict of Interest in Global, Public and Corporate Governance (2012); The Constitutionalization of International Law (2011); Non-State Actors as Standard Setters (2009); and Women, Quotas and Constitutions (1999).

Roland Portmann is Head of the Public International Law Section in the Directorate of International Law at the Swiss Ministry of Foreign Affairs. Prior to his current position, he served as the Legal Adviser at the Embassy of Switzerland in the United States in Washington, D.C. Being part of the Swiss diplomatic service, he served as an attorney-adviser in the Directorate of International Law in Berne and as a legal and diplomatic attaché to the Swiss Embassy in the Republic of Kosovo. Mr. Portmann studied in St. Gallen and in Geneva, Switzerland, as well as in Cambridge, United Kingdom. He holds master degrees in international affairs as well as in law and a doctorate in international law. His recent publications include Legal Personality in International Law (2010 and 2013). He is also a Lecturer in International Law and Constitutional Law at the University of St. Gallen, Switzerland.

Alejandro Rodiles is Associate Professor of International Law and Global Governance at the Law School of ITAM, in Mexico City. Before this position, he was a Research Fellow at the Chair for Public Law, Public International Law, and European Law at the Humboldt University of Berlin, and a Lecturer at the Law Faculty of the National Autonomous University of Mexico (UNAM). Professor Rodiles worked at the Ministry of Foreign Relations of Mexico and served on the Permanent Mission of Mexico to the United Nations in New York (2009–2011) as Legal Adviser. He also worked at the Office of the Legal Adviser and the Policy Planning Staff of the Foreign Minister. He has served at the Commission of Admissions to Mexico's Foreign Service. Professor Rodiles earned his law degree (LL.B.) from UNAM, did postgraduate studies at the Law Faculty of Ludwig-Maximilians University of Munich, and earned his Ph.D. (*summa cum laude*) from Humboldt University, Berlin. His research and teaching interests include the law of global governance, global security law, Latin American approaches to international law, and the geopolitics of international law. He is the author of

Coalitions of the Willing and International Law–The Interplay between Formality and Informality (2018). Professor Rodiles wishes to thank Ambassador Joel Hernández and Professor Helmut Aust for inspiring suggestions on previous drafts. Special thanks are due to Curtis A. Bradley for his careful and constructive engagement with the chapter.

Robert Schütze is Professor of European Union Law at Durham University (United Kingdom), where he also co-directs the Global Policy Institute together with the political scientist Professor David Held. He is a Visiting Professor at the School of Government of LUISS Guido Carli University (Rome) and at the College of Europe (Bruges). Schütze is a constitutional scholar with a particular expertise in the law of the European Union and comparative federalism. He has published extensively and his work has been translated into a number of languages. He is one of the co-editors of the *Yearbook of European Law*, the *Oxford Principles of European Union Law*, and the "Comparative Constitutionalism" book series by Oxford University Press. He is the author of Foreign Affairs and the EU Constitution, a collection of his well-known essays on the external affairs powers and principles of the European Union.

Paul B. Stephan is the John C. Jeffries, Jr., Distinguished Professor of Law and the John V. Ray Research Professor of Law at the University of Virginia. He has taught at the University of Virginia since 1979, and during that time has been a Visiting Professor at Duke Law School, Columbia Law School, the Peking University School of Transnational Law, Melbourne University, Sydney University, Paris II, Paris I, Sciences Po, the Interdisciplinary Center Herzliya, Lausanne University, the University of Vienna, Münster University, and the Moscow State Institute for International Relations and the World Economy. He served as Counselor on International Law in the Office of the Legal Adviser of the U.S. State Department during 2006–2007 and advised the U.S. Department of the Treasury on tax reform in the former socialist states of Europe from 1993 to 1998. He was an adviser to the law firm of Wilmer Cutler and Pickering from 1990 to 1994 and a scholar-in-residence in the London office of Wilmer Hale in 2014. He was a Coordinating Reporter for the American Law Institute's Restatement (Fourth) of the Foreign Relations Law of the United States.

David P. Stewart is Professor from Practice at Georgetown University Law Center in Washington, D.C., where he teaches Public and Private International Law, Foreign Relations Law, International Law in Domestic Courts, International Criminal Law, and International Human Rights. He co-directs the Global Law Scholars Program and directs the Center for Transnational Business and the Law. He joined Georgetown's faculty in 2008, following a career with the Office of the Legal Adviser at the U.S. Department of State, where he served as Assistant Legal Adviser in a number of areas, including private international law, diplomatic law and litigation, African affairs, human rights and refugees, law enforcement and intelligence, and international claims and investment disputes. He is former President (and now Chair of the Board of

Directors) of the American Branch of the International Law Association, an Honorary Editor on the Board of Editors of the American Journal of International Law, and a member of the American Law Institute. He served as one of the Reporters working on the immunities section of the Restatement (Fourth) of the Foreign Relations Law of the United States.

Hennie Strydom is Professor in Public International Law at the University of Johannesburg and holds the National Research Foundation Chair in International Law. He is the President of the South African Branch of the International Law Association and his research is focused on general international law, international human rights law, international humanitarian law, and international environmental law. He serves on the editorial board of the *South African Yearbook of International Law*, the *African Yearbook on International Humanitarian Law*, and the *Law Journal* of the Faculty of Law, Palacky University, Olomouc, Czech Republic.

René Urueña is an Associate Professor and Director of Research at the Universidad de Los Andes School of Law (Colombia). Twice an expert witness before the Inter-American Court of Human Rights, Professor Urueña served as an adviser of the Selection Committee of the Special Jurisdiction for Peace (Colombia), has published extensively on international law and global governance, and serves on the editorial board of the *International Organizations Law Review*, *Law and Practice of International Courts and Tribunals*, and *Latin American Law Review*. He holds a doctoral degree (*exima cum laude*) from the University of Helsinki, was President of the Colombian Academy of International Law, and has been a Visiting Professor at the University of Tel-Aviv and the University of Utah, a docent at the Institute for Global Law and Policy at Harvard Law School, and a research fellow at New York University and at the Max Planck Institute for Comparative Public and International Law in Heidelberg.

Gib van Ert is a litigation lawyer practicing in Ottawa and Vancouver. From 2015 to 2018 he was the Executive Legal Officer to two successive chief justices of Canada, the Rt. Hon. Beverley McLachlin PC and the Rt. Hon. Richard Wagner PC. The Executive Legal Officer is the chief justice's principal adviser in matters concerning the administration of the Supreme Court of Canada, the Canadian Judicial Council, and the National Judicial Institute. Prior to that Mr. van Ert had a broad civil litigation practice in Vancouver, B.C. He is the author of Using International Law in Canadian Courts and other works on the reception of international law in Canada. He is an annual contributor to the *Canadian Yearbook of International Law*. He served as law clerk to Justices Charles Gonthier and Morris Fish of the Supreme Court of Canada and Madam Justice Joanne Prowse of the Court of Appeal for British Columbia. Mr. van Ert has a B.A. (Hons.) from McGill, an M.A. in law from the University of Cambridge, and an LL.M. from the University of Toronto.

Carlos M. Vázquez is a Professor of Law at the Georgetown University Law Center in Washington, D.C., and he currently co-directs the Center for Transnational Legal

Studies in London. From 2012 to 2016, he was a member of the UN Committee for the Elimination of Racial Discrimination. From 2000 to 2003, he was a member of the Inter-American Juridical Committee of the Organization of American States. He has served on the board of editors of the *American Journal of International Law* and on the executive council of the American Society of International Law. He is a member of the American Law Institute, where he has advised on the RESTATEMENT (FOURTH) OF FOREIGN RELATIONS LAW OF THE UNITED STATES and the RESTATEMENT (THIRD) OF CONFLICT OF LAWS. He served as a law clerk to the Honorable Stephen R. Reinhardt. He has written extensively in the areas of public and private international law, foreign relations law, and constitutional law.

Pierre-Hugues Verdier is a Professor of Law at the University of Virginia. He specializes in public international law, banking and financial regulation, and international economic relations. Professor Verdier is a graduate of the joint civil law and common law program of the Faculty of Law, McGill University, and obtained LL.M. and S.J.D. degrees from Harvard Law School. Prior to joining the faculty at the University of Virginia, he was a law clerk for the Supreme Court of Canada, an associate with Cleary Gottlieb Steen & Hamilton in New York City, and a Visiting Assistant Professor at Boston University School of Law. He has also been a Visiting Professor at the University of Chicago Law School and Harvard Law School.

Mila Versteeg is Professor of Law and the Director of the Human Rights Program at the University of Virginia School of Law. Her research and teaching interests include comparative constitutional law, public international law, and empirical legal studies. Her publications have, among others, appeared in the *California Law Review*, the *New York University Law Review*, the *University of Chicago Law Review*, the *American Political Science Review*, the *American Journal of Political Science*, the *Journal of Legal Studies*, the *American Journal of International Law*, and the *Journal of Law, Economics and Organizations*. Versteeg earned her B.A. in public administration and first law degree from Tilburg University in the Netherlands in 2006, her LL.M. from Harvard Law School in 2007, and a D.Phil. in sociolegal studies in 2011 from Oxford University. Prior to joining UVA Law, Versteeg was an Olin Fellow and lecturer in law at the University of Chicago Law School. Versteeg previously worked at the UN Interregional Crime and Justice Research Institute in Turin and at the Southern Africa Litigation Centre in Johannesburg.

Philippa Webb is Associate Professor in Public International Law at the Dickson Poon School of Law, King's College London. She joined the Law School in 2012 after a decade in international legal practice. She has served as the Special Assistant and Legal Officer to President Higgins of the International Court of Justice, the Judicial Clerk to Judges Higgins and Owada, and Associate Legal Adviser at the International Criminal Court. Dr. Webb was on the International Advisory Panel for the American Law Institute's project RESTATEMENT FOURTH, FOREIGN RELATIONS LAW OF THE UNITED STATES.

She is a board member of the European Society of International Law, co-chair of the editorial committee of the *Journal of International Criminal Justice*, and on the editorial boards of *The Leiden Journal of International Law* and *The British Yearbook of International Law*. Her publications include OPPENHEIM'S INTERNATIONAL LAW: THE UNITED NATIONS (2017, with Dame Rosalyn Higgins, Dapo Akande, Sandy Sivakumaran, and James Sloan), THE LAW OF STATE IMMUNITY (2015, with Lady Hazel Fox), and INTERNATIONAL JUDICIAL INTEGRATION AND FRAGMENTATION (2013, paperback 2016). She is also a barrister at 20 Essex Street Chambers in London.

Hannah Woolaver is an Associate Professor in Public International Law at the Law Faculty of the University of Cape Town. Her research and teaching interests lie in public international law, especially the relationship between international law and domestic law, the law on the use of force, and international criminal law. Prior to joining the UCT Law Faculty in 2012, she completed her Ph.D. in international law at the University of Cambridge, a B.C.L. at the University of Oxford, and an LL.B. at the University of Durham. Dr. Woolaver has been a Visiting Professor at the Faculty of Law, University of New South Wales, Australia, and a Visiting Scholar at the Faculty of Law, University of Toronto.

Ernest A. Young holds the Alston & Bird Chair at Duke Law School, where he co-directs the Program in Public Law. His scholarship has focused on the law of American federalism, constitutional theory, and foreign relations law, and he has undertaken comparative projects in each of these areas. A graduate of Dartmouth College and Harvard Law School, Professor Young clerked for Judge Michael Boudin of the U.S. Court of Appeals for the First Circuit (1993–1994) and Justice David Souter of the U.S. Supreme Court (1995–1996). He also practiced law at Cohan, Simpson, Cowlishaw, & Wulff in Dallas, Texas (1994–1995) and at Covington & Burling in Washington, D.C. (1996–1998).

Katja S. Ziegler is the Sir Robert Jennings Professor of International Law at the University of Leicester and Director of the Centre of European Law and Internationalisation (CELI). Her research spans the areas of international, European, and comparative law, with a particular focus on the interaction of legal orders. Current research themes include, first, the constitutionalization and intersection of legal orders in an international, European, and comparative law context, in particular in the area of human rights and through the vehicle of general principles of law; and, second, limits on executive power to resort to military force from a comparative constitutional and international law perspective. She received grants from the European Commission (Jean Monnet actions) and the British Academy for these research themes. Publications from recent research include THE UK AND EUROPEAN HUMAN RIGHTS—A STRAINED RELATIONSHIP? (2015); *Beyond Pluralism and Autonomy: Systemic Harmonisation as a Paradigm for the Interaction of EU Law and International Law*, 35 YEARBOOK OF EUROPEAN LAW 667 (2016); and CONSTRUCTING LEGAL ORDERS IN EUROPE: THE GENERAL PRINCIPLES OF EU LAW (forthcoming).

PART I

COMPARATIVE FOREIGN RELATIONS LAW AS A FIELD

CHAPTER 1

WHAT IS FOREIGN RELATIONS LAW?

CURTIS A. BRADLEY

THIS first chapter considers what is potentially encompassed by the term "foreign relations law," and what it might mean to think about it as a distinct field of law that can be compared and contrasted across national jurisdictions. The chapter begins by outlining some differences between foreign relations law and international law. It then describes the development of foreign relations law as a field of study within the United States and considers why, at least until recently, it has not been treated as a field in many other countries. Finally, the chapter highlights a central question for foreign relations law, which is the extent to which it (or at least some parts or elements of it) should be treated differently than other types of domestic law—a debate referred to in the United States as one over "foreign affairs exceptionalism."

I. FOREIGN RELATIONS LAW AND INTERNATIONAL LAW

Before comparing and contrasting the foreign relations law of various nations, we first need to have a sense of what, precisely, we mean by "foreign relations law." For purposes of this book, the term is used to encompass the domestic law of each nation that governs how that nation interacts with the rest of the world.[1] These interactions include most centrally those that occur between nations, but they can also encompass interactions between a nation and the citizens or residents of other nations and

[1] As noted below, the European Union, as a supranational institution that in some ways resembles a nation, also has a developed body of foreign relations law. *See also* Joris Larik, *Regional Organizations' Relations with International Institutions: The EU and ASEAN Compared*, ch. 25 in this volume.

with international institutions. The law governing these interactions can take a variety of forms, including constitutional law (written and unwritten), statutory law, administrative regulations, and judicial decisions. Because many disputes concerning foreign relations law are addressed outside the courts, a full study of the topic also requires attention to domestic "conventions" (or customs) of proper political behavior that may or may not have legal status.

Many issues of foreign relations law concern allocations of authority between political actors, such as the authority to represent the nation in diplomacy, to conclude and terminate international agreements, to recognize foreign governments and their territories, and to initiate or end the use of military force. In federal systems, these allocation issues are not only horizontal but also vertical, extending to the relations between national and subnational institutions. But foreign relations law also encompasses issues relating to the role of the courts in transnational cases, such as whether certain issues are "nonjusticiable" and thus subject entirely to political branch determination, whether courts should take into account considerations of international comity when interpreting and applying domestic law, and whether and to what extent courts can apply international law directly to decide a particular case. Because much of foreign relations law addresses how authority is allocated among governmental actors, its topics are most salient for constitutional democracies that separate power and have independent judiciaries (and such democracies are the principal focus of this book), but the topics also have some relevance to other forms of government.[2]

For the purposes of this book, the term "foreign relations law" is not meant to encompass "pure" questions of international law—that is, a nation's obligations under treaties and customary international law on the international plane. While such international law governs in part how a nation conducts its foreign relations, it is both too vast, and in many respects too undifferentiated in its application to each nation, to be included in a working definition that will be useful for a study of comparative foreign relations law. So, when this book refers to foreign relations law, it is referring to various forms of domestic law. This means, among other things, that the field of foreign relations law makes no claim of universality; it accepts that nations can and will have different approaches. This feature makes foreign relations law especially ripe for comparative analysis.

To be sure, nations also have differing international law obligations, and that fact might also be of potential comparative interest. Perhaps most obviously, nations have differing treaty commitments, and variations in commitments can exist even for customary international law, because it is possible that some nations will have opted out of particular rules through persistent objection, or that particular sets of nations are subject to "regional custom." In addition, even when international law obligations are ostensibly equal, nations may interpret them differently. Given the limits on

[2] For additional discussion of some of the potential functions served by foreign relations law, *see* Campbell McLachlan, *Five Conceptions of the Function of Foreign Relations Law*, ch. 2 in this volume.

centralized international adjudication, these differences of interpretation will often persist. While it may be fruitful to study differing national approaches to international law, and there is important work that does so,[3] this book involves a different project.

This book recognizes, however, that there are important interconnections between international law and foreign relations law. Some international law is converted into domestic law, either by the courts or through legislative or executive branch directive. Moreover, even when international law is not incorporated into a domestic legal system, courts may construe domestic law in light of international legal obligations, and the executive branch may exercise its discretion with such obligations in mind.[4] At times, courts may even do the opposite and construe international law in light of domestic law. A domestic court might presume when construing a treaty, for example, that in making the treaty its government would not have intended to override certain aspects of domestic law. This book's definition of foreign relations law includes the domestic rules governing these interconnections, but not the substance of the underlying international law.[5]

A country's foreign relations law can also have important effects on the content and operation of international law. Foreign relations law can influence how nations form treaties and what they agree to in treaties, and it can also affect the state practice that forms the foundation for rules of customary international law. In addition, by regulating allocations of domestic authority, foreign relations law can affect a nation's compliance with international law because different domestic institutions may have differing levels of commitment to (or capacity for) ensuring compliance.

As illustrations of the distinction between international law and foreign relations law, consider these seven examples, involving different countries and different types of domestic law:

- In 2017, the Supreme Court of Ghana held that Ghana's president had acted unconstitutionally in concluding an agreement with the United States to receive and resettle two detainees who had been held by the United States at the

[3] *See, e.g.*, COMPARATIVE INTERNATIONAL LAW (Anthea Roberts, Paul B. Stephan, Pierre-Hugues Verdier, & Mila Versteeg eds., 2018).

[4] In the United States, courts apply the *Charming Betsy* canon of construction, whereby federal statutes are construed, where possible, so that they do not violate international law. *See* Murray v. The Schooner Charming Betsy, 6 U.S. (2 Cranch) 64, 118 (1804) ("[A]n act of Congress ought never to be construed to violate the law of nations if any other possible construction remains. . . . "). Many other countries have a similar canon of construction. *See* ANDRÉ NOLLKAEMPER, NATIONAL COURTS AND THE INTERNATIONAL RULE OF LAW 73–81 (2011).

[5] *See also* Thomas Giegerich, *Foreign Relations Law* (Jan. 2011), *in* MAX PLANCK ENCYCLOPEDIA OF PUBLIC INTERNATIONAL LAW, *available at* http://opil.ouplaw.com/view/10.1093/law:epil/9780199231690/law-9780199231690-e937 ("The concrete form and content of a State's foreign relations law is within its domestic jurisdiction and thus beyond the range of international law. . . . Nevertheless, international law cannot be completely indifferent to the foreign relations law of its subjects, which, after all, forms the legal link connecting their internal to the international sphere.").

Guantánamo Bay naval base.[6] The court reasoned that Article 75 of Ghana's constitution required that such an agreement be approved by the Parliament, and the court expressly distinguished Ghana's constitutional law and practice concerning treaty-making from that of the United States.

- Also in 2017, the Supreme Court of the United Kingdom held that the U.K. government was required to obtain authorization from Parliament before it could initiate withdrawal from the European Union.[7] The Court reasoned that withdrawal would result in "a fundamental change in the constitutional arrangements of the United Kingdom," and that such a change "must be affected in the only way that the UK constitution recognises, namely by Parliamentary legislation."[8] The Court was addressing only U.K. constitutional law, not the international law governing withdrawal from the European Union, which is regulated by Article 50 of the Treaty on European Union.
- In 2010, the Supreme Court of Canada held in *Canada (Prime Minister) v. Khadr* that, although the United States was violating a Canadian citizen's rights by holding him at the Guantánamo Bay detention facility, how Canada should respond to this violation was a matter for determination by the executive branch, not the courts.[9] The court therefore declined to order the Canadian executive branch to request the citizen's repatriation to Canada. The court based its decision on "the separation of powers and the well-grounded reluctance of courts to intervene in matters of foreign relations."[10]
- Also in 2010, the United Kingdom enacted a statute that, for the first time, gave Parliament the formal authority to block the ratification of treaties. Although the United Kingdom has long had a constitutional convention—known as the "Ponsonby Rule"—whereby treaties will be laid before Parliament for a period of time prior to ratification, Part 2 of the Constitutional Reform and Governance Act of 2010 gave the House of Commons the authority to indefinitely block ratification.[11]
- In 2008, the U.S. Supreme Court held in *Medellín v. Texas* that the U.S. obligation under Article 94 of the UN Charter to comply with decisions of the International Court of Justice (ICJ) was not "self-executing" in the U.S. legal system and thus that an ICJ decision could not be applied to override domestic law absent

[6] *See* Banful v. Attorney General, J1/7/2016, [2017] GHASC 10 (June 22, 2017), *available at* https://ghalii.org/gh/judgment/supreme-court/2017/21.

[7] R (on the Application of Miller and another) v. Secretary of State for Exiting the European Union, [2017] UKSC 5, *available at* https://www.supremecourt.uk/cases/docs/uksc-2016-0196-judgment.pdf.

[8] *Id.*, para. 82.

[9] [2010] 1 SCR 44, *available at* https://scc-csc.lexum.com/scc-csc/scc-csc/en/item/7842/index.do.

[10] *Id.*, para. 2.

[11] *See* Arabella Lang, *Parliament's Role in Ratifying Treaties* (House of Commons Library, Briefing Paper No. 5855, Feb. 17, 2017); *see also* Paul Craig, *Engagement and Disengagement with International Institutions: The U.K. Perspective*, ch. 22 in this volume.

congressional implementation of the decision.[12] The court did not question that the ICJ decision was binding on the United States as a matter of international law.

- In 2005, Germany enacted a Parliamentary Participation Act to regulate the use of its armed forces.[13] Under the Act, the executive branch is generally required to obtain legislative authorization before deploying armed forces, and the Act specifies in detail the information that the executive must provide to the Bundestag in its requests for authorization. The Act does not address the circumstances under which such deployments are consistent with international law governing the use of force.
- Since 1973, Japan's executive branch has followed the "Ohira Principles" (named after the foreign minister who initially promulgated them) in deciding whether to seek legislative approval of international agreements.[14] Under these principles, which might be viewed as a nonbinding "constitutional convention,"[15] legislative approval is to be sought in three general circumstances: (1) when new legislation will be needed or existing legislation will have to be maintained in order to comply with the agreement; (2) when the agreement affects fiscal obligations; and (3) when the agreement involves politically important obligations. These principles do not purport to determine whether an agreement is binding on Japan as a matter of international law.

In each of these examples, the relevant domestic law, whether in the form of a constitutional provision, statute, judicial doctrine, or customary practice, regulates how the nation interacts with the rest of the world, but the law does not itself purport to determine the nation's international rights or duties. Such law is what this book refers to as foreign relations law. There are important commonalities and variations in this foreign relations law across national jurisdictions, and those commonalities and variations are the focus of this book. This book also explores whether there are general trends in foreign relations law—for example, a growth in legislative involvement in some aspects of foreign relations decision-making (such as with respect to treaty-making, treaty withdrawal, or the use of military force), or an increasing use of international law by domestic courts to constrain executive authority.[16]

It is important to note that, even though the focus of foreign relations law is on domestic law rather than international law, there is nothing inherent in such a focus

[12] 552 U.S. 491, 508–509 (2008).

[13] For an English translation, *see* Memorandum by Dr. Katja S. Ziegler, Annex II to *The Model of a "Parliamentary Army" Under the German Constitution*, *available at* https://www.publications.parliament.uk/pa/ld200506/ldselect/ldconst/236/5120707.htm.

[14] *See* Tadaatsu Mori, *The Current Practice of Making and Applying International Agreements in Japan*, ch. 11 in this volume.

[15] Constitutional conventions are "maxims, beliefs, and principles that guide officials in how they exercise political discretion." Keith E. Whittington, *The Status of Unwritten Constitutional Conventions in the United States*, 2013 U. Ill. L. Rev. 1847, (1860).

[16] This book does not, however, attempt to determine from an international relations standpoint how particular forms of government may affect or be correlated with particular national behavior in foreign relations, although the book's coverage may intersect with that inquiry.

that requires valuing domestic law over international law or resisting the domestic incorporation of international law. Nations vary in the extent to which their foreign relations law places them on the "monist" or "dualist" ends of the spectrum with respect to the incorporation of international law.[17] Domestic doctrines that call for the direct incorporation of treaties or customary international law into the domestic legal system, or that give international law primacy over some forms of domestic law, or that look to international law when interpreting domestic law, are themselves part of foreign relations law.

There are many reasons why the content of foreign relations law might vary even among constitutional democracies. Countries have differing constitutional histories. It would not be surprising, for example, to find differences between constitutional arrangements developed after World War II and those developed earlier. Parliamentary and presidential systems may have also somewhat different approaches to questions of the separation of powers.[18] In addition, understandings of the judicial role might differ among countries, including as between civil law and common law countries (as well as those countries that have a mix of civil and common law). The particular domestic politics of a country can also have an important influence on the content of its domestic law, including its foreign relations law. Finally, if foreign relations law is affected by a nation's geopolitical status, this will obviously vary, both among individual countries and over time. Despite these points, differences in foreign relations law also sometimes reflect differences in policy choices, and an awareness of both the existence and potential ramifications of such choices can be illuminating for nations when evaluating their own foreign relations law.

II. Foreign Relations Law as a "Field"

At least until recently, what this book is defining as foreign relations law was not thought of as a "field" of study outside the United States. Instead, in most countries, it was thought that there were various fields of domestic law, such as constitutional law and administrative law, and that these fields sometimes had international components. These domestic fields, in turn, were sharply distinguished from the field of international law, both analytically and in terms of the individuals who focused on them.

[17] *See generally* Curtis A. Bradley, International Law in the U.S. Legal System xii (2d ed. 2015); Pierre-Hugues Verdier & Mila Versteeg, *International Law in National Legal Systems: An Empirical Investigation*, 109 Am. J. Int'l L. 514 (2015).

[18] *Cf.* Miriam Fendius Elman, *Unpacking Democracy: Presidentialism, Parliamentarism, and Theories of Democratic Peace*, 9 Security Stud. 91, 93 (2000) (discussing "how presidential, coalitional parliamentary, Westminster parliamentary, and semipresidential democratic systems . . . influence the autonomy of foreign policymakers, and pose different sets of constraints and opportunities for foreign security policy making").

Like the character in the Molière play who discovers that he has been speaking prose all his life without realizing it, these nations of course have had foreign relations law even if they did not describe it as a field. Most obviously, foreign relations law as defined by this book encompasses a lot of the law that is practiced, and has long been practiced, by lawyers in foreign ministries. But unlike in the United States, most nations did not treat it as a discrete field of study.[19]

That is starting to change. In 2014, Campbell McLachlan—one of the authors for this volume—published an extensive treatise on Commonwealth foreign relations law.[20] This is an important volume, and it was cited in the U.K. Supreme Court's 2017 decision concerning Brexit. There have also been recent books on the foreign relations law of the European Union, which address issues such as the process for concluding international agreements and the role of federalism that are somewhat comparable to the foreign relations law issues confronted by individual nations.[21] Some non-U.S. universities are also starting to offer courses on foreign relations law.[22]

The United States never actually had a monopoly on the field anyway. One substantial component of foreign relations law concerns the role of domestic courts in applying international law and in adjudicating transnational cases that implicate governmental interests. That topic has long received attention outside the United States. The British scholar and lawyer Cyril Picciotto published a study of the relationship between international law and both British law and U.S. law in 1915.[23] The British lawyer F. A. Mann was writing about the topic as early as the 1940s, long before he published his important 1986 volume on *Foreign Affairs in English Courts*.[24] There also

[19] Germany may be a partial exception. "Staatsrecht [Law of the State] III" encompasses that country's constitutional law relating to external relations, as well as the incorporation of international law within the German legal system.

[20] *See* CAMPBELL MCLACHLAN, FOREIGN RELATIONS LAW (2014).

[21] MARISE CREMONA & BRUNO DE WITTE, EU FOREIGN RELATIONS LAW: CONSTITUTIONAL FUNDAMENTALS (2008); ROBERT SCHÜTZE, FOREIGN AFFAIRS AND THE EU CONSTITUTION (2014); *see also* BART VAN VOOREN & RAMSES A. WESSEL, EU EXTERNAL RELATIONS LAW: TEXT, CASES AND MATERIALS (2014).

[22] *See, e.g.*, *Foreign Affairs and the Canadian Constitution* (David Dyzenhaus & Karen Knop), University of Toronto School of Law, *listed at* https://handbook.law.utoronto.ca/courses/international-comparative-transnational-ict-courses; *Foreign Relations Law in Comparative Perspective* (Roland Portmann), University of St. Gallen, *available at* http://tools.unisg.ch/Handlers/public/CourseInformationSheet.ashx?Semester=FS17&EventNumber=8,492,1.00; *Foreign Relations Law* (Campbell McLachlan), Victoria University of Wellington, *available at* http://www.victoria.ac.nz/courses/laws/547/2017/offering?crn=8592; *Foreign Relations Law* (Joris Larik), University of Leiden, *available at* https://studiegids.leidenuniv.nl/courses/show/63049/Foreign-Relations-Law. For courses on EU Foreign Relations Law, *see, e.g.*, University of Amsterdam, *available at* http://studiegids.uva.nl/web/uva/sgs/en/c/9964.html.

[23] *See* CYRIL M. PICCIOTTO, THE RELATION OF INTERNATIONAL LAW TO THE LAW OF ENGLAND AND OF THE UNITED STATES OF AMERICA (1915). *See also* H. Lauterpacht, *Is International Law Part of the Law of England?*, 25 TRANSACTIONS GROTIUS SOC. 51 (1939).

[24] *See, e.g.*, F. A. Mann, *The Sacrosanctity of the Foreign Act of State*, 59 L.Q. REV. 42 (1943). For a more recent volume concerning international law in British courts, *see* SHAHEED FATIMA, USING INTERNATIONAL LAW IN DOMESTIC COURTS (2005). For a study of international law within the U.S. legal system, *see* BRADLEY, INTERNATIONAL LAW IN THE U.S. LEGAL SYSTEM, *supra* note 17. For discussion of

has been some recent focus in other countries on how federalism can affect allocations of foreign relations authority.[25]

It is not entirely clear why the field of foreign relations law has a much more extensive history in the United States than in other countries. The United States has the oldest written Constitution in the world, and accommodating that Constitution to a radically changed international environment, as well as a substantially different U.S. role in that environment, may present unique challenges. The Constitution's inclusion of treaties in the Supremacy Clause, which infuses a degree of monism into U.S. constitutional law, may also present particular challenges for U.S. law, especially as treaty-making has changed over time. In addition, the United States has a unique brand of federalism that tends to generate difficult legal issues as globalization has blurred the line between foreign and domestic affairs. Law schools in the United States also may have a more flexible structure than in many other countries, allowing faculty to more easily cross historic subject matter divides. Finally, many internationally focused U.S. academics have experience in the Legal Adviser's Office of the State Department, the work of which is often centered around foreign relations law.

Nor is it clear when to date the emergence of such a field in the United States. One might be tempted to date it to Louis Henkin's magisterial treatise, *Foreign Affairs and the Constitution*, the first edition of which was published in 1972.[26] Since then, U.S. casebooks specifically dedicated to the study of foreign relations law emerged: initially the Franck and Glennon casebook, the first edition of which was published in 1987,[27] and then the Bradley and Goldsmith casebook, the first edition of which was published in 2002.[28] There have also been a number of additional monographs on the topic.[29]

The timing, however, is more complicated than that. For example, some of Henkin's most important foreign relations law work dates to well before his 1972 book and includes a number of articles from the 1950s and 1960s,[30] as well as a 1958 book that,

international law in Canadian courts, *see* GIB VAN ERT, USING INTERNATIONAL LAW IN CANADIAN COURTS (2d ed. 2008). Some comparative studies of aspects of foreign relations law have emerged in recent years. *See, e.g.*, THE ROLE OF DOMESTIC COURTS IN TREATY ENFORCEMENT: A COMPARATIVE STUDY (David Sloss ed., 2009).

[25] *See, e.g.*, FOREIGN RELATIONS IN FEDERAL COUNTRIES (Hans Michelmann ed., 2009).

[26] *See* LOUIS HENKIN, FOREIGN AFFAIRS AND THE CONSTITUTION (1972).

[27] The casebook, with new authors, is currently in its fifth edition. *See* SEAN D. MURPHY, EDWARD T. SWAINE, & INGRID WUERTH, U.S. FOREIGN RELATIONS LAW: CASES, MATERIALS, AND PRACTICE EXERCISES (5th ed. 2018).

[28] The casebook is now in its sixth edition. *See* CURTIS A. BRADLEY & JACK L. GOLDSMITH, FOREIGN RELATIONS LAW: CASES AND MATERIALS (6th ed. 2017).

[29] *See, e.g.*, HAROLD HONGJU KOH, THE NATIONAL SECURITY CONSTITUTION: SHARING POWER AFTER THE IRAN-CONTRA AFFAIR (1990); MICHAEL J. GLENNON, CONSTITUTIONAL DIPLOMACY (1991); THOMAS M. FRANCK, POLITICAL QUESTIONS/JUDICIAL ANSWERS: DOES THE RULE OF LAW APPLY TO FOREIGN AFFAIRS? (1992); MICHAEL D. RAMSEY, THE CONSTITUTION'S TEXT IN FOREIGN AFFAIRS (2007).

[30] *See, e.g.*, Louis Henkin, *The Treaty Makers and the Law Makers: The Niagara Reservation*, 56 COLUM. L. REV. 1151 (1956); Louis Henkin, *The Foreign Affairs Power of the Federal Courts: Sabbatino*, 64 COLUM. L. REV. 805 (1964).

despite its narrower focus, was in many ways a precursor to his 1972 book.[31] Moreover, in 1965, the American Law Institute published the *Restatement (Second) of the Foreign Relations Law of the United States*,[32] based on work that began in the mid-1950s.[33] Restatements are nonbinding but influential efforts by groups of legal experts that describe the state of the law in a particular field. The first Restatement of Foreign Relations Law was labeled the *Restatement (Second)* because it was part of the second series of Restatements published by the American Law Institute. A more expansive *Restatement (Third)* was published (in two volumes) in 1987, and Henkin was its Chief Reporter.[34] In 2012, a *Restatement (Fourth)* project was initiated, and materials on treaties, jurisdiction, and immunity have now been completed; several of the Reporters for that project are authors in this volume. The key point for present purposes is that foreign relations law has been conceived of as a field within the United States at least since the initial development of the *Restatement (Second)* project in the 1950s.

But the field of foreign relations law in the United States also predates the *Restatement* projects. As Henkin made clear in the Preface to his 1972 book, he was writing against the backdrop of earlier generations of work, and he noted that he was "much indebted" to Quincy Wright's book, *The Control of American Foreign Relations*, which was published in 1922.[35] Even prior to that, some of the earliest publications in the *American Journal of International Law*, which was initiated in 1907, were focused on issues of U.S. foreign relations law.[36]

Henkin also made several perceptive suggestions about why there had been a long gap in scholarly attention to U.S. foreign relations law, and some of these suggestions

[31] *See* LOUIS HENKIN, ARMS CONTROL AND INSPECTION IN AMERICAN LAW (1958). In the Introduction to this book, Henkin described it as "essentially a memorandum of law, an examination of problems which arms control and inspection may raise under the Constitution and laws of the United States." *Id.* at 3. But the study was wide-ranging and included, for example, a consideration of legal issues that might be entailed for the United States if it joined an international criminal court. In his 1972 book, Henkin noted that he was drawing on his earlier writings, including the 1958 book. *See* HENKIN, *supra* note 26, at x.

[32] RESTATEMENT (SECOND) OF THE FOREIGN RELATIONS LAW OF THE UNITED STATES (1965).

[33] As the Introduction to the *Restatement (Second)* notes, the work on it "was made possible by a grant from the Ford Foundation awarded in 1955, after a preliminary study financed by the Rockefeller Foundation." *Id.* at vii. For additional discussion of the genesis of the *Restatement (Second)*, *see* DAVID L. SLOSS, THE DEATH OF TREATY SUPREMACY 271–280 (2016).

[34] Unlike the focus of this *Handbook*, the *Restatement (Second)* and the *Restatement (Third)* defined foreign relations law to include international law, although their coverage of the international law applicable to the United States was very selective. Although focused on the United States, the Restatements are of potential interest to other national jurisdictions, in part because they describe U.S. views and practices that may contribute to the development of customary international law. *See, e.g.*, The Freedom and Justice Party v. Secretary of State, [2018] EWCA Civ 1719, paras. 32, 65, 97 (UK Ct. App., July 19, 2018), *available at* http://www.bailii.org/ew/cases/EWCA/Civ/2018/1719.pdf (considering the Restatements in analyzing whether there is immunity under customary international law for members of "special missions").

[35] *See* QUINCY WRIGHT, THE CONTROL OF AMERICAN FOREIGN RELATIONS (1922).

[36] *See* David J. Bederman, *Appraising a Century of Scholarship in the American Journal of International Law*, 100 AM. J. INT'L L. 20, 25 (2006) (noting that "in its first years, the [*Journal*] acknowledged a distinctive field of foreign relations law").

may be relevant to why foreign relations law has been less developed as a field outside the United States. First, he observed that the field of constitutional law in the United States had become heavily focused on Supreme Court decision-making, and that the Court was not frequently engaging with foreign affairs cases during the post–World War II period.[37] Second, he speculated that as both constitutional law and international law had expanded as part of the general growth of public law, they may have "developed into separate expertise of different experts."[38] Finally, he suggested that foreign relations law "fell between the constitutional lawyer and the international lawyer, perhaps nearer to the latter, but his credentials in constitutional law were not universally accepted and he was himself less than wholly comfortable with its matter and manner."[39]

During the pre–World War II period that Henkin saw as an earlier time of vibrancy in foreign relations law, the United States was emerging as a major world power. Not coincidentally, the presidency was also becoming a more robust institution, including in foreign affairs. In addition, there were efforts in this period to increase the scope and effectiveness of international law and institutions—through, for example, expansions of inter-state arbitration. These developments generated intense discussions within the United States about the limits of presidential authority, the extent to which the government could conclude international agreements without obtaining the advice and consent of a supermajority of the Senate, the relevance of federalism to the government's foreign affairs powers, the constitutionality of delegating U.S. "sovereignty" to international institutions, and the proper role of the courts in evaluating the government's foreign affairs decisions and actions.[40] There was particular reflection on these issues in the wake of World War I and the Senate's rejection of the Versailles Treaty, and Quincy Wright's 1922 book was written against the backdrop of these events.[41]

By the end of World War II, by contrast, the central debates in foreign relations law had been at least temporarily resolved.[42] The debate between nationalism and federalism had been resolved in favor of nationalism. The debate over executive power had been resolved in favor of the President. The Senate's role in the treaty process was weakened. Courts largely deferred to the political branches. These debates would later reopen, of course—first after Vietnam,[43] then after the end of the Cold War, and then

[37] Henkin, *supra* note 26, at vii–viii. [38] *Id.* at viii. [39] *Id.*

[40] *See, e.g.*, Edward S. Corwin, The President's Control of Foreign Relations (1917); Louis L. Jaffee, Judicial Aspects of Foreign Relations (1933); Harold W. Stoke, The Foreign Relations of the Federal State (1931).

[41] In the Preface to his book, Wright described the genesis of his thinking that ultimately led him to write the book: "In the winter of 1920, with the Treaty of Versailles still unratified and unrejected by the Senate," he discussed with colleagues "a subject then in the front of everyone's mind—the American system or lack of system for controlling foreign relations." Wright, *supra* note 35, at ix.

[42] *See generally* G. Edward White, *The Transformation of the Constitutional Regime of Foreign Relations*, 85 Va. L. Rev. 1 (1999).

[43] Henkin's treatise was self-consciously written "in the quicksands of Vietnam." Henkin, *supra* note 26, at viii.

again after the 9/11 terrorist attacks. Exogenous shocks in international relations, in other words, have tended periodically to revitalize the field of U.S. foreign relations law.

There has been an especially high level of contestation in the field of foreign relations law in the United States during the past several decades, with various "revisionist" challenges to orthodoxy.[44] Some of these challenges have pressed for more attention to structural constitutional considerations that may limit or filter the domestic application of international law. The U.S. Supreme Court during this period has been receptive to some of this revisionist thinking.[45] Whatever one's views about these critiques and the responses they have generated, this dialogue has helped to give vibrancy to the field of foreign relations law in the United States. Scholars of U.S. foreign relations law today (a number of whom are authors in this volume) vary significantly in their ideological orientation, and the dialogue among them is generally perceived to have strengthened the overall quality of the work in this area.

III. Foreign Affairs Exceptionalism

Early in my academic career, I coined the term "foreign affairs exceptionalism."[46] This term as I used it refers to "the view that the federal government's foreign affairs powers are subject to a different, and generally more relaxed, set of constitutional restraints than those that govern its domestic powers."[47] This might mean, to take a few examples, that the federalism constraints that apply to the government's exercise of domestic authority are weaker in the area of foreign affairs; that the usual separation of powers understandings that apply in the domestic arena (such as the proposition that the President is not a lawmaker) apply less strictly when foreign affairs are implicated; and that the judicial role is more constrained in cases implicating foreign affairs than in cases involving domestic affairs. Debates over whether and to what extent there should be such foreign affairs exceptionalism have been a core part of scholarship relating to U.S. foreign relations law.

[44] Professor Jack Goldsmith and I authored one of the initial challenges, concerning the domestic status of customary international law. *See* Curtis A. Bradley & Jack L. Goldsmith, *Customary International Law as Federal Common Law: A Critique of the Modern Position*, 110 HARV. L. REV. 815 (1997).

[45] *See* Curtis A. Bradley, *The Supreme Court as a Filter Between International Law and American Constitutionalism*, 104 CAL. L. REV. 1567 (2016).

[46] *See* Curtis A. Bradley, *A New American Foreign Affairs Law?*, 70 U. COLO. L. REV. 1089, 1104–1107 (1999); Curtis A. Bradley, Breard, *Our Dualist Constitution, and the Internationalist Conception*, 51 STAN. L. REV. 529, 539 n.51, 555–556 (1999); Curtis A. Bradley, *International Delegations, the Structural Constitution, and Non-Self-Execution*, 55 STAN. L. REV. 1557, 1582–1586 (2003).

[47] Bradley, *A New American Foreign Affairs Law?*, *supra* note 45, at 1096. For a slightly different definition, *see* Ganesh Sitaraman & Ingrid Wuerth, *The Normalization of Foreign Relations Law*, 128 HARV. L. REV. 1899, 1900 (2015) (defining it as "the belief that legal issues arising from foreign relations are functionally, doctrinally, and even methodologically distinct from those arising in domestic policy").

Probably no Supreme Court decision reflects this concept of exceptionalism more than *United States v. Curtiss-Wright Export Corporation.*[48] This case concerned what is known in U.S. law as the "nondelegation doctrine." The idea is that Congress is not allowed to transfer its legislative authority to the executive branch, and thus, when it grants authority to that branch, it must provide sufficient standards to guide the exercise of that authority. The modern Supreme Court does not apply this doctrine vigorously and allows even very broad delegations as long as there is an "intelligible principle" in the legislation.[49] But the Court was enforcing the doctrine more strictly during the 1930s when *Curtiss-Wright* was decided, and the Court invalidated some domestic New Deal legislation on that basis.

At issue in *Curtiss-Wright* was legislation relating to the Chaco War between Bolivia and Paraguay. Congress passed a statute providing that it would be a crime for U.S. citizens and corporations to sell arms or munitions to either of the two countries in the war if the President determined that a ban on such sales "may contribute to the reestablishment of peace between those countries." President Franklin Roosevelt immediately made such a determination, and the executive branch subsequently sought to prosecute the Curtiss-Wright Export Corporation and its officers for selling machine guns to Bolivia. The defendants argued that the statute under which they were being prosecuted was invalid because it delegated too much discretion to the President.

The Supreme Court explained that it was "unnecessary to determine" whether the statute in this case would constitute an unlawful delegation of authority if it "had related solely to internal affairs."[50] The Court then proceeded to describe the "fundamental" differences between "the powers of the federal government in respect of foreign or external affairs and those in respect of domestic or internal affairs."[51] Among other things, it reasoned that, unlike its domestic powers, the federal government's foreign affairs powers "did not depend upon the affirmative grants of the Constitution" and would in any event have "vested in the federal government as necessary concomitants of nationality."[52] As a result, claimed the Court, "[t]he broad statement that the federal government can exercise no powers except those specifically enumerated in the Constitution, and such implied powers as are necessary and proper to carry into effect the enumerated powers, is categorically true only in respect of our internal affairs."[53]

The Court in *Curtiss-Wright* also emphasized the "very delicate, plenary and exclusive power of the President as the sole organ of the federal government in the field of international relations."[54] It noted that the President often has access to information relating to foreign affairs that is not available to Congress. As a result, reasoned the Court, it is often necessary for Congress to grant to the President "a degree of discretion

[48] 299 U.S. 304 (1936).

[49] *See*, e.g., Whitman v. Am. Trucking Assn's, 531 U.S. 457, 472 (2001).

[50] 299 U.S. at 315. [51] *Id.* [52] *Id.* at 318. [53] *Id.* at 315–316.

[54] *Id.* at 320.

and freedom from statutory restriction which would not be admissible were domestic affairs alone involved."[55]

The author of the Court's opinion in *Curtiss-Wright* was Justice George Sutherland. Sutherland had been thinking about the distinction between foreign and domestic affairs for many years prior to the decision. In 1909, when serving as a senator from Utah, Sutherland wrote an essay entitled "The Internal and External Powers of the National Government."[56] In this article, Sutherland sharply distinguished between the constitutional law of domestic affairs and that of foreign affairs. About a decade later, Sutherland delivered a series of lectures on this topic at Columbia Law School and subsequently published a book based on them.[57] Like his earlier article, and his later opinion in *Curtiss-Wright*, the book takes the position that "[t]he rules of construction, which apply when the government undertakes to deal with *internal* matters, may not apply, in the case of *external* matters, in the same way, or to the same degree, or, conceivably, in some cases, may not apply at all."[58] As one commentator observed, Sutherland in *Curtiss-Wright* was "in the happy position of being able to give [his] writings and speeches the status of law."[59]

The analysis in *Curtiss-Wright* has been heavily criticized. Commentators have especially resisted the idea that the foreign relations powers of the government are "extra-constitutional,"[60] and it seems unlikely that the Supreme Court today would endorse that proposition. But the more general idea of foreign affairs exceptionalism—that is, the idea that legal issues implicating foreign affairs are to be treated differently than legal issues implicating domestic affairs—runs throughout much of U.S. foreign relations law. One way that such exceptionalism has tended to manifest itself is through heightened judicial deference to the executive branch in the foreign affairs area—on issues ranging from treaty interpretation, to foreign official immunity, to predictions about likely diplomatic consequences. Part of the justification for such heightened deference is functional: that the executive branch has more expertise and access to relevant information relating to foreign affairs than the other branches of government and that it is desirable for the United States to speak with "one voice" in foreign affairs where possible.

[55] *Id.*

[56] 191 N. Am. Rev. 373 (1910). The essay was first printed as a Senate document in 1909. *See* S. Doc. No. 61-417 (1909).

[57] *See* George Sutherland, Constitutional Power and World Affairs (1919).

[58] *Id.* at 29.

[59] David M. Levitan, *The Foreign Relations Power: An Analysis of Mr. Justice Sutherland's Theory*, 55 Yale L.J. 467, 476 (1946). For additional discussion of the decision, *see*, e.g., Charles A. Lofgren, *United States v. Curtiss-Wright Export Corporation: An Historical Reassessment*, 83 Yale L.J. 1 (1973), and H. Jefferson Powell, *The Story of Curtiss-Wright Export Corporation*, *in* Presidential Power Stories 195 (Christopher H. Schroeder & Curtis A. Bradley eds., 2009).

[60] *See*, e.g., Michael D. Ramsey, *The Myth of Extraconstitutional Foreign Affairs Power*, 42 Wm. & Mary L. Rev. 379 (2000).

Some commentators contend that the U.S. Supreme Court has been shifting away from foreign affairs exceptionalism since the end of the Cold War,[61] although this claim has been contested.[62] Recent Supreme Court decisions, such as the 2015 decision in *Zivotofsky v. Kerry*, suggests that the Court is still attentive to the comparative advantages of the presidency in the foreign affairs arena.[63] In that case, the Court held that the President had the exclusive authority to determine the U.S. position with respect to the status of Jerusalem and that Congress had unconstitutionally interfered with that authority in attempting to require the State Department to designate in the passports of U.S. citizen children born in Jerusalem that the birthplace was "Israel." While discounting some of the broad dicta from *Curtiss-Wright*, the Court emphasized that the nation needs to speak with one voice on the issue of recognizing foreign sovereigns and their territories and that "[b]etween the two political branches, only the Executive has the characteristic of unity at all times."[64] The Court also explained that "[t]he President is capable, in ways Congress is not, of engaging in the delicate and often secret diplomatic contacts that may lead to a decision on recognition" and that he "is also better positioned to take the decisive, unequivocal action necessary to recognize other states at international law."[65]

Whatever one may think about foreign affairs exceptionalism, it should be kept in mind that it does not mean isolationism or resistance to international law. Indeed, many Supreme Court decisions that seem exceptionalist with respect to federalism or executive power have made it easier for the national government to make and implement international commitments and engage in international relations. For example:

- In *Missouri v. Holland*, the Supreme Court held that the national government is not constrained by the federalism limits that apply to federal legislation when it enters into and implements treaties.[66] The Court made clear that it did "not mean to imply that there are no qualifications to the treaty-making power," but it said that "they must be ascertained in a different way."[67] For the migratory bird protection treaty at issue in that case, the Court explained that "[h]ere, a national interest of very nearly the first magnitude is involved," and "[i]t can be protected only by national action in concert with that of another power."[68]
- In *United States v. Belmont*, the Court (with Justice Sutherland authoring the opinion) upheld President Roosevelt's use of an executive agreement to settle

[61] *See* Sitaraman & Wuerth, *supra* note 47.

[62] *See*, e.g., Curtis A. Bradley, *Foreign Relations Law and the Purported Shift Away from "Exceptionalism,"* 128 HARV. L. REV. F. 294 (2015); Carlos M. Vázquez, *The Abiding Exceptionalism of Foreign Relations Doctrine*, 128 HARV. L. REV. F. 305 (2015).

[63] *See* 135 S. Ct. 2076 (2015). *See also* Curtis A. Bradley, *Introduction: The Irrepressible Functionalism in U.S. Foreign Relations Law*, *in* 1 FOREIGN RELATIONS LAW (Elgar 2019).

[64] *Id.* at 2079. [65] *Id.* at 2086. [66] 252 U.S. 416 (1920). [67] *Id.* at 433.

[68] *Id.* at 435. For additional discussion of the relationship between federalism and foreign relations law in the United States, *see* Ernest A. Young, *Foreign Affairs Federalism in the United States*, ch. 15 in this volume.

claims with the Soviet Union as part of his recognition of that government, and it allowed such an agreement to displace otherwise applicable state law.[69] Because of what it described as the national government's "complete power over international affairs," the Court reasoned that "all international compacts and agreements" are free from "any curtailment or interference on the part of the several states."[70]

- In *Zschernig v. Miller*, the Court held that an Oregon inheritance law was invalid because, by in effect disallowing inheritance of Oregon property by heirs living in Communist countries, it had the potential to "affect[] international relations in a persistent and subtle way."[71] While acknowledging that the states have traditionally regulated inheritance issues, the Court said that state laws in this area "must give way if they impair the effective exercise of the Nation's foreign policy."[72]

Of course, exceptionalism might also cut in the other direction—for example, by limiting the judicial role in a way that reduces enforcement of international law. Perhaps that is how to view *Banco Nacional de Cuba v. Sabbatino*.[73] In that case, the Court held that, because of the danger of disrupting the executive branch's management of foreign relations, "the Judicial Branch will not examine the validity of a taking of property within its own territory by a foreign sovereign government, extant and recognized by this country at the time of suit, in the absence of a treaty or other unambiguous agreement regarding controlling legal principles, even if the complaint alleges that the taking violates customary international law."[74] In dissent, Justice White complained that the Court had "with one broad stroke, declared the ascertainment and application of international law beyond the competence of the courts of the United States in a large and important category of cases."[75]

Some degree of exceptionalism is probably inevitable, if for no other reason than that the legal materials relating to foreign affairs sometimes have no precise analogue in domestic law. For example, although treaties are similar in some ways to statutes in the U.S. legal system, they are also different in that they are made through a separate process, and more importantly, they can create both international law and domestic U. S. law and thus implicate issues of reciprocity not implicated by mere domestic legislation. Similarly, although it is surely an overstatement to suggest that for the purposes of foreign affairs the states "do not exist,"[76] state actions relating to foreign affairs can create externalities for the entire nation that need to be considered in evaluating the proper

[69] 301 U.S. 324 (1937). [70] *Id.* at 331.

[71] 389 U.S. 429, 440 (1968). [72] *Id.* [73] 376 U.S. 398 (1964). [74] *Id.* at 428.

[75] *Id.* at 439 (White, J., dissenting). The Supreme Court's sovereign immunity decisions prior to the enactment of the 1976 Foreign Sovereign Immunities Act may be another example of how foreign affairs exceptionalism will not necessarily promote compliance with or incorporation of international law. *See*, e.g., Republic of Mexico v. Hoffman, 324 U.S. 30, 38 (1945) ("[I]t is the duty of the courts . . . not to enlarge an immunity [of a foreign government] to an extent which the [U.S.] government, although often asked, has not seen fit to recognize.").

[76] Louis Henkin, Foreign Affairs and the US Constitution 149–150 (2d ed. 1996).

application of federalism doctrines. And, while it is an overstatement to suggest that the President is the only important actor for the United States in foreign affairs, the President does possess unique access to information relating to foreign affairs and is able to act more quickly and in a more coordinated way in responding to foreign affairs developments than Congress, which faces both collective action limitations and internal partisan competition.

These observations are certainly not intended to suggest that the legal understandings that apply to domestic affairs have no application to foreign affairs. In many instances, these understandings very likely should apply—for example, with respect to the protection of individual rights within the country. But part of the vibrancy of the field of foreign relations law in the United States stems from the dialogue and contestation over when foreign affairs genuinely merit different legal treatment.

IV. Conclusion

There is a certain amount of arbitrariness in any attempt to define a "field" of legal study. When deciding whether to consider foreign relations law as a field, the ultimate question is whether valuable insights can be obtained by focusing on its particular collection of legal materials and doctrines.[77] For U.S. scholars, the answer has long been yes, and scholars in other countries are now increasingly finding that such a focus can be useful.[78] This book in turn asks another question: whether valuable insights can be obtained by comparing these bodies of foreign relations law across national jurisdictions, and with international organizations like the European Union. The chapters that follow explore that question, both generally and with respect to a variety of specific foreign relations law topics.

As hopefully will become apparent, there are a number of ways in which such comparisons can be valuable. Legal reform efforts can of course benefit from seeing how other jurisdictions have attempted to address similar issues. In addition, studying how other systems operate with respect to engaging in foreign relations might facilitate international cooperation, by making clearer the legal and political constraints faced by counterparts in international negotiations. Such knowledge could also potentially help us understand our own systems better, by showing that what we

[77] *Cf.* Todd S. Aagaard, *Environmental Law as a Legal Field: An Inquiry in Legal Taxonomy*, 95 Cornell L. Rev. 221, 242 (2010) ("At a minimum, a legal field must exhibit two characteristics: commonality and distinctiveness."); Lawrence Lessig, *The Law of the Horse: What Cyberlaw Might Teach*, 113 Harv. L. Rev. 501, 502 (1999) ("By working through these examples of law interacting with cyberspace, we will throw into relief a set of general questions about law's regulation outside of cyberspace.").

[78] For potential trade-offs associated with conceiving of foreign relations law as a field, *see* Karen Knop, *Foreign Relations Law: Comparison as Invention*, ch. 3 in this volume.

might take for granted is not necessarily inevitable and that there might be reasonable alternate approaches.

Moreover, as will become evident in these chapters, common issues can be perceived when studying foreign relations law across multiple jurisdictions. For example, a number of countries have struggled with whether and to what extent their legislatures should become more involved in foreign relations decision-making. On the one hand, executives have certain advantages in foreign relations, such as a unitary voice, better access to relevant information, and the ability to act quickly. On the other hand, foreign relations decisions sometimes entail potential risks or trade-offs for the nation that are sufficiently serious that they might seem to warrant full democratic deliberation.

Another common issue concerns the proper role of the courts in foreign affairs. Courts are likely to be sensitive to the danger that their interventions could undercut their government's effectiveness in foreign relations or create unnecessary friction with other countries. But they may also perceive that the political process relating to foreign affairs is not by itself sufficient to ensure vindication of fundamental principles of either domestic or international law.

Comparative foreign relations law overlaps with comparative constitutional law, although it is broader in some respects and narrower in others. Foreign relations law encompasses a wide range of public law materials, not just constitutional law, but it does not extend to all of the issue areas that fall within the domain of constitutional law. Moreover, the constitutional law relating to foreign relations law tends to be less "judicialized" than other areas of constitutional law, and in part for that reason is often given much less attention than domestic affairs in studies of comparative constitutional law.[79]

As others have noted, studying comparative public law may be more challenging than studying comparative private law, given the significant differences among countries in institutional structures.[80] Moreover, the public law of a country may be substantially different in practice from what appears in its formal written law (that is true in the United States, for example), making it difficult for outside observers to have

[79] Only one of the sixty-four chapters in the *Oxford Handbook of Comparative Constitutional Law* directly concerns an issue of foreign relations law—the chapter by Yasuo Hasebe on war powers—although some of the other chapters touch on the relationship between domestic law and international law. Of the thirty-three chapters in *Comparative Constitutional Law* (Tom Ginsburg & Rosalind Dixon eds., 2011), only two directly focus on foreign relations law, and on only one aspect of it—national security law. In his 1985 Hague lectures on comparative approaches to international law, W. E. Butler noted that comparative law "has traditionally overlooked this realm" of comparative foreign relations law. 1 Recueil des Cours 83 (1986).

[80] *See* Michel Rosenfeld & András Sajó, *Introduction*, *in* The Oxford Handbook of Comparative Constitutional Law 1, 2 (Michel Rosenfeld & András Sajó eds., 2012) ("Traditionally, comparison in private law has been regarded as less problematic than in public law. Thus, where it seems fair to assume that there ought to be great convergence among industrialized democracies over the uses and functions of commercial contracts, that seems far from the case in constitutional law.").

an accurate sense of it.[81] Despite these challenges, there is a rich literature on not only comparative constitutional law but also comparative administrative law. That literature has become analytically and methodologically sophisticated, and some of the concepts and approaches developed in that literature may be of value when focusing on comparative foreign relations law.[82]

[81] For discussion of this point, *see* Oona A. Hathaway, *A Comparative Foreign Relations Law Agenda: Opportunities and Challenges*, ch. 5 in this volume.

[82] For a description of some of the approaches to comparative constitutional law, *see* Vicki Jackson, *Comparative Constitutional Law: Methodologies, in* THE OXFORD HANDBOOK OF COMPARATIVE CONSTITUTIONAL LAW, *supra* note 80, at 54–74.

CHAPTER 2

FIVE CONCEPTIONS OF THE FUNCTION OF FOREIGN RELATIONS LAW

CAMPBELL McLACHLAN

AT the heart of the comparative enquiry to which this *Handbook* is devoted is a conundrum. "Foreign relations law" is not a legal term of art. It is not a synonym for public international law. Nor is it a category of the law with wide acceptance across national legal systems in contrast to, say, contract, crime or public law. On the contrary, outside the United States, the term enjoys only limited currency and no commonly accepted scope. Path-finding scholars have often remarked on the "peculiar difficulties" in trying to make sense of a field in which "the law displays much confusion of thought."[1]

Despite this, the set of problems that foreign relations law investigates are ones that all states must resolve. They sit at the interface between the internal constitutional order of each state and its relations with other states within the international legal system in which all states participate. In the present era that boundary has become increasingly porous, generating legal issues of increasing frequency and intensity. Yet, as David Armitage has written, it has frequently resisted investigation, since "there has been a fundamental assumption that there were two distinct realms, called variously the internal and the external, the domestic and the foreign or (in a more legalistic idiom) the municipal and the international. That dichotomy remains perhaps the least investigated of all the fundamental divisions in our political lives."[2]

By contrast, the comparative study of the relation between the domestic and the foreign is not at all neglected in the field of private law relations. On the contrary, the field of private international law retains an identity within national legal systems that is distinct from the particular categories of private law to which it applies. Despite the

[1] FRANCIS A. MANN, FOREIGN AFFAIRS IN ENGLISH COURTS vi (1986).

[2] DAVID ARMITAGE, FOUNDATIONS OF MODERN INTERNATIONAL THOUGHT 10 (2013).

diversity of national solutions, it has long been the subject of detailed comparative enquiry and international codification.[3] But the study of foreign relations law adds two dimensions to the enquiry that are not present in private cross-border legal relations. Private international law is classically understood as engaging the legal systems of two states. Whether in the assumption of jurisdiction or the determination of applicable law, its rules are concerned primarily with the horizontal relationship between two national legal systems. By contrast, foreign relations law also directly implicates a vertical legal relationship between the national legal system and the international legal system. Further, the subject matter of foreign relations law is public and therefore a part of the political life of the state both internally and in its external relations with foreign states. It is inescapably both constitutional and international.

The term "foreign relations" in this context is capable of capturing only part of the enquiry. Of course, from the vantage point of the home state, all other states are foreign. The exercise of powers within a constitution to engage outward with foreign states is a matter of foreign relations, and the department of state that conducts such relations will frequently be called a Department of Foreign Affairs. But the addition of the word "law" to foreign relations is apt to mislead to the extent that it suggests that the law in this field can be derived solely from the internal perspective of national law, treating all references to law outside the home state as foreign, whatever their source. On the contrary, the field has from the outset been concerned with the relationship between the constitution and the obligations of international law that directly bind the home state.

As a result, "foreign relations law forms that part of internal law that is most closely linked with international law."[4] It draws its sources both from international law as applicable to the relevant state and national law, in particular constitutional law, governing that state's foreign relations.[5] It must always be "double facing":[6] looking outward to the relations of the state with others beyond its borders and looking inward at the impact of the international upon the domestic sphere. This forms the starting place for any comparative enquiry. It means that international law forms a constant lodestar against which comparison of different national responses may be assessed. But it tells one little about precisely where the boundary is drawn within any particular national legal system.

The twin sources—national and international—of the legal norms that may bear upon the subject requires scholarship that straddles both fields. This poses particular difficulties in an increasingly specialized legal academy. As Louis Henkin remarked in publishing the first edition of his groundbreaking *Foreign Affairs and the Constitution*, "[t]he law of foreign affairs fell somewhere between the constitutional lawyer and the

[3] ALEX MILLS, THE CONFLUENCE OF PUBLIC AND PRIVATE INTERNATIONAL LAW (2009).

[4] Thomas Giegerich, *Foreign Relations Law*, *in* MAX PLANCK ENCYCLOPEDIA OF PUBLIC INTERNATIONAL LAW (last updated 2011).

[5] RESTATEMENT (THIRD) OF THE FOREIGN RELATIONS LAW OF THE UNITED STATES § 1 (1987).

[6] The writer is indebted to David Dyzenhaus (University of Toronto) for this illuminating expression.

international lawyer."[7] It is not the primary focus of either field, offering neither the appeal of universality inherent in international lawyer's endeavor,[8] which aims to subject all states to a common legal system, nor the constitutional lawyer's appeal to the internal coherence of a single national legal system.

Field definition here is not only a matter of demarcating the respective roles of internal law and international law. It is also a matter of determining a special function for the conduct of the foreign relations of a state that is distinct from other internal matters.[9] What is it that is special about the conduct of foreign relations that might justify different legal rules within the domestic constitution? The special status of foreign relations has been a deeply held strain in legal philosophy that is in turn reflected in constitutional provisions and in judicial decisions. But it may also be asked whether such a distinction is consistent with the basic principles that underpin a system of constitutional government under law. Is it possible for foreign relations law to be "normalized" and subjected to the same disciplines as other applications of constitutional law?[10]

The argument presented here is that, in searching for what it is that is distinctive about foreign relations law, we would do better to focus on functions than on definitions. We should ask: what is "foreign relations law" for? What functions does it perform? Yet it is apparent from the many contributions to the conferences on different continents in which scholars have debated comparative foreign relations law in preparation for the present volume that there is no single answer to this question. Rather, the issues that the jurist identifies as central to their specific enquiry in turn depend upon their particular conception of the function of the field. These conceptions retain a powerful hold on the legal imagination, and thus on the way that a particular legal system may view itself vis-à-vis the rest of world, even where they do not represent actual practice.[11]

In order to elucidate what foreign relations law does, it is first necessary to isolate the various conceptions that operate often as unstated major premises underlying the way in which the field is characterized. These conceptions may be grouped into five categories:

1. *Exclusionary.* The exclusionary conception captures the idea that the function of foreign relations law is to separate the internal from the external, excluding, so far as possible, any outward facing application of the constitution, such that the external actions of the state are shielded from internal purview; concentrating the exercise of the foreign relations power in the hands of a single executive organ of

[7] LOUIS HENKIN, FOREIGN AFFAIRS AND THE CONSTITUTION viii (1972) (preface, reproduced in the second edition in 1996).

[8] *But see* ANTHEA ROBERTS, IS INTERNATIONAL LAW INTERNATIONAL? (2017).

[9] Helmut Aust, *Foreign Affairs*, *in* MAX PLANCK ENCYCLOPEDIA OF COMPARATIVE CONSTITUTIONAL LAW (2017).

[10] Ganesh Sitaraman & Ingrid Wuerth, *The Normalization of Foreign Relations Law*, 128 HARV. L. REV. 1897 (2015).

[11] Pierre-Hugues Verdier & Mila Versteeg, *International Law in National Legal Systems: An Empirical Investigation*, 109 AM. J. INT'L L. 514 (2015).

government; and leaving the international engagements of the state with foreign states as the exclusive province of public international law.

2. *Internationalist.* The internationalist conception of foreign relations law embodies a strong countervailing strain: that the function of foreign relations law is to mediate the inward reception of international law into the domestic legal system, providing both the rules and processes of reception and extending also to those substantive elements of international law that are themselves directly applicable within the national legal system.
3. *Constitutional.* A constitutionalist focus within foreign relations law places its primary emphasis within the domestic constitution. It sees the field as concerned with the classic concerns of constitutional law—the separation of powers and the rule of law—as applied to the specific subject matter of foreign relations. That is to say, it is devoted to the distribution of the foreign relations power between the organs of government—executive, legislative, and judicial—and to the regulation of the exercise of the foreign relations power where it infringes the rights of the private individual.
4. *Diplomatic.* A fourth conception of foreign relations law focuses on its diplomatic functions. This approach sees the primary focus of the law in this field as facilitating the external relations of the state with foreign states. This is partly a matter of positive rules of law (international and domestic) that facilitate the intercourse of states. It also calls for a focus on state practice and for the discretionary consideration of diplomatic relations in the application of positive law.
5. *Allocative.* A fifth conception of foreign relations law views its function as allocative: as a set of rules of jurisdiction and applicable law. Such rules allocate competence and determine which law (whether national or international) is to be applied to determine issues concerning the external exercise or enforcement of the public power of states. In this way foreign relations law performs a function akin to that of private international law within the different context of public law.

Characterizing the different approaches to foreign relations law in this way is not meant to suggest that any particular legal system adopts only one of these conceptions. On the contrary, as will be seen, traces of each of these conceptions may be found in many different legal systems, despite otherwise major differences in their respective legal traditions.

I. The Exclusion of Foreign Relations from Domestic Law

The roots of the idea that the constitutional state exists to protect itself and its citizens from the chaos of relations beyond its border run very deep in political philosophy.

This is expressed most trenchantly in Hobbes' proposition that "in all times, Kings and Persons of Soveraigne authority, because of their independency, are in continuall jealousies, and in the state and posture of Gladiators; having their weapons pointing, and their eyes fixed on one another."[12]

The conclusion drawn by John Locke from the state of nature that otherwise exists outside an organized constitutional state is that the public power of dealing with relations outside the state—the "*security and interest of the publick without*"—must be concentrated in the single hands of the executive.[13] Locke coined the term "federative" for this distinct element of the executive power, which "contains the Power of War and Peace, Leagues and Alliances, and all the Transactions, with all Persons and Communities without the Commonwealth."[14] He argued that the exercise of this power "is much less capable to be directed by antecedent, standing, positive Laws . . . and so must be left to the Prudence and Wisdom of those who hands it is in, to be managed for the publick good."[15] Any division of the federative power internally "would be apt sometime or other to cause disorder and ruine."[16]

In English law, the powerful influence of Locke's idea of the concentration of the foreign affairs power in the hands of the executive is felt in the continuing emphasis on the prerogative as the legal source of the foreign affairs power. For Dicey, the prerogative power, defined as "the residue of discretionary or arbitrary authority, which at any given time is legally left in the hands of the Crown,"[17] had a particular application to "all foreign affairs." Though Ministers and not the Monarch in fact exercised this power, they did so "free from Parliamentary control."[18]

The idea that the international and the domestic are two distinct realms also justifies dualism in the relationship between the treaty-making acts of the executive on the international plane and the sovereignty of Parliament to prescribe the law of the land. If treaties can have no effect within domestic law, Parliament's legislative supremacy within its own polity is secure. If the executive must always seek the sanction of Parliament in the event that a proposed action on the international plane will require domestic implementation, parliamentary sovereignty is reinforced at the very point at which the legislative power in engaged. The significance of the "fundamental principle of the Constitution that, unless primary legislation permits it, the Royal prerogative does not enable Ministers to change statute law or the common law" was underscored as recently as 2017 in the context of the litigation over the United Kingdom's decision to withdraw from the European Union.[19]

[12] THOMAS HOBBES, LEVIATHAN 90. On the philosophical foundations and influence of the exclusionary approach in the common law tradition, *see generally* THOMAS POOLE, REASON OF STATE: LAW, PREROGATIVE AND EMPIRE (2015), especially pages 56–60.

[13] JOHN LOCKE, TWO TREATISES OF GOVERNMENT 147 (orig. 1690) (Peter Laslett ed., 2d ed. 1967).

[14] *Id.* at 146. [15] *Id.* at 147. [16] *Id.* at 148.

[17] ALBERT V. DICEY, LECTURES INTRODUCTORY TO THE STUDY OF THE LAW OF THE CONSTITUTION 348 (1885).

[18] *Id.* at 390.

[19] R (Miller) v. Secretary of State for Exiting the European Union, [2017] UKSC 5, [2018] A.C. 61, [50].

The exclusion of foreign affairs from the domestic realm also limits the scope of the judicial role in foreign affairs. Contemporary British and Commonwealth courts have accepted that the exercise of the foreign affairs power is derived from the prerogative[20] and that this limits the scope for judicial review.[21]

The state is conceived as a unity in all its relations without. Locke saw it as "one Body . . . in respect of all other States or Persons out of its Community."[22] One conclusion drawn from this unity on the international plane has been that there has to be a corresponding internal unity in foreign relations matters between the organs of state, since the "State cannot speak with two voices . . . the judiciary saying one thing, the executive another."[23]

The idea of foreign relations as a zone of nonlaw within the municipal legal system finds its highest expression in the doctrine of act of state, defined by Harrison Moore as an act which "whether it be regulated by international law or not, and whether the acts in question are or are not in accord with international law, is not a subject of municipal jurisdiction."[24] In the application of this doctrine, the executive retains the ability to exclude from domestic adjudication some common law claims in respect of its actions affecting foreigners abroad (at least in situations of armed conflict).[25]

A cognate doctrine in U.S. jurisprudence is that of the political question: that "[t]he conduct of the foreign relations of our Government is committed by the Constitution to the Executive and Legislative—'the political'—Departments of the Government, and the propriety of what may be done in the exercise of this political power is not subject to judicial inquiry or decision."[26]

The notion that foreign affairs are excluded from the municipal realm is not unique to the common law tradition. On the contrary, marked elements of an exclusionary doctrine may also be found in the legal systems of some civil law states, notably those in the French tradition.[27] In France, the theory of the *acte de gouvernement* traditionally limited the extent to which the administrative courts would review the international or diplomatic activities of the executive.[28] Though the *Conseil d'Etat* has moderated this

[20] Khadr v. Canada (Prime Minister), 2010 SCC 3, [2010] 1 S.C.R. 44, [34].

[21] Council of Civil Service Unions v. Minister for the Civil Service, [1985] 1 A.C. 374, 418 (HL per Lord Roskill).

[22] Locke, *supra* note 13, at 145.

[23] The Arantzazu Mendi, [1939] A.C. 256, 264 (HL per Lord Atkin).

[24] W. Harrison Moore, Act of State in English Law 1–2 (1906).

[25] Serdar Mohammed v. Ministry of Defence, [2017] UKSC 1, [2017] A.C. 649.

[26] Oetjen v. Central Leather Co., 246 U.S. 297, 302 (1918). *But see* Louis Henkin, Foreign Affairs and the United States Constitution 143–148 (2d ed. 1996); Thomas M. Franck, Political Questions/Judicial Answers: Does the Rule of Law Apply to Foreign Affairs? (1992).

[27] Daniele Amoroso, *A Fresh Look at the Issue of Non-Justiciability of Defence and Foreign Affairs*, 23 Leiden J. Int'l L. 933 (2010); Daniele Amoroso, *Judicial Abdication in Foreign Affairs and the Effectiveness of International Law*, 14 Chinese J. Int'l L. 99 (2015); Elizabeth Zoller, Droit des Relations Extérieures 298 ff (1992).

[28] Paul Duez, Les Actes du Gouvernement (1935, repr. 2006); Moncef Kdhir, *La Théorie de l'Acte de Gouvernement dans la Jurisprudence du Conseil d'Etat relative aux Relations Internationales de la France à l'épreuve du Droit International*, 4 J.D.I. 1059 (2003).

exclusionary doctrine by developing the notion of an *acte detachable*,[29] it remains a viable plea.[30] In Italy, the equivalent doctrine (*atto politico*) precludes the court from reviewing the manner in which political decisions of the state that are directed toward the international plane are taken and implemented.[31]

The imprint of the exclusionary doctrine continues be found in the constitutional thought of many states. The exclusionary doctrine captures two essential structural features of foreign relations law that continue to be of contemporary relevance. The first is the sovereign equality and independence of states, which in turn supports the independent domestic jurisdiction of states. The world is divided into separate national legal systems each of which has the capacity to determine for itself its relations with others.[32] The second is the central importance of the executive branch within constitutional systems in the actual conduct of foreign relations. Only the executive may *act* on the international plane, representing the state in its relations with other states. When it does so, the executive is not necessarily directly engaging rights and duties within the domestic sphere. This fact in turn has implications for the roles of the legislative and judicial branches.

However, to the extent that the exclusionary doctrine seeks to create a zone of nonlaw filled only by executive discretion, it fails to explain other key features of the legal regulation of foreign relations. First, it leaves out of account the real impact of international law upon the practice of states, an impact that falls most directly on the executive. The exclusionary doctrine put at its highest suggests that the exercise of the executive function in foreign affairs is a pure matter of discretion unbound by legal constraints.[33] Yet both the historical record[34] and contemporary practice continue to demonstrate the importance of the point made by Bethlehem that "[l]egality is paramount.... Governments may stand or fall by reference to considerations of legality."[35] The impact of international law on the practice of states has both an external and an internal aspect. Externally it constrains and in turn determines the legality of the external exercise of state power on the international plane. Internally, it operates to

[29] Described as "*mesures qui peuvent être appréciées indépendamment de leurs origines ou de leurs incidences internationales*": DALLOZ, LES GRANDS ARRÊTS DE LA JURISPRUDENCE ADMINISTRATIVE 9 (17th ed. 2009).

[30] CE 23 Sept. 1992, Nos. 120,437 and 120,737, *GISTI et MRAP* (Conseil d'Etat) [1992] A.J.D.A. 752, (1992) 106 I.L.R. 198; CE 29 Sept. 1995 No. 171277, *Association Greenpeace France* (Conseil d'Etat) [1995] A.J.D.A. 749, (1995) 106 I.L.R. 231.

[31] President of the Council of Ministers v. Marković (Court of Cassation, Decision No. 8157/2002) (2002) 128 I.L.R. 652; held not contrary to art. 6 European Convention on Human Rights: Marković v. Italy (ECtHR (GC), App No. 1398/03, (14 December 2006).

[32] Art. 2 Charter of the United Nations (signed 26 June 1945, entered into force 24 October 1945) 1 U.N.T.S. 16.

[33] JENS D. OHLIN, THE ASSAULT ON INTERNATIONAL LAW (2015).

[34] ISABEL HULL, A SCRAP OF PAPER: BREAKING AND MAKING INTERNATIONAL LAW DURING THE GREAT WAR (2014).

[35] Daniel Bethlehem, *The Secret Life of International Law*, 1 C.J.I.C.L. 23, 33 (2012) (Principal Legal Advisor FCO UK, 2006–11).

constrain the decisions of the executive. This is no less regulation according to law, whether or not it is also subject to domestic judicial review.

Second, the exclusionary doctrine does not explain essential aspects of the dynamics of the relations *between* states. It presents a one-sided view of foreign relations as concerned only with the position of the home state. This is, as Crawford has put it, a distorted conception of international law through "the sound of one hand clapping,"[36] since it fails to take account of the fact that international relations and in turn international law are made through the relations of two or more states, each with their own distinct interests. Nor can the relations between states be confined to the international plane and excluded from domestic purview. On the contrary, the legal relations between states involve multiple interactions at the domestic level, including in diplomatic relations and where states sue or are sued in the domestic courts of other states.

Third, the exclusionary doctrine does not account for the constitutional role of the judiciary in the protection of the individual from the abuse of executive power. The separation of powers exists not as a license for executive impunity, but in order that the judiciary may hold in check the power of the executive branch, where the latter's actions infringe the legal rights of individuals. This is a basic attribute of the rule of law in constitutional systems. Since executive actions abroad are as susceptible of infringing individual rights as its actions at home, any theory of foreign relations law must hold in balance the executive's right of action with a correlative protection of the individual.

Fourth, the exclusionary doctrine fails to explain the multifaceted role of international law within national legal systems, including those that adhere to a dualist approach. Why should the domestic judiciary concern itself at all with international law if the latter regulates only the world outside? Yet there is abundant evidence of reference to international law in domestic judicial decisions across a broad spectrum of different national legal systems.

II. The Domestic Reception of International Law

Whatever may be its continuing salience, the exclusionary approach does not explain a critically important means by which national legal systems mediate their relationship with the international sphere, namely, through rules of reception and recognition of international law. "Each legal system has its own rules of recognition: that is what it is to be a legal system."[37]

[36] James Crawford, *International Law as a Discipline and a Profession*, 106 Am. Soc. Int'l L. Proc. 471, 484 (2012).

[37] James Crawford, *International Law in the House of Lords and the High Court of Australia 1996–2008: A Comparison*, 28 A.Y.I.L. 1, 6 (2009).

The response of many scholars invited to participate in the present comparative exercise has been to view foreign relations law through the lens of the domestic reception of international law. Karen Knop refers to this in her introductory essay here as "the inward-looking perspective of international law in domestic law."[38] This question in turn invites separate consideration of (1) the national mechanisms for the conclusion and incorporation of treaty obligations;[39] and (2) the domestic law status of customary international law, including jus cogens norms.[40]

These issues fit the foreign relations law rubric not simply because they concern the interaction of international and national law. They also engage the functions of the organs of government within a constitutional state. The process for the ratification and incorporation of treaties concerns the relation between the executive and the legislature. The status of customary international law within the domestic legal system engages the function of the judiciary in the direct application of international law as a source of the applicable law.

The way in which particular legal systems determine the status and applicability of international law is not solely determined by the extent of adoption of an exclusionary approach: by whether the state regards itself as "dualist"—excluding the direct application of international law norms that have not been incorporated by Parliament into the domestic legal system. As Verdier and Versteeg conclude in their comparative survey: "the traditional monist-dualist distinction, which originally arose out of theoretical debates on the nature of international law, has limited value for the purpose of classifying actual legal systems or examining their policy and normative implications."[41]

This point is striking in the case of common law systems that have been traditionally treated as dualist. This description does not account for the direct application of customary international law within a common law legal system. Such a role may be traced to Blackstone's famous dictum:

> In arbitrary states [international] law, wherever it contradicts or is not provided for by the municipal law of the country, is enforced by the royal power: but since in England no royal power can introduce a new law, or suspend the execution of the old, therefore the law of nations (wherever any question arises which is properly the object of its jurisdiction) is here adopted in its full extent by the common law, and is held to be a part of the law of the land.[42]

Blackstone's point here is that the judiciary has a unique function within a constitutional state to apply international law when it is confronted with an issue for the

[38] Karen Knop, *Foreign Relations Law: Comparison as Invention*, ch. 3 in this volume, at p.53.

[39] *See*, e.g., Jaemin Lee, *Incorporation and Implementation of Treaties in South Korea*, ch. 13 in this volume; Tadaatsu Mori, *The Current Practice of Making and Applying International Agreements in Japan*, ch. 11 in this volume.

[40] *See*, e.g., Gib van Ert, *The Domestic Application of International Law in Canada*, ch. 28 in this volume.

[41] Verdier & Versteeg, *supra* note 11, at 532.

[42] William Blackstone, Commentaries on the Laws of England 67 (9th ed. 1783).

resolution of which international law is the applicable law. This principle originated in cases that directly affected foreign relations being concerned with the immunities of foreign states and diplomats.[43] But the power of the judiciary to apply customary international law directly has a much more general application, since, as a broad comparative analysis has shown, "in virtually all states, [customary international law] rules are in principle directly applicable without legislative implementation."[44]

The status of treaties within the domestic legal system is a matter of constitutional design that may also implicate the role of the courts. A provision that "all Treaties . . . shall be the supreme Law of the Land"[45] has broad implications not only for the sources of law within the domestic legal system but also for the power of the judiciary to determine the validity of other provisions of the law vis-à-vis the other organs of government.[46]

The general rules of recognition and incorporation of international law adopted within a particular national legal system affect the sources of law applicable to foreign relations questions that may come before the courts, because they determine to what extent and in what circumstances the courts may refer directly to international law rules. The internationalist approach to foreign relations law may, at its most expansive, seek to restate large parts of the substantive provisions of international law that are of direct application in the relevant state.[47]

The internationalist conception of foreign relations law is valuable precisely because it directly confronts the other part of the equation, the regulation of which is the central function of the field. In contrast to the exclusionary approach, it does not cast international law into a black hole of matters of no legal relevance to the domestic legal system. It enables consideration of the rules of international law that take into account the interests of other states as well as that of the home state. It also captures an important part of the practice of national courts in the direct application of international law to the decision of the claims of individual litigants before them.

However, an exclusive focus on the reception of international law may also leave important functions of foreign relations law out of account. In the first place, foreign relations law must accommodate the reception of international law within the constitutional constraints of a national legal system. A national court is bound to interpret its function within its own constitution. Constitutional doctrines that may

[43] Triquet v. Bath (1764) 3 Burr 1478, 97 ER 936 (Lord Mansfield); *see* CAMPBELL McLACHLAN, FOREIGN RELATIONS LAW 2.40 ff (2014).

[44] Verdier & Versteeg, *supra* note 11, at 528.

[45] U.S. CONST. art. VI; *see* CURTIS A. BRADLEY, INTERNATIONAL LAW IN THE U.S. LEGAL SYSTEM ch. 2 (2d ed. 2015).

[46] RESTATEMENT OF THE LAW FOURTH, THE FOREIGN RELATIONS LAW OF THE UNITED STATES § 310 (2018). For comparative discussion of the status of treaties in domestic legal systems, *see* DUNCAN B. HOLLIS, MERRITT R. BLAKESLEE, & L. BENJAMIN EDERINGTON, NATIONAL TREATY LAW AND PRACTICE (2005); and DINAH SHELTON, INTERNATIONAL LAW IN DOMESTIC LEGAL SYSTEMS (2011).

[47] *See, e.g.*, RESTATEMENT (THIRD) OF THE FOREIGN RELATIONS LAW OF THE UNITED STATES (1987); vol. 61 *International Relations Law*, *in* HALSBURY'S LAWS OF ENGLAND (5th ed. 2010).

limit the extent to which a court may properly give effect to international law are not to be summarily dismissed as "evidence of political limitations of the exercise of judicial independence,"[48] since "the domestic interpretation of international law is not simply a conveyor belt that delivers international law to the people."[49] Foreign relations law has to explain when and why international law is to be received and what function it is to perform within the domestic legal system.

In the second place, the rules of recognition that enable international law to be applied or taken into account in national legal systems play a much wider role than the conduct of foreign relations. The engagement of states in treaty-making now covers almost every aspect of human activity. This means that the contexts in which national legislatures and courts have had to examine the relevance of treaties reaches deep into almost every aspect of the domestic legal system. The influence of international law within the contemporary domestic sphere is pervasive. It affects many issues between citizen and state that are otherwise purely domestic, and has broad implications for the process of judicial interpretation.[50]

An internationalist conception captures more than is strictly necessary for the resolution of issues arising within domestic legal systems concerning the external exercise of public power in the relations between states, which remains the central concern of foreign relations law. These issues have to be disaggregated from the broader questions of the relation between national and international law to facilitate effective comparison and analysis.

III. Foreign Relations Law as Constitutional Law

A third way of looking at foreign relations law is to see it as a branch of constitutional or public law: as principally concerned with regulating the distribution of the foreign relations power between the organs of government. In this way, foreign relations are conceived primarily as an issue of internal governance, albeit that the subject matter of the enquiry concerns relations with the world outside.

To some extent this is an inevitable consequence of the need in constitutional states to organize and regulate the exercise of this particular type of power. As Hersch Lauterpacht put it, "limitations upon the freedom of judicial decision, far from amounting to a

[48] Andre Nollkaemper, National Courts and the International Rule of Law 53 (2011).

[49] Karen Knop, *Here and There: International Law in Domestic Courts*, 32 NYU J. Int'l L. & Pol. 501, 516 (2000).

[50] Helmut P. Aust & Georg Nolte, The Interpretation of International Law by Domestic Courts (2016).

suspension of the rule of law, are the expression of a differentiation of functions, which for reasons of obvious expediency is unavoidable in the modern State."[51]

The fact that foreign relations law must concern itself with the internal as well as the external, means that the unity of the state, a fundamental principle in international law,[52] cannot be simply transposed into the domestic framework, since "the identification of the judicial and other organs of the state with the state itself is a principle of international law. But it has no place in the domestic jurisprudence of the state. The legal relationships of the different branches of government depend on its internal constitutional arrangements."[53] For this reason, where a state organizes its internal constitutional arrangements in a manner that aims to separate the executive from the legislative and the judicial function, it is often a matter of great moment, in principle as in practice, to determine which branch holds particular elements of the foreign relations power and to what extent this may effectively be checked by other branches.

The allocation of such powers between the executive and the legislature may be a matter of conscious constitutional design, as, for example, in the case of the U.S. Constitution, which confers power upon the president "by and with the Advice and Consent of the Senate, to make treaties."[54] This "intermixture of powers" was deliberate, since, as Madison recognized, "[t]he qualities elsewhere detailed as indispensable in the management of foreign negotiations, point out the Executive as the most fit agent in those transactions; while the vast importance of the trust, and the operation of treaties as laws, plead strongly for the participation of the whole or a portion of the legislative body in the office of making them."[55]

A shared responsibility between the executive and the legislature may also be found in other constitutional systems.[56] In Commonwealth states, the role of Parliament in the treaty ratification process has been significantly extended in recognition of the significance of treaties in the law making process.[57] There has been a parallel debate about the role of the legislature in the decision of the state to engage in armed conflict.[58]

[51] HERSCH LAUTERPACHT, THE FUNCTION OF LAW IN THE INTERNATIONAL COMMUNITY 397 (1933, rev. ed. 2011).

[52] Art. 4(1) ILC Draft Articles on Responsibility of States for Internationally Wrongful Acts, [2001] 2(2) YB ILC 26.

[53] R v. Lyons, [2002] UKHL 44, [2003] 1 A.C. 976, [105] per Lord Millett.

[54] U.S. CONST. art. II, § 2.

[55] THE FEDERALIST NO. 75 (Madison), *in* ALEXANDER HAMILTON, JAMES MADISON, & JOHN JAY, THE FEDERALIST PAPERS (1788, republished 2008).

[56] *See, e.g.*, art. 73(3) of the Japanese Constitution, discussed in Tadaatsu Mori, *The Current Practice of Making and Applying International Agreements in Japan*, ch. 11 in this volume; arts. 60 and 73 of the Korean Constitution, discussed in Jaemin Lee, *Incorporation and Implementation of Treaties in South Korea*, ch. 13 in this volume.

[57] Pt. 2 Constitutional Reform and Governance Act 2010 (UK); MCLACHLAN, *supra* note 43, at 5.37–5.90,

[58] *See* Katja S. Ziegler, *The Use of Military Force by the United Kingdom: The Evolution of Accountability*, ch. 43 in this volume; MCLACHLAN, *supra* note 43, at 4.46–4.83.

A constitutional approach also engages the proper role of the judiciary in foreign relations matters.[59] It seeks to explain the doctrines applied by the courts in terms of the proper province of the judicial function vis-à-vis the executive. In this way, the courts may either find foreign relations cases nonjusticiable as "beyond the constitutional competence assigned to the courts under our conception of the separation of powers;"[60] or adjudicate them where they engage private rights or public law duties cognizable within the domestic legal system.

A core element of the judicial function in a constitutional state is the protection of the individual against the abuse of the executive power of the state, whether such power is exercised internally or externally. The constitutional approach can therefore also serve to articulate a common public law spine to the state's conduct of its foreign relations where such conduct trenches upon the fundamental rights of the individual—a spine that links national law with international law. This link is particularly apparent in states that have given domestic effect to international human rights norms, making them domestically enforceable and at the same time affording individuals a subsequent right of recourse to an international tribunal, as in the case of the European Convention on Human Rights.[61]

More generally, a focus on the shared elements of public law and public international law can serve what F. A. Mann has called "the ultimate unity of the law"[62] by promoting the shared disciplines of constitutionality at both the national and the international level. This is a particular feature of the German approach, which both seeks to subject the foreign relations power to public law disciplines at the domestic level and has developed the concept of the constitutional function of international law.[63] The consequence of this approach for the domestic judicial function is that in general foreign affairs is not excluded from judicial review. Rather, the courts determine such cases through the substantive interpretation of constitutional standards of control. Nevertheless, the judiciary may be expected to exercise judicial self-restraint on the merits in such cases, according the executive a higher degree of discretion in light of the nature of the issues.[64]

A constitutional conception of the primary function of foreign relations law may still, when translated into comparative law terms, result in an outward-facing focus: on those aspects of the distribution of powers internally within constitutional systems that concern the state's international engagements. Hathaway argues that a constitutional focus to the comparative enquiry may in this way benefit our understanding of international law since "it is the states themselves that decide when and how they

[59] Hiromichi Matsuda, *International Law in Japanese Courts*, ch. 30 in this volume.

[60] Shergill v. Khaira, [2014] UKSC 33, [2015] A.C. 359, [42].

[61] Convention for the Protection of Human Rights and Fundamental Freedoms, 213 U.N.T.S. 221 (signed 4 November 1950, entered into force 3 September 1953).

[62] Francis A. Mann, *The Consequences of an International Wrong in International and National Law*, 48 BRIT. Y.B. INT'L L. 1 (1976), *reprinted in* FRANCIS A. MANN, FURTHER STUDIES IN INTERNATIONAL LAW 141 (1990).

[63] ROBERTS, *supra* note 8, at 105–107.

[64] FRANCK, *supra* note 26, ch. 7.

will consent—and they do so through their own domestic legal and political institutions. Accordingly, examining domestic institutions that states use to create international law is essential to our understanding of international law."[65]

But an exclusive focus on the internal constitutional dimension of foreign relations law runs the risk of leading to an inward focus in which "international law is taught as just another aspect of the domestic public law."[66] This is particularly so where the foreign relations issues and the international law rules that they engage are subordinated to the study of "national security law," a field that has achieved particular prominence since 9/11 and which prioritizes the study of the protection of the nation according to principles of national law over international law norms.

At its most expansive such an approach can seek to rewrite the international relations of a particular state with the international community in exclusively domestic terms,[67] or to serve as a justification for the exercise of broad executive power abroad.[68] Such an interpretation of the function of foreign relations law can engender isolationism, cutting off the foreign relations law of a particular state from the engagement with other states and with the system of international law, which is the other side of the relationship that it exists to regulate.

IV. The Diplomatic Function of Foreign Relations Law

The fourth conception of foreign relations law stands in contrast to the constitutional model. It rather sees the principal function of foreign relations law to be diplomatic, that is to say: to promote the conduct of foreign relations *between* states. Such a conception views foreign relations law as operating in an horizontal dimension, neither inward-looking nor outward-looking, but rather reflecting the actual conduct of diplomatic relations, which operates in both directions, with each state seeking through those relations to promote its own foreign policy objectives.

Karen Knop has illuminatingly suggested that there may be different conceptions of the function of diplomacy itself at work here: whether it is conceived as "an instrument and background condition of foreign policy," as "including the substance of foreign policy," or "as simply describing relations conducted through negotiations."[69] However

[65] Oona A. Hathaway, *A Comparative Foreign Relations Law Agenda: Opportunities and Challenges*, ch. 5 in this volume, at p.79.

[66] Martti Koskenniemi, *Foreword*, *in* ROBERTS, *supra* note 8, at xiv.

[67] James Crawford, *International Law as a Discipline and a Profession*, 106 AM. SOC. INT'L L. PROC. 471, 484 (2012).

[68] JENS D. OHLIN, THE ASSAULT ON INTERNATIONAL LAW, ch. 2 (2015).

[69] Knop, *supra* note 38, at p.60.

the practice of diplomacy is itself conceived, it was early linked with foreign relations *law*. Early works in the field sought to capture this link, by expounding both the law applicable to the conduct of diplomatic relations and the practice of diplomacy by the relevant states.[70] In present times, much of the law relating to the conduct of diplomatic relations has been codified in conventions of wide acceptance, such that it has become international law properly so called.

The immunity of states from the domestic jurisdiction of other states is another key part of the conduct of bilateral relations between states that is regulated by international law. Immunity is a rule of customary international law rooted in the practice of states.[71] State immunity "derives from the sovereign equality of States, which, as Article 2, paragraph 1, of the Charter of the United Nations makes clear, is one of the fundamental principles of the international legal order."[72] The rules of immunity also serve a diplomatic function, since they "promote comity and good relations between States through the respect of another State's sovereignty."[73]

Nevertheless national legislatures and national courts retain a vital function in determining the precise scope of the immunity of states. The law on state immunity is derived from international law, but it must be interpreted and applied by national courts. State practice differs widely in the extent to which states have accepted exceptions to the principle of immunity.

Diplomatic relations may also be engaged in the protection of individual rights. International law recognizes the right of states to exert diplomatic protection where the actions of foreign states affecting the nationals of the home state give rise to an international delict.[74] Such a right is vindicated on the international plane.[75] But each state must also resolve for itself, as a matter of domestic law, the extent to which the state has a *duty* to protect its nationals, when they are subject to gross abuses of their rights at the hands of a foreign state.

Beyond the law of diplomatic relations and immunity *stricto sensu*, a conception of foreign relations law as diplomatic in function may have wider implications for the approach of national courts in deciding cases that engage the interests of foreign states and, in turn, may affect the foreign relations interests of the home state. The idea that "comity" should guide the extent to which each sovereign state takes account of the interests of other states may be traced to the seventeenth-century Dutch jurist Ulrich Huber.[76] In common law legal systems the notion of comity has exerted a powerful

[70] *See* Sir Ernest Satow, A Guide to Diplomatic Practice (1922); John W. Foster, The Practice of Diplomacy as Illustrated in the Foreign Relations of the United States (1906).

[71] Jurisdictional Immunities of the State (Germany v. Italy), [2012] I.C.J. Rep. 99, 123, [56].

[72] *Id.* at [57].

[73] Al-Adsani v. United Kingdom (App No. 35763/97, 21 November 2001), 34 E.H.R.R. 11, 123 I.L.R. 24, 54 (ECtHR GC).

[74] International Law Commission, Draft Articles on Diplomatic Protection, [2006] 2(2) Y.B. I.L.C. 22.

[75] Diallo (Guinea v. Democratic Republic of the Congo) (Merits), [2010] I.C.J. Rep. 639.

[76] Ulrich Huber, *De Conflictu Legum* (1686, trans. Ernest Lorenzen *in* Wigmore, Celebration Legal Essays 199 (Albert Kocourek ed., 1919)).

influence across a wide range of cases involving foreign elements.[77] Though used in a number of different senses, it is frequently deployed to explain the court's view that the interests of a foreign state must be taken into account.

A particular manifestation of this is the foreign act of state doctrine, expressed in the general proposition that "the courts of one country will not sit in judgment on the acts of the government of another done within its own territory."[78] Though subject to sustained criticism and much qualified by later decisions, the idea that the judicial function may properly be limited by diplomatic considerations of comity between nations still exerts a powerful hold in common law jurisprudence.[79]

The diplomatic conception of foreign relations law sees foreign relations law as not merely the concern of the constitution of one state. It performs the important function of focusing attention on the application of the law governing the relations *between* states when such issues arise within domestic legal systems.

On the other hand, the diplomatic conception has shortcomings of its own to the extent that it substitutes general references to comity or foreign act of state for a proper analysis of "the issues that arise in each case at a more particular level than is achieved by applying a single, all-embracing formula."[80] The doctrine of foreign act of state does not form part of international law, so as to preclude courts generally from reviewing the legality or effectiveness of foreign acts of state—a proposition confirmed in both German[81] and French law.[82] Rather, it is necessary to analyze what law is applicable to the claim before the court, which may, depending upon the nature of the issue, be the law of the forum, foreign law, or international law.

V. The Allocative Function of Foreign Relations Law

A fifth conception of foreign relations law is that it performs an allocative function: providing a set of rules that allocate jurisdiction and determine applicable law in cases involving the external exercise of the public power of states.[83] It does so in three dimensions: (1) between the organs of government within the national constitution; (2) between states; and (3) between the municipal and the international plane.

[77] William S. Dodge, *International Comity in Comparative Perspective*, ch. 39 in this volume; Lawrence A. Collins, *Comity in Modern Private International Law*, *in* Reform and Development of Private International Law: Essays in Honour of Sir Peter North 89 (James Fawcett ed., 2002).

[78] Underhill v. Hernandez, 168 U.S. 250, 252 (1897).

[79] Belhaj v. Straw, [2017] UKSC 3, [2017] A.C. 964. For discussion, *see* Campbell A. McLachlan, *The Foreign Relations Power in the Supreme Court*, 134 L.Q.R. 380 (2018).

[80] Moti v. The Queen, [2011] HCA 50, 52, 245 C.L.R. 456 (2011).

[81] Border Guards Prosecution, 100 I.L.R. 364 (BGHst 39, 1) & BVerfGE 95, 98 (1992).

[82] Patrick Kinsch, Le Fait du Prince Étranger 406 (1994).

[83] Campbell A. McLachlan, *The Allocative Function of Foreign Relations Law*, 82 Brit. Y.B. Int'l L. 349 (2012); Jörg Menzel, Internationales Öffentliches Recht (2011).

What is meant by an allocative function? Within the constitutional order of a nation-state, the idea of allocation serves a similar function to that of the distribution of the foreign relations power between the three organs of government: executive, legislative, and judicial. In states where the conduct of foreign relations has, as a matter of traditional doctrine, been seen as highly concentrated in the exercise of prerogative power by the executive, asking where the exercise of a particular power is allocated facilitates clearer analysis than blanket doctrines of judicial exclusion, deference or "speaking with one voice." It distinguishes, for example, matters that are plainly within the competence of the executive, such as the recognition of states, from matters concerning the protection of the rights of the individual affected by an exercise of the foreign relations power, where the judiciary may have power to intervene.

If this were the only dimension of allocation, one might reasonably conclude that a modern approach to constitutional analysis can perform the same task. However the resolution of foreign relations law issues requires the analysis of two other dimensions that lie outside the state: its relations with other states and its engagement with public international law. The first of these describes a *horizontal* dimension of allocation that is especially applicable to questions of legislative jurisdiction and state immunity. The second describes a *vertical* dimension, namely the question whether a particular issue is in fact properly capable of resolution within the national legal system at all or must rather be decided on the plane of international law or subject to its rules.

These considerations require an internationalist perspective. Why then is it necessary to interpose an intermediate set of rules of allocation between public international law, whose central concern is the relations between states, and the substantive rules of municipal law? Undoubtedly, the outlines of the solutions to problems of foreign relations law are supplied by public international law. But a law of foreign relations requires more than the simple transposition of such principles. An internationalist approach that seeks to address the external dimensions of foreign relations law solely through rules of reception of international law into the municipal legal system cannot address *when* reference is to be made to international law in the resolution of specific issues before the domestic court or when the domestic court of the forum must defer to the international legal system to determine the dispute.

Nor are the answers to these problems sufficiently to be found from an internal examination of the reach of municipal laws, since they engage the *interaction* of different legal systems (international law and the laws of other states). It is necessary to work out a much more fine-grained set of rules consistent with international law principles in order to provide workable solutions to current problems. In short, the allocative approach enables the task done for cross-border private law relations by the rules of the conflict of laws to be done for public law as well.[84]

One might object that such an approach transposes a methodology from private international law that is not capable of adaptation for public law issues. Indeed

[84] For a related argument for the application of conflict of laws techniques to explain the relationship between national law and international law, *see* Karen Knop, Ralf Michaels, & Annelise Riles, *International Law in Domestic Courts: A Conflict of Laws Approach*, 103 AM. SOC. INT'L L. PROC. 269 (2010).

private international law has itself traditionally sought to exclude direct consideration of public law issues from its scope.[85] Indeed, the prime function of choice of law in private international law has no direct analogue in public law matters. Neither the exercise of the external public power of the home state nor the treatment in domestic law of the foreign state necessarily involves the systematic application of choice of law rules leading to the application of either domestic or foreign law. Moreover, determinations of jurisdiction and applicable law in this sphere are not, as in private international law, primarily two-dimensional: determining horizontally the application of two competing systems of municipal law. They may also involve a three-dimensional vertical consideration: both of the application of public international law and its systems of dispute settlement; and internally within the state, determining the competence of the respective organs of government.

Seen in this light, an allocative conception of foreign relations law is not a mere transposition of a conflicts methodology developed for private law cross-border relations into the field of public law. Rather, it is an attempt to explain and synthesize key elements of a number of the other conceptions of foreign relations within a single coherent framework.

Such an approach provides a clearer explanation of the issues involved in determining the scope of prescriptive jurisdiction in public law cases.[86] An approach that seeks to analyze the reach of a domestic statute without reference to the interests of other states could, if unconstrained in its extraterritorial reach, result in serious conflict with the reserved domestic jurisdiction of other states. At the same time, a simple reference to the presumption of territoriality will not on its own suffice to determine what is the relevant connection to the territory, nor to deal with conduct that spans national borders and is "both here and there."[87] Principles of international law delimit the outer boundaries of permissible exercises of state jurisdiction. But on their own they do not resolve the interactions between the public laws of different states, when the exercise of jurisdiction overlaps. Nor are the international law principles of jurisdiction capable of resolving the liability of the state to individuals affected by its conduct when it has in fact already acted outside its own territorial borders.[88]

By contrast, an allocative approach asks how to balance the jurisdiction of the home state with the reserved jurisdiction of other states. Common law courts frequently invoke "international comity" in order to explain a process that is more accurately understood as an identification and application of the factors that connect given

[85] LORD COLLINS ET AL., DICEY, MORRIS, & COLLINS ON THE CONFLICT OF LAWS (15th ed. 2012), Rule 5: "English court have no jurisdiction to entertain an action . . . for the enforcement . . . of a penal, revenue or other public law of a foreign State."

[86] *See* MENZEL, *supra* note 83; MCLACHLAN, *supra* note 43, at 5.113–5.190.

[87] Libman v. The Queen, [1985] 2 S.C.R. 178, 208, 84 I.L.R. 672, *per* La Forest J.

[88] As the Supreme Court of Canada found when it sought to apply such principles to the extraterritorial conduct of Canadian officials in breach of fundamental human rights norms in *Khadr v. Canada (No. 1)*, 2008 SCC 28, [2008] 2 S.C.R. 125. *See* van Ert, *supra* note 40; MCLACHLAN, *supra* note 43, at 8.87–8.90.

conduct to a foreign state or to the home state, so as to identify whether there is a "sufficiently close connection to justify [the home] state in regulating the matter and perhaps also to override any competing rights of other states."[89]

So, too, the doctrines of state immunity and the foreign act of state have been explained as performing an allocative function. Hazel Fox writes that a principal function of the rules of state immunity is to serve "as a method of *allocating* jurisdiction between States relating to the prosecution of crimes and the settlement of claims by private litigants relating to State activities.... [I]t serves both as a sorting device between competing jurisdictions and as a holding device by which confrontation between States is avoided."[90] Mann argued that "the foreign act of State ought to be recognized and allowed effects... if it is done subject to or is recognized by that legal system which governs the legal relationship concerned."[91]

VI. Application in Cases Engaging Jus Cogens Norms

Analyzing foreign relations law problems as ones of allocation also provides a more coherent explanation for long-standing apparent inconsistencies in the application of international law at the domestic level, including in the hardest cases, such as the application of jus cogens norms by national courts.

Why, for example, was it that a peremptory norm could be applied directly to defeat a claim of immunity in the criminal claim against Pinochet, but not in subsequent civil claims brought before national courts?[92] In this enquiry "the jus cogens nature of the rule alleged to have been infringed does not provide an automatic answer."[93] Rather it is necessary to disaggregate the general issue depending upon the proper extent of jurisdiction and applicable law.

Where the peremptory norm speaks directly to the responsibility or the rights of the individual, the forum court may be able to give effect to it, provided that international law accords that court jurisdiction. So in *Pinochet* the House of Lords was concerned with a criminal application for extradition of Pinochet on charges of, inter alia, torture.

[89] Robert Jennings & Arthur Watts (eds.), Oppenheim's International Law (9th ed. 1992) vol. 1 "Peace" at 457–458; *see also* Vaughan Lowe & Christopher Staker, *Jurisdiction*, *in* International Law 313, 320 (Malcom D. Evans ed., 3d ed. 2010).

[90] Hazel Fox, The Law of State Immunity 2, 751 (2d ed. 2008) (emphasis added).

[91] Francis A. Mann, *The Sacrosanctity of the Foreign Act of State*, 59 L.Q.R. 42 (1943), *reprinted in* Francis A. Mann, Studies in International Law (1973), 420, 438; *see also* Lord Collins et al., Dicey, Morris & Collins on the Conflict of Laws (15th ed. 2012), at 5-047.

[92] R v. Bow Street Metropolitan Stipendiary Magistrate, ex p Pinochet Ugarte (No. 3), [2000] 1 A.C. 147 (HL); *cf.* Jones v. Ministry of Interior of the Kingdom of Saudi Arabia [2006] UKHL 26, [2007] 1 A.C. 270; Jurisdictional Immunities of the State (Germany v. Italy), [2012] I.C.J. Rep. 99.

[93] Jones v. Saudi Arabia, [49] *per* Lord Hoffmann.

The House held that "[t]he jus cogens nature of the international crime of torture justifies states in taking universal jurisdiction over torture wherever committed."[94] But the fact that an assumption of universal jurisdiction may be justified was not sufficient to answer the question whether the exercise of such jurisdiction was barred by another set of rules of customary international law: those relating to state immunity. On this crucial question, the decisive factor in the reasoning of the House was implied waiver by treaty. States (including in this case Chile) that had become party to the Convention against Torture (CAT) had implemented the prohibition on torture by expressly conferring jurisdiction on the state where an alleged offender was found and, by consenting to its exercise, necessarily waived immunity.[95] Once the House had decided that international law was the law applicable to the issue before it, the distinction (otherwise so fundamental to the reception of international law in the constitutional conception within a dualist state) between custom and treaty was simply incapable of addressing the issue. The House had to apply international law as a whole—custom and treaty—to determine whether immunity had been waived as a consequence of the treaty's conferral of universal jurisdiction upon national courts.

By contrast, the jus cogens character of the norm is not in itself sufficient to confer jurisdiction upon a national court in a civil claim against a foreign state or its officials. This would be to conflate the content of the substantive law with the prior question of whether the court seised has jurisdiction. In *Jurisdictional Immunities*, the International Court of Justice specifically held that "the rules which determine the scope and extent of jurisdiction and when that jurisdiction may be exercised do not derogate from those substantive rules which possess *jus cogens* status."[96] The common law courts have taken the same approach. So, in *Jones v. Saudi Arabia*, the House of Lords held that a civil claim of torture against a foreign state is barred by state immunity, despite the jus cogens nature of the norm. It found that there is no waiver of immunity in the CAT in civil cases akin to that in criminal cases that could operate to confer jurisdiction on the forum court, as states did not agree to confer universal jurisdiction upon each other's courts for civil claims, as they had in criminal cases.[97] An essential step in the reasoning in *Jones* is that the state asserting immunity is assuming state responsibility for the act. It follows from this that, if there is a denial of justice in the foreign state, its responsibility will be engaged on the international plane.

The position is different where the nature of the norm itself is one that can only properly be adjudicated on the international plane, because it concerns the relations

[94] *Pinochet*, 198 per Lord Browne-Wilkinson, citing *Demjanjuk v. Petrovsky*, 603 F. Supp. 1468 (N.D. Ohio 1985); 776 F. 2d 571 (6th Cir. 1985).

[95] *Id.*, 205; Convention against Torture and Other Cruel, Inhuman or Degrading Treatment or Punishment (CAT), 1465 U.N.T.S. 85, art. 5(2) (signed 10 December 1984, entered into force 26 June 1987).

[96] *Id.*, 141, [95].

[97] Jones v. Saudi Arabia, [25] *per* Lord Bingham: "article 14 of the Torture Convention does not provide for universal civil jurisdiction." *See also* Kazemi Estate v. Islamic Republic of Iran, 2014 SCC 62, [2014] 3 S.C.R. 176, [153]: "the peremptory norm prohibiting torture has not yet created an exception to state immunity from civil liability in cases of torture committed abroad."

between states. A national court does not adjudicate such a claim because the enforcement of the rule is allocated to the international plane. This is the case where the claim engages the rule against the use of force. As Lord Hope explained in *Gentle*: "The issue of legality in this area of international law belongs to the area of relations between states."[98] In *Margaret Jones*, the House of Lords was concerned with whether the prevention of an act of aggression could constitute a defense to a criminal charge. The crime of aggression could not be invoked before a domestic court, since it is "intrinsically and inextricably linked to the commission of aggression by a state,"[99] which involves the actions of the states on the international plane.[100]

Where a national court does have jurisdiction and is called upon to apply foreign law to a civil claim, it may be required to give effect to international law, where the rule of foreign law offends a peremptory norm. In allocative terms, this is because the peremptory norm is applicable as a super choice of law rule. In *Oppenheimer v. Cattermole*, the House was faced with determining the applicability of a Nazi decree that had deprived Jews of their German citizenship on emigration. It held that ordinarily the court must give effect to the jurisdiction of a foreign state over its own nationals and assets situate within its territories.[101] But the law in question in this case was different. As Lord Cross put it, such a law "constitutes so grave an infringement of human rights that the courts of this country ought to refuse to recognise it as a law at all," it being "part of the public policy of this country that our courts should give effect to clearly established rules of international law."[102]

The same principle was extended to other breaches of the mandatory provisions of international law in *Kuwait Airways*.[103] In that case, the House held that, although Iraqi law was otherwise applicable to the claim, an Iraqi decree purporting to validate all acts arising from Iraq's invasion of Kuwait could not be applied. It was contrary to the express provisions of a UN Security Council resolution.

The common feature of both of these cases is that the norm of international law in question was one that has a peremptory character—either in customary international law (as in the case of rule against discrimination in *Oppenheimer*) or by virtue of Article 103 of the UN Charter. It is this special feature that distinguishes both of these cases from the ordinary rule (referred to under the rubric of the foreign act of state doctrine) requiring the court to give effect to the jurisdiction of a foreign state within its own territory, a rule frequently applied by English courts to cases of expropriation in foreign states.[104] The ordinary rule is premised upon the international law rule of the sovereign equality of states. But the forum court is entitled to decide that the obligation of respect owed to the act of the foreign sovereign is dislodged by a higher norm within the international legal system that claims peremptory application.

[98] R (Gentle) v. Prime Minister [2008] UKHL 20, [2008] 1 A.C. 136, [24].

[99] R v. Jones (Margaret) [2006] UKHL 16, [2007] 1 A.C. 136, [64].

[100] *Id.*, [30]. [101] [1976] A.C. 249, 282. [102] *Id.*, 278.

[103] Kuwait Airways Corp v. Iraqi Airways Co. (Nos. 4 & 5), [2002] UKHL 19, [2002] 2 A.C. 883.

[104] Williams & Humbert Ltd. v. W & H Trade Marks (Jersey) Ltd., [1986] 1 A.C. 368.

So too the foreign act of state doctrine finds its limits where the officials of the home state are sued for their alleged complicity in the acts of foreign states outside their own territory, where those acts constitute breaches of peremptory norms. This point came to the fore in the recent judgment of the U.K. Supreme Court in *Belhaj v. Straw*,[105] in which a British Minister and high officials were sued for their alleged complicity in acts of torture committed by U.S. officials outside the territory of either state.

One way of explaining the foreign act of state doctrine, developed by Bjorge and Miles in their chapter for this *Handbook*,[106] is through a constitutional law analysis: that the doctrine is primarily concerned with the separation of powers between the judiciary and the executive within the domestic constitutional order. Undoubtedly such a conception provides part of the answer. However, on its own, this does not explain (as those authors conclude[107]) when the courts will find the claim to be admissible and when not. When should the constitutional function of the judiciary in the protection of the rights of the individual take precedence over the constitutional power of the executive to conduct foreign affairs? A constitutionalist conception cannot in any event address all dimensions of the issues raised by the justiciability of claims involving the conduct of foreign states, since of their nature these also engage both the external relations of the home state with foreign states and the role of public international law.

Lord Sumption in his minority judgment sought to explain the distinction by setting up the jus cogens character of the norm as an exception to what he saw as the ordinary rule requiring judicial abstention in all other cases of what he termed as "international law act of state."[108] Such an approach, however, conflates jurisdiction with applicable law, by treating the substantive law character of the norm as the determinant of jurisdiction.[109]

An allocative approach analyzes the issue more directly, by asking, as Lord Mance did in his leading judgment, why the English Court, which undoubtedly had jurisdiction over the British government officials, should not require them to answer for their alleged complicity in such serious breaches of fundamental norms.[110] No deference to a foreign state can derogate from the principle that officials are answerable before their own courts and may not escape liability at home for fundamental breaches of peremptory norms simply because they are complicit with the illegal acts of the officials of other states. Such claims are properly allocated to the courts of the home state. Otherwise those claims "could not be pursued anywhere in the world."[111]

[105] [2017] UKSC 3, [2017] A.C. 964. *See* Eirik Bjorge & Cameron Miles, *Crown and Foreign Acts of State before British Courts:* Rahmatullah, Belhaj, *and the Separation of Powers*, ch. 40 in this volume; McLachlan, *supra* note 79.

[106] *See* Bjorge & Miles, *supra* note 105.

[107] *Id.* at pp.730–731.

[108] Belhaj v. Straw, [2017] UKSC 3, [2017] A.C. 964 at [234–240].

[109] For detailed critique, *see* McLachlan, *supra* note 79, at 398–400.

[110] *Id.* at [81–102] (approving Habib v. Commonwealth of Australia, [2010] FCAFC 12, (2010) 265 A.L.R. 50; Moti v. The Queen, [2011] HCA 50, (2011) 245 C.L.R. 456).

[111] *Id.* at [102].

The cases in which the foreign act of state doctrine has justified the abstention of the domestic court are not explained simply on the basis, as Lord Sumption thought, that all acts of a foreign state outside its own territory are nonjusticiable (unless falling with his exception). Rather, they concern situations in which the issue engages a rule that of its nature can only be determined on the international plane and according to public international law, such as a boundary dispute between two sovereign states[112] or the liabilities of states for the debts of an international organization of which they were members.[113] Such cases are allocated to the international plane.

VII. Conclusion

It is remarkable that the relation between public international law—the legal system that all states have in common—and national legal systems in the exercise of foreign relations has to date proved so resistant to comparative investigation. One reason for this has been that the approach that one takes depends upon one's conception of the function of the law in this field. Differences in starting points can result in whole elements of the field being excluded from the enquiry as legally irrelevant. It is only by exposing those conceptions to critical examination that legal scholars can move beyond a mere exchange of differences and begin to analyze the actual legal problems that arise.

Seen in this light the present comparative investigation offers the prospect of saving the study of foreign relations law from isolationism. Instead it may promote engagement between states in the exploration of a common issue of great importance in our times: the regulation of the interface between international law and national constitutions in the control of the external exercise of public power.

[112] Buttes Gas v. Hammer (No. 3), [1982] A.C. 888 (HL).

[113] J H Rayner (Mincing Lane) Ltd. v. Department of Trade and Industry, [1990] 2 A.C. 418 (HL).

CHAPTER 3

FOREIGN RELATIONS LAW

Comparison as Invention

KAREN KNOP

I. Introduction

THIS *Handbook* considers the prospect of comparative foreign relations law. All legal systems deal with foreign relations issues, but few have a field of "foreign relations law." Given that comparison is necessarily generative, one question for scholars from legal systems without such a field is what the trade-offs of introducing foreign relations law might be—in particular, for international law.

The two starting points for this chapter are that fields of law are inventions, and that fields matter as analytical frames. Take family law as an example. There was no such thing as U.S. family law in the early nineteenth century. The law of husband and wife was proximate to the law of parent and child. But, as legal topics, they were equally closely related to the law of master and servant because the social order of the time assumed that the head of the household was husband, father, and master. Only later was family law separated from labor law, coinciding with "the emancipation of the servant from indenture and slavery and with the emergence of the laborer and employee selling his work for a wage."[1] The invention of family law also illustrates why framing matters. Its parameters have been challenged at various points, including by scholars who think that the household would be a better unit of analysis than the sentimental idea that there is something exceptional about the intimate family. We can see from the family law example how a new field of law can reorganize laws and issues, include or exclude different actors, foreground or background different facts, change what principles are relevant to the analysis, and so on. This carries risks. Indeed, there has been strenuous resistance to the introduction of some fields of law for such reasons.

[1] Janet Halley, *What Is Family Law?: A Genealogy Part I*, 23 YALE J.L. & HUM. 1, 2 (2011).

The adoption of administrative law in England is a good illustration. Viewed as a continental concept—and contrary to Dicey's rule-of-law principle of equality that subjected all alike to the ordinary law and the ordinary courts—administrative law was long rejected as "an exotic brand of un-English anti-law" and even "an almost unqualified evil."[2] Only in the second half of the twentieth century did it become an accepted field of English law. And more recently, in proposing "global administrative law" as a field, its originators recognized that "casting global governance in administrative terms might lead to its stabilization and legitimation in ways that privilege current power-holders and reinforce the dominance of Northern and Western concepts of law and sound governance."[3]

Creating a new field of law may not simply be additive. Even if fields of law need not be mutually exclusive—as they are in the classical division of private law into persons, things, and actions—a new field may intentionally or unintentionally jostle, compete with, or annex existing fields.[4] By far the best-known example of foreign relations law, the U.S. field is sometimes understood as a threat to international law. An international lawyer outside the United States may therefore be apprehensive about introducing foreign relations law into legal thought in her country where a constitutional or an administrative lawyer might not be. As the best-stocked cabinet of issues and ideas, U.S. law would be likely to generate the field elsewhere in the process of comparison. But anecdotal evidence suggests that some scholars, particularly outside the United States, see the nationalist or sovereigntist strains of U.S. foreign relations law, and perhaps even just its use as a template, as demoting international law.[5]

Because "comparative foreign relations law" is a new project, these concerns are somewhat free floating and inchoate. In this chapter, I try as a Canadian international lawyer interested in the potential of a Canadian field of foreign relations law to identify what the anxieties and opportunities are relative to public international law. The chapter begins by asking whether, for comparative purposes, international lawyers' puzzlement or apprehension about the field can be alleviated by using international law to inventory its issues. Finding that international law is not sufficient, the chapter turns next to comparative constitutional law and comparative administrative law as existing domestic-law launch pads that have already addressed the perennial problem of standpoint in comparative law. These too are found wanting. Why not, then, profit

[2] Jason N. E. Varuhas, *Taxonomy and Public Law*, *in* THE UNITY OF PUBLIC LAW? DOCTRINAL, THEORETICAL AND COMPARATIVE PERSPECTIVES 39, 42 (Mark Elliott, Jason N. E. Varuhas, & Shona Wilson Stark eds., 2018) (quoting from a 1943 book review).

[3] Benedict Kingsbury, Nico Krisch, & Richard B. Stewart, *The Emergence of Global Administrative Law*, 68 LAW & CONTEMP. PROBS. 15, 27 (Summer 2005). *See also* Karen Knop, *Elegance in Global Law: Reading Neil Walker*, Intimations of Global Law, 8 TRANSNAT'L L. THEORY 330 (2017) (book review).

[4] On methods of legal classification, *see*, e.g., Emily Sherwin, *Legal Taxonomy*, 15 LEGAL THEORY 25 (2009). *Compare* David Kennedy, *The Disciplines of International Law and Policy*, 12 LEIDEN J. INT'L L. 9 (1999) (analyzing the biases and blind spots that emerge from interactions among the fields of public international law, international economic law, comparative law, and international relations).

[5] *See* René Urueña, *Domestic Application of International Law in Latin America*, ch. 32 in this volume, at p.581.

from the well-developed field of U.S. foreign relations law as an initial set of parameters and rely on the dynamics of the comparative process to reveal any national preconceptions and adjust the parameters accordingly? The chapter goes on to sketch three types of concerns that the U.S. experience with the field has raised or might raise for international lawyers. The primary focus here is on foreign relations law as a frame: what it makes comparable, what its starting point is, what it relates to one another. One response to the U.S. experience indeed might be that a frame is not a picture: foreign relations law can accommodate internationalism as well as nationalism, more law or more politics, and so on. Hence, comparison can promote, as well as demonstrate, the field's substantive openness.[6] In contrast, the response sketched in this chapter turns on two aesthetic qualities of the frame: greater breadth and greater detail. Drawing on Campbell McLachlan's innovative "allocative" conception of foreign relations law, the chapter suggests that this conception might be adapted so as to turn anxieties about international law into opportunities.[7]

II. Invention—Where to Start?

On the assumption that we need to define a field of foreign relations law for some purposes of comparison, the task is to find a suitable standpoint from which to define the field. An obvious candidate is public international law. Thus the inward face of foreign relations law would equate with the generally recognized area known as "international law in domestic legal systems" or, more narrowly, "international law in domestic courts." Campbell McLachlan describes such a conception as internationalist: "to mediate the inward reception of international law into the domestic legal system, providing both the rules and processes of reception and extending also to those substantive elements of international law that are themselves directly applicable within the national legal system."[8] A purely internationalist conception of foreign relations law in McLachlan's sense would lend itself readily to comparison because the rules and processes of reception have received extensive national, international, and comparative attention over the past decade and a half. Public international law could also generate the outward face of foreign relations by identifying the domestic law relevant to interstate issues such as entry into treaties or the use of force. Unlike international law in domestic legal systems, however, this outward face has received only issue-specific comparative attention to date.

[6] *See* Oona A. Hathaway, *A Comparative Foreign Relations Law Agenda: Opportunities and Challenges*, ch. 5 in this volume (including "large-n" empirical studies among the methods of correcting for the usual overrepresentation of North America and Europe in comparative law projects).

[7] Campbell McLachlan, *Five Conceptions of the Function of Foreign Relations Law*, ch. 2 in this volume, at p.36; Campbell McLachlan, Foreign Relations Law 7–10 (2014); Campbell McLachlan, *The Allocative Function of Foreign Relations Law*, 82 Brit. Y.B. Int'l L. 349 (2012).

[8] McLachlan, *Five Conceptions*, *supra* note 7, at 24.

But public international law would inventory only a subset of a state's foreign relations issues. First, foreign relations issues can operate below international law's radar. Public international law does not recognize substate actors as legal subjects and therefore does not register the potential for actors such as cities to conduct their own foreign policy unless that policy places the state in violation of its substantive international obligations. However, the scope of this possibility in domestic law is attracting increasing attention as global networks of cities take coordinated action on such issues as climate change, sometimes with reference to international laws not binding on their own state.[9] Second, public international law overlooks domestic law issues that reflect internationalization by "policy consciousness" as opposed to the application of international law, as Robert Wai describes the Supreme Court of Canada's approach to private international law (conflict of laws).[10] Notably, U.S. scholars consider private international law to be a potential part of foreign relations law,[11] but public international law captures only those aspects where public international law is in play: for example, where there is an applicable treaty on private international law, where the foreign law in question violates public international law, or where inter-state legal relations are a reason for the government to intervene against jurisdiction on foreign relations grounds. Third, public international law does not readily generate foreign relations issues for which it merely sets the background conditions. For instance, international law does not impose a duty on states to exercise their right of diplomatic protection under international law on behalf of their nationals, whereas domestic law may require states to act.[12]

Thus international law cannot generate the entirety of foreign relations law. We might therefore proceed instead from the comparison of each of the national fields of law that contribute to foreign relations law: comparative constitutional law as applied to foreign relations, for instance, might capture a great deal.[13] But the relevant fields may vary with the state. U.S. foreign relations law is mainly housed in constitutional law, while in other legal systems, administrative law may be more relevant. To continue with the cities example, U.S. constitutional law determines whether a city can conduct foreign policy, whereas administrative law may govern the issue in other countries as a matter of the city's statutory grant of power.[14] Thus the field cannot simply be launched

[9] *See* Ernest A. Young, *Foreign Affairs Federalism in the United States*, ch. 15 in this volume, at p.264.

[10] Robert Wai, *In the Name of the International: The Supreme Court of Canada and the Internationalist Transformation of Canadian Private International Law*, 39 CAN. Y.B. INT'L L. 117, 120 (2001).

[11] *See* William S. Dodge, *International Comity in Comparative Perspective*, ch. 39 in this volume, at p.701.

[12] *See* Draft Articles on Diplomatic Protection, Report of the International Law Commission on the work of its fifty-eighth session (UN Doc. A/61/10), in *Yearbook of the International Law Commission 2006*, vol. 2, part 2 (New York: UN, 2006), at 28–29, 53–55 (UN Doc. A/CN.4/SER.A/2006/Add.1) (commentary on draft arts. 2 and 19).

[13] *See* Tom Ginsburg, *Comparative Foreign Relations Law: A National Constitutions Perspective*, ch. 4 in this volume, at p.64.

[14] *See* Michael Taggart, *Globalization, "Local" Foreign Policy, and Administrative Law*, *in* INSIDE AND OUTSIDE CANADIAN ADMINISTRATIVE LAW: ESSAYS IN HONOUR OF DAVID MULLAN 259 (Grant Huscroft & Michael Taggart eds., 2006).

as a subfield of comparative constitutional law, comparative administrative law, or another body of existing comparative domestic law in which issues of standpoint may already have been tackled.

Why not then use U.S. foreign relations law as the starting parameters on the view that any structural bias in those parameters would be corrected through the iterative process of comparative law? Comparison does not imply similarity or harmonization, and, in any event, the parameters could be recursive and self-reflexive.[15] Indeed, comparative law can be, and has been, deployed as a way of generating critical distance: recognizing that one's own legal approach is not universal. From this perspective, comparative foreign relations law may prompt reflection on the U.S. field as well, rather than making it the de facto index.

Comparative law's capacity for subversiveness—its ability to unsettle by showing a given legal system's assumptions and approaches to be a matter of choice rather than simply common sense—is one reason that critical international law scholars on the left have been drawn to "comparative international law." In the West, Anthea Roberts's *Is International Law International?*, together with several recent collections, has brought the spotlight back to comparative international law.[16] In previous periods, comparison waxed and waned with the Cold War divide between Western and Soviet approaches to international law, and the divide between developed and developing world perspectives in the post-decolonization period. Roberts's 2017 book coincides with the prominence of China and Russia and documents differences in outlook between the five permanent members of the UN Security Council. Critical international law scholars took up comparative international law a decade earlier as a form of critique,[17] and several have welcomed her book.[18]

In the United States, Samuel Moyn approaches Roberts's data as a way to substantiate the parochialism of U.S. approaches to international law. For Moyn, however, the salutary deprovincializing effect of comparative international law goes hand in hand with reservations about the dominant position of foreign relations law in U.S. law

[15] *See, e.g.*, Gerhard Dannemann, *Comparative Law: Study of Similarities or Differences*, *in* The Oxford Handbook of Comparative Law 383 (Mathias Reiman & Reinhard Zimmermann eds., 2006).

[16] Anthea Roberts, Is International Law International? (2017); Comparative International Law (Anthea Roberts, Paul B. Stephan, Pierre-Hugues Verdier, & Mila Versteeg eds., 2018); Anthea Roberts, Paul B. Stephan, Pierre-Hugues Verdier, & Mila Versteeg, *Comparative International Law: Framing the Field*, 109 Am. J. Int'l L. 467 (2015).

[17] *See, e.g.*, Symposium: *Comparative Visions of Global Public Order*, 46 Harv. Int'l L.J. 387 (2005) (Part I) and 47 Harv. Int'l L.J. 223 (2006) (Part II); Boris N. Mamlyuk & Ugo Mattei, *Comparative International Law*, 36 Brook. J. Int'l L. 385 (2011) (including a brief history of comparative international law).

[18] *See* Martti Koskenniemi, *Foreword* to Roberts, *supra* note 16, at xiii; Miriam Bak McKenna, Book Review, 87 Nordic J. Int'l L. 221 (2018); Samuel Moyn, *The Parochialism of American Cosmopolitanism*, Sept. 15, 2017, Lawfare, *available at* https://www.lawfareblog.com/parochialism-american-cosmopolitanism (book review).

schools. In other words, U.S. foreign relations law is *why* U.S. international lawyers need comparative international law. Moyn writes:

> Many of our debates about international law seem to be little more than local debates about how to wield our country's power, refracted into an ostensibly non-local rhetoric. . . . how nationalist in their outlook even our cosmopolitans usually are, wittingly or unwittingly. None of this is necessarily a matter of intention, let alone of malice. . . . But Americans today benefit structurally from the centrality and power of our country, and can expect others to engage with our framing of debates . . .
>
> [M]ost American practitioners and scholars of international law—unlike those in other places—cannot actually train in [international law], except through the portal and as an offshoot of constitutional law and especially foreign affairs law, or nowadays through so-called "national security law." Even for liberals, international law is sociologically a topic that many have reached through the indirect path of other fields, especially at the major law schools. This is most certainly true of human rights law, in the tradition of Louis Henkin, long a constitutional and foreign affairs scholar and later an icon of human rights law American-style.[19]

In a similar vein, Roberts, then based in the United Kingdom, describes a reaction that I also have heard among non-U.S. international lawyers. A "left-leaning US international lawyer" warned her against developing a field of foreign relations law in the United Kingdom because "[t]he turn from international law to foreign relations law was an inherently conservative move."[20] Roberts does not pursue the matter, but registers doubts both about this account of the U.S. field and about whether it would hold for other countries as well because the field "encouraged you to look at international law from a particular national perspective instead of from the perspective of the international community? Or did that depend on the nation in question?"[21]

Several points in this vignette are worth drawing out. The first is the starting point of this chapter that analytical frames such as fields of law matter. Hence, the creation of a field—even as a rough byproduct of comparison in the case of this *Handbook*—rightly attracts scrutiny. Second, the assumption is that the development of foreign relations law is a turn away from international law. In the United States, this assumption might be questioned—foreign relations law is a potential gateway to international law where none might otherwise exist—but it might be accurate for countries like the United Kingdom. As Roberts also notes, the turn away from international law may be intended by some but not other U.S. foreign relations scholars. Regardless, new fields of law exist in relation to existing fields and have effects on them, conceptual and sociological, intended and unintended.

A third point follows from the overall message of Roberts's book that the "international" differs from one country to another. For instance, she describes how, unlike the international law students she taught in the United States, her U.K. students would not

[19] Moyn, *supra* note 18. [20] Roberts, *supra* note 16, at xx. [21] *Id.*

think to ask of an international law rule whether it was in their state's political interests and, if not, whether their state should comply.[22] It is not only, then, the constitutional, administrative, and other areas of domestic law relevant to foreign relations that vary with the country. The international law that combines with them to make up the field of foreign relations law is a national view of international law, as Moyn observes even of U.S. cosmopolitanism. Thus if we are imagining what anxieties international lawyers elsewhere might have about a field of foreign relations law, the apprehensiveness might also be related to the predominant example as a reflection of and carrier for U.S. approaches to international law.

III. Anxieties

Relative to public international law, then, we can imagine three types of anxieties about a field of foreign relations law.

Displacing International Law

First is the possible substitution effect that foreign relations law might have on public international law in the production of legal knowledge. Depending on how a curriculum is determined, the introduction of a foreign relations law course or the addition of a foreign relations component to the basic constitutional law or administrative law course could displace the study of public international law as a field. Transnational law might be a precedent for this effect. In some North American law schools that instituted a first-year course in transnational law, anecdotal evidence suggests that demand for public international law has dropped in the upper years. More students now receive the basics of international law, but fewer know it in depth, and they are less likely to approach public international law as a legal system than instrumentally as one possible tool in the legal toolkit for solving transnational problems.

As regards scholarship, Roberts flags the U.S. system of student-edited law reviews, which creates a greater incentive for U.S. scholars to write on foreign relations law than on international law.[23] Whereas articles on international law subjects tend to be accepted by specialized student-edited law reviews (such as the *Harvard International Law Journal*), foreign relations law articles are of interest to the higher ranked and more prestigious generalist student-edited law reviews (such as the *Harvard Law Review*). Elsewhere, international law journals are not necessarily less prestigious, on the one hand, and, on the other, generalist law journals do not disfavor certain subject matters. Hence, the professional incentives for international law scholars to shift into foreign relations law are not the same.

[22] *Id.* at xviii. [23] Roberts, *supra* note 16, at 97–98.

Introducing foreign relations law as a field may also have the effect of displacing international law by routinely putting it side by side with domestic law as alternative means to an end. The rise of interest in "international law in domestic courts" was partly due to the notion that domestic courts could improve on or replace international compliance processes, but foreign relations law might introduce and normalize soup-to-nuts comparability and substitutability. On the one hand, as Tom Ginsburg argues from a national constitutions perspective in this *Handbook*, substitutability would be an advance in institutional design and could go either way.[24] On the other hand, as he also discusses, the process of horizontal diffusion and borrowing of constitutional ideas is not purely a matter of local needs or demands. Constitutions often end up with rules that reflect fashions and trends among perceived peer countries,[25] while imposed constitutions can implement outsiders' foreign policy priorities for the country in question.[26]

What would current trends predict about introducing comparability? Constitutions increasingly refer to particular treaties and international organizations, but the U.S. Constitution has also been highly influential abroad.[27] The upshot is that introducing comparability through foreign relations law is not cleanly detachable from the U.S. field's legacy of looking to constitutional law *as such* rather than considering international law. McLachlan identifies a "constitutional" conception of foreign relations law, in which the field "is devoted to the distribution of the foreign relations power between the organs of government . . . and to the regulation of the exercise of the foreign relations power where it infringes the rights of the private individual."[28] Louis Henkin's impetus for establishing the field in the 1970s can be classified as primarily constitutionalist. Henkin sought to educate U.S. public officials, lawyers, students of foreign affairs, and citizens alike that when their country acted in the world, its foreign policy had to comply with the Constitution, by which he had in mind both the structures of government—separation of powers, federalism—and the bill of rights.[29] The perspective here is not simply that constitutional law sometimes safeguards human rights better than international law. That lesson was internalized by international lawyers after 9/11, when the UN counterterrorism campaign ended the sunny assumption of the 1980s and 1990s uniting international lawyers, new constitution drafters, and human rights activists that international law provides equivalent or better protection

[24] Ginsburg, *supra* note 13; Tom Ginsburg, *Constitutions and Foreign Relations Law: The Dynamics of Substitutes and Complements*, 111 AJIL UNBOUND 326, 328–330 (2017).

[25] Ginsburg, *supra* note 13, at p.70.

[26] The term is from Noah Feldman, *Imposed Constitutionalism*, 37 CONN. L. REV. 857 (2005).

[27] Ginsburg, *supra* note 13, at p.68.

[28] McLachlan, *Five Conceptions*, *supra* note 7, at p.24.

[29] LOUIS HENKIN, FOREIGN AFFAIRS AND THE CONSTITUTION 7 (1972). Foreign relations law was also of interest to U.S. scholars earlier in the twentieth century. *See* Curtis A. Bradley, *What Is Foreign Relations Law?*, ch. 1 in this volume, at p.11.

to individuals.[30] Rather, a constitutionalist conception of foreign relations law always looks to the extraterritorial projection of the national bill of rights.[31]

Discounting International Law

A second, related anxiety is the discounting effect of foreign relations law on public international law: does promoting a field of foreign relations law reinforce the idea that international law is not real law? Alejandro Lorite Escorihuela helpfully distinguishes between dualism in the sense of the monism/dualism debate familiar to international lawyers and what he describes as "deep dualism" with reference to one group of prominent U.S. scholars who span international law and foreign relations law.[32] The familiar debate decides whether international law and domestic law are one system (monism) or two (dualism). As part of a single legal system, both are law. Dualism conventionally takes both international law and domestic law as legal systems and concentrates attention on whether and how one system recognizes the law of the other. The debate is most often studied from the inward-looking perspective of domestic law, the main question being whether the domestic legal system requires international law to be transformed into domestic law by statute or otherwise. But whatever the answer, international law, like foreign law, is understood to be law somewhere else.

In the work on international law and foreign relations law by the authors whom he calls the "nationalist school of international law in the United States," Lorite Escorihuela points to a deeper version of dualism or "dualism taken to its ultimate consequence." Logically, a domestic legal system "can actually transform anything into law through its internal mechanisms, or sources." In other words, dualist domestic law can take account of international law while withholding from it partially or entirely the status of law.[33] Thus, looking outward onto the realm of inter-state relations, as opposed to inward, a deep dualist can find that:

> Methodologically speaking, the world of "international law" . . . is really the world of international politics, and so we should, and will, talk about international legal questions as part of the dynamics of international relations. The proper methodological tools are those of political science and political theory, since approaching international law with a legal eye, as if it were actual law, is either a scientific mistake, or a cunning ideological maneuver aimed at hiding the realities of international relations . . . [34]

[30] *See*, e.g., Antonios Tzanakopoulos, *Mapping the Engagement of Domestic Courts with International Law*, Final Report of International Law Association Study Group on Principles on the Engagement of Domestic Courts with International Law, 10–11 (2016), *available at* http://www.ila-hq.org/index.php/study-groups.

[31] *See*, e.g., Louis Henkin, *The Constitution as Compact and as Conscience: Individual Rights Abroad and at our Gates*, 27 WM. & MARY L. REV. 11 (1985).

[32] Alejandro Lorite Escorihuela, *Cultural Relativism the American Way: The Nationalist School of International Law in the United States*, 5 GLOBAL JURIST (Issue 1, Article 2) 26 (2005).

[33] *Id.* [34] *Id.*

Deep dualism correlates with the two realms and a border that Lorite Escorihuela identifies in this scholarship: an outer, or inter-state, realm of politics and anarchy (in which international law is not law) and an inner realm of law and order (in which law is not international) with a borderland in between where international law exists. Regardless of whether one accepts Lorite Escorihuela's account of these authors, his point is structurally apposite. As others have also noted, the field of foreign relations law is structured as a divide between an internal realm in which law is the default and an external realm in which foreign relations is the default.[35]

Let us return to comparative international law for a moment. It functions as a critique of international law not only because it exposes the situatedness of international lawyers in their own national contexts, but because it exposes the politics of international law. In the conceptual world to which international lawyers are accustomed, relations between states are governed by law, and politics is notionally assigned to the domestic jurisdiction of states. Instead, comparative international law demonstrates empirically the political inflection of all universal norms. Politics is the punch line of the critique. In contrast, the outward face of foreign relations law begins with foreign relations, that is, with politics. Its origins story is the battle to limit the executive's power or the royal prerogative for foreign affairs. The origin is McLachlan's "exclusionary" conception of foreign relations law: "the external actions of the State are shielded from internal purview; concentrating the exercise of the foreign relations power in the hands of a single executive organ of government."[36] From an international law perspective, foreign relations law dualism threatens to return foreign relations to a world in which the outside of the state is presumptively a political space unless constrained by (domestic) law. The emergence of domestic-law limits may be progressive from the perspective of constitutional or administrative law. Indeed, international law was not straightforwardly available to control colonial governance, and thus any kind of law that availed was progressive.[37] Nonetheless, creating a field of foreign relations law risks restoring the factory settings for international law, so to speak, because its conceptual starting point is the unconstrained discretion of the executive, the Crown, to act externally in the world.

Distorting International Law

Finally, comparative foreign relations law could also change or distort the internal workings of international law. One example is the effect that a new baseline of knowledge about domestic law could conceivably have on the law of treaties. Under the Vienna Convention on the Law of Treaties (VCLT), states have no need

[35] *See also* Urueña, *supra* note 5, at p.581; Thomas Poole, *The Constitution and Foreign Affairs*, 69 Current Leg. Probs. 143 (2016).

[36] McLachlan, *Five Conceptions*, *supra* note 7, at pp.23–24.

[37] *See* Thomas Poole, Reason of State: Law, Prerogative and Empire (2015).

to inform themselves about their negotiating partners' constitutional arrangements for treaty-making. They are entitled to assume that heads of state, heads of government, ministers of foreign affairs, and several other categories of foreign official represent their state for the purpose of expressing that state's consent to be bound by a treaty.[38] And, more generally, a state's internal law cannot provide a justification for its failure to perform a treaty.[39] The state is bound under international law, and any internal-law obstacles are up to that state to surmount. When a state's consent to be bound by the treaty has been expressed in violation of its internal law, however, the VCLT makes an exception if that violation was "manifest" and concerned an internal rule of "fundamental importance." To be manifest, the violation must be "objectively evident to any state conducting itself in the matter in accordance with normal practice and good faith."[40] What is manifest, then, depends on what is ordinarily known about the internal law of the state in question. The rules most often invoked before domestic courts adjudicating the validity of a treaty are those requiring legislative participation in the treaty-making process.[41] In the *Case concerning the Land and Maritime Boundary*, however, the International Court of Justice (ICJ) rejected Nigeria's argument that an agreement with Cameroon signed by the Nigerian head of state was invalid because its Supreme Military Council had not ratified the agreement as required by the Nigerian Constitution. While the constitutional rules on treaty-signing authority are of fundamental importance, the ICJ found that the violation was not manifest because the limitation was not properly publicized, particularly given that the VCLT recognizes heads of state as representing their state by virtue of their functions. The Court stated that "there is no general legal obligation for states to keep themselves informed of legislative and constitutional developments in other States which are or may become important for the international relations of those States."[42]

By collecting constitutional law and practice on treaties across a range of states, comparative foreign law would change, and potentially equalize, what is known about states' internal law. At present, the VCLT rules incentivize a state to comply with its constitutional process for treaty-making because the state can be held to a treaty even if it does not. This also favors the efficiency of the international legal order over the constitutional order and the principle of democracy in the case of a violation. Greater awareness of internal law would shift the incentives to other states negotiating with that

[38] Vienna Convention on the Law of Treaties art. 7(2), May 23, 1969, 1155 U.N.T.S. 331.

[39] *Id.*, art. 27.

[40] *Id.*, art. 46. *See generally* Michael Bothe, *1969 Vienna Convention: Article 46*, *in* 2 The Vienna Convention on the Law of Treaties: A Commentary 1090 (Olivier Corten & Pierre Klein eds., 2011); Thilo Rensmann, *Article 46*, *in* Vienna Convention on the Law of Treaties: A Commentary 837 (Oliver Dörr & Kirsten Schmalenbach eds., 2d ed. 2018).

[41] *See* Benedetto Conforti & Angelo Labella, *Invalidity and Termination of Treaties: The Role of National Courts*, 1 Eur. J. Int'l L. 44, 52–55 (1990).

[42] Land and Maritime Boundary between Cameroon and Nigeria (Cameroon v. Nigeria), 2002 I.C.J. 303, paras. 258, 265–266. *See also* Maritime Delimitation in the Indian Ocean (Somalia v. Kenya), Preliminary Objections, 2017 I.C.J. 3, para. 49.

state and away from holding a state to the treaty because a violation would be more likely to be "manifest." In this respect, comparative foreign relations law would effectively bring the VCLT closer to a 2017 judgment by the Supreme Court of Ghana, which held that democratic constitutions should be promoted and thus foreign states entering into an international agreement with Ghana have a duty to conduct basic due diligence to ensure that the agreement complies with its constitutional law and is therefore enforceable: "A State, with all the resources at its disposal, cannot absolve itself from its failure to perform this basic inquiry."[43]

The interpretation of international law by domestic courts offers another example of the potential for a field of foreign relations law to distort the workings of international law by introducing the separation of powers—and thereby deliberately national interest—into what international law means.[44] Recent comparative and country studies of the interpretation of international law by domestic courts reveal interesting national variations in how fully or accurately courts apply the VCLT rules of interpretation (whether as a treaty binding on the state or as customary international law).[45] Some courts apply them without citation or do so more in spirit. Others rely more on international or foreign jurisprudence than on the VCLT rules themselves. Yet others merge international law's rules with the state's canons of interpretation for domestic law. Two generalizations can nevertheless be made. One is that the courts of most states recognize broadly that international law's rules of interpretation apply. The other, as significant, is that any national considerations that enter into the interpretation tend to be those of national law as opposed to national interest.

In contrast, U.S. courts often defer to the executive on what a treaty means. By introducing the logic of the separation of powers, U.S. foreign relations law opens the

[43] Mrs. Margaret Banful & Henry Nana Boakye v. Attorney-General & Minister of Interior, Writ number J1/7/2016 (June 22, 2017) (Supreme Court of Ghana) (per Akuffo, C.J.), *available at* https://ghalii.org/gh/judgment/supreme-court/2017/21, discussed in Ernest Yaw Ako & Richard Frimpong Oppong, *Foreign Relations Law in the Constitution and Courts of Commonwealth African Countries*, ch. 33 in this volume, at p.595.

[44] My hypothetical is that national interest might lead a state to adopt a highly strained interpretation of a treaty that differs from the interpretation(s) of all other state parties and even one inconsistent with all of its earlier positions, but one that is nonetheless among those possible under the applicable international law rules for the interpretation of treaties.

Why domestic courts should apply the international law rules of interpretation is a complex question. *See* André Nollkaemper, *Grounds for the Application of International Rules of Interpretation in National Courts*, *in* The Interpretation of International Law by Domestic Courts: Uniformity, Diversity, Convergence 34 (Helmut Philipp Aust & Georg Nolte eds., 2016).

[45] In this *Handbook*, *compare* Shaheed Fatima, *The Domestic Application of International Law in British Courts*, ch. 27 in this volume, at p.494, *with* Amichai Cohen, *International Law in Israeli Courts*, ch. 29 in this volume, at p.528. *Compare also* Michael P. Van Alstine, *The Role of Domestic Courts in Treaty Enforcement: Summary and Conclusion*, *in* The Role of Domestic Courts in Treaty Enforcement: A Comparative Study 555, 612 (David Sloss ed., 2009) ("almost irrespective of the fundamental approach, domestic courts have applied basic principles of interpretation that largely conform to the norms in the VCLT"), *with* Helmut Philipp Aust, Alejandro Rodiles & Peter Stabauch, *Unity or Uniformity? Domestic Courts and Treaty Interpretation*, 27 Leiden J. Int'l L. 75, 84 (2014) (using the United States, Mexico, and the European Union to argue that this is an open question).

door for domestic courts to favor the executive's interpretation of international law for political reasons. This detracts from the persuasiveness of their interpretation under Article 38(1)(d) of the Statute of the International Court of Justice, which provides that judicial decisions are subsidiary means for the determination of rules of international law. Deference to the executive in treaty interpretation thereby also detracts from the role of domestic courts in international law. This is not, I should note, inevitable. Alternative reasons for U.S. courts' deference to the executive on treaty interpretation can be, and have been, imagined; notably, the State Department's greater expertise in international law.[46] Nonetheless, this rationale would come into tension with the separation of powers rationale in cases where the administration changes its position on what a treaty means for political reasons.[47]

IV. Opportunities

This chapter began with the likelihood that the U.S. field of foreign relations law, including its systematized and meticulous Restatements of the Foreign Relations Law of the United States, would play a strong practical role in any project on comparative foreign relations law. As just seen, U.S. foreign relations law compounds anxieties that even as a frame of analysis, foreign relations law could displace, discount, or distort public international law. One line of response might be that *comparative* foreign relations law can ward off some of these effects. René Urueña's chapter on Latin America in this *Handbook* can be read in this mode.

A different line of response can be glimpsed in Andrea Bianchi's chapter on cases of "system closure," in which a domestic court refuses to recognize an international judgment, law, or other act because it conflicts with domestic constitutional values. For a "committed international law generalist," this closure is a mistake, while the domestic constitutional lawyer or foreign relations scholar interprets such instances as evidence of the domestic legal system's superiority in the hierarchy of systems. Bianchi adds a third standpoint, from which system closures illustrate the episodic communication between a plurality of legal orders that coexist and interact in contingent ways. Citing Gunther Teubner on legal pluralism, he writes that "the range of interactions . . . is symptomatic of a wide array of postures not always amenable within

[46] *See, e.g.*, Julian Arato, *Deference to the Executive: The US Debate in Global Perspective*, *in* The Interpretation of International Law by Domestic Courts: Uniformity, Diversity, Convergence 198 (Helmut Philipp Aust & Georg Nolte eds., 2016).

[47] *See, e.g.*, Migratory Bird Treaty Act—More Information, Environmental Law at Harvard, *available at* http://environment.law.harvard.edu/2018/07/migratory-bird-treaty-act-information/ (last visited Aug. 12, 2018) (history of the U.S. administration's interpretation of federal act implementing a series of bilateral treaties to protect migratory birds and litigation challenging a recent change to its interpretation).

clear-cut and straightforward rationalities."[48] Implicit in Bianchi's analysis is that international lawyers' concerns about foreign relations law need not re-entrench traditional models of international law by way of opposition, but might lead the idea of foreign relations law to develop in conversation with other currents of thought about law and globalization.

In pursuing this line of response, we might recognize that the task of defining foreign relations law for purposes of comparison is just as temporally contingent as the creation of the U.S. field was. It is occurring in the midst of a multitude of paradigms for law and globalization, including Third World Approaches to International Law, transnational law, global administrative law, global constitutionalism, global legal pluralism, and private international law as global governance. In this vein, Paul Stephan argues that the challenge that the rise of foreign relations law poses for international law should be understood together with challenges posed by the emergence of comparative international law and by anxieties about the fragmentation of international law into overlapping and potentially contradictory regimes. Stephan sees the spread of foreign relations law as productive, rather than threatening, for international law, but he also pulls no punches as he argues that contemporary U.S. foreign relations law comes with an embedded critique of international law.[49]

One way forward may lie in noticing and questioning the strong law/politics distinction at play in both foreign relations law and the international law that it threatens to displace, discount, or distort. Scholarship on U.S. foreign relations law—markedly unlike U.S. scholarship on international law, even by the same authors—has tended to develop around U.S. case law and be closely tied to the work of the judiciary.[50] This has given the U.S. field a relatively positivist and statist orientation as regards both international and domestic law.

To see why this need not be the case, let us return to why neither public international law nor comparative public law of one kind or another is entirely satisfactory as a way to cordon off the field of foreign relations law for comparative purposes. Relative to a field generated by inward and outward-facing international law, foreign relations law casts both a broader and a finer normative net in an era of globalization. Relative to a field generated by comparative constitutional law governing external relations or by comparative administrative law, comparative foreign relations law involves a more heterogeneous body of law that will vary in composition and proportion from one state to another. These ways in which the problem of definition defies easy solution are also a window onto what makes comparative foreign relations law a compelling project with regard to international law. The concrete examples from that earlier discussion—cities,

[48] Andrea Bianchi, *Jurisdictional Immunities, Constitutional Values, and System Closures*, ch. 38 in this volume, at p.699.

[49] Paul B. Stephan, *Comparative International Law, Foreign Relations Law, and Fragmentation: Can the Center Hold?*, *in* COMPARATIVE FOREIGN RELATIONS LAW 53, 57, 68–69 (Anthea Roberts, Paul B. Stephan, Pierre-Hugues Verdier, & Mila Versteeg eds., 2018).

[50] *See* Lorite Escorihuela, *supra* note 32, at 33–34.

private international law, and diplomatic protection—serve to illustrate what this broader and finer normative net and the actors it catches might look like.

Hard local/soft international law: San Francisco's "implementation" of the Convention on the Elimination of All Forms of Discrimination Against Women (CEDAW), a treaty to which the United States is not a party, is often cited as an example of why international lawyers should be interested in studying cities. There is, though, no obvious way for international law to capture the legal composition of this strategy—"informal" international law does not do it justice because the city is legally bound. Although San Francisco's adoption of the treaty is invisible to the CEDAW Committee, which monitors only the compliance of state parties, the treaty is binding domestically insofar as the city has passed its principles as municipal law. Moreover, the San Francisco model and its requirement of gender-responsive budgeting have been showcased by the UN Development Fund for Women (UNIFEM, now part of UN Women) in its literature on compliance.[51] And at the same time that San Francisco's implementation of CEDAW is regulated by hard local law and a soft international feedback cycle on treaty implementation, it is also vulnerable to a future constitutional challenge.[52]

Internationalist legal underpinnings in domestic courts: As noted earlier, the significance of private international law for foreign relations law is not solely as a conduit for public international law into domestic law. Its significance is also the foreign relations implications of private-law relationships across borders. Furthermore, in common-law countries, private international law is fertile ground for judicial conceptions of international relations; notably, reliance on comity, which is neither binding law nor pure politics. Public international lawyers tend to be dismissive of comity because they encounter it most often as a consolation prize for a domestic court's failure to recognize the existence of a legal obligation. U.S. courts, for instance, use it at least in part as the basis for sovereign immunity, as opposed to regarding immunity as a doctrine of international law.[53] In private international law, however, the principle of comity comes into play where no international law alternative exists. Moreover, it can ground private international law rules not only in laissez-faire respect for sovereignty but also in a more diffuse and solidaristic idea of international cooperation than strict tit-for-tat reciprocity.

Diplomacy as expertise: The aim of returning to these examples is to show that foreign relations law might uncover a more complex internationalist normativity and thus

[51] *See* Karen Knop, *International Law and the Disaggregated Democratic State: Two Case Studies on Women's Human Rights and the United States*, *in* We, the People(s): Participation in Governance 75, 96 (Claire Charters & Dean R. Knight eds., 2011).

[52] *See*, e.g., Judith Resnik, *Foreign as Domestic Affairs: Rethinking Horizontal Federalism and Foreign Affairs Preemption in Light of Translocal Internationalism*, 57 Emory L.J. 31, 71–87 (2007).

[53] *See* Philippa Webb, *International Immunities in English Law*, ch. 36 in this volume, at p.661. *See also* Dodge, *supra* note 11.

contribute to a richer understanding of international law. My last example springs from the possibility that some countries may distinguish diplomacy from politics more sharply than the United States does. British and continental European scholars traditionally conceived of diplomacy as an instrument and background condition of foreign policy, whereas U.S. scholars and policymakers from the outset tended to understand diplomacy either as including the substance of foreign policy or as simply describing relations conducted through negotiations.[54] McLachlan identifies a diplomatic conception of foreign relations law, which sees its primary focus

> as facilitating the external relations of the State with foreign States. This is partly a matter of positive rules of law (international and domestic) that facilitate the intercourse of States. It also calls for a focus on State practice and for the discretionary consideration of diplomatic relations in the application of positive law.[55]

The question for foreign relations law is not only whether other states understand the role of diplomacy differently, but whether their courts appreciate it differently. Thus, courts might be inclined to defer to the executive in administrative-law contexts like requests for diplomatic protection partly on the view that diplomacy is a practice with its own norms, a relationship with a given state to be maintained, and an envelope of effectiveness for the remedy requested.

The decentering of international law, a realm outside the state in which international law is not the default, more diversified international actors—in other words, the anxieties raised earlier—take on a potentially positive complexion as qualities of foreign relations law when they are not tightly tied to a strong and fixed law/politics opposition. I read Campbell McLachlan's "allocative" conception of foreign relations law in this light. This conception

> views its function as . . . a set of rules of jurisdiction and applicable law. Such rules allocate competence and determine which law (whether national or international) is to be applied to determine issues concerning the external exercise or enforcement of the public power of states. In this way foreign relations law performs a function akin to that of private international law within the different context of public law.[56]

Although what I have suggested is not McLachlan's conception, it can be seen as an extension or variation. An allocative conception of foreign relations law is a sort of legal space of possibility. It is national law, but it is not a body of substantive rules and thus stands apart, somewhat like private international law and perhaps not unlike older

[54] *See* Megan Donaldson, From Secret Diplomacy to Diplomatic Secrecy: Secrecy and Publicity in the International Legal Order c 1919–1950 136, n. 83 and accompanying text (Apr. 2016) (JSD dissertation, New York University School of Law). *See also,* e.g., Paul Sharp, Diplomatic Theory of International Relations (2009).

[55] McLachlan, *Five Conceptions*, *supra* note 7, at p.24.

[56] *Id.* at p.24.

bodies of law that once occupied such a position, such as admiralty law or lex mercatoria.[57] Unlike the internationalist, constitutionalist, and exclusionary conceptions that he identifies, which work mainly with binaries, an allocative conception admits of a larger variety of relevant bodies of law. It also has the potential to develop a more complex account of dualism, a desideratum for a number of contributors to this *Handbook*.[58] Indigenous issues are one important reminder that transnational law and nonstate law are also relevant to foreign relations. The foreign relations law relevant to indigenous issues in North America might involve, for instance, domestic-law developments in Canada and the United States respectively relating to the status of indigenous rights under the 1794 Jay Treaty, cross-border relations between indigenous peoples guaranteed by the UN Declaration on the Rights of Indigenous Peoples, possibly Canadian implementing legislation, Canadian constitutional guarantees of aboriginal customary rights, and traditional inter-indigenous forms of diplomacy.[59]

In short, one possible comparativist response to international lawyers' concerns about foreign relations law would be that it will look different in different places and, in particular, more internationalist. Empirical data shows, for instance, that states increasingly give treaties greater domestic status than ordinary laws.[60] The alternative response sketched here is to explore an allocative conception or some variation thereon that would lift out foreign relations law as a legal space of possibility and one that holds open the field to insights from other ideas of legal normativity under conditions of globalization.

[57] *See*, e.g., Nikitas E. Hatzimihail, *The Many Lives—and Faces—of* Lex Mercatoria*: History as Genealogy in International Business Law*, 71 LAW & CONTEMP. PROBS. 169 (Summer 2008).

[58] *See*, e.g., Ako & Oppong, *supra* note 43; Ginsburg, *supra* note 13.

[59] *See*, e.g., Charles-Emmanuel Côté, *Federalism and Foreign Affairs in Canada*, ch. 16 in this volume, at p.293; Douglas Sanderson, *Toward an Aboriginal Grand Strategy*, June 17, 2013, GLOBAL BRIEF, *available at* http://globalbrief.ca/blog/2013/06/17/toward-an-aboriginal-grand-strategy/.

[60] *See* Pierre-Hugues Verdier & Mila Versteeg, *International Law in National Legal Systems: An Empirical Investigation*, 109 AM. J. INT'L L. 514, 525 (2015).

CHAPTER 4

COMPARATIVE FOREIGN RELATIONS LAW

A National Constitutions Perspective

TOM GINSBURG

ANY field has to define its boundaries, and comparative foreign relations law is no exception. Curtis Bradley helpfully defines the field as including "the domestic law of each nation that governs how that nation interacts with the rest of the world."[1] This a good starting point, and invites us to consider domestic constitutional law, statutes, cases, and also norms of judicial and administrative practice, which condition the operation of formal rules.

As with all other fields of law, however, the boundaries are not self-defining, and so there are questions of the outer limits. In a world of low transaction costs, transborder interaction is ubiquitous, and many legal fields that might, in prior eras, have been seen as exclusively domestic can now implicate foreign relations. A divorce case in Illinois may implicate foreign relations law, as might an inheritance dispute in Oregon or a criminal prosecution in Pennsylvania.[2] The field is thus expanding in scope, even as its boundaries may be becoming less sharp.

This chapter starts with a reflection on what might be learned methodologically from the comparative study of national constitutions, an increasingly large and vital field, and sets out an agenda for future work in the area. It then, by way of example, provides some basic data from a comparative examination of formal constitutional provisions relevant to foreign relations. In doing so, it argues that a "foreign relations lens" helps elucidate an underappreciated core purpose of these foundational texts. That is, one of the central functions of national constitutions is to structure international relations.

[1] Curtis A. Bradley, *What Is Foreign Relations Law?*, ch. 1 in this volume, at p.3.

[2] *See* Zschernig v. Miller, 389 U.S. 429 (1968) (Oregon); Bond v. United States, 564 U.S. 211 (2011) (Pennsylvania).

The chapter next turns to normative considerations, showing how the shifting boundaries of constitutional design with regard to foreign relations serve to allocate lawmaking authority. There is a potential for complementarity between international and domestic regulation of some problems, but also the potential that international and domestic norms serve as substitutes for each other. An optimal constitutional design of foreign relations law would take these considerations into account.

I. Comparative Constitutional Law and Foreign Relations Law

Comparative constitutional law has experienced something of a renaissance in recent years.[3] It has advanced through a mix of positive and normative inquiry, focusing on different sites of legal production and activity. How might its experience as a field inform the development of comparative foreign relations law?

A comparative constitutional perspective would first explore the distribution of institutions, rules, and interpretations across countries. We lack basic data on foreign relations law in many countries, and learning about the arrangements and their operation is a first step. Next, we would search for an account of variation. Why is it that countries differ in their institutional arrangements and doctrine? What is the role of functional considerations, as opposed to diffusion of institutions? Do ideas, culture, or political traditions explain variation? Finally we would like to understand the consequences of different arrangements. Are particular foreign relations schemes "better" for dealing with particular kinds of problems or political environments? What normative advice would we give a new country just writing a constitution? All these questions are central to comparative constitutional studies and must be asked about foreign relations law as well.

Another relevant consideration is methodological. Comparative constitutional law has proceeded, to some degree, by ignoring disciplinary boundaries and drawing on relevant knowledge wherever it is found. It has also been willing to expand the focus beyond courts as the only source of legal knowledge, and to complement judicial studies by looking at legislatures and popular movements as sources of constitutional norms and understandings. Reflecting this methodological pluralism, Professor Hirschl has called for the replacement of comparative constitutional law with comparative constitutional studies as the name for the field.[4] The breadth and ecumenicalism has paid dividends, and might be pursued as well in the foreign relations field.

Finally, comparative constitutional law has faced the question of boundaries.[5] In thinking about fields of law, one can take a nominal definition or a functional one.

[3] Ran Hirschl, Comparative Matters: The Renaissance of Comparative Constitutional Law (2014).

[4] *See id.*

[5] *See also* Thomas Poole, *The Constitution and Foreign Affairs*, 69 Current Leg. Probs. 143 (2016).

Professor Hirschl's shift away from "law" as the target of inquiry reflects a very broad idea of what counts as "constitutional" and so tends toward the functional. A standard distinction is between the Constitution, with a capital C, that refers to formal legal text enacted to structure government and its relations with citizens; and the constitution, with a lower case c, that refers to all the various rules and norms that play a similar function. My co-authors and I have drawn on this to distinguish the constitution-as-form from the constitution-as-function.[6]

Foreign relations law faces some of the same boundary problems of defining the scope of the field. For one thing, it occupies a liminal space between international law and domestic law, and so depends on a defensible conceptual boundary between the two. This boundary is increasingly murky. A key analytic point that I wish to demonstrate is that many of the domestic legal rules that structure a country's relations with the rest of the world are themselves transnational in origin. The very structure of domestic legal rules, encapsulated at the highest level in a written constitution, are informed by and frequently determined by international forces. But the reverse is also the case, in that domestic rules that are not conventionally considered to be within the field of foreign relations law may have a powerful effect on the international environment.

Another way to think about comparative foreign relations law is as a subfield of comparative constitutional law. While not all the rules of the former are formally constitutional, they are arguably so in a functional sense, in that they condition the operation of government in the important sphere of international relations.

One can thus think about the space of comparative foreign relations law, comparative constitutional law, and international law as being shared. One reason the very label of "foreign relations law" is so rarely used outside the United States is that for many other countries, the topic is simply that of international or constitutional law. What is at stake by starting with one or another perspective? By using the frame of foreign relations, we might be privileging the local over the international, emphasizing the dualist idea that it is only through some act of incorporation that the international becomes legally binding. If one were to start with a normative perspective that privileges international law, one might think about the space of domestic regulation as being the residual that the international allows. In our increasingly unified world, in which there is a single global public law, we may need new frames that bridge the domestic and international.

In short, the boundary problem in foreign relations law is one that has been faced by other fields, including comparative constitutional law, with which it overlaps. The methodological questions of comparative constitutional law as a field are a good starting place for the foreign relations scholars to pursue. A comparative constitutional lens can help in that effort, and, as we shall argue in the next section, a foreign relations lens on national constitutions can elucidate their purposes as well.

[6] Zachary Elkins, Tom Ginsburg, & James Melton, The Endurance of National Constitutions 38–40 (2009).

II. A National Constitutions Lens on Foreign Relations Law: What Do They Say?

This section provides basic descriptive data on how written constitutions—the constitution-as-form—deal with the topics of foreign relations law. As we shall see, foreign relations functions are essential to the very operation of national constitutions.

International Signaling Function

Law professors and political theorists speak grandly of the role of constitutions in ordering power, in limiting government, and in expressing the fundamental values of a people. But even prior to these "internal" governance functions, constitutions have a more primal "external" role on the international plane: they signal independence, and clearly define who it is that can speak authoritatively on behalf of the state. This allows *other* states to be able to recognize a legitimate government, and to deal with it. This may be one reason that rebel groups, governments-in-exile, and others who do not fully wield territorial authority nevertheless take steps to adopt putative constitutions. These days, adopting a written constitution is the very first act of a new state on the international plane. A constitution signals a desire for admission to the club of nations, whether or not such admission is actually forthcoming.

This international signaling function has been central to the very constitutional form since it first emerged. The constitution of Corsica, to take one early example, was adopted by rebels trying to set up an independent country breaking away from Genoa, with at least some factions seeking to gain protection of a new foreign power.[7] The U.S. Constitution was adopted with a purpose of securing independence from foreign influence, and with careful consideration to how international commitments ought to be made.[8] And the short-lived Polish Constitution of 1791 was adopted "free of the ignominious dictates of foreign coercion," to secure "external independence and internal liberty of the people."[9]

Treaty-Making

The international signaling function may help explain why it is that national constitutions spend a good deal of time articulating rules for treaty formation: such rules allow other

[7] Dorothy Carrington, *The Corsican Constitution of Pasquale Paoli (1755–1769)*, 88 English Hist. Rev. 481, 485–486 (1973).

[8] Federalist No. 75, The Federalist Papers 378 (Ian Shapiro ed., 2009).

[9] Const. Poland (1791), preamble.

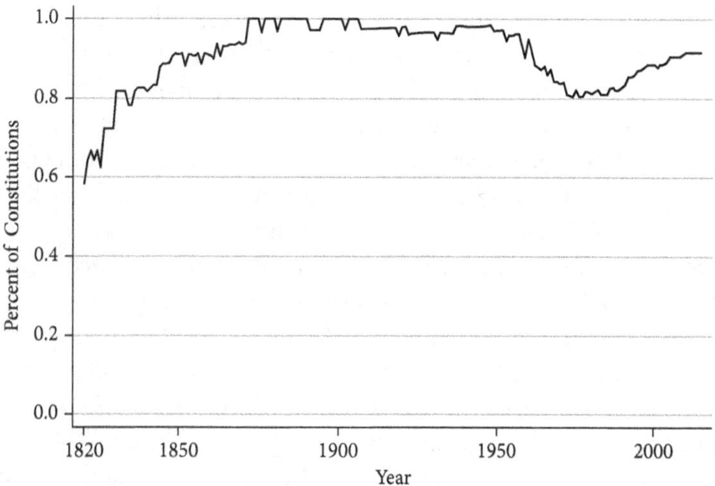

FIGURE 1. Constitutional References to International Treaties

states to know when a treaty has been authoritatively concluded and therefore may be relied on. Indeed, some 90 percent of all written constitutions ever adopted by nation-states include provisions for how treaties are adopted (see Figure 1).[10] Along with such features as defining how the head of state is selected and who is in charge of the military, treaty-formation rules are part of the constitutional core, definitional of the form.[11] Designating who speaks for and can bind the nation makes international communication possible, and is an essential if underappreciated function of national constitutions.

A clear pattern is that rules about treaty formation are well articulated in constitutional texts, and typically provide for an intricate set of arrangements involving legislature and executive. These tend to be articulated with greater specificity in presidential systems than in parliamentary ones. As Alexander Hamilton put it in *Federalist 75*:

> The essence of the legislative authority is to enact laws, or, in other words, to prescribe rules for the regulation of the society; while the execution of the laws, and the employment of the common strength, either for this purpose or for the common defense, seem to comprise all the functions of the executive magistrate. The power of making treaties is, plainly, neither the one nor the other. . . . They are not rules prescribed by the sovereign to the subject, but agreements between sovereign and sovereign.[12]

This sharing of authority requires careful drawing of boundaries, and rules about how treaties are made have become more elaborate over time as government structures have become more complicated. Hamilton's binary of executive and legislative must now contemplate additional actors. For example, in semi-presidential systems, there

[10] All data on file with author from the Comparative Constitutions Project, *available at* http://www.comparativeconstitutionsproject.org (last accessed Sept. 15, 2017).

[11] Tom Ginsburg, James Melton, & Zachary Elkins, Writing Rights (forthcoming 2021).

[12] The Federalist Papers 378 (Ian Shapiro ed., 2009).

may be distinct roles for the president and prime minister. Importantly, the growing presence of constitutional courts (now found in roughly half of constitutional systems in the world) has affected foreign relations law, as these bodies often have a role in examining treaties for constitutionality before promulgation. While only 6 percent of constitutions have historically given this power to such courts, the percentage approaches 23 percent of those in force. Constitutional court involvement changes the process of treaty-making, and likely its content, in ways that have not been fully explored to date.

The mechanisms of producing treaties vary across time and space. Some constitutions are vague, while others have a good deal of detail. Carlos Esposito, for example, elaborates how the Spanish Constitution differentiates legislative and executive roles depending on the subject matter of the treaty.[13] While that constitution provides for no role for the autonomous regions, Stefan Kadelbach documents a role for the Länder in approving certain treaties in Germany.[14] Pierre-Hugues Verdier and Mila Versteeg document further variation,[15] as do Ernest Ako and Richard Oppong in their contribution.[16]

What might drive such variation? Scholars of constitutional texts note that some features are best explained, not as a result of rational processes of design, but of chance, borrowing, and diffusion.[17] Certain texts, including the U.S. Constitution, became very influential on subsequent constitutions.[18] Choices made by accident or chance can have profound influence, and this is true of both inclusions and omissions. The U.S. Constitution provides for details on how treaties are adopted, but is silent on withdrawal from treaties.[19] While in the United States rules have developed as a result of practice and "historical gloss,"[20] it is the text that most foreign drafters first look at in designing their own arrangements. We have noted above that subsequent national constitutions have a good deal of detail on how treaties are adopted, and sometimes on the status of treaties vis-à-vis domestic law, but relatively few (roughly 20 percent) say anything about revocation or withdrawal.[21] This might simply reflect optimism that treaties will be enduring, but more likely it reflects a drafting convention that developed early on in the history of constitution-making. Path dependency is a powerful force in the drafting of constitutional text. As Laurence Helfer notes in his chapter in this

[13] Carlos Esposito, *Spanish Foreign Relations Law and the Process for Making Treaties and Other International Agreements*, ch. 12 in this volume.

[14] Stefan Kadelbach, *International Treaties and the German Constitution*, ch. 10 in this volume.

[15] Pierre-Hugues Verdier & Mila Versteeg, *Separation of Powers, Treaty-Making, and Treaty Withdrawal: A Global Survey*, ch. 8 in this volume.

[16] Ernest Yaw Ako & Richard Frimpong Oppong, *Foreign Relations Law in the Constitutions and Courts of Commonwealth African Countries*, ch. 33 in this volume.

[17] Zachary Elkins, *Diffusion and the Constitutionalization of Europe*, 43 COMP. POL. STUD. 969 (2010).

[18] GEORGE ATHAN BILLIAS, AMERICAN CONSTITUTIONALISM HEARD ROUND THE WORLD 1776–1989 (2009).

[19] Laurence Helfer, *Exiting Treaties*, 91 VA. L. REV. 1579 (2005).

[20] Curtis A. Bradley, *Treaty Termination and Historical Gloss*, 92 TEX. L. REV. 773 (2014); Jean Galbraith, *International Agreements and U.S. Foreign Relations Law: Complexity in Action*, ch. 9 in this volume.

[21] Data on file with author from the Comparative Constitutions Project, *available at* http://www.comparativeconstitutionsproject.org (last accessed Sept. 15, 2017).

Handbook, this gap opens up the possibility of complex relationships between domestic and international obligations.[22]

War-Making

Consider another critical aspect of international relations often discussed in national constitutions: making war. There is a good deal of variation in the allocation of war powers in national constitutions.[23] The most common approach is to divide authority between an executive that declares war and a legislature with the power to approve the declaration.[24] This approach was self-consciously avoided by the American Founding Fathers, notwithstanding the dangerous international environment that motivated their constitutional convention. Instead, they allocated the power to declare war to Congress, leaving the president with the power to command the armed forces. The functional defects of their choice have led to various workarounds, crystallizing in the debates over the War Powers Resolution in the 1970s.[25]

Outside the United States, an important global trend has been to give the legislature the power to approve the actions of the executive as commander in chief. There are interesting regional variations: constitutions in the relatively peaceful region of Oceania say little about war, whereas those in Latin America and the Middle East provide much more detail.[26] And there are also variations by regime type: semi-presidential regimes tend to say a lot about war, whereas parliamentary ones do not.[27]

As Monica Hakimi notes in her contribution to this *Handbook*, variation may in part reflect the myriad purposes that war powers serve.[28] A particularly important purpose, evident in Mathias Forteau's discussion of France in this *Handbook*, is collective security.[29] But given its importance in international law, the rules governing collective security are not always adequately reflected in national constitutions. This is a specific example of the phenomenon that Helfer identifies of potential gaps between the two levels of law.

Diffusion and Borrowing

The topic of war powers illustrates the diffusion dynamic in writing constitutions. Constitutional texts frequently contain rules that do not respond to local demands but

[22] Laurence R. Helfer, *Treaty Exit and Intrabranch Conflict at the Interface of International and Domestic Law*, ch. 20 in this volume.

[23] Tom Ginsburg, *Chaining the Dogs of War: Comparative Data*, 15 Chi. J. Int'l L. 493 (2014).

[24] *Id.*

[25] 50 U.S.C. §§ 1541–1548 (1973).

[26] Ginsburg, *supra* note 23, at 508.

[27] *See id.* at 508–509.

[28] Monica Hakimi, *Techniques for Regulating Military Force*, ch. 41 in this volume.

[29] Mathias Forteau, *Using Military Force and Engaging in Collective Security: The Case of France*, ch. 45 in this volume.

instead reflect fashions and trends among perceived peers. Since World War II, formal declarations of war are very rare, and have no legal effect on the international plane, since the UN Charter refers to "armed conflict" without regard to the earlier laws of war and peace. Despite having no legal significance, constitution makers dutifully continue to provide for declarations of war. The world's youngest generally recognized country, South Sudan, grants the president the power to declare war.[30]

Comparative constitutional law scholarship also suggests that the contents of relevant rules are driven by trends and borrowing as much as by function. Professors Goderis and Versteeg have shown how provisions on rights in national constitutions are often borrowed from abroad.[31] Even the parts of constitutions most associated with the expression of national values, the preambles, use language borrowed from abroad, and often mention international rules, norms, and institutions.[32] The reason for this borrowing is rooted in the complexities of constitutional drafting, which often takes place in fairly urgent circumstances. As a result, region and era drive contents. A quick perusal of the constitution of Abkhazia reveals a good deal in common with the charters of Georgia and Russia, while the constitution of the Confederate States in the United States borrowed large portions of text from the federal constitution.

If constitutional provisions are generally subject to processes of diffusion and borrowing, then we cannot assume that the texts respond to felt local needs. The structure of foreign relations law that regulates international engagement is itself foreign in origin. And form does not follow function. This observation undermines simplistic assertions of sovereignty—instead of thinking of our constitutional schemes as being produced by "We the People," we ought instead consider them to be the rules borrowed by the elites in power at the time of drafting the constitution, ideally but not necessarily based on some assessment of what might work.

Customary International Law

What other patterns do we observe in the contents of national constitutional texts? If treaties are nearly universal, a smaller number of constitutions—some 19 percent historically—make reference to customary international law or the law of nations. As Figure 2A shows, this number has risen slightly in recent decades and reaches 32 percent of those in force as of 2015. Such references vary in detail and effect. The U.S. Constitution, somewhat cryptically, provides that Congress has the power to "define and punish offenses against the law of nations." More common is a provision

[30] Const. South Sudan (2011), art. 101.

[31] Benedikt Goderis & Mila Versteeg, *The Diffusion of Constitutional Rights*, 39 Int'l Rev. L. & Econ. 1 (2014).

[32] Justin O. Frosini, Constitutional Preambles at a Crossroads Between Law and Politics (2012); Tom Ginsburg, Daniel Rockmore, & Nick Foti, *We the Peoples: The Global Origins of Constitutional Preambles*, 46 Geo. Wash. Int'l L. Rev. 305 (2014).

FIGURE 2A Constitutional References to Customary International Law

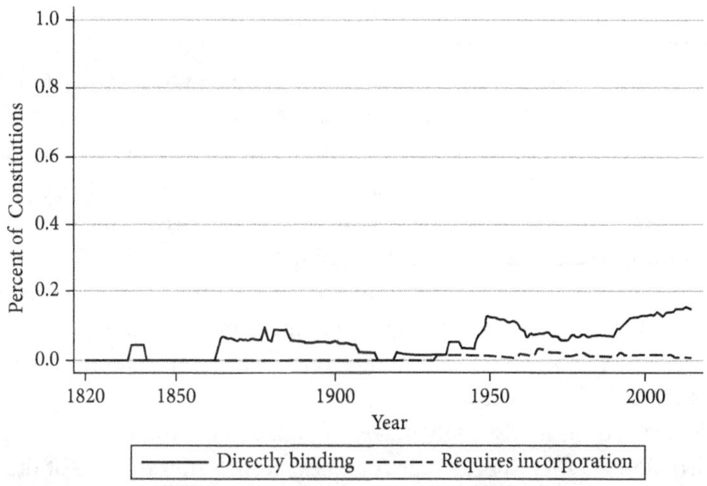

FIGURE 2B Constitutional References to the Status of Customary International Law

like that of Estonia, stating that "[g]enerally recognized principles and rules of international law are an inseparable part of the Estonian legal system."[33] Some of the other chapters in this *Handbook* document how courts have used relatively vague constitutional language to expand—and contract—the application of customary international law in particular contexts. While the monism indicated in the Estonian provision is still a minority position, it is rising in popularity, as Figure 2B demonstrates: while

[33] Const. Estonia (1992) art. 3. *See also* Const. Germany (1949), art. 25 ("The general rules of international law shall be an integral part of federal law. They shall take precedence over the laws and directly create rights and duties for the inhabitants of the federal territory"); Const. Austria (rev. 2013) art. 9.1 ("The generally recognized rules of international law are regarded as integral parts of Federal law.").

8 percent of all national constitutions historically have so provided, some 15 percent of those in force (as of 2015) make customary international law directly applicable in the domestic legal order. We seem to be in an era of growing, if sometimes grudging, constitutional recognition of international norms as a source of law.

Additional Trends

Two other aspects of the relationship of international and constitutional law deserve mention. First, there is an increasing trend to refer to or incorporate specific international treaties or other instruments into the national constitution. Fully one quarter of national constitutions adopted after 1948 make reference to the Universal Declaration of Human Rights somewhere in their text.[34] These references can range from a mere passing statement to an explicit commitment to uphold the values in the Declaration. Other human rights treaties are often mentioned, such as the American Convention of Human Rights, and especially the African Charter on Human and Peoples' Rights, now found in over 40 percent of constitutions in sub-Saharan Africa. Ako and Oppong, in their contribution to this *Handbook*, provide numerous examples.[35] These treaties are sometimes even incorporated as either directly binding or as rules to guide interpretation.[36] This produces a complicated configuration, with some treaties incorporated through a constitution, others left to ratification by an elected legislature, and others perhaps incorporated through judicial doctrines. These trends make the old monist-dualist dichotomy seem simplistic, and invite new ways to characterize the relationships between domestic and international law. Most importantly, the constitutional incorporation of treaties squeezes the space for the exercise of foreign relations law, as regulatory discretion may be limited by the very document that empowers particular national actors with their basic authority.

Second, constitutions increasingly make reference to the international organizations that have proliferated after World War II and especially after the end of the Cold War. Of constitutions in force today, fifty-two refer to the United Nations, for example. Regional organizations also are frequently mentioned. Many of these references are symbolic or expressive, but some may be more legally cognizable.

[34] Data on file with author from the Comparative Constitutions Project, *available at* http://www.comparativeconstitutionsproject.org (last accessed Sept. 15, 2017).

[35] Ako & Oppong, *supra* note 16.

[36] *See*, e.g., CONST. ANGOLA (2010), art. 12 ("The Republic of Angola shall respect and implement the principles of the United Nations Charter and the Charter of the Organisation of African Unity."), and art. 26 ("Constitutional and legal precepts relating to fundamental rights must be interpreted and incorporated in accordance with the Universal Declaration of the Rights of Man, the African Charter on the Rights of Man and Peoples and international treaties on the subject ratified by the Republic of Angola.").

Table 1 Selected Regional Variation in Constitutional Texts

Region	Mention of Customary International Law	Mention of International Organizations	Legislative Approval of Treaties
East Europe/post-Soviet	0.30	0.45	0.77
East Asia	0.12	0.24	0.60
Latin America	0.21	0.17	0.88
Middle East/N. Africa	0.09	0.44	0.67
Oceania	0	0.44	0.28
South Asia	0.18	0.18	0.32
Sub-Saharan Africa	0.13	0.61	0.57
W. Europe/U.S./Canada	0.25	0.23	0.64
TOTAL	0.19	0.35	0.70

Variations in Foreign Relations Law

These features are not equally distributed among regions. Table 1 provides some examples of the frequency (measured on a scale of 0 to 1, with the latter indicating universal adoption) of constitutional references relevant to foreign relations law, illustrating some regional variations.

Many questions arise from the observation of regional and temporal variation. What types of designs are more functional for particular political circumstances or to advance particular values? Does legislative involvement in war-making have consequences for war policy?[37] Should treaty powers mirror the domestic order of lawmaking? What consequences flow with alignment or mismatch of legislation and treaties? When do states incorporate customary international law, and does it matter? We are only beginning to answer these and other questions about comparative foreign relations law, and comparative constitutional law has a good deal to offer in terms of how we approach them.

III. The Possibility of Substitutes, Complements, and Duplicates

Comparative constitutional law is also a normative discipline, providing tools to understand how institutional design can be manipulated, or ways in which the law can be interpreted, to advance various policy goals. Of course, these goals depend on normative theories exogenous to the field. Similarly, foreign relations law is the terrain

[37] Tom Ginsburg, *War and Constitutional Design* (manuscript) (suggesting that the answer is yes).

for a variety of normative debates related to sovereignty, democracy, rights, and other small-c constitutional issues.

How might a comparative constitutional perspective inform foreign relations law? One simple way to start is to view constitutions as devices facilitating the creation of public goods for a political community. Government is required to produce public goods, and we need to design institutions of government to maximize the possibility that we get a set of public goods that matches the preferences of the citizenry. We are familiar with this perspective from discussions of federalism or local government: some public goods are best produced at a local level, while others might better be produced at the level of the nation state. An optimal constitutional design will allocate decisions over public goods to the level at which they are best produced.

Of course, there are also some public goods that require cooperation outside a nation's borders. There are certain things a people might want that can *only* be obtained through international cooperation. Climate regulation, international security, and free trade are all goods that the democratic state cannot achieve on its own. To the extent that constitutions allow international cooperation, they may allow the achievement of democratically demanded goals, even as they bypass the machinery of democratic control. In practice this often involves the delegation of decision-making power outside of the state, in the same way that regulatory law delegates to agencies inside the state. How might we ensure that states are cooperating when they need to and not cooperating when they should not be doing so? This is the normative task for a constitutional design of foreign relations law.

One way to organize the inquiry into the functions of foreign relations law is to think about international institutions as either substitutes or complements for domestic ones.[38] Sometimes, a rule on the international plane can complement a similar rule in the domestic sphere. For investment law, for example, a country with both credible domestic institutions and credible international commitments would presumably be even more attractive as an investment site than a country that was defective on either dimension. In this case, international arrangements complement domestic ones. Similarly, many national constitutions duplicate rights protections found in international agreements. The proliferation of rights on multiple levels can lead to complex jurisprudential tangles of different bodies interpreting different versions of the same right. But by and large, the duplication is complementary toward the overall goal of rights protection. Public goods production is enhanced through duplication.

In other areas, an international agreement can substitute for domestic law. The U.S. case of *Missouri v. Holland*, in which an international treaty to protect migratory birds served to bypass limits on domestic legislation, illustrates the substitution dynamic.[39] A coalition that loses in the "normal" processes of domestic politics can seek to shift levels, so as to advance its goals through international machinery.

[38] Eli Salzberger & Stefan Voigt, *Choosing Not to Choose: When Politicians Choose to Delegate Powers*, 55 KYKLOS 281 (2002).

[39] Missouri v. Holland, 252 U.S. 416 (1920).

With increasing frequency, international institutions can substitute for domestic ones. The Inter-American Court, for example, has an active jurisprudence reviewing states of emergencies that have passed muster in local constitutional schemes.[40] This is not merely backstopping local institutions; it is providing an alternative forum to review local processes.

The example of *Missouri v. Holland* illustrates that in federal countries, in particular, international arrangements can have profound consequences for the internal balance of power as between the national and state level governments. This has been a powerful theme of U.S. foreign relations scholarship and practice, and it remains a major issue in American politics, as states pursue policies on climate change, immigration, and other issues that are at odds with those of the federal government.[41] Substitution facilitates reallocation of power, with profound normative consequences for constitutional law and theory.

In particular, the availability of international substitutes suggests the possibility of strategic behavior in choosing to use one level of governance or the other.[42] While from a democratic point of view, one might fear bypassing local institutions for international ones, there are countervailing considerations. Because they bind the state itself rather than the government of the day, international commitments may be more difficult to revise or escape. This makes them more credible as commitment devices, allowing the people's representatives to potentially achieve more than can be done through domestic legislation. Giving up control can actually help people to achieve things they otherwise might not be able to.

The strategic analysis, however, suggests that this functional story might be too good to be true. Besides serving as complements and substitutes, shifts from one lawmaking device to another allow for the aggrandizement of some actors over others—perhaps most commonly, the aggrandizement of executive power over legislative power, or the privileging of center over state mentioned above. Foreign relations law allocates powers among different domestic actors, and so shifts in one direction or the other can shape the domestic incentives to use particular institutions. It can thus affect the operation of the domestic constitution.

Note how this view is at odds with the traditional international law view of a state as a unified entity with a single voice on the international plane. Expanding international power over particular policy areas may implicate domestic power struggles, and may privilege one coalition over another. Neither the international nor the domestic level of governance is "better" in the abstract; it depends on a normative theory as to what problems should be allocated to what levels. If one thinks that international institutions

[40] Edel Hughes, *Entrenched Emergencies and the "War on Terror": Time to Reform the Derogation Procedure in International Law?*, 20 N.Y. Int'l L. Rev. 1, 39–49 (2007).

[41] Daniel Abebe & Aziz Z. Huq, *Foreign Affairs Federalism: A Revisionist Approach*, 66 Vand. L. Rev. 723 (2013); Michael J. Glennon & Robert D. Sloane, Foreign Affairs Federalism: The Myth of National Exclusivity (2016).

[42] Rachel Brewster, *The Domestic Origins of International Agreements*, 44 Va. J. Int'l L. 501 (2004).

tend to be more aligned with the public interest because they are neutral, then one ought to favor an expansive view of delegation to international actors. On the other hand, if one thinks that international institutions are misaligned with local demands for public goods, a narrower structure of delegation is desirable. While argument in the field of foreign relations law tends to sound in grand terms like sovereignty and democracy, it may be more nuanced to ask, what allocation of powers will best align with preferences for public goods production over time?

A full elaboration of the possibilities of complements and substitutes is beyond the scope of this chapter. But it is important to note that whether something is perceived as a complement or substitute might vary with political attitudes. As a general matter, Europeans tend to be more comfortable with international delegations and supranational government than do, say, Americans or Japanese. Examining the political program of any major party in a democracy will tend to produce nuanced answers in this area, that vary with the field of law. President Donald Trump does not like international trade institutions, but presumably likes investment law where treaties can complement local protections for his hotels. Human rights advocates want international complements for local machinery, but sometimes view trade as undermining human rights, and so might prefer to restrict delegations in that area.

Furthermore, we are in an era of populist backlash against international commitments in many countries. Paul Craig's chapter in this *Handbook*, for example, grapples with the disengagement triggered by the Brexit referendum in the United Kingdom.[43] Populism is a complex phenomenon, with myriad causes, but one theme that unites its various exponents is a distrust of elites, including foreign policy elites. The call for a return to democracy invites closer scrutiny of international arrangements. Might this herald a slowdown of such arrangements? Or a fundamental reallocation of authority to make commitments in the first place? These questions are now salient in ways that were not the case even just a few years ago.

IV. Conclusion

Constitutions are central structures in foreign relations law, and they increasingly provide for detailed rules that condition its operation. As in most areas of constitutional design, the observed allocation of powers in a given system is unlikely to reflect an optimal one. Diffusion and path dependencies tend to lead to stickiness in constitutional design. The actual day-to-day working of a foreign affairs scheme will often involve searches for workarounds and pathways within a scheme of constitutionally assigned powers. In this regard, the shift of power to constitutional courts in recent

[43] Paul Craig, *Engagement and Disengagement with International Institutions: The U.K. Perspective*, ch. 22 in this volume.

decades, a development in constitutional design that has affected many countries, has made them central players in the operation of any scheme of foreign affairs law.

Juxtaposing the academic field of comparative constitutional law with that of foreign affairs law provides insights into both. The foreign affairs frame highlights the international functions of constitutional texts, even as an understanding of the production of those texts shows that they are more international than we would otherwise assume. For any country, the internal structures of lawmaking and the external structures of treaties interact to provide for the production of public goods, but are also the site of intense power politics among actors who understand that regulation at one level can sometimes substitute for the other. Elaborating on how these structures and politics to produce law interact requires an interdisciplinary perspective.

CHAPTER 5

A COMPARATIVE FOREIGN RELATIONS LAW AGENDA

Opportunities and Challenges

OONA A. HATHAWAY

INTERNATIONAL law is generally understood to be made up of the rules that states accept as binding in their relations with one another. But international law is the product not only of a political and legal process that takes place *between* states—as this common understanding implies—but also of processes that take place *within* them. Consider treaties. States are not committed to an international treaty obligation unless and until they ratify that treaty or otherwise indicate their consent.[1] It is that act of consent that transforms a treaty from a piece of paper devoid of any legal force into law that binds. But it is the states themselves that decide when and how they will consent—and they do so through their own domestic legal and political institutions. Accordingly, examining domestic institutions that states use to create international law is essential to our understanding of international law. And yet to date there has been remarkably little cross-national work examining the role of domestic politics and law in the creation of treaties and other international law.

Part of the reason for this gap is the difficulty of conducting cross-national studies of foreign relations law on a large scale. The specific requirements for treaty ratification, for example, are determined by domestic law and hence vary immensely across states.[2]

[1] *See* Oona A. Hathaway, *Between Power and Principle*, 72 U. CHI. L. REV. 469 (2005). *See also* RESTATEMENT (THIRD) OF FOREIGN RELATIONS LAW OF THE UNITED STATES 18 (1987) ("Modern international law is rooted in acceptance by states which constitute the system."); Vienna Convention on the Law of Treaties, art. 19, May 23, 1969, 1155 U.N.T.S. 331, 8 I.L.M. 679, entered into force Jan. 27, 1980 ("A treaty does not create either obligations or rights for a third State without its consent."); LOUIS HENKIN, INTERNATIONAL LAW: POLITICS AND VALUES 28 (1995) ("For treaties, consent is essential. No treaty, old or new, whatever its character or subject, is binding on a state unless it has consented to it.").

[2] *See* Vienna Convention on the Law of Treaties, arts. 11–17.

Some domestic legal systems provide that the chief executive officer's agreement is sufficient for a treaty to be ratified, while others require that the treaty be approved through the same process used to pass regular legislation, and yet others adopt some other process altogether. The United States, for example, has a process for approving treaties that is different from its ordinary domestic lawmaking process for treaties in several respects: whereas ordinary legislation is presented to two houses of Congress and then presented to the president for signature, treaties are submitted by the president to the Senate alone, which then must consent by an affirmative vote of two-thirds of its members, after which the president may ratify.[3]

To the extent there have been comparative studies done of foreign relations law, they have been largely limited to relatively small-scale case studies. More comprehensive examination of the differences across nations in the ways in which they make international commitments is rare. This chapter aims to contribute to an emerging conversation about how best to carry out a more comprehensive examination of differences between states in the law governing their engagement in the world around them.

This chapter maps out five areas that offer opportunities and challenges for the study of comparative foreign relations law: First, the choice of methodology, whether quantitative or qualitative. Second, the underrepresentation of certain states in existing foreign relations scholarship. Third, the domestic political and institutional structures that shape the interplay between the legislative, executive, and judicial functions within states. Fourth, the role of geopolitics. Fifth, the chapter sounds a cautionary note about approaching international law through domestic law.

This is meant as a proposed agenda for a fledgling field. Many of these issues are taken up in the chapters of this book; some remain as yet largely unexplored. The challenge for scholars the world over will be to fill out this agenda and then begin to tackle it.

I. Qualitative and Quantitative Work

One set of questions that researchers in the new field of comparative foreign relations law must consider is *how* to study the topic. This may seem simple and obvious, but it reflects a deep challenge for the field.

There are, as of this writing, 193 member states of the United Nations. Any comparative study of foreign relations law thus faces a choice: choose a small number or particular subset of states for deep and careful comparison or take a narrow slice of the problem and assess it across the full range of states (or at least a large number of them).

[3] Oona A. Hathaway, *Treaties' End: The Past, Present, and Future of International Lawmaking in the United States*, 117 Yale L.J. 1238 (2008).

Of course, this is not necessarily an either/or dilemma—different studies will take different approaches and, gradually, the field will develop both deep and broad knowledge. But it is important, as we set out, to be cognizant of the blind spots of each methodological approach, and mindful of the importance of using diverse methodologies to fill in the unavoidable gaps.

To date, comparative foreign relations law has largely focused on side-by-side comparisons. This takes advantage of the scholarship and knowledge bases within each country. After all, sophisticated studies abound of the particular institutional foundations of international lawmaking in individual states. These have occasionally been collected together in volumes that permit readers to consider similarities and differences between countries. One of the earliest—and extraordinarily valuable—such collections is *A Comparative Approach to Treaty Law and Practice*.[4] It collected together a "representative group of nineteen states" and compared their treaty laws and practices with respect to four core questions: "(1) How do states define treaties as a matter of domestic law and practice? (2) What is the scope of the executive's authority over treaty making? (3) What role does the legislature play in treaty making? and (4) How are treaties incorporated into national law?"

But such studies, as valuable as they are, have serious limits. The same countries are often included in these studies (the United States, the United Kingdom, Canada, France, and Germany are frequent repeat players, with less frequent but common appearances from the Netherlands, South Africa, India, Israel, and Japan). (More on this point below.) True, these states likely have the most developed law, hence they are attractive subjects of study, but focusing on them again and again leaves big blanks in our understanding—and limits the capacity to generalize beyond this small set. Are there important regional differences in the approach to comparative foreign relations law? That is a difficult question to answer when North America and Europe are so overrepresented and South America, Africa, and Asia so underrepresented. Why do some states *not* develop expansive rules regarding foreign relations—is it that they are less engaged in the international system or that they have less complex but effective techniques for incorporating international law domestically? Again, we cannot be confident of the answer if we focus our studies on the small set of states that have a robust foreign relations law tradition.

Quantitative studies offer one tool for filling this gap. They do not rely on individual expertise for deep comparison, instead providing studies of large number of states on particular identified criteria. Opening up the scope to a wider range of states has the potential to expand the collective sense of institutional possibilities, enables better understanding of the consequences of institutional choices, and makes it possible to

[4] National Treaty Law & Practice (Duncan B. Hollis, Merritt R. Blakeslee, & L. Benjamin Ederington eds., 2005). *See also* J. Denis Derbyshire & Ian Derbyshire, Political Systems of the World (2d ed. 1996); J. D. Huber, *The Vote of Confidence in Parliamentary Democracies*, 90 Am. Pol. Sci. Rev. 269 (1996); George Tsebelis & Jeanette Money, Bicameralism (1997); Giovanni Sartori, Comparative Constitutional Engineering 110 (2d ed. 1994).

develop an understanding of the nature of foreign relations law that does not unduly reflect the institutional choices of one state or one small set of states. This comparative analysis of state institutions has the potential, as well, to expand our understanding of how states "bring international law back home." Creating a census of the world's constitutions also enables "large-n" empirical studies that can check against inadvertent parochialism. Quantitative cross-national analysis also has the potential to allow scholars to observe a global evolution of constitutional techniques for making international law.

In the last decade, there have been important developments in enabling both qualitative and quantitative studies of global constitutions. The Constitute Project allows viewers to read constitutions from around the world in a variety of languages,[5] and the Comparative Constitutions Project provides comprehensive data about the world's constitutions, including on variables directly relevant to foreign relations—such as the ways in which the constitutions provide for making and enforcing treaties and decisions to go to war.[6] This resource has, in turn, given rise to a rich array of scholarship.[7] Indeed, several chapters in this volume rely on the data.[8]

The availability of comprehensive information on state constitutions has already begun to open up a wide variety of research in comparative politics, international relations, and international law. The global political and legal order is an extremely complex network of interlocking institutions and practices. States use constitutions as means to order, to the extent possible, their part in that network according to their political and legal commitments. Constitutions are not the only means of such ordering, they are not always the most important means, and of course they have many other important purposes. Nevertheless, constitutions generally represent significant attempts to formally relate a state to its international environment. International law cannot be properly understood without understanding them.

But there are downsides to this approach as well. Examining large numbers of states at once means ignoring much of the fine-grained institutional detail that may be essential to deep understanding of how international law is made.[9] The vast majority of quantitative scholarship in the field has a specific shortcoming: it is based on the

[5] The Constitute Project, *available at* https://constituteproject.org (last visited Apr. 2018).

[6] Comparative Constitutions Project, *available at* https://comparativeconstituitonsproject.org (last visited Apr. 2018).

[7] *See*, e.g., Articles, Comparative Constitutions Project, *available at* http://comparativeconstitutionsproject.org/articles/# (last visited Apr. 2018).

[8] Tom Ginsburg, *Comparative Foreign Relations Law: A National Constitutions Perspective*, ch. 4 in this volume.

[9] It is also worth noting that constitutions may influence one another and therefore are not necessarily independent data points. This process of influence could itself be an interesting topic of study. Digital Text Analysis has been used in other contexts to examine the process of overlap, borrowing, and diffusion, and could be used with constitutional texts as well. *See*, e.g., Kellen Funk & Lincoln Mullen, *The Spine of American Law: Digital Text Analysis and U.S. Legal Practice*, 123 Am. Hist. Rev. 132 (2018).

written constitutions (or, in the absence of a constitution, the basic laws) of states. But *much of what matters in foreign relations law is not reflected in written constitutions.*

There are two specific reasons that large scale quantitative analysis of foreign relations law based on data drawn from constitutional text is an imperfect—or, at least a partial—guide to comparative foreign relations law. The first is the possibility of institutional drift: practice grows and changes over time. The U.S. Constitution's Treaty Clause, for example, specifies an international lawmaking process that has almost entirely fallen into disuse.[10] Instead, much modern international lawmaking by the United States happens through processes never expressly mentioned in the constitution—through executive agreements and congressional-executive agreements, as well as "nonbinding" commitments. Meanwhile, the Supremacy Clause, which makes treaties the "supreme law of the land," has also been diluted, if not contradicted, by subsequent judicial decisions.[11] Perhaps the U.S. Constitution is an extreme case. It is, after all, the oldest written constitution (and has only been rarely amended) and thus the most susceptible to the drift of practice away from the text. But it is possible, if not likely, that other states will have practices that depart from a bare reading of the text.

There is a second reason that data drawn from constitutions may be imperfect guides as well: states may specify some formal rules in the constitution, but much of what matters in foreign relations law may not be specifically detailed in the constitution. For example, my own quantitative analysis based on constitutional texts finds that states rarely specifically mention customary international law or general law in their constitutions.[12] A majority of constitutions (162) do not mention customary international law; a small minority of constitutions (23) specify that customary international law is part of the state's domestic legal system. Similarly, although nearly all constitutions specify the process by which a state joins a treaty, many are silent on treaty withdrawal.[13] It is nonetheless unlikely that this silence is properly understood to mean that customary international law has no legal status in those states where

[10] Hathaway, *Treaties' End*, *supra* note 3; Oona A. Hathaway, *Presidential Power over International Law*, 119 YALE L.J. 140 (2009).

[11] Oona Hathaway, Sabria McElroy, & Sara Solow, *International Law at Home*, 37 YALE J. INT'L L. 51 (2012).

[12] Working with a team of researchers, I spent several years collecting every constitution that has been in force since 1980. My team then read each constitution and coded its domestic and international lawmaking processes. We recorded in detail the procedures each constitution establishes for treaty negotiation and ratification, and the domestic legal status the constitution accords to international law. We also recorded the constitutional procedures for ordinary domestic legislation, to provide a baseline against which to understand a state's international lawmaking. A small portion of this dataset was the basis for my comparative study in *Treaties End*, *supra* note 3.

[13] *See*, e.g., Pierre-Hugues Verdier & Mila Versteeg, *Separation of Powers, Treaty-Making, and Treaty Withdrawal: A Global Survey*, ch. 8 in this volume, at p.150 ("While explicit constitutional provisions of this sort remain the exception, a deeper investigation of infraconstitutional law reveals that binding parliamentary approval requirements for withdrawal are common."); Laurence R. Helfer, *Treaty Exit and Intrabranch Conflict at the Interface of International and Domestic Law*, ch. 20 in this volume, at p.358 ("According to the Comparative Constitutions Project, 43 out of 190 written constitutions currently in force contain provisions on treaty withdrawal, denunciation, or termination.").

the constitutions are silent, or that there is no domestic law governing treaty exit. Hence, while quantitative analysis for constitutional text offers a useful starting point for large-scale study of comparative foreign relations law, it is not a substitute for in-depth nuanced assessment of practices by those intimately familiar with the law as it is practiced.

II. Underrepresented States

The fledgling field of comparative foreign relations law reflects a broader imbalance in the global study of international law. Non-Western states, particularly those in the Global South, tend to be radically underrepresented in Western international law scholarship and jurisprudence. As Anthea Roberts argues in her book, *Is International Law International?*, sources and actors from Western states in general, and from the United States, the United Kingdom, and France, in particular, are privileged in the field of international law.[14] This extends to foreign relations law: when citing foreign court decisions, Western states heavily cite Western national cases and largely ignore non-Western cases.[15]

To be sure, one might argue that this imbalance is less of a concern with foreign relations law than it is with international law. International law aspires to be universal, whereas foreign relation law does not. It may therefore be appropriate for states to look to states with similar political systems or values for a foreign relations law issue. But if that is the case, then this should be done self-consciously. Instead, it appears that much of the narrow focus of foreign relations law study is less about intentional focus on states based on acknowledged areas of similarity that are relevant to the borrowing project and more a reflexive recourse to the familiar sites of comparison—or perhaps even just those on which information is available.

There are a number of reasons for this reflexive imbalance. English has become the dominant language in the scholarly field of international law, and that likely helps produce a heavier reliance on cases and materials from English-speaking countries. Moreover, the flow of students is lopsided: many more students flow into Western countries to study international law than flow out of them.[16] This dynamic spills over into the professional networks that generate comparative foreign relations law: the few existing foreign relations law studies that exist are produced by and involve networks of scholars who speak English. They also tend to involve scholars who have time to focus significant time on scholarship and funding to travel to conferences where they can meet other scholars with related expertise and interest—both more likely in wealthy Western countries.

[14] Anthea Roberts, Is International Law International? 210 (2017).

[15] *Id.* at 167–169.

[16] *Id.* at 52–72.

To be clear, this phenomenon is not limited to the study of comparative foreign relations law. Large research universities are primarily located in wealthy Western states, and scholarship generated by these universities sets the agenda for fields as diverse as physics and philosophy. A ranking of top global universities based on research output and research impact included not a single university located in a non-English-speaking country in the top thirty universities. Only six universities located in a non-English-speaking country were in the top fifty.[17] A similar imbalance is found among leading international law firms, which are primarily located in the United States, the United Kingdom, and France.

This means that gaining a truly global perspective on comparative foreign relations law will not occur without intentional effort to correct the imbalance. Allowing scholarship to simply emerge organically will inevitably favor the same small subset of countries that are already well represented. That will lead to an incomplete picture of the true shape of comparative foreign relations law.

One might respond to this concern by arguing that a critical mass of the most involved states is enough to get a clear picture of foreign relations law—or at least of the foreign relations law of the states that are significant players in the international legal order. But a key problem with the current state of scholarship is that scholars do not know what we do not know. We do not know if the unstudied states of the Global South are different in important respects from the better studied states mostly located in the north. Yes, it can be appropriate to study a subset of states that have certain key shared characteristics. But to only study those states and to assume that they are representative of foreign relations law around the globe is to make an assumption that may be entirely inaccurate. For the field to mature, those blind spots need to be filled in.

Let us take one example: comparative studies of domestic law for authorizing the use of military force abroad tend to focus on states that deploy force abroad on a frequent basis. It is understandable why this would be so: a scholar would naturally be interested in understanding how the decision to use force are regulated in states that regularly do use force. But focusing on these states alone can be misleading. It is entirely possible that these states place less rigorous checks on the power of the executive to use force than do states that less frequently use force abroad. If a study of separation of powers regarding use of force focuses on states that more readily use force (which make up a high percentage of the frequently studied states), that study will learn less about effective separation of powers constraints than it would if it took a broader perspective—one that includes states that less frequently deploy military forces outside their own borders.

Hence a clear goal for the field of comparative foreign relations law as it expands must be to reach out to experts in states that are less well represented in scholarship

[17] Scholarset, "2016 Research Ranking of Global Universities," *PR Newswire* (Mar. 1, 2016). Scholarset, which produced the ranking, is identified as "the leading academic social network of scientists, engineers, and scholars based in China."

and academic circles so that a fuller picture of the comparative landscape can emerge. That may require, moreover, reaching out to those who are not already part of the global scholarly conversation.

III. Domestic Political and Institutional Context

The working definition of foreign relations law for this volume is, "the domestic law of each nation that governs how that nation interacts with the rest of the world."[18] But it is difficult—if not impossible—to understand that domestic law without first understanding the domestic political institutions that generate, interpret, and enforce that law.

Some legal scholars have approached the question by classifying states into "monist" and "dualist" legal systems.[19] In this view, dualist states are states in which the rights and obligations created by international law have no effect in domestic law unless legislation is in force to give effect to them.In contrast, monist states directly incorporate international law into domestic law: once an international legal obligation comes into place, it automatically triggers a domestic legal commitment.

There are at least two difficulties with this approach, however: first, the categories are not, in fact, analytically distinct. Both assume that domestic law determines when and how international law has force as a matter of domestic law. The only question is whether domestic law provides that international law automatically has a particular domestic legal status or not. The few states that on first glance appear to be "monist" turn out to be much closer to the "dualist" approach in practice (including the United States, where the U.S. Constitution's Supremacy Clause is highly qualified by the doctrine of non-self-execution). Second, even if the categories were analytically distinct, they include states with wildly different practices. Arguably the variation within the categories is more interesting than the variation between them.

There is a robust comparative political science literature devoted to the broader, but related, issue of political differences across nations. Unfortunately, this literature has two shortcomings for these purposes. First, it rarely connects with foreign relations law. It does not address, for example, the ways in which international law is incorporated into domestic law. Second, and more important, the categories that have thus far been used to categorize political systems are much too categorical—missing an immense amount of important institutional detail. A careful look at the institutional structures that underlie international lawmaking therefore has the potential to ground theoretical

[18] Curtis A. Bradley, *What Is Foreign Relations Law?*, ch. 1 in this volume, at p.3.

[19] Anthony Aust, Modern Treaty Law and Practice 181–195 (2007); David Sloss, *Treaty Enforcement in Domestic Courts: A Comparative Analysis*, *in* The Role of Domestic Courts in Treaty Enforcement: A Comparative Study (2009).

accounts. This is particularly true when it comes to understanding the relationship between the legislature and executive.

In 1990, Juan Linz published two essays: "The Perils of Presidentialism"[20] and "The Virtues of Parliamentarism,"[21] initiating the modern debate about how to classify, define, and analyze different constitutional systems.[22] Although Linz limited his discussion to parliamentarism and presidentialism, he acknowledged the existence of institutional variety not captured by the dichotomy.[23] Subsequent scholarship introduced "hybrid" categories, including semi-presidentialism,[24] semi-parliamentarism,[25] and constrained parliamentarism.[26] More recent scholarship, including by a contributor to this book, Tom Ginsburg, has further challenged the traditional categories, demonstrating that even though the presidential-parliamentary distinction has remained foundational to comparative politics, there is a "fair degree of heterogeneity within these categories with respect to important institutional attributes."[27]

The broad categorical studies that have characterized much of the literature to date have immeasurably advanced our understanding of law and politics. And yet tethering research to grand categories has limited scholars' ability to analyze causal relationships and the political and legal consequences of institutional design. Empirical research driven by these categories almost inevitably involves broad ex ante decisions as to which constitutional variables are relevant to the category definition, and to that extent involves analytical prejudgment.

As comparative foreign relations law emerges as a field, it will be important to develop more detailed understandings of the multitude of institutional dynamics

[20] Juan J. Linz, *The Perils of Presidentialism*, 1 J. of Democracy 51 (1990).

[21] Juan J. Linz, *The Virtues of Parliamentarism*, 1 J. of Democracy 84 (1990).

[22] Scholars credit Linz as the most influential writer on the topic. His article to have the "most far-reaching" impact is *Presidential or Parliamentary Democracy: Does It Make a Difference?*, which Linz wrote in 1985. *See* Scott Mainwaring & Matthew S. Shugart, *Juan Linz, Presidentialism, and Democracy: A Critical Appraisal*, 29 Comp. Pol. 449 (1997). Linz presented the paper at academic conferences, and it served as the basis of his 1990 essays. He eventually published it in 1994. Juan J. Linz, *Presidential or Parliamentary Democracy: Does It Make a Difference?*, *in* The Failure of Presidential Democracy 3 (Juan J. Linz & Arturo Valenzuela eds., 1994).

[23] Linz, *supra* note 22, at 5.

[24] *See*, e.g., Thomas Sedelius & Jonas Linde, *Unravelling Semi-Presidentialism: Democracy and Government Performance in Four Distinct Regime Types*, 25 Democratization 136 (2017); Mark Freeman, *Constitutional Frameworks and Fragile Democracies: Choosing Between Parliamentarianism, Presidentialism, and Semi-Presidentialism*, 12 Pace Int'l L. Rev. 253 (2000); Alfred Stepan & Ezra N. Suleiman, *The French Fifth Republic: A Model for Import? Reflections on Poland and Brazil*, *in* Politics, Society, and Democracy: Comparative Studies 393, 398 (H. E. Chehabi & Alfred Stepan eds., Westview Press 1994).

[25] *See*, e.g., Philipp Dann, *Looking through the Federal Lens: The Semi-Parliamentary Democracy of the EU* (Jean Monnet Program, Working Paper No. 5/02) (2002).

[26] *See*, e.g., Bruce Ackerman, *The New Separation of Powers*, 113 Harv. L. Rev. 633 (2000); George Tsebelis, Veto Players: How Political Institutions Work 70 (2002); Jose Antonio Cheibub, Presidentialism, Parliamentarism, and Democracy (2007).

[27] Jose Antonio Cheibub, Zachary Elkins, & Tom Ginsburg, *Beyond Presidentialism and Parliamentarism*, 44 Brit. J. Pol. Sci. 515 (2014).

states have employed, moving beyond broad, general categorization of state institutions—democratic or nondemocratic, liberal or nonliberal, presidential or parliamentary, and so on—to record and analyze particular institutional forms. By examining the individual legal and institutional components of these concepts, scholars can elucidate the microfoundations of political power and law. Microfoundational provision-by-provision study of the foundations of international law minimizes this prejudgment and enables an ex post empirical analysis that may better serve the goals of political and legal inquiry. In particular, what is needed is fine-grained understanding of when and how domestic political and legal institutions are involved in the formation and enforcement of international law.

Ginsburg, founder of the Constitution Project database and leading figure in the quantitative study of comparative constitutions, has already made important progress on precisely this project. His own work, and the work of those who draw on the Constitution Project's database, has set this agenda for the field.[28] Pierre-Hugues Verdier and Mila Versteeg have developed yet another dataset covering 101 countries with more detailed data drawn not just from analysis of constitutional texts but from surveys as well. Their latest work drawing on this data set, Chapter 8 in this volume, illustrates the insights to be gleaned from this kind of work.[29] They find a sustained trend toward greater parliamentary involvement in treaty-making, important constraints on executive agreements and other alternative routes through which the executive can conclude internationally binding agreements, and a rise of parliamentary constraints on treaty withdrawal or termination. These are exciting findings that offer novel insights into the interplay between the branches of government in the creation of international law—as well as into how the relationship between them has changed over time.

My own research into the varied roles of the executive and legislative branches in the formation and enforcement of international law is much more limited, but it aims to illustrate the challenges—and the potential promise—of this effort. Here I outline findings based on an analysis of the constitutional text of 185 constitutions regarding three topics: (1) executive control over the creation of treaty obligations, (2) legislative control over the creation of treaty obligations, and (3) the legal status of international law, both treaties and custom, in the domestic legal system. This work faces some of the limitations outlined in Section I—in particular, it relies exclusively on constitutional text. But it aims to open the door to more fine-grained analysis of the political processes involved in the formation and enforcement of international law.

Table 1 summarizes the findings, which are explained in more detail below.

[28] See the many works listed at http://comparativeconstitutionsproject.org/articles/.

[29] Verdier & Versteeg, *supra* note 13. For more on their rich data set and its construction, *see* Pierre-Hugues Verdier & Mila Versteeg, *International Law in National Legal Systems: An Empirical Investigation*, 109 Am. J. Int'l L. 467 (2015); Pierre-Hugues Verdier & Mila Versteeg, *Modes of Domestic Incorporation of International Law*, *in* Handbook on the Politics of International Law (Wayne Sandholtz & Christopher A. Whytock eds., 2016).

Table 1 The Creation and Legal Status of International Law in 185 Constitutions

Executive Control		
	Yes	No
Specifies Government's Role in Negotiating and Concluding Treaties	61	124
Requires Government's Approval of Treaties	79	106
Specifies Chief Executive's Role in Negotiating and Concluding Treaties	112	73
Requires Chief Executive's Approval of Treaty	135	50
Legislative Control		
	Yes	No
Requires Legislative Approval of Treaties of Some or All Treaties	95 (some treaties) 53 (all treaties)	36
Requires Lower House Approval (If There Is a Lower House)	112 (majority of those present) 24 (majority of all members) 3 (supermajority)	39
Requires Upper House Approval (If There Is an Upper House)	41 (majority of those present) 10 (majority of all members) 4 (supermajority)	26
Legal Status of International Law in the Domestic Legal Order		
	Yes	No
Specifies that Some or All Approved Treaties Are a Part of the State's Domestic Legal System	80	105
Specifies that Supremacy of Some or All Treaties over Domestic Law	64	121
Specifies that Customary International Law Is a Part of the State's Internal Law	23	162
Specifies Some Relationship between Customary International Law and Ordinary Legislation	11	174

Executive Control

Government Role in Negotiating and Concluding Treaties

Political actors play a variety of roles in negotiating and concluding treaties. The power to negotiate and conclude treaties is important for two related reasons. First, the agent that concludes the treaty "sets the agenda" for the treaty vote—it determines (along with other parties to the treaty) the content of the treaty to be voted on, usually with no possibility of unilateral textual amendment. Second, an actor with the power to conclude a treaty has an implicit veto on a treaty[30]—it can choose not to conclude

[30] "Conclusion" refers here to the negotiation and finishing up of a treaty, as well as the requirement of formal approval. This leaves open the possibility that other agents within the executive branch would also need to give formal approval to the treaty before it can be ratified.

any given treaty, and its conclusion is tantamount to its acceptance (at least provisionally) of the treaty. Noting an actor's power to conclude treaties is particularly important in cases where that actor has no (further) formal role in approving the treaty—for instance, in a parliamentary system where a government concludes treaties, but ratification occurs through parliament and signature through the head of state.[31] In such cases, the variables documenting power to conclude treaties capture the implicit veto power that is ignored by variables documenting formal powers to sign and ratify. (This turns out to be an exclusively executive power. While it is possible to conceive of an extreme form of "assembly government"[32] in which the legislature itself negotiates and concludes treaties, no constitution examined here provides for such a government.)[33]

The majority of constitutions (124) do not explicitly permit or require the government or cabinet to play a role in negotiating or concluding treaties, but a significant minority (61) do.

Government Approval of Treaties

A number of constitutions formally require the government's approval of treaties. Specifically, the majority of constitutions (106) do not require the government's approval of treaties; a minority of constitutions (79) do require the government's approval.

In some cases, this requirement is redundant with power to conclude treaties, because "concluding" a treaty amounts to giving formal approval. But some constitutions require the formal approval of a treaty from an agent that does not possess the power to conclude treaties, or that exercises only partial or joint power in the conclusion process. For example, a constitution can invest the negotiation and conclusion powers in the government, but also require that the president ratify a treaty subsequent to legislative passage; or it might provide a role for both the government and the president in concluding a treaty, but only require the ultimate approval of one or the other.

Chief Executive's Role in Negotiating and Concluding Treaties

The chief executive frequently plays a key role in negotiating and concluding treaties. The "chief executive" is often the president or prime minister of a country, though occasionally (notably in Communist countries) the role of the chief executive is undertaken (at least formally) by a collective body separate from the ministries. The majority of constitutions (112) in the study do specify a role for the chief executive, but a significant minority (73) do not.

[31] The term "government" is used here to refer to the cabinet of ministers or other executive officials, not including the chief executive.

[32] Giovanni Sartori, Comparative Constitutional Engineering 110 (2d ed. 1994).

[33] Because the analysis here is based on constitutional text, it does not include informal involvement. For example, in a presidential system, the cabinet or ministries often do the actual work of negotiating and concluding treaties, but if the constitution assigns the power of negotiation and conclusion to the president, and makes no mention of the role of the cabinet or ministries in this regard, the cabinet has no constitutionally mandated role in negotiating or concluding treaties.

Chief Executive's Approval of Treaties

The majority of constitutions (135) explicitly require the chief executive's approval of treaties; a minority (50) do not.

Legislative Control

Legislative Approval of Treaties

Many constitutions establish a general requirement that some or all treaties, whatever the type or subject matter, receive legislative approval for ratification. A minority of constitutions (36) do not explicitly provide that any treaties are subject to legislative approval. A plurality (95) provide that some treaties are subject to legislative approval, and a strong minority (53) explicitly provide that all treaties are subject to legislative approval. In short, the vast majority of constitutions provide that some or all treaties are subject to legislative approval.

Looking at requirements that apply specifically to lower legislative houses, a number of constitutions (39) do not provide for any involvement by the legislature in treaty ratification. The majority of constitutions require a majority of all present members (112) or all members (24) to approve a treaty. Only a small minority require a supermajority of two-thirds or three-quarters of all members or present members (3 total).

Looking at requirements that apply to upper legislative houses, a moderate number of states have an upper house, but their constitutions do not specify any involvement in treaty approval (26). A plurality of constitutions require a majority of those present (41) or of all members (10) to approve a treaty. A minority of constitutions require a supermajority (4 in total).

Legal Status of International Law in the Domestic Legal Order

Treaties as Law

The approval of a treaty does not always render that treaty binding law from the perspective of a state's domestic legal system. As Duncan Hollis notes,[34] some states adhere to the "incorporation doctrine" regarding treaties, according to which treaties become binding in the domestic legal system at the same time that they become binding under international law. Other states adhere to the "transformation doctrine," according to which further domestic procedures are required before the treaties become binding in the domestic legal system.

[34] Duncan B. Hollis, *A Comparative Approach to Treaty Law and Practice*, *in* National Treaty Law and Practice 40–41 (Duncan Hollis et al. eds., 2005).

The majority of constitutions (105) do not specify that approved treaties are a part of the state's domestic legal system. A small number (4) specify that human rights treaties are part of the state's domestic legal system. A slightly larger (but still small) number (10) specify that treaties are part of the domestic legal system if the legislature has separately consented, and a significant number (37) specify that approved or ratified treaties are a part of the state's domestic legal system. A significant number (29) do not directly state that a treaty is a part of domestic law, but they specify a relationship to ordinary domestic legislation that implies a legal status.

Treaties' Relative Legal Status

A key question is not only whether a treaty is law, but what relationship it has to ordinary domestic legislation. The majority of constitutions (121) do not specify the relationship between treaties and ordinary legislation. A number of constitutions (13) provide that human rights treaties are supreme over ordinary legislation. A somewhat smaller number (9) provide for the supremacy of treaties to which the legislature has consented over ordinary domestic legislation. A significant portion of constitutions (42) establish general supremacy of treaties over prior domestic legislation.

Customary International Law as Law

Some constitutions address the legal status of customary international law (CIL) (often referred to as "international law," or "general international law" or "common principles" of international law). A majority of constitutions (162) do not mention customary international law; a small minority of constitutions (18) specify that customary international law is a part of the state's internal, domestic legal order—that is, CIL is viewed as "law" domestically.[35] A small number (5) do not directly state that CIL is a part of domestic law, but they specify a relationship to ordinary domestic legislation that implies a legal status.

Customary International Law Relative Legal Status

Again, for those states that identify customary international law as law, there is a question of what its status is relative to ordinary legislation. The vast majority of constitutions (174) do not specify a relationship between customary international law and ordinary legislation; a small number (11) specify some relationship between customary international law and ordinary legislation.

These data offer some insight into the institutional dynamics within and across states as they make and enforce international law. They help us identify outliers (e.g.,

[35] As in the case of treaties, this variable captures explicit and direct statements of the domestic legal status of customary international law. For example, the constitution of Austria declares that "[t]he generally recognized rules of International Law are valid parts of Federal law." Articles 9 and 11 of the Cape Verde Constitution states that "[i]nternational Law shall be an integral part of the Cape Verdian judicial system." Statements of supremacy of customary international law or interpretive rules regarding customary international law are coded in the next variable (Customary International Law Relative Legal Status).

the United States is unusual in several respects), and it can identify areas in which more fine-grained analysis is warranted. But because the data are based exclusively on the constitutional text, caution is also warranted: as noted earlier, much that matters in comparative foreign relations law is not reflected in the formal text but has instead emerged over time. These quantitative data should be regarded as a starting point for deeper inquiry into the roles of domestic actors in the creation and enforcement of international law.

IV. The Influence of Geopolitics

A final area that deserves attention from scholars working on comparative foreign relations law is the role of geopolitics. There are two topics in particular that are worthy of careful consideration—regional or geographic influence and the influence of a state's geopolitical status.

Regional or geographic influence. A state's foreign relations law may be influenced by the foreign relations law of states surrounding it. Political scientists have documented so-called "neighborhood effects" in democratization, economic interdependence, and conflict.[36] They have looked, as well, at the regional dimensions of war economies and the impact they have on sustainable peace and development.[37] On a domestic level, political scientists have shown that a U.S. state is more likely to adopt a law if its neighboring states have already done so.[38] Others have found regional standards of behavior might even affect a state's willingness to commit to and comply with international treaties.[39] These are suggestive that there may be similar regional or geographic effects on states' foreign relations law.

In earlier work, Tom Ginsburg has found that constitutional war powers are driven at least in part by copying from neighboring countries.[40] René Urueña's chapter in this volume on the domestic application of international law in Latin America offers an example of the insights such scholarship can provide.[41] Urueña shows that there are regional similarities that can be traced at least in part to events in the region's history—particularly its emergence from a period of brutal dictatorships in the 1970s and 1980s and the creation of the Inter-American regional treaties and courts, which have pressed

[36] *See* Kristian Skrede Gleditsch, All International Politics is Local: The Diffusion of Conflict, Integration, and Democratization (2002).

[37] Michael Pugh & Neil Cooper, War Economies in a Regional Context (2004).

[38] Christopher Z. Mooney, *Modeling Regional Effects on State Policy Diffusion*, 54 Pol. Res. Q. 103 (2001).

[39] *See* Beth Simmons, *International Law and State Behavior: Commitment and Compliance in International Monetary Affairs*, 94 Am. Pol. Sci. Rev. 819 (2000).

[40] Tom Ginsburg, *Chaining the Dog of War: Comparative Data*, 15 Chi. J. Int'l L. 138, 147 (2014).

[41] René Urueña, *Domestic Application of International Law in Latin America*, ch. 32 in this volume.

for further incorporation of international law—especially international human rights treaties—into domestic legal systems.

Geopolitical status. A state's relative status within the geopolitical space may also influence its posture toward international law. It is frequently hypothesized that weaker states are more likely to favor international law, as it provides them with a tool for influencing the behavior of more powerful states. The flip side of the hypothesis is that more powerful states are more likely to disfavor international law, as it allows weaker states to exercise influence over them. There are, of course, many reasons to think that these claims are untrue. To begin with, more powerful states may have played a significant rule in constructing the legal order in the first place—for example, the United States was key to the creation of nearly every significant international legal institution that came to life in the immediate post–World War II period. Such states may favor these international legal institutions because they serve their interests or support their values, even if they provide some voice or power to less powerful states.[42]

Relatedly, political scientists have hypothesized that newer states, particularly newly established democracies, are more likely to favor strong international legal regimes than are either dictatorships or strong democracies. That is because newly established democracies have the greatest interest in stabilizing the domestic political status quo against nondemocratic threats, and they regard binding international law—particularly international human rights law—as a tool for "locking in" credible domestic politics.[43]

This work generally focuses on the willingness of states to create and join strong international legal institutions. But does it have an impact on their foreign relations law as well? One could imagine that newly democratic regimes, in the process or revising their constitutions for the new political order, might revise the constitutions and other relevant legal institutions to be more favorable toward the incorporation of international law. For instance, South Africa's constitution, revised in the wake of the fall of the apartheid government, includes some of the strongest constitutional provisions incorporating international law into the domestic legal regime.[44] Similarly, the constitutions of a number of Latin American countries (including several that relatively recently democratized) directly incorporate international human rights law into their domestic law. A recent study of Argentina, Bolivia, Brazil, Colombia, and El Salvador found that all five have "constitutionalized" international human rights law in various ways.[45] Are these outliers or indicative of a broader trend?

Domestic law governing the use of force may also be influenced by geopolitics. States with large militaries—and large military budgets—may have a different posture toward

[42] A hypothesis worth exploring is whether growing geopolitical power encourages growth in executive power as well.

[43] Andrew Moravcsik, *The Origins of Human Rights Regimes: Democratic Delegation in Postwar Europe*, 54 INT'L ORG. 217 (2000).

[44] John Dugard, *International Law and the South African Constitution*, 1 EUR. J. INT'L L. 77 (1997).

[45] *See* Edgar Melgar, *Human Rights as Constitutional Rights: The Constitutionalization of International Human Rights Law in Latin America* (unpublished working paper 2018).

authorizing the use of military force than those without. States' historical geopolitical status may also play an important role. Notably, the states that lost World War II (Germany, Japan, and Italy) incorporated the prohibition on use of force into their constitutions after the war. As we can see from the chapters in this volume by Anne Peters (Germany) and Tadashi Mori (Japan),[46] these postwar constraints remain in place today, though there is new pressure to revisit them in light of changes in the geopolitical context.

V. A Cautionary Note: Approaching International Law through Domestic Law

As we aim to launch a field of comparative foreign relations law, it is important to be mindful—and perhaps even critical—of the nature of the enterprise. Implicit in the study of "the domestic law of each nation that governs how that nation interacts with the rest of the world" may be a suggestion of primacy of domestic law over international law. Certainly many studies of foreign relations law seem to approach the topic from this perspective—with the assumption that international law does not have the status of law in the domestic legal system unless domestic law provides it that status. But that is not the only possible relationship between the two legal orders.[47]

I do not mean to suggest that foreign relations law is not a proper subject of study. Clearly, it is important to understand when and how domestic law recognizes and incorporates international law into the domestic legal order. But we should not make the mistake of assuming that international law *only* has legal effect when domestic law gives it legal status. International law's juridical relationship to domestic law—and its independent juridical status—are separate subjects of study. It is important to recognize that comparative foreign relations law does not answer the question: when is international law legally effective? Comparative foreign relations law can instead answer only the question, when and how does domestic law recognize international law as legally effective.

This insight is far from new. In 1938, J. G. Starke engaged in what he called a "strictly theoretical treatment of the relation between international law and municipal law."[48] In it, he observed that, "[r]educed to its lowest terms, the doctrine of state primacy

[46] Anne Peters, *Military Operations Abroad under the German Basic Law*, ch. 44 in this volume; Tadashi Mori, *Decisions in Japan to Use Military Force or to Participate in Multinational Peacekeeping Operations*, ch. 46 in this volume.

[47] Karen Knop's chapter in this volume compellingly articulates a similar discomfort. *See* Karen Knop, *Foreign Relations Law: Comparison as Invention*, ch. 3 in this volume.

[48] J. G. Starke, *Monism and Dualism in the Theory of International Law*, 17 Brit. Y.B. Int'l L. 66 (1936).

is a denial of international law as law, and an affirmation of international anarchy."[49] He worried that under the approach of what he called the doctrine of state primacy, international law only has meaning insofar as it is given meaning by state law, making international law entirely contingent.

As the project of comparative foreign relations law commences, scholars participating in the enterprise should be thoughtful about the broader implications of approaching international law from the domestic law perspective. We should be careful to acknowledge that comparative foreign relations law, as important as it is, addresses one piece of the puzzle of international law's legal effect. When, whether, and how international law has legal effect independent of domestic law is not answered by comparative foreign relations law. Certainly, the fact that comparative foreign relations law does not address international law's independent effect does not mean that such an effect does not exist. It is, instead, a separate and independent question.[50]

VI. Conclusion

The emergence of the field of comparative study of foreign relations law opens up a number of new questions for scholars to tackle. But there is reason for caution as well. There is much to be learned from studying how states have solved shared legal dilemmas. Yet individual legal rules and practice on particular legal topics cannot be divorced from the broader context within which they are found. These rules are necessarily embedded in and intertwined with a given state's unique legal, historical, political context. As we compare practices across states, it can sometimes be easy to lose sight of these differences. The effort to engage in comparative foreign relations law should therefore not be understood as an effort to identify outliers and encourage conformity—though there may be instances in which a state may learn from another and adopt a similar practice as a result. It can and should also be seen as an opportunity to understand the sources of—and reasons for—differences across states.

[49] *Id.* at 77.

[50] It is worth noting that studying comparative foreign relations law can help to counteract some of the parochialism that otherwise might plague the field.

CHAPTER 6

THE CONSTITUTIONAL ALLOCATION OF EXECUTIVE AND LEGISLATIVE POWER OVER FOREIGN RELATIONS

A Survey

JENNY S. MARTINEZ

In respect to foreign relations, the executive branch of government is given a preeminent role in many constitutional systems. There are a number of practical and theoretical reasons for this allocation of authority: the ability of the head of government to interact and negotiate with foreign leaders; the speed with which the executive can make decisions as compared to a legislative body; and the executive's advantage in access to classified information. Nevertheless, countervailing interests related to democratic accountability, the rule of law, and the value of deliberative process lead many systems to allocate significant authority to the legislative branch of government as well. Even in parliamentary systems where the head of government presumably enjoys the support of a majority of the legislature, the great majority of constitutions specifically call for legislative participation in important decisions such as making war or undertaking significant international legal obligations through treaty ratification.

This chapter explores the allocation of authority between executive and legislative branch officials with respect to three areas: general foreign relations powers such as reception of ambassadors and recognition of foreign governments; treaty negotiation, ratification, and implementation; and war powers. The chapter begins with a theoretical account of the concerns motivating constitution drafters in determining how to allocate foreign affairs powers. Then, with respect to each area of foreign affairs power, the discussion continues with a descriptive analysis of world constitutions, based on the constitutions included in the Comparative Constitutions Project online database.[1] This approach has been chosen in order to move beyond mere anecdote and impression and provide a more solid empirical grounding for descriptive observation. Of course, the text of a constitution is only a part of the picture, for in many cases, actual practice may deviate. For example, a constitution may allocate the power to declare war to the legislature, while study of actual practice would show the executive branch more often initiating military action. To a limited extent, the chapter also examines practice and case law from a few jurisdictions, but this inquiry is limited by space constraints. It is nevertheless instructive to observe the patterns in constitution drafters' aspirations. Written constitutions are designed to set up structures of government, but also to signal normative values to both domestic and international audiences.

Overall, it appears that most modern constitutions contemplate the sharing of foreign relations authority between the executive and legislative branches, with the precise boundaries of power more often determined by practicalities, politics, and particular circumstances than abstract theories. In particular, constitutional design choices are often influenced by the history and political context of a particular country and region, and provide a lens into what a given society views as important, dangerous, or problematic. The variations in design choices refute the notion that most foreign relations powers are inherently "executive" or "legislative" in nature, and instead highlight the ways in which design choices are embedded in broader social and political contexts.

I. Design Choices and Relative Institutional Competence

The classic explanation for the preference for executive power in foreign relations is that given by Alexander Hamilton in Federalist No. 70: "[d]ecision, activity, secrecy and dispatch will generally characterise the proceedings of one man in a much more eminent degree than the proceedings of any greater number; and in proportion as the number is increased, these qualities will be diminished."[2] The U.S. Supreme Court in the *Curtiss-Wright* decision, reflecting a maximalist view of executive power in foreign affairs, similarly explained that the president, "not Congress, has the better opportunity of knowing the conditions which prevail in foreign countries, and especially is this true in time of war. He has his confidential sources of information. He has his agents in the form of diplomatic, consular and other officials. Secrecy in respect of information

[1] The analysis is based on material from the Comparative Constitutions Project, as published in the https://constituteproject.org database as of August 2017. This data set includes constitutions in force through September 2013 for "nearly every independent state in the world."

[2] The Federalist, No. 70.

gathered by them may be highly necessary, and the premature disclosure of it productive of harmful results."[3]

At the same time, the legislature is often given a role in decisions concerning foreign affairs as a matter of democratic legitimacy. For example, in one of several decisions concerning the role of parliamentary approval of military deployments, the German Constitutional Court explained that "[t]he Basic Law has entrusted the decision as to war or peace to the German *Bundestag* as the body representing the people."[4] Likewise, South Korea's constitutional court stated:

> [I]t is desirable that such a decision is to be made by the institution representative of the constituents that can be held politically responsible toward the constituents therefor, by way of prudent decision-making through an expansive and extensive deliberation with the experts in the relevant fields. The Constitution in this vein endows such authority onto the President who is directly elected by the constituents and is responsible directly for the constituents, while authorizing the National Assembly to determine whether or not to consent to a decision to dispatch the Armed Forces, in order to ensure prudence in the President's exercise of such authority.[5]

Legislative approval for treaties and international agreements is often required to ensure democratic legitimacy for measures that will require changes to domestic law or entangle the nation in foreign obligations that could lead to costly consequences down the road. Legislative authorization is also thought to reduce the chances of treaty breach, since it signifies a broad base of domestic political support for the obligation and willingness to take the necessary steps to fulfill treaty obligations.

Because of the tendency of constitutions to prescribe the sharing of foreign affairs powers, there is considerable ambiguity at the interstices of executive and legislative power in many of these areas. Much of the complexity in implementation comes from drawing the line between actions that are permissible and impermissible for the executive to undertake unilaterally: decisions to deploy troops that are of a minor or noncombat nature, or in situations of time-sensitive urgency, or pursuant to multilateral mutual defense treaties previously approved by the legislature; adherence to international agreements of a minor or technical nature, or those which will not necessarily require actions in the domestic legal system, or those which are concluded in haste by the executive to resolve imminent crises. Other ambiguities arise in relation to actions that fall generally into the category of foreign relations without implicating a typically enumerated or well-defined power; actions in this netherworld can include the power to withdraw from or decide deliberately to breach treaties previously ratified (although many constitutions actually do, in fact, address withdrawal, such provisions are not nearly as widespread as those discussing ratification); the power to recognize

[3] United States v. Curtiss-Wright Export Corp., 299 U.S. 304, 320 (1936).

[4] Bundesverfassungsgericht [BVerfG] [Federal Constitutional Court], Judgment of 7 May 2008, 2 BvE 1/03, para. 57.

[5] Case Concerning the Presidential Decision to Dispatch Korean National Armed Forces to Iraq, 16–11 KCCR 601, 2003Hun-Ma814, Apr. 29, 2004.

foreign governments when there is a dispute concerning the legitimate government of a particular territory, for example following a coup d'etat or independence movement leading to territorial secession; and the imposition of sanctions of various sorts on other nations. Resolution of such questions may take place in the political or judicial spheres, and may involve more or less candor about the balance between practical considerations and theoretical constraints on government power.

As a general matter, these issues of foreign relations law rest at the intersection of international law and domestic constitutional law; domestic rules in this realm do not exist in a vacuum, but are formed under the influence of and in dialogue with the world outside a country's borders. As other chapters in this book suggest, comparative constitutional analysis is useful for untangling the threads of influence and connection.[6]

II. General Foreign Affairs Powers

As explained in later sections of this chapter, an examination of world constitutions reveals that the majority of constitutions specifically address war powers and treaty powers explicitly, and a majority of constitutions that do address these powers in some way divide these powers between the executive and legislative branches of government. At the same time, a significant number of constitutions refer to more generic foreign affairs powers, such as the power to represent the nation in foreign affairs. Many constitutions also specifically address the power to send and receive ambassadors or otherwise to maintain relations with other nations and international bodies. This section addresses these general foreign affairs powers, while later sections discuss treaty and war powers.

Power to Represent the State Internationally

A large number of constitutions—at least 86 out of the 192 constitutions examined[7]—explicitly vest an executive official or the executive branch with general powers to

[6] *See,* e.g., Tom Ginsburg, *Comparative Foreign Relations Law: A National Constitutions Perspective,* ch. 4 in this volume.

[7] Constitutions with such provisions granting some form of general foreign affairs power (such as the power to represent the state) to the chief executive or executive branch include: Algeria, Angola, Armenia, Austria, Azerbaijan, Belgium, Bhutan, Bolivia, Bosnia-Herzegovina, Brazil, Bulgaria, Burundi, Cameroon, Cape Verde, Childe, China, Colombia, Comoros, Costa Rice, Croatia, Cuba, Czech Republic, Denmark, Dominican Republic, Ecuador, Egypt, El Salvador, Equatorial Guinea, Estonia, Finland, Gambia, Georgia, Germany, Greece, Guatemala, Guinea-Bissau, Honduras, Hungary, Ireland, Japan, Kazakhstan, North Korea, South Korea, Kosovo, Kyrgyzstan, Latvia, Liberia, Liechtenstein, Lithuania, Maldives, Marshall Islands, Mauritania, Mexico, Micronesia, Moldova, Monaco, Mongolia, Montenegro, Mozambique, Nicaragua, Oman, Panama, Qatar, Romania, Russian Federation, Rwanda, Sao Tome, Serbia, Sierra Leone, Slovakia, South Sudan, Spain, Sudan, Suriname, Switzerland, Taiwan, Tajikistan, Tunisia, Ukraine, United Arab Emirates, Uruguay, Uzbekistan, Venezuela, and Vietnam.

represent the state in foreign affairs. For example, South Korea's constitution states that: "[t]he President shall be the Head of State and represent the State vis-a-vis foreign states,"[8] while in Mexico the president is "to lead the foreign policy."[9] In a similar vein, the Russian Constitution provides that the "President of the Russian Federation, as the Head of State, shall represent the Russian Federation within the country and in international relations,"[10] while in Egypt "[t]he President of the Republic represents the state in foreign relations."[11] Somewhat cryptically, the U.S. Constitution vests "the executive Power" in the president, an allocation that has long led to debates about precisely which foreign affairs prerogatives, if any, are encompassed within this general executive power and therefore granted to the president.[12]

Some nations with more complex forms of executive structure divide general foreign affairs powers among various individuals or bodies. For governments that include both a president and a prime minister, for example, powers over international relations are sometimes divided between the two officials. In some instances, the president is given a formal role as head of state that translates to some form of international representation. Thus, the German Basic Law provides that "[t]he Federal President shall represent the Federation for the purposes of international law."[13] These powers are largely formal, however, as the German chancellor as head of government actually directs foreign policy. Finland's constitution provides that "[t]he foreign policy of Finland is directed by the President of the Republic in co-operation with the Government,"[14] while at the same time "[t]he Prime Minister represents Finland on the European Council" and "[u]nless the Government exceptionally decides otherwise, the Prime Minister also represents Finland in other activities of the European Union requiring the participation of the highest level of State."[15] In France's semi-presidential system, the president both nominally and in practice enjoys greater powers with respect to foreign affairs than the prime minister, though in periods of "co-habitation" when the president and prime minister are from different parties, prime ministers have also significantly participated in foreign policy and attended international meetings to represent the state.[16]

In some constitutional monarchies, the monarch is still recognized as head of state with a formal role in international relations, even while the elected government functionally exercises day-to-day foreign affairs powers. For example, Spain's constitution provides that "[t]he King is the Head of State, the symbol of its unity and permanence. He arbitrates and moderates the regular functioning of the institutions, assumes the highest representation of the Spanish State in international relations, especially with the nations of its historical community, and exercises the functions expressly conferred on him by the Constitution and the laws."[17] In Norway, "[t]he King

[8] South Korea, art. 66(1) (1948, rev. 1987). [9] Mexico, art. 89 (1917, rev. 2015).

[10] Russia, art. 80(4) (1993, rev. 2014). [11] Egypt, art. 151 (2014).

[12] Jenny S. Martinez, *Inherent Executive Power: A Comparative Perspective*, 115 Yale L.J. 2480, 2484 (2006).

[13] Germany, art. 59 (1949, rev. 2014). [14] Finland, sec. 93 (1999, rev. 2011).

[15] Finland, sec. 66 (1999, rev. 2011). [16] *See* Martinez, *supra* note 12, at 2488.

[17] Spain, sec. 56 (1) (1978, rev. 2011).

has the right to call up troops, to engage in hostilities in defence of the Realm and to make peace, to conclude and denounce conventions, to send and to receive diplomatic envoys."[18] In democratic constitutional monarchies like Spain or Norway, the allocation of more substantive foreign affairs powers to the elected head of government or to the legislature renders these nominal allocations of power to the monarch largely symbolic. In more traditional monarchies, the allocation of broad powers to the monarch is real; Qatar's constitution, for example, provides that the "Prince represents the State inside and outside the State and in all international relations," and that is indeed so.[19]

Sometimes the executive branch of government as a whole, rather than the chief executive alone, is given general authority. For example, in Japan "[t]he Cabinet, in addition to other general administrative functions, shall perform the following functions: . . . [m]anage foreign affairs."[20] Nations with unusual plural executive structures, like the three-person presidency of Bosnia and Herzegovina, have developed their own unique arrangements; Bosnia and Herzegovina's constitution provides that "[t]he Presidency shall have responsibility for: . . . [c]onducting the foreign policy of Bosnia and Herzegovina."[21] In South Korea, while the president and legislature are assigned formal powers, there is also provision for deliberation within the executive branch, as the constitution directs that "[t]he following matters shall be referred to the State Council for deliberation: Declaration of war, conclusion of peace and other important matters pertaining to foreign policy."[22] In Switzerland, "[t]he Federal Council is responsible for foreign relations, subject to the right of participation of the Federal Assembly; it represents Switzerland abroad."[23]

Aside from rare instances like Switzerland, it is not common for constitutions to grant generic foreign relations authority to a legislative body. Thus, at least in the category of generic foreign relations authority, it seems common for constitutions to view it as desirable for one person or at most a handful of people to serve as the symbolic main representative of the state when interacting with other states; in a sense, these provisions allow a nation to speak with one voice and thus, perhaps, increase its chances of being heard clearly.

Power over Reception, Recognition, and Appointment of Ambassadors

In a related vein, a large number of constitutions—at least 83 out of the 192 constitutions reviewed for this chapter—also contain specific provisions with respect to selection of ambassadors to serve abroad and reception of foreign ambassadors and

[18] Norway, art. 26 (1814, rev. 2015). [19] Qatar, art. 66 (2003). [20] Japan, art. 73 (1946).

[21] Bosnia and Herzegovina, art. V.3 (1995, rev. 2009). Other examples include Libya's "national transitional council" and the United Arab Emirates "Federal Supreme Council."

[22] South Korea, art. 89 (1948, rev. 1987). [23] Switzerland, art. 184 (1999, rev. 2014).

ministers. Most of these provisions grant such powers to the executive branch.[24] In one typical provision, in Brazil "[t]he President of the Republic has the exclusive powers to: . . . maintain relations with foreign States and accredit their diplomatic representatives."[25] Similarly, in South Korea, the president is empowered to "accredit, receive or dispatch diplomatic envoys."[26]

In a minority of constitutions, the executive power over appointing ambassadors is constrained in some way. For example, while the three-person presidency of Bosnia and Herzegovina has power over diplomatic representatives, in "[a]ppointing ambassadors and other international representatives of Bosnia and Herzegovina, no more than two-thirds of whom may be selected from the territory of the Federation."

In the U.S. Constitution, the president "shall nominate, and by and with the Advice and Consent of the Senate, shall appoint Ambassadors, other public Ministers and Consuls," though the power to "receive Ambassadors and other public Ministers" is vested in the president with no mention of the legislature.[27] In the *Zivotofsky* case, these and other provisions of the Constitution led the Supreme Court to conclude that "[t]he text and structure of the Constitution grant the President the power to recognize foreign nations and governments" and that this power was exclusively vested in the executive branch, not Congress. The Court explained that:

> Put simply, the Nation must have a single policy regarding which governments are legitimate in the eyes of the United States and which are not. Foreign countries need to know, before entering into diplomatic relations or commerce with the United States, whether their ambassadors will be received; whether their officials will be immune from suit in federal court; and whether they may initiate lawsuits here to vindicate their rights. These assurances cannot be equivocal. Recognition is a topic on which the Nation must "speak . . . with one voice."[28]

The Court further explained that the "President is capable, in ways Congress is not, of engaging in the delicate and often secret diplomatic contacts that may lead to a decision on recognition . . . He is also better positioned to take the decisive, unequivocal action necessary to recognize other states at international law."[29]

[24] Constitutions with provisions concerning executive power to send and/or receive ambassadors include Afghanistan, Albania, Angola, Argentina Bahrain, Belarus, Bolivia, Brazil, Burkina Faso, Cambodia, Chad, Colombia, Comoros, Croatia, Cyprus, Djibouti, Dominican Republic, Ecuador, Equatorial Guinea, Estonia, Ethiopia, France, Gabon, Gambia, Georgia, Germany, Ghana, Guyana, Haiti, Hungary, Iran, Iraq, Israel, Italy, North Korea, Kosovo, Kuwait, Kyrgyzstan, Lebanon, Libya, Madagascar, Mali, Mauritania, Micronesia, Moldova, Montenegro, Morocco, Mozambique, Myanmar, Namibia, Nepal, Niger, Norway, Oman, Panama, Poland, Portugal, Rwanda, Santa Lucia, Saudi Arabia, Senegal, Seychelles, Sierra Leone, Slovenia, Somalia, South Sudan, Sri Lanka, Sudan, Swaziland, Syrian Arab Republic, Timor-Leste, Tonga, Turkey, Uganda, UAE, United States, Vietnam, Zambia, and Zimbabwe.

[25] Brazil, art. 84 (1988, rev. 2015). [26] South Korea, art. 73 (1948, rev. 1987).

[27] United States, art. 2, §§ 2 and 3 (1789, rev. 1992).

[28] Zivotofsky v. Kerry, 135 S. Ct. 2076, 2086 (2015). [29] *Id.*

III. Treaties

The large majority of world constitutions contain provisions related to treaty ratification, and of these, most specify a role for the legislative as well as the executive branch of government. As Verdier and Versteeg discuss more extensively in their chapter in this book, the percentage of countries requiring legislative approval for treaties has varied over time, with an increase in recent decades.[30] Currently, at least 149 out of the 192 constitutions examined require legislative participation in the ratification of at least some treaties. A smaller number of constitutions also explicitly require legislative participation in the decision to withdraw from treaties. Some constitutions require even more elaborate procedures, such as popular referenda, for a small subset of treaties.

Legislative Participation

As Alexander Hamilton argued in Federalist No. 75, "the operation of treaties as laws, plead strongly for the participation of the whole or a portion of the legislative body in the office of making them." At least eighty-seven constitutions require legislative participation in treaty ratification on a blanket basis, without formally distinguishing among treaties based on subject matter or the importance of the agreement; in practice, not all of these countries may actually require legislative approval for every international agreement, but such exceptions are not obvious from the face of the constitutional text. At the same time, another very common pattern is for constitutions to require legislative ratification of a subset of treaties addressing particular topics deemed of significance. For example, the French Constitution vests the power to "negotiate and ratify" treaties in the president, while also providing that some treaties "may be ratified or approved only by virtue of an Act of Parliament." In France, the treaties that require legislative approval include "[p]eace treaties, commercial treaties, treaties or agreements relating to international organization, those that commit the finances of the State, those that modify provisions which are matters for statute, those relating to the status of persons, and those that involve the cession, exchange or addition of territory."[31] In a similar vein, Germany's Basic Law provides "[t]reaties that regulate the political relations of the Federation or relate to subjects of federal legislation shall require the consent or participation, in the form of federal law, of the bodies responsible in such a case for the enactment of federal law."[32] South Korea requires legislative approval for treaties "pertaining to mutual assistance or mutual security; treaties concerning important international organizations, treaties of friendship, trade

[30] *See* Pierre-Hugues Verdier & Mila Versteeg, *Separation of Powers, Treaty-Making, and Treaty Withdrawal: A Global Survey*, ch. 8 in this volume.

[31] France, arts. 52, 53 (1958, rev. 2008).

[32] Germany, art. 59 (1949, rev. 2014).

and navigation; treaties pertaining to any restriction on sovereignty, peace treaties, treaties which will burden the State or people with an important financial obligation; or treaties related to legislative matters."[33]

Common treaty types specifically identified in constitutions as requiring legislative approval include those involving national sovereignty and membership in international organizations (34 constitutions), those requiring changes to domestic law (30 constitutions), those that will necessitate the expenditure of funds (31 constitutions), peace (27 constitutions), territorial changes (26 constitutions), trade (19 constitutions), alliances (16 constitutions), the status of people (15 constitutions), the military (12 constitutions), human rights (11 constitutions), natural resources (7 constitutions), and national security (4 constitutions). The patterns in this regard seemingly reflect a concern over treaties covering matters typically addressed by legislatures (e.g., changes to law and expenditure of funds), as well as topics of significant importance to the nation (e.g., peace treaties, territorial changes).[34]

While there are certain types of treaties for which a significant number of countries require legislative approval, other countries have more idiosyncratic provisions, which appear to reflect concerns about treaty engagement based on national and regional history including any history of colonialism, and provide a lens into what a given society views as concerning or potentially troubling its foreign relations. For example, Ecuador adds to the typical list of treaties requiring legislative ratification those that "bind the State's economic policy in its National Development Plan to conditions of international financial institutions or transnational companies" and "compromise the country's natural heritage and especially its water, biodiversity and genetic assets."[35] Italy requires legislative approval for treaties requiring international arbitration or legal settlement of disputes.[36] Petroleum exporters Bahrain, Chad, Ecuador, and Kuwait contain provisions related to natural resources.

Some nations require a legislative supermajority or even a popular referendum before ratification of certain types of treaties, typically those involving matters it considers of widespread popular importance, such as territorial boundary changes, alliances or mutual defense pacts, or accession to regional or international organizations that involve some transfer of power to the supranational organization. Again, national and regional history as well as more abstract notions of political theory appear to play a role in these institutional design choices. For example, in Costa Rica, "public treaties and international agreements, that attribute or transfer specific competences to a community juridical order, with the purpose of realizing regional and common objectives, will require the approval of the Legislative Assembly, by a vote of no less than the two-thirds of the totality of its members."[37] Croatia's constitution requires that "[i]nternational agreements which grant international organization or alliances

[33] South Korea, art. 60 (1948, rev. 1987). *See also* Jaemin Lee, *Incorporation and Implementation of Treaties in South Korea*, ch. 13 in this volume.

[34] *See also* Verdier & Versteeg, *supra* note 30.

[35] Ecuador, art. 419(5), (8) (2008, rev. 2015).

[36] Italy, art. 80 (1947, rev. 2012).

[37] Costa Rica, art. 121 (1949, rev. 2011).

powers derived from the constitution of the Republic of Croatia, shall be subject to ratification by the Croatian Parliament by two-thirds majority vote of all representatives."[38] El Salvador requires varying supermajorities for certain types of treaties. In that country, "ratification of all extradition treaties shall require the affirmative vote of two-thirds of the elected Deputies"[39] and "for the ratification of any treaty or pact for which any question related to the limits of the Republic are submitted to arbitration, a vote of at least three-quarters of the elected Deputies shall be necessary."[40]

Other constitutions go even further in requiring a popular vote for certain types of treaties. For example, Bolivia requires a popular referendum concerning "questions of borders, monetary integration, structural economic integration," or the "grant of institutional authority to international or supra-national organisms, in the context of processes of integration."[41] Bolivia's constitution also allows for a referendum on treaty ratification "when it is requested by five percent of the citizens registered on the voting rolls, or thirty five percent of the representatives of the Pluri-National Legislative Assembly." Moreover, "[t]hese initiatives can be used also to request that the Executive Organ sign a treaty."[42] Similarly, Egypt requires that "with regards to any treaty of peace and alliance, and treaties related to the rights of sovereignty, voters must be called for a referendum, and they are not to be ratified before the announcement of their approval in the referendum."[43] Finally, a number of countries require that their constitutional courts review the constitutionality of treaties before they are ratified.[44]

Sole Executive Agreements

Some constitutions also specifically refer to international agreements that may be concluded by the executive alone. For example, in Honduras "[t]he Executive branch may, in matters of its exclusive competence, enter into, ratify or adhere to international conventions with foreign states or international organizations without the previous requirement of approval by congress, which it must inform immediately."[45] Sweden's constitution provides that "[t]he Government may instruct an administrative authority to conclude an international agreement in a matter in which the agreement does not require the participation of the Riksdag or the Advisory Council on Foreign Affairs."[46] Similarly, the German Basic Law notes that "[i]n the case of executive agreements the provisions concerning the federal administration shall apply mutatis mutandis." Colombia generally requires legislative ratification for treaties, but provides: "the President of the Republic may give temporary effect to treaties of an economic or commercial nature agreed upon in the context of international organizations which so

[38] Croatia, art. 140 (1991, rev. 2010). [39] El Salvador, art. 28 (1983, rev. 2014).
[40] El Salvador, art. 147 (1983, rev. 2014). [41] Bolivia, art. 257 (2009).
[42] Bolivia, art. 259 (2009). [43] Egypt, art. 151 (2014).
[44] *See*, e.g., Madagascar, art. 137 (2010). [45] Honduras 1982, art. 21 (rev. 2013).
[46] Sweden, art. 2 (1974, rev. 2012).

provide. In such a case, as soon as a treaty enters into force provisionally, it shall be sent to Congress for its approval. If Congress does not approve the treaty, its application shall be suspended."[47] Swaziland's constitution provides that the provisions governing legislative approval of treaties "do not apply where the agreement is of a technical, administrative or executive nature or is an agreement which does not require ratification or accession."[48] While the constitution of the United States does not specifically refer to agreements concluded solely by the executive branch, as a matter of constitutional interpretation, the U.S. Supreme Court has approved the validity of agreements concluded solely by the president in certain types of areas, such as settlement of claims with foreign governments.[49]

Negotiation of Treaties

Some constitutions specify a unique role for the executive in negotiating treaties, even if legislative approval is required for ratification.[50] For example, in Chile the president is given power to "conduct political relations with foreign powers and international organizations, and conduct negotiations."[51] Likewise, the Russian president "shall hold negotiations and sign international treaties of the Russian Federation."[52] In Iraq, the Council of Ministers has the power "[t]o negotiate and sign international agreements and treaties, or designate any person to do so."[53]

The likely rationale for such provisions privileging executive power is explained by the U.S. Supreme Court in the *Curtiss-Wright* decision, which, in endorsing a maximalist view of executive power, argued that "[i]n this vast external realm, with its important, complicated, delicate and manifold problems, the President alone has the power to speak or listen as a representative of the nation. He makes treaties with the advice and consent of the Senate; but he alone negotiates. Into the field of negotiation the Senate cannot intrude, and Congress itself is powerless to invade it."[54] The Court quoted President George Washington regarding the negotiation of the Jay Treaty and refusal to submit the papers respecting that negotiation to the House of Representatives, explaining that "[t]he nature of foreign negotiations requires caution, and their success must often depend on secrecy, and even when brought to a conclusion, a full disclosure of all the measures, demands, or eventual concessions which may have been

[47] Colombia, art. 224 (1991, rev. 2015). [48] Swaziland, art. 238 (3) (2005).

[49] United States v. Belmont, 301 U.S. 324 (1937); United States v. Pink, 315 U.S. 203 (1942).

[50] Constitutions containing provisions referring to the executive's power to negotiate treaties include: Bangladesh, Benin, Bosnia Herzegovina, Burundi, Cape Verde, Chile, Comoros, Guinea, Guinea-Bissau, Haiti, Iraq, Kazakhstan, Kyrgyzstan, Lebanon, Madagascar, Malawi, Mali, Myanmar, Namibia, Nicaragua, Niger, Panama, Paraguay, Romania, Russian Federation, Rwanda, Sao Tome, Senegal, Slovakia, Timor-Leste, Togo, Ukraine, Uzbekistan, and Zambia.

[51] Chile, art. 32(15) (1980, rev. 2015). [52] Russia, art. 86(b) (1993, rev. 2014).

[53] Iraq, art. 80(6) (2005).

[54] United States v. Curtiss-Wright Export Corp., 299 U.S. 304, 319 (1936).

proposed or contemplated would be extremely impolitic, for this might have a pernicious influence on future negotiations or produce immediate inconveniences, perhaps danger and mischief, in relation to other powers."[55]

Some contemporary constitutions reflect concerns about secrecy in detailed provisions. In Chile, for example, the president can ask that "discussions and deliberations on these matters [of treaty ratification] shall be secret if the President of the Republic so demands it."[56] In the United States, the Senate had a practice, until the twentieth century, of debating treaties in private session.

At the same time, some constitutions allow for the legislature or even the public to play a role in initiating the process of treaty ratification. For example, Ecuador's constitution provides that the ratification of treaties "can be requested by referendum, citizen initiative or the President of the Republic."[57] Such provisions may have been drafted with the ratification of existing multilateral treaties in mind rather than the negotiation of new treaties—for example, to encourage the ratification of an existing multilateral human rights treaty.

Treaty Reservations

A smaller number of constitutions specifically refer to the power to enter into treaty reservations. In Mexico, for example, the president has the power "to make and execute international treaties; as well as to end, condemn, suspend, modify, amend, withdraw reservations and make interpretative declarations relating such treaties and conventions, requiring the authorization of the Senate."[58] Meanwhile, in Chile, "[t]he Congress may suggest the formulation of reservations and interpretative declarations to an international treaty, during the process of its approval, as long as they proceed in conformity to what is established in the treaty itself or in the general rules of international law."[59] In Colombia, "[w]hen one or several provisions of a multilateral treaty are declared unenforceable by the Constitutional Court, the President of the Republic may declare consent, formulating the pertinent reservation."[60] In the United States, which lacks any specific provision on treaty reservations, the Senate has adopted a practice of providing reservations, understandings, and declarations along with its advice and consent.

Implementation of Treaties

Not surprisingly, constitutions also vary in the allocation of power with regard to implementation of treaty obligations. Some explicitly provide for legislative

[55] *Id.* at 321 (quoting 1 Messages and Papers of the Presidents, at 194).
[56] Chile, art. 32 (15) (1908, rev. 2015).
[57] Ecuador, art. 420 (2008, rev. 2015).
[58] Mexico, art. 89 (1917, rev. 2015).
[59] Chile, art. 54(1) (1980, rev. 2015).
[60] Colombia, art. 241 (1991) (rev. 2015).

implementation of some obligations, while allowing the executive alone to implement others. Finland, for example, provides: "[t]he provisions of treaties and other international obligations, in so far as they are of a legislative nature, are brought into force by an Act. Otherwise, international obligations are brought into force by a Decree."[61] In Chile, "[t]he measures that the President of the Republic adopts or the agreements that he celebrates to comply with a treaty in force will not require new congressional approval, unless they concern matters of law. The treaties celebrated by the President of the Republic in exercise of his regulatory authority [potestad reglamentaria] will not require congressional approval."[62]

In the United States, implementation of treaties is complicated by the self-executing treaty doctrine, which asks courts to examine the treaty text for indications as to whether it is meant to have domestic effect of its own force. The Supreme Court has said that non-self-executing treaties must be implemented by Congress through the legislative process. In *Medellín v. Texas*, the Court explained: "[t]he requirement that Congress, rather than the President, implement a non-self-executing treaty derives from the text of the Constitution, which divides the treaty-making power between the President and the Senate."[63] Because the U.S. Constitution vests the president with the authority to "make" a treaty, the Court reasoned, "[i]f the Executive determines that a treaty should have domestic effect of its own force, that determination may be implemented in 'mak[ing]' the treaty, by ensuring that it contains language plainly providing for domestic enforceability."[64] But "[o]nce a treaty is ratified without provisions clearly according it domestic effect, however, whether the treaty will ever have such effect is governed by the fundamental constitutional principle that '[t]he power to make the necessary laws is in Congress; the power to execute in the President.'"[65] Thus, "the terms of a non-self-executing treaty can become domestic law only in the same way as any other law—through passage of legislation by both Houses of Congress, combined with either the President's signature or a congressional override of a Presidential veto."[66]

Treaty Withdrawal

Some constitutions specifically address treaty withdrawal, with many requiring that the same process used for treaty ratification be used for withdrawal.[67] As Verdier

[61] Finland, art. 95 (1999, rev. 2011). [62] Chile, art. 54(1) (1980, rev. 2015).

[63] 552 U.S. 491, 526 (2008). [64] *Id.* [65] *Id.*

[66] *Id. See also* Duncan B. Hollis & Carlos M. Vázquez, *Treaty Self-Execution as "Foreign" Foreign Relations Law*, ch. 26 in this volume.

[67] Constitutions containing provisions for legislative approval of treaty withdrawal or termination include Afghanistan, Albania, Angola, Armenia, Azerbaijan, Belarus, Cape Verde, China, Cuba, Denmark, Estonia, Finland, Georgia, Kyrgyzstan, Laos, Lithuania, Mexico, Moldova, Mongolia, Mozambique, Myanmar, Peru, Spain, Timor-Leste, Ukraine, Uzbekistan, and Vietnam.

and Versteeg note, the trend has been toward increased mandates for legislative participation.[68] In Spain, for example, "the procedure provided for in section 94 for entering into international treaties and agreements shall be used for denouncing them."[69] In Denmark, the constitution provides that "nor shall the King, except with the consent of the Folketing, terminate any international treaty entered into with the consent of the Folketing."[70] In Armenia, the legislature can "ratify, suspend or denounce the international agreements of the Republic of Armenia" on enumerated topics,[71] while the president may "approve, suspend or annul the international agreements for which no ratification is required."[72]

Other constitutions allocate the power to withdraw from treaties in the executive branch. Chile, for example, provides that "it corresponds to the President of the Republic the exclusive power to denounce a treaty or withdraw from it, for which he shall ask for the opinion of both branches of the Congress, in the case that the treaties have been approved by it" and "[i]n the case of the denunciation or withdrawal from a treaty that was approved by Congress, the President of the Republic shall inform of that to it within fifteen days of effecting the denunciation or withdrawal." In rare instances, constitutions require a popular referendum for treaty withdrawal. For example, Bolivia's constitution requires that "treaties approved by referendum must be submitted to a new referendum prior to their repudiation by the President of State."

The U.S. Constitution does not directly address the power to withdraw from treaties. When President Jimmy Carter unilaterally withdrew from the defense treaty with Taiwan as part of the establishment of diplomatic relations with mainland China, members of congress tried to challenge his decision. In *Goldwater v. Carter*,[73] a fractured Supreme Court left the question of the president's authority to withdraw unilaterally from treaties unresolved, as some justices believed that the case, at least in the procedural posture in which it reached the court, was nonjusticiable.

IV. War Powers

With respect to the power to authorize and initiate the use of armed force, there is again substantial variation in national constitutions. As Curtis Bradley notes in chapter 1, caution is required in comparing laws and practices that are ultimately grounded in quite different systems legally and historically;[74] practices from a parliamentary system may not be easily compared to those in presidential systems, and those from states that are frequently involved in military action overseas may not be well matched to those of states that have rarely been involved in armed conflict. At the same

[68] *See* Verdier & Versteeg, *supra* note 30.
[69] Spain, art. 96 (1978, rev. 2011).
[70] Denmark, art. 19 (1953).
[71] Armenia, art. 81 (1995, rev. 2015).
[72] Armenia, art. 55 (1995, rev. 2015).
[73] 444 U.S. 996 (1979).
[74] *See* Curtis A. Bradley, *What Is Foreign Relations Law?*, ch. 1 in this volume.

time, war powers may be one of the areas in which state practice deviates most strongly from formal constitutional provisions, insofar as many states require legislative participation, but unilateral executive action is not so uncommon in practice, leading to the need for particular caution in taking formal allocations of power at face value.

Legislative Authorization

Most constitutions that explicitly mention war powers require some kind of legislative consultation, approval, or involvement in the decision to participate in significant armed conflict. Out of 124 world constitutions that refer specifically to war powers, 98 include some provision relating to the involvement of the legislature. Only 14 explicitly grant war powers solely to a chief executive, and most of the remainder require involvement by some other entity such as a cabinet or council.

In one fairly typical formulation, Mexico's constitution provides that the legislature has the power to "[d]eclare war, based on the information submitted by the President of the Republic,"[75] while the president has authority "[t]o declare war in the name of the United Mexican States, having the previous authorization of the Congress."[76] In Spain, "[i]t is incumbent upon the King, following authorization by the Cortes Generales, to declare war and to make peace."[77]

Formal declarations of war are not as common in the contemporary world as they were prior to the mid-twentieth century, and many contemporary constitutions reflect this reality. Many constitutions allow for exceptions to the requirement of legislative authorization based on exigent circumstances. For example, Sweden's constitution provides that "[t]he Government may not declare war without the consent of the Riksdag except in the case of an armed attack on the Realm."[78] The Netherlands similarly states that "[a] declaration that the Kingdom is in a state of war shall not be made without the prior approval of the States General" but that "[s]uch approval shall not be required in cases where consultation with Parliament proves to be impossible as a consequence of the actual existence of a state of war."[79] Turkey's constitution provides that "[i]f the country is subjected to sudden armed aggression, while the Grand National Assembly of Turkey is adjourned or in recess, and it thus becomes imperative to decide immediately on the use of the armed forces, the President of the Republic can decide on the use of the Turkish Armed Forces."[80] In Brazil, the President has exclusive powers to "declare war, in the event of foreign aggression, when authorized by the National Congress or, upon its ratification if the aggression occurs between legislative sessions, and decree full or partial national mobilization under the same conditions."[81]

[75] Mexico, art. 73 (1917 rev. 2015).
[76] Mexico, art. 89 (1917 rev. 2015).
[77] Spain, art. 63(3) (1978, rev. 2011).
[78] Sweden, art. 14 (1974, rev. 2012).
[79] Netherlands, art. 96 (1815, rev. 2008).
[80] Turkey, art. 92 (1982, rev. 2011).
[81] Brazil, art. 84 (1988, rev. 2017).

Some constitutions refer explicitly to military actions short of war, such as stationing troops abroad or allowing foreign troops to enter the country. For example, in Turkey, "[t]he power to authorize the declaration of a state of war in cases deemed legitimate by international law and except where required by international treaties to which Turkey is a party or by the rules of international courtesy to send the Turkish Armed Forces to foreign countries and to allow foreign armed forces to be stationed in Turkey, is vested in the Grand National Assembly of Turkey."[82] In South Korea, "[t]he National Assembly shall also have the right to consent to the declaration of war, the dispatch of armed forces to foreign states, or the stationing of alien forces in the territory of the Republic of Korea."[83] In Brazil the congress has the exclusive power "to authorize the President of the Republic to declare war, make peace, permit foreign forces to pass through national territory or remain therein temporarily, with the exception of cases provided for by complementary law."[84]

Historical precedents, court decisions, and legislative actions may add an additional gloss to the framework set out in formal constitutional provisions. In the United States, for example, the legislatively enacted War Powers Resolution calls upon the president to inform Congress (typically within forty-eight hours) when U.S. armed forces are deployed into situations of hostilities or while equipped for combat, and calls for the termination of such use of troops after a sixty-day period if not by then authorized by Congress, with certain exceptions and the possibility of an extension.[85] The constitutionality, scope, and application of the War Powers Resolution have been the subject of extensive debate in the United States. As Bradley discusses in this volume, recent examples such as the U.S. use of force in Syria highlight the degree to which the actual application of the War Powers Resolution and the scope of the president's Article II powers continue to be contentious.[86]

Perhaps the most elaborate judicial explanations of the role and contours of legislative participation in decisions about the use of force have come from the German Constitutional Court.[87] In the Military Deployment Case of 1994,[88] that court considered the use of German troops in connection with, among other things, the North Atlantic Treaty Organization (NATO) forces in the Balkans enforcing a UN no-fly zone. The court held that such actions were covered under the provisions of the Basic Law Article 24, allowing Germany to participate in systems of "collective security." The court further held that "deployments of armed forces are constitutionally subject to the

[82] Turkey, art. 92 (1982, rev. 2011).

[83] Korea, art. 60(2) (1948 rev. 1987).

[84] Brazil, art. 49 (1988, rev. 2017).

[85] 50 U.S.C. §§ 1541–1548.

[86] *See* Curtis A. Bradley, *U.S. War Powers and the Potential Benefits of Comparativism*, ch. 42 in this volume.

[87] *See* Anne Peters, *Military Operations Abroad under the German Basic Law*, ch. 44 in this volume.

[88] Bundesverfassungsgericht [BVerfG] [Federal Constitutional Court], Judgment of 12 July 1994 BVerfGE 90, 286.

essential approval of the German *Bundestag*, which in principle must be obtained in advance."[89] Moreover, the court has explained:

> Without parliamentary approval, a deployment of armed forces is as a general rule not permissible under the Basic Law; only in exceptional cases is the Federal Government entitled—in the case of imminent danger to provisionally resolve the deployment of armed forces in order that the defence and alliance capacities of the Federal Republic of Germany are not called into question by the requirement of parliamentary approval. In such an exceptional case, however, the Federal Government must without delay refer the deployment resolved in this way to parliament and at the request of the *Bundestag* recall the forces.[90]

In addition, since 2005, Germany has had its own statutory framework regarding the use of force.[91]

Mutual Defense Treaties and Multilateral Organizations

Participation by states in treaty systems for mutual defense adds another layer of complexity, since the legislature may previously have approved the treaty under which military action is obligated. German constitutional court decisions have elaborated on the particularities of multilateral operations, with the court opining that "it is not compatible with the principle of the separation of powers if every routine deployment of German soldiers in the lead-up to possible armed conflicts and without any contact with a military opponent is subjected to the approval of the *Bundestag*."[92] Furthermore, the court explained that modern warfare as practiced in conjunction with multilateral treaty organizations and alliances like NATO presents practical difficulties for legislative involvement. In this regard, the German court explained that "[t]he exercise of parliamentary responsibility, which is constitutionally required, for the further development of a system of mutual collective security may, however, encounter practical difficulties because the Federal Government has the advantage of the entity acting

[89] Bundesverfassungsgericht [BVerfG] [Federal Constitutional Court] Judgment of 7 May 2008, BVerfGE 121, para. 47, describing Judgment of 12 July 1994 BVerfGE 90, 286, 383.

[90] Bundesverfassungsgericht [BVerfG] [Federal Constitutional Court], Judgment of 7 May 2008, BVerfGE 121, 135, 2 BvE 1/03, para. 57; *see also* BVerfG, Order of the Plenary of 03 July 2012, 2 PBvU 1/11 ("Even in the event of an emergency, deployments of the armed forces under Article 35 section 3 sentence 1 of the Basic Law are permissible only on the basis of a decision by the Federal Government as a collegial body."); BVerfG, Judgment of the Second Senate of 23 September 2015, 2 BvE 6/11 (holding that requirement of parliamentary approval applies to basically to all deployments of German armed military forces abroad, although in cases of imminent danger, the government may deploy troops but must immediately bring the continuing deployment to the attention of the legislature, and, upon request by the Bundestag, withdraw the armed forces).

[91] For discussion of this provision, *see* Bradley, *supra* note 86, and Peters, *supra* note 87.

[92] Judgment of 7 May 2008, *supra* note 90, 2 BvE 1/03, para. 38.

directly, by reason of its superior knowledge and of its experience of the conditions of cooperation in the NATO system."[93] Because it "is only the Federal Government that participates in the coordinated decision-making, for example in the United Nations Security Council or in the decision-making bodies of NATO," as a practical matter the "Parliament may not subsequently and unilaterally deviate from the decisions made there without causing political damage to NATO and thus to the Federal Republic of Germany."[94] Thus, "[f]or this reason, the German *Bundestag* is often forced to monitor the political actions in an alliance of systems which is shaped by the executives of the member states, within the bounds of the amendment of the treaty on the one hand and the integration programme of the treaty on the other hand, limiting itself to the indirect exercise of influence described."[95] In summary, the court concluded:

> The appropriate division of state power in the field of foreign, with regard to systems of mutual collective security, is thus structured in such a way that parliament, through its participation in the decision, assumes fundamental responsibility for the treaty basis of the system on the one hand, and for the decision on the concrete deployment of armed forces on the other hand, whereas in other respects the specific structure of alliance policy, as responsibility for the concept, and concrete planning of deployments are both the responsibility of the Federal Government.[96]

V. Conclusion

The vast majority of world constitutions, with the exception of a few remaining monarchies or authoritarian states, at least nominally distribute power over foreign relations between the executive and legislative branches of government. Executive officials are most commonly given general foreign affairs powers to represent the country in international relations and to send and receive ambassadors. Most nations require treaties of significance to be approved by the legislature. In addition, most nations require legislative participation in the decision to go to war, at least absent exigent circumstances like an armed attack. These provisions attempt to strike a balance between values of democratic accountability and deliberative decision-making and practical considerations like the need for speed, secrecy, and unified action. Beyond these broad contours, however, there are nuanced distinctions in approach. Many of these stem from national history and politics, reflecting particular national concerns or priorities. These variations refute the notion that most foreign relations powers are inherently "executive" or "legislative" in nature, and instead reveal that allocations of authority reflect a balancing of interests that often depends on time, place, and circumstance.

[93] *Id.*, para. 67. [94] *Id.* [95] *Id.* [96] *Id.*, para. 71.

CHAPTER 7

EXECUTIVE POWER IN FOREIGN AFFAIRS

The Case for Inventing a Mexican Foreign Relations Law

ALEJANDRO RODILES

I. Introduction

MEXICAN international lawyers, in academia and practice, do not tend to use the expression "foreign relations law" (*derecho de las relaciones exteriores*). Foreign relations law as such is not taught in law schools in the country, nor is there any specialized literature on it. In other words, there is no established legal "field" on foreign relations law in Mexico,[1] as there is no such field in most, if not all, Latin American countries.[2] However, this does not mean that there is no set of legal principles and rules that regulate the ways in which Mexico relates to the outside world, how it is to take part in international legal processes, and how international law operates within the national legal order, i.e., what is usually understood in the United States, the United Kingdom, Germany, and the European Union, for example, as "foreign relations law."[3]

As a matter of comparative analysis, it is first important to raise the question of why it is that, despite the existence of a quite developed set of positive legal rules on external affairs, legal scholarship, judicial practice, and other practitioners (in the government,

[1] On the notion of foreign relations law as a "field of law," *see* Karen Knop, *Foreign Relations Law: Comparison as Invention*, ch. 3 in this volume.

[2] *See* René Urueña, *Domestic Application of International Law in Latin America*, ch. 32 in this volume.

[3] *See*, e.g., CURTIS A. BRADLEY & JACK L. GOLDSMITH, FOREIGN RELATIONS LAW: CASES AND MATERIALS (6th ed. 2017) (for the United States); CAMPBELL MCLACHLAN, FOREIGN RELATIONS LAW (2014) (for the United Kingdom and other Commonwealth countries). For a comparative analysis, *see* Helmut Aust, *Foreign Affairs*, *in* THE MAX-PLANCK ENCYCLOPEDIA OF COMPARATIVE CONSTITUTIONAL LAW (Rüdiger Wolfrum, Frauke Lachenmann, & Rainer Grote eds., 2017).

for instance) have not deemed it necessary to study the issues and problems raised in this area comprehensively as a separate legal field? There are, of course, many plausible answers to this, from a simple attention deficit, to a rather strict separation of the constitutional and international legal communities in the country, to the sovereigntist dogma that views foreign affairs as an exclusive domain of the executive and accordingly reduces the field to the idiosyncrasy of Mexican diplomatic elites that have put their hopes in the construction of one international legal order, which might be threatened by several national approaches to international law.[4] All of these reasons have played a role until today, but they have also started to change.

The next crucial question is whether it is desirable, at all, to have this field of law in the country? I intentionally use the rather vague verb "to have" in this context, because it is one thing to promote a foreign relations law in Mexico, based on previous, transplanted understandings of it, and a different one to try to create, indeed to "invent"[5] the field of Mexican foreign relations law. One could dwell on this issue at quite some length, relating the question to the relationship between comparative foreign relations law and comparative international law, and ultimately to the fundamental issue of the desirability and viability of one international law that is truly international.[6]

However, another way of addressing the question of the desirability of a Mexican foreign relations law is through a more pragmatic, functionally oriented lens that focuses on whether there is something to gain from such an invention. Even though the field as such is rare outside of countries like the United States, the United Kingdom, and Germany, the problems that constitute it are common to many countries in the world. A key question is whether there are compelling practical reasons to analyze these problems in Mexico differently from the way that they have been studied until now.[7] My short answer to this is yes. Taking executive power as an example, I will describe in this chapter some of the outstanding legal problems related to foreign policy as designed and implemented by the Mexican government. These problems have escaped the attention of lawyers in Mexico precisely because executive power over foreign relations has been analyzed through rationales that are not well shaped for addressing it and which remain unconnected among themselves.

[4] On the perception of foreign relations law as a fragmentation threat, *see* Paul B. Stephan, *Comparative International Law, Foreign Relations Law, and Fragmentation—Can the Center Hold?, in* Comparative International Law 53–70 (Anthea Roberts et al. eds., 2017). On Latin American approaches to international law based on a "generalist" tradition, *see* Alejandro Rodiles, *The Great Promise of Comparative Public Law for Latin America: Toward Ius Commune Americanum?, in* Comparative International Law, *supra*, at 501–526.

[5] *See* Knop, *supra* note 1.

[6] *See* Anthea Roberts, Is International Law International? (2017); Martti Koskenniemi, *The Case for Comparative International Law*, 20 Fin. Y.B. Int'l L. 1–8 (2009).

[7] This relates to the "trade-offs" discussed by Karen Knop in her chapter. *See* Knop, *supra* note 1, at p.45.

These rationales are tantamount to what Campbell McLachlan describes as the "diplomatic" and the "internationalist" conceptions of foreign relations law,[8] which in Mexico inform what is commonly known as the study about "international law in the domestic legal order," considered a sub-area of international law.[9] These studies have focused on the prerogatives of the executive in the conduct of foreign policy, on the one hand, and on treaty-making and the role of treaties within national law, on the other hand—unfortunately, customary international law still plays little to no role in the Mexican legal system.

The problem with this approach is that it has been piecemeal, and therefore it has led to an incoherent account of the broader issue of how the country relates to the outside world, with all its nuances. The diplomatic approach mainly understands its function as providing a defense-shield for executive discretion and as elucidating to the internal audiences how international law works. For its part, the internationalist perspective has not been sensitive to politics.[10] Especially in a political system the epicenter of which was until recently (2000) the head of state and government, foreign policy had more to do with those "domestic 'conventions' (or customs) of proper political behavior"[11] mentioned in the introduction to this volume, than with the formal separation of powers.

Recent studies on the role of international law in the domestic legal order have been captured by the discourse of global constitutionalism and its particular regional version called "*ius constitutionale commune* in Latin America (ICCLA)."[12] This has allowed for a contemporary reading that puts an end to the "exclusionary" paradigm that dominated prior to the democratic turn of the country,[13] but it has reduced the "field" to interactions between national constitutional law and the Inter-American human rights system. While this interaction is of the utmost importance, this new focus on the relationship between international law and national law has been unable to capture the innovative, mainly informal means of external executive action.

Sections II and III will describe the set of rules and principles of the domestic legal order that structure the relations of Mexico with the rest of the world, focusing on

[8] Campbell McLachlan, *Five Conceptions of the Function of Foreign Relations Law*, ch. 2 in this volume.

[9] *See* CÉSAR SEPÚLVEDA, DERECHO INTERNACIONAL 67–81 (26th ed., first reprint, 2013); LORETTA ORTIZ AHLF, DERECHO INTERNACIONAL PÚBLICO 56–75 (2004); MODESTO SEARA VÁZQUEZ, DERECHO INTERNACIONAL PÚBLICO 41–43 (2000); as well as GABRIELA RODRÍGUEZ HUERTA, LA INCORPORACIÓN DEL DERECHO INTERNACIONAL EN EL ORDEN JURÍDICO MEXICANO (2015).

[10] For important exceptions, *see* Antonio Gómez Robledo, *Directrices Fundamentales de la Política Exterior Mexicana*, 6 FORO INTERNACIONAL 271–287 (1966); Alonso Gómez Robledo-Verduzco, *La Política Exterior Mexicana: Sus Principios Fundamentales*, 1 AMDI 197–297 (2001); and Bernardo Sepúlveda, *Política Exterior y Orden Constitucional: Los Fundamentos de una Política de Estado*, *in* LOS SIETE PRINCIPIOS BÁSICOS DE LA POLÍTICA EXTERIOR DE MÉXICO 25–52 (Emilio O. Rabasa ed., 2005).

[11] *See* Curtis A. Bradley, *What Is Foreign Relations Law?*, ch. 1 in this volume, at p.4.

[12] *See* TRANSFORMATIVE CONSTITUTIONALISM IN LATIN AMERICA. THE EMERGENCE OF A NEW *IUS COMMUNE* (Armin von Bogdandy et al. eds., 2017). For a critique, *see* Rodiles, *supra* note 4.

[13] For this function of foreign relations law, which reduces the field to politics, *see* McLachlan, *supra* note 8.

executive power. Section IV will make the case for a Mexican foreign relations law that is attentive to persistent and novel problems that emerge from the executive's external actions.

II. Foreign Policy and the Constitution: From an Executive Unbound to a Tense Relationship

Executive Authority in Foreign Relations

Until recently, the area of study most commonly known as "the relationship of international law with the national legal order" was rather simple. International law in Mexico was for a long time largely reserved to the executive, and the diplomatic elites in particular. The country's political system was not only formally a presidential one that mirrors to a great extent the U.S. Constitution—as it still is today—but it was completely centered on the head of state, in what became known as "Mexican presidentialism." This peculiar political system was tied to the rule of one political party for over seven decades (the Revolutionary Institutional Party (PRI), from 1929 to 2000), coming thus very close to what Mario Vargas Llosa called "the perfect dictatorship."[14] There was thus little room for other actors like courts and the legislature, not to mention civil society, to get involved in an area that was conceived to be the political prerogative of the head of state.

The main constitutional norm in terms of executive power in foreign relations is Article 89 of the 1917 national constitution, which establishes the faculties and duties of the president. According to its paragraph x, the president shall conduct the country's foreign policy and sign treaties. Although both cannot be really separated from each other—treaty-making is an essential component of foreign policy, and the original text of the constitution actually talked about the president's authority to "direct diplomatic negotiations and sign treaties with foreign powers"[15]—legal scholarship has tended to analyze the two components separately,[16] producing one stream of writings on "foreign policy and the constitution," and another one on "the incorporation and application of international law in the national legal order."

[14] The novelist coined this catchphrase during a Mexican television programme, in 1990; *see Vargas Llosa: México es la dictadura perfecta*, El País (Sept. 1, 1990), *available at* https://elpais.com/diario/1990/09/01/cultura/652140001_850215.html.

[15] *See* Diario Oficial del Gobierno Provisional de la República Mexicana (Feb. 5, 1917), *available at* http://www.diputados.gob.mx/LeyesBiblio/ref/cpeum/CPEUM_orig_05feb1917_ima.pdf.

[16] For an attempt to bring both together, *see* Gabriela Rodríguez Huerta, México en el mundo: Constitución y Política Exterior (2017).

The executive's power to "direct the foreign policy" of the country, as Article 89, paragraph x states today, comprises almost everything that has to do with how the nation relates to the outside world, not only with other countries but also, and very important for Mexico, with the international community as organized through multilateral organizations. Political science and historical literature in Mexico has documented and commented in depth how this foreign policy has materialized over time through diplomatic practice and the articulation and interpretation of foreign policy doctrine. In contrast, legal scholarship was long silent on this, perhaps because until 1977 the president had the unrestricted power to "direct diplomatic negotiations" (Art. 89, para. x), i.e., without any oversight from other constitutional organs. Thus, "the exclusionary conception" of foreign relations dominated, and the area was practically reduced to politics—and its study to political scientists and historians.[17]

Since the political reform of December 1977,[18] the Senate has been entitled to "analyze the foreign policy developed by the federal executive, based on the annual reports that the President of the Republic and the corresponding Secretary of State delivers to Congress."[19] Although this remained a pure formality for quite some time, substantial discussions on foreign policy started to take place with the overall democratization of the country, which many date back to the elections for Congress of 1997, in which the PRI lost for the first time the majority.[20] Today, the practice is that the secretary of foreign relations explains in detail the foreign affairs part of the president's annual report to Congress, and in these hearings sensitive political issues are routinely raised. This review function of the Senate is not restricted to the annual debates, but can be exercised at any time and the Commission on Foreign Relations is the specialized body in this regard. It is important to underline that the Senate's review function is a political one; it has no legal means to challenge before the Mexican Supreme Court the constitutionality of the executive's foreign policy decisions and actions, apart from the constitutionality control of treaties already in force, and in cases in which the executive encroaches on the Senate's legal powers,[21] which in foreign affairs are limited to the approval of treaties and the authorization of the sending of troops outside the country.[22]

[17] El Colegio de México became the leading academic institution in this regard.

[18] Diario Oficial de la Federación (DOF) (Dec. 6, 1977), *available at* http://dof.gob.mx/nota_detalle.php?codigo=4664439&fecha=06/12/1977.

[19] Constitución Política de los Estados Unidos Mexicanos (CPEUM), art. 76 (i).

[20] For an excellent account of Mexico's transition to democracy, *see* José Woldenberg, Historia Mínima de la Transición Democrática en México (2012).

[21] The Senate has two judicial means at its disposal before the Supreme Court in relation to foreign relations: the "action of unconstitutionality" (*acción de inconstitucionalidad*) of a treaty in force, i.e., an a posteriori constitutional norm control, and the "constitutional controversy" (*controversia constitucional*), i.e., a proceeding whereby the Supreme Court resolves disputes on legal powers between the different branches of the federal government, or between the different subnational entities and the federation. *See* CPEUM, art. 105, I (c), and II (b).

[22] In relation to war powers properly, the Congress of the Union (i.e., the Senate and the Deputy Chamber together) is the constitutional organ entitled to "declare war," in light of the information

A case that illustrates the strictly political nature of the Senate's review function in foreign policy concerns the participation of Mexican troops in UN peacekeeping missions. Long-lasting resistance on behalf of leftist factions in Congress prevented a constitutional amendment that would have explicitly allowed the president to decide on such contributions. After several such initiatives failed, President Enrique Peña Nieto (PRI, 2012–2018), declared the nation's intention to contribute to UN peacekeeping missions during his speech at the sixty-ninth UN General Assembly,[23] and then announced this new foreign policy to the national audience in the "presidency's blog," contending that the Constitution need not be amended since Article 76, paragraph iii already allows the sending of troops abroad.[24]

Although such action must be approved by the Senate, on a case-by-case basis, such authorization is not required, it was claimed, for the general foreign policy decision that Mexico would participate in blue-helmet operations. The faction of the Labour Party (*Partido del Trabajo*) in the Senate protested and argued that the decision was unconstitutional because it violated Mexico's foreign policy principle of nonintervention,[25] but this remained a political protest. Now, the Senate bears the burden of disapproving specific participations, contradicting the unilateral declaration of the head of state made in the UN General Assembly.[26] The Labour Party's opposition can only be understood by analyzing the constitutional principles on foreign policy, one of the most interesting aspects of Mexico's foreign relations law.

Constitutional Principles on Foreign Policy

In 1988, a ground-breaking constitutional reform added "the constitutional principles of Mexico's foreign policy" to Article 89(x).[27] This amendment introduced seven principles that the president shall observe in the conduct of foreign policy. These are:

provided by the executive. *See* art. 73, para. xii, of the Constitution. In this sense, it is the Congress of the Union that could challenge a declaration of war made unilaterally by the executive.

[23] *See* Noticias ONU, *Enrique Peña Nieto en la 69 Asamblea General* [Video] (Sept. 24, 2014), *available at* https://news.un.org/es/audio/2014/09/1406801.

[24] Presidencia de la República, *Participación de México en Operaciones para el Mantenimiento de la Paz* [Blog] (Sept. 24, 2014), *available at* https://www.gob.mx/presidencia/articulos/participacion-de-mexico-en-operaciones-para-el-mantenimiento-de-la-paz.

[25] *See* Senado de la República, *Participar en operaciones de los cascos azules de la ONU, viola la Constitución: Grupo Parlamentario del PT* (Oct. 9, 2014), *available at* http://comunicacion.senado.gob.mx/index.php/informacion/boletines/15970-participar-en-operaciones-de-los-cascos-azules-de-la-onu-viola-la-constitucion-grupo-parlamentario-del pt.html.

[26] This move by the government of Peña was made only after it was assured sufficient political support in Congress, and, more importantly perhaps, the consent of the Mexican army and navy. *See* Juan Manuel Gómez Robledo Verduzco, El Principio de No Intervención en la Política Exterior de México 66–69 (2017).

[27] DOF (May 11, 1988), *available at* http://dof.gob.mx/nota_detalle.php?codigo=4735026&fecha=11/05/1988.

nonintervention, self-determination, peaceful means of dispute settlement, the proscription of the threat and use of force in international relations, sovereign equality, international cooperation for development, and the struggle for international peace and security. As can be seen, these principles were directly imported from the purposes and principles of the UN Charter (Arts. 1 and 2). In 2011, on the occasion of a major constitutional reform on human rights, the respect, protection, and promotion of human rights was added to the list.[28]

Commentators generally agree that the introduction of the constitutional principles was not necessary, because Mexico is obliged to respect these by virtue of the UN Charter, other treaties like the Charter of Bogotá of 1948, and customary international law, so that these rather serve as a "reminder" to the president to follow them in the conduct of foreign affairs.[29] It is often said that "elevating" these principles to constitutional status will help to disseminate them in the country and to promote a better understanding and respect for the fundaments of the international legal order inside the national legal system.[30] Nobody disagrees with these general affirmations, and the legal literature for a long time reduced its analysis to explaining what these principles mean in accordance with international law. But when it comes to their role as actual constraints on the executive's prerogative in foreign relations, opinions diverge. The following examples illustrate the tensions that the constitutional principles have caused between the executive and other branches, and sometimes even within the government.

The government of President Vicente Fox, who in 2000 became the first democratically elected president in over seventy years, changed Mexico's traditional diplomacy of friendship and dialogue with Cuba. After several episodes of tension—if not conflict—with the regime in La Habana, the secretary of foreign relations at the time, Jorge G. Castañeda Gutman, entered into a heated debate with the left in Congress and beyond. For several members of Congress and some public intellectuals on the left, the government was not observing the constitutional principles in the conduct of its renewed foreign policy toward the Castro regime, and it was disregarding a whole diplomatic tradition based on nonintervention in the internal affairs of other states.[31] Castañeda thus openly advocated for interpreting the constitutional principles, in particular nonintervention, in line with contemporary developments in international law, and the world.[32] Within the Foreign Ministry, especially inside the Policy Planning Staff, it was considered desirable to have the Supreme Court pronounce itself on the

[28] DOF (June 10, 2011), *available at* http://www.dof.gob.mx/nota_detalle.php?codigo=5194486&fecha=10/06/2011.

[29] *See* Gómez-Robledo Verduzco, *supra* note 10, at 199.

[30] *Id.*

[31] This is in clear relation with Mexico's main foreign policy doctrine, the "Estrada doctrine," *see infra* note 43 and accompanying text.

[32] Jorge G. Castañeda, *Los Ejes de la Política Exterior en México*, NEXOS (Dec. 1, 2001), *available at* https://www.nexos.com.mx/?p=10240.

"evolutionary nature" of these principles, but this did not occur, again because the Senate has no legal means at its disposal to challenge the executive's foreign policy.[33]

The constitutional principles also played an important role in face of the Iraq War of 2003. Mexico was an elected member of the UN Security Council at that time, so the possibility of having to vote on a resolution on the use of force against Iraq became a crucial issue for Mexico, in particular vis-à-vis its relations with the United States. While a broad majority in Congress and the Mexican public was clearly against a U.S.-led intervention,[34] Fox's administration was divided. In the end, the issue became the subject of a disagreement between Castañeda and Adolfo Aguilar Zínser, then Mexico's ambassador to the United Nations, a former national security adviser to President Fox, and a leading foreign policy thinker of the country, who clearly opposed an intervention.[35] As it is well known, it never came to that vote in the Security Council. But the debates on the issue centered on the constitutional principles and again on nonintervention as well as the prohibition on the use of force in international relations, which to the majority of the actors involved in the debate limited the ability of Fox's government to lend its support to the United States, both as matter of international law and national law. In the end, Aguilar Zínser won the battle inside the administration, based on international and constitutional legal arguments as well as on Mexico's diplomatic tradition.[36] Before Castañeda left the Foreign Ministry, in early 2003, Mexico stated its disapproval of any military action outside a clear authorization on the use of force by the Security Council.[37]

Evolutionary Approach to the Constitutional Principles?

Today, the diplomatic community increasingly regards the constitutional principles on foreign relations as an unnecessary and uncomfortable straitjacket on foreign policy decision-making, especially because many international lawyers outside the Foreign Ministry, not to mention members of Congress, tend to favor a rather literal and static interpretation of them.[38] In what can be viewed as an attempt to raise awareness about

[33] This is based on the recollections of the author as former junior advisor at the Policy Planning Staff of Foreign Minister Jorge G. Castañeda Gutman (2001–2003).

[34] *See* Olga Pellicer, *¿Por qué la ONU?*, *in* EL MUNDO DESDE MÉXICO: ENSAYOS DE POLÍTICA INTERNACIONAL. HOMENAJE A OLGA PELLICER 211–212 (Arturo C. Sotomayor Velázquez & Gustavo Vega Cánovas eds., 2008); *see also La crisis de Irak y la posición de México*, PROCESO (Mar. 1, 2003), *available at* https://hemeroteca.proceso.com.mx/?p=249890.

[35] Fernando González Saiffe, *Adolfo Aguilar Zínser y el Consejo de Seguridad*, PROCESO (June 13, 2005), *available at* https://www.proceso.com.mx/227549/adolfo-aguilar-zinser-y-el-consejo-de-seguridad.

[36] On this, *see* Alejandro Rodiles, *La Nueva Responsabilidad Global y la Doctrina Estrada*, ESTE PAÍS 39–44 (Sept. 2013).

[37] *See supra* note 34.

[38] According to the faction of the Labour Party in the Senate, the undersecretary of multilateral affairs and human rights of the Foreign Ministry mentioned during the debates on Mexico's participation in

the evolution that the principles have experienced over time, the Foreign Ministry recently published a series on them—one book per each principle, written by former and current high-ranking diplomats. There, the effort to transmit to the national audience how these principles have evolved in international law through state practice is quite clear. In the common preface to the series, then-secretary of foreign relations Luis Videgaray wrote that "in times when political, economic, technological, and social paradigms change rapidly, the principles do not represent dogmas but criteria of orientation that must be interpreted in light of new developments and dynamics."[39]

The constitutional principles on foreign relations were incorporated into Article 89(x) in 1988 with the intention of consolidating a diplomatic tradition that took pride in its role in the promotion of the international rule of law. As a semiperipheral nation and major player from the Third World, the construction of an international order based on law was associated with Mexico's reaffirmation as an independent and sovereign country, especially in face of its "special relationship" with the United States.[40] As explained by a former foreign secretary and one of Mexico's most prestigious international lawyers, international law should not be conceived of as separated from foreign policy but as the most powerful instrument of a foreign policy that seeks foremost to defend Mexico's independence—it is, in this light, "pure realism, not legalism."[41] It is precisely in this sense that the said principles enshrine Mexico's main foreign policy doctrine: the Estrada doctrine.[42]

In 1930, then secretary of foreign affairs Genaro Estrada instructed Mexican diplomats as follows:

> . . . the Mexican Government is issuing no declarations in the sense of grants of recognition, since that nation considers that such a course is an insulting practice and one which, in addition to the fact that it offends the sovereignty of other nations, implies that judgment of some sort may be passed upon the internal affairs of those nations by other governments, inasmuch as the latter assume, in effect, an attitude of criticism, when they decide, favorably or unfavorably, as to the legal qualifications of foreign regimes.[43]

UN peacekeeping missions that "it was a mistake to include these principles in the constitution." *See supra* note 25.

[39] Luis Videgaray Caso, Prefacio a los Principios Constitucionales de Política Exterior (2017).

[40] Mario Ojeda, a student of Hans Morgenthau, described Mexico's foreign policy in terms of its possibilities vis-à-vis the "special relationship with the U.S." *See* Mario Ojeda, Alcances y límites de la Política Exterior de México (1977).

[41] Jorge Castañeda, *México y el Nuevo Orden Mundial: Actualidad y Perspectivas*, *in* México y los Cambios de Nuestro Tiempo 263–264 (CONACULTA ed., 1992). This is Jorge Castañeda y De la Rosa, the father of Jorge G. Castañeda Gutman.

[42] On the Estrada doctrine and its importance for Mexico's role in the international legal order, *see* Alejandro Rodiles, *Il Ruolo Del Messico Nell'Ordine Mondiale (E Accanto Agli USA)*, 8 LIMES Rivista Italiana di Geopolitica 141–147 (2007).

[43] English version in 25 Am. J. Int'l L. (Supplement) 203 (1931).

It is not difficult to see that the essence of the Estrada doctrine is the principle of nonintervention in the internal affairs of other states. That principle, which became a building block of the postwar legal system, anchored in the UN Charter, was, at the time of its articulation as the Mexican foreign policy doctrine, still not a universally recognized rule of positive international law. Remember the history of abuses by the United States and European powers, which regarded it as their unquestionable right to exercise aggressive diplomatic protection of their citizens in Latin American countries, in order to protect the economic interests of the latter. Military intervention was also contemplated by those powers as a legitimate and legal means of collecting public debt. Mexico was no exception to this situation, as a series of claims and the Franco-Mexican wars in the nineteenth century demonstrate. It is in this historical context that the Estrada doctrine stood in line with other major international legal developments of the region, most notably the Drago and Calvo doctrines.[44] And it also honored the maxim of Mexico's great liberal patriot, Benito Juárez, who defended his country successfully against France and ended the reign of Maximilian of Habsburg: "among individuals, as among nations, respect for the rights of others is peace."[45]

By attaching nonintervention to the theme of state and government recognition, the Estrada doctrine went beyond the reaction of a nation to alien intrusion. Banning recognition from Mexican diplomatic practice was an assertive move in the reconstruction of the international law post-*jus publicum europaeum*. In Carl Schmitt's words, the Estrada doctrine "had the dialectical value of a consistent antithesis"[46]—an antithesis to the old system of subjective value judgments about which states deserved to be recognized as part of the family of "civilized nations," i.e., the constitutive thesis of recognition. The synthesis of this process became the declaratory thesis of recognition, stipulated in the Montevideo Convention on the Rights and Duties of States of 1933, according to which states that fulfill the formal criteria of territory, population, government, and the capacity to enter into foreign relations, are to be recognized as such.[47]

[44] Both doctrines stem from Argentinean international lawyers (Luis María Drago and Carlos Calvo) and date back to the early twentieth century. The Drago doctrine establishes that no foreign power has the right to use force against an American state in order to collect public debt. The Calvo doctrine states that domestic remedies shall be exhausted before resorting to diplomatic protection in cases of the protection of foreign property. On the relationship of the Drago, Calvo, and Estrada doctrines, *see* Jorge L. Esquirol, *Latin America*, *in* THE OXFORD HANDBOOK OF THE HISTORY OF INTERNATIONAL LAW 553, 568 (Bardo Fassbender & Anne Peters eds., 2012).

[45] Benito Juárez pronounced this phrase on the occasion of his triumphant entrance to Mexico City after overthrowing the Habsburg Empire, on July 15, 1867, *see* H. Congreso de la Unión, LX Legislatura, *Letras de Oro* (2006), *available at* http://www.diputados.gob.mx/LeyesBiblio/muro/pdf/respeto.pdf. On Juárez's foreign policy, *see* Daniel Cossío Villegas, *La Doctrina Juárez*, HISTORIA MEXICANA 527–530 (1962).

[46] CARL SCHMITT, DER NOMOS DER ERDE IM VÖLKERRECHT DES JUS PUBLICUM EUROPAEUM 282 (2d ed., 1974). The American international lawyer Philip Jessup also drew attention to the importance of this doctrine. *See* Philip C. Jessup, *The Estrada Doctrine*, 25 AM. J. INT'L L. 719 (1931).

[47] For the importance of the Montevideo Convention in the universalization of international law, *see* ARNULF BECKER LORCA, MESTIZO INTERNATIONAL LAW—A GLOBAL INTELLECTUAL HISTORY 1842–1933, at 249–252 (2014).

Although it is true that Mexican diplomatic practice has not always been consistent with the Estrada doctrine,[48] its anti-interventionist nucleus informed the country's foreign policy until the democratic turn in 2000. But it is also true that the Estrada doctrine and the static interpretations of Article 89(x) based on the former served as a shield for an authoritarian regime that did not wish to be subjected to international scrutiny and judged by the outside world on its human rights record. Once the country's diplomatic elites felt more inclined to support the values of liberal democracy, it became increasingly hard to remain attached to the Estrada doctrine. It was actually Foreign Secretary Castañeda who tried to force a rupture with it, declaring it an outdated foreign policy doctrine that fulfilled its function in the 1930s but did not make sense in a post–Cold War and post-9/11 global environment.[49] The denial of the Estrada doctrine became known as the Castañeda doctrine,[50] and with it the principles on foreign relations enshrined in the constitution became seriously under strain, at least in their traditionalistic reading informed by the Estrada doctrine. However, the tensions described in this section go beyond old and contemporary readings of the international law principles established in Mexico's constitution. They also reflect the fundamental question for Mexico's foreign policy of what kind of rule of law the country should promote at the international level, a question that is intrinsically tied to Mexico's comprehension of the international legal order and the role it is to play therein.

III. Domestic Treaty Law and Informal International Lawmaking

Role of the Senate in Treaty-Making

Part and parcel of the executive's power to direct foreign policy is its treaty-making power. According to Article 89(x) of the Constitution, the president shall sign treaties, terminate and denounce them, and formulate and retire reservations and interpretive declarations.[51] Somewhat like in the United States, the internal constitutional approval procedure is exercised by the Senate, which is related to the federal pact and the representation of the thirty-one states and Mexico City in the Upper House. An important reform of 2007 significantly broadened the Senate's role, and today it also has the power to approve the termination and denunciation (withdrawal) of treaties on

[48] Clear exceptions were Mexico's nonrecognition of Franco's Spain and the military coup of Augusto Pinochet in Chile. *See* Gómez Robledo Verduzco, *supra* note 26, at 36–52; Ana Covarrubias, *La Política Exterior "Activa"... Una Vez Más*, 48 Foro Internacional 13 (2008).

[49] *See* Castañeda, *supra* note 32.

[50] *See* Rodiles, *supra* note 42.

[51] CPEUM, art 89, para. x.

behalf of the executive,[52] as well as the decision of the latter "to suspend, to modify, to amend, to withdraw reservations and to formulate interpretive declarations."[53]

In 2014, the Mexican Senate approved the withdrawal proposed by the executive in 2013 of a reservation previously made to the 1994 Inter-American Convention on Forced Disappearance (the "Belém Convention"),[54] that precludes in Article 9 the resort to any kind of "special jurisdiction, in particular the military one." Mexico signed the convention with a reservation to this norm, "because the Constitution recognizes military jurisdiction whenever a member of the armed forces has committed a wrongful act during service."[55] As mentioned in the letter to the Senate containing the executive's proposal of withdrawal, this was motivated by the ruling of the Inter-American Court of Human Rights (IACtHR) in the *Radilla Pacheco* case, which disapproved Mexico's reservation as a violation of "the principle of a competent tribunal," and therefore declared it contrary to the convention.[56] The executive's proposal was also supported by a decision of the Supreme Court of Mexico, regarding the obligatory nature of the judgments of the IACtHR, and the unconstitutionality/unconventionality of military jurisdiction in cases related to human rights violations by military personnel.[57]

This withdrawal was clearly in line with the 2011 human rights reform. This major amendment of Mexico's basic law introduced a new rights paradigm, in fact changing the effect of the supremacy clause contained in Article 133 of the constitution. According to the clause, which was transplanted from the U.S. Constitution as part of Mexico's 1857 liberal constitution,[58] treaties are considered "supreme law of the Union." The Supreme Court had repeatedly clarified that international obligations are to be located beneath the constitution in the internal norm hierarchy. The 2011 reform, without changing Article 133 and thus opening the door to constitutional inconsistencies, amended Article 1 by elevating "human rights contained in treaties to which Mexico is a party" to constitutional status.[59] Thus, a differentiated hierarchy in regard

[52] On the distinction between these concepts, *see* Laurence R. Helfer, *Terminating Treaties*, *in* The Oxford Guide to Treaties 634–649 (Duncan Hollis ed., 2012).

[53] *See* CPEUM (as amended on Feb. 12, 2007).

[54] Presidencia de la República, *Letter to Congress regarding the elimination of the reservation made to the Inter-American Convention on Forced Disappearance of Persons* (Oct. 21, 2013), *available at* http://sil.gobernacion.gob.mx/Archivos/Documentos/2013/10/asun_3025238_20131022_1382539116.pdf.

[55] Department of International Law, OAS, Multilateral Treaties, *Inter-American Convention on the Forced Disappearance of Persons*, *available at* http://www.oas.org/juridico/english/sigs/a-60.html.

[56] *See* IACtHR, Series C No. 209, *Case Radilla Pacheco v. United Mexican States* (Preliminary Objections, Merits, Reparations and Costs), Judgment Nov. 23, 2009, para. 282.

[57] *See* Expediente Varios 912/2010, Pleno de la Suprema Corte de Justicia de la Nación [SCJN], Semanario Judicial de la Federación y su Gaceta, Ninth Epoch, Book I, Vol. I, Oct. 2011.

[58] *See* Fernando Serrano Migallón, Historia Mínima de las Constituciones en México 263–285 (2013).

[59] CPEUM, art 1.

to treaties within the national legal system was created, which does not correspond with international law.[60]

While this reform represents an interesting case of comparative international law,[61] what matters most in the present context is that the reform, along with the initial case law of the Supreme Court following suit, has been treated as part of a regional trend known as "*ius constitutionale commune* in Latin America (ICCLA)."[62] According to this narrative, which is one of global public law,[63] domestic treaty law has moved beyond the dualism/monism debate, focusing instead on dynamic interactions between national constitutional law and the Inter-American human rights system. As a consequence of these evolutions, much of the "international law in the domestic legal order" literature has been captured by ICCLA discourse, and international human rights, in particular those derived from the Inter-American System, are treated as "constitutionalized." It must be recalled that the same 2011 reform added "the respect, protection, and promotion of human rights" to the list of constitutional principles on foreign relations.[64] Thus, taken together, the amendments to Articles 1 and 89(x) have brought executive power in foreign relations better in line with rule of law demands, also in the sense "that 'foreign entanglements' are not working to the detriment of established constitutional guarantees,"[65] including those of an international origin.

Inter-Institutional Agreements and Informal Arrangements

There is still an important remnant of Mexican presidentialism in domestic treaty law: the 1992 Law on the Making of Treaties,[66] which increased executive powers by allowing the government to conclude some international agreements without the Senate's approval. It is true that the so-called "inter-institutional agreements" are constrained to the areas of competences of particular ministries or government agencies (Art. 2, para. ii), and thus are prima facie about agency-to-agency cooperation. But even if this distinction were persuasive (it has been questioned by several scholars[67]), the 1992 Law stands in stark contrast with the 2004 Law on the Approval of Economic Treaties, which reinforced the duties of the executive to inform the Senate on negotiation processes, as well as the right of civil society, with an emphasis on the private sector and labor unions, to be heard and to present proposals for the negotiation of such treaties.[68] Actually, shortly after the 2004 Law entered into force, members of

[60] *See* Francisca Pou Giménez & Alejandro Rodiles, *Mexico*, *in* Duelling for Supremacy: International Law Versus National Fundamental Principles (Fulvio Maria Palombino ed., 2019).

[61] *See* Roberts et al. eds., *supra* note 4. [62] *See* von Bogdandy et al. eds., *supra* note 12.

[63] *See* Rodiles, *supra* note 4. [64] *See supra* note 28. [65] *See* Aust, *supra* note 3.

[66] Ley sobre Celebración de Tratados, DOF (Jan. 2, 1992).

[67] *See* Juan De Dios Gutiérrez Baylón, Derecho De Los Tratados 35–42 (2010). For a nuanced critique, *see* Rodríguez Huerta, *supra* note 9, at 130–131; *contra see* Jorge Palacios Treviño, Tratados: Legislación y práctica en México 78–106 (2007).

[68] Ley sobre la Aprobación de Tratados Internacionales en Materia Económica, DOF (Sept. 2, 2004).

Congress and scholars started to make the case that the 1992 statute should be amended or replaced with a new one that would be more in line with the democratic evolutions of the country, and the 2007 constitutional reform in particular. Most convincing is the proposal to eliminate both the 1992 and 2004 statutes, substituting them with one single statute on the making of treaties, which would set aside the division between economic and other agreements.[69] This initiative better defines "inter-institutional agreements" and limits the ambit of those government agencies entitled to sign them. It also introduces a scheme of coordination on behalf of the Ministry of Foreign Relations, in order to reinforce its central role in treaty-making, which has been seriously reduced since the early 1990s as a consequence of the several processes of disaggregation of the state that have also been very present in Mexico. But the new law on treaties is still pending, in part because many lawyers keep insisting that the only way to properly regulate inter-institutional agreements would require constitutional amendments. Such a course would probably be an unduly risky enterprise for the executive as it would open spaces to those voices in Congress and society that prefer to do away with these constitutionally doubtful instruments altogether.

However, what is more worrisome from the perspective of constitutional controls on executive power in foreign relations than the existence of inter-institutional agreements is the increasing tendency in Mexico, as in many other parts of the world, to avoid the making of treaties altogether, resorting instead to informal arrangements that are negotiated and signed by the executive alone, without any intervention of other constitutional organs. These arrangements, whether called "declarations of intent," "declarations of principles," or just "partnerships," or "initiatives," are nonlegally binding and informal, but they entail important commitments on the transnational plane to which the executive adheres to without any internal law that establishes oversight, review, or accountability mechanisms.[70] Through them, executives act across the globe, thus configuring "global administrative spaces"[71] that regulate a variety of areas, therefore having a regulatory impact inside national jurisdictions. This trend has gone completely unnoticed by the Mexican literature on "international law in the national legal order," both in its more formalistic approach based on the separation of powers as well as in the eulogistic writings about *ius commune*.

Consider, for example, the Mérida Initiative. Signed as a joint political declaration of Presidents George W. Bush and Felipe Calderón (2006–2012), in Mérida, Yucatán, on March 14, 2007, this bilateral partnership foresees strengthened cooperation between Mexico and the United States in the fight against organized crime. Read in isolation, the initiative does not say much. It is, indeed, a "little paper," as former foreign

[69] Proposed in 2009 by the late Senator (PRI) and former Secretary of Foreign Relations, Rosario Green Macías. *See* Rodríguez Huerta, *supra* note 9, at 121–132.

[70] *See* Alejandro Rodiles, Coalitions of the Willing and International Law—The Interplay Between Formality and Informality (2018).

[71] *See* Benedict Kingsbury, *The Concept of "Law" in Global Administrative Law*, 20 Eur. J. Int'l L. 23, 25 (2009).

secretary and senator Rosario Green (PRI) put it, in clear disapproval of its informal nature, lack of transparency, and the bypassing of parliamentary participation along the process. However, the Initiative has evolved over the years through bilateral consultation mechanisms, like the High Level Consultative Group on Bilateral Cooperation against Transnational Organized Crime, the Policy Coordination, and the Bilateral Coordination Groups. These working groups function similar to those binational commissions established in bilateral treaties for the purposes of developing their rather general provisions over time. According to treaty law, the agreements reached in these commissions may constitute subsequent agreements in terms of Article 31(3)(a) of the Vienna Convention on the Law of Treaties (VCLT), which amount to authentic interpretations of the treaty text.[72] Subsequent practice and agreements have the potential of transforming rigid treaties into quite flexible treaty-governance regimes. In a similar fashion, subsequent joint political declarations and action plans have turned the Mérida Initiative into a very broad framework arrangement that now goes well beyond bilateral cooperation in the field of enhanced law enforcement and includes, among other things, recommendations that have been crucial in Mexico's criminal law reform of 2008, which transformed an inquisitorial criminal justice system into an adversarial one.[73]

IV. Conclusion

Legal scholarship in Mexico has treated the set of constitutional and administrative rules and principles that regulate how the nation relates to the outside world as a subfield of international law. These studies have focused on two main themes: the foreign policy conducted by the executive, on the one hand, and domestic treaty law, on the other. The former has become the terrain of diplomats trying to explain to the national constituencies that the constitutional principles on foreign policy, established in the national constitution in 1988, have evolved over time, mainly through the subsequent practice of the UN Charter.[74] Their main point is that the static interpretations of these principles are outdated and misguided, and hence so are many of the internal debates which concern the constitutionality and international legality of the executive's decisions and actions on the matter. In regard to domestic treaty law,

[72] *See* Georg Nolte, Special Rapporteur, International Law Commission, *Fourth report on subsequent agreements and subsequent practice in relation to the interpretation of treaties*, A/CN.4/694 (2016).

[73] These lines are based on Alejandro Rodiles, *The Tensions between Local Resilience-Building and Transnational Action—US-Mexican cooperation in crime affected communities in Northern Mexico, and what this tells us about global urban governance*, *in* The Globalisation of Urban Governance—Legal Perspectives on Sustainable Development Goal 11 (Helmut Aust & Anèl du Plessis eds., 2019).

[74] *See* Joel A. Hernández García, La lucha por la paz y seguridad internacionales 15–18 (2017).

international legal scholars in the country have engaged in positivistic analyses of the checks and balances on executive treaty-making powers, which have been gradually but forcefully introduced through a series of constitutional reforms tied to the democratization process of the country. Today, there is a strong mechanism in place for the participation of the Senate, which comprises the "whole life-span of treaties," meaning that the Upper House not only plays a pivotal role in the ratification procedure but also in the suspension, termination, as well as formulation and withdrawals of interpretive declarations and reservations. Concerning the internal norm hierarchy and the place of treaties within it, discussions have moved from formalistic, inward-looking analyses that basically portrayed a dualistic picture, to a cosmopolitan legal narrative according to which international human rights law, in particular that pertaining to the Inter-American System, and constitutional law are conceived as part of a regional common public law. This shift was clearly facilitated by the 2011 human rights reform that places human rights contained in treaties to which Mexico is a party at a constitutional level.

These two approaches within "the international law in the domestic legal order" literature remain unconnected, mainly because each one is tied to a particular rationale, that of the "diplomatic function," on the one hand, and the "internationalist approach," on the other.[75] While the first focuses on the relations of the state with its foreign peers and international organizations, reflecting classical, inter-state international law, the second puts the individual at its core, following a discourse of global public law which sees the in-and-outside divide as superseded. Although each approach portrays important aspects of the contemporary relationship of international law with national law, both fail to comprehend that the national legal rules and principles that regulate the relationship of the country with the outside world operate at the interstices of these legal orders, and that they are informed by both at the same time. For instance, the diplomatic approach is inattentive to the changing character of international law within the national legal system, the ever-more important role of national courts in this regard, and even to the fact that state practice is not a matter for the executive alone.

In their anxiety to release the conduct of foreign policy by the executive from the real or perceived constraints established in the constitutional principles, diplomatic elites have become oblivious to the fact that these principles were introduced as a means of reflecting Mexico's diplomatic tradition of promoting an international rule of law based on the basic principles of postwar international law, and nonintervention in particular, a tradition based on the Estrada doctrine. It is true, of course, that the world has changed dramatically since the articulation of that doctrine and also since the incorporation of the principles in the constitution. Moreover, the role of Mexico in the world inevitably changed, especially once the country transited to democracy. However, it is far from clear that it is in the interest of the nation to set aside, or lessen,

[75] *See* McLachlan, *supra* note 8.

the promotion of the international rule of law and to focus instead exclusively on the promotion of the internationalization of rule of law values attached to liberal democracies.[76]

The fundamental question for Mexican foreign policy of what kind of rule of law diplomats should promote, i.e., the international rule of law or the internationalization of the rule of law, is one that concerns the nation's geopolitical recalibrations in times of a rapidly shifting and uncertain world (dis)order. This requires a broad debate involving the country's foreign policy circles beyond diplomatic elites. Such a debate would be meaningful only if it were sensitive to the constitutional principles and their relationship with foreign policy doctrine, and, at the same time, to the evolution of these principles according to international law and beyond the understanding of them by the executive. It would have to integrate constitutionalist, diplomatic, and internationalist approaches to foreign relations, for only from the dialogue among them can the constitutional norms on foreign relations be properly understood. Hence, such a debate would be about setting the foundations of a Mexican foreign relations law, understood as a legal field axiomatically concerned with the kind of rule of law that the country should promote at the international level.

The second argument in favor of inventing a Mexican foreign relations law has to do with the myopia of domestic treaty law that is oblivious to everything that does not formally concern treaties. On the one hand, this reflects old dualistic vices of the traditional approach to "the international law in the domestic legal system" account, where international law is basically reduced to treaties in force in Mexico. On the other hand, and quite paradoxically, the more recent discourse about ICCLA, which explains the relationship of treaty law within the national legal system as a postnational public law narrative of pluralism and anti-formalism, has been equally insensitive to the many flexible ways through which the executive acts globally today and engages in commitments that, their informality notwithstanding, bear important consequences inside the country. In sum, informal international lawmaking[77] has practically gone unnoticed in domestic treaty law, both in its traditionalist, formalistic version, as well as in its contemporary, anti-formalistic variety. There are, of course, many different possible explanations for this. I believe that one of these reasons is related, again, to the disconnection between the dominant approaches to foreign relations in the country, i.e., the internationalist and diplomatic ones. Informal international lawmaking happens at the interstices between law and nonlaw,[78] and between national constitutional

[76] On the distinction between the international rule of law and the internationalization of the rule of law, *see* SUNDHYA PAHUJA, DECOLONISING INTERNATIONAL LAW—DEVELOPMENT, ECONOMIC GROWTH AND THE POLITICS OF UNIVERSALITY 176–185 (2011); *see also* Alejandro Rodiles, *Non-Permanent Members of the UN Security Council and the Promotion of the International Rule of Law*, 5 GOETTINGEN J. INT'L L. 333, 344–347 (2013).

[77] For discussion of this phenomenon internationally, *see* the contributions to the edited volume, INFORMAL INTERNATIONAL LAWMAKING (Joost Pauwelyn, Ramses A. Wessel, & Jan Wouters eds., 2012).

[78] *See* RODILES, *supra* note 70.

law and international, or perhaps more appropriately, transnational law. Indeed, one of the main reasons why executives resort to informal lawmaking at the global level is precisely to circumvent the internal approval and control procedures in place in most democratic constitutions in regard to treaty-making.[79] Hence, the adoption by the executive of legally nonbinding standards, best practices, guidelines, declarations of principles, and the like, represents not only a challenge for international law's doctrine of sources, but very concretely for the national law on foreign relations. Understanding these challenges requires an approach that is both sensitive to how international law is being made today, and to how these new trends at the global level affect the constitutional and administrative national legal frameworks that regulate the executive's conduct of foreign policy, and the problems these may raise in terms of separation of powers, transparency, and accountability.[80]

[79] *See* Eyal Benvenisti, *Coalitions of the Willing and the Evolution of Informal International Law*, *in* COALITIONS OF THE WILLING: AVANTGARDE OR THREAT? (Christian Calliess, Georg Nolte, & Peter-Tobias Stoll eds., 2007); *see also* RODILES, *supra* note 70.

[80] For an assessment of the ways the executive in the United States exercises control over different forms of international law, and engages in different kinds of international lawmaking, including nonbinding political commitments, *see* Curtis A. Bradley & Jack L. Goldsmith, *Presidential Control over International Law*, 131 HARV. L. REV. 1203, 1217–1220 (2018).

PART II

MAKING TREATIES AND OTHER INTERNATIONAL AGREEMENTS

CHAPTER 8

SEPARATION OF POWERS, TREATY-MAKING, AND TREATY WITHDRAWAL

A Global Survey

PIERRE-HUGUES VERDIER
AND MILA VERSTEEG

THE Donald Trump administration's belligerent outlook on international law and institutions has renewed interest in the process by which the United States makes international agreements, and in the scope and limits of the president's power to terminate them. In June 2017, the president announced that the United States would withdraw from the Paris Agreement on climate change mitigation, and in August the country delivered a notice of intent to do so.[1] In addition to withdrawing from negotiations for the Trans-Pacific Partnership, the president also threatened to terminate major trade agreements such as the North American Free Trade Agreement (NAFTA) and U.S.-Korea Free Trade Agreement, and even U.S. membership in the World Trade Organization (WTO). In May 2018, the president announced that the United States would withdraw from the Joint Comprehensive Plan of Action (JCPOA) on the Iranian nuclear program.

The power to terminate treaties is only one of several increasingly salient questions regarding the separation of powers with respect to international agreements. These questions—who is empowered to bind the country to international obligations, to make these obligations binding in domestic law, and to terminate them—are a key concern of comparative foreign relations law, the topic of this volume, and they are closely linked to each other.[2] In the United States, for example, the manner in which

[1] This was not formally a withdrawal notice, as Article 28 of the Paris Agreement provides that parties may not withdraw until three years have elapsed since the Agreement entered into force with respect to them.

[2] *See* Curtis A. Bradley, *What Is Foreign Relations Law?*, ch. 1 in this volume.

individual agreements were concluded and implemented may have implications for the president's power to terminate them. For example, some scholars have argued that since NAFTA was entered into as a congressional-executive agreement, the president lacks the authority to terminate it unilaterally, while others contest this argument.[3] Both the Paris Agreement and JCPOA, however, are generally considered to fall within the president's discretion to terminate.[4]

While these questions have attracted considerable attention in the United States,[5] they are far from unique to it. Over time, national constitutions have become more explicit in allocating responsibility for the state's international obligations. They have steadily expanded the legislature's role in treaty-making, requiring more intrusive approval procedures for more treaties. In this, they follow the model set by the United States, whose constitution "provided for the first time that the head of state could not enter into treaties alone."[6] This growing legislative role in approving international agreements has been called a "democratization" of treaty-making.[7] But the U.S. Constitution's strict treaty-making process soon collided with the realities of expanded international trade, commerce, and alliances, leading the government to seek ways to circumvent Article II's "advice and consent" requirement. As Oona Hathaway has shown, reliance on international agreements concluded without Senate approval increased dramatically in the twentieth century.[8] The emergence of "workarounds" is also not unique to the United States. In countries following the British tradition, the executive was of course always free to conclude agreements without parliamentary approval. In civil law jurisdictions, which almost universally adopted parliamentary approval requirements, agreements in simplified form (*accords en forme simplifiée*) emerged as an alternative procedure.[9] Until recently, treaty withdrawal was almost universally considered an exclusive executive power.

[3] *See* Joel Trachtman, *Trump Can't Withdraw from NAFTA Without a "Yes" from Congress*, The Hill Blog (Aug. 16, 2017, 8:00 a.m.), *available at* http://thehill.com/blogs/pundits-blog/international-affairs/346744-trump-cant-withdraw-from-nafta-without-a-yes-from; John Yoo & Julian Ku, *Trump Might Be Stuck with NAFTA*, L.A. Times (Nov. 29, 2016, 4:00 a.m.), *available at* http://www.latimes.com/opinion/op-ed/la-oe-yoo-ku-trump-nafta-20,161,129-story.html; *but see* Curtis A. Bradley, *Exiting Congressional-Executive Agreements*, 67 Duke L.J. 1615 (2018).

[4] David A. Wirth, *While Trump Pledges Withdrawal from Paris Agreement on Climate, International Law May Provide a Safety Net*, Lawfare Blog (June 2, 2017, 8:30 a.m.), *available at* https://lawfareblog.com/while-trump-pledges-withdrawal-paris-agreement-climate-international-law-may-provide-safety-net (emphasizing procedural constraints on withdrawal in the Agreement itself, rather than domestic legal constraints).

[5] *See* Jean Galbraith, *International Agreements and U.S. Foreign Relations Law: Complexity in Action*, ch. 9 in this volume.

[6] Luzius Wildhaber, Treaty-Making Power and Constitution: An International and Comparative Study 9 (1971).

[7] *Id.*

[8] *See* Oona A. Hathaway, *Treaties' End: The Past, Present and Future of International Lawmaking in the United States*, 117 Yale L.J. 1236, 1300–1302 (2008).

[9] *See* Wildhaber, *supra* note 6, at 125–129 (describing the rise of such agreements in France).

There is thus reason to question the extent to which the ostensible "democratization" of treaty-making truly represents a shift of treaty-related authority from the executive to other branches, and to investigate the consequences of these changes. While these questions have been studied extensively in a handful of salient jurisdictions, there is relatively little information on the broader landscape of national allocation of powers relating to treaty-making and withdrawal. In this chapter, we aim to provide a more comprehensive survey, drawing from a global data set on international law in domestic legal systems that currently covers 101 countries for the period 1815–2013.[10] While the breadth of our sample limits our ability to analyze and interpret developments in individual jurisdictions, it comes with several benefits: we can confirm and quantify the global prevalence of specific rules and practices, identify large-scale trends over time, and draw attention to innovations outside the limited circle of well-documented jurisdictions. Indeed, our data support several findings that would be difficult to identify, or at least to substantiate, without a large data set.

First, we confirm a sustained trend toward greater parliamentary involvement in treaty-making. Many countries insist on parliamentary approval prior to the executive formally expressing state consent to be bound by a treaty, and the categories of treaties that require such approval have expanded over time. In virtually all "monist" countries—those that give direct effect to ratified treaties in the domestic legal order without legislative implementation—parliamentary approval requirements now cover all treaties that modify domestic law, thus upholding the separation of powers between the legislature and the executive and blurring the traditional line between "monist" and "dualist" regimes.[11] In addition, a growing number of countries require supermajority approval of particularly sensitive treaties, such as those transferring authority to international organizations. Finally, although it appears that in many countries the legislative approval process consists of an "up or down" vote, about one-fifth allow the legislature to introduce modifications or reservations, thus giving it a more active role in shaping the substantive content of treaties.

Second, while many countries recognize executive agreements and other alternative routes through which the executive can conclude internationally binding agreements without parliamentary approval, these "workarounds" are subject to important limitations. In countries whose constitution or laws provide for parliamentary approval of specific categories of treaties—a common approach—the executive may not conclude executive agreements that fall within these categories. Some countries, like the United States, provide the executive with more discretion to choose among treaty-making procedures regardless of the agreement's subject matter. However, in virtually all those countries, the resulting agreements do not have the same domestic legal status as treaties concluded through the parliamentary procedure. They may not be incorporated in domestic law at all, and where they are, they enter the legal system with a status inferior to treaties and ordinary domestic legislation. This being said, a few countries provide alternative routes—such as referenda

[10] The data set remains a work in progress. We continue to add more countries to the data.

[11] We develop this point in Pierre-Hugues Verdier & Mila Versteeg, *International Law in National Legal Systems: An Empirical Investigation*, 109 AM. J. INT'L L. 514 (2015).

or emergency powers—that allow the executive to conclude treaties with full domestic legal status without parliamentary approval.

Third, an important and little-noticed development is afoot with respect to treaty withdrawal or termination, long considered a purely executive power in virtually all jurisdictions. In recent decades, several national legal systems have introduced constraints on that power, usually by requiring parliamentary approval of withdrawal from treaties whose conclusion required such approval. This may reflect the growing realization—expressed in the U.K. Supreme Court's recent Brexit case[12] and in the South African High Court decision on the government's attempted withdrawal from the Rome Statute of the International Criminal Court[13]—that treaty withdrawal can have momentous implications, including extensive changes in domestic law, and accordingly should be subject to greater parliamentary control. More demanding domestic requirements for treaty withdrawal also have important implications for theories of international credibility and compliance.

Finally, we find a growing role for the judicial branch in treaty-making. No less than 40 percent of countries in our sample require prior judicial review of proposed treaties for conformity with the constitution. Thus, the judicial branch is given a role in enforcing procedural constraints on treaty-making and, more significantly, in ensuring the substantive consistency of new treaty obligations with fundamental constitutional commitments such as the protection of individual rights and freedoms. This development has attracted little attention from U.S. and Commonwealth scholars, perhaps because their jurisdictions lack a tradition of ex ante (or abstract) judicial review and have not espoused court involvement in treaty-making. In addition to ex ante review, national courts have become increasingly active in reviewing the constitutionality of treaties after ratification, sometimes blocking their implementation or even confronting the government with a choice between withdrawing from the treaty or attempting to modify the constitution.

I. Legislative Power and the Democratization of Treaty-Making

According to Luzius Wildhaber, "treaty-making remained an exclusively executive domain until the end of the [eighteenth] century," reflecting absolutist doctrines under which the power to bind the state was an incident of sovereign power that rested in the hands of monarchs.[14] Indeed, until the nineteenth century the distinction

[12] R (Miller) v. Secretary of State for Exiting the European Union, [2017] UKSC 15 (appeal taken from Eng. & Wales).

[13] Democratic Alliance v. Minister of International Relations and Cooperation 2017 (3) SA 212 (GP) (S. Afr.).

[14] Wildhaber, *supra* note 6, at 9.

between the legal titles and claims of states and those of monarchs themselves was not always clear.

Early written constitutions—the U.S. Constitution of 1789, the French Constitutions of 1791 and 1793, and the Belgian Constitution of 1831—pioneered legislative constraints on the executive's treaty-making power, while adopting different approaches.[15] Article II, Section 2 of the U.S. Constitution appeared to make all treaties subject to the advice and consent of two-thirds of the U.S. Senate—which the Framers expected to act as a quasi-Cabinet rather than a legislative chamber.[16] By requiring a supermajority vote, this provision set a high bar for treaty-making, which most subsequent constitution makers declined to follow. The French revolutionary constitutions required legislative "ratification" of a closed list of treaties: those of peace, alliance, and commerce, implicitly leaving the conclusion of other treaties to the executive's discretion.[17] The Belgian Constitution took a more expansive approach, requiring parliamentary approval of "treaties of commerce and those that could financially oblige the state or bind Belgians individually," thus introducing a distinction apparently premised on protecting the legislative function of the parliament against executive lawmaking through treaties.[18]

Our data show that the requirement of legislative approval of treaties rapidly gained widespread acceptance. Figure 1 depicts the percentage of countries with such a requirement, without distinguishing for now among its various manifestations. The requirement was common from the mid-nineteenth to the mid-twentieth century, with a significant but temporary decline in the post–World War II era as many former

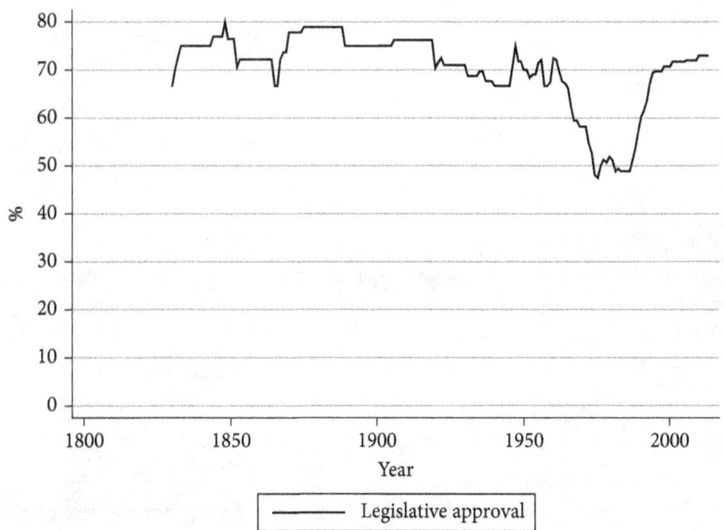

FIGURE 1

[15] *Id.* at 9–13. [16] Hathaway, *supra* note 8, at 1278–1281.
[17] Wildhaber, *supra* note 6, at 11–12. [18] *Id.* at 12–13.

colonies enter the sample. Interestingly, many of these countries later adopted such requirements, presumably out of concern with unconstrained executive power. The adoption of such requirements coincided in many countries with the wave of democratization and constitution-making of the late 1980s and the end of the Cold War. As we showed in previous work, they are particularly common among countries with monist legal systems, where ratified treaties become part of the domestic legal order without implementing legislation and often are considered hierarchically superior to ordinary laws.[19] In such systems, prior approval requirements may seem necessary, as otherwise the executive would possess the power not only to bind the state but also to make generally applicable domestic law without parliamentary participation.[20]

The data also show several, generally more recent, developments that have so far failed to attract much attention but confirm the growing role of legislatures in treaty-making. First, among countries that—following the French and Belgian models described above—set forth a list of treaties whose ratification requires legislative approval, this list has expanded considerably over time. While many earlier constitutions, following the French model, required approval for treaties with particularly serious implications for foreign relations—war and peace, alliances, territorial cessions, and the like—the requirement now frequently extends to several other categories, including trade treaties, treaties that affect domestic spending, and treaties that affect the rights and obligations of citizens, especially human rights. (See Table 1.)

A notable development is widespread acceptance, especially post–World War II, of the Belgian model requiring parliamentary approval of treaties that modify domestic

Table 1

Treaty Type	Percentage of countries with legislative approval requirements that require legislative approval for this type
Treaties that modify domestic law	60%
Military treaties	49%
Treaties that involve the joining of international organizations	46%
Territorial treaties	46%
Treaties affecting domestic spending	32%
Trade treaties	31%
All treaties	30%
Treaties affecting citizens	27%
Friendship treaties/alliances	20%
Treaties affecting human rights	14%

[19] Verdier & Versteeg, *supra* note 11, at 519–520, 525.

[20] At the same time, some countries in which treaties require legislative implementation have recently adopted prior parliamentary review mechanisms, the most salient example being the U.K. Constitutional Reform and Governance Act, 2010. *See id.* at 521.

law. Among countries with any requirement of parliamentary approval for treaty ratification, no less than 60 percent now specifically include this category. When added to the 30 percent whose requirement applies—at least on its face—to all treaties, in 90 percent of countries with such requirements the executive is prohibited from creating or modifying domestic law without prior parliamentary approval. Since most of the countries without parliamentary approval requirements have dualist systems in which ratified treaties do not become domestic law unless they have been implemented by legislation, it seems clear that separation of powers concerns animate the rise of these constraints.[21] This development is unsurprising, given the global proliferation of treaties and the extension of their subject matters to areas that traditionally fell within the realm of domestic law and regulation.

Second, while the United States' choice to require supermajority approval was long unpopular, a growing number of countries now require supermajority votes for certain categories of treaties. Aside from the United States, only the Philippines generally requires two-thirds approval of treaty ratification by a legislative chamber. However, 17 percent of the countries in our data (and 23 percent of countries with a legislative approval requirement) now require supermajority approval of some treaties, up from 6 percent in 1946. For example, several European countries now require supermajority approval of treaties that grant powers to international organizations, a requirement that likely reflects a desire to retain control over incremental transfers of authority to European institutions.[22] Indeed, in Germany and Slovakia the supermajority requirement applies specifically to grants of powers under EU treaties, and apparently not to other international organizations.[23] It also worth noting that in some European countries, EU treaties require approval by referendum.[24] Besides these countries, others require supermajority approval of treaties that imply changes to the constitution (Austria, Belgium, Chile), human rights treaties (Argentina, Brazil), and in a few cases, the traditional "core" of important treaties such as territorial cessions (Iran, Egypt).

Finally, another little-noticed form of parliamentary participation in treaty-making is the ability of legislatures to require reservations or modifications to treaties as part of the approval process, thus directly affecting the content of the agreement. In the United States, the Senate has long asserted the right to attach reservations to its approval of treaties, but in many countries—especially in the civil law world—the prevailing rule is

[21] By contrast, approval requirements for treaties that fall within more traditional areas of international relations (military, friendship, boundaries and trade) have remained more constant over time. *Id.* at 519–520.

[22] Those countries are Croatia, the Czech Republic, Greece, Luxembourg, the Netherlands, and Poland.

[23] On Germany, *see* Stefan Kadelbach, *International Treaties and the German Constitution*, ch. 10 in this volume.

[24] The Irish Constitution requires approval of new EU treaties by referendum, as did the United Kingdom's European Union Act 2011 (which applied to treaties that modified or replaced EU treaties). On mandatory treaty requirements for EU accessions and treaty modifications, *see* Referendums on EU Matters, Eur. Parl. Doc. PE 571.402 (2017), *available at* http://www.europarl.europa.eu/RegData/etudes/STUD/2017/571402/IPOL_STU(2017)571402_EN.pdf.

that parliament can only vote "up or down" on treaties proposed by the executive. Today, about 21 percent of all countries (and 29 percent of countries with legislative approval requirements) allow legislatures to attach reservations to treaties, and this number has been relatively stable over time.[25]

The overall picture that emerges from our data is one of increasingly robust parliamentary participation in treaty-making. As noted above, this development protects the traditional separation of powers, but does it amount to—in Wildhaber's formulation—"democratization" of treaty-making? After all, one might argue that since the executive is often elected directly (as in the United States or France) or responsible to parliament (as in South Africa or Norway), the shift merely transfers responsibility from one democratically accountable branch to another—and might dilute the executive's electoral accountability for foreign affairs. Instead of speaking of "democratization," it might be more accurate to say that parliamentary participation may bring into the treaty-making process desirable features associated with liberal democracy: transparency (the executive likely has to explain the factual basis and reasons for its decision to ratify the treaty), debate (the parliamentary opposition has an opportunity to challenge these reasons), and broader participation (legislature may hold hearings and solicit the views of interested parties). The South African decision on withdrawal from the International Criminal Court invoked precisely such reasons for requiring parliamentary participation, quoting an earlier Supreme Court case stating that, among other benefits, "participation by the public on a continuous basis . . . promotes a spirit of democratic and pluralistic accommodation calculated to produce laws that are likely to be widely accepted and effective in practice."[26]

II. Executive Power and the Emergence of Workarounds

The robust and growing role of legislatures in treaty-making likely responds to the expansion of international relations and the increasingly intrusive nature of treaties in policy areas traditionally regulated at the domestic level. However, as the United States soon found out as its international entanglements grew in the twentieth century, demanding treaty-making procedures protect the separation of powers and democratic accountability at the cost of erecting steep obstacles to international cooperation.

[25] These numbers reflect countries in which the legislature's authority to require reservations is documented in the constitution, laws, or other sources we have found. Because legislatures in other countries may be able to secure amendments or reservations as a condition of ratification without explicit authority do so, the numbers likely understate the authority of legislatures in this area.

[26] Democratic Alliance v. Minister of International Relations and Cooperation 2017 (3) SA 212 (GP) at 28 para. 61 (S. Afr.) (quoting Doctors for Life International v. Speaker of the National Assembly 2006 (6) SA 416 (CC)).

These obstacles were famously illustrated by the failure of the Covenant of the League of Nations in the U.S. Senate in September 1919, and more recently by the executive's inability to secure approval for ratification of important multilateral treaties such as the UN Convention on the Law of the Sea and the Convention on the Rights of Persons with Disabilities. Aside from the inherent difficulty of obtaining two thirds of the votes, the U.S. Senate is beset with multiple responsibilities, slow procedures, and weak interest in many areas of international cooperation. Even uncontroversial treaties languish for years. As of its latest update, the U.S. State Department listed forty-one treaties currently pending approval by the Senate—the oldest one dating back to 1949.[27]

It is therefore unsurprising that, from the early days of the United States, the executive has resorted to international agreements—"treaties" in the Vienna Convention sense—that are not considered "treaties" for U.S. constitutional purposes and therefore do not trigger Article II's advice and consent requirement. Thus, so-called congressional-executive agreements (CEAs) are authorized or approved by the U.S. Congress through the same process used for ordinary legislation, namely majority votes in the House of Representatives and Senate. Sole executive agreements (SEAs), for their part, are binding international agreements entered into without express authorization by either House of Congress, relying on authority arising from an existing agreement or on the president's own constitutional authority.[28] In the first decades of U.S. foreign relations, treaties outnumbered CEAs and SEAs, but the balance began to shift in the mid-nineteenth century. In the twentieth century, the latter became dominant. Between 1939 and 2012, the United States concluded 17,189 CEAs and SEAs, but only 1,068 treaties.[29]

The Constitution provides little guidance as to which international agreements should be concluded as treaties, CEAs, or SEAs. In practice, the decision is made by the U.S. State Department, based on a list of factors that effectively creates substantial discretion in the executive as to the choice of mechanism.[30] Congress could resist the rise of these alternative mechanisms, but it has generally acquiesced in the president's choice of procedure, and courts to date have held that choice to be an unreviewable political question.[31] While the president's choice of procedure is therefore largely discretionary, there are important differences among the three categories. For example, while Article I's limits on federal legislative authority apparently do not apply to treaties, they unquestionably apply to CEAs; and while both treaties and CEAs create binding federal law, the status of SEAs as sources of binding U.S. federal

[27] *Treaties Pending in the Senate (updated as of Jan. 2, 2019)*, U.S. DEP'T OF STATE, *available at* https://www.state.gov/s/l/treaty/pending/.

[28] Hathaway, *supra* note 8, at 1255.

[29] Curtis A. Bradley & Jack L. Goldsmith, *Presidential Control over International Law*, 131 HARV. L. REV. 1201, 1210 (2018).

[30] Hathaway, *supra* note 8, at 1250.

[31] *See*, e.g., Made in the USA Found. v. United States, 242 F.3d 1300 (11th Cir. 2001).

law is debated.[32] But for international law purposes, all are "treaties" that bind the United States.

One might think that the rise and widespread use of alternatives to the formal treaty-making process would be a phenomenon unique to the United States. While its Constitution requires a supermajority vote for treaties, most others require only majority votes, the same as for domestic lawmaking. The country often has divided government, making it difficult for the president to obtain Senate approval of treaties. In addition, the United States' uniquely central role in international governance after World War II creates constant demand for international agreements, putting great strain on the traditional treaty-making process. Yet, our data set reveals that many of the countries with parliamentary approval requirements have also developed alternative mechanisms allowing the executive to enter into international agreements outside the formal treaty-making process. In other words, the rise of legislative involvement in treaty-making has been accompanied by that of exceptions to that rule, which calls into question whether there has overall been a true "democratization" in this area.

More specifically, most countries now allow the executive to conclude at least some executive agreements, that is, binding international agreements that do not require parliamentary approval. In many countries, like in the United States, the practice of executive agreements evolved on an informal basis, while in a handful it is explicitly codified in the constitution or legislation. For example, in France and several other civil law countries, the term *accords en forme simplifiée* is used to designate international agreements that become effective upon signature. Because they do not require ratification, these agreements may be concluded by the executive without parliamentary approval.[33] No less than 70 percent of countries in our sample recognize some form of executive agreement. (Figure 2). These exceptions have grown in popularity during the same period as parliamentary approval requirements became more common, which suggests that, like in the United States, they likely constitute a response to demands on the legislature to approve many international agreements, often in areas of routine international cooperation considered unworthy of attention by the legislature. Nevertheless, the rise of these exceptions potentially paves the way for executive treaty-making outside the strictures of parliamentary review and approval. It is thus worth examining them in more detail.

It is important to note that executive agreements, while increasingly common, do not completely bypass the normal treaty-making process. First, in virtually all countries whose constitution lists the categories of treaties whose ratification requires parliamentary approval, the rule is that agreements falling within that list may not be entered into as executive agreements. For example, an international agreement that falls within

[32] Older cases such as United States v. Belmont, 301 U.S. 324 (1937), and United States v. Pink, 315 U.S. 203 (1942), appear to hold that sole executive agreements, like treaties, are supreme federal law. However, the constitutional basis for that status is unclear and the authority of these cases remains a matter of debate.

[33] The reasoning appears to be that the constitution requires parliamentary approval of the deposit of an instrument of ratification (or accession) but not of signature, so that if a treaty enters into force following signature the executive can effectively bind the state without prior approval.

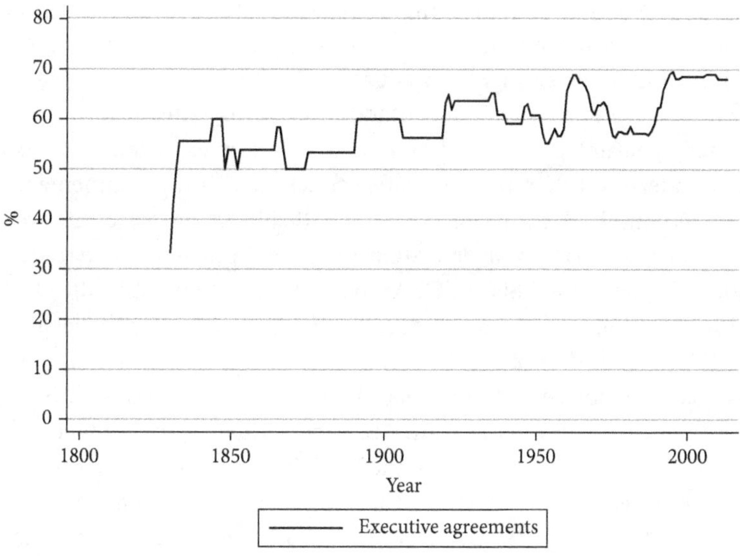

FIGURE 2

the topics listed in Article 53 of the French Constitution may not be concluded in simplified form; it must receive parliamentary approval. However, this is not universally the case. As seen above, the U.S. Constitution does not provide guidance as to which international agreements may be entered into as treaties, CEAs, and SEAs. In other words, the U.S. system provides the executive with a substantial choice between procedures, constrained not by legal rules and judicial review but by political considerations. Thus, the U.S. approach provides what we label a true alternative route, under which the executive wields discretion to conclude on its own at least some international agreements that would normally require parliamentary approval.

As seen in Figure 3, a significant minority of countries similarly provide what we call a true alternative route. For example, the Norwegian Constitution limits the parliamentary approval requirement to "[t]reaties on matters of special importance," giving the executive considerable discretion as to whether a particular agreement requires legislative approval.[34] The Zimbabwean Constitution requires international agreements to be approved by Parliament, but goes on to carve out agreements "the subject-matter of which falls within the scope of the prerogative powers of the President . . . in the sphere of international relations."[35] These systems, like the U.S.

[34] Kongeriket Norges Grunnlov [Constitution], May 17, 1814, art. 26 (Nor.). *See* Norwegian Ministry of Foreign Affairs, NOU 2012: 2, Outside and Inside: Norway's Agreements With the European Union (2012), *available at* https://www.regjeringen.no/contentassets/5d3982d042a2472eb1b20639cd8b2341/en-gb/pdfs/nou201220120002000en_pdfs.pdf.

[35] Constitution of Zimbabwe, Apr. 18, 1980, art. 111B(3)(b). Note that a new constitution was adopted in 2013, which is not reflected in our data set.

one, confer substantial discretion to the executive as to the appropriate procedure. In both cases, however, the constitution specifically excludes agreements that modify domestic law from the alternative procedure.[36]

Second, executive agreements and other agreements entered into through alternative routes typically possess a lesser status in domestic law. For example, in France it is understood that, unlike treaties concluded with parliamentary approval, agreements in simplified form are not automatically incorporated in domestic law with hierarchical superiority over ordinary statutes pursuant to Article 55 of the Constitution. In the United States, CEAs are generally adopted in the same manner as federal laws and have the same status, but there is considerable debate about the status of SEAs, which do not receive congressional approval. In some cases, courts have appeared to displace state-level legislation that conflicted with SEAs, but the legal basis for these decisions is contested, and courts have stopped well short of giving them the status of federal legislation. In some countries, executive agreements are considered to have the same status as subordinate (administrative) legislation, which means that the legislature—and perhaps the executive itself—may displace them. Thus, while national practice differs considerably in its details, in most systems the legal framework for executive agreements (and other agreements concluded through alternative procedures) maintains consistency with the separation of powers between the legislative and executive branches by giving these agreements a domestic legal status inferior to that of agreements concluded with parliamentary approval.

This being said, in a significant minority of countries, agreements concluded through an alternative route appear to have the same domestic legal status as treaties. These countries are shown by the dashed line in Figure 3. Closer examination reveals that some of these exceptions constitute relatively minor inroads into the principle of separation of powers. Thus, the Brazilian and Indonesian legal systems allow the executive to conclude agreements without parliamentary approval with the same legal status as treaties, but only where these agreements are authorized by prior agreements, or are of a relatively minor administrative nature. Other exceptions, however, widen executive powers to such an extent as to raise fears of undermining the role of the legislature. For example, the constitution of Cameroon allows the executive to secure treaty ratification via a referendum, thus bypassing parliamentary approval.[37] In Papua New Guinea, the executive may bypass parliamentary approval where the Speaker of Parliament and the prime minister consider that consent to the

[36] Alongside "[t]reaties on matters of special importance," Article 26 of the Norwegian Constitution specifically requires approval "in all cases, treaties whose implementation, according to the Constitution, necessitates a new law or a decision by the Storting." Article 111B(3) of the Zimbabwean Constitution excludes from the carveout agreements that require "the withdrawal or appropriation of moneys from the Consolidated Revenue Fund" or "any modification of the law of Zimbabwe."

[37] Constitution of the Republic of Cameroon, Jan. 18, 1996, art. 36.

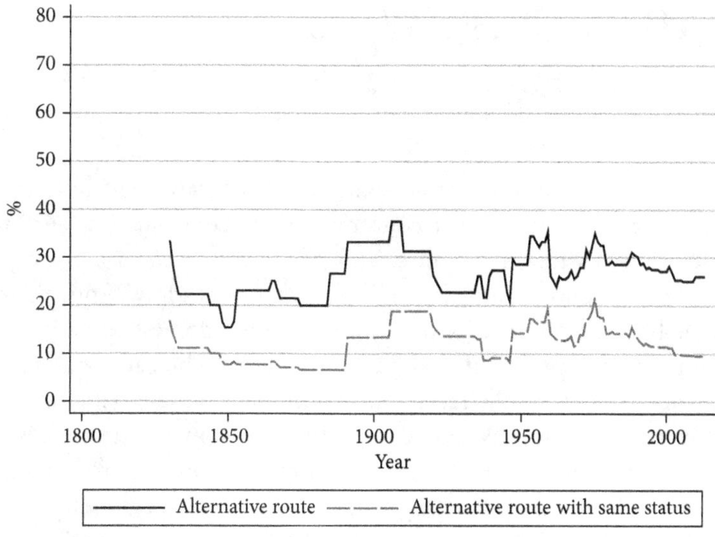

FIGURE 3

agreement must be given urgently.[38] The Egyptian Constitution likewise allows the executive to conclude treaties without parliamentary approval while a state of emergency is in effect.[39]

The separation of powers concerns may be most acute in systems in which agreements concluded using alternative procedures that bypass parliamentary approval—and usually place extensive discretion in the executive—possess the same domestic legal status as treaties concluded using the normal procedure. The Venezuelan Constitution provides that the National Assembly must approve treaties, "with the exception of those by means of which it is attempted to execute or perfect preexisting obligations of the Republic, apply principles expressly recognized in it, execute ordinary acts in the international relations, or exercise powers that the law expressly attributes to the National Executive."[40] Agreements concluded under the broad exceptions appear to become part of domestic law with the same status as those approved by the National Assembly. This also appears to be the case for agreements concluded pursuant to a state of emergency in Egypt.

[38] CONSTITUTION OF THE INDEPENDENT STATE OF PAPUA NEW GUINEA, Sept. 16, 1975, § 117(5)(b); *see* Eric Kwa, *Treaty Making Law in Papua New Guinea: After Two Decades, Yumi Stap We?*, 25 MELANESIAN L.J. 43 (1997).

[39] CONSTITUTION OF THE ARAB REPUBLIC OF EGYPT, Jan. 18, 2014, art. 156 (allowing the president to adopt decrees having the force of law during a state of emergency; under prior constitutions, similar provisions were used to ratify treaties without parliamentary approval).

[40] CONSTITUCIÓN DE LA REPÚBLICA BOLIVARIANA DE VENEZUELA [Constitution], Dec. 15, 1999, art. 154 (Venez.).

III. Treaty Withdrawal and the Separation of Powers

Many of the most contentious recent debates on democratic control of international commitments concern not whether countries should conclude new agreements, but whether they should withdraw from existing ones. As noted in the introduction to this chapter, the Trump administration's threats to withdraw from various agreements have led to extensive debate on the constraints—domestic and international—that may apply to the president's withdrawal powers. The same questions arise in other countries, and in some recent and prominent cases, national courts have curtailed the ability of the executive to withdraw from treaties. Thus, in a case brought by opponents of U.K. withdrawal from the European Union, the U.K. Supreme Court determined that legislation was necessary to effect such withdrawal.[41] Likewise, the High Court of South Africa held that the national executive's purported notice of withdrawal from the Rome Statute of the International Criminal Court was invalid, as Parliament had neither approved it nor repealed the Rome Statute's implementing legislation.[42]

How do national legal systems regulate withdrawal from treaties? Historically, the decision to withdraw has generally been considered an executive prerogative that could be exercised without legislative approval. This is true not only in constitutional traditions—like the United Kingdom's—which grant the executive wide prerogative powers over treaty-making and foreign affairs, but also in countries where treaty ratification is constrained by parliamentary approval requirements. The executive's unilateral authority to withdraw is usually not specifically granted in the constitution, but established by long-standing practice. In such systems, the assumption appears to be that withdrawal is fundamentally an executive power, which does not require parliamentary participation unless such a constraint is specifically imposed by the constitution or legislation. In the United States, the Constitution does not expressly regulate withdrawal, but in practice presidents have routinely withdrawn from treaties without any formal participation by Congress. The U.S. Supreme Court has declined to decide whether the Constitution imposes constraints on the president's authority to withdraw from treaties, with a number of Justices labeling it a nonjusticiable political question.[43]

According to our data, in most countries today the executive retains the authority to withdraw from treaties without parliamentary approval. At the same time, as described

[41] R (Miller) v. Secretary of State for Exiting the European Union, [2017] UKSC 15 (appeal taken from Eng. & Wales).

[42] Democratic Alliance v. Minister of International Relations and Cooperation 2017 (3) SA 212 (GP) (S. Afr.).

[43] Goldwater v. Carter, 444 U.S. 996 (1979).

above, most national legal systems require parliamentary approval for ratification of virtually all significant treaties. This means that in many countries, it is easier for the executive to withdraw from treaties than to conclude them—new governments can, at the stroke of a pen, reverse legal commitments concluded after extensive negotiations and parliamentary review. Because in most countries ratified treaties are part of domestic law but remain so only as long as they are in force for that country, the executive's unilateral decision to withdraw can effectively result in extensive and virtually instantaneous changes to domestic law.

This asymmetry between domestic constraints on ratification and the lack of such constraints on withdrawal appears incongruous from a domestic accountability perspective.[44] Indeed, concerns regarding this incongruity featured prominently in the recent U.K. and South African decisions imposing parliamentary approval requirements on withdrawal from—at least some—treaties. These decisions may prove a watershed, attracting political and scholarly attention to domestic law regimes governing treaty withdrawal, and perhaps creating pressure to reform them. At the same time, there may be sound policy reasons to afford the executive the authority to act unilaterally in withdrawing from treaties. For example, scholars have suggested that emergency situations or material breaches by other parties to a treaty may require prompt withdrawal, or that the executive's ability to credibly threaten to terminate a treaty may be essential in order to effectively renegotiate it.[45]

This being said, our data also reveal a trend observers have largely missed: several countries already mandate parliamentary involvement in treaty withdrawal, and their numbers have been growing substantially in the past four decades. As Figure 4 shows, the proportion of countries in which the executive can withdraw from treaties unilaterally has declined significantly since the 1970s, from a high of 89 percent to the current level of 72 percent. In most of these countries, the new constraints take the form of a requirement that the executive obtain parliamentary approval prior to withdrawing from treaties whose ratification required such approval. In some, this requirement is codified in the constitution itself. For example, Article 19(1) of the Danish Constitution requires the king to obtain legislative consent prior to "terminat[ing] any international treaty entered into with the consent of the Folketing." Article 91(1) of the Dutch Constitution provides that the country "shall not be bound by treaties, nor shall such treaties be denounced without the prior approval of the States General."[46]

[44] For a discussion of the merits of this asymmetry, *see* Laurence R. Helfer, *Treaty Exit and Intrabranch Conflict at the Interface of International and Domestic Law*, ch. 20 in this volume.

[45] The ease with which withdrawal can be accomplished as a matter of domestic law also has important implications for the design and credibility of treaty commitments. *See*, e.g., Laurence R. Helfer, *Exiting Treaties*, 91 VA. L. REV. 1579 (2005); Barbara Koremenos, *Contracting Around International Uncertainty*, 99 AM. POL. SCI. REV. 549 (2005).

[46] The Belgian Constitution also requires parliamentary approval of treaty ratification and withdrawal, although the authority to approve is split between the center and regions within a complex federal system. In China, withdrawal from treaties is subject to a vote by the Standing Committee of the

FIGURE 4

While explicit constitutional provisions of this sort remain the exception, a deeper investigation of infraconstitutional law reveals that binding parliamentary approval requirements for withdrawal are common. In several countries, especially in Eastern Europe and the former Soviet Union, treaty-making is governed by organic laws that require parliamentary approval of both ratification of, and withdrawal from, most treaties.[47] In several others, such a requirement is understood to apply as a matter of constitutional interpretation, or is embodied in a presidential decree, government regulation, or established administrative practice.[48] While these requirements do not enshrine as robust a role for the legislature as explicit constitutional provisions, they reveal the resilience of the notion of separation of powers in an environment where international treaties increasingly shape domestic policy and the power to withdraw is becoming equivalent to that of repealing laws.[49]

National People's Congress. The Chilean Constitution requires consultation with the legislature prior to withdrawal.

[47] This is the case in Belarus,* Bosnia and Herzegovina, Estonia, Latvia, Lithuania, Mexico,* the Russian Federation, Slovenia, Tajikistan,* Turkmenistan,* and Ukraine. (The stars denote countries in which the legislature's role in treaty withdrawal is mentioned in the constitution itself, but the treaty-making law fills in the details.).

[48] This is the case in Austria, the Czech Republic, Ethiopia, Hungary, Iran, Japan (apparently only for treaties without termination clauses), Norway, Slovakia, and South Africa.

[49] Consistently with Helfer, *supra* note 44, at pp.367–378, our data set reveals no clear instance where the legislative branch is given the authority to force withdrawal from a treaty.

IV. Judicial Involvement in Treaty-Making

While foreign relations law scholars have long noted the importance of courts in implementing and enforcing treaty obligations, treaty-making is traditionally seen as outside the purview of the judicial branch. This perception may be particularly salient because courts in the United States and the United Kingdom, where foreign relations law first emerged as a field, have played virtually no role in reviewing the constitutionality of treaty commitments.

However, there may be good reasons to expect courts to become more involved in the treaty-making process. First, as national constitutions increasingly regulate treaty-making, for example by requiring parliamentary approval of certain categories of treaties, judicial intervention to police the new boundaries may increase. Second, as treaties intrude upon ever-greater areas of domestic law and policy, treaty-making becomes more likely to implicate the judiciary's function of protecting fundamental constitutional commitments such as individual rights and freedoms—a function recognized in virtually all constitutions.

Indeed, despite this lack of attention by Anglo-American foreign relations law scholarship, our data reveal a clear worldwide trend toward greater judicial involvement in treaty-making. Figure 5 shows that since the 1950s, a growing number of countries require their constitutional court, highest court, or another judicial or quasi-judicial mechanism to review whether treaties conform to the constitution prior to ratification. No less than 40 percent of all countries in our sample currently impose such an ex ante

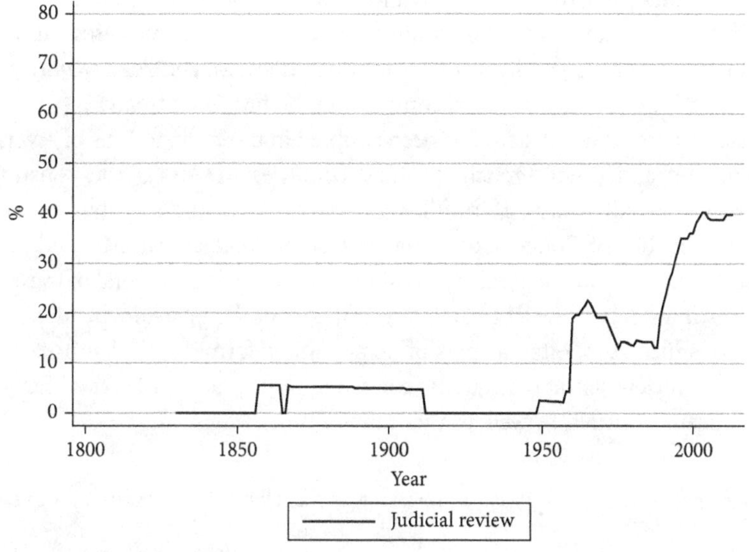

FIGURE 5

judicial review requirement. As judicial review of legislation has proliferated around the world, so has judicial review of proposed treaties for conformity with the constitution.

An illustrative and influential example of ex ante constitutional review of treaties is Article 54 of the 1958 French Constitution, which provides:

> If the Constitutional Council, on a referral from the President of the Republic, from the Prime Minister, from the President of one or the other Houses, or from sixty Members of the National Assembly or sixty Senators, has held that an international undertaking contains a clause contrary to the Constitution, authorization to ratify or approve the international undertaking involved may be given only after amending the Constitution.

The Constitutional Council is a peculiarly French institution, whose main function is to control the constitutionality of proposed statutes and treaties. It consists of nine members, three of which are appointed by each of the President of the Republic, the President of the National Assembly, and the President of the Senate for nonrenewable nine-year terms. Proposed treaties are routinely referred to the Council under Article 54.

In recent decades, the Council has blocked the ratification of important treaties, including the Maastricht Treaty (1992), the Rome Statute of the International Criminal Court (1999), the European Constitution (2004), the Second Optional Protocol to the ICCPR (2005), and the Lisbon Treaty (2007), on grounds that some of their provisions contradicted the French Constitution.[50] In each case, the constitution had to be amended to allow France to ratify; the European Constitution's ratification was eventually defeated in a national referendum. In the other cases, the government appears to have been able to secure the required constitutional amendments without substantial obstruction or delay. Nevertheless, France provides an example of an active system of ex ante review that subjects treaties to a probing examination of their compatibility with fundamental constitutional norms, and at least in some cases can pose a real obstacle to ratification, especially if the government does not control a majority sufficient to easily amend the constitution to accommodate the proposed treaty.

A similar ex ante review system has been adopted in the constitutions of several former French colonies and other French-speaking countries in Africa: the constitutions of Algeria, Benin, Burkina Faso, Burundi, Cameroon, Chad, the Republic of Congo, the Democratic Republic of Congo, Côte d'Ivoire, Gabon, Madagascar, Mali, Niger, Senegal, Togo, and Tunisia all contain similar provisions. Interestingly, in several of these countries ex ante constitutional review of treaties was not part of the post-independence constitution but was added later, often as part of democratic reforms in the late 1980s and early 1990s. Ex ante review also appears in the constitutions or practice of several European and Latin American countries, as well as a handful of other states.[51]

[50] For a complete history, *see* Patrick Daillier et al., Droit International Public 172–176 (8th ed. 2009).

[51] These countries are Austria, Belarus, Belgium, Bulgaria, Chile, Colombia, Czech Republic, France, Germany, Hungary, Indonesia, Iran, Ireland, Latvia, Lithuania, Mexico, Mozambique, Poland, Portugal,

Among these states that have adopted ex ante review, the process varies along two main dimensions: who can initiate it, and the institution that carries it out. In some countries, the process may only be initiated by the president, by the government, or by officials typically belonging to the party in power, which clearly reduces its impact as a constraint on the executive. For example, the Chadian Constitution provides that only the President of the Republic and the President of the National Assembly may refer a treaty to the Constitutional Council for review.[52] Many states, however, adopt a broader approach, allowing a minority in one or both legislative houses (usually one-tenth, one-fourth, or one-third) to refer a treaty.[53] This approach significantly broadens the applicability of ex ante review, as it is much more likely to allow opposition parties to challenge treaties proposed by the executive. Other countries allow yet broader access to the process, for example by requiring all international agreements to be referred for constitutional review (e.g., Madagascar), allowing provincial or regional authorities to request review of treaties that affect their interests (e.g., Cameroon), or allowing anyone to challenge a treaty prior to its ratification, at least in certain circumstances (e.g., Latvia).[54]

In most countries with constitutional review of treaties, such review is conducted by a constitutional court rather than by a hybrid council on the French model. Indeed, several of the French-speaking countries whose constitutions incorporated provisions modeled closely on Article 54 have themselves abandoned the council form in favor of a court,[55] and courts are also favored in virtually all other countries in our data set that allow ex ante review.[56] Like for constitutional review of statutes, the structure of the

Russia, Slovakia, Slovenia, Spain, Tajikistan, Ukraine, and Venezuela. A recent article by Mario Mendez, *Constitutional Review of Treaties: Lessons from Comparative Constitutional Design and Practice*, 15 Int'l J. Const. L. 84 (2017), provides a list that includes some additional countries not currently included in our data set: Albania, Angola, Bolivia, Dominican Republic, Ecuador, Georgia, Guatemala, Mauritania, and Romania.

[52] Constitution de la République du Tchad [Constitution], Mar. 31, 1996, art. 220 (Chad). Likewise, Mendez, *supra* note 51, at 107, reports that a similar procedure in Poland has never been used.

[53] *See*, e.g., Constitution du Burkina Faso [Constitution], June 11, 1991, art. 157 (Burk. Faso) ("The Constitutional Council may be seized by: the President of Faso; the Prime Minister; the President of the Senate; the President of the National Assembly; one-tenth of the members of each House of Parliament.").

[54] Latvia appears to allow anyone to challenge a treaty that allegedly violates certain fundamental constitutional rights. *See* Constitutional Court Law, Latvijas Vēstnesis [Official Gazette], No. 103 (588), June 14, 1996, § 17(1) (Lat.). Germany and Ireland also appear to provide broad constitutional standing to challenge treaties, although such review is not expressly provided for in the constitution. *See* Bundesverfassungsgericht [BVerfG] [Federal Constitutional Court], 2 BvR 1390/12, Sept. 12, 2012, *available at* https://www.bundesverfassungsgericht.de/SharedDocs/Entscheidungen/EN/2012/09/rs20120912_2bvr139012en.html (Ger.); Crotty v. An Taoiseach [1987] IR 713 (Ir.); Case C-370/12, Pringle v. Gov't of Ireland, [2012] IESC 47 (Ir.).

[55] Benin, Burundi, the Republic of Congo, the Democratic Republic of Congo, Madagascar, Mali, Niger, Togo, and Tunisia have all adopted constitutional courts, while Algeria, Burkina Faso, Cameroon, Chad, Côte d'Ivoire, and Senegal have constitutional councils.

[56] A notable exception is Iran, where ex ante review of treaties is conducted by the Council of Guardians.

reviewing institution may influence the effectiveness of the procedure as a check on the executive. Regardless of its formal institutional framework, the potency of treaty review likely depends on many factors that differ among countries, including de facto judicial independence.

While we have not systematically collected instances where constitutional courts or councils have exercised their authority to block the ratification of proposed treaties, anecdotal evidence suggests that the constitutional review procedure is not toothless. As noted above, the French Constitutional Council has often declared proposed treaties unconstitutional, requiring constitutional amendments prior to their adoption.[57] In September 2012, Germany's Federal Constitutional Court held that, in order for the country's ratification of the Treaty Establishing the European Stability Mechanism (ESM) to be constitutional, the government had to enter specific reservations imposing limits on Germany's financial exposure and requiring information about ESM activities to be provided to the Bundestag for oversight purposes.[58] The same year, the Irish Supreme Court held that the ESM Treaty could be ratified consistently with the Irish Constitution—a decision that came as a relief to the government and the rest of Europe, as a contrary decision would have required Ireland to hold a referendum prior to ratification.[59] In countries as diverse as Benin and Colombia, scholars report that constitutional courts have reviewed the constitutionality of numerous treaties,[60] although there appear to be few examples outside Europe in which courts have rejected proposed treaties.

Of course, ex ante treaty review is not the only mechanism through which the compatibility of treaties with the constitution may be controlled. In several countries, courts may review the constitutionality of treaties as a result of challenges brought after the treaty has been ratified. In some countries, such review is not expressly provided for in the constitution, being considered part and parcel of the court's authority to implement the hierarchy of norms and find that a treaty provision that has become part of the domestic legal order is overridden by a constitutional norm. In other countries, such as Austria, ex post treaty review is specifically codified.[61] While we have not systematically coded the availability of ex post treaty review and its use by courts, a recent study notes that there are few instances of courts declaring treaties unconstitutional after their ratification.[62] This seems unsurprising, given the significant

[57] However, for an extensive analysis concluding that Art. 54 has failed as a constraint on treaty-making, *see* Gerald Neuman, *The Brakes that Failed: Constitutional Restriction of International Agreements in France*, 45 CORNELL INT'L L.J. 257 (2012).

[58] BVerfG, 2 BvR 1390/12, Sept. 12, 2012. (Ger.).

[59] Pringle v. Gov't of Ireland, [2012] IESC 47 (Ir.).

[60] *See*, e.g., Bernadette Codjovi, *Communication de la Cour Suprême du Bénin*, *in* CAHIERS DE L'AOA-HJF: LES ACTES DU COLLOQUE INTERNATIONAL SUR « L'APPLICATION DU DROIT INTERNATIONAL DANS L'ORDRE JURIDIQUE INTERNE DES ETATS AFRICAINS FRANCOPHONES » at 131–161 (2003); Ricardo Abello Galvis, *La Corte Constitucional y el Derecho Internacional. Los tratados y el control previo de constitucionalidad 1992–2007*, 7 ESTUD. SOCIO-JURÍD 305 (2005).

[61] BUNDES-VERFASSUNGSGESETZ [B-VG] [CONSTITUTION], Oct. 1, 1920, art. 140a (Austria).

[62] Mendez, *supra* note 51, at 84.

intrusion in foreign affairs that would result, potentially placing the executive (and legislature) in the position of having to denounce or withdraw from a treaty, possibly in violation of the treaty's own provisions or other international law rules governing treaty termination.[63]

V. Conclusion

This chapter has outlined four trends in foreign relations law relating to treaty-making and withdrawal: (1) greater parliamentary participation in approving treaty ratification; (2) the emergence of "workarounds" that allow the executive to bypass parliamentary approval for certain agreements, but usually result in those agreements having lesser domestic legal status; (3) an emerging trend toward parliamentary approval of treaty withdrawal, usually for those treaties whose ratification required such approval; and (4) a more active role of the judiciary in policing treaties through both ex ante and ex post constitutional review. These trends emerge from analysis of our large-*n* data set documenting national doctrines governing the relationship of international law and domestic legal systems.

All four trends represent moves away from the executive-dominated world of traditional treaty relations. While some have already attracted notice, our data set provides a more precise idea of their prevalence and timing. Others, such as the rise and impact of constitutional review of treaties, had until recently largely escaped the attention of foreign relations scholars rooted in the Anglo-American tradition. Mapping these developments is an important first step in developing a more comprehensive research agenda, which would encompass their causes and consequences, questions of constitutional design, and how they interact with each other and with emerging mechanisms at the international level to promote greater participation and accountability in international lawmaking and governance.

[63] *See*, e.g., Vienna Convention on the Law of Treaties, art. 56, May 23, 1969, 1155 U.N.T.S. 331. Indeed, in some countries ex post review has been explicitly rejected by courts or prohibited in the constitution. *See* Mendez, *supra* note 51, at 99. For other examples of such "judicially compelled exit," *see* Helfer, *supra* note 44, at pp.369–370.

CHAPTER 9

INTERNATIONAL AGREEMENTS AND U.S. FOREIGN RELATIONS LAW

Complexity in Action

JEAN GALBRAITH

U.S. foreign relations law with respect to international agreements is fraught with complexity. The U.S. Constitution provides that the president "shall have power, by and with the advice and consent of the Senate, to make treaties, provided two thirds of the Senators present concur" and that these treaties "shall be the supreme law of the land."[1] Yet over its constitutional history, the United States has developed several other processes for entering into international agreements. Not only do these processes differ with respect to how agreements are made, but they can also vary regarding what these agreements may cover, how they will be implemented within the United States, and how they can be terminated. The president has considerable flexibility in choosing which process to pursue—a fact that in turn enhances executive power.

In general, U.S. foreign relations law on international agreements is insular. Even its vocabulary differs from world norms: the word "treaty" typically refers only to international agreements that receive the advice and consent of the Senate, rather than to the broader category of "treaty" under international law.[2] In its substance, U.S. practice has developed mostly on its own rather than consciously borrowing from practice abroad. Yet though insular, U.S. foreign relations law on international agreements is not entirely isolated. It has had some influence on the foreign relations law of other countries and in turn has been influenced indirectly by comparative

[1] U.S. CONST. art. II, § 2, cl. 2 (the Treaty Clause) & art. IV, cl. 2 (the Supremacy Clause).

[2] E.g., RESTATEMENT (FOURTH) OF THE FOREIGN RELATIONS LAW OF THE UNITED STATES, Part III, Introductory Note (2018) ("In U.S. domestic law, . . . the term 'treaties' refers . . . to international agreements concluded by the President with the advice and consent of two-thirds of the Senate.").

practice in several ways. Looking to the future, comparative practice is unlikely to affect U.S. constitutional law with respect to international agreements, but it might hold insights for legislative or administrative reforms.

I. Practice and Treaties

In the most famous U.S. Supreme Court case involving treaties, *Missouri v. Holland*, Justice Oliver Wendell Holmes, Jr., reflected on the importance of experience to constitutional interpretation. He wrote:

> [W]hen we are dealing with words that also are a constituent act, like the Constitution of the United States, we must realize that they have called into life a being the development of which could not have been foreseen completely by the most gifted of its begetters. It was enough for them to realize or to hope that they had created an organism; it has taken a century and has cost their successors much sweat and blood to prove that they had created a nation. The case before us must be considered in the light of our whole experience, and not merely in that of what was said a hundred years ago.[3]

These words are often read as a normative claim about living constitutionalism.[4] Yet at least as to U.S. foreign relations law on treaties, they also reflect practical necessity. The simple and seemingly straightforward words of the Treaty Clause and the Supremacy Clause left much unresolved. When was the president to seek the advice and consent of the Senate? Could treaties address issues that the federal government otherwise lacked the constitutional authority to regulate? Would the president need the advice and consent of the Senate or the support of Congress in order to withdraw from a treaty? Under what circumstances, if any, would congressional legislation be needed in the course of implementing treaty obligations? These questions all emerged early in U.S. constitutional history. Still others emerged later, tied to the rise of regional and worldwide multilateral treaties, such as whether the Senate needed to advise and consent to the addition of each new treaty party.

The answers to all these questions were left in the first instance to the president and the Senate. During George Washington's presidency, the process of answering many of them began.[5] But to the extent that lasting solutions now exist, their formation took

[3] 252 U.S. 416, 433 (1920).

[4] *See*, e.g., Bruce Ackerman, *Oliver Wendell Holmes Lectures: The Living Constitution*, 120 Harv. L. Rev. 1737, 1800 (2007).

[5] *See*, e.g., George Washington, Message to the House of Representatives, Declining To Submit Diplomatic Instructions and Correspondence (Mar. 30, 1796) (asserting that the House of Representatives has no role in treaty-making and that the Jay Treaty "exhibits in itself all the objects requiring legislative provision"); Thomas Jefferson, Notes on Cabinet Meeting of Feb. 26, 1793, *in* IX The Writings of Thomas Jefferson 135–138 (H. A. Washington ed., 1854) (describing a debate in

far longer to crystallize. Later political actors built upon or moved away from the precedents of the Washington administration, as well as addressing questions that the Washington administration never faced. In answering these questions, presidents, senators, and their advisers engaged in constitutional interpretation but also inevitably considered which answers would be politically feasible and would advance their policy goals. Some of their choices in turn have come to the Supreme Court for review, although others have never been adjudicated. For the most part, however, the decisions of the Supreme Court have validated choices made by the political branches.[6]

In the 230 years since the drafting of the Constitution, the political branches have developed a predictable treaty-making process. The president or subordinate executive branch officials negotiate a treaty, often in consultation with members of Congress. Following negotiation and signature, the president submits the treaty to the Senate for its advice and consent. The Senate Foreign Relations Committee holds hearings on the treaty and can vote it forward for consideration by the full Senate, accompanied by a report. If a floor vote is held, the Senate will vote on a resolution of advice and consent to the treaty. This resolution will typically specify how the treaty is to be implemented into the United States and may also include other reservations, understandings, declarations, conditions, and reporting requirements. If two-thirds of the Senate vote in favor of the resolution, then the president may ratify the treaty at his or her discretion once any preconditions set out in the resolution of advice and consent have been satisfied. If legislation is needed to implement the treaty, then the president will typically wait to ratify the treaty until Congress has passed this legislation.[7]

Washington's Cabinet over the scope of the treaty power); *Edmond Randolph on the British Treaty*, 1795, 12 AM. HIST. REV. 587, 591 (1907) (containing the view of Washington's attorney general on the extent to which the Constitution required the Senate's advice and consent to be obtained at a particular time or times in the treaty-making process).

[6] The Supreme Court has addressed the scope of the treaty power and the process of treaty implementation in various decisions. As to scope, to date it has never found a treaty obligation to exceed the constitutional authority of the federal government. *Missouri v. Holland* is the case most associated with this conclusion (though far from the only case in which the Supreme Court has recognized the broad reach of the Treaty Power). With regard to treaty implementation, the Supreme Court has emphasized that the intent of the president and the Senate, as demonstrated through the text of a treaty, shapes whether a treaty requires implementing legislation in order to be enforceable by the courts. Medellín v. Texas, 552 U.S. 491, 519 (2008) ("we have held treaties to be self-executing when the textual provisions indicate that the President and Senate intended for the agreement to have domestic effect"). In *Goldwater v. Carter*, the Court dismissed as nonjusticiable the question of whether President Jimmy Carter could terminate a treaty with Taiwan, in accordance with its termination provision, without also having the approval of either two-thirds of the Senate or of Congress. 444 U.S. 996, 1002 (1979) (plurality opinion of Rehnquist, J.) (finding the case to present a political question); *id.* at 996 (opinion of Powell, J.) (finding the case unripe).

[7] Some aspects of this process go back far in constitutional history. Others are much more recent. Only since the Supreme Court's 2008 decision in *Medellín*, for example, has the Senate come to specify with regularity in its resolutions of advice and consent whether or not a treaty is self-executing. *See* S. EXEC. REP. NO. 111-3, at 5 (2010) (introducing this policy).

This process is clear, but very difficult to complete. The need for two-thirds of the Senate effectively mandates strong bipartisan cooperation and has vexed presidents pursuing internationalist agendas throughout constitutional history. (Theodore Roosevelt's frustrated secretary of state famously likened a treaty in the Senate to "a bull going into the arena: no one can say just how or when the blow will fall—but one thing is certain—it will never leave the arena alive."[8]) And even if two-thirds of the Senate might vote in favor of a treaty, procedural hurdles can prevent a vote from taking place. Especially since the mid-1990s, with the rise of partisanship and procedural gridlock, it has been difficult for any treaty to make it through the Senate unless it has little to no opposition. The Law of the Sea Convention, for example, made it out of the Senate Foreign Relations Committee unanimously in 2004, but the Senate leadership never scheduled a floor vote.[9] During the Obama administration, a single Senator effectively held up the passage of all tax treaties.[10]

II. Practice and Other Types of International Agreements

As much as practice has shaped U.S. foreign relations law in relation to treaties, it has done so even more with respect to other kinds of international agreements. The Constitution does not identify any way for the federal government to make international agreements other than through the process specified in the Treaty Clause, although it does not specifically bar such agreements either.[11] Over time, however, other ways of making international agreements have developed, in part due to administrative efficiency and in part due to presidential interest in making important international agreements in situations where two-thirds of the Senate would be unobtainable.

Foreign relations law scholars typically categorize these agreements based on whether and when Congress is involved in their making. An ex post congressional-executive agreement (ex post CEA) receives the express approval of Congress after it is negotiated and typically before it is ratified. Trade agreements like the North American Free Trade Agreement (NAFTA) are now made as ex post CEAs, generally facilitated by preexisting "fast track" legislation that guarantees them an up-or-down vote if

[8] W. Stull Holt, Treaties Defeated by the Senate 209 (1933) (quoting John Hay).

[9] Scott G. Borgerson, The National Interest and the Law of the Sea 12 (2009).

[10] Alison Bennett, *Can Senate Reach Compromise on Tax Treaty Logjam? Maybe*, Bloomberg BNA (Dec. 2, 2016), *available at* https://www.bna.com/senate-reach-compromise-n73014448001.

[11] Language in clauses addressing the ability of U.S. states to make commitments with foreign nations suggests that the Framers were aware of the existence of international commitments other than "treaties." *See* U.S. Const. art. I, § 10, cls. 1 & 3 (barring states from making "any treaty, alliance, or confederation," and further from making "any agreement or compact . . . with a foreign power" without the consent of Congress).

certain prerequisites are met.[12] An ex ante congressional-executive agreement (ex ante CEA) is one that Congress has authorized to some degree prior to its negotiation, usually through a statutory provision signaling support for international cooperation on a particular issue. An early example of such a congressional authorization is a statutory provision passed in 1792 that authorizes the postmaster general to make agreements with international counterparts for mail delivery.[13] Finally, a sole executive agreement is negotiated and ratified by the president or subordinate executive branch officials without statutory support. An example is the Litvinov Assignment, which settled various claims between the United States and the Soviet Union in conjunction with U.S. recognition of the Soviet Union.[14]

Although ex ante CEAs and sole executive agreements are conceptually distinct, in practice they can blur together. The Paris Agreement on climate change illustrates this point. President Barack Obama made the United States a party to this agreement without receiving any post-negotiation approval from Congress or the Senate. Supporters could point to some preexisting indicia of legislative support, including the preexisting framework treaty on climate change and provisions in Congress's Global Climate Protection Act and Clean Air Act,[15] yet these indicia are far from compelling signals of legislative preapproval. Regardless of whether the Paris Agreement is categorized as an ex ante CEA, a sole executive agreement, or something in-between, it did not receive express and explicit approval from Congress. Nonetheless, existing congressional laws placed meaningful constraints on how the Paris Agreement could be implemented and thus on what President Obama could commit the United States to during the negotiations.

Ex post CEAs, ex ante CEAs, and sole executive agreements all have precedential roots that go back into the mid-nineteenth century or earlier. Their reach has grown since, in part through the accretion of minor precedents and in part through the deployment of bold new ones. The existence of all these processes is now well established, and U.S. international relations depend heavily upon them. By Oona Hathaway's calculations, between 1980 and 2000 the United States entered into almost 4,000 agreements through these processes, compared with 375 treaties.[16]

[12] Fast-track legislation typically comes with sunset provisions. The currently applicable fast-track legislation will sunset on July 1, 2021. Bipartisan Congressional Trade Priorities and Accountability Act of 2015 § 103, Pub. L. 114–26, 129 Stat. 320, 333.

[13] Act of Feb. 20, 1792, ch. 7, § 26, 1 Stat. 232, 239. Similar to an ex ante CEA, a treaty can explicitly or implicitly authorize the executive branch to make further agreements related to the treaty.

[14] *See* United States v. Belmont, 301 U.S. 324 (1937) (upholding the domestic implementation of this agreement).

[15] *See* Harold Hongju Koh, *Triptych's End: A Better Framework to Evaluate 21st Century International Lawmaking*, 126 Yale L.J. F. 338, 350–351 (2017); Daniel Bodansky & Peter Spiro, *Executive Agreements +*, 49 Vand. J. Transnat'l L. 885, 916–919 (2016).

[16] Oona A. Hathaway, *Presidential Power over International Law: Restoring the Balance*, 119 Yale L.J. 140, 150, 152–153 (2009). Almost all of these agreements were ex ante CEAs or sole executive agreements. *See id.* at 150 n.16 (identifying only nine ex post CEAs).

Yet there remain significant open legal questions about these agreements. One set of questions relates to their permissible scope. Can ex post or ex ante CEAs address issues that would otherwise lie outside the power of the federal government to regulate? To what extent is the president limited in the power to make sole executive agreements with respect to subject matter, importance, or duration? Another set of questions relates to the extent to which the executive branch can implement agreements domestically in ways that affect the rights of private actors or of state governments. To date, the Supreme Court has not addressed the permissible scope of these agreements.[17] As to implementation, it has upheld the domestic implementation of sole executive agreements focused on claims settlement.[18] While the Supreme Court has not explicitly addressed domestic implementation outside the claims settlement context, preexisting or subsequent congressional legislation is presumably essential in most other circumstances.[19]

As these alternatives to treaties have become integral to U.S. foreign relations practice, some regularized processes have developed with respect to their use. This is true both internally within the executive branch and in its dealings with Congress. Internally, the State Department employs a process, known as the C-175 Procedure, for determining what agreement should follow what pathway—and more generally for making sure that all agreements are reviewed by the State Department prior to their completion.[20] Externally, Congress has mandated in the Case-Zablocki Act of 1972 that any international agreements other than treaties be reported to Congress within sixty days of their entry into force.[21]

Separate from the types of international agreements described above, much of U.S. cooperation abroad involves "soft law": nonbinding political commitments by the executive branch. These commitments are not a source of international law

[17] The Supreme Court declined to review an appellate decision which dismissed on justiciability grounds a challenge to the constitutionality of NAFTA. Made in the USA Foundation v. United States, 242 F. 3d 1300 (11th Cir. 2001), *cert. denied* 534 U.S. 1039 (2001).

[18] E.g., United States v. Belmont, 301 U.S. 324 (1937); *see also* Dames & Moore v. Regan, 453 U.S. 654 (1981).

[19] In *Medellín v. Texas*, the Supreme Court described the claims settlement context as "a narrow set of circumstances" and rejected an argument that the president's foreign affairs powers entitled him to obedience from states on an issue within their traditional police powers. 552 U.S. at 531–532. In practice, executive branch actors typically assume that legislation is needed for implementation and therefore work to structure their agreements so that implementation lies within the scope of preexisting statutes. E.g., 11 FAM § 723.3 (identifying "[w]hether the agreement can be given effect without the enactment of subsequent legislation by Congress" as a relevant factor in determining what process to follow in making the agreement); U.S. Department of State, Press Release, United States Joins Minamata Convention on Mercury (Nov. 6, 2013), archived at http://perma.cc/66VU-SNSJ (noting that this agreement, which was joined without the subsequent approval of either the Senate or Congress, could be implemented "under existing legislative and regulatory authority").

[20] 11 FAM §§ 720–727; *see also* 22 CFR § 181.

[21] Pub. L. No. 92-403, 86 Stat. 619 (1972), codified as amended at 1 U.S.C. § 112b.

obligations, but in practice they can be enormously important. One of President Obama's signature foreign policy achievements—the Joint Comprehensive Plan of Action (JCPOA) reached between various major powers and Iran—was such a commitment. Such commitments can also be made by actors within the executive branch who have considerable operational freedom from presidential control. The Basel Accords on financial regulation, for example, are soft law commitments that the Federal Reserve Bank takes the lead in negotiating and implementing.[22] Because soft law commitments are traditionally thought to raise little or no constitutional concerns, they offer the president a pathway for pursuing international cooperation that is uncomplicated as a matter of constitutional law.[23] As with other alternatives to the treaty process, however, their implementation into domestic law will generally need to be done through preexisting or subsequent legislation. Soft law commitments are presently subject to very limited oversight mechanisms, although this may be starting to change.[24]

The chart at the end of this section summarizes the various pathways that are available for making international commitments and the law that surrounds these pathways. It is meant as a map of the landscape—as best this author understands it—rather than as a precise description of every feature of it. Thus, for example, it combines ex ante CEAs and sole executive agreements given the interests of space, the difficulties that can arise in assigning certain agreements to one category or the other, and certain overlapping features. The chart uses "domestic implementation" as a shorthand for implementation that directly affects the rights of private domestic actors or state governments (as opposed to implementation that occurs within the executive branch), and "President" as a shorthand for both the president and subordinate actors in executive branch agencies. And it does not attempt to explain the difference between self-executing and non-self-executing treaties.[25] What this chart does make clear, however, is that important commitments can be made—and have been made—through each of the given categories.

[22] *See* Michael S. Barr & Geoffrey P. Miller, *Global Administrative Law: The View from Basel*, 17 Eur. J. Int'l L. 15, 32–33 (2006).

[23] Some recent scholarship now urges constitutional scrutiny for soft law commitments. *See* Duncan B. Hollis & Joshua J. Newcomer, *"Political" Commitments and the Constitution*, 49 Va. J. Int'l L. 507 (2009); Michael D. Ramsey, *Evading the Treaty Power?: The Constitutionality of Nonbinding Agreements*, 11 Fl. Int'l U. L. Rev. 371 (2016).

[24] An attempt to increase oversight within the executive branch was undertaken by President Obama in 2013 with respect to international regulatory cooperation, which in turn can take the form of soft law commitments. Executive Order 13609, 3 CFR § 255 (2013) (increasing interagency coordination and establishing reporting requirements in relation to international regulatory cooperation).

[25] For this and other treaty issues, the best source for mainstream answers is the recent Restatement (Fourth) of Foreign Relations Law, *supra* note 2.

Table 1

	Binding Agreements under International Law			Nonbinding Political Commitments
	Treaties	Ex post CEAs	Other Executive Agreements	
Potential Scope	Exceedingly broad.	Very broad but likely narrower than treaties.	Broad and continuing to expand.	Presumably very broad.
Process of Formation	President negotiates and then ratifies with the advice and consent of 2/3 of the Senate.	President negotiates and then ratifies after receiving approval from Congress via a statute or joint resolution.	President makes, sometimes with prior indicia of legislative approval. Subject to reporting requirements.	President or independent agencies make.
Domestic Implementation	Comparable to a statute if the treaty is deemed self-executing. Non-self-executing treaties require intervening implementation.	Congress's approval during formation provides for whatever implementation Congress considers is needed.	Outside certain contexts like claims settlement, implementation presumably requires a preexisting or subsequent congressional statute.	Implementation will typically require a preexisting or subsequent congressional statute.
Exit	President can presumably trigger exit if consistent with international law.	Unclear whether president needs Congress's approval to trigger exit.	President can presumably trigger exit, at least if consistent with international law.	President can trigger exit (as can independent agencies for commitments they formed).
Examples	UN Charter; ICCPR	SALT I; NAFTA	Algiers Accords; Paris Agreement	Basel Accords; JCPOA w/Iran

III. International Agreements and Presidential Power

Benjamin Franklin once told a parable about a snake with two heads. "She was going to a brook to drink and . . . a twig . . . opposed her direct course; one head chose to go on the right side of the twig, the other on the left; so that time was spent in the contest, and, before the decision was completed, the poor snake died with thirst."[26]

[26] 10 The Complete Works of Benjamin Franklin 188 (John Bigelow ed., 1888). Franklin used this story to express wariness about Pennsylvania's bicameral legislature.

A scholar in the 1930s began his book on treaties with this cautionary tale, deeming the president and the Senate "condemned" to fight over treaty-making.[27] Yet in the years since, the United States has not died of thirst. The Senate has advised and consented to important treaties negotiated by the president, including many major treaties in the years between the end of World War II and the mid-1990s. The alternative pathways discussed above have also become increasingly available as a matter of constitutional practice. Crucially, it is the president who has the power to choose which option to pursue, conditional on it being deemed constitutional.[28]

Given these available pathways and the president's power to choose between them, the president is easily the dominant head with respect to the making of international commitments. And as a matter of constitutional practice, this flexibility is likely to continue growing over time. Presidents of both parties have incentives to value this flexibility and use it with expediency.[29] The Obama administration took advantage of this flexibility in crafting the Paris Agreement and the JCPOA with Iran. While President Donald Trump has yet to make any comparably creative moves, he believes that, "[a]s President, I can make far better deals with foreign countries than Congress."[30]

Yet for all the growth in presidential power with respect to the making of international commitments, considerable constraints exist as well. Some of these constraints remain tied to constitutional law and congressional power, while others stem from other types of law and other institutional actors.

One such constraint is that the president's power to choose is limited by more than constitutional law. If the president wishes to make a soft law commitment rather than a binding one, he or she must obtain the consent of negotiating partners. For binding agreements, the C-175 Procedure imposes an administrative process for selecting the path that considers factors besides constitutionality.[31] Finally, members of Congress can persuasively voice objections to the use of certain pathways, as occurred when

[27] Holt, *supra* note 8, at 1.

[28] *See* Jean Galbraith, *From Treaties to International Commitments: The Changing Landscape of Foreign Relations Law*, 84 U. Chi. L. Rev. 1675 (2017) (further discussing the president's power to choose and the various constraints that can limit how he or she uses this power). The current section draws upon themes developed in this article. For another recent article emphasizing strong presidential powers with respect to the making of international commitments, *see* generally Curtis A. Bradley & Jack L. Goldsmith, *Presidential Control over International Law*, 131 Harv. L. Rev. 1201 (2018).

[29] *See* Curtis A. Bradley & Trevor W. Morrison, *Historical Gloss and the Separation of Powers*, 126 Harv. L. Rev. 411, 442 (2012) (noting that "Presidents . . . enjoy a greater share of the power of their institution than members of Congress, and thus have more incentive to expend resources protecting and enhancing this power").

[30] Statement by President Donald J. Trump on Signing the "Countering America's Adversaries Through Sanctions Act" (Aug. 2, 2017), *available at* https://www.whitehouse.gov/the-press-office/2017/08/02/statement-president-donald-j-trump-signing-countering-americas.

[31] 11 FAM 723.3 (identifying eight factors as "considerations for selecting among constitutionally authorized procedures," including "[p]ast U.S. practice as to a particular type of agreement," "[t]he preference of the Congress as to a particular type of agreement," and "[t]he general international practice as to similar agreements").

President George W. Bush sought to make a nonbinding arms control commitment with Russia.[32] None of these constraints is impossible to surmount: the president can persuade negotiating partners, ramrod the C-175 process (conditional on defensible constitutionality), and ignore members of Congress. Yet collectively they limit the practical reach of the president's power to choose.

Still other constraints relate to the substance of what the president can include in international commitments that do not receive the specific approval of the Senate or Congress. As to the negotiated content of these commitments, there are strong incentives to keep them consistent with the existing superstructure of international law, which in turn is built by international agreements that have received the advice and consent of the Senate or the approval of Congress.[33] As to the implementation of these commitments, if the president does not wish to seek legislative approval then he or she must limit their contents to commitments that can be implemented without further legislation. Thus, in the JCPOA the United States only agreed to lift sanctions on Iran that the president had the previously delegated power to waive; U.S. negotiators could not and did not promise to waive other kinds of sanctions.[34] The Paris Agreement similarly contained obligations that were crafted to be within the boundaries of what the Environmental Protection Agency and other executive branch actors could already accomplish under the preexisting Clean Air Act.[35]

A final pragmatic limit on the president's power is the possibility that a future president will disavow an international commitment made by his or her predecessor. The legal power to terminate international commitments is an issue on whose merits the Supreme Court has been silent, but except perhaps with respect to ex post CEAs, it is generally thought to lie with the president.[36] Yet future presidents will have an

[32] *See* Jack L. Goldsmith & Eric A. Posner, *International Agreements: A Rational Choice Theory*, 44 VA. J. INT'L L. 113, 122–125 (2003) (describing how, following pressure from leading senators, President Bush moved from pursuing a handshake commitment to a treaty and analyzing why both President Putin and President Bush accepted this transition).

[33] This constraint is largely a political one: it is very difficult to obtain the international consensus needed to renegotiate framework treaties. But it has legal dimensions as well. A soft law commitment cannot formally alter this superstructure. And the president would face considerable resistance on legal as well as political grounds if he or she tried to terminate an international agreement that had received the express consent of the Senate or Congress in order to substitute a different agreement that would lack legislative consent.

[34] For an overview of the statutory scheme, *see generally* DIANNE E. RENNACK, CONG. RES. SERV. REP., IRAN; U.S. ECONOMIC SANCTIONS AND THE AUTHORITY TO LIFT RESTRICTIONS (Jan. 22, 2016).

[35] *See* Galbraith, *supra* note 28, at 1734–1739.

[36] For how presidents have come to claim this power with respect to treaties, *see generally* Curtis A. Bradley, *Treaty Termination and Historical Gloss*, 92 TEX. L. REV. 773 (2014). For ex post CEAs, it is an open and interesting question whether the president needs congressional approval to terminate these agreements and, if not, whether and under what conditions the legislation implementing these agreements is effectively suspended by their termination. For international commitments made by the executive branch without subsequent legislative approval, it is only logical that the executive branch can also terminate these commitments.

easier time exercising this power with respect to international commitments that have not received the subsequent blessing of the Senate or Congress. Commitments that have received legislative approval are likely to be harder to abandon as a matter of politics and more difficult to disassociate from as a matter of law, especially if legislation specifically implementing these commitments has been passed. The ability of a future president to back away from his or her predecessor's commitment is enhanced by the fact that international commitments take time both to negotiate and to implement. The Paris Agreement, for example, was finalized toward the end of President Obama's second term and was in the early stages of implementation when he left office. These factors, along with the absence of specific legislative approval, eased President Trump's path in announcing the future U.S. withdrawal from this agreement and in ceasing its implementation.[37] Similarly, in the spring of 2018, President Trump withdrew the United States from the JCPOA with Iran, another commitment reached in 2015 by the administration of President Obama.[38] These examples illustrates the greater fragility of international commitments made without specific legislative approval.

For U.S. negotiating partners, U.S. foreign relations law with respect to international commitments can lead to considerable confusion and frustration. With respect to treaties, the fact that the president cannot confidently promise the advice and consent of the Senate has bemused and dismayed foreign leaders since at least the failure of the Treaty of Versailles. John Bellinger, the Legal Adviser to the State Department for part of the George W. Bush administration, has noted that "our negotiating partners have no confidence that the executive branch will be necessarily be able to get a potentially controversial treaty through the Senate."[39] President Trump's repudiation of the Paris Agreement now highlights the limits on the president's ability to credibly commit the United States through pathways that do not involve specific legislative approval. Nonetheless, the position of the United States on the world stage can sometimes leave other countries with little choice but to risk these frustrations and to endure them when they arise.

[37] For the announcement of future withdrawal, *see* Statement by President Trump on the Paris Climate Accord (June 1, 2017), *available at* https://www.whitehouse.gov/the-press-office/2017/06/01/statement-president-trump-paris-climate-accord.

[38] Presidential Memorandum, Ceasing U.S. Participation in the JCPOA and Taking Additional Action to Counter Iran's Malign Influence and Deny Iran All Paths to a Nuclear Weapon (May 8, 2018), *available at* https://www.whitehouse.gov/presidential-actions/ceasing-u-s-participation-jcpoa-taking-additional-action-counter-irans-malign-influence-deny-iran-paths-nuclear-weapon.

[39] Interview by Toni Johnson with John B. Bellinger III (July 9, 2010), *available at* https://www.cfr.org/interview/us-trouble-start-and-other-treaties. President Trump's decision to abandon the Trans-Pacific Partnership trade agreement negotiated during the Obama administration, rather than to seek congressional approval for it as an ex post CEA, similarly illustrates how negotiations laboriously completed under one president can be abandoned prior to ratification.

IV. The Role of Comparativism

U.S. foreign relations law on international agreements is largely but not entirely self-contained. International law has helped to shape it over time, as has the march of world events.[40] In turn, U.S. foreign relations law on international agreements has affected the structure of particular international agreements and may even have influenced international law more generally.[41] This kind of back-and-forth is less obvious in the comparative context, but is still present if one looks closely. After identifying several forms of influence, I consider other ways in which comparative law and U.S. law could affect each other.

Constitutional Borrowing. Constitutional drafting is a well-recognized locus for the influence of foreign law. The Framers of the Constitution drafted the Treaty Clause partly in conscious opposition to British practice. As Alexander Hamilton wrote in *The Federalist Papers*, "[T]he king of Great Britain . . . can of his own accord make treaties of peace, commerce, alliance, and of every other description . . . there is no comparison between the intended power of the President and the actual power of the British sovereign. The one can perform alone what the other can do only with the concurrence of a branch of the legislature."[42] The Supremacy Clause, by contrast, was asserted by supporters of the Constitution to be consistent with British practice.[43]

In turn, U.S. constitutional provisions on treaties have influenced clauses in some other constitutions. The constitution of Mexico, for example, has a Supremacy Clause

[40] *See, e.g.*, Jean Galbraith, *International Law and the Domestic Separation of Powers*, 99 VA. L. REV. 987, 1027–1033 (2013) (describing how executive branch actors drew on international legal principles in defending the presidential power to make sole executive agreements); RESTATEMENT (FOURTH), *supra* note 2, § 313(1) (suggesting that the legality of treaty withdrawal under international law is relevant for determining whether the president has the constitutional power to trigger withdrawal); Bruce Ackerman & David Golove, *Is NAFTA Constitutional?*, 108 HARV. L. REV. 799, 802–803, 873–875 (1995) (showing how that political reaction within the United States to World War II helped trigger the rise of ex post CEAs).

[41] *See, e.g.*, Galbraith, *supra* note 28, at 1734–1741 (describing how the Paris Agreement was influenced by the U.S. need for an agreement that could be made and implemented without subsequent legislative approval); J. MERVYN JONES, FULL POWERS AND RATIFICATION: A STUDY IN THE DEVELOPMENT OF TREATY-MAKING PROCEDURE 12–17 (1946) (describing how U.S. practice helped lead to the erosion of the eighteenth-century doctrine of obligatory ratification, according to which a nation was obligated to ratify a treaty negotiated by an agent acting within his full powers).

[42] THE FEDERALIST NO. 69, at 418 (Alexander Hamilton) (Clinton Rossiter ed., 1961).

[43] E.g., 2 DOCUMENTARY HISTORY OF THE RATIFICATION OF THE CONSTITUTION 460–461 (Merrill Jensen ed., 1976) (containing notes of a debate in the Pennsylvania ratification convention over British practice with respect to self-execution); 10 DOCUMENTARY HISTORY OF THE RATIFICATION OF THE CONSTITUTION 1382–1393 (John P. Kaminski & Gaspare J. Saladino eds., 1993) (containing notes of a similar debate in the Virginia ratification convention). British practice was in fact far less similar to the Supremacy Clause than supporters of the Constitution acknowledged during these debates.

that is modeled on the one in the U.S. Constitution.[44] Even where such textual influences exist, however, they do not necessarily translate into similarities in practice. To continue with the above example, the Supreme Court of Mexico has interpreted its Supremacy Clause in ways that differ sharply from how the U.S. Supreme Court has approached the Supremacy Clause.[45] The practical importance of constitutional borrowing in the treaty context is thus modest at best (and in any event does not extend to nontextual developments like the other processes for making international agreements).

Indirect Influences. Comparative practice can affect the content of international agreements, which in turn can affect the development of U.S. practice. Such indirect influence is most evident with respect to treaties, particularly the issue of treaty self-execution. Because some countries have formally dualist systems requiring implementing legislation to translate treaty obligations into domestic law, the language of international agreements made with these countries must accommodate this dualism. The use of such language in turn has increased the likelihood that treaties will be deemed non-self-executing within the United States. In *Medellín v. Texas*, the Supreme Court concluded that in determining whether or not a treaty is self-executing, the focus should be on the text of the treaty.[46] The Court did not discuss how comparative practice in turn affects the text of a treaty. By contrast, in his dissent Justice Breyer noted that "the issue whether further legislative action is required before a treaty provision takes domestic effect in a signatory nation is often a matter of how that nation's domestic law regards the provision's legal status. And that domestic status-determining law differs markedly from one nation to another."[47] He added that, because of this, "the absence or presence of language in a treaty about a provision's self-execution proves nothing at all."[48]

Comparative practice may also have indirectly affected other aspects of U.S. foreign relations law with respect to treaties. With regard to the scope of the treaty power, for example, the Supreme Court has remarked in dicta "[t]hat the treaty power of the United States extends to all proper subjects of negotiation between our government and the governments of other nations is clear."[49] Yet what "proper subjects of

[44] Mexico's Constitution of 1917, as amended through 2015, at art. 132, available in translation at https://www.constituteproject.org/constitution/Mexico_2015.pdf?lang=en (providing as translated that "This Constitution, the laws derived from and enacted by the Congress of the Union, and all treaties made and executed by the President of the Republic, with the approval of the Senate, shall be the supreme law of the country").

[45] *See* Alejandro Lopez-Velarde, *Trademark in Mexico: The Effects of the North American Free Trade Agreement*, 17 Hous. J. Int'l L. 49, 85–86 (1994) (describing how, unlike in U.S. practice, the Supremacy Clause of Mexico's constitution is interpreted to put treaties on a higher footing than legislation).

[46] 552 U.S. 491, 506, 514 (2008).

[47] *Id.* at 547 (Breyer, J., dissenting) (going on to give examples of practice in Britain and the Netherlands).

[48] *Id.* at 549 (Breyer, J., dissenting).

[49] Geofroy v. Riggs, 133 U.S. 258, 296 (1890) (adding the caveat that it "would not be contended that [this power] extends so far as to authorize what the Constitution forbids, or a change in the character of

negotiation" are will inevitably depend not only on the judgment of U.S. negotiators but also of the judgment of their negotiating partners—which in turn will depend on the presence or absence of their own constitutional limits. The fact that treaties now cover not only peace, commerce, and alliance but also subjects like health, human rights, and the environment illustrates collective as well as individual judgments by nations regarding what are issues of international importance.

Direct Influences. Perhaps the most obvious way in which comparative practice could influence U.S. foreign relations law is by serving as a direct point of comparison. Political actors, courts, and scholars could look to the practice of other countries in concluding what U.S. law is or should be. Yet aside from the constitutional borrowing discussed above, there has not been much direct influence to date. Members of Congress have occasionally referred to comparative law in their debates,[50] but there has been relatively little sustained consideration of comparative practice by any branch.

Some scholarship does look to comparative law in offering analysis or prescriptions with respect to U.S. practice. In part of an important article on the process by which the United States makes international agreements, Oona Hathaway surveys comparative practice and shows that the Treaty Clause, with its unicameral supermajority requirement, "stands out as a remarkably unusual method of making international law."[51] Hathaway draws on this comparative practice not in making constitutional arguments, but rather in suggesting that the United States would do well to abandon treaties in favor of congressional-executive agreements.[52] Where scholarship does look to comparative law for constitutional purposes, it may well find that comparative law has little to offer.[53] The complexities of the U.S. processes for making international agreements, their strong grounding in historical practice, and the overall structure of the U.S. presidential system make it largely impermeable to direct comparative influence.

Future Influences. The future of foreign relations law with respect to international agreements rests not only on constitutional law but also on statutory and administrative processes. The fast-track legislation that exists for trade agreements, the Case-Zablocki Act, and the C-175 Procedure are all examples of statutory or administrative developments that affect U.S. foreign relations law with respect to international

the government, or in that of one of the states, or a cessation of any portion of the territory of the latter, without its consent").

[50] E.g., 5 ANNALS OF CONG. 617 (statement of Rep. Tracy); *id.* at 752 (statement of Rep. Harper); *id.* at 1253 (statement of Rep. Ames) (all considering comparative practice with respect to self-execution and focusing specifically on the 1713 Treaty of Utrecht).

[51] Oona A. Hathaway, *Treaties' End: The Past, Present, and Future of International Lawmaking in the United State*, 117 YALE L.J. 1236, 1271 (2008).

[52] *See id.* at 1274, 1309.

[53] *See, e.g.*, Curtis A. Bradley & Laurence R. Helfer, *Treaty Exit in the United States: Insights from the United Kingdom or South Africa?*, 111 AJIL UNBOUND 428, 428 (2018) (concluding that comparisons of recent court rulings on treaty exit from the United Kingdom and South Africa "are unlikely to offer much guidance" for U.S. practice, in part "because of differences in the three countries' constitutions").

agreements. To the extent that the political branches are interested in further reforms, then the practice of other countries might serve as reference points.

To give only one example, if Congress or the executive branch are interested in increasing transparency with respect to international commitments, then the practice of other countries might be helpful in assessing options. Marisa Cremona's chapter in this volume describes how the European Council is experimenting with making its negotiating directives public.[54] In the United States, some information about negotiating positions is already public, such as the broad instructions contained in fast-track trade legislation or specific agendas set by various agencies in certain contexts.[55] If the U.S. political branches are considering greater transparency and specificity with respect to negotiating positions, then consideration of EU practice might prove useful. With regard to soft law commitments, Carlos Espósito's chapter in this volume explains how Spain's Treaties Act requires the registry of nonbinding commitments and observes that "the obligation to publish these agreements in an official public registry creates a strong incentive to establish a better practice on MOUs."[56] This practice is one that Congress and the executive branch could look to if they wish to bring more transparency to soft law commitments.

V. Conclusion

U.S. foreign relations law on international agreements owes as much or more to precedents and practice as it does to the text of the Constitution. Layers upon layers have built an edifice that no one would have initially chosen but which enables the United States to engage in international cooperation while retaining some meaningful domestic checks on presidential power. The complexity and path dependency of the current system limits the likelihood of future comparative influence on constitutional issues. Nonetheless, comparative practice might hold lessons for statutory or administrative reforms.

[54] Marise Cremona, *Making Treaties and Other International Agreements: The European Union*, ch. 14 in this volume, at p.249.

[55] For example, Congress requires that the Food and Drug Administration, in participating in the Codex Alimentarius, publish yearly notice of "the agenda for the United States participation" and "provide an opportunity for public comment." *See* Uruguay Round Agreements Act § 491, Pub. L. No. 103–465, 108 Stat. 4809, 4970–4971 (1994).

[56] Carlos Espósito, *Spanish Foreign Relations Law and the Process for Making Treaties and Other International Agreements*, ch. 12 in this volume, at p.216.

CHAPTER 10

INTERNATIONAL TREATIES AND THE GERMAN CONSTITUTION

STEFAN KADELBACH

MOVING from the philosophies of state of Hobbes, Locke, Montesquieu, and Hegel, who placed foreign relations in the hands of the monarch's cabinet,[1] the U.S. Constitution was the first to open treaty-making to parliamentary influence.[2] European nineteenth-century constitutionalism gradually extended the rights of the legislature in general, including in the treaty-making process.[3] In modern constitutions, treaty-making is a function of the state in which different institutions have their share: The head of state who represents the commonwealth as a whole; the executive branch, which is responsible for the administration of state routine; and the legislative branch, which may need to be consulted for consent on important treaties and on questions of war and peace. To varying degrees, the judiciaries have a competency of constitutional review, often so before a treaty is ratified. Thus, the term "treaty-making power," like foreign relations power in general, does not denote a specific responsibility of one state organ alone, but a matter of distribution of powers, of co-operation between the different branches, and of checks and balances.

This chapter will discuss the interrelationship of the different constitutional institutions in treaty-making from a German point of view. Some references will be made to other continental systems, but the author is conscious of the fact that the ensuing impressions remain isolated and are embedded within particular legal and

[1] THOMAS HOBBES, LEVIATHAN pt. 2, ch. 18, sec. 6 and 9 (1651); JOHN LOCKE, TWO TREATISES OF GOVERNMENT II, § 148 (1690); MONTESQUIEU, De L'Esprit des lois, XI 6 (1784); GEORG WILHELM FRIEDRICH HEGEL, GRUNDLINIEN DER PHILOSOPHIE DES RECHTS §§ 321, 329 (1821).

[2] For the impact of Swiss and Swedish practice, their reception by Vattel, and his influence on the founding fathers, *see* Peter Haggenmacher, *Some Hints on the European Origins of Legislative Participation in the Treaty-Making Function*, 67 CHI.-KENT L. REV. 313 (1991).

[3] *See* Werner Heun, *Artikel 59*, *in* GRUNDGESETZ KOMMENTAR §§ 1–4 (Horst Dreier ed., 2015).

historical contexts.[4] However, these references may shed light on some similar features and show if and where a debate across the systems about the constitutional principles of treaty-making might be sensible. After discussing various aspects of treaty-making, the chapter will conclude with some observations about the impact and potential of a comparative approach.[5]

I. Treaty-Making Power

Scholars have disagreed since the 1950s about the answer to the question, who has the foreign relations power in Germany?[6] In terms of vertical allocation of competencies, Article 32(1) of the German Constitution, the *Grundgesetz* (GG), explicitly entrusts the maintenance of foreign relations with other states to the federal government. Although it has remained unclear what precisely this means for the capability of the states, the *Länder*, to conclude treaties, the matter was settled by a compromise between the federal and the state governments in 1957. Pursuant to this compromise, the states will not oppose treaty-making if most of the subject matter lies within the reach of federal legislative powers, but consent by the state governments must be sought as early as possible.[7] With respect to the horizontal distribution of powers, different schools of thought exist, and the position of the Federal Constitutional Court (FCC) on the matter is less easy to assess than it appears at first sight. Treaty-making power plays a decisive role in the debate. The central provision is Article 59 GG.

External Representation

According to the wording of Article 59(1) GG, the president of the Federal Republic represents the German state externally. The provision emerged over time from an article that placed foreign relations power with the emperor and, during the Weimar

[4] On the difficulties of "bilegalism," *see* Vicki C. Jackson, *Comparative Constitutional Law: Methodologies, in* The Oxford Handbook of Comparative Constitutional Law 54, 70 (Michel Rosenfeld & András Sajó eds., 2012).

[5] Since EU law, under the German constitution as well as under some other European constitutions, is not considered to be public international law, but an area of its own, its relationship with domestic law will not be dealt with in this chapter.

[6] The dispute goes back to a controversy between Wilhelm G. Grewe and Eberhard Menzel, *Die auswärtige Gewalt der Bundesrepublik, in* 12 Veröffentlichungen der Vereinigung Deutscher Staatsrechtslehrer [hereinafter VVDStRL] 129 and 179, respectively (1954).

[7] So-called Lindau Accord of 14 November 1957; for the comparatively stronger position of the Autonomous Communities in Spain, *see* Carlos Espósito, *Spanish Foreign Relations Law and the Process for Making Treaties and Other International Agreements*, ch. 12 in this volume.

republic, with the president of the empire.[8] Under the *Grundgesetz*, the president has a primarily representative role to play, but also functions as the state's notary public in that he finally and formally ratifies treaties.[9] The president's powers extend to unilateral acts like the accrediting of ambassadors, the recognition of states and governments, protests, the establishment or disruption of diplomatic relations, and the proclamation of maritime zones. With respect to treaties, it is argued that the president is also responsible for their termination or suspension. A narrow reading of Article 59(1) GG demands that any unilateral act under international law by the government or its members must be traced back to the president,[10] although actual practice is not that strict.

The president only formally declares the will of the state. It lies in the domains of the executive branch and the legislature how this will constitutes itself. The government is not expressly mentioned in the Constitution with respect to external affairs, except in the context of the European Union, which is also an exception to the rule of representation by the president (Art. 23 GG, read together with Arts. 15 and 16 of the Treaty on European Union). However, it is implicit that the executive branch's prerogatives encompass relations with other subjects of international law. Thus, these prerogatives include negotiating and signing treaties, and agreeing to their preliminary application (Art. 25 VCLT). Moreover, state practice largely ignores the president's powers of external representation in that the chancellor or the foreign minister often declares the accession to or the termination of treaties. This practice constitutes a constant source of creative construction to bridge the gap in the Constitution's wording, the most convincing explanation for which is that the Constitution's attribution of representative functions to the president in that field is not exclusive.[11]

In presidential systems, by comparison, the representative function is tied to executive powers. Thus, the French President of the Republic, according to the wording of the Constitution, negotiates treaties.[12] In Switzerland, the government (*Bundesrat*) as a collective body represents the state in external relations, so that also in that country representative function and executive powers are joined.[13]

Treaties That Require Approval by the Parliament

Article 59(2) GG requires that the legislative bodies give their assent to two types of treaties, those regulating "political relations of the federation" (political treaties) and

[8] *See* CONST. of 1849, sec. 75; CONST. of 1871, art. 11, § 1; CONST. of 1919, art. 45, § 1.

[9] The position of the Federal President in Austria is similar, *see* AUST. CONST., art. 65, § 1.

[10] Hermann Mosler, *Die auswärtige Gewalt im Verfassungssystem der Bundesrepublik Deutschland, in* VÖLKERRECHTLICHE UND STAATSRECHTLICHE ABHANDLUNGEN 243, 280 (Hermann Mosler ed., 1954).

[11] Dietrich Rauschning, *Artikel 59, in* BONNER KOMMENTAR ZUM GRUNDGESETZ §§ 28–33, 59 (Wolfgang Kahl et al. eds., 2009); for the parallel debate in Italy, *see* Giovanni Bognetti, *The Role of the Italian Parliament in the Treaty-Making Process*, 67 CHI.-KENT L. REV. 391, 396–397 (1991).

[12] FRENCH CONST., art. 52, § 1; OLIVIER DUHAMEL, DROIT CONSTITUTIONNEL ET INSTITUTIONS POLITIQUES 561–563 (2d ed. 2011).

[13] *See* SWISS CONST., art. 184, § 2.

treaties concerning "matters of federal legislation" (legislative treaties). Unilateral acts do not fall under the scope of Article 59 GG.[14] Both types of treaties mentioned in Article 59(2) GG are so-called state treaties (*staatsverträge*), which means that they are concluded by the state as a whole.[15] The "legislative bodies" referred to are the federal Parliament (*Bundestag*) and the assembly of state governments (*Bundesrat*). Political treaties, the first category, are agreements that define the position of the Federal Republic in the international system of states such as, above all, military alliances, disarmament obligations, landmark treaties of friendship after World War II, and treaties drawing state borders.[16] The term "treaties governing matters of federal legislation," which denotes the second and more important category, aims at the powers of the legislative branch as opposed to those of the executive. To executive agreements, the section of the GG on the federal administration applies. Such executive agreements may either be concluded by the whole government (governmental agreements) or by the responsible ministry (*ressort* agreements).

This approach of reserving certain categories of treaties for parliamentary assent is common in Europe.[17] The constitutions of Austria, Denmark, Italy, Poland, Spain, and Sweden follow an approach similar to the *Grundgesetz* in that they distinguish between politically important and other treaties and attribute particular significance to legislative treaties.[18] As for other European countries, France and Greece define certain subject matters,[19] the Swiss Constitution establishes a presumption in favor of parliamentary approval,[20] and Belgium and the Netherlands subject all treaties to approval by Parliament.[21]

[14] The recognition of the jurisdiction of the ICJ was declared unilaterally, without parliamentary participation, by Declaration of 1 May 2008; reprinted 68 HEIDELBERG J. INT'L L. 776 (2008). The same rationale applied to the decision to station Pershing 2 and cruise missiles on German territory in 1983, *see* the judgment by the German Federal Constitutional Court (FCC), *in* 68 ENTSCHEIDUNGEN DES BUNDESVERFASSUNGSGERICHTS [hereinafter BVerfGE] 1, at 80–89 (1984).

[15] The provision applies to agreements with states and other subjects of international law alike. Concordats with the Holy See, however, are in the powers of the states, 6 BVerfGE 309 (1957). Contracts under private law, like purchase or rental of premises for an embassy, even though concluded by the state, do not come under the purview of Article 59 GG; however, if private contracts function as EU law, Article 23 GG is applicable, which triggers the duty to keep the Parliament informed in all EU matters, *see* 129 BVerfGE 124 (2011) on the European Finance Stabilisation Facility, which was established as a corporation under Luxembourg law.

[16] 1 BVerfGE 372 (1952); 90 BVerfGE 286, 359 (1994).

[17] For comparative observations, *see* Ulrich Fastenrath & Thomas Groh, *Artikel 59*, *in* BERLINER KOMMENTAR ZUM GRUNDGESETZ §§ 148–159 (Karl Heinrich Friauf & Wolfram Höfling eds., 2016); Heun, *supra* note 3, § 11.

[18] AUST. CONST., art. 50, § 1; DAN. CONST., sec. 19, § 1; ITAL. CONST., art. 80; POL. CONST., art. 89; SPAN. CONST., art. 94, § 1 (a); SWED. CONST., ch. 10, sec. 2, § 3.

[19] FRENCH CONST., art. 53, § 1; GREEK CONST., art. 37, § 2.

[20] SWISS CONST., art. 166, § 2; in practice, most agreements are of minor importance and can be concluded by the executive alone.

[21] *Cf.* BELG. CONST., art. 167, § 2; Neth. Const., art. 91, § 1. Tacit approval is permissible under NETH. CONST., art. 91 § 2; *see* the guidelines by the first chamber of Parliament, Notitie "Criteria voor de beoordeling van verdragen," 01/LD (23 July 2009), at 13–16 and C.A.J.M. KORTMANN,

The German concept looks like a clear notion of rule and exception: executive action is the rule, and parliamentary participation is the exception. One school of thought derives from this distribution of powers an argument that foreign relations power is a domain of the executive. The opposing view sees in Article 59(2) GG only one of the cases in which Parliament has a powerful position, next to the declaration of a "case of tension" or a "case of defense" under the threat of an armed attack (Arts. 80a and 115a GG, respectively), the transfer of powers to the European Union (Art. 23(1) GG), and the dispatch of armed forces abroad according to the jurisprudence of the FCC. For this view, all these cases form a principle of "combined foreign relations powers" lying in the hands of the executive together with Parliament in important cases. The position with respect to the degree of participation of Parliament in treaty-making under Article 59(2) GG, at least for some authors, depends on the view taken on the matter.

For traditionalists, Article 59(2) GG is to be construed narrowly. Accordingly, "treaties governing matters of federal legislation" are treaties that can only be fulfilled if Parliament amends existing statute law, the rationale being that Article 59(2) GG is a safeguard to guarantee implementation. The Federal Republic has thus become a member of important international organizations, like the Food and Agriculture Organization (FAO), International Labour Organization (ILO), International Maritime Organization (IMO), UN Educational, Scientific and Cultural Organization (UNESCO), and World Health Organization (WHO), without a statute of incorporation. In one of its first decisions ever, dating back to 1952, the FCC had subscribed to this approach.[22] Since then, the Court has kept insisting on the rule/exception rhetoric,[23] but it has modified its position in substance. According to its current view, the Constitution requires that government and Parliament co-operate in foreign relations,[24] but it is left open what exactly this principle of co-decision entails.[25]

The combined powers theory, by contrast, defines legislative powers in abstract terms, without reference to existing statute law: whenever the subject matter falls into the prerogative of Parliament, a treaty would need parliamentary assent. In more recent contributions, the requirement is tied to the doctrine of essentiality in general constitutional law according to which the *Bundestag* must take care of all essential affairs itself and cannot leave them to the executive to regulate.[26] What is essential, in turn, is controversial, but is supposed to cover matters that have an impact

CONSTITUTIONEEL RECHT 167–168 (7th ed. 2016); as a result, the ratio of express approval appears to be comparable to other systems.

[22] 1 BVerfGE 372 (1952)—German-French economic agreement.

[23] 68 BVerfGE 1, 85 (1984)—Pershing; 90 BVerfGE 286, 357 (1994)—AWACS/Somalia.

[24] 104 BVerfGE 151, 194, 207–209 (2001)—NATO; 118 BVerfGE 244, 258–260 (2007)—ISAF.

[25] In 49 BVerfGE 89, 127 (1978), the Court even held, if *obiter*, that art. 59, § 2 GG was an emanation of the principle of essentiality.

[26] *See*, for instance, Fastenrath & Groh, *supra* note 17, § 60; for a similar debate on the role of the Parliament in Italy, *see* Vincenzo Atripaldi, *I trattati internazionali nell'ordinamento costituzionale italiano tra forma die Governo e forma di Stato*, *in* ATTUAZIONE DEI TRATTATI INTERNAZIONALI E COSTITUZIONE ITALIANA 55, 68–69 (Giuliana Ziccardi Capaldo ed., 2003).

on personal rights and freedoms. Thus, treaties that have a bearing on rights or duties of the individual would need parliamentary approval, most clearly, but not necessarily, if they are self-executing.[27] Following the executive view, however, the doctrine of essentiality would not apply to treaty-making.

The consequences of the controversy are not necessarily merely theoretical. The question of which view better reflects the law arises, for instance, for so-called parallel treaties, agreements which, at the time of their conclusion, correspond (and are therefore "parallel") to statute law, but would bind the legislative branch for the future. A related issue is the informal modification of a treaty by dynamic practice or secondary law agreed to by the parties. Likewise, the discussion as to which institutions have to be involved in the declaration of unilateral acts like memoranda of understanding; the declaration, withdrawal, and rejection of reservations; and the suspension or termination of a treaty depends for some authors on the position taken in the controversy on the nature of treaty-making power.[28] Furthermore, genuine joint responsibility of government and Parliament would demand early and comprehensive information and consultation of the Parliament, probably as early as during negotiations.[29]

Many arguments have been exchanged between the two camps during the past decades. Executivists point to the needs of the government to act flexibly, the reliability of the state as a party to international treaty systems, the complexity of an often technical subject matter which requires administrative expertise rather than public debate, and the limited capacities of Parliament. Adherents to the combined powers theory claim that the dominance of the government in foreign affairs is a relic from the nineteenth century that does not comply with requirements of democratic legitimacy as they have developed after World War II, that expertise is not a privilege of the executive, that the line between the internal and the external has been blurred, and that more and more fields formerly covered within a state have become internationalized but still require public debate.

The principal antagonism of the approaches notwithstanding, there have been rapprochements in practice that have mitigated some of the effects mentioned. German state practice construes Article 59(2) GG broadly. It is undisputed that intrusions into

[27] Fastenrath & Groh, *supra* note 17, § 61.

[28] *See*, for instance, Rüdiger Wolfrum, *Kontrolle der auswärtigen Gewalt*, 56 VVDStRL 38, 50 (1997). For the FCC, it follows from a narrow construction of Article 59 GG that unilateral acts do not require parliamentary participation, *see* 68 BVerfGE 1, 86 (1984); 90 BVerfGE 286, 358 (1994). In Austria, unilateral acts related to treaties are subject to approval by the Parliament (*Nationalrat*), *see* THEO ÖHLINGER, VERFASSUNGSRECHT § 115 (9th ed. 2012). Similarly, DAN. CONST., sec. 19, § 1, NETH. CONST., art. 91, § 1, and POL. CONST., art. 89, § 1 expressly demands approval for the termination of treaties adopted by Parliament; for treaty termination under the U.S. Constitution, *see* Laurence R. Helfer, *Treaty Exit and Intrabranch Conflict at the Interface of International and Domestic Law*, ch. 20 in this volume.

[29] As it is possible, albeit not common practice under the NETH. CONST., *see* C. B. Modderman, *De Staten-Generaal en de totstandkoming van verdragen*, 6 TIJDSCHRIFT VOOR CONSTITUTIONEEL RECHT 34 (2015).

personal freedoms by the state are not permissible without an explicit empowerment by a statute, so that a treaty alone would not suffice. Furthermore, a pragmatic view would stress that opt-outs, reservations, suspension, and termination do not create, but limit or end international obligations and are therefore not subject to approval for lack of a conflict with prerogatives of the legislature.[30] However, it lies within the powers of Parliament to allow ratification only if a reservation is declared.[31] Parallel agreements are in practice presented to Parliament for approval. Whether binding secondary law created within a treaty regime or the possibility of an opt-in into further treaty obligations trigger the need for parliamentary approval depends on whether the treaty could be interpreted ex ante as to empower such lawmaking, as is considered to be the case, for example, with the participation of the Federal Republic in the International Monetary Fund (IMF) system of special drawing rights;[32] otherwise, such law is at risk of being declared inapplicable for German state organs. Parliament may also empower the government to accept later modifications; without such authorization, formal treaty amendments must be approved. Furthermore, treaties that incur financial obligations would need assent since the budget must be enacted by a formal statute (Arts. 110(2) and 115 GG); however, this requirement is satisfied if expenditures are foreseen in general terms or authorized in advance. This is often the case with specific agreements, such as on development aid, that merely execute the budget plan.[33]

Providing early information to Parliament about treaty-making is not only a requirement of an abstract notion of foreign relations powers, but of democracy itself. This matter has become a subject of public debate with respect to the negotiations of trade and investment agreements between the European Union and Canada (with the Comprehensive Economic and Trade Agreement, known as "CETA"), and the United States (with the Transatlantic Trade and Investment Partnership, known as "TTIP"), respectively. Both are mixed agreements that the European Union as well as its member states must ratify.[34] Such treaties are negotiated by the EU Commission, and the process was criticized for being insufficiently transparent to the *Bundestag* and the general public. From the perspective of constitutional law, mixed agreements

[30] Hermann Butzer & Julia Haas, *Artikel 59*, *in* KOMMENTAR ZUM GRUNDGESETZ §§ 63, 65 (Bruno Schmidt-Bleibtreu et al. eds., 14th ed. 2014); with the same result for France, *see* Francois Luchaire, *The Participation of Parliament in the Elaboration and Application of Treaties*, 67 CHI.-KENT L. REV. 341, 353 (1991); for Italy, *see* Bognetti, *supra* note 11, at 404; *but see* Fastenrath & Groh, *supra* note 17, who demand approval for all unilateral declarations concerning state treaties, as it is provided for in the Netherlands, *see* Pieter van Dijk & Bahiyyih G. Tahzib, *Parliamentary Participation in the Treaty-Making Process of The Netherlands*, 67 CHI.-KENT L. REV. 413, 431–435 (1991).

[31] Ondolf Rojahn, *Artikel 59*, *in* GRUNDGESETZ KOMMENTAR I § 57 (Ingo von Münch & Philipp Kunig eds., 6th ed. 2012).

[32] *Id.* § 73.

[33] Rauschning, *supra* note 11, §§ 78–84; *see* 132 BVerfGE 195, 135, 317 (2011)—European Stability Mechanism. For similar, express provisions, *see* FRENCH CONST., art. 53, IT. CONST., art. 80, and SPAN. CONST., art. 94, § 1.

[34] For the European Union's treaty-making powers, *see* Marise Cremona, *Making Treaties and Other International Agreements: The European Union*, ch. 14 in this volume.

are to be split along the lines of powers between the European Union and its member states. Whereas the European Union part falls into the ambit of surveillance and information rights of the *Bundestag* over governmental participation in EU legislation (which is regulated in Article 23 GG and bylaws thereto), the portions for which the state level has retained powers are dealt with like any international treaty. The prevailing view holds that for the question whether such an agreement would be a political or legislative treaty under Article 59(2) GG, the whole treaty must be evaluated, including the sections for which the European Union is competent. Since the integration clause of Article 23(2) GG grants early information rights to the Parliament about mandates, subjects, guidelines, and initiatives, and arguably also about drafts and positions of delegations,[35] participatory rights appear to be codified in a far-reaching manner, the more so as compared to other agreements of the German state.

For the general delimitation of governmental and legislative powers, the "treaty set on wheels"—a treaty that departs from the original consent given by Parliament and lives a life of its own—plays an important role in the jurisprudence of the FCC. The decisive thresholds so far have been the will of the parties, contents, and (legal) form. Recent jurisprudence places weight on objective criteria like the integrity of the essentials of the treaty and the legally binding character.[36] Since the Washington Accords defining the new strategic orientation of the North Atlantic Treaty Organization (NATO) were seen to be within the general framework of the original treaty and not agreed in legal terms, the FCC did not find an obligation to seek the consent of Parliament.[37] After the Court had derived a principle of parliamentary prerogatives over military affairs from the Constitution, however, it had provided the ground for a more intensive monitoring by the *Bundestag*, which compensates for the lack of participation in laying down strategic objectives for NATO. As to soft law in general, the requirement of parliamentary approval did not apply. In a similar vein, in its case law on the European Union's rescue policies in the eurozone, the FCC has repeatedly reinforced the *Bundestag*'s powers—and duties—regarding expenditures beyond a threshold that would unduly limit legislative freedom to act on other areas.[38] However, the areas of defense and EU policies hardly suffice to take them as indicators of a new trend with respect to a general democratization of treaty-making powers, the less so since they have always been considered special areas.

[35] Wolfgang Weiß, *Informations- und Beteiligungsrechte des Deutschen Bundestags bei gemischten Abkommen wie TTIP*, 69 Die Öffentliche Verwaltung 661 (2016), with reference, who also rightly holds that the practice of allowing Members of Parliament only review under restrictive circumstances in a "reading room" was unconstitutional, since no statement of Parliament could be prepared on that basis.

[36] Doubts still exist if this applies if the original treaty had required approval, as it is done in practice, *cf.* sec. 1.1.3. (e) Guidelines of the Ministry of Justice, or only if the amendment would change the substance of the treaty, as it was held in 37 BVerfGE 363, at 380 (1974).

[37] 104 BVerfGE 151, at 199 (2001).

[38] *See supra*, note 34.

For treaties that confer powers on the European Union and other supranational organizations, special rules exist (Arts. 23 and 24 GG), as in most European constitutions.[39] Such treaties change the attribution of powers foreseen in the *Grundgesetz* and may amount to implicit constitutional revision. They therefore demand a majority of two-thirds in both the *Bundestag* and *Bundesrat*. In all EU matters the *Grundgesetz* (Art. 23(2) GG) expressly requires a constant and comprehensive flow of information from the executive to the legislative branch so that enactment of secondary law may become the subject of debate at an early stage. The Constitution requires a specialized EU Committee in Parliament (Art. 45 GG). Details are regulated in special statutes on the co-operation between government and Parliament and on the co-operation between the federal and the state levels in EU matters.[40] No such legislation exists with respect to international law and international organizations. Whether members of Parliament would be inclined to pursue such participation actively, however, is often doubted.[41]

To conclude this section, it can be said that the requirement of parliamentary approval of certain types of treaties serves different functions. It is part of the legislative prerogatives, it complies with the rule of law in that the administration and courts have a legislative basis on which to act if treaties have an impact on individual rights, and it is a stone in the mosaic of checks and balances between the different branches of state authority. This latter function, control of government, also requires constant involvement of Parliament with foreign affairs, for which the Constitution expressly provides that a foreign relations committee and a committee of defense are established (Art. 45 a GG); all treaty matters, also as far as they concern defense politics, are under the primary responsibility of the foreign relations committee.[42] Additionally, a committee on human rights and humanitarian assistance is set up on a regular basis in each election period. Parliament has the right to demand the presence of any member of government at any time (Art. 43 GG), may use its budgetary powers, and can adopt

[39] See AUST. CONST., art. 23a to 23 f, FRENCH CONST., art. 88, HUNG. CONST., art. 2a; *cf. also* POL. CONST., art. 90; SPAN. CONST., art. 93 (transfer of powers to international organizations, without mentioning the European Union); SWED. CONST., ch. 10, § 5; some constitutions contain clauses on European integration without specific provisions on transfer of powers, others like those of Italy and the Netherlands use the constitutional provisions on general international law. For a detailed account, *see* contributions in HANDBUCH IUS PUBLICUM EUROPAEUM II chs. 14 to 26 (Armin von Bogdandy et al. eds., 2008).

[40] Found in Bundesgesetzblatt (Federal Law Gazette, hereinafter BGBl.) 2013 I, 2170 and BGBl. 1993 I, 313, as amended BGBl. 2009 I, 3031, respectively; *see also* the statute on the responsibilities of the *Bundestag* and *Bundesrat* in EU matters (*Integrationsverantwortungsgesetz*) BGBl. 2009 I, 3022.

[41] The plea by Tom Barkhuysen, *Parlement moet minder (stil)zwijgen bij sluiting, wijziging en opzegging van verdragen*, [2015] NEDERLANDSE JURISPRUDENTIE 551, could be addressed to most continental systems.

[42] VOLKER PILZ, DER AUSWÄRTIGE AUSSCHUSS DES DEUTSCHEN BUNDESTAGES UND DIE MITWIRKUNG DES PARLAMENTS AN DER AUSWÄRTIGEN UND INTERNATIONALEN POLITIK (2006); for Italy, *see* FABIO LONGO, PARLAMENTO E POLITICA ESTERA—IL RUOLO DELLE COMMISSIONI (2011).

resolutions on any matter it desires and thereby try to influence foreign policy.[43] Such a weak concept of "combined powers" appears to be realized in several states, even though such a labeling is disputed even where Parliament has a stronger position than in Germany.[44]

II. The Process of Making Treaties and Executive Agreements

There have been cases in which Parliament took the initiative to encourage treaty negotiations, but usually the government acts of its own motion. According to its rules of procedure, negotiations must not be started without the consent of the Foreign Office; if it so requests, it must be included in the negotiating process.[45] A ministry whose jurisdiction is particularly affected may coordinate the process and function as the head of delegation, but needs authorization by the Foreign Office.[46] The ministries of Home Affairs and of Justice participate from an early stage to safeguard the constitutionality of the procedure and the substance of the agreement. The signing of the treaty, which requires authorization by the president, completes this stage. The Foreign Office considers itself as being generally empowered by the president for signature in all cases to which Article 59(2) GG does not apply.[47] Without presidential approval the plenipotentiaries may merely initial the text. If Parliament must yet give its consent, signature is done on condition of later ratification.

The government does not act on any parliamentary guidance or even instructions. If parliamentary approval is necessary, it is done only after signature of the treaty, basically in a take-it-or-leave it fashion.[48] Treaties are usually adopted within one to three months, even though there is no express provision on time limits. Since the political coalitions that make up the government usually have the majority and have no

[43] Such resolutions are not formally binding, but hard to ignore; a recent and prominent example is the decision of the *Bundestag* to denote the large number of Armenian victims under Turkish responsibility in 1915/16 as genocide, *see* Resolution of 2 June 2016, Bundestags-Drucksache 18/8613 (31 May 2016).

[44] Daniel Thürer et al., Verfassungsrecht der Schweiz—Droit Constitutionnel Suisse (2001) sec. 11, § 52.

[45] As provided for by sec. 11, § 2 of the Rules of Procedure of the Federal Government (21 November 2002).

[46] The internal procedure is codified in sec. 72–73 of the Common Rules of Procedure of the Federal Ministries (1 September 2011); the Guidelines of the Federal Ministry of Justice on the formulation of treaty statutes and treaty-related orders (2007); and the Guidelines of the Foreign Office for the treatment of international agreements (10 March 2014).

[47] *See* sec. 28, § 2 (a) of its Guidelines, *supra* note 46.

[48] Amendments are not permitted, *see* sec. 81, § 4 and sec. 82, § 2 Rules of Procedure of the Bundestag (2 July 1980, as revised 3 April 2014).

interest in seeing the treaty fail,[49] the control function is to a considerable degree fulfilled by the opposition.

In the course of the ratification of state treaties, the *Bundesrat*, the chamber of the *Länder*, also has to be involved. In most areas, consultation is sufficient. Approval must be sought only in matters explicitly spelled out in the Constitution, which is not the case for political treaties, but in certain areas of legislation. Thus, in most cases the *Bundesrat* may only voice objections, which can be overruled in an ensuing reconciliation procedure. As far as assent is needed, the *Bundesrat* has a veto, which, however, does not play a significant role in external affairs.

The formal approval of state treaties by the two chambers empowers the president to conclude the treaty, upon countersignature by the government,[50] to publish it in the official journal, and to convey the instrument of ratification to the depositary of the treaty.[51]

As opposed to this so-called composite procedure, executive agreements follow a so-called simplified, or one-phase procedure, which means that the negotiating institution concludes the agreement alone. Differences are that, apart from lacking parliamentary involvement, practice does not require the president's participation. Negotiations are coordinated by the Foreign Office, but often done by the responsible ministry; if more than one of them is competent, they or the cabinet may nominate a representative and empower him or her to sign the treaty. Such executive agreements are mostly, but not necessarily, published.

If the president has doubts about the constitutionality of the procedure because of evident conflicts with the Constitution or with general international law, which is superior to the statute of incorporation (Art. 25 GG), he may halt the procedure and refer the treaty back to the responsible bodies. The question whether he has the power to deny ratification is part of a general debate concerning the president's powers as the state's notary public in the process of lawmaking. Theoretically, the government or the Parliament could sue the president before the FCC for failure to ratify, but they have never done so.

The FCC has wide opportunities for judicial review, in part created by the law and in part developed by its jurisprudence. Thus, any institution or parts thereof may initiate proceedings for violation of their constitutional competencies (*organstreit*). This is the procedure in which the requirement of parliamentary approval has repeatedly been

[49] It very rarely happens that a treaty is not approved; an example is the German/French treaty on the delimitation of borders of July 31, 1962. Informal debate is influential, but hard to verify, *see* Felix Arndt, *Völkerrechtsfreundlichkeit und Völkerrechtsskepsis in der politischen Praxis des Deutschen Bundestages*, *in* DER „OFFENE VERFASSUNGSSTAAT" DES GRUNDGESETZES NACH 60 JAHREN 99, at 110 (Thomas Giegerich ed., 2010),

[50] Countersignature (art. 58 GG) is necessary to secure the involvement of an institution of the state directly legitimated by the electorate. It is, however, considered to be implicit in the request by the government or the Foreign Office to grant authorization.

[51] As opposed to occasional practice in Italy (*see* Bognetti, *supra* note 11, at 398–400), parliamentary approval after ratification is not possible.

raised by Parliament as a whole or by its fractions. Furthermore, the federal and state governments as well as one-quarter of the members of the *Bundestag* can initiate proceedings for full judicial review (*abstrakte normenkontrolle*),[52] as can any court hearing a case in which the constitutionality of a treaty statute is decisive for the outcome of a lawsuit and the court considers it unconstitutional (*konkrete normenkontrolle*).[53] Likewise, individuals may challenge treaties for violations of fundamental rights (*verfassungsbeschwerde*).[54] The usual hurdle, that a law must be in force before a complaint is accepted for review, does not apply. The FCC may also issue preliminary orders. In such cases, the president will suspend the completion of the ratification process until the end of proceedings. At times he is asked to do so by the FCC itself, as it has recently done with respect to the European Patent agreement. The Court may reject the suit, declare the treaty incompatible with the Constitution, or may order that a reservation to the treaty be registered.

III. The Status of Treaties in Domestic Law

Treaties for which approval by Parliament is necessary are incorporated by a federal statute, as expressly spelled out in Article 59(2) GG. Treaties account for about 25 percent to 28 percent of federal legislation.[55] Even if the entry into force of the statute of incorporation, theoretically, can be determined for the day after its publication, its domestic applicability does not take effect before the entry into force of the treaty at the international level.

Whether the German approach is dualist or monist has been disputed for decades, without a clear result.[56] In any event, mere approval does not suffice, which is different

[52] For historic examples, *see* 4 BVerfGE 157 (1955)—Saar Treaty; 36 BVerfGE 1 (1973)—Treaty between FRG and GDR.

[53] This has been done repeatedly on request by the Federal Court of Finance, for an example, *see infra*, note 62.

[54] 84 BVerfGE 133 (1991) and 85 BVerfGE 360 (1992)—Treaty of German Unity; standards for the substantiation of a complaint are high, however, *cf.* BVerfG, 17 Neue Juristische Online Zeitschrift 599 (2017)—Cybercrime Convention.

[55] Arndt, *supra* note 49, at 116.

[56] The concept appears at first sight to be in the dualist tradition (*see* the classic exposition in Heinrich Triepel, Völkerrecht und Landesrecht (1899), defended for the *Grundgesetz* by Walter Rudolf, Völkerrecht und deutsches Recht (1967)), but can better be explained by a mitigated monist approach, which would consider the treaty statute as a directive of application; the courts are undecided, which seems to advocate in favor of the view that the two concepts do not differ substantially in practice. A monist concept can explain why domestic effects depend on the entry into force of the treaty, and it makes the integration of treaty practice and interpretation by competent international bodies into the domestic sphere easier, *see* Karl-Josef Partsch, *Die Anwendung des Völkerrechts im innerstaatlichen Recht*, 6 Berichte der Deutschen Gesellschaft für Völkerrecht 13 (1964).

than in more clearly defined monist systems like in France and the Netherlands.[57] In contrast to these two systems, in which adopted treaties take precedence over statute law, statutory approval in Germany means that such treaties are placed at the same level as ordinary federal statute law. Secondary law can be implemented by executive order, provided that a statute empowers the government to do so.[58]

To resolve conflicts between treaties and statute law, the last in time rule applies, provided that the treaty provision at stake has not crystallized into customary international law, which would prevail (Art. 25 GG). However, courts are under an obligation to avoid a collision with domestic laws by means of consistent interpretation. The underlying presumption that Parliament had no will to violate treaty obligations is reinforced by the principle of friendliness toward international law (*völkerrechtsfreundlichkeit*), which is according to long-standing jurisprudence of the FCC a *leitmotiv* of the whole Constitution.[59] In a much-disputed recent judgment, however, the FCC established the doctrine of so-called treaty override.[60] The case arose with respect to a double taxation agreement with Turkey after the *Bundestag* had adopted a bill that tightened the requirements of documentation for income abroad. Without trying to reconcile this statute with the treaty, the FCC decided that the Parliament had the right to enact laws in conflict with treaty law, with the express exception of human rights treaties. The decision can be read as a reconstitutionalization of foreign relations law, by placing democratic will above international obligations, while keeping fundamental rights intact.[61]

The Italian Constitution after a constitutional reform in 2001 avoids such effects, since its Article 117(1) obliges the legislature to observe international obligations.[62] Also under French and Polish law treaties prevail over statute law, on condition of reciprocity (Art. 55 French Constitution, Art. 91(2) Polish Constitution).[63] In France, such conflicts are addressed not by the *Conseil constitutionnel*, but by the ordinary courts.

The European Convention of Human Rights and Fundamental Freedoms has a special status. The requirement of consistent interpretation demands not only that statute law be construed in the light of international treaties but also the *Grundgesetz* itself. That means that the fundamental rights catalogue and the rule of law principle

[57] French Const., art. 55; Neth. Const., art. 91.

[58] At least according to 1 BVerfGE 372, at 393 (1952).

[59] For the debate on a consistent interpretation of the Japanese Constitution, *see* Hiromichi Matsuda, *International Law in Japanese Courts*, ch. 30 in this volume.

[60] 145 BVerfGE 1 (2015).

[61] *Cf.* Matthias Kumm, *Democratic Constitutionalism Encounters International Law: Terms of Engagement*, *in* The Migration of Constitutional Ideas 256 (Sujit Choudhry ed., 2006).

[62] The Constitutional Court, therefore, considers any violation of treaty law as a violation of the Constitution, *see* dec. no. 349, [2008] Foro it. I, 39/57—Commune di Avellino (2007); as to the effects of the amendment, *see* Giuliana Ziccardi Capaldo, *Verso una riforma del rapporto tra ordinamento italiano e trattati internazionali—Contenuti di una riforma possibile dopo le modifiche al Titolo V della Parte seconda della Costituzione*, *in* Attuazione dei Trattati Internazionali e Costituzione Italiana (note 26), 17–53; Atripaldi, *supra* note 26, 76–85.

[63] Louis Favoreu et al., Droit constitutionnel § 230 (20th ed. 2018).

of the Constitution must be construed in harmony with the Convention. Thus, even though the Convention's guarantees may not be invoked directly before the FCC, they find an indirect way into the Court's case law. The presumption of innocence as enshrined in Article 6(2) of the Convention, for instance, is not expressly mentioned in the Constitution, but must be considered as part of the rule of law.[64] So far, the question has been left open whether these requirements also apply to other human rights treaties, since the Convention system is by far more frequently used by German applicants.[65]

Executive agreements do not require a specific form of law; it suffices that they are implemented in administrative practice. Practice distinguishes independent and dependent, as well as normative and administrative agreements.

Independent agreements regulate a subject matter that has no context with a state treaty in the meaning of Article 59(2) GG. The pertinent examples are administrative co-operation in regions near the state frontier, but also remission agreements with third states aiming at the repatriation of migrants who are not granted a title of residence.[66] Dependent administrative agreements aim at implementing objectives that are agreed upon in the framework of a state treaty; examples are the stationing of NATO troops and standby agreements for UN peacekeeping missions, or common technical standards agreed upon in international organizations. Internally, these agreements often form the only legal basis and do not entail further legal acts.

Normative agreements are incorporated by legal ordinance or another formal act of a general nature. Administrative agreements may be adopted in administrative circulars, which are only binding on the authorities, or simply be applied by the competent agencies, police co-operation with Interpol being an example. Interests protected by such agreements, or secondary acts taken within the treaty system, are to be taken into account by the responsible executive, but do not necessarily prevail. A prominent case was the *Waldschlösschen* bridge in Dresden: A local plebiscite opted for a new bridge, which spoiled the view at a landscape that was on the UNESCO list of cultural heritage. The courts made an effort to balance out the diverging interests, but decided in favor of the democratic will, at the price of removal of the Elbe Valley from the list.

IV. Treaty Interpretation

Even though the statute of incorporation is a domestic legal act and the German version also plays a certain role in court practice if German is not one of the authentic

[64] 74 BVerfGE 358, 370 (1987).

[65] For a treaty-consistent interpretation of fundamental rights of the Constitution, the provisions of such a treaty do not have to be self-executing.

[66] 91 BVerwGE 150 (1992).

treaty languages, it is undisputed that the international rules of interpretation apply (Arts. 31, 32 VCLT). The federal courts mostly use the English, often also the French, treaty version and take practice of competent bodies into account.

As compared to other legal systems, such as that of the United States, it is interesting to note the interpretive role played by international courts and tribunals in litigation in German courts. In cases about the right to consular assistance of an accused with foreign nationality, the FCC repeatedly stressed that the interpretation given to the Vienna Convention on Consular Relations by the International Court of Justice (ICJ) must be followed by German courts.[67] This also applies to the interpretation of the European Convention on Human Rights (ECHR) by the European Court of Human Rights (ECtHR); the fundamental freedoms of the Constitution must be construed in the light of the Convention's guarantees. Even though not formally, the ECHR in effect participates in the German legal order at the rank of constitutional law. The German system thus is in line with many constitutions and pertinent domestic jurisprudence according to which human rights treaties have a special domestic status. In the spectrum between systems that attribute human rights treaties a rank coequal to the constitution, such as in some Latin American countries,[68] the Netherlands, or, as far as the ECHR is concerned, in Austria, on the one hand, and legal orders that transform them at the level of statute law, Germany takes an intermediate position.

Additionally, the FCC has developed the custom of ensuring that its interpretation of the Constitution is in harmony with the jurisprudence of the ECtHR, even if its decisions concern cases in which Germany was not a party. Judgments in which the ECtHR found that Germany has violated the Convention must be executed in good faith. This is the more remarkable since the FCC, because of the requirement to exhaust all domestic remedies before an application can be brought before the ECtHR, is necessarily involved in every successful complaint.

However, the FCC made caveats in the famous *Görgülü* judgment. Accordingly, in rare cases, as the Court puts it, implementation of ECtHR judgments can constitute a violation of the Constitution if a complex balancing out of colliding interests is necessary which the ECtHR fails to assess properly. The Court explicitly mentions family law cases, immigration law, and conflicts between the tabloid press and privacy. With the latter category, the FCC alludes to a decision in which it had given more weight to the freedom of speech than to the protection of the private sphere of a celebrity than the ECtHR seized of the case later.[69] Even though this caveat has not materialized so far, the *Görgülü* case was invoked by other courts, most prominently by the Constitutional Court of the Russian Federation, which expressed much more severe reservations concerning the ECtHR than the FCC ten years later and subjected the

[67] BVerfG (Chamber), 60 NEUE JURISTISCHE WOCHENSCHRIFT 499, at 502 (2007).

[68] *See* René Urueña, *Domestic Application of International Law in Latin America*, ch. 32 in this volume.

[69] 111 BVerfGE 307 (2004); for a similar approach, *see* the *controlimiti* doctrine of the Italian Constitutional Court, dec. no. 238/2014 (22 October 2014), concerning a judgment by the ICJ.

implementation of ECtHR judgments to review of the president of the Russian Federation.[70] The relevance in practice is limited, since the FCC so far has followed the ECtHR and even adapted its own case law to its judgments.[71]

Interpretation, obviously, is particularly relevant to assess the self-executing character of treaty provisions, especially if they are invoked by individuals before courts.[72] Whereas the domestic courts can submit the question of direct effect of EU law to the European Court of Justice (ECJ), they are acting without such guidance with respect to international law. And while ordinary courts may refer the assessment of direct effect of customary international law to the FCC (Art. 100(2) GG), there is no procedure of treaty interpretation before the constitutional court. Many provisions granting individual rights, particularly civil and political rights, run parallel to constitutional guarantees. However, economic, social, and cultural rights, as well as labor law rights as they are spelled out in human rights conventions of the United Nations, the Council of Europe, and the International Labour Organization every now and then play a role before the ordinary courts. Thus, administrative law courts were seized of the question whether or not state governments are entitled to introduce university fees, which was claimed to be in conflict with Article 13(2)(c) of the International Covenant on Economic, Social and Cultural Rights (ICESR); some courts decided on that basis, so that the ICESR, as federal law, prevailed over conflicting state law. By and large, however, the prevailing tendency is to declare provisions about social rights as non-self-executing.[73] In contrast, double taxation agreements are mostly held directly applicable.

In some situations, treaties may have an indirect effect on rights, through provisions or concepts in domestic law. For a tort claim against the German state, for example, the law violated by state officials must have the objective of protecting rights of the individual. For lawsuits brought against the army, be it for acts during the Second World War or measures taken in the course of NATO or UN missions abroad, the question has arisen how far conventions on the regulation of armed conflict have that purpose. At first sight, the answer appears to be clear, but courts have repeatedly ruled that the obligations of humanitarian law are directed toward states and do not entitle individuals.[74] In a similar vein, the Federal Administrative Court decided that owners of premises near a U.S. air base used for drone attacks in the Middle East have no

[70] Constitutional Court of the Russian Federation, Resolution No. 21-P/2015 on request of *State Duma deputies* (14 July 2015), Engl. translation available at http://transnational-constitution.blogspot.de/2015/08/russian-constitutional-court-decision.html.

[71] For an example, *see* 128 BVerfGE 326 (2012)—ordering of preventive detention after final judgment.

[72] On the relationship between the monism/dualism debate and the self-executing character of treaties, *see* Jean Galbraith, *International Agreements and U.S. Foreign Relations Law: Complexity in Action*, ch. 9 in this volume.

[73] *See* the Federal Administrative Court in 91 BVerwGE 327 (1992)—European Social Charter; 92 BVerwGE 116 (1993)—Treaty against Statelessness.

[74] BVerfG (Chamber), 2 BvR 2660/06 (13 August 2013)—Bridge of Varvarin.

standing to sue for breaches of international law since the norms at stake do not protect them, but rather protect foreign states or third persons.[75]

V. Comparative Aspects and Conclusions

The distinctions of common law and civil law, of dualism and monism, of presidential and parliamentary systems, and of federal and unitary states do not lend themselves as fruitful paradigms for the comparative analysis of the making, effect, and status of treaties. Differences and common features are independent of these dichotomies. Rather, such analysis is of interest as a contribution to studies of comparative government, with the guiding question whether developments on the global level have brought about universal trends and institutions or whether adherence to historically grown settings of decision-making persist.[76] With that interest, the focus is on constitutional change and judicial review.

Constitution-making has rarely paid attention to treaties in recent years. As for Germany, the relevant provisions have only been amended with a view towards the European Union (Art. 23 GG) and with the transfer of powers to international cross-border institutions of a regional nature (Art. 24(1a) GG) in 1992. Thus, impulses gained by a comparative view might be more interesting for constitutional practice; parliaments may profit from interparliamentary exchange with respect to the flow of information, early consultation procedures, and the internal structuring into committees.

As to the role of the judiciary, the spectrum of approaches is wide. Whereas the courts of some countries are largely unaffected by foreign influences, others like the South African Constitutional Court, to name an example outside Europe, make ample use of the jurisprudence of courts in other legal orders.[77] The German FCC very rarely resorts to courts of other states, and, if so, mostly in the EU context. This attitude is in contrast to the role the FCC plays for many constitutional courts, which regularly cite its case law. The "migration of constitutional ideas"[78] in the area of foreign relations law appears to go only one way.

However, there is common ground on which constitutional practice by the responsible institutions might bring about similar features. In various continental systems the

[75] 154 BVerwGE 328 (2016).

[76] For the approaches to comparative constitutional scholarship, *see* Jackson, *supra* note 3, at 55–67.

[77] Constitutional Court of the Republic of South Africa, S v. Makwanyane and Mchunu, [1995] ZACC 3, § 35 (1995).

[78] *See* The Migration of Constitutional Ideas, *supra* note 61; for further reference, *see* Gabor Halmai, *The Use of Foreign Law in Constitutional Interpretation*, *in* Rosenfeld & Sajó, *supra* note 4, at 1328–1348.

roles of the heads of state, of governments, and of parliaments are described in a comparable way. Discretion of the government can be limited as to when to refer treaties for approval, the more so since the rationale is the same: guaranteeing that treaties comply with the domestic legal order so that they can be implemented and international obligations fulfilled, and that practice reflects the constitutional principles of democratic legitimacy and the rule of law.

Set against this background is the question whether the provision in the German Constitution for making treaties lives up to the role that treaties also play on the domestic plane. It has its roots in the nineteenth century and has not been changed since 1949. The world, however, has. Whereas some observers hold that Article 59 GG has passed the test of history,[79] others plead for reform. They note that Article 59 GG does not even mention the most important actor, the government as an institution separate from the head of state, and that the line between the domestic domain and external relations is blurred.[80] And whereas parliamentary rights have been continuously redefined with respect to EU matters, they lag behind this development with respect to international relations beyond Europe.[81] This development appears to be similar in many European states. A comparison of constitutional experience could contribute to further debate and reflection.

[79] Rauschning, *supra* note 11, §§ 214–218.

[80] Rojahn, *supra* note 31, §§ 96–98; Fastenrath & Groh, *supra* note 17, § 164; for Italy, *see* Ziccardi Capaldo, *supra* note 62.

[81] For this observation, *see* with regard to the Netherlands, Modderman, *supra* note 29, at 34.

CHAPTER 11

THE CURRENT PRACTICE OF MAKING AND APPLYING INTERNATIONAL AGREEMENTS IN JAPAN

TADAATSU MORI

I. Introduction

EACH country has its own historic background, which forms a basis for the practice of making treaties and other international agreements. Before World War II, Article 13 of the Meiji Constitution stipulated, "The Emperor declares war, makes peace, and concludes treaties." This provision indicated that the power to conclude treaties resided in the head of state, which, in those days, was the common understanding.

Today, Article 73 of the Constitution of Japan, which came into effect in 1947, ensures democratic control by the Diet in approving treaties and other international agreements, while giving the power to conclude treaties to the Cabinet. The detailed rules concerning which treaties require an approval by the Diet were shaped over time through the Diet discussions, and the government of Japan set forth specific criteria regarding the democratic control over treaty-making through a statement by Foreign Minister Masayoshi Ohira in 1974. The so-called Ohira Principles continue to serve as guidance in treaty-making.

In recent years, the international community has become more complex and diverse and the sheer volume of international agreements has grown significantly. The number of treaties and other international agreements concluded by Japan in recent years is:

333 in 2013, 288 in 2014, 320 in 2015, and 291 in 2016.[1] As those legal instruments address a wide range of areas from security and trade to outer space and cyberspace, there remains a greater need for concluding international agreements in an effective manner as a way to manage foreign affairs.

The current practice of making and applying international agreements in Japan reflects dynamics between the executive branch and the Diet. Such practice is also an outcome of efforts in the postwar Japanese democratic process to strike the right balance between democratic control and effective management of foreign affairs. At the same time, the following practice reflects traditions of Japan's politics, which attach importance to the spirit of *Wa* (harmony).

II. Process for Concluding Treaties and Other International Agreements

Responsibility for Managing Foreign Affairs

Article 73 of the Constitution stipulates, "The Cabinet, in addition to other general administrative functions, shall perform the following functions," including managing foreign affairs.[2] As such, management of foreign affairs is regarded as one of the important functions of the Cabinet. Functions of the Cabinet are divided by each ministry and agency based on the principle of "division of duties."[3] Item 1, Article 4 of

[1] The number of the treaties and other international agreements concluded by Japan in 1993 was 828, hitting its peak mainly due to the increase of the number of Exchange of Notes to extend Official Development Assistance (ODA) to developing countries. In the past ten years (2007–2016), the number of treaties and other international agreements concluded by Japan fluctuates between around 280 and 630.

[2] The Cabinet, in addition to other general administrative functions, shall perform the following functions:

Administer the law faithfully; conduct affairs of state.
Manage foreign affairs.
Conclude treaties. However, it shall obtain prior or, depending on circumstances, subsequent approval of the Diet.
Administer the civil service, in accordance with standards established by law.
Prepare the budget, and present it to the Diet.
Enact cabinet orders in order to execute the provisions of this Constitution and of the law. However, it cannot include penal provisions in such cabinet orders unless authorized by such law.
Decide on general amnesty, special amnesty, commutation of punishment, reprieve, and restoration of rights. http://japan.kantei.go.jp/constitution_and_government_of_japan/constitution_e.html.

[3] Article 3, paragraph 1, of the Cabinet Act stipulates: "The Ministers shall divide among themselves administrative affairs and be in charge of their respective share thereof as the competent Minister, as provided for by other law." Article 5, paragraph 1, of the National Government Organization Act stipulates: "The Heads of the Prime Minister's Office and of each Ministry shall be, respectively, the Prime Minister and the Minister of each Ministry (hereinafter referred to as 'each Minister'), who as competent Ministers referred to in the Cabinet Law (Law No.5 of 1947) shall have charge and control of

the Act for Establishment of the Ministry of Foreign Affairs (MOFA) (hereinafter referred to as the Act) stipulates that "issues related to foreign policy" fall under the purview of the MOFA. Item 5, Article 4 of the Act stipulates that interpretation and implementation of treaties and other international agreements as well as established international law falls under the purview of the MOFA, explicitly defining the MOFA's full and unique responsibility in this regard. The Act also stipulates that the MOFA is in charge of the conclusion of treaties and other international agreements. In accordance with the principle of division of duties, only the MOFA has the authority to conclude treaties and other international agreements.

Item 3, Article 73 of the Constitution stipulates that the conclusion of treaties is a function of the Cabinet, with the reservation that "it shall obtain prior or, depending on circumstances, subsequent approval of the Diet." That is, "treaties" in Item 3, Article 73 of the Constitution means "treaties for the Diet approval."[4]

There are also international agreements that do not require the Diet approval and can be concluded within the authority of the executive branch. Those international agreements are called "administrative arrangements" (the equivalent of "sole executive agreements" concluded by the U.S. president without approval by the U.S. Congress). As part of managing foreign affairs, a large number of administrative arrangements are concluded by the Cabinet, without the Diet approval.

Examination by the Cabinet Legislation Bureau

After fixing the text in negotiations, an international agreement is subject toexamination by the Cabinet Legislation Bureau (CLB). The Japanese text and the draft

their respective administrative affairs." As such, each ministry and agency is in charge of administrative affairs as provided for by relevant law, which serves as the foundation for the establishment of each ministry and agency.

[4] Article 98, paragraph 2, of the Constitution stipulates: "This Constitution shall be the supreme law of the nation and no law, ordinance, imperial rescript or other act of government, or part thereof, contrary to the provisions hereof, shall have legal force or validity. The treaties concluded by Japan and established laws of nations shall be faithfully observed," *available at* http://japan.kantei.go.jp/constitution_and_government_of_japan/constitution_e.html.

Therefore, legally speaking, "treaties" stipulated in Item 3, Article 73 of the Constitution means "treaties for the Diet approval," whereas "treaties" stipulated in Article 98, paragraph 2, of the Constitution includes so-called "administrative arrangements." As such, the word "treaties" in the Constitution has two different meanings.

In contrast, Article 60 of the Constitution of the Republic of Korea identifies specific types of treaties for which the National Assembly must provide its consent before the president ratifies them. However, it still invites active debates and controversies as to which treaty should obtain consent from the National Assembly. *See* Jaemin Lee, *Incorporation and Implementation of Treaties in South Korea*, ch. 13 in this volume. Reserving certain categories of treaties for parliamentary assent is also common in Europe, but each constitution takes a different approach in stipulating the scope of such treaties. *See* Stefan Kadelbach, *International Treaties and the German Constitution*, ch. 10 in this volume, and Carlos Espósito, *Spanish Foreign Relations Law and the Process for Making Treaties and Other International Agreements*, ch. 12 in this volume.

legislation for the implementation of the international agreement are subject to the CLB's examination, which is extremely detailed and requires a considerable amount of time. There are frequent interactions between the CLB and the MOFA, and other ministries and agencies as necessary, during the examination.

With regard to domestic measures of implementation, bills are drafted for those treaties that require new legislation or legislative amendments prior to their submission to the Diet. The legislation and amendments are drafted, in principle, by those ministries and agencies in charge of the relevant administrative affairs. As for "administrative arrangements," the CLB, consistent with the Ohira Principles, confirms that the arrangement does not involve legislative or budgetary actions.

Cabinet Decision for Signing a Treaty

Prior to the signing of a treaty or an international agreement, the minister for foreign affairs requests a decision concerning the signing in a Cabinet meeting, which is normally convened every Tuesday and Friday. The authority of the minister for foreign affairs for concluding international agreements is ensured through such procedures.

Signing Authority

Persons automatically considered as representing a state in virtue of their functions, namely, heads of state, heads of government, ministers for foreign affairs, and heads of diplomatic missions[5] are considered to have signing authority in accordance with international law. In accordance with Article 7 of the Vienna Convention on the Law of Treaties, a person producing appropriate full powers also has signing authority.

In actual practice, Japan recognizes signing authority for a person if he or she carries a power of attorney signed by persons automatically considered as representing a state in virtue of their functions, or if he or she is legally authorized to sign a treaty in accordance with relevant law of the nation that he/she represents.

Treaty Approval Process in the Diet

The Constitution does not specifically define what kind of treaties and international agreements shall be approved by the Diet in accordance with Item 3, Article 73. In this regard, the government of Japan specified three categories of treaties for the Diet

[5] In the case of Japan, the Ambassador Extraordinary and Plenipotentiary has signing authority but only limited to a treaty between the accrediting state and the state to which they are accredited.

approval through Foreign Minister Masayoshi Ohira's statement at the Committee on Foreign Affairs in the House of Representatives in 1974, as follows:

> *Category 1: International agreements including so-called "legislative issues"*
>
> International agreements which require Japan to develop new legislation or maintain existing legislation[6] for the purpose of implementing such agreements, as long as the said agreements are in effect.
>
> *Category 2: International agreements including so-called "budgetary issues"*
>
> International agreements which create additional fiscal obligation for Japan on top of already-approved fiscal obligation as provided for by law or as included in the budget.
>
> *Category 3: Other important international agreements*
>
> International agreements which do not fall under either Category 1 or Category 2 but are politically important in a sense that those agreements stipulate basic relations between/among countries and therefore require ratification for their entry into force.

It is the executive branch that determines whether or not an international agreement falls under any of these three categories. If an agreement is regarded as not falling within any of these categories, it is regarded as falling within the authority of the executive branch and therefore is concluded without Diet approval.

The above-mentioned criteria set by Foreign Minister Ohira in 1974 reflected a number of actual practices regarding the conclusion of international agreements that had crystallized since World War II.[7] Since then, there have been instances in which members of the Diet have had heated discussions as to the application of the Ohira Principles. For example, some members of the Diet claimed that an Exchange of Notes (E/N) of Official Development Assistance (ODA) projects should be approved by the Diet and not be treated as administrative arrangements. Those members argued that, since yen loan projects usually amount to more than 10 billion yen and some ODA is grant aid that does not have to be paid back, those ODA projects should be subject to careful examination by the Diet even before the signing of E/Ns. In response, the government of Japan repeatedly explained to the Diet that ODA projects are implemented within the already approved budget and thus that the E/Ns of ODA projects do not fall under Category 2 of the Ohira Principles.[8]

Another example was the 1997 "Guidelines for Japan-U.S. Defense Cooperation" (Guidelines). The Guidelines are not an international agreement. They only provide a general framework and policy direction for the roles and missions of Japan and the

[6] If a treaty is concluded on the assumption that relevant domestic laws are already in place to ensure legal commitment, those treaties are regarded as requiring Japan to maintain such domestic laws. This is because if those exiting laws are amended or abolished, Japan cannot fulfill its legal commitment under the treaty.

[7] Similarly, in the Republic of Korea, accumulated practice of the government and the National Assembly plays a key role in managing the conclusion and implementation of treaties. For additional discussion, *see* Lee, *supra* note 4.

[8] For example, the discussion in the Investigation Committee on International Affairs of the House of Councilors, Nov. 21, 1997.

United States, as well as ways of cooperation and coordination. However, some members of the Diet argued that the Guidelines virtually amended the Japan-U.S. Security Treaty in a substantial way and that the Guidelines should be approved by the Diet. The government explained to the Diet that, despite its political importance, the Guidelines do not create any legal obligations between Japan and the United States, and that this document had been consistently treated as a political document, instead of an international agreement.[9]

Arguments are sometimes made in favor of changing the Ohira Principles. Most recently, one member of the Foreign Affairs Committee of the House of Representatives argued in 2017 that the Ohira Principles should be revised and that only politically important treaties should be approved by the Diet. Referring to treaties such as investment treaties and social security treaties as somewhat "technical" ones, this member argued that, in order to expedite the process of concluding such agreements, approval of the Diet should not necessarily be required.[10]

Cabinet Decision on Requesting the Diet Approval for Treaties

There will be a Cabinet decision if the Cabinet decides to request the Diet approval for treaties prior to submitting those treaties to the Diet. The Diet is to decide whether to approve the conclusion of a treaty or not. As such, it is the government's long-standing position[11] that the Diet does not have authority to add amendments to the submitted treaties and that it only makes a decision whether to approve or disapprove treaties.

Prior Explanation to Ruling and Opposition Parties

Before submitting a treaty to the Diet, the government goes through necessary procedures within ruling parties to obtain their support for the submission, with a view to

[9] For example, the discussion in the Foreign Affairs Committee of the House of Representatives on June 11, 1997, and the discussion in the Plenary Session of the House of Representatives on December 2, 1997.

[10] Foreign Affairs Committee of the House of Representatives on May 17, 2017.

[11] *See*, e.g., Foreign Minister Masahiko Komura's statement at the Special Committee on the Guidelines for Japan-U.S. Defense Cooperation in the House of Representatives on April 20, 1999:

> Item 3, Article 73 of the Constitution stipulates that concluding treaties is one of the functions performed by the Cabinet. The executive branch decides which treaty with what content is to be concluded. What the executive branch requests Diet approval for is the conclusion of a treaty whose content has been decided by the executive branch. The Diet has the authority to approve or disapprove the conclusion of the said treaty, but does not have the authority to conclude them. Therefore, the Diet cannot decide the content of the treaty nor has the authority to amend it. (provisional translation).

ensuring a collective decision by the government and the ruling parties. There are some opposition parties that have similar processes to decide their position vis-à-vis the submission of a treaty to the Diet before the Diet actually starts deliberation.

Multiple treaties are often bundled into one package when they go through a party process among ruling and opposition parties. Each treaty has to be cleared in various processes within parties, and the MOFA is held accountable for each treaty. Usually, the MOFA goes through a similar process simultaneously for multiple treaties.

Diet Approval Process

Treaties require a majority of votes to be approved both in the House of Representatives and the House of Councillors. Except for some cases where the House of Councillors first deliberates on a treaty, the normal sequence of Diet deliberation is as follows: first, the Committee on Foreign Affairs in the House of Representatives; second, the Plenary Session in the House of Representatives; third, the Committee on Foreign Affairs and Defense in the House of Councillors; and finally the Plenary Session of the House of Councillors.

There are some key concepts in relation to Diet deliberation on treaties such as the "thirty-day rule" and supremacy of the decision by the House or Representatives. In Japan, the House of Representatives and the House of Councillors have equal status in principle, but the House of Representatives is exceptionally accredited superiority on some issues, including approval for the conclusion of treaties.

According to Article 60, paragraph 2[12] and Article 61[13] of the Constitution, when the conclusion of a treaty is approved by the House of Representatives, and in the case of failure by the House of Councillors to take action within thirty days, the decision of the House of Representatives becomes the decision of the Diet.

Therefore, while it is important to make thorough preparations for the deliberations in both Houses, it is also necessary to gain a decision by the House of Representatives well in advance, considering the Diet schedule, so as to be able to successfully apply the "thirty-day rule."

[12] "The budget must first be submitted to the House of Representatives. Upon consideration of the budget, when the House of Councillors makes a decision different from that of the House of Representatives, and when no agreement can be reached even through a joint committee of both Houses, provided for by law, or in the case of failure by the House of Councillors to take final action within thirty (30) days, the period of recess excluded, after the receipt of the budget passed by the House of Representatives, the decision of the House of Representatives shall be the decision of the Diet," *available at* http://japan.kantei.go.jp/constitution_and_government_of_japan/constitution_e.html.

[13] "The second paragraph of the preceding article applies also to the Diet approval required for the conclusion of treaties," *available at* http://japan.kantei.go.jp/constitution_and_government_of_japan/constitution_e.html.

During the Diet deliberation, treaties do not necessarily go through the Diet process one by one. Multiple treaties of a similar nature (e.g., investment agreements, tax conventions) are bundled into one package and considered together. The way of bundling of treaties is to be coordinated in the Diet and is determined through negotiations between ruling parties and opposition parties. While ruling parties try to bundle as many treaties as possible to have them approved within limited days of the Diet session, opposition parties may attempt to divide treaties into many groups so that they will need longer deliberations in the Diet to be approved. As a result, there were cases in which treaties were grouped in a different manner in each chamber.

For example, at the 190th Session of the Diet in 2016, investment agreements with Iran and Oman as well as a treaty with Iran on the transfer of sentenced persons were bundled into one and approved together in the House of Representatives. Similarly, agreements for air services with Cambodia and Laos as well as an agreement on social security with the Philippines were bundled into one and approved together in the House of Representatives. These treaties were grouped into one bundle, respectively, taking into account the fact that they were negotiated with countries in the same region. However, the treaty with Iran on the transfer of sentenced persons and the agreement on social security with the Philippines were unbundled and went through the deliberation in the House of Councillors one by one as a result of the negotiation between the ruling parties and the opposition parties.

At the same session of the Diet, conventions for the elimination of double taxation with Germany and Chile as well as an amendment protocol of the convention for the elimination of double taxation with India were bundled into one and approved together in the House of Representatives. These treaties were grouped into one bundle because of their similar nature. At the 129th Session of the Diet in 1994, as many as seven air services agreements (i.e., with Brunei, Mongolia, Hungary, South Africa, Jordan, Singapore, and Vietnam) were bundled into one and approved.

In Case of Different Decisions by the Two Legislative Houses

For both the Guam International Agreement between Japan and the United States (at the 171st Session in 2009), and the Host Nation Support Agreement between Japan and the United States (at the 169th Session in 2008), the treaties were approved in the House of Representatives but could not get approval in the House of Councillors, which was then controlled by the opposition parties. After the treaties were rejected by the House of Councillors, a joint committee of both Houses was held but did not reach a compromise. Eventually, the decisions by the House of Representatives prevailed and became a decision of the Diet, in accordance with the provisions of the Constitution (i.e., Art. 60, para. 2, and Art. 61).

Application of the Thirty-Day Rule

The House of Councillors generally prefers to avoid the application of the "thirty-day rule." As a result, there are many instances in which treaties have been successfully approved just before the thirty-day deadline or on the thirtieth day after the approval by the House of Representatives.

The followings are actual cases in the past in which treaties were approved just before the thirty-day deadline:

- In 2014: Geneva Act of the Hague Agreement Concerning the International Registration of Industrial Designs; Locarno Agreement Establishing and International Classification for Industrial Designs Signed at Locarno on October 8, 1968, as Amended on September 28, 1979
- In 2008: Agreement on Comprehensive Economic Partnership among Japan and Member States of the Association of Southeast Asian Nations
- In 1977: Agreement between Japan and the Republic of Korea Concerning the Establishment of Boundary in the Northern Part of the Continental Shelf Adjacent to the Two Countries; Agreement between Japan and the Republic of Korea Concerning Joint Development of the Southern Part of the Continental Shelf Adjacent to the Two Countries
- In 1960: Treaty of Mutual Cooperation and Security between Japan and the United States of America; Agreement under Article VI of the Treaty of Mutual Cooperation and Security between Japan and the United States of America, Regarding Facilities and Areas and the Status of United States Armed Forces in Japan

The following are examples of treaties approved by the House of Councillors on the thirtieth day after the approval by the House of Representatives:

- In 2013: Convention on the Civil Aspects of International Child Abduction
- In 2011: Agreement between the Government of Japan and the Government of the Republic of Korea on the Transfer of Traditional Archives of Korean Origin Stored in Japan to the Republic of Korea
- In 2010: Protocol Amending the Agreement between the Government of Japan and the Government of the Republic of Singapore for the Avoidance of Double Taxation and the Prevention of Fiscal Evasion with Respect to Taxes on Income; Protocol Amending the Agreement between the Government of Japan and the Government of Malaysia for the Avoiding of Double Taxation and the Prevention of Fiscal Evasion with Respect to Taxes on Income

Report to the Diet on Administrative Arrangements

Foreign Minister Masayoshi Ohira explained the practice of providing information to the Diet about administrative arrangements as follows:

> As a long-standing practice, administrative arrangements that are simultaneously concluded for the implementation and operation of a treaty or for providing details of a treaty are submitted to the Diet for its reference when the Diet conducts deliberations on the said treaty. This is to respect the Diet's right of deliberation. The Government will further make sure to follow the practice by submitting relevant information about the administrative arrangements made after the conclusion of a treaty for the Diet approval to the Committee on Foreign Affairs if those administrative arrangements are considered important and necessary for the Diet to keep track of how the said treaty is being implemented or operated. Such information will be provided to the Diet as soon as those administrative arrangements are concluded.[14]

As such, there are a number of administrative arrangements that were submitted to the Diet or reported to the Diet for its reference in the past. Recent examples include:

(1) E/N between Japan and the United States concerning cash contributions under the protocol amending the Guam International Agreement in 2016; and

(2) Japan-U.S. Supplementary Agreement on Environment.

Both were reported to the Committee on Foreign Affairs of the House of Representatives on March 4, 2016, and to the Committee on Foreign Affairs and Defense of the House of Councillors on March 7, 2016. Reports are made by providing members of relevant committees with texts of administrative arrangements.

The Guam International Agreement (hereinafter referred to as the GIA) and the Protocol amending the GIA (hereinafter referred to as the Protocol) were concluded in order to implement the projects related to the relocation of U.S. Marine Corps and their family members from Okinawa. Both the GIA and the Protocol were submitted to the Diet for its approval. Under the GIA and the Protocol, the amount of Japanese cash contributions has to be agreed in "further arrangements" between Japan and the United States.

Those "arrangements" are made in the form of E/Ns between the governments of Japan and the United States, in which the amount of cash as well as the concrete projects for which those cash contributions will be spent are specifically described. The amount of cash contributions constitutes a part of the sum pledged by Japan in the GIA and the Protocol. Since such E/Ns are essential for the Diet to keep track of how the GIA and the Protocol are being implemented, the government of Japan reported them to the Diet.

The Supplementary Agreement on Environment establishes a framework to strengthen cooperation in the field of environmental stewardship in relation to the U.S. armed forces in Japan. The agreement stipulates measures in the field of environmental stewardship to be taken by the U.S. armed forces inside the facilities and areas provided from Japan to the United States under the Status of Forces Agreement (SOFA). Since this agreement does not fall into any categories of the Ohira Principles, it was concluded as an administrative arrangement without an approval by the Diet.

[14] Statement by Foreign Minister Ohira at the Committee on Foreign Affairs of the House of Representatives on February 20, 1974.

Precisely speaking, the agreement was not concluded for the implementation and operation of the Diet-approved SOFA or for providing details of the SOFA. However, in essence this agreement addresses bilateral cooperation in the field of the environment, which is not covered by the SOFA. In other words, the agreement supplements the SOFA. Taking that into account, the government considered it to be an important administrative arrangement that has to be reported to the Diet.

In this way, the government decides which administrative arrangements are to be reported to the Diet on a case-by-case basis, taking into account the content and significance of the arrangements.

III. Domestic Legal Effect of Treaties and Other International Agreements

Bills for Implementation

The MOFA, in coordination with other relevant ministries and agencies, including the CLB, identifies whether the conclusion of a treaty or other international agreement requires domestic legislation. Depending on the nature of a treaty, some treaties are regarded as so-called "self-executing treaties," which are suitable for domestic application without implementing legislation and/or are applied by courts. Whether a treaty is regarded as "self-executing" or not will depend on the purpose of a treaty or intention of the parties to a treaty, the nature of the rights and obligations set forth by a treaty, as well as the degree of specificity of its provisions.[15]

In principle, when new bills or amendments to existing legislation are required, they will be submitted to the Diet together with the treaties or other international agreements concerned. The following are some specific examples:

1. Agreement between the Government of Japan and the Government of the United States of America concerning Reciprocal Provision of Logistic Support, Supplies and Services between the Self-Defense Forces of Japan and the Armed Forces of the United States of America (ACSA):

[15] In this regard, Mr. Shuichi Akamatsu, then Counsellor of the CLB, referred to two additional elements as follows: whether or not a treaty includes provisions to create systems or procedures which require new domestic legislation; and whether or not a treaty is consistent with the existing domestic legal system and each individual law. Mr. Jota Yamamoto, then Counsellor of the CLB, wrote how the Bureau concluded that the Convention for the Unification of Certain Rules for International Carriage by Air of 1999 could be directly applied in the Japanese legal system in his article, *Nihonto Kokusaihono 100nen: Riku, Sora, Uchu*, *in* Japan and International Law in the Past One Hundred Years, Vol. 2: Land, Air, and Space (2001). *See also* Yuji Iwasawa, International Law, Human Rights, and Japanese Law: The Impact of International Law on Japanese Law (1998).

The Japan-U.S. ACSA enables the provision of logistic support, supplies, and services between the Self-Defense Forces and the U.S. armed forces. The agreement stipulates that either party may provide logistic support, supplies, and services "within its competence," but once a party decides to provide logistic support, supplies, and services, it has to be done in accordance with the settlement procedures set out in the agreement.

In other words, the agreement does not require either party to develop or maintain domestic legislation so as to allow the Self-Defense Forces or the U.S. armed forces to provide logistic support, supplies, and services under certain circumstances. It only requires the parties to enable the settlement procedures set out in the agreement. This agreement requires Japan to maintain relevant domestic laws on settlement procedures. Therefore, it corresponds to an international agreement for the Diet approval as it includes legislative issues.

More concretely, Section 1, Article 9 of the Public Finance Law stipulates that "[n]ational property, unless otherwise in compliance with the laws, shall not be exchanged to use for payment purposes or transferred without [payment of] proper price or rent." Accordingly, in order to follow the settlement procedures set out in the agreement, relevant laws that enable the transfer of national property "without [payment of] proper price or rent" had to be developed and maintained. Article 100-7 of the Self-Defense Forces Law was added for such purpose.

There are other unique cases in which the government took a different approach in concluding treaties and other international agreements:

2. Japan-U.S. Status of Forces Agreement:

With regard to the application of domestic laws and regulations to foreign armed forces, the position of the government of Japan is as follows: "under customary international law, the laws and regulations of the receiving state are not applied to foreign armed forces stationed under the consent of the receiving state, unless it is stipulated otherwise. This is also applicable to the U.S. armed forces. Having said that, it is also understood that under customary international law, the armed forces of the sending state has the obligation to respect the laws and regulations of the receiving state. The United States is also under such obligation."

The application of domestic laws and regulations to the U.S. armed forces can be categorized as follows:

(a) Laws and regulations directly applied to the U.S. armed forces:

These laws and regulations are explicitly stipulated in the Japan-U.S. SOFA or relevant documents. Such examples are those related to the movement of forces in the receiving state (Agreed Minutes with regard to Article 5 of Japan-U.S. SOFA), labor issues (Art. 12, para. 5, of Japan-U.S. SOFA), and foreign exchange (Art. 19, para. 1, of SOFA).

(b) The laws and regulations not applied to the U.S. armed forces:

There are a number of Special Measures Laws through which the U.S. armed forces are exempted from its obligation to comply with or respect the laws and regulations of

Japan. Such examples include those related to the application of the Aviation Law, Road Transportation Law, Wireless Radio Act, Telecommunications Business Act, and Postal Act.

(c) Laws and regulations for the implementation of the Japan-U.S. SOFA:

Examples of such laws and regulations include those related to the National Property Act (Art. 2 of SOFA), Customs Law (Art. 11 of SOFA), National Public Service Act (Art. 12 of SOFA), Code of Criminal Procedures (Art. 17 of SOFA), and Code of Civil Procedures (Art. 18 of SOFA).

3. United Nations Convention against Transnational Organized Crime:

Japan signed the UN Convention against Transnational Organized Crime in December 2000 and obtained the approval by the Diet in May 2003 to conclude the Convention. Lack of relevant domestic legislation prevented Japan from concluding the Convention until recently.

One of the reasons those bills have not been passed by the Diet was the heated argument over criminalizing "conspiracy" (punishing an act of agreeing with one or more other persons to commit a serious crime in para. 1(a) (i) of Art. 5 of the Convention). One of the main arguments against criminalizing conspiracy is that the definition was too broad and ambiguous and that it might lead to criminalization of thought-crime. The government of Japan continued its careful consideration on the draft bill to fulfill the requirements of the Convention and to simultaneously protect human rights for over ten years. Finally, the new bill was drafted in a restrictive manner and submitted in March 2017. The bill was passed in the Diet in June 2017, and Japan concluded the Convention in July of the same year.

IV. Conclusion

The Ohira Principles established a stable balance between the executive branch and the Diet. All in all, it was an extremely well-crafted formula. The formula has not changed since 1974, although it has been challenged by the growing needs for effective management over a wide range of issues in foreign affairs. The procedure of the Diet deliberation consists of multiple steps, involving many members of political parties and the Diet, which contributes to producing a sense of harmony.

Historically, national security issues were treated as the most contentious in the Diet deliberations. As we have seen, the Japan-U.S. Security Treaty and the SOFA were approved by applying the "thirty-day rule" in 1960. The Host Nation Support Agreement in 2008 and the Guam International Agreement in 2009 were exceptional examples where different decisions were made by the two Houses. In recent years, however, we can also observe heated discussions over trade issues, such as the

Trans-Pacific Partnership, or human rights issues, including the crime of conspiracy in the context of the UN Convention against Transnational Organized Crime.

The existing Japanese treaty-making practice will continue to face a question of how to strike the right balance, between producing necessary international agreements in a timely manner over various and more specialized issues while also maintaining a sufficient level of democratic control by the Diet.[16]

[16] In the Republic of Korea, the spread of democracy has invited the general public and scholars to inspect the treaty conclusion system from various angles. The case of the Republic of Korea also gives us an interesting perspective as to how to strike the right balance between managing foreign affairs and ensuring democratic control. *See* Lee, *supra* note 4.

CHAPTER 12

SPANISH FOREIGN RELATIONS LAW AND THE PROCESS FOR MAKING TREATIES AND OTHER INTERNATIONAL AGREEMENTS

CARLOS ESPÓSITO

THE concept of foreign relations law is strange to Spanish law. This chapter, however, suggests that the Spanish domestic law governing international interactions may well be described as foreign relations law. The first part discusses scholarly texts, case law, and legislation as evidence of a Spanish foreign relations law. The rest of the chapter deals with a particular area of foreign relations law: the process under Spanish law for making treaties and other international agreements. It offers an account of the constitutional design of the treaty-making process in Spain, and an explanation of the regulation of other international agreements as set forth in the 2014 Treaties and Other International Agreements Act.[1] It also discusses controversies stemming from the conclusion and enforcement of the law of treaties in relation to autonomous communities. The chapter concludes with thoughts relating to the Spanish conception of foreign relations law.

[1] Ley 25/2014, 27 November 2014, Tratados y otros Acuerdos Internacionales, *available at* http://www.boe.es/boe/dias/2014/11/28/pdfs/BOE-A-2014-12326.pdf [hereinafter the Treaties Act]. *See* COMENTARIOS A LA LEY DE TRATADOS Y OTROS ACUERDOS INTERNACIONALES (Paz Andrés Sáenz de Santa Maria, Javier Díez-Hochleitner, & José Martín y Pérez de Nanclares eds., 2015).

I. Is There Spanish Foreign Relations Law?

Spain has a number of complex and diverse rules of domestic law that may be included in the concept of foreign relations law as defined in this *Handbook*, i.e., "the domestic law of each nation that governs how that nation interacts with the rest of the world."[2] Legal scholars and practitioners, however, have not yet openly considered foreign relations law as a distinctive discipline of Spanish law. With the exception of EU law,[3] the rules typically associated with foreign relations law have been usually taught in law schools as part and parcel of public international law, either in relation to the treaty-making power and domestic treaty procedures, or in connection with the reception of international law in Spain and its application by the Spanish administrative officials and the judiciary.[4]

Nevertheless, the Spanish domestic law regulating foreign affairs may be described as a field of domestic law related to international relations. There is evidence that the stakeholders are not unaware of this reality, whether scholars, executive officers, legislators, judges, or practitioners. A few examples relating to scholarly texts, laws, and judicial decisions will support this suggestion.

Scholarly Texts. In the United States, where foreign relations law is an established field, experts usually cite to some titles that have shaped the discipline, particularly the first edition of the classic book by Louis Henkin, *Foreign Affairs and the Constitution*, published in 1972,[5] and several textbooks that started to appear in those years.[6] Although Spain lacks such a systematic approach, it does have some titles that respond well to the object of foreign relations law. The book by Antonio Remiro, *La Acción Exterior del Estado (The External Action of the State)*, published in 1984, is a good example, which contains essential elements of foreign affairs law.[7] Javier Roldán published a comprehensive monograph on the external relations of Spain in 2001,

[2] Curtis A. Bradley, *What Is Foreign Relations Law*, ch. 1 in this volume, at p.3. *See also* Thomas Giegerich, *Foreign Relations Law* (Jan. 2011), *in* Max Planck Encyclopedia of Public International Law, *available at* http://opil.ouplaw.com/view/10.1093/law:epil/9780199231690/law-9780199231690-e937; Campbell McLachlan, Foreign Relations Law (2014).

[3] Spain has been a member of the European Union since 1986, and European Law became a discipline of its own in most law schools during the 1990s, usually taught by scholars with backgrounds on international law, administrative law, and constitutional law. *See*, e.g., Daniel Sarmiento, El Derecho de la Unión Europea (2016); *see also* Marise Cremona, *Making Treaties and Other International Agreements: The European Union*, ch. 14 in this volume.

[4] *See*, e.g., Antonio Remiro-Brotóns et al., Derecho Internacional 629–668 (2007); Oriol Casanovas & Angel J. Rodrigo, Compendio de Derecho Internacional Público 145–162 (Tecnos, 7th ed. 2018).

[5] Louis Henkin, Foreign Affairs and the US Constitution (2d ed. 1996).

[6] *See* Bradley, *supra* note 2, at p.10.

[7] Antonio Remiro Brotóns, La Acción Exterior del Estado (1984).

which covers most matters related to foreign affairs law.[8] To be sure, the analyses of these texts take the perspective of international law instead of a primarily domestic law approach.[9] However, the themes and objects of the books are mainly foreign relations law.

Legislation. Legislation relating to both executive and legislative powers has recently shown a notable awareness of foreign relations law. Since 2014, Spain has adopted new important pieces of foreign relations legislation, including legislation addressing the law of treaties and other international agreements,[10] the law of foreign state immunities,[11] and the law of external action policy and service.[12] These laws are ambitious in their scope, dealing with detailed matters of foreign relations law. Each responds to different normative and practical needs. The law of foreign state immunities is a good example. It was probably the least needed because the adjudication of jurisdictional immunities of the states has been dealt with by the judiciary on the basis of customary international law without major interpretative problems.[13] Indeed, the case law of the Spanish Supreme Court on jurisdictional immunities of foreign states since 1986 established well-defined exceptions to the rule of immunities and left behind the absolute interpretation of the principle.[14] This case law was supported and further developed by the Constitutional Court when the rule of foreign state immunities was contested from the perspective of the right to a fair trial.[15] The lack of Spanish legislation was therefore not an impediment to applying and developing the law of foreign state immunities in Spain. The new legislation on foreign state immunities, less usual in continental law than in common law countries, does not differ much from the UN Convention on Jurisdictional Immunities of States and Their Property. The incorporation of customary international law in this field offers, nevertheless, an extra

[8] Javier Roldán Barbero, Las Relaciones Exteriores de España (2001).

[9] *See* Jorge Cardona-Llorens, *Book Review*, 2 REEI (2012), *available at* http://www.reei.org/index.php/revista/num4/recensiones/roldan-barbero-javier-relaciones-exteriores-espana-editorial-dykinson-madrid.

[10] *See supra* note 1.

[11] Ley 16/2015, of 27 October 2015, on privileges and immunities of foreign states, international organizations with headquarters or offices in Spain, and international conferences and meetings, available at https://www.boe.es.

[12] Ley 2/2014, of 24 May 2014, de la Acción y del Servicio Exterior del Estado (BOE-A-2014-3248), *available at* https://www.boe.es/.

[13] Spain has deposited the instrument of accession to the Convention of the United Nations on Jurisdictional Immunities of States and of Their Property, adopted by the General Assembly of the United Nations on 2 December 2004. But the Convention is not yet in force. *See* General Assembly Resolution 59/38, annex, Official Records of the General Assembly, Fifty-ninth Session, Supplement No. 49 (A/59/49). On the law of foreign states immunities in Spain, *see* Fernando Gascón-Inchausti, Inmunidades Procesales y Tutela Judicial Frente a Estados Extranjeros (2008).

[14] Judgment of the Supreme Court of 1 December 1986 (STS 6699/1986), *available at* http://www.poderjudicial.es/.

[15] Judgments of the Constitutional Court SSTC 107/1992 (Sala Segunda), 1 July 1992; 292/1994 (Sala Primera), 27 October 1994; 18/1997 (Sala Segunda), 10 February 1997; 176/2001 (Sala Segunda), 17 September 2001, all *available at* https://www.tribunalconstitucional.es/.

layer of certainty for national judges applying the law of foreign state immunities, and allows officials to solve thorny administrative issues in a rather simple manner, such as providing for timely appropriate immunities to attendants of international conferences taking place in Spain without having to conclude a new international treaty for each and every conference.[16]

Judicial Decisions. The case law on foreign relations law was rather scarce in Spain, but it has become much more common in recent times. The case law on jurisdictional immunities has already been mentioned, showing a proper judicial handling of both customary international law[17] and international treaties.[18] The best and most famous example of judicial practice related to foreign relations law in Spain is the series of cases relying on the principle of universal jurisdiction that started in 1996.

Criminal prosecutions based on universal jurisdiction were possible because, in the beginning, the law governing universal jurisdiction was extremely broad in scope. Indeed, the original Spanish model of universal jurisdiction, as established in Article 23(4) of the 1985 law governing the judiciary,[19] was based purely on the nature of the crimes persecuted, without any kind of limitations or requirements, such as the nationality of the victims or the presence of the alleged authors of the crimes in Spanish territory. Moreover, the Spanish model, unlike many other types of universal jurisdiction, was not constrained by rules providing for the intervention of political authorities with the power to correct or impede the operation of the judiciary. This structure paved the way for the idea that universal jurisdiction was not only for "low-cost defendants,"[20] and could actually become a suitable tool to fight impunity worldwide even against high-cost and mid-cost defendants.[21] The Constitutional Court did not agree with the opinion of the Supreme Court[22] and supported the broad understanding of the provision in its 2005 judgment on the Mayan genocide case,[23] holding that the principle of universal jurisdiction was designed to have an

[16] *See* arts. 42–48 of the Spanish law on privileges and immunities of foreign States, *supra* note 11.

[17] *Supra* note 16.

[18] *See* the Judgment of the Constitutional Court 140/95, 28 Sept. 1995. *See* Carlos Espósito & Francisco J. Garcimartín Alférez, *El Artículo 24 de la Constitución y la inmunidad civil de los agentes diplomáticos extranjeros (comentario a la sentencia del Tribunal Constitucional 140/1995)*, 47 REVISTA ESPAÑOLA DE DERECHO CONSTITUCIONAL 257 (1996).

[19] Organic Law N° 6/1985, 14 March 1985, *available at* http://www.boe.es/.

[20] *See* Maximo Langer, *The Diplomacy of Universal Jurisdiction: The Political Branches and the Transnational Prosecution of International Crimes*, 105 AM. J. INT'L L. 1, 2–3 (2011).

[21] The actual record of the application of the principle of universal jurisdiction in Spain has, however, been rather scant if assessed from the point of view of the number of final judgments that it has produced—i.e., there have been many investigations but only one, rather controversial, guilty verdict in the Scilingo case. *See* Judgement of the National Court 16/2005, 19 April 2005, finding the Argentinian Adolfo Scilingo guilty of crimes against humanity during that last dictatorship in Argentina. The practice, however, has triggered significant legal and political consequences worldwide, as happened, for example, with the *Pinochet* case.

[22] Judgment of the Supreme Court (Criminal Chamber) N° 327/2003, 25 Feb. 2003.

[23] Judgment of the Constitutional Court 237/2005, 26 Sept. 2005.

"absolute" character, based only on the particularly grave nature of the crimes that are the object of its persecution.

The Spanish government, with the support of the opposition and under pressure from foreign governments,[24] introduced several restrictions to the provision on universal jurisdiction in 2009, but the amendment was poorly drafted and consequently did not prove effective in restricting the scope of the universal basis of jurisdiction.[25] A more effective restrictive amendment was passed on March 14, 2014, marking what one scholar has called "the end of the Spanish model of universal jurisdiction."[26] This sweeping reform, again stimulated by external pressure from powerful foreign countries reacting against judicial investigations by the National Court,[27] established new requirements regarding the alleged authors of the crimes, who now have to be Spaniards or reside in Spain, together with the strict application of the principle of subsidiarity, and the limitation of the *actio popularis*. The Supreme Court held that the new conception of the principle of universal jurisdiction, as amended in 2014, was both in conformity with international law and with constitutional law in a long and thoroughly researched judgment concerning China's alleged genocide and crimes against humanity against the people of Tibet.[28]

Foreign relations law is distinctive in all these examples. All of them, however, are far from any idea of exclusionism from international law;[29] on the contrary, both the norms and the stakeholders insist on the idea that domestic law shall be applied and interpreted in conformity with international law. This mandate is explicitly incorporated in the Constitution, which establishes in Article 96(1) that international treaties "may only be repealed, amended or suspended in the manner provided for in the treaties themselves or in accordance with the general rules of international law." The Constitution also provides that its provisions relating to the fundamental rights and liberties "shall be construed in conformity with the Universal Declaration of Human Rights and international treaties and agreements thereon ratified by Spain."[30] The rest of

[24] For instance, the protests of authorities of Israel against the decision of Judge Fernando Andreu to pursue investigations into a 2002 Israeli bombing in the Gaza Strip.

[25] Organic Law 1/2014, 13 March 2014, amending Organic Law 6/1985 on the Judicial Power in relation to universal justice, BOE, Nº 63, 14 March 2014, at 23,026, *available at* http://www.boe.es/.

[26] Angel Sánchez Legido, *El fin del modelo español de jurisdicción universal*, 27 REEI (2014), *available at* http://www.reei.org/index.php/revista/num27/articulos/fin-modelo-espanol-jurisdiccion-universal. *See also* Agora on Universal Jurisdiction after the entry into force of the Organic Law 1/2014, 13 March 2014, 18 Span. Y.B. Int'l L. 223 (2013–2014), *available at* http://www.sybil.es/archive/vol18/.

[27] Particularly, the Chinese government's discontent with respect to the judicial investigations regarding the Tibet and the Falung Gong cases before the National Court, which included two former presidents of the People's Republic of China, Jiang Zemin and Hu Jintao.

[28] Judgment of the Supreme Court (Criminal Chamber), Nº 296/2015, 6 May 2015.

[29] *See* Campbell McLachlan, *Five Conceptions of the Function of Foreign Relations Law*, ch. 2 in this volume. *Cf.* Curtis A. Bradley, *A New American Foreign Affairs Law?*, 70 U. Colo. L. Rev. 1089 (1999) (discussing the concept of foreign relations law exceptionalism).

[30] *See* art. 10(2) of the Spanish Constitution regarding the interpretation in conformity with international law of human rights. Alejandro Saiz-Arnaiz, La Apertura Constitucional al Derecho Internacional y Europeo de los Derechos Humanos. El Articulo 10.2 de la Constitucion

this chapter deals with the treatment of treaties and nonbinding political commitments in Spanish law. Therefore, it can be read as a continuation of this line of reasoning.

II. Treaties and the Spanish Constitution

Spanish constitutional democracy was established on December 6, 1978. Throughout most of the life of the 1978 Constitution,[31] treaties and other nonbinding agreements were governed by a few norms provided for in the Constitution, together with rules and practices that endured from preconstitutional times. In 2014, however, an ambitious piece of legislation on treaties and other international agreements was enacted.[32] The new legislation sets forth a comprehensive regulation of the law of treaties and other international agreements in Spain and also addresses the role of the Spanish Autonomous Communities in international legal affairs, excluding only the EU law dimension of external legal affairs.

The original problem with the regulation of the treaty process in Spain after the adoption of the 1978 Constitution was that the rules in force were only half democratic. In 1972, under the Franco regime, Spain acceded to the 1969 VCLT[33] and at the same time regulated its domestic treaty process through a Decree.[34] This Decree reproduced and adapted the wording of the VCLT on matters such as negotiation, adoption, and authentication of the text of a treaty, and expression of consent to be bound by a treaty, and it mentioned the possibility of provisional application of treaties. It also added provisions on the registration and publication of treaties. The Spanish Constitution of 1978 derogated from many of those provisions, but not all of them, and the Decree of 1972 continued to govern many practical administrative matters related to the conclusion of treaties by Spain.[35]

Espanola (1999); *Comentario del artículo 10.2 CE La interpretacion de los derechos fundamentales y los tratados internacionales sobre derechos humanos, in* Comentarios a la Constitucion 193 (María Emilia Casas & Miguel Rodríguez-Piñero eds., 2008).

[31] For a general introduction to the 1978 Spanish Constitution, *see* Víctor Ferreres-Comella, The Constitution of Spain: A Contextual Analysis (2013). The following text elaborates from thoughts on the Spanish regulation of treaties published in the Boletim da Sociedade Brasileira de Direito Internacional (2017).

[32] *See supra* note 1.

[33] The Spanish instrument of accession to the Vienna Convention on the Law of Treaties was deposited on 16 May 1972. *See* Vienna Convention on the Law of Treaties, 23 May 1969, 1155 UNTS 331 [hereinafter VCLT].

[34] Decree 801/1972, of 24 March 1972, regulating the activity of the administration of the state in matters of international treaties (in force until 18 December 2014), *available at* http://boe.es/.

[35] The Ministry of Foreign Affairs had its own internal regulation on treaty procedures: Ministerial Order of 17 February 1992 of the Under-Secretariat for Foreign Affairs establishing rules for the

The Spanish Constitution has provisions concerning the conclusion of treaties, the treaty-making power, the process of democratic control of treaties by the Congress and the Senate, and incorporation of validly concluded treaties into the Spanish legal system.[36] The Constitution also provides for the exclusive powers of the national government ("the State" in the terms of the Constitution) over the Autonomous Communities with regard to foreign affairs.[37]

With regard to the treaty-making process, the executive has the discretion to start negotiations, to conclude a treaty, and to ratify such treaties. However, the Constitution requires that the government obtain legislative authorization prior to expressing the consent to be bound to certain categories of treaties.[38] As provided for in Article 93 of the Constitution, an overall majority vote, through the adoption of a statute, is required for treaties that transfer constitutional powers to international organizations.[39] This provision was adopted with a view to Spain becoming a member of the European Communities, and that explains the mere absolute majority requirement in this provision. History proved that it was not necessarily a wise decision, and that a larger majority would have probably been appropriate, such as the supermajority required for the "advice and consent" of the Senate in the U.S. Constitution.[40]

All other international treaties must be authorized by the legislature in accordance with Article 94 of the Constitution. The first paragraph of that provision contains a list of the treaties that need authorization by a simple majority of the Houses: "(a) Treaties of a political nature, (b) Treaties or agreements of a military nature, (c) Treaties or agreements affecting the territorial integrity of the State or the fundamental rights and duties established under Part 1 [of the Constitution], (d) Treaties or agreements which imply financial liabilities for the Public Treasury, (e) Treaties or agreements which involve amendment or repeal of some law or require legislative measures for their execution." Article 94 of the Constitution also provides in its second paragraph that "[t]he Congress and the Senate shall be informed forthwith of the conclusion of any other treaties or agreements," although in practice this option is almost never used

procedure to be followed for international treaties by the agencies of this department. Official Bulletin of the Ministry of Foreign Affairs, Nº 592, Feb. 1992.

[36] Spanish Constitution, 6 December 1978, arts. 56, 63(2), 93–96.

[37] Spanish Constitution, arts. 97 and 149(1)(3).

[38] An accessible account of the Spanish treaty process provided for in the Constitution may be found in Cristina Izquierdo-Sanz, *Parliamentary Procedure in the Conclusion of International Treaties in Spain*, 5 SPAN. Y.B. INT'L L. 1 (1997), *available at* http://www.sybil.es/documents/ARCHIVE/vol5/Izquierdo.pdf.

[39] Article 93: "Authorization may be granted by an organic act for concluding treaties by which powers derived from the Constitution shall be transferred to an international organization or institution. It is incumbent on the *Cortes Generales* [i.e., the Congress and the Senate] or the Government, as the case may be, to ensure compliance with these treaties and with resolutions originating in the international and supranational organizations to which such powers have been so transferred."

[40] *See* Antonio Remiro-Brotóns, *De los tratados internacionales (arts. 93–96 de la Constitución), in* COMENTARIOS A LA CONSTITUCIÓN ESPAÑOLA DE 1978, vol. VII 491–651 (Oscar Alzaga ed., 2d ed. 1999).

due to the very broad list of treaties included in the first paragraph, and also because "treaties of a political nature" may cover almost any kind of agreement.

An advisory function of the Constitutional Court is also provided for in Article 95(2), but not a specific referendum procedure for the conclusion of treaties.[41] The advisory function is meant to solve problems of nonconformity of treaty clauses with the Constitution.[42] This prior constitutional control has been used twice to elucidate whether the EU amendments were in conformity with the Spanish Constitution. On one occasion, the Constitution had to be amended, allowing European citizens to vote in local elections, in order to express the consent of Spain to the Maastricht Treaty;[43] in the other case, the Constitutional Court declared that the proposed treaty establishing a constitution for Europe was not incompatible with the Spanish Constitution.[44]

International treaties validly concluded by Spain prevail over domestic law, "except for constitutional provisions."[45] Therefore, the validity of treaties under the Constitution may also be assessed by the judiciary after the treaties are validly concluded by Spain. A finding against the constitutional legality of treaty provisions would of course have only domestic effects as regards the validity of such provision, notwithstanding the consequences on international responsibility. Article 96(1) of the Constitution confirms this interpretation when it establishes that the provisions of "validly concluded treaties" are part of the Spanish legal order but "may only be repealed, amended or suspended in the manner provided for in the treaties themselves or in accordance with the general rules of international law."

The Constitution does not cover administrative aspects of the treaty process, which until the entry into force of the 2014 Treaties Act were governed partially by the Decree of 1972, along with numerous internal administrative orders known as Ministerial Circulars. This was one of the main reasons for adopting a comprehensive law regulating international treaties, a legislative ambition that had been on the desk of almost all Spanish governments since 1979.[46]

[41] Referenda have been used twice under the 1978 Constitution: on the permanence of Spain as a member of the NATO on 12 March 1986, and on the establishment of an EU Constitution on 20 February 2005. Both referenda were voluntarily called by the government on the basis of Article 92 of the Constitution. *See* the commentary by Nicolás Pérez Sola in COMENTARIOS A LA CONSTITUCION 1551 (María Emilia Casas & Miguel Rodríguez-Piñero eds., 2008).

[42] Article 95(1) ("The conclusion of an international treaty containing stipulations contrary to the Constitution shall require prior constitutional amendment. (2) The Government or either House may request the Constitutional Court to declare whether or not such a contradiction exists.").

[43] Declaration of the Constitutional Court 1/1992, 1 July 1992, on the existence or inexistence of a contradiction between Article 13(2) of the Spanish Constitution and Article 8(B)(1) of the Constitutive Treaty of the European Economic Community as drafted in Article 10 of the Treaty of the European Union.

[44] Declaration of the Constitutional Court 1/2004, 13 Dec. 2004, on the constitutionality of the Treaty establishing a Constitution for Europe.

[45] Article 31 of the Spanish Treaties Act on Prevalence of treaties: "The legal provisions contained in validly concluded and officially published international treaties shall prevail over any other domestic law provisions in the event of conflict with them, except for constitutional provisions."

[46] *See*, e.g., LA CELEBRACIÓN DE TRATADOS INTERNACIONALES POR ESPAÑA: PROBLEMAS ACTUALES (1990), with a series of papers presented at a conference organized by the Spanish Diplomatic School to

III. Regulating Other International Agreements

The other main reason for the adoption of a law of treaties was the need to deal with the vast conventional practice by the executive and the Autonomous Communities affecting foreign affairs, particularly through Memoranda of Understanding (MOUs), but also through the use of different sorts of international administrative agreements.[47] These matters are now governed by the Treaties Act, which in Article 1 establishes that its purpose is the regulation of Spain's "conclusion and implementation of international treaties, international administrative arrangements and non-binding international agreements."[48] The Treaties Act does not introduce substantial changes in the treaty process of international treaties,[49] but instead brings about a set of new legal provisions regulating international administrative agreements (IAAs) and MOUs.

An IAA is defined in Article 2(b) of the Treaties Act as an agreement of an international character that does not constitute a treaty, concluded by public bodies concerning a subject of international law, within the scope of an underlying treaty, and governed by international law.[50] The requirement of not being a treaty may be confusing, because IAAs are treaties under international law. The difference with international treaties according to the Treaties Act is that they need not be submitted to the Congress and the Senate before the government expresses consent to be bound by the agreement, and they may be concluded by public organs or entities of the state to develop or execute matters within the scope of an underlying treaty.[51] The Act specifies, however, that an IAA may only be concluded "to implement and specify the terms of an international treaty when the treaty itself so provides."[52]

discuss the draft act on the law of treaties of April 15, 1985. The most comprehensive account on the law of treaties in Spanish is still Antonio Remiro-Brotóns, Derecho de los Tratados (1986).

[47] Curtis A. Bradley, International Law in the U.S. Legal System (2d ed. 2015), *see particularly* ch. 3 on executive agreements; Anthony Aust, Modern Treaty Law and Practice (2000), esp. ch. 3.

[48] The provisions of the Treaties Act shall be without prejudice to EU agreements, *see* Spanish Treaties Act, Additional Provision Two on the regime of the external action of the European Union.

[49] Title II of the Treaties Act. *See* José Martín y Pérez de Nanclares, *La Ley de Tratados y otros acuerdos internacionales: una nueva regulación para disciplinar una práctica internacional difícil de ignorar*, 76 REDI 1 (2015).

[50] According to Article 2(b) of the Treaties Act, an IAA is "an agreement of an international nature which does not establish a treaty and is concluded by bodies, agencies or entities of a subject of international law with powers in the matter, the conclusion of which is set forth in the treaty that it implements or specifies the terms of. The usual content of such an arrangement is technical in nature, whatever its denomination, and it is governed by international law."

[51] Art. 38(1) Treaties Act ("*Los órganos, organismos y entes de las Administraciones Públicas podrán celebrar acuerdos internacionales administrativos en ejecución y concreción de un tratado internacional cuando el propio tratado así lo prevea.*").

[52] Art. 38(1) of the Treaties Act.

The Treaties Act establishes in its Title III an obligation to ask for the legal opinion of the Legal Advisor of the Ministry of Foreign Affairs as to whether the draft agreement is a true international administrative agreement, and also to check with the Treasury about its budgetary commitment.[53] It also provides that international administrative agreements should be published in order to become part of the Spanish legal system.[54] The Treaties Act also provides for additional transparency in directing the Ministry of Foreign Affairs to regularly publish a collection of international administrative treaties.[55]

Title IV of the Treaties Act regulates nonlegally binding agreements.[56] These agreements are not treaties: they are neither governed by international law nor constitute sources of legal obligations per se.[57] The Treaties Act, however, requires that each body or organ with the authority to sign an MOU shall ask its own legal services for an opinion on the legal nature of the agreement. These bodies or organs shall also assure themselves that the necessary budgetary needs for the implementation of the MOU are guaranteed. The Treaties Act requires that copies of all MOUs be sent to the Ministry of Foreign Affairs in order to keep a register of these international nonlegal agreements.

The focus of the Treaties Act is on domestic requirements for international treaties and other international agreements.[58] The distinction among different kinds of agreements does not affect their international legality.[59] Moreover, domestic classifications and definitions of agreements have not had a major influence in the case law of the International Court of Justice.[60] The question then is why the Spanish legislature thought it necessary and wise to regulate these three categories of international agreements instead of only proper international treaties as defined in Article 2(1) of the VCLT. As mentioned above, there was a wide consensus on the need to replace the old preconstitutional regulation with a new law of treaties. The extensive scope of the Treaties Act was, however, more controversial. Indeed, some thought that it was unnecessary (and even wrong) to include IAAs and MOUs,[61] while others thought that

[53] Art. 39. [54] Art. 41. *Cf.* Case-Zablocki Act, 1 U.S.C. § 112b. [55] Art. 42.

[56] In Spanish, MOUs are called "non-normative international agreements." This imprecise term was coined in the 1980s and has been used since then in ministerial circulars and other texts. *See* the chapter by Antonio Remiro-Brotóns in LA CELEBRACIÓN DE TRATADOS INTERNACIONALES POR ESPAÑA: PROBLEMAS ACTUALES, *supra* note 46. On MOUs, *see* Anthony Aust, *Alternative to Treaty-Making: MOUs as Political Commitments, in* THE OXFORD GUIDE TO TREATIES 4, 6–72 (Duncan B. Hollis ed., 2012).

[57] Arts. 2(c) and 43.

[58] *See* BRADLEY, *supra* note 47, at 74 ("The distinction between treaties and executive agreements is one of U.S. law, not international law").

[59] Art. 26 VCLT.

[60] *Maritime delimitation and territorial questions between Qatar v. Bahrain*, ICJ Reports 1994, at 112. *See also Land and Maritime Boundary between Cameroon and Nigeria (Cameroon v. Nigeria: Equatorial Guinea intervening)*, ICJ Reports 2002, at 303; JAN KLABBERS, THE CONCEPT OF TREATY IN INTERNATIONAL LAW (1996).

[61] Antonio Fernández-Tomás, *Parliamentary Control of "Other International Agreements" in the New Spanish Treaties and Other International Agreements Act (TOIAA)*, 18 SPAN. Y.B. INT'L L. 61 (2013–2014), *available at* http://www.sybil.es/documents/ARCHIVE/vol18/4_Fernandez_Tomas.pdf.

it was insufficient in scope as the trilogy of categories left some relevant international agreements out of the picture.[62]

Both critiques make interesting points. The latter, which may be called the critique of incompleteness, may prove right in cases of sole executive agreements, since the definition of IAA only seems to cover agreements based on a principal treaty providing for the authority to execute its provisions through further administrative agreements.[63] The drafters of the Treaties Act were not persuaded by this critique. They seemed to understand that sole executive agreements fall under the category of international treaties, and so require the normal treaty process for their conclusion,[64] or they are international agreements governed by national law and therefore not international treaties. In any case, both fall outside of the IAA definition.

The critique that there was no need to include the new categories of international agreements is more complex. A general point affecting both IAAs and MOUs is that for some authors the treaty system had functioned rather well with the Decree plus the Ministerial Circulars, so allegedly there was no need to adopt a law with such a comprehensive scope.[65] The legislature was not impressed by this argument and believed that the legal system could not continue to avoid the proper regulation of the rich practice of international agreements.[66]

Regarding IAAs, there have been concerns about the avoidance of control by the legislature, and the consequences of their vague legal nature. Let us recall that IAAs are not to be submitted to the treaty process provided for in the Constitution for international treaties, which requires the authorization (and therefore the control) of the Congress and the Senate prior to the government's expression of consent to be bound by the treaty. The Treaties Act requires a consultation to the Legal Advisor of the Ministry of Foreign Affairs on the nature of the agreement,[67] and its publication in the Official Journal.[68] The practice has been criticized on the ground that what matters for the determination of a treaty in the Spanish constitutional system is its substance, not its form.[69] Concerns about this issue may have been particularly intense in light of the controversial decision by the International Legal Advisory Department of the Ministry of Foreign Affairs holding that the agreement on the financial sector adjustment program for Spain of the Memorandum of Understanding between the European Commission and Spain on Financial Sector Policy was an "international administrative

[62] Opinion of the Spanish Council of State 808/2013, of 3 October 2013, *available at* http://www.boe.es/.

[63] For example, art. 3 of the Second Protocol of Amendment of the Agreement between the United States and Spain on defense cooperation, of 1 December 1988, signed in 10 October 2012 (authorizing the conclusion of administrative agreements in conformity with the agreement and the national legislations of the parties).

[64] *Cf.* Judgment of the Constitutional Court 155/2005, 9 June 2005 (sustaining the unavoidable necessity of Parliamentary control for certain international agreements with the IMF), *available at* http://hj.tribunalconstitucional.es/en/Resolucion/Show/5415.

[65] Fernández-Tomás, *supra* note 61, at 64.

[66] Preamble of the Treaties Act. *See also* Martín y Pérez de Nanclares, *supra* note 49.

[67] Art. 39(1) Treaties Act. [68] Art. 41(1) Treaties Act.

[69] *See* Fernández Tomás, *supra* note 61, at 79.

agreement."[70] The huge amount of debt contracted by Spain for the restructuring and recapitalization of the Spanish banking sector was a key element in support of the argument that the MOU was in fact an international treaty requiring the procedure provided for in Article 94 of the Constitution.[71] In the view of the Legal Advisor, the agreement was founded in the previous Framework Agreement on the European Financial Stability Facility of 2010,[72] and therefore was properly considered an IAA.[73] The rest of Spanish practice on IAAs has been less controversial.

There has been substantial criticism regarding the extensive use of MOUs by the executive. The Treaties Act intends to tackle "hidden treaties"[74] made as MOUs with the following two requirements: first, MOUs should be submitted to the legal advisers of the bodies or organs intending to sign them;[75] second, MOUs should be communicated to the Ministry of Foreign Affairs in order to be included in a special Registry of MOUs.[76] In theory, these requirements should be helpful, especially the obligation to register these nonbinding agreements, which may prove beneficial for a better practice on MOUs and their transparency. Until now, the practice was dispersed and chaotic, and the International Law Department of the Ministry of Foreign Affairs was able to check only a few of those agreements.[77] Moreover, some public bodies and ministries used and abused MOUs, particularly in certain areas, such as defense and foreign aid. The very broad capacity to make MOUs remains problematic,[78] and of course the registry to be kept by the Ministry of Foreign Affairs will not solve the difficulties arising from treaties wrongly qualified as "non-normative agreements." Having said that, such risk already existed before the Treaties Act, and it is likely that the obligation to publish these agreements in an official public registry creates a strong incentive to establish a better practice on MOUs.

The measures intended to increase transparency and control over the conventional activities of diverse organs and bodies negotiating IAAs and MOUs are significant. The challenges, however, remain considerable, and they may not necessarily arise from the functioning of the law but from entrenched practices, deficiencies, and equilibriums of

[70] Memorandum of Understanding on Financial Sector-Policy Conditionality, Brussels and Madrid, 23 June 2012, published in the BOE nº 296, 10 December 2012. *See also* Martín y Pérez de Nanclares, *supra* note 49, at 43.

[71] *See* Fernández Tomás, *supra* note 61, at 79.

[72] The Framework Agreement is *available at* http://www.efsf.europa.eu/attachments/20111019_efsf_framework_agreement_en.pdf.

[73] Martín y Pérez de Nanclares, *supra* note 49, at 43, n.119.

[74] Javier González-Vega, *¿Tratados ocultos?, sobre ciertas manifestaciones de la acción concertada no convencional en el marco de las competencias reservadas a los tratados internacionales*, *in* El Derecho Internacional en el Mundo Multipolar del Siglo XXI. Obra Homenaje al Profesor Luis Ignacio Sánchez Rodríguez 75 (S. Torres-Bernárdez et al. eds., 2013) (studying "hidden treaties" affecting the categories included in the list of treaties of art. 94(1) of the Spanish Constitution, which need a parliamentary authorization).

[75] Art. 45 Treaties Act.

[76] Art. 48 Treaties Act.

[77] A Circular of the Ministry of Foreign Affairs was applicable for the determination of the legal nature of "non-normative agreements." Circular 3.286 of the Ministry of Foreign Affairs, 19 July 2010.

[78] Art. 44 Treaties Act.

power within the Administration. In this sense, there is room to doubt the ability of the incentives to do away with "hidden treaties" and to strengthen the role of the legislature. The main problem concerns not those mechanisms of control, which function well when they are followed,[79] but rather the minimal involvement of the Spanish legislature in the treaty-making process. The formal rules of the Constitution, and now the Treaties Act, are structurally sound. Nevertheless, the role of the Congress and the Senate in the scrutiny and democratic control over treaties is scarce and deficient—as a general rule, it is a "low intensity intervention" at best.[80] The Foreign Affairs Committee of the Congress is prone to discussing controversial political issues, but it does not have a practice of thorough examination of the treaty-making process. The Congress and the Senate usually authorize the government to express consent to be bound by treaties without any discussion or debate at all. When legislators are asked about this deficiency, some would allege a lack of resources. There is some truth to that, of course, but it is not a very persuasive argument since such democratic control has never been a legislative priority—a culture of democratic scrutiny of treaties is simply absent from the Spanish parliamentary practice. A more sophisticated response to that fact is based on the existence of a sort of consensus on foreign policy in the Parliament. From this perspective, the lack of debate would not be a mere blank check, but a recognition of all legislatures since the Spanish transition that foreign affairs policy is a state policy. This explanation is not convincing, however, given that there have been situations of vast dissent on foreign affairs policy, and in any case the legislative power has a constitutional democratic mandate to control the treaty-making practice of the government.

IV. The Role of the Autonomous Communities in the Treaty Process

One of the bodies with the capacity to make IAAs and MOUs are the Autonomous Communities of Spain.[81] The Treaties Act regulates this power in Title V on Autonomous Communities, Cities of Ceuta and Melilla, and Local Entities. A long road has led Spain into this intricate landscape. In fact, most observers believe that the projects to regulate treaties failed due to the lack of consensus on the role of the Autonomous

[79] The mandatory reports on the legal nature of treaties of the Legal Advisor of the Ministry of Foreign Affairs and the Council of State are highly appreciated.

[80] Antonio Remiro Brotóns, Política Exterior de Defensa y Control Parlamentario 137 (1988).

[81] *See* Ferreres Comella, *supra* note 32, ch. 7 on regional decentralization, at 167–200. For a discussion on the Spanish system from a federalist point of view, *see* Roberto S. Blanco Valdes, Los Rostros del Federalismo (2012). *See also* Foreign Relations in Federal Countries (Hans Michelmann ed., 2009).

Communities in the treaty-making process.[82] This is not totally true as the lack of will to coordinate the different ministries and other organs of the central government was responsible for those failures as well—they did not want to give up the power to control their foreign relations portfolio, which in some cases means a huge deal of power. The zeal to keep a capacity to project domestic powers externally will not disappear, but it may be less problematic if there is a substantive positive contribution of the new Inter-Ministerial Coordination Commission for treaties and other international agreements established by the Treaties Act to deal with the coordination of treaties and other international agreements.[83]

According to the Spanish Constitution, the treaty-making power is an exclusive competence of the Spanish national government.[84] Article 149(1)(3) of the Constitution clearly establishes that "[t]he State holds exclusive competence over . . . international relations." This provision may be read in a strict manner, as shown by the first judgments of the Constitutional Court dealing with controversies over foreign relations competences between the state and the Autonomous Communities, which upheld the exclusion of the Autonomous Communities from the treaty-making process.[85] The participation of Autonomous Communities was also restricted by the fact that they did not have effective indirect ways to participate in the treaty-making process. Indeed, in other countries, the Senate would represent rather well the interests of the territorial entities of the state, whether federal states, *Länder*, or regions. This would satisfy, at least with regard to solemn treaties, the legitimate quest for participation of the basic territorial entities of the state. This is not the case in Spain, where the Senate is weaker than the Congress, and it represents not the interests of the Autonomous Communities, but those of the provinces of Spain.[86] Moreover, the Autonomous Communities did not have clear rules to participate in the negotiations and implementation of agreements affecting their own constitutional competences, a problem that was evident in transfrontier relations and also in the EU sphere.[87]

This situation has changed considerably over the years. First, the Constitutional Court accepted, soon after its initial judgments on the role of Autonomous Communities with regard to international agreements, that these entities had a relevant role in "international relations," an expression that should be constructed in a less exclusive manner. Therefore, while affirming the exclusive competence of the state to conclude

[82] Carlos Espósito, *Reflexiones sobre la reforma del servicio exterior de España*, FRIDE Working Paper (2005).

[83] Art. 6 Treaties Act.

[84] For comparable provisions in other national constitutions, *see*, e.g., Article I, Section 10 of the U.S. Constitution; Article 117(1) of the Constitution of México; and Article 59 of the Constitution of Germany. For a comparative study, *see* DINAH SHELTON, INTERNATIONAL LAW AND DOMESTIC LEGAL SYSTEMS (2011) (with twenty-seven country studies, not including Spain).

[85] Constitutional Court, Judgment 137/1989, 20 July 1989 (denying the power of the Autonomous Community of Galicia to conclude a «Communiqué of Collaboration» with Denmark, which was signed on Nov. 2, 1984). *See also* Judgment 149/1991, 4 July 1991.

[86] ANTONIO REMIRO BROTÓNS ET AL., DERECHO INTERNACIONAL 400 (2010).

[87] *Cf.* arts. 23 and 24(1)(a) of the German Constitution.

solemn international treaties, the Court recognized the power of the Autonomous Communities to make some international agreements and even establish offices abroad to deal with matters of their competence.[88] Second, many statutes of the Autonomous Communities, particularly after their recent amendments, include different kinds of external competences.[89]

Title V of the Treaties Act regulates Autonomous Communities and takes into account this complex and sometimes awkward legal and political panorama. There are several rights and obligations concerning the participation of Autonomous Communities in the treaty process.[90] The Autonomous Communities now have the right to request that the central government open negotiations of treaties on subject matters of their own jurisdiction or affecting in a special manner their territorial scope. They may also ask to be part of the Spanish delegation charged with such negotiation. The government is under the obligation to give a reasoned answer to these requests. The Autonomous Communities may submit comments on the negotiation of those treaties, which shall be taken seriously by the government. Furthermore, the government shall inform the Autonomous Communities about the negotiation and ratification of treaties affecting their subject matter jurisdiction.

The Treaties Act also regulates the power of the Autonomous Communities to conclude IAAs and MOUs.[91] The Autonomous Communities may conclude IAAs executing or crystallizing an international treaty on subject matters of their own jurisdiction with due regard to the provisions of such international treaty. IAAs negotiated by Autonomous Communities must be submitted to the Ministry of Foreign Affairs before their conclusion in order to obtain the opinion of the International Legal Advisory Department of the Ministry of Foreign Affairs, which will decide on whether they are IAAs or treaties. MOUs may also be signed by the Autonomous Communities on subject matters of their own jurisdiction, and the draft of the agreements shall also be submitted to the International Legal Advisory Department, which shall produce

[88] Constitutional Court, Judgment 165/1994, of 26 May 1994 (on the right of the Basque Government to establish an office in Brussels). *See, however,* Judgment 198/2013, of 5 December 2013 (affirming the exclusive jurisdiction of the state under Article149.1.3 of the Constitution to make treaties with other countries, and nullifying the Fishing Agreement of September 21, 2003 between the Regional Minister of Fisheries of the Basque Country and the Minister of Fisheries of the Republic of Mauritania).

[89] *See,* e.g., Articles 192–200 of the Organic Law 6/2006, of 19 July 2006, on the Reform of the Statute of Autonomy of Catalonia, *available at* http://www.parlament.cat/porteso/estatut/estatut_angles_100506.pdf. *See also* Xavier Pons & Eduard Sagarra, *La acción exterior de la Generalitat en el nuevo Estatuto de autonomía de Cataluña,* 12 Revista Electrónica de Estudios Internacionales (2006), *available at* http://www.reei.org; Catarina García, Sílvia Morgades y Angel J. Rodrigo, *Las relaciones exteriores de la Generalitat en el Estatuto de Autonomía de Cataluña de 2006,* Anuario español de Derecho Internacional, 2006, Vol. XXII, at 23–52.

[90] *See* José Martín y Pérez de Nanclares, *Commentary to Articles 49–51, in* Comentarios a la Ley de Tratados y Otros Acuerdos Internacionales, *supra* note 1, at 875–909.

[91] *See* José Martín y Pérez de Nanclares, *Commentary to Articles 52–53, in* Comentarios a la Ley de Tratados y Otros Acuerdos Internacionales, *supra* note 1, at 913–946.

"a report on their nature, procedure and most appropriate implementation under international law."

The greatest challenge, however, lies in the political tensions created by the will of the Autonomous Communities (particularly, but not only, the Basque Country and Catalonia) to acquire more and more foreign relations power, as expressed in the letter of their Statutes of Autonomy, and of the will of some of them to have a foreign affairs power of their own. The aspirations of the Treaties Act to coordinate the practice of Autonomous Communities concerning international agreements would become sterile without a minimum respect for the federal loyalty principle.

V. Conclusion

This chapter has provided evidence to affirm that there is foreign relations law in Spain. Spanish foreign relations law, borrowing from Campbell McLachlan's categories,[92] may be described as predominantly internationalist, with elements of allocative, constitutional, and diplomatic functions. Spanish foreign relations law, however, is not exclusionary. The discussion of both the constitutional norms and the provisions of the Treaties Act support this assertion. Indeed, the constitutional design favors an internationalist conception of Spanish foreign affairs law through norms that incorporate international law in a direct and fully operative manner as it considers customary international law and validly concluded international treaties as part of the Spanish legal order. Moreover, constitutional rights are to be interpreted in conformity with international human rights conventions. At the same time, the Constitution respects the international legal order as far as international treaties can only be denounced, amended, or suspended as provided for in the treaties themselves or in accordance with the general rules of international law. The Treaties Act of 2014 aims at putting order in a complex area of practice concerning Spanish foreign affairs law. In order to do that, it regulates the domestic life of international treaties and creates internal categories of agreements, i.e., international administrative agreements and nonbinding agreements, always respecting the internationalist constitutional design.[93] The Treaties Act, of course, also has the legal and political goal of more effectively controlling the power to make international treaties and agreements within Spain, particularly the power of the Autonomous Communities, which have demonstrated a strong desire to have a greater or even an independent role in international relations.

[92] *See* McLachlan, *supra* note 29.

[93] Article 30 of the Treaties Act even goes beyond international law requirements, prescribing that "international treaties are directly applicable" unless there is textual evidence that the application shall be conditional. *Cf.* Javier Díez-Hochleitner, *Commentary to Article 30*, *in* Comentarios a la Ley de Tratados y Otros Acuerdos Internacionales, *supra* note 1, at 532–560.

CHAPTER 13

INCORPORATION AND IMPLEMENTATION OF TREATIES IN SOUTH KOREA

JAEMIN LEE

THIS chapter reviews South Korea's approach to incorporating and implementing treaties within its domestic legal system. As will be discussed, although South Korea follows a "monistic" approach whereby treaties are automatically deemed to be part of Korean domestic law, there are a number of legal complexities associated with this approach depending on the type of treaty at issue and how it is concluded. These complexities have been especially evident with respect to recent free trade agreements and in legislation relating to such agreements. The relationship between treaties and domestic legislation is receiving renewed attention and stimulating robust discussion in South Korea. Recent judicial decisions have attempted to clarify outstanding issues, and fine-tune related jurisprudence. The executive and legislative branches are also providing their own views on these issues. Continued effort and active interaction relating to the incorporation and implementation of treaties are likely to be observed in South Korea in the coming years.

I. South Korea's Monistic Approach to Incorporating Treaties

In terms of incorporating treaties into municipal law, Korea adopts a so-called "monistic" approach. The monistic approach is reflected in Article 6, paragraph 1 of the Korean Constitution, which states:

> Treaties duly concluded and promulgated under the Constitution and the generally recognized rules of international law shall have the same effect as the domestic laws of the Republic of Korea.

This provision has been understood to codify monism in a straightforward manner. As such, under the Korean constitutional regime, treaties concluded in accordance with relevant constitutional rules and statutory requirements ("duly concluded and promulgated") and customary international law ("generally recognized rules of international law") have the same legal status as domestic laws of Korea.[1] So, under this provision, both treaties and customary international law are treated as domestic law as well as sources of international law that bind Korea as long as proper consent is given by Korea in due course. With respect to treaties, this provision means that upon entry into effect they are automatically incorporated into the domestic legal system without any particular domestic procedure to "transform" the treaty into a domestic law.

This monism principle has been reflected in the Korean Constitution since its inception in 1948. The Constitution was most recently amended in 1987.[2] The monistic approach was imported from Japan that had been in turn affected by European jurisprudence. In this regard, Article 6, paragraph 1 is the most important provision in the Constitution dealing with international law in the Korean domestic legal system and has been invoked frequently in legal disputes involving treaties and international agreements of various sorts.

It should be noted, however, that the monistic approach does not necessarily mean that implementing legislation is never needed. Despite the monism principle, sometimes it is necessary to adopt implementing legislation in such cases where a treaty itself requires adoption of such legislation or where a treaty contains provisions contrary to existing Korean law, thus making amending legislation mandatory.[3] As a matter of fact, an increasing number of treaties do require attendant or companion domestic legislation for proper implementation. Consequently, the "automaticity" element of monism is not as evident in Korea as it used to be.

[1] The majority view among Korean constitutional law scholars opines that the Korean Constitution itself is not included in the "domestic law" mentioned in this provision. In other words, in terms of hierarchy, the Constitution stays above international law or treaty. In a case where a person was charged by customs officials because of the alleged criminal violation of a tariff rate regulation that had been introduced as a result of the Marrakesh Agreement (WTO Agreements) and where the defendant claimed that it constituted illegal punishment without an applicable statute pronounced in advance, the Korean Constitutional Court rejected the defendant's argument and stated that because the Marrakesh Agreement constitutes part of the Korean law according to Article 6 of the Constitution, it was indeed punishment in accordance with preexisting statutes. *See* Korean Constitutional Court, Case No. 97 Hunba 65 (Nov. 26, 1998).

[2] *See* Korean Culture and Information Service, *Government: Executive, Legislature and Judiciary* (May 9, 2017), *available at* http://www.korea.net/Government/Constitution-and-Government/Executive-Legislature-Judiciary.

[3] For a general overview of monistic and dualistic approaches to international law in domestic courts in the Korean context, *see* Daesoon Kim, *The Relationship between International Law and Municipal Law: Is There Any Change in the Attitude of Municipal Law Towards International Law?*, 35 KOREA INT'L L. REV. 4, 10 (2012) (in Korean).

As regards the phrase "treaties duly concluded and promulgated under the Constitution" in the article, there are other provisions in the Constitution that are relevant to the interpretation and understanding of the wording. By way of example, a proposed treaty must be considered by the State Council (i.e., a cabinet meeting presided over by the president). Before the State Council deliberation, vice ministers and high-ranking officials of various ministries and agencies involved should conduct internal discussions regarding the proposed treaty. The Ministry of Legislation also conducts its own review of the proposed treaty because it is regarded as a type of proposed bill under the operation of Article 6 of the Constitution.

In addition, a group of important treaties require prior consent from the National Assembly. This legislative consent is codified in the Constitution as a consent to presidential ratification of a treaty. It applies only to certain enumerated types of treaties that are considered important for and critical to the national interest.

The president, as the head of the state, possesses the right of ratification. In this respect, Article 73 of the Constitution provides:

> The *President* shall conclude and ratify treaties. (Emphasis added.)

Article 60 of the Constitution in turn sets forth specific types of treaties for which the National Assembly must provide its consent before the president ratifies them in accordance with Article 73. Article 60 states:

> The National Assembly shall have the right to consent to the conclusion and ratification of treaties pertaining to *mutual assistance or mutual security*; treaties concerning *important international organizations*; treaties of *friendship, commerce, and navigation*; treaties pertaining to any *restriction in sovereignty*; *peace treaties*; treaties which will burden the State or people with an *important financial obligation*; or treaties related to *legislative matters*. (Emphasis added.)

As this provision has not been changed in essence since the inception of the first Constitution in 1948, while the Korean society has undergone dramatic changes since then, the scope of the treaties subject to legislative consent has become a rather controversial issue these days. For instance, countries, including Korea, no longer conclude treaties of friendship, commerce, and navigation (FCN treaties). In addition, the terms "legislative matters" or "restriction on sovereignty" are arguably vague, so that they could easily invite debates and controversies each time.

Other than these rather skeletal provisions in the Constitution, Korea does not have a separate statute on the procedure of treaty conclusion and implementation. Over the years, the government has proposed that a separate statute should be adopted to respond to the increasing legal and practical issues, but this has not happened. Political sensitivities and different views of relevant ministries have been major obstacles. It has also been argued that any elaboration of these provisions, in order to be done correctly, should be preceded by constitutional amendment—a daunting and challenging project. Such being the case, at this point treaty conclusion and implementation are largely regulated by the accumulated practice of the government (such as the Ministry of Foreign Affairs) and the National Assembly.[4] At any rate, once this procedure is completed and the treaty at issue is brought into effect, it instantly becomes part of domestic law of Korea as set forth in Article 6, paragraph 1 of the Constitution.

II. Hierarchy of Treaties in the Domestic Legal System

As to the hierarchy of treaties in the domestic legal system, the situation has not been as clear as it should be.[5] Article 6, paragraph 1 only provides that "[treaties] shall have the same effect as the domestic laws." A natural question that follows is what types of domestic law it refers to. In the Korean legal system, the hierarchy of legal norms is as follows: at the highest in echelon stands the Constitution, followed by acts (statutes), presidential decrees (enforcement decrees), prime minister's ordinances, and then ministerial ordinances. The prevailing view among Korean constitutional law scholars is that the term "shall have the same effect as the domestic laws" means that treaties ratified under Article 60 of the Constitution have the same effect as acts or statutes. The main reason behind this view is that both Article 60 treaties and acts/statutes undergo a process of deliberation and approval (consent) by the National Assembly. On the other hand, other types of treaties that do not require consent by the National Assembly for ratification or that do not require ratification in the first place (together, called "treaties in simplified form" in Korea) are considered to have the same legal effect as presidential decrees or enforcement decrees under acts/statutes. The latter category of treaties are negotiated and concluded by the executive branch on its own initiative without the supervision or intervention by the legislature, so on the surface they are quite similar to the adoption of a presidential decree. As for this category of treaties, the Foreign Ministry conducts the negotiation in cooperation with other related ministries, and once completed it is the president who makes the final decision to conclude them. Most of the time, these treaties do not require ratification: in this instance only signature provides Korea's "consent to be bound by the treaties." In the absence of "ratification," therefore, there is no need for "consent" for ratification from the legislature. This process could reduce the time for the conclusion of a treaty by almost a half-year or so. That said, even with respect to this second category of treaties, from time to time there is "consultation" between the executive branch and the legislative branch when there is an important treaty or agreement being negotiated. But such consultation is distinct from supervision or consent by the legislature. In this consultation, the executive branch does not have to seek consent or approval from the legislature.

[4] For the specific procedures of treaty conclusion, *see* Seokwoo Lee & Hee Eun Lee, The Making of International Law in Korea: From Colony to Asian Power 4–6 (2016) (in Korean).

[5] *Id.* at 3–4.

As a matter of fact, this second category of treaties (i.e., those in simplified form) take up the vast majority of treaties that Korea concludes these days. On average, Korea concludes roughly fifty to one hundred treaties each year, and approximately 90 percent of them fall under this category. In other words, relatively few treaties are considered to fall under Article 60 of the Constitution where the legislature's consent for ratification is required. A majority of treaties and agreements in Korea these days are negotiated and concluded by the executive branch (the president) on its own accord and enter into force with "signature" only. It should be noted, however, that this tendency is now changing due to the increasing domestic interest and political sensitivity of recent free trade agreements (FTAs), as discussed below.[6] Needless to say, this issue is entirely about the "domestic" legal effect. Whatever status an international instrument holds within the Korean domestic legal system, the instrument's legal effect under international law vis-à-vis their respective foreign counterparts is unaffected and remains the same.[7] Treaties under the second category have the same effect under international law as those in the first category (those concluded with ratification together with the consent from the National Assembly when necessary), as mandated under Article 27 of the Vienna Convention on the Law of Treaties (VCLT).

Under this understanding of hierarchy, it follows logically that a treaty, whether understood to be at a statutory level or presidential decree level, should be subject to constitutional review by the Constitutional Court of Korea. The Constitutional Court has exclusive jurisdiction over constitutional challenges such as the constitutionality of a statute, impeachment of the president, dissolution of a political party, constitutional petitions filed by individuals, and jurisdictional conflicts between government agencies.[8] To the extent that treaties are regarded as statutes or presidential decrees, they also fall under the constitutionality review jurisdiction of the Constitutional Court. So far, only a few challenges have been lodged at the Constitutional Court regarding the constitutionality of treaties, and none of them has succeeded. If there is a constitutional challenge against a treaty in the future and if the Constitutional Court accepts the claim, the treaty will be declared unconstitutional and invalid within Korea. But the treaty will still remain valid toward the other contracting party under international law unless and until it is terminated in accordance with the relevant provisions of the treaty.

In case of a conflict between a ratified treaty and a statute, or between a nonratified treaty (treaty concluded through a simplified form) and a decree, the resolution of this conflict falls under the jurisdiction of the judiciary (ordinary court). In these disputes, the principles of *lex posterior* and *lex specialis* would apply.

[6] *See* section V *infra*.

[7] *See* Jaemin Lee, *Domestic Law Superiority Provision Contained in Implementing Legislations for Trade Agreements and Article 27 of the Vienna Convention*, 28 Hanyang L. Rev. 66–68 (2011) (in Korean).

[8] *See* Supreme Court of Korea, *The Judiciary: Introduction* (Mar. 2, 2018), *available at* http://eng.scourt.go.kr/eng/judiciary/introduction.jsp.

III. Issues Relating to South Korea's Monistic Approach

While the monistic approach has enabled Korea to incorporate treaties in a relatively simple manner, there are also ensuing questions being raised under the general rubric of monism. Recent cases have propelled Korea to confront these questions more directly.

Increasing Instances of Implementing Legislation

As noted above, through the operation of monism, treaties duly concluded by the Korean government are automatically incorporated into the domestic legal system of Korea.[9] It follows, therefore, that the Korean legislature need not enact legislation to implement a treaty. As such, it was traditionally rare to see Korea adopting implementing legislation upon conclusion of a treaty.

This situation is changing fast, however. This is not because there is any change in the monistic stance but rather because the nature of recent treaties requires attendant legislation and/or amendment. It has become increasingly common these days that a package of legislation is passed before or at the time the Korean National Assembly provides its consent to ratification to a treaty under Article 60 of the Korean Constitution.[10] Thus, on the surface, it looks as if a dualistic approach were followed here. In fact, this phenomenon results from the new reality that treaties have become more detailed and specific, such that Korea is required to adopt or amend existing domestic law to comply with the provisions of treaties. Consequently, these treaties still become part of Korean law instantly and automatically through the operation of monism. Yet at the same time, legislative action is nonetheless undertaken to comply with the terms of the treaties. In other words, these companion statutes are derived from the specific provisions of the treaties demanding such legislative action, and not by the operation of monism or dualism. Nonetheless, it should be noted that the treaties at issue are valid and applicable per se domestically, regardless of companion domestic legislation: they become part of the Korean domestic law instantly and automatically through the operation of monism.

This recent phenomenon is increasingly observed in trade agreements and investment agreements where agreed terms between contracting parties mandate rather massive changes in domestic laws and regulations. FTAs and international investment agreements (IIAs) with major trading and investment partners have presented this new phenomenon most acutely. Legislative changes under these circumstances have also become politically sensitive topics, rendering the treaty conclusion process more difficult and time-consuming than before. Legislative changes in the aftermath of treaty

[9] *See* Korean Constitution, art. 6, para. 1. [10] *Id.*

conclusion have not historically been a common feature in Korean politics, and as a result these new changes could easily incite arguments of sovereign infringement and stoke political discussion on a particular treaty.

Self-Executing vs. Non-Self-Executing Treaties

While Korea adopts a rather clear-cut monist approach, this does not necessarily mean that all treaties are "self-executing" in Korea. Determining whether a treaty is self-executing or non-self-executing requires an inquiry into the specific content of the treaty in question. If it is determined that the intention of the drafters of a certain treaty is to directly apply the treaty at issue to the contracting parties as it stands, the treaty is then considered self-executing and will apply to Korean government agencies and entities directly. Many of the treaties that Korea concludes are in fact of this nature. If, on the other hand, a treaty is not intended for direct application but instead anticipates application through implementing legislation, it is considered non-self-executing. Some treaties that Korea concludes have this nature.

In other words, even if a treaty is incorporated into Korean law based on Article 6 of the Constitution (i.e., monism), when the treaty itself is considered to be non-self-executing, further action or legislation by Korea would still be needed. Depending on the specific terms and wording of the treaty at issue, the absence or lack of specific action or legislation may or may not constitute a violation of the treaty. This issue becomes important in a domestic court proceeding where a presiding judge in a given case must determine whether the treaty is directly applicable as it currently stands. The judge in the domestic court proceeding may decide, upon close inspection of the contents of the treaty and the intention of contracting parties, that the treaty may not be directly applicable to specific entities and agencies on its own, although it is still legally valid and binding on Korea as a state.

By way of example, almost all trade agreements and investment agreements that Korea has concluded are considered self-executing. At the same time, recent FTAs increasingly include provisions that envision adoption of, and implementation through, legislation. This obligation to adopt implementing legislation, however, does not necessarily change the status of these agreements as self-executing ones. The obligation to undertake legislative changes is a task mandated by a treaty, the failure of which would lead to violation of the treaty, whereas the nature of self-execution means that the treaty at issue can be directly applicable as it presently stands. In other words, they are two different questions in Korean treaty practice.

Private-Party Claims under Treaties

Yet another issue is whether an individual (natural or legal person) can invoke a treaty before a Korean court to make his or her claim. As a treaty is automatically incorporated into Korean domestic law, disputing parties are often tempted and even compelled to refer to a treaty provision as part of their reasoning and argument. This particular issue is also separate from the adoption of monism. Again, the issue is not about whether a particular treaty is valid for and binding on Korea. The answer to that question is always in the affirmative, because of the operation of the monism in Article 6. Rather, the question here is whether the particular treaty permits an individual to invoke a treaty provision before a Korean court. In other words, this issue concerns whether the treaty in question provides "standing" to individuals in Korean courts. This question also entails a treaty-specific inquiry. Determinative factors include the intention of the contracting parties of the treaty in question and the relevant wording of the treaty as interpreted in accordance with Article 31 of the VCLT.

If a treaty is interpreted to provide individuals with the right to refer to the provisions of the treaty before domestic courts when there is an alleged violation, those individuals are then able to refer to them in their respective domestic legal proceedings, either in lieu of or in addition to relevant domestic statutes. In contrast, if a treaty is phrased or interpreted to provide rights and obligations only to the governments of contracting parties, then natural persons or corporations are not allowed to invoke the provisions of the treaty before a domestic court. Rather, they would have to invoke comparable provisions of domestic statutes that have been adopted to implement the treaty or that are otherwise relevant to the issue.

As it is sometimes difficult to ascertain the intent of treaty drafters, a more recent practice that is growing in popularity in Korea is to stipulate such intent in treaty texts themselves to preempt any future controversy on this point. For instance, recent FTAs of Korea contain stand-alone provisions that explicitly state that these agreements are not intended to provide legal rights to individuals and corporations affected by these FTAs. It is the contracting parties, these agreements state, that have the rights and obligations under these FTAs.

IV. Recent Court Cases

As the number of treaties that Korea concludes increases, foreign attention is also being directed to how Korean judges incorporate and apply treaties when they are brought before Korean courts. Recently, the Korean Supreme Court rendered key judgments in this respect, which confirmed or established that: (1) treaties that have been ratified with approval from the National Assembly possess the same status as statutes in Korea, and (2) unless explicitly stipulated, treaties themselves do not entitle private individuals and entities to refer to the provisions of trade agreements as a direct cause of action in Korean courts. These recent decisions are largely related to the interpretation and application of FTAs that have become increasingly sensitive in Korea.

Monism in the Constitutional Structure

One of the leading cases that clarify the monistic approach of Korea involves World Trade Organization (WTO) Agreements. In a case where a local government of Korea filed a statutory violation claim against its counterpart local legislative assembly when the latter had enacted an ordinance arguably inconsistent with the WTO Agreements, the Korean Supreme Court applied the General Agreement on Tariffs and Trade 1994 (GATT 1994) and found the ordinance in violation of GATT 1994 and the Agreement on Government Procurement (GPA).[11] The court clarified that GATT 1994 and the GPA have been transformed into domestic statutes by the monism in Article 6 of the Constitution, and that any local assembly ordinance in violation of these agreements should be struck down.

Furthermore, in several cases involving taxation of international corporations and interpretation of tax treaties, the Korean Supreme Court has found that: (1) international treaties have the same effect as domestic law under Article 6 of the Constitution, and (2) the principle of "substantial taxation" as defined under the Framework Act on National Taxes is equally applicable in the interpretation of these treaties, unless the treaties contain specific provisions barring application of this principle.[12] This pronouncement again shows that the court regards treaties as part of domestic law, and also that the legal status of these treaties is considered comparable to a statute adopted by the National Assembly.

Likewise, the Korean Constitutional Court has consistently taken a similar position on the legal status of treaties. For instance, a defendant of a criminal case claimed that the punishment imposed on him because of his violation of customs law was unconstitutional because his punishment was made possible due to the change in tariff rates, which in turn was caused by Korea's accession to the WTO Agreements in 1995. He then claimed that the accession to the international organization did not constitute pronouncement of the criminal penalty provision in advance in accordance with the rule of *nullum crimen sine lege*. The Constitutional Court rejected the claimant's constitutional claim, reasoning that the Marrakesh Agreement (establishing the WTO) constitutes part of Korean law, such that criminal punishment for a customs law violation based on the Marrakesh Agreement should still count as punishment based on prior law, satisfying the criminal law principle.[13]

Similarly, in a case involving the constitutionality of the Assembly and Demonstration Act's restriction on public demonstrations near diplomatic missions in Seoul, the Constitutional Court found that the 1961 Vienna Convention on Diplomatic Relations,

[11] *See* Supreme Court of Korea, Compatibility of Ordinance of Jeollabukdo-province with GATT 1994, Case No. 2004 Chu 10 (Sept. 9, 2005).

[12] *See*, e.g., Supreme Court of Korea, Case No. 2010 Du 11948 (Apr. 26, 2012); Supreme Court of Korea, Case No. 2015 Du 55134 (July 11, 2017); and Supreme Court of Korea, Case No. 2017 Du 59253 (Dec. 28, 2017).

[13] *See* Korean Constitutional Court, *supra* note 1.

to which Korea is a party and which requires contracting parties to take protective measures for diplomatic missions within their jurisdiction, is still part of the Korean Law because of Article 6, paragraph 1 of the Constitution.[14]

In accordance with the views of the Supreme Court and the Constitutional Court, the Seoul Administrative Court, in its judgment of December 2007,[15] held that an antidumping duty determination of the Korea Trade Commission (KTC) was appropriate because it was consistent with the Customs Act, the Enforcement Decree of the Customs Act, and the WTO Antidumping Agreement. Thus, the court explicitly referred to the Antidumping Agreement as a legal basis for judicial review of an antidumping duty imposition determination. The same court previously took the same position in September 2005 regarding judicial review of another antidumping determination of the KTC.[16]

Ambiguities Involving Disposal of Individual Claims

Recently, a new complexity has arisen in this regard. The Korean Supreme Court opined in a January 2009 judgment that the WTO Agreements may *not* directly apply to the review by the Korean court of an agency determination, because the agreements were not supposed to confer rights on individual plaintiffs.[17] Therefore, according to the court, these treaties can directly apply to agency-to-agency disputes, but not to disputes involving claims of individuals. The precise relationship of this judgment to monism and to issues relating to private rights was not entirely clear.

A Supreme Court decision from November 2015 again underscored the rather fluid nature of the jurisprudence here. The case was brought by owners of large retailers operating in Seoul, called Super-Super Markets (SSMs), subject to a biweekly mandatory close-down requirement of the local governments at issue (the "measure").[18] Under the requirement, these stipulated SSMs are ordered to close their shops twice a month. The measure at issue stemmed from the Act on the Development of Distribution Service Business of 2013 (the Act), and its enforcement decree (Enforcement Decree of the Act on the Development of Distribution Service Business (the Enforcement Decree)). The Act and the Enforcement Decree provide a general mandate concerning the protection of small retailers, while leaving specific regulatory options to the discretion of heads of respective local governments.

[14] *See* Korean Constitutional Court, Case No. 2010 Hunma 111 (Oct. 28, 2010).

[15] *See* Seoul Administrative Court, Case No. 2006 Guhab 29782 (Dec. 24, 2007).

[16] *See* Seoul Administrative Court, Case No. 2005 Guhab 5911 (Sept. 1, 2005).

[17] *See id.*

[18] *See* Supreme Court of Korea, Case Concerning Revocation of Limitation of Operating Hours for Certain Retailers, Case No. 2015 Du 295, at 18 (Nov. 10, 2015), *available at* http://www.scourt.go.kr/supreme/news/NewsViewAction2.work?currentPage=5&searchWord=&searchOption=&seqnum=5035&gubun=4 (in Korean).

The plaintiff SSMs argued that the ordinances of the local governments pronounced under the Act and the Enforcement Decree violated Korean Administrative Law principles (i.e., abuse of discretion and disproportionate regulation), the WTO's General Agreement on Trade in Services (GATS), and the Free Trade Agreement between Republic of Korea and the European Union (Korea–EU FTA) (i.e., regulation not authorized in the schedules of specific commitments applicable to services trade).[19] As the measure attempts to regulate retail distribution service providers operating in the Korean market, and as one of the plaintiffs is owned by an EU corporation (called Home Plus, a joint venture between Tesco and Samsung), the dispute involved the schedules of specific commitments of the GATS and the Korea–EU FTA.

The local governments, as the defendants, were various district offices of the Seoul Metropolitan City Government. The defendants issued respective ordinances following the enactment of the Act and the Enforcement Decree in 2013. The Act and the Enforcement Decree were designed to maintain "good order in the distribution service industry," "health rights of employees working in the distributions service industry," and "the co-prosperity of large corporations and Small and Medium Enterprises ('SMEs')," among other things.[20] In particular, the Act authorizes the heads of respective local governments to impose a close-down requirement not exceeding twice a month.[21] The local governments in turn adopted their respective ordinances mandating two close-downs per month for SSMs operating within their jurisdiction.

In a nutshell, the objective of the Act, the Enforcement Decree, and the ordinances is to protect small retailers who stand to lose sales due to the penetration and expansion of large retail shops, both Korean and foreign. Thus, the legal scheme aims to protect the interest of the SMEs in the retailing industry from fierce competition caused by large retailers. It has been argued that the new scheme will ensure even distribution of wealth in the society in general. Arguably, no one would challenge the noble cause of equality in society, but the issue remained whether such a measure is compatible with Korean Administrative Law and international agreements that Korea has concluded.

In the proceeding of the Seoul Appeals Court, the plaintiffs prevailed: the court decided that the ordinances of the local governments constitute a violation of Korean Administrative Law principles because they constitute abuse of discretion on the part of the agency and place a disproportionate burden on certain corporations in the industry. In addition, the court also found that the measure constituted a violation of the GATS and the Korea–EU FTA by deviating from the schedules of specific commitments that Korea has submitted.

In its decision of November 10, 2015, however, the Supreme Court reversed the decision of the Seoul Appeals Court on both counts. In the decision, the Supreme Court held that the challenged ordinances are within the discretion of the local governments as empowered by the Act and the Enforcement Decree,[22] and that they manage to

[19] *See id.* at 3–5, 6, 8.

[20] *See* Act on the Development of Distribution Service Business of 2013, art. 12-2.

[21] *See id.*

[22] *See* Supreme Court of Korea, *supra* note 18, at 14–15.

maintain a balance between the conflicting interests of those regulated and that of the society at large.[23] Thus, the Supreme Court found the ordinances to be compatible with the principle of "reasonable regulation" in administrative law.

With respect to the issue of a possible violation of international trade agreements, the Supreme Court basically held that these trade agreements create rights and obligations *only* for the contracting parties (i.e., governments and state entities of the contracting parties).[24] Consequently, the plaintiffs, as corporations, do not possess the right to bring a legal action before the Korean domestic court based on the trade agreements at issue, according to the court's decision.[25] The court thus dismissed the claim of the plaintiffs to the extent that it referred to trade agreements, without deciding whether or not the said measure constituted a violation of schedules of specific commitments. Thus, in a sense, in this high-profile dispute attracting attention from the European Union and the United States, the Supreme Court managed to avoid evaluating the measures from the perspective of trade agreement obligations.

These recent judgments arguably create confusion in terms of treaty incorporation and implementation. Criticism can be raised that these judgments conflated the concept of monism on the one hand and direct applicability to individuals (standing) on the other hand. In the two disputes above, the plaintiffs were arguably not attempting to exercise their rights under the trade agreements, a situation that the courts describe in their judgments. Rather, it seems that the plaintiffs were mentioning the Antidumping Agreement, GATS, and the Korea–EU FTA simply in an effort to point out that the domestic legislation and enforcement decrees should be interpreted in a way that is consistent with obligations under international agreements. If that is the case, it may not be appropriate to dismiss these treaties simply because the plaintiffs were alluding to or relying upon them in their domestic claims. In both cases, the plaintiffs were also invoking domestic statutes separately.

According to the rationale of the courts, only the governmental agencies can cite Korea's trade agreements in domestic court proceedings, unless a foreign government claims a violation of trade agreements in Korean courts. Given the existence of the WTO and FTA dispute settlement proceedings, this would be highly unrealistic. In other words, the Korean court's interpretation of the nature of the obligation of trade agreements of Korea would run the risk of rendering trade agreements virtually unreachable or unchallengeable by interested parties. This understanding would not dovetail with the provision of the Korean Constitution that stipulates "treaties concluded and promulgated according to the Constitution shall possess the same legal effect as domestic law."[26] As a matter of fact, regardless of the issue of "standing," the issue raised by the plaintiffs in these disputes was whether the measure at issue could be found to be compatible with major trade agreements. Arguably, the courts are obligated to review the issue and render judgments. Other examples may shed light on this issue.

[23] *See id.* at 15–17.
[24] *See id.* at 17.
[25] *Id.*
[26] *See* Korean Constitution, *supra* note 9.

V. New Challenges in Treaty Conclusion and Implementation

While Korea tries to clarify and develop its jurisprudence on treaty conclusion and implementation, new challenges are arising that are likely to make the situation even more complicated.

Dissecting and Spreading of Treaty Obligations

One question being raised is how to address a situation where obligations arising from a treaty are compartmentalized, dissected, and spread over different categories of domestic laws and regulations. Obligations from the same treaty are inserted into different instruments within the hierarchy of the domestic legal system. What usually happens in Korea is that core elements (provisions) of a treaty are included in domestic statutes, either existing or newly adopted, and elements or provisions of an implementing nature considered less important are included in enforcement decrees or sometimes enforcement regulations that are inferior to statutes in the domestic echelon. The decision is usually made by an agency or ministry at issue, sometimes in consultation with the National Assembly. There is no clear constitutional basis for this consultation. This would basically mean that obligations from the same treaty would have different legal status domestically, depending upon where they ended up through domestic implementation proceedings and consultation.

While this domestic grouping would not change the quantity and quality of treaty obligations for Korea internationally,[27] the governmental agencies would often face confusion in domestic implementation of these treaties. Also, if treaties are not found to be self-executing or to permit individual claims, the presiding judge will find governing law only from domestic laws and domestic regulations on point. In this case, whether a particular provision is codified in a statute or an enforcement decree would matter significantly. Interested parties and individuals may be subject to domestic laws and regulations that are not entirely consistent with the treaties at issue. In addition, having treaty obligations in lower ranked enforcement decrees or regulations would make it more difficult for government agencies to comply with the treaties when conflicting statutes exist or emerge. This phenomenon is now raising a new challenge for the Korean government when it comes to treaty negotiation, conclusion, and implementation.

[27] *See* Vienna Convention on the Law of Treaties, art. 27.

FTA Implementation Act and Increasing Legislative Intervention

The recent treaty law development and controversies in Korea have been mainly triggered by domestic reaction toward a series of major FTAs that Korea has concluded. The sheer workload entailed in the course of negotiating, concluding, and implementing the FTAs has increased substantially. Concurrently, domestic controversies surrounding these FTAs have intensified. These controversies have led to the enactment of a new legislative scheme to address the practice of treaty negotiation, conclusion, and implementation.[28] This new legislation aims to regulate the "entire" process of concluding an FTA.[29] The concerns and opposition of the executive branch were brushed off and the need for more heightened legislative oversight over the FTAs has prevailed.

This legislative effort led to the enactment of the Act on Governing Procedures of Conclusion and Implementation of Trade Agreements (FTA Implementation Act, or Act). This Act was passed by the National Assembly on December 30, 2011[30] and went into effect on July 18, 2012, after the grace period of roughly six months. The Act applies to all sorts of trade agreements including FTAs in the entire segments of the life cycle of trade agreements, from negotiation to implementation.[31] This legislation deviates from the existing treaty conclusion practice so much that its compatibility with the relevant provisions of the Constitution has been heavily debated. In any event, the introduction of the FTA Implementation Act has had a significant impact on the negotiation, conclusion, and implementation of the FTAs and potentially other treaties as well.

The FTA Implementation Act is the first attempt of this kind in Korea, and it is difficult to find comparable legislation in other countries. There are domestic statutes in Korea and other countries addressing the implementation of trade agreements, but few of them aim to provide for tight legislative monitoring and supervision from the negotiation and continuing for a decade after enforcement. According to the scheme of the statute, a broadly defined "trade agreement" is only to be concluded and implemented with the consultation of the National Assembly. More than anything else, it is not clear whether such direct and longstanding intervention by the legislature is practically feasible. In particular, the new statute even requires the government to take remedial action when it becomes apparent that Korea's national interest is not adequately guaranteed through the implementation of a trade agreement.[32] If a remedial action is indeed taken under this provision in the future, it may even raise the legal question of compliance with an FTA at issue or with the WTO Agreements.[33]

[28] *See* Act on Governing Procedures of Conclusion and Implementation of Trade Agreements, at art. 1 (Objective).

[29] *See id.*, arts. 7–8.

[30] *See* Jaechul Lee, *Interview with the New Trade Minister, Taeho Bark*, MAEIL BUSINESS NEWSPAPER (Jan. 4, 2012), *available at* http://news.mk.co.kr/newsRead.php?year=2012&no=9278 (in Korean).

[31] *See supra* note 28, arts. 5–15.

[32] *See supra* note 28, arts. 17, 20.

[33] *See*, e.g., Agreement Establishing the World Trade Organization, art. XVI, para. 4.

Among many traits, two aspects stand out with respect to the new legislation. One of the fundamental traits of the Act is the participation of the National Assembly in virtually all procedural stages, such as negotiation, conclusion, and implementation of trade agreements.[34] The objective of the legislation is provided in Article 1 of the Act as follows:

> Article 1 (Objective) – This Act aims to achieve, by stipulating necessary details concerning the conclusion and implementation process of trade agreements, improvement of transparency in the conclusion process of trade agreements by ensuring understanding and participation of the general public, pursuit of effective trade negotiation, and contribution to the development of the sound national economy by guaranteeing the rights and interest of Korea in terms of implementation of trade agreements.[35]

The three key words of the Act can be summarized as "transparency," "participation," and "national economic interest." The first two terms stand for wider participation of the general public in the treaty negotiation process, and the third term signifies the focus on political and economic consideration of Korea's long-term interest with respect to particular trade agreements at issue. All of these items thus stand to require more direct and broader participation of the National Assembly. Not surprisingly, this objective constitutes a key underpinning of the Act.

The second trait is that the definition of a "trade agreement" itself is unclear. Article 2 of the Act provides:

> Article 2 (Definition) – Definitions of the terms used in this Act are as follows:
>
> 1. A "trade agreement" means a treaty, as set forth below, which Korea concludes with other countries or by which Korea accedes to international organizations such as the World Trade Organization or other economic unions, and which is subject to the consent of the National Assembly for ratification in accordance with Article 60, paragraph 1 of the Korean Constitution.
>
> A. A treaty whose objective is to open up domestic market comprehensively thorough conclusion at the level of international organizations such as the World Trade Organization.
>
> B. A treaty concluded at the regional or bilateral levels, whose objective is to open up domestic market comprehensively.
>
> C. Other treaties that stand to cause a significant impact on the national economy through the market opening in various sectors of economy.[36]
>
> 2. "Trade negotiation" is negotiation that Korea conducts with other countries in order to conclude trade agreements.

[34] *See* the flow of measures in sequence required under the FTA Implementation Act as stipulated in Articles 5–15 of the Act.

[35] This English translation has been prepared by the author. An official translation of the Act does not exist as of this writing.

[36] This English translation has been prepared by the author. An official translation of the Act does not exist as of this writing.

As can be seen from the above article, the Act is supposed to apply to a "trade agreement," but the definition of the term is arguably not as clear as it should be. Therefore, the door is open to the coverage of a variety of agreements by the Act. A typical FTA is an easy example, and it certainly falls under the definition of the trade agreement. What is less clear is what kind of "trade agreements" other than FTAs are covered by the Act. Likewise, what kind of amendments of existing trade agreements the Act covers is not clear. The uncertainty becomes greater in cases where the original agreements were concluded before the effective date of the Act, which is July 18, 2013.

With the unclear definition of trade agreements, in principle, *any* agreement with a comprehensive market opening effect, which is also subject to the National Assembly's consent for ratification under Article 60, paragraph 1 of the Korean Constitution, is to be covered by the Act.[37] At the same time, *any* agreement that may significantly affect the national economy, which is subject to the National Assembly's consent for ratification under Article 60, paragraph 1 is also covered by the Act. However, the qualifiers on the nature of eligible agreements, such as "comprehensive market opening" or "national economy," are potentially vague and amorphous. Notably, there are no definitions for these two key terms in the statute. A range of different situations could be found to satisfy these requirements. Consequently, not only FTAs or WTO Agreements, as classic trade agreements, but also other treaties and agreements with trade elements could still be regarded as "trade agreements" covered by the Act.[38]

The combination of these two traits means that the Korean National Assembly is now authorized to intervene in the negotiation, conclusion, and implementation of a wide range of trade-related agreements of Korea. FTAs are the main targets of the Act, but other forms of agreements are also within the scope. Motivated by this development, similar legislative effort seems to seep into treaties in other sectors as well. The National Assembly thus either reviews, approves, or discusses issues relating to broadly defined "trade agreements" throughout the entire segments of trade negotiation procedures.[39] In fact, the monitoring continues as late as ten years after the effective date of a covered trade agreement.[40]

Of course, legislative participation itself is not new. As noted above, under the Korean Constitution, the National Assembly's participation in treaty matters is guaranteed in the form of legislative consent to ratification with respect to certain key treaties.[41] What is noteworthy about the FTA Implementation Act is the scope of such participation by the National Assembly. While the constitution only envisages the National Assembly providing "consent to ratification" of certain treaties, the scheme of the Act covers proceedings both prior to and after such ratification procedures.

[37] *See supra* note 28, art. 2.

[38] For instance, the Trade in Services Agreement (TISA), a plurilateral agreement on trade in services currently being negotiated by twenty-two states outside the scope of the WTO Agreements' framework, may also be found to be a "trade agreement" within the meaning of the Act.

[39] *See supra note* 28, arts. 6, 10, 12, 13, 15.

[40] *See id.* art. 15.

[41] *See* Korean Constitution, *supra* note 9.

Consequently, the newly proposed participation of the National Assembly far exceeds the boundaries of legislative participation prescribed by the Constitution. Setting domestic constitutional issues attendant to the new statutory scheme aside, such attempt for intensive participation of the National Assembly in treaty matters is a new challenge to the government.

It is not clear whether the government can report all the issues being discussed on the negotiating table to the National Assembly or whether the National Assembly is in the position of approving or rejecting specific issues on the table. It is no secret that many issues on the trade agreement negotiation tables are technical and complex, which would render legislative intervention either impractical or unfeasible. It is one thing that legislative supervision is appropriate in a democratic state, but quite another that the legislative body itself participates in the negotiation. This model departs from the previous structure in Korea and those of many other countries wherein the executive branch makes key decisions for a trade agreement.

In short, for better or worse, the National Assembly has become a key decision maker under the new statutory scheme of Korea when it comes to trade agreement negotiations and conclusions.[42] In particular, it should be noted that FTAs are viewed as an ongoing process even after their conclusion.[43] Constant surveillance has thus become one of the key components of FTA implementation.[44] The National Assembly is supposed to stay vigilant to the effects of FTAs on domestic industries in the practice of postconclusion monitoring. Furthermore, the National Assembly has the authority to request that the government take remedial action vis-à-vis the trading partner, once it determines the difficulties in domestic industries resulting from the conclusion of an FTA.[45] All in all, this new legislation of 2011 heralds a changing domestic landscape in terms of treaty negotiation, conclusion, and implementation. Its compatibility with the provisions in the Constitution and prior treaty practice of Korea is still not clear. It is hoped that the accumulation of more practice and experience regarding this unique statute will be able to provide clarification.

VI. Conclusion

Korea has been a faithful follower of the monistic approach when it comes to incorporation of treaties into the domestic legal system. Its Constitution stipulates this principle in a clear manner. This monistic approach has been able to address, rather successfully, various legal issues and disputes over the years. Since its inception in 1948, the Constitution has operated as an efficient legal tool for Korea to implement its obligation under treaties and agreements. Within the monistic stance, Korea has also distinguished between self-executing and non-self-executing treaties, depending on

[42] *See supra* note 28, arts. 6, 10, 12, 13, 15. [43] *See id.*, art. 15. [44] *See id.*

[45] *See id.*, arts. 17, 20.

their contents and the intentions of the parties. The latter category requires specific implementing legislation to fulfill treaty obligations. Likewise, some treaties in Korea are considered to provide legal standing to natural persons or corporations before Korean courts, while others are not. Contents of the treaties and intention of drafters are the key to the final decision.

Since early 2000s, however, new questions and challenges have been presented. This development is a reflection of the increase in the number of treaties and the advent of politically sensitive and economically important treaties, thereby inviting acute domestic debates and controversies. The rise and spread of democracy has also played an important role in having the general public and scholars inspect the treaty conclusion system from a different angle. Under these circumstances, questions have been raised in various legal disputes involving specific treaties and entities as to the relationship among monism, self-executing and non-self-executing treaties, and standing of individuals. These three issues are closely related but address different aspects of treaty conclusion and implementation. Up until now, the Korean judiciary has sometimes conflated the three and pronounced ambiguous and conflicting judgments. Individual decisions and judgments may have reached the correct outcome for respective disputes under the circumstances. But they have apparently failed to view these issues from a structural point of view, as reflected in the Constitution and in accordance with Korea's treaty practice and relevant international law. Fortunately, judicial efforts to clarify and fine-tune the jurisprudence on treaty conclusion and implementation are increasingly visible. In a larger perspective, the judiciary's effort to elaborate its jurisprudence on foreign relations law in general is also being observed. This is a reflection of the new reality: as Korea's economic influence has increased by becoming the world's seventh largest trading nation, foreign governments and corporations seem to watch the Korean legal system and judgments with heightened interest and scrutiny.

CHAPTER 14

MAKING TREATIES AND OTHER INTERNATIONAL AGREEMENTS

The European Union

MARISE CREMONA

THIS chapter examines EU foreign relations law concerning the making of treaties and other international agreements. It will first outline the sources of EU law on treaty-making and the legal and constitutional context in which EU treaty-making takes place before turning to the law relating to the process of treaty negotiation and to the signature, provisional application, and conclusion of treaties. Because the focus is on treaty-making, the chapter will not discuss the law relating to decision-making within bodies established by treaty,[1] nor will it discuss the suspension or denunciation of treaties. For reasons of space, the chapter will concentrate on the general law on EU treaty-making and will not discuss the sector-specific rules that exist for agreements in the field of Economic and Monetary Union, or Euratom.

I. SOURCES OF EU LAW ON TREATY-MAKING

The focus of this book is on foreign relations law in the sense of domestic rather than international law.[2] For the European Union, "domestic" law includes the EU Treaties:

[1] On the participation of the European Union in international organizations, *see* Joris Larik, *Regional Organizations' Relations with International Institutions: The EU and ASEAN Compared*, ch. 25 in this volume.

[2] *See* Curtis A. Bradley, *What Is Foreign Relations Law?*, ch. 1 in this volume.

the Treaty on European Union (TEU), the Treaty on the Functioning of the European Union (TFEU), and the Euratom Treaty, which together with their protocols and the Charter on Fundamental Rights are known as EU primary law. Domestic EU law also includes secondary legislation made under the Treaties, but although such law may be relevant to the making of treaties (e.g., the adoption of a Council decision authorizing the signature of a treaty), the rules governing treaty-making are almost entirely found in primary law.

EU law on treaty-making includes the grant of express powers in specific policy fields, together with procedural rules for negotiating and concluding treaties that establish the roles of the institutional actors. EU law also includes more general constitutional rules and principles that govern and guide the implementation of the provisions on treaty-making—such as, for example, the duty of "mutual sincere cooperation" imposed on the institutions by Article 13(2) of the TFEU. All these rules are subject to the interpretation of the European Court of Justice, which has played an important role in developing EU law on treaty-making. In fact, the law as currently expressed in the EU Treaties contains a number of provisions (the duty of cooperation imposed on the institutions being one) that originated with judgments of the Court of Justice.[3] International law, although not the focus of this contribution, does affect EU law on treaty-making. The European Union is not a party to the Vienna Convention on the Law of Treaties of 1969, but, insofar as the Convention codifies customary law, the Court has held its rules to be applicable also to the European Union and uses them to interpret EU treaties with third countries.[4]

These are the central legal sources, but two other sources of norms that help to determine treaty-making procedures for the European Union should also be taken into account. Neither source may alter the roles of the institutions as laid down in the primary law, but they do establish norms of practice and may create legal effects. First is the inter-institutional agreement between the Commission and the European Parliament of 2010, which puts some flesh on the bones of the basic procedural rules contained in the EU Treaties.[5] Such agreements, now expressly sanctioned by the EU Treaties,[6] are one way of giving effect to the duty of inter-institutional cooperation.[7] According to its preamble, the 2010 agreement "does not affect the powers and prerogatives of Parliament, the Commission or any other institution or organ of the Union, but seeks to ensure that those powers and prerogatives are exercised as effectively and transparently as possible." Despite this assurance, doubts were

[3] C-65/93 European Parliament v. Council, EU:C:1995:91, para. 23.

[4] C-162/96 *Racke*, EU:C:1998:293, para. 45; C-386/08 *Brita*, EU:C:2010:91, para. 42; Opinion 2/15, EU:C:2017:376, para. 161.

[5] Framework Agreement on relations between the European Parliament and the European Commission OJ 2010 L304/47, paras. 23–29 and Annex III.

[6] Art. 295 TFEU.

[7] C-25/94 Commission v. Council, EU:C:1996:114, para. 49.

expressed by the Council over its compatibility with the Treaties.[8] The agreement has not been directly assessed by the Court but some of the questions raised by the Council—for example those concerning the provision to the European Parliament of information on international negotiations—have since arisen indirectly in litigation.

The second source of norms are administrative procedures to which the EU institutions commit themselves. An example particularly relevant to EU treaty-making is the commitment to conduct sustainability and human rights impact assessments before concluding trade agreements.[9] While nonbinding, these procedural commitments may form the basis of a finding of maladministration by the European Ombudsman.[10]

II. The Constitutional Background

In Opinion 2/13, the Court of Justice referred to the "essential characteristics of EU law [which] have given rise to a structured network of principles, rules and mutually interdependent legal relations linking the EU and its Member States, and its Member States with each other."[11] In order to understand EU law on treaty-making, we need to briefly highlight the "essential characteristics" of the European Union's constitutional structure, in particular the principle of conferral of powers and the institutional framework.

Conferral of Powers

The European Union's treaty-making powers are governed by the principle of conferral: they must find their basis in the EU Treaties either expressly or impliedly.[12] Nevertheless, the European Union's treaty-making powers are now so extensive that it is hard to imagine a treaty that would fall outside them. On only two occasions has the European Court of Justice had to declare that an international treaty fell outside European Community (EC) or EU competence. The first was when it held that the European Community lacked competence to accede to the European Convention

[8] Opinion of the Council legal service, 18 October 2010, Council doc. 15018/10; Council statement of 21 October 2010, Council doc. 15172/10, p.17.

[9] EU Strategic Framework and Action Plan on Human Rights and Democracy, 25 June 2012, Council doc. 11855/12, point I/1.

[10] Art. 228 TFEU and Art. 43 of the Charter of Fundamental Rights. Decision of the European Ombudsman on the European Commission's failure to carry out a prior human rights impact assessment of the EU–Vietnam free trade agreement, case 1409/2014/MHZ, 26 February 2016.

[11] Opinion 2/13, EU:C:2014:2454, para. 167.

[12] Art. 5(1) and (2) TEU; Opinion 2/94, EU:C:1996:140, paras. 24–25.

on Human Rights,[13] a deficit now remedied by Article 6 TEU.[14] The second concerned the treaty with the United States on the collection of airline passenger name records, and related to the now abolished separation—including separation of treaty-making capacity—between the European Community and European Union.[15]

The power-conferring provisions in the Treaties are both substantive and procedural, and every international agreement therefore requires a substantive and a procedural legal basis in the EU Treaties. The European Union has extensive express treaty-making powers, concerning: trade and investment; development cooperation; association agreements (which can encompass all fields covered by the EU Treaties[16]); general economic, financial, and technical cooperation with third countries; the common foreign and security policy (CFSP). Although the latter is potentially very broad, covering "all areas of foreign policy and all questions relating to the Union's security,"[17] in practice it is currently used mainly to cover agreements relating to specific CFSP actions, such as status of forces agreements with third countries hosting EU military missions, or agreements on the participation of third countries in EU military and civilian missions. However it is now sometimes also used to cover the "political" dimension of broader association or partnership agreements.

In addition to these general external powers, some sectoral provisions of the Treaties explicitly include treaty-making powers.[18] Others do not, and yet external powers may be implied. Since the landmark decision in *Commission v. Council* (AETR),[19] the derivation of treaty-making powers from an internal competence has been one of the defining features of EU foreign relations law. Despite the growth of express external powers in successive EU Treaty revisions, implied powers are still important in some sectoral fields, notably transport, energy, migration, private international law, and criminal justice.

The principle of conferral, as well as defining the substantive scope of EU competence, governs the degree to which the European Union replaces its member states as an international actor.[20] The member states remain sovereign subjects of international law, but as a matter of EU constitutional law, EU treaty-making powers may be exclusive (thereby precluding the member states from acting) as well as shared. Exclusive EU competence may be established by the EU Treaties for a whole policy

[13] Opinion 2/94, EU:C:1996:140.

[14] In Opinion 2/13, EU:C:2014:2454, the Court found that a proposed treaty of accession to the European Convention on Human Rights was incompatible with the EU Treaties, but not on the ground of lack of competence.

[15] Joined Cases C-317/04 and C-318/04 European Parliament v. Council and Commission, EU: C:2006:346. *See* Opinion 1/15, EU:C:2017:592.

[16] Case 12/86 *Demirel*, EU:C:1987:400.

[17] Art. 24 TEU.

[18] E.g., Art. 191(4) TFEU, on environmental protection.

[19] Case 22/70 Commission v. Council, EU:C:1971:32. *See* Art. 216(1) TFEU.

[20] *See* Robert Schütze, *Foreign Affairs Federalism in the European Union*, ch. 19 in this volume.

field, such as trade,[21] or may arise case-by-case, most commonly as a result of internal legislative action.[22]

Any discussion of the European Union's treaty-making powers is therefore likely to center not on whether the European Union possesses the necessary competence but rather on the choice of legal basis, or the implications of the exercise of the European Union's powers on the member states. Legal basis, as the Court of Justice has often remarked, has a constitutional significance.[23] It may affect decision-making procedures and determine whether the European Union's competence is exclusive or shared with the member states. Sometimes the appropriate legal basis is clear from the start, but sometimes it will be left open during the negotiation stage and clarified at the time when the Commission submits the proposal for a decision to sign a treaty. The Court of Justice's position on choice of legal basis may be summarized briefly as follows:

— Choice of legal basis should be based on objective factors amenable to judicial review, and is not simply a matter of institutional choice.
— The relevant factors are the aim or purpose, and the content of the agreement. The Court will look at the text of the agreement to determine these, and will focus on the agreement itself rather than the putative aims of the European Union in concluding the agreement.
— Where possible, a single legal basis should be chosen that represents the main or predominant purpose of the agreement. Subsidiary or incidental purposes or content do not need to be reflected in a separate legal basis.
— A multiple legal basis for an agreement is thus unusual; it is necessary where there is more than one main or predominant purpose, and neither can be regarded as subsidiary, as long as the legal bases proposed are procedurally compatible.[24]

If there is a choice between two single legal bases for the conclusion of a particular treaty, it will be a matter of deciding which one expresses its predominant purpose. If, on the other hand, an agreement contains a number of different elements, a single legal basis (such as development cooperation, trade, or the CFSP) may be sufficient, although additional legal bases may be required to cover specific commitments. Here the questions will be, first, whether these specific elements can be included under the primary legal basis (i.e., whether all the operative elements serve the purpose of the primary legal basis); and, second, whether they impose specific and distinct obligations on a particular matter that are neither secondary nor indirect in relation to the objectives of the primary legal basis.[25] It will thus be matter of weighing the objectives and content of the specific clause against the agreement as a whole. Since legal basis is not a description of the content of a measure but establishes competence

[21] Art. 3(1) TFEU. [22] Art. 3(2) TFEU. [23] Opinion 1/15, EU:C:2017:592, para. 71.
[24] On procedural compatibility, *see id.*, paras. 105–118.
[25] Case C-377/12, EU:C:2014:1903, para. 59.

to act, only those legal bases should be included that are necessary and sufficient to ground competence.

Choice of legal basis may also affect the relative powers of the institutions. The European Parliament, for example, has a restricted role to play in the conclusion of international agreements in the field of the CFSP. One of the peculiarities of the EU system, therefore, as compared to treaty-making in national jurisdictions, is that the precise procedural rules and powers of the institutions (and member states) will vary according to which specific power-conferring provision is used as a legal basis. Since the EU Treaty provisions granting treaty-making powers allow considerable latitude to the policy choices of the EU institutions, the rules governing who makes policy, and how, are of central importance. That said, we should not underestimate the importance of the general external objectives and principles governing EU external action introduced by the Lisbon Treaty.[26] To date, these have been largely used to enable rather than constrain action: for example, the inclusion of sustainable development among the European Union's general external objectives was relied on by the Court of Justice in concluding that sustainable development commitments in a trade agreement could legitimately be based on trade policy powers.[27] However, they also form the basis for the obligation to comply with international law and human rights.[28] EU treaty-making is thus constrained by general rules of the primary law: a decision signing or concluding an international treaty may be annulled on the ground that it contravenes a substantive or procedural provision of the EU Treaties.[29]

The procedural rules are now contained in a single provision, Article 218 TFEU, which with a very few exceptions now covers all EU treaty-making, and which will be a central reference point for the remainder of this chapter. According to the Court of Justice, Article 218 TFEU "constitutes, as regards the conclusion of international treaties, an autonomous and general provision of constitutional scope, in that it confers specific powers on the EU institutions' and establishes a balance between those institutions."[30] Agreements concluded by the Union are binding on the institutions of the Union and on its member states.[31] As expressed by Alan Dashwood, "The special constitutional significance of Article 218 TFEU lies in the fact that international agreements provide one of the sources of the EU's positive law."[32] The adoption of

[26] *See* in particular Arts. 3(5) and 21 TEU.

[27] Opinion 2/15, EU:C:2017:376, para. 147ff.

[28] C-366/10 *Air Transport Association of America*, EU:C:2011:864, para. 101; T-512/12 Front populaire pour la liberation de la saguia-elhamra et du rio de oro (Front Polisario) v. Council, EU:T:2015:953, paras. 223–228; C-104-16P Council v. Front Polisario, opinion of AG Wathelet, EU:C:2016:677, paras. 220–237.

[29] E.g., C-122/95 Germany v. Council, EU:C:1998:94.

[30] C-425/13 Commission v. Council, EU:C:2015:483, para. 62.

[31] Art. 216(2) TFEU. *See* Mario Mendez, *The Application of International Law by the Court of Justice of the European Union*, ch. 34 in this volume.

[32] Alan Dashwood, *EU Acts and Member State Acts in the Negotiation, Conclusion and Implementation of International Agreements*, *in* EU LEGAL ACTS—CHALLENGES AND TRANSFORMATIONS 190 (Marise Cremona & Claire Kilpatrick eds., 2018).

nonbinding instruments is not covered by Article 218 TFEU,[33] and the roles of the different institutions in such cases will be governed by the specific sectoral and general institutional provisions of the EU Treaties.[34]

Article 218 of the TFEU applies to the negotiation and conclusion of "agreements between the Union and third countries or international organisations." The concept of "agreement"—the generic term used in the article—is a broad one, which should be "understood in a general sense to indicate any undertaking entered into by entities subject to international law which has binding force, whatever its formal designation."[35] The Court of Justice has on occasion referred to the Vienna Convention on the Law of Treaties to assist in determining the concept of "agreement," for example, in holding that it may be constituted by two or more related instruments which express a "convergence of intent" between the parties. Thus the adoption of a unilateral act that is intended to form part of an agreement, such as a unilateral offer to a third country that will become binding on acceptance by that third country, or a decision on the acceptance of the accession of new parties to an international convention, falls within the scope of Article 218 TFEU.[36]

Article 218 of the TFEU covers agreements concluded by the European Union, and therefore excludes member state agreements. This appears to be stating the obvious, but it deserves a brief comment. First, it might not always be clear whether it is the Union acting or the member states acting collectively.[37] Second, there are circumstances in which a treaty cannot be concluded by the European Union, despite falling within exclusive EU powers, because it is open only to states. In such cases the European Union may authorize the member states to conclude the agreement on its behalf, and Article 218 TFEU will be used as the procedural legal basis for the authorizing act.[38]

Institutional Framework

At a general level, the EU Treaties give the Council the role of establishing policy and "elaborat[ing] the Union's external action on the basis of strategic guidelines laid down

[33] Case C-233/02 France v. Commission, EU:C:2004:173, para. 45.

[34] Case C-660/13 Council v. Commission, EU:C:2016:616, paras. 32–34.

[35] Joined cases C-103/12 and C-165/12 European Parliament and Commission v. Council, EU:C:2014:2400, para. 83. *See also* Opinion 1/75, EU:C:1975:145, p. 1360; C-327/91 France v. Commission, EU:C:1994:305, para. 27.

[36] For an example of the former, *see* joined cases C-103/12 and C-165/12 European Parliament and Commission v. Council, EU:C:2014:2400, paras. 68–73 and 83; for an example of the latter, *see* Opinion 1/13, EU:C:2014:2303, paras. 37–41, referring to Art. 2(1)(a) of the Vienna Convention.

[37] *See,* e.g., the orders of the General Court in cases T-192/16, EU:T:2017:128; T-193/16, EU:T:2017:129; T-257/16, EU:T:2017:130 (under appeal: C-208/17 P NF v. European Council, pending).

[38] C-399/12 Germany v. Council, EU:C:2014:2258; Opinion 1/13, EU:C:2014:2303.

by the European Council,"[39] while the European Commission has a right of initiative and is (with the exception of the CFSP) to "ensure the Union's external representation."[40] In terms of treaty-making procedures, this translates into a division of responsibility whereby the Council decides to initiate negotiations, sets the parameters of the negotiation, and signs and concludes the treaty, whereas the Commission proposes the negotiating directives to the Council and conducts the negotiations. The European Parliament does not have a formal say in the opening of negotiations or the drafting of the directives, but is to be kept informed throughout the procedure, and (most important) its consent is now required for the conclusion of most treaties.

From this it will be seen that the Council will be taking decisions at crucial points during the procedure. These are taken by qualified majority,[41] except in a number of defined cases where unanimity is required: association agreements; agreements with states that are accession candidates; the agreement on accession of the Union to the European Convention on Human Rights; and cases when the agreement covers a field for which unanimity is required for the adoption of a Union act (for example, the CFSP, family law, or taxation).[42] The wording of Article 218(8) TFEU would suggest that where unanimity is required, it is required throughout the Article 218 procedures, and not only at the stage of signature and conclusion, but there is some doubt about this.[43]

The European Court of Justice has a general jurisdiction to ensure that the law is observed.[44] As far as judicial review of treaty-making is concerned, the Court has both ex ante and ex post jurisdiction. First, prior to conclusion of a treaty there is the possibility of ex ante review, where the Court is asked for an Opinion on the compatibility of an "envisaged" treaty with the EU Treaties.[45] Compatibility includes questions of competence as well as substantive compatibility.[46] The purpose of this procedure has been explained by the Court in terms of the interests of third countries as well as EU constitutional law, its aim being to "[forestall] complications which would result from legal disputes concerning the compatibility with the Treaties of international agreements binding upon the EU."[47] Although called an "opinion," the Court's ruling is binding; an adverse Opinion means that the "envisaged agreement" cannot enter into force unless either it is amended or the EU Treaties are revised. The request for an Opinion may be presented, framed in the form of question(s), by a member state, the European Parliament, the Council, or the Commission—not, therefore, by a private

[39] Art. 16(1) and (6) TEU. [40] Art. 17(1) TEU.

[41] A qualified majority (QMV) is defined as at least 55 percent of the members of the Council, comprising at least fifteen of them and representing member states comprising at least 65 percent of the population of the Union; *see* Art. 16(4) TEU and Art. 238 TFEU.

[42] Art. 218(8) TFEU.

[43] According to C-81/13 UK v. Council, EU:C:2014:2449, the QMV rule in Art. 218(9) TFEU is not displaced by the unanimity rule for association agreements established in Art. 218(8) TFEU; see however C-244/17 Commission v. Council, EU:C:2018:662, paras. 25–34.

[44] Art. 19 TEU. [45] Art. 218(11) TFEU. [46] Opinion 1/75, EU:C:1975:145.

[47] Opinion 2/13, EU:C:2014:2454, para. 145.

actor. These "privileged applicants"[48] do not need to show any interest in bringing the case. The agreement must be "envisaged" by "one or more EU institutions on which powers are conferred for the purposes of the procedure provided for in Article 218 TFEU."[49] The procedure may therefore be set in motion in cases where the Council (e.g., because of disagreement over allocation of competence) has not accepted the Commission's proposal to conclude the agreement. Since the agreement must be "envisaged," once it has been concluded this procedure can no longer be used;[50] in practice, therefore, the procedure will be started at some point during the Article 218 TFEU treaty-making process.[51] The request for an Opinion does not have an automatic suspensory effect, so it would be possible for the Council to proceed to conclude an agreement while an Opinion is still pending.[52]

Second, the Court has jurisdiction by way of ex post review over any institutional act adopted during the treaty-making procedure that is designed to have legal effects.[53] This includes decisions adopting a negotiating position,[54] decisions appointing an advisory committee,[55] as well as decisions on signature and conclusion of the agreement.[56] It is thus possible for the Commission, the Parliament, or a member state to challenge the validity of the Council decision concluding the agreement, which may lead to the annulment of the decision on grounds of lack of competence (rare but not unknown[57]), incorrect legal basis, breach of an essential procedural requirement, or substantive incompatibility with primary law. This procedure is also in principle open to natural and legal persons, but rules of standing require the individual applicant to demonstrate that the decision is of "direct and individual concern," and this requirement is difficult to satisfy given that the applicant is not an addressee of the decision under challenge. Recently, for the first time, the General Court accepted that a non-privileged applicant had standing to challenge a Council decision on the signature of an international agreement.[58] The judgment was reversed by the Court of Justice on grounds of lack of standing; its judgment leaves open the possibility in future cases, but the standing requirements are likely to prove a difficult hurdle to surmount.[59]

[48] *Cf.* Art. 263 TFEU, 2nd para. [49] Opinion 1/13, EU:C:2014:2303, para. 45.

[50] Opinion 3/94, EU:C:1995:436.

[51] If the agreement is not yet in final form, the Court may not be able to answer all questions: Opinion 2/94, EU:C:1996:140.

[52] E.g., Opinion 1/04, requested by the Parliament but withdrawn when the Council concluded the treaty in question; the Parliament then brought a successful ex post challenge to the Council decision: joined cases C-317/04 and C-318/04 European Parliament v. Council, EU:C:2006:346. This scenario is much less likely now that Parliamentary consent to the conclusion of most treaties is required.

[53] Art. 263 TFEU. [54] E.g., case 22/70 Commission v. Council, EU:C:1971:32.

[55] E.g., C-425/13 Commission v. Council, EU:C:2015:483.

[56] E.g., joined cases C-103/12 and C-165/12 European Parliament and Commission v. Council, EU:C:2014:2400; C-377/12 Commission v. Council, EU:C:2014:1903; C-660/13 Council v. Commission, EU:C:2016:616.

[57] E.g., joined cases C-317/04 and C-318/04 European Parliament v. Council, EU:C:2006:346.

[58] T-512/12 Front populaire pour la liberation de la saguia-elhamra et du rio de oro (Front Polisario) v. Council, EU:T:2015:953, paras. 61–114.

[59] C-104-16P Council v. Front Polisario, EU:C:2016:973.

The annulment of the decision concluding a treaty does not affect the validity of the treaty in international law, but it will no longer be binding on the institutions and member states as a matter of EU law.[60] Depending on the nature of the defect, the legal effects of the decision may be preserved in the interests of legal certainty until the defect has been remedied and the decision readopted.[61]

III. Process of Treaty Negotiation

The formal procedure starts with a recommendation to the Council to authorize the opening of negotiations. This will come from the Commission except where the projected agreement relates exclusively or principally to the CFSP, in which case the recommendation is made by the High Representative.[62] The Council adopts a decision authorizing the opening of negotiations and appointing the Union negotiator or head of the negotiating team. This decision produces legal effects between the European Union and its member states,[63] and between Union institutions, and may be subject to legal challenge.[64] Even the Commission's recommendation to the Council may create obligations for the member states to refrain from unilateral action.[65] Although not expressly stated, it is clear that the Commission may subsequently recommend that the Council withdraw the authorization to negotiate.[66]

The Union negotiator is generally the Commission (one of the Commission's tasks under Article 17 TEU is to represent the Union internationally). CFSP agreements, exceptionally, are negotiated by the High Representative, and in some cases the team might include both the Commission and High Representative. The Parliament–Commission inter-institutional agreement provides that the Commission will "at Parliament's request, facilitate the inclusion of a delegation of Members of the European Parliament [MEPs] as observers in Union delegations." The agreement acknowledges that MEPs may not participate directly in the negotiations, but the Commission may, "subject to the legal, technical and diplomatic possibilities," grant them observer status.[67]

[60] *Cf.* Art. 216(2) TFEU. C-266/16 *Western Sahara Campaign UK*, EU:C:2018:118, paras. 49–50.

[61] Art. 264 TFEU; *see*, e.g., C-137/12 Commission v. Council, EU:C:2013:675, paras. 78–81.

[62] Art. 218(2) and (3) TFEU. The High Representative of the Union for Foreign Affairs and Security Policy chairs the Foreign Affairs Council and is also a Vice-President of the Commission; his or her responsibility is to "conduct" the CFSP on behalf of the Union (Art. 18(2) TEU) and to "ensure the consistency of the Union's external action" (Art. 18(4) TEU).

[63] Once negotiations have been authorized the member states are under an obligation of cooperation based on Art. 4(3) TEU: C-433/03 Commission v. Germany, EU:C:2005:462, para. 66.

[64] T-754/14 Efler v. Commission, EU:T:2017:323, para. 34; *see*, e.g., C-114/12 Commission v. Council, EU:C:2014:2151, para. 40; C-425/13 Commission v. Council, EU:C:2015:483, para. 28.

[65] C-433/03 Commission v. Germany, EU:C:2005:462, para. 65.

[66] T-754/14 Efler v. Commission, EU:T:2017:323.

[67] Framework Agreement, 20 October 2010, para. 25.

This commitment is presented as an expression of the Parliament's right to be kept informed at all stages of the procedure.[68] The Parliament's right to be informed applies also to CFSP agreements, even though it does not participate in the ultimate conclusion of such an agreement.[69] This indicates that the right to be informed is not simply an adjunct to the right to consent to the final version of the agreement; rather it enables the Parliament more generally to "exercise democratic control over the European Union's external action," helping to ensure its consistency and constitutionality.[70] In the case of CFSP agreements, where the High Representative is the negotiator, the duty to inform the Parliament falls on the Council.[71]

As well as authorizing the opening of negotiations, the Council may also "address directives to the negotiator" and "designate a special committee in consultation with which the negotiations must be consulted."[72] In practice, the Commission's recommendation will generally contain draft "negotiating directives" outlining the objectives and parameters of the negotiation. The Council's directives reflect its policymaking role and may contain considerable detail but should not tie the hands of the Commission to such a degree that its role as negotiator is compromised.[73] Likewise, the special committee, where there is one, has a consultative role and should not be empowered to direct the negotiations. This point is worth highlighting since it illustrates one of the features of EU treaty-making: each of the institutions in the procedure has its own autonomy and prerogatives; the Commission is the representative of the Union and not the mouthpiece of the Council or a diplomatic service answerable to the Council.

The line between the Council's right to set policy and the Commission's rôle as negotiator is a fine one and may be difficult to draw. In one recent case, the Court held that the Council was entitled to require the Commission to keep it informed as to the progress of negotiations, as well as to establish procedures for the consultation of the special committee, but that the Council should not empower the special committee to issue ongoing instructions to the Commission by establishing detailed negotiating positions;[74] this, the Court reasoned, would encroach upon the Commission's powers and breach the principle of institutional balance contained in Article 13(2) TEU.

Until recently the Council and Commission both sought to keep the negotiating directives confidential on the ground that to publish them would prejudice the Union's negotiating position. This was carried to an extreme in some cases where there was no conceivable leverage to be gained by secrecy, but has overall been upheld by the Court

[68] Art. 218(10) TFEU.

[69] C-658/11 European Parliament v. Council, EU:C:2014:2025; C-263/14 European Parliament v. Council, EU:C:2016:435.

[70] C-263/14 European Parliament v. Council, EU:C:2016:435, para. 71.

[71] *Id.*, para. 73. [72] Art. 218(4) TFEU.

[73] The term "negotiating mandate" is quite often used, but has been argued to be incorrect and misleading: *see* C-425/13 Commission v. Council, opinion of AG Wathelet, EU:C:2015:174, paras. 157–163.

[74] C-425/13 Commission v. Council, EU:C:2015:483.

of Justice.[75] Legally there is a distinction between the provision of information to the European Parliament, and to ordinary members of the public. The Parliament, as we have seen, has a right to be informed under Article 218(10) TFEU, and in the inter-institutional agreement the Commission has undertaken to provide the Parliament with information on international negotiations "including the definition of negotiating directives."[76] Some MEPs have been dissatisfied with the degree of information provided and have resorted to individual requests for access to documents under the European Union's transparency regulation.[77] However, the approach has been changing under pressure from the public over some high-profile negotiations, as well as from the Ombudsman.[78] For the first time, the negotiating directives for the Transatlantic Trade and Investment Partnership (TTIP) were released to the public in October 2014,[79] and the Commission's Directorate-General for Trade has now taken the position that negotiating directives should generally be published, though the ultimate decision to publish lies with the Council.[80]

The Union's negotiator (usually the Commission) will agree and initial the final text; no formal procedure is provided for this purpose as it is treated as a part of the negotiation. In cases where the European Union is negotiating alongside its member states (a "mixed" agreement), the member states are not a formal part of the European Union's negotiating team—indeed mixed agreements are invisible as far as Article 218 TFEU is concerned. However, as might be expected, the European Union and member states will adopt a common negotiating position (legally speaking, this is an expression of the duty of cooperation, based on Article 4(3) TEU), and the final text will be agreed by all parties.

IV. Signature, Provisional Application, and Conclusion of Treaties

Once the text is agreed, the Council adopts a decision authorizing the signature of an agreement, and if necessary, its provisional entry into force, on the basis of Article 218(5) TFEU. The negotiator proposes the decision, which also requires a substantive legal basis,

[75] E.g., T-331/11 Besselink v. Council, EU:T:2013:419.

[76] Framework Agreement, 20 October 2010, para. 23.

[77] Regulation No. 1049/2001 on the right of public access to documents, Art. 4(1)(a); T-529/09 In 't Veld v. Council, EU:T:2012:215, appealed in C-350/12 P, EU:C:2014:2039.

[78] Decision of the European Ombudsman in case OI/10/2014/RA, Transparency and public participation in relation to the Transatlantic Trade and Investment Partnership (TTIP) negotiations, 6 January 2015.

[79] Council document 11103/13.

[80] European Commission, *Trade for all—Towards a more responsible trade and investment policy*, 14 October 2015, at 18–19, *available at* http://trade.ec.europa.eu/doclib/docs/2015/october/tradoc_153846.pdf.

and it may be at this stage that conflict will emerge as to the proposed legal basis, followed by either a request for an opinion of the Court under Article 218(11) TFEU or—if the decision has already been adopted—an action to annul the decision on signature.[81] The choice of legal basis will affect the voting in the Council, since although qualified majority voting is the norm, some require unanimity. The Commission's proposal will suggest the legal basis, but it is not unknown for the Council to alter this. It is at this stage too, if not already decided, that the question will be settled regarding whether the agreement will be signed and concluded by the European Union alone or also by the member states as a mixed agreement; again, the Commission will propose, but its views may be overridden in the Council. For example, it is known that in the case of the European Union's trade and investment agreement with Canada (CETA), the Commission accepted the Council's insistence that the agreement should be mixed; however, in the case of the trade agreement with Singapore, the Commission asked for an opinion from the Court of Justice as to whether member state participation was required.[82]

Article 218(5) now explicitly includes the possibility that the decision on signature will include provision for provisional entry into force,[83] and this procedure is quite commonly used in the case of mixed agreements so as to bring into force more quickly aspects of the agreement (such as trade provisions) that do not need member state ratification, a process that generally takes some time. As this decision is taken simply by the Council, and as provisional application may both include significant commitments and last for some time, other actors—Parliaments in the member states and the European Parliament—have found ways to assert their interests.[84] Although the European Parliament does not have a formal role in the adoption of the decision on signature and provisional application, the Commission has undertaken not to propose important trade agreements for signature until it has Parliamentary consent.[85] In some member states, too, constitutional requirements, including votes in regional parliaments, may need to be complied with before the Council vote.

The agreement will be concluded by the Council, again on a proposal from the negotiator; the decision will state that the President of the Council is authorized to designate the person empowered to conclude the agreement on the Union's behalf. Like the decision on signature, the decision on conclusion must be published in the

[81] As an example of the former, *see* Opinion 1/94, EU:C:1994:384; of the latter, *see* C-28/12 Commission v. Council, EU:C:2015:43.

[82] Opinion 2/15, EU:C:2017:376.

[83] Before this provision was introduced in 1997, it was common practice to conclude a separate interim agreement containing the trade provisions, which would automatically terminate once the full agreement entered into force.

[84] David Kleimann & Gesa Kübek, *The Signing, Provisional Application, and Conclusion of Trade and Investment Agreements in the EU. The Case of CETA and Opinion 2/15*, RSCAS Research Paper 2016/58, *available at* http://cadmus.eui.eu/bitstream/handle/1814/43948/RSCAS_2016_58.pdf?sequence=1.

[85] Statement by Trade Commissioner Malmström to the European Parliament: P-004200/2016.

European Union's Official Journal.[86] There is no category of "executive" or similar agreements that may be concluded by the Commission. The decision on conclusion is subject to the same voting rules in the Council as the authorization of signature. But in contrast to the decision on signature, the European Parliament must give consent to the conclusion of the majority of agreements, most importantly, agreements covering fields to which the ordinary legislative procedure applies (this includes trade and investment) and Association Agreements.[87] In other cases the Parliament must be consulted. The only exception is for agreements "relating exclusively" to the CFSP, where the Parliament does not have even the right to be formally consulted; this applies to all agreements whose sole substantive legal basis is the CFSP, a reminder of the importance of legal basis.[88]

Where the Parliament only has the right to be consulted, it only has limited leverage. The Council may set a time limit and has been known to conclude an agreement without waiting for the Parliament's opinion if it sees the agreement as urgent and the Parliament's requests for delay as unreasonable; in such cases the only recourse for Parliament is to challenge the legality of the Council decision.[89] The Parliament has used its power of consent to reinforce its role in the negotiation of treaties, and has been prepared to reject a proposed treaty. This is a powerful weapon; it may lead to the reopening of negotiations or to the effective abandonment of the treaty. Nonetheless it is a blunt weapon and of limited use by itself: a take-it-or-leave-it consent procedure at the end of a negotiation is no substitute for involvement in shaping the content of a complex agreement. Hence the importance of practice involving the Parliament more closely in the actual negotiation.

The Council decision concluding the agreement may also designate the procedures for appointing Union representation in committees established by the agreement and may "authorise the negotiator to approve on the Union's behalf modifications to the agreement where it provides for them to be adopted by a simplified procedure or by a body set up by the agreement."[90]

There may be situations in which the member states will conclude a treaty on behalf of the European Union. On occasion the Council has delegated the conclusion of a treaty to a specific member state.[91] In addition, as already mentioned, if a proposed treaty falls within the European Union's exclusive competence but the European Union is not able to become a party, then the member states may be authorized by Council decision to sign and conclude it on the European Union's behalf. This gives rise to legal obligations within EU law but does not, of course, affect the position of the member states as parties in international law. Just as the European Union may conclude treaties,

[86] As a nonlegislative act that does not specify to whom it is addressed. *See* Art. 297(2) TFEU.

[87] Art. 218(6) TFEU.

[88] C-658/11 European Parliament v. Council, EU:C:2014:2025.

[89] Joined cases C-317/04 and C-318/04 European Parliament v. Council, EU:C:2006:346.

[90] Art. 218(7) TFEU.

[91] For example, monetary agreements on the use of the euro with San Marino and Vatican City, concluded by Italy on behalf of the European Union.

parts of which will be implemented by the member states, so the member states may conclude treaties that may need to be implemented by the European Union.

There is another, more common, way in which the member states may be involved with EU treaty-making. As has already been mentioned, the agreement may be "mixed," i.e., concluded by the European Union and its member states together. Practice as to the conclusion of a mixed agreement varies depending on whether it is essentially bilateral or multilateral in nature. Where the European Union and member states are concluding a multilateral treaty as a mixed agreement (e.g., a multilateral environmental convention), they will each sign and conclude or ratify it according to their own procedures. Where the mixed agreement is bilateral in nature (i.e., the European Union and its member states of the one part and a third state of the other part), then the European Union will coordinate its signature and conclusion process with the member states, and will not conclude the agreement until it has been ratified by all member states. The member states in such cases need to follow their own national constitutional procedures, but, especially in the case of signature and provisional application, they may seek to coordinate by adopting a decision of the "Representatives of the Governments of the Member States." This is not a Council decision and any legal force it has derives from international, not EU, law.

In recent years a practice developed whereby the Council and the "Representatives of the Governments of the Member States" (in practice, the same people exercising different roles) would combine their decisions on signature into a single joint, or "hybrid," decision. This practice has now been declared illegal under EU law by the Court of Justice on the grounds that it interferes with the voting rules in the Council (the "Representatives of the Governments of the Member States" act collectively and therefore unanimously), and that for the member states to take part in a Council decision alters the decision-making procedures for international agreements set out in Article 218 TFEU.[92] Although the Council presented the hybrid decision as an effective way of dealing with mixed agreements and an expression of unity and the duty of cooperation between the European Union and member states, the Court held that the duty of cooperation "cannot justify the Council setting itself free from compliance with the procedural rules and voting arrangements laid down in Article 218 TFEU."[93] The problem that this case illustrates is that the rules on EU treaty-making are "blind" to mixed agreements and proceed as if every agreement was concluded by the European Union alone. The Council may wish to establish procedures for handling mixed agreements, but these must not alter the rules set out in Article 218 TFEU for the negotiation and conclusion of treaties by the European Union. These decision-making rules "are laid down in the Treaties and are not at the disposal of the Member States or of the institutions themselves."[94]

[92] C-28/12 Commission v. Council, EU:C:2015:43.

[93] C-28/12 Commission v. Council, EU:C:2015:43, para. 55.

[94] C-28/12 Commission v. Council, EU:C:2015:43, para. 42.

V. Conclusion

In common with national jurisdictions, the European Union possesses a set of rules on treaty-making as part of its foreign relations law. These rules are found in EU primary law (in the EU Treaties). They are supplemented by institutional practice, which may be formalized in inter-institutional agreements, but such practice may not alter the institutional balance or the relationship between EU and member state powers established in the Treaties, which have been termed the European Union's "constitutional charter." In common with a state, the European Union's law on treaty-making contains rules establishing the roles of the different actors in the process of negotiating and concluding treaties. Nevertheless, the European Union has a number of important characteristics as a treaty-maker that distinguish it from a state.

The EU Treaties grant the European Union the capacity to enter into treaties, and this capacity has been accepted by third state treaty partners; the European Union's treaty-making practice is extensive. Indeed it can be argued that treaty-making is at least or even more important as an instrument of foreign policy for the European Union as for the modern state. But unlike a state, the scope of the European Union's treaty-making power is inherently limited since it has only those powers that are conferred by the EU Treaties, expressly or impliedly. For the European Union, treaty-making is not a manifestation of sovereignty and cannot be regarded as simply a matter of executive discretion. As a matter of practice, these conferred powers are very broad and limitations are political more than legal; nonetheless the legal reality of conferred powers impacts the European Union's law of treaty-making. This is seen in the requirement that there must be a basis in the Treaties for every EU legal act ("legal basis"), including acts authorizing the signature or conclusion of a treaty. The Treaties do not contain a general treaty-making power, so although the European Union has extensive policy discretion as to the substantive content of the treaties it concludes, there is still a need to demonstrate a link to a specific Treaty-based power, tied to the aim and content of each treaty. The policy balance of a projected treaty and its relation to the European Union's general objectives thus becomes a matter of institutional debate and potential judicial assessment.

The European Union acts through its institutions, and these institutional actors operate in a different legal framework than those involved in treaty-making as branches of the state. The relationship between them is not hierarchical, nor is treaty-making ultimately the prerogative of any one institution. Thus, for example, the Commission as negotiator is not simply carrying out instructions and cannot be dictated to by the Council. Each EU institution has a degree of autonomy and a specific role in the treaty-making process; the EU Treaties (and the Court of Justice) protect the "institutional balance," i.e., the balance of power between the institutions. The corollary of this balance of power is that the institutions are themselves subject to the principle of conferral. They cannot ignore, even in the interests of efficiency or cooperation, the rules established by the Treaties. These rules are part of the "structured network of principles, rules and mutually interdependent legal relations linking the EU and its Member States, and its Member States with each other,"[95] and are not "at the disposal" of the institutions (or the member states).[96] Inter-institutional litigation over treaty-making is quite common, and whereas in earlier years institutional litigation was often a proxy for disagreements between member states and the EU, since the adoption of the Treaty of Lisbon the institutions have litigated more on their own behalf, seeking to defend their prerogatives and establish the new institutional balance of powers.

In comparison with national jurisdictions, the frequency with which questions of treaty-making are brought before the Court of Justice is striking. Legal control of the process is not just potential, it is often invoked, by member states and by institutions. In fact, the European Parliament's exercise of legal as well as political control over treaty-making is a distinctive feature of the EU system. Prior constitutional review of treaties (or of the law approving a treaty) exists in some jurisdictions, such as France and Germany; in the EU system this specialized jurisdiction of the Court of Justice has proved to be an important mechanism for determining the scope and nature (exclusive or shared) of external powers and the substantive and procedural constraints on EU treaty-making.

The degree of direct and indirect Parliamentary oversight of treaty-making is now also a distinctive feature of EU treaty-making, having been strengthened considerably in recent years. Whereas under the original Treaty of Rome, the Parliament did not have a formal role in treaty-making, almost all treaties now require the consent of the European Parliament, and it has been prepared to exercise its power of veto. Parliamentary consent applies to the Council's decision on conclusion, and is therefore granted case-by-case and to an already finalized text; Parliament itself does not mandate, or approve, future treaty negotiations. Its indirect monitoring of treaty negotiations has also increased, facilitated by its inter-institutional agreement with the Commission, by a practice of greater transparency on the part of both the Commission and the Council in the case of significant negotiations, and of course by the latter's awareness that Parliamentary consent to the final text will be required. However, the Parliament is absent from some elements of the procedure, notably the adoption of negotiating directives, and the conclusion of CFSP agreements, and in other cases (e.g., provisional application) its involvement depends on the Commission's political will.

The legal conceptualization of the European Union's treaty-making powers has evolved away from the type of federal model that would place all treaty-making competence at federal level.[97] The member states remain sovereign subjects of international law. The European Union's external powers may—as a matter of EU law—displace those of the member states, but often they do not and powers are shared, to be

[95] Opinion 2/13, EU:C:2014:2454, para. 167.

[96] C-28/12 Commission v. Council, EU:C:2015:43.

[97] *See* Schütze, *supra* note 20.

exercised subject to mutual duties of cooperation. As a result, the European Union and member states will often enter into treaties together. Although such "mixed agreements" are common, there are no formal rules in the EU system, apart from the general duty of cooperation, governing their negotiation and conclusion. The EU Treaties ignore their existence, creating problems when member state actions (e.g., failure to ratify a mixed agreement) impinge on EU treaty-making. For third state partners, treaty negotiations may thus be complicated by the foreign relations law of twenty-eight member states, as well as of the European Union itself.

PART III

FEDERALISM AND FOREIGN AFFAIRS

CHAPTER 15

FOREIGN AFFAIRS FEDERALISM IN THE UNITED STATES

ERNEST A. YOUNG

THE American federal relationship with respect to foreign affairs was supposed to be simple, but it isn't. Our Founders conceived of foreign affairs as exclusively national; even Thomas Jefferson acknowledged that the states should be made "one as to all foreign concerns," albeit "several as to all merely domestic."[1] And yet federalism has come to complicate American foreign affairs just as it adds a layer of complexity to all other aspects of American governance. Nor is this complexity a remnant of a more decentralized past. Earl Fry recently observed that "[o]ver the past quarter-century, there has a been a sharp acceleration in the foreign relations of US state and municipal government"; moreover, "[t]his trend . . . is likely to continue as state and municipal leaders act to protect the interests of their local populations in an era of expanding globalization and rapid technology change."[2]

To be sure, the national government dominates the core of foreign affairs: the conduct of foreign policy toward other nations. Yet even here, states and municipalities intrude from time to time. More broadly, state and local governments remain important players in areas such as immigration and commercial regulation that have important international dimensions. Federalism constrains—legally and especially politically—the international agreements that the national government can enter into, and central authorities remain dependent on state and local officials to implement many important international commitments.

[1] Letter from Thomas Jefferson to George Washington, Aug. 14, 1787, *available at* National Archives, *Founders online*, *available at* https://founders.archives.gov/documents/Jefferson/01-12-02-0040.

[2] Earl H. Fry, *The United States of America*, *in* FOREIGN RELATIONS IN FEDERAL COUNTRIES 296, 296 (Hans Michelmann ed., 2009).

Internal and external forces have combined to make a multilayered approach to foreign affairs inevitable in the United States. Internal forces include the constitutional structure itself, which stops short of giving exclusive foreign affairs powers to the national government and reserves important authority to the states, as well as the more contemporary impact of polarization in American political life. On the external side, globalization has blurred the very distinction between foreign and domestic affairs, and international law's increasing preoccupation with nations' treatment of their own citizens has rendered many traditional areas of state governance subjects of international concern.

I. The Founding Conception and the Slow Death of Dual Federalism

A variety of dissatisfactions with the Articles of Confederation—America's original governing framework—led the Founders to draft a new constitution in 1787, but concerns about the Confederation's inability to conduct a coherent foreign policy played a prominent role.[3] Because the Articles reserved such important powers to the states, the Confederation Congress "could not raise revenue, could not bargain effectively, could not assure other nations that any agreements it made would actually be observed by the states, could not develop a unified commercial policy to extort concessions from other countries, could not maintain an effective military or naval force."[4] In particular, the young nation could not secure commercial access to foreign markets, guarantee rights of navigation on the Mississippi River, or compel the British to vacate their western forts pursuant to the peace treaty that had ended the Revolutionary War.[5]

The 1789 Constitution, which replaced the Articles, aimed both to centralize the conduct of foreign policy in the national government and to enable that government to bring the states into line.[6] Writing in the *Federalist*, James Madison emphasized "the advantage of uniformity in all points which relate to foreign powers"[7] and insisted that "[i]f we are to be one nation in any respect, it clearly ought to be in respect to other nations."[8] Instead of simply declaring a monopoly over foreign affairs for the national government, the U.S. Constitution enumerated particular foreign affairs powers—e.g.,

[3] *See, e.g.*, The Federalist No. 3, at 13–18 (J. Cooke ed., 1961) (John Jay); *see also* George C. Herring, From Colony to Superpower: U.S. Foreign Relations Since 1776, at 48–55 (2008); David C. Hendrickson, Peace Pact: The Lost World of the American Founding (2003).

[4] Bradford Perkins, The Creation of a Republican Empire, 1776–1865, at 56 (1993).

[5] *See* Herring, *supra* note 3, at 48–49.

[6] *See* Perkins, *supra* note 4, at 58.

[7] The Federalist No. 44, at 299 (J. Cooke ed., 1961).

[8] The Federalist No. 42, at 279 (J. Cooke ed., 1961).

to declare war and command the armed forces, to regulate foreign commerce, to hear judicial cases involving foreign citizens and officials—and allocated them among the branches of the new federal government.[9] It also forbade the states from exercising certain foreign affairs powers; they could not, for example, enter into agreements with foreign powers or undertake various military activities without Congress's consent.[10]

The new structure left ample room for states to do things that might impact foreign affairs.[11] Nonetheless, the Framers plainly envisioned a division of labor under which the national government would be responsible for external relations and the states would have primary authority over domestic matters.[12] This division eventually hardened into a regime of "dual federalism" contemplating "two mutually exclusive, reciprocally limiting fields of power—that of the national government and of the States."[13] This paradigm dominated American constitutional law for over a century; courts invalidated state regulation impinging on interstate commerce and limited national legislation regulating intrastate affairs.[14] The Great Depression in the 1930s spurred broad demand for more active government, however, and the U.S. Supreme Court accepted broad *concurrent* jurisdiction for federal and state regulation of the domestic economy.[15]

Notwithstanding this general abandonment of dual federalism's separate spheres of state and federal regulatory authority, vestiges of the old demarcation persist in foreign affairs.[16] Lawyers, courts, and commentators sometimes treat foreign affairs as if they remain exclusively federal. But dual federalism is unsustainable in foreign affairs for the same reasons it failed in domestic life: the expanding responsibilities of government at all levels and increased integration of economic life across all jurisdictional lines have

[9] *See* Michael D. Ramsey, The Constitution's Text in Foreign Affairs 7 (2007). *Compare* Roland Portmann, *Foreign Affairs Federalism in Switzerland*, ch. 17 in this volume (noting that the Swiss Constitution does confer a general foreign affairs power on the central government).

[10] *See* U.S. Const. art. I, § 10.

[11] *See*, e.g., Curtis A. Bradley & Jack L. Goldsmith, *The Abiding Relevance of Federalism to U.S. Foreign Relations*, 92 Am. J. Int'l L. 675, 677 (1998).

[12] *See*, e.g., The Federalist No. 45, at 313 (J. Cooke ed., 1962) (James Madison).

[13] Alpheus Thomas Mason, *The Role of the Court*, *in* Federalism: Infinite Variety in Theory and Practice 8, 24–25 (Valerie A. Earle ed., 1968); *see also* Anthony J. Bellia Jr., Federalism 183 (2011) ("The *dual federalism* paradigm understands federal and state governments to operate in different spheres of authority."). "Dual federalism" ought not to be conflated with "dual sovereignty," a more capacious term connoting any arrangement that divides sovereignty between two levels of government. *See* Ernest A. Young, *The Puzzling Persistence of Dual Federalism*, *in* Nomos LV: Federalism and Subsidiarity 34, 36–38 (James E. Fleming & Jacob T. Levy eds., 2014).

[14] *See*, e.g., Wabash, St. Louis, & Pacific Ry. Co. v. Illinois, 118 U.S. 557 (1886) (striking down state regulation of interstate railroad traffic); Hammer v. Dagenhart, 247 U.S. 251 (1918) (striking down national legislation banning child labor).

[15] *See*, e.g., NLRB v. Jones & Laughlin Steel Corp., 301 U.S. 1 (1937); Wickard v. Filburn, 317 U.S. 111 (1942); *see also* Edward S. Corwin, *The Passing of Dual Federalism*, 36 Va. L. Rev. 1 (1950); Young, *Puzzling Persistence*, *supra* note 13, at 53–54. For an argument that a similar jurisprudential transition has occurred in European law, *see* Robert Schütze, From Dual to Cooperative Federalism: The Changing Structure of European Law (2009).

[16] *See generally* Young, *Puzzling Persistence*, *supra* note 13, at 57–59.

rendered impracticable any allocation of governmental authority turning on a sharp divide between foreign and domestic concerns.[17]

II. The States in Foreign Affairs

In *United States v. Belmont*,[18] Justice Sutherland rejected any notion that New York state law could interfere with a presidential agreement to settle conflicting claims arising out of the Russian Revolution. "In respect of all international negotiations and compacts, and in respect of our foreign relations generally," he wrote, "state lines disappear. As to such purposes the State of New York does not exist."[19] One finds similar statements in other decisions both before and since,[20] and *Belmont* is frequently invoked by contemporary commentators seeking to avoid state law or suppress state interests in foreign relations contexts.[21] But "sweeping, absolutist pronouncements" like that in *Belmont* "have only the flimsiest connection with what modern state and local governments actually *do*."[22]

Consider, for example, state and local authorities' administration of the criminal law with respect to crimes committed within their own territory. If there *were* exclusive state and national spheres, this would plainly be a state function.[23] Yet its exercise frequently affects diplomatic relations. When Texas executed Karla Faye Tucker—a Texan who hacked two other Texans to death with a pickax in Texas—the European Parliament adopted a resolution condemning the execution.[24] Capital cases in the United States have attracted international criticism dating at least to the Sacco and Vanzetti case in the 1920s, and European criticism of George W. Bush's administration of the death penalty as governor of Texas soured his first goodwill trip abroad as president.[25] State enforcement of criminal law requires state and local officials to be the primary implementers of international agreements like Article 36 of the Vienna

[17] *See generally* Jack L. Goldsmith, *Federal Courts, Foreign Affairs, and Federalism*, 83 Va. L. Rev. 1617 (1997); Ernest A. Young, *Dual Federalism, Concurrent Jurisdiction, and the Foreign Affairs Exception*, 69 Geo. Wash. L. Rev. 139 (2001).

[18] 301 U.S. 324 (1937).

[19] *Id.* at 331.

[20] *See*, e.g., United States v. Pink, 315 U.S. 203, 222–223 (1942); Chae Chan Ping v. United States, 130 U.S. 581, 606 (1889); Holmes v. Jennison, 39 U.S. 540, 575, 14 Pet. 470, 501–502 (1840).

[21] *See*, e.g., Harold Hongju Koh, *Is International Law Really State Law?*, 111 Harv. L. Rev. 1824, 1847 (1998); Louis Henkin, Foreign Affairs and the US Constitution 150 (2d ed. 1996).

[22] Michael J. Glennon & Robert D. Sloane, Foreign Affairs Federalism: The Myth of National Exclusivity xiv (2016).

[23] *See*, e.g., United States v. Lopez, 514 U.S. 549, 561 n.3 (1995) ("Under our federal system, the States possess primary authority for defining and enforcing the criminal law.").

[24] *See* Resolution on the Death Sentence Passed on Karla Faye Tucker in the United States, 1998 O.J. (C 34) 168.

[25] *See* Mark Warren, *Death, Dissent and Diplomacy: The U.S. Death Penalty as an Obstacle to Foreign Relations*, 13 W. & M. Bill of Rts. J. 309, 309–10, 332–333 (2004).

Convention on Consular Relations,[26] which requires law enforcement to notify foreign nationals upon arrest of their right to speak to their consulate. Failures by state and local police to comply have repeatedly led to diplomatic protests and judgments against the United States in the International Court of Justice.[27]

Or consider American states' actions bearing on immigration. National law determines who can enter the country legally and dominates direct enforcement actions against unlawful immigrants.[28] But state policy on education, employment, welfare benefits, and other matters critically influences the attractiveness of a particular jurisdiction to immigrants, as well as the prospects of immigrants who settle there. State policies on these matters are generally *not* preempted by federal law[29] but may substantially affect population flows across borders. They may also significantly undermine U.S. foreign relations with immigrant-sending countries. When California adopted Proposition 187, making undocumented aliens ineligible for state public benefits, Mexico threatened economic retaliation.[30] As these examples illustrate, states performing their ordinary *domestic* functions often affect the whole nation's foreign relations.

Other state actions are deliberately directed abroad. American states and localities frequently enter into agreements with foreign jurisdictions to address problems affecting border regions.[31] Acting through the organization of New England Governors and Eastern Canadian Premiers (NEG/ECP), northeastern states have concluded agreements on education, tourism, trade, and the environment.[32] Northwestern states have joined western Canadian provinces to create the Pacific Northwest Economic Region, focusing on economic development and environmental protection.[33] As of 1998, more than four hundred agreements existed between U.S. states and Canadian provinces, involving forty-six U.S. states.[34] Numerous cross-border agreements exist on the southern border as well. Texas, New Mexico, Arizona, and California have

[26] Apr. 24, 1963, U.S.T. 77, 596 U.N.T.S. 261.

[27] *See, e.g.*, Case Concerning Avena and other Mexican Nationals (Mex. v. U.S.), 2004 I.C.J. 12 (Mar. 31); Lagrand (F.R.G. v. U.S.), 2001 I.C.J. 466 (June 27); *see also* Breard v. Greene, 523 U.S. 371 (1998) (rejecting Paraguay's suit in U.S. federal court on behalf of its national set to be executed in Virginia). *See generally* Ernest A. Young, *Institutional Settlement in a Globalizing Judicial System*, 54 DUKE L.J. 1143, 1163–1170 (2005); Peter J. Spiro, *Foreign Relations Federalism*, 70 U. COLO. L. REV. 1223, 1262–1264 (1999).

[28] *See, e.g.*, Arizona v. United States, 567 U.S. 387 (2012).

[29] *See, e.g.*, Chamber of Commerce v. Whiting, 563 U.S. 582 (2011).

[30] *See* Spiro, *supra* note 27, at 1261–1262.

[31] *See, e.g.*, JULIAN KU & JOHN YOO, TAMING GLOBALIZATION: INTERNATIONAL LAW, THE U.S. CONSTITUTION, AND THE NEW WORLD ORDER 166–168 (2012).

[32] *See* EARL H. FRY, THE EXPANDING ROLE OF STATE AND LOCAL GOVERNMENTS IN U.S. FOREIGN AFFAIRS 73 (1998).

[33] *See id.* at 73–74. *See also* Conference of Great Lakes and St. Lawrence Governors and Premiers, *About Us, available at* http://www.cglslgp.org/about-us/ (visited Sept. 1, 2017).

[34] *See* FRY, *supra* note 32, at 73; *see also* Duncan B. Hollis, *Unpacking the Compact Clause*, 88 TEX. L. REV. 741, 750 (2010) (using different criteria and finding "at least 340 [foreign-state agreements] since 1955").

cross-border agreements with Mexico and Mexican states on trade, infrastructure, and other issues.[35] Such agreements have generally been assumed to be insufficiently important to require scrutiny under the Compact Clause, although that assumption may not withstand examination.[36] For example, these relationships occasionally provide an avenue for foreign states to try to influence U.S. foreign policy, sometimes at odds with the president's own foreign policy.[37]

States' international agreements reach beyond regional arrangements. Nearly six hundred American cities have entered into "sister city" arrangements with cities all over the world.[38] Durham, North Carolina, for example, has no less than *five* sister cities (Arusha, Tanzania; Kostroma, Russia; Toyama, Japan; Durham, England; Zhuzhou, China) and one "friendship city" (Kunshan, China).[39] Activities include cultural exchanges, promotion of tourism and trade, and quirkier institutions such as the annual Liberal, Kansas–Olney, England "Pancake Day Race."[40] These agreements, while generally innocuous, have the potential for diplomatic conflict; a number of U.S. cities, for example, have considered ending sister-city relationships with Russian cities over anti-gay laws in that country.[41] Other agreements have greater political and practical significance. In 2014, for example, California Governor Jerry Brown signed a pact with Mexico to cooperate in fighting climate change.[42] And Massachusetts contracted with Venezuela's state-owned oil company to provide heating oil to low-income

[35] *See* Office of the Governor, *Governor Abbott Signs Transportation Agreement with Mexico; Announces Energy Task Force*, Sept. 8, 2015, *available at* https://gov.texas.gov/news/post/governor_abbott_signs_transportation_agreement_with_mexico_announces_energy; Fry, *supra* note 32, at 74.

[36] *See generally* Hollis, *supra* note 34, at 745–746 (arguing that Congress should scrutinize state agreements with foreign nations more regularly). The U.S. Constitution's Compact Clause provides that states may not enter into any "Agreement or Compact" with a foreign nation without the consent of Congress. *See* U.S. Const. art. I, § 10.

[37] *See*, e.g., Sean Collins Walsh, *Mexico's Top Diplomat for North America: "Texas is the NAFTA State,"* Austin American-Statesman, Mar. 9, 2017, *available at* http://www.mystatesman.com/news/national-govt-politics/mexico-top-diplomat-for-north-america-texas-the-nafta-state/PRgHmmTBXRkyDYAPVlHbjK/ (recounting Mexican efforts to enlist Texas officials to influence Trump administration's stance on NAFTA renegotiation).

[38] *See What Is a Sister City?*, Sister Cities International, *available at* http://sistercities.org/what-sister-city (visited Sept. 1, 2017).

[39] *See Interactive City Directory*, Sister Cities International, *available at* http://sistercities.org/interactive-map/Durham,%20North%20Carolina (visited Sept. 1, 2017).

[40] *See* Kansas Historical Society, *Liberal pancake race*, kansaspedia, *available at* https://www.kshs.org/kansapedia/liberal-pancake-race/18238 (visited Sept. 1, 2017); *see also* Miranda Kaplan, *11 Surprising Pairs of Sister Cities, Mental Floss*, Oct. 11, 2013, *available at* http://mentalfloss.com/article/53064/11-surprising-pairs-sister-cities.

[41] *See*, e.g., Nicole Saidi, *Michigan city council votes to sever ties with Russian "sister city" over anti-gay law*, CNN, Aug. 13, 2013, *available at* http://www.cnn.com/2013/08/13/us/michigan-sister-city-russia-gay-policies/index.html; Karen Ocamb, *Will Los Angeles Sever "Sister City" Ties to Anti-Gay St Petersburg, Russia?*, Huffington Post, July 30, 2013, *available at* http://www.huffingtonpost.com/karen-ocamb/will-los-angeles-sever-sister-city-ties-to-anti-gay-st-petersburg-russia_b_3673511.html.

[42] *See* Rory Carroll, *California and Mexico Sign Pact to Fight Climate Change*, Scientific American, July 28, 2014, *available at* https://www.scientificamerican.com/article/california-and-mexico-sign-pact-to-fight-climate-change/?print=true.

Massachusetts families—notwithstanding tensions between the Chavez government in Venezuela and the United States.[43] Such agreements may afford state and local governments an opportunity to implicitly criticize national policy.

States actively pursue their interests through diplomatic activities abroad. While governor of Texas, George W. Bush famously met with Mexican President Ernesto Zedillo and future President Vicente Fox, then governor of the border state of Guanajuato.[44] More commonly, states have established foreign missions to promote their commercial interests. As of 2009, states operated 230 trade offices around the world,[45] and governors and mayors also lead trade delegations abroad.[46] These activities rest in part on a perception that the national government inadequately promotes trade and foreign direct investment.[47] Although the American states' efforts pale beside the Canadian provinces—which depend more on foreign trade[48]—they are nonetheless a significant category of foreign affairs activity.

Although trade missions are generally unlikely to undermine national foreign policy, they sometimes involve foreign nations or organizations with which the nation has sensitive relations. Texas, for example, has sent observers to Organization of the Petroleum Exporting Companies (OPEC) meetings and organized shipment of hormone-free beef to Britain at a time when the United States was engaged in a dispute over shipments of hormone-treated beef to Europe.[49] Many states maintain relationships with Taiwan notwithstanding the potential for conflict with U.S. policy toward China; then-governor Bill Clinton of Arkansas, for example, visited Taiwan in the same year that the United States broke off official diplomatic relations with it.[50] And Kansas Governor Kathleen Sebelius agreed to lobby Congress to repeal federal sanctions against Cuba in exchange for Cuban purchases of Kansas products.[51]

Other state activities are even more directly analogous to the sort of political foreign policy that a nation-state might conduct. State foreign offices abroad occasionally seek to improve overall relations or secure the release of persons detained abroad.[52] Local governments have distanced themselves from national foreign policy by holding referenda on the Vietnam war, declaring themselves "nuclear-free zones," or establishing sister-city relationships with cities in countries at odds with the United States.[53] National authorities generally—but not always—ignore these efforts.[54] More commonly, states and cities take stands in areas where national authorities have not

[43] *See* Glennon & Sloane, *supra* note 22, at 61.

[44] *See, e.g.*, Kevin Sullivan, *Bush's Relations With Mexico Rooted in Symbols, Friendship*, Wash. Post, Feb. 13, 2001, *available at* https://www.washingtonpost.com/archive/politics/2001/02/13/bushs-relations-with-mexico-rooted-in-symbols-friendship/50ccbc3c-f778-411e-944d-be0009206548/?utm_term=.33e550774343.

[45] *See* Glennon & Sloane, *supra* note 22, at 64–65.

[46] *See id.* at 65.

[47] *See* Fry, *supra* note 2, at 309.

[48] *See id.* at 318.

[49] *See* Fry, *supra* note 32, at 95–96.

[50] *See id.* at 96.

[51] *See* Hollis, *supra* note 34, at 741–742.

[52] *See* Glennon & Sloane, *supra* note 22, at 67–68.

[53] *See* Fry, *supra* note 32, at 92–93.

[54] For example, when Oakland, California—the site of an important naval supply depot—purported to forbid the manufacture or storage of nuclear weapons, the U.S. Department of Justice successfully

adopted a firm policy. Roughly 150 states, cities, and counties divested themselves of investments in apartheid South Africa or penalized companies doing business in that country.[55] Some states adopted similar policies concerning Burma. Some—but by no means all—of these state policies have been struck down on the ground that they conflict with federal policy toward the relevant foreign state.[56]

Finally, states sometimes adopt nonbinding international law—that is, international treaties that the United States has not ratified at the national level. At least 185 local jurisdictions have taken measures designed to implement the Kyoto Protocols on preventing climate change.[57] In so doing, they have frequently expressed frustration at a lack of action by Washington, D.C.[58] Similarly, the Coalition of Northeastern Governors announced that "[r]egardless of the [Donald Trump] administration's recent decision to withdraw the United States from the Paris Climate Agreement, the Northeast states will continue to build on their successful efforts to reduce greenhouse gas emissions."[59] Other jurisdictions have announced that they will implement the Convention on the Elimination of All Forms of Discrimination Against Women (CEDAW) and the Convention on the Elimination of All Forms of Racial Discrimination.[60] To the extent that these measures do not *bind* U.S. entities internationally and are not preempted by affirmative federal legal requirements, it is difficult to object on constitutional grounds. Nonetheless, the effect—and often the purpose—may well be to embarrass national foreign policy by highlighting its inaction on these issues.

III. National Limits on the States in Foreign Affairs

This survey belies any notion that national foreign affairs are exclusive. Rather, "[t]he Constitution empowers the federal government to exercise *potentially plenary* authority in foreign relations, but it does not contemplate *exclusive* authority in this realm by *default*."[61] The old dual federalism regime—under which federal spheres of authority excluded all state and local activity, even in the absence of action by the national

sued to enjoin the local ordinance on the ground that it undermined national defense policy. *See id.* at 93–94.

[55] *See* Glennon & Sloane, *supra* note 22, at 70–71.

[56] *See* Crosby v. National Foreign Trade Council, 530 U.S. 363 (2000).

[57] *See* Glennon & Sloane, *supra* note 22, at 62.

[58] *See id.*

[59] Coalition of Northeastern Governors, *Statement on U.S. withdrawal from Paris Climate Agreement*, June 2, 2017, *available at* http://coneg.org/Data/Sites/1/media/paris-agreement-statement-6-2-17.pdf. *But see, e.g.*, Eugene Kontorovich, *The U.S. can't quit the Paris climate agreement, because it never actually joined*, Volokh Conspiracy, June 1, 2017, *available at* https://www.washingtonpost.com/news/volokh-conspiracy/wp/2017/06/01/the-u-s-cant-quit-the-paris-climate-agreement-because-it-never-actually-joined/?utm_term=.31a48794164d.

[60] Glennon & Sloane, *supra* note 22, at 63–64.

[61] *Id.* at xix–xx.

political branches—was thus inconsistent with the constitutional text. Although dual federalism retains some influence in foreign affairs,[62] American law now acknowledges concurrent national and state jurisdiction over many areas that affect foreign relations.

The Constitution does restrict state foreign affairs activity in two ways, however. *Dormant* restraints operate to restrict state activity even in the absence of affirmative action by the national political branches. These limits are largely vestigial in contemporary law. More importantly, affirmative actions by the national legislature or executive can preempt state governmental activity under the Supremacy Clause. The primacy of preemption is consistent with the general notion that our Constitution leaves it to the federal political branches to decide how much foreign affairs activity by subnational governments to permit.[63]

Dormant foreign affairs preemption reached its apogee in the 1968 case of *Zschernig v. Miller*.[64] That case concerned an Oregon probate statute providing that foreign citizens could inherit under Oregon law only if their country provided reciprocal rights to U.S. citizens and the foreign heirs could take the property in question "without confiscation."[65] State judges applying the statute tended to rule against heirs from communist bloc countries on the ground that the inherited property would be vulnerable to seizure. These cases frequently generated inflammatory judicial commentary. One Pennsylvania judge applying a similar statute, for example, opined that "[a]ll the known facts of a Sovietized state lead to the irresistible conclusion that sending American money to a person within the borders of an Iron Curtain country is like sending a basket of food to Little Red Ridinghood in care of her 'grandmother.'"[66] The U.S. Supreme Court found it "inescapable" that such laws affect international relations "in a persistent and subtle way."[67] Even though "[t]he several States . . . have traditionally regulated the descent and distribution of estates," the Court found that "those regulations must give way if they impair the effective exercise of the Nation's foreign policy."[68]

Zschernig did not specify the degree to which a state policy must "impair" national foreign policy in order to be unconstitutional. Indeed, the Court ignored the representation of the U.S. Solicitor General that the Oregon statute did *not* "unduly interfere[] with the United States' conduct of foreign relations."[69] But if, as the Court suggested,[70] a *potential* impairment of diplomatic relations is enough, then it is hard to imagine why nearly any of the state and local activities catalogued earlier would not be unconstitutional. One could imagine, for example, a court finding severance of sister-city ties over a disagreement with a foreign government's gay rights policy[71] quite comparable to the

[62] *See* Young, *Dual Federalism*, *supra* note 17, at 167–185.

[63] *See* GLENNON & SLOANE, *supra* note 22, at xx.

[64] 389 U.S. 429 (1968).

[65] *Id.* at 430–431.

[66] *Id.* at 437 n.8 (*quoting* In re Belemecich's Estate, 192 A.2d 740, 742 (Pa. 1963)).

[67] *Id.* at 440.

[68] *Id.*

[69] *See id.* at 443 (Stewart, J., concurring) (quoting the SG's representation as *amicus curiae*).

[70] *See id.* at 441 (majority opinion); *id.* at 443 (Stewart, J., concurring).

[71] *See supra* notes 40–43 and accompanying text.

commentary elicited by the Oregon law in *Zschernig*. Certainly, the damage to American policy from state enforcement of the death penalty is far more evident than the potential disruption occasioned by the Oregon probate statute.[72]

No subsequent Supreme Court decision has ever struck down a state or local law on *Zschernig*'s ground.[73] Lower courts have read the decision narrowly,[74] and the Supreme Court has upheld state actions that seem to present considerably clearer threats to national foreign relations. *Barclay's Bank v. Franchise Tax Board of California*[75] rejected a challenge to California's idiosyncratic method of taxing foreign multinational corporations, and *Medellín v. Texas*[76] affirmed a state court's right to ignore orders from both the International Court of Justice and the president of the United States to reexamine the case of a capital murderer claiming violation of his rights under the Vienna Convention on Consular Relations. In both cases, the international outcry was significantly greater than in *Zschernig*.[77]

The closest the Court has come to relying on *Zschernig* is its decision in *American Insurance Association v. Garamendi*,[78] which struck down California's Holocaust Victim Insurance Relief Act (HVIRA), a statute designed to facilitate suits by Holocaust survivors and their heirs to recover insurance proceeds either stolen by the Nazis or simply unpaid by the insurers. Noting that the U.S. government had entered into executive agreements with Germany, Austria, and France concerning the lost insurance money, the Court held California's act invalid.[79] Justice Souter's majority opinion discussed *Zschernig* at some length but determined that "the express federal policy" embodied in the executive agreements, which aimed to solve the problem through negotiation rather than to facilitate litigation, and "the clear conflict raised by the state statute" with that policy "are alone enough to require state law to yield."[80] *Garamendi*

[72] *See generally* Warren, *supra* note 25. In 2004, a prominent international law scholar who later became State Department Legal Adviser told this author that, in his view, state administration of the death penalty *was* unconstitutional under *Zschernig*. The U.S. Supreme Court is unlikely to issue any such holding any time soon.

[73] *See* Ku & Yoo, *supra* note 31, at 155.

[74] *See* Glennon & Sloane, *supra* note 22, at 116–118.

[75] 512 U.S. 298 (1994).

[76] 552 U.S. 491 (2008).

[77] *See* Goldsmith, *supra* note 17, at 1699–1701 (noting that the plaintiffs in *Barclays* relied heavily on *Zschernig* and that the California scheme had provoked "enormous diplomatic controversy," and concluding that the opinion in *Barclays* "undermine[d] much of the logic of [*Zschernig*]"); Ku & Yoo, *supra* note 31, at 156–157 ("[T]he Court's decision [in *Medellín*] to permit Texas to act in conflict with express federal policy set by the President further confirms the end of the *Zschernig* conception of federal exclusivity over all matters affecting foreign affairs.").

[78] 539 U.S. 396 (2003).

[79] *See id.* at 427.

[80] *Id.* at 417–20, 427. *But see, e.g.*, Glennon & Sloane, *supra* note 22, at 121–145 (arguing that the Court applied preemption doctrine more broadly than in domestic cases); Brannon P. Denning & Michael D. Ramsey, American Insurance Association v. Garamendi *and Executive Preemption in Foreign Affairs*, 46 Wm. & Mary L. Rev. 825 (2004) (arguing that *Garamendi* violated separation of powers by according preemptive force to an executive agreement).

reflects current law's focus on affirmative acts by the national political branches that may preempt state actions affecting foreign relations.[81]

Preemption doctrine addresses the central question of any concurrent powers regime: How are conflicts between measures adopted by one level of government and those of another to be identified and resolved?[82] The Supremacy Clause subordinates state law to federal constitutional provisions, treaties, and statutes,[83] but identification of conflicts is considerably more difficult. American law makes this primarily a function of Congress's intent.[84] Where that intent is ambiguous, there is a presumption against preemption,[85] although courts often apply that presumption inconsistently and sometimes neglect to mention it at all.[86]

The central question concerning preemption in American foreign relations law is whether courts should find preemption more readily in foreign affairs cases.[87] Several recent cases suggest that the Supreme Court thinks they should. In *Crosby v. National Foreign Trade Council*,[88] for example, the Court struck down a Massachusetts law imposing trade sanctions on Myanmar (formerly Burma) in protest of that country's human rights record. Although Congress had also enacted a law concerning trade sanctions on Myanmar, the case for preemption was relatively weak: there was no express preemption clause in the federal law, Massachusetts' policy pointed in the same direction as Congress's, and although Congress had delegated to the president broad authority to control sanctions policy, he had not exercised that authority to preempt Massachusetts' own measures.[89] Although the Court purported not to decide whether the presumption against preemption should apply in foreign affairs cases,[90] its analysis hardly seems faithful to such a presumption.[91] Likewise, in *Garamendi*, the Court found California's statute preempted notwithstanding that Congress had taken no action, and even the president's executive agreement made no mention of preemption

[81] *See, e.g.*, Ku & Yoo, *supra* note 31, at 156 (concluding that "the *Garamendi* approach implicitly rejected the sweeping version of federal exclusivity adopted by the *Zschernig* majority").

[82] *See generally* Daniel J. Meltzer, *Preemption and Textualism*, 112 Mich. L. Rev. 1 (2013); Stephen A. Gardbaum, *The Nature of Preemption*, 79 Cornell L. Rev. 767 (1994); Ernest A. Young, *"The Ordinary Diet of the Law": The Presumption Against Preemption in the Roberts Court*, 2011 Sup. Ct. Rev. 253 (2012).

[83] *See* U.S. Const. art. VI, cl. 2.

[84] *See, e.g.*, Medtronic, Inc. v. Lohr, 518 U.S. 470 (1996) ("The purpose of Congress is the ultimate touchstone in every pre-emption case.").

[85] *See* Rice v. Santa Fe Elevator Corp., 331 U.S. 218, 230 (1947) (stating that "the historic police powers of the States" are not to be superseded "unless that was the clear and manifest purpose of Congress").

[86] *See* Young, *Ordinary Diet*, *supra* note 82, at 307–310.

[87] *Compare, e.g.*, Jack L. Goldsmith, *Statutory Foreign Affairs Preemption*, 2000 Sup. Ct. Rev. 175 (arguing that there should be no presumption against preemption in foreign affairs cases), *with* Young, *Dual Federalism*, *supra* note 17, at 174–176 (arguing that the ordinary presumption against preemption should apply across the board).

[88] 530 U.S. 363 (2000).

[89] *See* Young, *Dual Federalism*, *supra* note 17, at 170–172.

[90] *See* 530 U.S. at 374 n.8.

[91] *See* Young, *Dual Federalism*, *supra* note 17, at 168–173.

or the California law.[92] Had *Garamendi* been a domestic case, it surely would have come out the other way.

Crosby and *Garamendi* were both cases, however, in which the states were quite deliberately seeking to pursue their own policies on the international stage. The Court has less readily found preemption in cases where the states seemed more intent on governing activity within their own jurisdictions, even though the states' actions might significantly impact foreign affairs. *Chamber of Commerce v. Whiting*,[93] for example, upheld an Arizona law making it more difficult for undocumented aliens to obtain employment within the state. And *Barclays Bank*[94] upheld California's tax on multinational corporations in the face of considerable international protest.

A distinction between "direct" or "purposeful" effects on foreign relations, on the one hand, and "incidental" or "inadvertent" effects, on the other, seems unlikely to prove stable or coherent over the long haul. The Supreme Court relied for a time on a similar distinction between "direct" and "indirect" effects to police the boundary between state and federal authority in the domestic realm,[95] but that doctrine ultimately foundered in a sea of incoherence.[96] The crucial point is simply that the Court has not yet reached equilibrium on the standard for preemption in foreign affairs cases, and it is unlikely to do so as long as the Court applies different rules in the foreign and domestic contexts. That is because, as discussed further in this chapter's Conclusion, foreign and domestic affairs pervasively overlap in the modern world.

IV. Federalism-Based Limits on National Foreign Policy

American federalism limits both state and national authority. Limits on national power have not been as salient in foreign relations law, but they do exist. Moreover, the existence of the states as distinct power centers with traditional interests and prerogatives has imposed important *political* limits on the nation's conduct of its external affairs.

The most important legal limits on national action stem from the principle, basic to American federalism, that the national government is one of limited and enumerated powers. That principle has sometimes been contested in foreign affairs. An important

[92] *See* 539 U.S. at 438 (Ginsburg, J., dissenting) (noting that not only did the executive agreement not specifically address preemption, it also failed to mention public disclosure—which the California law required—as a concern under the agreement).

[93] 563 U.S. 582 (2011).

[94] Barclay's Bank v. Franchise Tax Board of California, 512 U.S. 298 (1994).

[95] *See*, e.g., United States v. E.C. Knight Co., 156 U.S. 1 (1895).

[96] *See*, e.g., Lawrence Lessig, *Translating Federalism*: United States v. Lopez, 1995 Sup. Ct. Rev. 125, 176–178.

line of cases, for example, maintained that power over immigration stems from the United States' existence as a sovereign state, not from the enumerated authority of the Constitution, and was therefore not limited by constitutional constraints—not only federalism limitations but also the Bill of Rights.[97] This notion of "powers inherent in sovereignty" survives in much-attenuated form in the doctrine of Congress's "plenary power" over immigration,[98] as well as in the *Curtiss-Wright* decision[99] suggesting that constraints on legislative delegation of authority to the president are lessened in foreign affairs. But the inherent powers notion is fundamentally inconsistent with contemporary understandings of limited government.[100]

The enumerated powers of the national government in foreign affairs are very broad but not unlimited. The most important limitations go not to the *subjects* on which national power may operate—virtually any interaction between domestic actors and the outside world will, for example, fall within Congress's power "to regulate commerce with foreign nations"[101]—but to the *means* that the national government may employ and the institutions that must participate in policy formation. For example, Congress has broad power to "define and punish . . . offenses against the law of nations."[102] But because the Constitution requires that *Congress* make the laws,[103] attempts to get federal *courts* to incorporate customary international law into federal law without legislative authorization have been highly controversial.[104] Congress plainly may regulate immigration, yet the anticommandeering doctrine—which forbids Congress to "commandeer" state officials and require them to implement federal law—limits Congress's ability to require state and local law enforcement to police illegal immigrants.[105] The constitutionally protected sovereign immunity of the states from lawsuits may well complicate Congress's ability to provide remedies against state

[97] *See,* e.g., Fong Yue Ting v. United States, 149 U.S. 698 (1893); Chae Chan Ping v. United States, 130 U.S. 581 (1889).

[98] *Compare,* e.g., Kleindienst v. Mandel, 408 U.S. 753 (1972) (holding that Congress's plenary power over immigration sharply limits First Amendment rights in the immigration context), *with* Zadvydas v. Davis, 533 U.S. 678, 695 (2001) (insisting that the immigration power is "subject to important constitutional limitations").

[99] United States v. Curtiss-Wright Export Corp., 299 U.S. 304 (1936).

[100] *See generally* Sarah H. Cleveland, *Powers Inherent in Sovereignty: Indians, Aliens, Territories, and the Nineteenth Century Origins of Plenary Power over Foreign Affairs*, 81 Tex. L. Rev. 1 (2002).

[101] U.S. Const. art. I, § 8, cl. 3.

[102] *Id.*, art. I, § 8, cl. 10.

[103] *See* Erie Railroad Co. v. Tompkins, 304 U.S. 64 (1938).

[104] *Compare,* e.g., Curtis A. Bradley & Jack L. Goldsmith, *Customary International Law as Federal Common Law: A Critique of the Modern Position*, 110 Harv. L. Rev. 815 (1997), and Ernest A. Young, *Sorting Out the Debate over Customary International Law*, 42 Va. J. Int'l L. 365 (2002), *with* Koh, *supra* note 21.

[105] *See,* e.g., County of Santa Clara v. Trump, 250 F. Supp. 3d 497, 533–534 (N.D. Cal. 2017) (entering a preliminary injunction against President Trump's executive order purporting to cut off federal funds to "sanctuary cities" declining to enforce federal immigration laws). Litigation continues over the sanctuary cities order as this chapter goes to press.

governments for violations of certain treaties.[106] And despite the president's broad authority to conduct foreign affairs, he may not—without legislative authorization—issue orders to state courts requiring that they comply with the mandates of international tribunals.[107]

One much-contested question is whether Congress may implement treaties by legislation that cannot be grounded in one of Congress's enumerated powers.[108] *Missouri v. Holland*,[109] which involved legislation implementing a treaty that protected migratory birds, held that Congress has such authority. *Holland* has been read to suggest that Congress has freestanding power to legislate on any subject the national government might choose to make a treaty about.[110] The potential impact of that holding has grown as treaty-making has come to concern subjects that the Constitution's Framers would have considered purely domestic.[111] Recently, in *Bond v. United States*,[112] three justices questioned *Holland*. Justice Scalia, joined by Justice Thomas, took the view that Congress's power, under the Necessary and Proper Clause, "to help the President *make* treaties is not a power to *implement* treaties already made.... To legislate compliance with the United States' treaty obligations, Congress must rely upon its independent (though quite robust) Article I, § 8 powers."[113] And Justice Thomas, joined by Justices Scalia and Alito, also suggested that power to make treaties is limited to matters of international concern.[114] Although the *Bond* majority avoided reaching these questions,[115] *Holland* faces an uncertain future.

The scope of the national treaty power remains unresolved precisely because the most important restraints on national foreign affairs actions that encroach on state prerogatives are political, not judicial, in nature. In foreign affairs as elsewhere, American federalism relies primarily on the political representation of the states in

[106] *See*, e.g., Breard v. Greene, 523 U.S. 371 (1998) (holding that state sovereign immunity barred a suit by Paraguay to enforce U.S. obligations under the Vienna Convention on Consular Relations); Carlos Manuel Vazquez, *Treaties and the Eleventh Amendment*, 42 VA. J. INT'L L. 713 (2002).

[107] *See* Medellín v. Texas, 552 U.S. 491 (2008).

[108] *See* Curtis A. Bradley, *The Treaty Power and American Federalism*, 97 MICH. L. REV. 390 (1998) (arguing that federalism limits the treaty power), *with* David M. Golove, *Treaty-Making and the Nation: The Constitutional Foundations of the Nationalist Conception of the Treaty Power*, 98 MICH. L. REV. 1075 (2000) (rejecting this view).

[109] 252 U.S. 416 (1920).

[110] Ironically, Canada (on behalf of whom Great Britain had signed the treaty at issue in *Holland*) lacks such a general national implementation power. *See* Charles-Emmanuel Côté, *Federalism and Foreign Affairs in Canada*, ch. 16 in this volume.

[111] *See* Bradley, *supra* note 108, at 396–399.

[112] 134 S. Ct. 2077 (2014).

[113] *Id.* at 2099 (Scalia, J., concurring in the judgment). *See also* Nicholas Roskenkranz, *Executing the Treaty Power*, 118 HARV. L. REV. 1867 (2005).

[114] 134 S. Ct. at 2077, 2103–2110 (Thomas, J., concurring in the judgment).

[115] *See id.* at 2091–2092 (majority opinion) (construing the treaty-implementing statute not to reach a wholly domestic crime).

Congress and the procedural difficulty of making federal law.[116] For example, Congress almost never tests the limits of its treaty-implementing power under *Holland*; on the contrary, the Senate has generally served as a zealous guardian of state prerogatives by refusing to ratify or attaching reservations to international conventions that intrude into traditional state spheres.[117] And the national executive also weighs federalism concerns—at least sometimes—in deciding not to pursue or sign particular treaties.[118] These same political and procedural forces tend to limit the extent to which national preemption threatens the states' own foreign initiatives.

V. Conclusion: Looking Forward

The federal relationship in U.S. foreign affairs is likely to face increasing pressure going forward from globalization and the polarization of American domestic politics. Three aspects of globalization are important here. The first is the pervasive overlap between foreign and domestic concerns, including not only increasing integration of domestic markets into the global economy but also the increasing salience of cross-border problems like pollution and terrorism. This has been going on for some time; Senator William Fulbright, former chairman of the Senate Foreign Relations Committee, observed in 1974 that "[i]t has ceased to be useful, if it ever was, to deal with foreign policy as a category distinct from domestic policy."[119] Classically diplomatic problems like dealing with the acquisition of nuclear weapons by Iran or North Korea may remain distinct, but foreign relations are now pervasively concerned with other sorts of issues—trade, climate change, human rights, and terrorism—whose international dimensions are not readily separable from the domestic.

A second and related aspect of globalization is the continuing domesticization of international law. The international law known to the American Founders focused primarily on the relationship of one state to another—the determination of boundaries, the predicates and conduct of wars, and the conduct of diplomatic nations.[120] When it focused on individuals, they tended to be foreign nationals, especially diplomats, so

[116] *See, e.g.*, Bradford R. Clark, *Separation of Powers as a Safeguard of Federalism*, 79 Tex. L. Rev. 1321 (2001); Herbert Wechsler, *The Political Safeguards of Federalism: The Role of the States in the Composition and Selection of the National Government*, 54 Colum. L. Rev. 543 (1954).

[117] *See* Peter Spiro, *The Waning Federal Monopoly over Foreign Relations*, Lawfare, Jan. 9, 2017, *available at* https://www.lawfareblog.com/waning-federal-monopoly-over-foreign-relations-0 (book review).

[118] *See* Duncan B. Hollis, *Executive Federalism: Forging New Federalist Constraints on the Treaty Power*, 79 S. Cal. L. Rev. 1327 (2006).

[119] *Quoted in* Glennon & Sloane, *supra* note 22, at xvii.

[120] *See, e.g.*, Ku & Yoo, *supra* note 31, at 35–37.

that norms governing such treatment were an extension of one nation's obligations to another.[121] In the twentieth century, however, international law came to be significantly concerned with nations' treatment of their own citizens.[122] This, after all, was a central lesson of the Nuremberg trials. As a result, international law now covers matters like education, family law, and criminal justice that, a century ago, would have been considered wholly domestic.[123] This means that state and local governments cannot help being *international* actors, and conflicts proliferate between state and international law.

The third important aspect of globalization is the "disaggregation of the state" in international affairs—that is, "the rising need for and capacity of different domestic government institutions to engage in activities beyond their borders, often with their foreign counterparts."[124] Because central problems of governance—crime, pollution, economic instability—no longer respect national borders, state and local leaders must look not only to Washington, D.C., but also abroad. As Ivo Duchacek has observed, "the well-being of the subnational electorates, and therefore their leaders' own staying power, has clearly begun to depend on these leaders' ability to couple their primary links with the national centre and its funding agencies with their new lines to foreign sources of economic, financial, and industrial power."[125] Hence Texas governors seek good relations with the Mexican border states, and Great Lakes states form organizational networks with their Canadian counterparts.

The increasing polarization of American politics is also likely to encourage autonomous foreign relations activities by American states and municipalities in the coming years. The two major American political parties were once "big tents"; they each had conservative and liberal wings, and party identification corresponded only loosely with ideology. Bipartisan cooperation was often possible as politicians could reach across the party divide to persons with similar ideological preferences.[126] In recent decades, the parties have each become more ideologically coherent; conservative Democrats switched parties to become Republicans and liberal Republicans became Democrats. At the same time, the ideological distance between the median Republican and the

[121] Customary international law did once govern commercial relations among some merchants. That law raised federalism problems of its own. *See generally* William A. Fletcher, *General Common Law and Section 34 of the Judiciary Act of 1789: The Example of Marine Insurance*, 97 HARV. L. REV. 1513 (1983). But that general commercial law bore little relationship to the customary international law at the center of modern debates. *See* Emily Kadens & Ernest A. Young, *How Customary Is Customary International Law?*, 54 WM. & MARY L. REV. 885, 914–920 (2013).

[122] *See, e.g.*, KU & YOO, *supra* note 31, at 37–38.

[123] *See* Spiro, *supra* note 117.

[124] ANNE-MARIE SLAUGHTER, A NEW WORLD ORDER 12 (2004).

[125] Ivo D. Duchacek, *Perforated Sovereignties: Towards a Typology of New Actors in International Relations*, *in* FEDERALISM AND INTERNATIONAL RELATIONS: THE ROLE OF SUBNATIONAL UNITS 1, 6 (Hans J. Michelmann & Panayotis Soldatos eds., 1990).

[126] *See, e.g.*, RONALD BROWNSTEIN, THE SECOND CIVIL WAR: HOW EXTREME PARTISANSHIP HAS PARALYZED WASHINGTON AND POLARIZED AMERICA (2008).

median Democrat has grown. The result is a highly polarized politics in which bipartisan cooperation is unlikely.[127]

One consequence of polarization is gridlock at the national level. These conditions encourage presidents to act unilaterally, but such actions may be ephemeral if control of the executive shifts to the other party. Hence President Barack Obama's agreement to the Paris Climate Accords and his refusal to deport large classes of undocumented aliens were both rescinded by President Trump. But most *state* governments are not so closely divided; as of August 2017, nearly two-thirds of the states had unitary party control.[128] National gridlock thus encourages state governments to act, including in areas that affect foreign affairs. When states adopt international standards as their own despite nonratification by Washington, or when they enter into agreements on subjects like climate change with foreign governments, they are taking advantage of their own superior capacity for action in an era of polarized national politics.[129] And national gridlock will likely make it far more difficult for the national political branches to rein in such actions.

For all these reasons, arising from both globalization and polarization, the intersection of federalism and foreign affairs in American law and politics will likely remain complex for the foreseeable future. It is too late in the day to cling to *Belmont*'s mantra that states "do not exist" in foreign affairs. The task for politicians, lawyers, and scholars going forward is to find ways to ensure that states' engagement with foreign affairs is constructive, rather than destructive, of the national interest.

Comparative foreign relations law could illuminate this ongoing domestic conversation by exploding some enduring myths about the necessity of national exclusivity in foreign relations law. The European Union, for example, continues to grope toward a common foreign policy while recognizing that its member states will often go their own way.[130] The results have not always been pretty, but Europe manages to play an effective role in world affairs. Likewise, Canadian provinces have demonstrated that subnational units may play a low-key but effective role without fatally undermining national policy.[131] As frequently happens in comparative law, the lesson is not so much that American law should take this form or that, but rather that the world is frequently more complicated—and more interesting—than long-standing assumptions have recognized.

[127] *See id.*; *see also* Thomas E. Mann, *Foreword*, *in* AMERICAN GRIDLOCK: THE SOURCES, CHARACTER, AND IMPACT OF POLITICAL POLARIZATION xxi, xxii (James A. Thurber & Antoine Yoshinaka eds., 2015).

[128] *See State Government Trifectas*, Ballotpedia, *available at* https://ballotpedia.org/State_government_trifectas (visited Sept. 5, 2017).

[129] Polarization occurs not only among states, but also *within* states between urban and rural communities. Hence many incidences of subnational foreign policy involve municipal governments, not states. This is particularly true of subnational efforts to implement international standards like the Kyoto Protocols or the Convention on the Elimination of All Forms of Discrimination Against Women.

[130] *See* Robert Schütze, *Foreign Affairs Federalism in the European Union*, ch. 19 in this volume.

[131] *See* Côté, *supra* note 110.

CHAPTER 16

FEDERALISM AND FOREIGN AFFAIRS IN CANADA

CHARLES-EMMANUEL CÔTÉ

It is impossible to study the foreign relations law of Canada without dealing with federalism. Preservation of the federal principle in the construction of the Canadian Constitution by the courts and its operation by governments has had and continues to have a significant impact on the rules dealing with foreign affairs. Unlike the United States, the issue has not materialized in preemption cases involving provincial legislation that would encroach on foreign affairs.[1] Contrary to Switzerland, participation of provinces in foreign affairs is not channeled through the upper chamber of the federal parliament.[2] As opposed to India, the written Constitution does not recognize a strong role for the federal government in foreign affairs.[3] The effect of federalism on foreign affairs in Canada has varied over time due to various external and internal factors, each of which corresponds to a period in its development. Following this chronological approach allows for a better understanding of how the law addresses the issues of treaty-making, treaty implementation, and provincial participation to international conferences and organizations. This chapter will consider those issues during the time of Confederation and the process of acquisition of statehood by Canada (Section I); during the debates on constitutional reform and in the aftermath of the Quiet Revolution in Quebec (Section II); and finally, in the age of globalization and free trade (Section III).

[1] *See* Ernest A. Young, *Foreign Affairs Federalism in the United States*, ch. 15 in this volume.

[2] *See* Roland Portmann, *Foreign Affairs Federalism in Switzerland*, ch. 17 in this volume.

[3] *See* Anamika Asthana & Happymon Jacob, *Federalism and Foreign Affairs in India*, ch. 18 in this volume.

I. Confederation and Acquisition of Statehood

Colonial Period and Section 132 of the Constitution Act, 1867

A striking feature of the Constitution Act, 1867[4] is the absence of any comprehensive treatment of foreign affairs. The Fathers of Confederation did not intend to draft the Constitution of a sovereign state, but rather that of a united colony still connected to her mother country.[5] Thus, little is said in the Act concerning foreign affairs, treaty-making, or the interplay between international law and Canadian law. A significant exception to this is the exclusive power to implement certain treaties granted to the federal parliament by Section 132.

The Canadian Constitution being "similar in principle to that of the United Kingdom,"[6] principles found in the foreign relations law of Great Britain may be imported into Canada, as long as they are compatible with its federal structure. Under the British Constitution, only parliament may amend domestic law in order to implement a treaty.[7] The pressing issue at the time of Confederation was that of the power to implement treaties signed by London. Section 132 provides the following:

> The Parliament and Government of Canada shall have all Powers necessary or properfor performing the Obligations of Canada or of any Province thereof, as Part of the British Empire, towards Foreign Countries, arising under Treaties between the Empire and such Foreign Countries.[8]

This means that the federal parliament acquired the power to legislate in the provincial jurisdictions once London signed a treaty with a foreign country, even if the parliament could not do so otherwise. The Migratory Birds Convention Act[9] is probably the last federal legislation adopted under this power to be still in force, raising the question of the permanency of federal jurisdiction if the treaty is

[4] *Constitution Act, 1867*, 30 & 31 Vict., c. 3 (U.K.), reprinted in R.S.C. 1985, App. II, No. 5.

[5] *See* Province of Canada, Parliamentary Debates on the Subject of the Confederation of the British North American Provinces 136, 367–369 (1865) (statements of Thomas D'Arcy-McGee and Hector Louis Langevin); U.K., H.L., Parliamentary Debates, vol. 185, 557 (Feb. 19, 1867) (statement of Viscount Charles Stanley Monck).

[6] *Constitution Act, 1867*, *supra* note 4, Preamble.

[7] *See* Walker v. Baird, [1892] A.C. 491, 496–497 (P.C.); Parlement Belge (1879), 4 P.D. 129, 154–155 (Ad. Ct.), reversed for other reasons by (1880) 5 P.D. 197 (C.A.).

[8] *Constitution Act, 1867*, *supra* note 4, § 132.

[9] S.C. 1994, c. 22.

amended by Canada.[10] It aims to implement a treaty signed in 1916 by the United Kingdom.[11]

Two observations are in order about Section 132. First, it was drafted in the nineteenth century, at a time when treaties dealt mostly with issues of war and peace, international trade, or immigration—all matters falling within federal jurisdiction. It is telling that this federal power was not controversial in the preconfederation debates, from its insertion in the Quebec Resolutions to the drafting of Section 132 in London.[12] It was in accordance with the desire of the United Kingdom to speak with a unified colony when it came to its foreign affairs. Nevertheless, the British government developed the practice of consulting with the provinces whenever it contemplated signing a treaty falling under their jurisdiction.[13]

Second, it is worth noting that the language of the provision evolved in the preparatory works from the power to implement "Treaties between Great Britain and [Foreign] Countries"[14] to that to implement "Treaties between the Empire and . . . Foreign Countries."[15] This led to uncertainties as to which treaties fall within the purview of Section 132. All treaties signed by Great Britain that are applicable to Canada? Treaties signed by Great Britain but not those signed by Canada in the name of Great Britain? Only treaties applicable to the whole Empire? Moreover, Section 132 is not included in the provisions on distribution of powers, but rather with the miscellaneous provisions at the end of the Constitution Act, 1867.

Treaty-Making Power and Government Practice

The process by which Canada reached statehood was incremental and culminated with the severing of the jurisdiction of the British Parliament over Canada by the Statute of

[10] In Directeur des poursuites criminelles et pénales v. Frégeau (Sept. 10, 2015), Montmagny, 300-61-021781-139 (C.Q.), a hunter found to have used ammunition prohibited under this legislation challenged its constitutionality based on Section 132. The hunter argued that the federal legislation could no longer be valid under this provision, since the original treaty was amended by a subsequent treaty signed by Canada. The Crown eventually dropped the charges thus avoiding going to the merits of the constitutional issue.

[11] This is the very same treaty as the one in dispute in the landmark U.S. case *Missouri v. Holland*, 252 U.S. 416 (1920).

[12] *See* Conference of Delegates from the Provinces of Canada, Nova Scotia, and New Brunswick, and the Colonies of Newfoundland and Prince Edward Island, *Resolutions*, Quebec, Oct. 10–27 1864, No. 30, at 38 [*Quebec Resolutions*], *in* CONFEDERATION: BEING A SERIES OF HITHERTO UNPUBLISHED DOCUMENTS BEARING ON THE BRITISH NORTH AMERICA ACT (Joseph Pope ed., 1895); Conference of Delegates from the Province of Canada, Nova Scotia, and New Brunswick, *Resolutions*, London, Dec. 4–14, 1866, No. 29, at 98 *in* Pope, *id.*

[13] Arthur B. Keith, *The Privy Council Decisions: A Comment from Great Britain*, 15 CAN. BAR REV. 428, 430–431 (1937).

[14] *Quebec Resolutions*, *supra* note 12, No. 30.

[15] *Constitution Act, 1867*, *supra* note 4, § 132.

Westminster, 1931.[16] Before the legal recognition of its independence, Canada had already started to sign treaties with foreign powers, most notably at the Paris Peace Conference in 1919, as a part of the British Empire, and later in its own capacity.[17] Under the British Constitution, there is a clear distinction between the conclusion of treaties and their implementation; the government has the exclusive power to conclude treaties without the assent of parliament.[18] This power derives from the common law of England, which attributes the prerogative to conduct foreign affairs to the Crown on the advice of her ministers. The British Parliament has not legislated to take away or reduce the treaty-making power of the government.

The systematic practice in Canada has been that the federal government concludes treaties for Canada, despite the fact that no constitutional provision deals explicitly with treaty-making power.[19] Ottawa considers that this exclusive federal treaty-making power stems implicitly from the devolution of the royal prerogative from the king to the governor general of Canada concerning all powers that it exercised over its former colony.[20] The Department of Foreign Affairs, Trade and Development Act[21] does not refer explicitly to treaty-making, but it provides that the minister of foreign affairs is to "conduct and manage international negotiations as they relate to Canada."[22]

Treaty Implementation and the *Labour Conventions* Case

While it was expected that an evolutionary interpretation of the Constitution of Canada would maintain the exclusive federal power to implement treaties now signed by Canada, the Privy Council took a different view in the landmark *Labour Conventions* case.[23] It was decided against the backdrop of two earlier cases from the early 1930s, dealing respectively with the power of the federal parliament to pass legislation to implement the 1919 aerial navigation convention and the 1927 radiotelegraph

[16] 22 Geo. 5, c. 4 (U.K.), reprinted in R.S.C. 1985, App. II, No. 27, §§ 2 and 4. With the notable exception of amendment to the Constitution of Canada, which remained within the jurisdiction of the British Parliament until 1982. The federal parliament also gained exclusive extraterritorial jurisdiction (*id.* § 3).

[17] ALLAN E. GOTLIEB, CANADIAN TREATY-MAKING 6–10 (1968).

[18] Canada (A.G.) v. Ontario (A.G.), [1937] A.C. 326, 347 (P.C.) [*Labour Conventions*]; ARNOLD D. MCNAIR, THE LAW OF TREATIES 68–69 (1961).

[19] *See* Léonard H.J. Legault, *Canadian Practice in International Law during 1979 as Reflected Mainly in Public Correspondence and Statements of the Department of External Affairs*, 18 CAN. Y.B. INT'L L. 301, 314 (1980).

[20] PAUL MARTIN, SECRETARY OF STATE FOR EXTERNAL AFFAIRS, FEDERALISM AND INTERNATIONAL RELATION 13–15 (1968). *See* George R., *Letters Patent Constituting the Office of Governor General of Canada*, Oct. 1, 1947, reprinted in R.S.C. 1985, App. II, No. 31.

[21] S.C. 2013, c. 33 § 174.

[22] *Id.* § 10(2)(c).

[23] *Labour Conventions*, *supra* note 18. *See* Vincent C. MacDonald, *Canada's Power to Perform Treaty Obligations. Part I*, 11 CAN. BAR REV. 581, 599 (1933); A. W. Rogers, *Some Aspects of Treaty Legislation*, 4 CAN. BAR REV. 40, 43 (1926).

convention. A key element of these cases was that jurisdiction over these topics was not clearly assigned to the federal government or the provinces. The Privy Council found both federal statutes constitutionally valid for various reasons, blurring more than clarifying the law on treaty implementation.

In *Aeronautics Reference*,[24] the Privy Council considered Section 132 applicable because London signed the 1919 aerial navigation convention for the whole British Empire. Nevertheless, it mentioned that an evolutionary interpretation of Section 132 could maintain the federal power to implement treaties signed by Canada.[25] Adding to the complexity of its reasoning, it stated that the federal legislation could also be valid under the general power to make laws for the "Peace, Order and Good Government" (POGG) of Canada, because of the national dimensions of aeronautics.[26] The reasoning of the Privy Council in *Radio Reference*[27] was equally obscure. Unlike *Aeronautics Reference*, this case dealt with a treaty concluded by Canada, not by London. The Privy Council found that the federal parliament had the exclusive power to implement treaties signed by Canada based on both the residuary branch and the national dimension branch of POGG.[28] Finally, it reasoned that the topic of radiotelegraphic communications fell under federal jurisdiction following an evolutionary interpretation of its power over telegraph, works, and extraprovincial undertakings.[29]

The *Labour Conventions* case arose out of the decision of Ottawa in the mid-1930s to legislate directly in the provincial jurisdiction of labor law to implement a series of conventions adopted at the International Labour Organization (ILO). In addressing the validity of this legislation, the Privy Council first distinguished the case from *Aeronautics Reference* and *Radio Reference*.[30] Regarding the former, the Council recalled that the implementing legislation fell squarely within Section 132 since London signed the treaty for the whole British Empire. In the latter case, it considered that the federal parliament had jurisdiction over radiotelegraphic communications not because it implemented a treaty, but because the topic itself fell within federal jurisdiction following an evolutionary interpretation. It considered all other statements on federal powers to be *obiter* and thus concluded that neither case had settled the law on implementation of treaties signed by Canada in provincial jurisdiction. Having dissipated the ambiguities left by its previous judgments, the Privy Council found that Section 132 was now obsolete as it only concerned treaties signed by London.[31] It privileged a teleological interpretation of the Constitution of Canada

[24] Re the Regulation and Control of Aeronautics in Canada, [1932] A.C. 54, 74 (P.C.) [*Aeronautics Reference*].

[25] *Id.* at 73.

[26] *Id.* at 77. *See Constitution Act, 1867*, *supra* note 4, § 91 *intro*.

[27] Re Regulation and Control of Radio Communication in Canada, [1932] A.C. 304 (P.C.) [*Radio Reference*].

[28] *Id.* at 312–314.

[29] *Id.* at 314–315. *See Constitution Act, 1867*, *supra* note 4, §§ 91(29) and 92(10).

[30] *Labour Conventions*, *supra* note 18, at 349–351.

[31] *Id.* at 349–350.

over an evolutionary one, aiming at preserving the Constitution's key objective to establish a federal state.

The Privy Council ruled that there is no autonomous, exclusive power to implement treaties signed by Canada under the Constitution.[32] Rather, the normal distribution of powers remains applicable when it comes to treaty implementation: only the federal parliament may legislate to implement a treaty dealing with matters falling within its jurisdiction, and the same is true for provincial parliaments as regards their own jurisdiction.

Aware of the consequences of its ruling in *Labour Conventions*, the Privy Council stressed the importance of cooperation between Ottawa and the provinces in conducting the foreign affairs of Canada:

> It must not be thought that the result of this decision is that Canada is incompetent to legislate in performance of its treaty obligations. In totality of legislative powers, Dominion and Provincial together, she is fully equipped. But the legislative powers remain distributed and if in the exercise of her new functions derived from her new international status she incurs obligations they must, so far as legislation be concerned when they deal with provincial classes of subjects, be dealt with by the totality of powers, in other words, by co-operation between the Dominion and the Provinces.[33]

Thus, the rationale of *Labour Conventions* is grounded in the federal principle, later identified as one of the fundamental unwritten principles of the Constitution of Canada.[34]

II. Constitutional Reform and Quiet Revolution

Failed Attempts to Revisit the *Labour Conventions* Case

The *Labour Conventions* case generated criticism immediately after its issuance. Scholars, the federal government, and even the courts expressed their discontent with the solution found by the Privy Council to accommodate federalism with treaty implementation. The fear was that Canada would be impotent in conducting its foreign affairs, Ottawa being unable to guarantee the implementation of treaties that it signs.

The Supreme Court of Canada has explicitly criticized the *Labour Conventions* case on two occasions. In *Francis v. R*,[35] Chief Justice Kerwin stated in *obiter* that "it may be necessary in connection with other matters to consider in the future the judgement of

[32] *Id.* at 351–352. [33] *Id.* at 354.

[34] *See* Reference re Secession of Quebec, [1998] 2 S.C.R. 217, paras. 55–60.

[35] [1956] S.C.R. 618.

the Judicial Committee in the Labour Convention Case."[36] Chief Justice Laskin went beyond mere criticisms twenty years later in *MacDonald v. Vapor Canada Ltd.*,[37] again in *obiter*, going as far as proposing new detailed treaty implementation rules:

> In my opinion, assuming Parliament has power to pass legislation implementing a treaty or convention in relation to matters covered by the treaty or convention which would otherwise be for provincial legislation alone, the exercise of that power must be manifested in the implementing legislation and not be left to inference. The Courts should be able to say, on the basis of the expression of the legislation, that it is implementing legislation. Of course, even so, a question may arise whether the legislation does or does not go beyond the obligations of the treaty or convention.[38]

Despite these criticisms, the Supreme Court of Canada never overturned the *Labour Conventions* case, and the courts continue to apply it routinely.[39]

In parallel with these judicial criticisms, the lengthy discussions on constitutional reform from the late 1930s to the early 1990s never resulted in any agreement on the issue of treaty implementation, whether to reverse the *Labour Conventions* case or to entrench it in the written constitution. The Constitution Act, 1982[40] that repatriated the full power to amend the Constitution of Canada does not deal with foreign affairs at all; neither did the failed 1971 Victoria Charter or 1987 Meech Lake Accord.[41] The issue of treaty implementation was on the agenda of the constitutional talks that resulted in the ill-fated 1992 Charlottetown Accord,[42] but the negotiators were unable to reach a consensus on the issue.[43] Over time, a score of scholars pleaded for the reversal of the *Labour Conventions* case and were critical of the provincial power to implement treaties,[44] with notable exceptions, especially from Quebec.[45] None of the

[36] *Id.* at 621. It is generally understood that Chief Justice Kerwin meant "reconsider" the case.

[37] [1977] 2 S.C.R. 134. [38] *Id.* at 171.

[39] Charles-Emmanuel Côté, *La réception du droit international en droit canadien*, 52 SUP. CT. L. REV. (2d) 483, 518–521 (2010). *See*, e.g., Health Services and Support—Facilities Subsector Bargaining Assn v. British Columbia, [2007] 2 S.C.R. 391, 433; Thomson v. Thomson, [1994] 3 S.C.R. 551, 611–612, L'Heureux-Dubé JA, concurring.

[40] *Constitution Act, 1982*, being Schedule B to the *Canada Act 1982* (U.K.), 1982, c. 11, reprinted in R.S.C. 1985, App. II, No. 44. The 1982 constitutional reform also added the *Canadian Charter of Rights and Freedom* to the Constitution of Canada and enshrined the rights of Aboriginal peoples.

[41] CANADA, MEETING OF FIRST MINISTERS ON THE CONSTITUTION, 1987 CONSTITUTIONAL ACCORD, (1987); CANADA, MEETING OF THE CONSTITUTIONAL CONFERENCE, CANADIAN CONSTITUTIONAL CHARTER, 1971 (1971).

[42] CANADA, CONSENSUS REPORT ON THE CONSTITUTION. CHARLOTTETOWN, AUGUST 28, 1992: FINAL TEXT (1992).

[43] *Id.* at 20.

[44] *See*, e.g., PETER W. HOGG, CONSTITUTIONAL LAW OF CANADA, § 11.5(c) (5th ed. 2007); Ronald St. John MacDonald, *The Relationship between International Law and Domestic Law in Canada*, *in* CANADIAN PERSPECTIVES ON INTERNATIONAL LAW AND ORGANIZATION 88, 129 (Ronald St. John MacDonald, Gerald L. Morris, & Donald M. Johnston eds., 1974).

[45] *See*, e.g., HENRI BRUN, GUY TREMBLAY, & EUGÉNIE BROUILLET, DROIT CONSTITUTIONNEL 595–598 (6th ed. 2014); HUGO CYR, CANADIAN FEDERALISM AND TREATY POWERS. ORGANIC CONSTITUTIONALISM AT WORK 217–218 (2009).

attempts at revisiting the *Labour Conventions* case were successful, and it appears that alteration of the provincial power to implement treaties should only be achieved through constitutional amendment.

The Gérin-Lajoie Doctrine and Provincial Treaty-Making

The dramatic development of the French-speaking majority in the province of Quebec in the 1960s is characterized by an accelerated modernization of its government and institutions. The need for the people of Quebec to have better and deeper contacts with foreign nations and especially other French-speaking ones has been a vital concern ever since. Dissatisfied with the inattention of Ottawa to the Francophone world, especially regarding culture and education, the Quebec government decided to conduct directly its foreign affairs in that field. The Gérin-Lajoie doctrine asserts the constitutional basis on which Quebec claims to have the power to sign treaties, to have direct diplomatic relations with foreign countries, and to participate in international conferences and forums dealing with matters falling under its jurisdiction. Paul Gérin-Lajoie, Deputy Premier of Quebec, enunciated the doctrine in 1965, in a famous speech to the Montreal consular corps.[46] He went as far as affirming that it is no longer admissible "for the federal state to exert a kind of supervision and adventitious control over Quebec's international relations."[47]

The idea that provinces may conclude agreements with foreign states is not new and the Supreme Court of Canada even recognized their validity under Canadian law in *Ontario (A.G.) v. Scott*.[48] However, those agreements are typically informal technical or administrative arrangements, not treaties under international law. The Gérin-Lajoie doctrine pushes constitutional interpretation further, claiming that the provinces may in addition conclude treaties binding under international law.[49] Public international law recognizes that federal constitutions may grant treaty-making power to federated units.[50] In the absence of an explicit provision in the Constitution of Canada and of any binding precedent affirming the exclusivity of the federal treaty-making power, the

[46] Paul Gérin-Lajoie, *Speech to the Members of the Montréal Consular Corps* (Speech delivered in Montreal, 12 April 1965), *reprinted in* QUÉBEC, SECRÉTARIAT DU QUÉBEC AUX RELATIONS CANADIENNES, *QUÉBEC'S POSITION ON CONSTITUTIONAL AND INTERGOVERNMENTAL ISSUES FROM 1936 TO 2001*, at 130, *available at* https://www.sqrc.gouv.qc.ca/documents/positions-historiques/positions-du-qc/part2/PaulGuerinLajoie1965_en.pdf.

[47] *Id.* at 133.

[48] [1956] S.C.R. 137; GOTLIEB, *supra* note 17, at 30–32.

[49] *See* QUÉBEC, MINISTÈRE DES RELATIONS INTERNATIONALES ET DE LA FRANCOPHONIE, DOCTRINE GÉRIN-LAJOIE. LES 50 ANS DE LA DOCTRINE, *available at* http://www.mrif.gouv.qc.ca/fr/ministere/historique/doctrine-paul-gerin-lajoie/50-ans-doctrine; QUÉBEC, MINISTÈRE DES AFFAIRES INTERGOUVERNEMENTALES, DOCUMENT DE TRAVAIL SUR LES RELATIONS AVEC L'ÉTRANGER 15–21 (1969) [unpublished, archived at the Library of Université Laval].

[50] *See* International Law Commission, *Draft Articles on the Law of Treaties with Commentaries*, art. 5:2, *reprinted in* [1966] 2 Y.B. INT'L L. COMM'N 203.

Gérin-Lajoie doctrine resorts to general principles of law to assert the existence of a provincial power.

Since a first education agreement signed with France in 1965, Quebec has signed over seven hundred international agreements with foreign states or subnational units.[51] The magnitude of the international practice of Quebec and the solemn form of some agreements depart significantly from the earlier practice of Canadian provinces. In 2008, for instance, the Premier of Quebec signed a landmark agreement with the French President on the mutual recognition of professional qualifications.[52] According to scholars like Arbour[53] and Morin,[54] the existence of this practice would establish materially the limited international personality of Quebec, distinct from that of Canada. All Quebec governments have endorsed the Gérin-Lajoie doctrine and the provincial parliament acknowledged the treaty-making power of Quebec in two statutes.[55] To this day, however, the legal qualification of the international agreements of Quebec remains controversial in Canada.

The federal government has systematically opposed the existence of a provincial treaty-making power. The most elaborate exposition of its views is the white paper *Federalism and International Relations*.[56] The main thrust of the argument of Ottawa is that only the federal government inherited from London the royal prerogative to make treaties at the independence of Canada.[57] The objection to any provincial power to make treaties binding under international law is shared by scholars like Laskin,[58] later Chief Justice of Canada, and Hogg.[59]

Canadian courts have had very few occasions to consider the legal status of international agreements signed by provinces. The Supreme Court of Canada ruled in *Scott* that reciprocal legislation arrangements between a province and a foreign jurisdiction are not treaties binding under international law.[60] Regarding international agreements

[51] *See* Québec, Ministère des Relations Internationales et de la Francophonie, *International Agreements, available at* http://www.mrif.gouv.qc.ca/en/ententes-et-engagements/ententes-internationales. This open database contains the integral text of all international agreements signed by Quebec since 1965.

[52] *Entente entre le Québec et la France en matière de reconnaissance mutuelle des qualifications professionnelles*, Oct. 17, 2008, No. 2008-12.

[53] JEAN-MAURICE ARBOUR & GENEVIÈVE PARENT, DROIT INTERNATIONAL PUBLIC 201–202 (7th ed. 2017).

[54] Jacques-Yvan Morin, *La personnalité internationale du Québec*, 1 QC. J. INT'L L. 163, 261, 274–275 (1984).

[55] Act Respecting the Ministère des Relations Internationales, L.R.Q. c. M-25.1.1, § 19; Act Respecting the Exercise of the Fundamental Rights and Prerogatives of the Québec People and of the Québec State, L.R.Q. c. E-20.2, § 7.

[56] *Supra* note 20. *See also* GLOBAL AFFAIRS CANADA, POLICY ON TABLING OF TREATIES IN PARLIAMENT, Annex C, *available at* http://www.treaty-accord.gc.ca/procedures.aspx?lang=eng.

[57] FEDERALISM AND INTERNATIONAL RELATIONS, *supra* note 20, at 13–15.

[58] Bora Laskin, *The Provinces and International Agreements*, *in* 1 BACKGROUND PAPERS AND REPORTS, E-1 (Ontario Advisory Committee on Confederation ed., 1967).

[59] HOGG, *supra* note 44, § 11.6.

[60] *Supra* note 48, at 142.

signed by Quebec, the Court of Appeal of the province ruled in *Bazylo v. Collins*[61] that an agreement regarding mutual aid in judicial matters was not a treaty under international law.

Even umbrella treaties by which Canada allows its provinces to sign agreements raise questions as to their precise legal effects.[62] From time to time, Ottawa authorizes foreign jurisdictions to sign agreements with Canadian provinces in a treaty, in matters such as education, culture, or social security. The legal effect of umbrella treaties could be to make Canada bound under international law by the provincial agreement.[63] However, recent practice tends to show that their effect could rather be simply to authorize a foreign country to have direct relations with a province.[64] In retrospect, most of the debate surrounding the international agreements of Quebec occurred during times of constitutional controversy over the rise of the independence movement in the province. Save for any international dispute regarding the violation of such agreements, the issue is now essentially academic and it is fair to say that a *modus vivendi* has taken place between Ottawa and Quebec despite legal uncertainties.

Occasionally, the lack of clarity of the law and the absence of institutionalization of federal-provincial cooperation regarding provincial agreements can still create diplomatic problems. A good example is the case of the 2006 international adoption agreement between Quebec and Vietnam.[65] Ottawa stalled the planned signing of the provincial agreement until Vietnam concluded an umbrella treaty with Canada, and a reference to it was added in the agreement. Surprisingly, similar agreements were signed by Quebec before without umbrella treaties and it had not been problematic. The lack of predictability of federal-provincial cooperation in this regard may put foreign countries in an uneasy place.

Provincial Paradiplomacy and Participation in International Organizations or Conferences

An old practice of Canadian provinces is to carry out foreign visits and economic missions or to send permanent representatives abroad, with status depending on the

[61] [1984] R.J.Q. 194, paras. 10–11, 18 (Qc CA).

[62] *See* Charles-Emmanuel Côté, *Le Canada et la capacité des entités infra-étatiques de conclure des traités*, *in* REFLECTIONS ON CANADA'S PAST, PRESENT AND FUTURE IN INTERNATIONAL LAW 96, 111–113 (Oonagh E. Fitzgerald, Valerie Hugues, & Mark Jewett eds., 2018).

[63] *See* Laskin, *supra* note 58, at E-17, E-18.

[64] *See* Charles-Emmanuel Côté, *L'affaire des droits de scolarité des étudiants français au Québec*, *in* LES VISAGES DE L'ÉTAT. LIBER AMICORUM YVES LEJEUNE 187, 195–196 (Pierre d'Argent, David Renders, & Marc Verdussen eds., 2017).

[65] *See* Daniel Turp, *La doctrine Gérin-Lajoie et l'émergence d'un droit québécois des relations internationales*, *in* LES RELATIONS INTERNATIONALES DU QUÉBEC DEPUIS LA DOCTRINE GÉRIN-LAJOIE (1965–2005) 49, 58–59 (Stéphane Paquin ed., 2006) [hereinafter Turp, *Doctrine*].

law of the foreign jurisdiction.[66] This provincial "paradiplomacy" is mostly uncontroversial since it does not involve issues of "high politics." Again, Quebec maintains the most extensive network abroad, but Alberta, Ontario, New Brunswick, and British Columbia are also active to a lesser extent on the international stage, mostly for economic purposes. Federal law envisages that Ottawa may reach agreements with provinces respecting the carrying out of programs related to the powers, duties, and functions of the minister of foreign affairs;[67] a recent agreement deals with hosting of provincial agents within the premises of Canadian embassies or consular posts.[68]

A related issue is that of provincial participation in international organizations or conferences active in their fields of jurisdiction. This other aspect of the Gérin-Lajoie doctrine was more controversial and even triggered a genuine diplomatic crisis when Quebec attended a diplomatic conference of French-speaking ministers of education in Libreville in 1968 at the invitation of the host country.[69] Canada had not been invited, and Ottawa retaliated by suspending its diplomatic relations with Gabon. At another session of the conference of the ministers of education held in 1969 at Niamey, Niger, Canada, and Quebec, invited separately, participated uneasily in a joint delegation. The "Gabon Crisis" led the federal government to clarify its position in a supplement to the aforementioned white paper, entitled *Federalism and International Conferences on Education*.[70] The position of Ottawa was that all discussions in international organizations and conferences involve foreign policy, even those that may appear technical, and that Canada must speak with one voice on the international stage.[71]

Two important intergovernmental agreements in the field of culture and education eroded this rather orthodox view from the late 1960s. A first agreement, signed in 1985, deals with participation in the Summit of the Francophonie and more broadly with all the activities of the *Organisation internationale de la francophonie* (OIF), the international organization of French-speaking countries.[72] Quebec is to participate in the Summit and the OIF as a distinct delegation under the name "Canada-Quebec." It may only act as an interested observer regarding discussions on world politics, but, with the agreement of the Canadian delegation, it can intervene in concert with the delegation

[66] *See* André Lecours, *Canada*, *in* FOREIGN RELATIONS IN FEDERAL COUNTRIES 115, 126–133 (Hans Michelmann ed., 2009).

[67] *Department of Foreign Affairs, Trade and Development Act*, *supra* note 21, § 12.

[68] *Protocole d'entente de cooccupation de locaux avec les provinces et les territoires dans les missions diplomatiques et consulaires à l'étranger*, Aug. 1, 2016, No. 2016-2045 (Alberta, British Columbia, New Brunswick, Ontario, and Quebec), *available at* https://francophonie.sqrc.gouv.qc.ca/VoirDocEntentes/AfficherDoc.asp?cleDoc=228016163130236007241012167075179233252114160044.

[69] *See* Edward McWhinney, *Canadian Federalism and the Foreign Affairs and Treaty Power. The Impact of Quebec's Quiet Revolution*, 7 CAN. Y.B. INT'L L. 3, 12–16 (1969).

[70] MITCHELL SHARPE, SECRETARY OF STATE FOR EXTERNAL AFFAIRS, FEDERALISM AND INTERNATIONAL CONFERENCES ON EDUCATION. A SUPPLEMENT TO FEDERALISM AND INTERNATIONAL RELATION (1968).

[71] *Id.* at 11–12.

[72] *Entente Canada-Québec relative au sommet des pays francophones*, Nov. 7, 1985, No. 1985–031, *reprinted in* 2 QC. J. INT'L L. 395 (1985).

as regards discussions on the world economy of special interest to it. The province may fully participate in discussions on cooperation and development. Ottawa applies a similar arrangement to the provinces of New Brunswick and Ontario to allow them to participate to the Summit and the OIF.

A second agreement, signed in 2006, applies exclusively to the participation of Quebec in the United Nations Education, Science and Culture Organization (UNESCO).[73] A delegate of the Quebec government is to be a member of the permanent delegation of Canada to UNESCO at Paris; the Quebec delegate reports to the government of the province but works under the direction of the Canadian ambassador. Canada must immediately transmit all official documents circulated by UNESCO to Quebec. The province has the right to intervene in all discussions at UNESCO to supplement the Canadian position and express the voice of Quebec. The Canadian delegation should reach consensus on all votes, resolutions, or draft instruments; if this is not possible, Quebec is at liberty to decide whether it will implement the measure or not. A last provision worth mentioning is that Canada and Quebec agree to apply their best efforts to expand the role of federated units at UNESCO. Those two examples show that the rationale of the *Labor Conventions* case remains strong in government practice.

III. Globalization and Free Trade

Institutionalization of Federal-Provincial Cooperation in Foreign Affairs

Globalization intensified the foreign relations of Canada not only in trade but in every aspect of government activities. International rules now have a bearing on all fields of provincial jurisdiction, and there is a pressing need for federal-provincial cooperation. Despite the fundamental constitutional role of provinces in treaty implementation, no general, systematic process exists to facilitate discussion on Canadian positions over issues within provincial jurisdiction. Ottawa puts into place, from time to time, ad hoc, informal mechanisms, mostly in the field of international trade, labor, and environment.[74] Since the Tokyo Round in the 1970s, nontariff barriers to trade have been the focus of international trade negotiations, and provincial involvement became crucial. Federal-provincial administrative networks were set up, especially in connection with the negotiation of the Canada–United States free trade agreement[75] (CUSFTA) in the

[73] *Accord Canada-Québec relatif à l'Organisation des Nations Unies pour l'éducation, la science et la culture (UNESCO)*, May 5, 2006, No. 2006-018.

[74] *See* Lecours, *supra* note 66, at 122–125.

[75] Free Trade Agreement between the Government of Canada and the Government of the United States of America, Jan. 2, 1988, Can. T.S. 1989 No. 3 (CUSFTA).

late 1980s. The negotiation of the Canada–European Union comprehensive economic and trade agreement[76] (CETA) in the 2010s stands as an exception. The European Union insisted on the participation of the provinces in the negotiation, in order to secure commitments on the removal of provincial trade barriers. This resulted in an unprecedented level of involvement of provinces in trade negotiations, with them literally sitting at the table dealing with issues in their fields of jurisdiction.[77]

The key problem with the lack of formal institutionalization of provincial participation is the ease with which Ottawa may revert to other processes. A good example of this is the negotiation of the Trans-Pacific Partnership[78] (TPP), in which provinces did not sit at the table even though it was contemporaneous with CETA negotiation. This absence of formalization of federal-provincial cooperation remains a serious shortcoming in the conduct of Canada's foreign affairs, where provincial involvement depends on the will of the federal government of the day, or even of the foreign country concerned as shown with CETA. Ratification of the Kyoto protocol on climate change without any provincial consultations provoked a serious political crisis in 2002 between Edmonton and Ottawa. Oil-rich Alberta formally threatened to file a constitutional challenge against the implementation of the protocol if Ottawa were to ratify it without proper consultation with the provinces.[79]

Provinces prioritized work on institutionalization of federal-provincial cooperation on the conduct of foreign affairs at the Council of Federation from its inception. This new institution on the Canadian intergovernmental landscape replaced the annual meeting of provincial premiers and aims at promoting interprovincial cooperation.[80] In 2004, the premiers agreed that a written agreement on the role of provinces "in

[76] Comprehensive Economic and Trade Agreement between Canada, of the one part, and the European Union and its Member States, of the other part, Oct. 30, 2016 (provisionally applied since Sept. 21, 2017), *available at* http://www.international.gc.ca/trade-commerce/trade-agreements-accords-commerciaux/agr-acc/ceta-aecg/text-texte/toc-tdm.aspx?lang=eng (CETA).

[77] *See* Christopher J. Kukucha, *Canadian Sub-Federal Governments and CETA: Overarching Themes and Future Trends*, 68 INT'L J. 528 (2012–2013); Stéphane Paquin, *Federalism and the Governance of International Trade Negotiations in Canada: Comparing CUSFTA with CETA*, 68 INT'L J. 545 (2012–2013).

[78] Trans-Pacific Partnership, Feb. 4, 2016 (Australia, Brunei Darussalam, Canada, Chile, Japan, Malaysia, Mexico, New Zealand, Peru, Singapore, United States, Vietnam) (ratification process abandoned), *available at* http://international.gc.ca/trade-commerce/trade-agreements-accords-commerciaux/agr-acc/tpp-ptp/text-texte/toc-tdm.aspx?lang=eng (TPP). The TPP was replaced and incorporated into the Comprehensive and Progressive Agreement for Trans-Pacific Partnership after the United States decided not to ratify it. Comprehensive and Progressive Agreement for Trans-Pacific Partnership, Mar. 8, 2018 (entered into force Dec. 30, 2018), *available at* http://international.gc.ca/trade-commerce/trade-agreements-accords-commerciaux/agr-acc/cptpp-ptpgp/text-texte/cptpp-ptpgp.aspx?lang=eng (CPTPP).

[79] Canada, Alberta, News Release, *Klein releases open letter to PM on Alberta's opposition to Kyoto ratification* (Sept. 3, 2002). *See* Lecours, *supra* note 66, at 124–125.

[80] Council of Federation Founding Agreement, Dec. 5, 2003 (Ontario, Quebec, Nova Scotia, New Brunswick, Manitoba, British Columbia, Prince Edward Island, Saskatchewan, Alberta, Newfoundland and Labrador, Yukon, Northwest Territories, and Nunavut), *available at* http://www.canadaspremiers.ca/en/.

Canada's international negotiations, agreements and other fora is essential."[81] However, the premiers were quickly disappointed with the failure of the federal government to develop a detailed agreement on the question as it had committed to do.[82] Five years later, the provinces reiterated the need for such an agreement and identified key elements to be addressed—i.e., the role of provinces in the negotiation process; the management of agreements and the institutional mechanisms established to implement them; the means to signify formally provincial consent to agreements; and an arrangement to ensure the flow of information.[83] The Council of Federation scaled down its ambitions since then and now focuses on provincial involvement in trade negotiations, after the successful experience with CETA, especially in the context of renegotiation of the North American Free Trade Agreement (NAFTA).[84]

To this day, only a handful of federal-provincial agreements deal with the implementation of specific treaties signed by Canada in the fields of human rights, labor, and environment. The first one deals with provincial participation in the implementation of the UN human rights covenants. It was formalized by an exchange of letters between Quebec City and Ottawa and was instrumental in allowing Canada to accede finally to the covenants.[85] The main feature of the agreement is that Ottawa must consult with the provinces on all issues regarding the covenants, including composition of the Canadian delegation to the meetings of the parties or nomination of Canadians on treaty bodies. Provinces must have the opportunity to defend their measures in case of challenge, including being part of the Canadian delegation appearing before the international body hearing that challenge. Provinces are responsible for drafting parts of the Canadian report dealing with their jurisdiction regarding implementation of the covenants. The other federal-provincial agreements deal with the implementation of the North American side agreements on labor and the environment[86] accompanying NAFTA. These side-agreements include a rare federal clause according to which Canada must provide a list of the covered provinces.[87] Ottawa and the covered provinces signed an intergovernmental agreement setting up

[81] Canada, Council of the Federation, News Release, *Premiers Announce Progress on Key Initiatives* (July 30, 2004).

[82] Canada, Council of the Federation, News Release (Aug. 12, 2005).

[83] Canada, Council of the Federation, News Release, *Strengthening International Trade Relationships* (Aug. 6, 2010).

[84] North American Free Trade Agreement Between the Government of Canada, the Government of Mexico and the Government of the United States, Dec. 17, 1992, Can. T.S. 1994 No. 2 (NAFTA); Canada, Council of the Federation, News Release, *Premiers Collaborate to Strengthen Canada—U.S. Relations* (July 18, 2017).

[85] *Modalités et mécanismes de participation à la mise en œuvre du Pacte international relatif aux droits économiques, sociaux et culturels, du Pacte international relatif aux droits civils et politiques et du Protocole facultatif se rapportant aux droits civils et politiques*, May 18, 1976, No. 1976-015 (Canada, Quebec). *See* Luc Bergeron, *Le rôle du gouvernement du Québec dans la mise en œuvre du droit international des droits de la personne*, 2 Qc. J. Int'l L. 257(1985).

[86] North American Agreement on Labor Cooperation, Sept. 14, 1993, Can. T.S. 1994 No. 4 (NAALC); North American Agreement on Environmental Cooperation, Sept. 14, 1993, 32 I.L.M. 1480 (NAAEC).

[87] NAALC, *id.* art. 46 & Annex 46; NAAEC, *id.* art. 41 & Annex 41.

a governmental committee responsible for developing and managing Canada's involvement with the side-agreements.[88] Ottawa and Quebec City extended this model to other side agreements on labor concluded by Canada together with free trade agreements.[89] All these intergovernmental agreements led to orderly implementation of the treaties.

Parliamentary Control over Treaty-Making

While the legislative branch does not play a formal role in treaty-making in Canada, the federal parliament has been historically involved in the process to a varying extent. From 1926 to 1966, the federal government submitted important treaties to the federal parliament for a symbolic approval prior to their ratification.[90] This practice concerned only a small proportion of all treaties entered into by Canada, since it left aside treaties not needing ratification.[91] It fell into disuse in the late 1960s, and approval of treaties by the federal parliament became occasional, as was the tabling of treaties in parliament.[92]

In 2008, Ottawa announced a new policy inspired by the practice of Australia and the United Kingdom, providing for the tabling of all treaties in the House of Commons for review at least twenty-one sitting days prior to finally binding Canada.[93] An explanatory memorandum must accompany the treaty, dealing notably with federal-provincial implications and determining whether "the obligations in the treaty relate in whole or in part to matters under provincial constitutional jurisdiction."[94] The new policy has a wider scope than the previous practice as it is not limited to important treaties or treaties that need ratification but instead covers all treaties governed by public international law. Conversely, the tabling of a treaty does not necessarily imply that the House will hold a debate on the treaty, examine it, or approve it. This process does not take seriously into account the federal principle and the provincial power to

[88] Canadian Intergovernmental Agreement regarding the North American Agreement on Labour Cooperation, Feb. 10, 1997 (Canada, Quebec, Nova Scotia, Manitoba, Prince Edward Island, and Alberta), *available at* https://www.canada.ca/en/employment-social-development/services/labour-relations/provincial-territorial/north-american-agreement.html; Canadian Intergovernmental Agreement regarding the North American Agreement on Environmental Cooperation, Dec. 2, 1996 (Canada, Quebec, Manitoba, and Alberta) [unpublished, archived with the author].

[89] Canadian Intergovernmental Agreement regarding the Implementation of International Labour Cooperation Agreements, Jan. 23, 2008 (Canada, Quebec), *available at* https://www.canada.ca/fr/emploi-developpement-social/services/relations-travail/provinciales-territoriales/accord-intergouvernemental.html.

[90] *See* Joanna Harrington, *Redressing the Democratic Deficit in Treaty Law Making: (Re-)Establishing a Role for Parliament*, 50 McGill L.J. 465, 476–478 (2005); Gotlieb, *supra* note 17, at 15–19.

[91] *See* Harrington, *supra* note 90, at 477.

[92] *See id.* at 480–481.

[93] Canada, News Release No. 20, *Canada Announces Policy to Table International Treaties in House of Commons* (Jan. 25, 2008); Policy on Tabling of Treaties in Parliament, *supra* note 56.

[94] Policy on Tabling of Treaties in Parliament, *supra* note 56, at para. 6.4 b.

implement treaties. The federal parliament may review treaties that it does not have jurisdiction to implement, while provincial parliaments are totally left aside. Moreover, it is not legally binding on the government.

The only jurisdiction in Canada to have legislated to enhance parliamentary control over treaty-making is Quebec. The Summit of the Americas held in Quebec City in 2001 and the protestations against the proposal for a free-trade area of the Americas increased the need for more transparency and democratic debates on international agreements negotiated by Canada. The Quebec Act Respecting the Ministère des Relations Internationales[95] was amended in 2002 to set up a compulsory process of parliamentary approval of international agreements.

Since 1974, the legislation aimed to protect the provincial power to implement treaties signed by Canada in providing that the Quebec minister responsible for international relations "shall recommend the ratification of international treaties . . . to the [provincial] Government in fields within the constitutional jurisdiction of Québec."[96] The 2002 amendments replaced this process of provincial ratification by that of assent of Quebec to the conclusion of treaties by Canada on matters within provincial jurisdiction.[97] The legal effects of the assent by Quebec to treaties signed by Canada are ambiguous. As Harrington rightly put it, provincial legislation cannot impair the capacity of Ottawa to conclude treaties under Canadian law or international law.[98] However, its effects on Quebec are less obvious. Is it only a political signal that Quebec will implement the treaty, as some authors believe?[99] Or does it legally bind the government to implement the treaty, as a technical guide published by the government of Quebec seems to indicate,[100] in which case a legal remedy could exist in case of failure to do so? At the very least, it is certainly an indication that Quebec considers that it has jurisdiction to implement the treaty and that it intends to do so.

More significantly, the 2002 amendments conditioned the power of the Quebec government to assent to important agreements signed by Canada or Quebec on their prior approval by the provincial parliament.[101] It also obliged the government to table these agreements in parliament, accompanied with an explanatory note.[102] Important agreements are those requiring implementing legislation, relating to human rights or

[95] *See supra* note 55.

[96] Act Respecting the Ministère des Relations Internationales, L.R.Q., c. M-25.1, § 15, para. 1 (replaced by L.R.Q., c. M-25.1.1).

[97] Act Respecting the Ministère des Relations Internationales, *supra* note 55, § 22.1, para. 3. In addition, the Minister "may" agree to the signature of such treaties by Canada. *Id.* at para. 2.

[98] Harrington, *supra* note 90, at 507.

[99] Turp, *Doctrine*, *supra* note 65, at 62; Morin, *supra* note 54, at 253.

[100] François LeDuc, Ministère des Relations internationale, Guide de la Pratique des Relations Internationales du Québec 75 (revised ed. 2009). *See also* Bergeron, *supra* note 85, at 262.

[101] Act Respecting the Ministère des Relations Internationales, *supra* note 55, § 22.3. It only refers to agreements signed by Canada on matters within provincial jurisdictions.

[102] *Id.* § 22.2 para. 1.

international trade, and those that are important according to the minister.[103] As Turp observes, this new process of compulsory parliamentary approval raised the awareness of legislators on international agreements signed by Canada and Quebec, and forced the provincial government to clarify its position on various international issues.[104] At the same time, he notes that short delays and simultaneous tabling of multiple agreements hindered the quality of the debates, while the fact that parliament intervenes after the negotiation and signature of the agreements greatly limits its role.

Toward Consultation with Aboriginal Peoples on Foreign Affairs

Globalization is also characterized by the increasing attention given to Aboriginal issues under international and domestic law. An obligation to consult with Aboriginal peoples on foreign affairs is emerging from the constitutional protection of their rights in Canada. This protection and especially the right to self-government contribute to the creation of a new level of governance that is akin to federalism in substance, if not in form.

Ottawa undertook to sign comprehensive land claim agreements with Aboriginal peoples to deal with the unfinished clarification of the scope of their rights on their ancestral territories.[105] The first agreements signed in the 1970s do not impose an obligation to consult, but a mixed Aboriginal-government expert body has the power to submit recommendations to Ottawa regarding Canada's international position on wildlife management.[106] Subsequent agreements signed in Yukon impose a best effort obligation to ensure representation of Aboriginal peoples' interests in international negotiations of treaties relating to fish and wildlife management.[107] Another model

[103] *Id.* § 22.2 para. 2.

[104] Daniel Turp, *L'approbation des engagements internationaux importants du Québec: la nouvelle dimension parlementaire à la doctrine Gérin-Lajoie*, 2016 Qc. J. Int'l L. 9, 24–25.

[105] *See* Aboriginal Affairs and Northern Development Canada, Renewing the Comprehensive Land Claims Policy: Toward a Framework for Addressing Section 35 Aboriginal Rights (2014). An open database managed by the federal government contains the integral text of all comprehensive land claim agreements. Indigenous and Northern Affairs Canada, *Final Agreements and Related Implementation Matters*, *available at* http://www.aadnc-aandc.gc.ca/eng/1100100030583/1100100030584.sc

[106] James Bay and Northern Quebec Agreement, Nov. 11, 1975, art. 24.4.27. *See also* Northeastern Quebec Agreement, Jan. 31, 1978 (not providing for a mixed expert body).

[107] Carcross/Tagish First Nation Final Agreement, Oct. 22, 2005, art. 16.3.5; Kwanlin Dun First Nation Final Agreement, Feb. 19, 2005, art. 16.3.5; Kluane First Nation Final Agreement, Oct. 18, 2003, art. 16.3.5; Ta'an Kwach'an Council Final Agreement, Jan. 13, 2002, art. 16.3.5; Tr'ondëk Hwëch'in Final Agreement, July 1, 1998, art. 16.3.5; Little Salmon/Carmacks First Nation Final Agreement, July 21, 1997, art. 16.3.5; Selkirk First Nation Final Agreement, July 21, 1997, art. 16.3.5; Champagne and Aishihik First Nations Final Agreement, May 29, 1993, art. 16.3.5; First Nation of Nacho Nyak Dun Final Agreement, May 29, 1993, art. 16.3.5; Teslin Tlingit Council Final Agreement, May 29, 1993, art. 16.3.5; Vuntut Gwitchin First Nation Final Agreement, May 29, 1993, art. 16.3.5; Umbrella Final Agreement between the

applied in Nunavut and Northern Quebec obliges Ottawa to include representatives of the Aboriginal peoples concerned in discussions leading to formulation of the position of Canada on international negotiations of treaties relating to their rights to harvest wildlife.[108] Their representation in these discussions must be greater than that afforded to nongovernmental organizations. A slightly different model consists of requiring Ottawa to consult with the Aboriginal peoples in relation to international negotiations of treaties dealing with wildlife, fisheries, and migratory birds.[109]

The most recent model of comprehensive land claim agreement goes far beyond this and takes into account the right to self-government of Aboriginal peoples.[110] First, Ottawa has a general obligation to consult with Aboriginal peoples before it signs a new treaty with a foreign country that could adversely affect their rights. Second, Ottawa must inform the Aboriginal people if they have adopted a measure causing Canada to be unable to perform an international obligation and both must discuss the remedial measures needed. Disagreement as to the need for the Aboriginal people to take remedial measures or the adequacy of the measures taken must be resolved by arbitration, or by the Federal Court in one case. Third, Ottawa must consult with Aboriginal peoples in relation to the development of positions taken by Canada before an international tribunal that is dealing with an Aboriginal measure. If that international tribunal finds the measure to be contrary to Canada's international obligations, the Aboriginal people must take remedial measures to perform the obligations at the request of Ottawa. As noted by Van Ert and Matiation, the institutionalization of cooperation between the Crown and Aboriginal peoples in the conduct of foreign affairs is more legally stringent than that with provinces and departs from the rationale of *Labour Conventions*.[111]

Government of Canada, the Council for Yukon Indians and the Government of the Yukon, May 29, 1993, art. 16.3.5.

[108] Agreement between the Crees of Eeyou Istchee and Her Majesty the Queen in Right of Canada concerning Eeyou Marine Region, 2011, art. 17.2; Nunavik Inuit Land Claims Agreement, Dec. 1, 2006, art. 5.8.2; Nunavut Land Claims Agreement, May 25, 1993, art. 5.9.2.

[109] Nisga'a Final Agreement, Apr. 27, 1999, chap. 8, art. 115, ch. 9, art. 96; Sahtu Dene and Metis Comprehensive Land Claim Agreement, Sept. 6, 1993, art. 13.6.7, 13.10.1; Gwich'in Comprehensive Land Claim Agreement, Apr. 22, 1992, art. 12.6.7, 12.10.1; Western Arctic Claims. Inuvialuit Final Agreement, June 5, 1984, art. 14:38.

[110] Déline Final Self-Government Agreement, Feb. 18, 2015, art. 2.13; Tla'amin Final Agreement, Apr. 11, 2014, arts. 24–29; Sioux Valley Dakota Nation Governance Agreement and Tripartite Governance Agreement, Aug. 30, 2013, art. 36.0; Yale First Nation Final Agreement, 2012, art. 2.8; Maa-nulth First Nations Agreement, Apr. 9, 2009, art. 1.7.0; Labrador Inuit Land Claim Agreement, Jan. 22, 2005, art. 17.27; Tlicho Agreement, Aug. 25, 2003, art. 7.13.

[111] Gib Van Ert & Stefan Matiation, *Labour Conventions and Comprehensive Claim Agreements: A New Model for Subfederal Participation in Canadian International Treaty-Making*, *in* The Globalized Rule of Law: Relationships between International and Domestic Law 203, 230–231 (Oonagh Fitzgerald ed., 2006).

The constitutional duty of the Crown to consult with Aboriginal peoples could also have a bearing on foreign affairs.[112] In *Hupacasath First Nation v. Canada (Foreign Affairs and International Trade Canada)*,[113] a small Aboriginal community located on Vancouver Island invoked the breach of this duty to prevent Ottawa from ratifying the Canada–China foreign investment promotion and protection agreement. The Federal Court of Appeal concluded that the alleged impacts of the agreement on the rights asserted by the Aboriginal community on their territory were nonappreciable and speculative in nature, thus not triggering the duty to consult in that case.[114] Nevertheless, it would seem possible that under another set of facts, ratification of a treaty without consultation of Aboriginal peoples could violate the constitutional duty of the Crown to do so, especially with a treaty likely to have a direct impact on the use of the land.

IV. Conclusion

Since Confederation and after lengthy constitutional talks and the coming of the age of globalization, the interplay between federalism and foreign affairs in Canada remains characterized by the absence of written constitutional rules, the lack of institutionalization, and the important role of government practice in filling that void. Despite past controversies over the *Labour Conventions* case, the provincial power to implement treaties did not cause any serious foreign relations difficulties, and Canada was able to play an active role as a middle power on the international stage. Nevertheless, the current political and legal framework is such that problems can arise from time to time in the conduct of foreign affairs, if international obligations are incurred without substantial provincial support. Prior consultations with provinces are crucial and the formulation of treaty reservations may be necessary in some cases. The insufficient political will to better institutionalize cooperation between Ottawa and the provinces in the conduct of foreign affairs continues to be surprising, especially in the light of positive sectoral or ad hoc initiatives. The positive role that provincial paradiplomacy may play in expanding the global influence of Canada could also be better embraced. The emerging obligation to consult with Aboriginal peoples stands in stark contrast with the lack of institutionalization of federal-provincial cooperation on foreign affairs.

[112] *See* Mikisew Cree First Nation v. Canada (Minister of Canadian Heritage), [2005] 3 S.C.R. 388, 405–406; Haida Nation v. British Columbia (Minister of Forest), [2004] 3 S.C.R. 511, 522–530; Taku River Tlingit First Nation v. British Columbia (Project Assessment Director), [2004] 3 S.C.R. 550, 562–563; Hogg, *supra* note 44, § 28.8(j).

[113] 2015 F.C.A. 4, 379 D.L.R. (4th) 737, *aff'g* 2013 F.C. 900, [2014] 4 F.C.R. 836 (F.C.T.D.).

[114] *Id.* at paras. 89, 99–101, 118 (F.C.A.).

CHAPTER 17

FOREIGN AFFAIRS FEDERALISM IN SWITZERLAND

ROLAND PORTMANN*

FEDERALISM is one of the organizing principles of Swiss statehood. Napoléon Bonaparte, on the height of his power in Europe, memorably remarked of Switzerland in 1802: "*Nature made your state a federation. No man in his right mind would want to change this.*"[1] Napoléon came to this conclusion after a failed attempt to transform Switzerland into a centralized state from 1798 to 1803, the so-called "Helvetian Republic." This was the only time in Swiss history that it was not a federation made up of its constituent entities, the Cantons.[2] Today, Article 1 of the Swiss Constitution declares the twenty-six Cantons, along with the population, as the constituent entities (*pouvoirs constituants*) of the Swiss Confederation.[3] Napoléon's dictum about federalism is thus firmly part of today's Swiss polity and one of its key organizing principles, along with direct democracy,

* The views expressed in this chapter are personal and do not represent the official position of the Swiss Ministry of Foreign Affairs.

[1] Napoleon's speech to the Consulta, Dec. 10, 1802. Translated as included in JEAN-FRANÇOIS AUBERT, TRAITÉ DE DROIT CONSTITUTIONNEL SUISSE (1967) (« *La nature a fait votre Etat fédératif. Vouloir la vaincre ne peut pas être d'un homme sage* ».).

[2] For a succinct overview of early Swiss constitutional history, *see* ZACCARIA GIACOMETTI, SCHWEIZERISCHES BUNDESSTAATSRECHT (1949), and, for a more current view, *see* Andreas Kley, *Geschichtliche Einleitung*, *in* DIE SCHWEIZERISCHE BUNDESVERFASSUNG, ST. GALLER KOMMENTAR (2d ed. 2014).

[3] Constitution of Switzerland of Apr. 24, 1999. The original Constitution of Switzerland of 1848 had been completely revised in 1874. The 1999 Constitution is the second completely revised version. As part of direct democracy, the Constitution can be amended at any time on the initiative of 100,000 voters or the government and parliament. The amendment takes effect if a majority of the population and—of particular relevance here—a majority of the Cantons approve of it. The Swiss Constitution is thus a living document in the sense that it is constantly amended and modified through the processes foreseen by the Constitution itself.

individual rights, separation of powers, and—especially relevant from a foreign affairs perspective—its international law status of permanent neutrality.[4]

As will be seen throughout this chapter, the role of federalism in Swiss foreign affairs is closely connected to these other main constitutional principles, especially to aspects of direct democracy and the popular referenda that are a major characteristic of the Swiss polity. Direct democracy itself contains federalist elements because the Cantons are the voting districts for popular referenda, and, if certain conditions stated by the Constitution are fulfilled, a majority of these Cantonal voting districts (and not only a majority of the overall population) must approve of a particular foreign policy decision in order for it to take effect. In the area of foreign affairs, this may involve a particular decision or the approval of a specific international agreement. The same holds true for the link between federalism and the separation of power between the executive and the legislature: whenever the legislature is involved in foreign policy, federalist principles are more prominently discussed via the bicameral system in which one of the chambers is constituted of equal representatives of the Cantons, thus naturally providing a perspective from the individual Cantons in view of foreign affairs issues. Federalism thus plays an important role in foreign affairs in Switzerland not only as an isolated constitutional principle but also through its interplay with additional peculiar aspects of the Swiss polity.

Though idiosyncratic as a product of particular historical developments and circumstances, Swiss federalism is akin in several respects to its American "sister republic," in particular with regard to the principle of enumerated powers of the federal government and the bicameral system of the legislature, with one chamber representing the Cantons in equal terms (two representatives for every Canton regardless of its population size). To a much more limited extent, there are some similarities of Swiss federalism to structural features present in the EU treaties (of which Switzerland is not a member). Of course, there are also some similarities with other federalist systems such as in Canada, Belgium, and Germany. A description of issues of federalism related to foreign affairs in the Swiss system may thus be of relevance also from a comparative foreign relations law perspective. It is with this objective in mind that the present chapter outlines how federalism relates to the conduct of foreign affairs in the Swiss constitutional system and aims to provide some observations that are of interest outside the Swiss polity and to those dealing with it as a partner in foreign affairs issues.

Federalism plays an important role in Swiss foreign policy in three respects. First, the Cantons have a role through their general powers in policymaking in the Swiss constitutional system. This reflects an indirect role of the Cantons in foreign affairs, as it requires foreign policy to be part of the overall constitutional system, wherein federalism is one of the key organizing principles. It will thus be called *indirect foreign affairs federalism* for present purposes. Second, the Swiss Constitution expressly

[4] For further elaboration on the key constitutional principles of the Swiss polity, *see* PHILIPPE MASTRONARDI, STRUKTURPRINZIPIEN DER BUNDESVERFASSUNG? ZEITSCHRIFT FÜR SCHWEIZERISCHES RECHT (1988).

preserves a residual treaty-making capacity and autonomous foreign policy competence for the Cantons. This may be called *autonomous foreign affairs federalism*, as it reflects the express constitutional direction to preserve a limited international legal capacity of the Cantons. Third, the Cantons have specific participation rights in the definition of Swiss foreign policy, i.e., in foreign policy decisions by the federal government. These rights are peculiar to the foreign policy realm and thus translate the more general role of Cantons in the Swiss polity into the sphere of Swiss diplomacy in more specific terms. This aspect may be coined *direct foreign affairs federalism*, as it relates to specific Cantonal rights in the immediate conduct of foreign affairs by the federal government.

This chapter first presents the basic principles of Swiss federalism as relevant for present purposes. It then discusses indirect, autonomous, and direct foreign affairs federalism in the Swiss polity. In all these areas, as a response to the increasing internationalization of many policy areas that historically were seen as domestic issues, the role of Cantons in foreign affairs has been strengthened in recent decades, at least on a theoretical level. In practice, there are several challenges when it comes to foreign affairs federalism, most of them related to developments in the international realm and to the need for the federal government to act quickly and decisively in a dynamic international environment in order to safeguard Swiss interests. Given these challenges, the chapter concludes with observations on recent challenges in practice, thereby aiming to come to conclusions that are of more general relevance from a comparative perspective outside the Swiss polity.

I. Basic Principles of Swiss Federalism Relevant to Foreign Affairs

Swiss federalism as it exists today is the product of a particular historical context and development.[5] The Swiss Cantons had been sovereign entities in an evolving Swiss Federation based on treaty relationships from the late thirteenth century onward until the creation of Swiss statehood in 1848. Starting with the first Swiss Constitution in 1848, the Cantons, along with the population, became the composite entities of the Swiss Confederation.

Article 3 of the current Swiss Constitution provides that the Cantons are sovereign entities to the extent that their sovereignty is not limited by the Constitution. The allocation of competencies between the federal government and the Cantons is based on the principle of enumerated powers. As in the U.S. version of federalism, the federal

[5] For a more detailed presentation of Swiss federalism, *see* Jean-François Aubert, Traité de Droit Constitutionnel Suisse (1967).

government only possesses those powers expressly granted to it by the Constitution; all matters that are not referred to the federal level in the Constitution remain in the realm of the Cantons. Even when a power is allocated on the federal level, this does not necessarily mean that the Cantons are excluded from being active in this particular area. With certain exceptions, they are allowed to legislate as long as they do not interfere with existing federal law. To the extent that the federal government does not make use of a power granted to it by the Constitution, the Cantons remain free—subject to general limits set by the Constitution and applicable international law—to continue to regulate these areas. In addition, there also exist strictly parallel competencies, authorizing the federal government and the Cantons both to be active in certain areas (e.g., concerning education and research at the university level).

Concerning the implementation of federal law, there is a constitutional presumption that this is taken care of by the Cantons. To a large extent, implementation of federal law thus falls into the powers of the Cantons and their authorities. As one of the effects of the system of monism concerning the relationship of domestic law and international law in Switzerland, federal law includes international agreements to which Switzerland is a party. It follows that many international obligations are put into effect in the Swiss polity by the Cantons, either directly (in the absence of implementing legislation on the federal level) or indirectly (through the general competence to implement federal legislation). Of course, a particular statute on the federal level can always rebut the presumption for implementation by the Cantons and assign it to a federal agency. However, the latter is rather the exception than the norm in the Swiss system.

Foreign affairs is one of the federal competences enumerated in the Constitution. However, it is not an exclusive federal competence. According to Article 54 of the Swiss Constitution, the federal government is in charge of foreign affairs, and the same provision spells out policy guidelines for the conduct of foreign affairs. The nonexclusivity of the competence is expressly defined in Articles 55 and 56, which regulate participatory rights of the cantons in the conduct of foreign policy by the federal government (Art. 55) and authorize the Cantons to conduct their own foreign policy in areas where they remain competent according to domestic federalism and to conclude international agreements in the same realm (Art. 56). Already on this level of fundamental constitutional principle, the foreign affairs power in Switzerland is thus divided between the federal government and the Cantons, albeit with the federal government in a leading role.[6]

Based on Article 54 of the Constitution, the federal government is authorized to take domestic and international action. It follows that the federal government, by relying on the foreign affairs competence in the Constitution, can enter in international obligations or can regulate domestic matters that have a link to international affairs without being granted this specific competence in the overall system of competencies. For

[6] *See* Bernhard Ehrenzeller, Roland Portmann, & Thomas Pfisterer, *Article 54*, *in* Die Schweizerische Bundesverfassung, *supra* note 2.

example, the federal government could regulate domestic security issues on the federal level even though the police power is generally vested in the Cantons according to the overall system of competencies. If an expansive view is taken, the federal government could thus encroach on Cantonal rights via the foreign affairs competence. It is also broadly accepted that treaties concluded under a broad reading of the foreign affairs competence of the federal government—and thus to a certain extent infringing of the distribution of competencies in the overall system of federalism—are principally valid and to be applied by the Swiss and Cantonal authorities.[7] At the same time, it is generally agreed that the federal government is not allowed to circumvent the overall system of competencies via the foreign affairs power. As a result, the Swiss position in this regard is somewhat similar to the situation under the U.S. Constitution and the leading cases of *Missouri v. Holland* and, more recently, *Bond v. United States*.[8]

Apart from the vertical allocation of competencies, the principle of federalism is present in domestic and international lawmaking procedures prescribed by the Constitution. First, based on the bicameral system, the Swiss Senate is empowered with equal competencies as the Swiss version of the House of Representatives, the National Council (this is obviously in contrast to the superior competencies of the U.S. Senate). To become law, every constitutional amendment and statute—including those having an effect on foreign affairs—must be approved by both chambers of parliament. The Swiss Senate thus always has a role whenever the legislature has to approve a treaty. This gives the Senate as the "federalist" Chamber of parliament—and through it the Cantonal representatives—a say not only in domestic lawmaking, but also in treaty-making.

Second, related to the Swiss form of direct democracy, there is an additional role of the Cantons in domestic and international lawmaking. Constitutional amendments, statutes, and certain kinds of treaties can be put to a popular vote if they fulfill certain conditions and if 50,000 voters or eight Cantons ask for such a vote. In certain cases deemed by the Constitution to be of particular importance, not only must a majority of the population approve of these acts, a majority of the Cantons also has to do so (whereby the vote of one Canton is also determined based on the principle of direct democracy, i.e., the Cantonal population votes on it).

Third, there is a final mechanism of Swiss federalism that is relevant. For the acts of parliament described above, before a vote in parliament takes place, under certain conditions again spelled out in the Constitution, a consultation process with all relevant stakeholders has to take place. The Cantons are always consulted in this context. They can thus influence the discussion already before parliament considers a bill or an international treaty. This is one of the main entry points for Cantons to also influence foreign affairs decisions by the federal government.

[7] *See* the overview provided by ROBERT BAUMANN, DER EINFLUSS DES VÖLKERRECHTS AUF DIE GEWALTENTEILUNG 352 (2002).

[8] Missouri v. Holland, 252 U.S. 416 (1920); Bond v. United States, 564 U.S. 211 (2011). *See also* Ernest A. Young, *Foreign Affairs Federalism in the United States*, ch. 15 in this volume.

II. Indirect Foreign Affairs Federalism: The Role of Cantons in Foreign Affairs Based on the General Constitutional Framework

Federalism plays a role in three ways in foreign affairs through the overall constitutional system. First, it is generally relevant through the so-called "normalization of foreign affairs," that is, the incorporation of foreign affairs into the overall constitutional system, including the constitutional principle of federalism. Second, there are specific constitutional rules regarding the treaty-making power of the federal government that give Cantons a peculiar role in foreign policy via the general constitutional framework, especially on the basis of its interplay with instruments of direct democracy and separation of power. Third, the general constitutional principle according to which Cantons (and not primarily federal agencies) execute federal law implies an important role of Cantons in treaty implementation by Switzerland.

The Role of Federalism as a Result of the "Normalization of Foreign Affairs" in General

As in other legal systems, foreign affairs had long been viewed as exceptional by constitutional law scholars and practitioners in Switzerland, and thus to fall outside of the general constitutional framework.[9] In more recent times, however, foreign policy has been perceived more to be part of the overall framework, thus ascribing a general role to constitutional principles like federalism in foreign affairs.[10] To use a phrase coined in the context of the American constitutional law, foreign affairs has been "normalized," and in so doing, constitutional principles such as federalism play a more important, if only indirect, role in foreign affairs.

A *first instance* for the normalization of foreign affairs in the case of Switzerland is that its Constitution contains several explicit foreign policy objectives in its Articles 2 and 54. These objectives include preserving Swiss independence and economic well-being as well as Swiss engagement for international peace and security, sustainable development, and human rights. Though not a foreign policy objective in itself, the Constitution, in Articles 174 and 185 related to the foreign policy authorities of

[9] For an authoritative treatment contesting this perspective, *see* Bernhard Ehrenzeller, Legislative Gewalt und Aussenpolitik (1992).

[10] *See* Roland Kley & Roland Portmann, *Vorbemerkungen zur Aussenverfassung*, *in* Die Schweizerische Bundesverfassung, *supra* note 2.

the legislative and the executive branches, respectively, also makes reference to the principle of neutrality, without however defining its content and role any further. Given the mechanisms by which the Constitution comes into being and is amended as well as the role of Cantons therein—a majority of them has to agree to any constitutional change—Swiss foreign policy objectives and the foreign policy instrument of neutrality cannot be modified without the Cantons having a say in it through their role as *pouvoirs constituent*. The main direction of Swiss foreign policy as prescribed by the Constitution can thus only be changed if a majority of the Cantons so agree. With regard to neutrality, this holds true with regard to its abolition—it is theoretically possible as a matter of international law (as far as the principle of good faith is respected), because Switzerland is under no obligation to remain neutral, but its neutrality is recognized by the international community of states—as well as with regard to its inclusion into the foreign policy objectives.

A *second instance* of the normalization of foreign affairs is the increasing amount of statutes in Switzerland dealing with foreign affairs. For example, there are statutes regulating activities of the Swiss army in international peacekeeping operations, defining Swiss judicial action in cases of international corruption, and setting principles for Swiss development aid. As part of the general lawmaking process in Switzerland, Cantons play a major role in consultation processes by the federal government when a draft statute is discussed. Through the Senate chamber and the option for a minority of eight Cantons to demand a popular referendum on any statute passed by the federal parliament, Cantons are among the major actors influencing and approving such foreign affairs legislation.

A *third instance* is the increasing role of the legislature in foreign affairs decision-making (apart from crafting statutes). This also contributes to federalist principles being more present, especially through the Senate chamber. Parliamentarian consultation rights have been strengthened in recent times. So have approval rights by parliament with regard to international treaties. In accordance with Article 24 of the Act on Parliament, any major foreign policy issue has to be brought before the foreign relations committees in both chambers of parliament. The committees can make recommendations to the executive branch. Although these recommendations are not binding in a legal sense, they have considerable political weight. In these parliamentary deliberations on foreign affairs issues, especially, by its very nature, in the foreign relations committee in the Senate, considerations related to federalism are usually more present than inside the executive branch whose main focus is preserving the interests and values of Switzerland as a whole.

Finally, a *fourth instance* of the normalization of foreign affairs and its corresponding inclusion in the general constitutional system in Switzerland is the role that courts play in foreign affairs. This role has always been present as an effect of monism, i.e., the direct incorporation of international treaties into the Swiss legal system. To the extent that these treaties have been deemed to contain direct rights and obligations of individuals, Swiss courts have always played a role in foreign affairs through the interpretation and application of treaties. This general role has increased in recent years to encompass foreign policy issues more broadly. Two main factors have contributed to this development. On the one hand, as an effect of the increasing internationalization of issues of daily life, many issues brought before the courts by litigants involve some relation to foreign affairs (e.g., a bilateral treaty with the European Union, an implementation issue of a UN Security Council Resolution, or simply a general practice out of international comity toward one the neighboring countries of Switzerland). On the other hand, through the jurisprudence of the European Court on Human Rights with regard to access to a court (Art. 6 of the European Convention on Human Rights), it has become untenable to exclude relevant foreign affairs issues from review by the courts as has been historically the case in the Swiss system. Accordingly, federal procedure statutes now explicitly state that although issues of foreign affairs are in principle excluded from the competence of the courts, this does not apply in cases for which Article 6 of the European Convention on Human Rights grants access to a court. In the latter case, Swiss courts will also adjudicate foreign affairs issues.

In the Swiss system, the courts are organized in federalist terms, i.e., in principle all matters are first adjudicated by the competent Cantonal courts. The Cantonal courts thus apply federal law, including treaty law, and in so doing may hand down decisions that have a foreign policy effect. A recent example in this context are decisions by a variety of Cantonal courts on transfer of data on bank employees that allegedly have played a role in advising American clients in tax issues. As part of a political agreement between the U.S. Department of Justice and the Swiss Finance Department of 2013,[11] this transfer was possible in the framework of applicable Swiss data protection and employment law. This also entails a right of those bank employees affected to ask for review by a court. This review is undertaken by Cantonal courts, which then have to balance the foreign policy interest of Switzerland with regard to its relations with the United States and the individual interests of the employees

The Role of Federalism via the Treaty-Making Power and Popular Referenda on Treaties

Apart from these instances of normalization of foreign affairs from the perspective of constitutional law, Cantons play a role in foreign affairs through more specific constitutional provisions related to the treaty-making power. The Swiss Constitution essentially distinguishes three types of international agreements subject to approval by the legislature, and, depending on the type, assigns different roles to the Cantons in the approval process. This particular role of the Cantons is in addition to the one they already play as a part of the legislative approval process of these international agreements, in which federalist considerations enter especially through necessary approval

[11] Joint Statement between the U.S. Department of Justice and the Swiss Federal Department of Finance of Aug. 29, 2013, *available at* https://www.newsd.admin.ch/newsd/message/attachments/31815.pdf.

by the Swiss Senate. It is also in addition to the consultation rights they enjoy in advance of the parliamentary process.

- *International agreements on joining supranational organizations and on acceding to international institutions on collective security.* Article 140(1)(b) of the Swiss Constitution prescribes that an international agreement on joining a supranational organization, or on acceding to an international institution on collective security, is subject to a referendum requiring a majority of the popular vote and a majority of the Cantons in order to be approved. The obvious example for a supranational organization is the European Union, in which member states transfer competencies to the organs of the Union. The main example for an international institution on collective security is the North Atlantic Treaty Organization (NATO). The decision to join either the European Union or NATO would have pivotal repercussions for the Swiss polity: EU membership would lead to changes in the order of competencies among the different levels and branches of the Swiss state, and accession to NATO would be inconsistent with the Swiss international law status of permanent neutrality. Given the extraordinary importance of such foreign policy decisions for the Swiss polity, they are considered to be on a level with constitutional norms for the sake of the necessary approval process. In consequence, as is the case with any change in the Constitution, such a decision is partly in the hands of the Cantons, which must agree by a majority in order for Switzerland to join the European Union or NATO.
- *International agreements that cannot be terminated, provide for the accession to an international organization, or contain substantial rules of a statutory nature.* In the case of international agreements falling into this category, Article 141(1)(c) provides that eight Cantons can call for it to be made subject to a popular referendum. In this case, Cantons thus cannot block Switzerland from entering such agreements, but they can make it harder for the federal government to do so.
- *Other international agreements the conclusion of which is not delegated by statute or treaty to the executive branch.* All other international agreements, for which, in accordance with Article 166 of the Swiss Constitution, there is no statutory or treaty delegation to the executive, are to be approved by both chambers of parliament without subsequent referendum. In this case, there is no direct role of Cantons in the approval process, but federalist considerations enter as part of deliberations in the Swiss Senate.

The Role of Federalism via the General Principle of Cantonal Execution of Federal Law, Including International Treaties

Finally, in the overall constitutional system in Switzerland, implementation of federal legislation is generally a matter for the Cantons (if not specifically assigned to a federal agency). This holds true for treaties entered into by the federal government. In principle, it is up to the Cantons to put them into effect. However, as a result of the monist system in Switzerland regarding incorporation of international treaties into the Swiss legal order, implementation does not generally involve legislation. Often Cantonal authorities apply international treaties directly in addressing concrete administrative issues for which they are competent.

However, in case a Canton does not implement an international agreement properly (either by not directly applying it in the proper way or by not implementing it through necessary legislation), the executive branch of the federal government, based on Article 186(4) of the Constitution, is in principle authorized to take the necessary measures on behalf of the Canton. The underlying rationale for this principle is that the federal government will incur international responsibility in case a Canton, in accordance with the internal distribution of competencies, does not comply with a treaty obligation of Switzerland. Within this system, a situation similar to the *Medellín v. Texas* case in the United States, in which the U.S. Supreme Court denied the president the authority to order Texas to comply with an obligation under the UN Charter to implement a decision by the International Court of Justice, could thus in principle be avoided in Switzerland. Under the Swiss system, the executive branch of the federal government would have the constitutional authority to issue such an order to a Canton. It also has the authority to take measures on behalf of the Canton—for example, if the Canton, on the basis of an international treaty obligation in the realm of double taxation, fails to process payments to a treaty partner of Switzerland.[12] However, given the delicacy of such a step in the overall constitutional framework of federalism, it is only taken by the federal government in extraordinary circumstances as it involves fundamental issues of Swiss federalism and the autonomy of the Cantons.

All of the above instances show the range of areas in which federalism plays a role in Swiss foreign affairs based on the overall constitutional system. Even though this role has been increased as an effect of normalization of foreign affairs from the perspective of constitutional law, the role of Cantons in Swiss foreign affairs goes beyond this general framework. There are specific autonomous foreign affairs competencies of Cantons as well as specific participation rights of Cantons in the conduct of foreign affairs by the federal government in order to further strengthen the federalist principle

[12] An important discussion in recent Swiss practice concerns the Treaty between Switzerland and Italy of 1974 on the Taxation of Cross-Border Employees (i.e., Italian residents commuting daily to neighboring Swiss Cantons for work). As part of the treaty obligations, it is stipulated that the neighboring Cantons of Graubünden, Tessin, and Wallis are required to tax the income earned by Italian residents in their Cantons at their source and then to redistribute part of the tax-substrate to Italy on behalf of the relevant neighboring communities (which would otherwise lack tax income as a result of the large number of residents earning their income in neighboring Switzerland). In case one of the Cantons does not conform to this obligation, the Swiss federal government would be in noncompliance vis-à-vis the Italian government. In order to resolve this legal issue, the Swiss federal government would have the competence to transfer the necessary amounts directly to Italy and then to take internal recourse vis-à-vis the relevant Canton.

in the particular area of foreign affairs. These two more specific aspects are dealt with in the ensuing two sections.

III. Autonomous Foreign Affairs Federalism: The Limited International Personality of Cantons

Given the historical role of the Cantons until 1848, especially their substantial treaty practice throughout the centuries, it has been a constant in Swiss constitutional law and practice that the Cantons continue to have a limited international legal personality granted by the Constitution. This international legal personality allows the Cantons to conduct an autonomous foreign policy as long as they do not infringe on the interests of the federal government. As part of this competence, in accordance with Article 56 of the Swiss Constitution, the Cantons are allowed to enter into international treaties and to conduct their proper foreign policy.

The treaty-making power of the Cantons is, however, limited in several respects related to both substance and possible treaty partners:

- *The subject matter of a treaty must fall into the Cantonal competencies in accordance with the distribution of powers in the Constitution.* It follows that many treaties entered into by Cantons relate to police and education matters. As part of increasing initiatives in Europe for more regional cooperation across borders, a number of treaties entered into by Cantons also cover environmental or transportation issues. The Cantons are also allowed to create regional institutions by treaty.
- *The possible partners to enter into treaty relationships by Cantons are substate entities*, i.e., local or regional institutions of the neighboring countries, as well as administrative agencies of the federal level in foreign states. Excluded are the political institutions of the central government. In case the central government of one of the neighboring countries is to be involved in the negotiation, the Swiss federal government must be involved as well. A treaty with the central government of a neighboring country can only be concluded by the Swiss federal government, not the Cantons.

In order to ensure that treaties entered into by Cantons do not infringe on the interests of the federal government or other Cantons, the following procedure is prescribed by the Constitution and by statute:

- Before entering into a treaty, the Cantons have to *inform the federal government about their intention*. The federal government announces this intention in the federal register.

- The federal government as well as the other Cantons have two months in order to *raise any objections* with regard to the treaty being contrary to federal law or federal as well as Cantonal interests.
- In case such objections are raised, the relevant Canton and the objecting parties are required to attempt an *amicable solution*.
- In case no amicable solution is possible, *both Chambers of the federal parliament assume a role in the settlement of the dispute*. If no settlement is possible, the federal parliament has to decide whether to approve the treaty intended to be concluded by the Canton.

Before the current procedure just described came into effect, there was a requirement of explicit approval by the federal government of treaties entered into by the Cantons. This requirement has been waived, in this way facilitating the process of Cantonal treaty-making. Today, there are more than four hundred treaties in force entered into by Cantons.[13] It is important to note that, as a matter of international law, these treaties bind Switzerland as a state. In case of nonperformance, it is the Swiss federal government that is internationally responsible.

Autonomous Cantonal foreign policy is not restricted to treaty-making. There is a rich and versatile foreign policy practice of most Swiss Cantons below the level of treaty-making, especially by those bordering a neighboring state of Switzerland. Most of these Cantons have assigned representatives for foreign policy matters and are active in cross-border regional fora (which are partly based on treaties and partly simply on practice). In these cross-border regional fora and commissions—such as the Commission on Fishing Rights in Lake Geneva or the Commission on Protection of Water Quality in the Rhein—usually, on the Swiss side, the Cantonal representatives are joined by members of the federal administration representing the interests of the federal government. There is thus in large part a collaboration between Cantons and the federal government as part of these cross-border commissions, including with regard to questions of international law, which the federal government usually covers on behalf of the Cantons.

In recent years, the collaboration between the federal government and the Cantons with regard to Cantonal foreign policy has increased. There is an ambassador-at-large in the federal government specifically in charge of facilitating regional foreign policy on the different levels. This reflects the increasing interlinkages and need for coordination between regional foreign policy by the Cantons with their partners across the region (e.g., the neighboring *Bundesländer* in Germany or Austria or the regions in Italy and the provinces in France) and the classic foreign policy between the Swiss federal government and the central governments of the neighboring states.

[13] *See* the collection of current international agreements concluded by Cantons in BARDO FASSBENDER & RAFFAEL GUEBELI, DIE GEGENWÄRTIG GÜLTIGEN VÖLKERRECHTLICHEN VERTRÄGE DER KANTONE, SCHWEIZERISCHES ZENTRALBLATT FÜR STAATS- UND VERWALTUNGSRECHT (2018). The authors count 436 international agreements concluded by Cantons that are currently in force.

IV. Direct Foreign Affairs Federalism: The Specific Rights and Obligations of Cantons in the Conduct of Swiss Foreign Affairs

Apart from the competencies of Cantons to conduct an autonomous foreign policy, subject to the substantive as well as procedural limits outlined above, Cantons have specific rights relating to participation in foreign policy decisions by the federal government. These rights are enumerated in Article 55 of the Swiss Constitution and are also further codified in a specific statute to this effect on the Participation of Cantons in Foreign Policy Decisions. These rights are in addition to the general role of Cantons in the overall constitutional framework that, as part of the normalization of foreign affairs, is relevant for foreign policy decisions as well.

Though there had always been some constitutional practice regarding specific participation rights of Cantons, these specific rules were brought about by the specific question of the relationship of Switzerland to the European Union in the early 1990s. Switzerland not being a member of the European Union, it is today a party to more than 120 treaties with the European Union, often related to access to the European Common market and thus to regulatory issues. It was in this context of the bilateral relationship between Switzerland and the European Union—and the manifold issues regarding constitutional structure it entails in Switzerland—that this specific framework of Cantonal participation in Swiss foreign policy was elaborated and put into practice.

In accordance with the constitutional guidelines and the statute, the specific participatory rights of Cantons in foreign policy decisions by the federal government are:

- *The federal government must inform the Cantons whenever it intends to be active on the international field in an area affecting the competencies of the Cantons or their interests.* The Cantons have a right to comment on the intention or mandate drafted by the federal government. Although these comments are not legally binding upon the federal government, the federal government is required to specifically justify its decision if it does not modify its foreign policy intention or negotiation mandate for its diplomats in response to Cantonal comments.
- *In the course of international negotiations affecting the Cantons, the Cantons are to be involved in the preparation of these negotiations as well as in their conduct.* It is thus not unusual that a Swiss delegation conducting an international negotiation includes representatives by the Cantons. Often, these representatives are part of the so-called "Conference of the Cantonal Governments," i.e., a coordinating organization under Swiss law assembling the Cantons and their interests vis-à-vis the federal government.

- After a negotiation has been concluded, the Cantons—in accordance with the internal order of competencies—are *in charge of implementing the treaty concluded by the federal government.*
- These participatory rights of the Cantons are subject to *the federal government's capacity to act in the international sphere.* In a case in which the safeguard of Swiss national interests thus requires the federal government to act quickly—e.g., by negotiating a treaty in order to settle a foreign policy crisis-situation—the participatory rights of the Cantons may not be taken into account, at least not to their full extent. This situation is specifically outlined in the relevant statute on Cantonal participation in foreign policy decisions by the federal government.

In specific areas of importance to the Cantons where Switzerland is part of an international regulatory mechanism, as is most prominently the case in the area of Schengen-Dublin (wherein Switzerland participates with decision-shaping rights on the EU-level based on a particular association agreement with the European Union), these participation rights of Cantons are even further specified on the basis of an agreement by the Cantons with the federal government.[14] Through this agreement, there are specific rules and how the Cantons are associated by the federal government in any decision in the Schengen-Dublin area as far as development of new regulations, their application, and their implementation are concerned. This represents an even further concretization of Cantonal participation rights in one specific area of foreign affairs.

As might be expected, the first main issue in practice regarding the participation of Cantons in foreign policy decisions by the federal government arises when the federal government, notwithstanding critical comments by the Cantons on a specific matter, continues its initial course of action without accommodating the Cantonal concerns. However, given the Cantonal role in the overall constitutional framework, e.g., with regard to treaty-approval or implementation, the Cantons will be able to make their concerns heard (and felt) at later stages. In turn, this means that the federal government, in the normal course of events, will try to accommodate Cantonal comments to the extent possible in any important foreign policy decision.

The second main issue is under what circumstances the federal government is allowed not to involve the Cantons in order to preserve its own capacity to act in the national interest under time pressure. In recent years, the matter has been primarily discussed in Swiss constitutional law as part of the so-called Libya Hostage Crisis of 2008–2010, when two Swiss citizens were held as hostages by the Muammar Gaddafi regime in Libya in response to an incident in Geneva involving a law enforcement action by the Cantonal police of Geneva and one of the sons of the Libyan ruler.[15]

[14] Agreement of 20 March 2009 between the Federal Government and the Cantons, *available at* https://www.admin.ch/opc/de/official-compilation/2009/1139.pdf.

[15] For this discussion, *see* the report by the parliamentary committee, «*Verhalten der Bundesbehörden in der diplomatischen Krise zwischen der Schweiz und Libyen*» of 2011, *available at* https://www.admin.ch/opc/de/federal-gazette/2011/4215.pdf.

In order to resolve the crisis, the federal government at one point attempted to enter into a settlement agreement with the Libyan government, thereby, given the time pressure, not immediately and formally consulting the relevant Cantons. There were conflicting legal views about whether this particular issue fulfilled the statutory criteria for not consulting the Cantons, but the general principle is undisputed.

V. Concluding Observations from a Practical and Comparative Perspective

From a comparative perspective, neither the "normalization of foreign affairs" nor the autonomous foreign policy competencies of the Swiss Cantons is unique. Similar constitutional designs and practices are present in, for example, the constitutional systems of Germany, Belgium, Canada, and the United States. Most of these federal systems ascribe a role in the overall internal decision-making framework on foreign affairs and international agreements to their component parts or the representatives thereof. The more that foreign affairs is perceived as a part of this overall constitutional framework, the more the principle of federalism influences foreign affairs decisions. The one aspect in which the Swiss system is more unique in this context is through the interplay of federalism with other organizing principles in its Constitution, especially the peculiar system of direct democracy. It is in this regard that the Swiss system contains some unique features related to foreign affairs federalism, including through the role of Cantons as part of the treaty-making power of the federal government (although such a role, in a different format however, also exists in Belgium and the respective role of its constituent parts in treaty-approval). In addition, most of these federalist states mentioned allow their substate entities to have some form of autonomous foreign policy and even treaty practice and thus a limited international legal personality. In this regard, the exact procedures and criteria as to when and how such autonomous foreign policy initiative are possible of course vary, and it may be in this respect that further comparative analysis would prove useful.

Of a more idiosyncratic nature in the Swiss system are the specific participation rights of Cantons in foreign affairs decision-making by the federal government. Though lacking the peculiar nature of the Swiss relationship with the European Union, this setup may be of interest also in different constitutional systems, including for states that are members of the European Union. The more that regulatory issues that historically formed part of the competencies of the component parts of a federalist system are transferred to international levels of governance, the more there seems to be a need to associate these component parts of federalism into the decision-making process on the international level. Without such association, principles of federalism as contained in various constitutions are at risk of being weakened through international governance.

Related to these broader considerations from a comparative perspective, there are three interrelated conclusions to be drawn from this chapter on Swiss foreign affairs federalism for foreign relations law more generally in this area:

The *first conclusion* is that the inclusion of federalist principles into foreign affairs depends on foreign affairs being to a large extent a formalized process on the international level through the conclusion of international agreements and work inside formal international organizations with a specifically defined mandate. It is in this context that most constitutions—including the Swiss one—incorporate foreign affairs into their general framework of organizing principles, including federalism. However, the more that international governance issues are dealt with in informal settings—through soft law standards set by international institutions or political agreements lacking the force of international law—the less the general constitutional framework takes account of these international developments and the less also the principle of federalism plays an important role. "Normalization of foreign affairs" is hence often limited to what could be called "foreign affairs in the classic or formal sense"; as soon as more recent aspects of foreign affairs like the rise of soft law standards are considered, the more principles of federalism are again sent to the background.

The *second conclusion* is that the idiosyncratic Swiss aspect of specific participation rights of Cantons in foreign affairs may be one possible model in order to counterbalance developments such as increasing informal international decision- and lawmaking processes. Given that the overall constitutional framework is often at pains to incorporate more informal international processes, the direct participation of the component parts in foreign affairs decisions that concern their competencies may help in preserving the role of these substate levels not only formally but substantially in foreign affairs. In a comparative perspective, some aspects of the Swiss model will be difficult to apply in a different constitutional system, especially those aspects of federalism that are closely intertwined with direct democracy. Of interest, however, could be the attempt in Switzerland to regulate Cantonal consultation and participation in important international negotiations. With such mechanisms, implementation problems of international agreements as a result of the federalist structure—that are sometimes present in different systems—are largely avoided.

The *third conclusion* is that there has to be a balance between the rights of the component parts in foreign affairs decisions by the federal government and their obligations to implement international obligations that result from these decisions. In the Swiss model, these two sides are included in the specific framework on Cantonal participation in foreign affairs. Though always a delicate issue in any federal system, there is a sounder justification for the federal government to order a government of a component part to bring itself into compliance with an international obligation when this component part has been involved in negotiating the international obligation at issue in the first place.

Finally, there may be an even more general observation to be taken into account. Even (or rather especially) with states that, as Napoléon Bonaparte put it in the citation at the outset of this chapter for the case of Switzerland, are a federation by nature, the practical effect and meaning of federalism in foreign affairs may from time to time require practical adjustments in light of new developments on the international plane, in particular with regard to new means of international regulation. As in other constitutional domains, foreign affairs federalism, in order to have a meaningful content, must not only be understood as a static set of competencies and procedures, but also as a more dynamic overall principle.

CHAPTER 18

FEDERALISM AND FOREIGN AFFAIRS IN INDIA

ANAMIKA ASTHANA
AND HAPPYMON JACOB

This chapter locates India's foreign affairs within the federal structure of the country's constitution. As the chapter explains, India's foreign policymaking processes do not strictly correspond to either a unitary or a federal model. As a formal matter, India's constitution strongly favors the central government's authority. However, the central government has, over time, pursued a pragmatic approach in dealing with subnational engagement in the country's foreign policymaking. This has been especially evident in the area of international trade. Moreover, despite the constitutional preeminence of the central government in matters of foreign policy and defense, state entities in the era of coalition politics have successfully deployed extraconstitutional means, mostly through bargaining and pressure tactics, to influence the central government's foreign policy processes.

I. The Central Government's Authority over Foreign Affairs

The Constitution of India came into force on January 26, 1950, more than two years after India's independence in August 1947. Since then, the country's constitution has undergone over a hundred amendments. At present, the Republic of India consists of twenty-nine states and seven union territories, including the national capital of Delhi. Both the preamble to the constitution and Article 1, which defines India as a "union of states," reflect the intention of the constitution makers to accord more and definite powers to the central government vis-à-vis the state governments. In the formative years of independence, the country not only witnessed the perils of partition, resulting in loss of territory, population, and resources, but also the difficulties of unifying a newly independent country. The years of colonial rule also left the country mired in poverty, underdevelopment, unemployment, and chaos in general. Against this backdrop, a unitary bias in the constitution was a deliberate act on the part of the constitution makers to cope with the contextual need of the hour as reflected in the constituent assembly debates on various provisions. Dr. Ambedkar, the leading architect of the Indian constitution, explained that the constitutional scheme was meant to be federal in normal times, while enabling a unitary state in emergency situations (Arts. 352, 356 of the constitution). The Supreme Court pronounced "federalism" as one of the basic features of the Indian constitution.[1]

Indian federalism, often described as "quasi-federal,"[2] leans strongly in favor of the center.[3] For example, India has a single citizenship, the union parliament has the power to alter the territorial area or names of the constituent states without constitutional amendment (Art. 3), the central government has emergency powers that enable it to dismiss the elected state governments, and (unlike under the American and Canadian constitutions) the Rajya Sabha—the House of States—does not have residential criteria for election of the members.[4]

The legislative mandates of the central and the state legislatures are specified in lists, under the seventh schedule of the constitution: List I sets forth the areas in which the union parliament has exclusive competence to legislate, List II sets forth the predominant (although not exclusive) competence of the state legislatures, and List III sets forth the concurrent jurisdiction of both the center and the states, although in cases of conflict the central law prevails.[5] The entries in the state list can be legislated upon by the parliament in the "national interest" if approved by a two-thirds majority of present and voting members of the upper house, for a period not exceeding one year at a time (Art. 249). Proclamations of emergency similarly grant wide-ranging powers to the parliament in matters in the state list (Art. 250). Unlike the American or the Australian constitutions, powers not mentioned in any of the lists (the residuary powers) lie within the exclusive legislative authority of the parliament.

The nature of the Indian constitution translates into federal supremacy in matters of foreign affairs law. The story was somewhat different during the colonial era, which was characterized by limited authority of the provinces to participate in matters of

[1] The concept of "basic features of constitution" essentially means that parliamentary amendment powers cannot be exercised to violate the basic essence of the constitution. Secularism, rule of law, federalism, free and fair elections, and so on are a few among them.

[2] *See* Kenneth C. Wheare, Federal Government (1953).

[3] *See* State of West Bengal v. Union of India, 1963 AIR 1241.

[4] *See* Kuldip Nayar v. Union of India and Ors, 22 August 2006. *See also* Mahendra P. Singh, *The Federal Scheme*, *in* The Oxford Handbook of the Indian Constitution (Sujit Choudhry, Madhav Khosla, & Pratap Bhanu Mehta eds., 2016).

[5] An exception to such a super-imposition is made in cases where there has been a prior presidential approval for the prevalence of state laws, even in the face of contradictory parliamentary legislation. For details, *see The Constitution of India* 1950, art. 254; *see also* Gujarat University v. Krishna Ranganath Mudholkar, 1963 AIR 703.

foreign affairs and treaty-making. Post-independence, however, such federal distribution of power in foreign affairs was eliminated.[6] The constitution makers believed that there was no place for subnational confrontations in the realm of foreign policy, which needed to be projected in a single, coherent manner. As a result, matters pertaining to foreign affairs, international law, international conventions, foreign trade, citizenship, and more have been placed in the union list, and therefore are exclusively within the jurisdiction of the union parliament (Art. 246(1)). Under Article 253, the union legislature, i.e., the parliament, enjoys exclusive and complete authority to legislate on such matters.[7] The words "notwithstanding anything in the foregoing provisions of this Chapter" in the beginning of Article 253 in effect grant the parliament the power to legislate on any matter related to foreign policy, even if placed in the state list, in order to carry out the implementation. The scope of this article, which covers "any decision made at any international conference, association or other body" (Art. 253), implies that the extension of parliamentary legislative powers extends even to the implementation of soft law or other nonbinding international actions.

Unlike the American system, there is no mandatory requirement of parliamentary ratification of treaties in India. Consistent with common law practices, the Union executive (the central government), and not the Union parliament, performs such treaty-making functions, except in cases involving infringement of an individual's fundamental rights,[8] imposition of financial obligations on the country, or where alterations in national laws are required. This reduces what otherwise might be an opportunity for state involvement through the upper chamber of the parliament.

The idea of such an overwhelming authority in the center for matters of treaty-making and implementation encountered resistance during the constituent assembly debates.[9] It is noteworthy that for the purposes of treaty implementation, the Government of India Act 1935 had required the federal government to seek the consent of the provinces when the matter belonged to the provincial list. Two members of the Constituent Assembly, Sir V. T. Krishnamachari and Mr. Nazir Ahmed, proposed amendments to the draft item no.14 (now item 13 in the union list of schedule VII), relating to the central executive's "participation in international conferences and implementation of decisions taken thereat," as it undermined the provincial authority

[6] *See* M. Frank L. M. Van de Craen, *The Federated State and Its Treaty Making Power*, RBDI (1983).

[7] *See* art. 253 of the Indian Constitution: "[N]otwithstanding anything in the foregoing provisions of this chapter, Parliament has power to make any law for the whole or any part of the territory of India for implementing any treaty, agreement or convention with any other country or countries or any decision made at any international conference, association or other body."

[8] *See* D K Basu v. State of West Bengal, 1 SCC 416 AIR 1997 SC 610.

[9] Existing rules under the Government of India Act 1935 provided that, although the implementation of treaties and agreements was within the jurisdiction of the federal government, the federal legislature was required to obtain the prior consent of the governor before making those laws applicable to the provinces [Section 106(1)]. The federal provisions concerning international treaties, however, did not enter into force before independence.

in the matters of the state list, if the express consent of the provinces was not sought beforehand.

K.T. Munshi, N. Gopalaswami Ayyangar, M. S. Aney, and B. L. Mitter opposed these amendments. Munshi argued that if the representatives of India at such conferences would not have the power to implement their decisions, then their opinions would not be valued internationally. Also, he contended that it did not make sense that decisions agreed upon by most of the countries at such conventions and consented to by most states within India could be withheld because of a few states. Hriday Nath Kunzru suggested that at such conferences, where the subjects of the state list are discussed, state representatives could be included along with those from the central legislature or secretariat. The suggestion was not accepted, however.

Item no.16 (now item 14 of List I of schedule VII), relating to "entering into and implementation of treaties and agreements with foreign countries," was also contested by Nazir Ahmed on the ground that it was a blatant violation of provincial rights. Responding to this, A. K. Ayyar cited the constitutional precedents of other federal countries like the United States and Australia, where despite stronger federal characteristics (because residuary powers lie with the states/provinces), foreign treaty decisions remain under the central prerogative. M. A. Ayyangar proposed the establishment of an Inter-Provincial Council or an All India Council, which could choose the representatives to be sent to such international platforms, provide them directions, and seek reports on the progress.

Both amendments were dropped, however, and the entries were adopted as originally proposed. The constitutional framers explicitly rejected the 1935 Act model that envisaged a fragmented treaty implementation power when the matter related to the provincial list. In due course, the Supreme Court further reaffirmed the Union executive's prerogative even in matters relating to the state list in compliance with treaty obligations.[10]

In effect, the treaty-making power of the central government is largely unfettered,[11] subject only to a few express and implied limitations,[12] to the disadvantage of the subnational units. For instance, despite the opposition from the state governments and the Standing Committee of the Parliament attached to the commerce ministry, the

[10] *See* P. B. Samant And Others v. Union of India and Anr, AIR 1994 Bom 323, 1994 (4) BomCR 491. *See also* Maganbhai Ishwarbhai Patel v. Union of India and Anr, AIR 783, 1969 SCR (3) 254. The Court cited the discussion in the constituent assembly of a Canadian precedent, in which the Privy Council declared invalid a parliamentary statute giving effect to international obligations while regulating certain matters in the provincial list. The Court noted that Article 253 may have been worded the way it was in order to avoid having the Canadian precedent occur in India. For details, *see* CONSTITUTIONAL PRECEDENTS, FIRST SERIES (Government of India Press, 1946).

[11] In practice, there are rules of international law, for example, under the UN Charter, and Article 53 of the Vienna Convention on the Law of Treaties, that constrain the treaty-making powers of a state, but these are not the subject matter of this chapter. For details, *see* Prem Varma, *Position Relating to Treaties Under the Constitution of India*, 17 J. INDIAN L. INST. 1 (1975).

[12] Article 53 of the Indian constitution provides that such power should be exercised in accordance with the constitution.

government of India signed the Trade-Related Aspects of Intellectual Property Rights (TRIPS) agreement in 1994. Such pursuits of the central executive have been more prominent in the trade-related agreements pertaining to the matters of the state list, like agriculture. States do not have a constitutional right to review the agreements before they are signed by the central government, as it is not obligatory on the latter to place the treaties before the parliament unless the treaty specifically calls for it.

On several occasions, the individual MPs put the notice of intention for a constitutional amendment to make ratification a precondition for implementation of treaties, but all of those proposals eventually lapsed.[13] The idea was to have a constitutional mechanism for the parliamentary oversight of treaty-making by the central executive. The national commission to review the working of the constitution, in 2002, proposed greater executive accountability through higher parliamentary involvement in treaty-making functions through the establishment of a parliamentary committee to review the need for ratification on a case-by-case basis. It proposed that some sort of arrangement be devised in order to categorize the treaties as (1) those that could be concluded by the executive on its own, (2) those requiring parliamentary ratification, and (3) those requiring parliamentary involvement at the negotiation stage as well. This proposal, however, was not taken up by the parliament. The recommendation of the Justice Venkatchalliah Committee report (2002) on the desirability of prior consultation between the Union government and the Inter-State Council on matters of vital interests to the states was ignored as well.[14] The Inter-State Council, the only constitutional body created to ensure center-state coordination and cooperation on matters concerning the states, remains mostly nonoperational since the body rarely meets and its recommendations are not legally binding. The constitutional prerogative of the executive in treaty-making, the legislative apathy with respect to enlarging parliamentary involvement in the matters of foreign relations law,[15] and the strong "whip-based" party system in the legislature limit the role of parliament and states in foreign policy-related matters.

II. Subnational Engagement in Foreign Affairs

In contrast to the permissive conditions under the Canadian, Swiss, and German constitutions, where the provinces are allowed to engage in foreign affairs within

[13] In February 1992, MP M. A. Baby introduced the constitution amendment bill in the Rajya Sabha to make provisions for the parliamentary ratification of treaties. In March 1993, MP George Fernandes, in July 1994, MP Chitta Basu, and in October 2008, MP Brinda Karat introduced similar proposals, but all eventually lapsed.

[14] *See* Ministry of Law, Justice and Company Affairs, *Department of Legal Affairs, National Commission to Review the Working of the Constitution (NCRWC)*, 2002.

[15] *See* Lavanya Rajamani, *International Law and the Constitutional Schema, in* The Oxford Handbook of the Indian Constitution, *supra* note 4.

certain restrictions, the Indian constitution does not provide for subnational engagement in foreign affairs. Despite the constitutionally sanctioned preponderance of the Union over foreign policy matters, however, the center has often been restrained by states from making foreign policy decisions unilaterally. In the Indian case, there is a wide scholarly consensus that the involvement of federal units in foreign affairs has increased over the last few years. The extent and nature of such participation, however, remains contested. Mattoo and Jacob point out the following four factors that contribute to evolving federalization of foreign policymaking in India: (1) the special constitutional status given to some of the states, like Jammu and Kashmir (J&K), empowering the state leadership; (2) the political weight of certain state leaders, albeit indirectly; (3) the phenomenon of coalition politics empowering regional parties; and (4) globalization-induced changes.[16] The following sections examine these factors in detail, along with others.

Special Constitutional Status for Certain States

India presents an example of both political asymmetry (constituent states do not have an equal footing in the upper house of the parliament and their seat share corresponds to their respective population size) as well as constitutional asymmetry (as reflected in the provisions for special legislative and executive powers of some of the states).[17] The special constitutional status accorded to certain states, like Jammu and Kashmir (Art. 370) and Nagaland (Art. 371 A), and special provisions for schedule six states (Assam, Meghalaya, Tripura, and Mizoram) provide greater autonomy to these states in matters of local governance. Theoretically, the concerns of foreign affairs and defense would supersede local priorities if there is a conflict. On the ground, however, the situation is more complex. Leaders whose states are provided with special powers/provisions have expressly resented the central deployment of military and paramilitary forces in their states, which have often been mired in controversies over the extensive and unjust use of force in the region. West Bengal, for example, investigated cases of rape against the Border Security Force (BSF) personnel, an action that was upheld by the Kolkata High Court, despite the fact that the BSF Act empowers the force to conduct such investigations.[18]

During times of good relations between India and Pakistan, i.e., during the 2004 to 2007 period, the J&K state leadership, thanks to the special status of the state and due to the dynamics of coalition politics, was instrumental in persuading the central government to initiate several confidence-building measures with Pakistan that would benefit

[16] *See* Amitabh Mattoo & Happymon Jacob, *Foreign Relations of India: The Federal Challenge, in* SHAPING INDIA'S FOREIGN POLICY: PEOPLE, POLITICS AND PLACES (Amitabh Mattoo & Happymon Jacob eds., 2012).

[17] *See* Rekha Saxena, *Is India a Case of Asymmetrical Federalism?*, 47 ECON. & POL. WKLY. 2 (2012).

[18] *See* TNN, *State to Probe BSF Rape Case*, TIMES O.I. (Mar. 11, 2004).

the J&K state. The state's involvement in foreign affairs thus, in a sense, emanates from its own existential and local factors.

While the special status given to such states under the constitution may not result in autonomous powers of decision-making, it does ensure their participation in the matters of foreign policy corresponding to their territorial areas, albeit with limitations.

Role of the Individual State Leaders

State leaders in India mostly voice their opinions in cases where a foreign policy matter seems to have a substantial impact on the local population. For instance, the Kerala chief minister (CM) reprimanded the center in 2013 for not ensuring for the return of two Italian marine officers who were on trial in India and were allowed to go back to their country for a short while. They were charged with killing two fishermen in the waters adjacent to Kerala. Forced to take action due to pressure from the state government, the center got into a face-off with the Italian government, and, as a result, the latter blocked India's entry into the Missile Technology Control Regime (MTCR) in 2015.[19]

In another instance of state involvement in foreign policy, Narendra Modi, as the CM of Gujarat, complicated the ongoing India-Pakistan negotiations over Sir Creek, a body of water adjacent to the Gujarat border, by making it seem like a handover of the territory to Pakistan. Though the cessation of territory is a sovereign authority of the government of India, such a declaration by the state leadership politicized the issue and, in effect, forestalled the negotiations for a possible solution.

Most such cases of federalization, or the "regionalization" as scholar M. P. Singh terms it, have been in states with strong and influential leaders who have even been re-elected to a second term in their respective states. Such instances of foreign policy dispute between the center and the state leadership have been more common when the ruling governments at the two levels belong to different political parties, spilling their domestic tussle into the realm of foreign affairs.

Coalition Dynamics

One of the most significant factors responsible for the increased assertions of authority by subnational entities in foreign affairs in India is coalition dynamics. With the decline of the powerful Congress party in the 1990s and a parallel rise of coalition politics, both at the center and in the states, regional state leaders and parties have become

[19] *See* Tom Kington & Vivek Raghuvanshi, *Italy Blocks Indian Application to MTCR*, DEF. NEWS (Oct. 17, 2015).

prominent. Concerned more about their local voters, regional parties are more assertive of their local interests when part of the central coalition.

For instance, the Tamil Nadu–based Dravida Munnetra Kazhagam (DMK), an important coalition partner in the United Progressive Alliance (UPA)-II government that was in power in the center at the time, was able to exert pressure on the latter to vote against Sri Lanka in the UN Human Rights Council (UNHRC) in 2013.[20] The DMK had eighteen seats in the central coalition, which became significant given the central government's deteriorating relations with the Trinamool Congress (TMC), another coalition partner. As the DMK was not in the government in the state, it was not dependent on the central alliance for power sharing purposes. This gave it more leeway to pursue a more unrestrained and populist policy, which eventually succeeded.

Coalition dynamics also played an important role in the Indo-U.S. nuclear deal, where the opposition of the Left parties, a major coalition partner at the center, almost jeopardized the deal in 2008. The government had to face a no-confidence motion in the parliament when the Left withdrew its support for the government.

The absence of coalition dynamics since the arrival of the BJP-led National Democratic Alliance's (NDA) central government in 2014 seems to be favoring a more "New Delhi–centric" approach to foreign policymaking. For example, reversing her earlier stand of opposition during the UPA government, Mamata Banerjee agreed to support the Land-Boundary agreement during the NDA regime. Having lost its leverage as a coalition partner, the state government agreed to support the deal, albeit only after getting substantial funds for the transformation.

Role of the Border States

There are several ways in which border states influence foreign policy. India's border states have shown keen political interest when there are co-ethnic populations in neighboring countries. For example, Tamil Nadu has been voicing its opinions about the treatment meted out to the co-ethnic and co-linguistic Tamil population in Sri Lanka. Punjab and J&K have been vocal about India-Pakistan relations, being the first in the line of defense along India's western border. The J&K leadership under the PDP government in 2002, as a coalition partner at the center, managed to carry out its agenda, such as facilitating a dialogue between separatist groups in Kashmir and the government at the center and releasing suspected militants in Kashmir. In response to the center's objection,[21] it agreed to put the cases before the screening committee with

[20] The resolution was critical of the Sri Lankan government for gross violations of human rights while suppressing the minority Tamil insurgency on its soil. The Tamil regional parties have been very sensitive about the treatment of the Sri Lankan Tamil population by the government there.

[21] *See* Rafiq Dossani & Srinidhi Vijaykumar, *Indian Federalism and the Conduct of Foreign Policy in Border States: State Participation and Central Accommodation Since 1990*, Asia-Pacific Research Centre (2005).

one central nominee in it. The state government also disbanded and refused to re-establish the Special Operations Group (SOG), much to the chagrin of the central government.[22]

West Bengal and other border states of the northeast have played a similar role in New Delhi's policy formation toward countries along India's eastern border. The West Bengal government has often been at loggerheads with the center on the question of deportation of illegal migrants from Bangladesh.

The center has often conceded to the states' demands. For instance, the center sought the assistance of Jyoti Basu, the former CM of West Bengal, in concluding the Ganga water treaty with Bangladesh in 1996. In 2011, the West Bengal state government prevented the central government from signing the Teesta water treaty between India and Bangladesh, accusing the center of not consulting the state well ahead of the deal, the terms of which were inimical to the interests of the West Bengal farmers. Threatened by the withdrawal of another coalition partner (the DMK), the Manmohan Singh government at the center decided to heed to the state government, and the deal was called off at the last moment, turning it into a national embarrassment. West Bengal's opposition also led to the stalling of the Land-Boundary Agreement in 2011, which aimed at the transfer of 111 Indian enclaves in Bangladesh and 51 Bangladeshi enclaves in India.

Sometimes the center takes on board a state's objections even when there are no coalition compulsions. The NDA government, despite being a majority government and unconstrained by coalition compulsions, has decided not to impose the Teesta water-sharing agreement on West Bengal and has recognized the latter as a party to any such arrangement between New Delhi and Dhaka.[23] West Bengal's concurrence for the Land-Boundary agreement in 2014 was achieved because of the diplomatic efforts of the Bangladesh government under Sheikh Hasina, which reached out to Mamata Banerjee.

Another border state with significant engagements with Bangladesh is Tripura. Prime Minister Sheikh Hasina thanked the CM of Tripura, Manik Sarkar, for his constructive role in the India-Bangladesh land boundary agreement. The state has engaged in mutual, courteous diplomatic visits to Bangladesh under the Sheikh Hasina regime. In its efforts to manage the law and order situation in the state emanating from the transnational security threats, the Sarkar government leveraged its goodwill across the border and conducted police operations on insurgent bases and safe houses within Bangladesh, with the help from the central intelligence agencies.[24] Sheikh Hasina's government also cracked down on insurgents in its territory and handed over the rebel leaders to the Tripura government in 2009.

[22] Though established by the state, it was favored by the center in antiterror operations.

[23] *See* IANS, *Teesta Issue: Will Take Mamata on Board, Says Sushma*, BUSINESS STANDARD (June 5, 2017).

[24] *See* Subir Bhaumik, *Tripura: Ethnic Conflict, Militancy and Counter-Insurgency*, 52 MAHANIRBAN CALCUTTA RESEARCH GROUP, POLICIES AND PRACTICES (Aug. 23, 2012).

Defense-Related Mandates

National defense remains the center's prerogative in India. None of the security-related institutional mechanisms involve the state leaders. States do not normally challenge the center's mandate when it comes to defense-related issues. Internal security, on the other hand, has been a thorny domain. With the increasing conflation of issues related to insurgency, terrorism, and law and order, the distinction between internal and external security threats has become fuzzy, leading to conflicts between the center and the states.

While the subject "criminal law" appears in the concurrent list, the term "terrorism" per se does not appear in any of the lists, thereby creating confusion. As a consequence of such ambiguity, the enactment of the Terrorist and Disruptive Activities (Prevention) Act (TADA) by the center came to be challenged in the *Kartar Singh v. State of Punjab* (1994) case on grounds, among others, that being a matter of "public order," which is mentioned in the state list, the parliament lacked the legislative competence.[25] The court, however, set aside the challenge and upheld the constitutionality of the law on the ground that the center's predominance applies in the matters of both the concurrent and the residuary list. Furthermore, the court reasoned that terrorist activities are serious dangers to the security and integrity of the country and cannot be categorized as "disorders of lesser gravity having an impact within the boundaries of the state." This makes them a matter of the union list within the ambit of entry 1, namely, "defence of India."

Differences of opinion between the states and the center have also overshadowed the creation and shaping of the country's National Counter-Terrorism Centre (NCTC). It was envisaged with the authority not only for information collection and sharing but also for conducting enquiries and making arrests without the prior permission of the state governments in such cases. However, several non-Congress CMs during the UPA-II regime opposed the proposals for a nationwide mandate of the NCTC as a violation of the federal structure of the country. They feared that the center could politically misuse such an institution to trouble the state governments that refused to comply with the center.[26] The dissenting states proposed a parliamentary enactment for creating it, in order to avoid central predominance if created by the executive order alone. Even the diluted draft proposing the operation of the NCTC "through or in conjunction with the state police," was opposed by a few CMs like Modi, Banerjee, and Jayalalitha, arguing that a proliferation of institutions, rather than addressing the gaps in the existing system, would only destabilize it and weaken the federal trust.[27]

[25] *See* Kartar Singh v. State of Punjab 1994, SCC (3) 569, JT 1994 (2) 423; *see also* Naga People's Movement of Human Rights v. Union of India 1988 (2) SCC 109.

[26] *See* PTI, *NCTC a Poorly Conceived* Idea: *Modi*, THE HINDU (June 5, 2013).

[27] *See* Surabhi Malik, *P Chidambaram vs Narendra Modi Over Proposed Anti-Terror Body, the NCTC*, NDTV (June 5, 2013).

In 2015, after the Gurdaspur terror attack, the Punjab government under CM Praksah Singh Badal went against the Union directive and insisted on conducting the investigation by state agencies rather than handing over the probe to the National Investigation Agency (NIA), which under the NIA Act has the independent power to probe the terror-related incidents.[28] This bone of contention between the center and the state was resolved later when the Union government transferred the case to the NIA, citing "international ramifications."[29]

In short, while there is some flexibility when it comes to states' engagement in foreign affairs matters, national defense remains entirely under the central command despite resistance from states.

III. Subnational Engagement in Foreign Trade

The Indian state, in its formative years up to the early 1980s, aimed for limited foreign trade expansion, focusing on import substitution and self-sufficiency. The trade regime was not only inflexible but also highly centralized. Cumbersome procedures under the permit system or the "license-permit-raj," as it was widely called, dissuaded foreign companies from investing substantially in the Indian markets. By implication, the states were not heavily involved.

This situation started changing in the late 1980s, when the balance of payment situation became too precarious and the lacunae of state planning and its failures became too glaring to be avoided anymore. A series of procedural and legal changes were introduced in 1991 to overhaul the Indian economic structure. With the progressive liberalization of the economic regulations over the years, the ease of conducting business with foreign companies has grown substantially, and this has helped the states carve out an important space for themselves. Today, important state dignitaries from abroad make it a point to visit some of these high-potential investment destinations in the Indian states.

The center has not pursued a conscious strategy of promoting foreign investment in subnational units, but it has accommodated the states' concerns by not vetoing such trade pursuits unless for specific reasons, such as security concerns or limitations of international trade regimes to which India is a signatory. As treaties and agreements are within the exclusive domain of the union, the central government, in the spirit of cooperative federalism, has facilitated state agreements by acting as guarantor.

[28] *See* Mail Today, *Gurdaspur Terror Attack: Punjab Reluctant to Hand Over Probe to NIA*, India Today (Aug. 19, 2015).

[29] *See* Rajesh Ahuja, *Centre May Hand Over Gurdaspur Terror Attack Probe to NIA*, Hindustan Times (July 30, 2015).

This means that the center could still veto such arrangements if it wanted to do so. However, it has generally avoided doing so.

In the absence of a constitutional mandate, the asymmetry between the states in terms of their access to emerging economic opportunities is apparent. A few states exhibit self-limitations in terms of poor economic potential and backwardness. Left to fend for themselves, the states with proactive leadership and greater industrial bases are on the forefront of subnational diplomacy in foreign-trade-related matters. For instance, Narendra Modi, as Gujarat's CM, started the "Vibrant Gujarat" initiative to showcase the economic potential and achievements of the state. Success of this initiative also inspired other states like Maharashtra, Madhya Pradesh, and Rajasthan to undertake similar initiatives in their bid to compete for foreign investments.

The enabling power of globalization for the subnational entities is not without its share of disputes. Scholars like Jenkins argue that the limited exposure of states to multilateral fora like the World Trade Organization (WTO) has not granted them corresponding access and leverage to influence the policy decisions.[30] Unlike Canada, where provincial delegations formally attend designated multilateral meetings, no such formal arrangement exists in India at present. Also, several multilateral agreements have increasingly led to the erosion of the legislative jurisdiction of states in matters such as agriculture and land. The WTO negotiations during the late 1990s and 2000s became a serious bone of contention between the center and the states. The center disregarded the states' insistence on prior discussions before concluding the agreements.

Over the years, the center faced criticism from various quarters, prompting it to adopt a more flexible and accommodating approach. The political uproar and dissent from domestic quarters have been successful in putting pressure on the central government to conduct broader discussions with domestic stakeholders. Post-2000, Indian engagements with the WTO and other such multilateral institutions have shown increasing instances of references to the subnational sensitivities while considering the trade-related proposals.

External Financing

Article 293(1) of the Indian constitution places territorial limits on the borrowing power of the constituent states in India, implying their non-access to foreign loans on their own accord. As a result, the center has been borrowing on behalf of the states and disbursing the funds as grants and loans. But states like Andhra Pradesh and Maharashtra approached the World Bank directly for development loans, and in 1997, Andhra Pradesh became the first Indian state to receive a structural adjustment loan

[30] *See* Robert Jenkins, *India's States and the Making of Foreign Economic Policy: The Limits of the Constituent Diplomacy Paradigm*, 33 PUBILUS 4 (2003).

directly from the World Bank.[31] Recently, with the center's consent, it also borrowed an infrastructure development loan from the World Bank for the rejuvenation of the Amaravati city. In general, the Department of Economic Affairs within the Ministry of Finance has been assisting the states in accessing the external financial assistance. The external donors like the World Bank and others have come up with a mechanism to assess the nature of economic performance of major states in order to decide on their credibility. This, in a way, has made these engagements between the subnational entities and the external agencies more direct.[32]

Moreover, in order to address the fiscal burdens arising out of lending to the states, as part of the fiscal reforms management, the twelfth finance commission in 2004 recommended that the prevailing system of central loans and grants be done away with and the external financial assistance be transferred to states, including the full exchange rate risk, on the same terms and conditions as those attached to such assistance by external funding agencies and borne by the center till now.[33] More significantly, in April 2017, the central government approved guidelines to allow the "financially sound" states to borrow directly from the bilateral Official Development Assistance (ODA) partners for implementation of vital infrastructure projects.[34] The idea was to externally facilitate greater fund availability to the states, which otherwise, when borrowed domestically, could exhaust the borrowing limits of the state governments, drying up funds for other projects. Consequently, in 2017, the Mumbai Metropolitan Region Development Authority, a state government entity, approached the Japan International Cooperation Agency for ODA loans for the Mumbai Trans Harbour Link project.

The center has also formulated a set of guidelines facilitating such loans, subject to the fulfillment of certain conditions and borrowing limits under the Fiscal Responsibility and Budget Management Law.[35] All the consequent repayment of loans and interests would be made directly by the concerned state government. The borrowing state will furnish the guarantee for the loan, while the government of India will be the counter guarantor for the loan.[36]

The center's flexible interpretation of the borrowing conditionality has been approached with caution. In order to prevent excess borrowing by the states, there

[31] *See* BSCAL, *Andhra First State to Get Direct World Bank Loan*, BUSINESS STANDARD (Apr. 8, 1997).

[32] *See* Kripa Sridharan, *Federalism and Foreign Relations: The Nascent Role of the Indian States*, 27 ASIAN STUDIES REVIEW 463 (2003).

[33] *See* Ministry of Finance, Government of India, *Explanatory memorandum on the Action Taken on the Recommendations of the Various Finance Commissions, available at https://fincomindia.nic.in/writereaddata/html_en_files/oldcommission_html/memorandum/12memorandum.htm.*

[34] *See* Special Correspondent, *States Can Seek Overseas Loans for Projects*, THE HINDU (Apr. 19, 2017).

[35] *Id.* at 34.

[36] *See* Press Information Bureau, *Cabinet Approves Permission to Avail External Assistance by State Government Entities from Bilateral Agencies for Implementation of Vital Infrastructure Projects*, GOVT. OF INDIA, CABINET (Apr. 19, 2017), *available at* http://pib.nic.in/newsite/PrintRelease.aspx?relid=161135.

are national regulations, and the finance ministry also instructs the lending agencies to make sure that the grants are not misused by the recipient states.[37]

Institutional Mechanisms

The central governments have been facilitating subnational engagements in foreign trade, albeit with regulatory caution. The institutional mechanisms to strengthen center-state coordination, however, remain woefully inadequate. There is no specifically designated institution to work on center-state coordination in economic matters. As it is not obligatory on the part of the center to introduce the agreements in the parliament before signature, states may not be aware of the specific details beforehand. The WTO cells formed in the background of center-state tussles in matters involving agriculture, patents, and so on have not been very effective. Set up by some of the state governments, these cells are concerned mostly with compliance with such rules as already acceded to by the center under the WTO provisions.[38]

This, however, does not mean that states are completely marginalized in trade-related matters. As the implementation is to be done mostly through states' cooperation, the central government often makes efforts to consult them beforehand. Apart from such voluntary gestures, opinion-seeking is performed at the industry level. Institutions like the Federation of Indian Chambers of Commerce and Industry (FICCI) have state bodies that analyze the impact of trade arrangements on the state economies and recommend on the merits of the deals. The opinions of such bodies are not binding in nature but are often valued by the central government.[39]

Another important forum that caters to state concerns, albeit indirectly, is the Department Related Parliamentary Standing Committee on Commerce, attached to the Ministry of Commerce and Industry.[40] It has twenty-one members from the Lok Sabha and ten members from the Rajya Sabha. It conducts a detailed analysis of trade-related proposals of the central government and offers recommendations pertaining to multiple aspects, including the impact on states' economies.

However, the lack of institutionalized channels of communication to deal with trade-related matters prompts the state governments to approach the center with their concerns, demands, and recommendations. Since there are no specifically designated authorities for the same, much of this remains ad hoc.

[37] *See* Sridharan, *supra* note 32.

[38] Dipankar Sengupta, interviewed by Anamika Asthana, 2017, Telephone Interview, Delhi-Jammu and Kashmir.

[39] Reji Joseph, interviewed by Anamika Asthana, 2017, Institute for Studies in Industrial Development, New Delhi.

[40] Debasish Chakraborty, interviewed by Anamika Asthana, 2017, Telephone Interview, Delhi-Kolkata.

There are scholars who think that the argument about economic federalization is often overstated. Dipankar Sengupta points out that an argument for the economic federalization can be misleading as it is not the "states" but the "stakeholders" that are able to influence the central policies.[41] These could be state parties or corporate lobbies, or both. Certain states, such as Gujarat and Maharashtra, have higher stakes and a higher bargaining power because of their greater industrial potential, streamlined investment procedures, and better infrastructure.

In general, however, both the center and the states seem to acknowledge the need for and advantages of subnational economic engagements in foreign trade. Borrowing from his own experiences as the CM of Gujarat, Narendra Modi, as the prime minister since 2014, has pushed his agenda of providing more opportunities to the subnational entities in matters of foreign policy, in particular foreign trade policy. Parting ways from the traditional practice of inviting the foreign state leaders to New Delhi, Modi met with the Japanese Prime Minister Shinzo Abe in Varanasi and the Chinese President Xi Jinping in Ahmedabad, in order to promote the investment potential of these cities.[42]

In 2014, a "States Division" was established within the Ministry of External Affairs (MEA). It facilitates meetings of Indian officials with foreign delegations in India and abroad. It also advises the states on attracting investments and conducting humanitarian operations. This division has not only facilitated the signing of sister-state agreements between Karnataka-Sichuan, Chennai-Chongqing, Hyderabad-Qingdao, and Aurangabad-Dunhuang but also the Kyoto-Varanasi Partner City Agreement during Prime Minister Modi's visit to Japan in 2015.

In another interesting move, foreign service officers of the country are now being tasked with specializing in at least one Indian state and evaluating its economic potential for the purposes of international trade.[43] These Indian envoys are also supposed to advertise and promote the trade and tourism potential of these states in the countries of their posting.[44] There are also proposals for assigning diplomats to certain major states where they would advise the local government on means and opportunities in matters of foreign trade. In the light of this expanded mandate of the foreign office, it is difficult to ascertain the level of central outreach to the states, given the existing shortage of manpower in the MEA. There are also proposals for establishing "Videsh Bhavans" in state capitals, which would house MEA branch secretariats, regional passport offices, and Protector of Emigrants offices.[45] How much of this, if at

[41] *See* Sengupta, *supra* note 38.

[42] There have been just these two instances so far, where the highest-level foreign dignitaries have been invited by the prime minister to meet in the cities other than the capital city. It, therefore, remains too soon to be viewed as a new norm of standard operating procedure in India.

[43] *See* Charu S. Kasturi, *Land Hunt in States for MEA Hubs*, THE TELEGRAPH (Feb. 12, 2017).

[44] *See* Express News Service, *South Block Initiative: Indian Envoys to Facilitate Trade Links Between States and Countries of Posting*, THE INDIAN EXPRESS (May 28, 2016).

[45] *See* Jabin Jacob, *Govt Planning Videsh Bhavans in States to Help Passport Seekers, Migrant Workers*, HINDUSTAN TIMES (Feb. 15, 2107).

all, will translate into federalization of foreign policy is difficult to predict. The branch secretariats would still house the central bureaucrats from the MEA, and there is no proposal for inducting state officials in either the states division or the branch offices as yet. The existing MEA branch secretariats in cities like Hyderabad and Kolkata are more in the nature of decentralization measures to ease the burden of the main office at Delhi and have limited mandates. While states are now proactively negotiating with the foreign entities, they are still not allowed to establish their own offices in foreign countries, and their inclusion in international negotiation panels is subject to the will of the center.

Trade and Border States

While the central governments have been flexible on the issue of state involvement in foreign trade in general, they have exercised more restraints with respect to the border states like Punjab, Arunachal Pradesh, and so on. There still have been a few instances of subnational engagement in foreign economic affairs. In the case of Punjab, for instance, the state leadership has mostly supported the border trade with Pakistan. Prakash Singh Badal, building on cultural diplomacy of the past, managed to convince the center of the inauguration of the Integrated Check-Post (ICP) at Attari in 2012. The center also facilitated his proposal of selling 500 megawatts of power to Pakistan.

The eastern border, too, reflects subdued foreign collaboration by the state entities. The importance of the northeastern states is undisputed as they serve as a gateway to the Southeast Asian markets. Economic development in these states is significantly is linked to their role in the facilitation of international trade as they share more international boundary with Bangladesh, Myanmar, Bhutan, Nepal, and China than with the rest of India. The incomplete and disputed nature of boundary demarcation, however, severely constrains the regulatory power of these states in border management.

Moreover, since the South Asian region is a hotbed of terrorism, insurgency, and ethnic violence, compounded by issues of smuggling, illegal trade, and cross-border trafficking, it becomes a securitized zone with stringent border monitoring and control being prioritized over open and flexible trade arrangements. The imperatives of the inter-state and the transboundary nature of both the trade opportunities and security threats complicate the center-state relations in this region all the more.

Three-way trade-related negotiations (between the center and the state, between the center and the neighboring countries, and among the states of the region) often lead to prolonged talks and delays. The North Eastern Regional Council, comprising the chief minsters of the northeastern states, remains primarily advisory in nature and does not enjoy any substantial power of decision-making.

This, however, has not prevented cross-border trade altogether. Local traders continue to carry out small-scale cross-border trade despite the center's apprehensions. Apart from this, in a few cases, there have been interactions between the neighboring countries and the Indian border-state governments, over and above the involvement of the central government. Tripura, for example, not only convinced the center to allow the sale of electricity to Bangladesh through its Paltana ONGC power plant but also managed to obtain reciprocal cooperation from Bangladesh, which allows the transport of heavy equipment and food grains to Tripura through the Chittagong and Asuganj ports.[46]

One can also find instances of border states frustrating the efforts of the center toward the promotion of foreign trade. The BJP government in Rajasthan, for example, thwarted the attempts of the UPA government at the center and opposed the opening up of the Munabao-Khokhrapar land route between Rajasthan and Sindh, fearing Sindhi migration from across the Pakistan border.[47] In general, however, geopolitical tensions with neighboring countries and transnational security threats constrain the potential of border states in entering into trading relations with their neighbors.

IV. Conclusion

Changes in the politics and political economy of India have far exceeded the gradual evolution of the constitutional scheme. Contemporary dynamics have necessitated increasing subnational engagements in matters of foreign affairs. However, with the lack of a constitutional mandate and limited political will on the part of both the center and the states, federalization of foreign affairs in India remains very limited. To date, the central government has been willing to provide more space for subnational diplomacy in matters of foreign trade than in political and strategic affairs.[48] The jury is still out on how much of this is inspired by a genuine interest in the federalization of foreign policymaking. The center's flexibility and willingness to accommodate states' opinions appears to reflect at this point more of an instrumental approach. The absence of a strong momentum for foreign policy federalization in the Indian political landscape, however, has not obstructed the introduction of ad hoc arrangements to facilitate the same, in cases where the constituent states have significant domestic stakes in the country's foreign policy pursuits. India, however, has a long way to go to introduce the federalization of foreign policymaking as a conscious policy.

[46] *See* Subir Bhaumik, *The Agartala Doctrine*, Tripura Infoway (2014), *available at* http://www.tripurainfoway.com/column-details/60/the-agartala-doctrine.html.

[47] *See* Tridivesh S. Maini, *Opening up the Munabao Khokhrapar Crossing*, The Hindu (Apr. 11, 2014), *available at* http://www.thehindu.com/opinion/op-ed/opening-up-the-munabaokhokhrapar-crossing/article6105073.ece.

[48] *See* Happymon Jacob, *Putting the Periphery at the Centre: Indian States' Role in Foreign Policy*, Carnegie Endowment for International Peace (2016).

CHAPTER 19

FOREIGN AFFAIRS FEDERALISM IN THE EUROPEAN UNION

ROBERT SCHÜTZE

I. Introduction

The federal principle stands for a duplex regime—the existence of two levels of government within a compound polity. Within federal states, powers are divided between a general government and particular governments, and there are therefore potentially two governments that could engage in foreign relations with third parties. Yet classic international law has principally responded to the emergence of federal states "by ignoring their constitutional characteristics and assimilating them to other sovereign States."[1] In light of its unitary vision, international law has indeed long remained ambivalent toward the foreign affairs powers of member states within a federation. Modern doctrine today holds that they can enjoy international personality "[i]f the federal constitution grants them the right to deal separately with foreign States and such States agree to deal with them."[2] Chapters in this *Handbook* describe some specific approaches taken by a number of federal states.

But what about classic international organizations or unions of states, like the European Union? Here, the problem has traditionally been the reverse: with the member states presumed to be sovereign, the capacity of international organizations to conduct foreign affairs of their own has long been in doubt. And even if the capacity of international organizations to engage in treaty making was expressly recognized in 1949,[3] international

[1] Ivan Bernier, International Legal Aspects of Federalism 1 (1973). [2] *Id.* at 81.

[3] *Cf.* Reparation for Injuries Suffered in the Service of the UN, Advisory Opinion [1949] ICJ 174, at 179: "Accordingly, the Court has come to the conclusion that the Organization is an international person. That is not the same thing as saying that it is a State, which it certainly is not, or that its legal personality and rights and duties are the same as those of a State. Still less is it the same thing as saying that it is 'a super-State,' whatever that expression may mean. It does not even imply that all its rights and duties must be upon the international plane, any more than all the rights and duties of a State must be upon that plane.

law has nonetheless remained ambivalent about the nature and scope of the foreign affairs powers of international organizations.Their external relations raise fundamental challenges to the traditional conception of international law as a law based on the sovereign equality of its subjects because "[i]nternational organizations are neither sovereign nor equal."[4] The foreign affairs powers of international organizations have thus been attacked from two sides: "from the outside world, where historically only States have held 'full powers,' and also from within, where member states are constantly on guard against both loss of sovereignty and against any consequences the activities of the organization might bring for them."[5]

What was the outcome of this dual challenge for the foreign affairs powers of the European Union? The European Union was born with the genetic code of an international organization. The 1957 Treaty of Rome formed part of international law, although the European Court of Justice was eager to emphasize that the Union "constitutes a new legal order of international law."[6] With time, this new legal order has indeed evolved into a true "federation of States."[7] How would the foreign affairs powers of this new supranational entity be divided? Would the European Union gradually replace the member states, or would it preserve their distinct and diverse foreign affairs voices? As discussed below, in light of its international origins, the European legal order has remained an "open federation": both the Union and its member states are entitled to conduct their own foreign affairs autonomously. Yet bound together in a compound polity, the Union's foreign affairs federalism nevertheless had to be organized in a way that would enable coordination and cooperation between the Union and its states. Both of these *federal* strategies will be discussed below. But first we need to quickly explore the limits of the Union's foreign affairs powers.

II. The Union's Enumerated Foreign Affairs Powers

The Treaty of Rome acknowledged the legal personality of the European "Union";[8] and the international *capacity* of the Union would thereby stretch "over the whole field of

What it does mean is that it is a subject of international law and capable of possessing international rights and duties, and that it has capacity to maintain its rights by bringing international claims."

[4] Paul Reuter, *Question of Treaties Concluded Between States and International Organizations or Between Two or More International Organizations*, 27 Y.B. ILC (vol. 2) 119, 120 (1975).

[5] Neri Sybesma-Knol, *The New Law of Treaties: The Codification of the Law of Treaties Concluded between States and International Organizations or between Two or More International Organizations*, Ga. J. Int'l & Comp. L. 425, 428 (1985).

[6] Case 26/62 NV Algemene Transporten Expeditie Onderneming van Gend & Loos v. Netherlands Inland Revenue Administration [1963] ECR 1, 12.

[7] On this point, *see* Robert Schütze, European Constitutional Law ch. 2 (2015).

[8] Ex-Art. 210 EEC: "The Community shall have legal personality."

[its] objectives."[9] But what about the Union's treaty-making *powers*? In accordance with the federal principle of enumeration or conferral, the Union must act "within the limits of the competences conferred upon it by the Member States in the Treaties."[10] The European Court of Justice has clarified that this principle applies to "both the internal action and the international action of the [Union]."[11]

Under the 1957 Rome Treaty, the Union's foreign affairs powers were originally confined to the Common Commercial Policy (CCP) and Association Agreements with third countries or international organizations.[12] This restrictive attribution of external powers protected a status quo in which the member states were to remain the principal players on the international relations scene. Yet this picture has changed dramatically in the past forty years: the Union has expanded its foreign affairs powers significantly, both through the doctrine of implied external powers and by the significant widening of its express external powers.

The Doctrine of Implied External Powers

The doctrine of implied external powers is the single most important foreign affairs doctrine of EU law. While not completely unknown to the early Treaties,[13] it is best understood as a constitutional invention offered by the European Court of Justice in its famous *ERTA* decision.[14]

The European Road Transport Agreement (ERTA, or under its French acronym, AETR) had been intended to harmonize certain aspects of international road transport and involved a number of member states as potential signatories. The negotiations had restarted in 1967 and were conducted without involvement of the Union. The member states involved in the ERTA negotiations agreed to coordinate their positions within the Council, with the presiding member state acting as a spokesman. The Commission felt excluded from its role as the Union's external broker and insisted on being involved in the negotiations and finally brought the matter before the European Court.

The Commission argued that the Union's internal power over transport policy—set out today in Article 91 TFEU—included the external power of treaty-making. This broad teleological interpretation was justified by reference to the argument that "the full effect of this provision would be jeopardized if the powers which it confers, particularly that of laying down 'any appropriate provisions,' within the meaning of subparagraph (1)(c) of the article cited, did not extend to the conclusion of agreements with third countries."[15] The Council opposed this interpretation, contending that "Article [91] relates only to measures *internal* to the [Union], and cannot be interpreted as authorizing the conclusion of international agreements." The power to enter

[9] Case 22/70 Commission v. Council (ERTA) [1971] ECR 263, para.14.

[10] Art. 5(2) TEU.

[11] Opinion 2/94 (Accession to the ECHR) [1996] ECR I-1759, para. 24.

[12] *Cf.* Ex-Arts. 113 and 238 of the original EEC Treaty.

[13] *Cf.* Ex-Art. 101 Euratom Treaty.

[14] Case 22/70 Commission v. Council (ERTA) [1971] ECR 263.

[15] *Id.*, para. 7.

into agreements with third countries, argued the Council, "cannot be assumed in the absence of an express provision in the [Treaties]."[16]

In its judgment, the European Court sided with the Commission's expansive approach, explaining:

> To determine in a particular case the [Union's] authority to enter into international agreements, regard must be had to the whole scheme of the [Treaties] no less than to its substantive provisions. Such authority arises not only from an express conferment by the [Treaties]—as is the case with Article [207] for tariff and trade agreements and with Article [217] for association agreements—but may equally flow from other provisions of the [Treaties] and from measures adopted, within the framework of those provisions, by the [Union] institutions...
>
> Article [91(1)] directs the Council to lay down common rules and, in addition, "any other appropriate provisions"... This provision is equally concerned with transport from or to third countries, as regards that part of the journey which takes place on [Union] territory. It thus assumes that the powers of the [Union] extend to relationships arising from international law, and hence involve the need in the sphere in question for agreements with the third countries concerned.[17]

This passage spoke the language of teleological interpretation: in light of the general scheme of the Treaties, the Union's power to adopt "any other appropriate provision" to give effect to the Union's transport policy objectives must be interpreted as including the legal power to enter international agreements.[18] This was subsequently confirmed by the Court in *Opinion 1/76*.[19] There, the Court declared that "whenever [European] law has created for the institutions of the [Union] powers within its internal system for the purpose of attaining a specific objective, the [Union] has authority to enter into the international commitments necessary for the attainment of that objective even in the absence of an express provision in that connexion."[20] The reasoning of the Court created the idea of a parallel treaty-making power running alongside the internal legislative powers of the Union. In its most extensive format, this doctrine of parallel external powers means that the Union's foreign affairs powers are "coextensive with its internal domestic powers."[21]

The doctrine of parallel external powers has had a complex and contradictory history.[22] The Lisbon Treaty tried to codify it in Article 216 TFEU.[23] The provision today states:

[16] *Id.*, paras. 9–10 (emphasis added). [17] *Id.*, paras. 15–16 and 23–27.

[18] In the words of the *ERTA* Court: "With regard to the implementation of the [Treaties] the system of internal [Union] measures may not therefore be separated from that of external relations." *Id.*, para. 19.

[19] Opinion 1/76 (Draft Agreement for the Laying-up Fund for Inland Waterway Vessels) [1977] ECR 741.

[20] *Id.*, para. 3.

[21] Eric Stein, *External Relations of the European Community: Structure and Process*, *in* COLLECTED COURSES OF THE ACADEMY OF EUROPEAN LAW (vol. I-1) 115, 146 (1990).

[22] *See* ROBERT SCHÜTZE, FOREIGN AFFAIRS AND THE EU CONSTITUTION ch. 7 (2014).

[23] *See* European Convention, *Final Report Working Group VII—External Action* (CONV 459/02), para. 18: "The Group saw merit in making explicit the jurisprudence of the Court[.]"

> The Union may conclude an agreement with one or more third countries or international organisations where the Treaties so provide or where the conclusion of an agreement is necessary in order to achieve, within the framework of the Union's policies, one of the objectives referred to in the Treaties, or is provided for in a legally binding Union act or is likely to affect common rules or alter their scope.[24]

While recognizing the express treaty-making competences of the Union conferred elsewhere by the Treaties, this provision grants the Union a residual competence to conclude international agreements in three situations.

The first alternative mentioned in Article 216(1) TFEU confers a treaty-making power to the Union "where the conclusion of an agreement is necessary in order to achieve, within the framework of the Union's policies, one of the objectives referred to in the Treaties." Textually, this competence seems much wider than the judicial doctrine of parallel external powers as espoused in *ERTA*. For, as we saw above, the Court had insisted that an external Union competence only derived from an internal *competence*, and that meant that no external competence could be derived from an internal *objective*. By contrast, the first alternative in Article 216 suggests exactly that. The Court has recently clarified, however, that this implication reflects sloppy drafting and that Article 216 TFEU in fact codifies the doctrine of parallel powers from *ERTA*.[25]

Article 216 mentions two additional situations. The Union will also be entitled to conclude international agreements where this "is provided for in a legally binding act or is likely to affect common rules or alter their scope." Both alternatives make the existence of an external competence dependent on the existence of internal Union law. Two objections may be launched against this view. Theoretically, it is difficult to accept that the Union can expand its competences without Treaty amendment through the simple adoption of internal Union acts, and practically, it is hard to see how either alternative will ever go beyond the first alternative.

The Union's Express Foreign Affairs Competences

The express foreign affairs competences of the Union are grouped into two constitutional sites: Title V of the Treaty on European Union deals with the "Common Foreign and Security Policy" (CFSP),[26] and Part V of the Treaty on the Functioning of the European Union enumerates various specific policies within which the Union is entitled to act. Perhaps the best way to make sense of the constitutional division is to identify the Union's CFSP competence as a *lex generalis* to the specific external competences found in the TFEU.

[24] Art. 216(1) TFEU. [25] Opinion 1/13 (Hague Convention), EU:C:2014:2303, para.67.

[26] The TEU's common provisions also contain two external competences for the Union. Article 6(2) TEU empowers the Union to accede to the European Convention for the Protection of Human Rights and Fundamental Freedoms. The Union's "Neighbourhood Policy" (ENP) finds its constitutional basis in Article 8 TEU.

The general competence over the CFSP can be found in Article 24 TEU, which states:

> The Union's competence in matters of common foreign and security policy shall cover all areas of foreign policy and all questions relating to the Union's security, including the progressive framing of a common defence policy that might lead to a common defence.

This competence includes the power to adopt unilateral decisions and, as Article 37 TEU clarifies, the power to "conclude agreements with one or more States or international organisations." The Common Security and Defence Policy (CSDP) is thereby generally seen to form "an integral part" of the CFSP.[27] The latter "shall provide the Union with an operational capacity," which the Union may use "on missions outside the Union for peace-keeping, conflict prevention and strengthening international security in accordance with the principles of the United Nations Charter."[28] The CSDP will—in the future—also include the "progressive framing of a common Union defence policy,"[29] yet Article 42 TEU here contains a constitutional guarantee not to prejudice the neutrality of certain member states, and to respect other member states' obligations within the North Atlantic Treaty Organization (NATO).[30]

The Union's general CFSP competence is complemented by a number of special foreign affairs competences listed in Part V of the TFEU. The latter contains seven titles. Title II deals with the Union's Common Commercial Policy (CCP). This is the external expression of the Union's internal market. Here, the Union is tasked with representing the common commercial interests of the member states on the international scene and with contributing to "the harmonious development of world trade."[31] Under Article 207 TFEU, the Union is entitled to adopt unilateral legislative acts,[32] and to conclude bilateral or multilateral international agreements.[33] The scope of the CCP covers all matters relating to trade in goods and services, commercial aspects of intellectual property, and foreign direct investment.[34]

Title III deals with three related but distinct external policies in three chapters. All three policies allow the Union to adopt unilateral measures,[35] and to conclude international agreements with third states.[36] Chapter 1 concerns "Development Cooperation," whose primary objective is "the reduction and, in the long term, the eradication of poverty" in developing countries.[37] Chapter 2 extends various forms of assistance to "third countries other than developing counties."[38] The Union's competence in respect of humanitarian aid can be found in Chapter 3 of this Title. It permits the Union to provide "ad hoc assistance and relief and protection for people in third countries who are victims of natural or man-made disasters, in order to meet the humanitarian needs resulting from these different situations."[39]

[27] Art. 42(1) TEU. [28] *Id.* [29] Art. 42(2) TEU, first indent. [30] *Id.*, second indent.
[31] Art. 206 TFEU. [32] Art. 207(2) TFEU. [33] Art. 207(3) TFEU.
[34] Art. 207(1) TFEU. [35] *See* Arts. 209(1), 212(2), 214(3) TFEU.
[36] *See* Arts. 209(2), 212(3), 214(4) TFEU. [37] Art. 208(1) TFEU. [38] Art. 212(1) TFEU.
[39] Art. 214(1) TFEU.

Finally, Title IV confers on the Union a competence to adopt economic sanctions against third states and nonstate actors. These are unilateral acts with a "punitive" character. This competence has had an eventful constitutional history,[40] and still constitutes a strange animal. For, according to Article 215 TFEU, the Union is not entitled to act on the basis of this competence alone. It can only exercise this competence *after* the Union has exercised its CFSP competence. The provision constitutes the central platform for the implementation of resolutions of the Security Council of the United Nations.

In addition to these three main competence titles, we also find some special foreign affairs competences in the institutional provisions of this Part of the TFEU. Title V grants the Union a residual competence to conclude international agreements in Article 216 as well as a special competence to conclude "association agreements."[41] Title VI grants the Union a competence to establish and maintain cooperative relations "as are appropriate" with international organizations, in particular the United Nations and the Council of Europe.[42] Even outside Part V of the TFEU, external competences can be found.[43]

Voting in the Council: The Political Safeguards of Federalism

The central organ responsible for the Union's external relations is the Council. While increasingly required to obtain the consent of the European Parliament, the Council has remained the "primus" in the foreign relations apparatus of the Union. Representing the member states, it constitutes the intergovernmental organ of the Union, and, as such, it constitutes the most important political safeguard of foreign affairs federalism of the Union.

Within the Council, the most powerful way to protect particular member state interests is unanimity voting. This voting arrangement still predominates the CFSP, where Article 31 TEU states that the Council generally acts by unanimity.[44] In stark contrast to the remarkably strong political safeguards of federalism under the CFSP, in

[40] For a good account of that constitutional history, *see* PANOS KOUTRAKOS, TRADE, FOREIGN POLICY AND DEFENCE IN EU CONSTITUTIONAL LAW: THE LEGAL REGULATION OF SANCTIONS, EXPORTS OF DUAL-USE GOODS AND ARMAMENTS (2001), ch. 3.

[41] *See* Art. 217 TFEU. These agreements are special agreements in that they create "special, privileged links with a non-member country which must, at least to a certain extent, take part in the [Union] system." *See* Case 12/86, Demirel v. Stadt Schwäbisch Gmünd [1987] ECR 3719, para. 9.

[42] Art. 220 TFEU. The European Union is a full or partial member of a number of international organizations. For a comparative perspective here, *see* Joris Larik, *Regional Organizations' Relations with International Institutions: The EU and ASEAN Compared*, ch. 25 in this volume.

[43] A number of legal bases outside Part V of the TFEU also grant the Union external competences. For example, Article 168(3) TFEU confers the power to adopt measures that foster cooperation with third countries and competent international organizations in the context of the Union's Public Health policy.

[44] Exceptionally, and in derogation from the unanimity rule, Article 31(2) enumerates a number of situations in which qualified majority voting applies. The CFSP also recognizes the option of a "constructive abstention."

many other areas of EU foreign affairs the Council increasingly operates on the basis of a qualified majority.[45] This voting arrangement is set out in Article 16(4) TEU:

> As from 1 November 2014, a qualified majority shall be defined as at least 55 per cent of the members of the Council, comprising at least fifteen of them and representing Member States comprising at least 65 per cent of the population of the Union. A blocking minority must include at least four Council members, failing which the qualified majority shall be deemed attained. The other arrangements governing the qualified majority are laid down in Article 238(2) of the Treaty on the Functioning of the European Union.[46]

In a Union of twenty-eight states, 55 percent of the Council members corresponds to sixteen states. This near simple majority rule is, however, "qualified" by an additional criterion as the bigger member states have insisted on a population majority in addition to the state majority. (The population threshold of 65 percent theoretically means that any three of the four biggest states of the Union could block a Council decision.) By contrast, the smaller member states have insisted that a qualified majority will be "deemed attained" where fewer than four states try to block a Council decision. Thus, as under the past system of weighted votes in the Council,[47] the EU constitutional order does not adopt the sovereign equality solution that can be found in classic international law or the U.S. Senate. Instead, it distinguishes between bigger and smaller states, and this distinction makes the voting in the Council not just a direct political safeguard of federalism but also an indirect safeguard of democracy.

III. Dual Federalism: Originally and Subsequently Exclusive Powers

From a classic international law perspective, the member states of the European Union enjoy full treaty-making powers as equal and sovereign subjects. Yet this perspective is not shared by the European legal order. Here, the member states enjoy only limited foreign affairs powers, and these Union limits are set in two ways. First, the EU Treaties may themselves grant the Union a constitutionally exclusive competence over external relations. Even where this is not the case, the Union can preempt the member states in areas of shared foreign affairs competences.

[45] For an analysis of the treaty-making procedure within the Union legal order, *see* Marise Cremona, *Making Treaties and Other International Agreements: The European Union*, ch. 14 in this volume.

[46] The Treaty recognizes an express exception to this in Art. 238(2) TFEU.

[47] On the old arrangement of weighted votes, *see* Schütze, European Constitutional Law, *supra* note 7, at 179.

Originally Exclusive External Powers: The Common Commercial Policy

Exclusive powers are constitutionally guaranteed monopolies: only one governmental level is entitled to act autonomously. For the Union legal order, exclusive competences are defined as areas in which "only the Union may legislate and adopt legally binding acts." The member states will only be able to act "if so empowered by the Union or for the implementation of Union acts."[48]

With regard to foreign affairs, the core exclusive competence of the Union is its competence over the Common Commercial Policy (CCP). The first signs of such a constitutionally exclusive power began to take shape in the form of the "succession" doctrine established by the Court in *International Fruit*.[49] But the constitutional exclusivity thesis only fully emerged in *Opinion 1/75*.[50] The European Court had here been asked to clarify the scope and nature of the Union's power under Article 207 TFEU in the context of an Organisation for Economic Co-operation and Development (OECD) agreement on export credits. In denying that the member states had a shared competence over the issue, the Court explained:

> Such a policy is conceived in that Article in the context of the operation of the common market, for the defence of the common interest of the [Union], within which the particular interests of the Member States must endeavour to adapt to each other. Quite clearly, however, this conception is incompatible with the freedom to which the Member States could lay claim by invoking a concurrent power, so as to ensure that their own interests were separately satisfied in external relations, at the risk of compromising the effective defence of the common interests of the [Union] . . . To accept that the contrary were true would amount to recognizing that, in relations with third countries, Member States may adopt positions which differ from those which the [Union] intends to adopt, and would thereby distort the institutional framework, call into question the mutual trust within the [Union] and prevent the latter from fulfilling its tasks in the defence of the common interest.[51]

The harmonious operation of the institutional framework of the Union and the solidarity among its members would, according to the Court, be called into question if the member states retained a shared competence to engage autonomously in commercial activities with third countries. The judgment was affirmed a year later in *Donckerwolcke*,[52] where the Court again held that "full responsibility in the matter

[48] Art. 2(1) TFEU.

[49] Joined Cases 21–24/72, International Fruit Company NV v. Produktschap voor Groenten en Fruit [1972] E.C.R. 1219.

[50] Opinion 1/75 (Draft understanding on a local cost standard) [1975] E.C.R. 1355.

[51] *Id.* at 1363–1364.

[52] Case 41/76, Suzanne Criel, née Donckerwolcke and Henri Schou v. Procureur de la République au tribunal de grande instance de Lille and Director General of Customs [1976] E.C.R. 1921.

of commercial policy was transferred to the [Union] by means of Articles [207 (1)]," with the consequence that "measures of commercial policy of a national character are only permissible after the end of the transitional period by virtue of specific authorization by the [Union]."[53] Under the CCP, the member states therefore no longer enjoyed any autonomous foreign affairs powers, and the exclusive nature of the CCP is today firmly established in European constitutionalism.[54]

Subsequently Exclusive Powers: Dual Federalism on the Move

Early on, the Union legal order insisted that the member states will be deprived of their treaty-making powers to the extent that their exercise would affect internal European law. This first limit was spelled out in *ERTA* and became known as the "ERTA doctrine." It states that each time the Union "adopts provisions laying down common rules, whatever form these may take, the Member States no longer have the right, acting individually or even collectively, to undertake obligations with third countries which affect those rules."[55]

The original *ERTA* ruling had thereby left in suspense the question of *when* the exercise of external powers by the member states would be incompatible with European law, and it was up to subsequent jurisprudence to clarify the extent to which the member states would lose their treaty-making power. In *Opinion 1/94*,[56] the Court voted against the automatic field preemption of the member states. And, according to *Opinion 1/2003*,[57] a finding in favor of exclusive Union powers indeed requires "a comprehensive and detailed analysis" of the relationship between internal legislation and the international treaty that must prove that "it is clear that the conclusion of such an agreement is capable of affecting the [European] rules."[58]

The second constitutional principle is the *Opinion 1/76* doctrine.[59] The Court here wished to extend the exclusionary effect to situations where the "external powers may be exercised, and thus become exclusive, without any internal legislation having first been adopted."[60] An external Union power could thus become exclusive by exercising that very power through the conclusion of an international agreement. The exclusivity here is neither purely legislative, since the member states are prevented from autonomous action

[53] *Id.*, para. 32.

[54] Art. 3(1) (e) TFEU. On the rise and fall of partial exclusivity of the CCP from Opinion 1/94 to the Lisbon Treaty, *see* Schütze, Foreign Affairs, *supra* note 22, at 411.

[55] *ERTA*, *supra* note 14, para. 18.

[56] Opinion 1/94 *(WTO)* [1994] ECR I-5267, para. 96.

[57] Opinion 1/2003 (Lugano) [2006] ECR I-1145.

[58] *Id.*, para. 124.

[59] On the transformation of the *Opinion 1/76* ratio decidendi, *see* Schütze, Foreign Affairs, *supra* note 22, at 258.

[60] Opinion 1/94, *supra* note 56, para. 85.

at a time when no European secondary law exists, nor purely constitutional, for it is through the subsequent exercise that the competence becomes exclusive.

The scope of this hybrid exclusivity has, however, always been very restricted. It was confined to "the situation where the conclusion of an international agreement is necessary in order to achieve Treaty objectives which cannot be attained by the adoption of autonomous rules."[61] The Union would therefore only enjoy an exclusive external power where the achievement of an internal objective was "inextricably linked" with the external sphere.[62]

Lastly, in *Opinion 1/94* the Court added a third constitutional principle limiting the treaty-making powers of the member states, known as the "WTO Principle."It states that "[w]henever the [Union] has included in its internal legislative acts provisions relating to the treatment of nationals of non-member countries or expressly conferred on the institutions powers to negotiate with non-member countries, it acquires exclusive external competence in the spheres covered by those acts."[63]

These three judicial doctrines have, with the 2007 Lisbon Treaty, been imperfectly codified in Article 3(2) TFEU. The provision states:

> The Union shall also have exclusive competence for the conclusion of an international agreement when its conclusion is provided for in a legislative act of the Union or is necessary to enable the Union to exercise its internal competence, or in so far as its conclusion may affect common rules or alter their scope.

According to the first situation mentioned here, the Union enjoys an exclusive treaty-making power when the conclusion of an international agreement "is provided for in a legislative act." This formulation corresponds to the "WTO Doctrine," yet the codification is more restrictive, as it excludes the first alternative ("provisions relating to the treatment of nationals of non-member countries") from its scope.

The second situation mentioned in Article 3(2) TFEU grants the Union an exclusive treaty power, where this "is necessary to enable the Union to exercise its internal competence." This formulation aims to codify the "Opinion 1/76 Doctrine,"[64] yet unlike the original version, Article 3(2) TFEU seems much wider. The almost identical wording of Article 3(2) and Article 216 TFEU indeed suggested that "implied shared competence would disappear," yet as Marise Cremona notes, this would be "a wholly undesirable departure from the case law."[65]

Finally, the third situation in Article 3(2) appears to refer to the Court's *ERTA* doctrine. But it strangely breaks the link between a *member state agreement* and

[61] Opinion 2/92 *(OECD)* [1996] ECR I-1759, § V, para. 4.

[62] Case 476/98 Commission v. Germany (Open Skies) [2002] ECR I-9855, para. 87.

[63] Opinion 1/94, *supra* note 56, para. 95.

[64] Opinion 1/76 (Laying-up Fund) [1977] ECR 741. On the evolution of the Opinion 1/76 doctrine, *see* Schütze, *supra* note 22, at 258.

[65] Marise Cremona, *A Constitutional Basis for Effective External Action? An Assessment of the Provisions on EU External Action in the Constitutional Treaty*, EUI Working Paper 2006/30, 10.

internal European law, and replaces it with an analysis of the effect of a *Union agreement* on European rules. This is an "editorial mistake," and the Court has clarified that the "old" *ERTA* case law fully applies here.[66]

As a practical matter, the most important situation within Article 3(2) is the third situation. To what extent does the *ERTA* doctrine "preempt" the member states from concluding international agreements on their own? The following criteria have guided the Court in its analysis. First, Article 3(2) TFEU is only triggered once the Union has adopted secondary law. The reference to "common rules" being affected does not include primary law.[67] Second, in order to see if Article 3(2) applies, the Court will investigate the extent to which internal Union law covers the scope of the envisaged international agreement. If that is the case "to a large extent," the Court will then, as a third step, look to what extent there exists a risk that the Union common rules will be affected.[68]

What happens to international agreements, originally concluded by the member states, that subsequently cover an area in which the Union has assumed an exclusive competence? The Union has answered this question by means of a doctrine of functional succession.[69] Treaty succession is here not based on a transfer of territory, but rather on a transfer of functions. The European Court originally announced this European doctrine in relation to the General Agreement on Tariffs and Trade in *International Fruit*.[70] Formally, the Union was not a party to the GATT, but the Court nonetheless found as follows:

> [I]n so far as under the [European] Treat[ies] the [Union] has assumed the powers previously exercised by Member States in the area covered by the General Agreement, the provisions of that agreement have the effect of binding the [Union].[71]

Functional succession here emanated from the exclusive nature of the Union's powers under the Common Commercial Policy (CCP). Since the Union had assumed the "functions" previously exercised by the member states in this area, it was entitled and obliged to also assume their international obligations.

For a long time after *International Fruit*, the succession doctrine remained quiet. In the last decade, however, it has experienced a constitutional revival. This allowed the Court to better define the doctrine's contours. Three principles have traditionally governed functional succession in the European legal order. First, for the succession

[66] Case C-114/12 Commission v. Council, EU:C:2014:2151, para.66.

[67] This was recently confirmed, beyond doubt, in Opinion 2/15 (Singapore), EU:C:2017:376, paras. 234 and 235.

[68] *See* Opinion 1/13 (Hague Convention), EU:C:2014:2303, paras. 83–84.

[69] *See* Pierre Pescatore, L'Ordre Juridique des Communautés Européennes 147–148 (Presse Universitaire de Liège, 1975) (my translation): "[B]y taking over, by virtue of the Treaties, certain competences and certain powers previously exercised by the Member States, the [Union] equally had to assume the international obligations that controlled the exercise of these competences and powers[.]"

[70] Joined Cases 21–24/72, International Fruit Company NV v. Produktschap voor Groenten en Fruit [1972] ECR 1219.

[71] *Id.*, paras. 14–18.

doctrine to come into operation, all the member states must be parties to an international treaty.[72] Second, when the international treaty is concluded is irrelevant. It will thus not matter whether the international treaty was concluded before or after the creation of the European Community in 1958.[73]

Third, the Union will only succeed to international treaties where there is a "full transfer of the powers previously exercised by the Member States."[74] The Union will thus not succeed to all international agreements concluded by all the member states, but only to those where it has assumed an exclusive competence. Would the European succession doctrine thereby be confined to the sphere of the Union's *constitutionally* exclusive powers, or would *legislative* exclusivity generated by Article 3(2) TFEU be sufficient? The Court has shown a preference for a succession doctrine that includes legislative exclusivity. In *Bogiatzi*,[75] the Court indeed found that a "full transfer" could take place where the member states were completely preempted within the substantive scope of the international treaty.

A fourth and potentially radical principle has recently been suggested in *Opinion 2/15*.[76] The Court here controversially found that where the Union has succeeded the member states according to principles one through three, it also "has competence to approve, by itself, a provision of an agreement concluded by it with a third State which stipulates that the commitments . . . in bilateral agreements previously concluded between Member States of the European Union and that third State must, upon entry into force of that agreement concluded by the European Union, be regarded as replaced by the latter."[77] If that means what it seems to mean, then the doctrine of functional succession would no longer only have purely "internal" effects within the Union legal order. It would, on the contrary, seem to entitle the *Union* to *externally* terminate the international agreements of the member states previously concluded with a third state.

IV. Cooperative Federalism: Sharing Power between the Union and the States

How has the EU legal order coordinated the potentially dual presence of the Union and its member states? The Union has followed two mechanisms. The first mechanism is a political safeguard of federalism that brings the Union and its member states to the same negotiating table for an international agreement. This technique of cooperation is called a mixed agreement. A second mechanism is "internal" to the Union and

[72] Case C-188/07, Commune de Mesquer v. Total [2008] ECR I-4501.

[73] Case 308/06, Intertanko and others v. Secretary of State for Transport [2008] ECR I-4057.

[74] *Id.*, para. 4.

[75] Case C-301/08, Bogiatzi v. Deutscher Luftpool and others [2009] ECR I-10185.

[76] Opinion 2/15, *supra* note 67.

[77] *Id.*, para. 249.

imposes a "duty of cooperation" so as to guarantee "unity in the international representation of the [Union]."[78]

Mixed Agreements: An International and Political Safeguard

Who can conclude international agreements that do not entirely fall into the competence sphere of the Union or the member states? The traditional answer to that question has been that the Union *and* the member states combine their foreign affairs competences in the form of a *mixed* agreement—that is, an agreement to which both the Union and some or all of its member states appear as contracting parties. Mixity was originally designed for a specific sector of European law,[79] yet it soon spread to become the hallmark of the European Union's foreign affairs federalism.[80]

The growth and success of mixed agreements in Europe's foreign affairs federalism may be accounted for by a number of reasons internal and external to the Union legal order. First, mixed agreements would allow the Union and its member states to combine their competences into a unitary whole that matched the external sovereignty of a third state. The division of treaty-making powers between them could then be reduced to an "internal" Union affair.[81] Second, the uncertainty surrounding the nature and extent of the treaty-making powers of the young Union under international law originally provided an additional reason.[82] As long as it remained uncertain whether or how the Union could fulfill its international obligations, mixed agreements would provide legal security for third states by involving the member states as international "guarantors" of the Union obligation.[83]

The constitutional developments within the European legal order in the last four decades have weakened both rationales. Not only have the external powers of the Union been significantly expanded through the development of the doctrine of implied powers—now codified in Article 216 TFEU—its internal powers have been sharpened to guarantee the autonomous enforcement of Union agreements within the European

[78] Opinion 1/94, *supra* note 56, para. 108.

[79] Art. 102 Euratom Treaty.

[80] For a now slightly outdated registry, *see* Joni Heliskoski, Mixed Agreements as a Technique for Organizing the International Relations of the European Community and Its Member States 252–277 (2001) (listing 154 mixed agreements concluded between 1961 and 2000).

[81] *See* Ruling 1/78 (IAEA Convention) [1978] ECR 2151, para. 35 ("It is sufficient to state to the other contracting parties that the matter gives rise to a division of powers within the Community, it being understood that the exact nature of that division is a domestic question in which third parties have no need to intervene.").

[82] Pierre Pescatore, *Les Relations extérieures des communautés européennes: contribution à la doctrine de la personnalité des organisations internationales*, 103 Recueil des Cours 1, 105 (1961).

[83] Maurits J. Dolmans, Problems of Mixed Agreements: Division of Powers within the EEC and the Rights of Third States 95 (1985).

legal order.[84] Today, the dominant reason behind mixed agreements appears to be of a purely political nature: member states insist on participating in their own name so as to remain "visible" on the international scene. Even for matters that fall squarely into the Union's competence, the member states dislike being enclosed behind a supranational veil.

How has the European Union reacted to the member states' demand for mixed agreements? Shared competences should not, constitutionally, require mixed action. For within shared competences, the Union or the member states can both act autonomously and conclude independent agreements; or, if they so wish, they may act jointly.[85] Indeed, it originally seemed that the European Court would demand specific constitutional justification for mixed external action in place of a pure Union agreement.[86] However, in the last three decades, the Court of Justice has given its judicial blessing to the uncontrolled use of mixed agreements in areas of shared competences. And in *Opinion 2/15*, the Court even alluded to the idea that shared competences required joint action by the Union and its member states under a mixed agreement.[87]

The widespread use of mixed external action evinces a remarkable Union tolerance toward the member states' international powers, as the practice of mixed agreements entails a significant anti-Union consequence. For, according to a European "constitutional convention," the Council generally concludes mixed agreements on behalf of the Union only once all the member states have themselves concluded the agreement in accordance with their constitutional traditions.[88] The convention thus boils down to requiring unanimous consent before the Union can exercise its competence. The conventional arrangement thus prolongs the infamous Luxembourg Compromise in the external sphere. The constitutionally uncontrolled use of mixed agreements under the Union's shared powers has, unsurprisingly, been criticized as "a way of whittling down systematically the personality and capacity of the [Union] as a representative of the collective interest."[89]

On the other hand, mixed agreements can also be seen more positively as a way of safeguarding the role of national parliaments in EU treaty-making. For once the Union uses a mixed agreement, the conclusion of this agreement will not only require

[84] On the direct and indirect effects of international agreement in the Union legal order, *see* Mario Mendez, *The Application of International Law by the Court of Justice of the European Union*, ch. 34 in this volume.

[85] *See* Case 316/91, Parliament v. Council [1994] ECR I-625, para. 26 ("The [Union's] competence in that field is not exclusive. The Member States are accordingly entitled to enter into commitments themselves vis-à-vis non-member States, either collectively or individually, or even jointly with the [Union].").

[86] Opinion 1/76 (Laying-up Fund) [1977] ECR 741, paras. 6–8.

[87] In Opinion 2/15, *supra* note 67, para.244 the Court found that because the Union "only" had a shared competence, "the envisaged agreement cannot be approved by the European Union alone."

[88] The inspiration for this constitutional convention appears to lie in Article 102 of the Euratom Treaty.

[89] Pierre Pescatore, *Opinion 1/94 on "Conclusion" of the WTO Agreement: Is There an Escape from a Programmed Disaster?*, 36 CML Rev. 387 fn.6 (1999).

ratification by the European Parliament, but also—subject to the constitutional traditions of the member states—the ratification by every single national parliament and sometimes even regional parliaments. How complex and uncertain this makes the EU ratification process can be seen in the drama surrounding the conclusion of the EU-Canada Trade Agreement that had originally been blocked by the Belgian region of Wallonia.[90] Yet the constitutional principles governing an "incomplete" ratification of a mixed agreement have hardly been explored.[91]

The Duty of Cooperation: An Internal and Judicial Safeguard

The member states' duty to cooperate loyally informs all areas of European law.[92] The duty is particularly important in the external sphere.[93] Unlike the internal sphere, the duty has here been predominantly used to facilitate the autonomous exercise of the Union's external competences. This facilitating role has been expressed in a positive and a negative manner. The positive aspect of the duty here demands that the member states act as "trustees of the Union interest." By contrast, the negative aspect of the duty can place a limit on the member states exercising their shared external competences.

Classic international law is still built on the idea of the sovereign state. The European Union is a union of states, and, as such, still encounters legal hurdles when acting on the international scene. These hurdles have become fewer, but there remain situations in which the Union cannot externally act due to the partial blindness of international law toward compound subjects. And where the Union is—internationally—"disabled" from exercising its competences, it will have to authorize its member states to act on its behalf. This positive manifestation of the duty of cooperation is called the "trustees doctrine."[94]

A good illustration of the trustees doctrine may be found in the context of the Union's inability to participate in international organizations. Many of these organizations still only allow states to become active members, and hence the European Union finds itself unable to exercise its competences in these international decision-making

[90] *See Belgium's Walloon Parliament blocks EU-Canada free-trade deal*, FINANCIAL TIMES, Oct. 14, 2016.

[91] *But see* Guillaume van der Loo & Ramses Wessel, *The Non-Ratification of Mixed Agreements: Legal Consequences and Solutions*, 54 CML REV. 735 (2017).

[92] For the general duty, *see* Art. 4(3) TEU.

[93] For a special expression of the general duty of Article 4(3) TEU in the CFSP area, *see* Art. 24(3) TEU; and for even more specific duties of cooperation, *see* Art. 32 TEU (consultation and coordination of national policies within the European Council and the Council), and Art. 34 TEU (coordination of member states in international organizations).

[94] For a first analysis of this doctrinal construction in the external sphere, *see* Marise Cremona, *Member States as Trustees of the Union Interest: Participating in International Agreements on Behalf of the European Union*, *in* A CONSTITUTIONAL ORDER OF STATES: ESSAYS IN HONOUR OF ALAN DASHWOOD 435 (Anthony Arnull et al. eds., 2011).

forums. An example of this state-centered membership is the International Labour Organization (ILO). Here, the Union cannot itself conclude international conventions and must thus rely on its member states. The obligation to act as trustee of the Union thereby derives from the duty of cooperation:

> In this case, cooperation between the [Union] and the Member States is all the more necessary in view of the fact that the former cannot, as international law stands at present, itself conclude an ILO convention and must do so through the medium of the Member States.[95]

The Union must thus exercise its external competences indirectly, that is, through the member states "acting jointly in the [Union's] interest."[96] This idea was recently confirmed in the context of the International Organisation of Vine and Wine.[97] The Court here expressly clarified that the Union is entitled to adopt a common position for all the European Union that would subsequently need "to be adopted on its behalf in the body set up by that agreement, in particular through the Member States which are party to that agreement acting jointly in its interest."[98]

In an area of shared competence, both the Union and the member states are entitled to act externally by, for example, concluding an international agreement with the United States. But due to the various procedural obstacles in the Union treaty-making power, the member states might be much quicker in exercising their shared competence, and third parties might also be more interested in twenty-eight bilateral agreements than one Union agreement on a matter.[99] Thus, in order to safeguard the "unity in the international representation of the [Union],"[100] the Court has therefore developed a "negative" aspect to the duty of cooperation. Where the international actions of a member state might jeopardize the conclusion of a Union agreement, the Court has imposed specific obligations on the member states.

We find a good illustration of the negative duties imposed on the member states when exercising their shared external competences in *Commission v. Luxembourg*.[101] Luxembourg had exercised its international treaty power to conclude a number of bilateral agreements with Eastern European states. The Commission was incensed, as it had already started its own negotiations for the Union as a whole. It thus complained that even if Luxembourg enjoyed a shared competence to conclude the agreements, "[t]he negotiation by the Commission of an agreement on behalf of the [Union] and its subsequent conclusion by the Council is inevitably made more difficult by interference from a Member State's own initiatives."[102] The Union's position was claimed to have

[95] Opinion 2/91 (ILO Convention 170) [1993] ECR I-1061, para. 37.

[96] *Id.*, para. 5.

[97] Case C-399/12, Germany v. Council (OIV), EU:C:2014, 2258. [98] *Id.*, para.52.

[99] This approach might be inspired by the classic Roman strategy of *divide et impera*, that is, divide and rule.

[100] Opinion 1/94 (WTO Agreement) [1994] ECR I-5267, para. 108.

[101] Case 266/03, Commission v. Luxembourg [2005] ECR 4805. [102] *Id.*, para. 53.

been weakened "because the [Union] and its Member States appear fragmented."[103] The Court adopted this view, but only partly:

> The adoption of a decision authorising the Commission to negotiate a multilateral agreement on behalf of the [Union] marks the start of a concerted [Union] action at international level and requires, for that purpose, if not a duty of abstention on the part of the Member States, at the very least a duty of close cooperation between the latter and the [Union] institutions in order to facilitate the achievement of the [Union] tasks and to ensure the coherence and consistency of the action and its international representation.[104]

Importantly, the Court did not condemn the exercise of Luxembourg's foreign affairs power as such. Endowed with shared external power, Luxembourg could very well conclude bilateral agreements with third states. However, since the Commission had started a "concerted [Union] action" for the conclusion of a Union agreement in this area, the member state was under an obligation to cooperate and consult with the Commission. And in not consulting the Union, Luxembourg had violated the duty of cooperation.[105] The duty of cooperation was thus primarily seen as a duty of information. It appeared to be a *procedural* duty of conduct, and not a substantive duty of result.

The purely procedural character of the duty was subsequently put into question in *Commission v. Sweden.*[106] The Union institution brought proceedings against Sweden for "splitting the international representation of the [Union] and compromising the unity achieved... during the first Conference of the Parties to [the Stockholm Convention on Persistent Organic Pollutants]."[107] What had happened? Sweden had not abstained from making a proposal within the international conference, and the Commission claimed that this unilateral action violated the duty of cooperation. Sweden responded that it had given sufficient information to and consulted with the Union and the other member states.[108]

But this time, information and consultation were not enough. After duly citing its case law, the Court moved to examine whether there existed a Union "strategy" not to make a proposal.[109] In finding that such a Union strategy existed, and that Sweden had "dissociated itself from a concerted common strategy within the Council,"[110] the Court concluded that Sweden had violated the duty of cooperation. In a remarkable feat of judicial creativity, the Court now found that its past case law stood for the proposition that:

> Member States are subject to special duties of action *and abstention* in a situation in which the Commission has submitted to the Council proposals which, although

[103] *Id.* [104] *Id.*, para. 60. [105] *Id.*, para. 61.

[106] Case C-246/07, Commission v. Sweden [2010] ECR I-3317. For an extensive analysis, *see* Geert de Baere, *"O, Where Is Faith? O, Where Is Loyalty?" Some Thoughts on the Duty of Loyal Co-operation and the Union's External Environmental Competences in the Light of the PFOS Case*, 36 ELR. 405 (2011).

[107] Commission v. Sweden, *supra* note 106, para. 44. [108] *Id.*, para. 63.

[109] *Id.*, para. 76. [110] *Id.*, para. 91.

> they have not been adopted by the Council, represent a point of departure for concerted [Union] action.[111]

This case represents the beginning of a *substantive* duty of cooperation. Because the Court was not satisfied with the procedural obligation to inform and consult, it prohibited the very exercise of a shared external competence by a member state.

V. Conclusion

The European Union is not a federal state. It was born as an international organization at a time when international law betrayed an impressive ambivalence toward the treaty powers of international organizations. In the past sixty years, the Union has nevertheless significantly sharpened its foreign affairs powers. While still based on the idea that it has no plenary power, the Union's external competences have expanded dramatically, and today it is hard to identify a nucleus of exclusive foreign affairs powers reserved for the member states.

How do the Union and the member states coordinate their foreign affairs powers? In contrast to a classic international law perspective, the Union's member states only enjoy limited treaty-making powers under European law. Their foreign affairs powers are limited by the exclusive powers of the Union, and they may be preempted through European legislation. The Union thereby prefers to gradually preempt the member states through the adoption of internal legislation. And where this has happened exhaustively (or to a large extent), the Union may even functionally succeed the member states in their international commitments.

There are, however, moments when both the Union and its states enjoy overlapping foreign affairs powers. For these situations, the Union legal order has devised a number of cooperative mechanisms to safeguard a degree of "unity" in the external actions of the Union. Mixed agreements constitute an international mechanism that brings the Union and the member states to the negotiating table. The second constitutional device is internal to the Union legal order. It is the duty of cooperation. The duty of cooperation has thereby been given a positive and a negative aspect. Positively, the member states might be obliged to act as "trustees of the Union interest" in international forums. Negatively, the duty has imposed obligations on the member states when exercising their shared competences.

[111] *Id.*, para. 103 (emphasis added).

PART IV

ENGAGING WITH, AND DISENGAGING FROM, INTERNATIONAL INSTITUTIONS

CHAPTER 20

TREATY EXIT AND INTRABRANCH CONFLICT AT THE INTERFACE OF INTERNATIONAL AND DOMESTIC LAW

LAURENCE R. HELFER

THE rise of nationalist populism around the world has triggered a range of backlashes against existing laws and institutions. Included among these are calls for states to unilaterally withdraw from treaties and international organizations. The legal and political stakes of exit are especially high when a state leaves a treaty that is deeply embedded in its national legal system (such as the United Kingdom's "Brexit" from the European Union), that creates a multilateral institution (such as African states withdrawing from the Rome Statute creating the International Criminal Court (ICC)), or that is widely viewed as a pillar of the global legal order (such as the United States' notice of intent to withdraw from the Paris Agreement on Climate Change and statements by President Donald Trump that he may consider withdrawing from the World Trade Organization (WTO), North American Free Trade Agreement (NAFTA), and North Atlantic Treaty Organization (NATO)).[1]

These and other treaty denunciations raise important and unresolved questions of foreign relations and international law. These legal issues can be charted along two distinct axes. The first concerns whether treaty obligations end or continue under international and domestic law. In many instances, a state's withdrawal affects the treaty's status in both legal systems in the same way. For example, Parliament's approval of Brexit following the U.K. Supreme Court's decision in *R (Miller) v. Secretary*

[1] Laurence R. Helfer, *Introduction to Symposium on Treaty Exit at the Interface of Domestic and International Law*, 111 AJIL UNBOUND 425 (2017).

of State for Exiting the European Union,[2] and the legislation to be enacted prior to the United Kingdom's departure from the European Union, together mean that the Treaty on European Union will no longer have legal force—under either international or domestic law—on the date that the withdrawal takes effect. Conversely, *Democratic Alliance v. Minister of International Relations and Cooperation*,[3] the South African High Court ruling abrogating the executive's notice of withdrawal from the ICC, resulted in the continuation of South Africa's obligations under both the Rome Statute and its domestic implementing legislation.

The domestic and international status of a treaty do not always shift in tandem as a result of exit. As examples discussed in this chapter reveal, withdrawal can bifurcate a treaty's legal status, abrogating obligations in domestic law that continue to bind the state under international law. And the converse situation—in which a state validly quits a treaty according to its terms but remains bound as a matter of domestic law—is also plausible.

A second dimension of treaty exit concerns the relationship among the branches of government. In most instances, the executive decides whether to denounce a treaty. But the impetus for withdrawal—or actions that make exit more likely—can also originate with judges and legislators. In several cases, courts have invalidated the executive's prior accession to a treaty, or a declaration relating to it, forcing the political branches to choose between exiting the treaty, curing the violation, or breaching its international obligations. In other instances, the legislature has enacted laws that require or pressure the executive to leave a treaty.

Conflicts involving both dimensions of treaty exit stem from a common source—the different objectives underlying domestic and international rules governing how states enter into and leave treaties. In domestic law, these rules balance multiple policy goals, such as enhancing democratic deliberation and preserving flexibility to make or unmake compacts to achieve national interests or in response to changes in international affairs.[4] One indicator of the diversity of these goals is the wide variation in the constitutional texts, legislation, and historical practices that determine how different countries enter into and leave international agreements.

The rationales that inform international rules governing treaty entry and exit are categorically different. These rules aim to prescribe clear, stable, and objective rules to determine whether a state is or is not a party to a treaty on a particular date. These rules also reinforce sovereignty by making it unnecessary for government officials to evaluate the constitutional details of how other nations enter into or terminate their international obligations.[5]

The remainder of this chapter analyzes the different types of conflicts that arise from mismatches between international and domestic rules governing treaty exit and the

[2] [2017] UKSC 5 (Jan. 24, 2017). [3] 2017 (3) SA 212 (G.P).

[4] Michael Bothe, *Article 46, Convention of 1969*, *in* The Vienna Conventions on the Law of Treaties: A Commentary 1090, 1091 (Olivier Corten & Pierre Klein eds., 2011).

[5] *Id.* at 1097; Mark E. Villiger, Commentary on the 1969 Vienna Convention on the Law of Treaties 591 (2009).

divergent policies that underlie them. Section I summarizes international and domestic law governing treaty withdrawals. Section II draws on a wide range of contemporary examples to explain how treaty withdrawal can produce convergent or divergent outcomes in domestic and international law. Section III explores different contestations among the branches of government that can arise over treaty exit. Section IV explains that international law takes little if any account of violations of domestic treaty-making procedures, generating the controversies described in the previous two sections. A brief conclusion follows.

I. Treaty Exit Rules in International and Domestic Law

A brief primer on the international and domestic rules governing treaty withdrawals is necessary in order to set the stage for analyzing the full spectrum of conflicts that exit can engender.

The vast majority of treaties contain withdrawal or denunciation clauses that authorize a state to exit simply by announcing its intention to leave and providing the advance notice—often six months or one year—indicated in those clauses.[6] A relatively small number of treaties are silent regarding the possibility of exit.[7] The Vienna Convention on the Law of Treaties (VCLT) creates a presumption against leaving these agreements unless it is "established that the parties intended to admit the possibility of denunciation or withdrawal; or [a] right of denunciation or withdrawal may be implied by the nature of the treaty."[8]

The formal mechanics of exit are simple. A high-level executive official—usually the foreign minister—sends a brief statement notifying the treaty depository that the state will no longer be a party to the agreement as of a specified future date. Most notices do not explain the decision to withdraw, and the handful of treaties that require an explanation are easily satisfied. If no action is taken to abrogate the denunciation during the notice period, the withdrawal takes effect on the date indicated. This ends the state's prospective legal obligations under the treaty as well as its membership in any institutions that the treaty creates.

In contrast to international law, the domestic procedures governing exit are more complex, uncertain, and vary widely from country to country. According to the Comparative Constitutions Project, 43 out of 190 written constitutions currently in

[6] Barbara Koremenos, The Continent of International Law: Explaining Agreement Design 140–144 (2016); Laurence R. Helfer, *Exiting Treaties*, 91 Va. L. Rev. 1579, 1592–1595 (2005).

[7] Several treaties protecting human rights and creating international organizations are prominent examples.

[8] Vienna Convention on the Law of Treaties [VCLT], art. 56 (1), *opened for signature* May 23, 1969, 1155 U.N.T.S. 331.

force contain provisions on treaty withdrawal, denunciation, or termination.[9] All but four[10] of these 43 constitutions require the national legislature to approve exit from at least some treaties. In several countries, the legislature authorizes withdrawal from all international agreements.[11] In others, the constitution lists the subject matter of treaties for which exit requires parliamentary assent,[12] or provides that ratification and denunciation are governed by the same procedures.[13] Statutes or administrative rules in approximately a dozen countries specify the domestic procedures governing treaty exit, often clarifying the executive's powers vis-à-vis the legislature.[14]

The remaining 140 or so nations lack constitutional or subconstitutional rules governing exit. In these states, it is unclear which actors can withdraw from international agreements, although in most countries the executive alone has exercised this function.[15] Some courts and commentators have argued, however, that the rules governing ratification are equally applicable to denunciation and, as a result, that both political branches must agree to withdraw from treaties whose ratification requires legislative assent.[16]

[9] Comparative Constitutions Project, *available at* http://comparativeconstitutionsproject.org/.

[10] Three countries appear to authorize unilateral executive withdrawal. CONST. OF BOSNIA AND HERZEGOVINA, Dec. 14, 1995 (rev. 2005), art. V; CONST. OF GUATEMALA, Jan. 14, 1986 (rev. 1993), tit. IV, ch. III, art. 183; CONST. OF THE SYRIAN ARAB REPUBLIC, Feb. 26, 2012, tit. II, ch. II, art. 107. Chile requires the executive to consult with the legislature. CONST. OF CHILE, Sept. 11, 1980 (rev. 2015), ch. V, art. 54.

[11] E.g., CONST. OF MOLDOVA, tit. III, Aug. 27, 1994 (rev. 2016), ch. IV, § 1 (66) (granting the Parliament the power "to ratify, terminate, suspend and repeal . . . international treaties").

[12] E.g., CONST. OF ESTONIA, June 28, 1992 (rev. 2015), ch. IX, art. 121 ("Riigikogu [Parliament] shall ratify and denounce treaties . . . which alter state borders; the implementation of which requires the passage, amendment or repeal of Estonian laws; by which the Republic of Estonia joins international organizations or unions; by which the Republic of Estonia assumes military or proprietary obligations; in which ratification is prescribed").

[13] E.g., CONST. OF KOSOVO, June 15, 2008 (rev. 2016), ch. I, art. 18 ("withdrawal from international agreements follows the same decision-making process as the ratification of international agreements").

[14] E.g., Law No. 421-Z on Treaties of the Republic of Belarus (July 23, 2008), art. 41 (listing different categories of treaties whose denunciation may be carried out by, respectively, the National Assembly, the President, and the Council of Ministers); Treaty-Making Procedures Proclamation 25/1988, art. 11(2) (Eth.) (providing that the Council of State approved the denunciation or termination of political and economic agreements, while other treaties were denounced or terminated by the Council of Ministers). I am grateful to Pierre-Hugues Verdier and Mila Versteeg for sharing their research on national laws governing treaty withdrawal.

[15] In this *Handbook*, Verdier and Versteeg analyze a data set on international law in domestic legal systems that covers 101 countries between 1815 and 2013 and includes treaty withdrawal rules in both constitutions and legislation. The authors find that treaty exit has "long [been] considered a purely executive power in virtually all jurisdictions," but that "the proportion of countries in which the executive can withdraw from treaties unilaterally has declined significantly since the 1970s, from a high of 89% to the current level of 72%." Pierre-Hugues Verdier & Mila Versteeg, *Separation of Powers, Treaty-Making, and Treaty Withdrawal: A Global Survey*, ch. 8 in this volume, at pp.138, 149.

[16] E.g., Democratic All. v. Minister of Int'l Relations and Cooperation 2017 (3) SA 212 (G.P), at para. 56; GIULIANA ZICCARDI CAPALDO, LA COMPETENZA A DENUNCIARE I TRATTATI INTERNAZIONALI 63 (1983). Some constitutions expressly recognize international agreements that the executive alone can make and unmake. E.g., CONST. OF ARMENIA, July 5, 1995 (rev. 2015), art. 132 (2) (the president shall "by proposal of the Government, approve, suspend or renounce international treaties not requiring ratification").

The extent to which this "mirror image" analogy is followed in practice is uncertain, however. In authoritarian states, the executive is likely to make all decisions relating to treaty withdrawal regardless of the constitution's formal rules. Executive withdrawals also appear to be common even in democracies whose constitutions require legislative approval of treaties.[17] Functional considerations also militate in favor of unilateral executive exit. The executive is often better placed to determine whether exit is factually or legally justified, it can act quickly in response to rapidly evolving events, and it can weigh the risks and benefits of withdrawal in light of other foreign relations concerns.

In sum, whereas the international law of treaty exit is simple, uniform, and objectively well defined, the domestic rules governing the topic vary widely from state to state and often do not indicate which actors have the power to withdraw. The divergence between the two legal systems creates a range of actual and potential conflicts over treaty exit.

II. A Typology of Treaty Exit Conflicts in International and Domestic Law

This section sets forth a typology of conflicts that can arise from differences in how international and domestic law regulate treaty exit. The analysis begins with exits that are valid in both legal systems, then considers withdrawals that are valid internationally but contrary to domestic law, and then turns to treaty exits that comply with domestic law but are ineffective internationally. The final section discusses withdrawals that are invalid under both legal systems. Table 1 provides an overview of this typology and several real and hypothetical examples in each category.

A few words of caution are in order before turning to this analysis. I selected the examples discussed below to illuminate the basic features of the typology and the types of legal conflicts that can arise in each category. I omitted other examples that were less suited to these goals and glossed over details that may interest scholars, such as when a conflict arises or how procedures governing exit evolve over time. In addition, some cases emphasize the enhanced potential for exit, even if the state did not in fact quit a treaty. Finally, the typology does not address all of the ways that a treaty's status can be bifurcated in international and domestic law. In particular, it does not consider bifurcations unrelated to exit, such as when a state enacts legislation that is inconsistent with its treaty obligations.

[17] *See, e.g.*, Giovanni Bognetti, *The Role of Italian Parliament in the Treaty-Making Process—Europe*, 67 Chi. Kent. L. Rev. 391, 404 (1991); Curtis A. Bradley, *Treaty Termination and Historical Gloss*, 92 Tex. L. Rev. 773, 788 (2014); Luzius Wildhaber, *Parliamentary Participation in Treaty-Making: Report on Swiss Law*, *in* Parliamentary Participation in the Making and Operation of Treaties: A Comparative Study 131, 139 (Stefan A. Riesenfeld & Frederick M. Abbott eds., 1994).

Table 1

	Treaty exit valid under domestic law	Treaty exit invalid under domestic law
Treaty exit valid under int'l law (State no longer a party; prospective obligations end)	**Actual examples:** • Ecuador and Romania: denunciation of multiple BITS (2017) • Bolivia: denunciation of 1961 Single Convention on Narcotic Drugs (2011) • US: unilateral executive termination of mutual defense treaty with Taiwan following *Goldwater* (1978) • UK: Notice of withdrawal from the EU following *Miller* and parliamentary approval of Brexit (2017)	**Actual and hypothetical examples:** • US: If President Trump attempts to unilaterally exit from NAFTA and negate the NAFTA Implementation Act • South Africa: aborted attempt to withdraw from the ICC, abrogated after *Democratic Alliance* (2016–2017) • Venezuela: denunciation of American Convention on Human Rights contrary to the constitution (2012–2013)
Treaty exit invalid under int'l law (State remains a party; obligations continue)	**Actual and hypothetical examples:** • North Korea: purported denunciation of the ICCPR (1997) • Dominican Republic: if executive seeks to withdraw declaration accepting jurisdiction of IACtHR following 2014 Constitutional Tribunal ruling finding declaration unconstitutional • Peru: legislative resolution approves president's withdrawal from IACtHR jurisdiction (1999)	**Hypothetical examples:** • Poland: if executive had attempted to withdraw unilaterally from the EU (prior to the 2009 Treaty of Lisbon) contrary to legislative approval requirement in the constitution • US: if president unilaterally attempts to denounce one of the four Geneva Conventions during an ongoing armed conflict with a terrorist organization

Treaty Exits Valid under International and Domestic law

Several types of treaty exit are effective both internationally and domestically. Perhaps the least controversial pattern involves the executive receiving legislative assent before filing a notice of withdrawal. Such approval may be mandated by the constitution or sought as a matter of political expediency. In either case, when the notice period expires, so too does the treaty's status as a legal instrument that binds the state under domestic and international law. Examples of this type of exit include 2017 approvals by the legislatures of Ecuador and Romania to terminate bilateral investment treaties,[18]

[18] Kate Cervantes-Knox & Elinor Thomas, *Ecuador terminates 12 BITs—a growing trend of reconsideration of traditional investment treaties?*, INT'L ARB. ALERT (May 15, 2017); Volterra Fietta, *Romania set to terminate its intra-EU BITs* (Mar. 27, 2017), *available at* https://www.lexology.com/library/detail.aspx?g=89abdc5f-4749-4f27-9edb-a4714c09dfc4.

and the Bolivian parliament's 2011 authorization to the president to denounce the UN Single Convention on Narcotic Drugs.[19]

Another common pattern involves treaties incorporated into domestic law via implementing legislation. Such statutes may include a "self-destruct" clause that abrogates the statute when the executive terminates the treaty, such as the U.S.-Korea Free Trade Agreement Implementation Act.[20] Some constitutions appear to require a similar result.[21] Absent such provisions, the executive may ask the legislature to abrogate the implementing statute before the notice of withdrawal is filed or takes effect.[22]

Another straightforward scenario involves unilateral executive exit from an international agreement adopted without legislative approval. President Trump's announced intention to withdraw from the Paris Agreement on Climate Change arguably falls into this category.[23] If the executive can enter into these commitments on its own authority, it seems plausible that it can also exit from those same obligations unilaterally.[24]

The situation is somewhat more complicated when the executive files a notice of withdrawal without involving the country's legislature, engendering opposition from that institution, from some of its members, or from interest groups. Where such objections trigger litigation, the consequences of withdrawal may depend on timing.

Consider President Jimmy Carter's termination of a mutual defense treaty between the United States and Taiwan. Carter filed a notice of termination on December 15, 1978, triggering a lawsuit that the U.S. Supreme Court dismissed as nonjusticiable on December 13, 1979—two days before the termination's effective date.[25] With the federal litigation over, the end of the notice period abrogated the treaty as a matter of both international and domestic law.

With regard to Brexit, a referendum endorsing the United Kingdom's withdrawal from the European Union was held in June 2016. The next month, Prime Minister Teresa May announced that she would unilaterally pull the country out of the Treaty

[19] *See* Sven Pfeiffer, *Rights of Indigenous Peoples and the International Drug Control Regime: The Case of Traditional Coca Leaf Chewing*, 5 GOETTINGEN J. INT'L L. 287, 304 (2013).

[20] Section 107(c) of the statute provides: "On the date on which the [United States-Korea Free Trade Agreement] terminates, this Act . . . shall cease to have effect."

[21] E.g., CONST. OF CHILE, Sept. 11, 1980 (rev. 2015), ch. V, art. 54 ("Once [a] denunciation or withdrawal has produced its effects in conformity with the provisions of the international treaty, it shall cease to have effect in the Chilean legal system.").

[22] *See, e.g.*, Democratic All. v. Minister of Int'l Relations and Cooperation 2017 (3) SA 212 (G.P), at para. 5.

[23] Michael D. Shear, *Trump Will Withdraw U.S. from Paris Climate Agreement*, N.Y. TIMES (June 1, 2017). It is uncertain, however, whether President Trump has the constitutional authority to withdraw the United States from the Paris Agreement in contravention of its notice and waiting periods.

[24] *See*, e.g., CONG. RESEARCH SERV., 106th Cong., TREATIES AND OTHER INTERNATIONAL AGREEMENTS: THE ROLE OF THE UNITED STATES SENATE 208 (Comm. Print 2001) ("the President's authority to terminate executive agreements, in particular sole executive agreements, has not been seriously questioned").

[25] Goldwater v. Carter, 444 U.S. 996 (1979).

on European Union (TEU), triggering a lawsuit. The U.K. Supreme Court held that parliamentary approval was constitutionally required in January 2017. Parliament then approved the withdrawal, and the prime minister filed the formal notice of withdrawal on March 29, 2017.[26]

In both examples, the executive's power to exit unilaterally from the treaties was uncertain. Litigation challenging that authority led to opposite results. In the United States, judicial refusal to adjudicate the president's action resulted in de facto approval of unilateral withdrawal authority. In the United Kingdom, the courts reviewed the constitutional claims on the merits and ruled against the executive. Yet in both countries, the litigation ended prior to the effective date of withdrawal, allowing each state to resolve the domestic legal issues before the withdrawal took effect at the international level. The timing of these events is not always so felicitous, however, creating conflicts between international and domestic law.

Treaty Exits Valid under International Law But Invalid under Domestic Law

The VCLT identifies heads of state, heads of government, ministers for foreign affairs, and officials with full powers as authorized to bind the state to international commitments and to withdraw from those same commitments.[27] As Section IV explains, this authority exists as a matter of international law regardless of whether domestic law empowers those officials to make or unmake treaties. Thus, if the executive files a notice of withdrawal in contravention of the constitution, a statute, or a judicial ruling, and if the executive does not cure the violation—for example, by securing legislative approval or deciding not to withdraw[28]—the state will no longer be a party to the treaty under international law, but it will remain bound by the treaty or by its implementing legislation as a matter of domestic law.

Such bifurcations can arise in a number of ways. Perhaps the most obvious involves treaties incorporated into domestic law via implementing statutes. In most countries, it is axiomatic that the executive does not possess legislative power. As a result, even if the executive has the authority to withdraw from a treaty unilaterally, he or she cannot abrogate the statute that gives domestic effect to the treaty without agreement of the legislature. Debates over the continuation of the NAFTA Implementation Act

[26] Simon Kennedy, *Brexit Timeline: From the Referendum to Article 50*, Bloomberg News (Mar. 20, 2017).

[27] VCLT, arts. 7, 67(2).

[28] The VCLT permits unilateral revocation of notices of withdrawal. *Id.* art. 68. It is unsettled whether treaty parties can contract around the VCLT and make withdrawal notifications irrevocable, an issue the CJEU addressed in the context of Brexit. *See* CJEU, Judgment in Wightman v. Secretary of State for Exiting the European Union [2018], C-621/18, EU:C:2018:999 (ruling that a Member State may unilaterally revoke its notice of withdrawal from the TEU at any time before the withdrawal enters into force).

following a possible future decision by President Trump to withdraw from NAFTA focus on precisely this issue.[29]

South Africa's aborted exit from the ICC illustrates a different type of bifurcation. The government filed a notice of withdrawal on October 19, 2016. The High Court judgment of February 22, 2017 held the notice unconstitutional, and the executive complied with the court's order to revoke the notice.[30] But what if the government had chosen a different course? If the executive had defied the High Court (or the Constitutional Court, after an unsuccessful appeal) and refused to revoke the notice, South Africa would have no longer been a party to the Rome Statute as of October 19, 2017. Yet the treaty would not have been abrogated in domestic law, and the ICC implementation statute would have remained in effect. A similar outcome would occur in countries where the executive unilaterally quits a treaty in contravention of a constitutional requirement that the legislature approve withdrawal.

A more fundamental conflict can arise where a treaty is embedded in the constitution. Such a possibility arose following Venezuela's 2013 withdrawal from the American Convention on Human Rights—a treaty that includes an express denunciation clause.[31] Like several Latin American countries, Venezuela considers ratified human rights treaties as part of a "constitutional block" that national courts are authorized to enforce.[32] According to a lawsuit challenging the withdrawal, the hierarchically superior status of these international agreements means that "any act of public power that violates or impairs the rights guaranteed in those treaties is void."[33] According to

[29] *See* Brandon J. Murrill, *U.S. Withdrawal from Free Trade Agreements: Frequently Asked Legal Questions*, CONG. RESEARCH SERV., 13–17 (2016). For a recent example involving Australia, *compare* Maria O'Sullivan, *Nauru's Renunciation of Appeals to the High Court—Lawfulness and Implications*, Castan Centre for Human Rights Law (Apr. 5, 2018) (arguing that the Nauru Appeals Act, which implements a 1976 agreement between Australia and Nauru authorizing appeals from the Nauru Supreme Court to the Australian High Court, continues in force following the Nauru executive's denunciation of the agreement), *with* Ben Ye, *Can once valid legislation 'become' invalid? A case study of the High Court's (now-lost) Nauru jurisdiction*, AUSPUBLAW (Nov. 28, 2018), *available at* https://auspublaw.org/2018/11/can-once-valid-legislation-become-invalid (arguing that Nauru Appeals Act is no longer in force following denunciation of 1976 agreement).

[30] Democratic All. v. Minister of Int'l Relations and Cooperation 2017 (3) SA 212 (G.P), at para. 84. In a similar constitutional challenge to Philippine President Duterte's withdrawal from the ICC, the Supreme Court of the Philippines declined to block the withdrawal from taking effect on March 17, 2019, although the suit challenging the withdrawal remains pending. *See* Edu Punay, *Sans Supreme Court action, withdrawal from ICC to take effect*, The Philippine Star (Mar. 13, 2019), *available at* https://www.philstar.com/headlines/2019/03/13/1901025/sans-supreme-court-action-withdrawal-icc-take-effect.

[31] Diego Germán Mejìa-Lemos, *Venezuela's Denunciation of the American Convention on Human Rights*, 17:1 ASIL INSIGHTS (Jan. 9, 2013).

[32] CONST. OF THE BOLIVARIAN REPUBLIC OF VENEZUELA, Dec., 1999 (rev. 2009), tit. III, ch. 1, art. 23 (ratified human rights treaties "have a constitutional rank . . . and shall be immediately and directly applied by the courts").

[33] Carlos Ayala Corao, *Inconstitucionalidad de la Denuncia de la Convención Americana Sobre Derechos Humanos por Venezuela*, 10 ESTUDIOS CONSTITUCIONALES 643, 650 (2012) (author's unofficial translation).

the complainants, it follows that the executive's "denunciation, which disregarded the constitutional hierarchy of the American Convention and arbitrarily dis-incorporated the treaty from the constitutional block," is invalid.[34] Although the fate of this litigation is unknown, the case illustrates how a withdrawal expressly permitted by a treaty and carried out by a state's authorized representative can be fully effective on the international level but have no effect in the domestic legal order.

Treaty Exits Valid under Domestic Law But Invalid under International Law

As previously explained, most treaties expressly authorize denunciation or withdrawal. However, a small number of treaties lack such clauses and have been interpreted, under VCLT Article 56, as presumptively prohibiting exit.[35] When a state nonetheless attempts to quit the agreement in conformity with national law, the result may bifurcate the treaty's legal status, with the state's obligations continuing in international law but not in domestic law.

This possibility is illustrated by a 2014 ruling of the Constitutional Tribunal of the Dominican Republic (DR) invalidating the acceptance of the jurisdiction of the Inter-American Court of Human Rights (IACtHR).[36] In the DR, the national congress must assent to treaties negotiated by the executive. In 1978, the congress ratified the American Convention on Human Rights, which does not require states parties to accept the IACtHR's jurisdiction. Such recognition can occur later by filing a declaration, which the DR's president did in 1999.

Inter-American case law was subsequently incorporated into the DR legal system by legislation, executive action, and judicial decisions.[37] This deep domestication of regional human rights norms ruptured following an IACtHR judgment condemning a Constitutional Tribunal ruling that upheld the decision to abrogate the citizenship of thousands of Dominicans of Haitian descent. After the government rejected the regional court's judgment, the Tribunal received a petition challenging the

[34] *Id.* at 654 (author's unofficial translation).

[35] A prominent example is North Korea's purported denunciation of the International Covenant on Civil and Political Rights (ICCPR).

[36] Relativo a la acción directa de inconstitucionalidad incoada contra el Instrumento de Aceptación de la Competencia de la Corte Interamericana de Derechos Humanos, Judgment No. TC/0256/14 (Trib. Const. Dom. Rep. Nov. 4, 2014), *available at* https://www.tribunalconstitucional.gob.do/consultas/secretar%C3%ADa/sentencias/.

[37] Dinah Shelton & Alexandrea Huneeus, *In re Direct Action of Unconstitutionality Initiated Against the Declaration of Acceptance of the Jurisdiction of the Inter-American Court of Human Rights*, 109 AM. J. INT'L L. 866, 869 (2015).

president's acceptance of the IACtHR's jurisdiction without congressional approval. Interpreting the declaration as equivalent to a treaty, the Tribunal held the executive's action unconstitutional. Yet the judges also acknowledged that the government could not lawfully withdraw the declaration while remaining a party to the American Convention—a conclusion the IACtHR had reached in an earlier case against Peru.[38]

The Constitutional Tribunal did not order the DR to denounce the American Convention. However, its ruling, which scholars have labeled as a "court-led treaty exit,"[39] produced similar bifurcated effects: "Under international law, the Dominican Republic remains subject to the Inter-American Court's jurisdiction, bound to appear before the Court and to comply with its rulings. Internally, however, the effect of the judgment may be to bar authorities . . . from domestic actions to implement the Court's judgments."[40]

Whether compelled by the judiciary or authorized by the political branches, domestically-valid-but-internationally-prohibited withdrawals have a distinctive foreign relations valence. From the perspective of other member states, international secretariats, and monitoring bodies, the exiting nation remains a member of the treaty or organization. These actors continue to communicate with the state and invite it to resume full participation. Such was the response to purported withdrawals from the World Health Organization (WHO) by the Soviet Union, China, and several Eastern European countries in the late 1940s and early 1950s, and from UNESCO by Czechoslovakia, Hungary, and Poland a few years later. All of these states soon returned to full membership, but only after settling their arrears for contributions not paid during periods of nonparticipation.[41]

Negotiating a return to a treaty or international organization raises unresolved questions. Can the executive recharacterize a denunciation as a temporary cessation of participation? Or is a fresh ratification required? And must the legislature approve the payment of overdue financial contributions for years when the state had purportedly exited? The examples discussed above do not shed much light on these questions, since they involve socialist regimes in which executive decisions and communist party policy were tightly aligned and legislative approval of such decisions, even if required, was rarely if ever withheld.

[38] Constitutional Court v. Peru, Inter-Am. Ct. H.R. (ser. C) No. 55, paras. 49–50 (1999).

[39] Alexandra Hunneus & Renè Ureña, *Treaty Exit and Latin America's Constitutional Courts*, 111 AJIL UNBOUND 456, 458 (2017).

[40] Shelton & Huneeus, *supra* note 37, at 868.

[41] N. Feinberg, *Unilateral Withdrawal from an International Organization*, 39 BRIT. Y.B. INT'L L. 189, 204–211 (1963).

Treaty Exits Invalid under International and Domestic Law

The final category of the typology concerns treaty exits that contravene both domestic and international law. I am unaware of any real-world examples of such withdrawals, although one can imagine a range of plausible hypotheticals.

A straightforward illustration of dual invalidity would be a unilateral attempt by the executive to denounce, in contravention of a legislative approval requirement, a treaty from which exit is presumptively barred under VCLT Article 56. Prior to entry into force of the Treaty of Lisbon in 2009, it was widely accepted that EU treaties "did not permit unilateral withdrawals, in view of express provisions stating that these treaties were concluded for unlimited periods."[42] In Poland, an EU member since 2004, the constitution requires legislation to join or leave treaties involving "membership in an international organization."[43] Thus, a 2007 executive decree purporting to pull Poland out of the European Union would have been invalid under domestic and international law.

Executive withdrawals from treaties approved by the U.S. Senate present a more complex scenario. Commentators generally agree that the president's unilateral authority to quit such agreements applies only to withdrawals consistent with the treaty's terms or otherwise justified in international law, such as in response to another state's breach.[44] The Geneva Conventions of 1949 provide a plausible example of a unilateral executive exit that would be doubly illegal.

Common Article 63 provides that a denunciation of one of the conventions takes effect one year after notification. However, when notice is "made at a time when the denouncing Power is involved in a conflict," the denunciation "shall not take effect until peace has been concluded, and until after operations connected with the release and repatriation of the persons protected by the present Convention have been terminated."[45] Given the U.S. Supreme Court's conclusion that a core provision of the Geneva Conventions applies to armed conflicts between the United States and nonstate terrorist groups,[46] and that the threat of terrorist attacks from such groups is unlikely to end soon,[47] the president would likely be precluded under U.S. and international law from exiting one of the conventions unilaterally.

[42] Oliver Dörr & Kirsten Schmalenbach, Vienna Convention on the Law of Treaties: A Commentary 985 (2011).

[43] Const. of Poland, Oct. 17, 1997 (rev. 2009), ch. III, art. 89 (1) (3).

[44] *See*, e.g., Restatement (Fourth) of the Foreign Relations Law of the United States § 313 (2018); *see also* Bradley, *supra* note 17, at 823–824 (discussing Office of Legal Counsel memoranda and other materials relating to whether the president can unilaterally suspend or exit from an Article II treaty in contravention of international law).

[45] E.g., Geneva Convention for the Amelioration of the Condition of the Wounded and Sick in Armed Forces in the Field, art. 63, Aug. 12, 1949.

[46] Hamdan v. Rumsfeld, 548 U.S. 557, 630 (2006) (concluding that common Article 3 of the Geneva Conventions applies to armed conflict between the United States and al Qaeda).

[47] Boumediene v. Bush, 553 U.S. 723, 793 (2008) ("The real risks, the real threats, of terrorist attacks are constant and not likely soon to abate.").

III. Intrabranch Conflicts over Treaty Exit

Given the executive's preeminent role in foreign relations, it is unsurprising that most treaty exit decisions are initiated by the executive. But the other branches of government sometimes push for withdrawal. For example, the legislature may adopt a law or resolution that purports to exit from a treaty or demands that the executive do so. Or a judicial ruling may invalidate a ratification, making withdrawal a plausible response. Such legislatively and judicially compelled treaty exits have received little attention from scholars.

Legislatively Compelled Exit

There are two distinct but interrelated facets of legislative efforts to compel a state to exit from a treaty. The first relates to whether the legislature can force a withdrawal over the executive's objection. The second concerns the rationales that animate legislative exit.

None of the thirty-nine constitutions (discussed in Section II) that expressly require legislative approval of exit appears to give that body the power to initiate a withdrawal.[48] Rather, the issue appears to be regulated by historical practice and by ordinary legislation. The United States and Kenya provide contrasting illustrations.

There is a longstanding debate in the United States over whether Congress can compel the president to denounce a treaty. The competing constitutional arguments have never been conclusively settled, but the weight of historical practice and commentary suggests that Congress cannot itself abrogate a treaty but can direct the executive to do so by enacting legislation over the president's veto.[49] The most recent example involved the imposition of sanctions against South Africa. As part of the Comprehensive Anti-Apartheid Act of 1986, Congress directed President Ronald Reagan to terminate a tax treaty and an air services agreement with South Africa. The president promptly terminated both treaties notwithstanding his prior veto of the legislation.[50]

[48] Several constitutions require the executive to submit a proposal to the legislature to withdraw from a treaty. E.g., Const. of Armenia, July 5, 1995 (rev. 2015), art. 116 (2). Others authorize the legislature to ratify and denounce treaties without indicating which branch initiates withdrawal. E.g., Const. of Estonia, June 28, 1992 (rev. 2015), ch. IX, art. 121.

[49] James J. Moriarty, *Congressional Claims for Treaty Termination Powers in the Age of the Diminished Presidency*, 14 Conn. J. Int'l L. 123 (1999).

[50] David "Dj" Wolff, *Reasserting Its Constitutional Role: Congress' Power to Independently Terminate a Treaty*, 46 U.S.F. L. Rev. 953, 983–986 (2012).

In Kenya, the legislature's role in treaty withdrawals is regulated by statute. The Treaty Making and Ratification Act (2012), sets forth procedures for negotiating, ratifying, and denouncing treaties. In essence, these procedures authorize the executive to initiate the treaty making process and the National Assembly to approve or deny ratification of treaties submitted to it. With regard to denunciation, the Act requires the preparation of a memorandum indicating the reasons for withdrawal, but expressly excludes any role for the Assembly in initiating or objecting to such withdrawal.[51]

Notwithstanding these statutory provisions, in 2013 the parliament adopted a motion urging Kenya's immediate withdrawal from the Rome Statute and resolving to introduce a bill to repeal the International Crimes Act. President Uhuru Kenyatta, then under indictment by the ICC, did not act on the motion. As a result, Kenya continues to be a member of the Rome Statute and the legislation implementing its ICC obligations remains in force.[52]

Turning from de jure authority to justification, why might the legislature seek to denounce a treaty when the executive opposes such a move? In some instances, the political branches may have different substantive views regarding the treaty and its obligations. In others, the executive and legislature may share the same goals but disagree about the propriety of using exit to achieve them. In still other cases, the parliament may call for withdrawal to contribute to ongoing political debates with little hope—or even desire—that the executive will actually quit the treaty.

The apartheid legislation is an example of the second rationale while the ICC withdrawal motion provides an illustration of the third. Both the U.S. Congress and president disfavored South Africa's practice of systematic racial segregation but differed over how (and how hard) to pressure the country's white minority government to abandon it. Terminating bilateral tax and air services treaties added little to this disagreement, but was a symbolic way to isolate South Africa and demonstrate solidarity with other nations that had cut legal ties to the country.

The Kenyan parliament's withdrawal motion contributed to a wider backlash against the ICC, a strategy that included urging all African states to withdraw from the Rome Statute and enabling Kenya's political leaders to feign cooperation with the criminal prosecutions while shoring up domestic political support for blocking the trials from proceeding. Seen in this light, the National Assembly's motion "facilitated the generation of regional support for the [executive's] masse withdrawal proposal and also allowed the two officials to simultaneously mobilize—but divorce themselves from—other anti-ICC lobbying efforts."[53]

[51] Treaty Making and Ratification Act (2012) Sec. 17. An earlier draft of the Act authorized the Assembly to approve or deny withdrawal. The Treaties Bill (2011) Sec. 9 (on file with author).

[52] *See* Laurence R. Helfer & Anne E. Showalter, *Opposing International Justice: Kenya's Integrated Backlash Strategy Against the ICC*, 17 INT'L CRIM. L. REV. 1, 18–21 (2017).

[53] *Id.* at 21.

Judicially Compelled Exit

In two recent rulings, high courts in Ghana and Sri Lanka invalidated international agreements that contravened constitutional treaty-making procedures. Although neither court ordered the government to denounce the constitutionally invalid treaty, the decisions highlight the possibility of judicially compelled exit in future cases, as well as the different approaches to treaty invalidity in international and domestic law.[54]

In 2017, the Supreme Court of Ghana invalidated a bilateral agreement between the United States and Ghana to resettle two Yemeni detainees from the Guantánamo Bay detention camp.[55] The president did not submit the agreement to Parliament for ratification pursuant to Article 75 of the Ghanaian Constitution.[56] In response to a suit challenging the resettlement deal, the government characterized the agreement as a note verbale, a type of executive agreement that, as shown by the practice of other states, does not require legislative approval. Alternatively, the government claimed that international law "estopped Ghana from resiling" (i.e., pulling out from or abrogating) a previously concluded agreement.[57]

The Supreme Court held the agreement unconstitutional. The court concluded that Article 75 does not distinguish between international agreements based upon their formality or their designation as executive or nonexecutive. And it reasoned that the practice of entering into executive agreements in other countries—including the United States and South Africa—had no bearing on the interpretation of Ghana's constitution. Finally, the court rejected the estoppel argument, contending that other states are "duty bound to conduct the necessary due diligence when entering into international agreements with Ghana to ensure that such agreements are in consonance with our Constitution."[58]

Subsequently, the Supreme Court ordered the executive to submit the resettlement agreement to Parliament within three months or return the detainees to the United States. The legislature ratified the agreement in August 2017, avoiding the abrogation of the note verbale.[59]

A 2006 ruling of the Supreme Court of Sri Lanka invalidating the state's accession to the First Optional Protocol to the International Covenant on Civil and Political Rights (ICCPR) reached a similar conclusion.[60] The Optional Protocol creates a mechanism

[54] *See also* Namah v. Pato [2016] PGSC 13, para. 39 (Papua N.G.) (holding unconstitutional the detention of asylum seekers and refugees pursuant to a memorandum of understanding between PNG and Australia and ordering the government to cease the illegal detention, in effect rendering the memorandum domestically unenforceable).

[55] Banful v. Att'y Gen. [2017] Accra-A.D. 1 (Ghana).

[56] CONST. OF GHANA, Apr. 28, 1992 (rev. 1996), ch. VII, art. 75(2) ("A treaty, agreement or convention executed by or under the authority of the President shall be subject to ratification by (a) Act of Parliament; or (b) a [majority] resolution of Parliament.").

[57] *Banful*, [2017] Accra-A.D., at 7–12.

[58] *Id.* at 13–15. This statement conflicts with a 2002 ICJ judgment, discussed in Section IV, *infra*.

[59] Press release, *Ghana: Parliament Extends Stay of Gitmo 2* (Aug. 2, 2017), *available at* http://allafrica.com.proxy.lib.duke.edu/stories/201708020865.html.

[60] Singarasa v. Att'y Gen., No. 182/99 (2006), 138 I.L.R. 451.

for individuals to file complaints with a quasi-judicial treaty body, the UN Human Rights Committee, against states that have accepted the Protocol, which Sri Lanka's president did in a 1997 declaration.[61]

The petitioner in the case sought to overturn a criminal conviction, relying on a decision of the Committee finding that his rights had been violated.[62] The government opposed the petition, arguing that the president's declaration was unconstitutional. The Supreme Court interpreted the declaration as usurping both a legislative power—conferring on individuals the rights recognized in the ICCPR and the right to submit complaints to the Committee—and a judicial function—recognizing the Committee's authority to review complaints alleging violations of those rights.[63] Since the executive was not authorized to exercise these powers, the court held that Sri Lanka's accession to the Optional Protocol was unconstitutional and "does not bind the Republic qua state and has no legal effect within the Republic."[64]

Notwithstanding this ruling, the government has not sought to withdraw the declaration and individuals continue to file complaints against Sri Lanka alleging violations of the ICCPR. The government has, however, refused to respond to any of these cases, relying on the 2006 ruling. In 2014, the Committee chastised this "lack of cooperation" and urged the state to establish a procedure to implement its decisions.[65]

IV. The Mismatch between Domestic and International Treaty Procedures and Their Consequences

This chapter illustrates the wide cross-national variation in how states make and unmake treaties. This variation is partly the result of different views about the appropriate functions of, and relationship between, the political branches of government. Although there are compelling justifications for executive primacy in foreign affairs, these are counterbalanced by the desire to bolster the democratic legitimacy of international commitments. The widespread inclusion of national legislatures in the approval and domestication of treaties reflects this democratic impulse. At the same time, many states recognize the executive's sole authority to make (and unmake) at least some international agreements. These two categories of international agreements coexist uneasily in many countries, even as the precise boundary between them varies from state to state.

[61] *See* Office of the High Commissioner for Human Rights, Human Rights Committee, *available at* https://www.ohchr.org/EN/HRBodies/CCPR/Pages/CCPRIndex.aspx.

[62] Singarasa, No. 182/99 (2006), at 1–2. [63] *Id.* at 8. [64] *Id.*

[65] U.N. Human Rights Committee, Concluding observations on the fifth periodic report of Sri Lanka, CCPR/C/LKA/CO/5 (Nov. 21, 2014), at 2.

How does international law take account of the diversity of domestic procedures governing how states enter into and leave treaties? The short and perhaps surprising answer is hardly at all. The VCLT makes it exceptionally difficult for a state to invoke a violation of its internal treaty-making rules to invalidate its consent to be bound. Article 46 precludes a state from raising this issue "unless that violation was manifest and concerned a rule of its internal law of fundamental importance."[66] The article further provides that "[a] violation is manifest if it would be objectively evident to any State conducting itself in the matter in accordance with normal practice and in good faith."[67]

On its face, Article 46 applies only to the act of joining a treaty. Yet the policy rationales underlying the VCLT, as articulated in the ICJ's 2002 judgment in *Land and Maritime Boundary (Cameroon v. Nigeria)*,[68] favor applying the same approach to treaty withdrawals. A key instrument in that case was a declaration signed by both heads of state. Nigeria challenged the binding status of the declaration, arguing that it should have been "objectively evident" to Cameroon that, under the Nigerian constitution then in force, the head of state did not have authority to enter into a treaty without the approval of the Supreme Military Council.[69]

The ICJ rejected Nigeria's argument. The Court first explained that while some treaties specify "a two-step procedure consisting of signature and ratification," others "enter[] into force immediately upon signature," and states are free to choose "which procedure they want to follow."[70] As for domestic law limitations on the executive's authority to bind the state, the ICJ accepted that such limits were of "fundamental importance" under Article 46. They were not, however, "manifest" for two reasons—first, "because Heads of State belong to the group of persons who . . . '[i]n virtue of their functions and without having to produce full powers' are considered as representing their State,"[71] and second, because "there is no general legal obligation for States to keep themselves informed of legislative and constitutional developments in other States which are or may become important for the international relations of these States."[72]

The ICJ's reasoning applies with equal force to treaty withdrawals. As the International Law Commission commentary on the draft articles of the VCLT explains, "the rule concerning evidence of authority to denounce, terminate, etc., should be analogous to that governing 'full powers' to express the consent of a State to be bound by a treaty."[73] The VCLT thus recognizes that the same high-level executive officials are authorized both to bind the state and to effectuate treaty withdrawals.[74] In addition, functional rationales for permitting other nations to rely on the apparent authority of state agents and not imposing on those nations a duty to investigate internal treaty-making procedures are equally applicable to facially valid exit notices. As a result, just

[66] VCLT, art. 46(1). [67] *Id.* art. 46(2). [68] 2002 ICJ Reports 303. [69] *Id.* para. 258.
[70] *Id.* para. 264. [71] *Id.* para. 265 (*quoting* VCLT Article 7(2)). [72] *Id.* para. 266.
[73] *Draft Articles on the Law of Treaties with Commentaries*, II Y.B. INT'L L. COMM'N (1966), at 264; *see also Second Report on the Law of Treaties by Sir Humphrey Waldock*, II Y.B. INT'L L. COMM'N (1963), at 85 ("The power to annul, terminate, withdraw from or suspend treaties, no less than the power to conclude treaties, forms part of the treaty-making power of the State.").
[74] VCLT, art. 67(2).

as a treaty entered into by an authorized executive official in violation of a constitution does not invalidate the state's consent to be bound,[75] so too a notice of withdrawal by that same official will end the state's status as a treaty party, even if the withdrawal is contrary to the constitution.

V. Conclusion

International and domestic law adopt different rules for how states enter into and exit from treaties. These rules, their interrelationship, and the divergent policies underlying them have received inadequate attention from scholars. The rules also create the possibility of bifurcating the status of treaties in international and domestic law. This chapter develops a typology to categorize these divergences, drawing upon recent examples of exit and actions by the executive, legislature, and judiciary that make such withdrawals more likely.

The chapter also suggests several topics for future research. First, national courts are quite willing to invalidate treaty ratification and treaty withdrawal decisions by the executive that contravene legislative approval requirements. This is hardly surprising, since national judges regularly review other constitutional provisions that allocate authority between the political branches. Yet these courts have given insufficient attention to the foreign relations implications of their decisions, presuming—incorrectly, as this chapter shows—that abrogating a treaty on constitutional grounds is also effective in international law. Once apprised of how a treaty's legal status can be bifurcated, national judges may consider whether new doctrines are needed to take account of these foreign relations concerns.

Second, the VCLT lacks a bespoke provision identifying when, if at all, violations of domestic law may be invoked to abrogate a facially valid notice of withdrawal. The VCLT's drafting history and a key ICJ judgment support a strong presumption against invoking such domestic violations to invalidate denunciations. This interpretation of existing law is premised on the belief that recognizing the executive's apparent authority to bind or unbind the state is the same in both contexts. That assumption merits further investigation and need not control how international law evolves in the future.[76]

Finally, governments and scholars may wish to consider whether it is desirable to narrow the divergence between domestic and international rules governing treaty entry and treaty exit. The bifurcation of a treaty's legal status that these divergent rules engenders creates foreign relations frictions for governments that might be avoided, or at least mitigated, if the two sets of rules were more closely aligned.

[75] Villiger, *supra* note 5, at 589.

[76] *See* Hannah Woolaver, *State Engagement with Treaties: Interactions between International and Domestic Law*, ch. 24 in this volume; Hannah Woolaver, *From Joining to Leaving: Domestic Law's Role in the International Legal Validity of Treaty Withdrawal*, 30 Eur. J. Int'l L. (forthcoming 2019).

CHAPTER 21

CONSTITUTIONALISM AND INTERNATIONALISM

U.S. Participation in International Institutions

PAUL B. STEPHAN

EARLY in its history, international law helped the United States to maintain its status as a new state created over the objections of its imperial master. A thread running through the foundational period, dated roughly from the establishment of the Confederation in 1776 to the conclusion of the War of 1812, is the use of the law of nations to gain acceptance as a peer of European states.[1] Until the modern era, this pattern largely held.

Beginning with U.S. entry into World War II, there emerged a body of U.S. foreign relations law that reflected radically different needs and ambitions. The term "foreign relations law" itself is a postwar phenomenon, indicating a distinction between international law as such and the domestic law that governs domestic participation in international lawmaking and the incorporation of international law into the domestic legal system.[2] From 1941 on, the United States, rather than trying to fit in with other powers, took on the role of a preeminent superpower seeking to promote globally its version of liberal democracy. International law became an instrument in this project. Where it impeded the project, international law, not U.S. goals, gave way.

This transformation of purposes as well as sources rewrote the script for courts as well. Instead of trying to mimic what foreign peers would do in cases involving mostly private litigants, U.S. courts invoking international law in the modern era more often confronted disputes with public authorities, either federal or state. These cases frequently implicated the constitutional separation of powers, both the relationship between the executive and Congress and the particular role of the judiciary, in novel ways.

[1] *See* ANTHONY J. BELLIA, JR. & BRADFORD R. CLARK, THE LAW OF NATIONS AND THE UNITED STATES CONSTITUTION 13–18, 73–90 (2017).

[2] *See* Curtis A. Bradley, *What Is Foreign Relations Law?*, ch. 1 in this volume (tracing history of concept).

A profound change in the form and function of international law accompanied this transformation of U.S. foreign relations law. Much of this transformation involved the rise of international institutions. Having stayed out of the bodies created in the wake of World War I, the United States took the lead in forming the principal post–World War II structures. Not only the United Nations, but the International Bank for Reconstruction and Development, the International Monetary Fund, and the General Agreement on Tariffs and Trade (GATT) took shape under U.S. leadership and, at least for the first decade after the war, largely reflected U.S. geopolitical interests.

The end of the Cold War presented dual challenges for these institutions. On the one hand, they had to adapt to the absorption of the former socialist world into the U.S.-led international order. This involved not only bringing in new members but also rethinking the purposes of the institutions in light of what seemed a new consensus about liberal internationalism. On the other hand, the collapse of bipolarity in the international structure not only gave greater room for promotion of U.S. values (especially the so-called "Washington consensus") but also for undertaking new initiatives, both regional and multilateral, not necessarily reflecting U.S. goals and interests. Examples include the conversion of the European Communities into the European Union and the GATT into the World Trade Organization (WTO), as well as the establishment or extension of new regional tribunals to promote economic integration and human rights.[3] A deeper and broader theme was the freeing of Europe from its strategic dependence on the United States and the emergence of significant differences between these powers over the resources and goals of the international system.

The 9/11 terrorist attacks and U.S. response led to a reconsideration of fundamental national interests and international commitments, further widening the gap with Europe. Military operations in Afghanistan and Iraq, although multilateral, strained traditional alliances. The 2008 financial crisis disrupted and discredited the existing global financial architecture. Calamitous international interventions in Libya and Syria further undermined U.S. confidence in the purposes and capacities of multilateral military interventions. The 2016 federal elections produced a victory for a nationalist populist agenda that rejected the assumptions of the existing liberal international order. Comparisons with the isolationism that drove U.S. international relations from 1919 to 1941 are overblown, but growing uncertainty about U.S. involvement with international institutions seems beyond doubt.

This chapter considers the larger patterns found in legal norms derived from U.S. engagement with international institutions during the modern period. It first outlines a conceptual framework for assessing engagement. It draws on the "two-level game" concept proposed by Robert Putnam as a means of understanding the connections between domestic legal questions, particularly separation-of-powers doctrines, and choices about the nature and extent of international engagement. Next, it reviews modern U.S. participation in international institutions, including joint military activities, economic regulation, trade

[3] Paul B. Stephan, *The New International Law—Legitimacy, Accountability, Authority, and Freedom in the New Global Order*, 70 U. Colo. L. Rev. 1555 (1999).

and investment liberalization, and dispute settlement. It examines legal doctrine expressed in judicial decisions that has addressed, confirmed, and limited U.S. participation.

This chapter demonstrates that U.S. doctrine fits plausibly within the Putnam two-level framework. The executive faces structural limits on its power to make international commitments, including to international organizations. Some degree of legislative consent is required both as a means of joining such organizations and to enable the actions of those organizations to take effect in the domestic legal system. Courts enforce these limits, and do not themselves apply international actions in the absence of endorsement by a responsible domestic political actor. Whether the outcomes of particular cases are optimal is debatable, but the general mix of executive, legislative, and judicial authority can be seen as striking a plausibly desirable balance between international flexibility and domestic constitutional entrenchment.

I. The Political Economy of International Institutions: A Two-Level Game

A substantial literature exists addressing the purposes and efficacies of international institutions.[4] For political scientists working on international relations, three perspectives, reductively speaking, seem to dominate. Realists focus on the security interests of states and doubt the ability of international institutions to exercise a meaningful influence over state behavior. Constructivists believe that institutions not only reflect but shape the preferences of states and other significant actors within the international system. Rational-interest theorists assert that states make international institutions to maximize the satisfaction of salient goals, which in turn reflect the preferences of domestic actors with the capacity to influence international-relations decisions.[5] Conceptually, the rational-interest approach of international relations theorists overlaps substantially with that of economists, who study goal maximization of social groups under conditions of selective pressure, limited resources, transactions costs, and information asymmetry. My own work on international law falls within the last tradition, and this chapter will go down that path.

No defensible rational-choice theory maintains that the current arrangement of any institution represents the best possible outcome. Social life is too complex and contingent to be reduced to Panglossian simplicities. Rather, the theory posits the existence of selective pressure that, absent some intervening accident or disruption, pushes institutions toward better realization of the interests of those whom the institution serves and

[4] Gillian K. Hadfield & Barry R. Weingast, *Microfoundations of the Rule of Law*, 17 Ann. Rev. Polit. Sci. 21, 26 (2014).

[5] Others approaches exist, but these seem the most important.

to whom it answers. It does not promise that decision makers, in particular the current leadership of the branch of government that both deals with foreign governments and shapes the domestic political and legal agenda, will either accurately assess the contingencies latent in events or choose wisely. It is instead a theoretical construct that seeks to look past the noise of posturing politics to find more durable explanations for institutional actions. That it cannot always achieve this goal does not make it useless. Whether it does better than other models depends ultimately on its ability to generate plausible guesses about future events that stand up to empirical testing.

In his 1988 article, Robert Putnam modeled the entanglement of domestic politics and international relations by drawing on game theory to posit a two-level game, with each level affecting play at the other level:

> At the national level, domestic groups pursue their interests by pressuring the government to adopt favorable policies, and politicians seek power by constructing coalitions among those groups. At the international level, national governments seek to maximize their own ability to satisfy domestic pressures, while minimizing the adverse consequences of foreign developments.[6]

In most states, representatives of the head of government (executive branch) appear at both levels. The moves that the government makes reflect a complex calculus of offsetting domestic and international incentives and constraints.

Putnam's rational-choice/law-and-economics perspective supports both a positive prediction and a normative goal for foreign relations law. It predicts that rules of foreign relations law that over the long haul maximize a state's welfare will endure, and rules that do not will fall into desuetude. A state's welfare in turn will depend on the satisfaction of domestic interests given the opportunities presented and constraints imposed by the international environment. The normative goal is to design rules that will maximize the satisfaction of domestic interests in light of the international environment, which in turn may involve altering the international environment in pursuit of those interests.

Two extreme examples of hypothetical foreign-relations rules illustrate how a rational-interest analysis plays out in a two-level model. Imagine first a domestic constitution that makes international engagement very difficult. Let's call this a high-entrenchment regime.[7] It would impose great costs on entering into, as well as altering, international commitments. It might, for example, require that any agreement with another state, or any official act that has an impact on the foreign relations of the state,

[6] Robert Putnam, *Diplomacy and Domestic Politics: The Logic of Two-Level Games*, 42 INT'L ORG. 427, 434 (1988).

[7] I assume here something that would need to be proved empirically, namely, that assigning a rule or structure to a constitution substantially increases the level of domestic entrenchment. This is not always the case. *See* Mila Versteeg & Emily Zackin, *Constitutions Un-Entrenched: Towards an Alternative Theory of Constitutional Design*, 110 AM. POL. SCI. REV. 657 (2016). As a general matter, constitutionalization increases entrenchment, but in some systems the relative increase might not be much.

satisfy a unanimous voting requirement (applicable to the parliament or, in an even more extreme instance, a nationwide referendum). The same rule would apply to amendments to and withdrawals from such commitments.

The high-entrenchment regime would make it hard at the domestic level for a state to engage in legally sustained international cooperation, but exactly for that reason it also would make any commitments that such a state made more credible at the international level. An ongoing failure to engage the outside would entail significant opportunity costs, to use a term beloved of economists. Over time the people of the state would bear these costs, both politically and economically. Offsetting these costs, however, would be higher returns from the few deals made. To the extent that international commitments bring benefits, and that durability (albeit coupled with inflexibility) might enhance those benefits, the people of the state might do better.[8] If the international environment changes rapidly and in unforeseen directions, however, inflexibility might be a curse, not a boon.

Second, imagine a constitution that allows the executive to make binding international commitments and to override domestic legislation whenever it deems that its interests require such a move. Lapdog parliaments and courts could bring about such a system even in states with formal checks on executive actions. Call this the easy-access regime.

At the domestic level, such a state could respond quickly and decisively to changes in the international environment and harvest gains that it could dispense throughout the population. The absence of internal checks on the executive, however, might be problematic. Absent parliamentary or judicial accountability, the executive might choose to enrich itself at the expense of the nation. In the extreme case, the state could become a kleptocracy.

At the international level, foreign partners might be ambivalent. They would welcome the low barriers to international agreements, but be wary of commitments that are as easy to undo as they are to make. The absence of domestic institutional structures that might hold the executive to its obligations would reduce the value of its promises, and thus of international cooperation.

Each of these regimes seems obviously suboptimal. A state that mostly stays outside the international system will miss many chances to undertake valuable projects, to the detriment of its people as well as its leaders. It may even lose the capacity to stave off existential threats. Moreover, an inability to revise its commitments in the face of changed circumstances might cost such states more than it would gain from the increased credibility of its commitments. Conversely, a state that makes its looting easy and its international promises dubious will find it hard to cope over the long run. Authoritarian regimes that concentrate international relations in a few hands, such as the German Reich under National Socialism or the contemporary Democratic

[8] Pierre-Hugues Verdier & Mila Versteeg, *Separation of Powers, Treaty Making, and Treaty Withdrawal: A Global Survey*, ch. 8 in this volume (documenting trend toward relatively greater entrenchment, although not necessarily high entrenchment).

People's Republic of Korea, do not seem to offer stable solutions to the challenges of today's world.

If the rational-interest perspective has any traction, then, one would expect states to have rules governing foreign relations that avoid these extremes. The costs imposed by domestic institutional checks, whether legislative or judicial, might be substantial but not too large. Domestic institutions would reinforce international commitments, but not to the point where the state is shackled in the face of a fluid international environment. The obvious question is whether these theoretical conjectures bring us closer to observed practice.

In the case of the United States, several aspects of its general constitutional arrangements constrain the formation of foreign relations law, and therefore its optimization. First, the United States uses first-past-the-post rules for selection of its parliamentarians as well as of the electors who in turn choose the president. This feature promotes competition between only two, rather than many, political parties. Second, the president dominates the executive and is elected separately from the parliament (Congress). The independence of the selection of these branches makes it possible, and perhaps even likely, that the president and his government will come from a different party than that enjoying a majority in one or both houses of Congress. These party characteristics reinforce other institutional forces that can drive a wedge between the executive and Congress. Third, the judiciary as a whole has the authority to carry out constitutional review of all laws, federal and state. Any court, federal or state, can apply the federal Constitution to invalidate any inferior legal act. Moreover, the members of the federal judiciary enjoy lifetime tenure that insulates them from overt political pressure. Most federal judges regard their post as a terminal position, which means that they mostly do not decide cases with a view to professional advancement outside the judiciary. The judiciary as a whole, rather than a specialized tribunal with limited jurisdiction, exercises significant supervisory power over the other branches of government. Anxiety about this power in turn plays a significant part in legal decision-making.

In sum, the development of U.S. participation in international institutions takes place against a background of political contestation between two principal parties, competition between the executive and Congress based on both political and institutional factors, and ongoing tension between political accountability and judicial authority. These constitutional structures frame two fundamental issues that U.S. foreign relations law must resolve, namely, the shared lawmaking role of the executive and Congress (the political branches) and the role of the judiciary in both policing interbranch conflicts and asserting independent lawmaking authority.

First, to what extent do choices made by the executive require the endorsement of the Congress? Because these branches often are led by different parties, the issue has great political salience. Endorsement might be implicit or explicit, and either before or after the fact. Due to the peculiarities of the U.S. Constitution, legislative approval might take the form of simple majorities of both Houses (for nontreaties), or a two-thirds vote of the Senate alone (for treaties). The executive might have unilateral competence to decide whether to make a treaty (in the U.S. domestic law sense of the term) or instead to reach international agreements (treaties in the international law sense of the term) based on prior legislative authorization or subsequent confirmation. Alternatively, the executive might be held to an objective, judicially enforced standard as to when the treaty process must be used. Foreign relations law must address each of questions.

The second fundamental issue is the tension between judicial authority and the autonomy of the political branches (both the executive and Congress). To what extent will the courts resolve conflicts between the political branches, or instead allow the political process to run its course? To what extent will the judiciary decide cases based on liberal principles of statutory interpretation and common-law decision-making, or instead demand clear instructions from the political branches before acting? Throughout, foreign relations law in the United States turns on choices between judicial innovation and judicial deference to the political branches.

II. U.S. Participation in International Institutions

The United States throughout the modern period has organized, supported, and engaged with international institutions. As already noted, it was instrumental in the creation of the United Nations, the World Bank, the International Monetary Fund, and the General Agreement on Tariffs and Trade shortly after World War II. Not long afterward, it organized the North Atlantic Treaty Organization (NATO) and supported the creation of the Council of Europe. It early on accepted the compulsory jurisdiction of the International Court of Justice (ICJ). After the end of the Cold War, it promoted the creation of the World Trade Organization and generally supported the conversion of the European Communities into the European Union as well as the establishment of the international criminal tribunals for the former Yugoslavia and Rwanda.

A commitment to international institutions, however, is only part of the story. The United States withdrew its consent to the compulsory jurisdiction of the ICJ in the 1980s and has not accepted any new jurisdictional commitments. It refused to join the 1998 Rome Statute and thus to submit to the jurisdiction of the International Criminal Court. In 2003 it organized a multilateral coalition to invade and occupy Iraq without obtaining clear authority from the Security Council or working through NATO.[9] In the 2008 WTO ministerial talks, it failed to find a way to bridge the gap between rich states and the rising economic powers over the future legal regime for the world economy, effectively killing off the Doha Round. Clearly, the relationship between the United States and international institutions is complicated.

[9] The United States worked through NATO to bomb Serbia in 1999, even though that operation also lacked the support of the Security Council.

That said, the United States retains a number of international institutional commitments that rest on and manifest the specifics of foreign relations law. This brief section describes four areas where these commitments do significant work: use of armed force; financial, economic, and environmental regulation; trade and investment; and dispute resolution.

Multilateral Military Operations

Foreign relations law normally does not require, but rather permits, U.S. forces to operate within international structures. The strongest and most controversial example in which the United States did so is the Korean War, where the Harry Truman administration argued that neither a declaration of war (in a time before adoption of the War Powers Resolution) nor an express congressional authorization was needed for U.S. participation in military operations authorized by the Security Council.[10] More recently, in the major interventions of the twenty-first century, the United States has mostly used ad hoc multilateral coalitions to carry out the mission and only episodically sought Security Council endorsement.[11]

International Regulatory Cooperation

The modern economy is characterized by increasing returns to scale, reflected in the expansion of global markets, breakthroughs in communications and information-processing technologies, and the dissolution of geographical, state-based barriers to flows of people, goods, services, and capital. With these technological and institutional developments have come greater exposure to threats that also transcend national boundaries. Some are physical byproducts of the enlarged global economy, including environmental (air and water pollution, threats to the ozone layer, global warming) and public health (pandemics). Others are institutional problems created by economic interdependence (fiscal stability, financial market stability, competition policy, worker protection, social solidarity). A common thread in each of these cases is externalities that make national-level regulatory choices ineffective and demand some form of international cooperation.

The United States belongs to, and sometimes leads, a variety of international organizations and informal clubs that address these regulatory challenges. Its participation in the Montreal Protocol to combat ozone depletion has been significant, even if

[10] Congress did fund these operations, even though it did not adopt a separate authorization law.

[11] Even in the Libyan intervention in 2011, where the U.S. executive acted without congressional endorsement and argued that the War Powers Resolution did not apply, the government still had a Security Council resolution in hand.

it has lagged in the effort to contain global warming. It supports the World Health Organization in its efforts to monitor and respond to pandemics, although proposed funding cuts might put these activities at risk. The International Monetary Fund and the Bank for International Settlements provide a formal structure for fiscal operations and bank regulation, while the G7, G11, and G20 have functioned as informal means of coordinating these measures. The United States has been the foremost norm entrepreneur in attacking bribery of foreign officials and money laundering, using the Organisation for Economic Co-operation and Development (OECD) and its associated Financial Action Task Force as the principal platforms for coordination of international measures. It has promoted informal institutions that encourage cooperation in competition policy and securities market regulation, including the OECD, the International Competition Network, and the International Organization of Securities Commissions.

Trade and Investment

Since the end of World War II, the United States has promoted liberalization of goods, services, and capital flows through multilateral (the GATT, transformed into the WTO) and bilateral institutions, typically resting on free trade agreements (FTAs). Some of these agreements contain dispute resolution mechanisms, including in the case of the North American Free Trade Agreement (NAFTA) a means for importers to bypass normal judicial review of certain tariff assessments in favor of international arbitration.[12] The U.S. record of complying with the outcome of these proceedings has been good. The United States also led the way in adopting investment treaties that provide for investor-state (rather than state-state) arbitration of disputes.

The last decade, however, has seen a shift in emphasis, if not yet direction, on the part of the United States. It has renounced no trade commitments already in force, but it no longer aspires to expand them. Conflicts between the executive and Congress blocked approval of new agreements during the Barack Obama administration, and President Donald Trump announced that the United States would not join the Trans-Pacific Partnership, the one multilateral trade agreement that his predecessor has negotiated, instead of submitting it to Congress for its endorsement.[13] The current administration also has started negotiations intended to revise NAFTA and the Korea-U.S. Free Trade Agreement, with uncertain prospects and unclear consequences.[14]

[12] North American Free Trade Agreement, ch. 19.

[13] Both presidential candidates in 2016 opposed the Trans-Pacific Partnership.

[14] *See* Verdier & Versteeg, *supra* note 8 (listing episodes); *cf.* Laurence R. Helfer, *Treaty Exit and Intrabranch Conflict at the Interface of International and Domestic Law*, ch. 20 in this volume (general problem of exit from international commitments); Hannah Woolaver, *State Engagement with Treaties: Interactions between International and Domestic Law*, ch. 24 in this volume (discussing treaty exit in comparative perspective). The United States-Mexico-Canada Agreement, designed to supersede

Dispute Resolution

While (until recently) the United States promoted binding international dispute settlement of trade and investment matters, in other areas its record has been more complicated. In the first two decades of the post–World War II era, the United States was a leading advocate of the International Court of Justice, both submitting to its jurisdiction and hectoring the socialist states for not doing likewise. It frequently joined treaties calling for ICJ dispute settlement. Beginning in the 1980s, however, it changed direction. It withdrew its acceptance of general ICJ jurisdiction, stayed out of optional protocols in human rights treaties calling for ICJ dispute resolution, and declined to join the UN Convention on the Law of the Sea, in part because of concerns about its tribunal. Although taking the lead in creating ad hoc international criminal tribunals through the Security Council, it declined to join the Rome Statute, largely because of what it saw as excess discretion on the part of the International Criminal Court to determine its own jurisdiction.[15] Throughout this period and up to the present, the executive argued, largely successfully, against domestic judicial enforcement of ICJ decisions.

III. U.S. Foreign Relations Law and International Institutions

U.S. foreign relations law raises two structural issues about U.S. participation in international institutions. First, to what extent must Congress approve actions undertaken at the international level before the United States can implement them? Is it enough for Congress to endorse U.S. participation in the international structure in contemplation of particular actions, or must Congress endorse the action after the fact as a condition of U.S. implementation? Second, to what extent will the judiciary review and supervise these actions? The courts might invoke constitutional limitations, especially to constrain actions that have a direct effect on the liberty or property of persons. They also might act as agents of Congress by blocking actions of the executive that lack a satisfactory legislative foundation, or instead defer to the executive in the absence of clear legislative proscriptions. In this section, I discuss how the U.S. courts have resolved these structural areas in the four areas of institutional participation that the previous section described.

NAFTA, was signed in November 2018 but as of March 2019 had not yet obtained the ratification of any of the parties.

[15] Paul B. Stephan, *US Constitutionalism and International Law: What the Multilateralist Move Leaves Out*, 2 J. Int'l Crim. Just. 11 (2004).

Joint Military Operations

The success of the American Revolution depended fundamentally on a treaty of alliance with France, which provided crucial military support and played the principal role in the decisive victory at Yorktown. Yet the U.S. Constitution has nothing particular to say about joint military operations or the possibility of subordinating U.S. armed forces to international authority. It does require that the Senate consent to treaties by a supermajority vote, a measure motivated in part by concerns about military alliances. It provides that the Congress may declare war, issue letters of marque and reprisal, and provide rules for captures (the latter two significant aspects of warfare at the time, but anachronisms today), while the president serves as commander in chief of the armed forces.[16] Congress alone can "raise and support" armies and provide for a navy, a specific instance of the power of the purse.[17] The Constitution does not indicate, however, whether the president as commander in chief may delegate his authority to an international structure or whether Congress must approve any decision to do so.

Congress has not exercised its power to formally declare war since the commencement of World War II, but the United States has engaged in military operations abroad almost continuously since the end of that conflict. Litigants have asked the judiciary to review the legality of the use of armed force, but the courts have refused to do so.[18] This reticence is controversial, but justifications do exist. One argument regards the willingness of Congress to enact an authorization of the use of military force as an adequate substitute for a declaration of war.[19]

Because the modern U.S. Supreme Court has not addressed the legality of the use of force (*jus ad bellum*) on any terms, it necessarily has not considered whether actions supported by international organizations, such as a Security Council decision or an invocation of Article V of the NATO treaty, is either necessary or sufficient to justify the use of force by the United States. What it has done with some frequency, however, is determine whether particular actions undertaken in the context of armed conflict that interfere with the property or liberty of persons fall within the limits permitted by the law of war (*jus in bello*). In addressing these cases, it has distinguished between actions undertaken by the United States on its own authority, on the one hand, and steps taken on behalf of other states or an international organization, on the other hand.

The first case, *Hirota v. MacArthur*,[20] involved a challenge to punishment (including capital sentences) imposed by the International Military Tribunal for the Far East, a body "set up by General MacArthur as the agent of the Allied Powers."[21] This circumstance,

[16] U.S. Const. art. I § 8, cl. 11; art. II § 2, cl. 1. [17] *Id.* art. I § 8, cls. 12–13.

[18] Paul B. Stephan, *Treaties in the Supreme Court, 1946–2000*, *in* International Law in the U.S. Supreme Court: Continuity and Change 317, 326–327 (David L. Sloss, Michael D. Ramsey, & William S. Dodge eds., 2011).

[19] Curtis A. Bradley & Jack L. Goldsmith, *Congressional Authorization and the War on Terrorism*, 118 Harv. L. Rev. 2047, 2057–2066 (2005).

[20] 338 U.S. 197 (1948). [21] *Id.* at 198.

reasoned the Court, meant that it was "not a tribunal of the United States" and hence U.S. courts lacked the power to review its sentences.[22]

The second, *Munaf v. Geren*,[23] was decided sixty years later. It considered the legality of detention by U.S. military forces acting on behalf of Iraq of U.S. nationals accused of committing crimes on Iraqi territory. In *Munaf*, the petitioners sought a court order forbidding the United States from handing them over to Iraqi authorities for trial for kidnappings and other criminal acts allegedly carried out within Iraq. The Court ruled that they were being held by the United States, not by an international entity to which U.S. forces were subordinated, and thus were entitled to seek judicial review of their detention. On the merits, however, they were found to lack any substantive legal basis for opposing a turnover to Iraqi authorities.

In distinguishing *Hirota* on the jurisdictional issue, the *Munaf* Court indicated that principles of agency would distinguish actions subject to judicial review from those that were not. Where U.S. military forces serve as subordinates of an international authority, the courts will decline to act. Where the chain of command between U.S. armed services personnel and the president as commander in chief is unbroken, however, the acts of those personnel will count as those of the United States, and thus must submit to U.S. judicial scrutiny, even where the commander in chief cooperates and coordinates with foreign powers and relies on the Security Council for legal authority. That the U.S. forces detaining Munaf and Omar participated in a coalition endorsed by the Security Council, then, did not rob them of their status as U.S. actors. By implication, however, replication of the kinds of structures that governed the allies in the European and Pacific Theaters in World War II might insulate detentions and punishments from judicial review, even when the U.S. military does most of the work.

Regulation

The U.S. federal government regulates a wide range of economic activity, and in the contemporary world most regulatory issues have international dimensions. Many kinds of pollution, such as the release of carbon into the atmosphere, affect others beside the state where the release occurs. Pandemic pathogens do not respect national boundaries. One could go on. The point is that the power to regulate necessarily implies the authority, as well as the obligation, to grapple with international problems.

The conventional form of domestic regulation in the United States involves a legislative delegation of authority to an administrative agency, which might adopt regulations, investigate and sanction offenders, grant or withhold licenses, or otherwise implement the authority bestowed by Congress. Several general statutes, most prominently the Administrative Procedure Act, impose additional procedural requirements for administrative actions. Courts thus will determine whether regulatory agencies act

[22] *Id.* [23] 553 U.S. 674 (2008).

within the scope of authority granted them by Congress as well as whether they meet the procedural obligations that Congress has imposed.

An open question is whether Congress may delegate regulatory authority not to a domestic agency, but instead to an international organization. Domestic decision makers are subject to formal and informal checks, including freedom of information obligations to the general public and congressional budgetary supervision. International bodies by their nature cannot submit to a single state's supervisory power, even if that state is richer and more powerful than any other.

Two cases in the D.C. Circuit, the principal appellate court for review of administrative agencies, illustrates the approach that courts take to the delegation issue. *George E. Warren Corporation v. EPA*[24] upheld a domestic agency regulation that made it easier for foreign refiners to meet U.S. clean air standards in the wake of a WTO decision declaring a prior regulation inconsistent with U.S. treaty obligations. Domestic refiners argued that Congress had not given the Environmental Protection Agency (EPA) the authority to consider U.S. international obligations when determining the optimal standard for air quality. The court ruled that legislation did give the EPA the flexibility to take these obligations into account, although it did not mandate that the agency do so.

NRDC v. EPA[25] involved an attack on EPA regulations limiting production of a chemical covered by the Montreal Protocol on Substances that Deplete the Ozone Layer. The attackers argued that the regulations were inconsistent with more stringent decisions made at the regular meetings of the parties to the Protocol. The court ruled that Congress had required the EPA to implement only the Protocol itself, not decisions made at the international level that interpreted it. Accordingly, the case did not present a question of delegation of downstream regulatory authority to an international decision maker. The court strongly hinted, however, that such a delegation, had it occurred, would face serious constitutional obstacles.

NRDC's hint seems to rest on a belief that public regulation requires the blessing of a domestic decision maker, even if that decision maker faces a take-it-or-leave-it proposal from an international body. Prior authorization to act does not suffice, even though such delegations to domestic agencies are an accepted part of the regulatory landscape.[26] The differences between domestic and international agencies, the court intimated, require in the case of the latter a second step, an after-the-fact ratification by the legislature, that does not apply to domestic agencies.

The D.C. Circuit's intimation is only that. What is interesting, however, is how hard Congress and the courts try to avoid testing the constitutional waters. As *Warren* illustrates, the United States allows domestic administrative agencies to implement regulatory choices reached through international institutions if their preexisting statutory authority permits the agency's action, but Congress normally does not compel international agencies to fulfill international decisions. *NRDC* indicates that an agency

[24] 159 F.3d 616 (D.C. Cir. 1998). [25] 464 F.3d 1 (2006).

[26] Chevron U.S.A., Inc. v. NRDC, 467 U.S. 837 (1984); Skidmore v. Swift & Co., 323 U.S. 134 (1944).

must go back to Congress for permission to take action mandated by an international agency that goes beyond what its preexisting authority allows. Curtis Bradley has usefully suggested that this approach is analogous to a decision to make a treaty obligation non-self-executing.[27] In both instances, the United States makes binding international commitments while protecting the structural norms of lawmaking embedded in the Constitution. Requiring a domestic actor operating under the direct authority of the executive, and also subject to legislative pressure through hearings and the budgetary process, to own the outcome of international regulation reconciles international commitment and domestic accountability.

The practical consequence of this approach, whether constitutionally mandated or not, is to limit the scope of judicial oversight of regulatory decisions and thus to increase the policy space available to regulatory agencies in the executive branch relative to that of the judiciary. As *NRDC v. EPA* illustrates, a reviewing court must determine whether the agency action came within the legislative mandate, but cannot conduct an additional inquiry as to whether the agency action complies with decisions reached at the international level that have not been subsequently incorporated into domestic law. As a result, individual litigants cannot invoke international law as an independent means of constraining agency actions.[28]

One might ask whether this approach sacrifices individual interests that an international commitment might be intended to protect. It is far from clear, however, that judicial intervention will provide a satisfactory response to this problem. Within the U.S. system, litigation based on claims of international law present two interrelated problems. As noted above, courts face inherent information deficiencies. Courts do not interact with foreign states and thus cannot update their assessments of international law in light of the expectations and reactions of other states. Some scholars have posited a growing network of judicial contacts that fill this gap, but the claim lacks empirical support.[29]

Judges can learn about the world from many sources, but the structure of ligation in the United States requires them to confront first the representations of the parties, on which they have must rely disproportionately. Parties to litigation have structural as well as particular biases that skew the kinds of evidence they present and the arguments they make.[30] Attempts to overcome these biases are both costly and likely to reflect

[27] Curtis A. Bradley, *International Delegations, the Structural Constitution, and Non-Self-Execution*, 55 STAN. L. REV. 1557, 1587–1595 (2003).

[28] Compare the British approach, which pursuant to statute allows the judiciary to interpret and apply European law to review the acts of domestic officials. Paul Craig, *Engagement and Disengagement with International Institutions: The U.K. Perspective*, ch. 22 in this volume. U.S. law contains nothing like the European Communities Act 1972 or the Human Rights Act 1998, and U.S. courts have declined to imply such authority in the absence of clear legislation.

[29] Paul B. Stephan, *Courts on Courts: Contracting for Engagement and Indifference in International Judicial Encounters*, 100 VA. L. REV. 17, 75, 78, 86–87, 94, 99–102 (2014) (documenting lack of evidence).

[30] Paul B. Stephan, *The Political Economy of Extraterritoriality*, 1 POL. & GOVERNANCE 92, 94–95 (2013).

other, if different, biases. As a result, were courts to make determinations about the scope and meaning of international determinations, they might surprise other states.

The informational problem is exacerbated by the inability of courts to negotiate with other states to adjust and refine interpretations of international obligations in light of what other states expect. Compare, as a counterexample, the procedure created by the North American Free Trade Agreement to permit the governments of the three parties to issue downstream interpretations of the Agreement. Wielding this authority, the governments revised the treaty's rules implementing the obligation of fair and equitable treatment of foreign investors in reaction to a decision of an arbitral tribunal that, the governments believed, incorrectly stated the law.[31] Nothing like this exists for most international obligations.[32]

The general strength of these arguments, and the need for and possible scope of exceptions to a general rule of judicial deference, need not detain us here. The important point is that U.S. lawmakers, including the judiciary, to date have avoided any constitutional confrontation over the permissibility of delegating regulatory authority to international bodies. Rather, such delegations as they make are inevitably contingent on implementation by authorized domestic actors, either an administrative agency acting within the scope of its legislative authority or Congress through adoption of after-the-fact implementing legislation.

Trade and Investment

The manner in which the United States implements its trade and investment commitments refines the point made in the previous section. To the extent that trade agreements alter substantive domestic law, whether through tariff changes or other forms of regulation, their legal effect depends on legislative confirmation after the signing of the agreement. In this respect, U.S. practice resembles that of the European Union, which typically does not give direct effect to trade agreements with other states.[33]

Before the 1970s, Congress had delegated to the executive the authority to enter into trade agreements that could take direct effect in domestic law without requiring either Senate consent or implementing legislation. This process did not delegate authority to

[31] NAFTA FTC, Notes of Interpretation of Certain ch. 11 Provisions, § B (July 31, 2001), *available at* http://www.international.gc.ca/trade-agreements-accords-commerciaux/topics-domaines/disp-diff/NAFTA-Interpr.aspx?lang=eng; Charles H. Brower, II, *Why the FTC Notes of Interpretations Constitute a Partial Amendment of NAFTA Article 1105*, 46 VA. J. INT'L L. 347 (2006).

[32] An important counterexample to the point in text is the European Union, the organs of which may adopt law that binds its members without resort to domestic legislative ratification and which participate in international institutions on behalf of its members. *See* Joris Larik, *Regional Organizations' Relations with International Institutions: The EU and ASEAN Compared*, ch. 25 in this volume.

[33] *Cf.* Duncan B. Hollis & Carlos Vázquez, *Treaty Self-Execution as "Foreign" Foreign Relations Law*, ch. 26 in this volume (discussing EU treatment of self-execution of some treaties, but omitting non-self-execution of trade agreements).

international institutions, but did give the executive discretion, subject to prescribed limits, to make new law based on agreements with other states. During the 1950s a court of appeals ruled, as a matter of statutory interpretation more than constitutional mandate, that Congress had not conveyed the discretion that the executive exercised. The Supreme Court then reversed that decision, but its narrow opinion shed no light on the underlying separation-of-powers questions.[34] The Trade Act of 1974 mooted the point by mandating post hoc legislative approval of all trade agreements made by the executive.[35]

With respect to investment protection, a more complex pattern emerges. The United States does not enter into treaties that allow international institutions—typically ad hoc arbitral tribunals—to assess the validity of domestic law and to proscribe actions that violate treaty obligations. U.S. legislation, however, authorizes the payment of any and all arbitral awards against the United States, subject only to the certification of the Attorney General.[36] In the case of awards arising under the Convention on the Settlement of Disputes Between States and Nationals of Other States (Washington Convention), this certification is dispensed with.[37] Payment of money, in other words, does not require any legislative confirmation or, in the case of awards under the Washington Convention, even approval by an executive agency. The action of an international actor—an arbitral tribunal issuing an award against the United States—has direct effect in U.S. law to the extent it requires the payment of money, but not otherwise.

What makes money different? One might think of an arbitral agreement as equivalent to a contract for services, which binds the purchaser (here the United States) to pay for the service obtained (here dispute resolution). Allowing states to pay for purchases without after-the-fact approval makes sense for many reasons. Critically, an arbitral award does not have a direct effect in a state's legal regime, even if it may affect the cost-benefit analysis of undertaking particular state actions. As a result, paying an award does not implicate the constitutional structure of domestic lawmaking in the same manner as does automatic implementation of international decisions invalidating or changing domestic law.

Dispute Resolution

The discussion of investment tribunal awards raises a more general point. Although the United States accepts the jurisdiction of various international dispute-settlement tribunals, it does not give direct effect to the decisions of those bodies, awards of money against the United States or parties to arbitration agreements aside. Indeed, the

[34] United States v. Guy W. Capps, Inc., 348 U.S. 296 (1955).

[35] Trade Act of 1974 §§ 151–154. The current rules are in Trade Act of 2002, §§ 2103–2105.

[36] 28 U.S.C. § 2414. [37] 22 U.S.C. § 1650a.

Supreme Court has intimated that the interpretations of U.S. treaty obligations by international tribunals cannot bind U.S. courts, even if these interpretations have full effect at the international level.

Two modern Supreme Court decisions are relevant here. In *Dames & Moore v. Regan*,[38] the Court upheld a mandatory stay of domestic litigation involving Iranian defendants so that the U.S.-Iran Claims Tribunal, the creature of an international agreement, could resolve these disputes. The newly created international body was foisted upon the claimants, who had brought in U.S. courts mostly contract and property claims not based on federal law. The Court determined that existing legislation did not provide a clear basis for this stay, but that a long tradition of congressional support for executive settlement of these kinds of disputes between U.S. private actors and foreign governments sufficed to legitimize the executive's order terminating domestic litigation.[39] Although the issue was not before the Court, it was the expectation of the United States that decisions of the Tribunal would be binding in the United States on the same basis as contracted-for arbitration.[40]

On its face, then, *Dames & Moore* appears to indicate that delegation to an international body of authority to resolve a broad range of private disputes with a foreign state and its agencies and instrumentalities passes constitutional muster.[41] One might detect some tension between this outcome and the Court's decision a year later in *Northern Pipeline Construction Co. v. Marathon Pipe Line Co.*,[42] which invalidated as an infringement of the judiciary's exclusive powers the delegation of private-law dispute resolution to bankruptcy courts, domestic tribunals that lacked the characteristics of regular federal courts. Why may a class of cases be nondelegable to bankruptcy tribunals, but exactly the same kind of cases (excepting the nature of the parties) be delegable to an international tribunal? The *Northern Pipeline* Court did not address the discrepancy, but one might speculate that the foreign-affairs dimension provides a ground for distinction.[43]

Muddying the waters, however, is *Sanchez-Llamas v. Oregon*.[44] The case involved the binding effect of treaty interpretations made by the International Court of Justice. In ruling that the ICJ's reading of a treaty would be accorded deference, but not regarded as authoritative, the Court explained that to do otherwise would encroach on the

[38] 453 U.S. 654 (1981). [39] *Id.* at 686–688.

[40] As the lower courts subsequently held. E.g., Ministry of Defense of the Islamic Republic of Iran v. Gould Inc., 887 F.3d 1357 (9th Cir. 1989).

[41] The Algiers Accords also covers interstate disputes, and these have kept the Tribunal going up to the present. The United States has not challenged the enforceability of this commitment, which would seem to come under the umbrella of 28 U.S.C. § 2414.

[42] 458 U.S. 50 (1982).

[43] Arguably contracts and property disputes with foreign persons fall within the "public rights" exception to Northern Pipeline's requirement of an Article III court. Oil States Energy Services, LLC v. Greene's Energy Group, LLC, 138 S. Ct. 1365 (2018).

[44] 548 U.S. 331 (2006).

constitutional authority of the federal judiciary "'to say what the law is.'"[45] At least when the issue involved a state's criminal justice process, rather than private rights to contract and to own property, the decision suggests that Congress may lack the power to authorize an international tribunal to make binding determinations of U.S. domestic law. *Medellín v. Texas* then held that a U.S. court could not order compliance with the ICJ's order to provide further review of a criminal defendant's case, absent a clear basis for that order in domestic law, such as a self-executing treaty.[46] Implicit in that decision, however, is the suggestion that, with appropriate domestic legal authority, a U.S. court may implement a judgment of an international tribunal, even if it cannot be bound by such a tribunal's interpretations of U.S. law.[47]

From one perspective, one might think of the *Sanchez-Llamas/Medellín* position on nondelegability as protecting judicial power. It enables courts to reject particular legislative determinations that would deprive them from hearing certain kinds of cases. It thus limits political control over judicial jurisdiction. From a different perspective, however, *Sanchez-Llamas/Medellín* reduces judicial discretion and thus power. It makes out of bounds a particular kind of argument—claims based on treaty interpretations originating in international tribunals—and thus cuts back on the kinds of arguments that litigants are allowed to raise and courts are permitted to embrace.

IV. Conclusion

Two tendencies emerge from a review of U.S. involvement in international institutions since 1941. First, the United States historically played a leading role in creating many of these institutions. As policy areas such as anticorruption and money laundering indicate, the United States even in recent times has sought to organize international cooperation around institutional structures to respond to new challenges. Second, U.S. attitudes toward specific institutions and cooperative projects has shifted in ways that resonate with the two-level game model.

U.S. foreign relations law accommodates these institutional commitments in a way that the two-level-game model predicts. The U.S. Constitution, as interpreted by the judiciary, gives the president considerable flexibility to make international

[45] *Id.* at 353 (*quoting* Marbury v. Madison, 5 U.S. (1 Cranch) 137, 177 (1803)). Compare the German approach, which also reserves the authority of the *Bundesverfassungsgericht* to review the international-law interpretations of international tribunals, but in practice accords greater deference to (at least some of) those bodies than does the U.S. Supreme Court. *See* Andreas L. Paulus & Jan-Henrik Hinselmann, *International Integration and Its Counter-Limits: A German Constitutional Perspective,* ch. 23 in this volume.

[46] 552 U.S. 491 (2008).

[47] The persons seeking to invoke the ICJ judgment in *Sanchez-Llamas* were not covered by that judgment. Accordingly, the Court addressed only the question of the binding effect of the ICJ's treaty interpretations, and not of the judgment itself.

commitments, but also requires some level of congressional authorization before those commitments can have domestic legal consequences. This check reduces the risk of rent-seeking while preserving flexibility.

The courts also have made it difficult for litigants to invoke the actions of international institutions as an independent source of law. Instead, they look to domestic law to determine the authority of these actions within the domestic legal system. An exception applies to arbitral awards that produce money judgments. One can reconcile this practice with the general rule by arguing that such awards may affect the incentives of lawmakers but do not alter the validity of domestic law as such. More importantly, the general rule requiring domestic legal authority as a basis for enforcing international actions serves as a check on the already considerable power of domestic courts to review and revise domestic law. This constraint may enhance participation in international institutions by reducing the risk that courts, prodded by litigants, may rewrite bargains reached at the international level.

CHAPTER 22

ENGAGEMENT AND DISENGAGEMENT WITH INTERNATIONAL INSTITUTIONS

The U.K. Perspective

PAUL CRAIG

I. Introduction

This chapter considers the U.K. legal rules that govern engagement and disengagement with international institutions. The discussion begins with consideration of the rules that shape initial treaty engagement with such institutions. The United Kingdom is fundamentally a dualist system, such that the basic starting point is that statutory incorporation of treaties is a condition precedent to their application in U.K. law, although the breadth of this rule has been questioned, as will be seen from the analysis. U.K. law also contains statutory provisions that, subject to certain conditions, accord a veto power to the House of Commons to prevent the executive ratifying a treaty, thereby preventing the United Kingdom from being bound by international law obligations. This analysis concludes with discussion of the limits of dualism, as manifest in the making and application of rules at the global level that can have an impact, de jure or de facto, on the nation-state.

The focus in the second part shifts to what is termed continuing engagement. This concerns constraints flowing from national law while the United Kingdom is a member of an international organization. The nature and content of such constraints can vary, as can their conceptual foundation. The discussion considers three types of constraint: statutory, common law, and those grounded in the desire for autochthony.

The final part of the chapter addresses the U.K. rules concerning disengagement from an international organization. The starting point is that the executive, acting pursuant to prerogative power, negotiates disengagement from an international organization, and Parliament then enacts or repeals the legislation to make this a legal reality in national law. There are, however, limits to the prerogative: it cannot be used to alter the law of land or affect rights, and it cannot be deployed to circumvent a statute that covers the same ground. There was contestation as to the meaning of these precepts in litigation concerning the United Kingdom's exit from the European Union.

II. Initial Engagement

The United Kingdom adopts a dualist perspective to the relationship between national law and international law, which frames the way in which the United Kingdom engages with international institutions.

Dualism: Treaties, Parliamentary Authorization, and National Law

International treaties are negotiated and signed by the U.K. executive. This executive authority is derived from the royal prerogative, which is a species of nonstatutory discretionary power. Historically, prerogative power resided in the monarch, and some personal prerogatives continue to do so. However, most prerogative power is exercised by the executive. The courts make the ultimate determination as to whether a prerogative power exists; they also determine the extent thereof[1] and the manner of exercise.[2] There is no doubt that there is a prerogative power in relation to the making of treaties and the conduct of foreign affairs, and it would require something extraordinary for a court to intervene in relation to the manner of exercise of this power.

Parliamentary sovereignty is, however, the cornerstone of the unwritten U.K. constitution. There is a proximate normative connection between sovereignty thus conceived, and the dualist perspective on the relationship between domestic law and international treaties that prevails in U.K. law. The latter is designed to protect the former. The executive, as noted above, negotiates and signs treaties on behalf of the United Kingdom. If, however, the treaty thus signed could impose rights and obligations in national law without statutory authorization, then Parliamentary sovereignty would be undermined. The executive would be able to "legislate" through conclusion of

[1] Case of Proclamations (1611) 12 Co. Rep. 74; Prohibitions del Roy (1607) 12 Co. Rep. 63.

[2] Council of Civil Service Unions v. Minister for the Civil Service [1985] AC 374.

such treaties, thereby bypassing Parliament. The U.K. courts have, therefore, held that an unincorporated treaty has no effect in domestic law.[3]

Treaties must be transformed or adopted into national law in order to be enforceable in national courts, and will not generate rights unless this has been done. In *Rayner*, Lord Oliver held that an unincorporated treaty provision was irrelevant as a source of rights and obligations.[4] Lord Templeman explained the doctrine in the following manner:

> A treaty is a contract between the governments of two or more sovereign states. International law regulates the relations between sovereign states and determines the validity, the interpretation and the enforcement of treaties. A treaty to which Her Majesty's Government is a party does not alter the laws of the United Kingdom. A treaty may be incorporated into and alter the laws of the United Kingdom by means of legislation. Except to the extent that a treaty becomes incorporated into the laws of the United Kingdom by statute, the courts of the United Kingdom have no power to enforce treaty rights and obligations at the behest of a sovereign government or at the behest of a private individual.[5]

This view was reiterated by Lord Millett, giving judgment for the Privy Council, in the *Baptiste* case:

> Their Lordships recognise the constitutional importance of the principle that international conventions do not alter domestic law except to the extent that they are incorporated into domestic law by legislation. The making of a treaty, in Trinidad and Tobago as in England, is an act of the executive government, not of the legislature. It follows that the terms of a treaty cannot effect any alteration to domestic law or deprive the subject of existing legal rights unless and until enacted into domestic law by or under authority of the legislature. When so enacted, the courts give effect to the domestic legislation, not to the terms of the treaty. The many authoritative statements to this effect are too well known to need citation.[6]

The principle was reiterated more recently in *Miller*,[7] where Lord Neuberger held that although unincorporated treaties were binding on the United Kingdom in international law, they were not part of U.K. law, and gave rise to no legal rights or obligations in domestic law. His Lordship repeated this view in *Belhaj*, stating that "domestic

[3] Brownlie's Principles of Public International Law 50 (James Crawford ed., 8th ed. 2012); Philip Sales QC & Joanne Clement, *International Law in Domestic Courts: The Developing Framework*, 124 L.Q.R. 388 (2008).

[4] JH Rayner (Mincing Lane Ltd) v. Department of Trade and Industry [1990] 2 AC 418, 500.

[5] *Id.* at 477–478.

[6] Thomas v. Baptiste [2000] 2 AC 1, 23. *See also* The Parlement Belge (1879) 4 PD 129; R v. Home Secretary, ex p. Brind [1991] 1 AC 696; John Junior Higgs v. Minister of National Security [2000] 2 AC 228, 241.

[7] Miller v. Secretary of State for Exiting the European Union [2017] UKSC 5, [55].

courts should not normally determine issues which are only really appropriate for diplomatic or similar channels."[8]

The corollary is that decisions of international courts and tribunals that find the United Kingdom in breach of an international obligation flowing from an unimplemented treaty do not have effect in national courts, since this would indirectly undermine the need for Parliament to transform the treaty into domestic law. Thus, in the *Lyons* case, Lord Hoffmann held that:

> The argument that the courts are an organ of state and therefore obliged to give effect to the state's international obligations is in my opinion a fallacy. If the proposition were true, it would completely undermine the principle that the courts apply domestic law and not international treaties. There would be no reason to confine it to secondary obligations arising from breaches of the treaty. The truth of the matter is that, in the present context, to describe the courts as an organ of the state is significant only in international law. International law does not normally take account of the internal distribution of powers within a state. It is the duty of the state to comply with international law, whatever may be the organs which have the power to do so. And likewise, a treaty may be infringed by the actions of the Crown, Parliament or the courts. From the point of view of international law, it ordinarily does not matter. In domestic law, however, the position is very different. The domestic constitution is based upon the separation of powers. In domestic law, the courts are obliged to give effect to the law as enacted by Parliament. This obligation is entirely unaffected by international law.[9]

There are, however, some judicial statements questioning the generality of the preceding orthodoxy. Thus Lord Steyn took the view that the rationale for dualist theory was that any exception to it would risk abuse by the executive to the detriment of citizens, but that it was "difficult to see what relevance this has to international human rights treaties which create fundamental rights for individuals against the state and its agencies."[10] His Lordship felt that there might be a need to re-examine this aspect of the law in the future. More recently, Lord Kerr in *J.S.* reasoned in a similar vein, and opined that there should be an exception to traditional dualist theory for human rights conventions to be recognized in domestic law, even if they had not been incorporated.[11] More recently yet again, Lady Hale held that the possibility that a domestic statute should be interpreted consistently with an unincorporated treaty obligation, such as Article 3 of the Convention on the Rights of the Child, should be examined in an appropriate case.[12]

The possibility of such exceptions to dualist theory has, however, been criticized by Sales and Clement, who take issue with Lord Steyn's dictum, arguing that the

[8] Belhaj v. Straw [2017] 2 WLR 456, [123].

[9] R v. Lyons [2003] 1 AC 976, 995.

[10] McKerr [2004] UKHL 12, [52].

[11] R. (J.S.) v. Secretary of State for Work and Pensions [2015] UKSC 16, [254].

[12] Nzolameso v. City of Westminster [2015] UKSC 22, [29].

underlying rationale for the orthodox dualist position is not to guard against abuse by the executive to the detriment of citizens, but to buttress parliamentary sovereignty, by preventing the executive from altering the law through recourse to the prerogative and the making of an international treaty. This argument has, in turn, been criticized by Bjorge, who contends that, viewed historically, the test as to whether an unincorporated treaty obligation could have effect in domestic law was whether the treaty obligation effected a change of domestic law that infringed the existing legal rights of the subject. Bjorge is careful to make clear that he is not countenancing the wholesale import of unincorporated treaty obligations into domestic law, but advocates a more nuanced approach, whereby the focus is squarely on the particular obligation at stake in the particular case, and whether it can be allowed to have effect, assuming that it did not affect the legal rights of subjects.[13]

It remains to be seen whether the courts will countenance any exceptions to the general dualist position adumbrated at the outset of this section. The answer will depend, explicitly or implicitly, on the policy underpinning the dualist perspective. Insofar as that is taken to be the protection of parliamentary sovereignty, it would lend force to the conclusion that there should be no exceptions, this being predicated on the assumption that it is for Parliament to decide on domestic law, including the rights and obligations of individuals. Insofar as the rationale is taken to be protective of executive abuse, there is more room for some limited exceptions whereby unincorporated treaty obligations might have effect in national law, provided that rights of the subject are not infringed.

Dualism: Treaties, Parliamentary Authorization, and International Law

The preceding doctrine is directed toward preventing unincorporated treaties taking effect in national law. U.K. law also possesses constitutional doctrine designed to prevent the executive from ratifying a treaty, and thereby committing the United Kingdom at the international level, in circumstances where Parliament does not accept the treaty. This area is interesting, since it reveals a shift from practice, to a convention, and then to a statutory obligation.[14]

It had been the practice, since 1892, to present to Parliament the texts of treaties binding the United Kingdom. The mode of presentation was through a numbered series of Command Papers known as the Treaty Series. However, treaties were thus published only when they had entered into force for the United Kingdom, and therefore there was no room for Parliamentary approval at that stage.

[13] Eirik Bjorge, *Can Unincorporated Treaty Obligations Be Part of English Law?*, PUBLIC LAW 571 [2017].

[14] House of Lords, Select Committee on the Constitution, 15th Report (HL 236-I, 2006), Appendix 5.

The origin of the constitutional convention that Parliament would have the opportunity to consider a treaty prior to ratification is to be found in the statement by Ponsonby, who was Under-Secretary of State for Foreign Affairs in Ramsay MacDonald's first Labour Government, on April 1, 1924, during a debate concerning a peace treaty with Turkey. He stated that the government would lay on the table of both Houses of Parliament every treaty, when signed, for a period of twenty-one days, after which the treaty would be ratified and published and circulated in the Treaty Series. If there was demand for discussion, time would be found.[15] Ponsonby made it clear that resolutions expressing Parliamentary approval of every Treaty before ratification would be too cumbersome, and therefore the absence of disapproval should be accepted as sanction. The catalyst for the statement was concern among government supporters about secret treaties of the kind that were felt to have helped bring about the First World War, although the practice of secret treaties had, by 1924, been largely abolished through changes in diplomatic practice, coupled with obligations in the Covenant of the League of Nations. The Ponsonby Rule was withdrawn during the subsequent Baldwin government, but reinstated in 1929. It assumed the status of a constitutional convention through adherence by successive governments. The Ponsonby Rule applied to treaties that were subject to ratification, and this was interpreted by the Foreign and Commonwealth Office to include acceptance, approval, and accession as well as ratification.

The shift from convention to statute came with the enactment of the Constitutional Reform and Governance Act 2010, which was part of a broader governmental program to place conventions on a more secure statutory footing. The principal provisions are contained in Section 20. The basic regime is as follows. The minister lays a copy of the treaty before Parliament, including an Explanatory Memorandum.[16] The onus is on Parliament to object to a treaty[17] to prevent ratification. If neither the House of Commons nor the House of Lords objects within twenty-one days,[18] the treaty can be ratified. If the House of Commons resolves that the treaty should not be ratified,[19] irrespective of whether the House of Lords has also so resolved, then the minister is, in effect, given a second opportunity to present the treaty, with arguments as to why it should be ratified. The onus is then once again on the House of Commons to resolve that the treaty should not be ratified within a further twenty-one-day period.[20] It is, moreover, open to a minister to do this more than once.[21] Where the House of Commons does not object to the treaty, but the House of Lords does, then the

[15] HC Deb (1924) 171 c. 1999–2005.

[16] Constitutional Reform and Governance Act 2010, § 24.

[17] The definition of treaty includes an agreement between the United Kingdom and an international organization. *Id.*, § 25(1).

[18] This period can be extended. *Id.*, § 21.

[19] Ratification includes accession, approval, acceptance, and also deposit or notification of completion of domestic procedures. *Id.*, § 25(4).

[20] *Id.*, § 20(4). [21] *Id.*, § 20(6).

government's position is stronger, since it can, in effect, override the House of Lords, and ratify the treaty, giving reasons why it has chosen to do this.[22]

There are certain qualifications to the preceding regime. A minister may, exceptionally, take the view that a treaty should be ratified without complying with Section 20, although this cannot happen if either House has already resolved, pursuant to Section 20(1)(c), that the treaty should not be ratified.[23] If the minister ratifies the treaty pursuant to this power, there are then obligations to lay the treaty before Parliament, to publish it, and to give reasons for this course of action. There are also certain categories of treaties that are not subject to Section 20,[24] although the rationale for these exceptions is that the treaties listed are subject to greater parliamentary scrutiny through, for example, an obligation to secure positive statutory authorization before the treaty takes effect.

It is important to stand back from the detail, in order to assess the legal and political impact of the Constitutional Reform and Governance Act 2010. The legislation affords the House of Commons an ultimate veto. The minister may, after the House of Commons has resolved that the treaty should not be ratified, attempt to persuade it that this should occur by re-presenting it, thereby forcing the House of Commons to pass a further resolution against the treaty. However, if the House of Commons remains firm, it retains the ultimate veto, and the treaty cannot be ratified. It therefore prevents the executive from committing the United Kingdom at the international level through ratification of a treaty of which Parliament disapproves. This is in addition to the dualist requirement that an Act of Parliament is necessary to give effect in domestic law to matters embodied in such an agreement. The two operate as "constitutional belt and braces," the former ensuring that Parliament has voice before the executive commits the country on the international plane, the latter preventing the executive making binding rules at national level independent of the legislature.

The veto power accorded to the House of Commons should, however, be seen against the backdrop of the U.K. party system, which is dominated by the executive. There are occasions when the government's backbench Members of Parliament (MPs) rebel against aspects of government policy. The reality is, nonetheless, that party discipline remains strong, and it would be exceptional for the legislature to block ratification of an international treaty. This is especially so, given that the onus is on Parliament to pass the resolutions preventing ratification; it is not for the minister to secure a positive resolution in favor of the treaty.

The Limits of Dualism: Treaties, Transnational Organization, and Globalization

While the preceding picture is relatively clear, there is, nonetheless, something resembling a black hole that is pertinent to this study. The doctrinal rules adumbrated above

[22] *Id.*, § 20(7)–(8). [23] *Id.*, § 22. [24] *Id.*, § 23.

apply to formal treaties. They do not cover all global regulatory rules, which can impact, de jure or de facto, on the United Kingdom. There is a very considerable body of such rules.[25]

Prominent examples include rules made by nongovernmental regulatory organizations, such as the ISO,[26] the International Organization for Standardization, the IEC, the International Electrotechnical Commission,[27] and the ISAB,[28] the International Accounting Standards Board. These bodies produce rules and standards for a range of products, and compliance will often be required either to secure market access, or because the regulatory requirements are incorporated in national laws, directly or indirectly.[29]

In other instances, there will be transnational networks and coordination arrangements, which may, but need not be, embedded in a treaty, and where the principal objective is cooperation among state regulators, as exemplified by the Basel Committee on Banking Supervision.[30] In yet other instances there is "hybrid intergovernmental-private administration," as exemplified by the Codex Alimentarius Commission,[31] where the food standards are adopted through a decision-making process that includes participation by nongovernmental actors as well as government representatives, and by ICANN, the Internet Corporation for Assigned Names and Numbers,[32] which although founded as a nongovernmental body, now includes government representatives.

The rules made by such bodies shape, de jure or de facto, national regulatory strategies, whether those are run by state agencies, private standardization organizations, or an admixture of the two. Thus, even if the foundational document of the organization is subject to the preceding gatekeeping doctrine as to the applicability of treaties in national law, this is not normally so for the rules made thereafter. This is so notwithstanding the fact that Parliament may, in reality, be bypassed by the application of such global rules at the national level.

It is increasingly common for national administrative discretion to be constrained by global standards developed by bodies such as the World Trade Organization, created pursuant to a classic international treaty, and also by norms fashioned by transnational regulatory networks, or international standardization organizations.[33]

[25] *See*, e.g., Kal Raustiala, *The Architecture of International Cooperation: Transgovernmental Networks and the Future of International Law*, 43 Va. J. Int'l L. 1 (2002); Walter Mattli & Tim Büthe, *Setting International Standards: Technological Rationality or Primacy of Power*, 56 World Politics 1 (2003); Anne-Marie Slaughter, A New World Order (2004); Benedict Kingsbury, Nico Krisch, & Richard Stewart, *The Emergence of Global Administrative Law*, 68 Law & Contemp. Probs. 15 (Summer/Autumn 2005); Tim Büthe & Walter Mattli, The New Global Rulers: the Privatization of Regulation in the World Economy (2011); Sabino Cassese, The Global Polity: Global Dimensions of Democracy and the Rule of Law (2012).

[26] http://www.iso.org/iso/home.html. [27] http://www.iec.ch.

[28] http://www.iasplus.com/en/resources/ifrsf/iasb-ifrs-ic/iasb.

[29] *See* Mattli & Büthe, *supra* note 25; Büthe & Mattli, *supra* note 25.

[30] http://www.bis.org/bcbs/. [31] http://www.codexalimentarius.org/.

[32] https://www.icann.org/.

[33] Daphne Barak-Erez & Oren Perez, *Whose Administrative Law Is It Anyway? How Global Norms Reshape the Administrative State*, 46 Cornell Int'l L.J. 455 (2013).

In some instances national administrative authorities directly adopt standards developed by international organizations, and in others this is done voluntarily by private firms. There are, moreover, issues raised by the disjunction between transfer of regulatory responsibility and responsibility for enforcement.[34]

It is, however, important to dispel any idea that the blame for problems concerning regulatory interaction between the global, regional, and national should be placed solely at the door of the global order. This will not withstand examination. The reality is more complex, there being issues of accountability that relate to the national/regional level, and to the global level.

From the national perspective, regulators are limited in what they can achieve, since they can only regulate conduct that falls within their jurisdiction, but there is also a disjunction between what Scott has aptly termed "regulatory jurisdiction and regulatory impact."[35] States are often not accountable to other states affected by their domestic regulation, thereby creating a horizontal accountability gap, since the affected states have no voice in such measures. In a similar vein, Aman notes that a democracy deficit can arise from the fact that individuals may be affected by decisions that have significant adverse impact, which are made by jurisdictions beyond the reach of those affected.[36] Viewed from this perspective, global regulatory regimes can help to reduce this accountability gap in national regulation, by encouraging horizontal and vertical integration of domestic regulatory systems, and by requiring national regulators to take into account all affected interests, including those of other states.[37]

From the global perspective, there are, however, accountability problems that pertain to the global regulatory regimes established to ameliorate the effect of domestic regulation.[38] Thus while some such regimes are accountable to national governments through national representatives on such bodies, this is indirect and of limited efficacy. This is, moreover, only applicable to certain global regulatory regimes, and "reconnects each member of the global bodies only to its own national community."[39] The development of precepts of global administrative law is one way of alleviating the accountability problem at the global level, but this must be complemented by recourse to, and reform of, domestic administrative law. This duality has been succinctly captured by Stewart, who notes that global administrative law must ensure that "domestic interests are properly considered in global regulatory decisions and their

[34] *Id.* at 486.

[35] Joanne Scott, *Cooperative Regulation in the WTO: The SPS Committee*, Global Law Working Paper, 3/06, Hauser Global Law School Program-NYU School of Law.

[36] Alfred C. Aman, Jr., The Democracy Deficit, Taming Globalization Through Law Reform 3 (2004)

[37] Stefano Battini, *The Proliferation of Global Regulatory Regimes*, *in* Research Handbook on Global Administrative Law ch. 2 (Sabino Cassese ed., 2015).

[38] Paul Craig, UK, EU and Global Administrative Law: Foundations and Challenges chs. 5–6 (2015).

[39] Battini, *supra* note 37.

domestic implementation, and . . . that global interests are likewise properly considered in domestic administrative decisions."[40]

III. Continuing Engagement

The discussion thus far has been concerned with U.K. constitutional constraints as to initial engagement with treaty regimes. This section considers the constitutional constraints that limit the national applicability of a treaty regime that the United Kingdom has ratified.

Statutory Constraints

Parliament may impose constraints on delegation, which condition the legal reception in U.K. law of changes made by an international organization. This is exemplified by the European Union Act 2011, which introduced a regime of statutory and referendum "locks." It contains far-reaching limits to the acceptance of treaty change and certain other EU decisions within the United Kingdom. There are serious issues concerning the compatibility of the 2011 Act with EU law,[41] although they will be rendered moot when the United Kingdom leaves the European Union pursuant to Brexit.

The Act embodied a regime of referendum and statutory locks. Section 2 dealt with treaty amendment pursuant to the ordinary revision procedure in Article 48(2)–(5) of the Treaty on European Union (TEU), and specified that there must be an Act of Parliament plus a positive vote in a national referendum, unless the exemption condition applies. Section 3 sets the same conditions for treaty change undertaken through the Simplified Revision Procedure in Article 48(6) TEU, unless the exemption or significance condition applies.[42] These statutory provisions related to constitutional constraints on the acceptance of EU treaty amendment in the United Kingdom. The 2011 Act, however, went considerably beyond this. It imposed limits before changes in EU voting rules could be accepted by the United Kingdom, and prevented a minister from approving certain EU decisions without approval via an Act of Parliament.

[40] Richard B. Stewart, *The Global Regulatory Challenge to U.S. Administrative Law*, 37 N.Y.U. J. Int'l L. & Pol'y 695, 750 (2005).

[41] Paul Craig, *The European Union Act 2011: Locks, Limits and Legality*, 48 CML Rev. 1881 (2011).

[42] European Union Act 2011, § 4(1)(i): the conferring on an EU institution or body of power to impose a requirement or obligation on the United Kingdom, or the removal of any limitation on any such power of an EU institution or body; (j) the conferring on an EU institution or body of new or extended power to impose sanctions on the United Kingdom.

The obligation to hold a referendum was determined by Section 4(1), which covered almost every conceivable case of extension of competence and/or conferral of power, and even more so because Section 4(2) states that extension of competence includes the removal of a limitation on a competence.

Common Law Constitutional Constraints

The United Kingdom does not have a written constitution, and there are therefore no written constitutional limits on delegation to international organizations of the kind that exist in other countries. There are, nonetheless, constitutional constraints fashioned by the courts, which can affect the acceptance of rules or decisions made by an international organization, to which the United Kingdom is a party, within the U.K. legal order. This will be more especially so where U.K. courts feel that such a rule of decision can impact adversely on U.K. constitutional identity. This can provoke an interpretive and/or substantive response from U.K. courts.

The courts used interpretive precepts in order to read, for example, EU law in a manner that was consonant with the relevant precept of U.K. constitutional identity. The idea that national courts should, in the spirit of cooperation, read Court of Justice of the European Union (CJEU) judgments so as to avoid an interpretation that conflicted with valued national principles, or that placed in question the identity of the national constitutional order, gained force from Article 4(2) TEU, which was added to the Lisbon Treaty.[43]

The idea that national constitutional identity can be protected, in part, through interpretation is exemplified by the *HS2* case.[44] The Supreme Court held that CJEU judgments should be interpreted, whenever possible, so as to avoid conflict with national law, more especially where that could be serious. This interpretive precept was used when considering whether EU law should be construed so as to require a national court to undertake the kind of in-depth review of the quality of the legislative process that would be problematic from the perspective of U.K. constitutional law. The Supreme Court when developing this reasoning drew on the approach of the *Bundesverfassungsericht*. This was evident in the judgment of Lord Neuberger and Lord Mance.[45] It was apparent once again in the judgment of Lord Reed:

> [I]t appears unlikely that the Court of Justice intended to require national courts to exercise a supervisory jurisdiction over the internal proceedings of national legislatures of the nature for which the appellants contend. There is in addition much to be said for the view, advanced by the German Federal Constitutional Court in its

[43] National Constitutional Identity and European Integration (Alejandro Saiz Arnaiz & Carina Alcoberro Llivina eds., 2013); Elke Cloots, National Identity in EU Law (2015).

[44] R (on the application of HS2 Action Alliance Ltd) v. Secretary of State for Transport [2014] UKSC 3.

[45] *Id.* at [202].

> judgment of 24 April 2013 on the Counter-Terrorism Database Act, 1 BvR 1215/07, para. 91, that as part of a co-operative relationship, a decision of the Court of Justice should not be read by a national court in a way that places in question the identity of the national constitutional order.[46]

There may also be substantive consequences of a finding that a measure from an international organization impacts on U.K. constitutional identity. The Supreme Court in the *HS2* case confirmed that there was a category of constitutional statutes in U.K. law. Lord Neuberger and Lord Mance put the matter in the following way:

> The United Kingdom has no written constitution, but we have a number of constitutional instruments. They include Magna Carta, the Petition of Right 1628, the Bill of Rights and (in Scotland) the Claim of Rights Act 1689, the Act of Settlement 1701 and the Act of Union 1707. The European Communities Act 1972, the Human Rights Act 1998 and the Constitutional Reform Act 2005 may now be added to this list. The common law itself also recognises certain principles as fundamental to the rule of law. It is, putting the point at its lowest, certainly arguable (and it is for United Kingdom law and courts to determine) that there may be fundamental principles, whether contained in other constitutional instruments or recognised at common law, of which Parliament when it enacted the European Communities Act 1972 did not either contemplate or authorise the abrogation.[47]

If the statute is so regarded, then a later Parliament may still choose to amend or repeal it expressly and unequivocally. If, however, there is mere inconsistency, with no express repeal, and nothing to indicate that Parliament intended for the earlier constitutional statute to be amended or repealed, then the U.K. courts will conclude that implied repeal is not applicable in this instance because of the normative importance of the earlier statute.

The consequence of recognition of a statute as capturing part of the United Kingdom's constitutional identity is, therefore, that in the event of a clash between it and a rule or decision flowing from an international organization, such as the European Union, the U.K. courts will not readily accept that the constitutional statute has been impliedly overruled, qualified, or displaced. While it would be difficult to maintain that implied repeal has no application at all in the realm of constitutional statutes,[48] the standard of proof would be very high, along the lines suggested by Laws LJ, who stated that in the absence of express repeal there would have to be words in the later statute "so specific that the inference of an actual determination to effect the result contended for was irresistible."[49]

[46] *Id.* at [111]. [47] *Id.* at [207].

[48] Alison L. Young, Parliamentary Sovereignty and the Human Rights Act ch. 2 (2009).

[49] Thoburn v. Sunderland City Council [2003] QB 151 [63].

Autochthonous Constraints

The preceding discussion should be viewed against the more general backdrop of how national legal orders respond to the legal interaction flowing from membership in international organizations, and more generally from being part of a world where regulatory norms are increasingly globalized. This issue has featured prominently in legal and extralegal discourse, primarily in relation to the legal consequences of U.K. membership in the European Convention on Human Rights (ECHR) and European Union. There are various dimensions to the jurisprudence, but there is nonetheless a discernible theme, which is the judicial desire to assert some degree of independence in the relations between the United Kingdom and other legal orders, consistent with our obligations as signatories of the respective treaties. There is thus an autochthonous strain within U.K. jurisprudence, connoting the descriptive and normative ideal of attachment to indigenous or native values.[50] It stands in counterpoise to themes of globalization, expressive of the desire to maintain some degree of national control.[51]

This can be exemplified by the approach of U.K. courts to membership in the ECHR, which imposes obligations on signatory states to comply with the rights therein. The Supreme Court has, nonetheless, emphasized that the common law should be regarded as the first source in assessing how the demands of membership should be met in a particular case. This was evident in *Osborn*,[52] where the Supreme Court considered whether the Parole Board had breached the ECHR by not providing an oral hearing to three prisoners whose sentences it reviewed.

Lord Reed gave judgment for the Supreme Court. He held that protection of human rights was not a distinct area of the law, based solely on the jurisprudence of the European Court of Human Rights (ECtHR), but permeated the domestic legal system. Compliance with the ECHR should initially be determined through relevant rules of domestic law. This was especially so given that the ECHR rights were set out at a high level of generality. It followed that "the values underlying both the Convention and our own constitution require that Convention rights should be protected primarily by a detailed body of domestic law."[53] The courts could, pursuant to the Human Rights Act 1998, take account of ECHR obligations in the development of the common law and in the interpretation of legislation.

While the importance of the HRA was unquestionable, it did not "however supersede the protection of human rights under the common law or statute, or create a discrete body of law based on the judgments of the European court," with the consequence that "human rights continue to be protected by our domestic law, interpreted and developed in accordance with the Act when appropriate."[54]

[50] Vincent J. Rosivach, *Autochthony and the Athenians*, Classical Quarterly 294 (1987); Peter Geschiere, The Perils of Belonging: Autochthony, Citizenship, and Exclusion in Africa & Europe ch. 1 (2009).

[51] Craig, *supra* note 38, at 271–300.

[52] Osborn v. Parole Board [2013] UKSC 61.

[53] *Id.* at [56].

[54] *Id.* at [57].

The same approach has been adopted in other cases.[55] Lord Reed's approach coheres with the legitimate desire for subsidiarity in application of Convention precepts. It enables U.K. courts to fashion a solution that is consistent with the ECHR, and consistent also with common law traditions in the United Kingdom. Lord Reed acknowledged that if there was an inconsistency between the demands of the ECHR and received common law wisdom, then the latter would have to give way, in accord with the dictates of the Human Rights Act 1998. It does not, however, undermine the value of the methodology in the preceding cases. This is because in most instances the common law will cohere with Convention demands, or can be adapted to do so, and because the Convention requirements can be met in more than one way in accord with ECHR conceptions of subsidiarity.

IV. Disengagement

The legal precepts that govern disengagement from international institutions are, to a certain degree, symmetrical with those that govern initial engagement. The basic starting point is that the executive, acting pursuant to prerogative power, negotiates withdrawal or disengagement from an international organization, and Parliament then enacts or repeals the requisite legislation to make this a legal reality in national law.

Matters can, however, be more complex, as exemplified by the litigation concerning the United Kingdom's exit from the European Union. The exit process is governed by Article 50 TEU, and Article 50(1) TEU stipulates that a state can withdraw in accord with its constitutional requirements. The government argued that it could trigger the beginning of exit through the royal prerogative, and that it did not require statutory approval from Parliament to authorize the start of this process. The question was simple and sharply defined. The answer proved to be more contentious. The litigation process was attended by countless blogs, the case became the most discussed prior to the court's ruling, and the hearing before the Supreme Court was televised. The ensuing analysis is a bare summation of the contending views of the majority and the dissent in *Miller*. The contrasting arguments were considerably more complex. I regard the majority decision as correct and my views can be found in detail elsewhere.[56]

The Supreme Court in *Miller*[57] upheld the Divisional Court,[58] and decided that the government could not trigger Article 50 TEU to begin withdrawing from the European Union without statutory authorization from Parliament. The case concerned structural

[55] A v. BBC [2014] UKSC 25.

[56] Paul Craig, *Miller, Structural Constitutional Review and the Limits of Prerogative Power*, Public Law 48 [2017].

[57] *Miller*, *supra* note 7.

[58] R. (on the application of Miller) v. The Secretary of State for Exiting the European Union [2016] EWHC 2768 (Admin).

constitutional review, in which the Supreme Court demarcated the ambit of legislative and executive power, the latter being exercised through the prerogative. While there is indubitably a prerogative power that covers foreign affairs and treaties, there are also limits to the prerogative: it cannot be used to alter the law of land or affect rights, and it cannot be deployed so as to circumvent a statute that covers the same ground. It was contestation as to the meaning of these precepts that divided the majority and the dissent in *Miller*, and disagreement in this regard also underpinned academic discourse.

The first limit on the prerogative power is that it cannot alter the law of the land, or effect rights, a proposition derived from the *Case of Proclamations*. It concerned the legality of two proclamations made by the king: one prohibited new buildings in London, the other the making of starch from wheat. The court held that the king cannot by his proclamation change "any part of the common law, or statute law or customs of the realm."[59] Nor could the king create any new offence by way of proclamation, for that would be to change the law. It was, moreover, for the courts to determine the existence and extent of prerogative powers. These principles were reinforced by the Bill of Rights 1688, which provided that "the pretended power of suspending of laws or the execution of laws by regall authority without consent of Parlyament is illegall"[60] and that "the pretended power of dispensing with laws or the execution of laws by regall authoritie as it hath beene assumed and exercised of late is illegall."[61]

The application of the principle from *Proclamations* in *Miller* raised difficult issues concerning the meaning of "the law" that could not be changed through the prerogative, and the nature of the rights that could not be affected by use of the prerogative. The majority of the Supreme Court regarded EU law as a novel source of law within the U.K. legal order.[62] EU law, and the rights emanating from it, was therefore part of the law of the land that could not be altered through recourse to the prerogative. The majority acknowledged that the EU rights brought into U.K. law through the European Communities Act (ECA 1972) could vary from time to time, and that this would cease when the United Kingdom withdrew from the European Union. This did not, however, mean that withdrawal, with the consequential impact on rights, could be done through the prerogative without Parliamentary authorization. There was, said the majority, no indication that Parliament intended this. There was a vital difference between changes in domestic law resulting from variations in EU law arising from new EU legislation, and changes in domestic law resulting from withdrawal by the United Kingdom from the European Union.[63]

The principal dissent was by Lord Reed, who held that the prerogative over the making and unmaking of treaties was a fundamental part of the U.K. constitutional

[59] 12 Co. Rep. 74 at 75 (1611).

[60] Bill of Rights 1688, 1 Will. and Mar. Sess. 2, c. 2, art. 1.

[61] Bill of Rights 1688, 1 Will. and Mar. Sess. 2, c. 2, art. 2; Sir Stephen Sedley, *The Judges' Verdicts*, *available at* https://www.lrb.co.uk/2017/01/30/stephen-sedley/the-judges-verdicts.

[62] Miller, *supra* note 7, at [65].

[63] *Id.* at [76]–[78], [83].

order, which could only be curtailed expressly or by necessary implication. The ECA 1972 contained no express limitation on the Crown's prerogative power, nor were there any words through which to infer that this was the necessary implication of the statute.[64] Lord Reed denied that triggering Article 50 TEU would impact on rights. Parliament had, he said, recognized in the ECA 1972, Section 2(1), that rights given effect under the ECA could be altered or revoked from time to time without the need for a statute, and he rejected the distinction drawn by the majority between such changes in rights and that resulting from withdrawal from the European Union.

The second constraint on the prerogative power is that it cannot be exercised if a statute covers the same area. The seminal case was *Attorney General v. De Keyser's Royal Hotel*,[65] which arose out of the Crown's decision, acting under the Defence of the Realm Regulations, to take possession of a hotel to accommodate personnel of the Royal Flying Corps. The Crown contended that the hotel owners had no legal right to compensation. The Defence Act 1842 gave broad powers to the Crown to take possession of land, subject to compensation. The Crown maintained that the taking was, however, justified by the prerogative, which was said to warrant temporary seizure of property in time of emergency, without any legal right to compensation.

Their Lordships were unpersuaded by the argument. Lord Atkinson held that it would be absurd to construe a statute so as to enable the executive to disregard limits contained therein by reliance on the prerogative. Lord Parmoor was equally clear in this respect: when executive power had been directly regulated by statute, the executive could no longer use the prerogative, but had to observe the restrictions that Parliament imposed in favor of the subject.[66]

The decision in *Miller* did not turn on application of the *De Keyser* principle as such, but the Supreme Court nonetheless said some important things about it. The majority accepted the principle from *De Keyser*, and its application in subsequent cases. It held, moreover, that it was highly improbable that Parliament had the intention that ministers could subsequently take the United Kingdom out of the European Union without the approval of the constitutionally senior partner, which was Parliament.[67] If that had been the intent it was, in accord with the principle of legality, incumbent on Parliament to have made this clear, and thus pay the political cost of the choice. There was, said the majority, no evidence that the ECA 1972 was intended to clothe the executive with that far-reaching choice.[68]

Lord Reed also accepted the principle in *De Keyser*, but did not believe that it was applicable to this case. It was central to *De Keyser* that Parliament had regulated the area in relation to which the executive sought to exercise the prerogative. This was not so here. The 1972 Act did not regulate withdrawal from the European Union. It merely recognized the existence of Article 50 TEU, but said nothing as to who should take the decision to invoke Article 50.[69]

64 *Id.* at [160], [177], [194], [197].

65 Attorney General v. De Keyser's Royal Hotel [1920] AC 508.

66 *Id.* at 575.

67 Miller, *supra* note 7, at [85]–[90].

68 *Id.* at [87]–[88].

69 *Id.* at [233].

It is important not to lose sight of the value that underpins the twin constraints on prerogative power in *Proclamations* and *De Keyser*, which is the sovereignty of Parliament. It is Parliament that is the legitimate legislator within the United Kingdom, and the limits on prerogative power protect that authority from being undermined. If the executive could change the law of its own volition, it could thereby bypass legislation without the need for amendment and repeal, hence the principle in *Proclamations*. If the executive could use the prerogative where Parliament had already addressed the issue in a statute it could then avoid the legislation crafted by Parliament, hence the principle in *De Keyser*, and its extension to cases where the prerogative would frustrate the legislation. *Proclamations* protects Parliamentary sovereignty directly, by preventing recourse to the prerogative where it would change the law; *De Keyser* protects sovereignty indirectly, by precluding use of the prerogative where the formal law is left intact, but the executive seeks to circumvent it by use of the prerogative.

It is also important not to lose sight of the value underlying the prerogative power over treaties, which was identified by William Blackstone:

> This is wisely placed in a single hand by the British constitution, for the sake of unanimity, strength, and despatch. Were it placed in many hands, it would be subject to many wills, if disunited and drawing different ways, create weakness in a government; and to unite those several wills, and reduce them to one, is a work of more time and delay than the exigencies of state will afford.[70]

For Lord Reed, "the value of unanimity, strength and dispatch in the conduct of foreign affairs are as evident in the 21st century as they were in the 18th,"[71] and Timothy Endicott voiced strong views to the same effect.[72] It can be readily acknowledged that unanimity, strength, and dispatch are important values in the conduct of international relations. It is accepted that the executive has primary responsibility for negotiation of treaties, which cannot be done in a collective.

The reality was, however, that the rationale for according the executive prerogative power over treaty making had scant if any relevance to the issue in *Miller*, which was whether Parliament should have to give statutory approval before triggering Article 50 TEU. It is not self-evident that unanimity, strength, or dispatch should be regarded as the principal values in this determination; it is not self-evident that the executive has advantages in making this decision over Parliament; and it is not self-evident that the executive values would be placed in jeopardy by requiring a vote in Parliament. Consider these issues in turn.

The decision to trigger Article 50 and leave the European Union ranks among the most significant peacetime treaty determinations ever made by the United Kingdom.

[70] Sir William Blackstone, Commentaries on the Laws of England, Bk. 1, ch. 7 (1765–1769) ("Of the King's Prerogative").

[71] Miller, *supra* note 7, at [160].

[72] Timothy Endicott, "*This Ancient, Secretive Royal Prerogative*," UK Const. L. Blog, Nov. 11, 2016, *available at* https://ukconstitutionallaw.org/.

It is an issue on which the country was fiercely divided, notwithstanding the referendum. The U.K. constitutional tradition is one of parliamentary as opposed to popular sovereignty, which is why the referendum was not legally binding, although it was clearly important in political terms. The values that matter here are those that are fundamental to a parliamentary democracy—in particular that major decisions are not made without approval by Parliament.

It is not self-evident that the executive would have any advantages over Parliament when making this determination. The executive may claim epistemic advantages and experience in relation to some aspects of foreign policy. The reality is that such advantages were not relevant to the current determination, or to analogous decisions of this nature. MPs knew the issues concerning EU membership as well as the executive.

Nor is it self-evident that requiring a vote in Parliament placed the executive's strategy for triggering Article 50 TEU in jeopardy. To the contrary, the date chosen by the executive, the end of March, had no special magic; it was not jeopardized by the parliamentary vote, which was accomplished in a matter of weeks; and if the government had not contested the issue in litigation, parliamentary approval would have been secured earlier.

V. Conclusion

It is readily apparent that every legal system will determine the legal rules that govern engagement and disengagement with international organizations. There will, in addition, commonly be legal rules or principles that govern continuing engagement with such organizations. It is, moreover, axiomatic that the legal rules will reflect deeper values concerning the relationship between the legislature and the executive in the national polity, embodying assumptions as to the legitimate locus of power for the making of certain decisions. The legal rules also reflect values as to the relationship between that national polity and the international organization that it has joined. The constraints on continuing engagement speak to the limits of consent through initial engagement, combined with the dynamic nature of treaty interpretation. They serve thereby to protect the national legal order from claims made by the international organization that are felt to have no warrant in the treaty, or are felt to infringe fundamental national values that could not, from a national constitutional perspective, be given up.[73]

[73] *See, e.g.*, the jurisprudence of the *Bundesverfassungsgericht* concerning the limits of EU law, discussed in Paul Craig & Gráinne de Búrca, EU Law: Text, Cases, and Materials ch. 9 (6th ed. 2015).

CHAPTER 23

INTERNATIONAL INTEGRATION AND ITS COUNTER-LIMITS

A German Constitutional Perspective

ANDREAS L. PAULUS
AND JAN-HENRIK HINSELMANN

THE German Constitution (*Grundgesetz*, hereinafter "Basic Law") is "inspired by the determination to promote world peace as an equal partner in a united Europe."[1] While euphoria in preambles is common, its materialization in the operative part is not necessarily so. The Basic Law specifically regulates and mandates international engagement. In this way, it accommodates the pluralist international legal landscape, in which domestic constitutional orders are embedded. In practice, this constitutional configuration is complemented by a strong role of the Federal Constitutional Court (*Bundesverfassungsgericht*), which exercises judicial control over the constitutional mandate for international integration and its limits.

I. Engaging with International Institutions under German Constitutional Law

Under the Basic Law, constitutional readiness to engage with international institutions stems from an integration-friendly attitude that nevertheless accommodates popular sovereignty and rests upon distinct constitutional foundations.

[1] GRUNDGESETZ [Basic Law] [GG] Preamble (Christian Tomuschat et al. trans., 2014) (Aug. 15, 2018), *available at* https://www.gesetze-im-internet.de/englisch_gg/index.html. For an overview of the German Constitution, *see* WERNER HEUN, THE CONSTITUTION OF GERMANY—A CONTEXTUAL ANALYSIS (2010).

The Concept of "Open Statehood"

The integration-friendly normative environment under the German Basic Law is commonly conceptualized as "Open Statehood" (*Offene Staatlichkeit*).[2] Open Statehood manifests an early constitutional recognition of international interdependence. The framers of the Basic Law made a conscious decision in 1949 to mandate international engagement. Whereas such constitutional readiness to international engagement finds some of its roots in concepts of the interwar period, much of the Basic Law is to be viewed as an antithesis to the totalitarian abyss of the following time.[3]

Besides idealistic recalibration, Open Statehood also manifests practical considerations. International integration provided a natural escape for an occupied and morally, as much as financially, bankrupt state, which, as an enemy state, had been sidelined by the newly institutionalized international community. Open Statehood promised the end of occupation and integration into the Western world (*Westbindung*) as well as a perspective to end the German division into two states in opposed military alliances. Likewise, international law promised to serve as a means of recovery through economic integration.

As a doctrinal concept, Open Statehood is not explicitly mentioned within the Basic Law. Yet, constitutional jurisprudence developed from it other relevant doctrines, most prominently the friendliness toward international law (*Völkerrechtsfreundlichkeit*) and the friendliness toward European law (*Europarechtsfreundlichkeit*),[4] which serve as interpretative rules to avoid collision between international and domestic law. Ultimately, Open Statehood requires taking into account international law to the extent that it supersedes, reshapes, or influences the interpretation and application of the Basic Law.

Sovereignty and International Integration

Open Statehood seeks to overcome the supposed dichotomy between state sovereignty and international integration. To fulfill the constitutional mandate for international cooperation and European integration, the Basic Law partially renounces the claim to

[2] Initially coined by Klaus Vogel, Die Verfassungsentscheidung des Grundgesetzes für eine internationale Zusammenarbeit 42–44 (1964). *See also* Udo Di Fabio, Das Recht offener Staaten (1998). Compare the recent decision of the German Federal Constitutional Court, ECLI:DE:BVerfG:2018:rs20180724.2bvr196109 – European Schools, [2018] para. 28. For translation of selected judgments since 1998, *see* http://www.bundesverfassungsgericht.de/en. The sole authoritative versions are the German originals.

[3] 124 Decisions of the German Federal Constitutional Court [hereinafter BVerfGE] 300—Wunsiedel [2009] headnote 1, paras. 64–65.

[4] The German terms "Völkerrechts-" and "Europarechts*freundlichkeit*" are often translated as "openness" toward international or European law. However, this translation comes at the cost of obscuring the distinctly sympathetic undertone of the term "friendliness."

the exclusivity of national self-government. Open Statehood in that way prominently allowed Germany, as the strongest European economy, to take an active part in the establishment of the European (Economic) Community. It shows how the "pooling" of domestic resources may result not in a loss, but in a (re-)gain of democratic decision-making power over the (economic) forces of globalization. Law provides the means as well as the limits of such functional "Integration Through Law."[5]

Skepticism persists, however. In its judgments regarding the Maastricht and Lisbon treaties establishing the European Union, the Federal Constitutional Court rejected the idea of a complete transfer of domestic democracy onto a supranational body, in spite of the common value system embraced by the Union, because it lacked the required democratic legitimacy, in particular a common public opinion.[6] Even critics of this jurisprudence[7] will agree that the mere establishment of a supranational parliament alone does not suffice for multilevel democracy, and that deliberation is a component of, but not a substitute for, democratic *decision*-making.[8]

However, the supposed choice between national democracy and international legality establishes a false dichotomy. Hardly any constitution admits of the direct applicability of international norms without a process of legislative and/or executive review. Rather, in most countries, important agreements—in particular multilateral, quasi lawmaking treaties—require the consent of both the executive and legislative branches. This is the case in Germany with regard to so-called highly political treaties as well as treaties with direct applicability in the domestic legal system (Art. 59(2) Basic Law).[9] It is the domestic legal order that ultimately determines if international commitments are undertaken and how they are implemented.

Regulation by international institutions thus appears acceptable to democratic states when it meets at least two conditions: representation and subsidiarity.[10] In general, contemporary international law and institutions meet these criteria, with the latter being more problematic than the former. It appears as true as ever that international engagement is an expression of, and not a contradiction to, sovereignty.[11] However, subsidiarity often lies in the eye of the beholder. It is difficult to implement against the

[5] *Cf.* MAURO CAPPELLETTI ET AL., INTEGRATION THROUGH LAW (1986).

[6] 89 BVERFGE 155—Maastricht/Brunner in: [1994] 1 CMLR 57, paras. 41–45; 123 BVERFGE 267—Lisbon Treaty [2009], para. 251.

[7] *See* JOSEPH H. WEILER, CONSTITUTION OF EUROPE 345 (1999); *cf.* Samantha Besson, *Institutionalizing Global Demoi-cracy, in* INTERNATIONAL LAW, JUSTICE AND LEGITIMACY 58 (Lukas H. Meyer ed., 2009) (embracing a pluralist theory of multiple *demoi*).

[8] BVerfG, Lisbon Treaty, *supra* note 6, para. 272.

[9] For further analysis, *see* Stefan Kadelbach, *International Treaties and the German Constitution*, ch. 10 in this volume.

[10] Andreas L. Paulus, *Subsidiarity, Fragmentation and Democracy: Towards the Demise of General International Law?, in* THE ALLOCATION OF AUTHORITY IN INTERNATIONAL LAW 193–213 (Tomer Broude & Yuval Shany eds., 2008).

[11] PCIJ, The SS Wimbledon, United Kingdom v. Germany, [1923] PCIJ Series A no. 1, ICGJ 235, at 25.

political will of the executive branch and tends to exclude the legislature and substate entities.[12] Disobedience is thus far too often the real control that member states—and occasionally regional courts—exercise with regard to international regulation that they deem beyond the transferred powers or simply materially or politically too costly.

Article 24(1) Basic Law—From Delegation to Integration

The basic provision of the Basic Law regulating the engagement with international institutions is found in its Article 24(1). Its genesis was inspired by the French as well as the Italian constitutions of the time,[13] and the provision eventually was labeled, in more figurative fashion, as "lever of integration" (*Integrationshebel*[14]), or simply as "hinge provision" (*Scharniernorm*[15]). What distinguishes treaties under Article 24(1) from those exclusively based on the treaty-making provision of Article 59[16] is that Article 24(1) allows for the integration of secondary laws, subsequently made by the international body, into the domestic legal sphere. Integration thus goes considerably beyond the mere incorporation of self-executing treaties where only the provisions of the treaty itself are directly applied within domestic law.[17]

The text of Article 24(1) of the Basic Law provides: "The Federation may by a law transfer sovereign powers to international organizations."[18] This provision is susceptible to specification through state practice and legal doctrine. In the first place, Article 24(1) grants German public authority wide discretion as to whether or not to engage with an international institution, on the timing and the scope of its engagement,

[12] Thus, in the European Union, the principles of "conferral" (e.g., enumerated powers) and subsidiarity are enshrined in Article 5(1) TEU but difficult to implement partly because their judicial control is entrusted to a Court (art. 19 TEU) that regards itself as a pillar of the Union rather than an institution balancing community and member states' rights. For the ECHR, compare the theory of the domestic "margin of appreciation." CETS 213—Convention for the Protection of Human Rights (Protocol No. 15), 24.VI.2013, art. 1.

[13] Section 15 of the 1946 Preamble of the French Constitution; Article 11 of the Italian Constitution. Other European constitutions contain similar provisions, *see* HANDBUCH IUS PUBLICUM EUROPAEUM II Chapters 14–26 (Armin von Bogdandy et al. eds., 2008). For further analysis, *see* MATTIAS WENDEL, PERMEABILITÄT IM EUROPÄISCHEN VERFASSUNGSRECHT 144–164 (2011).

[14] HANS PETER IPSEN, EUROPÄISCHES GEMEINSCHAFTSRECHT 58 (1972).

[15] For further analysis of both the domestic and international "opening clauses," *see* Andreas L. Paulus, *Zusammenspiel der Rechtsquellen aus völkerrechtlicher Perspektive*, 46 BERICHTE DER DEUTSCHEN GESELLSCHAFT FÜR INTERNATIONALES RECHT, INTERNATIONALES, NATIONALES UND PRIVATES RECHT: HYBRIDISIERUNG DER RECHTSORDNUNGEN—IMMUNITÄT (2014) [including English summary].

[16] For further analysis, *see* Kadelbach, *supra* note 9.

[17] Note how the ambit of Article 24(1) thus excludes, for instance, the kind of "transnational organizations" with *de facto*, but not *de jure*, impact (ISO, IEC, ISAB, ICANN, etc.) referred to by Paul Craig, *Engagement and Disengagement with International Institutions: The U.K. Perspective*, ch. 22 in this volume.

[18] Original: "Der *Bund* kann durch Gesetz Hoheitsrechte auf zwischenstaatliche Einrichtungen übertragen."

and on its participation in the decision-making process of the receiving organization.[19] For "delegation," Article 24(1) uses the language of "*trans*fer" of sovereign powers to international institutions (*übertragen*). This term must not be understood in a literal sense, but rather is to be interpreted as "to *con*fer," in the sense that the member states jointly establish a new organization with its own powers and competences with direct effect in the domestic legal order.[20]

Delegating sovereign rights under the Basic Law, as a specific form of international engagement, is most aptly understood as a process that is procedurally uniform, but materially multipart: The first part of that process establishes the international institution with corresponding authoritative competences. The second part consists in the "opening" of the German legal order to the regulatory acts of the institution, allowing them to have direct effect. Correspondingly, the Federal Constitutional Court understands the delegation less as a transfer of jurisdiction than as the suspension of the state's claim to regulatory exclusivity within the ambit of the Constitution, in order to give way to the direct effect of regulations issued by the international institution.[21]

Figuratively speaking, Article 24(1) voices constitutional consent to opening the "armor of sovereignty"[22] to international regulation. In that sense, delegation of national competences presents itself as *integration* of supranational regulation based on *conferred* competences. This result fits in the overarching concept of Open Statehood. Open Statehood signals readiness to international engagement: it issues a standing invitation, it holds an option, and it expresses an intention, but it does not completely subordinate the German legal order to international law. Rather, it makes a reservation to domestically control the scope of its binding effect.[23]

Such doctrinal construction allows the exercise of non-German legal authority to be held against the yardstick of the German legal order (see discussion in Section II below). The construction allows for the attachment of conditions to the recognition of the direct effect of international regulation. Absent permission, the domestic legal order "snaps back" into the default mode reclaiming regulatory exclusivity. In that way, the inherent tension between retaining sovereignty and enabling international regulation can be moderated.

International and European Integration: From Unity via Divergence to Convergence?

The Basic Law contains a two-tiered structure when it comes to engagement with international institutions, depending on whether engagement occurs with genuinely

[19] 58 BVERFGE 1, 28—Eurocontrol I [1981], summary in English language in: [1983] CMLR 20: 87–95.

[20] *Cf.* art. 1(1) TEU. For a comprehensive analysis of similar European constitutional conceptions, *see* WENDEL, *supra* note 13, at 163–196.

[21] 37 BVERFGE 271, 280—Solange I [1974].

[22] Albert Bleckmann, *Zur Funktion des Art. 24 Abs. 1 Grundgesetz*, 35 ZAÖRV 79, 81 (1975).

[23] 141 BVERFGE 1—Treaty Override [2016], para. 69.

international institutions (Art. 24(1)) or with the European Union (Art. 23). Both provisions apply to instances of supranational institutions. But Article 23 (the "Europe-Article"), introduced together with the approval of the Maastricht treaty in 1992, applies as *lex specialis* to Article 24(1) in all matters pertaining to the European Union, including those not formally part of its legal regime.[24] Article 23 has built on Article 24(1) but also contains both substantial limits to integration and provisions for the participation of the national legislature and the Federal Council composed of representatives of the federal units, the *Länder*, in decision-making on the European level, thus modifying the traditional executive prerogative in international affairs.

By constitutionalizing the goal of a united Europe, Article 23 has, at least in principle, also approved of the specific integrating features of European law that makes it a legal order of special characteristics, namely, its supremacy[25] (rather, in the language of the German Federal Constitutional Court, precedence[26]) and its direct effect.[27] Direct effect means that European primary and secondary law needs implementing legislation only if it explicitly says so (as in the directives, Art. 288, subparagraph 3 Treaty on the Functioning of the European Union (TFEU)), turning the exception in international law into a rule; precedence renders contrary national law, including constitutional law, not invalid, but *inapplicable*,[28] albeit only within the EU sphere of competences.

In principle, the substantive and procedural safeguards of parliamentary democracy and federalism contained in Article 23, in particular the requirement of a two-thirds majority for the transfer of most if not all competences, are not limited to European integration. Indeed, the German Federal Constitutional Court has extended its application to the European Stability Mechanism (ESM) in spite of its basis in an international treaty separate from EU law.[29] Those international institutions exhibit a great institutional and material proximity to the European Union and its normative framework. This legal grey zone is referred to as (intergovernmental) European International Law,[30] as opposed to regular (supranational) EU law.

A similar pattern of convergence emerges with a view to specific forms of judicial review ("counter-limits," discussed in Section II below) developed originally in the context of the European Union then regulated by Article 24(1) that is now reflected in

[24] 135 BVerfGE 317—European Stability Mechanism (Judgment) [2014], para. 232.

[25] Case 6/64 Costa v. ENEL [1964] ECR 1251; Case 11/70 Internationale Handelsgesellschaft [1970] ECR 1125; Case 106/77 *Simmenthal* [1978] ECR 629; Declaration No. 17 to the Lisbon Treaty, OJ C 115, 9 May 2008, pp. 344–344.

[26] *Cf.* Peter M. Huber & Andreas L. Paulus, *Cooperation of Constitutional Courts in Europe*, *in* Courts and Comparative Law 281, 286–287 (Mads Andenæs & Duncan Fairgrieve eds., 2015).

[27] *Cf.* European Court of Justice, Case 26/62 van Gend & Loos [1963].

[28] 129 BVerfGE 78—Le Corbusier [2011], paras. 81; 126 BVerfGE 286—Honeywell [2010], paras. 53–55; BVerfG, Lisbon Treaty, *supra* note 6, paras. 335–339 ("primacy of application").

[29] 132 BVerfGE 195—European Stability Mechanism (Preliminary Reference) [2012], para. 182. In the long run, both institutions are to be integrated into European Union law. *Cf.* art. 16 of the Treaty on Stability, Coordination and Governance in the Economic and Monetary Union [2012].

[30] Christian Calliess, *Art. 24 Abs. 1*, *in* Grundgesetz-Kommentar, para. 216 (Theodor Maunz & Günter Dürig eds., 2018).

Article 23. These counter-limits can be applied *mutatis mutandis* also in the ambit of Article 24(1) to international institutions other than the European Union.[31]

Constitutional Competence and Separation of Powers

Constitutional provisions on the foreign affairs of the Federal Republic are dispersed throughout the text of the Basic Law. The federal state's competences, instruments, concepts, and norms in the area of foreign affairs are subsumed under the heading of "foreign affairs power" (*auswärtige Gewalt*), and they are said to be exercised in common by the executive and legislative branches (*Gesamthand*).[32] To put it pointedly, the competence in the area of foreign relations resides with all of the constitutional organs within the parliamentary system of government—with some executive prerogative, however, at least in the original conception.

In the years of German division, the Federal Constitutional Court emphasized executive control, to the point where it opposed an identification of democracy with "parliamentary monism."[33] Rather, it was to be recognized how the executive was uniquely equipped to adequately address foreign relations.[34] The case law is reminiscent of the parallel argument of the U.S. Supreme Court in *Curtiss-Wright*.[35]

Today, more caution seems warranted, as the so-called "essentiality" (*Wesentlichkeit*) doctrine of the separation of powers that requires parliamentary approval by legislation for all "essential" decisions ("legislative reservation"), in particular those affecting individual rights,[36] has spilled over into foreign affairs. This is most visible in the requirement of parliamentary approval for military operations abroad,[37] which the Court first derived from a—quite original—reading of German constitutional history,[38] but has now—correctly—anchored in the essentiality doctrine, whether based on the risk to the existential rights of individual soldiers or on the political importance of foreign entanglements.[39] In sum, the *Bundestag* as legislature is developing more and more into a coequal branch in foreign affairs.[40]

[31] BVerfG, European Schools, *supra* note 2, paras. 27–32.

[32] *Cf.* Ernst Friesenhahn, *Parlament und Regierung, in* 16 VVDStRL 38 (1957).

[33] 68 BVerfGE 1, 86–87—Pershing 2 and Cruise Missile II [1984].

[34] *Id.* at 87; (Mahrenholz, E. G., dissenting, 111–132); 143 BVerfGE 101—NSA Selectors List [2016], paras. 129–136.

[35] United States v. Curtiss-Wright Export Corp., 299 U.S. 304 (1936). *Cf.* Curtis A. Bradley, *What Is Foreign Relations Law?*, ch. 1 in this volume.

[36] 49 BVerfGE 89, 126–127—Kalkar I [1978]. The doctrine is rooted in the both the principle of democracy and the principle of *Rechtsstaat*. *Cf.* Kadelbach, *supra* note 9.

[37] For analysis in greater detail, *see* Anne Peters, *Military Operations Abroad under the German Basic Law*, ch. 44 in this volume.

[38] 90 BVerfGE 286, 381—AWACS/Somalia [1994].

[39] 121 BVerfGE 135—AWACS II [2008], para. 71. In this regard, the U.S. Supreme Court displays greater reticence, *see* Paul B. Stephan, *Constitutionalism and Internationalism: U.S. Participation in International Institutions*, ch. 21 in this volume.

[40] For the United Kingdom, *see* Craig, *supra* note 17.

Drawing on these considerations of "essentiality," the Basic Law also addresses the general problem of predictability of dynamics of international institutions. The original conception of an international treaty as intended by its parties—and also the legislator when consenting to its ratification or approval under Article 24(1)—gives way to new secondary acts often not contemplated at the origins. Taking up a term coined by Georg Ress, this constellation is commonly referred to as "treaty on wheels" (*Vertrag auf Rädern*[41]). The legislature can only wave in the train station at the founding. Thus, the requirement of legislative consent merely to the founding treaty often proves ineffective in limiting the future institutional practice of international organizations. Hence, with regard to the European Union, the Federal Constitutional Court has established the "responsibility for integration" that is shared among all branches of government,[42] and the following case law emphasizes the need for parliamentary approval in particular with regard to huge monetary and financial decisions by EU organs, in particular in the framework of the European Monetary Union.[43]

Responsibility for integration is meant to ensure an appropriate role for parliament in the domestic process of developing the program of integration against the backdrop of prevailing executive lawmaking (*Exekutivföderalismus*). The Court has gone on to emphasize another dimension of responsibility for integration, according to which the legislature, if need be, must be enabled to exercise effective control over the limits of whatever program of integration it initially approved.[44] The concept's practical merits, however, remain disputed,[45] and so does the de facto status of the *Bundestag* as a truly coequal branch.

Procedural Limits

Article 24(1) of the Basic Law requires an ordinary federal statute (*durch Gesetz*). Such delegating act (*Übertragungsgesetz*) has to be one of parliament itself. The article does not contain further procedural requirements. But the delegating act refers to an international commitment in the form of an international treaty, and that delegation must sufficiently specify the competences to be conferred.[46] If this is not the case,

[41] Georg Ress, *Verfassungsrechtliche Auswirkungen der Fortentwicklung völkerrechtlicher Verträge*, *in* 2 Festschrift Zeidler 1779 (1987).

[42] BVerfG, Lisbon Treaty, *supra* note 6, headnotes 2 lit. a, 2 lit. b, paras. 236–251. In case of the United Kingdom, the European Union Act 2011 serves similar functions. For further analysis, *see* Craig, *supra* note 17.

[43] BVerfG, European Stability Mechanism (Judgment), *supra* note 24, paras. 159–160, 165, 194–212, 223–242; 142 BVerfGE 123—OMT (Judgment) [2016], paras. 163–173.

[44] BVerfG, OMT (Judgment), *id.*, para. 165.

[45] Michael Tischendorf, Theorie und Wirklichkeit der Integrationsverantwortung Deutscher Verfassungsorgane (2016).

[46] BVerfG, Pershing 2 and Cruise Missile II, *supra* note 33, paras. 98–100; Maastricht/Brunner, *supra* note 6, paras. 52, 71.

Germany must reserve a veto power, and the vote of the German member in the international body must follow parliamentary guidance.[47]

In effect, formal delegation of competences onto an international institution amounts not to a formal but to a material amendment of the constitutional order.[48] Such assumption bears the risk of creating a significant procedural hurdle for integration, because constitutional amendments require a two-thirds majority in not only the *Bundestag* but also the Federal Council representing the *Länder* in the federation, the *Bundesrat*.[49] Constitutional practice sticks closely to the text of Article 24(1), ultimately allowing for greater political flexibility, the precise limits of which are controversial.[50] The parallelism to Article 23(1), sentence 3 militates for the requirement of a constitutional amendment for every transfer of competences, albeit without some of the usual requirements such as the explicit citation of the affected constitutional rights. Others regard Article 24(1) as enabling a conferral by regular statutory law.[51] At least those core constitutional principles set out by Articles 79(3) and 23(1), which are not subject to revision, e.g., human dignity, democracy, the rule of law, subsidiarity, and federalism, also constitute an absolute bar to contrary international obligations. But note that these categories are broad, and thus leave much leeway for interpretation.

II. Disengaging from International Institutions

From the perspective of democratic governance, delegation of sovereign competences onto international institutions must, in principle, be revocable.[52] Otherwise, international law could prevent democratic change and overturn the result of democratic elections. International integration is well advised to respect the democratic will of member state constituents. Is it really imaginable that an organization integrating democratic member states would simply ignore a popular referendum repudiating membership?

On the other hand, many international obligations do not explicitly allow for revocation or are even expressly designed to be permanent. Article 46 of the Vienna Convention on the Law of Treaties (VCLT) does not, in general, accept the invocation

[47] BVerfG, Lisbon Treaty, *supra* note 6, para. 320 (in the context of the European Union).

[48] Amendment is assumed because of derogation from the constitutional division of competences. *See* BVerfG, Eurocontrol I, *supra* note 19, at 36.

[49] Art. 79(2) Basic Law.

[50] For critique, *see* Frank Schorkopf, Staatsrecht der Internationalen Beziehungen § 2 paras. 147–149 (2017).

[51] Georg Erler, 18 VVDStRL 7, 19 (1960); *see* Vogel, *supra* note 2, at 5–7; Christian Tomuschat, *Art. 24*, para. 34, *in* Bonner Kommentar zum Grundgesetz (Wolfgang Kahl et al. eds., 2018).

[52] With a view to the European Union, *see* BVerfG, Maastricht/Brunner, *supra* note 6, para. 55; BVerfG, Lisbon Treaty, *supra* note 6, para. 233.

of domestic grounds for the invalidation of treaties for which treaty law requires special reasons (Arts. 46–53 VCLT), as well as for termination or suspension (Arts. 54–64 VCLT). This apparent contradiction can be resolved by interpretation—the Vienna Convention contemplates the possibility of an implied right of denunciation by the intention of the parties or the nature of a treaty (Art. 56(1) VCLT), and also accepts, in exceptional situations, termination because of a fundamental change of circumstances.[53] The German Federal Constitutional Court has closed the remaining gap by pointing to two devices: on the one hand, it has referred to the possibility of using the just mentioned international law means for termination of a treaty;[54] on the other, it has allowed the national legislature, under narrow conditions, to override the implementation of treaty commitments in domestic law.[55] While the first solution does not suffice when international law does not permit such termination and, in principle, falls under the executive prerogative, the latter may result in a violation of international law and thus trigger the international responsibility of Germany.

Until the recent past, disengaging from international institutions was not a major concern meriting a separate subchapter in a handbook on international institutions. The current backlash against globalization and the special case of "Brexit" of the United Kingdom from the European Union[56] have revealed that such "disentanglement"[57] is fraught not only with enormous practical but also legal problems.[58] Contemporary international law does not involve only rights and duties of states but also those of individuals. These rights cannot simply be taken away and need to be protected both by as well as against international institutions.[59] Recent practice has shown that the emphasis is moving away from the executive privilege of terminating treaties of integration toward a strengthened role for parliaments and a certain involvement of the judicial branch that has developed brakes known as "counter-limits" to the overreach of international institutions.

[53] Art. 62 VCLT. *But see* the narrow interpretation advanced in *Gabčíkovo-Nagymaros Project (Hungary/Slovakia)* [1997], ICJ Rep. 1997, 7, para. 104.

[54] BVerfG, European Stability Mechanism (Preliminary Reference), *supra* note 29, para. 215.

[55] BVerfG, Treaty Override, *supra* note 23.

[56] *See*, in particular, art. 50 TEU on exiting the European Union as well as Miller v. UK [2016] UKSC 5, [2016] EWHC 2768 (Admin), [2016] NIQB 85.

[57] *Cf.* George Washington, *The Address of General Washington To The People of The United States on his Declining of the Presidency of the United States, in* David C. Claypoole's American Daily Advertiser on 19 September 1796.

[58] For a "typology of treaty exit conflicts in international and domestic law," *see* Laurence R. Helfer, *Treaty Exit and Intrabranch Conflict at the Interface of International and Domestic Law*, ch. 20 in this volume.

[59] *See*, in particular, Bosphorus v. Ireland [GC], no. 45036/98, Eur. Ct. H.R. 2005, paras. 149–157; Avontiņš v. Latvia [GC], no. 17502/07, Eur. Ct. H.R. 2016, paras. 101–127; Charter of Fundamental Rights of the European Union of 12 December 2007, OJ C 303 p 1, art. 51(1). With regard to the United Nations, the protection is more limited. *But see* Anne Peters, *Article 25, in* The Charter of the United Nations paras. 172–174 (Bruno Simma et al. eds., 3d ed. 2012); *see also* Andreas L. Paulus & Johann Leiss, *Article 103, in* The Charter of the United Nations, *supra*, at paras. 37–65, 71–73.

Disengaging as Executive Privilege—Between Competence and Practice

Traditionally, the act of revocation, at least with a view to disengagement from international treaties, falls under executive privilege. The legislature does not enjoy constitutional authority to repudiate international treaties made by the executive.[60] In accordance with Article 59(2), legislative approval is only required for the *conclusion* of treaties concerning "high politics" and self-executing treaties with legislative content. Crucially the wording encompasses engagement, but not disengagement.[61] Such narrow construction may be due to practical considerations such as the necessity to accommodate short-term changes in foreign relations,[62] but it is also due to the hitherto rarity of unilateral termination of treaty obligations.[63]

While constitutional jurisprudence seems consistent and unequivocal, the higher the stakes the more the support for executive privilege wanes. More specifically, this shift occurs when disengagement is not only international but supranational, as in the case of treaties of integration under Article 24(1), in particular when it not only concerns the state but also abrogates or limits individual rights, in particular those contained in human rights treaties and treaties of integration. The following subsection demonstrates how crossing that systemic line changes the constitutional calculus.

Disengaging through the Legislature

Altering pervasive legal effects on individuals through disengagement may be of an essential (*wesentlichen*) character so as to require parliamentary approval for the sake of democracy and the rule of law. It is the essence of the democratic rule of law that regulating and abrogating rights of individuals is the province of parliaments and not of the executive branch. Statutory law enacted to revoke the delegation of sovereign powers needs at least to abide by the same constitutional standard as the ordinary federal statute underlying the initial delegation.[64]

In any case, regardless of whether parliament *must* be involved in cases of disengagement, parliament still *may* take matters of foreign relations into its own hands by

[60] BVerfG, Treaty Override, *supra* note 23, para. 89.

[61] BVerfG, Pershing 2 and Cruise Missile II, *supra* note 33, paras. 84–85. For the similar situation in the South African constitution, *see* Hannah Woolaver, *State Engagement with Treaties: Interactions between International and Domestic Law*, ch. 24 in this volume.

[62] BVerfG, NSA Selectors List, *supra* note 34.

[63] For an overview of recent instances of disengagement from international obligations, *see* James Crawford, *The Current Political Discourse Concerning International Law*, 81 MLR 1 (2018).

[64] Such "*acte contraire* theory" was adopted, for instance, in Democratic Alliance v. Minister of International Relations and Cooperation and Others, ZAGPPHC [2017] High Court (83145/2016), where this theory was held applicable for *any* treaty subject to ratification, *see* Woolaver, *supra* note 61.

domestically overriding international treaty obligations. However, it then must also accept responsibility for an eventual breach of international obligations.

Constitutional Democracy and International Responsibility

A domestic override of international obligations can be undertaken through the legislature single-handedly.[65] Under the German Basic Law, the enactment of ordinary federal statutes derogating from prior international legal commitments are not held per se unconstitutional, at least in the rather specific cases of international double taxation agreements.[66]

The corresponding debate revolves around the collision of two major constitutional principles: rule of law versus democracy. On the one hand, legal obligations stemming from international treaties are accorded the rank of ordinary statutes. On the other hand, the principle of democracy demands that subsequent legislatures must have the power to revise, within the limits set by the Basic Law, legislative acts enacted by previous legislatures in accordance with the will of the people expressed through elections. From the perspective of domestic law, the case of such collision of a prior international legal obligation in the form of an ordinary statute with a subsequent statute is governed by the principle of *lex posterior derogat legi priori*. Thus far democracy prevails.

However, the openness of the Constitution toward international law and the principle of the *Rechtsstaat* based on the rule of law point in the opposite direction. For this openness requires public authorities, first, to comply with international legal obligations binding upon the Federal Republic. Second, the federal legislature must guarantee that respective violations are rectified. Third, public authorities are obliged to advance compliance with international obligations even by other states.[67]

But the *Rechtsstaat* principle also demands legal certainty, which would be ill-served by the balancing test proposed by the dissent in the Treaty Override judgment.[68] Furthermore, denying the legislature the power to modify the domestic effect of treaties would run counter to the Basic Law's separation of powers.[69] Rather, another solution to the tension between international law and domestic democracy suggests itself: according to international law, the domestic separation of powers does not generally absolve a nation from fulfilling its treaty commitments (Art. 46 VCLT). Thus,

[65] The Court has emphasized for a long time that such a derogation from international treaty commitments cannot be implied, but must be explicit, 74 BVERFGE 358, 370—Presumption of Innocence [1987], confirmed in 128 BVERFGE 326—Preventive Detention [2011], para. 82; BVerfG, Treaty Override, *supra* note 23, paras. 58, 72.

[66] BVerfG, Treaty Override, *supra* note 23.

[67] 112 BVERFGE 1—Land Reform III [2004], para. 93.

[68] BVerfG, Treaty Override, *supra* note 23; König, D., dissenting, paras. 1–26.

[69] BVerfG, Treaty Override, *supra* note 23, para. 69, *citing* Land Reform III, *supra* note 67, para. 25.

parliament can indeed deny direct effect to a self-executing treaty provision by passing a law contrary to Germany's international commitments. But it then also carries the burden of international responsibility if such internal disobedience cannot be rectified internationally through treaty interpretation, amendment, or abrogation. Disengagement comes at a price.

Human Rights and Disengagement: A Special Case?

Constitutional democracy under the German Basic Law faces certain absolute limits.[70] For the Basic Law differentiates not only between international treaty law (Art. 59(2)) and general international law (Art. 25), the latter of which is accorded the rank *beneath* the Basic Law, but *above* federal legislation. Rather, the Basic Law also differentiates between imperative provisions that the legislature cannot modify even by constitutional amendment, and "other" law, including international law.[71]

As much as the contours of the latter category—"*other* law"—remain somewhat unsettled, the former category—"imperative provisions that may not be modified"—is less indeterminate: Prominently, Article 1(2) recognizes "inviolable and inalienable human rights as the basis of every community, of peace and of justice in the world." This avowal stands in direct connection to Article 1(1) with its guarantee of the inviolability of human dignity. Though its exact reach remains subject to debate, Article 1(2) echoes the 1948 Universal Declaration of Human Rights that was on the minds of the original drafters[72] and also the 1950 European Convention on Human Rights (ECHR). As to international integration, Article 23 mandates the participation of Germany in the establishment of the European Union under the conditions of democracy, human rights, federalism, and subsidiarity. In addition, Article 24(2) calls for limitations of sovereign rights for the peaceful and permanent order in Europe and between the peoples of the world referring to the systems of collective security of the United Nations and collective defense of NATO;[73] Article 24(3) demands the accession to a permanent system of binding international dispute settlement. Finally, Article 26 determines the unconstitutionality of preparations for an aggressive war and demands their criminalization. The constitution thus distinguishes between different international norms and levels of commitment. Constitutional jurisprudence on disengaging from international treaties in one area is not readily applicable in another. Where the Basic Law itself requires adherence to international rules and international or regional integration, ordinary federal legislation will not suffice for disengagement.

[70] Somewhat similarly, in the *Democratic Alliance* case in South Africa, the applicants argued in favor of limitations of treaty disengagement based on constitutional rights. *See* Woolaver, *supra* note 61.

[71] 111 BVerfGE 307—Görgülü [2004], paras. 61–62; BVerfG, Preventive Detention, *supra* note 65, paras. 87–90.

[72] Dr. von Mangoldt, *in* 5/II Eberhard Pikard & Wolfram Werner, Der Parlamentarische Rat 1948–1949: Ausschuss für Grundsatzfragen 592, 596, 599 (1993).

[73] BVerfG, AWACS/Somalia, *supra* note 38. On this, *see* Peters, *supra* note 37.

The Case of Exit from the European Union

Neither Article 24(1) nor Article 23 Basic Law provide for criteria regulating acts of disengagement from international institutions. As per Article 50(1) TEU, however, any member state may decide to withdraw from the European Union, subject only to its own constitutional requirements. The consequence of disengaging from the Union after withdrawal is that EU Treaties cease in due course to apply, depriving individuals of formerly available legal rights. With regard to the European Union, however, the Basic Law explicitly commits German public authority to European integration.[74] In line with the friendliness toward international law, the Federal Constitutional Court based on this provision the *topos* of friendliness toward European law (*Europarechtsfreundlichkeit*).[75] The exercise of the right to withdraw from the European Union hence faces a rather high threshold, which may only be reached when the Union is agreed to have failed definitively as such or the conditions posed by Article 23(1) are no longer met.[76]

The UK Supreme Court's *Miller* judgment concerning "Brexit" confirms that contemporary treaties of integration create—far beyond traditional inter-state treaties—individual rights and duties demanding at the very least parliamentary involvement and authorization for their revocation (and may be further protected by constitutional rights, e.g., against the retroactive effect of a withdrawal). By that token, the traditional executive prerogative gives way to a joint responsibility of the executive and legislative branches when treaties of integration are concerned.

This insight similarly underpins the Basic Law's differentiation between treaties of integration under Articles 24(1) and 23 and ordinary treaties falling only under Article 59. This has consequences not only for engaging but also for disengaging. In addition, the detailed scheme for the involvement of the federal units and national parliament in European legislation as contained in the provisions of Article 23 could *mutatis mutandis* be transferred to international integration falling under Article 24, too, at least in cases involving the protection of individual rights. This would also protect the rights of citizens from the whims of a dictatorial executive, even if democratically elected.

Disengaging through the Judiciary ("Counter-Limits")

In many respects, disengagement remains more of a theoretical possibility and less of a practical reality. The rarity of actual disengagement is due not only to political exigencies but may also be explained by the principle of "mutual respect" between

[74] BVerfG, Lisbon Treaty, *supra* note 6, para. 225.

[75] *Id.*; 129 BVERFGE 124—European Rescue Package [2011], para. 172.

[76] *Cf.* BVerfG, Lisbon Treaty, *supra* note 6, para. 233: "[Withdrawal] is not a secession from a state union (*Staatsverband*) . . . , but merely the withdrawal from an association of sovereign states (*Staatenverbund*) which is founded on the principle of reversible self-commitment."

different authoritative legal regimes. Such a principle prescribes a judicial practice that prefers harmonious interpretation, which can stretch to the outermost limits of interpretation, over resort to confrontation, renegotiation, or overall disengagement. International and national courts first and foremost bear the responsibility for accommodating necessarily diverse multilayered decision-making processes.[77] However, in a multilevel governance system this is only possible if courts navigate the inevitable conflicts that are the flipside of permeable constitutional orders.

Mechanisms for such a type of dialogue[78] have been developed by national courts primarily in the light of European court decisions. Following the Italian example, European and national constitutional and supreme courts, which may be conceived of as an informal European association of constitutional courts (*europäischer Verfassungsgerichtsverbund*),[79] have developed three specific "counter-limits"[80] to tackle a lack of democratic legitimization of supranational decisions. These devices have developed into important instruments of dialogue between the highest national and European jurisdictions.[81] *Mutatis mutandis*, these mechanisms can be applied to the relationship between different international legal orders. However, as international courts are rare and of limited jurisdiction, the dialogue of courts is often, but not exclusively, a regional phenomenon, for example with regard to the European and the Inter-American Human Rights[82] systems. Globally, the UN Committee system[83] and the Human Rights Council are also engaging in such dialogue, even if their effect is at times of a more limited nature than that of their regional European counterparts. Thus, the German Federal Constitutional Court has distinguished between the respect for the European Court of Human Rights, which under Article 1(2) of the Basic Law requires, if possible, an interpretation of the Basic Law in line with the Convention as interpreted by the European Court of Human Rights ("orientation and guidance"),[84]

[77] *Cf.* Andreas L. Paulus, *International Adjudication*, *in* PHILOSOPHY OF INTERNATIONAL LAW 207–224 (John Tasioulas & Samantha Besson eds., 2010).

[78] Term used by Anne-Marie Slaughter, *A Global Community of Courts*, 44 HARV. INT'L L.J. 191 (2003).

[79] Andreas Voßkuhle, *Multilevel Cooperation of the European Constitutional Courts—Der Europäische Verfassungsgerichtsverbund*, 6 EUR. CONST. L. REV. 175 (2010). *See also* the *Conference of European Constitutional Courts, General Report of the XVIth Conference*, *in* DIE KOOPERATION DER VERFASSUNGSGERICHTE IN EUROPA (Verfassungsgerichtshof ed., 2015).

[80] The term "counter-limits," by all accounts, stems from Paolo Barile, *Ancora su diritto comunitario e diritto interno*, VI STUDI PER IL XX ANNIVERSARIO DELL'ASSEMBLEA COSTITUENTE 49 (1969), cited in accordance with Giuseppe Martinico, *Is the European Convention Going to be "Supreme"?: A Comparative-Constitutional Overview of ECHR and EU Law Before National Courts*, 23 EUR. J. INT'L L. 401 (2012).

[81] *Cf.* Huber & Paulus, *supra* note 26, at 291–295.

[82] EL DIÁLOGO ENTRE LOS SISTEMAS EUROPEO Y AMERICANO DE DERECHOS HUMANOS (Javier García Roca et al. eds., 2012), in particular Chapter IX 3.2.

[83] Anja Seibert-Fohr, *Judicial Engagement in International Human Rights Comparitivism*, *in* 5 SELECT PROCEEDINGS OF THE EUROPEAN SOCIETY OF INTERNATIONAL LAW 7–24 (August Reinisch et al. eds., 2016).

[84] This "*de facto* function of orientation and guidance for the interpretation" of international decisions extends to all events, thus even beyond the specific individual case, but only to the extent

and the respect for the views of the UN treaty bodies, which requires dialogue, but not necessarily implementation.[85]

Effectiveness of Human Rights Protection—"Solange"

Constitutional jurisprudence on Article 24(1) developed the first counter-limit that has come to be enshrined in Article 23(1) sentence 1 of the Basic Law, namely, that a supranational institution (in this context: the European Union) must ensure effective human rights protection equivalent to that under the German Basic Law. "So long as" the international institution lives up to this constitutional expectation, the Federal Constitutional Court is willing to abstain from judicial review of respective secondary laws using the yardstick of the Basic Law. Thus, when legal analysis shows that a matter is completely regulated by European law, the Court will not exercise its jurisdiction[86] "so long as" human rights are adequately protected at the centralized (mostly European) level.

The "Solange" jurisprudence has developed into a general *topos* of the interrelationship of different legal orders. Equivalence rather than identity of human rights protection not only describes an existing relationship between legal orders but also circumscribes the conditions for their reciprocal acceptance. In its *Kadi* jurisprudence, the Court of Justice of the European Union has adopted that approach at least to some extent with regard to the relationship between the Court and the UN Security Council.[87] A Chamber of the European Court of Human Rights (ECtHR) in *Al-Dulimi* also applied the *Solange* concept to the Terror Lists of the UN Security Council.[88]

By demanding a satisfactory system of human rights protection from any international organization of integration, the respect of individual rights of the citizens is guaranteed and controlled by the domestic constitutional court.[89] The emphasis here is on the systemic protection of individual rights, not on individual guarantees.[90] But

that Germany has submitted to the jurisdiction in question. As to decision of the ECtHR, *see* BVerfG, Preventive Detention, *supra* note 65, para. 89. Regarding decisions of the ICJ, *see* BVerfG (Chamber ECLI:DE:BVerfG:2006:rk20060919.2bvr211501—Consular Notification Decision [2006], para. 61.

[85] 142 BVERFGE 313—Coercive Medical Treatment [2016], para. 90.

[86] 142 BVERFGE 74—Sampling [2016], paras. 112–124; 118 BVERFGE 79—Emission Trading [2007], para. 73.

[87] Caution is thus due in assuming the case fits the logic of *Solange*. *See* Juliane Kokott & Christoph Sobotta, *The Kadi Case—Constitutional Core Values and International Law—Finding the Balance?*, 23 EUR. J. INT'L L. 23, 1015 (2012).

[88] Al-Dulimi v. Switzerland, no. 5809/08, Eur. Ct. H.R. 2013, paras. 111–121 ("equivalent protection test"), though the issue was rendered "nugatory" by the following Grand Chamber of 21 June 2016, Al-Dulimi v. Switzerland [GC], no. 5809/08, Eur. Ct. H.R. 2016, para. 149.

[89] BVerfG, Maastricht, *supra* note 6, headnote 7: "Protection of fundamental rights in Germany and insofar not only against Germany, but also in Germany."

[90] 73 BVERFGE 339—Solange II, [1986] CMLR 25: 201-206; 102 BVERFGE 147—Banana Market Regulation [2000], para. 39.

mutual respect as a guiding principle requires, before finding nonequivalence and invoking a counter-limit, thorough engagement with the foreign legal order at issue. In the course thereof, as shown for example by the *Nada* case before the Grand Chamber of the ECtHR,[91] material equivalence may eventually crystallize, even if this stretches the methodological confines near the breaking point.

Domestic Control of the Limits of International Jurisdiction—Ultra Vires

A legal order of integration can exist next to the domestic legal order only if both stay within the limits of their respective scope of jurisdiction. The conferral of powers to an international organization or institution is prescribed by the jurisdictional clauses of the treaty. The limit of acceptance, Open Statehood notwithstanding, is reached when an international institution acts beyond these competences or powers conferred on it, in other words when it acts *ultra vires*. In effect, finding an act to be *ultra vires* can lead to disengagement in the forms of divergence and denial of implementation. The purpose of this legal tool is to delimit the powers as contained in the delegating act according to Article 24(1) and—explicitly—Article 23(1), sentence 2 of the Basic Law, and to protect democracy.[92] The Federal Constitutional Court does not consider this domestic reservation to be a violation of Article 19 TEU, which gives the task of interpretation and application of the European treaties to the Court of Justice of the European Union. Rather, the Constitutional Court asks whether the powers in question have been "transferred" in the sense of Article 23(1) in the first place and are thus a legitimate means of international action. According to the most recent rendition, "ultra vires acts of institutions, bodies, offices and agencies of the European Union violate the European integration agenda laid down in the Act of Approval pursuant to Article 23 sec. 1 sentence 2 of the Basic Law and thus also the principle of sovereignty of the people (Article 20 sec. 2 sentence 1 of the Basic Law). The ultra vires review aims to protect against such violations of the law.[93]"

The European law principle of conferral (or enumerated powers) is thus partly under the control of domestic courts, albeit only with regard to the general program of integration, not in every detail.[94]

Open Statehood and, more specifically, the principle of friendliness toward European Union Law ensure that the counter-limit of *ultra vires* is to be used in a Union-friendly manner. That is to say, the counter-limit of *ultra vires* control is activated only in instances of certain qualified transgressions: "Ultra vires review . . . is contingent on the act of the authority of the European Union being manifestly in breach of competences

[91] Nada v. Switzerland, no. 10593/08, Eur. Ct. H.R. 2012.

[92] BVerfG, OMT (Judgment), *supra* note 43, headnote 1, para. 123.

[93] *Id.*, headnote 2.

[94] BVerfG, Honeywell, *supra* note 28, para. 61.

and the impugned act leading to a structurally significant shift to the detriment of the Member States in the structure of competences."[95] In addition, before declaring an act of the European Union *ultra vires*, the Federal Constitutional Court requires a preliminary reference of the underlying legal question to the Court of Justice of the European Union pursuant to Article 267 TFEU.[96] Thus, the Court of Justice will always have the possibility of self-correction. Thereby, before any action is taken, a dialogue between the national court and the European Court takes place.

Indeed, the Court has thus far referred two matters regarding the exercise of the competences of the European Central Bank (ECB) to the Court of Justice. In one instance, regarding the Outright Monetary Transactions (OMT) program on maintaining the transmission effects of the monetary policy of the ECB, the Federal Constitutional Court has accepted the limitations put forward by the Court of Justice as sufficient although not completely in line with its views.[97] The Court of Justice has recently decided on the second reference regarding the ECB's Quantitative Easing program.[98] It will now be for the Federal Constitutional Court to respond.

Intrinsic Limits of International Legal Integration—Constitutional Identity

The third counter-limit is the most difficult one. It demands not only a system of human rights protection but also the substantive respect of core constitutional provisions of member states. The Treaty on European Union seems to recognize this to a certain extent.[99]

However, constitutional identity seems to run contrary to the international law principle according to which domestic law cannot be invoked against international treaties if its violation is not manifest (*cf.* Art. 46 VCLT). But the indeterminacy of "constitutional identity" will almost certainly mean that its violation will be difficult to

[95] *Id.*, headnote 1; recently confirmed in BVerfG, OMT (Judgment), *supra* note 43, paras. 148–154.

[96] BVerfG, Honeywell, *supra* note 28, headnote 1 lit. b.

[97] BVerfG, OMT (Judgment), *supra* note 43, para. 193: "If the conditions specified by the Court of Justice are applied, the policy decision regarding the OMT Programme and its possible implementation do not exceed, at least not manifestly, the competences attributed to the European Central Bank."

[98] Weiss et al., Case No. C-493/17, ECLI:EU:C:2018:1000 [2018]. For the reference, see 146 BVerfGE 216—Public Sector Purchase Programme [2017] ("Quantitative Easing").

[99] *Cf.* art. 4(2) TEU: "The Union shall respect the equality of Member States before the Treaties as well as their national identities, inherent in their fundamental structures, political and constitutional, inclusive of regional and local self-government. . . . " Note the methodological difference between ECJ and *Bundesverfassungsgericht*: while the ECJ understands constitutional identity as relative limit subject to balancing, *see* Case C-208/09, Sayn-Wittgenstein, 2010 E.C.R. I-13693; Case C-36/02, Omega, 2004 E.C.R. I-9609, the Federal Constitutional Court regards it as an absolute limit, *see* 134 BVerfGE 366—OMT (Preliminary Reference) [2014], para. 29.

show. In addition, rare will be the cases where the constitution itself determines those core principles, as is the case in Article 79(3) Basic Law. However, even this explicit Basic Law provision is very sweeping: it includes principles as broad as human dignity, democracy, and rule of law. A mere constitutional custom running counter to constitutional law will also not suffice. Nevertheless, the Italian Constitutional Court held, without an explicit textual basis in the Italian Constitution, that according immunity to past violations of international humanitarian law and thus denying adjudication of claims for damages for human rights violations amounted to the violation of a core principle of Italian law.[100]

Thus, identity control must be exercised with great care. On the other hand, it does not seem appropriate to bind a state by a content it never could have conceivably chosen—in other words, a decent interpretation of state consent will, as a rule, preclude the necessity of invoking identity control. This also cautions, however, against too sweeping a use of constitutional identity to deny application of international commitments. Interestingly, the German Constitutional Court that invented this "brake" has never used it to invalidate a judgment or a provision of secondary law under a treaty of integration, let alone a provision of a treaty itself. Some other Courts of member states of the European Union[101] and state parties to the European Convention[102] have not been so circumspect.

However, a domestic court cannot be expected to abandon the core provisions of its constitutional system,[103] unless there is a compelling reason. Herein lie the core problems of dealing with numerous systems of law and respective subsystems: how much mutual respect is tenable and at what point is disengagement unavoidable. The judicial key is to avoid respective incompatibilities in the first place by means of a sensible interpretation and application of one's own law as well as the law of the integrated other legal system. In our postmillennium pluralist world of multiple legal systems, we thus expect from contemporary judges an equivalent degree of methodological sensitivity.

[100] Corte Costituzionale, Sentenza No. 238/2014.

[101] ECJ, Joined Cases C-143/15 and C-147/15, Hungary and Slovak Republic v. Council of the European Union, 2017. The case initiated actions for annulment by the Slovak Republic and Hungary of Decision (EU) 2015/1601, which had set out provisional measures in the area of international protection for the benefit of the Hellenic Republic and the Italian Republic, in order to address the emergency situation characterized by a sudden inflow of nationals of third countries into certain EU member states.

[102] OAO Neftyanaya Kompaniya Yukos v. Russia (CC Decision in Yukos) [2017] 1-П/2017.

[103] Similarly, the U.K. Supreme Court in *R (on the application of HS2 Action Alliance Ltd) v. Secretary of State for Transport* [2014] UKSC 3, in the judgments of Lords Reed (para. 111), Neuberger, and Mance (para. 202) drew on the approach adopted by the *Bundesverfassungsgericht*. For further analysis, *see* Craig, *supra* note 17. The "autochthonous strain . . . , connoting the descriptive and normative ideal of attachment to indigenous or native values," identified by Craig, finds a certain equivalent in the German jurisprudence.

III. Conclusion

Specific clauses of the German Basic Law concerning international engagement establish an elaborate framework allowing for, at the same time, constitutional integration of primary and secondary law of international institutions as well as for the cooperation and coordination of the branches of government in international decision-making. It is by such effort that competing constitutional writs of engaging with international institutions and retaining national sovereignty are reconciled while ensuring continuous mutual deference. In other words, Open Statehood is being put into practice.[104]

On the other hand, these clauses remain largely silent on questions of disengagement. This void used to be filled by the traditional model of executive prerogative for foreign affairs. Yet, in Germany,[105] this model increasingly reflects an understanding of international integration as a common task of all branches of government, in particular whenever the protection of individual rights is in question—including with respect to the actions of state agents such as soldiers in military operations abroad. The British *Miller* case on Brexit and the South African *Democratic Alliance* case on exiting the International Criminal Court have shown the resilience of these international institutions, in particular, due to the acquired rights of citizens conferred to them by international integration.

As the most densely integrated organization, the European Union demands outright direct effect in and supremacy over domestic law. As an alternative to exit, constitutional courts have developed brakes on the overreach of international institutions, otherwise referred to as "counter-limits"—namely, the existence of an international system of protection of human rights, the rejection of acts *ultra vires*, and finally the absolute protection of constitutional identity, thus trying to combine membership with protection of sovereign prerogatives. Ideally, such limitations of the law of integration may render the option of exit unnecessary while maintaining the benefits of membership. Of course, dialogue within the system—for instance by reference of a question to the Court of Justice of the European Union—is preferable to exit. International and European integration being an essential goal of the German Constitution, the main challenge consists in striking the right balance between engagement and disengagement, as well as between international integration and the protection of individual rights. It may be the essence of the German experience since 1949 that these contradictions are more apparent than real.

[104] *See*, however, for the identification of an integration-skeptic trend in German constitutional jurisprudence, Helmut Aust, *The Democratic Challenge to Foreign Relations Law in Transatlantic Perspective*, *in* The Double-Facing Constitution: Legal Externalities and the Reshaping of the Constitutional Order (David Dyzenhaus et al. eds., forthcoming 2019).

[105] For the somewhat contrary development in the United States, *see* Curtis A. Bradley & Jack L. Goldsmith, *Presidential Control over International Law*, 131 Harv. L. Rev. 120 (2018).

CHAPTER 24

STATE ENGAGEMENT WITH TREATIES

Interactions between International and Domestic Law

HANNAH WOOLAVER

TREATY engagements are an important exercise of a state's conduct of its foreign relations. As defined in this volume, foreign relations law is the "domestic law of each nation that governs how that nation interacts with the rest of the world."[1] Treaty membership is a key mechanism by which a state interacts with foreign actors, including other states, intergovernmental organizations, nongovernmental organizations, and foreign nationals. The identity of the domestic actors that are empowered to make decisions on treaty entry and exit is therefore a crucial reflection of whose voice is accounted for in the state's foreign relations. As a result, the domestic allocation of responsibility for the making and unmaking of treaties is a significant question of the constitutional separation of powers in the realm of foreign relations law. Increasingly, certain states have sought to augment democratic participation in the exercise of their foreign relations by moving away from giving unilateral and absolute treaty engagement authority to the executive, and instead providing a role for the legislature and even the judiciary in the state's decision to join and leave treaties. These developments have often been precipitated by national electoral campaigns or referenda highlighting the important ramifications for state sovereignty of belonging to international treaty regimes.

In addition to being expressions of domestic foreign policy, treaties are also the primary tool of international law for facilitating international engagement and cooperation. Treaties are used to create and codify rules of international law, and to establish and modify international organizations, among a number of other indispensable functions in the international legal sphere. The international law and domestic law of treaties

[1] *See* Curtis A. Bradley, *What Is Foreign Relations Law?*, ch. 1 in this volume.

are therefore inextricably linked. However, while both systems of law concern the very same treaty commitments undertaken by states, each has its own set of rules for the allocation of the state's treaty-making capacity. Given this substantive overlap, the way in which the international law and domestic law of treaties relate to each other can either support or undermine respect for the rule of law in the other domain.

This chapter will explore the interactions between international and domestic law in relation to the allocation of states' authority to engage with treaties. In doing so, it sets out and compares examples from different jurisdictions, seeking to draw out global constitutional developments in reallocating aspects of treaty-making authority from the executive to other branches of government. It also considers how international law takes account of these constitutional developments, if at all. Despite the increasing division of authority for entering and exiting treaties between the executive and other branches of government at the domestic level, the general rules of international law currently have limited recognition of these constitutional requirements when testing the international validity of the state's treaty consent. The chapter concludes by considering possibilities for change in this area, particularly through states' exercise of their international law power to determine the conditions for valid entry to and exit from treaty regimes.

I. The Allocation of Treaty-Making Power

Domestic Allocation of Treaty-Making Powers

Given the multiplicity of states in modern international society, and the different constitutional traditions around the world, it is unsurprising that there are many ways that states have chosen to regulate the government's authority to join treaties. As noted above, this is a reflection of the state's internal allocation of authority to conduct its foreign relations. The domestic regulation of the treaty-making power of the state determines which organs are ultimately given the power to decide which treaties reflect and further the state's foreign policy choices, and to bind their state to those international engagements.

A wide variety of approaches to such regulation is taken, ranging from vesting the executive with unilateral authority to bind the state to treaties, to the requirement of legislative authorization, or, less commonly, judicial branch involvement in such decisions. As noted by Verdier and Versteeg in this volume, there is a clear global trend reflecting increased involvement of both parliamentary and judicial branches in treaty-making in constitutional systems.[2] While the involvement of the latter is less

[2] *See* Pierre-Hugues Verdier & Mila Versteeg, *Separation of Powers, Treaty-Making, and Withdrawal: A Global Survey*, ch. 8 in this volume, at p.137.

widespread, civilian jurisdictions lead the way in this regard. For example, the French *Conseil Constitutionnel* can review the constitutionality of a treaty on referral by the President of the Republic, the prime minister, the president of one or the other Houses, or from sixty Members of the National Assembly or sixty senators. If the treaty is held to be unconstitutional, it cannot be ratified unless the constitution is amended.[3] A number of other civilian countries, including some countries that were formerly colonies administered by France, have similar provisions.[4]

In addition, many states have different legal requirements depending on the type of treaty in question. For instance, in South Africa, most treaties require the approval of Parliament to be binding on the state, while treaties of a "technical, executive, or administrative nature" require only signature by the executive.[5] In the United States, domestic law distinguishes between treaties that require the executive to obtain the approval of a supermajority of the Senate, as opposed to "executive agreements" (which are nonetheless treaties under international law) that may be entered into by the executive alone or with the majority approval of Congress, depending on the agreement in question.[6] Further, in some states, the relevant rules are set out in the constitutional text, while in others the rules have developed based on practice or judicial determinations. In the United Kingdom, for instance, while treaty consent is considered to be an aspect of unfettered executive prerogative, the Ponsonby Convention, developed through practice, required parliamentary consideration prior to the executive's ratification of treaties.[7] Domestic disagreements as to the precise requirements for treaty consent in the abstract and in particular cases are therefore not uncommon.

We can see in these examples, and others around the world, an effort to extend the domestic separation of powers into the realm of the state's foreign relations. While the executive is still generally solely empowered to speak on behalf of the state internationally, the dispersal of authority between several branches of government in the decision-making process to take on treaty obligations can be observed in many states. In these states, the executive's unilateral authority to determine the state's foreign engagements is limited, requiring input and approval by the legislative and/or judicial branches. Such constitutional requirements therefore can have the effect of increasing democratic participation in the state's foreign relations, or at least increasing the transparency and public involvement in treaty engagement decisions, and thus in the foreign relations of the state more generally.

[3] *See* art. 54, Constitution of the Republic of France (Oct. 4, 1958).

[4] *See*, e.g., art. 122, Constitution of Côte d'Ivoire (2016).

[5] Sec. 232, South African Constitution (1996).

[6] Restatement (Third) of the Foreign Relations Law of the United States §§ 301–303 (1987).

[7] *See* R (on the Application of Miller and another) v. Secretary of State for Exiting the European Union, [2017] UKSC 5, *available at* https://www.supremecourt.uk/cases/docs/uksc-2016-0196-judgment.pdf. The Ponsonby Convention is now codified in Sec. 20 of the Constitutional Reform and Governance Act 2010.

International Allocation of Treaty-Making Power

As noted previously, the domestic allocation of treaty-making power is only one side of the equation. The other side is the allocation of this authority on the international plane. In international law, the Vienna Convention on the Law of Treaties (VCLT) assigns authority to bind the state to become a party to treaties to two categories of domestic officials. First, there are officials who are presumed to be vested with this authority, without any proof being necessary: the head of state, head of government, and minister of foreign affairs.[8] Such representatives hold "ostensible authority" to express the consent of their state to be bound by a treaty. Second, the VCLT provides that other state representatives may validly express consent on behalf of their state, but that they must prove their authority to do so either by providing full powers, or as evidenced by the practice of their state.[9] This provision therefore establishes an international legal assumption that the foreign relations of the state, in terms of its expression in treaty-making, will be conducted by those specified officials, regardless of the internal allocation of this foreign relations power in domestic law.

However, the VCLT does integrate a limited form of recognition of the domestic allocation of treaty-making authority in its provisions on the "Invalidity of Treaties," regulated by Section II of the VCLT. In particular, Article 46 of the VCLT, entitled "Provisions of internal law regarding competence to conclude treaties," states:

1. A State may not invoke the fact that its consent to be bound by a treaty has been expressed in violation of a provision of its internal law regarding competence to conclude treaties as invalidating its consent unless that violation was manifest and concerned a rule of its internal law of fundamental importance.
2. A violation is manifest if it would be objectively evident to any State conducting itself in the matter in accordance with normal practice and in good faith.

Thus, in the case of a "manifest violation" of an "internal law of fundamental importance" concerning the capacity to conclude treaties, the state whose domestic law was violated when becoming a party to a treaty (and only that state) may choose to invalidate its prior consent by invoking the violation. Doing so would have the effect of ending the state's membership of the treaty, and freeing it retrospectively of any obligations under the treaty. However, significant barriers to the successful reliance on this ground of invalidity are included in the provision. Most challengingly, in order to be sufficiently "manifest," the violation of the domestic law must be objectively obvious to other treaty parties acting in good faith. Since states are not assumed to know the domestic constitutional requirements of their treaty partners, it has been held that this will normally require that a "specific warning" have been given to the other treaty parties concerning the violated rule in question, or that the rule was unusually "publicised."[10]

[8] Art. 7(2)(a), VCLT. [9] Art. 7(1), VCLT.

[10] Land and Maritime Boundary between Cameroon and Nigeria (Cameroon v. Nigeria; Equatorial Guinea Intervening) ICJ Reports (2002), para. 265.

If this can be established, Article 46 acts as an exception to the general rule that treaty consent given by the representatives set out in Article 7 of the VCLT—either those members of the executive with ostensible authority, or those who have substantiated their authority—will be effective in international law.

As this provision constitutes customary international law,[11] the domestic allocation of foreign relations powers can indeed override the international allocation thereof, though only in the narrowly defined circumstances of Article 46 of the VCLT. The narrowness of this provision is illustrated by the fact that it has not yet been successfully invoked before an international court in order to free a state from otherwise validly undertaken international treaty obligations. Thus, in most instances, it is the international allocation of treaty-making authority that will take precedence, potentially undermining respect for the applicable distribution of this power in domestic law, and consequently also the rule of law in that domain.

Special Cases

The rule set out in Article 46 of the VCLT—possibly vitiating a state's treaty consent on the basis of a violation of domestic constitutional requirements only if that violation is "manifest" and of an internal rule of "fundamental importance"—applies as the default position. Presumably, if a treaty specifies that an augmented role will be given to the requirements of internal law when determining the international validity of the state's consent, that alternative position will apply to the treaty in question. When drafting treaties, states have an unrestricted right in international law to establish the requirements for the expression of consent to be bound by the treaty. As put in Article 11 of the VCLT, "[t]he consent of a State to be bound by a treaty may be expressed by signature, exchange of instruments constituting a treaty, ratification, acceptance, approval or accession, or by any other means if so agreed." Given this freedom to determine the applicable means of expressing consent to become party to the particular treaty, there is no reason that the drafters cannot also specify that the parties' consent must be expressed in compliance with the constitutional requirements of each state.

Treaty practice illustrates that there are examples in which such provision has been made. Most prominently, Article 110 of the UN Charter states that "[t]he present Charter shall be ratified by the signatory states in accordance with their respective constitutional processes."[12] Article 110 applies only to the "original Members of the United Nations," namely, the "States which, having participated in the United Nations

[11] *Id.* at para. 303 (applying art. 46 even though the dispute in question occurred before the VCLT came into force); Thilo Rensmann, *Article 46: Provisions of Internal Law Regarding Competence to Conclude Treaties, in* Vienna Convention on the Law of Treaties: A Commentary 785 (Oliver Dörr & Kirsten Schmalenbach eds., 2012); The Vienna Conventions on the Law of Treaties: A Commentary 1092 (Oliver Corten & Pierre Klein eds., 2011).

[12] Art. 110, UN Charter.

Conference on International Organization at San Francisco, or having previously signed the Declaration by United Nations of 1 January 1942."[13] Admission of subsequent members is regulated by Article 4 of the Charter, in relation to whom no equivalent obligation of constitutional ratification is specified. Thus, by the terms of the Charter, the original members were bound to ratify the Charter in such a way as to comply with the requirements set out in their own constitutional laws in order to become a party thereto in international law.

Kelsen argued that this provision clearly made the fulfillment of constitutional requirements in the ratification of the UN Charter internationally relevant. As put by Kelsen, per Article 110 of the Charter, "an unconstitutional ratification is not valid; and a valid ratification is the essential condition of original membership."[14] Kelsen argued that, while in ordinary circumstances the state itself would be responsible for ensuring that its ratification took place according to its constitution, given that the treaty here unusually "expressly prescribes observance of the respective constitutional process," in this case "the constitutional problem was not merely an internal matter; it was also a concern of the Organisation." Thus, the body that was tasked with applying Article 110, namely, the treaty depositary (the U.S. government) must consider whether the ratifications it received were concluded in accordance with the relevant state's constitutional requirements. Kelsen therefore concluded that:

> [T]he authority which had to apply this Article was competent to decide the constitutional question.... This provision may be interpreted to mean that the government of the United States, acting in service of this Organisation, had to accept the deposit of a ratification only if the latter was in conformity with the provision of Paragraph 1 of Article 110 and, consequently, had to decide on behalf of the Organisation whether or not the ratification fulfilled the requirements of this paragraph when this question became doubtful.[15]

Writers such as Kopelmans, Dahm, and Verdross also supported the view that Article 110 made the international validity of ratifications of the UN Charter conditional on compliance with domestic constitutional requirements.[16]

Other commentators, however, reject the above interpretation of Article 110, asserting instead that this provision is in line with the usual international law practice—that treaty ratification is expected to be carried out in accordance with the state's internal law, but only the state itself is competent to assess such compliance, which does not have a bearing on the international validity of the state's consent.[17] In rejecting Kelsen's approach, Simma's view was that:

[13] Art. 3, UN Charter.

[14] Hans Kelsen, The Law of the United Nations: A Critical Analysis of Its Fundamental Problems 57 (1951).

[15] *Id.* at 58–59.

[16] *See* Bruno Simma, The Charter of the United Nations: A Commentary 1374 (2d ed. 2002).

[17] *Id.*

> [T]o read into Article 110(1) an expression of the so-called "relevance theory" [that only those ratifications executed in accordance with the respective constitutional law were valid under international law] would be an excessive interpretation of the wording. Article 110's language only reflects the general precept of international law that ratifications must be effected according to national constitutional provisions in this regard.[18]

Simma noted that there was no evidence in the *travaux préparatoires* to support Kelsen's interpretation, and neither did the U.S. government as treaty depositary in practice actually examine whether the ratifications of the original UN members had been done according their constitutional requirements.[19]

A similar provision was included in the Treaty Constituting the European Coal and Steel Community (the ECSC Treaty). Article 99 of the ECSC Treaty provides: "the present Treaty shall be ratified by all the member States in accordance with their respective constitutional rules." Subsequent to the coming into force of the treaty, this provision was the subject of judicial interpretation. In the *Acciaierie San Michele* case,[20] the applicant argued that the case before the European Court of Justice (ECJ) should be adjourned until an Italian domestic case on the constitutionality of the ECSC Treaty was resolved. The domestic case involved an examination of whether the ratification of the ECSC Treaty was constitutional, and therefore binding on Italy. The ECJ, however, rejected this argument, holding that they could not decline to enforce the treaty for one member state. Ratification of the treaty by Italy meant that no Italian citizen could avoid the "complete and uniform application" of the ECSC Treaty. While Article 99 of the treaty was not directly cited by the Court, this reasoning indicates that the ECJ was not of the view that it had the authority to examine the constitutionality of Italy's ratification, despite Article 99.[21]

Nonetheless, whatever the position in relation to the UN Charter and the ECSC Treaty, provisions such as these illustrate one possible model for how international law could develop to provide for more protection for compliance with constitutional procedures and the domestic rule of law. As noted above, the VCLT recognizes states parties' rights to determine the necessary procedures and formalities to validly consent to a treaty, which could include an internationally verifiable requirement to abide by the state's established constitutional procedures. By incorporating such provisions in individual treaties, and perhaps including more specific wording than that in the UN Charter and the ECSC Treaty, expressly indicating that the constitutionality of ratification will be subject to international verification, states could condition the international validity of treaty ratifications on the fulfillment of constitutional criteria, beyond the limited scope of application of the manifest violation exception in Article 46 of the VCLT. Furthermore,

[18] *Id.* [19] *Id.*

[20] Acciaierie San Michele Spa (in Liquidation) v. High Authority of the ECSC, European Court of Justice 22 June 1965, at 29.

[21] *See* Anna Wyrozumska, *Article 50*, *in* THE TREATY ON EUROPEAN UNION: A COMMENTARY 1406 (Hermann-Josef Blanke & Stelio Mangiameli eds., 2013).

such provisions could authorize international actors—particularly the treaty depositary but perhaps also the other treaty parties—to examine the constitutionality of the ratification process. While such inquiries might normally constitute unlawful intervention, this would not be so where the state has freely undertaken international obligations to abide by its own constitutional processes.[22] Thus, international law could develop as a buttress to the state's constitutional allocation of its foreign relations authority on a treaty-by-treaty basis.

II. The Allocation of Treaty Exit Power

Domestic Allocation of Treaty Exit Powers

As noted above, the state's decision to terminate or withdraw from a treaty is equally important to the exercise of its foreign relations as the decision to join treaties. A decision to leave a treaty can be a crucial expression of a change in the state's foreign policy, or a reflection that the treaty is no longer serving the state's foreign policy goals. It should be the case, then, that the constitutional separation of powers concerning foreign relations runs through both treaty entry and exit.

In comparison with the domestic allocation of authority to join treaties, though, there are far fewer examples of explicit domestic regulation on withdrawal. It has been noted elsewhere in this volume that an increasing number of states are adopting constitutional or "infraconstitutional" laws concerning the power to leave treaties, and particularly requiring legislative approval of treaty withdrawal. Nonetheless, in most states, the power to withdraw remains unregulated, and by default, vests in the executive.[23] For example, while the U.S. and South African constitutions expressly set out the requirements to join a treaty under their domestic law, as discussed above, neither contains a provision on withdrawal.

The lack of explicit constitutional regulation of treaty withdrawal has sometimes led to litigation concerning the question. In the United States, for example, several cases have been brought concerning the constitutional requirements for treaty exit—though without authoritatively deciding the matter, instead holding that this was a political question inappropriate for judicial resolution.[24] Two jurisdictions—namely, the United Kingdom and South Africa—have recently decided landmark cases regulating the

[22] *See* Military and Paramilitary Activities in and against Nicaragua (Nicaragua v. United States of America), Merits, Judgment, I.C.J. Reports 1986, p. 14, at para. 259.

[23] *See* Verdier & Versteeg, *supra* note 2, at p.148. *See also* Laurence R. Helfer, *Treaty Exit and Intrabranch Conflict at the Interface of International and Domestic Law*, ch. 20 in this volume, for further discussion of these domestic provisions regulating withdrawal.

[24] *See*, e.g., Goldwater v. Carter, 444 U.S. 996 (1979); Kucinich v. Bush 236 F. Supp. 2d 1 (2002).

domestic allocation of treaty withdrawal powers. These decisions will be discussed below, highlighting the proposed procedural and substantive limitations on treaty withdrawal powers examined by the courts.

Procedural Limitations

In both the United Kingdom and South Africa, courts have recently established procedural limitations on the executive's power of treaty withdrawal. The U.K. Supreme Court in the *Miller* case, and the South African High Court in the *Democratic Alliance* case, held that the executive's withdrawal from the Treaty on European Union (TEU), and the Rome Statute of the International Criminal Court, respectively, could not take place without receiving prior legislative approval from the countries' parliaments. In both cases, these limitations were established despite the absence of textual bases in the constitution or elsewhere. Instead, the courts extrapolated from the constitutional separation of powers between the executive and the legislature in relation to the exercise of the state's foreign relations and domestic lawmaking powers.

Following a 2016 referendum in which a majority of voters supported the United Kingdom's withdrawal from the European Union, the U.K. executive planned to act unilaterally to trigger the withdrawal provision of the TEU, Article 50. This action was challenged in a judicial review proceeding, however, in which the applicants argued that withdrawal could not be initiated without prior parliamentary approval in the form of legislation. The U.K. Supreme Court ultimately ruled in favor of the applicants, holding that domestic law required Parliament to pass legislation to authorize the triggering of Article 50 TEU by the executive.

The domestic legal requirements for treaty withdrawal in the United Kingdom are not based on textual provisions, and this case provided the first judicial consideration of these rules. As noted above, treaty-making capacity in the United Kingdom is considered to be part of the executive's unilateral prerogative to conduct foreign relations of the state, although constitutional convention has required notice to Parliament prior to treaty ratification. The Court held that treaty withdrawal is equally part of the prerogative, and therefore in principle can be exercised unilaterally.[25] However, the Court reasoned that this does not extend to instances in which treaty withdrawal would result in a change to the constitutional framework in the United Kingdom, which it concluded was the case here. After the United Kingdom joined the European Union, Parliament had enacted legislation establishing EU law as a source of domestic law with "overriding supremacy in the hierarchy of domestic law sources." Removing this source of domestic law through withdrawal from the TEU would therefore result in a "fundamental change in the constitutional arrangements of the United Kingdom." The exercise of the prerogative here would therefore cause alterations to domestic law

[25] *Miller*, *supra* note 7, at para. 5.

that only Parliament had the authority to enact. Therefore, the prerogative power had to be exercised with parliamentary authorization.[26] The Supreme Court also barred the unilateral exit from the TEU on the basis that it would result in the loss of certain individual rights vested in domestic law that would be removed by virtue of the withdrawal from the treaties in question.[27]

The South African High Court was faced with a question similar to that decided by the U.K. Supreme Court in the *Miller* case: Can the executive withdraw from an international treaty, which had been ratified and domesticated by Parliament, without prior parliamentary approval? The question is not directly addressed by the South African Constitution, which contains no explicit provision on treaty withdrawal, and had not yet received judicial attention. Like the U.K. Supreme Court, the South African High Court answered in the negative.[28] It held that since Section 231(2) of the South African Constitution requires Parliamentary approval for treaties subject to ratification, this section also by implication requires the consent of Parliament to withdraw from such treaties. Therefore, the notice of withdrawal was unconstitutional and invalid.

The government had argued that the executive's authority to negotiate and sign international treaties (per Sections 231(1) and (3) of the Constitution) necessarily included the power to withdraw from treaties, and that Parliament's role was confined to that explicitly provided for in the Constitution in Sections 231(2) and (4), that is, to approve signed treaties subject to ratification and to pass domesticating legislation if it so chose. The Court, however, held that, because parliamentary approval is required to ratify treaties, "there is a glaring difficulty in accepting that the process of withdrawal should not be subject to the same parliamentary process." Furthermore, the Court emphasized the importance of public participation when withdrawing from treaties. The Court held that "[i]t must be assumed that parliament will comply with its constitutional obligation [when considering legislation authorizing treaty exit], for example, to facilitate public participation, which is its own process, and not of the executive. Any legislation which has potential impact on the bill of rights passed without such participation could be susceptible to a constitutional challenge against parliament."[29] Thus, the need for public participation in such treaty withdrawal decisions indicated that allocation of domestic authority in this regard needed to include Parliament, which is the only body with public participation processes.

The South African court's reasoning is wider than that of the U.K. Supreme Court in the Brexit case. In the latter, it was held that withdrawal from the European Union required parliamentary approval due to the significant constitutional change that would result: eliminating EU law as a source of domestic U.K. law and negating certain

[26] *Id.*, paras. 80–81.

[27] *Id.*, para. 83. In addition, there were issues of devolution that were addressed by the court, but will not be addressed here.

[28] *See* Democratic Alliance v. Minister of International Relations and Cooperation and Others (Council for the Advancement of the South African Constitution Intervening) (83145/2016) [2017] ZAGPPHC 53, *available at* http://www.saflii.org/za/cases/ZAGPPHC/2017/53.pdf.

[29] *Id.*, para. 76.

rights of U.K. citizens vested in domestic law by virtue of EU law. Since Parliament alone can make domestic law, Parliament alone could approve these changes to domestic law. The South African decision, by contrast, held that *any* treaty subject to ratification required parliamentary approval for withdrawal—whether or not withdrawal would result in a change to South African domestic law.

Substantive Limitations

In both the U.K. and South African cases, the courts established procedural limitations on the power of the executive to withdraw unilaterally from certain treaties. As noted above, such restrictions are increasingly common in states around the world. Interestingly, the South African court also considered substantive limitations on treaty withdrawal. The development of such limitations would give domestic courts a greater level of involvement in treaty withdrawal decisions, allowing the judicial invalidation thereof on the basis of the substantive effect of leaving the treaty, regardless of whether the necessary legislative approval, or other established procedures had been satisfied.

The applicants in the *Democratic Alliance* case argued not only that the executive had violated certain procedural requirements for exiting from the Rome Statute, but also that, ultimately, the executive could not withdraw from the Rome Statute at all. It was argued that this was so even if parliamentary approval had been obtained prior to initiating the process in Article 127(1) of the Rome Statute. In essence, the applicants argued that the South African government was constitutionally barred from withdrawing from the Rome Statute, due to Section 7(2) of the Constitution, which provides that "the state must respect, protect, promote and fulfill the rights in the Bill of Rights." It was submitted that to withdraw from the Rome Statute would deprive both South Africans and foreign nationals of the human rights protections of the International Criminal Court (ICC), and thus that such a withdrawal would constitute a "retrogressive measure" in the protection of human rights contrary to Section 7(2).[30] As a result, regardless of whatever process was followed, any withdrawal from the ICC would inevitably violate the state's obligations in Section 7(2) of the Constitution and was therefore impermissible.

At first glance, it may appear that this claim is analogous to that recognized by the U.K. Supreme Court and the lower courts in the *Miller* case, which, as previously explained, held that unilateral withdrawal from the TEU could not proceed because it would negate vested rights held by EU citizens in British law by virtue of the United Kingdom's EU membership. This claim is also, at least superficially, similar to the "constitutional blocks" on treaty withdrawal seen in certain Latin American countries, such as the constitutional prohibition on withdrawal from ratified human rights treaties in Venezuela.[31]

[30] *Id.* at para. 72.

[31] *See* Helfer, *supra* note 23, at p.363.

However, the South African court was considering a claim that went beyond both kinds of rights-based limitations accepted in other jurisdictions. The claim concerning vested rights upheld in the *Miller* case was indeed a rights-based argument. Nonetheless, it remains a procedural rather than substantive limitation on withdrawal. The Court in *Miller* did not hold that such rights could not be removed, but simply that such rights had to be removed through parliamentary process, rather than exercise of ministerial prerogative. In contrast, in the *Democratic Alliance* case, the submission was that whatever process was satisfied, including the passing of legislation by Parliament, South Africa could not withdraw from the ICC because, once the human rights protections of the treaty had been accepted, the state could not "move backwards" from that level of protection. Further, unlike the South American examples, the Rome Statute was not a treaty that had been given constitutional status by explicit provision in the constitution itself, but was in effect argued to have been elevated to that status because of the enhanced human rights protections that membership to the treaty gave. Thus, this same argument could potentially apply to any treaty that is thought to augment the protection of human rights in South Africa.

The High Court ultimately chose not to rule on this potential ground of invalidity, holding that the procedural challenges were sufficient to render the withdrawal invalid and unconstitutional. Thus, this substantive argument was not extensively considered in this instance. However, it may reappear if efforts to withdraw from the Rome Statute are revived, and parliamentary approval in the form of legislation is obtained. Indeed, the Court indicated that if Parliament did pass legislation authorizing withdrawal from the ICC following proper procedure as determined in the *Democratic Alliance* decision, then a substantive challenge against that legislation may nonetheless be available before the Constitutional Court.[32] This is particularly relevant given that a bill seeking parliamentary approval for the executive's renewed action to end its membership of the ICC has been tabled in the South African parliament.[33] It is likely that if this legislation is passed, the same groups that challenged the initial withdrawal attempt will raise this substantive challenge afresh. Furthermore, if this argument is successful, it may influence developments in other jurisdictions. In fact, it is likely that such influence can already be detected. Litigants in the Philippines have recently challenged that country's withdrawal from the Rome Statute of the International Criminal Court in the Philippines' Supreme Court on the basis that, among other things, withdrawal constitutes "a violation of the Petitioners' right to ample remedies for the protection of their rights, and of their other fundamental rights, especially the right to life."[34]

[32] Democratic Alliance, *supra* note 28, at paras. 75 and 76.

[33] South Africa, International Crimes Bill 37 of 2017, *available at* http://www.justice.gov.za/legislation/bills/2017-b37-ICBill.pdf.

[34] Petition of the Philippine Coalition for the International Criminal Court in Philippine Coalition For The International Criminal Court (PCICC) et al. v. Office Of The Executive Secretary, The Department Of Foreign Affairs, and The Permanent Mission Of The Republic of The Philippines To The United Nations (2018), on file with the author.

If such an argument were accepted, it would be a significant augmentation of judicial involvement in the conduct of the state's foreign relations. In particular, it would give the courts the authority to determine that certain treaty obligations were not subject to termination by the executive or legislative branches of government, binding them to previously undertaken foreign policy commitments represented by these treaties—even if the treaties themselves give a right of withdrawal to states parties. While this may be laudable in certain instances, possibly safeguarding important international human rights protections, it also risks causing stagnation of the state's foreign policy, disabling the government of the day from ending membership in treaties that are no longer best suited to the state's foreign policy goals, unless they undertake the onerous process of constitutional amendment. Such developments may also discourage governments from becoming a party to treaties, for fear of being unable to leave at a future date, undermining the very type of international engagements that these substantive, human rights–based limitations on treaty withdrawal would seek to promote.

International Allocation of Treaty Exit Powers

As in the case of becoming a party to a treaty, international law allocates the authority to end a state's membership of international treaties to two designated categories of state representatives, in Article 67 of the VCLT.[35] First, the head of state, head of government, or minister of foreign affairs is vested with the power to execute the treaty exit on behalf of his or her state without the need for proof of his or her authority; and second, other representatives empowered by their government may exercise this power, though they may be requested to produce full powers by other treaty parties to verify their authority to do so. For an instrument of withdrawal to be effective, it must be in writing and signed by one of these categories of state officials.[36] Article 67, then, is the equivalent of Article 7 of the VCLT discussed above, which establishes those with "ostensible authority" to join treaties on behalf of their state. Therefore, as with the authority to bind the state to the treaty in Article 7, international law designates certain classes of state representatives as bearing the default authority to conclude an internationally effective treaty withdrawal. If these requirements are not

[35] The procedural requirements for treaty withdrawal are regulated by Art. 65–68 of the VCLT.

[36] There have been some views expressed that the Art. 67 instrument need not be in writing, but, as argued by Tzanakopoulous, it is difficult to understand how an instrument can be signed if it is not in writing. *See* Antonios Tzanakopoulos, *Article 67*, *in* Corten & Klein, *supra* note 11, at 1551. Furthermore, the drafting history of the provision indicates the intention for it to be in writing. The German delegation, who proposed the final wording, for instance, said that the drafting was motivated in part because of the importance of clarity and the problems that had been in the past been experienced as a result of informal and unwritten expressions of intent to withdraw from treaties. United Nations Conference on the Law of Treaties Conference Proceedings, Part II, at 156.

satisfied by the instrument of withdrawal—for instance, if it lacks the signature of one of the designated officials—then it will not take effect in international law.[37]

In contrast to Article 7, however, the authority of the state representatives listed in Article 67 of the VCLT is unqualified with any reference to the allocation of treaty exit powers under domestic law. It will be recalled that the powers of those under Article 7 to join treaties is limited by Article 46 of the VCLT, whereby their exercise of authority will be ineffective under international law if they act in manifest violation of an internal rule of fundamental importance relating to the conclusion of treaties. No such equivalent limitation is provided in relation to the domestic representatives' power to leave treaties. The VCLT then does not have any explicit provision allowing for the nullification of treaty withdrawal due to a "manifest violation" of domestic laws concerning treaty exit powers, whether procedural or substantive.[38]

Thus, when dissolving their treaty engagements under international law, domestic actors are even less restrained by internal allocations of treaty exit powers in their state's constitution or other domestic laws than they are in the context of entering into new treaty commitments. As such, despite the important development of procedural and substantive limitations on treaty withdrawal powers in certain jurisdictions, as discussed above, without a corresponding limit on the international legal authority to exit treaties, state representatives may circumvent their own constitutional limitations in the exercise of their foreign relations.

Special Cases

In light of the absence of any explicit recognition of the domestic allocation of treaty exit powers in the international law on treaty withdrawal, it is particularly important to explore alternative international legal mechanisms to support adherence to the domestic separation of powers in this sphere. As will be discussed in this section, just as in the case of joining treaties, there are instances in which specific provision has been made in particular treaties seeking to ensure that states do comply with their constitutional requirements when withdrawing therefrom. Furthermore, again echoing the international law regulating the requirements to become a party to a treaty, Article 54(1) of the VCLT confirms that particular conditions for treaty withdrawal can be set in the treaty itself, to diverge from the general rules of international law.[39] This then provides an

[37] *See* Sir Humphrey Waldock, *Summary Records of the Fifteenth Session*, I Y.B. INT'L L. COMM'N 166 (1963); Tzanakopoulous, *supra* note 36, at 1548.

[38] *But see* Hannah Woolaver, *From Joining to Leaving: Domestic Law's Role in the International Validity of Treaty Withdrawal*, EUR. J. INT'L L. 30 (1) (2019) (arguing that the relevant provisions should be interpreted to apply the VCLT "manifest violation" exception by analogy from the rules on joining treaties to the rules on treaty withdrawal).

[39] Art. 54(1)(a), VCLT ("The termination of a treaty or the withdrawal of a party may take place . . . in conformity with the provisions of the treaty.").

opportunity for treaty drafters to require that withdrawal take place in conformity with domestic constitutional rules.

In light of the controversy concerning the United Kingdom's exit from the European Union, it is interesting that the TEU itself provides an example of one such provision integrating internal law into the international requirements on withdrawal. Article 50(1) states: "Any Member State may decide to withdraw from the Union in accordance with its own constitutional requirements." Commentators have recognized that this requires that the state's decision to withdraw be done in a manner that complies with its domestic constitutional rules.[40] However, as with Article 110 of the UN Charter, discussed above, there is disagreement as to whether this compliance can be internationally verified. On the one hand, this provision has been criticized precisely on the basis that it makes the ECJ the final arbiter in a question of constitutional law, which is said to be an unprecedented abrogation on internal matters.[41] Others have argued, in contrast, that "the fulfilment of constitutional requirements can only be verified by the Member State itself, not by the CJEU or other Member States," pointing to the *Acciaierie San Michele* case outlined above to support this interpretation.[42] At the very least, though, where there is a clear and final domestic determination of the unconstitutionality of the triggering of Article 50, as in the *Miller* case, this should have the effect of invalidating a member state's instrument of withdrawal for the purposes of international law when that treaty provision specifies the requirement of constitutionality.

More generally, Article 54(1) of the VCLT enables treaty drafters to include in their withdrawal clauses wording to ensure that fulfillment of constitutional requirements is considered as a prerequisite to the international validity of a state's withdrawal from the treaty. Given the increasing provision under domestic law for the constitutional separation of powers to extend to both entry to and exit from treaties, such clauses may become more common. It would be logically consistent for actors who support such developments in the domestic legal arena to also encourage the inclusion of such clauses in treaties to which their states are party. Such clauses could be generally phrased, such as those in Article 50 TEU, or they could specifically provide that constitutional compliance will be subject to verification of the treaty depositary, other member states, or another body. However, it is submitted that specific provision is not necessary to enable such international verification. Rather, any conditions of withdrawal from a treaty—or indeed for becoming a party to a treaty—that are included in its text, or included in the general

[40] *See*, e.g., Wyrozumska, *supra* note 21, at 1406; Raymond Friel, *Providing a Constitutional Framework for Withdrawal from the EU: Art. 59 of the Draft European Constitution*, 53 INT'L & COMP. L.Q. 407 (2004). Moreover, the European Court of Justice has recently held that revoking an art. 50 notice of withdrawal must also be done according to the state's constitutional requirements. *See Wightman and others v. Secretary of State for Exiting the European Union*, Judgment of 10 December 2018, Case C-621/18 ECLI:EU:C:2018:999, at 66–67, *available at* http://curia.europa.eu/juris/document/document.jsf;jsessionid=328689FC3D67B59B6EFA51394331C7B9?text=&docid=208636&pageIndex=0&doclang=EN&mode=req&dir=&occ=first&part=1&cid=1384995.

[41] Friel, *supra* note 40, at 425.

[42] Wyrozumska, *supra* note 21, at 1406.

law of treaties, are presumptively applicable. For example, a state cannot simply unilaterally assert the existence of a fundamental change of circumstance in order to terminate a treaty—this is subject to examination by other states parties, and international courts if jurisdiction exists. Thus, it would seem that unless the treaty expressly provided that only the state party itself could determine compliance with international law, this would be a question for international decision. In light of the absence of any alternative role for domestic constitutionality in the international law of treaties on withdrawal, Article 54(1) of the VCLT provides an important opportunity to develop such recognition.

III. Conclusion

The VCLT rules, which are generally accepted to represent customary international law, protect the domestic rule of law and the state's internal separation of powers to a very limited extent when a state joins a treaty, and currently do not explicitly have even this limited level of protection concerning treaty withdrawal. By failing to integrate domestic rules on treaty-making, and instead giving international effect to treaty acts as long as they are duly consented to by the state executive, international law facilitates unilateral action taken by the executive in violation of their internal constitutional requirements. The established international law of treaties therefore provides only minimal support for the domestic allocation of authority over foreign relations and the exercise thereof in states' engagement with treaties.

There is room, however, to increase international law's protection of the domestic rule of law on issues of treaty relations. In particular, treaty drafters could include explicit requirements in the treaty text providing that, when joining or withdrawing from the treaty, states must comply with their domestic constitutional procedures. The law of treaties allows specific provisions to be made for the entry to and exit from particular treaties, and indeed examples are already found in practice. While this would of course only operate to protect democratic participation in treaty-making when the state itself has established such constitutional requirements, and only in relation to those individual treaties, it would at least act to buttress the constitutional separation of powers on a treaty-by-treaty basis, displacing the limited, and arguably outdated, rules of the VCLT. Finally, if such provisions become common in treaty practice, they may eventually become so widespread as to themselves establish a new rule of customary international law, thereby facilitating greater separation of powers in states' engagement with treaties.

CHAPTER 25

REGIONAL ORGANIZATIONS' RELATIONS WITH INTERNATIONAL INSTITUTIONS

The EU and ASEAN Compared

JORIS LARIK

STATE engagement with international institutions raises questions not only under international law but also under the domestic law of states participating in them.[1] In addition, it implicates broader policy issues about the extent to which states are comfortable setting up and cooperating within durable institutional frameworks, especially those with at least one organ with "a will of its own"[2] that can produce legally binding decisions.

This chapter addresses a more recent phenomenon, which further adds to the complexity of these legal and policy questions. Regional organizations have started to become active in treaty-making and in interacting systematically with international institutions, in some cases even joining international organizations as members alongside states. The engagement of regional organizations with international institutions raises a number of questions for comparative foreign relations law. Which rules govern the engagement—and disengagement—of regional organizations when they act within or interact with international institutions? What happens to the regional organizations' member states? Are they being replaced or do they keep their membership? What

[1] *See* the preceding chapters of Part IV, "Engaging With, and Disengaging From, International Institutions," in this volume.

[2] HENRY G. SCHERMERS & NIELS M. BLOKKER, INTERNATIONAL INSTITUTIONAL LAW: UNITY WITHIN DIVERSITY 44 (5th ed. 2011).

voting rights and other powers do regional organizations possess in the organs of an international institution, and how do they differ from those of states? More fundamentally, how does this direct engagement between "derivative" international legal persons affect our view of a state-based international system?

This chapter shows that there are two different models for the engagement of regional organizations with and within international institutions, illustrated, respectively, by the European Union (EU) and the Association of South East Asian Nations (ASEAN). Both are active internationally and have developed sets of internal norms for conducting their external relations and interacting with international institutions. The European Union uses a highly formalized approach in which it takes on a state-like position, but without always replacing its member states. ASEAN adopts an approach that reflects great sensitivity to the sovereignty of its member states not only *inter se* but also in external relations, so much so that the states and the Association never appear together; it is always either one or the other that engages internationally.

As a preliminary matter, this chapter provides definitions of the core concepts and the selection of the European Union and ASEAN as case studies. It then outlines their respective internal rules on engaging with international institutions. Turning to the substance of the analysis, the chapter delves into the different forms in which regional organizations engage with international institutions, followed by forms of disengagement, including situations in which regional organizations crowd out their member states in global fora.

I. Main Concepts and Focus

For the purposes of this chapter, international institutions consist of both formal international organizations (IOs) and more informal groupings such as the G20, but not nongovernmental organizations (NGOs). IOs can be defined by three elements: they must be founded on an international agreement, have at least one organ with a will of its own, and be established under international law.[3] This definition by Schermers and Blokker is more useful—for present purposes in any event—than that of the International Law Commission (ILC), which defines an IO as "an organization established by a treaty or other instrument governed by international law and possessing its own international legal personality,"[4] since that definition does not make explicit the element of a "will of its own," a *volonté distincte* of its members. At its maximum, such a will is formed in a way that includes overruling certain member states. At its minimum, it refers to a common identity and consistent practice when interacting with the outside world. Nonetheless, a useful addition from the ILC's definition is that

[3] *Id.* at 37.

[4] UN General Assembly Res. 66/100 (Dec. 9, 2011), Annex: Responsibility of international organizations, art. 2(a).

an IO "may include as members, in addition to States, other entities,"[5] thus hinting at the fact that not only states engage with international institutions. The elements of being founded on a treaty and having its own legal personality exclude informal settings such as the G20 from the definition of IOs. Thus, IOs are those entities that derive their international legal personality either directly from sovereign states or entities established by sovereign states. Since this chapter is concerned with the legal aspects, the focus is on IOs, though informal settings will be considered in passing.

Regional integration organizations (RIOs) are a subset of IOs. Defining them is a matter of degree. The qualifier "regional" is to set them apart from universal organizations. RIOs can encompass an entire world region or continent, or only a part of them, in which case they are sometimes referred to as subregional organizations.[6] The term "integration" signifies cooperation beyond a narrowly defined functional area. While in the past the category "regional economic integration organization" (REIO) was used in some treaties,[7] more recent usage has omitted the term "economic,"[8] recognizing that in many cases the scope of operation of such organizations extends to a range of policy areas such as security or the environment.[9]

While there exist numerous regional organizations today, this chapter uses the European Union and ASEAN as case studies. It does so for three reasons. First, the European Union and ASEAN are well established. In 2017, the former celebrated the sixtieth anniversary of the Rome Treaty, which first established the European Economic Community, while the latter celebrated the fiftieth anniversary of the Bangkok Declaration, which is regarded as its foundational moment. Second, both organizations are highly active internationally, providing many examples of international engagement. Third, and most importantly, insights can be gained by comparing them. ASEAN and the European Union represent two very different models of international engagement by regional organizations. While the European Union is based on a model of conferred powers and strong supranational institutions, ASEAN espouses a much more sovereignty-sensitive approach. Hence, the two open up a spectrum from the supranational to the intergovernmental, between which other RIOs would likely fall in terms of their international engagement.

A final clarification concerns the field of law under discussion. In the national context, this is referred to as "foreign relations law." However, in the case of the

[5] *Id.*

[6] For example, the Economic Community of West African States (ECOWAS) is referred to as a subregional organization, since it only covers a part of Africa, while the African Union (AU) is referred to as the regional organization. Anders Lidén, *United Nations after the Cold War: Power, Regions and Groups*, *in* REGIONAL ORGANIZATIONS AND PEACEMAKING: CHALLENGERS TO THE UN? 39–53, 49 (Peter Wallensteen & Anders Bjurner eds., 2015).

[7] E.g., United Nations Convention against Transnational Organized Crime, New York, 15 November 2000, art. 38(1).

[8] United Nations Convention on the Rights of Persons with Disabilities, New York, 30 March 2007, art. 44.

[9] Ramses Wessel, *The Legal Framework for the Participation of the European Union in International Institutions*, 33 EUROPEAN INTEGRATION 621, 625 (2011).

European Union, the term "external relations law" is the predominant one. The reason for this may be that "foreign policy" harbors a connotation with the Common Foreign and Security Policy, which is only one—historically kept separate—part of the full range of the European Union's external action.[10] Since the ASEAN Charter also refers consistently to its "external relations," that term will be used throughout this chapter.

II. Internal Rules and a Global Mandate

The present section introduces the European Union and ASEAN as international actors and makes three points. First, both the European Union and ASEAN are international legal persons, as made explicit in their respective foundational documents,[11] and confirmed by their practice on the international legal plane. Second, although they are nonstate entities, both have their own rules on external relations. Curtis Bradley defines foreign relations law as "the domestic law of each nation that governs how that nation interacts with the rest of the world," adding in a footnote that "the European Union, as a supranational institution that in some ways resembles a nation, also has a developed body of foreign relations law."[12] The body of EU external relations law consists chiefly of a wide range of provisions on objectives, competences, institutions, and procedures in the EU Treaties, which have been referred to as the Union's "constitutional charter"[13] by the Court of Justice of the European Union (CJEU) and which create a quasi-federal relationship between the Union and its members.[14] In addition, there are countless pieces of EU secondary legislation and CJEU judgments relating to external relations.[15]

ASEAN, by contrast, defines itself not as supranational but as an "intergovernmental" organization.[16] This difference will be important to keep in mind as it reflects both on its internal workings according to the "ASEAN Way" as well as its global interaction. Given the preponderance of the consensus principle (also known as *mufakat*) in ASEAN, and the absence of an "ASEAN legal order" distinct from international law with case law from an "ASEAN court," it would be misplaced to

[10] Geert De Baere & Kathleen Hutman, *Federalism and International Relations in the European Union and the United States: A Comparative Outlook*, *in* Federalism in the European Union 131, 136 (Elke Cloots, Geert De Baere, & Stefan Sottiaux eds., 2012).

[11] Art. 47 TEU; art. 3 ASEAN Charter.

[12] Curtis A. Bradley, *What Is Foreign Relations Law?*, ch. 1 in this volume, at p.3.

[13] CJEU, Case 294/83 Parti écologiste "Les Verts," EU:C:1986:166, para. 23.

[14] *See* Robert Schütze, *Foreign Affairs Federalism in the European Union*, ch. 19 in this volume.

[15] For commentary on some of the most important case law, *see*, e.g., The European Court of Justice and External Relations Law: Constitutional Challenges (Marise Cremona & Anne Thies eds., 2014).

[16] Art. 3 ASEAN Charter.

speak of a body of "domestic" foreign relations law. Nonetheless, a set of rules for the external relations of ASEAN exists in the ASEAN Charter,[17] as well as in other documents such as the 2011 Rules of Procedure for the Conclusion of International Agreements by ASEAN.[18] Hence, the European Union and ASEAN represent, respectively, maximalist and minimalist legal approaches to their external relations.

Third, not only do the European Union and ASEAN have internal rules that allow them to interact with the outside world, their foundational documents actually direct them to play an active role in wider regional and global governance. The EU Treaties make up arguably the most internationally oriented constitutional document currently in existence.[19] The Treaty on European Union (TEU) stipulates that the "Union shall seek to develop relations and build partnerships with third countries, and international, regional or global organisations" and that it, moreover, "shall promote multilateral solutions to common problems, in particular in the framework of the United Nations."[20] At the wider regional level, furthermore, the "Union shall develop a special relationship with neighbouring countries, aiming to establish an area of prosperity and good neighbourliness."[21] In both the global and regional context, this involves directly engaging with international institutions. According to Article 220 of the Treaty on the Functioning of the European Union (TFEU), the "Union shall establish all appropriate forms of cooperation with the organs of the United Nations and its specialised agencies, the Council of Europe, the Organisation for Security and Cooperation in Europe and the Organisation for Economic Cooperation and Development,"[22] as well as "maintain such relations as are appropriate with other international organisations."[23] In order to do so, the European Union has been given the explicit power to conclude international agreement not only with "third countries" but also with "international organisations."[24]

In the case of ASEAN, its Charter lists as one of its purposes "to maintain the centrality and proactive role of ASEAN as the primary driving force in its relations and cooperation with its external partners in a regional architecture that is open, transparent and inclusive."[25] Its list of principles furthermore includes "the centrality of ASEAN in external political, economic, social and cultural relations while remaining actively engaged, outward-looking, inclusive and non-discriminatory."[26] According to the Charter's Chapter XII on "External Relations," "ASEAN shall develop friendly relations and mutually beneficial dialogue, cooperation and partnerships" not only

[17] *See*, in particular, Chapter XII of the ASEAN Charter on "External Relations."

[18] Rules of Procedure for the Conclusion of International Agreements by ASEAN, adopted in Bali, Indonesia, 17 November 2011.

[19] Joris Larik, Foreign Policy Objectives in European Constitutional Law 124 (2016).

[20] Art. 21(1), first subpara. TEU. *See also* art. 21(2)(h), according to which the European shall "promote an international system based on stronger multilateral cooperation and good global governance."

[21] Art. 8(1) TEU. [22] Art. 220(1), first subpara. TFEU.

[23] Art. 220(2), first subpara. TFEU. [24] Art. 218(1) TFEU.

[25] Art. 1(15) ASEAN Charter. [26] Art. 2(2)(m) ASEAN Charter.

with states but also with "sub-regional, regional and international organisations and institutions."[27] To this end, ASEAN is empowered to "conclude agreements with countries or subregional, regional and international organisations and institutions."[28] According to Article 45 of the Charter, moreover, "ASEAN may seek an appropriate status with the United Nations system as well as with other sub-regional, regional, international organisations and institutions."[29]

III. Engaging with and within International Institutions

Having established that the European Union and ASEAN, although not states, have international legal personality, internal rules on external relations, and mandates to engage with international institutions, the question arises how the two make use of these powers, and how this use compares to state practice. In order to assess this, the present section distinguishes three principal ways in which an entity can engage with and within international institutions: (1) concluding international agreements with international organizations; (2) becoming a member of an international organization and founding new ones; and (3) taking part in the internal decision-making and dispute settlement procedures of the organization.

Concluding International Agreements with International Organizations

Regarding treaty-making, both the European Union and ASEAN have expressly been given the power to conclude international agreements, not only with states but also with other regional and international organizations. Both organizations possess detailed procedures on how to make treaties.[30] Both the European Union and ASEAN have been avid treaty-makers.[31] The main differences between the two are, first, in terms of the possibility of "mixity" and, second, in terms of the profile and substance of these agreements.

[27] Art. 41(1) ASEAN Charter. [28] Art. 41(7) ASEAN Charter.

[29] Art. 45(1) ASEAN Charter.

[30] Art. 218 TFEU; art. 41(7) ASEAN Charter and Rules of Procedure for Conclusion of International Agreements by ASEAN.

[31] ASEAN, or its member states acting under the ASEAN collective label, have concluded more than one hundred international agreements and memoranda to date. *See* Marise Cremona et al., ASEAN's External Agreements: Law Practice and the Quest for Collective Action 69 (2015). The European Union has concluded more than a thousand agreements. *See* European External Action Service, *Treaties Office Database*, *available at* http://ec.europa.eu/world/agreements/SimpleSearch.do.

One of the hallmarks of EU external relations is the use of mixed agreements, i.e., agreements with third parties concluded by both the Union and the member states. This is a result of the substantial but not complete transfer of sovereign powers to the European Union, meaning that in many cases neither Union nor member states have the power to conclude the agreement on their own. This is the case for some high-profile agreements, such as the World Trade Organization (WTO) agreements, the UN Convention on the Law of the Sea (UNCLOS), and the newer generation of trade agreements, including the EU-Canada Comprehensive Economic and Trade Agreement (CETA). By contrast, certain technical agreements falling fully within the European Union's competence are concluded without the member states, as are—perhaps counterintuitively—agreements under the Common Foreign and Security Policy.[32]

The European Union has concluded international agreements with international organizations such as UN agencies,[33] as well as regional organizations.[34] There are even cases of "double mixed" agreements, i.e., having two RIOs and both sets of member states as parties.[35] Nonetheless, the majority of the agreements that the European Union concludes (either mixed or by itself) are with states, not with international institutions.[36]

In terms of the internal procedures to be followed, Article 218 TFEU applies to all treaties concluded by the European Union with third parties.[37] Five key features should be noted here: First, the negotiator for the Union will be the European Commission except for those agreements relating "exclusively or principally to the common foreign and security policy,"[38] for which the High Representative will be the negotiator. Second, the Council of the European Union has the primary role of adopting the mandate and for monitoring the negotiations. Third, the Council will sign and conclude the agreement.[39] Fourth, for some agreements, the consent of the European Parliament is required, especially the more politically salient ones, including those that amount to engaging or creating international institutions such as association agreements or the accession to the European Convention on Human Rights (ECHR).[40]

[32] E.g., Acquisition and Cross-servicing Agreement between the European Union and the United States of America (ACSA) [2016] OJ L350/3.

[33] *See*, e.g., Memorandum of Cooperation between the European Union and the International Civil Aviation Organization providing a framework for enhanced cooperation [2011] OJ L232/2.

[34] Agreement between the European Community and the West African Economic and Monetary Union on certain aspects of air services [2010] OJ L56/16.

[35] Economic Partnership Agreement between the West African States, the Economic Community of West African States (ECOWAS) and the West African Economic and Monetary Union (UEMOA), of the one part, and the European Union and its Member States, of the other part (not in force, initialed June 30, 2014).

[36] European External Action Service, *Treaty Database, available at* http://ec.europa.eu/world/agreements/default.home.do.

[37] *See* Marise Cremona, *Making Treaties and Other International Agreements: The European Union*, ch. 14 in this volume.

[38] Art. 218(3) TFEU. [39] Art. 218(2) TFEU. [40] Art. 218(6), second subpara. (a) TFEU.

The Parliament's consent is also required for trade agreements,[41] the more recent ones of which tend to create sophisticated institutional structures such as the Investment Court System.[42] Fifth, the degree of control from the member states sitting in the Council varies, as there are a number of exceptions to the Qualified Majority default rule, based on which member states can be outvoted by others. For instance, association agreements require unanimity in the Council.[43]

In contrast to the European Union, ASEAN to date has not concluded any mixed agreements. The parties are always either ASEAN or its member states. Moreover, whenever ASEAN exercises its own treaty-making powers, it is normally with other international organizations, not with states. These are mostly of a low political profile, such as Memoranda of Understanding with UN agencies[44] or other regional bodies.[45] For treaties with states, ASEAN countries are the contracting parties. However, they like to stress their collective identity, denoting themselves as "collectively ASEAN" when concluding an agreement with a third state party.[46] An important exception here is the European Union, with which the ASEAN countries (but not ASEAN itself) have concluded a cooperation agreement.[47]

Nonetheless, in 2011 ASEAN adopted specific Rules of Procedure for the Conclusion of International Agreements. These rules apply to "any written agreement, regardless of its particular designation, governed by international law which creates rights and obligations for ASEAN as a distinct entity from its Member States."[48] The ASEAN Foreign Ministers Meeting appoints the negotiator.[49] The ASEAN Foreign Ministers Meeting, moreover, decides "on the signing of, and/or an act of formal confirmation of an international agreement."[50] All of these decisions are made by consensus, in contrast to the European Union where in many cases a minority of member states can be overruled in the Council. In contrast to the prominent role of the European

[41] Art. 218(6), second subpara. (v) TFEU in combination with art. 207(3) TFEU; *see* Piet Eeckhout, EU External Relations Law 203–204 (2d ed. 2011).

[42] *See*, respectively, chs. 8 and 26, Section F of the CETA.

[43] Art. 218(8), second subpara. TFEU.

[44] 2007 Memorandum of Understanding between the Association of Southeast Asian Nations (ASEAN) and the United Nations (UN) on ASEAN-UN Cooperation; 1998 Agreement of Co-operation between ASEAN and United Nations Educational, Scientific and Cultural Organization signed in Jakarta, Indonesia on 12 September 1998.

[45] 2012 Memorandum of Understanding between the Association of Southeast Asian Nations and the Asian Development Bank signed on 4 April 2012 in Phnom Penh, Cambodia.

[46] *See*, for instance, the 2010 Air Transport Agreement between the Governments of the Member States of the Association of Southeast Asian Nations and the Government of the People's Republic of China signed in Bandar Seri Begawan, Brunei Darussalam on 12 November 2010, which states at the outset "Governments of the Member States of the Association of Southeast Asian Nations (hereinafter referred to collectively as 'ASEAN' or 'ASEAN Member States', or individually as 'ASEAN Member State')," followed by a list of the ten members.

[47] Cooperation Agreement between the European Economic Community and Indonesia, Malaysia, the Philippines, Singapore and Thailand, member countries of the Association of South-East Asian Nations, signed on 7 March 1980 in Kuala Lumpur.

[48] Rules of Procedure for the Conclusion of International Agreements by ASEAN, rule 2.

[49] *Id.* rule 3.

[50] *Id.* rule 8(4).

Commission, the role of the ASEAN Secretariat is merely to "assist the representative(s) and relevant ASEAN organs throughout the process of conclusion of international agreements."[51] Moreover, practice based on these Rules of Procedure has thus far been very limited.[52]

Becoming a Member of an International Organization and Founding New Ones

In addition to interacting with IOs through treaty-making, RIOs can also become members of IOs or even be founders of new IOs. The European Union is active in several international organizations,[53] as well as gatherings such as the G20.[54] It is a full member of the Food and Agriculture Organization (FAO), the Codex Alimentarius Commission, certain fisheries commissions, and the World Trade Organization. Membership in an IO is obtained by concluding an international agreement. Here, the European Union's internal procedures as set out in the TFEU apply. However, its ability to join IOs is constrained, in the first place, by the internal division of powers with its member states and its constitutional principles, and—equally importantly—by barriers on the international level. Probably the most infamous example of internal obstacles is the decades-long saga of the European Union trying to join the European Convention of Human Rights and the European Court of Human Rights (ECtHR). Even though the Lisbon Treaty introduced a constitutional obligation for the EU to accede to the ECHR,[55] the CJEU ruled in 2014 that subjecting itself to ECtHR jurisdiction would be at odds with the EU Treaties, in particular the autonomy of EU law and the prerogatives of the CJEU.[56]

In terms of international barriers, many charters of international organizations, most prominently the United Nations, only allow for states to become members.[57] In the case of the FAO, EU membership only was made possible through an amendment to the FAO constitution. In the amended version, it allows for the admission "as a

[51] *Id.* rule 11.

[52] Pieter Jan Kuijper, James H. Mathis, & Natalie Y. Morris-Sharma, From Treaty-Making to Treaty-Breaking: Models for ASEAN External Trade Agreements 120 n.45 (2015).

[53] *See* Frank Hoffmeister, *Outsider or Frontrunner? Recent Developments Under International and European Union in International Organizations and Treaty Bodies*, 44 Common Mkt. L. Rev. 41 (2007).

[54] Jan Wouters, Sven Van Kerckhoven, & Jed Odermatt, *The EU at the G20 and the G20's Impact on the EU*, *in* The EU's Role in Global Governance: The Legal Dimension 259–271 (Bart Van Vooren, Steven Blockmans, & Jan Wouters eds., 2013).

[55] Art. 6(2) TEU. [56] CJEU, Opinion 2/13 (ECHR II), ECLI:EU:C:2014:2454, para. 258.

[57] Art. 4(1) UN Charter; *see also* Jan Wouters, Jed Odermatt, & Thomas Ramopoulos, *The EU in the World of International Organizations: Diplomatic Aspirations, Legal Hurdles and Political Realities*, *in* The Diplomatic System of the European Union: Evolution, Change and Challenges 94–111 (Michael Smith, Stephan Keukeleire, & Sofie Vanhooacker eds., 2015).

Member of the Organization of any regional economic integration organization."[58] The European Union joined the FAO in 1991 and remains the only "member organization" to date.[59] When existing members of an IO remain reluctant to open membership up to RIOs, they can keep the European Union out by maintaining state-only membership rules, as happened with the European Union's endeavors to join the International Labour Organization (ILO).[60] Where the European Union cannot become a full member, it strives for a form of "enhanced observer status," which it achieved at the UN General Assembly.[61] Moreover, if it has the relevant powers conferred upon it internally, the European Union can have its member states act in the Union's interest.[62] Conversely, the European Union can also implement binding decisions of international organizations of which only its member states are members if they fall within the Union's powers. A prominent example here for that is the implementation of sanctions adopted by the UN Security Council.[63]

In a more accommodating milieu, the members of the old General Agreement on Tariffs and Trade (GATT) allowed the then European Economic Community (the European Union's predecessor) to join and take over most of the functions of its member states in the 1970s. In 1994, moreover, the European Union became a founding member of the WTO. However, member states often remain members of IOs alongside the European Union, as is the case in the WTO and FAO, leading to mixity in membership. One could also argue that by concluding association agreements that establish internal rule-making procedures (e.g., with Turkey) and FTAs with permanent dispute settlement arrangements (e.g., CETA), the European Union creates, if not new, fully-fledged IOs, at least new international institutions.

[58] FAO Constitution, art. II(3). Additional criteria apply as specified in art. II(4) of the FAO Constitution. *See also* Eeckhout, *supra* note 41, 228–229.

[59] FAO, Legal Office, *Membership of FAO*, *available at* http://www.fao.org/legal/home/membership-of-fao/en/.

[60] *See* Paul O'Higgins, *The Interaction of the ILO, the Council of Europe and European Union Labour Standards*, *in* Social and Labour Rights in a Global Context: International and Comparative Perspectives 55–69, 62 (Bob Hepple ed., 2002).

[61] UN General Assembly Resolution A/65/276, 3 May 2011. This status allows it, among other things, to take part in the UNGA General Debate and to present common positions but does not confer upon it any voting rights.

[62] *See* CJEU, Opinion 2/91 (ILO), ECLI:EU:C:1993:106, para. 5: "In any event, although, under the ILO Constitution, the Community cannot itself conclude [ILO] Convention No 170, its external competence may, if necessary, be exercised through the medium of the Member States acting jointly in the Community's interest." *See also* Marise Cremona, *Member States as Trustees of the Union Interest: Participating in International Agreements on Behalf of the European Union*, *in* A Constitutional Order of States? Essays in EU Law in Honour of Alan Dashwood 435–457 (Anthony Arnull et al. eds., 2011).

[63] *See*, e.g., Council Decision (CFSP) 2017/1512 of 30 August 2017 amending Decision (CFSP) 2016/849 concerning restrictive measures against the Democratic People's Republic of Korea [2017] OJ L 224/118, which implements UN Security Council Resolution 2270 (2016) of March 2, 2016, for the entire European Union.

Taking Part in Internal Decision-Making and Dispute Settlement

Once a full member of an IO, the European Union can exercise voting rights and take part in institutionalized dispute settlement. For adopting positions in IOs, the TFEU provisions apply, according to which the "Council, on a proposal from the Commission or the High Representative of the Union for Foreign Affairs and Security Policy, shall adopt a decision . . . establishing the positions to be adopted on the Union's behalf."[64] In mixed settings, this leads to a number of constraints on the ability of member states to operate as members within these IOs, which are discussed in the next section. In terms of litigation in the WTO context, the European Union has been one of the most active participants alongside the United States, also taking up the defense of its Member States in cases launched against them.[65]

ASEAN, by contrast, is not a full member of any IOs, only having observer status in some organizations such as the United Nations.[66] The adoption of the Rules of Procedure on international agreements did not change that. As pointed out by Paruedee Nguitragool and Jürgen Rüland, the rules "sought to strengthen ASEAN as a negotiator not *in* but *with* international organizations."[67] As such, the Association cannot take part in IO decision-making through exercising voting rights. At the G20, while ASEAN is not one of the members, the ASEAN Chair used to be invited as a guest, although this did not happen at the 2017 G20 Summit in Hamburg.

Whereas ASEAN has not joined any formal IOs thus far, it plays an important role as a convener in the wider Southeast Asian and Pacific regional architecture.[68] This architecture consists of varying formats, such as ASEAN Plus Three (China, India, and South Korea), the ASEAN Regional Forum (ARF), and the Treaty of Amity and Cooperation in Southeast Asia (TAC). Nonetheless, these processes are driven by the member states, while ASEAN as a legal person stays in the background. The European Union, by contrast, takes part both in the ARF and acceded to the Treaty of Amity and Cooperation in 2012.[69] The TAC includes all ASEAN members but not ASEAN itself as parties, as well as third parties including the United States, China, and France. In order to accommodate the European Union's request to accede, a special protocol was adopted, which amended the TAC's article on accession to include "regional

[64] Art. 218(9) TFEU.

[65] For an overview of this practice, *see* Andrés Delgado Casteleiro & Joris Larik, *The "Odd Couple": The Responsibility of the EU at the WTO*, *in* THE INTERNATIONAL RESPONSIBILITY OF THE EUROPEAN UNION: EUROPEAN AND INTERNATIONAL PERSPECTIVES 233–255 (Malcolm Evans & Panos Koutrakos eds., 2013).

[66] UN General Assembly Res. (61/44) of 4 December 2006. Another example is Codex Alimentarius.

[67] PARUEDEE NGUITRAGOOL & JÜRGEN RÜLAND, ASEAN AS AN ACTOR IN INTERNATIONAL FORA: REALITY, POTENTIAL AND CONSTRAINTS 61 (2015) (emphases in the original).

[68] *See* CREMONA ET AL., *supra* note 31, at ch. 6.

[69] Council Decision 2012/308/CFSP of 26 April 2012 on the accession of the European Union to the Treaty of Amity and Cooperation in Southeast Asia [2012] OJ L 154/1.

organisations whose members are only sovereign States."[70] This highlights again the difference between the European Union acting as a quasi-state alongside (some of) its own members and ASEAN as a collective identity of a group of states.

IV. Disengaging from International Institutions

There are also a number of ways to disengage from international institutions, such as suspending or terminating agreements with IOs, leaving IOs, and refusing to participate or abide by the rules and decisions of dispute settlement mechanisms of IOs. The existence of RIOs raises two additional considerations. First, to the extent that RIOs start becoming active within international institutions, this may have a constraining effect on the ability of the member states to engage with IOs. Second, as illustrated by the decision of the United Kingdom to leave the European Union, there is a question of how a country's disengagement from an RIO affects the engagement of that country with international institutions.

Acts Contrary to Engagement

The European Union's internal procedure for suspending international agreements is set out in the TFEU, according to which the Council adopts a decision to that effect based on a proposal from the Commission or the High Representative.[71] No consent from the European Parliament is required. The procedure under international law is specified in the agreement in question—or by default in the law of treaties.[72] Termination is a possibility as envisaged in international agreements that the European Union has concluded with third parties, including international organizations.[73] By the same token, the European Union could leave international organizations of which it is a member.[74] There are a few occasions in which the European Union has suspended agreements with third parties, although sometimes only partially.[75] However, these

[70] Third Protocol Amending the Treaty of Amity and Cooperation in Southeast Asia, Ha Noi, Viet Nam, 23 July 2010, art. 1, amending art. 18(3) of the TAC.

[71] Art. 218(9) TFEU. Termination is not mentioned.

[72] Art. 56 Vienna Convention on the Law of Treaties.

[73] *See*, e.g., Memorandum of Cooperation between the European Union and the International Civil Aviation Organization providing a framework for enhanced cooperation [2011] OJ L232/2, art. 9.3.

[74] Constitution of the Food and Agriculture Organisation of the United Nations, art. XIX.

[75] *See*, e.g., 2011/523/EU: Council Decision of 2 September 2011 partially suspending the application of the Cooperation Agreement between the European Economic Community and the Syrian Arab Republic [2011] OJ L 228/19.

were all with states, and to date the European Union has not suspended or terminated any of its agreements with IOs. Nor has it left any IOs.

A similar picture emerges with regard to ASEAN. The Rules of Procedure for international agreements are to be applied "*mutatis mutandis*, to the amendment, suspension and termination of international agreements to which ASEAN is a party."[76] The agreements it has with international organizations include termination clauses.[77] However, it has not invoked them to date. Since it is not a member of any IO, leaving them is not currently a live issue.

A form of disengagement from international institutions short of leaving them is to cease participation in them, i.e., adopting a kind of "empty chair policy." Such cases are not known with respect to the European Union and cannot apply to ASEAN since it not a member of any IOs. However, since the European Union is an active litigator in the WTO, it faces the issue of compliance with panel and Appellate Body reports. In some of the more controversial cases, compliance by members that had been found to violate their obligations under WTO law was not immediate. They had to be prompted by follow-up procedures and suspension of concessions (sanctions) by complaining WTO members. An example of this is the *Bananas* dispute between the United States and others and the European Union, which lasted for sixteen years (from 1996 to 2012).[78] However, since the European Union is cooperating with its WTO partners and participating in the procedures, such temporary noncompliance does not amount to systematic obstruction or disengagement.

As a preliminary finding, it appears that both the European Union and ASEAN, to the extent that they interact directly with other IOs, are averse to stepping back from these engagements. Once they engage with international institutions, they seem to be there to stay.

Constraining the Member States

As has been noted, the European Union's and ASEAN's engagement with international institutions does not automatically lead to a replacement of the member states on the international scene. Nonetheless, the question arises whether and to what extent states' international scope of maneuver is affected, amounting in the extreme to their

[76] Rules of Procedure for the Conclusion of International Agreements by ASEAN, rule 10.

[77] E.g., Agreement of Co-operation between ASEAN and UNESCO, signed in Jakarta, Indonesia on 12 September 1998, art. VII.3.

[78] European Communities—Regime for the Importation, Sale and Distribution of Bananas—Second Recourse to art. 21.5 of the DSU by Ecuador—AB-2008-8, European Communities—Regime for the Importation, Sale and Distribution of Bananas—Recourse to art. 21.5 of the DSU by the United States—AB-2008-9, Reports of the Appellate Body, WT/DS27/AB/RW2/ECU, WT/DS27/AB/RW/USA, 26 November 2008.

disengagement from international institutions. Here, the European Union and ASEAN espouse radically different approaches.

In the case of the European Union, given its supranational setup and significant areas of power, this issue is particularly salient. As aptly formulated by Bruno De Witte, sovereignty has been pooled to such an extent within the European Union that both Union *and* its member states have become "strange subjects" of international law.[79] This manifests itself with regard to IOs in two main ways.

First, there are situations in which the member states are absent due to the fact that the European Union has "exclusive" powers over an area. Rather than disengagement, member states are legally barred from engaging in the first place. An example for this is the Convention on Future Multilateral Cooperation in North-East Atlantic Fisheries of 1981, which set up the North-East Atlantic Fisheries Commission. It includes the then European Economic Community and a number of third states, but no Community member states given that the latter had conferred powers upon the Community over fisheries as part of the Common Agricultural Policy.[80] The Convention of 1981 replaced the 1959 North-East Atlantic Fisheries Convention,[81] which had Belgium, France, Germany, and the Netherlands as parties rather than the European Community.[82] Thus, the Community replaced the member states in this instance, became a party itself, and set up an international organization of which it was a member. The member states, for their part, did not have to officially withdraw. They simply did not appear as parties to the successor convention. A similar development might occur with regard to the member states' numerous bilateral investment treaties (BITs) with third countries as the European Union moves into this area.[83]

It should be stressed that this does not happen against the will of the member states, which, despite relinquishing their international legal presence in these scenarios, maintain control inside the European Union through the Council and its committees. Depending on the particular area and situation, they either retain veto power or can be outvoted by a Qualified Majority.

[79] Bruno De Witte, *The Emergence of a European System of Public International Law: The EU and Its Member States as Strange Subjects*, *in* THE EUROPEANISATION OF INTERNATIONAL LAW: THE STATUS OF INTERNATIONAL LAW IN THE EU AND ITS MEMBER STATES 39–54 (Jan Wouters, André Nollkaemper, & Erika de Wet eds., 2008).

[80] Council Decision 81/608/EEC of 13 July 1981 concerning the conclusion of the Convention on Future Multilateral Cooperation in the North-East Atlantic Fisheries [1981] OJ L227/21.

[81] North-East Atlantic Fisheries Convention, signed in London, 24 January 1959.

[82] *See* UK Foreign and Commonwealth Office, UK Depositary Status list North-East Atlantic Fisheries Convention, *available at* https://www.gov.uk/government/uploads/system/uploads/attachment_data/file/600575/18._NE_Atlantic_Fisheries__1959___Status_list.pdf.

[83] *See* CJEU, Case C-284/16, *Slovak Republic v. Achmea*, ECLI:EU:C:2018:158, which found BITs between EU member states to be illegal. Whereas new EU trade agreements such as CETA include investment protection mechanisms, the CJEU ruled in *Opinion 2/15 (EU-Singapore FTA)*, ECLI:EU:C:2017:376 that nondirect investments and their protection remain a shared competence. In *Opinion 1/17 (CETA)*, which is still pending at the time of writing, the CJEU will determine whether the mechanism contained in CETA is compatible with the EU Treaties or not.

Second, in other cases, the member states are still present alongside the Union in international institutions, but the scope of their operation is limited, sometimes severely. In these mixed settings, having both the European Union and member states present requires close coordination between them in order to maintain a joint front in negotiations and in organs of the IO, and to make sure all obligations stemming from membership in the IO are observed. One way of doing this is by drawing up declarations of competence, which are required by some IOs as a condition for RIOs to join.[84] Depending on whether the RIO or its member states have the relevant competence, voting rights can be exercised.[85] However, given the dynamic nature of EU competences, the usefulness of such declaration is rather limited.[86]

In ensuring coherence between the European Union and its member states in IOs, the legally enforceable "duty of sincere cooperation" has been instrumental.[87] This duty also places constraints on how member states can operate in IOs. Instructive here are the *International Maritime Organization* (*IMO*) and *PFOS* cases. In both, a member state had submitted a proposal of its own in a forum of an international organization. Both times, the European Commission sued the member state for having violated its duty of sincere cooperation by undermining the "unity in the international representation" of the Union and the members. In the *IMO* case, the European Union was not even present in the international forum, due to barriers to membership at the IMO, but wielded exclusive competence over the subject matter.[88] Hence, rather than acting in their own right, the member states had to exercise the Union's powers in its stead. In the *PFOS* case, the European Union was present, but the matter concerned an area of competence shared between Union and member states.[89] In both cases, the member states were found in breach of their EU membership obligations. Hence, even though they are still present in international fora, the member states are under wide-ranging duties to desist from engagement if their acts could undermine concerted EU approaches.[90] The situation at the WTO is also indicative of this. Both the European Union and member states are still members, but the latter stay largely in the background given the wide scope of the European Union's exclusive competence in trade matters, which is supplemented by the duty of sincere cooperation.[91]

[84] *See*, e.g., Constitution of the Food and Agriculture Organisation of the United Nations, art. II(5).

[85] *See*, e.g., art. II(8) Constitution of the Food and Agriculture Organisation of the United Nations; and art. IX(1) Agreement Establishing the World Trade Organization.

[86] Andrés Delgado Casteleiro, *EU Declarations of Competence to Multilateral Agreements: A Useful Reference Base?*, 17 EUR. FOREIGN AFF. REV. 491 (2012).

[87] Art. 4(3) TEU. *See also* Christophe Hillion, *Mixity and Coherence in EU External Relations: The Significance of the "Duty of Cooperation," in* MIXED AGREEMENTS REVISITED: THE EU AND ITS MEMBER STATES IN THE WORLD 87–114 (Christophe Hillion & Panos Koutrakos eds., 2010).

[88] CJEU, Case C-45/07 Commission v. Greece *(IMO)*, ECLI:EU:C:2009:81.

[89] CJEU, Case C-246/07 Commission v. Sweden *(PFOS)*, ECLI:EU:C:2010:203.

[90] Andrés Delgado Casteleiro & Joris Larik, *The Duty to Remain Silent: Limitless Loyalty in EU External Relations?*, 36 EUR. L. REV. 522 (2011).

[91] Joris Larik, *Sincere Cooperation in the Common Commercial Policy: Lisbon, a "Joined-Up" Union, and "Brexit,"* 8 EUR. Y.B. INT'L ECON. L. 83, 105 (2017).

In the case of ASEAN, the question of crowding out the member states has been avoided by its "either/or" practice in international representation. When interacting with international institutions, whenever the member states engage, the Association is absent, and when the Association as a legal person engages, the member states are not present. In the former case, practice indicates that when a matter is taken up by the member states, the Association is barred from engaging in the first place. In the latter case, the member states were not engaged to begin with in the international setting in question. However, they do retain full control through the ASEAN bodies in which they are represented and in which the consensus rule applies.

"Brexit": Disengage to Re-engage?

The question of what happens if a member state of an RIO leaves has turned from theoretical to real due to "Brexit." One argument of those advocating the United Kingdom's withdrawal was that it could allow for international re-engagement under the heading "Global Britain." As Boris Johnson, a prominent figure in the campaign to leave, noted shortly after the EU referendum in June 2016, Brexit was a chance "to bring our uniquely British voice and values, powerful, humane, progressive, to the great global forums without being elbowed aside by a supranational body."[92] Legally, three scenarios need to be distinguished here, showing that, at least at first, Brexit leads to considerable disengagement from international treaties and the institutions they set up. Only subsequently does it open up the possibility for the United Kingdom to either disengage further or re-engage internationally.

First, where the United Kingdom is a member of an IO (or an informal institution for that matter) in its own right, exercising its own competences rather than the European Union's, Brexit will change virtually nothing. The prime example here is the United Nations and the United Kingdom's permanent seat on the Security Council. As an EU member, the duty of sincere cooperation also applies here in theory, but it is not justiciable due to the exclusion of the jurisdiction of the CJEU over matters pertaining to the European Union's Common Foreign and Security Policy.[93]

Second, there are the "mixed" settings in IOs as well as the situations where the member states act as the Union's "trustees." Here, the United Kingdom is already a full member of these IOs from the point of view of international law but is currently constrained in its freedom of action by obligations under EU law. The latter would disappear with Brexit, providing greater freedom of maneuver for the United Kingdom

[92] *See Boris Johnson dramatically rules himself out of Conservative election race*, THE TELEGRAPH (June 30, 2016), *available at* http://www.telegraph.co.uk/news/2016/06/30/boris-johnson-dramtically-rules-himself-out-of-conservative-elec/.

[93] Art. 24(1), second subpara. TEU. Note also that art. 27(7) TEU stresses "mutual political solidarity" in the CFSP and refers to the Council and High Representative to uphold it (i.e., not the Court or Commission).

in these institutions. Two examples here would be the WTO and the IMO. In the WTO in particular, a case of involuntary increased direct engagement may be observed, as the United Kingdom would have to defend itself in dispute settlement proceedings brought against it by other WTO members, instead of being defended by the European Union.

However, some new constraints may be placed on the United Kingdom in the form of the transitional and future agreements with the European Union.[94] An example here would be remaining (temporarily) in a customs union with the European Union. This would entail a commitment to adjust its tariffs and duties to those of the European Union as far as covered by such a customs union, and mimic trade agreements that the European Union is concluding with other third parties.[95] However, these constraints would be governed by public international law, rather than EU external relations law as a part of "domestic" EU law.

Third, there are the situations in which the European Union exercises exclusive competence and is the only entity represented. These are the cases where the United Kingdom would decrease its international engagement, hitherto exercised through the European Union, in particular the Council and its committees. According to some estimates, this could require the need to negotiate more than seven hundred treaties, including their institutional provisions.[96] Here, Brexit means in the first place a considerable international disengagement and the need for the United Kingdom to work its way back in.

A similar maze of legal complexities is currently inconceivable in the ASEAN context, although some problems would also be raised here. As noted earlier, "mixity" is not practiced by ASEAN and its members, and the Association's engagement as a legal person is limited in international treaty making and marginal in international institutions. But should one of the ten ASEAN members decide to leave, this would raise questions about its status in agreements concluded "collectively" by the member states with third countries. As a matter of the law of treaties, the withdrawing member could claim to remain a party in its own right given that it was a party all along and that the collective label "ASEAN" has no legal significance. At international institutions, the departing country would simply cast off its ASEAN identity and nothing more, since any hard legal constraints for its international engagement under a presumptive "ASEAN law" did not exist in the first place. As Reuben Wong aptly put it, "the depth of integration demanded of member states in Asean has been low" compared to the European Union, avoiding "politically sensitive, long-term commitments from

[94] For a discussion of Brexit's implications for treaty relations with the United States, including in multilateral settings, *see* Joris Larik, *The New Transatlantic Trigonometry: Brexit and Europe's Treaty Relations with the United States*, 40 U. PA. J. INT'L L. 1 (2018).

[95] This is the case currently for Turkey due to its customs union with the European Union, *see* Decision No. 1/95 of the European Community-Turkey Association Council of 22 December 1995 on implementing the final phase of the Customs Union (96/142/EC) [1996] OJ L 35/1, respectively arts. 14 (on aligning external tariffs) and 16 (on aligning external trade policy, including trade agreements).

[96] Paul McClean, Alex Barker, Chris Campbell, & Martin Stabe, *The Brexit treaty renegotiation checklist*, FIN. TIMES (Aug. 20, 2017), *available at* https://ig.ft.com/brexit-treaty-database/.

which disentanglement could be protracted and costly."[97] Since the ASEAN member states were never really overshadowed by the Association, they would not need to work their way back like the United Kingdom in its international engagement.

V. Conclusion

Comparative foreign relations law is not only about comparing the domestic laws of states but also those of regional organizations as increasingly active global players. Beyond traditional treaty-making, regional organizations also engage with international institutions in other ways. As a comparison of the European Union and ASEAN reveals, there are radically different modes of doing so, ranging from supranational "quasi-federal" to strictly intergovernmental.

While the European Union is more active than ASEAN, it rarely completely replaces its member states when it joins IOs, or even when creating new institutions such as the WTO. This makes interaction of the European Union within IOs a highly complex matter, often painstaking for both the European Union as well as third parties. ASEAN, by contrast, employs its consensus-based, intergovernmental "ASEAN Way" also in its relations with third parties. Its member states are always in the driver's seat, even on the occasions that use is made of ASEAN as a legal person. Once the European Union and ASEAN engage with international institutions, it seems they are there to stay. Some disengagement, however, can be seen on the part of the member states of the European Union, whose scope of action is often restrained while still retaining their seats within IOs. If states choose to leave the European Union, they regain this scope of action, but this does not automatically mean more active engagement within international institutions.

In sum, the fact that regional organizations engage with international institutions should not be seen as a sign of a "runaway regionalism." This chapter has shown that this inter-IO engagement is still limited, that its internal and international legal modalities are complex, and that becoming more active under a collective label in international institutions often leads back to "Westphalia," i.e., the idea of an international legal system comprising states. In the case of ASEAN, this means the prominent role of its member states; in the case of the European Union, it means acting more like a state itself alongside its own member states.

[97] Reuben Wong, *Brexit and the false analogies with Asean*, The Straits Times (Aug. 3, 2016), *available at* http://www.straitstimes.com/opinion/brexit-and-the-false-analogies-with-asean.

PART V

DOMESTIC APPLICATION OF INTERNATIONAL LAW

CHAPTER 26

TREATY SELF-EXECUTION AS "FOREIGN" FOREIGN RELATIONS LAW

DUNCAN B. HOLLIS
AND CARLOS M. VÁZQUEZ

In this chapter, we posit that in some cases a state's approach to a foreign relations problem may have an external origin, generating what might be called "foreign" foreign relations law (FFRL). Differentiating the exogenous and endogenous origins of foreign relations laws raises questions that can deepen and develop the nascent field of comparative foreign relations law.[1] Why do states accept (or reject) FFRL? How does FFRL enter a state's system? Who is doing the transporting? What happens to FFRL in its new site(s)—i.e., how static or dynamic does the concept prove in different settings? The answers to these questions may, in turn, set the table for more normative questions such as when states should seek (or resist) the importation of foreign relations law.

To illustrate the possibilities of FFRL, this chapter offers a case study of treaty self-execution. In Section I, we explain the doctrine's origins and its various manifestations in the United States and other national legal systems. We highlight some similarities between the forms the doctrine has taken in the United States and other states, including indications that the doctrine's origins and development in the latter states were influenced by U.S. case law and scholarship. In Section II, we introduce three sets of framing questions regarding the identification, causation, and evolution of FFRL. We conclude by highlighting several practical and normative implications of FFRL.

[1] A similar line of research already exists in many other areas of comparative law. *See*, e.g., Comparative International Law (Anthea Roberts et al. eds., 2018); Sujit Choudhry, The Migration of Constitutional Ideas 16 (2006); Mark Tushnet, *The Possibilities of Comparative Constitutional Law*, 108 Yale L. J. 1225, 1229 (1999); Alan Watson, Legal Transplants—An Approach to Comparative Law (2d ed. 1993). *But see* Pierre Legrand, *The Impossibility of "Legal Transplants,"* 4 Mastricht J. Euro. & Comp. L. 111 (1997).

I. Self-Execution through a Comparative Lens

The doctrine distinguishing self-executing from non-self-executing treaties originated in the United States,[2] and it is fair to say that few doctrines of U.S. foreign relations law have confounded U.S. courts and commentators as thoroughly.[3] It is therefore surprising that this distinction has been embraced in other states. It has, for example, found its way into the South African Constitution, where scholars have noted that this "unwise []" importation from U.S. jurisprudence[4] is "bound to create problems."[5] In some states, the term "direct effect" is used to describe the self-execution concept. Scholars appear to use the terms interchangeably.[6]

Commentators have argued that the U.S. term "self-executing" masks a number of distinct issues that should be addressed separately.[7] Some have gone so far as to claim that "[t]his word 'self-executing' is essentially meaningless and the quicker we drop it from our vocabulary the better for clarity and understanding."[8] Nonetheless, the adoption of the concept—and the term—by other states suggests that it serves a purpose that courts (and sometimes constitution writers) regard as useful. A comparative look at the doctrine of self-execution of treaties reveals, moreover, that the term has been as versatile outside the United States as inside it.

The U.S. Doctrine

In U.S. case law, the distinction between self-executing and non-self-executing treaties articulates a limit on the judicial power to enforce treaties notwithstanding a general

[2] *See* Yuji Iwasawa, *Domestic Application of International Law*, 378 Recueil des cours 9, 54 (2016).

[3] *See* United States v. Postal, 589 F.2d 862, 876 (5th Cir. 1979).

[4] Neville Botha, *Treaty Making in South Africa: A Reassessment*, 25 S. Afr. Y.B. Int'l L. 69, 91 (2000).

[5] John Dugard, International Law: A South African Perspective 62 (3d ed. 2005). Other scholars are less concerned. *See* Elias M. Ngolele, *The Content of Self-Execution and Its Limited Effect in South African Law*, 31 S. Afr. Y.B. Int'l L. 141 (2006); M. E. Olivier, *Exploring the Doctrine of Self-Execution as Enforcement Mechanism of International Obligations*, 27 S. Afr. Y.B. Int'l L. 99 (2002).

[6] *See, e.g.*, Christina Binder & Catherine M. Brölmann, *The Law of Treaties Before Domestic Courts and Human Rights Bodies, in* International Law in Domestic Courts: A Casebook (André Nollkaemper, August Reinisch, Ralph Janik, & Florentina Simlinger eds., 2018) (using the term "self-executing" interchangeably with "directly applicable" or "directly effective"); André Nollkaemper, *The Duality of Direct Effect of International Law*, 25 Eur. J. Int'l L. 105, 106 n.3 (2014) (referencing Jean-Marie Henckaerts, *Self-Executing Treaties and the Impact of International Law on National Legal Systems: A Research Guide*, 26 Int'l J. Legal Info. 56 (1998)). *See generally* Iwasawa, *supra* note 2.

[7] *See, e.g.*, Carlos Manuel Vázquez, *The Four Doctrines of Self-Executing Treaties*, 89 Am. J. Int'l L. 695, 695 (1996).

[8] *See, e.g.*, Myres S. McDougal, *Remarks at the Annual Meeting of the American Society of International Law* (Apr. 27, 1951), 45 Proc. Am. Soc'y Int'l L. 101, 102 (1951).

constitutional rule that treaties have the force of domestic law. That rule marked a shift from the constitutional law of Great Britain where treaties have never had the force of domestic law. U.K. courts only apply treaties if they have been given domestic legal force by statute. The U.S. Constitution, in contrast, declares that "all Treaties made, or which shall be made, under the Authority of the United States, shall be the supreme Law of the Land; and the judges in every State shall be bound thereby, any Thing in the Constitution or Laws of any State to the Contrary notwithstanding."[9]

The concept of a non-self-executing treaty first emerged (even though the Court did not use the term) in *Foster v. Nielson*.[10] In *Foster*, the U.S. Supreme Court recognized that some treaties require legislative implementation before they may be enforced by the courts despite the Constitution's declaration that all treaties have the force of domestic law. As the Court put it in *Percheman v. United States*, the paradigmatic non-self-executing treaty is one that "stipulat[es] for some future legislative act."[11] Thus, if a treaty text says its aims are to be accomplished through subsequent legislation, the courts may not enforce it until such legislation is enacted.

After *Percheman*, the Supreme Court did not address the self-execution doctrine again in any depth until 2008. In the interim, the Court routinely enforced treaties without pausing to consider whether they were self-executing. After the Second World War, U.S. lower courts invigorated the distinction between self-executing and non-self-executing treaties.[12] But rather than confine the concept to treaties that expressly "stipulate for" future legislation, the courts inferred the need for implementing legislation from various factors. The resulting case law has been aptly described as confounding, and the Supreme Court's 2008 decision in *Medellín v. Texas* did little to clarify matters.[13] U.S. courts have employed the non-self-executing concept to describe at least four reasons why particular treaties might not be judicially enforceable despite the Constitution assigning them the force of domestic law.

First, some U.S. cases indicate that a treaty requires implementing legislation if it purports to accomplish something that, under the U.S. Constitution, can only be accomplished by statute. Examples include treaties that purport to raise revenue, make conduct criminal, or appropriate money.[14] *The Restatement (Fourth) of the Foreign Relations Law of the United States* (hereinafter *Fourth Restatement*) recognizes this as a distinct category of non-self-executing treaties.[15]

[9] U.S. CONST. art. VI.

[10] Foster v. Nielson, 27 U.S. (2 Pet.) 253, 314 (1829). The Court first used the term "self-executing" in Bartram v. Robertson, 122 U.S. 116, 120 (1887).

[11] United States v. Percheman, 32 U.S. (7 Pet.) 51, 89 (1833).

[12] For analysis of these developments, *see* DAVID L. SLOSS, THE DEATH OF TREATY SUPREMACY: AN INVISIBLE CONSTITUTIONAL CHANGE (2016).

[13] Medellín v. Texas, 552 U.S. 491 (2008). On *Medellín*, *see generally* Carlos Manuel Vázquez, *Treaties as Law of the Land: The Supremacy Clause and the Judicial Enforcement of Treaties*, 122 HARV. L. REV. 599 (2008).

[14] For citations, *see* Vázquez, *supra* note 7, at 718 & nn.107–109.

[15] RESTATEMENT (FOURTH) OF THE FOREIGN RELATIONS LAW OF THE UNITED STATES § 310(3) cmt. f & reporters' note 11 (AM. LAW INST. 2018) [hereinafter RESTATEMENT (FOURTH)].

Second, numerous U.S. cases apply the distinction between self-executing and non-self-executing treaties to distinguish between treaty provisions that give private parties a cause of action and those that do not.[16] The *Third* and *Fourth Restatements* take the position that the existence of a private cause of action is distinct from the "self-execution" issue.[17] For present purposes, however, the important points are that (1) U.S. courts have often referred to this as a "self-execution" issue, and (2) this issue is conceptually distinct from the others that the courts use the term "self-executing" to describe.

A third category derives from the cases that originally introduced the distinction between self-executing and non-self-executing treaties, i.e., a non-self-executing treaty is one that must be implemented by legislation because it "stipulates for some future legislative act." This does not mean that a treaty's self-executing character is a matter of international law rather than U.S. foreign relations law. Treaties generally do not address the manner in which they are to be enforced in the courts of states parties, and it is clear that a treaty's self-executing character does not turn on whether the treaty requires direct judicial enforcement as a matter of international law.[18] Still, this domestic law distinction turns on the type of substantive obligation to which the parties agreed. In the words of Chief Justice Marshall in *Foster*, did the parties "pledge the faith" of the nation to accomplish certain aims through subsequent acts of domestic legislation, or, in his words in *Percheman*, did they "stipulate for a future legislative act"? According to the *Fourth Restatement*, "[a] treaty provision is more likely to be regarded as self-executing if it imposes obligations or creates authorities designed to have immediate effects, as opposed to contemplating additional legal measures."[19]

Finally, U.S. courts have recognized that treaty provisions require legislative implementation before they may be judicially enforced if they are framed in vague or aspirational terms. This category also encompasses precatory terms (i.e., requiring parties to use their "best efforts"). The *Fourth Restatement* recognizes that "whether a treaty provision is sufficiently precise or obligatory" is a "consideration" in determining if it is self-executing, but does not treat this as a distinct category of non-self-execution.[20]

Vague or aspirational treaty provisions might be unenforceable because such language suggests the parties contemplated that the provision's aims would be fleshed out

[16] *See* Vázquez, *supra* note 7, at 719–722.

[17] *See* Restatement (Fourth), *supra* note 15, § 310 cmt. b, § 111, § 111 cmt. a; Restatement (Third) of the Foreign Relations Law of the United States § 111 cmt. h (1987).

[18] *See* Vázquez, *supra* note 13, at 652–656. *Accord* Restatement (Fourth), *supra* note 15, § 310 cmt. c; *cf. Medellín*, 552 U.S. at 546–561 (Breyer, J., dissenting) ("whether further legislative action is required before a treaty provision takes domestic effect . . . is often a matter of how that Nation's domestic law regards the provision's legal status. And that domestic status-determining law differs markedly from one nation to another").

[19] Restatement (Fourth), *supra* note 15, § 310 & reporters' note 6.

[20] *Id.*, § 310, cmt. d.

through subsequent legislation.[21] If so, then this category might be regarded as a subset of the self-execution category recognized in *Foster* and *Percheman* (with stipulations for legislation inferred from—rather than expressed in—treaty text). Alternatively, these cases might reflect separation-of-powers concerns: to the extent a treaty provision leaves the parties with discretion regarding performance, the political branches—not the courts—are best suited to exercise that discretion. Under this alternative explanation, implementing legislation is required—not because of the parties' intentions—but due to constitutional principles allocating power between U.S. courts and the political branches.

We think the second explanation is more persuasive. Even treaties that "stipulate for a future legislative act" do not, technically, reflect the parties' preference that the treaty be unenforceable pending enactment of legislation. Such language may reflect *permission* for states parties not to apply the treaty as domestic law before further legislation is enacted. But even treaties phrased in precise and obligatory terms implicitly permit parties to enforce such provisions in the courts via implementing legislation. Otherwise, states following the British rule would not be able to become parties.

Self-Execution around the Globe

Looking at other states shows that (1) some have specifically imported self-execution in name or concept; (2) each of the foregoing U.S. types of non-self-execution has an analogue in one or more other states; and (3) virtually all states recognize some version of the distinction between self-executing and non-self-executing treaties. Moreover, even though the term is susceptible to multiple meanings, most states employing it fail to draw clear distinctions among the possible grounds of non-self-execution.

Constitutional Non-Self-Execution

Although the British constitutional rule—under which treaties may not be judicially enforced absent implementing legislation—predates the U.S. self-execution concept, courts and commentators outside the United States commonly use the term "non-self-executing" to describe the status of treaties in states that follow the British rule.[22] Thus, "[a]ccording to the government of India, treaties are not self-executing and therefore 'require enabling legislation, or constitutional and legal amendments in cases where existing provisions of law and the Constitution are not in consonance with the obligations arising from the treaty'."[23] In such strict dualist states, the rule reflects the

[21] *See* Iwasawa, *supra* note 2, at 173. [22] *See id.* at 25–26.

[23] Nihal Jayawickrama, *India*, *in* The Role of Domestic Courts in Treaty Enforcement: A Comparative Study 326, 341–369 (David Sloss ed., 2009).

idea that treaties are concluded by the executive, while enactment of domestic law is a matter for the legislature.[24]

For these states, the distinction between self-executing and non-self-executing treaties describes a general attribute of treaties under their domestic law. The terms are not used to distinguish some treaty provisions from others, as they are in states where treaties generally have direct effect as domestic law. As noted, the U.S. Constitution gives "all" treaties the force of domestic law. And, in the Netherlands—where the distinction between self-executing and non-self-executing treaties has also taken root[25]—treaties have a *higher* status in the domestic legal order than other forms of domestic law.[26] In states like the United States and the Netherlands, therefore, a treaty's "non-self-executing" character does not relate to its status as domestic law, but rather describes a treaty that—while having the force of domestic law—is not directly applicable in the courts (either in all cases or in a given case).

As noted, one type of U.S. non-self-executing treaty purports to accomplish what, under the U.S. Constitution, may only be done by the legislature. The need to enact legislation to implement such treaties results from the Constitution itself, which disables the treaty makers from accomplishing certain things directly. In light of the constitutional disability, treaties falling within this category of non-self-execution might be thought to lack domestic legal force by virtue of the Constitution itself. Treaties in states that follow the British rule are "non-self-executing" in exactly this sense. The difference is that, in the United States, this category includes very few treaties, whereas in states following the British rule, this category includes all treaties.

South Africa presents a hybrid situation. It has departed from the British rule, but its constitution appears to say that all non-self-executing treaties lack domestic legal force. Section 231(2) provides that some treaties "bind[] the Republic only after [they have] been approved by resolution in both the National Assembly and the National Council of Provinces."[27] Section 231(4) goes on to provide that "a self-executing provision of an agreement that has been approved by Parliament is law in the Republic unless it is inconsistent with the Constitution or an Act of Parliament."[28] A non-self-executing provision, therefore, does not have the force of domestic law (i.e., is not "law in the Republic"). South Africa thus employs the concept of self-execution to describe an attribute that some treaties possess and others lack, like the United States and the Netherlands, and unlike strict dualist states, which use non-self-execution to describe

[24] Attorney General for Canada v. Attorney General for Ontario, [1937] AC 326 (PC) [347] (appeal taken from Can.). *See generally* CAMPBELL MCLACHLAN, FOREIGN RELATIONS LAW 31, 81 (2014). Although these states can be described as "strict dualist" states with respect to treaties, we note that these same states are monist with respect to customary international law, which they regard as part of the law of the land without the need for legislative implementation.

[25] *See* Jan G. Brouwer, *The Netherlands*, *in* NATIONAL TREATY LAW AND PRACTICE 502–505 (Duncan B. Hollis et al. eds., 2005).

[26] *See id.* at 498 (noting that "the priority of treaty law over municipal law has never been seriously contested in the Dutch legal literature").

[27] S. AFR. CONST., 1996 § 231(2).

[28] *Id.* § 231(4).

all treaties in their legal systems. Unlike the United States and the Netherlands, however, the non-self-executing character of South African treaties always deprives them of domestic legal force.

Interestingly, states that do give treaties the force of domestic law have not followed the U.S. example of considering some treaties non-self-executing on the ground that they purport to accomplish something that, under their constitutions, may only be accomplished by law makers. This is likely because these states generally require legislative consent before a treaty's ratification, and thus the treaty makers and the law makers are the same entities.[29] Even in these states, however, the particular type of treaty obligation involved may, for constitutional reasons, impose additional constraints on the treaty provision's self-executing nature. For example, treaties that contemplate the criminalization of conduct will, in most states, require additional levels of specificity and clarity.[30]

Nonconstitutional Non-Self-Execution

In states that generally give domestic legal force to treaties, the term "non-self-executing" (and its cognate "no direct effect") describe an attribute of certain treaties. The term describes treaties that are not judicially enforceable in the absence of implementing legislation even though treaties generally have the force of domestic law. In some states, the distinction has its basis in explicit constitutional text. Thus, in the Netherlands, a constitutional amendment in 1956 clarified that "the power of the courts is restricted to treaties that are self-executing."[31] The constitution provides that "[s]tatutory regulations . . . [may not be applied] . . . if such application is in conflict with [treaty] provisions . . . that are binding on all persons."[32] The reference to treaties that are "binding on all persons" is generally understood to establish that the judicial power is limited to enforcing treaties that are self-executing.[33]

In most states that generally give treaties domestic legal force, however, courts have elaborated a similar distinction without relevant constitutional text. Courts applying the self-executing/non-self-executing distinction in these states appear to use it for issues similar to those addressed by the U.S. doctrine. One notable difference, however,

[29] *See* Duncan B. Hollis, *A Comparative Approach to Treaty Law & Practice*, *in* NATIONAL TREATY LAW AND PRACTICE, *supra* note 25, at 36, 41.

[30] *See*, e.g., André Nollkaemper, *The Netherlands*, *in* THE ROLE OF DOMESTIC COURTS IN TREATY ENFORCEMENT, *supra* note 23, at 357–358; Lech Garlicki et al., *Poland*, *in* THE ROLE OF DOMESTIC COURTS IN TREATY ENFORCEMENT, *supra* note 23, at 370, 403.

[31] Brouwer, *supra* note 25, at 502–503.

[32] *Id.* at 503 (*quoting* The Netherlands' Constitution, art. 94).

[33] *Id.* (citing Kemerstukken II, 1955–1956 4133 (R 19), No. 3, 5) ("The term 'self-executing treaty provision' was considered to be a synonym [for the constitutional language].").

is that non-U.S. courts rarely say that a treaty's self-executing character is a matter of intent.[34] This could be because these courts recognize that treaties rarely—if ever—address whether they are to be enforced directly by courts or through implementing legislation. Indeed, recognition of this fact may explain why the *Fourth Restatement* takes the position that self-execution turns on the U.S. treaty makers' intent or understanding rather than the intent of all parties.[35] In contrast, courts and commentators in other states have not taken the position that the self-executing nature of treaties turns on either the parties' intent or the unilateral intent of a given country's treaty makers regarding the treaty's self-executing character.

On the other hand, several non-U.S. courts echo the U.S. use of the concept of self-execution to assess "whether the provision was designed to have immediate effect, as opposed to contemplating additional measures by the [legislature]."[36] The Supreme Court of Poland, for example, has written that treaty provisions may be "qualified as self-executing" when they "creat[e] immediate entitlements for citizens."[37] It has also found a treaty provision to be non-self-executing because "[t]he wording of that provision indicates that it was directly addressed only to the State, establishing its obligation to adopt a corresponding penal norm."[38]

Like U.S. courts, other states' courts sometimes use self-execution to refer to treaties that confer remedies on private parties. Thus, the Supreme Court of Poland has stated that "international agreement provisions are effective not only with regard to the States, but may provide an independent ground of claims for damages raised before domestic courts (so-called self-executing norms)."[39]

By far the most common approach to self-execution for states that generally give treaties the force of domestic law is to regard treaties as self-executing when they are framed in sufficiently precise and obligatory terms for judicial application. Belgian legal scholar Marc Bossuyt describes this as the requirement that the treaty be "self-sufficient."[40] Judicial decisions from numerous states reflect this theme. Thus, Brouwer

[34] There are isolated exceptions, however. *See* Nollkaemper, *The Netherlands*, *supra* note 30, at 341 (citing Supreme Court, E.O. v. Public Prosecutor, Apr. 18, 1995, 28 N.Y.I.L. 1997, 336).

[35] Restatement (Fourth), *supra* note 15, § 310 cmt. c ("[T]reaties . . . typically do not address the issue of domestic implementation."); *id.* § 310 (2) ("Courts will evaluate whether the text and context of the provision are consistent with an understanding by the U.S. treatymakers that the provision would be directly enforceable in U.S. courts."). For a critique of the *Restatement's* emphasis on U.S. treaty maker's intent, *see* Carlos Manuel Vázquez, *Four Problems with the Draft Restatement's Treatment of Treaty Self-Execution*, 2015 BYU L. Rev. 1747, 1761 (2015).

[36] Restatement (Fourth), *supra* note 15, § 310(2).

[37] Garlicki et al., *supra* note 30, at 370, 402 (*quoting* I KZP 37/96, OSNKW 1997 no. 3–4, item 21). The court also suggested the provision must be "apt to be applied by the State bodies, especially by the courts and administrative organs," an apparent reference to the requirement, discussed below, that treaties be sufficiently precise and obligatory. *Id.*

[38] *Id.* at 403 (*quoting* V KKN 353/00, Lex 56863).

[39] *Id.* at 402 (*quoting* I CK 323/02, OSNC 2004 nr 6, item 103).

[40] *See* Marc Bossuyt, International Human Rights Protection: Balanced, Critical, Realistic 104 (2016). *Cf.* Iwasawa, *supra* note 2, at 175 (discussing view that treaty provisions "must be *complete* to be directly applicable" (emphasis in original)).

concludes that, "[e]xamining the [Netherlands Supreme] Court's case law, one may say that [a treaty will be deemed non-self-executing] if there is a lack of judicially manageable standards for resolving the question, or when the issue involved ought to be resolved by the legislator."[41] The Supreme Court of Poland has held that whether "a treaty may be regarded as self-executing" turns on "the completeness of the treaty provision that enables its operation without any additional implementation [in domestic legislation]."[42] The Hungarian Constitutional Court has stated that "[t]he precondition for applicability [of a treaty in domestic courts] is that those subject to the international treaty are precisely defined private entities and that the rights and obligations included in the treaty are specific enough so that the treaty is enforceable without any further domestic legislative action."[43] And the Swiss Federal Supreme Court held a treaty (the Lisbon Treaty) was "not self-executing," while noting that "[a]ccording to the relevant case law, a treaty norm is directly applicable if its content is sufficiently precise and clear to form the basis of a decision in a particular case."[44] In other words, "[t]he norm . . . has to be justiciable . . . "[45]

These cases do not explain the rationale for why insufficiently precise treaty provisions require legislative implementation. Bossuyt takes the position that a treaty's self-sufficient status "is a matter of international law."[46] The better view, we think, is that sufficiency issues are a matter of domestic—rather than international—law. A provision that may be too vague to be directly enforced in the courts of one state may well be enforceable in another. In a number of Latin American states, for example, there is a "constitutional block"—i.e., specific human rights treaties designated for direct effect by the constitution or a constitutional court.[47] For example, Article 75 of the Argentine Constitution lists treaties—including the Covenant on Economic, Social and Cultural Rights—as having a constitutional footing.[48] As a result, the Argentine

[41] Brouwer, *supra* note 25, at 504–505; Nollkaemper, *The Netherlands*, *supra* note 30, at 341 (reading the Dutch cases to establish that "a [treaty] provision can be applied [by the courts] only if it is sufficiently clear from its content that it can serve as objective law").

[42] Garlicki et al., *supra* note 30, at 402 (*quoting* I CK 323/02, OSNC 2004 no. 6, item 103). *See also id.* at 401–402 (noting that treaties are self-executing if they are "apt to be applied by the State bodies, especially by the courts and administrative organs").

[43] Alkotmánybíróság (AB) [Constitutional Court] Mar. 29, 2005, 964/A/2004, Decision No. 7/2005 (III. 31) (Hung.). [Preventive Review of Unconstitutionality of Statute, Determination of Unconstitutional Omission to Legislate]. This case is discussed in Binder & Brölmann, *supra* note 6, at [9].

[44] Bundesgericht [BGer] [Federal Supreme Court] Mar. 13, 2014, 2C_457/2013 (Switz.). [X v. University of Lucerne, Student Administration Office and Department of Education and Culture of the Canton of Lucerne]. This case is discussed in Binder and Brölmann, *supra* note 6, at [10].

[45] *Id.*; *see also* Liechtenstein, Addendum, Report of the Working Group on the Universal Periodic Review, UN Doc. A/HRC/23/14/Add.1 ¶24 (May 28, 2013).

[46] Bossuyt, *supra* note 40, at 105.

[47] *See* René Urueña, *Domestic Application of International Law in Latin America*, ch. 32 in this volume.

[48] Constitution of Argentina 1853 (reinst. 1983, rev. 1994), art. 75(22), English translation *available at* https://www.constituteproject.org/constitution/Argentina_1994?lang=en.

Supreme National Court has found provisions of the Covenant to be enforceable in Argentine courts.[49] In contrast, other states, such as Switzerland, view the same treaty's provisions as non-self-executing.[50] In our view, neither the Argentine nor Swiss approach violates the requirements of the Covenant. If the treaty is consistent with a constitutional rule (such as that of the United Kingdom) requiring implementing legislation in all circumstances, then it must also be consistent with an approach requiring implementing legislation because a state regards the treaty as too vague for direct judicial enforcement.

Nollkaemper offers a different rationale for the unenforceability of treaty provisions that are insufficiently clear or specific:

> The principal basis for the requirement that the content of a treaty provision must be clear for it to have direct effect lies in the boundaries of judicial competence. If a court were to enforce a treaty provision that is formulated too openly, it would effectively be taking over the task of the legislature.[51]

This rationale seems to us to align more closely with the language of the non-U.S. cases. And, as discussed above, it also may be the best explanation for the judicial unenforceability of vague or aspirational treaty provisions in U.S. courts. Indeed, the Dutch cases invoke the absence of "judicially manageable standards" as the reason for finding a treaty provision non-self-executing,[52] while the Swiss courts invoke the concept of justiciability.[53] The phrase "judicially manageable standards" comes directly from *Baker v. Carr*,[54] the leading case in the United States for the political question doctrine, which is a key justiciability doctrine. As one of us has argued, the notion that vague or aspirational treaty provisions are non-self-executing is best understood as the treaty-law equivalent of the political question doctrine.[55] Thus, these references to judicially manageable standards and justiciability are suggestive of the U.S roots of the "self-execution" doctrine in at least some states.[56]

[49] Corte Suprema de Justicia de la Nación [CSJN] [National Supreme Court of Justice], 24/04/2012, "SYQC v. Government of the City of Buenos Aires/review of facts motion before the Supreme Court," (Arg.). This case is discussed in Binder and Brölmann, *supra* note 6, [at 9].

[50] *Cf.* Bundesgericht [BGer] [Federal Supreme Court] Sept. 22, 2000, 2P.273/1999 (Switz.) [A and B v. Government of the Canton of Zurich].

[51] Nollkaemper, *The Netherlands*, *supra* note 30, at 342.

[52] *See supra* text accompanying note 41.

[53] *See supra* text accompanying note 45.

[54] *See* Baker v. Carr, 369 U.S. 186, 217 (1962) ("Prominent on the surface of any case held to involve a political question is . . . a lack of judicially discoverable and manageable standards for resolving it.").

[55] Vázquez, *supra* note 7, at 715–716.

[56] Like self-execution, moreover, the migration of the political question doctrine across legal systems could itself be another example of FFRL.

II. Self-Execution as "Foreign" Foreign Relations Law

It is not surprising that the distinction between self-executing and non-self-executing treaties first emerged in the United States. The United States was the first country to adopt a Constitution giving treaties automatic force as domestic law.[57] Its courts were thus among the first to determine whether that designation required judicial enforcement of *all* treaties, or, instead, permitted a doctrine limiting judicial enforcement to specific types of treaties.

But how did other states come to self-execution? Did they import the term (and the underlying concept) from the U.S. legal system? This is the central question that motivates our inquiry into "foreign" foreign relations law (FFRL). Time and space make a definitive response difficult, but we offer here three framing questions on the (1) *identification*; (2) *causation*; and (3) *evolution* of self-execution as FFRL. We believe that these questions may be generalized across comparative foreign relations law to improve our descriptive (and perhaps normative) understanding of the field.

Identification—What Constitutes FFRL?

First, the concept of FFRL involves *identification*—asking if a particular term (or rule, or allocation of authority) in foreign relations law has external origins. In some cases, that lineage is clear. As noted, South Africa's constitution explicitly references "self-executing treaties," and Botha notes that it "was taken over . . . from United States' jurisprudence."[58] In other cases identifying FFRL will not be so easy. One problem lies in identifying *what* is being imported—is it just terminology, functions, or both? The British rule, for example, predates the self-execution concept. Thus, the use of "non-self-executing treaties" in that context was—at least initially—the mere importation of the term; it did not include the original distinguishing function that motivated self-execution's creation.

Identification may also be problematic in cases of functional convergence, where states use different terminology. One might find that the evidence supports reading such cases as FFRL, or there may be instances where states, facing similar issues, reached the same solution independently. For example, even if the Netherlands'

[57] *See* Ware v. Hylton, 3 U.S. (3 Dall.) 199, 272 (1796) (Iredell, J., dissenting) (observing that the U.S. Constitution "affords the first instance of any government . . . saying, treaties should be the *supreme law of the land.*" (emphasis in original)).

[58] *See, e.g.*, Botha, *supra* note 4, at 91 (criticizing this borrowing).

category of treaties with "direct effect" functions similarly to that of self-executing treaties, further research is required to determine what—if any—role the U.S. doctrine of self-execution had in motivating the 1956 constitutional amendment that introduced that category.

Our comparative analysis of self-execution suggests, moreover, that FFRL may occur not just in whole, but also in part—some states appear to be adopting one particular thread of the U.S. self-execution concept without adopting all of them. Thus, Poland and Hungary have incorporated non-self-executing treaties involving vague or precatory terms without importing the idea of non-self-execution based on party intent or constitutional delegation to other branches of the government.

FFRL may even be pluralist. The South African Constitution, for example, was subject to multiple foreign influences, including from the United States, Canada, and Europe.[59] It is possible that the introduction of self-executing treaties owed its origin not just to the U.S. jurisprudence, as Botha suggests, but also to European conceptions of self-executing treaties. Indeed, Michèle E. Olivier (who participated in drafting South Africa's earlier, Interim Constitution) suggests that the current constitutional reference should be understood not only in light of U.S. doctrine, but also of EU experiences with self-execution.[60] In other words, FFRL might be constructed from multiple foreign sources rather than just one.[61]

This last point is worth emphasizing. Although self-execution's origins may trace back to the United States, not all instances of FFRL will do so. For example, domestic authority to forgo legislative approval of "executive agreements" has long been associated with U.S. foreign relations law.[62] But it also appears in other states. It is not clear if modern iterations of executive agreements derived from the U.S. experience or sprung up elsewhere out of functional necessity or expediency.[63] In other instances, U.S. foreign relations law concepts (e.g., the practice of concluding treaties among government agencies or ministries) appeared alongside similar practices elsewhere with no established timeline as to which state(s) originated the concept.[64] There are,

[59] *See, e.g.*, Dennis M. Davis, *Constitutional Borrowing: The Influence of Legal Culture and Local History in the Reconstitution of Comparative Influence: The South African Experience*, 1 INT'L J. CONST. L. 181, 187 (2003) (discussing American, Canadian, and German influences).

[60] Olivier, *supra* note 5, at 118 (criticizing Botha's objections to self-execution in South Africa for "not taking cognisance . . . of the increasing body of academic discussion and judicial consideration of self-executing treaties within the context of the European Union").

[61] Of course, multiple foreign sources might all trace back to a single, original source (if, for example, EU versions of self-execution came from the U.S. concept) or multiple sources (if, for example, several states arrived independently at functionally similar—or even equivalent—distinctions for their treaties' domestic enforceability).

[62] *See, e.g.*, J. MERVYN JONES, FULL POWERS AND RATIFICATION 53–56 (1949); FRANCIS O. WILCOX, THE RATIFICATION OF INTERNATIONAL CONVENTIONS 226 (1935); SAMUEL B. CRANDALL, TREATIES, THEIR MAKING AND ENFORCEMENT 102–140 (2d ed. 1916).

[63] On the widespread use of executive agreements today, *see* Hollis, *supra* note 29, at 19–29.

[64] *See id.* (surveying states that do—and do not—authorize interagency treaty-making); JONES, *supra* note 62, at 53–56 (noting practice of interdepartmental agreements).

of course, numerous examples where FFRL is *not* associated with U.S. foreign relations law. For example, the British practice of concluding legally nonbinding memoranda of understanding (MOUs) has been adopted in numerous other states, including many outside the Commonwealth.[65]

How then can we identify FFRL? More research could certainly do so, although it may be challenging. Differing languages will pose problems. Most states that give treaties domestic legal force are not English-speaking, while most English-speaking states follow the British rule. Still, if foreign states' courts cite U.S. cases on self-execution, that would permit us to attribute to its domestic incarnation the character of FFRL. Of course, certain foreign legal systems (e.g., those that track the civil law) often cite sources less frequently than common law opinions. In such cases, references to "foreign" foreign relations scholarship by legislators, government officials, or scholars may provide an alternative vehicle for identifying FFRL.[66]

Nor is FFRL work limited to tracing the path of ideas; the movement of people (e.g., graduate study in U.S. law schools by foreign decision makers) could assign FFRL status to a rule.[67] In some cases, historical and cultural materials may identify FFRL patterns. For example, the shared history of France and Mexico could explain why both states authorize the conclusion of inter-institutional agreements (or what the French call *arrangements administratifs*) that—unlike almost all other states—are viewed as only binding on the concluding agency and not the state as a whole.[68] More rigorous methods for investigating FFRL would engage in process tracing or elite-level interviews.[69]

Identification studies might even include a search for cases of FFRL failure. We predict that sometimes research will reveal de minimis foreign influence on a state's foreign relations law. In other cases, a state's legal system may reject an invitation to

[65] *See*, e.g., ANTHONY AUST, MODERN TREATY LAW AND PRACTICE, 26–28 (3d ed. 2013); Duncan B. Hollis, *Second Report on Binding and Non-Binding Agreements*, Inter-American Juridical Committee, 92nd Regular Session, OAS/Ser.Q, CJI/doc.542.17 (Feb. 25–Mar. 2, 2018) (Colombia, the Dominican Republic, Jamaica, Peru, and Uruguay report using MOUs to conclude nonbinding agreements).

[66] For example, Olivier's analysis of self-execution in South Africa shows a deep familiarity with U.S. and European scholarship on self-execution. *See* Olivier, *supra* note 5, at 100 n.4 (citing scholarship).

[67] *See* Vicki Jackson, *Comparative Constitutional Law: Methodologies*, *in* MICHAEL ROSENFELD & ANDRÁS SAJÓ EDS., THE OXFORD HANDBOOK OF COMPARATIVE CONSTITUTIONAL LAW 58 (2012). Anthea Roberts' studies of difference and dominance in international law similarly emphasize the role of academics and textbooks. *See* COMPARATIVE INTERNATIONAL LAW, *supra* note 1, chs. 3 and 4; ANTHEA ROBERTS, IS INTERNATIONAL LAW INTERNATIONAL? (2017).

[68] *Compare* Pierre Eisemann & Raphaële Rivier, *France*, *in* NATIONAL TREATY LAW AND PRACTICE, *supra* note 25, at 253, 255 (describing *arrangements administratifs* concluded by French governmental agencies and their counterparts which "do not bind the State, only the signatory agency"); *with* Law Regarding the Making of Treaties, *reprinted in* 31 ILM 390 (1992); CDLX, *Diario Oficial de la Federación* 2 (Jan. 2, 1992); Luis Miguel Diaz, *Mexico*, *in* NATIONAL TREATY LAW AND PRACTICE, *supra* note 25, at 450 (under its treaty law, Mexico's inter-institutional agreements are "only binding upon those agencies which have entered into them, and not upon the federation").

[69] *See*, e.g., Jackson, *supra* note 67, at 58–60 (surveying historical and migration methodologies and scholarship in comparative constitutional law).

adopt FFRL. In 2017, for example, the Supreme Court of Ghana was invited to adopt the U.S. concept of executive agreements to legitimate a bilateral treaty with the United States resettling two detainees from the Guantánamo naval base. The Court refused to endorse the executive agreements category, holding instead that all Ghanaian treaties require parliamentary approval. As a result, the Court ruled that the treaty was unconstitutional.[70]

Causation—Why Do States Import Self-Execution?

Assuming that we can identify self-execution or other examples as FFRL, the next question is what caused the state to import it? Why do states incorporate foreign rules, doctrines, or allocations of authority within their foreign relations laws? We envision at least four possible causes for FFRL: (1) function; (2) bricolage; (3) power; and (4) socialization.

First, FFRL may arise due to its *functional* appeal. With globalization, states increasingly must mediate the relationship between their internal law and international legal obligations. In doing so, they encounter new issues for which their internal law has yet to offer an answer. In such cases, the state's decision makers may survey solutions elsewhere and find one (or more) they believe will work best for their situation. Our survey above suggests that, in many states, the distinction between self-executing and non-self-executing treaties covers a wide range of reasons for why a treaty is not subject to judicial application. The attraction to judges of having discretion to enforce a treaty (or not) is one plausible explanation for the spread of the amorphous doctrine of self-execution among states that have (or, like South Africa, have shifted to) a system in which treaties have the status of domestic law.[71]

Second, FFRL may be the product of what Mark Tushnet identifies as *bricolage*.[72] Bricolage would explain the advent of FFRL as the result of happenstance rather than carefully calibrated functional analysis, where decision makers simply adopt concepts about which they have some awareness. To the extent the United States has the most robust (and certainly most written about) foreign relations law, its concepts may be the most likely candidates for FFRL.[73] Thus, an alternative explanation for self-execution's

[70] *See* Banful v. Attorney General, J1/7/2016 [2017] GHASC 10 (Ghana, June 22, 2017). The Ghanaian legislature subsequently approved the agreement. For a similar judicial approach in the Dominican Republic, *see* Judgement of Plenary of the Supreme Court of Justice, Aug. 10, 2005, B.J. 1 037 (Dom. Rep.).

[71] Alternatively, courts might find functional appeal in self-execution as a way to respect separation of powers, leaving to legislatures the implementation of vague/aspirational treaty provisions.

[72] Tushnet, *supra* note 1, at 1286.

[73] It would be interesting to assess by which networks FFRL moves. As a technical concept, self-execution would most likely migrate via intergovernmental networks of officials or academics. *See*, e.g., Anne-Marie Slaughter, A New World Order (2004). In contrast, for FFRL addressing fundamental values (e.g., human rights), Linos' policy diffusion theory suggests patterns of movement

global diffusion may be its visibility rather than its utility. Bricolage may explain why states adopted the terminology of self-execution rather than one or more of the four (more coherent) threads it contains.

Power offers a third—and very different—rationale for the existence of FFRL. Power can manifest itself in various efforts to impose FFRL on a targeted state. In some cases, international institutions might mandate the direct application of treaties. Thus, the European Court of Justice (ECJ) has held that certain treaty provisions and acts of EU institutions have "direct effect" in member states' legal orders.[74] And the Inter-American Court of Human Rights (IACtHR) insists that member states directly apply the American Convention on Human Rights—*and* the Court's interpretation of it—within their internal legal orders.[75] In other cases, power dynamics might be internal to the state—the result of interactions among executives, courts, and legislatures.

Power dynamics may also be less formal, resulting from spheres of influence or the long tail of colonialism. That Commonwealth states follow the British rule is a function of those states' historical relationship with the United Kingdom.[76] A similar rationale could explain the use of MOUs among Commonwealth states. But power also has limits; states can reject the attempted imposition of a rule. For example, states outside the British sphere (most notably the United States) have not adopted the linguistic cues or architectural artifacts of MOUs in concluding political commitments.[77] In any case, we have our doubts that the spread of the self-execution doctrine resulted from power dynamics; we would need to see further evidence of U.S. interests favoring the bifurcation of other states' judicial enforcement of treaties.

Fourth, forces of *socialization* may motivate the creation of FFRL. Some FFRL is likely the result of mimicry. Social scientists have long known that states sometimes conform their systems to those of other states whom they perceive as successful. The calculation can be instrumental (i.e., "we'll do what they do to get where they are") or affective (i.e., "to be regarded as responsible, we should do this too").[78] Under this view, self-execution might be adopted—as a term or concept—to mimic the U.S. doctrine.

Alternatively, FFRL may emerge for expressive purposes. A state might adopt a regime not because of its functions, but because of what it signals to other states about the nation and its identity.[79] For example, South Africa may have adopted the concept

originating from "large, rich, and culturally proximate countries." KATERINA LINOS, THE DEMOCRATIC FOUNDATIONS OF POLICY DIFFUSION 5 (2013).

[74] *See* Case C-26/62, Van Gend en Loos, 1963 E.C.R. 1, 13.

[75] *See* Urueña, *supra* note 47 (recounting direct effect for IACHR opinions under the heading "conventionality" in Brazil, Bolivia, Honduras, Mexico, and Peru, while noting resistance to doing so in Argentina, Chile, the Dominican Republic, and Venezuela).

[76] Of course, some former colonies (e.g., the United States, South Africa) rejected or varied the British rule, suggesting inertia may be at work alongside power dynamics.

[77] *See* AUST, *supra* note 65, at 38–39.

[78] *See, e.g.*, Paul DiMaggio & Walter W. Powell, *The Iron Cage Revisited: Collective Rationality and Institutional Isomorphism in Organizational Fields*, 48 AM. SOCIO. REV. 147, 151 (1983).

[79] *See, e.g.*, Jackson, *supra* note 67, at 66–67 (surveying expressivism in scholarship).

of self-executing treaties as much to signal its commitment to human rights and their enforcement as to making functional distinctions among treaties based on factors such as precision.[80] René Urueña's chapter in this volume provides another example, examining how Latin American states may forgo the very concept of foreign relations law because it is alien to their understanding of international law as something not outside, but inside, their internal law.[81]

These four causes should not be understood as exhaustive. Nor do we mean to suggest they will arise in isolation; FFRL may have not one, but perhaps multiple, causes. The spread of self-execution, for example, may be explained in functional terms and as the product of mimicry or bricolage. Other FFRL might result from different combinations of causal factors.

Moreover, FFRL can conceivably have different causes at different times. Self-execution might have originally spread for reasons of bricolage or mimicry. But it might be sustained within a system for functional reasons whether in terms of judicial discretion or separation of powers.[82] Similarly, the use of nonbinding MOUs might have been originally imposed by a metropolitan power, but other causes (perhaps the functional utility of coordinating nonbinding commitments around a common format) may explain their subsequent spread beyond the Commonwealth.

Evolution—How Does FFRL Evolve over Time?

Even after identifying FFRL and examining why it occurs, the story of its evolution remains. To begin, we should compare the similarities and differences of the FFRL to its original source. While self-execution in some states appears to track some of the features of the U.S. doctrine, some states do not appear to have adopted *all* the concepts subsumed under the U.S. self-executing heading. Differences in form may also prove significant. Consider, for example, self-execution's shift in South Africa and the Netherlands from a judicially developed doctrine to one specified in constitutional text. Doing so may affect the doctrine's status *within* the domestic legal order and, more importantly, trigger a different set of interpretative methodologies—i.e., those applicable to constitutions rather than judicial opinions.

Beyond comparing FFRL manifestations, we should also ask about its dynamic character. Does FFRL hew to its original boundaries or change over time? In the context of self-execution, the appeal to judges of the U.S. doctrine's malleability—evidenced by its amalgamation of a variety of distinct reasons why a treaty might not be

[80] *See,* e.g., Olivier, *supra* note 5, at 119 (emphasizing self-execution's role in advancing human rights).

[81] Urueña, *supra* note 47, at 16.

[82] In South Africa, in contrast, the self-execution concept has rarely been employed, suggesting that its utility has not been perceived as greater than obtaining parliamentary implementation for South Africa's treaties.

judicially enforceable—may suggest that the doctrine is unlikely to evolve (at least overtly) to any great extent. On the other hand, frustration among judges and scholars with the doctrine's indeterminacy may produce pressures for clarification.

Then there is the question of how FFRL affects the state's foreign relations law more generally. Following the British rule, for example, implicates a whole set of rules and allocations of authority (e.g., the plenary power of the executive in treaty-making). Similarly, as we have explained, self-execution not only implicates how international legal obligations enter the domestic legal system, but it also has broader implications for the separation of powers between a state's judiciary and legislature.

One might even ask about the impact of FFRL outside of the state in which it emerges. As FFRL evolves, it might become a source on which other states rely. To the extent that one instance of FFRL creates another, FFRL can operate as much as the influencer as the influenced. Indeed, it might even be possible for certain strains of FFRL to create a feedback loop influencing the evolution of the original rule or regime. To date, self-execution has not exhibited such a pattern—for the most part, U.S. self-execution doctrine still looks primarily to U.S. precedents. But there may be much for U.S. courts and scholars to learn from how this (possibly) transplanted doctrine has fared abroad. More generally, the experience of other states with FFRL might cause the originating state to rethink its own foreign relations law.

III. Conclusion

In 1829, the U.S. Supreme Court introduced the idea that, despite the constitution designating all U.S. treaties the "law of the land," U.S. courts would only enforce those treaties that are "self-executing."[83] In the twentieth century, this distinction evolved to identify different types of unenforceable U.S. treaties. Today, this concept of self-execution and the various doctrines it contains are no longer a uniquely U.S. feature (or, some would say, bug) of its foreign relations law. Various manifestations of self-execution—either in name, function, or both—are visible in other states' internal legal systems.

In at least some of these cases, we find indications that states have derived their version of self-execution from U.S. jurisprudence (i.e., as FFRL). This chapter offered an introduction to the FFRL concept and suggested ways to examine it along three different lines of inquiry. First, we suggest that there is value merely in identifying those parts of a state's foreign relations law that have external origins (whether in whole or in part, and whether from single or multiple sources), including cases where a state rejects proposed FFRL. Second, we ask what causes FFRL, and offer four potential rationales: function, bricolage, power, and socialization. Third, and finally, we inquire into how

[83] *See* Foster v. Nielson, 27 U.S. (2 Pet.) 253, 314 (1829).

FFRL converges or diverges from its source initially and over time, while evaluating FFRL's potential impact on the originating state's and other states' foreign relations law.

But why engage in this inquiry? What value can the inquiry have? Comparative law projects are usually celebrated for enhancing intellectual knowledge and improving self-reflection by increasing knowledge of other systems.[84] Both goals are served by FFRL. Appreciating that foreign relations law's origins lie not only in a state's history and internal dynamics inevitably increases our understanding of what law "is" and how it changes. Moreover, for scholars of foreign relations law, looking at how these concepts travel creates new opportunities to evaluate the system within which they reside. Some U.S. scholars have found the self-execution doctrine to be confusing and even incoherent. By looking at how other states engage with self-execution, U.S. foreign relations lawyers can gain a new appreciation not only of specific categories of self-execution, but their functional utility (especially when compared to foreign variations).

Understanding FFRL may also assist in mapping convergence and divergence across national systems. Our research suggests that—as a matter of national law—most states judicially enforce some, but not all, of their treaties. The more that states come to accept this reality, the more they may become sensitized to (or perhaps even accepting of) the reticence of other states' courts to empower themselves to enforce particular types of treaty provisions without additional guidance from the legislature. Conversely, where we see states rejecting FFRL, it may signal areas at risk of future tensions or conflict. Rejecting the idea of executive agreements in Ghana, for example, threatened the underlying agreement's validity and the goals motivating that deal. The U.S. refusal to import the Commonwealth MOU practice also produced some significant disputes over the legal status of certain defense MOUs it concluded with those states.[85]

FFRL may even have normative value. Certain rationales for adopting FFRL have greater normative purchase than others. Functionally motivated FFRL may be desirable, while FFRL that results from power dynamics, especially those with a colonial heritage, are more undesirable. In other words, a better understanding of FFRL may allow states to be more self-conscious in their choices of whether and when to import or export foreign relations laws.

Finally, FFRL may improve the normative appeal of comparative foreign relations law itself. At present, the field risks U.S.-centricity—not in the sense of distinguishing foreign relations law from other rules of internal law, but in pushing states to conceptualize their internal law along U.S. lines.[86] Our inquiry offers a more transparent approach to understanding where ideas and approaches originate and how they move across boundaries. In doing so, it offers the promise of a truly global field rather than one only indexed to U.S. versions of ideas like self-execution.

[84] Jackson, *supra* note 67, at 70–72.

[85] *See, e.g.*, John H. McNeill, *International Agreements: Recent U.S.-U.K. Practice Concerning the Memorandum of Understanding*, 88 Am. J. Int'l L. 821 (1994).

[86] *Accord* Karen Knop, *Foreign Relations Law: Comparison as Invention*, ch. 3 in this volume.

CHAPTER 27

THE DOMESTIC APPLICATION OF INTERNATIONAL LAW IN BRITISH COURTS

SHAHEED FATIMA Q.C.

THIS chapter considers the use and application of international law in British courts.[1] After an introductory overview of this use, the case law is contextualized within the British constitutional framework, and the dualist nature of the legal system is explained.[2] Further consideration is then given to the constitutional and common law framework within which international law may be used. This includes the use of treaties that are formally incorporated into domestic law (incorporated treaties), those that are not so incorporated (unincorporated treaties), and customary international law.

I. Use of International Law in British Courts

Case reports show that British courts were considering international law from at least 1673.[3] These early cases were diverse. For example, they covered immunities

[1] This chapter uses the terminology of British courts and British law because there is no material difference, in relation to the use and application of international law, as between the different parts of the United Kingdom, e.g., as between courts in England and Scotland.

[2] There is no written British constitution, so the relevant framework is found in constitutional law principles and practice. This is in contrast with some of the other jurisdictions addressed in this volume, where the written constitutions contain provisions on the role and status of international law.

[3] In Blad v. Bamfield 26 Car 2. Blad, a Danish subject sought to stay several actions that were brought against him in the British court arising out of his seizure of the defendants' goods in Iceland because (he

and privileges, issues of justiciability, the use of the law of nations, and treaty interpretation.[4]

From the late twentieth century, there was a gradual, but discernible, increase in the use and application of international law. By 2005, international law was frequently used and applied in British courts. As Lord Bingham observed at that time, "To an extent almost unimaginable even thirty years ago, national courts in this and other countries . . . consider and resolve issues turning on . . . international law . . . routinely, and often in cases of great importance."[5] Since 2005 that trend has continued, as illustrated by the cases that are described below. The subject matter of such cases frequently involves human rights, state immunity and diplomatic immunity, refugee law, extradition and deportation, and cases involving the rights of children.[6]

This increasing use and application of international law in British courts may be attributed to various political, social, and legal developments. However, two developments have been particularly influential. The first is the increasing use of treaties in international practice as a means of regulating "how [a] nation interacts with the rest of the world."[7] This has trickled into domestic law: numerous treaty provisions of this kind, to which the United Kingdom is bound on the international plane, have been given domestic legal effect.[8] Even where they have not been given direct effect, they have influenced the interpretation and application of domestic law. Second, the rapid development of international human rights law from the mid-twentieth century onward has contributed to increasingly visible, vertical international law obligations, which individuals have sought to enforce against the executive through litigation in British courts.

contended) the defendants' activities there were contrary to letters patent given to him by the King of Denmark. The defendants contended that they had a right to trade in Iceland and that if the King of Denmark had granted any patents of privilege contrary to the freedom of trade then they were illegal and a breach of the articles of peace agreed with Denmark. The court rejected the defendants' submissions and gave Blad a perpetual injunction staying the defendants' claim.

[4] *See*, e.g., Triquet v. Bath (1764) 97 ER 936; R v. Keyn (1876) 2 Ex D 63; Rustomjee v. The Queen (1876) 2 QBD 69; and The Parlement Belge (1879) 4 PD 129.

[5] Foreword in SHAHEED FATIMA, USING INTERNATIONAL LAW IN DOMESTIC COURTS (2005; 2d ed. forthcoming in 2019).

[6] This is similar to the profile of relevant Canadian case law. *See* Gib Van Ert, *The Domestic Application of International Law in Canada*, ch. 28 in this volume. In THE RULE OF LAW 119 (2011), Lord Bingham referred to FATIMA, *supra* note 5, "in which the author lists the main practice areas where issues of international law may arise in national courts: they are aviation law, commercial and intellectual property law, criminal law, employment and industrial relations law, environmental law, European treaties, family and child law, human rights law, immigration and asylum law, immunities and privileges, international organizations, jurisdiction, law of the sea, treaties and, finally, warfare and weapons law. In recent years the British courts have ruled on questions arising in most of these areas."

[7] *See* Curtis A. Bradley, *What Is Foreign Relations Law?*, ch. 1 in this volume and the definition of foreign relations law as "the domestic law of each nation that governs how that national interacts with the rest of the world."

[8] There are also other international treaties that have been domesticated, e.g., those that regulate the conduct of commercial relationships between private individuals and entities.

As a result of these and other developments, compliance with international law is now a central part of evaluating the lawfulness of executive actions. In his October 2015 speech, "The Importance of International Law for Government Lawyers," the U.K. Attorney-General commented, "So just how important is international law? The short answer is, very. I have been struck in my first year as Attorney General just how central it is to the daily work of government."[9] In his January 2017 speech, "The Modern Law of Self-Defence,"[10] he described the United Kingdom as a "world leader in promoting, defending and shaping international law." As Attorney-General he said that he followed in a tradition of "advocating, celebrating and participating in a rules-based international order" and that, "International law binds the UK, both as a central tenet of our constitutional framework and as a distinct legal regime at the constitutional level . . . We rightly pride ourselves on being advocates for, and acting within, a rules-based approach." His words reflect Lord Bingham's extracurial assertion that the rule of law requires compliance, by a state, with its obligations in international law as in national law.[11]

However, the words of the Attorney-General should be considered along with the controversy, and litigation, over the October 2015 amendment to the Ministerial Code. The Ministerial Code "sets out the standards of behaviour expected from all those who serve in Government."[12] The October 2015 amendment involved the deletion of the italicized words: "The Ministerial Code should be read alongside . . . the background of the overarching duty on Ministers to comply with the law *including international law and treaty obligations and to uphold the administration of justice* and to protect the integrity of public life." The amendment provoked commentary. For example, in a letter to *The Guardian*, a senior international lawyer and former legal adviser to the Foreign and Commonwealth Office observed: "It's impossible not to feel a sense of disbelief at what must have been the deliberate suppression of the reference to international law in the new version of the ministerial code." The former Treasury Solicitor and head of the government legal services wrote: "I saw at close hand in 2010 onwards the intense irritation these words caused the [Prime Minister] as he sought to avoid complying with our international legal obligations, e.g., in relation to prisoner voting."[13] It also led to litigation: a judicial review claim was issued challenging the amendment and seeking an explanation for

[9] *Available at* https://www.gov.uk/government/speeches/the-importance-of-international-law-for-government-lawyers.

[10] *Available at* https://www.gov.uk/government/uploads/system/uploads/attachment_data/file/583171/170111_Imminence_Speech_.pdf.

[11] *See* Bingham, *supra* note 6, ch. 10.

[12] Foreword by the Prime Minister from the January 2018 version of the Ministerial Code, *available at* https://assets.publishing.service.gov.uk/government/uploads/system/uploads/attachment_data/file/672633/2018-01-08_MINISTERIAL_CODE_JANUARY_2018__FINAL___3_.pdf.

[13] The letters are *available at* https://www.theguardian.com/law/2015/oct/25/international-law-and-the-ministerial-code.

the change in wording. The claim was rejected by the Court of Appeal on the basis that the amendment involved no change in substance.[14]

The existing importance of international law in the British legal system, especially as a vehicle for challenges to the lawfulness to executive conduct, is unlikely to diminish in the near future. Indeed, the relationship between domestic law and other sources of law, including international law, is arguably more important than ever before as a result of the vote to leave the European Union in June 2016 (the Brexit vote). This has already generated high-profile litigation, notably the *Miller* case, which is considered below,[15] and it will entail many more months, if not years, of debate. It is also likely to generate further litigation.

II. British Law as a Dualist System

Understanding and evaluating the use of international law in British courts requires an appreciation of the constitutional context.[16] Despite the increasing use of international law in British courts and the increasing complexity of the issues raised by recent cases, it remains a dualist legal system.[17] The primary underpinning of this dualism is the constitutional principle of Parliamentary sovereignty or supremacy and the corollary that an exercise of the royal, executive, prerogative—which includes the power to enter into treaties—does not enable ministers to change the law, unless such a power is expressly conferred by statute. It is, therefore, the framework of constitutional theory and practice—the role of, and relationships between, Parliament, the Crown/executive, and the courts—and, more subtly, political reality, that guide and shape British courts' engagement with international law.

Although this constitutional framework has long been clear as a matter of *principle*, it is the *application* of it, in discrete cases, that gives rise to continuing debate. The best recent illustration of this is *Miller*. The claim in *Miller* was brought after the Brexit vote. It involved a justiciable[18] question of statutory interpretation, concerning the European

[14] R (Gulf Centre for Human Rights) v. The Prime Minster and the Chancellor of the Duchy of Lancaster [2018] EWCA Civ. 1855.

[15] R (Miller) v. Secretary of State for Exiting the European Union [2018] AC 61 (*Miller*). *Miller* is also considered in Paul Craig, *Engagement and Disengagement with International Institutions: The U.K. Perspective*, ch. 22 in this volume.

[16] As a procedural matter, international law is a matter for submissions, not expert evidence. In contrast, foreign law is a question of fact in British courts to be adduced by way of expert evidence.

[17] It was recently described as such by the Supreme Court in R (Yam) v. Central Criminal Court [2016] AC 771, at para. 35, and in *Miller*, *supra* note 15, at paras. 57 and 79. For more detailed consideration of dualism and the respective roles of the executive and Parliament in concluding treaties, *see* Craig, *supra* note 15.

[18] This was common ground between the parties (as noted by the Divisional Court) and agreed upon by both the majority and minority Justices in the Supreme Court. *See Miller*, *supra* note 15, at paras. 3 and 276.

Communities Act 1972 (ECA).[19] The interpretative exercise required the balancing of two competing constitutional principles as well as consideration of the role of Parliamentary accountability.[20] The Divisional Court and then the Supreme Court considered what steps were required, as a matter of U.K. domestic law, before the process of leaving the European Union could be initiated. In particular, they considered whether a formal notice of withdrawal could lawfully be given by ministers without prior legislation passed in Parliament. Both courts concluded that prior legislation was necessary, the Supreme Court reaching this conclusion by a majority of 8 to 3.

The two constitutional law principles considered by the courts (and already mentioned above) were as follows: *first*, the principle that the conduct of the United Kingdom's foreign relations, including treaty-making, is part of the executive's prerogative power and, *second*, the principle that, unless permitted by primary legislation, the prerogative power does not enable ministers to change statute law or common law. The application of these principles to the interpretation of the ECA pulled in different directions: the Secretary of State relied on the former principle,[21] whereas the claimants relied on the latter.[22] The answer to the question of interpretation therefore turned, to

[19] The two key provisions requiring interpretation were Secs. 2(1) and 1(2). Sec. 2(1) provides: "All such rights, powers, liabilities, obligations and restrictions from time to time created or arising by or under the Treaties, and all such remedies and procedures from time to time provided for by or under the Treaties, as in accordance with the Treaties are without further enactment to be given effect or used in the United Kingdom shall be recognised and available in law, and be enforced, allowed and followed accordingly." Sec. 1(2) defines the expression "the Treaties" as including the pre-accession treaties (described in Part 1 of Schedule 1 of the ECA), other treaties listed in Sect. 1(2), and "any other treaty entered into by the EU . . . with or without any of the member States, or entered into, as a treaty ancillary to any of the Treaties, by the United Kingdom." The Courts also considered art. 50 of the EU Treaty, which provides: "1. Any member state may decide to withdraw from the Union in accordance with its own constitutional requirements. 2. A member state which decides to withdraw shall notify the European Council of its intention. In the light of the guidelines provided by the European Council, the Union shall negotiate and conclude an agreement with that state, setting out the arrangements for its withdrawal . . . 3. The Treaties shall cease to apply to the state in question from the date of entry into force of the withdrawal agreement or, failing that, two years after the notification referred to in paragraph 2, unless the European Council, in agreement with the member state concerned, unanimously decides to extend this period."

[20] Both the majority and dissenting judges referred to Parliamentary accountability. *See Miller*, *supra* note 15, at paras. 100 and 249.

[21] The Secretary of State submitted: "[T]he fact that significant legal changes will follow from withdrawing from the EU Treaties does not prevent the giving of Notice, because the prerogative power to withdraw from treaties was not excluded by the terms of the 1972 Act . . . More particularly, [the Secretary of State] contended that the 1972 Act gave effect to EU law only insofar as the EU Treaties required it, and that that effect was therefore contingent upon the United Kingdom remaining a party to those treaties. Accordingly, he said, in the 1972 Act Parliament had effectively stipulated that, or had sanctioned the result whereby, EU law should cease to have domestic effect in the event that ministers decide to withdraw from the EU Treaties." *See Miller*, *supra* note 15, at para. 37.

[22] The claimants submitted: "[W]hen Notice is given, the United Kingdom will have embarked on an irreversible course that will lead to much of EU law ceasing to have effect in the United Kingdom, whether or not Parliament repeals the 1972 Act. . . . In particular . . . some of the legal rights which the applicants enjoy under EU law will come to an end. This . . . means that the giving of Notice would preempt the decision of Parliament on the Great Repeal Bill. It would be tantamount to altering the law by

a significant degree, on judicial discretion regarding the relative weight that should be given to these principles and the manner of their application to the statutory framework.

The majority of the Supreme Court favored the claimants' approach.[23] They emphasized the "unprecedented"[24] constitutional effect of the ECA and, because of this characterization, gave greater analytical weight to the second principle that the executive's treaty-making (and withdrawing) power cannot alter domestic law. This led the majority to conclude that legislation was needed before a formal notice of withdrawal from the European Union could be given by ministers. The dissenting Supreme Court judges, on the other hand, gave greater significance to the first principle, that the conduct of the United Kingdom's foreign relations falls within the executive's prerogative power, and concluded that there were no restrictions on that power in the ECA, or other relevant statutes.[25]

Miller illustrates not only the continuing challenge posed by the practical application of settled constitutional principles but also the political significance of the issues that may arise in such cases.

III. Treaties

As noted above, in the United Kingdom, the treaty-making power vests in the executive. Since treaties are entered into by the executive, the constitutional position, pursuant to the principle of Parliamentary sovereignty, is that they do not—without more (e.g., statutory incorporation)—form part of, or alter the content of, British law. *Miller* contains a recent endorsement of this proposition.

ministerial action, or executive decision, without prior legislation, and that would not be in accordance with our law." *See Miller*, *supra* note 15, at para. 36.

[23] *See id.* at para. 81: "Accordingly, the main difficulty with the Secretary of State's argument is that it does not answer the objection based on the constitutional implications of withdrawal from the EU. . . . A complete withdrawal represents a change which is different not just in degree but in kind from the abrogation of particular rights, duties or rules derived from EU law. It will constitute as significant a constitutional change as that which occurred when EU law was first incorporated in domestic law by the 1972 Act. And, if Notice is given, this change will occur irrespective of whether Parliament repeals the 1972 Act. *It would be inconsistent with long-standing and fundamental principle for such a far-reaching change to the UK constitutional arrangements to be brought about by ministerial decision or ministerial action alone.* All the more so when the source in question was brought into existence by Parliament through primary legislation, which gave that source overriding supremacy in the hierarchy of domestic law sources." (emphasis added).

[24] *Id.* at para. 60.

[25] For example, Lord Reed commented: "[I]t is a basic principle of our constitution that the conduct of foreign relations, including the ratification of treaties, falls within the prerogative powers of the Crown. That principle is so fundamental that it can only be overridden by express provision or necessary implication, as is accepted in the majority judgment at para. 48. No such express provision exists in the 1972 Act. Nor do its provisions override that principle as a matter of necessary implication." *Id.* at para. 194.

Treaty-making is part of the traditional, nonjusticiable, royal prerogative. That means, for example, that a decision to sign or ratify a treaty is not amenable to judicial review. Neither is a decision that a particular treaty should not be signed or ratified.[26] This is because the "nature and subject-matter are such as not to be amenable to the judicial process."[27] The principle of nonjusticiability (an example of "system closure," to use Professor Bianchi's helpful term)[28] also informs the orthodox position that British courts lack the competence to "adjudicate upon or to enforce" or to interpret unincorporated treaties.[29] However, the more recent, and preferable, approach is for the court to ask whether it is necessary to interpret a treaty in order to determine rights or obligations under domestic law and, where the answer is "yes," for the court to interpret the relevant treaty provisions.[30] Even then, a British court is likely to be reluctant to interpret an unincorporated treaty "where the contracting parties have embraced an alternative means of resolving differences" or where there is "a live dispute on the meaning of an unincorporated provision on which there [is] no judicial authority."[31]

The judicial restraint that applies in the context of unincorporated treaties is unnecessary, or more limited, in the context of incorporated treaties i.e., treaties that are given the force of law in the United Kingdom by statute, either directly or indirectly. Courts may, more freely, interpret and apply such treaties. Before embarking on treaty interpretation, the court will need to consider the extent, and mode, of incorporation, i.e., the way in which the treaty has been incorporated into domestic law. Since "there is no rule specifying the precise legislative method of incorporation,"[32] Parliament may incorporate treaties into law in any way, and to whatever extent, that it sees fit. Perhaps the most common mode of incorporation is for a statute to expressly state that all or part of a treaty, which is often scheduled (i.e., annexed) to the statute, has the force of law.

The court will interpret the relevant incorporated treaty provision by applying international law principles, i.e., those in the Vienna Convention on the Law of Treaties (the VCLT). British courts use the VCLT as a source of law, even though it is not an incorporated treaty, because the primary provisions relating to interpretation, Articles

[26] JH Rayner (Mincing Lane) v. Department of Trade and Industry [1990] 2 AC 418 (*Tin Council*), at 499F-500C (Lord Oliver), and Lewis v. AG of Jamaica [2001] 2 AC 50, at 77B (Lord Slynn).

[27] Council of Civil Service Unions v. Minister for the Civil Service [1985] AC 374, at 418B-C (Lord Roskill).

[28] *See* Andrea Bianchi, *Jurisdictional Immunities, Constitutional Values, and System Closures*, ch. 38 in this volume.

[29] *See* Lord Oliver in the *Tin Council* case, *supra* note 26, at 499F-500C, and British Airways v. Laker Airways [1985] AC 58, at 85H (Lord Diplock).

[30] R (CND) v. Prime Minister [2002] EWHC 2777 (Admin), at para. 36 (Simon Brown LJ).

[31] R (Cornerhouse) v. Director of Serious Fraud Office [2009] 1 AC 756, at paras. 44 and 45 (Lord Bingham) (*Cornerhouse*).

[32] R (ERRC) v. Immigration Officer at Prague Airport [2005] 2 AC 1, at para. 42 (Lord Steyn).

31 and 32, are considered to have the status of customary international law (CIL).[33] Cases on treaty interpretation demonstrate a spectrum of engagement by British courts with international law.

At one end of that spectrum are those cases where Parliament's intent—as to the form and extent of incorporation—is clearly discernible from the statute. The role of the court in these cases is likely to focus on the meaning and scope of the particular incorporated treaty provision and its application to the facts in that case.[34] But the court still has discretion in the interpretative analysis. It may, for example, limit the sources to which it has regard in interpreting the treaty provision or it may limit the role or influence of those sources in the interpretative analysis.[35] Statutory provisions may themselves identify the sources that the domestic court may consider and indicate their status. For example, Section 2 of the Human Rights Act 1998 (HRA) gives domestic courts some discretion regarding the weight to give to judgments of the European Court of Human Rights.[36] Domestic courts may also interpret a particular treaty provision by reference to provisions in other international law instruments,[37] or they may have to consider the interrelationship between different systems—for example, between international law, the European Convention on Human Rights (ECHR), and domestic law.[38] The diverse approach of British

[33] *Id.* at para. 18 (Lord Bingham), and Fothergill v. Monarch Airlines [1981] AC 251, at 282D (Lord Diplock). For a recent example of the Supreme Court applying the VCLT principles, *see Al-Malki v. Reyes* [2017] 3 WLR 923, at paras. 10 and 11.

[34] Recent examples include Secretary of State for the Home Department v. Skripal [2018] EWCOP 6 (application of Sec. 63 and Schedule 3 of the Mental Capacity Act 2005, which give effect in England and Wales to the Convention on the International Protection of Adults), and R (Bancoult) v. Secretary of State for Foreign and Commonwealth Affairs (No. 3) [2018] 1 WLR 973 (consideration of the Diplomatic Privileges Act 1964, which gives effect to certain provisions of the Vienna Convention on Diplomatic Relations 1961).

[35] *See,* e.g., Lord Hoffmann's observation: "Parliament may pass a law which mirrors the terms of the treaty and in that sense incorporates the treaty into English law. But, even then, the metaphor of incorporation may be misleading. It is not the treaty but the statute which forms part of English law. And English courts will not (unless the statute expressly so provides) be bound to give effect to interpretations of the treaty by an international court, even though the United Kingdom is bound by international law to do so." R v. Lyons [2003] 1 AC 976, at para. 27.

[36] The HRA is an example of indirect incorporation: the ECHR was not made a part of English law but Sec. 6 makes it unlawful for a public authority to act incompatibly with the ECHR rights set out in the Schedule to the HRA. A recent case involving consideration of the effect of a judgment of the European Court of Human Rights (which clarified art. 3, ECHR principles previously laid down in an earlier ECtHR judgment, and applied in the United Kingdom) is *AM (Zimbabwe) v. Secretary of State for the Home Department* [2018] 1 WLR 2933, at paras. 29 and 30.

[37] For example, in R (Al-Saadoon) v. Secretary of State for Defence [2017] QB 1015, Lloyd Jones LJ, in the Court of Appeal, construed the scope of art. 5, ECHR by reference to a range of instruments and, in particular, the International Convention for the Protection of All Persons from Enforced Disappearance. *See id.* paras. 147–155.

[38] *See, in particular,* Al-Jedda v. UK (2011) 53 EHRR 23, and R (Serdar Mohammed) v. Ministry of Defence [2017] AC 271, and, for a recent summary of this case law, Alseran and others v. Ministry of Defence [2018] 3 WLR 95, at paras. 86–91. Note also the similar difficulties in the context of EU law. *See,* e.g., Kadi v. Council of the EU [2008] 3 CMLR 4; [2011] 1 CMLR 24. For a more recent

courts in this last group of cases defies general characterization: these are unique cases involving multiple levels of analyses, interpretations of different regimes of substantive law, and consideration of the relationships between these legal regimes. Indeed, these cases are so unique that detailed consideration of them may distort the accuracy of the general overview of the use of international law in the United Kingdom.

At the other end of the incorporated treaty spectrum are hybrid statutes—that is, statutes that do not directly or indirectly incorporate treaty provisions but which are intended to give effect to all or part of an unincorporated treaty. This intention will usually be clear from either the title or preamble of the statute[39] or extrinsic evidence.[40] It is now well established that a statute should be construed by reference to an underlying, unincorporated, treaty.[41] This could be construed as being a more ambitious use of international law by British courts, but it is not, in fact, qualitatively or materially different from the use that occurs in relation to incorporated treaties. That is because the construction of a hybrid statute by reference to the relevant unincorporated treaty is explicable by reference to the same constitutional rationale as that which applies when construing an incorporated treaty, i.e., to construe legislation so as to give effect to Parliament's intention. The construction of hybrid statutes also involves judicial discretion regarding interpretative sources and their weight.

The interpretation and application of incorporated treaties probably represents, in empirical terms, the single most common use of international law in English courts. That use defies easy characterization given the scope for judicial discretion in the interpretative analysis in relation to both incorporated treaties and hybrid statutes. However, the use of unincorporated treaties gives rise to an *additional* form of judicial discretion. Unincorporated treaties are those that the United Kingdom has either signed or ratified as a matter of international law but which have no formal status as a matter of domestic law.[42] While they may also require interpretation and application—like incorporated treaties—they involve the prior question of whether it is permissible to have recourse to them in the first place. That question arises in light of the constitutional principle noted above: that treaties signed or ratified by the executive

example of the interaction between English, EU, and international law, *see* R (Western Sahara) v. HMRC [2016] 1 CMLR 36 (Admin).

[39] *See*, e.g., the long title of the Suppression of Terrorism Act 1978, which states: "An Act to give effect to the European Convention on the Suppression of Terrorism." (The Convention is not given the force of law.)

[40] *See*, e.g., Section 134(1) of the Criminal Justice Act 1988, which gives effect to the United Kingdom's obligations under the UN Convention Against Torture and Other Cruel, Inhuman and Degrading Treatment or Punishment 1984.

[41] Salomon v. Commissioners of Customs and Excise [1967] 2 QB 116, at 144B-F (Diplock LJ).

[42] There is also an intermediate category: treaties that are not incorporated into domestic law by statute but are given effect by executive policy. For an example of this, *see* R (PK (Ghana)) v. Secretary of State for the Home Department [2018] EWCA Civ. 98, at para. 15, considering the executive policy, the National Referral Mechanism, that gives effect to the Council of Europe Convention on Action Against Trafficking in Human Beings.

do not, without more, alter domestic law. Despite this principle, British courts have long been open to the use of unincorporated treaties. This is illustrated by the fact that Lord Bingham chose to make his maiden speech in the House of Lords on the (then unincorporated), ECHR and the "six respects in which . . . [the ECHR] can, and in practice does, have an influence in our domestic proceedings."[43] The key issue is not, therefore, whether unincorporated treaties may be used and applied in cases before British courts, but rather the extent to which that use is permissible and the principles on which it is based.

In particular, there are two canons of interpretation that enable recourse to unincorporated treaties. The first is the presumption of compatibility (the POC).[44] The premise underlying the POC is that Parliament cannot have intended to legislate contrary to the United Kingdom's international law obligations as contained in unincorporated treaties. The POC applies to ambiguous or obscure provisions in primary or subordinate legislation and enables recourse to unincorporated treaties for the resolution of the ambiguity or obscurity in a way that is compatible with the United Kingdom's unincorporated treaty obligations.[45] The precondition of a statutory ambiguity or obscurity is malleable and may be deployed to justify a variety of different outcomes. For example, in *Brind*,[46] Lord Bridge defined an ambiguous provision in broad terms as being, "capable of a meaning which either conforms to or conflicts with the [ECHR]."[47]

The POC has also, occasionally, been applied outside the statutory context, to the common law: " . . . there is a strong presumption in favour of interpreting English law (whether common law or statute) in a way which does not place the United Kingdom in breach of an international obligation."[48] This enables the invocation of unincorporated treaty obligations where the common law is unclear or developing. In such cases, courts may define or develop the common law so as to be consistent with the United Kingdom's international law obligations. An example is *R v. G*,[49] where Lord Steyn considered the common law of recklessness by reference to the UN Convention on the Rights of the Child.

Although the POC illustrates that English courts are amenable to using and applying international law even where it has not been formally incorporated into domestic law, there are constitutionally imposed limits to such use. Thus, the POC has no application where the relevant statutory provision is clear and unambiguous, even if that clarity

[43] Hansard (House of Lords, July 3, 1996, Columns 1466–1467).

[44] For a similar principle in Canadian law, *see* Van Ert, *supra* note 6.

[45] R v. Secretary of State for the Home Department, ex parte Brind [1991] AC 696, at 747H–748A (Lord Bridge) and 760G (Lord Ackner). For a recent illustration of its invocation, *see* USA v. Nolan [2016] AC 463, at paras. 27–47.

[46] *Brind*, *supra* note 45, at 747H–748A.

[47] A recent example of a court concluding that the words in a statutory provision ("public interest" in Sec. 2(2)(a) of the Freedom of Information Act) were not ambiguous is Willow v. Information Commissioner [2017] EWCA Civ 1876, at paras. 48 and 49.

[48] *Lyons*, *supra* note 35, at para. 27.

[49] [2004] 1 AC 1034.

results in an outcome that is contrary to the United Kingdom's unincorporated treaty obligations.[50] Nor will the POC be applied in the common law context where there is prior statutory regulation or incorporated treaty obligations.[51] This means that, in reality, there is a fairly circumscribed ambit within which the POC may operate.

A second canon of interpretation is the principle of legality (the POL). In contrast with the POC, there is no precondition of statutory ambiguity or obscurity before the POL can be applied. The POL enables general words in primary and subordinate legislation to be construed compatibly with fundamental rights on the basis that Parliament cannot have intended, by using general words, to override such rights.[52] While the right in question must already be a part of domestic law,[53] the nature and scope of the right may be affected by either CIL or the content of unincorporated treaties. This means that the POL provides opportunities for using and applying international law, but, like the POC, the POL is displaced where, "the statute conferring the power makes it clear that such was the intention of Parliament."[54] One example of the limits of the POL is *Al-Saadoon*, in which the Court of Appeal rejected the submission that the United Kingdom's human rights obligations under Articles 10 and 11 of the UN Convention Against Torture are enforceable public law obligations owed by domestic public authorities in domestic law, provided that their violation has not been mandated or empowered by Parliament through clear primary legislation. The Court of Appeal rejected this submission on the grounds that the POL is a principle of statutory interpretation and not a broad principle as to how the courts should develop common law; the POL requires the fundamental rights in question to be part of the extant domestic law; and there is no room for the POL where Parliament has already entered the field to strike the appropriate balance.

Apart from these two specific interpretative mechanisms, British courts are often invited to consider unincorporated treaties and other, often nonbinding, international law materials in a range of other, softer, ways. For example, unincorporated treaties have been used as aids in construing legislation[55] and as illuminating the purpose and object of domestic legislation.[56] Such usage may be regarded as evidencing

[50] *Salomon*, *supra* note 41, at 143D–E (Diplock LJ).

[51] As recognized by both Lord Nicholls and Lord Hoffmann in *Re McKerr* [2004] 1 WLR 807, at paras. 30 and 71.

[52] R v. Secretary of State for the Home Department ex parte Simms [2000] 2 AC 115, at 131E (Lord Hoffmann).

[53] R (ERRC) v. Immigration Officer, *supra* note 32, at para. 29.

[54] R v. Secretary of State for the Home Department ex p Pierson [1998] AC 539, at 575D (Lord Browne-Wilkinson).

[55] *See*, e.g., A v. Secretary of State for the Home Department [2005] 2 WLR 87, in which Lord Bingham used a range of international materials when determining the validity of a derogation from art. 5, ECHR.

[56] *See*, e.g., McIntosh v. HM Advocate [2003] 1 AC 1078, where Lord Bingham referred to the policy underlying the Misuse of Drugs Act 1971/the Proceeds of Crime (Scotland) Act 1995 by reference to the United Nations Convention against Illicit Traffic in Narcotic Drugs and Psychotropic Substances, and ZH Tanzania v. Secretary of State for the Home Department [2011] 2 AC 166, para. 23, in which

the openness of British courts to the use of international law, but one should not read too much into such ad hoc, and often unexplained, usage. This is especially so in light of the following three points (in addition to the points already made above), which demonstrate the very real limits on the extent to which unincorporated treaties may be used.

First, English courts have rejected attempts to apply the POC to statutory conferrals of executive power.[57] Thus, the rule is as follows: where Parliament gives an executive decision maker a broad power, English courts will *not* apply the POC so as to *require* the decision maker to exercise his or her discretion in a way that is compatible with the United Kingdom's unincorporated treaty obligations.[58] This has been recently affirmed by the Supreme Court.[59]

Second, it is theoretically possible to judicially review a voluntary executive decision to take international law into account and the resulting self-direction regarding an unincorporated treaty obligation. However, a court may refuse to do so where it considers that there is inadequate judicial authority on the meaning of the provision in question. *R v. Secretary of State for the Home Department,* ex parte *Launder*[60] is an example of a case in which the court held that a voluntary executive self-direction (as to the then unincorporated ECHR) was subject to judicial review. However, that case was distinguished in *Cornerhouse*, where Lord Bingham refused to judicially review the decision of the Director of the Serious Fraud Office. This was because of the lack of judicial authority regarding the meaning of the provision in question (Article 5 of the OECD Convention on Combating Bribery of Foreign Public Officials in International Business Transactions), which the Director had, voluntarily, taken into account. As for the standard of review, in his opinion in *Cornerhouse*, Lord Brown said that when an executive decision maker voluntarily self-directed himself to take into account (unincorporated) international law and was challenged, then "the 'tenable view' approach is the furthest the court should go in examining the point of international law in question"—that is, the court should just ask whether the decision maker's view was a tenable one. However, the Supreme Court has, rightly, declined to follow this approach. It has held, "If it is necessary to decide a point of international law in order to resolve a justiciable issue and there is an ascertainable answer, then the court is bound to supply that answer."[61]

Baroness Hale noted: "In all actions concerning children the best interests of the child shall be a primary consideration. This is a binding obligation in international law, and the spirit, if not the precise language, has also been translated into our national law [Sec. 11 of the Children Act 2004]."

[57] There have been occasional judicial statements, however, that are not easy to reconcile with this proposition. *See*, e.g., R v. Secretary of State for the Home Department ex parte Venables [1998] AC 407, at 499.

[58] *Brind, supra* note 45, at 748.

[59] In R (Yam) v. Central Criminal Court, *supra* note 17, the Supreme Court held that a domestic decision maker exercising a discretionary common law power was not bound to have regard or give effect to the United Kingdom's purely international obligations, although he could have regard to those obligations if he considered appropriate.

[60] [1997] 1 WLR 839.

[61] Benkharbouche v. Embassy of the Republic of Sudan [2017] 3 WLR 977, at para. 35 (Lord Sumption JSC).

Third, unincorporated treaties do not give rise to legitimate expectations. This area of the law is not free from ambiguity and it may not be settled. On the basis of Australian authority,[62] British courts have held, on at least two occasions, that the ratification of an unincorporated treaty could give rise to a representation on which members of the public could rely as creating a legitimate expectation that future executive decision-making would be compatible with the unincorporated treaty obligations.[63] Against these two cases there are three others that doubt the proposition that mere ratification of a treaty can, without more, give rise to legitimate expectation.[64] These inconsistent decisions illustrate the tension at the fringes of the relationship between domestic law and international law.

This summary demonstrates the variety of ways in which unincorporated treaties are used and applied in British courts. A general explanation for this role is that unincorporated treaties may be used where the use is constitutionally permissible, pursuant to the principle of Parliamentary sovereignty. However, it is questionable whether that general explanation is consistent with the reality of decision-making in discrete cases. Even if that explanation does justify the role of unincorporated treaties in each case, it may not be the actual or primary rationale for the way in which unincorporated treaties are treated. Instead, there may be other rationales at play. For example, there may be a perceived, or real, lack of "relative institutional competence" (whether by reference to the distinct competences of the executive and the courts or as between domestic courts and international courts), which causes domestic courts to step away from the use and application of unincorporated treaty provisions.

IV. Customary International Law

It is sometimes said that customary international law (CIL) is automatically incorporated into domestic law.[65] However, it is more accurate to describe it as a source of domestic law.[66] In theory, the use of CIL is more straightforward than the use of unincorporated treaties because the reception of CIL into domestic law does not give

[62] Minister for Immigration and Ethnic Affairs v. Teoh (1995) 183 CLR 273.

[63] *See* R v. Secretary of State for the Home Department, ex parte Ahmed [1999] Imm AR 22 at 36, and R v. Uxbridge Magistrates' Court, ex parte Adimi [2001] QB 667, at 686.

[64] R (ERRC) v. Immigration Officer [2004] QB 811, at paras. 51 and 100 (the House of Lords' judgment does not address this issue); Chundawadra v. IAT [1988] Imm AR 161, at 173–174, and Behluli v. Secretary of State for the Home Department [1998] Imm AR 407, at 415.

[65] *See*, e.g., the majority of the Court of Appeal in *Trendtex Trading Corp v. Central Bank of Nigeria* [1977] QB 529, and, in particular, the following comment by Lord Denning MR: "rules of international law are incorporated into English law automatically and considered to be part of English law unless they are in conflict with an Act of Parliament . . . " *Id.* at 553.

[66] R v. Jones [2007] 1 AC 136, at para. 11. In *Jones*, the House of Lords held that although the crime of aggression was a crime under international law, it was not a part of domestic criminal law since it required a statute to incorporate it. In R (Al Rabbat) v. Westminster Magistrates' Court [2017] EWHC

rise to the constitutional difficulties posed by unincorporated treaties. CIL rules do not become binding on the United Kingdom as a consequence of the acts of the U.K. executive, although the executive may have contributed to their formation since its acts and omissions are, by definition, examples of state practice and may evidence opinio juris. This distinguishes CIL from treaties. It means that CIL may, prima facie, be treated as a source of common law without offending the principle of Parliamentary sovereignty. As a source of law, CIL may assist with the interpretation of statutes,[67] or it may assist with the development of the common law.[68]

In practice, the use of CIL is limited. There are not many cases in which rules of CIL have been successfully invoked and applied in British cases.[69] The likely reason for this is that it is difficult to show that a rule in question has attained the status of CIL. In any event, even if a rule has attained the status of CIL, it will only be drawn upon as source of common law if its use is consistent with the applicable constitutional constraints. Thus, where a rule of CIL exists, it may only be applied by a court if the application does not conflict with, or undermine, an Act of Parliament,[70] and if that application is otherwise permissible as a matter of English law concerning constitutional principles and judicial competence.[71]

V. Other Foreign Affairs Cases

In addition to cases that give rise to the use of treaties or customary international law, there are other cases that may raise issues of international law—for example, where a

1969 (Admin), the Divisional Court held that there was no prospect of the Supreme Court holding that the decision in *Jones* was wrong or the reasoning no longer applicable.

[67] For example, CIL principles regarding state/sovereign immunity are often considered by English courts in the context of interpreting the State Immunity Act 1978. For a recent example, *see Benkharbouche, supra* note 61.

[68] For example, in R (Freedom and Justice Party) v. Secretary of State for the Foreign and Commonwealth Office [2018] EWCA Civ. 1719, the Court of Appeal upheld the Divisional Court's finding that members of special missions visiting the United Kingdom with the approval of the Foreign Office enjoyed personal inviolability and/or immunity from criminal process as a matter of CIL and English common law.

[69] For recent unsuccessful attempts, *see Benkharbouche* (state immunity in an employment context to acts of a private character), *supra* note 61, and R (Al-Saadoon) v. SSD [2015] 3 WLR 503 (torture).

[70] *See*, e.g., R (Keyu) v. Secretary of State for Foreign and Commonwealth Affairs [2016] AC 1355 where Lord Neuberger PSC opined that it would be "quite inappropriate" for courts to develop the common law by reference to CIL (if there was a rule of CIL requiring a state to investigate deaths) in light of the express provision made by Parliament for the investigation of deaths. *Id.* at para. 117.

[71] *See*, e.g., R (Akarcay) v. Chief Constable of the West Yorkshire Police [2017] EWHC 159 (Admin), in which Burnett LJ commented: "Even if it could be shown that [CIL] imposed an obligation not to recognize Northern Cyprus, in my opinion it could not form part of the common law. To treat it as such would contravene the unequivocal constitutional principle that questions of recognition are for the executive. It is not for the courts to dictate to the executive whether they can, must, or cannot recognise a state." *Id.* at para. 23.

British court is invited to adjudicate on the lawfulness of a foreign state's conduct. In such cases, the alleged unlawfulness may stem from a breach of human rights or another cause of action that can be readily located against a backdrop of public international law principles. There have been a number of national security cases in the last decade that raise such issues. Much of this case law is difficult to describe in general terms, in part because it is highly fact-sensitive. However, there are two legal concepts that feature frequently: the principle of nonjusticiability (already referred to above), and the foreign act of state doctrine.

The scope and ambit of these principles was recently considered in *Belhaj v. Straw*.[72] The Supreme Court disaggregated the foreign act of state doctrine as follows. First, it requires a British court to recognize, and treat as valid, foreign legislation that affects movable or immovable property within the jurisdiction of the foreign state. Second, a British court will not normally question the validity of a foreign sovereign act in respect of property within that foreign jurisdiction. Third, a British court will refrain from adjudicating on, or questioning, certain categories of foreign sovereign acts even where they take place outside that the jurisdiction of the foreign state. The first two rules are qualified by a public policy exception that enables allegations of certain egregious conduct (for example, complicity in torture, unlawful detention, and rendition) to be pursued before British courts. Exceptions to the third rule are considered on a case-by-case basis, by reference to the separation of powers, the sovereign nature of the activities concerned, and the extent to which fundamental rights are engaged.

The third category of foreign act of state identified in *Belhaj* is often considered by reference to the principle of nonjusticiability, which explains the judicial restraint exercised in such cases. In *Buttes v. Gas and Oil v. Hammer (No. 3)*, Lord Wilberforce referred to the international law and inter-state issues that arose in that case and explained: "They have only to be stated to compel the conclusion that these are not issues upon which a municipal court can pass. Leaving aside all possibility of embarrassment in our foreign relations . . . there are . . . no judicial or manageable standards by which to judge these issues . . . the court would be in a judicial no-man's land."[73] In *Shergill v. Khaira*, the Supreme Court explained that this passage did not mean that judges were incapable of deciding questions of international law but that the issue was nonjusticiable because it was political and this was for two reasons. First, "it trespassed on the proper province of the executive, as the organ of the state charged with the conduct of foreign relations," and, second, there was a lack of judicial or manageable standards.[74]

Both of the concepts of foreign act of state and nonjusticiability therefore focus on relative institutional competence or, rather, the lack of judicial competence regarding the issues engaged by such cases. In that sense, both concepts hark back to the

[72] [2017] 2 WLR 456. *See also* Eirik Bjorge & Cameron Miles, *Crown and Foreign Acts of State before British Courts:* Ramatullah, Belhaj, *and the Separation of Powers*, ch. 40 in this volume, and Van Ert, *supra* note 6, for the Canadian position on similar issues.

[73] [1982] AC 888, at 938.

[74] Shergill v. Khaira [2015] AC 359, at para. 40.

constitutional tensions already addressed above in the sections considering the use of international treaties and customary international law in British courts.

VI. Conclusion

In general, British courts have a flexible and open approach to the possibility of using and applying international law obligations and standards, especially in the context of assessing the lawfulness of executive action. This use and application of international law by British courts is subject to the important caveat that it must be constitutionally permissible and institutionally appropriate. However, while the relevant principles relating to the role and status of international law in British courts are relatively uncontroversial and readily identifiable, their application to the facts of discrete cases continues to give rise to debate. This is generally attributable to either the legal complexity or the political significance of the issues raised by such case law, which continues to make it a rich topic for legal scholarship and practice.

CHAPTER 28

THE DOMESTIC APPLICATION OF INTERNATIONAL LAW IN CANADA

GIB VAN ERT

THE rules by which international law is received into Canadian domestic law originate in British constitutionalism and English common law. In recent times, however, the Supreme Court of Canada has put its own stamp on this inheritance with the introduction of a simple yet remarkable idea: Canadian enactments are to be interpreted in their entire context, including international law. The Court has affirmed that the "values and principles of customary and conventional international law form part of the context in which Canadian laws are enacted."[1] This conclusion "follows from the fact that to interpret a Canadian law in a way that conflicts with Canada's international obligations risks incursion by the courts in the executive's conduct of foreign affairs and censure under international law." The contextual significance of international law is "all the more clear" in, but seemingly not limited to, cases in which the provision to be construed "has been enacted with a view towards implementing international obligations." In keeping with Canadian legislation's international context, courts apply the interpretive presumption that it conforms with the state's international obligations. Courts construing domestic enactments are therefore "direct[ed] . . . to relevant international instruments at the context stage of statutory interpretation."[2]

The Supreme Court of Canada's identification of international law as part of the context in which Canadian laws are enacted orients Canadian reception law toward openness to internationally informed arguments. Consistently with this, the Federal

[1] R v. Hape, 2007 SCC 26 (*Hape*), para. 53; B010 v. Canada (Citizenship and Immigration), 2015 SCC 58 (*B010*), para. 47.

[2] *B010*, paras. 47–49.

Court of Appeal in 2005 identified the "expanding role that the common law has given to international law in the interpretation of domestic law" as "one of the signal legal developments of the last fifteen years" and criticized a trial judge for adopting "an unduly limited view of the effect of the burgeoning common law" in this area.[3] Openness to international sources and submissions does not always prevail in lower courts or even in the Supreme Court itself. But the trajectory is clear.

This spirit of openness to international law does not detract from the fact that Canada, as a Westminster-model state, remains significantly—but not wholly—dualist. Treaties are not directly effective in domestic law. The rule is otherwise for customary norms, which (as explained below) are directly effective in a monist way unless supplanted by inconsistent legislation. Furthermore, the capacity of the interpretive presumption of conformity with international law to give indirect effect to treaties cannot be ignored. These considerations warn us against too readily characterizing Canada as a dualist jurisdiction. It is, rather, a hybrid jurisdiction with dualist and monist elements.[4]

I begin this chapter with some recent illustrations of Canadian courts engaging with international law. Next I consider the reception rules applicable to treaties and customs, the interpretive presumption of conformity with international law, and the role of nonbinding international sources. I conclude with a 2010 case in which the Supreme Court of Canada pointedly neglected international law despite the rather sophisticated edifice of reception rules described here.

I. Areas of Engagement

Traditional international legal issues such as state immunity claims, enforcement and review of international arbitral awards, and questions surrounding extradition and deportation proceedings, are well represented in recent Canadian decisions. International labor law, refugee law, and child protection also figure prominently. Some examples are given below, but many others (from these and other areas) may be cited.

In a series of Ontario cases, claimants sued Iran for human rights violations. In *Bouzari*, the claimant was an Iranian national who alleged that Iran had tortured him. The courts dismissed Bouzari's argument that Canada had an international obligation to take universal jurisdiction.[5] In *Steen*, American claimants who had successfully sued Iran in the United States for terrorist acts attempted, without success, to enforce their judgments against Iranian assets in Canada.[6] A similar claim succeeded in *Tracy* due to

[3] De Guzman v. Canada (Minister of Citizenship and Immigration), 2005 FCA 436 (*De Guzman*), paras. 61 and 62.

[4] *See* Gib van Ert, *Dubious Dualism: The Reception of International Law in Canada*, 44 Val. U. L. Rev. 927 (2010).

[5] Bouzari v. Iran, [2002] OTC 297 (Ont SCJ); Bouzari v. Iran, 2004 CanLII 871 (Ont CA).

[6] Steen v. Islamic Republic of Iran, 2011 ONSC 6464; Steen v. Islamic Republic of Iran, 2013 ONCA 30.

Canada's subsequent enactment of State Immunity Act amendments specifically aimed at permitting such claims.[7] The possibility of similar results obtaining at common law was suggested by the Supreme Court of Canada in *Kuwait Airways*[8] but squarely rejected four years later in *Kazemi*.[9] There, an attempt to sue Iran in Canada for the rape, torture, and murder of a Canadian journalist by Iranian government officials failed. Parliament, the majority held, had chosen to uphold state immunity "as the oil that allows for the smooth functioning of the machinery of international relations" in priority over civil redress for torture.[10]

Arbitral awards frequently come before Canadian courts, usually for enforcement but sometimes for review. The Supreme Court has noted that the New York Convention[11] and UNCITRAL Model Law[12] regimes are implemented throughout the country.[13] In one notable case, the Court of Appeal for British Columbia overturned a decision setting aside a worldwide asset-freezing injunction where the application judge wrongly assumed that, given the parties' limited associations with British Columbia, the applicant must first resort to Pakistan's courts for enforcement of the award.[14] Several attempts to judicially review international arbitral awards made under the North American Free Trade Agreement (NAFTA)[15] have been rejected.[16] In *SD Myers*, the Federal Court dismissed Canada's attempt to set aside three NAFTA awards made against it, the chambers judge rightly noting that domestic legal principles "cannot be used to create a standard of review not provided for in article 34" of the Model Law.[17] The Court of Appeal for Ontario made this very mistake in *Karpa*, but nevertheless preserved the award.[18] That same court righted matters in *Cargill*, affirming that "importing and directly applying domestic concepts of standard of review... may not be helpful to courts when conducting their review process of international arbitration awards."[19]

[7] Tracy v. Iranian Ministry of Information and Security, 2016 ONSC 3759, 2017 ONCA 549.

[8] Kuwait Airways Corp v. Iraq, 2010 SCC 40 (*Kuwait Airways*), para. 24.

[9] Kazemi Estate v. Islamic Republic of Iran, 2014 SCC 62 (*Kazemi*), paras. 57 and 58.

[10] *Kazemi*, para. 46.

[11] Convention on the Recognition and Enforcement of Foreign Arbitral Awards 1958, [1986] CanTS no. 43.

[12] UNCITRAL Model Law on International Commercial Arbitration, UN Doc. A/40/17 ann 1 (1985).

[13] Yugraneft Corp v. Rexx Management Corp., 2010 SCC 19, paras. 10 and 11.

[14] Sociedade-de-fomento Industrial Private Limited v. Pakistan Steel Mills Corporation (Private) Ltd., 2014 BCCA 205. *See also*, e.g., West Plains Company v. Northwest Organic Community Mills Co-Operative Ltd., 2009 SKQB 162; Crystallex International Corporation v. Bolivarian Republic of Venezuela, 2016 ONSC 469.

[15] [1994] CanTS no. 2.

[16] One early judicial review of a NAFTA award that notoriously succeeded was United Mexican States v. Metalclad Corp., 2001 BCSC 664.

[17] Canada (Attorney General) v. SD Myers Inc. 2004 FC 38, para. 39.

[18] United Mexican States v. Karpa, (2005) 74 OR (3d) 180 (Ont CA). *See also* Bayview Irrigation District #11 v. Mexico, 2008 CanLII 22120 (Ont SCJ).

[19] United Mexican States v. Cargill Inc. 2011 ONCA 622, para. 30. *See also* Attorney General of Canada v. Mobil et al., 2016 ONSC 790.

International human rights law is often relied on, sometimes effectively, in challenges to extradition and deportation proceedings. In *Baker*,[20] the Supreme Court of Canada set aside a minister's decision to deport a woman who had overstayed her visa by eleven years. The majority found that a contextual approach to the minister's statutory discretion required close attention to the interests and needs of Ms. Baker's children, and that Canada's ratification of the Convention on the Rights of the Child 1989[21] (CRC) was an "indicator of the importance of considering the interests of children when making a compassionate and humanitarian decision."[22] In *Suresh*,[23] the Court considered the prohibition of *refoulement* in the Convention Against Torture 1984 (CAT) in the case of a Convention refugee who Canada sought to deport to Sri Lanka. Suresh won his appeal, but the Court's heavily qualified description of the prohibition of torture as merely an "emerging peremptory norm of international law which cannot be easily derogated from" was criticized.[24] In *Diab*, the Court of Appeal for Ontario held, based in part on the CAT and European jurisprudence, that once a fugitive establishes a plausible connection between evidence against him and an act of torture, the onus shifts to the Crown to show that there is no real risk that torture-derived evidence will be used against him.[25] In *Badesha*, the Supreme Court held that, in extradition cases, the constitutional guarantee of "life, liberty and security of the person" should be presumed to provide at least as great a level of protection as found in Canada's international commitments regarding non-refoulement to torture or other gross human rights violations, and that extraditing a person to face a substantial risk of torture or mistreatment in the requesting state contrary to Article 3(1) of the CAT will violate the principles of fundamental justice.[26]

International labor law has been central to Supreme Court of Canada decisions on the scope of freedom of association in Section 2(d) of Canada's Charter of Rights and Freedoms. In *Health Services*, the Court overturned its long-standing interpretation of Section 2(d) as excluding constitutional protection for collective bargaining based in part on the recognition of collective bargaining in international law.[27] In *Fraser*, the majority of the Court affirmed and expanded upon this conclusion in the face of a vigorous minority arguing that the majority had misconstrued Canada's international labor obligations.[28] The Court was similarly divided in *Saskatchewan Federation of Labour*, where the majority again pointed to international law (among other considerations) in

[20] Baker v. Canada (Minister of Citizenship and Immigration), [1999] 2 SCR 817 (*Baker*).

[21] [1992] CanTS no. 3. [22] *Baker*, para. 69; *see also* paras. 70 and 71.

[23] Suresh v. Canada (Minister of Citizenship and Immigration), 2002 SCC 1 (*Suresh*).

[24] *Suresh*, para. 65.

[25] France v. Diab, 2014 ONCA 374, especially paras. 229–249. *See also* Re Mahjoub 2010 FC 787, where again the state bore the burden.

[26] India v. Badesha, 2017 SCC 44, para. 38.

[27] Health Services and Support—Facilities Subsector Bargaining Assn v. British Columbia, 2007 SCC 27 (*Health Services*).

[28] Ontario (Attorney General) v. Fraser, 2011 SCC 20 (*Fraser*).

finding that the right to strike is protected by Section 2(d), while the dissent held that the international position was less clear than the majority allowed.[29]

Litigation involving children frequently prompts Canadian courts to look to international law. In *Canadian Foundation*,[30] the Supreme Court of Canada invoked the presumption of conformity with international law to narrow the ambit of a Criminal Code provision permitting parents and teachers to use reasonable force by way of correction of a child. In two notable first instance decisions, judges in family law proceedings resorted to out-of-court, face-to-face meetings with children to give effect to the requirement, in Article 12 of the CRC, to assure children the right to express their views in matters affecting them.[31] In *Inglis*, the Supreme Court of British Columbia ruled unconstitutional a government decision to cancel a program allowing incarcerated mothers to keep their infants with them in jail. The court relied in part on the CRC and other instruments.[32] Hague Convention[33] cases arise regularly, too. In *Office of the Children's Lawyer v. Balev*, the Supreme Court adopted the hybrid approach to habitual residence, as now favored in European and Australasian jurisdictions, explaining that it "should prefer the interpretation that has gained the most support in other courts and will therefore best ensure uniformity of state practice across *Hague Convention* jurisdictions."[34] The Court also noted the Convention's requirement that judicial authorities act expeditiously in child abduction proceedings and called on lower courts to "use their authority to expedite proceedings in the interest of the children involved."[35] *AMRI v. KER* was a Hague case in which a mother sought her child's return to Mexico after Canada had granted the child refugee status due to her mother's abuse. The application judge found that the child was wrongfully retained and ordered her return. The Court of Appeal for Ontario ordered a new hearing, finding that the Hague Convention did not require the *refoulement* of child refugees.[36]

Refugee claims may be the area of Canadian law in which international legal arguments are most frequently made. In *Németh*,[37] two Hungarian Roma refugees resisted their extradition to Hungary on the ground of non-*refoulement*. The unanimous Supreme Court of Canada affirmed that, at international law, protection from *refoulement* applies to expulsions by extradition and concluded that Canadian law fully satisfied this obligation by means of the Extradition Act. In *Febles*,[38] the Court divided on whether a Cuban refugee claimant who had served two U.S. criminal sentences was excluded from refugee status by Article 1F(b) (serious criminality) of the Convention Relating to the Status of Refugees 1951.[39] The majority held that Febles was excluded,

[29] Saskatchewan Federation of Labour v. Saskatchewan, 2015 SCC 4 (*Saskatchewan Federation*).

[30] Canadian Foundation for Children, Youth and the Law v. Canada (Attorney General), 2004 SCC 4.

[31] BJG v. DLG, (2010) 324 DLR (4th) 367; Haberman v. Haberman, 2011 SKQB 415, paras. 165ff.

[32] Inglis v. British Columbia (Minister of Public Safety), 2013 BCSC 2309.

[33] Hague Convention on the Civil Aspects of International Child Abduction 1980, [1983] CanTS no. 35.

[34] 2018 SCC 16 (*Balev*), para. 49.

[35] *Balev*, paras. 83–87, 89.

[36] AMRI v. KER, 2011 ONCA 417.

[37] Németh v. Canada (Justice), 2010 SCC 56 (*Németh*).

[38] Febles v. Canada (Citizenship and Immigration), 2014 SCC 68.

[39] [1969] CanTS no. 6; *see also* Protocol Relating to the Status of Refugees, [1969] CanTS no. 29.

while the dissent found that Article 1F(b) did not apply to criminally convicted claimants who had served their sentences. In *Ezokola*, the Supreme Court overturned lower court precedents on complicity in international crime to "rein in the Canadian approach to complicity"[40] and bring Canadian law in line with the Refugee Convention, the case law of other Convention states, and international criminal law.

II. The Reception of Treaties by Implementation

Canada takes a dualist approach to conventional international law.[41] "This means that . . . a treaty provision . . . will only be binding in Canadian law if it is given effect through Canada's domestic law-making process,"[42] i.e., statutory or regulatory implementation[43] by Parliament or the provincial legislatures. The classic statement of this principle remains Lord Atkin's 1937 dictum that "the making of a treaty is an executive act, while the performance of its obligations, if they entail alteration of the existing domestic law, requires legislative action."[44] The rationale for this rule is that the Crown is not a source of law.[45]

Canada's treaty-dualist posture may not prevent courts from allowing treaties some indirect domestic legal effects even without legislative implementation. The Supreme Court of Canada split on this issue in *Capital Cities*.[46] The question was whether a federal agency, the Canadian Radio-Television Commission, had the power to authorize Canadian cable television licensees to delete commercials from U.S. television broadcasts receivable in Canada and replace them with messages of their own. In response to the contention that doing so was contrary to Canadian telecommunications

[40] Ezokola v. Canada (Citizenship and Immigration), 2013 SCC 40, para. 30.

[41] An approach it shares with the United Kingdom. *See* Shaheed Fatima, *The Domestic Application of International Law in British Courts*, ch. 27 in this volume, and similarly constituted countries. *See*, e.g., Amichai Cohen, *International Law in Israeli Courts*, ch. 29 in this volume.

[42] *Kazemi*, para. 149.

[43] "Implementation" is the term used by Canadian legislatures and draftspeople to describe the domestic performance of a treaty obligation by legislative or regulatory means. The term "incorporation" is sometimes also used by Canadian judges, but this ignores parliamentary usage and risks confusing treaty implementation with its near opposite, the incorporation of custom (discussed below).

[44] Attorney General for Canada v. Attorney General for Ontario, [1937] AC 326 (PC), 347. *See also* Operation Dismantle Inc. v. Canada, [1985] 1 SCR 441, 484 per Wilson J: "A treaty . . . may be in full force and effect internationally without any legislative implementation and, absent such legislative implementation, it does not form part of the domestic law of Canada. Legislation is only required if some alteration in the domestic law is needed for its implementation."

[45] *See*, e.g., In re Employment of Aliens, (1922) 63 SCR 293, 339 per Brodeur J: "The bill of rights [Bill of Rights 1689 (UK) 1 William & Mary sess 2 c 2] having declared illegal the suspending or dispensing with the laws without the consent of parliament, the Crown could not in time of peace make a treaty which would restrict the freedom of parliament."

[46] Capital Cities Communications Inc. v. Canadian Radio-Television Commission, [1978] 2 SCR 141 (*Capital Cities*).

treaty obligations, Laskin CJ observed that a treaty gives rise to "no domestic, internal consequences unless they [arise] from implementing legislation giving [it] a legal effect within Canada."[47] In a strong dissent, Pigeon J (Beetz and de Grandpré JJ concurring) called it "an oversimplification to say that treaties are of no legal effect unless implemented by legislation."[48] The dissent would have taken judicial notice of the relevant convention and interpreted the Commission's powers in conformity with it.

The propriety of permitting unimplemented treaties domestic legal effects split the Court again in *Baker*.[49] This time, however, the majority accepted that a supposedly unimplemented treaty[50] could be used to control administrative decision-making. Concurring in the result, Iacobucci J pointedly observed that he did not share the majority's "confidence that the Court's precedent in *Capital Cities*... survives intact following the adoption of a principle of law which permits reference to an unincorporated convention during the process of statutory interpretation."[51]

Iacobucci J makes a strong argument that *Baker* undoes *Capital Cities*. Laskin CJ's dictum that treaties give rise to no domestic consequences without implementing legislation is difficult to reconcile with the important role the presumption of conformity with international law had come to play in Canadian jurisprudence even before *Baker* and certainly since. As we will see, the presumption can afford unimplemented treaties domestic consequences in some cases. Without denying Canada's treaty dualism, one can say that international conventions have no direct effect in domestic law without implementing legislation, but indirect interpretive effects are permissible. The distinction between impermissible direct effects and permissible indirect effects was drawn by Duff J nearly a century ago,[52] and has more recently been drawn in Australian[53] and English law.[54]

[47] *Capital Cities*, at 173. [48] *Capital Cities*, at 188.

[49] Baker v. Canada (Minister of Citizenship and Immigration), [1999] 2 SCR 817.

[50] It is an error to describe the CRC, or other UN human rights treaties, as unimplemented in Canada based solely on the absence of express implementing legislation. As Canada has explained to the UN treaty bodies: "It is not the practice in Canada for one single piece of legislation to be enacted incorporating an entire convention on human rights into domestic law, primarily due to the division of jurisdiction between federal and provincial/territorial levels. Rather, many different federal, provincial and territorial laws and policies together serve to implement Canada's international human rights obligations." Canada, *Core document forming part of the reports of States parties*, HRI/CORE/CAN/2013 (28 Jan. 28, 2013).

[51] *Baker*, para. 80.

[52] In *In re Employment of Aliens*, (1922) 63 SCR 293, 329, Duff J observed: "the Crown... possesses authority to enter into obligations towards foreign states diplomatically binding and, indirectly, such treaties may obviously very greatly affect the rights of individuals. But it is no part of the prerogative of the Crown by treaty in time of peace to effect directly a change in the law governing the rights of private individuals."

[53] In *Australian Competition and Consumer Commission v. P.T. Garuda Indonesia (No. 9)*, [2013] FCA 323 (Fed Ct Australia), para. 43, Perram J noted: "When... a court construes a statute to comply with a treaty obligation... international law then exerts a discernable influence on the content of local law."

[54] In *R (Miller) v. Secretary of State for Exiting the European Union*, [2016] EWHC 2768 (Admin), para. 33, the court observed: "... treaties can have certain indirect interpretive effects in relation to domestic law, such as those discussed in *R v. Lyons* [2002] UKHL 447; [2003] 1 AC 976 at [27]-[28]; but this does not affect the basic position that the Crown cannot through the use of its prerogative powers

Jurisdiction to implement Canadian treaty obligations is split between Parliament and the provincial legislatures according to the subject-matter distribution of legislative powers set out in Part VI of the Constitution Act, 1867.[55] While treaty implementation is formally a legislative matter, in practice the executive drives the process. The starting point is the federal government's decision to incur the obligation (an exercise of the royal prerogative over foreign affairs).[56] This involves careful consideration of what new laws or amendments (if any) would be needed to perform the obligation. Such legislative measures may be required at the federal level, the provincial level, or both. Once the federal executive decides to proceed, it will (in the case of multilateral agreements) sign on behalf of Canada but delay ratification, acceptance or approval until the needed implementing laws have been enacted. That way, Canada incurs no obligation until being able to perform it.[57] The upshot is that every Canadian treaty obligation is undertaken on the strength of an executive determination that Canadian laws suffice to perform it, whether because the treaty does not require domestic performance, or existing enactments suffice to perform it, or new provisions have been enacted to do so.

The element needed to affect implementation, rather than mere approval, of a treaty obligation is nowhere specified in Canadian laws or jurisprudence. Canadian legislatures use a variety of implementing techniques. A plain statement that the treaty has the force of law is the simplest.[58] Equally effective are laws giving legal force to specific treaty provisions.[59] Another form of implementation is to enact a law that (in the government's estimation) suffices to ensure performance of the treaty, but without directly adopting that treaty's wording.[60] Some laws empower the government to implement treaty obligations by regulation.[61] Others make no mention of the treaty

increase or diminish or dispense with the rights of individuals or companies conferred by common law or statute or change domestic law in any way without the intervention of Parliament." The reference to *R v. Lyons* is to what Lord Hoffmann called "a strong presumption in favour of interpreting English law (whether common law or statute) in a way which does not place the United Kingdom in breach of an international obligation."

[55] Constitution Act, 1867, 30 & 31 Vict, c 3 (UK); Attorney General for Canada v. Attorney General for Ontario [1937] AC 326 (PC); *Health Services*, para. 69. For a full account, *see* Charles-Emmanuel Côté, *Federalism and Foreign Affairs in Canada*, ch. 16 in this volume.

[56] *See generally* Canada (Prime Minister) v. Khadr, 2010 SCC 3 (*Khadr No. 2*), paras. 34–37.

[57] Maurice Copithorne, *National Treaty Law and Practice: Canada*, *in* NATIONAL TREATY LAW AND PRACTICE 5 (Duncan Hollis et al. eds., 2003).

[58] E.g., Tax Conventions Implementation Act 2013, SC 2013 c 27.

[59] E.g., Safeguarding Canada's Seas and Skies Act, SC 2014 c 29 s 74.01: "Articles 1 to 5, 7 to 23, 37 to 41, 45, 48 and 52 of the Hazardous and Noxious Substances Convention—that are set out in Part 1 of Schedule 9—have the force of law in Canada."

[60] E.g., Crimes Against Humanity and War Crimes Act, SC 2000 c 24 (full title: "An Act respecting genocide, crimes against humanity and war crimes and to implement the Rome Statute of the International Criminal Court, and to make consequential amendments to other Acts").

[61] In *Amaratunga v. Northwest Atlantic Fisheries Organization*, 2013 SCC 66, paras. 32–34 a statute authorized the Governor in Council, by order, to grant privileges and immunities according to the Convention on the Privileges and Immunities of the United Nations 1946, and Order SOR/80-64

at all; one must rely on extrinsic sources like Hansard or explanatory memoranda to ascertain that the provision was adopted to perform a treaty obligation.[62] Another, quite common, means of ensuring domestic performance of Canadian treaty obligations is to rely on existing laws. This technique stretches the usual definition of treaty implementation, but should not be overlooked.[63]

Once satisfied that a treaty is implemented, Canadian courts show little hesitation in considering and applying the underlying international obligations. In *World Bank*,[64] Moldaver and Côté JJ determined the meanings of "archive" and "inviolable" in the relevant treaties and applied them as Canadian law. In *Peracomo*,[65] Cromwell J considered at length the Convention on Limitation of Liability for Maritime Claims 1976[66] in order to decide whether Article 4 of that treaty limited liability for a damaged underwater cable. In both cases the treaties at issue were clearly implemented in federal law.

III. The Reception of Custom by Incorporation

Rules of customary international law may be given direct effect by Canadian courts without legislative implementation.[67] This doctrine, known as incorporation or adoption, is infrequently applied, seemingly because international customs are rarely directed at, or even pertinent to, states' internal laws. The exception is state immunity from proceedings in other states' courts; most Canadian incorporation cases arise from this context. In *Kuwait Airways*, LeBel J for the Supreme Court of Canada observed that the customary international rule of restrictive immunity formed part of the common law even before Parliament adopted it in the State Immunity Act.[68] La Forest J had made a similar observation eighteen years earlier.[69] Only a monist adoption of customary norms by the courts explains this conclusion.

(Northwest Atlantic Fisheries Organization Privileges and Immunities Order) made such a grant. *See also* the Civil International Space Station Agreement Implementation Act SC 1999 c 35, s 3 of which reads, "The purpose of this Act is to fulfil Canada's obligations under the Agreement." Sec. 9 then provides, "The Governor in Council may make regulations that the Governor in Council considers necessary for carrying out the purposes of this Act and giving effect to the Agreement . . . "

[62] E.g., Criminal Code RSC 1985 c C-46 s 269.1, which criminalizes the infliction of torture by officials as required by the CAT.

[63] *See* Elisabeth Eid & Hoorie Hamboyan, *Implementation by Canada of Its International Human Rights Treaty Obligations: Making Sense Out of the Nonsensical*, *in* The Globalized Rule of Law: Relationships Between International and Domestic Law 449, 450 (Oonagh E. Fitzgerald ed., 2006).

[64] World Bank Group v. Wallace, 2016 SCC 15.

[65] Peracomo Inc. v. Telus Communications, 2014 SCC 29. [66] 1456 UNTS 221.

[67] The doctrine is of British provenance and continues to apply there. *See* Fatima, *supra* note 41.

[68] *Kuwait Airways*, para. 13.

[69] Re Canada Labour Code [1992] 2 SCR 50, 73–74, calling the State Immunity Act "a codification that is intended to clarify and continue the theory of restrictive immunity, rather than to alter its substance."

The Supreme Court of Canada most recently considered the incorporation of custom in *Hape*. LeBel J for the majority reviewed the leading English decision, *Trendtex Trading*,[70] then observed that the Supreme Court itself had "implicitly or explicitly applied the doctrine of adoption in several cases."[71] While there were cases in which the Court had "not applied or discussed the doctrine of adoption of customary international law when it had the opportunity to do so," the doctrine had "never been rejected in Canada. Indeed, there is a long line of cases in which the Court has either formally accepted it or at least applied it."[72] LeBel J went on to affirm that, "following the common law tradition, it appears that the doctrine . . . operates in Canada such that prohibitive rules of customary international law should be incorporated into domestic law in the absence of conflicting legislation."[73] The phrase "should be" here may suggest some judicial discretion not to apply the doctrine. But no such discretion is allowed in the precedents LeBel J affirms, and to recognize one would be at odds with the "judicial policy"[74] of advancing internationally conforming interpretations of Canadian law. A better reading of *Hape* might emphasize LeBel J's observation that the incorporation of custom is "automatic . . . on the basis that international custom, as the law of nations, is also the law of Canada."

LeBel J's account of incorporation in *Hape* noted that the doctrine applies only in respect of "prohibitive rules of customary international law." In *Kazemi*, LeBel J elaborated on this point, explaining that "the mere existence of a customary rule in international law does not automatically incorporate that rule into the domestic legal order" if the customary rule at issue is permissive rather than mandatory.[75] Mandatory (or, in the language of *Hape*, "prohibitive") rules of customary international law are automatically incorporated, but permissive customs require legislative action.[76]

The reception of peremptory norms (jus cogens) appears to occur by incorporation. In *Kazemi*, LeBel J described such norms as "a higher form of customary international law"[77] and noted that Canada's treaty dualism "means that, unless a treaty provision expresses a rule of customary international law or a peremptory norm, that provision will only be binding in Canadian law if it is given effect through Canada's domestic law-making process."[78]

The incorporation of custom is a significantly monist element in a system too often depicted as dualist. But incorporation cases are rare. In particular, reliance on

[70] [1977] 1 QB 529 (Eng CA).

[71] *Hape*, para. 37, quoting from *The Ship "North" v. The King*, (1906) 37 SCR 385; Re Foreign Legations, [1943] SCR 208; Re Armed Forces, [1943] SCR 483; and Saint John (Municipality of) v. Fraser-Brace Overseas Corp., [1958] SCR 263.

[72] *Hape*, paras. 38 and 39. [73] *Hape*, para. 39. [74] *Hape*, para. 53.

[75] *Kazemi*, para. 61.

[76] This is in keeping with a prevalent reading of *R v. Keyn* (*The Franconia*), (1876) 2 Ex D 63 (Ct Crown Cas Res), in which a bare majority (7–6) of the Court of Crown Cases Reserved declined to incorporate the customary three-mile territorial sea in the absence of legislation abolishing the common law rule that the realm ends at the high water mark. *See* Gib van Ert, Using International Law in Canadian Courts 218–223 (2d ed. 2008), cited in *Kazemi*, para. 61.

[77] *Kazemi*, para. 151. [78] *Kazemi*, para. 149.

international custom to found a cause of action is theoretically possible but practically almost unheard of. Abrioux J of the Supreme Court of British Columbia recently noted that while "[c]ommon law courts have historically applied international custom to create private law obligations and, indeed, entire fields of private law" (such as bills of exchange, the law merchant, maritime law and the law of prize), "[n]o civil claims alleging breach of [customary international legal] norms, peremptory or otherwise have been successfully advanced in Canada."[79]

IV. The Presumption of Conformity with International Law

Since the start of the twenty-first century, the Supreme Court of Canada has endorsed or applied the interpretive presumption of conformity with international law[80] on an almost yearly basis. It frequently did so in the late twentieth century as well. I noted at the outset the Court's affirmation that "the values and principles of customary and conventional international law form part of the context in which Canadian laws are enacted,"[81] and its related observation that "to interpret a Canadian law in a way that conflicts with Canada's international obligations risks incursion by the courts in the executive's conduct of foreign affairs and censure under international law."[82] "These principles," said McLachlin CJ for the Court in *B010*, "direct us to relevant international instruments at the context stage of statutory interpretation."[83] They may also direct courts to customary international law, as the presumption applies to international law in all its forms.[84] The presumption "is based on the rule of judicial policy that, as a matter of law, courts will strive to avoid constructions of domestic law pursuant to which the state would be in violation of its international obligations, unless the wording of the statute clearly compels that result."[85]

A recent decision of the Supreme Court of Canada illustrates the presumption's application and potential importance. In *Thibodeau*, Air Canada breached Canada's Official Languages Act (OLA) by failing to provide in-flight services in French as well as English. The Thibodeaus sought damages under the OLA despite the limitation of air carrier liability established by the Montreal Convention[86] and implemented by the

[79] Araya v. Nevsun Resources Ltd., 2016 BCSC 1856, paras. 442 and 445.

[80] In U.S. law, this interpretive rule is known as the "Charming Betsy" doctrine. It is, as the Supreme Court of Canada recently noted, "a feature of legal interpretation around the world." *B010*, para. 48.

[81] *Hape*, para. 53. [82] *B010*, para. 47. [83] *B010*, para. 49.

[84] *Hape*, para. 53. An example of the presumption invoked in respect of custom is *114957 Canada Ltée (Spraytech, Société d'arrosage) v. Hudson (Town)*, 2001 SCC 40, para. 30.

[85] *Hape*, 2007 SCC 26, para. 53.

[86] Convention for the Unification of Certain Rules for International Carriage by Air 1999, 2242 UNTS 350.

Carriage By Air Act.[87] Cromwell J noted that the Thibodeaus' position "in effect is that Parliament . . . intended that courts should be able to grant damages even though doing so would be in violation of Canada's international undertakings as incorporated into federal statute law," contrary to the presumption of conformity.[88] He found it "impossible to discern any such intent in the broad and general language" of the OLA's remedial provision. "Instead, this provision should be understood as having been enacted into an existing legal framework which includes statutory limits, procedural requirements and a background of general legal principles—including Canada's international undertakings incorporated into Canadian statute law."[89]

The presumption of conformity is, by constitutional necessity, rebuttable.[90] Like the Parliament at Westminster, Canadian legislatures are recognized as "sovereign" to legislate in violation of international law. Parliamentary sovereignty in Canada is curtailed by the Constitution which, as defined in Section 52(2) of the Constitution Act, 1982, does not include public international legal norms. So while Canadian courts are empowered to invalidate laws for inconsistency with the constitution, they cannot do so for inconsistency with international law. An Act of Parliament or a provincial legislature that puts Canada in breach of its international obligations is not, for that reason alone, domestically unlawful. The presumption of conformity is not easily rebutted, however. What is needed is "an unequivocal legislative intent to default on an international obligation,"[91] statutory wording that "clearly compels" a nonconforming result,[92] or "unambiguous" statutory provisions.[93] While the standard is high, it remains true that the presumption cannot be applied to "override the clear words used in a statute."[94]

Some uncertainty remains about whether ambiguity on the face of an enactment is a precondition to interpretive recourse to international law.[95] The Supreme Court of Canada rejected a facial ambiguity requirement in *National Corn Growers*,[96] and expressly held in *Crown Forest* that "a court may refer to extrinsic materials which form part of the legal context . . . without the need first to find an ambiguity before turning to such materials."[97] Lower courts usually understand these decisions (correctly,

[87] RSC 1985 c C-26. [88] *Thibodeau*, para. 113.

[89] *Thibodeau*, para. 114; *see also id.*, para. 117.

[90] "Parliamentary sovereignty requires courts to give effect to a statute that demonstrates an unequivocal legislative intent to default on an international obligation." *Hape*, para. 53. "The presumption that legislation implements Canada's international obligations is rebuttable. If the provisions are unambiguous, they must be given effect." *Németh*, para. 35.

[91] *Hape*, para. 53. [92] *Hape*, para. 53. [93] *Németh*, para. 35.

[94] Fraser v. Janes Family Foods Ltd., 2012 FCA 99, paras. 15–19.

[95] Again the ambiguity requirement comes to Canada from the United Kingdom, where it appears to still apply (*see* Fatima, *supra* note 41). But it was not always thus in English law. *See* van Ert, *supra* note 76, at 135–139.

[96] National Corn Growers v. Canadian Import Tribunal, [1990] 2 SCR 1324, 1371.

[97] Crown Forest Industries Ltd. v. Canada, [1995] 2 SCR 802, para. 44. *See also* Najafi v. Canada (Public Safety and Emergency Preparedness), 2014 FCA 262, para. 61.

it seems to me) as consigning the ambiguity requirement to history.[98] Almost all Supreme Court of Canada invocations of the presumption of conformity since *National Corn Growers* have omitted any mention of ambiguity as a step in the interpretive process. Yet some lower courts persist in requiring facial ambiguity.[99] The better view is that courts need not find, and litigants need not show, ambiguity on the face of an enactment before considering its international context[100] and applying (unless rebutted) the presumption that it conforms to Canada's international obligations.

V. The Presumption of Minimum Protection

A variation on the presumption of conformity exists in respect of Canada's constitutionally entrenched human rights instrument, the Charter. In 1987, Dickson CJ argued in dissent for a rebuttable presumption that the Charter provides at least as great a level of protection as that afforded by similar provisions in Canada's international human rights agreements.[101] This refinement of the general presumption of conformity makes international human rights law a floor, but not a ceiling, for judicial development of constitutionally entrenched civil and political rights. A litigant can point to a human rights obligation of the state to elucidate the minimum content of a Charter right, but a government cannot rely on a human rights obligation to restrict the scope of such a right.[102]

Thirty years later, this interpretive presumption appears to be well established, having been repeatedly endorsed by Supreme Court majorities. Yet the Court's commitment to the presumption of minimum protection has, at times, seemed notably weaker than its commitment to the ordinary presumption of conformity.[103]

[98] *See,* e.g., Canada v. Seaboard Lumber Sales Co., [1995] 3 FCR 113, 120 ("It is now established that courts will look to relevant international documents to aid interpretation of implementing legislation from the outset of the investigation, and even absent ambiguity on the face of that legislation"); De Guzman v. Canada (Minister of Citizenship and Immigration) 2005 FCA 436 at paras. 63–64; Najafi v. Canada (Public Safety and Emergency Preparedness) 2014 FCA 262 at para. 61 (" . . . relevant international law . . . should ideally be taken into account before concluding whether or not a text is clear or ambiguous").

[99] *See,* e.g., Canadian Security Intelligence Service Act (Canada) (Re), 2008 FC 301, para. 38; Lum v. Alberta Dental Association and College (Review Panel), 2016 ABCA 154, paras. 52–54; Prophet River First Nation v. Canada (Attorney General), 2016 FCA 120, para. 12.

[100] *See* the cases cited at note 87.

[101] Reference re Public Service Employee Relations Act (Alta.), [1987] 1 SCR 313, 349.

[102] At least not at the right-defining stage of the analysis. International law can inform the rights-limitation stage. *See,* e.g., R. v. Oakes, [1986] 1 SCR 103, 140–141.

[103] E.g., *Kazemi*, para. 150.

VI. Judicial Notice of International Law

Canadian courts, like courts around the world, generally take judicial notice of public international law without requiring that it be proved in evidence. Indeed, judicial notice of international law is the unspoken foundation of the reception system's other rules. Express, recent case law on the point is wanting,[104] but the practice of the Supreme Court of Canada is clear,[105] and one cannot treat international law as "part of the context in which Canadian laws are enacted"[106] without permitting judicial recourse to that context—whether in the record or not. Expert evidence on points of international law has sometimes been admitted into evidence in recent years, but in each case without judicial consideration of its admissibility. Such decisions must be regarded as per incuriam.

VII. Deference and Nonjusticiability

Unlike their American counterparts,[107] Canadian courts do not defer to the executive on questions of international law. The Canadian position remains that set out by Lord Parker in 1916: "If the Court is to decide judicially in accordance with what it conceives to be the law of nations, it cannot, even in doubtful cases, take its directions from the Crown, which is a party to the proceedings. It must itself determine what the law is according to the best of its ability, and its view, whatever hesitation it be arrived at, must prevail over any executive order."[108] This position may be under threat, in Canadian administrative law at least, due to an ongoing judicial controversy about the role of deference to the executive in judicial review proceedings.[109]

Political questions, act of state, and similar doctrines touching the justiciability of certain kinds of foreign affairs controversies have mostly failed to gain much

[104] *See* The Ship "North" v. The King, (1906) 37 SCR 385, 394; R v. Appulonappa, 2014 BCCA 163, para. 62; Boily c Sa Majesté la Reine, 2017 CF 396 (FC).

[105] *See,* e.g., World Bank Group v. Wallace 2016 SCC 15; R v. Appulonappa, 2015 SCC 59.

[106] *B010*, para. 47.

[107] *See,* e.g., David Sloss, *United States*, *in* The Role of Domestic Courts in Treaty Enforcement: A Comparative Study 504, 524 (David Sloss ed., 2009).

[108] The Zamora, [1916] 2 AC 77, 97. Quoted with approval in *Reference re Japanese Treaty Act, 1913*, (1922) 29 BCR 136 (BCCA), at 147–148.

[109] *See* Gib van Ert, *The Reception of International Law in Canada: Three Ways We Might Go Wrong, in Canada in International Law at 150 and Beyond* (Paper No. 2—January 2018), *available at* https://www.cigionline.org/publications/reception-international-law-canada-three-ways-we-might-go-wrong.

traction in Canadian law. In *Operation Dismantle* (1985),[110] the Supreme Court doubted the U.S. political question doctrine and affirmed that the executive's exercise of the foreign affairs prerogative is not exempt from constitutional scrutiny. Judicial scrutiny on other-than-constitutional grounds is available as well, if in attenuated form.[111] The foreign act of state doctrine, as recently revived in U.K. law,[112] is virtually nonexistent in Canada. No Canadian decision applies it, and few have considered it. The doctrine seems inconsistent with the decision and result in *Badesha*. There, a judge of the Court of Appeal in extradition proceedings hesitated to "judge the laws and systems in place in another country" and worried that the fugitives' arguments amounted to "a general indictment of India's criminal justice system and the conditions in its prisons."[113] In upholding the extradition decision, Moldaver J. for the unanimous Supreme Court of Canada rejected these concerns as "too sweeping" and affirmed that the Minister (and, by extension, the reviewing court) can "consider evidence of the general human rights situation" in the receiving state.[114] This result seems consistent with the Court's observation, in the Quebec secession case, that it has sometimes been "necessary for this Court to look to international law to determine the rights or obligations of some actor within the Canadian legal system."[115]

VIII. Use of Nonbinding International Materials

No settled rules govern resort to nonbinding international materials by Canadian litigants and courts. Given their nonbinding nature, they are not incorporated by the common law like custom nor do they attract the presumption of conformity.[116] Rather, their use seems to depend on their relevance and persuasiveness in particular cases.

[110] Operation Dismantle v. The Queen, [1985] 1 SCR 441. *See also* Air Canada v. British Columbia (Attorney General), [1986] 2 SCR 539, and Canada (Prime Minister) v. Khadr, 2010 SCC 3, para. 36.

[111] Black v. Chrétien, (2001) 54 OR (3d) 215, affirming *Council of Civil Service Unions v. Minister for the Civil Service*, [1985] 1 AC 374 (HL). But some courts continue to assert the general nonjusticiability of foreign affairs prerogative powers in nonconstitutional cases. *See*, e.g., Turp v. Minister of Justice, 2012 FC 893, para. 19.

[112] *See* Eirik Bjorge & Cameron Miles, *Crown and Foreign Acts of State before British Courts:* Ramatullah, Belhaj, *and the Separation of Powers*, ch. 40 in this volume.

[113] India v. Badesha, 2016 BCCA 88, para. 125.

[114] India v. Badesha, 2017 SCC 44, para. 44. *See also* Suresh v. Canada (Minister of Citizenship and Immigration), 2002. SCC 1, paras. 124–125; Kindler v. Canada (Minister of Justice), [1991] 2 SCR 779, 849–850.

[115] Reference re Secession of Quebec, [1998] 2 S.C.R. 217, para. 22; *see also id.*, para. 23.

[116] Nothing, of course, prevents a legislature from implementing a nonbinding instrument despite the absence of legal obligation to do so. As noted above, the UNCITRAL Model Law on International Commercial Arbitration is implemented in every Canadian jurisdiction.

Some nonbinding sources are very highly regarded. The UNCITRAL Model Law[117] and the UNHCR Handbook[118] are examples.[119] More frequently, the weight given to such materials varies based on the apparent strength of international feeling around them,[120] their relevance to the case at hand,[121] and (a skeptic might say) judicial preference for a particular result.

The Supreme Court of Canada has repeatedly divided on the weight to be given to formally nonbinding international labor law sources in the interpretation of Charter Sec. 2(d) (freedom of association). In *Fraser*, Rothstein J criticized the Court's decision in *Health Services*[122] for giving weight to International Labour Organization (ILO) Convention No. 98[123] on the ground that Canada has not ratified it. The debate continued in *Saskatchewan Federation*. There the majority recognized the right to strike as an aspect of free association. Abella J relied in part on the opinions of ILO supervisory bodies such as the Committee on Freedom of Association, which "[t]hough not strictly binding . . . have considerable persuasive weight."[124] Rothstein and Wagner JJ took issue with this. In their view, while "obligations under international law that are binding on Canada are of primary relevance to this Court's interpretation of the Charter . . . other sources of international law can have some persuasive value in appropriate circumstances" but "should be granted much less weight than sources under which Canada is bound."[125]

IX. Postscript: *Khadr (No. 2)*

The somewhat sophisticated reception scheme described above offers little resistance to a court (or at any rate a Supreme Court) inclined to downplay the state's international obligations. In *Khadr (No. 2)*, the Supreme Court of Canada considered the case of fifteen-year-old Omar Khadr, a Canadian boy seized by American forces

[117] *See* Dell Computer Corp. v. Union des Consommateurs, 2007 SCC 34, paras. 44–46.

[118] *See* Canada (Attorney General) v. Ward, [1993] 2 SCR 689, 713–714; Chan v. Canada (Minister of Employment and Immigration), [1995] 3 SCR 593; Pushpanathan v. Canada (Minister of Citizenship and Immigration), [1998] 1 SCR 982; Hinzman v. Canada (Citizenship and Immigration), 2007 FCA 17, para. 23.

[119] *See also* the discussion of OECD materials in interpreting tax treaties in *Prévost Car Inc. v. Canada*, 2009 FCA 57.

[120] E.g., *Kazemi*, para. 147, where LeBel J concluded that the UN Committee Against Torture's General Comment No. 3, UN Doc. CAT/C/GC/3, "only indicate that there is an absence of consensus around the interpretation of art. 14."

[121] E.g., *Re Mahjoub*, 2010 FC 787, paras. 25–28, where the court relied on the work of the Committee Against Torture and other UN materials "to provide guidance as to the meaning of" cruel, inhuman or degrading treatment or punishment.

[122] *See supra* note 31.

[123] Convention (No. 98) Concerning the Application of the Principles of the Right to Organise and Bargain Collectively, 96 UNTS 257.

[124] *Saskatchewan Federation*, para. 69.

[125] *Id.*, para. 157.

in Afghanistan in 2002. He was charged with killing an American soldier and conspiring with al Qaeda, then sent to Guantánamo Bay, Cuba where he was held without trial for eight years. In 2009, Khadr went to Federal Court to challenge the federal government's refusal to seek his repatriation to Canada. O'Reilly J found that U.S. authorities, with the knowledge and participation of their Canadian counterparts, had subjected Khadr to an extended sleep deprivation program in "an effort to make him more amenable and willing to talk."[126] After a review of Canada's obligations under the CRC, that treaty's Optional Protocol on the Involvement of Children in Armed Conflict 2000,[127] and the CAT, O'Reilly J concluded that Canada "participated directly in conduct that failed to respect" Khadr's international human rights of freedom from torture and unlawful detention, particularly given Canada's heightened obligation to protect minors "drawn into hostilities before they can apply mature judgment to the choices they face."[128] To remedy these wrongs, O'Reilly J applied ordered Canada to request Khadr's repatriation. The majority of the Federal Court of Appeal dismissed Canada's appeal, relying on the trial judge's findings of Khadr's mistreatment contrary to international human rights law.[129]

On further appeal to the Supreme Court of Canada, the central issues of torture and child protection at international law vanished. The Court's judgment studiously avoided the word "torture," saying instead that Khadr's statements were obtained in "oppressive circumstances" contrary to "the most basic Canadian [not international] standards about the treatment of detained youth suspects."[130] Khadr's sleep-deprived interrogations by Canadian officials were dubbed "interviews."[131] On the all-important issue of remedy, the Court affirmed that Khadr's constitutional rights had been violated but overturned the repatriation order. In its place the Court granted a declaration that Canada had "actively participated in a process contrary to Canada's international human rights obligations" and "deprive[d] [Khadr] of his right to liberty and security of the person," but left it "to the government to decide how best to respond to this judgment in light of current information, its responsibility for foreign affairs, and in conformity with the *Charter*."[132] While this may seem appropriately deferential to the executive's conduct of foreign affairs, it was, at best, a weak application of authorities affirming that the conduct of foreign affairs was not immune from constitutional scrutiny.[133] Or, in Campbell McLachlan's stronger words, the Court draped Khadr's case in "the cloak of deference to the executive's exercise of the prerogative . . . simply to obscure the legal issues and to legitimise the will of the executive to take not steps

[126] Khadr v. Canada (Prime Minister), 2009 FC 405, para. 15 (*quoting* a Canadian government official).

[127] [2002] Can TS no. 5.

[128] Khadr v. Canada (Prime Minister), 2009 FC 405, paras. 64 and 68.

[129] Khadr v. Canada (Prime Minister), 2009 FCA 246.

[130] *Khadr No. 2*, paras. 20 and 25.

[131] *Khadr No. 2*, para. 24 (among others).

[132] *Khadr No. 2*, para. 39.

[133] Operation Dismantle v. The Queen, [1985] 1 SCR 441, 455; Canada v. Schmidt [1987] 1 SCR 500, 518, 520–521; Kindler v. Canada (Minister of Justice), [1991] 2 SCR 779, 799; United States v. Burns, 2001 SCC 7, para. 32.

to protect Mr Khadr."[134] The government responded to the Court's deferential declaration by promptly disclaiming any intention to seek Khadr's repatriation,[135] and indeed he was not returned to Canada until September 2012, nearly two years after pleading guilty and being sentenced to forty years in prison by the U.S. authorities. In 2017, a new Canadian government apologized to Khadr and paid him CDN$10.5 million in compensation.[136]

[134] Campbell McLachlan, Foreign Relations Law 9.75 (2014).

[135] *Government has no plans to bring back Khadr*, CBC News (Feb. 3, 2010), *available at* http://www.cbc.ca/news/canada/government-has-no-plans-to-bring-back-khadr-1.935533.

[136] *Canada Apologizes and Pays Millions to Citizen Held at Guantánamo Bay*, N.Y. Times (July 7, 2017), *available at* https://www.nytimes.com/2017/07/07/world/canada/omar-khadr-apology-guantanamo-bay.html.

CHAPTER 29

INTERNATIONAL LAW IN ISRAELI COURTS

AMICHAI COHEN

THE fact that many international obligations are relevant to Israel should occasion no surprise. After all, Israel has been almost constantly involved in armed conflicts from its birth. It also controls relatively large areas under the law of occupation. What is remarkable, however, is the extent to which Israeli judges and courts use and discuss international law, and do so in ways that are very rare elsewhere.

Three factors are important to understanding the role of international law in Israeli courts: first, there exists no general law or constitutional arrangement regarding the role of international law in domestic Israeli law. The Israeli Supreme Court (ISC), left with the task of creating Israel's foreign relations law, adopted the English common law tradition with regard both to customary international law (CIL), which is part of Israeli law, and concerning treaties, which are not.

The second factor is the general "activism" of the Israeli courts. Judicial activism is especially evident in the ISC, which is both Israel's highest court of appeal and its high court of justice, and which has the power of review of all administrative action and legislative activity. While Israel possesses no formal constitution, the Knesset, Israel's unitary legislature, has enacted "Basic Laws" that are designed to serve as possible building blocks for a future constitutional corpus. In 1995, the ISC decided that it has the power to invalidate statutes that contradict these laws.[1] The judicial activism of the ISC is also reflected in its willingness to interpret international law and interact with it, though not always to follow it.

The third factor affecting the jurisprudence of Israeli courts concerning international law is that international law is typically applied in the context of the Israeli-Palestinian conflict. Specifically, international law is frequently mentioned in judgments involving

[1] Civ. App. 6821/93, United Mizrahi Bank v. Migdal Cooperative Village, 49(4) PD 221(1995) [*translated at* http://versa.cardozo.yu.edu/sites/default/files/upload/opinions/United%20Mizrachi%20Bank%20v.%20Migdal%20Cooperative%20Village_0.pdf].

Israel's control of the "territories," an area lying beyond Israel's official borders, where the Court applies the international law of occupation.[2]

As I will show, the confluence of these factors means that while, as mentioned, the formal doctrine of Israeli law seems to follow the English tradition, in reality the role of international law in Israeli law follows a dynamic path of creating a "fusion" between international law and Israeli Law.

The remainder of this chapter will proceed as follows. Its first part will describe the formal Israeli doctrine of the role of international law in Israeli courts. The next part will describe and analyze the jurisprudence of Israeli courts about Israeli conduct in the territories. Finally, the third part will review the role of international law in other areas of concern to Israeli courts.

I. The Formal Doctrine

The Knesset has never clearly stated the way in which Israel accedes to international treaties, or the power of these treaties in domestic law. Hence, the law in these matters is judge-made. The formal Israeli doctrine in this area, as declared by several early ISC decisions, closely follows the dualist English tradition.[3] Ratification and accession to international treaties are tasks carried out by the government, which occupies the pinnacle of Israel's executive branch. There is no formal requirement for approval of treaties by the Knesset.[4]

Regarding the status of international law in Israeli courts, the situation can be summarized in four simple "rules." First, CIL is automatically part of domestic law.[5] The Court has supplied two explanations for this rule. One is that the adoption of English practice in these matters conformed with the general acceptance of English common law in the early days of Israeli independence. The other explanation is more general in nature, and refers to the requirement that all independent states respect international customs.[6]

[2] The question of the legality of Israel's control of the territories is so politically charged that even the name of the geographical area is in dispute. I here employ the somewhat colloquial term "the territories" in a destined-to-fail attempt to avoid these political sensitivities.

[3] In this sense, the Israeli doctrine is not dissimilar from the U.K. and Canadian doctrines. *See* Shaheed Fatima, *The Domestic Application of International Law in British Courts*, ch. 27 in this volume, and Gib Van Ert, *The Domestic Application of International Law in Canada*, ch. 28 in this volume. For a review of the status of international law in the Israeli legal system, *see* Ruth Lapidoth, *International Law within the Israel Legal System*, 24 Israel L. Rev. 451 (1990).

[4] *See* Crim. App. 131/67, Kamiar v. The State of Israel, 22 (2) PD 85 (1968). There is a tradition, however, that peace treaties are submitted by the government for approval by the Knesset.

[5] *See* Crim. App. 174/54, Shtamper v. Attorney General, 10 PD 5 (1954); Crim. App. 336/61, Eichman v. Attorney General, 16 PD 2033 (1962).

[6] For a discussion of these justification and their problems, *see* Eyal Benvenisti, *Judicial Misgivings Regarding the Application of International Law*, 4 Eur. J. Int'l L. 159, 176 (1993) (discussing the justification for automatic implementation of international customs in Israeli courts).

The second rule is that international treaties only become part of Israeli law when expressly incorporated by domestic legislation.[7] The justification for this doctrine is the principle of "separation of powers." Since ratification of a treaty is an action taken by the government, it cannot be accorded the status of law, because legislation is the prerogative of the Knesset. Furthermore, the Court justified this rule on the basis that international treaties are matters of government foreign and security policy, in which courts should not interfere. Both the positive and the normative justifications supplied by the Court are contestable. As a matter of positive law, it is unclear why international treaties would not be accorded legal status as secondary legislation, or at least as a government decision, both of which are legally binding in Israeli law. With regard to the normative claim, the proposition that international treaties deal only with matters of foreign affairs and security is difficult to sustain. Modern treaties concern almost every issue in which the state is involved, such as trade, environmental protection, and minorities' rights, and a gap between international obligations and judicial application in these issues is a problematic position for the state.[8]

Two further rules mitigate the dichotomy between CIL and treaty law. The first of these (and the third overall rule) is that whenever there exists a clear contradiction between Israeli and international law, Israeli law prevails in domestic courts.[9] The last rule posits the "presumption of compatibility," which closely resembles the American *Charming Betsy* doctrine.[10] According to this rule, Israeli legislation would be interpreted in line with Israel's international obligations, whether customary or treaty.[11]

In certain specific areas, such as intellectual property,[12] custom duties,[13] and diplomatic immunity,[14] the formal doctrine does describe how the courts implement international law in reality. However, these areas represent only the minority of cases in which Israeli courts refer to international law. The vast majority of discussions of international law in Israeli courts concern armed conflict, the law of occupation, and human rights. In these areas there is a need for a more nuanced discussion of the effects of international law in Israeli courts. The remainder of this chapter is designed to serve that purpose.

[7] Civ. App. 25/55, Custodian of Absentee Property v. Samra, 10 PD 1825 (1950).

[8] *See* Benvenisti, *supra* note 6, at 178. *See also*, e.g., his claim that with regard to the law of occupation the separation of powers claim is actually irrelevant because the sovereign is the military commander.

[9] *See Eichman*, *supra* note 5.

[10] *See* Curtis A. Bradley, *The Charming Betsy Canon and Separation of Powers: Rethinking the Interpretive Role of International Law*, 86 GEO. L.J. 479, 538 (1998).

[11] HCJ 302/72, Abu Chilu v. Gov't of Israel, 27(2) PD 169 (1973); HCJ 2599/00, Yated—Association for Children with Down Syndrome v. Ministry of Education, 56(1) PD 834 (2002) [*translated at* http://versa.cardozo.yu.edu/opinions/yated-v-ministry-education].

[12] E.g., Civ. App. 6316/03, Ilan Zagagut Rechev v. Baruch, 62(2) PD 749 (2007) [*translated at* http://versa.cardozo.yu.edu/opinions/ilan-car-glazing-ltd-v-baruch].

[13] E.g., Civ. 18199-06-10, Mavidex v. The State of Israel (Tel Aviv District Court) (2013).

[14] Civ. App. 4289/98, Shalom v. Attorney General (Tel Aviv District Court) (1999).

II. The Law Applied in the Territories

In 1967, Israel took control over the "territories," portions of the former mandate of Palestine that at the end of the Israeli war of independence in 1949 were controlled by Arab countries. After some internal Israeli discussions, which lie outside the scope of this chapter, the state presented the following position to the ISC: Israel did not formally, or de jure, recognize that the territories are occupied in the sense of Article 42 of the Hague Regulations[15] or Common Article 2 of the Geneva Conventions.[16] However, Israel committed internationally to the de facto application of the law of occupation: the full application of the Hague Regulations and the application of "humanitarian instructions" contained in the Fourth Geneva Convention (GC-IV).[17] Furthermore, the state never challenged the authority of the ISC, sitting as the high court of justice, to hear petitions submitted by Palestinian residents of the territories against actions taken by the Israeli military government. Hence, since the very early days of the Israeli occupation of the territories, the Court was open to petitions based on the international law of occupation.[18]

Customary International Law in the Territories

Early decisions of the ISC regarding the territories differentiated, at least formally, between the Hague Regulations and the GC-IV, both of which include articles laying down the international law of occupation. The Court determined that the Hague Regulations represent CIL, and hence are automatically part of the law applied in the territories. However, it also ruled that the GC-IV is treaty law (and not CIL), and hence inapplicable in Israeli courts. The Court did discuss the GC-IV, but only in the form of *obiter dicta*. Moreover, its discussion reflected the need to explain that Israeli policies are not in violation of international law, whether or not it is applicable in domestic law.[19] We shall return to the GC-IV and its effects below. For present purposes, what needs to be noted is that until the year 2000, no specific policy was declared to be in violation of the GC-IV, and so the question of its applicability remained somewhat academic.

[15] Laws and Customs of War on Land, Convention (IV) (1907).

[16] Common Art. 2, Geneva Convention Relative to the Protection of Civilian Persons in Time of War (Fourth Geneva Convention), 75 UNTS 287 (Aug. 12, 1949).

[17] Fourth Geneva Convention, art. 146.

[18] HCJ 302/72, Abu Chilu v. The Government of Israel, 27(2) PD 169 (1973). For a full discussion and critique of the position of the Israeli government, *see* David Kretzmer, The Occupation of Justice: The Supreme Court of Israel and the Occupied Territories 19–43 (2002). *See also* Amichai Cohen, *Administering the Territories: An Inquiry into the Application of International Humanitarian Law by the IDF in the Territories*, 38(3) Israel L. Rev. 24–79 (2005).

[19] HCJ 606/78, Ayyub v. Minister of Defense, 33(2) PD 113 [*English summary* at 9 Isr. YBHR 345 (1979)].

With respect to the Hague Regulations, the ISC has generally interpreted them in a manner that supports governmental and military policy. The ISC used Article 43 of the Hague Regulations to approve the government's policy of "benevolent occupant," declaring that according to Article 43, the occupying power should balance its military interest with the humanitarian needs of the occupied population. Furthermore, the Court explained that in a long-term occupation, such as the Israeli occupation of the territories, the local occupied population also has an interest in projects designed to develop infrastructure and promote its welfare.[20] On this basis, the Court approved Israeli policies such as the passage of laws regulating taxes, electricity supply, infrastructure, and employment.[21]

The Court also approved most of the security measures used by the Israeli military commander, which it declared to be legal under international law. It sanctioned the demolition of houses, a policy clearly intended to hurt not the actual perpetrators of terrorist acts but their close family, reasoning that demolitions did not constitute a form of "collective punishment," which is forbidden by Article 50 to the Hague Regulations (and Article 33 of the GC-IV), but rather were a measure of deterrence.[22] The Court allowed the government to deport Palestinian leaders from the occupied territories, and found that this action did not violate the clear international law prohibition on deportations.[23]

David Kretzmer summarized the pre-2000 record of the ISC as follows: "In its decisions relating to the Occupied Territories, the Court has rationalized virtually all controversial actions of the Israeli authorities, especially those most problematic under principles of international humanitarian law."[24]

In effect, the Court's behavior might be termed *Reverse Charming Betsy*. Instead of interpreting Israeli law in conformity with international law, it interpreted international law in ways that conformed with the domestic practices of the Israeli military government in the territories. Such limitations as the Court did impose on Israeli policies in the territories during this period were more connected to principles of Israeli administrative law. What it emphasized was the need for the right of fair hearing and for procedural safeguards in the use of the state's authority as an occupying power.

In one area, that of expropriation of private Palestinian property for the purpose of Israeli settlement construction, the ISC did use international law to limit the policies preferred by the Israeli government.[25] Based on Article 52 to the Hague Regulations, the Court prohibited all expropriation of private land that is not justified by military

[20] HCJ 393/82, Jam'iat Iscan v. The Commander of the IDF Forces in Judea and Samaria, 37(4) PD 785 (2003) [*translated at* http://www.hamoked.org/items/160_eng.pdf].

[21] *See* Kretzmer, *supra* note 18.

[22] HCJ 698/85, Dujlas v. IDF Commander in Judea and Samaria, 40(2) PD 42 (1985).

[23] HCJ 785/87, Afu v. IDF Commander in the West Bank, 42(2) PD 001 (1988) [*translated at* http://www.hamoked.org/files/2011/280_eng.pdf].

[24] Kretzmer, *supra* note 18, at 187.

[25] HCJ 390/79, Dawikat v. The Gov't of Israel, 34(1) PD 1 (1979) [*translated at* http://www.hamoked.org/files/2010/1670_eng.pdf].

necessity. This decision had only limited effect; the Court evaded the issue of the legality of the settlements project itself, relying on the "political question" doctrine,[26] and in essence allowed the continuance of the building of Israeli settlements on all "public" lands in the territories, which constitute the vast majority of land there.

After 2000—Justice Barak and the Application of the Fourth Geneva Convention

The period since the mid 1990s, and especially after the eruption of the second *intifada* in the summer of 2000, witnessed a significant increase in the use of international law in limiting specific Israeli policies. The background for this development should be explained.

In the aftermath of the failure of the negotiations held at Camp David, relationships between Israelis and Palestinians rapidly deteriorated. On September 29, 2000, they entered a new violent phase with the outbreak of the second *intifada*. Between 2000 and 2004, more than a thousand Israelis (soldiers and civilians) were killed by Palestinians, and over 8,000 injured. On the Palestinian side, the cost during the same period was even higher and amounted to some 5,000 fatalities and 25,000 injured.[27] It was in this unlikely environment that the ISC developed its most sophisticated jurisprudence regarding international law.

Most of the cases in which the Court reviewed security measures and intervened followed the same pattern. First, the ISC ceased resorting to vague statements about the applicability of the GC-IV. Instead, it clearly declared the entire corpus of the international law of occupation to be relevant and applicable to the situation in the territories.[28] Second, the Court always declared that, *in principle*, the *state possesses the authority* to employ the security measure under discussion. However, and this is the most important part of the decisions, the Court interpreted international law in a way that inserted a condition qualifying the authority of the state to use the measure under discussion, such as a requirement to use it proportionally and reasonably.[29]

The then president of the ISC, Justice Aharon Barak, first gave notice of the new direction in the 2002 *Ajuri* case.[30] Ostensibly, the issue in this case was hardly novel: an appeal against an Israel Defense Forces (IDF) decision to relocate the family of a

[26] HCJ 4481/91, Bargil v. The Gov't of Israel, 47(4) PD 210 (1993) [*translated at* http://versa.cardozo.yu.edu/sites/default/files/upload/opinions/Bargil%20v.%20Government%20of%20Israel_0.pdf].

[27] Stuart A. Cohen, Israel and Its Army: From Cohesion to Confusion 179 (2008).

[28] *See* HCJ 1661/05, Gaza Beach Regional Council et al. v. Knesset of Israel et al., 59(2) PD, 481 514 (2005).

[29] *Id.*

[30] HCJ 7015/02, Ajuri v. IDF Commander in the West Bank, 56(6) PD 352 (2002) [*translated at* http://versa.cardozo.yu.edu/sites/default/files/upload/opinions/Ajuri%20v.%20IDF%20Commander%20in%20West%20Bank_0.pdf].

deceased suicide bomber from the West Bank to the Gaza Strip. The decision, too, accorded with precedent, in that the ISC allowed this instance of "assigned residence" for one of the three people to whom the government sought to apply the policy. Where Barak broke new ground, however, was in the principles that he enunciated in his decision, with which all of his colleagues on the bench concurred. First, he declared the GC-IV (Article 78 of which relates to "assigned residence") to be applicable and enforceable by the courts—a position that had thereto been considered at best debatable, but was henceforth never questioned. Second, he interpreted Article 78 of the GC-IV far more strictly than had previously been conventional, limiting future cases of assigned residence to persons who could be proven to have been directly involved in a crime. The result of these strict limitations was that without explicitly announcing that such was his intent, Barak ensured that assigned residence would simply disappear from the IDF's repertoire of punishments. Indeed, since *Ajuri* it has never been used again.

Justice Barak used a similar judicial method in the 2004 *Beit Sourik* case.[31] This was one of a series of cases revolving around the "security/separation fence" that Israel began to construct in 2002 in an effort to impede the movement of terrorists intent on attacking Israeli civilian targets. Israeli military officials would persistently credit this "fence" as a key factor in the reduction the level of Palestinian incursions and attacks.[32] Its opponents highlighted, by contrast, the economic, social, and psychological hardships on Palestinians caused by what they termed "the separation barrier" or "apartheid wall."[33] In *Beit Sourik*, Justice Barak sought to balance the conflicting aspects of the case. Accepting the government's argument that the barrier was designed to serve security purposes, and not to promote a political program, Barak was prepared to sanction some infractions of human rights, such as the confiscation of private lands situated on the route of its construction. Where he drew a line, however, was on granting the military sole discretion in the determination of what actions could and could not be taken. As he wrote in Paragraph 48 of his judgment:

> The military commander is the expert regarding the military quality of the separation fence route. We are experts regarding its humanitarian aspects. The military commander determines where, on hill and plain, the separation fence will be erected. That is his expertise. We examine whether this route's harm to the local residents is proportional. That is our expertise.

Since *Beit Sourik*, almost every kilometer of the separation barrier has been subjected to judicial review.

[31] HCJ 2056/04, Beit Sourik Village Council v. the Government of Israel, 58(5) PD 807 (2004) [*English summery at* http://opil.ouplaw.com/view/10.1093/law:ildc/16il04.case.1/law-ildc-16il04?rskey=iMOam8&result=1&prd=ORIL].

[32] Doron Almog, *The West Bank Fence*, Policy Focus no. 47 (Washington Institute for Near East Policy, 2004).

[33] Aeyal Gross, The Writing on the Wall: Rethinking the International Law of Occupation 265–338 (2017).

Ten days after the ISC issued its *Beit Sourik* decision, the International Court of Justice (ICJ) published its *Advisory Opinion* regarding the legality of the barrier.[34] The two documents were in conflict on several essential points. Contradicting the ISC, the ICJ argued that the real goal behind the barrier (which is pointedly termed a "wall") is political, i.e., that it is designed to facilitate the annexation of some of the territories, an action forbidden by international law. Likewise, the ICJ declared the construction of the barrier to be in violation of international human rights laws and international humanitarian laws, a situation that it called upon all states to end. But not even this condemnation (incidentally, the first and thus far the only occasion on which the ISC has come into direct conflict with an international tribunal) caused the ISC to retract from its basic position with respect to the need to apply international law to matters related to security measures. On the contrary, in his judgment in the *Mara'be* case,[35] Justice Barak invested considerable energy in arguing that disputes between the ISC and the ICJ revolved around facts rather than the law per se. On the basic principle, the content of international law and its status, the two sides were, so he maintained, in complete agreement.

As some commentators noted, when reviewing security measures in the territories, the Court did not exactly apply international law in the traditional sense. Rather, it enriched international law with concepts of individual responsibility and proportionality that were adopted from the Court's own domestic human rights jurisprudence. In some cases, the Court explicitly used human rights conventions to interpret the meaning of the law of occupation.[36] Once again, it could be said that the ISC used the *presumption of compatibility* rule in a reverse manner. It was not that domestic law was interpreted according to international law, but rather the opposite. The difference from the earlier jurisprudence, however, was that after 2000 the Court did not interpret international law in a way that accorded with the government's policies, as had previously been its practice, but rather in accordance with domestic *legal concepts regarding the balancing of human right and security considerations.*[37]

[34] Advisory Opinion Concerning Legal Consequences of the Construction of a Wall in the Occupied Palestinian Territory, International Court of Justice (ICJ), July 9, 2004.

[35] HCJ 7957/04, Mara'abe v. the Prime Minister of Israel, 60(2) PD 477 (2005) [*translated at* http://elyon1.court.gov.il/Files_ENG/04/570/079/a14/04079570.a14.htm].

[36] For example, in the *Mar'ab* case, the Court determined that an order of the military commander limiting the ability of Palestinian detainees to meet with lawyers, and delaying their appearance in court was illegal. It based its decision on an interpretation of Article 9(3) to the International Covenant on Civil and Political Rights: "Anyone arrested or detained on a criminal charge shall be brought promptly before a judge or other officer authorized by law to exercise judicial power. . . . ". See HCJ 3239/02 Mar'ab v. Commander of the IDF forces in Judea and Samaria, 57(2) PD 349 (2003) [translated at http://versa.cardozo.yu.edu/opinions/marab-v-idf-commander-west-bank].

[37] As Aeyal Gross noted, by thus using domestic concepts of human rights and balancing, the Court did not always afford Palestinians more protection. Sometimes, the result was to provide protection to the settlers, who are not nominally protected under the GC-IV, and to sanction an infringement of the rights of Palestinians. Gross, *supra* note 33, at 16. *See*, e.g., HCJ 10356/02, Hass v. Commander of the IDF Forces in the West Bank, 58(3) PD 443 (2004) [*translated at* http://versa.cardozo.yu.edu/sites/default/files/upload/opinions/Hass%20v.%20IDF%20Commander%20in%20West%20Bank.pdf] (balancing the property rights of Palestinians against the rights of freedom of movement and of religious

The ISC also applied international law as a basis for reviewing the legality of specific military methods under the Laws of Armed Conflict (LOAC).[38] From the beginning of the second *intifada*, the IDF submitted a novel claim to the ISC. Given the number of troops now committed to suppressing the uprising, and the firepower that they had to employ, it no longer made sense to speak of IDF missions in the territories in terms of constabulary operations, designed merely to restore law and order. Rather, the campaign warranted categorization as a military confrontation or, in the formulation preferred by the IDF, "an armed conflict short of war."[39] After initial hesitations regarding whether the doctrine of nonjusticiability should be applied to actual conflict,[40] Justice Barak firmly rejected this claim, and declared that the Court would discuss petitions regarding the legality of the way the IDF conducts its operations, under the international law of armed conflict.

The development in this area was gradual. The first step was taken during the IDF's siege of the Church of the Nativity in Bethlehem (April–May 2002). The petition to the Court focused on the extent of the IDF's duty to deliver food, water, and additional necessities to the 180 clerics and other civilian personnel who were being held hostage in the Church by some forty armed Palestinians. Necessarily, all such deliveries weakened Israel's bargaining power vis-à-vis the hostage takers. In that case, Barak "brokered an agreement" (but in fact forced the government to agree) to allow delivery of foodstuff into the church, basing his position on Article 23 of the GC-IV.[41]

A further important milestone in this area was *Physicians for Human Rights* (2004).[42] The case involved military operations in the southern part of the Gaza strip in 2004, a year prior to Israel's disengagement from that region. IDF units entered certain neighborhoods in Rafah in order to detain suspects, locate weapons, and destroy underground tunnels bypassing Israeli checkpoints along the border with Egypt. The operation met with heavy Palestinian armed resistance. The petitioners claimed that various violations of LOAC were taking place and that the local population was being deprived of drinking water and medical supplies. Once again, regarding most claims, Barak was able to broker an agreement between the petitioners and the government in court. Only with respect to the right of Palestinians to participate in the funerals of their family members killed during the operations did Barak rule against the government. The importance of the decision lies, however, not in this specific

worship of Jewish settlers in the West Bank, who wanted to pray in the Cave of the Patriarchs in Hebron).

38 I prefer this term here to the term "International Humanitarian Law" in order to highlight the difference between the application of the law of occupation, which was discussed in the previous section, and the context of armed conflict, which is the focus of this section.

39 Amos Harel & Avi Isacharoff, The Seventh War 195 (2004) (Heb.).

40 E.g., HCJ 3022/02, Cannon Law v. IDF Commander in the West Bank, 56(3) PD 9 (2002).

41 HCJ 3451/02, Al-Madani v. Minister of Defense, 56(3) PD 30 (2002) [*translated at* http://versa.cardozo.yu.edu/sites/default/files/upload/opinions/Almandi%20v.%20Minister%20of%20Defense.pdf].

42 HCJ 4764/04, Physicians for Human Rights v. IDF Commander in Gaza, 58(5) PD 385 (2004) [*English summary at* http://opil.ouplaw.com/view/10.1093/law:ildc/17il04.case.1/law-ildc-17il04?rskey=gFSN3F&result=6&prd=ORIL].

ruling, but rather in the fact that it details the duties of armed forces operating in a civilian area. Based mainly on Articles 27 and 55 of the GC-IV, the Court also details the way in which the IDF should prepare for providing humanitarian needs, and emphasizes the need for it to supply the civilian population with information about the mechanisms put in place to provide this assistance. From a humanitarian law point of view, this is one of the most important legal judgments on the subject of humanitarian assistance to civilian population in an armed conflict.

A further development in the ISC's application of LOAC is discernable in two cases where the court actually discussed, and limited, specific methods of warfare. The first of these is the 2005 *Adalah* case,[43] colloquially known as the "early warning" decision. Once again handed down by Justice Barak, the Court in this decision declared unlawful the "neighbor practice"—a procedure whereby the IDF used civilians as intermediaries, tasked with persuading terrorists holed up in their neighborhood to give themselves up peacefully to the soldiers surrounding them. The judgment rested on an interpretation of Article 31 of the GC-IV, which forbids coercion against protected persons, and Article 51 of the same convention, which forbids the occupying power to force protected civilians to serve in its armed forces. The Court explicitly states that the consent of the civilians should be completely disregarded in this case.

The pinnacle of the ISC's intervention in actual methods of warfare, and perhaps its best known decision on matters of international law, is the *targeted killings* case.[44] In this decision, one of Justice Barak's last before his retirement, the Court dealt extensively with the legality of the targeted use of lethal force against active terrorists outside the battlefield. Space limitations do not allow a complete treatment of the impressive coverage of LOAC in this judgment. Suffice to say that Justice Barak's treatment of the issue was based on a novel interpretation of Article 51(3) of the first additional protocol to the Geneva Conventions,[45] which concerns civilians directly participating in hostilities. The judgment lays down the terms according to which targeted killings may be used, and orders the IDF to create a mechanism to evaluate the legality of their use.

Several authors, myself included, have advanced various explanations for the ISC's seemingly extreme, perhaps even unprecedented, reliance on international law.[46] One argument is that the Court's policy was driven by a concern that Israeli soldiers would be subject to procedures in the International Criminal Court, which began operating in 2002, and by national courts applying universal jurisdiction.[47] Another explanation is

[43] HCJ 3799/02, Adalah—The Legal Center for Arab Minority Rights in Israel v. OC Central Command, 60(3) PD 67 (2005) [*translated at* http://versa.cardozo.yu.edu/sites/default/files/upload/opinions/Adalah%20v.%20IDF%20Central%20Commander_0.pdf].

[44] HCJ 769/02, The Public Committee Against Torture in Israel v. The Gov't of Israel, 62(1) PD 507 (2006) [*translated at* http://elyon1.court.gov.il/Files_ENG/02/690/007/a34/02007690.a34.HTM].

[45] Protocol Additional to the Geneva Conventions of 12 August 1949, and Relating to the Protection of Victims of International Armed Conflicts (Protocol I), 1125 U.N.T.S. 3, 8 Jun. 1977.

[46] E.g., Amichai Cohen & Stuart A. Cohen, Israel's National Security Law: Political Dynamics and Historical Development 201–206 (2012).

[47] Indeed, these years saw a surge in the complaints against Israelis in various international courts, based on the universal jurisdiction doctrine.

that the use of international law simply enabled the ISC to gain some control over the behavior of the government, which under the pressure of terrorism evinced a tendency to resort to extreme measures.[48] Doubtless, the intervention had a lot to do with the personality and personal power of Justice Barak, who toward the end of his term as president of the ISC became one of the most important persons in Israeli public life. Whatever its cause, there can be no doubt that extensive review by the Court did indeed limit Israel's operational conduct. The ISC's decisions, and more importantly the potential for judicial intervention, served to mitigate the effect of armed conflict on Palestinian civilians.[49]

Note, once again, the changing logic of the application of international law by the courts. While the initial justification for the doctrine according to which international treaties are not applied by the courts is the attempt to avoid clashes with the government in matters of security and foreign policy, the later logic seemed entirely the opposite. Instead of avoiding political questions, the Court explicitly declared its wish to deal with them, and to do so precisely because they involve issues of morality in times of tension. Perhaps the best expression of this policy is Justice Barak's:

> The role of decision has been placed at our door, and we must fulfill it. It is our duty to preserve the legality of government, even when the decisions are difficult. Even when the cannons roar and the muses are silent, the law exists, and acts, and determines what is permissible and what is forbidden; what is legal and what is illegal. As the law exists, so exists the Court, which determines what is permissible and what is forbidden, what is legal and what is illegal. Part of the public will be happy about our decision; the other part will oppose it. It may be that neither part will read our reasoning. But we will do our job.[50]

A New Approach—Retreat?

Some scholars claim that since Barak's retirement in 2006, and especially since the retirement of his immediate successor, Justice Dorit Beinisch in 2012, the ISC has slowly retreated from its activist position in the application of international law regarding the territories.[51] One example of this "retreat" is the clearer emphasis now placed on the justiciability issue. In Justice Barak's latest decisions of 2005–2006, the court seemed to abandon the justiciability discussion altogether. Later opinions, however, make it clear that the Court will not intervene in areas in which the dominant

[48] Amichai Cohen, *Guardians and Guards: The Israeli Supreme Court's Role in Matters of National Security*, *in* Civil Military Relations in Israel 171 (Elisheva Rosman-Stollman & Aharon Kampinsky eds., 2014).

[49] David Kretzmer, *The Law of Belligerent Occupation in the Supreme Court of Israel*, 94 Int'l Rev. Red Cross 207, 236 (2012).

[50] HCJFH 2161/96, Sharif v. GOC Home Front Command, 50(4) PD 485, 491 (1996).

[51] Tamar Hostovsky Brandes, *The Declining Status of International Law in the Decisions of the Israel Supreme Court Concerning the Occupied Territories: Is the Golden Age Over?*, *available at* https://papers.ssrn.com/sol3/papers.cfm?abstract_id=3076843 (last revised Jan. 17, 2018).

character of the question is a military operational issue.[52] It was in accordance with this doctrine that in 2011 the ISC refused, on justiciability grounds, to review the use of shells in urban surroundings.[53] Another example is the set of decisions regarding house demolitions, which were renewed in 2014 after almost a decade of nonuse. Claims that the policy violates international law, and especially Article 33 of the GC-IV, were rejected almost without discussion.[54]

It seems that indeed the number of decisions in which the Court refers to international law when reviewing Israeli actions in the territories has declined. But that decline can at least partially be attributed to the ending of the second *intifada*, and Israel's disengagement from the Gaza Strip, and to the fact that most Palestinians in the territories are under the control of the Palestinian Authority. It remains to be seen whether this trend is a deeper one, signaling the retreat of the Court from this politically charged area of judicial review.

III. Applying International Law within Israel

International law, and especially international human rights law, does appear in the jurisprudence of the ISC in other cases as well. Here, too, the end of the 1990s signaled a rise in the use of international law. While the doctrine stating that international treaties cannot be independently implemented in Israeli courts remains the law, the *opportunities* for the application of international human rights increased. First, in 1992 the Israeli Knesset enacted *Basic Law: Human Dignity and Liberty*,[55] which strengthens the position of human rights in Israeli jurisprudence in general. Second, in the early 1990s Israel ratified many of the important human right treaties.

At least potentially, these developments created an opportunity for the ISC to use international human rights law in a more extensive manner. It did so in three clusters of cases not related to the Territories. The first cluster consisted of cases relating to the Arab-Israeli conflict, in which the court applied international law in a manner very similar to its behavior respecting security measures and life in the territories. The

[52] E.g., HCJ 4146/11, Hass v. Chief of the General Staff (July 9, 2013), Nevo Legal Database (by subscription, in Hebrew) [*translated at* http://versa.cardozo.yu.edu/sites/default/files/upload/opinions/Hess%20v.%20Chief%20of%20General%20Staff.pdf].

[53] HCJ 3261/06, Physicians for Human Rights v. Minister of Defense (Jan. 31, 2011), Nevo Legal Database (by subscription, in Hebrew).

[54] HCJ 8091/14, Hamoked—Center for the Defense of the Individual v. Minister of Defense (Dec. 31, 2014), Nevo Legal Database (by subscription, in Hebrew) [*translated at* http://versa.cardozo.yu.edu/sites/default/files/upload/opinions/HaMoked%2C%20Center%20for%20the%20Defense%20of%20the%20Individual%20v.%20Minister%20of%20Defense.pdf].

[55] Basic Law: Human Dignity and Liberty, *available at* https://www.knesset.gov.il/laws/special/eng/basic3_eng.htm.

second cluster of cases address purely Israeli matters. Here Court citations of international law seem designed merely to bolster a position that the Court would have reached even without international law. The third cluster of cases deal with the "other" in the Israeli society—asylum seekers, illegal immigrants, and foreign workers. Interestingly, it is here that the ISC uses international law in the most "extreme" manner.

Cases Involving the Arab-Israeli Conflict

Cases discussing Israel's actions in the context of the Arab-Israeli conflict within Israel deal with two main issues: investigations of suspected terrorists and their detention.

The question of the legality and morality of the use of force in the Israel Security Agency's (ISA) investigations of suspected terrorists has been part of the Israeli discussion of the balance between democracy and security needs since the early 1980s. In 1999, the Court issued its much-awaited decision in the *Public Committee Against Torture* case.[56] The petition challenged the Israeli policy of using "moderate" physical force in interrogations, a method approved by the Landau commission in 1987. The Court held that Israeli law as it stands does not provide authority for the ISA to use force in investigation. While the core of the decision is hence based on internal Israeli law, the Court discussed several international law instruments, and especially the Convention Against Torture.[57] It declared that torture and the use of cruel, inhuman, and degrading treatment is forbidden in Israeli law, as it is under international law. However, the Court allowed for an exception to the general prohibition in "ticking bomb" situations. Under the criminal exculpation of "necessity," the Court determined that the attorney general (AG) need not prosecute ISA interrogators suspected of resorting to physical pressure, if and when they had done so in circumstances requiring the immediate use of extreme methods in order to save lives.[58] Furthermore, the Court prohibited the creation of a system of ex ante authorization for the use of force in investigations (which was the main recommendation of the Landau commission). However, it did permit the AG to specify in writing the cases in which he would not prosecute on the grounds of the "necessity defense." The AG did

[56] HCJ 5100/94, Public Committee Against Torture v. Gov't of Israel, 53(4) PD 817 (1999) [*translated at* http://versa.cardozo.yu.edu/sites/default/files/upload/opinions/Public%20Committee%20Against%20Torture%20in%20Israel%20v.%20Government%20of%20Israel%281%29_0.pdf].

[57] Convention Against Torture and Other Cruel, Inhuman or Degrading Treatment or Punishment, Dec. 10, 1984, S. Treaty Doc. No. 100-20, 1465 U.N.T.S. 85 (1988).

[58] Sec. 34(11) of Israel's Penal Law provides:

> A person will not bear criminal liability for committing any act immediately necessary for the purpose of saving the life, liberty, body or property, of either himself or his fellow person, from substantial danger of serious harm, in response to particular circumstances during a specific time, and absent alternative means for avoiding the harm.

indeed publish such a directive.[59] This document expressly differentiated between torture—committing severe pain and ongoing damage, for which he proclaimed that no defense would be relevant—and lesser uses of force, where the necessity defense would be applied in appropriate cases.[60]

In the 2017 *Abu Gosh* decision,[61] the ISC rejected a petition to open a criminal investigation against ISA investigators who had used force when conducting an investigation. The Court seemed to accept the premise that had torture been employed, no defense would be applicable. However, it ruled that the methods used did not amount to actual torture, comparing those employed by the ISA with those used, for instance, in Guantánamo. The Court also judged reasonable the AG's decision to apply the necessity defense.

The *Abu Gosh* decision seems to strengthen the position of those scholars that claim that the *Public Committee Against Torture* case had only a limited effect.[62] To me, it seems clear that the ISC's decision in this matter has at least limited the use of force, and thus brought Israeli practice closer into line with international standards.

The second set of cases in which the ISC referred to international law is in the context of "bargaining chips"—a term used to describe the practice whereby enemy combatants are detained, even though they are not involved in any specific ongoing criminal case, for the purpose of exchanging them for Israelis held captive by the enemy. In the *Lebanese Detainees* case of 2000, the Court decided to release Lebanese nationals being held in Israel as "bargaining chips" in exchange for the return for the missing Israeli pilot Ron Arad, allegedly held by Hezbollah. The ISC judged this situation as tantamount to the holding of hostages, an action forbidden by Article 34 of the GC-IV and the International Convention Against the Taking of Hostages. Based on its understanding of international law, and applying the presumption of compatibility, the Court interpreted Israeli administrative detention law to permit administrative detention only where the detainee constitutes a specific threat. Hence, the detention of "bargaining chips" was prohibited.[63]

Similarly, in 2008 the court interpreted the "Illegal Combatants Detentions Act," allowing the detention of members of Hamas, as limited to persons against whom there is some proof that they represent a threat. The court based this interpretation on its

[59] Also, in 2002 the General Security Service Law was enacted. This law defined the positions and authorities of the Israeli General Security Service. For an English version, *see* https://knesset.gov.il/review/data/eng/law/kns15_GSS_eng.pdf.

[60] For a fuller description of these development, and a critical assessment of their compatibility with international law, *see* Yuval Shany, *Back to the "Ticking Bomb" Doctrine*, LAWFARE (Dec. 27, 2017), *available at* https://www.lawfareblog.com/back-ticking-bomb-doctrine.

[61] HCJ 5722/12, Abu Gosh v. Attorney General (Dec. 12, 2017), Nevo Legal Database (by subscription, in Hebrew).

[62] Itamar Mann & Omer Shatz, *The Necessity Procedure: Laws of Torture in Israel and Beyond, 1987–2009*, 6 UNBOUND: HARV. J. OF THE LEGAL LEFT 59 (2010).

[63] Crim. F.H. 7048/97, Does v. Minister of Defense, 54(1) PD 721 (2000) [*translated at* http://versa.cardozo.yu.edu/sites/default/files/upload/opinions/Does%20v.%20Ministry%20of%20Defense.pdf].

understanding of Articles 42 and 78 of the GC-IV.[64] In the recent *Alyan* case (2017),[65] the ISC refused to interpret Israeli law as authorizing government policy whereby corpses of terrorists were held as bargaining chips against the release of corpses of Israelis held by Hamas. While the Court stopped short of claiming that international law forbids this practice, it did strongly suggest that LOAC limits this possibility.

Human Rights in "Domestic" Cases

Israel has been a party to most international human rights treaties since the early 1990s. Do these instruments have a real impact on the jurisprudence of Israeli courts? Considering that the docket of the ISC sitting as the High Court of Justice is replete with petitions in which the petitioners claim violations of their rights, the use of international law is actually not that impressive. There are, of course, instances in which the Court cites international conventions on human rights, and especially the two main covenants: the International Covenant on Civil and Political Rights, and the International Covenant on Economic, Social and Cultural Rights. However, in most of these cases the Court appears to cite international law merely in support of decisions that it has reached based on other legal considerations.

More than a decade ago, Professor Daphne Barak-Erez (now a Supreme Court Judge) suggested that the main impact of international human rights law is felt in the Israeli domestic context with respect to social and economic rights, which are not covered by any Israeli Basic Laws.[66] One such example is the *Yated* case.[67] An organization representing parents of children with Down syndrome petitioned the Court to order the government to pay for the costs associated with "mainstreaming" their children in regular classrooms. Based on the International Covenant on Economic, Social and Cultural Rights, and the Convention on the Rights of the Child, the ISC determined that Israeli law should be interpreted in a way that reflects the right to education in a regular classroom.

Another case in which international law seems to have exerted even more impact is *Abu Mas'ad*.[68] At issue was whether Bedouins living in illegal settlements have a right to be connected to water. The Court determined that such a right could be inferred

[64] Crim. App. 6659/06, John Doe v. The State of Israel, 62(4) PD 329 (2008) [*translated at* http://versa.cardozo.yu.edu/sites/default/files/upload/opinions/A%20v.%20State%20of%20Israel%20%282%29.pdf].

[65] HCJ 4466/16, Alyan v. Military Commander in the West Bank (Dec. 14, 2017), Nevo Legal Database (by subscription, in Hebrew).

[66] Daphne Barak-Erez, *The International Law of Human Rights and Constitutional Law: A Case Study of an Expanding Dialogue*, 2 ICON—INT'L J. CONST. L. 611, 626 (2004).

[67] HCJ 2599/00, *Yated v. Ministry of Education*, *supra* note 11.

[68] Civ. App. 9535/06, Abu Mas'ad v. The Water Commissioner (May 6, 2011), Nevo Legal Database (by subscription, in Hebrew).

from the constitutional right to dignity of the person. The scope of the right to water was inferred from an international document interpreting the right to an adequate standard of living and the right to health.[69] The use of this interpretative document is telling. Although not a binding document, the Court nevertheless relied on it when positing the right to water as an Israeli constitutional right.

An important set of cases in which the ISC has referred to international law concerns foreign workers, asylum seekers or refugees, and illegal immigrants. Once again, the absence of Israeli law regarding many of the issues arising with regard to these persons seems to have prompted the Court to look to international law. Furthermore, these issues are "international" in nature, because they involve the movement of persons across borders, and thus affect the interests of many countries and cannot be treated as a purely domestic matter.

As early as 1995, the ISC determined that the Refugee Convention reflects CIL and that asylum seekers, whether or not they fulfill the exact conditions of that Convention for definition as refugees, will not be deported to countries where their lives will be endangered.[70] In a recent decision, the ISC discussed at length the right to deport asylum seekers to third countries, in which the government claimed that their lives would be protected according to an agreement between Israel and the other state.[71] Both the name of the "third state" (believed to be Rwanda) and the contents of the agreement with that state were kept secret. The holding of the Court is a complex one, and cannot be fully discussed here. Suffice it to say that, contrary to the position of many international lawyers, the court accepted the position of the government according to which the secret agreement provides sufficient protection to the deported persons. In defining what international law requires from Israel, the Court relied not only on the Refugee Convention (which might reflect CIL) but also on the interpretations of the UN High Commissioner for Refugees. On the one hand, we can see that for an issue that is at root "international," the Court is willing to accept a broad definition of international law, one that also includes interpretative statements of international bodies, even if these documents are not binding according to Israeli doctrine. On the other hand, based on its interpretation of international law, the Court approved a policy the legality of which is at best arguable. The Court did limit the authority of the government to deport in an important way, holding that if the agreement with the third country requires the consent of the deportee before transferring him to the third state, the deportee cannot be detained until he "consents." Once again, it seems that the court used a general principle of free consent in

[69] The court relied heavily on the UN Committee on Economic, Social and Cultural Rights (CESCR), General Comment No. 15: Substantive Issues Arising in the Implementation of the International Covenant on Economic, Social and Cultural Rights, UN Doc. E/C. (Nov. 26, 2002), a document that details the view of the committee with regard to the right to water.

[70] HCJ 5190/94, El Tay v. Minister of Interior, 49(3) PD 843 (1995).

[71] Admin. App. 8101/15, Zageta v. Minister of Defense (Aug. 28, 2017), Nevo Legal Database (by subscription, in Hebrew).

order to qualify the authority of the government to apply a policy that the Court approved in general.

The issue of illegal immigrants and asylum seekers also raises an important constitutional issue: the relevance of the presumption of compatibility (the *Charming Betsy* doctrine) to the interpretation of Basic Laws. The issue arose in the context of asylum seekers when the government amended the Entrance to Israel Act in a way that allowed the Ministry of the Interior to detain illegal immigrants for up to three years in a special detention center.[72] Since detentions of asylum seekers and illegal immigrants are extensively discussed in international law, the latter was cited by the petitioners, by the government, and in *amicus* briefs. The main claim *against* the application of the presumption of compatibility with regard to rights contained in *Basic Law: Human Dignity and Liberty* is that the application of this presumption would actually mean incorporating international human rights law into Israeli law without parliamentary authorization. The Basic Law is drafted in such an open-ended manner that applying the presumption of compatibility would actually mean that all rights are interpreted exactly as they are in international law.

The ISC did not expressly rule on this matter, but a careful reading of the judgment seems to suggest that at least with respect to the subject of asylum seekers and refugees, which as noted has a strong international component, the Court feels that the Basic Law should be interpreted in accordance with international law. Evidence for this view is provided by the way in which the Court struck down the amendment to the Entrance to Israel Act as incompatible with the right to freedom. Moreover, throughout the judgment many justices emphasized that Israel's law in this matter should be compatible with international law.

Presently pending before the ISC is a subject that might become one of the most important cases it has ever had to consider. In 2017, the Knesset passed the Land Regulation Act, which allows, in some cases, the expropriation of private Palestinian property upon which Israeli settlements have been constructed.[73] This law is intended to overturn the Court's earlier rulings, discussed in Part II of this chapter, which determined that such expropriations are incompatible with the international law of occupation. The principal claim presented to the Court by petitioners against the new law is that the right of property, enshrined in the *Basic Law: Human Dignity and Liberty*, should be interpreted according to international law, and that the Court should therefore declare the new law to be invalid. It remains to be seen whether or not the ISC will adopt this position.

[72] HCJ 7146/12, Adam v. The Knesset (Sept. 16, 2013), Nevo Legal Database (by subscription, in Hebrew) [*English summary at* http://versa.cardozo.yu.edu/sites/default/files/upload/opinions/Adam%20v.%20Knesset.pdf].

[73] For a description and analysis of the law, *see* Elena Chachko, *The Israeli Knesset Passes the Settlement Regularization Law*, LAWFARE (Feb. 7, 2017), *available at* https://www.lawfareblog.com/israeli-knesset-passes-settlement-regularization-law.

IV. Conclusion

Review of decisions of the ISC relating to international law shows that the formal doctrine does not exactly reflect the jurisprudence of the Court as practiced in reality. CIL, which is supposed to be implemented by the Court, has very little effect apart from the issues of LOAC. On the other hand, the ISC has implemented the GC-IV and other international treaties. Sometimes the Court has operated by interpreting Israeli law according to the presumption of compatibility, but in many cases the Court has implemented international treaties directly.

The presumption of compatibility has also been applied in a flexible manner. The Court has interpreted international law based on both domestic concepts of human rights and on nonbinding international documents. In addition, until recently the Court did not evade international law by resorting to such doctrines as justiciability.

Two observations can be made regarding these conclusions. First, as noted above, the use of international law by the ISC in the context of human rights and the law of occupation has endowed the Court with the ability to review and limit government actions, to a degree that would not otherwise have been possible. Second, Israel's Supreme Court does not simply implement international law. In many important areas, such as the international law of occupation, or LOAC, it also affects it. The *Targeted Killings* case, for example, serves as the baseline for any discussion of the legality of this policy in international law. In this, as in many other decisions, the ISC has been a participant in the dialogue that lies at the heart of international law, and which is the true source of its power.

CHAPTER 30

INTERNATIONAL LAW IN JAPANESE COURTS

HIROMICHI MATSUDA

INTERNATIONAL law and domestic law are becoming increasingly intertwined as domestic constitutional systems operate in an increasingly transnational legal environment.[1] Scholars have begun to focus on the role of national constitutions and constitutionalism in the international context, under a plurality of legal orders,[2] a "global community of courts,"[3] and "crosspollination and dialogue."[4] This chapter examines the Japanese perspective on this question of international law in domestic courts.

The Constitution of Japan was enacted in 1946 during the occupation after World War II. Reflecting upon the devastation of war caused by fascism, the preamble enshrines a strong commitment to internationalism.[5] Article 98(2) of the Constitution stipulates that "[t]he treaties concluded by Japan and established laws of nations shall be faithfully observed." The prevailing view in Japan maintains that both customary

[1] *See* VICKI C. JACKSON, CONSTITUTIONAL ENGAGEMENT IN A TRANSNATIONAL ERA 1 (2010).

[2] Neil Walker, *The* Idea *of Constitutional Pluralism*, 65 MOD. L. REV. 317, 337 (2002) (addressing the concept, development, and challenges of constitutional pluralism).

[3] *See,* e.g., Anne-Marie Slaughter, *A Global Community of Courts*, 44 HARV. INT'L L. J. 191 (2003) (discussing phenomena that reflect emerging global community of courts as both symptom and cause); ANNE-MARIE SLAUGHTER, A NEW WORLD ORDER 65–103 (2004) (examining the role of judges in constructing a global legal system).

[4] Claire L'Heureux-Dubé, *The Importance of Dialogue: Globalization and the International Impact of the Rehnquist Court*, 34 TULSA L.J. 15, 16 (1998) ("More and more courts, particularly within the common law world, are looking to the judgments of other jurisdictions, particularly when making decisions on human rights issues.").

[5] Preamble, The Constitution of Japan ("We, the Japanese people, . . . determined that we shall secure for ourselves and our posterity the fruits of peaceful cooperation with all nations and the blessings of liberty throughout this land, and resolved that never again shall we be visited with the horrors of war through the action of government. . . . ").

international law and treaty law acquire domestic effect through Article 98(2) of the Constitution[6] and are ranked higher than statutory law but lower than the Constitution.[7]

Since Japan has a unitary rather than federal judicial system, the jurisdiction of the courts is very simple: judicial power is vested in the Supreme Court, high courts, and district courts,[8] and these courts decide "all legal disputes."[9] However, Japanese courts are highly restrictive in exercising judicial power over cases concerning foreign affairs, except for cases where the judges use international norms as persuasive authority.

This chapter examines international law in Japanese courts in the context of separation of powers, treaty-making procedure, and transnational judicial dialogue under the Japanese Constitution. More specifically, this chapter analyzes international law in Japanese courts in the following four categories: (1) constitutional review of international law; (2) judicial application of international law; (3) consistent interpretation of statutory and constitutional law with international law; and (4) reliance on persuasive authority in constitutional interpretation.

I. Constitutional Review of International Law

The text of the Japanese Constitution is unclear about whether Japanese courts possess the competence to review the constitutionality of international law. Article 81 declares that "the Supreme Court is the court of last resort with power to determine the constitutionality of any law, order, regulation or official act." Article 98(1) stipulates that "this Constitution shall be the supreme law of the nation and no law, ordinance, imperial rescript or

[6] *See also* Shin Hae Bong, *Japan*, *in* International Law and Domestic Legal Systems: Incorporation, Transformation, and Persuasion 360, 365–376 (Dinah Shelton ed., 2011) (discussing domestic incorporation of international law in the Japanese legal system).

[7] Yuji Iwasawa, International Law, Human Rights, and Japanese Law: The impact of International Law on Japanese Law 28–36, 95–103 (1998). Professor Iwasawa further argues that international norms are divided into two types—directly applicable norms and not directly applicable norms—through subjective and objective criteria with a relative approach. *Id.* at 44–81; Yuji Iwasawa, *Domestic Application of International Law*, 378 Recueil des Cours 9 (2016). However, Japanese judicial and administrative practices do not necessarily follow this purely theoretical framework of subjective and objective criteria. For the practice of the Ministry of Foreign Affairs, *see* Tadaatsu Mori, *The Current Practice of Making and Applying International Agreements in Japan*, ch. 11 in this volume. To better explain Japanese practice, this chapter discusses the issues of self-executing and direct applicability from the perspective of the separation of powers and the competence of the judicial branch under Japanese constitutional law.

[8] *See* art. 76 of the Japanese Constitution ("The whole judicial power is vested in a Supreme Court and in such inferior courts as are established by law."). The district courts are the principal courts of first instance. There are 50 district courts with an additional 203 branches. Above the district courts are high courts located in eight big cities: Sapporo, Sendai, Tokyo, Nagoya, Osaka, Takamatsu, Hiroshima, and Fukuoka, with six branches.

[9] *See* art. 3(1) of the Court Act ("Courts shall . . . decide all legal disputes.").

other act of government, or part thereof, contrary to the provisions hereof, shall have legal force or validity." These provisions do not make reference to international norms.

In 1959, the constitutionality of the Japan-U.S. Security Treaty and the stationing of American military forces in Japan was challenged as a violation of Article 9(2) of the Constitution, which provides that "land, sea, and air forces, as well as other war potential, will never be maintained." The Supreme Court of Japan declared:

> The Security Treaty . . . is featured with an extremely high degree of political consideration, . . . and any legal determination as to whether the content of the treaty is constitutional or not is in many respects inseparably related to the high degree of political consideration or discretionary power on the part of the Cabinet which concluded the treaty and on the part of the Diet which approved it. . . . Accordingly, unless the said treaty is obviously unconstitutional and void, it falls outside the purview of the power of judicial review granted to the court.[10]

Although Japanese scholars have tried to explain this judgment by borrowing the French theory of *acte de gouvernement* or the American theory of the political question doctrine, the theoretical standpoint of this judgment is not very clear.[11] However, two points should be noted. First, the Supreme Court implicitly accepted that it has the competence to review some treaties when it held that this particular case "falls outside the purview of the power of judicial review granted to the court." Second, the Supreme Court actually made a constitutional decision by declaring that the Japan-U.S. Security Treaty is not "obviously unconstitutional and void." This would be contrary to the original purpose of the political question doctrine, which aims to keep the judicial function separate from politics.[12]

II. Judicial Application of International Law

Right of Action Based on International Law

In order for an international norm to give an individual a right of action in Japanese courts, the provision must be "clear and precise." In *Siberian Internment*, former

[10] The Supreme Court of Japan, Judgment, *Sunagawa*, December 16, 1959, 4 Japanese Annual of Int'l L. 103, 107 (1960). The English translation is available at the website of the Court at http://www.courts.go.jp/app/hanrei_en/detail?id=13.

[11] Many scholars find this judgment confusing because it mixes the political question doctrine with the theory of discretion. *See*, e.g., 高橋和之『立憲主義と日本国憲法』/Kazuyuki Takahashi, Constitutionalism and the Japanese Constitutional Law 436 (4th ed. 2017).

[12] *See* 樋口陽一『憲法 I』/Yoichi Higuchi, Constitutional Law I 477 (1998) (criticizing this judgment as recognizing "modified act of states doctrine with exceptions"). In 2016, the government of Japan used this judgment to justify the constitutionality of exercising the right of collective self-defense. *See* Tadashi Mori, *Decisions in Japan to Use Military Force or to Participate in Multinational Peacekeeping Operations*, ch. 46 in this volume.

prisoners of war who were detained in Siberia asked for compensation based on customary international law as reflected in Articles 66 and 68 of the 1949 Geneva Convention Relative to the Treatment Prisoners of War. The court declined, however, to recognize a right of action:

> The specific intent of the parties to a treaty is, of course, an important element, but moreover, the provisions must be precise. In particular, when an international rule imposes on states an obligation to act, when it involves appropriation of national expenditure, or when a similar system already exists in domestic law, then harmony with the system must be taken into full consideration, and therefore, the content needs to be all the more precise and clear. . . . If a customary international rule is not minutely detailed as to the substantive conditions on the creation, existence, and termination of a right, the procedural conditions on the exercise of the right, and moreover, the harmony of the rule with the existing various systems within the domestic sphere, and so forth, its domestic applicability must be denied.[13]

Similarly, in *Titherington and Others*, the Tokyo High Court rejected the plaintiff's claim of compensation for the damages they suffered as prisoners or civilian detainees of the Japanese army during World War II because Article 3 of the 1907 Hague Convention on Land Warfare was not clear enough about an individual right of action for damages.[14] This requirement of "clear and precise" provisions, which is very similar to the requirement for direct effect in EU law, is based on the separation of powers, because it would be difficult for courts to create an individual right based on unclear international law.[15]

Judicial Review of Statutory Law Based on International Law

This section discusses two issues. Do Japanese courts have the competence to review statutory law based on international law? If the courts do possess such a competence, what are its limitations?

The constitutional text is silent on the issue of competence. Article 98(2) only stipulates vaguely that "[t]he treaties concluded by Japan and established laws of nations shall be faithfully observed." However, most scholars argue that treaties prevail over statutory law because of Article 98(2), and that the courts have the competence of enforcing this higher status against statutory law.[16] Since Japan does not have an

[13] Tokyo High Court, Judgment, 1993 March 5, 37 JAPANESE ANN. INT'L L. 129 (1994).

[14] Tokyo High Court, Judgment, 2001 October 11, 45 JAPANESE ANN. INT'L L. 144 (2002).

[15] However, this requirement is not relevant when the court conducts legality review or consistent interpretation.

[16] IWASAWA, INTERNATIONAL LAW, *supra note* 7, at 95–96 (discussing the rank of international law in relation to statutes).

administrative or constitutional court system separate from its ordinary courts, there is no debate over which type of courts have the authority to conduct such a review.

The Supreme Court of Japan accepts the view that Japanese courts have the competence to review the legality of statutory law in light of international law, and that a statute that violates international law is invalid. For example, when asked whether a provision of the Act on Special Measures Concerning Taxation was in violation of a tax treaty, the Supreme Court conducted a legality review by declaring that "there may be some room to question the validity of such tax measures that are clearly incompatible with that purpose and objective of the treaty."[17] However, the Court found no violation of the treaty in that particular case.

Despite the fact that Japanese courts have such a competence, few cases have invalidated statutory law or declared a government action void in light of international law.[18] This observation corresponds with the highly restrictive approach in Japanese constitutional review:[19] in seventy years of its history, the Japanese Supreme Court struck down a statutory law only ten times. This highly restrictive approach is very different from other countries, such as the United States.

A principal reason for this restrictive approach is Japan's unique practice of *implementing-legislation-perfectionism* (*Kanzen Tampo Shugi*): every time that the Diet introduces a statute, the Legislation Bureau carefully checks the compatibility and consistency of the bill with the Constitution, existing law, and international obligations.[20] After strict review, the Bureau proposes necessary amendments or implementing legislation. Because of this pre-reviewing system, the legislature can eliminate unconstitutionality and unconventionality of statutory law in advance. Some even call the Legislation Bureau "the second Supreme Court,"[21] as its review is extremely strict and perfectionist.[22]

Another reason for this restrictive judicial attitude is that the requirements for congressional approval of treaties are lighter than those for statutory law. The

[17] The Supreme Court of Japan, Judgment, *Glaxo*, 2009 October 29, *available at* http://www.courts.go.jp/app/hanrei_en/detail?id=1030

[18] For example, an article in the Public Corporation and National Enterprise Labour Relations Law was declared void because it violated the 1949 ILO Convention and thus was contrary to art. 98(2) of the Constitution. Tokyo District Court, Judgment, 1966 September 10, 17 RÔMINSHÛ 1042, 1055. And the Tokyo High Court declared a government action of charging a defendant a fee of translation void because of a violation of ICCPR, art. 14.3(f). *See*, 1993 February 3, HANKETSU JIHÔ 44-1-12-11.

[19] *See* IWASAWA, INTERNATIONAL LAW, *supra* note 7, at 303 ("The courts' reluctance to find violations of international human rights law . . . is merely a reflection of the judicial restraint generally exercised by Japanese courts.").

[20] 松田浩道「憲法秩序における国際規範：実施権限の比較法的考察(4)」/Hiromichi Matsuda, *The Competence of Implementing International Norms in Constitutional Legal Systems: A Comparative Analysis (4)*, 130 (1–2) KOKKA GAKKAI ZASSHI 122, 37–41 (2017).

[21] 五十嵐敬喜『議員立法』/TAKAYOSHI IGARASHI, LEGISLATION BY DIET MEMBERS 106–107 (1994).

[22] This approach is different from the practice in many states. *See* Congyan Cai, *International Law in Chinese Courts*, ch. 31 in this volume (stating that failure of a transformation of an international obligation is not rare).

requirement for congressional approval of a statute is a simple majority in both Houses.[23] In contrast, approval from the upper House is not necessarily required for treaties; a simple majority of lower House members can suffice when no agreement can be reached in a joint committee of both Houses.[24] The Japanese courts probably tend to refrain from invalidating statutory law based on treaties because the democratic basis of a treaty is not as solid as statutory law. For example, the Supreme Court declined to conduct a legality review of statutory law in light of World Trade Organization (WTO) Agreements, based on considerations of "separation of powers, the situation of domestic legislation, and how the plaintiff construed the legal claim, based on the content and nature of the treaty."[25]

However, *implementing-legislation-perfectionism* is not always perfect. The Japanese legal system can conflict with international law, especially in the rapidly evolving field of human rights law.[26] If there is a gap between national legislation and international law, the Japanese courts could play a useful role in advising the legislature to address the issue,[27] even if it is not desirable under separation of powers to invalidate the law immediately.

III. Consistent Interpretation of International Law and Domestic Law

The doctrine of consistent interpretation, which corresponds to the *Charming Betsy* canon in the United States,[28] can be divided into interpretation of statutory law and interpretation of constitutional law. Since Japan does not have a federal system, there is no issue of consistent interpretation of state law.

[23] *See* art. 59 (1) ("A bill becomes a law on passage by both Houses. . . . ").

[24] *See* art. 60 (2) ("Upon consideration of the budget, when the House of Councillors makes a decision different from that of the House of Representatives, and when no agreement can be reached even through a joint committee of both Houses, provided for by law, or in the case of failure by the House of Councillors to take final action within thirty (30) days, the period of recess excluded, after the receipt of the budget passed by the House of Representatives, the decision of the House of Representatives shall be the decision of the Diet."). According to art. 61, this "applies also to the Diet approval required for the conclusion of treaties."

[25] Tokyo High Court, Judgment, 2013 November 27, 1406 Hanrei Times 273, 278 (2013).

[26] *See*, e.g., CCPR/C/JPN/CO/6 (2014).

[27] The Supreme Court of Japan sometimes takes this approach and calls for legislative action, especially in constitutional cases concerning the vote-value disparity. *See*, e.g., The Supreme Court of Japan, Judgment, 2012 October 17, 66–10 Minshû 3357.

[28] *See* Curtis A. Bradley, *The Charming Betsy Canon and Separation of Powers: Rethinking the Interpretive Role of International Law*, 86 Geo. L.J. 479 (1997).

Interpretation of Statutory Law Consistent with International Law

In light of Article 98(2) of the Japanese Constitution, as discussed, Japanese courts are required to interpret statutory law so as not to violate binding international law. If consistent interpretation is not possible, Japanese courts have the competence to invalidate a government action that is contrary to the spirit of a treaty. Some Japanese cases have endorsed this approach. For example, the Sapporo District Court, while rejecting the government's argument of denying the direct applicability of the Convention on Biological Diversity,[29] declared that "the government action can be illegal as outstepping its discretionary power, if the action is clearly against the spirit of the Treaty." The Tokushima District Court also declared that the Prison Law and its implementing regulations "should be interpreted in accordance with the International Covenant of Civil and Political Rights (ICCPR) and the Constitution," and that "if the provisions in the law and the regulations conflict with the ICCPR, the relevant part is null and void."[30] The Court ordered the government to pay damages because the warden had overstepped the scope of discretion allowed under law, when interpreted in light of ICCPR Article 14(1). In addition, in *Nibutani-dam*, expropriating the sacred land of the native Ainu people was declared illegal because the Sapporo District Court interpreted the Expropriation Act consistently with ICCPR Article 27.[31]

Interpretation of Constitutional Law Consistent with International Law

The theoretically more interesting question is whether the Court can or should interpret the Japanese Constitution consistently with international law. The attitude of the Japanese Supreme Court is still unclear. Some scholars only accept the obligation of consistent interpretation of treaties with the Constitution, not vice versa, because treaties are ranked lower than the Constitution.[32] However, one can argue that such ranking is not absolute in the context of interpretation, and that Article 98(2) allows Japanese courts to interpret the Constitution in line with international obligations.

[29] The court rejected using the framework of subjective and objective criteria of direct applicability. *See also supra* note 7.

[30] Tokushima District Court, 1996 March 15, 1597, Hanrei Jihô 115; Takamatsu High Court, 1997 November 25, 1653 Hanrei Jihô 117. Rejected by the Supreme Court, 2000 September 7, 1728 Hanrei Jihô 17.

[31] Sapporo District Court, Judgment, 1997 March 27, 1598 Hanrei Jihô 33. English translation of the full text is available in 38 I.L.M. 394(1999).

[32] 内野正幸「条約·法律·行政立法」高見勝利編『日本国憲法解釈の再検討』/Masayuki Uchino, *Treaties, Statutory law, and Administrative Legislation, in* Reconsidering Japanese Constitutional Law 429 (Katsutoshi Takami ed., 2004). *See also* the text accompanying *supra* note 7.

Because it is problematic to allow substantial constitutional amendment by using consistent interpretation, however, the most desirable approach is probably one of restrictive consistent interpretation, whereby a court would use international law as one of the interpretive tools, while considering the balance between other branches.

A good example of desirable consistent interpretation is Justice Izumi's concurring opinion in the *Nationality Act Case*. Under the *jus sanguinis* principle, the Nationality Act did not allow a child born out of wedlock to a Japanese father and a non-Japanese mother to acquire Japanese nationality without legal marriage of the parents. Article 3(1) of the Nationality Act provided that:

> A child who has acquired the status of a child born in wedlock as a result of the marriage of the parents and the acknowledgment by either parent . . . may acquire Japanese nationality . . . , if the father or mother who has acknowledged the child was a Japanese citizen at the time of the child's birth, and such father or mother is currently a Japanese citizen. . . .

The Court invalidated a part of Article 3(1) because it violated Article 14(1) (the equality clause) of the Constitution. Justice Izumi invoked the principle of desirable consistent interpretation in his concurring opinion:

> The gist of the provision of Article 3, para.1 of the Nationality Act is to grant Japanese nationality to children who were born to Japanese citizens as their fathers or mothers and are ineligible for application of Article 2 of said Act,[33] and the "marriage of the parents" is merely one of the requirements to be satisfied to achieve this. Therefore, said gist of the provision should be maintained to the greatest possible extent even if the part requiring the "marriage of the parents" is unconstitutional, and this is what the lawmakers would have intended. Furthermore, applying Article 3, para.1 of the Nationality Act in this manner conforms to the gist of Article 24, para.3 of the ICCPR which provides that "Every child has the right to acquire a nationality" and that of Article 7, para.1 of the Convention on the Rights of the Child (CRC).[34]

While conducting consistent interpretation with treaties, Justice Izumi also carefully paid attention to the relationship between the judiciary and the legislature, by mentioning that this construction "may not be permissible when there is a clear probability that the Diet, from the legislative perspective, will not maintain the provision of said paragraph."[35]

[33] Art. 2(1) of the then Nationality Act provided that a child was a Japanese citizen if the father or mother was a Japanese citizen at the time of birth.

[34] The Supreme Court of Japan, Judgment, 2008 June 4, 62–66 MINSHÛ 1367, ILDC 1814 (JP 2008) (Izumi, J., concurring). Full text *available at* http://www.courts.go.jp/app/hanrei_en/detail?id=955.

[35] *Id.*

IV. Reliance on Persuasive Authority in Constitutional Interpretation

In the *Nationality Act* case, the Supreme Court of Japan, when invalidating the nationality law based on constitutional grounds, referred to the situation abroad and human rights treaties as persuasive authority. The Court held that "other states are moving toward scrapping discriminatory treatment by law against children born out of wedlock, and in fact, the ICCPR and the CRC, which Japan has ratified, also contain such provisions to the effect that children shall not be subject to discrimination of any kind because of birth."[36] In 2013, when asked whether drawing a distinction between children born outside and within wedlock was contrary to the Constitution in light of Japan's obligations under the ICCPR and the CRC, the Supreme Court invalidated the statutory law by referring to the views and recommendations issued by the Human Rights Committee and the Committee of the Rights of the Child.[37]

Although one can surmise that the underlying assumption of these cases is that "the values reflected in international human rights law may help inform the contextual approach to statutory interpretation and judicial review,"[38] the Supreme Court of Japan did not discuss any theoretical basis for its reference to persuasive authorities.[39] Similar to the criticisms against *Atkins v. Virginia*[40] and *Roper v. Simmons*[41] in the United States,[42] many Japanese scholars criticized the decision.[43] In contrast, some theorists

[36] The Supreme Court of Japan, Judgment, 2008 June 4, 62–66 MINSHŪ 1367, ILDC 1814 (JP 2008).

[37] The Supreme Court of Japan, Judgment, 2013 September 4, 67–66 MINSHŪ 1320, ILDC 2060 (JP 2013).

[38] The Supreme Court of Canada, Baker v. Canada [1999] 2 S.C.R. 817, 861. *See also* Karen Knop, *Here and There: International Law in Domestic Courts*, 32 INT'L L. & POL. 501, 507–512 (2000).

[39] The situation might be similar in Canada. *See* Gib Van Ert, *The Domestic Application of International Law in Canada*, ch. 28 in this volume, at p.518 ("No settled rules govern resort to non-binding international materials by Canadian litigants and courts").

[40] 536 U.S. 304 (2002). [41] 543 U.S. 551 (2005).

[42] *See, e.g.*, Curtis A. Bradley, *The Juvenile Death Penalty and International Law*, 52 DUKE L.J. 485 (2002) (arguing that juvenile death penalty issue must be resolved through U.S. democratic and constitutional processes). *See also* Lawrence v. Texas, 539 U.S. 558, 598 (2003) (Scalia, J., dissenting) ("The Court's discussion of these foreign views . . . is therefore meaningless dicta. Dangerous dicta, however, since 'this Court . . . should not impose foreign moods, fads, or fashions on Americans'.") (*quoting* Foster v. Florida, 537 U.S. 990, n.990 (2002) (Thomas, J., concurring in denial of certiorari)).

[43] *See*, e.g., 蟻川恒正「婚外子法定相続分最高裁違憲決定を書く(2)」/Tsunemasa Arikawa, *Drafting Supreme Court Decision (2)*, 400 HOGAKU KYOSHITSU 132, 133 (2014) (emphasizing the distinction between *questions facti* and *question juris*).

have attempted to situate these references within the framework of *transnational human rights sources*,[44] or *transnational judicial dialogue*.[45]

In the present author's opinion, reference to persuasive authority in constitutional interpretation is desirable if the citation is "complete, careful and contextualized."[46] Although foreign experiences cannot by themselves decide the meaning of the Japanese Constitution, they are in many cases helpful in trying to find better solutions. However, Japanese courts should add more reasoning on the relevance of persuasive authorities, and distinguish foreign cases from Japanese ones when necessary. Otherwise, reliance on persuasive authority runs the risk of being ultra vires, because courts do not have the competence to substantially legislate nor amend the Constitution through interpretation.

V. Conclusion

Although Japanese courts are reluctant to use international law as binding law, the Supreme Court of Japan recently began actively referring to foreign and international sources as persuasive authorities. Because of the practice of *implementing-legislation-perfectionism* and the relative lack of democratic legitimacy of international law, Japanese courts will probably continue to take a restrictive approach toward applying binding international norms. In contrast, the Supreme Court of Japan is expressing a positive attitude toward transnational dialogue. In 2016, the Supreme Court of Japan started sending Justices to the U.S. Federal Judicial Center's program. The Supreme Court made the following comment: "it is important to explain the Japanese legal system to foreign judges. We try to make Japanese input toward 'common understanding' of judges."[47] Considering this strong motivation, Japanese courts will probably expand and enhance transnational judicial dialogue in and out of the courtroom.

At the same time, Japanese courts have the potential to be one of the interesting benchmarks for whether any existing "global community of courts" can really be global and universal. Although Japanese lawyers have always been eager to learn from Western experiences, especially since the *Meiji* period, this process is a one-way "reception" process rather than mutual "dialogue." However, it would sometimes be

[44] 山元一「グローバル化世界と人権法源論の展開」小谷順子ほか編『現代アメリカの司法と憲法⊠理論的対話の試ま』/Hajime Yamamoto, *Globalized World and the Theory over Sources of Human Rights Law*, *in* Judiciary and Constitutional Law in the U.S. Today 344 (Junko Kotani et al. eds., 2013).

[45] Akiko Ejima, *Emerging Transjudicial Dialogue on Human Rights in Japan*, 14 Meiji L. School Rev. 139 (2014).

[46] *See* Stephen Yeazell, *When and How U.S. Courts Should Cite Foreign Law*, 26 Const. Comment. 59, 71 (2009) ("'good' citation of foreign law will have the same characteristics as good citation of domestic law; they will be complete, careful, and contextualized.").

[47] Asahi Shimbun, Apr. 2, 2016, evening edition, at 6.

beneficial for courts in other jurisdictions to learn from Japanese experiences, because courts are encountering similar issues worldwide.[48] Since Japan is the first non-Western state in world history to modernize its nation by adapting the Western legal system to its traditional culture, Japan's successful (and sometimes unsuccessful) experiences can provide interesting lessons to many states. In this regard, Japanese lawyers should continue making more efforts to explain the Japanese legal system and cases to the world.

[48] The European Court of Human Rights has cited Japanese Supreme Court Judgments several times. *See*, e.g., ECtHR, Case of Jehovah's Witnesses of Moscow and Others v. Russia (Application no. 302/02), para. 88 (*citing* Supreme Court of Japan, Judgment, 2000 February 29, 54-52 MINSHU 582, which held the doctor liable for damages under tort law for providing a blood transfusion to a believer of Jehovah's Witnesses).

CHAPTER 31

INTERNATIONAL LAW IN CHINESE COURTS

CONGYAN CAI

I. Introduction

THE application of international law in Chinese courts has received little attention,[1] except perhaps with respect to the treaties regulating private relations like the UN Convention on Contracts for the International Sale of Goods (CISG),[2] which are not the focus of "public" international law. Some commentators thus look down on the role of the Chinese judiciary in the enforcement of international law. For instance, André Nollkaemper argued that Chinese courts did little in coordinating the international and national legal systems and in ensuring that China comply with international law.[3] This accusation is not unfounded because courts in China, a permanent member of the UN Security Council (UNSC), are quite moderate in their application of international law, especially when one considers that China might have the largest number of judges in the world.[4]

This chapter offers a perspective on how international law is understood and applied in a country with a unique history, ideology, and governance, and, more generally, to

[1] For instance, China is the only permanent member state of the UN Security Council that was not included in a large comparative survey on how domestic courts in thirteen countries enforce treaties. *See* THE ROLE OF DOMESTIC COURTS IN TREATY ENFORCEMENT: A COMPARATIVE STUDY (David Sloss ed., 2009).

[2] *See, e.g.*, Jie Huang, *Direct Application of International Commercial Law in Chinese Courts: Intellectual Property, Trade, and International Transportation*, 5 MANCHESTER J. INT'L ECON. L. 105 (2008); Xiao Yongping & Long Weidi, *Selected Topics on the Application of the CISG in China*, 20 PACE INT'L L. REV. 61 (2008).

[3] ANDRÉ NOLLKAEMPER, NATIONAL COURTS AND THE INTERNATIONAL RULE OF LAW 13, 55 (2011).

[4] It was reported that in 2013 there were about two hundred thousand judges in China, *available at* http://news.sohu.com/20130725/n382586635.shtml (in Chinese) (last visited Aug. 10, 2017).

add a Chinese perspective on comparative foreign relations law. The chapter aims not merely to present a piecemeal analysis based on concrete cases, which, although it might be useful, could mislead observers. Instead, the chapter will explore the context, dynamics, and emerging trends concerning the application of international law in Chinese courts.

The chapter begins in Section II by investigating several major factors relevant to the judicial application of international law in China. Section III explores how Chinese legal policy influences the judicial administration in regard to international law. A case study is presented in Section IV to illustrate the changing context in which Chinese courts apply international law and the delicate strategy that Chinese courts employ toward applying international law.

II. Major Factors Affecting the Application of International Law in Chinese Courts

Generally speaking, states under international law have great discretion to decide on issues like which organ is authorized, and which method is employed, to honor their international legal obligations. This implies that, in addition to the international legal rules themselves, there are domestic variants affecting the actual application of international law in domestic courts, including legal culture.[5] Therefore, it is necessary to investigate what these domestic variants are, thereby revealing the context in which, and dynamics underlying, how Chinese judges interact with international law. Three major factors will be addressed in turn.

This first factor concerns China's ambivalence toward international law. China's ambivalence can be attributed to its special state identity. On the one hand, during the first thirty years after the founding of People's Republic of China (PRC) in 1949, China, as a country with a century-long national humiliation since the nineteenth century and an orthodox socialist state, was critical of the international legal order that had been crafted by a handful of Western powers.[6] As a result, it had little interest in concluding treaties with foreign states except a limited number of other socialist states. Nor was it willing to accept international customs.[7] On the other hand, in order to implement the

[5] *See generally* Rosalyn Higgins, Problems and Process: International Law and How We Use It ch. 12 (1994).

[6] Congyan Cai, *International Law in Chinese Courts During the Rise of China*, 110 Am. J. Int'l L. 269, 272 (2016).

[7] Interestingly, although China, in defining the minimum standard of investment treatment in a recently concluded investment treaty, accepted the two recognized constituent elements of state practice and *opinio juris*, it avoided mentioning the phrase "international custom" or "customary international law." *See* China-Mexico BIT (2008), art. 5(2).

Reform and Opening-up Policy starting in the late 1970s with the aim of remedying the political, economic, and social catastrophe brought about by the "Cultural Great Revolution" (1966–1976), China had to attract political support and economic resources from the Western states by integrating itself into international legal order that it had condemned. For instance, since the 1980s, China has concluded more than one hundred investment treaties,[8] which increase the confidence of transnational corporations to make investment in China.

Moreover, as China is recently rising as a new great power, there is a clear trend of it seeking to rely more heavily upon international law to expand and protect its national interests. In 2014, China pledged to "actively participate in international rule-making" and to "increase China's power of discourse and influence in international legal affairs."[9]

Such an instrumental approach has led to an ambiguous and fragmented status of international law in Chinese domestic legal order. Sharply different from constitutions of most of other countries, China's Constitution provides nothing about the domestic status of international law. Instead, it leaves this issue to be decided on a case-by-case basis, based on nonconstitutional law. Such an omission in the Constitution discourages many secondary laws from defining the status of international law. As a matter of fact, many Chinese laws do not have provisions concerning international law. For instance, in preparing for the amendment of the Legislation Law (2000), several members of the Standing Committee of the National People's Congress (NPC) once suggested that the new law include a provision clarifying the status of treaties in the Chinese legal system, but the suggestion was rejected.[10] Similarly, although the General Principles of Civil Law adopted in 1986 (GPCL), in defining the applicable law to foreign-related civil relations, included a provision for international law,[11] a similar provision did not appear in the Choice of Law for Foreign-Related Civil Relations enacted in 2010.[12] Furthermore, some references to international law have been removed from particular laws. For instance, Article 72 of the Administrative Procedure Law (APL) adopted in 1990 provided, "If an international treaty concluded or acceded to by the People's Republic of China contains provisions different from those found in this law, the provisions of the international treaty shall apply, unless the provisions are ones on which the People's

[8] *See A List of Bilateral Investment Agreements Concluded by China*, *available at* http://tfs.mofcom.gov.cn/article/Nocategory/201111/20111107819474.shtml (last visited July 10, 2017).

[9] Central Committee of CCP, Decision on Some Major Issues Concerning Comprehensively Enhancing the Rule of State by Law (Oct. 23, 2014), Part VII.7, *available at* http://news.cnwest.com/content/2014-10/28/content_11767768_7.htm (last visited Aug. 24, 2017).

[10] Cai, *supra* note 6, at 272–273.

[11] GPCL (1986), art. 142(2).

[12] This provision, however, was included in a Judicial Interpretation issued by the Supreme People's Court (SPC) in 2012. *See* SPC, Interpretation (First) on Certain Issues Concerning the Application of the Choice of Law for Foreign-Related Civil Relations of the People's Republic of China, December 2012, art. 4, *available at* http://www.court.gov.cn/shenpan-xiangqing-5273.html (last visited Aug. 10, 2017).

Republic of China has announced reservations." But this provision was repealed in 2015 without any explanation.[13]

It should be stressed that those provisions of international law in laws like the APL (1990) and the GPCL (1986) refer to "treaties" only and do not include other sources of international law—for instance, international customs or decisions of international organizations. In recent years, however, some central-governmental organs, such as the Ministry of Foreign Affairs (MFA), have adopted a number of legal instruments requiring that the relevant governmental organs and private entities implement the sanction decisions approved by the UNSC. For instance, the MFA, in 2001, issued a note requiring the implementation of Resolution 1267 and Resolution 1333 of the UN Security Council.[14]

China's ambivalence toward international law appears to have discouraged judges from applying it. As a matter of fact, according to a Judicial Interpretation issued by the Supreme People's Court (SPC) in 2009, the normative instruments that can be invoked as the basis for "legal conclusions" do not include international law. Instead, international law belongs to "other normative instruments," which may be invoked to sustain "legal reasoning."[15] Although some judges still explicitly invoke certain treaty provisions as the basis for legal conclusions, many judges do not, even though the legal reasoning heavily relies on the relevant treaty provisions.

More seriously, the absence of a provision for international law in China's constitution and the above-mentioned Judicial Interpretation may be invoked by some judges to justify nonapplication of international law. In practice, it is believed that some treaties that should have been applied were not applied.[16] For instance, although China has ratified the International Convention against Torture and Other Cruel, Inhuman or Degrading Treatment or Punishment (CAT), China's representative to the Committee Against Torture stated explicitly that the CAT "could be invoked before the Chinese courts,"[17]

[13] Similarly, art. 46 of the Environmental Protection Law (1989), which provides, "If an international treaty related to the environmental protection, which have been concluded or acceded to by the People's Republic of China, contains provisions different from those found in Chinese laws, the provisions of the international treaty shall apply, unless the provisions are ones on which the People's Republic of China has announced reservations," was removed in its amendment in 2014. *See* the Environmental Protection Law (1989, as amended in 2014).

[14] *See*, e.g., MFA, Note on Imposing Financial Sanctions towards the Relevant Individuals and Entities in Order to Implement Resolution 1267 and Resolution 1333 of the Security Council, Oct. 17, 2001, *available at* http://www.gov.cn/gongbao/content/2002/content_61464.htm (last visited Aug. 10, 2017).

[15] SPC, Rules on the Invocation of Normative Instruments Including Law and Regulations in the Adjudicatory Decisions, art. 6 (July 3, 2009), *available at* http://www.court.gov.cn/fabu-xiangqing-73.html (last visited July 10, 2017).

[16] Yu Zhijing & Li, Jian, *On the Dilemma and Way out of Judicial Application of Treaties in China*, 8 Pol. & L. 138, 139–140 (2016).

[17] Committee Against Torture, Summary Record of the 419th Meeting, para. 9, UN Doc. CAT/C/SR.419 (May 12, 2000).

and torture has been rampant in China,[18] the CAT has never actually been applied by Chinese courts.[19]

The second factor is the role of the judiciary in Chinese national governance. According to China's Constitution (2004), courts "exercise judicial power independently, in accordance with the provisions of the law, and are not subject to interference by any administrative organs, public organizations or individuals."[20] The Law of Organization of Courts (2006) and the Judges Law (2001) have the same provisions.[21] However, the judiciary, together with the executive branch, is created by, and is supervised by, the People's Congress,[22] a parliamentary body. Furthermore, there is a "living constitution" established by, and centered on, the Chinese Community Party (CCP).[23] That is, although not being accorded with any special powers, the CCP has been declared as the sole ruling party in China.[24] In practice, the CCP controls the operation of legislative, executive, and judicial organs at both central and local levels through its Party committees or groups at these organs.[25] As a result, the CCP fully integrates itself with the state, creating the Chinese Party State constitutional order.[26] So, it comes as no surprise that all governmental organs in China are encouraged to implement the policies that the CCP proposes or supports.

As far as the judiciary is concerned, Chinese courts, in accordance with the Law of Organization of Courts (2006), shall "protect the regimes of dictatorship of the proletariat . . . and guarantee the successful conducting of the course of socialist revolution and socialist construction."[27] For this purpose, the SPC has taken numerous judicial measures to materialize and consolidate this supportive role. For instance, as China's President Xi Jinping proposed the "One Belt One Road" Initiative (BRI),[28] the

[18] *See* Committee Against Torture, Concluding Observations of the Committee Against Torture: China, para. 11, UN Doc. CAT/C/CHN/CO/4 (Dec. 12, 2008).

[19] Interestingly, the Ministry of Public Security (MPS) once explicitly required, perhaps rhetorically, that its local branches strictly abide by the CAT. Ministry of Public Security, Note on Strictly Implementing Provisions in International Conventions Related to Public Security (Mar. 24, 1989), *available at* http://www.chinalawedu.com/falvfagui/fg22598/22828.shtml (last visited Aug. 24, 2017).

[20] Constitution (1982, amended in 2004), art. 126.

[21] Law of Organization of Courts (1979, amended in 2006), art. 4; Judge Law (1995, amended in 2001), art. 8(2).

[22] Constitution (2004), arts. 3, 92, 96, 111, 128, and 133. *See also* Law of Organization of Courts (1979, amended in 2006), art.16.

[23] Xin He, *The Party's Leadership as a Living Constitution in China*, 42 HONG KONG L.J. 73 (2012).

[24] Constitution (2004), Preamble.

[25] Zhu Suli, *Political Parties in China's Judiciary*, 17 DUKE J. COMP. & INT'L L. 533, 535, 538 (2006–2007); Zhu Suli, *The Party and the Courts*, *in* JUDICIAL INDEPENDENCE IN CHINA ch. 4 (Randall Peerenboom ed., 2010).

[26] Shucheng Wang, *Emergence of a Dual Constitution in Transitional China*, 45 HONG KONG L.J. 819 (2015).

[27] Law of Organization of Courts (1979, as amended in 2006), art. 3(1).

[28] National Development and Reform Commission (NDRC), Ministry of Commerce (MOC) and Ministry of Foreign Affairs (MFA), Preamble, Vision and Actions on Jointly Building the Silk Road Economic Belt and the 21st-Century Maritime Silk Road, *available at* http://gb.cri.cn/42071/2015/03/28/6351s4916394.htm (last visited Aug. 2017).

SPC recently required that courts should "effectively serve and guarantee the successful implementation of 'One Belt One Road' Initiative" through, among other things, more active application of international treaties.[29] Judge He Rong, then vice president of the SPC, also wrote that, as China increases its international status and, in particular, advocates the BRI, Chinese courts should enhance their participation in the international economic rule-making through more active application of international law.[30]

According to the conventional wisdom in the Western world concerning the rule of law, the unique role of the Chinese judiciary in China's constitutional framework and public governance seriously damages the judicial independence and power indispensable to resolve disputes fairly and impartially.[31] A commentator once suggested that the lack of judicial independence is a major reason why Chinese courts fail to secure China's compliance with international law.[32] While the extent of judicial independence in China is debatable, there has been a consensus that it needs to be improved.[33]

The unique role of the Chinese judiciary has in fact greatly influenced the application of international law in Chinese courts. As examined below, Chinese courts follow a structural approach to international law, pursuant to which international legal rules are applied in a way that does not meaningfully challenge the executive.[34] Indeed, even in applying international legal rules that have little to do with executive authority—for instance, the Convention on the Recognition and Enforcement of Foreign Arbitral Awards (New York Convention)—judges sometimes are still not immune from the interference from the executive branch. This is because, for instance, although the application of the New York Convention in and of itself does not challenge executive authority, some local executive organs are still likely to intervene out of consideration of narrow interest, for instance, the protection of state-owned enterprises (SOEs). Presumably, this is one of the reasons why the SPC requires that the refusal of recognition and enforcement of foreign arbitral awards under the New York Convention must be finally decided by the SPC,[35] which helps reduce the "local protectionism" once rampant in China.

Nevertheless, as China enhances its rule of law[36] and increasingly embraces international regimes that either provide private rights (for instance, investment treaties or the UN Convention on Jurisdictional Immunities of States and Their Property[37]) or influence private interests (for instance, the UN sanction resolutions), international law

[29] SPC, Opinions on the Provision of Judicial Service and Guarantees to "One Belt One Road" Initiative (June 16, 2015), *available at* http://www.court.gov.cn/fabu-xiangqing-14900.html (last visited July 10, 2017).

[30] He Rong, *On China's Judiciary Participation in the Formation of International Economic Rules*, 1 INT'L L. STUD. 3 (2016).

[31] RANDALL PEERENBOOM, CHINA'S LONG MARCH TOWARD RULE OF LAW 280 (2002).

[32] NOLLKAEMPER, *supra* note 3, at 53–55.

[33] *See* JUDICIAL INDEPENDENCE IN CHINA, *supra* note 25, chs. 2, 4–6.

[34] *See infra* Part III.

[35] SPC, Note on the Dealing with Issues Concerning the Foreign-related Arbitration and Foreign Arbitration, Aug. 28, 1995.

[36] CHINA'S SOCIALIST RULE OF LAW REFORMS UNDER XI JINPING 208–221 (John Garrick & Yang Chang Bennett eds., 2016).

[37] China signed this convention on September 14, 2005, but has not yet ratified it.

is more likely to be applied in Chinese courts. Equally importantly, it appears that Chinese courts themselves seek to increase their role in national governance by applying international law more actively. For instance, Wang E'xiang, while acting as a vice president of the SPC, suggested that the role of Chinese courts in foreign relations should be enhanced—for instance, in deciding whether a treaty is self-executing or non-self-executing.[38] Recently, the SPC pledged that Chinese courts should increase their "international judicial power of discourse."[39]

The third factor is the professional competence of judges. A good judicial administration is preconditioned on judges with highly professional competence. Unfortunately, the Chinese judiciary has long been notorious for its lack of professionally competent judges. Prior to 1995 when the Judge Law was adopted, there were no compulsory qualifications required to be a judge in China. Officials from the executive branch, the CCP, and military units were often appointed as judges. Most judges did not have a law degree or sufficient legal knowledge.[40] The Judge Law (1995) for the first time provided that judges shall be appointed from those receiving education at law schools or receiving education at nonlaw schools but having legal knowledge. Those incumbent judges who did not meet such a requirement were to receive legal training.[41] The Judge Law (2001) provided even stricter qualifications. According to this law, any person who would be appointed as a judge shall receive a bachelor degree in law, or a nonlaw bachelor degree but having legal knowledge. More importantly, all would-be judges shall pass the Unified National Judicial Examination (UNJE). Still, those incumbent judges failing to meet such requirements could qualify themselves through receiving legal training.[42] The poor professional competence has often resulted in wrongly adjudicated cases, which seriously damaged the legitimacy of the judiciary.[43]

Application of international law is especially demanding for Chinese judges. First, language is a big obstacle for most Chinese judges. Many treaties that China has concluded either have no Chinese authentic texts or stipulate that English authentic texts prevail over Chinese authentic texts in case of any divergence. Most Chinese judges do not have a sufficient command of English to ensure a correct understanding of treaty provisions.[44] Second, the identification and interpretation of international legal rules is a complicated process.[45] It requires practical capability much more than legal theories. However, Chinese law school students were traditionally taught what international law was, not how international law was used. As the result, although some

[38] A Study on the Relationship between International Law and National Law 476–481 (Wang E'xiang et al. eds., 2011) (in Chinese).

[39] SPC, Opinions on the Provision of Judicial Service and Guarantees to "One Belt One Road" Initiative (June 16, 2015), *available at* http://www.court.gov.cn/fabu-xiangqing-14900.html (last visited July 10, 2017).

[40] Peerenboom, *supra* note 31, at 290.

[41] Judge Law (1995), art. 9.

[42] Judge Law (1995, as amended in 2001), arts. 9 and 12.

[43] Peerenboom, *supra* note 31, at 290.

[44] Qingjiang Kong, *International Law Teaching in China: Emerging in a Pedagogical Reform or Embracing Professionalism and Internationalization?*, 12 Cambridge J. China Stud. 11, 20 (2017).

[45] *See* Statute of the International Court of Justice, art. 38(1); Vienna Convention on the Law of Treaties of 1969 (VCLT), arts. 31 and 32.

Chinese judges know international legal theories well, they may find that the theories they learned in law schools are of little help in applying international law. Third, the fact that China, generally speaking, adopts the transformation method rather than automatic incorporation to enforce its international legal obligations, as examined below, discourages Chinese judges from learning international law. As noted by Rosalyn Higgins, however, this is a common phenomenon in many countries that embrace a dualist approach to international law.[46]

The issue is more serious in the vast Middle and Western areas of China. It is suggested that many judges in those areas do not consider international law as "law" and they should apply domestic law only.[47] In practice, nearly all the application of international law happens in the Eastern part of China, especially in Shanghai, Beijing, and Guangdong, and judges in the Western areas, for instance, Xinjiang and Yunan, hardly have the experience of applying treaties.[48]

The SPC recognized the lack of professional competence of judges and directed that judges shall improve their knowledge of international law.[49] It has also taken many additional measures to improve the competence of judges.[50] In particular, it proposed a variety of important measures in 2015—for instance, the establishment of Judicial Selection Committees (JSC) at the national and provincial levels, more appointment of attorneys, legal scholars as judges, and more cooperation with law schools.[51]

In short, there are some positive developments with respect to the major factors that once discouraged Chinese judges from applying international law.

III. Methods and Structure for the Application of International Law in Chinese Courts

Methods

Generally speaking, international law requires that a state enforce legal obligations imposed on it, leaving issues such as who are authorized to perform obligations and

[46] Rosalyn Higgins, Problems and Process: International Law and How We Use It 206 (1994).

[47] Zhijing & Jian, *supra* note 16, at 142.

[48] Du Jing, *The Application of International Treaties by Courts in Shanghai 1990–2012*, 2 Theory Learning 82 (2015); Zhijing & Jian, *supra* note 16, at 142.

[49] *See, e.g.*, SPC, Notice of the Supreme People's Court on Several Issues Concerning the Trial and Enforcement of Foreign-Related Civil and Commercial Cases, Apr. 17, 2000, *available at* http://www.tpan.cn/html/5196.htm (last visited Aug. 24, 2018).

[50] Peerenboom, *supra* note 31, at 292–293.

[51] SPC, Opinion on the Comprehensively Deepening the Reform in People's Courts—Outline of the Fourth Five-Year Reform (2014–2018), Feb. 2015, *available at* http://www.court.gov.cn/fabu-xiangqing-13520.html (last visited July 10, 2017).

how to perform obligations to be decided by the state. For instance, the Vienna Convention on the Law of Treaties of 1969 (VCLT) only provides that a contracting state perform a treaty that has come into force for it "in good faith,"[52] not stipulating which method it should choose.

As far as treaty obligations are concerned, there are two major methods to enforce them: automatic incorporation and transformation. Under automatic incorporation, domestic courts are empowered to directly give effect to a treaty without a further implementing legislation. By contrast, the transformation method requires a legislative action to be taken before domestic courts enforce treaty obligations. Each method has its own merits and weaknesses. It is therefore legitimate for a state to adopt automatic incorporation or transformation, and the choice is likely to be affected by a number of factors, such as the national constitutional order and the characteristics of particular treaties.[53]

According to incomplete statistics, the automatic incorporation method has been used for about eighty laws passed between 1978 and 2004 in China.[54] In this regard, a frequently mentioned example is Article 142 of the GPCL.[55] Article 142 provides that "[i]f any international treaty concluded or acceded to by the People's Republic of China contains provisions differing from those in the civil laws of the People's Republic of China, the provisions of the international treaty shall apply, unless the provisions are ones on which the People's Republic of China has announced reservations."

Since China's Constitution is silent on the status of international law and only a small number of secondary laws include provisions concerning international law, it is right to contend that transformation is the primary method for China to implement treaty obligations.[56] Interestingly, while doctrinal debates on the automatic incorporation and transformation had continued for years in China, it was not until China's accession to the World Trade Organization (WTO) in 2001 that there was heated discussion on the potential legal significance of adopting different methods of application of international law in China. At that time, most Chinese lawyers suggested that Chinese courts could directly apply at least some WTO rules.[57] The proposition failed, however, when the SPC adopted the Regulations on Issues Concerning the Trial of Administrative Cases Relating to International Trade (Trade Case Regulations) in 2002.[58] In introducing that judicial instrument, Judge Li Guoguang, the SPC's deputy president at that time, clarified that WTO rules could not be invoked by courts

[52] VCLT, art. 26. [53] NOLLKAEMPER, *supra* note 3, at 73–81.

[54] WANG YONG, FUNDAMENTAL THEORY OF THE APPLICATION OF TREATIES IN CHINA 146 (2007) (in Chinese).

[55] The GPCI was promulgated by the NPC on April 12, 1986, and came into force on January 1, 1987.

[56] Xue Hanqin & Jin Qian, *International Treaties in the Chinese Domestic Legal System*, 8 CHINESE J. INT'L L. 299, 308 (2009).

[57] *See* CAI CONGYAN, PRIVATE STRUCTURAL PARTICIPATION IN THE MULTILATERAL TRADE SYSTEM 265–268 (2007).

[58] SPC, Regulations of the Supreme People's Court on Issues Concerning the Trial of Administrative Cases Relating to International Trade, Aug. 27, 2002.

as the applicable law to decide disputes.[59] The judicial instrument has been affirmed in several cases. In the *Shengzheng Chengjie'er Trade Co., Ltd.* case (2012), for instance, the respondent, Tianjin Customs authority, detained the imported goods of Plaintiff, Chengjie'er. The plaintiff argued that the prolonged detention breached Article 55 of Agreement on Trade-Related Aspects of Intellectual Property Right (TRIPS Agreement). A Tianjin court ultimately held that, according to the Trade Case Regulations, Chinese laws rather than the TRIPS Agreement should be applied.[60] Similarly, in *Longines Co. v. Trademark Review & Adjudication Board*, a Beijing court affirmed that the defendant was justified in not relying directly in its decision upon the TRIPS Agreement because the relevant TRIPS provisions had been "included in the current Trademark Law."[61]

Obviously, automatic incorporation gives domestic courts ample opportunities to invoke international law while transformation seriously limits the ability of domestic courts in this regard. Notably, China several times clarified its position in favor of the method of transformation. For instance, in its second periodic report to the Committee on Economic, Social and Cultural Rights, China argued that human rights treaties "do not directly function as the legal basis for the trial of cases in Chinese courts, . . . ; rather, they are applied after being transformed into domestic law through legislative procedures."[62] Also, as noted above, the provision concerning international law was removed from the APL (2015). While it remains to be seen whether these events represent a trend, they are not an encouraging development for the role of Chinese courts in applying international law.

In case of the absence of legislative action, domestic courts still may apply international law by interpreting national law in conformity with an international obligation. This is the principle of consistent interpretation.[63] Chinese courts sometimes employ the principle even when the relevant domestic laws do not explicitly provide for it. For instance, in *Nanning XX Service LLC v. Nanning XX Bureau*, there was disagreement regarding the meaning of "workplace."[64] China's Work Injury Insurance Regulations of 2010 fail to provide a definition. A Chinese court held that the Regulations should be interpreted in conformity with Article 3(c) of the Convention Concerning Occupational Safety and Health and the Working Environment (to which China is a contracting party), which provides that "the term workplace covers all places where workers

[59] *See* Li Guoguang, A Speech given at the brief on the Regulations of the Supreme People's Court on Issues Concerning the Trial of Administrative Cases Relating to International Trade, *available at* http://www.lawxp.com/statute/s898388.html (last visited Aug. 24, 2018).

[60] Selected Collection of People's Court Cases 368 (Shen Deyong ed., 2013).

[61] Longqinbiao Co. Ltd. v. Trademark Review & Adjudication Bd., *available at* http://www.pkulaw.cn/case/pfnl_118497741.html?match_Exact (last visited Aug. 24, 2018).

[62] Committee on Economic, Social and Cultural Rights, Second Periodic Report Submitted by States Parties Under arts. 16 and 17 of the Covenant: China, UN Doc. E/C.12/CHN/2, at 9 (July 6, 2012).

[63] Nollkaemper, *supra* note 3, at 73–81.

[64] Nanning XX Serv. LLC. v. Nanning XX Bureau, *available at* http://www.pkulaw.cn/case/pfnl_118505863.html (last visited Aug. 24, 2018).

need to be or to go by reason of their work and which are under the direct or indirect control of the employer."

In addition, treaties that China has not entered into are still likely to be applied by Chinese courts. For instance, in a Judicial Interpretation issued in 2012, the SPC noted that Chinese courts, in determining the rights and obligations of parties to a contract, could rely on provisions of a treaty that has not come into effect but is invoked by parties to a dispute, except those provisions in breach of the public interest, laws, and compulsory provisions of administrative regulations in China.[65]

Structure

"Selective adaptation" was considered as a pragmatic strategy that China adeptly maneuvers to maximize the benefits and to minimize the risks arising from the engagement with international regimes.[66] I do not want to join in the debates over the legitimacy of this legal strategy, but instead will simply offer new evidence for this observation.

It has been found that more than thirty treaties have been applied in Chinese courts, including the Convention on the Contract for the International Carriage of Goods by Road (1955), the Convention on International Bill of Exchange and International Promissory Note (1988), and the International Convention for the Unification of Certain Rules of Law Relating to Bills of Lading (1924) to which China was not a Contracting Party.[67] Furthermore, according to my own survey in 2016, most of these treaties deal with relations between private actors, such as the CISG, and those are the types of treaties most frequently invoked. For instance, as of January 18, 2016, the CISG has been invoked in 198 cases; the New York Convention, 66 cases; the Paris Convention for the Protection of Industrial Property (Paris Convention), 381 cases; the Berne Convention for the Protection of Literary and Artistic Works (Berne Convention), 622 cases.[68] However, treaties that are concerned with executive authority have rarely been applied. For instance, Chinese courts have never applied any "core" human rights conventions that it entered into, such as the CAT or the International Covenant on Economic, Social and Cultural Rights (ICESCR).

This structure of treaties applied in Chinese courts is rooted in Chinese national development strategy in the past thirty years. That strategy, which has sometimes been

[65] SPC, Interpretation (First) on Certain Issues Concerning the Application of the Choice of Law for Foreign-Related Civil Relations of the People's Republic of China, Dec. 2012, art. 9, *available at* http://www.court.gov.cn/shenpan-xiangqing-5273.html (last visited Aug. 10, 2017).

[66] Pitman B. Potter, *Globalization and Economic Regulation in China: Selective Adaptation of Globalized Norms and Practices*, 2 Wash. U. Global Stud. L. Rev. 119 (2003); Pitman B. Potter, *Selective Adaptation and Institutional Capacity*, 61 Int'l J. 389 (2005–2006); Ljiljana Biukovic, *Compliance with International Treaties: Selective Adaptation Analysis*, 44 Can. Y.B. Int'l L. 451 (2006).

[67] Zhijing & Jian, *supra* note 16, at 138.

[68] *See* Cai, *supra* note 6.

called the Beijing Consensus,[69] is characterized by two core elements: (1) a focus on economic growth over political democracy and social justice, and (2) an authoritarian regime with an executive branch that can pursue public policies as efficiently as possible.[70] On the one hand, the primary consideration of the Reform and Opening-up Policy was to attract capital and technology from Western states to repair the collapsed economy that followed the Cultural Revolution (1966–1976). However, China's "command economy" as the basic economic regime of a socialist state[71] discouraged Western investors and traders who operated in market economies, and China could not create a legal regime to support a fully fledged market economy in a short period of time. Therefore, it became expedient for China to incorporate international regimes into its domestic legal system with the aim of increasing foreign confidence on Chinese business environment. The infusion of massive amounts of foreign capital and technology into China accelerated the country's rapid economic growth. On the other hand, "efficiency" has always been considered as a great advantage inherent in the socialist regime.[72] This efficiency advantage often justifies the maintenance of executive authority and discretion. As the result, it comes as no surprise that, on the one hand, treaties like the CISG are allowed and encouraged to be invoked in Chinese courts because those treaties merely provide rights between private individuals; on the other hand, Chinese courts are reluctant to apply treaties like the CAT, even though China entered into these treaties, because executive authority would thus be seriously challenged.[73]

Nevertheless, as China rises as a new great power, it is likely that Chinese courts will apply, in addition to those treaties dealing with relations between private actors, other treaties in order to protect China's increasingly expanding interests. For instance, whenever China eventually ratifies the State Immunity Convention, which it signed in 2005, it is expected that the Convention will be applied in Chinese courts in some manner.[74]

IV. Application of International Law in Chinese Courts in the Chinese Context of Foreign Relations Law: A Case Study

If we agree with the proposition that foreign relations law serves as "an internal constraint on the unilateral exercise of foreign relations powers through the distribution

[69] *See* Bradley Klein, *Democracy Optional: China and the Developing World's Challenge to the Washington Consensus*, 22 UCLA Pac. Basin L.J. 89 (2004).

[70] Cai, *supra* note 6, at 286–287.

[71] Constitution (1982), art. 15.

[72] Deng Xiaoping, Selected World of Deng Xiaoping, Vol. 3, at 187–183, 188 (1994).

[73] Cai, *supra* note 6, at 284.

[74] *Id.* at 279.

of authority within the national government,"[75] it appears that Chinese courts have failed to live up to the expectations of many persons. A recent case, however, might provide a new perception of the role of Chinese courts in the Chinese context of foreign relations law. This case was filed before a Beijing court by Chinese individuals against two Japanese companies, accusing them of involvement in forced labor organized or supported by the Japan government during World War II. This case merits a close examination because it concerns the interpretation of a Communiqué signed between China and Japan in 1972 (China-Japan Joint Communiqué), which deals with the war-related compensation arising from Japan's aggression in China.

Since the mid-1990s, some Chinese war victims and their descendants had begun to file lawsuits in Japan, arguing that Japan's government and some Japanese companies should be liable for using forced labor and "comfort woman" (i.e., sexual slavery) during World War II. Chinese plaintiffs did not win any of these cases. One of justifications given by Japanese courts for ruling against the plaintiffs was that China's government had waived the right of China's government and its nationals to claim compensation, in Paragraph 5 of the China-Japan Joint Communiqué.[76] Paragraph 5 provides that "the Government of the People's Republic of China declares that in the interest of the friendship between the Chinese and the Japanese peoples, it renounces its demand for war reparation from Japan." The *Nishimatsu Construction* case and the *Second Chinese "Comfort Women"* case[77] are decisive. In two judgments both issued on April 27, 2007, Japan's Supreme Court (JSC) held that "[i]t should be out of doubt that, all claims arising from the war, including the claims by private individuals, are abandoned mutually."[78] This was the first time that JSC came to such a definite conclusion. Chinese leaders argued, however, that China, under Paragraph 5 of the China-Japan Joint Communiqué, merely waived the right of the Chinese government to bring war reparations claims and that Chinese nationals could be not barred from bringing such claims.[79] Although China condemned the JSC's interpretation as "void" and "invalid" and asserted that the Japanese government should "take Chinese

[75] Daniel Abebe, *Great Power Politics and the Structure of Foreign Relations Law*, 10 Chi. J. Int'l L. 125, 125 (2009–2010).

[76] Zhang Xingjun, *Evolution of Compensation Claims by Chinese War Victims in Japanese Courts and the Response of China's Government*, 4 Tsinghua L.J. 96 (2007) (in Chinese); Guang Jianqiang, Equity, Justice, and Dignity—Legal Foundation of Claims against Japan by Chinese Victims of Japan's Aggression to China (2006) (in Chinese).

[77] For the description of the two cases, *see* Masahiko Asada & Trevor Ryan, *Post-War Reparations Between Japan and China and the Waiver of Individual Claims: Japan's Supreme Court Judgments in the Nishimatsu Construction Case and the Second Chinese "Comfort Women" Case*, 19 Italian Y.B. Int'l L. 207 (2009).

[78] 中国人強制連行広島訴訟等上告審判決, 平成17年（受）第1735号, 平成19年4月27日.

[79] *See Experts Advise Chinese WWII Laborers to File Class Action*, People's Daily Online (Jan. 15, 2002), *available at* http://en.people.cn/200201/15/eng20020115_88683.shtml (last visited Aug. 24, 2018).

concerns seriously and properly resolve this issue,"[80] it could not do anything to overturn the judicial decision of the JSC.

Chinese victims and their descendants shifted their focus back to China, seeking to bring claims against the Japanese government and the relevant companies before Chinese courts. For example, in September 2012, some Chinese victims of the Chongqing Grand Bombing by the Japanese air force from 1938 to 1945 brought claims against Japan at a Chongqing court.[81] Similarly, in March 2014, a group of Chinese forced laborers and their descendants filed cases against Japan and several Japanese companies at a Hebei court.[82] The Japanese government was a defendant in both proposed lawsuits, and the two Chinese courts declined to register the cases.

In March 2014, however, a Beijing court registered a case filed by thirty-seven Chinese forced workers and their descendants against two Japanese companies, arguing that Japanese companies should be liable for their involvement in forced working programs during World War II. This is the first time that Chinese courts have exercised jurisdiction over disputes arising from the aggression of Japan in China.[83] Interestingly, this time the plaintiffs did not add the Japanese government as a defendant. This case is still pending.

This case between private parties provides Chinese courts an opportunity to clarify the meaning of Paragraph 5 of the China-Japan Communiqué, potentially rebutting the interpretation of the JSC. It should also be noted that this case is taking place in the context of continuous confrontations between two great powers. In the past decade, China–Japan bilateral relations have tended to worsen. For instance, in September 2012, Japan's government decided to "buy" the Diaoyu Islands, concerning which both states claim their sovereignty from a Japanese family who, under Japanese law, is the owner. China has responded with a set of measures, including issuing a white paper on Diaoyu Islands,[84] establishing the East China Sea Air Defense Identification Zone (ADIZ),[85] and publicizing confessions by forty-five Japanese war convicts.[86]

[80] *China Strongly Opposes Japan's Supreme Court's Arbitrary Interpretation of the Relevant Provisions of China-Japan Communiqué*, XINHUANET (Apr. 28, 2007) (China), *available at http://www.cnr.cn/news/200704/t20070428_504454131.shtml* (last visited Aug. 24, 2018).

[81] *Fifteen Victims of "Chongqing Grand Bombing" Bring Lawsuit against Japan* (Sept. 11, 2012), *available at* https://news.qq.com/a/20120911/000158.htm?pgv_ref=aio2012&ptlang=2052 (last visited Aug. 24, 2018).

[82] *Following up Lawsuits Brought by Chinese Laborers against Japanese Government and Enterprises* (Mar. 27, 2014), *available at http://news.163.com/14/0326/17/9O9F6D4E00014JB5.html* (last visited Aug. 24, 2018).

[83] *Court Accepts Chinese WWII Forced Labors Lawsuit, available at* http://english.cri.cn/6909/2014/03/19/3521s818167.htm (last visited Aug. 15, 2017).

[84] State Council Information Office of the People of Republic of China, *Diaoyu Dao, an Inherent Territory of China*, Sept. 2012, *available at* http:// http://www.scio.gov.cn/zfbps/ndhf/2012/Document/1225271/1225271.htm (last visited Dec. 12, 2018).

[85] *Defense Ministry Spokesman on China's Air Defense Identification* Zone, *available at* http://www.mod.gov.cn/affair/2013-11/23/content_4476908.htm (last visited Dec. 12, 2018).

[86] *Confessions of Japanese War Criminals, available at http://jishi.cntv.cn/special/ribenzhanfanchanhuibeiwanglu/index.shtml* (last visited Dec. 12, 2018).

The Beijing court exhibited its judicial wisdom in this case. It is expected that the two Japanese defendants would defend themselves against the plaintiffs' claim by invoking the above-mentioned judicial decision made by the SPC concerning Paragraph 5 of China-Japan Joint Communiqué. The Beijing court would thus have a good opportunity to give its own interpretation, affirming the Chinese position and refuting the SPC's judgments. On the other hand, in contrast with the two lawsuits initiated in Hebei and Chongqing, Japan's government is not listed as a defendant in this case, which could reduce the risk of diplomatic confrontations between China and Japan.

According to an instrument jointly issued by the SPC, MFA, and several other Chinese governmental organs,[87] the Beijing court was not likely to hear this case without the consent from the SPC and the MFA. Thus, it is fair to suggest that this case was deliberately included by China in its systematic diplomatic "struggles" with Japan. In other words, Chinese courts were mobilized to coordinate with and support other Chinese governmental organs in conducting foreign relations.

V. Conclusion

Generally speaking, international law merely requires that a state honor its international legal obligations, leaving the issue of how to honor them to be decided by the state itself. Any state thus has the right to decide on the method of automatic incorporation or transformation in light of domestic considerations. The automatic incorporation approach, compared with the transformation approach, gives domestic courts more say in enforcing international law by directly invoking specific legal rules, but the preference for transformation in and of itself does not necessarily mean that a state is less willing to conform to international law. Nevertheless, if a state fails to transform its international obligations into the domestic legal order, domestic courts can do little to make their home state honor its commitments.

A close examination of the application of international law in Chinese courts might frustrate those who endeavor to build a theoretical edifice applicable to most, if not all, states.[88] This examination can be helpful, however, for understanding the diversity of judicial application of international law among states. The application of international law in Chinese courts has its own context and dynamic that has changed somewhat over time. Such a context and dynamic fundamentally affect the method that is chosen to enforce international law and the structure of international law that is judicially

[87] MFA, SPC, the Supreme People's Procuratorate (SPP), Ministry of Public Security (MPS), Ministry of State Security (MSS), and the Ministry of Justice (MOJ), *Rules on Concerning Resolving Foreign-Related Cases*, June 20, 1995, *available at* http://www.chinalawedu.com/news/1200/22598/22604/22717/2006/3/ga31631653541313600219936-0.htm (last visited Aug. 10, 2017).

[88] *See* Eyal Benvenisti & George W. Downs, *National Courts, Domestic Democracy, and the Evolution of International Law*, 20 Eur. J. Int'l L. 59 (2009).

applied. The Chinese example also provides a good illustration of how domestic courts function to contribute to national development through strategically applying international law, rather than of how domestic courts, by applying international law, enhance domestic governance and, in particular, enforce individual rights against public authority, which has become regular practice not only in many Western countries that were major crafters of international law but also in some other countries that were once less friendly to international law, such as Japan and South Africa. Furthermore, it should be noted that some factors discouraging the judicial application of international law in China might also exist in some other countries, including the lack of professional competence of judges. They merit serious consideration in a larger context of comparative foreign relations law.

CHAPTER 32

DOMESTIC APPLICATION OF INTERNATIONAL LAW IN LATIN AMERICA

RENÉ URUEÑA

INTERNATIONAL law plays a central role in domestic adjudication in Latin America. The region is, in that respect, close to the African Commonwealth countries and to South Africa, studied elsewhere in this volume, as they share a deep interaction of domestic constitutions with international law, and international human rights law in particular. This chapter explores the central elements of such an interaction, as a contribution to the emerging field of "comparative foreign affairs law." The first section of the chapter describes the *domestic* factors that facilitate such a deep integration with international law: open constitutional clauses, and the case law of domestic courts. The second section explores the *international* factors that explain the deep interaction, and focuses on the doctrine of "control of conventionality," developed by the case law of the Inter-American Court of Human Rights (IACtHR). The tide in the region, though, might be changing, and the third section describes some of the incipient resistance that the deep integration of international law in domestic systems seems to be inspiring. The final section concludes, by looking at the field of "foreign relations law" from the perspective of Latin America.

I. APPLICATION OF INTERNATIONAL LAW IN LATIN AMERICA: DOMESTIC FACTORS

The interaction between international and domestic laws in Latin America is facilitated by both domestic and international factors.[1] On the domestic side, "open"

[1] Speaking of "Latin America" as an analytical unit for comparative legal analysis poses methodological problems, as the differences among countries in the region are considerable, and any grouping

constitutional clauses have been important for the domestic application of international law in the region, providing in turn the basis for domestic case law that has made international law an important dimension of the practice of pubic law in Latin America. This section will explore each of these dimensions.

Open Clauses in Latin American Constitutions

Following a period of brutal dictatorships during the 1970s and 80s, several Latin American countries introduced major reforms to their existing constitutions.[2] These "opened" the constitutions to international law, in particular to international human rights law, featuring clauses that incorporated international law in domestic legal systems.

Such openness can be explained by the region's recent history. Extremely closed political institutions and dictatorial regimes made Latin American civil society highly reliant on international institutions to achieve some level of political change. Such is the well-known "boomerang effect," observed in the late 1990s by Keck and Sikkink in Argentina, Chile, and Mexico, in which domestic nongovernmental organizations directly sought international allies to try to bring pressure on their respective states from the outside.[3] Constitutional openness to international law can be read, in that context, as a continuation of the same strategy: a way of formalizing the hard-earned space for external pressure that activists had achieved in their struggle against arbitrary rule.

To be sure, as each constitution reflects a particular political project, such openness to international law is not uniform throughout the region. Regarding the domestic status of international law, the 2009 Bolivian Constitution adopted a strong form of integration, giving international human rights treaties the same status as the Constitution.[4] Other countries opted for a different kind of integration. The 2008 Ecuadorian Constitution provided for the integration of international human rights with a lower status than the constitutional text, while recognizing that human rights treaties that provide for more favorable rights than the Constitution prevail in the domestic order, over "any

could be artificial. Despite these problems, as this chapter will show, it is possible to describe shared trends and challenges in the region, particularly with regard to public law after the 1990s. One caveat, though, is in order: this chapter explores Spanish-speaking states and Brazil, and will not cover English- and French-speaking Latin American states.

[2] Constitutional reforms occurred in Costa Rica in 1989, Mexico in 1992, and Argentina in 1994, while other countries adopted new constitutions (Brazil in 1988, Colombia in 1991, Paraguay in 1992, Peru in 1993, Ecuador in 1998 and 2008, Venezuela in 1999, and Bolivia in 2009). *See* Rodrigo Uprimny, *The Recent Transformation of Constitutional Law in Latin America: Trends and Challenges*, 89 TEX. L. REV. 1587 (2010).

[3] KATHRYN SIKKINK & MARGARET KECK, ACTIVISTS BEYOND BORDERS 79–120 (1998).

[4] Constitution of the Plurinational State of Bolivia, arts. 257 and 410. On the Bolivian system, *see* José Ismael Villarroel Alarcón, *El Tratamiento del Derecho Internacional en el Distema Jurídico Boliviano*, *in* DE ANACRONISMOS Y VATICINIOS: DIAGNÓSTICO SOBRE LAS RELACIONES ENTRE EL EERECHO INTERNACIONAL Y EL DERECHO INTERNO EN LATINOAMÉRICA 29–66 (Paola Acosta Alvarado, Juana Inés Acosta López, & Daniel Rivas Ramírez eds., 2017).

other legal norm or act of public power."[5] Thus, in Ecuador, domestic law is forbidden from restricting international human rights. Brazil's 2004 constitutional amendment, in turn, established that human rights treaties approved by Congress by the same majority as a constitutional amendment would be considered as an actual amendment, and thus part of the Constitution.[6] In contrast, other constitutional arrangements, such as Chile's 1989 amendment, merely established the "duty of the organs of the State to respect and promote [essential] rights, guaranteed by this Constitution, as well as by international treaties," without any specific reference to their status.[7]

Regarding sources, most constitutions in the region refer only to treaties, and not to other sources of international law. The exception may be Argentina, where Congress has power to regulate jurisdiction over crimes against the "law of nations."[8] Outside of human rights treaties, international law is seldom mentioned. Potential exceptions include Colombia, which considers border treaties as part of its Constitution;[9] Nicaragua, which does the same with territorial decisions by the International Court of Justice (ICJ);[10] and Peru, whose Constitution gives domestic effects to *all* treaties.[11] Outside these cases, the overall landscape in Latin America is one of openness and deep integration of domestic constitutions with international human rights treaties, with varying solutions with regard to the domestic hierarchy of such treaties, and very little concern with other branches of international law.

Domestic Courts and the "Constitutionality Block"

The constitutional provisions discussed above have been applied extensively by domestic courts, effectively integrating domestic and international law in the region—at least

[5] Constitution of the Republic of Ecuador, art. 424. On the Ecuadorian system of integration, *see* Danilo Alberto Caicedo Tapia, *El Bloque de Constitucionalidad en el Ecuador: Derechos Humanos Más allá de la Constitución*, FORO REV. DERECHO 5–29 (2009).

[6] Constitution of the Federal Republic of Brazil, art. 5, as amended by Enmienda Constitucional N° 45.

[7] *See* Francisco Cumplido Cereceda, *Alcances de la Modificación del Artículo 5° de la Constitución Política Chilena en Relación a los Tratados Internacionales*, 23 REV. CHIL. DERECHO 255–258 (1996).

[8] *See* Constitution of the Argentinean Nation, art. 118.

[9] Constitution of the Republic of Colombia, art. 102. On the constitutional status of border treaties, *see* Colombian Constitutional Court, Decisions C-197 of 1998, C-400 of 1998, C-1022 of 1999. However, other sources of international law that define borders, such as international judicial decisions, are not part of the Constitution, and require domestic legislation to be locally binding. *See* Colombian Constitutional Court, Decision C-268 of 2014.

[10] Constitution of the Republic of Nicaragua, art. 10. That Nicaragua and Colombia have these norms in their constitutions is not coincidental. The constitutional status of ICJ territorial decisions was established in Nicaragua following that country's victory in a long-standing maritime dispute against Colombia before the ICJ. *See* ICJ, Territorial and Maritime Dispute (Nicaragua v. Colombia), Judgment, I.C.J. Reports 2012, p. 624; Republic of Nicaragua, Ley de Reforma Parcial A La Constitución Política N° 854 (Jan. 29, 2014).

[11] Constitution of the Republic of Peru, art. 55. *See* Victor Hugo Montoya Chávez & Raúl Feijóo Cambiaso, *El rango de los Tratados sobre Derechos Humanos*, 24 IUS VERITAS 314–343 (2015).

with regard to human rights. Perhaps the most elaborate doctrine of integration is the *bloque de constitucionalidad* (the "constitutionality block"), which plays a central role in Latin American law.[12]

Bloque de constitucionalidad generally refers to an expanded constitutional canon that includes norms not featured in the immediate text of the written constitution. In Latin America, though, constitutional tribunals systematically used international human rights instruments as part of their own expanded constitutional canon, thus inextricably linking the notion of constitutional block with the domestic application of international law.[13]

Thus, the "block" became shorthand in the region for giving direct effect and constitutional status to international human rights law, most often treaties.[14] The key developments in this regard came first in the Argentinean and Colombian Constitutional Courts, and then in Bolivia, Ecuador, and Peru. In Argentina, the 1994 Constitution recognized constitutional status for several human rights treaties, expressly named in the text. On that basis, the Argentinean Supreme Court has established the existence of a "constitutional block."[15] The list of the treaties that belong to the "block" can be expanded, if Congress approves by a two-thirds majority in each chamber, which means that, in practice, the executive lacks the power to denounce the treaties that are part of the "block," unless the same majority in Congress gives its authorization.

The "block" in Colombia is, in contrast, more flexible. There is no list of specific treaties that hold constitutional status. Instead, treaties recognizing human rights and prohibiting their limitation during states of emergency will "prevail" over other norms in the constitutional order,[16] something that was construed by the Constitutional Court to mean that such treaties enjoy constitutional status.[17]

[12] Compare with Kenya and South Africa, which also integrate international law and domestic constitutions, but do it through means different from the constitutionality block. For the Kenyan example, *see* Ernest Yaw Ako & Richard Frimpong Oppong, *Foreign Relations Law in the Constitution and Courts of Commonwealth African Countries*, ch. 33 in this volume.

[13] This description of the "constitutionality block" is based on René Urueña, *Global Governance Through Comparative International Law?: Inter-American Constitutionalism and the Changing Role of Domestic Courts in the Construction of the International Law*, N.Y. Univ. Jean Monnet Work. Pap. Ser. (2013).

[14] However, in some jurisdictions, the "block" is also used to make custom domestically binding. Thus, for example, the Colombian Constitutional Court has held that customary norms protecting fundamental rights belong to the constitutional block (*see* Decision C-1180 of 2000). The Colombian Court has also held that customary international humanitarian law (IHL) is part of the constitutional canon in and of itself, due to the direct reference made in art. 214.2 of the Constitution, which prohibits the derogation of IHL in times of emergency. *See* Decision C-269 of 2014.

[15] *See*, e.g., Supreme Court of Argentina, Verbitsky, Horacio s/habeas corpus, V. 856. XXXVIII, 9 February 2004, paras. 5, 13, 39, and 57. Even before the 1994 amendment, though, the Supreme Court had held that international human rights law had direct effect in Argentinean law. *See* Ekmekdjian v. Sofovich, E. 64. XXIII, July 7, 1992.

[16] Constitution of the Republic of Colombia, art. 93.

[17] Colombian Constitutional Court, Decision C-225 of 1995.

The Colombian case is a good example of the crucial role played by the "block" in the politics of constitutional adjudication. In general, this may be due to the political economy of domestic judicial independence:[18] in a region of strong presidencies and populist legislatures, courts may find in international law an ally to bolster their independence. But, more specifically, the constitutional block provides one further level of legal stability that the actual constitutional text is unable to provide. In Colombia, constitutional amendments are relatively easy to achieve: in the first 25 years of the 1991 Constitution, more the 41 constitutional amendments were passed, amending a total of 127 articles.[19] While most of these amendments were not substantive, they do show that constitutional norms are potentially unstable. In this context of relative ease of constitutional amendments, the "block" emerges as a guarantee of stability: constitutional norms that, given their dual national/international pedigree, are harder to amend.

Such was the case of the 2016 Colombian peace agreement with the *Fuerzas Armadas Revolucionarias de Colombia* (FARC). The FARC and the Colombian government originally agreed that the peace deal would be a "special agreement" in "terms of Article 3 common to all Geneva Conventions of 1949," which would "be part of the constitutional block."[20] The logic was that the guerrilla group had no actual legal guarantees that the government would keep its part of the deal—particularly, if a new administration opportunistically calculated that, once the FARC were demobilized, the agreement was not worth implementing.

In this context, a constitutional amendment was one obvious answer. However, considering the ease of amendment referred to earlier, and since the main opponents of the peace deal had already succeeded twice in reforming the constitution to allow for the re-election of their leader, a standard amendment failed to provide the assurances required by the guerrilla group. Enter thus the idea of making the peace deal an international humanitarian law instrument belonging to the constitutional block, which would have made it all but impossible to repeal (unlike a standard constitutional amendment).

Colombians rejected the peace deal in a referendum, in part precisely because the integration of the deal to the constitutional block was viewed as a back-door constitutional amendment.[21] After the rejection, the idea of total integration of the agreement

[18] Eyal Benvenisti, *Reclaiming Democracy: The Strategic Uses of Foreign and International Law by National Courts*, 102 Am. J. Int'l L. 241 (2008).

[19] Nestor Osuna, *Van 41 reformas a la Constitución, y vienen más*, El Espectador, July 7, 2016, *available at* https://www.elespectador.com/opinion/van-41-reformas-constitucion-y-vienen-mas (last visited Nov. 16, 2017).

[20] Fuerzas Armadas Revolucionarias de Colombia, Ejército del Pueblo—FARC-EP & Gobierno de Colombia, Acuerdo Final Para la Terminación del Conflicto y la Construcción de una Paz Estable y Duradera 249 (2016). Further, the Constitutional Amendment No. 1 of 2016 changed the Constitution to achieve such integration.

[21] *See* Laura Betancur, *The Legal Status of the Colombian Peace Agreement*, 110 AJIL Unbound 188 (2016).

to the constitutional block was dropped.[22] Once the Constitutional Court reviewed the deal, the matter was settled: the peace agreement was not part of the constitutional block,[23] and its amendment was certainly possible in the future.

Outside Colombia and Argentina, other jurisdictions are increasingly using the constitutional block. The constitutional tribunals of Guatemala and Peru have used it to give constitutional status to rights not explicitly included in their respective constitutions—such as the right to prior consultation to indigenous communities, recognized in International Labour Organization (ILO) Convention 169.[24] Similarly, since 2001, the Bolivian Constitutional Tribunal used the "block" to give constitutional status to international human rights instruments, absent an explicit constitutional provision[25] and, after 2009, when there was an explicit reference to the constitutional block, the Tribunal confirmed such constitutional status.[26]

Around the "Block"

Elsewhere in the region, though, the block is less useful as an analytical category. Such is the case in Brazil. Under the 1988 Constitution, international human rights law could recognize rights not granted under domestic law. However, while there was scholarly debate over a possible *bloco de constitucionalidade*,[27] the Supreme Federal Tribunal considered that there was not such a "block," and that human rights treaties had infraconstitutional status.[28]

In 2004, a constitutional amendment in Brazil established that human rights treaties approved in Congress by a more demanding procedure would have constitutional status. Such is the case of the Convention on the Rights of Persons with Disabilities.[29]

[22] Fuerzas Armadas Revolucionarias de Colombia, Ejército del Pueblo—FARC-EP & Gobierno de Colombia, Acuerdo Final Para la Terminación del Conflicto y la Construcción de una Paz Estable y Duradera (2016). Further, the Constitutional Amendment No. 2 of 2017 excluded the integration.

[23] *See* Constitutional Court of Colombia, Decision C-630 of 2017.

[24] Constitutional Court of Guatemala, Files 4783–2013, 4812–2013, 4813–2013, Apelación de Sentencia de Amparo, July 6, 2016; Constitutional Tribunal of Peru, Decision 05427-2009-PC/TC (Asociación Interétnica de Desarrollo de la Selva), para. 9. The Colombian Constitutional Court has also held that the right to prior consultation is part of the constitutional block. *See* Constitutional Court of Colombia, Decision T-955 of 2003.

[25] Constitutional Tribunal of Bolivia, Decision N° 95 of December 21, 2001.

[26] *See* art. 410 of the Constitutional of the Plurinational Republic of Bolivia. *See also* Plurinational Constitutional Tribunal of Bolivia, Decision 0110-R of May 10, 2010. In a similar line, *see* Decision 0212-R of May 24, 2010 and Decision 1227 of September 7, 2012.

[27] *See* Valério de Oliveira Mazzuoli, *Os Tratados Internacionais de Direitos Humanos Como Fonte do Sistema Constitucional de Proteção de Direitos*, 6 Rev. CEJ 120–124 (2002).

[28] Supreme Federal Tribunal of Brazil, Ação Direta De Inconstitucionalidade 1.480, 03/09/1997 (per Celso de Mello), which reviewed ILO Convention 158.

[29] *See* Decree 6949/2009 da Presidência da República. Note that, in any event, the treaty has direct effect in the domestic legal system. The unwritten tradition in Brazilian constitutional law is for the

In contrast, human rights treaties not approved through this procedure (including those adopted before the 2004 amendment) have a higher hierarchical status than acts of Congress, but are below the Constitution.[30] There is, though, a vocal minority, represented by Judge Celso de Mello, for whom human rights treaties not adopted by the special procedures have constitutional status, and would be part of a veritable constitutional block.[31]

In Mexico, the constitutional block is similarly subject to debate. A constitutional reform in 2011 established a system of "conforming interpretation" (*interpretación conforme*[32]), under which domestic law relating to human rights must be interpreted as "conforming" to the Constitution and to international treaties. Following the amendment, two readings of the applicability of international law in Mexico emerged. One group of scholars defended the existence of a veritable constitutional block, with international human rights having constitutional status.[33] Other commentators saw a hierarchy between constitutional rights and international human rights, the former featuring a higher status.[34]

The Mexican Supreme Court gave some clarification. Unlike the "block," the Court explained, the amendment was not a hierarchy clause, but a hermeneutic principle that introduced international human rights in constitutional adjudication, and required a case-by-case approach. This "parameter of constitutional regularity,"[35] as the Court called it, implies that international law has no inherent superior hierarchy in Mexican law, but may have primacy if it provides the best protection to human rights. In one dimension, though, domestic law retains supremacy: if the constitution establishes "express restrictions to the exercise of human rights," such restrictions will *always* have precedence over international human rights norms[36]—even they are in contradiction to more generous international standards.

president to enact treaties by domestic Executive Decree. However, the date of domestic entry into force of the treaty is that of ratification, and not that of the Decree. *See* Supreme Federal Tribunal of Brazil, ADI 1.480-MC, 18/05/2001 (per Celso de Mello).

30 *See* Supreme Federal Tribunal of Brazil, Recurso Extraordinário 466.343-1, 03/12/2008 (per Cezar Peluso). For Flávia Piovesan, human rights treaties adopted before 2004 also have that status. *See* Flávia Piovesan & Henrique Delavi Daum, *Controle da Convencionalidade: Experiência Brasileira*, *in* El Control de Convencionalidad: Un Balance Comparado de 10 Años de Almonacid Arellano vs. Chile 259–280 (Miriam Henriquez Viñas & Mariela Morales eds., 2017).

31 Supreme Federal Tribunal of Brazil, Recurso Extraordinário 466.343-1, 03/12/2008, at 129.

32 José Luis Caballero Ochoa, La Interpretación Conforme: El Modelo Constitucional ante los Tratados Internacionales sobre Derechos Humanos y el Control de Convencionalidad 27 (2015).

33 *See* Sergio García Ramírez, *El Control Judicial Interno de Convencionalidad*, 5 Rev. IUS 123–159 (2011).

34 *See* José Ramón Cossío D., *Primeras Implicaciones del Caso Radilla*, Cuest. Const. Rev. Mex. Derecho Const. 31–63 (2012).

35 Mexican Supreme Court of Justice of the Nation, Acción de Inconstitucionalidad 155/2007, decided on February 6, 2012.

36 Mexican Supreme Court of Justice of the Nation, Tesis Jurisprudencial P./J. 20/2014 (10a.).

II. Application of International Law in Latin America: International Factors

Differences notwithstanding, the general landscape in Latin America is one of openness toward international law—be it in the text of the constitutions, or in the ample case law of domestic courts. This, though, is only half of the story. Openness toward international in Latin America is complemented (and reinforced) by an expansive practice of the Inter-American Court of Human Rights (IACtHR), which, despite its relatively traditional jurisdiction, has developed innovative doctrines that further deepen the already deep integration between international and domestic laws in the region.[37]

Perhaps the most important of such innovations is the doctrine of "conventionality control" (*control de convencionalidad*), which has two effects: first, it creates the obligation of domestic authorities to interpret domestic norms in accordance with Inter-American human rights law and, in the case of unsolvable conflict, orders national authorities to refrain from applying domestic law, in order to avoid any violation of an internationally protected right.[38] And, second, it gives the IACtHR jurisdiction to review the compatibility of domestic laws with the American Convention of Human Rights. We now turn to explore each of these effects.

Domestic Conventionality Control

Judicial review of legislation has been a central characteristic of Latin American constitutionalism since the nineteenth century.[39] Often referred to as "constitutionality control" (*control de constitucionalidad*), it has played an important role as a check on executive and legislative abuses (with varying degree of success in each country[40]). Building on that experience, the IACtHR developed a "conventionality control," which creates the obligation of domestic authorities to interpret domestic norms in accordance with the Inter-American human rights law and, in the case of unsolvable conflict, orders national authorities to refrain from applying domestic law. While close to a

[37] *See generally* David Harris, *Regional Protection of Human of Human Rights: The Inter-American Achievement, in* The Inter-American System of Human Rights 1–30 (David Harris & Stephen Livingstone eds., 1998).

[38] *See* Eduardo Ferrer MacGregor, *Conventionality Control: The New Doctrine of the Inter-American Court of Human Rights*, 109 AJIL Unbound 93–99 (2015).

[39] Allan-Randolph Brewer Carías, Judicial Review in Comparative Law 89 (1989).

[40] In Mexico, *see* Matthew Campbell Mirow, *Marbury in Mexico: Judicial Review's Precocious Southern Migration*, 35 Hastings Const. L.Q. 41 (2007). In Colombia, Manuel José Cepeda-Espinosa, *Judicial Activism in a Violent Context: The Origin, Role, and Impact of the Colombian Constitutional Court*, 3 Wash. U. Glob. Stud. L. Rev. 529 (2004).

"conforming interpretation" clause, in the sense that it requires national authorities to construe domestic law in a way not contrary to Inter-American human rights law, "conventionality control" in fact goes much further: it creates the actual international obligation, on behalf of domestic authorities, not to apply domestic law if it contradicts international law.

In its most extreme version, "conventionality control" may even imply disregarding the very Constitution. In Honduras, for example, the Supreme Court decided to disregard (*inaplicar*) constitutional norms that limited the possibility of presidential re-election, because they contradicted the Honduran court's interpretation of Inter-American standards.[41] By doing so, the Supreme Court used Inter-American standards to undermine a central constitutional safeguard, which sought to limit the power of *caudillos* by limiting the possibility of their re-election.[42] Similarly, the Bolivian Constitutional Tribunal held that the American Convention of Human Rights had primacy (*aplicacion preferente*) over domestic constitutional norms limiting presidential re-election,[43] thus clearing the way for President Morales to run for a fourth term, despite a popular vote rejecting such an option.[44] These are, however, exceptional cases. For the most part, "conventionality control" provides the international legal basis for domestic judges to directly apply international law, and to use international human rights law as a parameter to review domestic legislation.

The exact scope of conventionality control has been the object of some controversy. A first difficulty is to determine who is responsible for undertaking the control of conventionality. In *Cabrera García*, et al. *v. Mexico*, the IACtHR held that such a review was an obligation of all state organs, and not only of judicial authorities.[45] This interpretation posed a major challenge for the system, as it risked an uncoordinated enforcement of Inter-American standards at the local level.[46] To solve this problem, the Court sought to limit the scope of the doctrine by clarifying that conventionality control should be exercised, *ex officio*,[47] by state authorities "evidently within the framework of their respective jurisdiction and the corresponding procedural rules."[48]

[41] Supreme Court of the Republic of Honduras, Constitutional Chamber, Decision of April 22, 2015.

[42] *See* Brian Sheppard & David Landau, *Why Honduras's Judiciary Is Its Most Dangerous Branch*, N.Y. Times, June 25, 2015, *available at* https://www.nytimes.com/2015/06/26/opinion/why-hondurass-judiciary-is-its-most-dangerous-branch.html (last visited Nov. 25, 2017).

[43] Plurinational Constitutional Tribunal of Bolivia, Decision 084 of November 28, 2017.

[44] Nicholas Casey & Monica Machicao, *Referendum to Let Bolivian President Seek a Fourth Term Appears Headed for Defeat*, N.Y. Times, Feb. 21, 2016, *available at* https://www.nytimes.com/2016/02/22/world/americas/bolivia-to-vote-on-term-limits-amid-growing-doubts-about-its-president.html (last visited Dec. 5, 2017).

[45] IACtHR, Cabrera García and Montiel-Flores v. Mexico, Decision of November 26, 2010 (Preliminary Objection, Merits, Reparations, and Costs), para. 225.

[46] Diego García-Sayán, Cambiando el Futuro 194 (2017).

[47] IACtHR, Case of the Dismissed Congressional Employees (Aguado—Alfaro et al.) v. Peru, Decision of November 24, 2006 (Preliminary Objections, Merits, Reparations and Costs), para. 128.

[48] *See* IACtHR, Case of the Dismissed Congressional Employees (Aguado—Alfaro et al.) v. Peru, Decision of November 24, 2006 (Preliminary Objections, Merits, Reparations and Costs), para. 128; IACtHR, Gelman v. Uruguay, Decision of February 24, 2011 (Merits and Reparations), para. 193.

In this context, conventionality control implies that domestic institutions have the duty to apply international law, as long as it is compatible with domestic norms of jurisdictions and procedure—a much less radical doctrine than would initially appear.

Notwithstanding the limitation of its scope, domestic conventionality control may imply incoherence in some countries—even if exercised only by courts and within their respective jurisdictions. Judicial review in some countries in the region is decentralized (or "diffuse," as it is often known in Latin America), in the sense that numerous courts have jurisdiction to perform judicial review of legislation using the Constitution as the relevant parameter.[49] Domestic conventionality control means, then, that such a review is also decentralized, such that different courts will have the jurisdiction to strike down domestic legislation by directly applying Inter-American human rights law. This situation may create confusion in domestic judges. Such was the case of Mexico, where the combination of control of conventionality and diffuse domestic constitutional review led to some confusion over whether, and to what extent, nonfederal judges would have to the power to perform conventionality control.[50]

A second difficulty is that it is not entirely clear what standards are to be used. To be sure, the first standard to be used to undertake conventionality control is the text of the American Convention of Human Rights. Beyond the Convention, as Inter-American Judge Ferrer MacGregor explains, there is also a "block of conventionality"—an Inter-American *corpus iuris* that includes other human rights treaties,[51] soft law instruments, and, importantly, the case law of the IACtHR.[52] From the perspective of "conventionality control," then, Inter-American case law has *erga omnes* effect, in the sense that that the standards it develops in its case law are binding upon all parties to the American Convention of Human Rights, and not only the parties to the dispute.[53]

The impact of conventionality control on the domestic application of international law will depend on each state's constitutional arrangements. For states with a constitutionality block system, there is little added value to be found, from a domestic point of view, in this doctrine. Indeed, undertaking the Inter-American "conventionality

[49] *See* Elena Highton, *Sistemas Concentrado y Difuso de Control de Constitucionalidad*, *in* HACIA UN IUS CONSTITUTIONALE COMMUNE EN AMÉRICA LATINA? (Armin von Bogdandy, Mariela Morales, & Eduardo Ferrer MacGregor eds., 2011).

[50] The Mexican Supreme Court ultimately clarified that federal judges, upon hearing constitutional disputes, can strike down norms that contravene the Federal Constitution or international treaties that recognize human rights. Other judges may disregard (*inaplicar*) norms that violate the Federal Constitution or international treaties that recognize human rights, only for the purposes of the specific case and without making a declaration of general invalidity of the provisions. Finally, other nonjudicial authorities should interpret norms in such a form that they conform with human rights; but are not empowered to strike down norms or to disregard them in specific cases. *See* Mexican Supreme Court of Justice of the Nation, Expediente Varios 912/2010. It remains unclear, however, precisely which are the treaties that "recognize human rights," and such the standards included the case law of the Inter-American Court.

[51] IACtHR, Familia Pacheco Tineo v. Bolivia, Preliminary Objections, Merits, Reparations, and Costs, Judgment, Inter-Am. Ct. H. R. (ser. C) No. 272, para. 143 (Nov. 25, 2013).

[52] *See* Ferrer MacGregor, *supra* note 38.

[53] IACtHR, Gelman v. Uruguay, Decision of February 24, 2011 (Merits and Reparations), para. 69.

control" by using this *corpus* as a parameter is indistinguishable from performing domestic review using as a parameter the constitutional block that includes Inter-American human rights law. For a system with a deep integration of international law with the constitution, conventionality control is just the international side of a constitutional openness toward international law. In other words, when a domestic court reviews domestic legislation using the constitutional block as a parameter, it is ultimately undertaking conventionality control.

The doctrine grows in importance, though, in legal systems with a less integral openness toward international law, such as Brazil. In those cases, the doctrine of "conventionality control" becomes crucial, because it creates the international obligation of domestic courts to directly apply Inter-American human rights law—even if their constitution features no such obligation. Thus, the Brazilian Supreme Federal Tribunal found that the crime of contempt (*desacato*) of authority was contrary to Inter-American standards, even if it was not in direct contradiction with the Constitution.[54] In those cases, "conventionality control" provides the basis for domestic courts to perform constitutional review using international law as a parameter, even if their own constitutional text remains silent on the domestic status of international law, or gives it infraconstitutional status.

The doctrine is also important with regard to the specific contents of Inter-American human rights law that are to be applied in domestic judicial review. As we have seen, the IACtHR considers that its case law has *erga omnes* effects, and constitutes a "conventionality block." Therefore, domestic courts that engage in conventionality control should apply the Court's case law as binding law, even if its respective state was not part of the dispute. Again, the added value of such a move depends on the domestic system of reception of international law. Some domestic courts in the region already consider Inter-American case law as part of their constitutional block, even with regard to cases involving third states. In those cases, there is little added value to the doctrine, as the IACtHR's conventionality block and the constitutional block would be one and the same thing. Thus, domestic courts that perform judicial review on the basis of a constitutional block that includes Inter-American case law are, by necessity, applying the conventionality block. Such is the case of Bolivia, where the Constitutional Tribunal held that case law by the Inter-American Court of Human Rights is "binding for domestic courts,"[55] as did the Guatemalan Constitutional Court.[56] In Peru, while no express reference is made to a constitutionality block, the Constitutional Tribunal did hold that Inter-American case law is "binding for all national public powers"[57]; and the

[54] Superior Tribunal of Justice of Brazil, Recurso Especial 1640084/SP (drafted by Ribeiro Dantas), fifth *turma*, Dec. 15, 2016.

[55] Plurinational Constitutional Tribunal of Bolivia, Decision 491-R of April 15, 2003. *See also* Expediente No. 2006-13381-27-RAC of May 10, 2010.

[56] Constitutional Court of Guatemala, Files 4783-2013, 4812-2013, 4813-2013, Apelación de Sentencia de Amparo, July 6, 2016.

[57] Peruvian Constitutional Tribunal, Case No. 27302006—PA/TC of July 21, 2006, Case No. 5854-2005—PA/TC, para. 30. *See also* Juan Andrés Fuentes, *Algunas Precisiones Sobre la Relación Entre el*

Colombian Constitutional Court, in turn, has also stated that Inter-American case law is binding and has primacy in Colombian law.[58] In these systems, domestic judicial review will necessarily apply the Inter-American case law as part of the domestic constitutional standard.

Elsewhere, direct application of Inter-American case law has been contested. In Mexico, the Supreme Court dealt with the implementation of an IACtHR decision ordering Mexican judges to review legislation giving military courts jurisdiction over human rights violations against civilians, among other orders.[59] The Mexican Court held that the Inter-American decision was binding, if Mexico had been a party to the case; if not, the international decision was a nonbinding "guiding principle."[60] This distinction was dropped later, when the Court decided that *all* IACtHR decisions were binding on domestic judges.[61] Some resistance, though, remained: if Mexico was not party to the dispute, domestic judges should "verify that the same reasoning applies" when directly applying IACtHR case law to domestic cases.[62]

In Chile, resistance is even clearer: Inter-American case law is a guide for interpretation, but is not binding upon domestic courts, if Chile was not part of the dispute. And in Colombia, the Constitutional Court has sometimes verged toward these more restrictive interpretations holding IACtHR case law as "relevant criteria for interpretation" of the constitutional norms,[63] and "authentic interpretation" of the Convention.[64] In those cases, conventionality control gives domestic courts the space to directly apply international human rights law—even if they are not constitutionally required to do so.

International Conventionality Control

Complementing the domestic dimension of conventionality control, the IACtHR has held that it has the power to directly review domestic norms, using as a parameter the Inter-American *corpus iuris*, composed, as we have seen, of the American Convention, other relevant treaties, and crucially, the Inter-American case law. At one level, this mode of conventionality control is just an exercise of the IACtHR's jurisdiction to adjudicate on state responsibility, as states may be in violation of the American

Derecho Internacional y el Derecho Nacional Peruano in Juana Acosta, in El Anacronismo y los Vaticinios. Diagnósticos Sobre las Relaciones Entre el Derecho Unternacional y el Derecho Interno en Latinoamerica (Paola Acosta & Daniel Rivas eds., 2017).

[58] Colombian Constitutional Court C-715 of 2012 and C-795 de 2014.

[59] *See* Mexican Supreme Court of Justice of the Nation, Expediente Varios 912/2010. The IACtHR's decision was *Radilla-Pacheco v. Mexico* (23 November 2009), Series C No. 209.

[60] *Id.*, para. 19.

[61] Mexican Supreme Court of Justice of the Nation, Contradicción de Tesis 293/2011.

[62] *Id.*

[63] Colombian Constitutional Court, Decision C-010 of 2000.

[64] Colombian Constitutional Court, Decision C-370 of 2006.

Convention in virtue of their domestic law, which entails, in effect, a conventionality control on behalf of the international court.

However, the IACtHR has gone farther, directly striking down domestic laws that it deemed in contravention of the Inter-American "block of conventionality." By doing so, the IACtHR has played the role of a veritable constitutional tribunal, by expressly holding that domestic laws that violate the Convention "lack legal effects," and have never produced them.[65] For the IACtHR, its decisions are "*ipso iure* part of domestic legal systems," and "wholly incorporated" in them.[66]

This doctrine implies an astonishing move[67] and a first of its kind in international law.[68] However, it might prove to be an exceptional decision at an exceptional moment of the region, never to be seen again in such a clear level of Inter-American judicial involvement with domestic law. The case dealt with amnesty laws adopted in Peru during Alberto Fujimori's government, which gave impunity to human rights violations during his mandate. After Fujimori's fall from power, transitional President Paniagua did not want to maintain the amnesties, but was tied by those domestically valid laws, and lacked the political majorities in Congress to immediately overturn them.[69] Peru was also recently returning to the jurisdiction of the Inter-American Court, after Fujimori had tried to withdraw. In that context, Peru's agent put forward before the Inter-American Court the question of what to do with these valid amnesty laws,[70] thus opening the space for the IACtHR to directly strike down a piece of legislation that was not only contrary to Inter-American human rights law but also inconvenient to the new administration.

The decision had clear effects in domestic politics: in 2008, based on the very decision being discussed here, Peruvian domestic courts sentenced the head of the powerful National Intelligence Service (SIN) under ex-President Fujimori to thirty-five years in prison for what happened at the University of La Cantuta.[71] Perhaps mindful of this fact, the Court has used this doctrine sparingly. While present in its most extreme form in cases dealing with amnesties and transitional justice,[72] the judicial

[65] *See* IACtHR, La Cantuta v. Peru, Decision of 29 November 2006 (Merits, Reparations and Costs), para. 189. In his separate opinion to this decision, Segio García Ramírez argues that domestic laws that violate the Convention are "basically invalid" (paras. 4 and 5).

[66] *Id.*, para. 186.

[67] *See generally* Alexandra Huneeus, *The Institutional Limits of Inter-American Constitutionalism*, *in* COMPARATIVE CONSTITUTIONAL LAW IN LATIN AMERICA (Rosalind Dixon & Tom Ginsburg eds., 2017).

[68] Antonio Cassese, *Y-a-t-il un Conflit Insurmontable entre Souveraineté des États et Justice Pénale Internationale?*, *in* CRIMES INTERNATIONAUX ET JURIDICTIONS INTERNATIONALES 13, 16 (Antonio Cassese & Mireille Delmas-Marty eds., 2002), *quoted in* Christina Binder, *The Prohibition of Amnesties by the Inter-American Court of Human Rights*, 12 GERMAN L.J. 1203 1212.

[69] GARCÍA-SAYÁN, *supra* note 46, at 172–173. [70] *Id.* at 173.

[71] *See* Human Rights Watch, "Boletín Informativo Human Right Watch," Apr. 10, 2008, *available at* http://www.hrw.org/doc/?t=spanish&c=peru.

[72] *See, e.g.*, IACtHR, *La Cantuta*, *supra* note 65. *See also* ICtHR, Barrios Altos v. Peru, Decision of 14 March 2001 (Merits).

control by the IACtHR of domestic law has sometimes led to an order to change national norms in a "reasonable period of time."[73]

III. Growing Resistance?

The integration of international and domestic law in Latin America has had a deep impact in the domestic constitutional landscape of the region. In this context, there seems to be some backlash in some states in the region, which suggests that the domestic application of international law in Latin America has gone beyond what some courts consider acceptable.

One example is Venezuela. In August 2008, the IACtHR decided in *Apitz Barbera Et Al.* that Venezuela had violated the American Convention when it removed three judges from the bench. The violation was committed when the Venezuelan Supreme Court dismissed the judges on the grounds of an alleged "inexcusable judicial error," without respecting their right to a due process. The Inter-American Court held that the Venezuelan Supreme Court had violated the judges' human rights and the principle of judicial independence.[74]

The Venezuelan Supreme Court decided that it would not comply with the IACtHR's decision, arguing that it represented a "usurpation of its functions." Moreover, it referred to "the impossibility of implementing the Inter-American Court decision," and issued a plea to the executive to denounce the American Convention, "in light of the clear usurpation of functions in which the Inter-American Court of Human Rights has incurred."[75] The Supreme Court's opinion came amid tensions between Venezuela's government and the IACtHR, which only became more serious when the Inter-American Court found that Venezuela had breached the American Convention when it prevented opposition leader Leopoldo López from running for office.[76] Ultimately, President Hugo Chávez denounced the American Convention in 2012, using the Supreme Court's decision as part of the grounds for his withdrawal.[77]

The Dominican Republic (DR) has also strongly rejected the IACtHR's strategy of strong integration. In 2014, the Inter-American Court ruled that the DR has breached the American Convention by adopting measures that discriminated against Haitians

[73] *See*, e.g., IACtHR, Suarez Rosero, Decision of 12 November 1997 (Merits); ICtHR, Castillo Petruzzi el al v. Perú, Decision of 30 May 1999 (Merits); IACtHR, Fermín Ramírez v. Guatemala, Decision of 20 June 2005 (Merits).

[74] IACtHR, Apitz Barbera et al. v. Venezuela, Decision of 5 August 2008 (Merits).

[75] Tribunal Supremo de Justicia de Venezuela (Sala Constitucional), Sentencia no. 1939 del 18 de Diciembre de 2008 (Exp. 08-1572).

[76] IACtHR, Case of Leopoldo Lopez v. Venezuela (merits, reparations, and costs), Sept. 1, 2011, Series C 233.

[77] Letter from Nicolás Maduro, Venezuelan Foreign Minister, to José Miguel Insulza, OAS Secretary General 171–175 (Sept. 6, 2012) (on file with author).

and those of Haitian descent—including a 2013 domestic court decision. The IACtHR ordered not only a proper compensation but also requested an appropriate system of civil registration, banned the expulsion of Dominican nationals of Haitian descent, and urged the nullification of all the regulations denying the nationality of any child born in the DR.[78]

The response was swift, with the Constitutional Tribunal declaring that the DR was not subject to the jurisdiction of the IACtHR, since the instrument by which Dominican Republic had seemingly accepted the Inter-American Court's jurisdiction was constitutionally invalid.[79] The Constitutional Tribunal considered that, according to the Constitution, a congressional vote was necessary to approve the treaty, and in this case the instrument was the product of a sole executive act.[80] The DR's acceptance of IACtHR jurisdiction was thus invalid, and domestic courts were under no obligation to follow its orders, or apply its case law.

A final example is Argentina. In 2011, the IACtHR ruled that Argentina was responsible for the violation of the right to expression of Jorge Fontevecchia and Héctor D'Amico, two journalists who were condemned by a national court to pay a substantial compensation to former president Menem, after publishing information about the president's alleged child, and the possible misappropriation of public funds in 1995. The IACtHR ordered Argentina to render the Supreme Court decision ineffective, and to reimburse costs and expenses to the petitioners.[81]

In 2017, the Supreme Court of Argentina rejected the IACtHR's ruling, arguing that the international tribunal had no jurisdiction to review their decisions, as the highest court in the judiciary. In an interesting reversal of roles, the Argentinean Supreme Court considered the IACtHR's decisions as incompatible with the American Convention on Human Rights, as the latter gave the IACtHR no jurisdiction to revoke national decisions. Moreover, the Argentinean agents before the IACtHR also claimed that, despite the fact that Argentina recognized the binding nature of the decisions taken by IACtHR, the Supreme Court should decide whether its own decision is null and void, as finding otherwise would collide with the Argentinean separation of powers by giving judicial powers to the executive branch.[82]

As can be gleamed from these examples, much of this resistance to the domestic application of international law in Latin America is part of a wider strategy to avoid compliance with international decisions. Overall, states in the region have tried to limit

[78] IACtHR, Case of Dominican And Haitian People Expelled v. The Dominican Republic (merits, reparations, and costs), 28 August 2014, Series C 282, at 512.

[79] Tribunal Constitucional de la República Dominicana, Sentencia TC/0256/14.

[80] Note, however, that of the twenty-two states that have accepted the Inter-American Court's jurisdiction, only two did so upon ratification; the remainder accepted the Court's jurisdiction at a later date through a sole executive act.

[81] IACtHR, Case of the Fontevecchia and D'amico v. Argentina (merits, reparations, and costs), 29 November 2011, Series C 238, at 137.

[82] IACtHR, Case of the Fontevecchia and D'amico v. Argentina (Resolución 18 October 2017—Supervisión De Cumplimiento de Sentencia), para. 8.

the Inter-American system's impact, for example, by withdrawing funding, which is to be expected from governments accused by an international organ of violating human rights.

However, other concerns do point to a reasonable disagreement over the democratic legitimacy of such a profound intervention in domestic public law,[83] which reflects a "maximalist" understanding of international adjudication that is not required by the American Convention.[84] While the deep integration of international and domestic public law has led to a stronger protection of human rights in the region, it is still the case that more work is required on behalf of both the IACtHR and domestic courts to give a normative account as to why such integration should continue in light of its risks and challenges, and why it is better to continue toward what some scholars are calling a veritable *Ius Commune* in Latin America.[85]

IV. Conclusion

Resistance to the integration of international human rights with domestic public law can be read as a reaction to a transformation that has occurred in Latin America at a speed, and to such a depth, that seems exceptional in the world. Such a tight network of domestic and international instruments, all continuously interacting, could help explain the absence of "foreign relations law" as a discrete field of study in Latin American legal scholarship. Most of the issues covered in the United States under such a label have been part of Latin American judicial and scholarly debates for at least a couple of decades; yet, they have been understood as part of the discussion on the status of international law in domestic systems.[86] Why is there no "foreign relations law" in Latin America?

To answer this question, perhaps the best place to start is to recall the emergence of Latin American "new constitutionalism" in the 1990s. As has been discussed in this chapter, such a constitutional framework had important practical impacts on the political landscape in the region, particularly with regard to human rights adjudication. For decades, the Inter-American system of human rights has yielded great influence on

[83] *See*, e.g., Roberto Gargarella, *La Democracia Frente a los Crímenes Masivos: Una Reflexión a la luz del Ccaso Gelman*, Rev. Latinoam. Derecho Int. (2015).

[84] Jorge Contesse, *The Final Word? Constitutional Dialogue and the Inter-American Court of Human Rights*, 15 Int'l J. Const. Law 414–435 (2017).

[85] Transformative Constitutionalism in Latin America: The Emergence of a New Ius Commune (Armin von Bogdandy et al. eds., 2017).

[86] For coverage of the issues understood in U.S. scholarship as belonging to "foreign relations law" (e.g., the status of international law in domestic systems, the role of courts and Congress in foreign affairs, war powers, and issues of federalism in foreign relations), *see* Curtis A. Bradley & Jack L. Goldsmith, Foreign Relations Law: Cases and Materials (6th ed. 2017). In Latin America, in contrast, these issues are typically covered as part of constitutional law. *See*, e.g., Darío Villarroel, Derecho de los Tratados en las Constituciones de América (2014).

domestic debates in Latin America. International human rights law and institutions are constantly covered in mainstream media in Latin America, and are taught as part of the mandatory course load in most law schools in the region.

In this context, the starting point for analyzing the legal dimensions of the interaction of a Latin America state with the rest of world is not domestic law *strictu sensu*, but rather this form of "transnational" or "monist" understanding of domestic law that includes international law as an inherent part of its DNA. Public law in Latin America after the 1990s is inherently transnational, in the sense that it already is permeated, both in the texts and in judicial practice, by international law—and continues to be permeated constantly by Inter-American adjudication.

From a Latin American perspective, the field of "foreign affairs law" seems, well, particularly *foreign*. It seems to build on the analytical premise of an effective separation between domestic and international laws that needs to be managed by courts or the legislatures, which is the exact opposite of the premise adopted by Latin American constitutions. As we have seen, much of the Inter-American human rights project consists of rejecting differing approaches to the domestic application of human rights law, and rather building a common human rights law in the region. To be sure, such a project has a distinct normative agenda and begins to raise controversy—this chapter has reviewed some of the critiques. However, it remains the default Latin American approach to the domestic application of international law, and may be at odds with the field of foreign relations law.[87]

In this sense, it is not that "foreign affairs law" has not been developed in Latin America *yet*—it is that, by starting off from a strictly national point of view, and then deciding "foreign" affairs from that national vantage point, the "foreign affairs" legal field builds on a premise that is not applicable to Latin American constitutions, which lack such a strictly national vantage point for public law, from where to look at the international.[88] In Latin American public law, looking outside, to international law, is in fact looking inside, to domestic constitutional law and looking inside, to constitutional law, necessarily means looking outside, to international law. Despite the expansion and consequent reaction to this common juridical space, such a transnational default starting point seems to be the central contribution of Latin American law to the comparative study of foreign relations law.

[87] Karen Knop argues that foreign relations law may trigger anxieties of displacement, discounting, and distortion of public international law. The Latin American approach to human rights may be an example of such anxieties. *See* Karen Knop, *Foreign Relations Law: Comparison as Invention*, ch. 3 in this volume.

[88] *But see* Alejandro Rodiles, *Executive Power in Foreign Affairs: The Case for Inventing a Mexican Foreign Relations Law*, ch. 7 in this volume (making the case for a foreign relations law in Mexico).

CHAPTER 33

FOREIGN RELATIONS LAW IN THE CONSTITUTIONS AND COURTS OF COMMONWEALTH AFRICAN COUNTRIES

ERNEST YAW AKO
AND RICHARD FRIMPONG OPPONG

I. Introduction

THIS chapter examines the laws and judicial decisions in eighteen Commonwealth African countries[1] that implicate the interaction of these individual states with the rest of the world, known as foreign relations law.[2] Using a qualitative comparative research approach, we analyze these laws mainly as reflected in national constitutions and through their interpretation and application in domestic courts. While an in-depth discussion of all eighteen countries is impossible for the purposes of this chapter, we

[1] Nineteen African countries are members of the Commonwealth, but we focus on eighteen of them in this chapter to the exclusion of South Africa. These are: Botswana, Cameroon, the Gambia, Ghana, Kenya, Lesotho, Malawi, Mauritius, Mozambique, Namibia, Nigeria, Rwanda, Seychelles, Sierra Leone, Swaziland (now the Kingdom of Eswatini), Uganda, United Republic of Tanzania, and Zambia. "The Commonwealth is a voluntary association of 53 independent and equal sovereign states," many of whom are former territories of the British Empire. *See* http://thecommonwealth.org/about-us.

[2] For the purposes of this book, Curtis Bradley notes, "The term foreign relations law is used to encompass the domestic law of each nation that governs how that nation interacts with the rest of the world." For a discussion of the meaning and scope of foreign relations law, and how it is distinct from international law, *see* Curtis A. Bradley, *What Is Foreign Relations Law*, ch. 1 in this volume.

endeavor to distill the laws and judicial decisions in a manner that is capable of reflecting a common trend in these countries.

Foreign relations law is an intriguing, yet under researched, aspect of the law in Africa in general, and Commonwealth Africa in particular. Even though many Commonwealth African countries have practiced this aspect of the law dating back to precolonial times, it may not have been labeled as such and may not have been taught as a distinct field of law in many law schools in Africa. Before the colonization of nations in Commonwealth Africa, their leaders followed certain protocols in their dealings with the leaders, communities, and even individuals of other nations states, which may be classified as belonging to the realm of foreign relations law.[3]

For instance, protocols were followed regarding trading with individuals, groups, and other states; the reception of visitors; and even the conduct of war with neighboring communities or states.[4] This pattern of dealings with other states, communities, and individuals continued during the colonial era. However, even though traditional leaders of the various communities interacted and negotiated agreements for and on behalf of their communities with the British colonial authority,[5] the British assumed the conduct of international relations on behalf of the colonized states.[6]

In the post-colonial era, these interactions with states are captured in the various constitutions and national laws. Specific organs of government are empowered to conduct this aspect of governance, which is largely reserved for the heads of state with some participation by the legislature and in rare instances by the judiciary. It is evident from the precolonial to the post-colonial context that while this branch of law was not acknowledged as such, and therefore as Curtis Bradley has noted, is akin to "the character in the Moliere play who discovers that he has been speaking prose all his life without realizing it,"[7] these Commonwealth African states have long practiced foreign relations law.

Apart from South Africa, which is discussed elsewhere in this book, there are eighteen African countries that belong to the Commonwealth. They comprise sixteen democracies[8] and two kingdoms.[9] With the exception of the United Republic of Tanzania, whose legal system is solely based on the common law tradition, the other seventeen states have a mixed legal system. Five countries have a mixed legal system of common law and customary law,[10] four others practice common law, civil law, and

[3] *See* Christian N. Okeke, *The Use of International Law in the Domestic Courts of Ghana and Nigeria*, 32 Arizona J. Int'l & Comp. L. 372, 386–387 (2015).

[4] *See* Basil Davidson, West Africa Before the Colonial Era: A History to 1850, at 26, 31 (1998).

[5] *See* Justice Modibo Ocran, *The Clash of Legal Cultures: The Treatment of Indigenous Law in Colonial and Post-Colonial Africa*, 39 Akron L. Rev. 465 (2006).

[6] *See* Okeke, *supra* note 3, at 388.

[7] *See* Bradley, *supra* note 2, at p.8.

[8] Botswana, Cameroon, the Gambia, Ghana, Kenya, Malawi, Mauritius, Mozambique, Namibia, Nigeria, Rwanda, Seychelles, Sierra Leone, Uganda, United Republic of Tanzania, and Zambia.

[9] Lesotho and Swaziland.

[10] Ghana, Malawi, Sierra Leone, Uganda, and Zambia.

customary law,[11] while three practice common law, Islamic law, and customary law.[12] Rwanda and Namibia have a mixed legal system based on civil and customary law; Mauritius has a civil and common law combination; while Mozambique's legal system comprises civil, customary, and Islamic law. It is important to note that these different legal systems influence a state's approach to foreign relations law.

In order to appreciate the different and similar approaches of states to this branch of law, we analyze the relationship between international law and the constitutions of Commonwealth African states, followed by an analysis of judicial decisions that have foreign relations implications, and we then conclude the chapter with a summary of its central message.

II. The Relationship between International Law and the Constitutions of Commonwealth African States

Internationalist Values in National Constitutions

Most constitutions of Commonwealth African states outline the values that motivate them to interact with the outside world. These values are usually expressed in the preambles to the national constitutions, the nonjusticiable provisions of the constitutions, or in provisions that relate to the duties and responsibilities of the head of state. The common theme that runs through these provisions, in more than half of the countries under review, is a desire first of all to "promote and protect the interest"[13] of their countries in their dealings with the outside world. There is, however, no express provision that such interest should be parochially placed first, that is, above and beyond the interests of all other countries in the world. Implicit in these provisions is an emphasis on cooperation and the need for mutually or multilaterally beneficial approaches to inter-state or international problems.

Quite apart from this, the national constitutions express a desire to abide by international law[14]; to resort to peaceful means to resolve disputes[15]; to strive for a just economic and social order[16]; and to adhere to the principles of regional and

[11] Botswana, Cameroon, Seychelles, and Swaziland.

[12] Kenya, Nigeria, and the Gambia.

[13] *See*, e.g., Constitution of Ghana, art. 40(a); Constitution of Nigeria, art. 19(a); Constitution of Sierra Leone, art. 10(a); and Constitution of Swaziland, art. 61(1)(a).

[14] Constitution of Gambia, art. 219(b); Constitution of Ghana, art. 40(b).

[15] Constitution of Swaziland, art. 61(1)(d); Constitution of Namibia, art. 96(b); and Constitution of Nigeria, art. 19(d).

[16] Constitution of Swaziland art. 61(1)(b); Constitution of Ghana, art. 40(b).

international organizations such as the African Union, the Commonwealth, the United Nations, and other international organizations that they have joined.[17] For instance, apart from seeking the promotion and protection of the national interest, the Constitution of Ghana states, among other things, that:

> In its dealings with other nations, the Government shall—
> (b) seek the establishment of a just and equitable international economic and social order.
> (c) promote respect for international law, treaty obligations and the settlement of international disputes by peaceful means.
> (d) adhere to the principles enshrined in or as the case may be, the aims and ideals of –
> (i) the Charter of the United Nations;
> (ii) the Charter of the Organisation of African Unity [now African Union]
> (iii) the Commonwealth
> (iv) any other international organisation of which Ghana is a member.[18]

Other countries are informed by a "policy of non-alignment"[19]; "opposed to all forms of domination, racism and other forms of oppression and exploitation"[20]; and support the "promotion of African integration and support for African unity"[21] in their dealings with other states.

A common feature of these provisions is that they reflect a historical past of most African countries. Constitutional provisions that emphasize a desire for a "just and equitable international economic and social order" and "opposition to all forms of domination and racism" respond to the past of many African states and project a future that many aspire to.

There is also a striking similarity between the values expressed in the constitutions of constitutional democracies and, for example, the Constitution of Swaziland, which is a monarchy. It states that in its dealings with other nations, the government shall:

1. promote and protect the interests of Swaziland;
2. seek the establishment of a just and equitable international economic and social order;
3. promote respect for international law, treaty obligations and the settlement of international disputes by peaceful means;
4. be opposed to all forms of domination, racism and other forms of oppression and exploitation.

[17] With the exception of Botswana, Cameroon, Kenya, Lesotho, Malawi, Mauritius, Seychelles, and Rwanda, all other Commonwealth African countries pledge commitments to various subregional, regional, and international organizations.

[18] Constitution of Ghana, art. 40.

[19] Constitution of Namibia, art. 96(a).

[20] Constitution of Swaziland, art. 61(e).

[21] Constitution of Nigeria, art. 19(b); Constitution of Ghana, art. 40(d)(ii).

It also states that "Swaziland shall actively participate in international and regional organisations that stand for peace and for the well-being and progress of humanity."[22]

These provisions in the Swaziland Constitution are similar to those in constitutions of constitutional democracies such as Ghana, Namibia, and Nigeria. The absence of such provisions in the constitutions of other democratic Commonwealth African countries suggests two things. First, it is not only the constitutions of monarchial governments that may lack provisions spelling out the values that inform the relationship with other states. Second, the constitutions of monarchical governments may in fact express values that are similar to those expressed in the constitutions of democracies.

Governance System and Allocation of Foreign Relations Authority

An important aspect of the constitutions of Commonwealth African states that is a catalyst for interaction with other states is the allocation of power among the various organs of government, especially in respect of the ratification and domestication of international treaties. The executive branch, legislature, and judiciary have varied roles in these countries in making international law part of their legal systems. In most countries, the executive is the only organ of state entrusted with the power to negotiate and enter into treaties with other states.[23] Some entrust power in the hands of the executive and the legislature to enter into treaties on behalf of the state,[24] while others delegate power to all three organs of government to conclude international treaties, for and on behalf of the state.[25]

For the legal systems that entrust treaty-making power in the hands of the executive only, the legislature is usually required to perform a further act of domesticating the treaty before it becomes part of the domestic legal system.[26] In rare instances, even in systems where the power to execute treaties is entrusted to the executive and the judiciary, the legislature is called upon to amend the national constitution before the treaty is ratified.[27]

The judiciary also occupies an important position in the application and interpretation of international treaties. In almost all the countries under review, the judiciary is the final arbiter in pronouncing on the meaning and application of international law. While some constitutions expressly recognize international law as part of the

[22] Constitution of Swaziland, art. 61(1) and (2).

[23] Constitution of Gambia, art. 79(1)(c); Constitution of Malawi [Amended by Act No. 6 of 1995], art. 89(1)(f); Constitution of Uganda, art. 123(1); Constitution of Zambia, art. 44(2)(d).

[24] Constitution of Rwanda, art. 189.

[25] Constitution of Cameroon, secs. 36 (1) and 47 (3).

[26] Constitution of Ghana, art. 75(2); Constitution of Nigeria, art. 12(1); and Constitution of Sierra Leone, art. 40(4)(i) and (ii).

[27] Constitution of Cameroon, sec. 44; Constitution of Rwanda, art. 145.

legal system,[28] other constitutions are silent, even though the judiciary has applied international law as a source of law or as an aid to interpreting some aspects of the national constitution.[29]

Scholars identify the monist and dualist theories as two main approaches for describing the reception and application of international law in domestic legal systems.[30] While monism is usually associated with civil law legal systems, dualism is associated with common law legal systems. However, a strict compartmentalization of countries in Commonwealth Africa into monist and dualist categories may not be an adequate way of looking at the issue. As noted above, all countries in Commonwealth Africa practice mixed legal systems, with some of them practicing a combination of civil and common law systems. Thus, a better way of looking at the approach of Commonwealth African countries to the application of international law in the domestic legal system is to examine the role of the organs of governments in presidential, parliamentary, and monarchical systems of government.

For countries that practice a presidential system of government, like Ghana, Nigeria, and Gambia, the power to negotiate and execute treaties on behalf of their countries lies in the domain of the executive while domestication is reserved for the legislature. Where the power to negotiate and execute treaties is not restricted to the executive only, in countries such as Rwanda, the legal system is civil law. Thus, for presidential systems that have a predominantly common law legal system, the executive is entrusted with negotiating and executing treaties, while presidential systems with a predominantly civil law system adopt a monist approach toward international law.[31] For the countries that practice the parliamentary system of government, the constitution requires the involvement of both the executive and the legislature in international lawmaking. In monarchical governments, the monarch and parliament are involved in the process of negotiating and executing international treaties for and on behalf of the state.[32]

Even though there is no clear reason assigned for the approaches adopted in the various constitutions, one explanation may be that those countries that restrict the negotiation of treaties to the executive are presidential systems of government, while the countries that have both the executive and legislature participate in the process of negotiation and ratification of treaties are parliamentary systems of government.

There might be benefits and disadvantages in the approaches adopted by the various countries. While strict separation of the process of negotiation and ratification of

[28] Constitution of Mozambique, art. 18(2).

[29] International law is not stated as one of the sources of law in the Ghanaian Constitution but the courts have applied international law in the determination of cases.

[30] *See* Richard Frimpong Oppong, *Re-Imaging International Law: An Examination of Recent Trends in the Reception of International Law into National Legal Systems in Africa*, 30 FORDHAM INT'L L.J. 296, 298–299 (2007).

[31] An exception to this is Kenya, which subscribes to the common law legal tradition but arguably adopts a monist system of international law.

[32] Constitution of Swaziland, art. 238(1).

treaties when limited to the executive alone may lead to inertia of domestication of treaties, it also symbolizes the fact that there are issues that should be entrusted to the executive only. On the other hand, having all three organs of government decide on the suitability of treaties before ratification allows for more certainty about what the country is entering into, but may lead to unnecessary delays because of the bureaucratic processes that accompany such an approach.

Treaty-Making in the Constitutions of Commonwealth Africa

A characteristic feature of all the constitutions of the Commonwealth states is that they contain provisions for treaty-making. These provisions outline the institutions of state that are involved in making these treaties, their specific functions, and the limitations on their powers. In most of the constitutions, the executive is assigned the power to negotiate and enter into treaties with foreign powers, while the legislature has the power to scrutinize these treaties and incorporate them into domestic legislation. The judiciary has the power, in disputes before the courts, to interpret and determine the applicability of these international agreements to domestic situations, their hierarchy in the laws of the domestic legal system, and whether or not they are superior to the constitution and other laws of the state. In some legal systems, the judiciary has to certify that the treaty is not inconsistent with the provisions in the national constitution before the executive ratifies the treaty.[33] Where a provision in the constitution is contrary to that particular international treaty, the constitution will need to be amended first before ratification of the international treaty takes place.

There are three main treaty-making approaches in Commonwealth Africa. The first approach empowers the executive, led by the president or his appointed representative, to exclusively negotiate and ratify treaties for and on behalf of the state. It is only after the treaty has been ratified that the legislature is called upon to enact the treaty that has been ratified into domestic law; before this, the treaty has no force of law in the domestic legal setting. For instance, in Ghana, the president is empowered by Article 75 of the Constitution to "execute or cause to be executed treaties, agreements or conventions . . . " in the name of the state without prior approval of parliament.[34] What this means is that without any prior consultation or involvement of the legislature, the president of Ghana can execute a bilateral or multilateral treaty binding on Ghana at the international level. For the same treaty to have binding effect in the domestic legal system, the Parliament of Ghana has two options to give effect to the law. It either has to pass an Act, in the normal course of its legislative duties, that reflects the contents of

[33] *See,* e.g., Constitution of Rwanda, art. 113; Constitution of Cameroon, sec. 44.

[34] Constitution of Ghana, art. 75(1); Constitution of Namibia, art. 32(3) (e); Constitution of Swaziland, art. 238 (1); Constitution of Zambia, art. 44 (2) (d).

the treaty or, by "a resolution of Parliament supported by the votes of more than one-half of all members of Parliament," pass the treaty into law.

The second approach vests power in both the executive and legislature to conclude international treaties for and on behalf of the state. Here, the process of negotiating and executing treaties for and on behalf of the state is the shared responsibility of both the executive and the legislature. This is evident in the Rwanda Constitution, which grants the president power to negotiate and enter into treaties on behalf of Rwanda generally. However, treaties that implicate peace, commerce, international organizations and those which commit state finances, modify provisions of laws already adopted by Parliament, or relate to the status of persons, can only be ratified after authorization by Parliament.[35]

A third approach of treaty-making in the Commonwealth, which is rare and restricted to only two countries, is the participation of all three organs of government in the negotiation and ratification of treaties. This approach of all three organs of state playing different roles to conclude treaties for the state is a feature of the Rwandan and Cameroonian Constitutions. For instance, the Constitution of Rwanda empowers the President of the Republic or his or her accredited representatives to be the body for the conduct of foreign relations[36] and to negotiate and ratify treaties on behalf of Rwanda[37] However, the constitution places important restrictions on these powers, with the legislature entitled to vote on "international treaties and agreements,"[38] while the judiciary has power to determine the constitutionality of international treaties and agreements if requested by the President of the Republic.[39] In an extreme situation, the president may resort to a referendum in order to execute a treaty "which is not inconsistent with the Constitution but has repercussions on functioning of state institutions."[40] Thus, in addition to the three organs of government, a fourth constituency that may be involved in the ratification of treaties in Rwanda is the ordinary citizen who participates through a referendum.

Similarly, the Cameroonian Constitution empowers the trio of the executive, legislature, and judiciary with various powers to make international treaties binding in the legal system of Cameroon. First, the president is empowered by the constitution to negotiate and ratify international treaties and agreements that fall outside the purview of legislative power,[41] while those treaties and international agreements that fall within the legislative power are required to be tabled before the legislature for authorization to be granted by parliament to the president before execution of the treaty can take place.[42] Meanwhile, the Constitutional Council, which is the highest judicial body in Cameroon, reserves the right to pronounce on the constitutionality of a provision in

[35] Constitution of Rwanda, art. 189. [36] Constitution of Rwanda, art. 114.

[37] *Id.*, art. 98. [38] *Id.*, art. 88. [39] *Id.*, art. 145. [40] *Id.*, art. 109.

[41] Constitution of Cameroon, sec. 43. The Constitution does not specify the list of treaties and agreements that the president is entitled to ratify on his own volition but provides in sec. 26 the list of laws that mostly have domestic implications that fall within the legislative power. Those not listed in sec. 26 are deemed to be within the powers of the president to ratify.

[42] *Id.*

a treaty and cause the ratification of the treaty to be deferred until the constitution is amended to be in sync with the treaty.[43]

On paper, all three organs of government in Rwanda and Cameroon are involved in the process of negotiating and executing treaties on behalf of the state, which appears to be the case because of their monist system of international law, but this has implications for foreign relations law. In the case of Rwanda, while all three organs of government are involved in the process of negotiating and ratifying international treaties, the president appears to have the upper hand because the constitution makes the president the "guardian" of international treaties and agreements,[44] and the president only refers matters to the legislature, judiciary, and the citizens in a referendum upon the advice of either his cabinet, the Supreme Court, the President and Speaker of Parliament, or one-fifth of members of parliament.[45] Thus, the Constitution of Rwanda grants the president the power to determine whether a treaty or international agreement is worth executing and only acts on the advice of other organs of government. In the case of Cameroon, however, the judiciary has the power to decide if a treaty or international agreement is unconstitutional without the prompting of the president and can order such treaty or agreement to be deferred until such time that the legislature amends the constitution to be compatible with such treaty or agreement.

Implementation of Treaties in Domestic Law

A contentious issue, which has engaged the attention of scholars in international law, is the implementation of treaties in domestic law once ratified by a state. There are at least two modes of implementation of treaties. The monist view is that once a state ratifies a treaty on the international plane it immediately has the force of law in the domestic legal system. The dualist view is to the effect that once a treaty is ratified by a state at the international level a further act of domestication is required, usually by that country's legislature in order for that treaty to have the force of law in the domestic legal system.

Of the eighteen constitutions of the Commonwealth African states under review, thirteen of them on their face are dualist, while the remaining five subscribe to the monist view of international law. Simply put, thirteen countries in Commonwealth Africa apply international treaties they have ratified domestically only after their respective legislatures have debated these laws and passed legislation to give effect to these international norms. Conversely, five of these countries on paper appear to embrace international law and make it part of their laws once the state ratifies an international treaty. Even in these five countries that adopt the so-called monist approach, international law does not automatically become part of the national law unless such law is either passed into domestic legislation or published. Thus, the effect

[43] *Id.*, sec. 44. [44] Constitution of Rwanda, art. 98.

[45] Constitution of Rwanda, arts. 109, 113, 145.

of this is that even though the constitution specifies that once ratified, international law becomes part of the domestic legal system, absent publication in a national gazette or enactment into a local legislation such international law is of no effect and a party to litigation before the domestic courts cannot rely on it.

While on paper it is not clear which theory, the monist or dualist, is more beneficial, in practice the choice of theory could have important implications for foreign relations law. For dualist countries like Ghana, the Constitution empowers the president to "execute or cause to be executed treaties, agreements or conventions in the name of Ghana."[46] The Constitution further states that such treaties, agreements, or conventions could either be domesticated by an "Act of Parliament or a resolution of Parliament supported by the votes of more than one-half of all the members of Parliament."[47] The implications of this provision in the Constitution of Ghana, which is repeated in other constitutions of Commonwealth African states,[48] are twofold. First, the provision does not specify whether there is a difference between the words, "treaties, agreements or conventions," or whether it uses these three words interchangeably. Second, it is not clear whether some international agreements are exempted from this provision.

Countries like Kenya that practice the monist system are also not spared the controversy surrounding the implementation of international treaties in the domestic system. While the Constitution of Kenya states that "any treaty or convention ratified by Kenya shall form part of the law of Kenya under this Constitution,"[49] there is no provision in the Constitution that distinguishes treaties, agreements, or conventions that the president can ratify on his own accord without recourse to parliament and those that require parliamentary approval to become part of the laws of Kenya.[50]

The examples above, from countries that either practice the dualist or monist system, suggest that the theory that underpins a country's treaty implementation may not be as important as the constitutional arrangement for making agreements. An example of this is the provision in the Constitution of Swaziland, which despite leaning toward a dualist approach to the implementation of international treaties, provides that parliamentary approval is not required in all circumstances to make an international agreement part of the domestic law of Swaziland. It states that an Act of Parliament or a resolution of Parliament is not required "where the agreement is of a

[46] Constitution of Ghana, art. 75(1).

[47] *Id.*, art. 75(2)(a) and (b).

[48] Constitution of Sierra Leone, art. 40(4)(h), (i), and (ii); Constitution of Swaziland, art. 238(1) and (2); Constitution of Tanzania, art. 63(3)(e); Constitution of Namibia, arts. 32(e), 63(2)(d) and (e).

[49] Constitution of Kenya, art. 2(6). *See generally* Archibold Ombongi Nyarango, *A Jigsaw Puzzle or a Map? The Role of Treaties under Kenya's Constitution*, 62 J. AFR. L. 25 (2018); Nicholas Wasonga Orago, *The 2010 Kenyan Constitution and the Hierarchical Place of International Law in the Kenyan Domestic Legal System: A Comparative Perspective*, 13 AFR. HUM. RTS. L. J. 415 (2010).

[50] *But see* Treaty Making and Ratification Act No. 45 of 2012 Revised Edition 2014 [2012] that lays down the procedure for treaty-making and ratification, and which attempts in art. 3(4)(a) and (b) to afford the executive an opportunity to enter into bilateral agreements.

technical, administrative or executive nature or is an agreement which does not require ratification or accession."[51] The import of this provision is that the executive can enter into some agreements that will not require parliamentary approval, a feature that could be adopted by both monist and dualist legal systems.

However, a critical look at the constitutions of Commonwealth African states reveals the use of similar phrases, sentences, and provisions relating to treaty-making and foreign relations. One possible explanation for this trend is that "the post-independence constitutions in Africa were the result of agreements reached at independence conferences which followed nationalist campaigns for independence.... The text of the constitutions bequeathed to the new states followed colonial models developed by the various colonial powers for newly independent states."[52]

While this assertion is true of some constitutions, many African countries have since independence enacted new constitutions on three or four occasions.[53] Thus, the similarity in the provisions suggests, apart from retention of colonial remnants, a borrowing from other constitutions that existed prior to enacting their own constitutions. Robert Seidman is therefore right that the constitution makers in Africa are prone to copying "sentences, paragraphs, whole sections and chapters... from one constitution to the next."[54] The effect of this borrowing of constitutional provisions among Commonwealth African states by constitutional drafters has potentially deprived many constitutions of the opportunity to rethink some of these issues relating to foreign relations law.

Status of International Law in the Hierarchy of Domestic Law

In Commonwealth African countries, three approaches to the domestic status of international law are discernible. The first involves constitutions that state clearly that international law is part of the laws of the country and identify the hierarchy of laws in the domestic legal system in relation to international law.[55] A distinguishing feature of this category is that once ratified and domesticated, international law is deemed to be part of the national law. After gaining recognition as part of national law

[51] Constitution of Swaziland, art. 238(3).

[52] M. Ndulo, *Constitution-Making in Africa: Assessing Both the Process and the Content*, 21 PUB. ADMIN. DEV. 1–1, 113 (2001).

[53] These include Ghana, Nigeria, and Uganda.

[54] Robert B. Seidman, *Perspectives on Constitution-making: Independence Constitutions of Namibia and South Africa*, 3 LESOTHO L.J. 45, 56 (1987).

[55] Constitution of Kenya, art. 2(5); Constitution of Mozambique, art. 18(1). This is different from constitutions that state that as part of their foreign policy objectives they will promote respect for "international law and treaty obligations," like the Constitution of Zimbabwe, art. 12(1), and the Constitution of Uganda, sec. XXVIII under the "national objectives and directive principles of state policy."

it may be recognized as being of equal status to ordinary legislation but inferior to the national constitution.[56]

Other constitutions are ambiguous and do not state the relationship between international law and the national constitution. These constitutional provisions simply state that international law is part of the laws of the state but do not state its hierarchy in the list of laws in the legal system. The effect is that the status of international law is not clear.

Still other constitutions are silent on the status of international law in relation to the national constitution. An example is the Constitution of Ghana, which does not state that international law is part of the sources of laws of Ghana and also fails to state the hierarchy of international law in the legal system and whether it should be applied in disputes in the domestic courts. Despite this lacuna, scholars generally agree that international law forms part of the laws of Ghana, and this is vindicated by its application by the judiciary in domestic court cases.[57]

Treatment of Customary International Law and General Principles

The Constitution of Malawi is the only constitution of the eighteen Commonwealth African states being reviewed here that explicitly mentions customary international law as a source of law. It states that "Customary International Law, unless inconsistent with this Constitution or an Act of Parliament, shall form part of the law of the Republic."[58] The effect of this provision is that even customary international law that is nonderogable is subordinated to the constitution and ordinary legislation in Malawi. The constitutions of Kenya, Namibia, and Mozambique state that general principles of international law form part of the laws of their domestic legal systems.

While the constitutions generally state that the norms, rules, or principles of international law shall form part of domestic legislation, they do not mention the hierarchy and manner of application of this source of law in domestic disputes. Thus, the status of customary international law and general principles of law in these national constitutions is unclear.

III. Commonwealth African National Courts and Foreign Relations Law

This section of the chapter examines the jurisprudence of Commonwealth African courts when issues arise concerning the domestic distribution of foreign relations

[56] Constitution of Mozambique, art. 18(2).

[57] Emmanuel Yaw Benneh, *The Sources of Public International Law and Their Applicability to the Domestic Law in Ghana*, 26 U. Ghana L.J. 67 (2013).

[58] Constitution of Malawi, art. 211(3).

authority. The central question is the extent to which courts in Commonwealth Africa are prepared to intervene or judicially review matters that may be deemed as pertaining to foreign relations.

As a preliminary matter, none of the constitutions in the countries under study grants their courts any express role in matters of foreign relations. In this respect, the situation is not different from what pertains in other legal systems. However, the jurisdiction often reserved exclusively for the Supreme Courts or Constitutional Courts to review executive actions and domestic legislation sometimes allows the courts to confront issues that may fall within the domain of foreign relations.

There are relatively few cases from the countries under study dealing with such issues.[59] The dominance of the executive branch in these legal systems, the underdeveloped nature of public law litigation, and the application of doctrines such as the "political question" doctrine[60] and act of state doctrine (which render certain matters nonjusticiable) are some of the reasons that can be proffered for this state of affairs.

The few cases discussed in this part provide some insights into the likely approaches of the courts when confronted with issues of foreign relations. The Ghanaian case of *Margaret Banful v. Attorney General*[61] involved an agreement between the government of Ghana and the United States of America, under which two former Guantánamo Bay detainees were transferred to and settled in Ghana. The plaintiffs contended that such an agreement fell within the scope of Article 75 of the Constitution of Ghana, which requires parliamentary approval of treaties, and therefore the president was required to bring the said agreement to Parliament for ratification. In the view of the plaintiffs, the failure to do so rendered the agreement unconstitutional. The defendants responded that the agreement at issue was "not the type of agreement contemplated by article 75" and that Article 75 only "covers treaties, agreements and conventions in more solemn form than mere diplomatic notes." The defendants cited examples of this practice from the jurisprudence of the courts of the United States.

The Supreme Court of Ghana acknowledged that there was a distinction in the United States between agreements executed by the president without the approval of Congress and others that required the approval of Congress. It held, however, that a similar case could not be made in Ghana because the Constitution of Ghana did not distinguish between various types of agreements. Accordingly, the majority held that the agreement in question was unconstitutional.[62]

[59] One fertile area for such issues that is not examined in this chapter is the law on sovereign, state, and diplomatic immunity. For a discussion, *see* RICHARD FRIMPONG OPPONG, PRIVATE INTERNATIONAL LAW IN COMMONWEALTH AFRICA 112–125 (2013).

[60] Centre for Health Human Rights & Development v. Attorney General (Constitutional Petition No. 16 of 2011) [2012] UGCC 4 (5 June 2012). This case, however, did not raise an issue of foreign relations law.

[61] Mrs. Margaret Banful & Henry Nana Boakye v. The Attorney-General & The Ministry of Interior, Writ number J1/7/2016 (June 22, 2017).

[62] *Id.*

This decision is remarkable given the extent to which the Supreme Court was prepared to intervene to ensure that the dictates of the Ghanaian Constitution are adhered to. First, the defendants' argument that the documents exchanged between the U.S. and Ghanaian governments that formed the basis of the relocation where "purely administrative and confidential in nature" and hence should not be disclosed was rejected by the court after holding an in-camera hearing to review the documents. This is an important ruling, which helped the plaintiffs to develop their case.[63] More importantly, the ability of citizens to access such governmental documents is important to ultimately holding the government accountable in its foreign relations. This is especially important in a country such as Ghana, where the scope of the right or freedom to information is ill-defined. The Constitution of Ghana provides for the right to information,[64] and the High Court has also held that "the individual does not need a Freedom of Information Act to enjoy the right to information in Ghana."[65] However, in the absence of such an Act, accessing government documents is a significant challenge. The willingness of the court to order access on such a controversial subject is thus commendable.

Second, the court rejected the international law argument that "there is no general legal obligation for States to keep themselves informed of legislative and constitutional developments in other States which are or may become important for the international relations of these States."[66] Rather, the court was emphatic that foreign states are "duty bound to conduct the necessary due diligence when entering into international agreements into international agreements with Ghana to ensure that such agreements are in consonance with our Constitution, and, therefore, enforceable." This decision not only appears to depart from an international law principle, but also appears to impose an obligation on states entering into agreements with the government of Ghana.

While the above jurisprudence is commendable, the majority of the Supreme Court appears to have read into Article 75 an obligation to submit *all* agreements for domestic ratification. In the words of the court, "the arrangement, as unique as it is, cannot be made without parliamentary ratification." If this is accepted, then it is likely to place a significant fetter on the ability of the executive to conduct foreign relations. Some Ghanaian scholars have been concerned about the number of treaties that have been signed by the government but have not yet been domesticated. One of us has observed that "bureaucratic inertia and lacuna . . . has beset the ratification of treaties

[63] The court expressly noted that the plaintiffs relied on the documents "to bolster their additional arguments in support of their case."

[64] Constitution of Ghana, art. 21(1)(f).

[65] Lolan Kow Sagoe-Moses v. Attorney General, Suit No. HR/0027/2015 (High Court of Ghana, 2016).

[66] Land and Maritime Boundary between Cameroon and Nigeria (Cameroon v. Nigeria: Equatorial Guinea intervening), Judgment, I.C.J. Reports 2002, at 303, para. 266.

executed by Ghana."[67] While such agreements are binding under international law, the prevailing view is that such agreements do not have the force of law in Ghana.[68] Accordingly, an individual cannot base a claim or assert a right on the basis of such undomesticated agreements.

Allowing individuals to acquire rights in domestic law on the basis of treaties concluded between or among governments has been the traditional purpose of domestically implementing treaties, i.e., to give them the force of law and allow individuals to benefit from them. It has never been the law that a government cannot otherwise domestically act or give effect to an international agreement except when the agreement has been first ratified by parliament. Indeed, many such agreements are given effect in the day-to-day operations of the government, even though they have not been ratified by Parliament.[69] In the *Banful* case, the plaintiffs were not asserting any right under the agreements.

Related to the above is the issue of whether the courts can review a government's decision to ratify a treaty at the international level. The signing or ratification of treaties at the international level is a quintessential act of a sovereign state. In the Kenyan case of *National Conservative Forum v. Attorney General*,[70] one of the issues the court had to decide was whether the Kenyan government's ratification of the Rome Statute for the establishment of the International Criminal Court was constitutional.[71] The High Court of Kenya held that it had no jurisdiction to declare acts of the state with regard to the ratification of treaties unconstitutional.[72] The court reasoned that "the Court would be encroaching on the Executive function were it to purport to direct the

[67] Ernest Yaw Ako, *Rethinking the Domestication of International Treaties in Ghana*, *in* A Commitment to Law, Development and Public Policy: A Fetschrift in Honour of Nana Dr. Samuel Kwadwo Boaten Asante 602 (Richard Frimpong Oppong & Kissi Agyebeng eds., 2016).

[68] Emmanuel Yaw Benneh, *The Sources of Public International Law and Their Applicability to the Domestic Law in Ghana*, 26 U. Ghana L.J. 67 (2013); Ako, *supra* note 66, at 587–604.

[69] For example, as Justice Atuguba pointed out in his dissent in *Republic v. High Court (Commercial Division), Accra;* Ex Parte *Attorney-General (NML Capital LTD & Republic of Argentina Interested Parties)* (2013–2014) 2 SCGLR 990 [hereinafter *NML Capital*], when an Argentine military vessel came to Ghana under a military exercise agreement between Ghana and Argentina and was detained by some private creditors of Argentina, no issue of parliamentary ratification was involved. It would have been unreasonable to argue that the vessel could not land in Ghana because there had been no parliamentary approval of the military exercise agreement.

[70] Petition No. 438 of 2013, High Court of Kenya at Nairobi, Constitutional and Human Rights Division.

[71] Kenya ratified the Statute in 2005, which is five years before the 2010 Constitution of the Republic of Kenya came into force.

[72] *But see* Law Society of South Africa v. President of the Republic of South Africa [2018] ZACC 51; 2019 (3) BCLR 329 (CC), where the court held that the President's participation in the decision-making process and his own decision to suspend the operations of the SADC Tribunal were unconstitutional, unlawful, and irrational. The court also held that the President's signature of the 2014 Protocol on the Tribunal in the Southern African Development Community was unconstitutional, unlawful, and irrational. The court directed the President to withdraw his signature from the 2014 Protocol.

Executive on how to perform its foreign relations, including the signing and ratification of treaties."[73]

This approach does not mean that the courts or national constitutional laws are irrelevant when it comes to treaties. The executive is certainly under an obligation to take into account the foreign policy objectives outlined in the respective constitutions (as discussed above) in deciding which treaties to ratify or sign at the international level. The role of the court becomes important after the relevant international treaty has been domestically implemented with appropriate legislation (as in dualist states) or has become part of domestic law (as in monist states). Once that occurs, the constitutionality of the domestic law that gives effect to the international treaty can be challenged.

The preceding Ghanaian and Kenyan cases demonstrate the potential impact of national constitutional laws on the conduct of foreign relations. The same is true of cases involving statutory laws and common law principles. Thus, for example, in the Ghanaian case of *Republic v. High Court (Commercial Division), Accra;* Ex Parte *Attorney-General (NML Capital LTD & Republic of Argentina Interested Parties),*[74] the Supreme Court was emphatic that it would not lightly depart from established domestic law on granting the remedy of certiorari simply to enable the Republic of Ghana to fulfill its obligations on the international plane. In the words of the court, certiorari "is not a tool of diplomacy, but rather a remedy available in respect of fundamental errors of a court below."[75] The government had sought the remedy to quash an earlier High Court decision in order to enable the government to comply with a subsequent ruling from the International Tribunal of the Law of the Sea (ITLOS). The ITLOS decision had ordered the immediate and unconditional release of an Argentinian warship, which, while on a diplomatic mission of promoting friendship between Argentina and other states, had been restrained from leaving Ghana following an application to the High Court by certain foreign judgment creditors of Argentina.

Ultimately, the Supreme Court, obviously taking into account the potential security and diplomatic implications of the situation, held that there should be no seizures of military assets of sovereign states by Ghanaian courts in execution of foreign judgments, even if the sovereign concerned had waived its immunity.[76] In other words, the court chose to focus on the nature of the asset that had been seized rather than on the nonenforceable ITLOS decision that had ordered the warship's immediate release.[77]

[73] National Conservative Forum v. Attorney General, Petition No. 438 of 2013 (High Court of Kenya at Nairobi, Constitutional and Human Rights Division, 2013), at para. 39.

[74] (2013–2014) 2 SCGLR 990. For a review of this case, *see* George A. Sarpong & Emmanuel Yaw Benneh, *The Doctrine of Sovereign Immunity in International Law: The Ara Libertad Case (Argentina v. Ghana)*, 28 U. Ghana L.J. 138 (2015).

[75] *NML Capital, supra* note 68, at 999.

[76] *NML Capital, supra* note 68, at 1028–1029.

[77] The court held that the ITLOS decision was not binding on Ghana because Ghana had not domestically implemented the relevant provisions of the Law of the Sea Convention. On the enforcement of judgments from international courts in national courts, *see* Richard Frimpong Oppong & Lisa C. Niro, *Enforcing Judgments of International Courts in National Courts*, 5 J. Int'l Dispute Settlement

Although issues of foreign relations law are more likely to arise in litigation against governments, they can also arise in the context of litigation between private persons as could be seen from the Ugandan case of *Techno Telecom Ltd. v. Kigalo Investments Ltd.*[78] In such a situation, the procedures the court adopts with respect to the issue as well as the substance of its determination are important. The *Techno Telecom Ltd.* case raised an issue with potentially significant foreign policy implications for the government of Uganda. For the purpose of this chapter, the main issue of contention between the parties was whether Hong Kong and China are one and the same country for purposes of trademark law in Uganda.[79] The trademark at issue had been registered in Hong Kong. The court held that, for purposes of reciprocity in Uganda's trademark legislation, China and Hong Kong are the same.

While the court may be right in its conclusion on this matter, it is how the court arrived at that conclusion that raises concern. Given the sensitive nature of the relationship between Hong Kong and China, one would have expected the court to seek the opinion of the minister of foreign affairs or the attorney general. Rather, the court relied solely on the submissions of counsel and on "the information obtained from the internet." It is submitted that this is inappropriate: issues relating to the legal status of states and territories within another state can have significant foreign relations implications for the latter's government, and require sensitive judicial treatment. It would have been useful for the Ugandan court to be more rigorous in its approach. It is unclear whether the court would have adopted the same approach to dealing with the issue had it been raised in respect of China and Taiwan. Without doubt the executive is often better equipped when it comes to matters of foreign relations, and seeking its views on the issue of the relationship between Hong Kong and China would have been useful.

IV. Conclusion

A critical analysis of the domestic application of international law in Commonwealth African states suggests that there are important commonalities and differences among these states. As the analysis above shows, all of the eighteen Commonwealth African states under review express the values that guide their relationship with the outside world in their various constitutions. Typical of these values is a commitment to world

344–371 (2014); Richard Frimpong Oppong, *The High Court of Ghana Declines to Enforce an ECOWAS Court Judgment*, 25 Afr. J. Int'l & Comp. L. 127–132 (2017).

78 (Miscellaneous Cause no. 0017 OF 2011) [2011] UGCOMMC 112 (28 November 2011).

79 Sec. 45(1) of Uganda's 2010 Trademarks Act provided for the removal of a trademark registered in Uganda where on defined conditions it is established that a trademark is identical with or nearly resembles a trademark that had previously been registered in "a country or place from which the goods originate."

peace, a just economic order, and the promotion of international law and human rights. However, these values that animate their gravitation toward international law are subject to the interests of the state concerned. Interestingly, the constitutional provisions not only suggest a pattern of commonalities but reveal the borrowing of phrases and whole sentences from one constitution to the other. It is not clear what informs this pattern but it is indicative of what scholars have suggested is an armchair approach to drafting of constitutions by many African states, relying heavily on the approach of other countries without regard to the specific national interests of their own countries.

It is also a feature of these constitutions that parliaments are granted enormous powers that have the potential to hold the executive accountable in the performance of its duties in foreign affairs. Yet in practice, the absence of a legislature that is completely independent of the executive means that almost every decision that the executive desires is promptly endorsed by the parliament, which in most cases have a majority of members who belong to the political party of the executive in charge of the country.

There is also a lacuna in most national constitutions in Commonwealth Africa regarding the distinction between whether and to what extent the executive can exercise its foreign relations powers without recourse to parliamentary scrutiny. The national constitutions generally do not distinguish between agreements that require parliamentary ratification and those that do not and could be executed at the discretion of the executive. This is seen in the Guantánamo Bay case decided by the Supreme Court of Ghana. There is therefore a need for the framers of the national constitutions of Commonwealth Africa to take account of this distinction and provide for it in the national constitutions. It is also the duty of the judiciary, as exemplified in the Kenyan Supreme Court case, to put on the hat of foreign relations law and attempt to segregate treaties and other agreements into categories that require parliamentary ratification and those that do not. If that is done, the courts will assist in developing an area of law that is fairly old but rarely distinguished and discussed.

CHAPTER 34

THE APPLICATION OF INTERNATIONAL LAW BY THE COURT OF JUSTICE OF THE EUROPEAN UNION

MARIO MENDEZ

I. Introduction

This chapter assesses key strands of the jurisprudence of the Court of Justice of the European Union (CJEU, or the Court) concerning a central dimension of foreign relations law, namely, the application of international law. Unlike the other chapters in this part of the *Handbook*, the focus is on the application of international law by an international court, itself created by a treaty, rather than by the courts of a municipal legal system. However, in its early foundational jurisprudence in the 1960s, the Court was already distancing the founding treaties of this international organization from "ordinary" international law.[1] And, with respect to the treatment of international law, excluding EU law itself, scholarship has long treated the Court like a municipal court in the sense that it is primarily addressing the same kinds of questions faced by domestic courts. These questions include, among others, whether international law, both treaties and general international law, can penetrate its legal order and under what conditions they can do so; whether binding treaties can be judicially reviewed; what conditions international law must meet to be judicially enforceable and what hierarchical status it will have; and how international law is to be interpreted.

How the CJEU deals with these and other questions pertaining to the application of international law is particularly significant. It is in effect the Supreme Court for a very

[1] For a recent careful analysis of the status of EU law, *see* Bruno de Witte, *EU Law: Is It International Law?*, *in* European Union Law (Catherine Barnard & Steve Peers eds., 2d ed. 2017).

powerful international organization, with extremely wide legislative and treaty-making powers, that is currently composed of twenty-eight member states with a combined population of over half a billion.[2] Its pronouncements can also affect how the courts in the member states might treat international law outside the field of EU law. Indeed, the Court's increasing stature in an era of a "Global Community of Courts," engaged in a transnational constitutional dialogue,[3] means that its pronouncements will likely be of influence well beyond the European Union.

This chapter is divided into three sections that seek to capture core strands of the Court's case law relating to the application of international law. The first and second sections focus on constitutional review and enforcement of treaties, and a brief third section focuses on the application of customary international law.

II. Constitutional Review of Treaties

Ex Ante Constitutional Review

Since an ex ante constitutional review of treaty-making power was first expressly included in the French Constitution of 1958, its presence in constitutional texts has spread rapidly.[4] Such a power was already included in the European Union's 1957 foundational text, the Treaty of Rome. This procedure, whereby the Court can currently be asked by a member state or the European Union's political institutions (the European Parliament, Commission, and Council) to review the compatibility of an envisaged agreement with the European Union's treaties, has given rise to over twenty opinions.[5] A few important points relating to international law have arisen that are worth highlighting.

First, the Court's initial opinion explained that the rationale for this jurisdiction is that it would forestall complications resulting from legal disputes as to the compatibility of binding EU agreements with the Treaty. The Court added that a ruling that a binding EU agreement was incompatible with the EU Treaty could not fail to provoke serious difficulties and might give rise to adverse consequences for all interested parties

[2] On the treaty-making powers, *see* Marise Cremona, *Making Treaties and Other International Agreements: The European Union*, ch. 14 in this volume, and Robert Schütze, *Foreign Affairs Federalism in the European Union*, ch. 19 in this volume.

[3] Anne Marie Slaughter, *A Global Community of Courts*, 44 HARV. INT'L L.J. 191 (2003).

[4] *See* Mario Mendez, *Constitutional Review of Treaties: Lessons for Comparative Constitutional Design and Practice*, 14 INT'L J. CONST. L. 84 (2017); *see also* Tom Ginsburg, *Comparative Foreign Relations Law: A National Constitutions Perspective*, ch. 4 in this volume, and Pierre-Hugues Verdier & Mila Versteeg, *Separation of Powers, Treaty-Making, and Treaty Withdrawal: A Global Survey*, ch. 8 in this volume.

[5] Art. 218(11) TFEU. Although labeled by the treaty text as an "opinion," they are binding. For more details, *see* Cremona, *supra* note 2.

including third countries.[6] As a result, many commentators saw *Opinion 1/75* as having confirmed that ex post review of EU agreements is possible.

Second, the ex ante review procedure can be pursued following signature of a treaty pending ratification. The Court rejected the argument that the signature of the final act embodying the Uruguay Round of Multilateral Trade Negotiations "entailed an obligation on the part of the signatories to submit them for approval of their respective authorities."[7] The argument that was rejected is sometimes thought to be grounded in Article 18 of the Vienna Convention on the Law of Treaties 1969 (VCLT). However, the obligation therein not to defeat the object and purpose of a treaty prior to its entry into force clearly does not preclude recourse to ex ante review, nor for that matter does it preclude a state from changing its mind and withdrawing its signature or consent to be bound.[8] The Court, making no mention of the VCLT, underlined that its opinion could be sought any time before the European Union's consent to be bound by the agreement is finally expressed.

Third, the ex ante review procedure can be used to contest the compatibility of an envisaged agreement with substantive provisions of the EU Treaty. On at least two occasions this has included contestation vis-à-vis the European Convention on Human Rights (ECHR),[9] and most recently led to a treaty signed with Canada on Passenger Name Record (PNR) data being held incompatible with EU data-protection standards.[10] Although this case law is not as such about applying international law, insofar as the European Union will not actually be bound by the envisaged agreements that arise, it is case law of considerable importance because it can determine the permissible substantive content of international agreements for EU purposes and whether the European Union can ratify already existing treaties.

The case law is increasingly criticized for exhibiting a marked aversion to accepting international dispute settlement mechanisms. Most recently and controversially this occurred with the Draft Accession Agreement to the ECHR,[11] notwithstanding that the European Union is now required by its own constitutional text to accede.[12] The overriding focus of *Opinion 2/13* was on preserving the autonomy of the European Union's legal order and the exclusivity of the Court's jurisdiction. There is some treaty basis to justify this focus as Article 344 TFEU provides that "Member States undertake not to submit a dispute concerning the interpretation or application of the Treaties to

[6] Opinion 1/75, EU:C:1975:145. [7] Opinion 1/94, EU:C:1994:384.

[8] On Art. 18 of the VCLT, *see* Anthony Aust, Modern Treaty Law and Practice 107–110 (3d ed. 2013).

[9] Opinion 1/04 concerned a Passenger Name Record Agreement with the United States. A request for an opinion by the Parliament was withdrawn when the Agreement was concluded notwithstanding the pending case before the Court.

[10] Opinion 1/15, EU:C:2017:592. For discussion of this opinion, which also has ramifications for similar PNR Agreements already in force with the United States and Australia, *see* Mario Mendez, *Opinion 1/15: The Court of Justice Meets PNR Data (Again!)*, 2 Eur. Papers 803 (2017).

[11] Opinion 2/13, EU:C:2014:2454. [12] Current art. 6(2) TEU.

any method of settlement other than those provided for therein."[13] But equally there are treaty provisions that can be seen to support EU participation in international dispute settlement systems.[14] The literature on *Opinion 2/13* is already vast and generally critical of the Court for having blocked, potentially indefinitely, the European Union's accession to this regional human rights system and thus the ability of the European Court of Human Rights to hold the European Union directly liable for human rights violations.[15]

Ex Post Constitutional Review

Constitutional review of already concluded treaties has rarely been expressly provided for in constitutional text. However, it has emerged in states as a matter of constitutional practice, and this is also true for the European Union. Debate as to whether ex post review of the European Union's treaty commitments would be possible began as early as 1960 and continued even in the wake of the 1975 opinion noted above (*Opinion 1/75*) in which the Court clearly committed itself to this form of review. Those against ex post review saw it as a fundamental threat to international law. It was underscored that a treaty binding in international law could not be annulled, and the possibility of annulling the internal EU act concluding the agreement was viewed as a threat to international law, with one commentator suggesting that this would lead to a catastrophic result with grave international consequences.[16] The Court first reviewed the act concluding an agreement in 1988, rejecting the challenge to it on the merits.[17] But concluding acts have since been annulled on a number of occasions with no such grave international consequences.[18] This is primarily because of devices used by the Court and the political institutions to ensure that while the relevant treaties are in force they continue to deploy their internal legal effects.[19] This offers a valuable lesson for

[13] This was also the basis for Ireland being found to have violated EU law by instituting UNCLOS dispute settlement proceedings against a member state in an area of EU competence. *See* C-459/03, *Commission v. Ireland*, EU:C:2006:345.

[14] *See* Christophe Hillion & Ramses Wessel, *The European Union and International Dispute Settlement: Mapping Principles and Conditions*, *in* The European Union and International Dispute Settlement (Marise Cremona et al. eds., 2017).

[15] *See, e.g.*, Adam Łazowski & Ramses Wessel, *When Caveats Turn into Locks: Opinion 2/13 on Accession of the European Union to the ECHR*, 16 German L.J. 179 (2015).

[16] Olivier Jacot-Guillarmod, Droit Communautaire et Droit International Public (1979).

[17] 165/87, *Commission v. Council*, EU:C:1988:458.

[18] Only one challenge concerning the content of an agreement, as opposed to the appropriate internal EU legal basis for concluding the relevant agreement, has been successful. *See* C-122/95 *Germany v. Council*, EU:C:1998:94.

[19] *See* Mario Mendez, The Legal Effects of EU Agreements: Maximalist Treaty Enforcement and Judicial Avoidance Techniques 81–82 (2013) (noting that the Court has limited the effects of its judgment so as to maintain in force measures such that the internal EU law applicability of a treaty is not affected, while the political institutions have adopted new acts to conclude the agreements with retroactive effect).

comparative foreign relations law, demonstrating that treaties can be found incompatible with constitutional rules without negatively affecting the domestic application of the treaty. Despite this lesson, there is evidence of ex post review of treaties being rejected because it is viewed as challenging international law.[20]

As a matter of international law, states and international organizations can only rely on their own law as invalidating their consent to be bound by a treaty where that consent was expressed in manifest violation of a provision of their internal law or organizational rules of fundamental importance regarding the competence to conclude treaties (VCLT 1969 and 1986, Article 46). It is unclear whether only procedural rules concerning competence to conclude treaties can be invoked, such as parliamentary approval requirements, or also substantive rules, such as fundamental rights.[21] In any event, the bar for manifest violation is set very high as the VCLT requires this to be objectively evident to any state or international organization conducting itself in accordance with the normal practice of states, and, where appropriate, of international organizations, and in good faith. The CJEU has not expressly commented on these rules. However, when it annulled the act concluding a PNR Agreement with the United States, it underscored that the European Union "cannot rely on its own law as justification for not fulfilling the Agreement."[22] This could be read as affirming Article 27 VCLT, namely, that parties cannot invoke their internal law as justifying failure to perform a treaty, and also as implicit rejection of the applicability of Article 46 VCLT to that PNR Agreement. Crucially, the Court effectively ordered the EU institutions to terminate the agreement in line with its termination clause,[23] an intrusion into foreign affairs that would be anathema in most constitutional systems; indeed, even where ex post review is possible in states, that does not mean treaties are in fact found unconstitutional,[24] much less that the executive has been required to denounce a treaty.[25]

[20] For examples from Luxembourg, Serbia, and Chile, *see* Mendez, *supra* note 4, at 99.

[21] For the view that it is only procedural rules, *see* Michael Bothe, *Article 46*, *in* The Vienna Conventions on the law of Treaties: A Commentary 1090, 1093–1094 (Olivier Corten & Pierre Klein eds., 2011). *But see* Thilo Rensmann, *Article 46*, *in* Vienna Convention on the law of Treaties: A Commentary 775, 789–790 (Oliver Dörr & Kirsten Schmalenbach eds., 2012). *See also* Hannah Woolaver, *State Engagement with Treaties: Interactions between International and Domestic Law*, ch. 24 in this volume.

[22] C-317/04, *European Parliament v. Council*, EU:C:2006:346, para. 73.

[23] On treaty termination generally, *see* Laurence R. Helfer, *Treaty Exit and Intrabranch Conflict at the Interface of International and Domestic Law*, ch. 20 in this volume, and Verdier & Versteeg, *supra* note 4.

[24] For a recent example in Ghana, *see* Helfer, *supra* note 23; Ernest Yaw Ako & Richard Frimpong Oppong, *Foreign Relations Law in the Constitutions and Courts of Commonwealth African Countries*, ch. 33 in this volume.

[25] Austria has had ex post treaty review since 1964, and it has been used without a treaty ever having been found to violate the constitution. With respect to Germany and Japan, *see* Stefan Kadelbach, *International Treaties and the German Constitution*, ch. 10 in this volume, and Hiromichi Matsuda, *International Law in Japanese Courts*, ch. 30 in this volume.

Finally, it is worth noting that challenges to EU-concluded agreements have alleged, unsuccessfully thus far, noncompliance with other international agreements and customary international law.[26]

Reviewing Member State Treaties

The Court will also review treaties concluded by its member states for their compatibility with EU law. Article 351 TFEU seeks to protect agreements concluded by member states and third countries before the European Union was created or before they acceded to the European Union. It does this by stipulating that the rights and obligations under such agreements shall not be affected by the EU Treaty. A leading scholar of this terrain has argued, however, that "the protection offered by Article 351 TFEU to the rights of third states is to a large extent illusory," pointing to several judicial techniques to preclude its application, including treating older treaties that have been amended as new treaties unprotected by Article 351.[27] Where Article 351 is applicable, member states are expressly required to "take all appropriate steps to eliminate the incompatibilities," interpreted as a duty to renegotiate or even terminate such agreements, and this has even been required where the conflict with EU law has not yet materialized.[28] It is not surprising, then, that some consider this prima facie international law friendly provision to have been somewhat neutered.[29]

Treaties concluded between member states, whether since EU membership or accession or prior, and posterior agreements with third states, do not fall within Article 351 TFEU. As concerns posterior agreements concluded with third states, the best known litigation saw a number of member states found in breach of EU law for concluding bilateral air transport agreements with the United States.[30] In the event of conflict, even potential rather than actual, both posterior agreements with third states, and agreements between member states, must give way to EU law supremacy such that member states will ordinarily be required to amend or terminate those treaties.[31]

[26] Examples include alleged breaches of WTO Agreements (C-149/96, *Portugal v. Council*, EU:C:1999:574), the ECHR (C-347/03, *ERSA*, EU:C:2005:285, C-231/04, *Confcooperative Unione Regionale della Cooperazione FVG Federagricole*, EU:C:2006:307, and C-317/04, *supra* note 22), and general international law, an Association Agreement with Morocco and UNCLOS (T-512/12, *Front Polisario v. Council*, EU:T:2015:953, appealed in C-104/16 P, *Council v. Front Polisario*, EU:C:2016:973).

[27] Jan Klabbers, The European Union in International Law 60–67 (2012).

[28] For recent valuable discussion, *see* Panos Koutrakos, EU International Relations Law 324–341 (2d ed. 2015).

[29] *See especially*, Klabbers, *supra* note 27.

[30] See Koutrakos, *supra* note 28, at 342–343.

[31] *See*, e.g., Allan Rosas, *The Status in EU Law of International Agreements Concluded by EU Member States*, 34 Fordham. Int'l L.J. 304 (2011).

In sum, review of member state treaties has given rise to significant intrusion into their foreign affairs and is the subject of heated discussion, particularly as to whether greater generosity toward international law was possible.[32]

III. Enforcing Treaties

The bulk of the case law concerning treaties that are in force ultimately involve their enforcement.[33] Before turning to the trends in this case law over time, judicial answers to some important general questions concerning treaties are discussed.

Automatic Incorporation of EU Agreements

In 1974, the Court gave its seminal *Haegeman* ruling concerning its jurisdiction over EU agreements, which profoundly shaped their enforceability.[34] A preliminary ruling was sought concerning the interpretation of an association agreement with Greece. The Court held that, as the agreement was concluded by the Council, it was "an act of one of the institutions . . . within the meaning of . . . Article [267 TFEU]" and that "[t]he provisions of the Agreement, from the coming into force thereof, form an integral part of [EU] law." The proposition that EU agreements are acts of the EU institutions and form an integral part of EU law has been repeated to this day.[35]

Essentially the *Haegeman* ruling attached the European Union to a model of "automatic treaty incorporation,"[36] whereby EU-concluded treaties will, upon their entry into force, automatically become part of EU law, and accordingly, all EU law enforcement machinery is potentially available for policing compliance. Crucially, this implied that EU agreements could possess those two central hallmarks of EU law within the legal orders of its member states, namely, direct effect and supremacy. This outcome was not preordained by the text and the advocate general felt sufficiently constrained by the reference in Article 267 TFEU to the CJEU's interpretative jurisdiction over the founding treaty and the validity and interpretation of acts of the EU institutions to rule out jurisdiction where it was not EU acts that were being interpreted or challenged. On that reading, individuals and national courts assisted by the Court

[32] *See, e.g.*, Klabbers, *supra* note 27.

[33] There is a voluminous body of case law concerning the ECHR that is not considered in this chapter. The European Union is not a party to this treaty, but the treaty has been channeled via judicially created general principles of EU law. *See* Paul Craig & Gráinne de Búrca, EU Law ch. 11 (6th ed. 2015).

[34] 181/73, *Haegeman v. Belgium*, EU:C:1974:41.

[35] *See*, most recently, C-266/16, *Western Sahara Campaign UK*, EU:C:2018:118, paras. 45 and 46.

[36] Frequently, the language used in this context is one of monism, but it is submitted that this language obscures more than clarifies the questions that still arise in any legal system where treaties automatically become part of the domestic legal order upon their entry into force.

could not be co-opted into ensuring enforcement of EU agreements vis-à-vis member state level action as contrasted with EU level action. In light of this, the recourse to textual acrobatics to assert that the agreements are themselves acts of the institutions was perhaps unsurprising, although arguably the Court could simply have invoked the unmentioned Article 216(2) TFEU, which stipulates that EU agreements are binding on the European Union's institutions and its member states.[37]

Non-EU Agreements and the Functional Succession Doctrine

Prior to the *Haegeman* ruling, the Court had been faced with a challenge to an EU measure for violating the 1947 General Agreement on Tariffs and Trade (GATT). In the *International Fruit* ruling, one of the conditions stipulated to be able to invalidate an EU act was that the European Union must be bound by the relevant international law rule.[38] This might have been thought an impossible hurdle for the GATT to surmount given that, although signed by all the member states, it predates the European Union's founding and was never signed by the European Union. However, with this ruling the functional succession doctrine was born, for the Court concluded that the European Union was indeed bound by the GATT insofar as it had assumed the powers previously exercised by the member states in areas governed by the agreement.[39] Functional succession is theoretically of great importance because it can allow for treaty enforcement vis-à-vis EU level action using EU law machinery where this would otherwise not have been possible due to the European Union not being a party. It can also potentially bolster the legal status of any such treaties in the member states insofar as the doctrines of direct effect and supremacy are applied to them. But whether any of this theoretical promise obtains depends on how the functional succession doctrine is applied in practice, which is addressed further below.

Judicially Applying Treaties: Rights, Direct Effect, and Consistent Interpretation

We have seen that in its *Haegeman* ruling, the Court concluded that EU agreements would form an integral part of EU law, and, via the earlier *International Fruit* ruling, that the European Union could be bound by agreements to which it was not a party.

[37] *See also* Giorgio Gaja, *Trends in Judicial Activism and Judicial Self-Restraint Relating to Community Agreements*, *in* THE EUROPEAN UNION AS AN ACTOR IN INTERNATIONAL RELATIONS 117, 119 (Enzo Cannizzaro ed., 2002).

[38] Joined Cases 21–24/72, *International Fruit Company*, EU:C:1972:115.

[39] For additional discussion of this doctrine, *see* Schütze, *supra* note 2.

But this did not mean that such agreements could without more be used to challenge action taken either by the European Union or at the domestic level within member states. This was first made clear with the challenges to the EU regulations in *International Fruit*, for as well as the need for international law to be binding, it was held that the relevant provision must also be capable of conferring rights. Although the Court did not use the label of direct effect, commentators viewed the test as analogous to that deployed in the relationship between EU and domestic law.[40]

As concerns EU agreements, their judicial application was not initially attached to a direct effect or rights-based test. In *Haegeman*, for example, the Court interpreted the association agreement in concluding that EU-imposed charges were compatible with it. But in the next EU agreement case, *Bresciani*, concerning charges imposed on Senegalese imports and their compatibility with the Yaoundé Convention, the Court used a rights-based analysis.[41] It held that in order to determine whether the relevant provision conferred the right to rely on it, "regard must be simultaneously paid to the spirit, the general scheme and the wording of the Convention and of the provision concerned." The language was strikingly reminiscent of that first employed in the famous *Van Gend en Loos* case when the direct effect of the Treaty of Rome first arose.[42] Some thirteen years on, the Court in *Bresciani* found a very similar provision to that at issue in *Van Gend en Loos* directly effective.

The Court has also created a *Charming Betsy*–style canon of interpretation, known as consistent interpretation, whereby secondary EU law and domestic law is interpreted compatibly with EU- and non-EU-concluded agreements without a direct effect or rights based hurdle, or even the European Union needing to be bound by the agreement.[43] This interpretive principle first emerged in a 1972 ruling when tariff agreements concluded within the GATT framework were drawn upon in interpreting the European Union's Common Customs Tariff.[44]

Questions of Hierarchy

The hierarchical status of EU agreements was not expressly addressed until a 1996 ruling asserted that they—and it was assumed by implication any treaty binding the European Union—took primacy over secondary EU legislation.[45] Some saw this

[40] *See, e.g.*, Stefan Riesenfeld, *The Doctrine of Self-executing Treaties and Community Law: A Pioneer Decision of the Court of Justice of the European Communities*, 67 AM. J. INT'L L. 504 (1973).

[41] 87/75, *Bresciani*, EU:C:1976:18.

[42] 26/62, *van Gend & Loos*, EU:C:1963:1.

[43] For detailed discussion, *see* Federico Casolari, *Giving Indirect Effect to International Law Within the EU Legal Order: The Doctrine of Consistent Interpretation*, *in* INTERNATIONAL LAW AS LAW OF THE EUROPEAN UNION (Enzo Cannizzaro et al. eds., 2012). On the *Charming Betsy* canon in the United States, *see* CURTIS A. BRADLEY, INTERNATIONAL LAW IN THE U.S. LEGAL SYSTEM 15–18 (2d ed. 2015).

[44] 92/71, *Interfood*, EU:C:1972:30.

[45] C-61/94, *Commission v. Germany*, EU:C:1996:313, para. 52.

question being answered by the language of "binding" used in Article 216(2) TFEU,[46] but clearly textually more explicit language is possible and many constitutional texts expressly refer to treaties having superiority, or taking precedence, over statutes, or that treaties are the supreme law of the land, nation, or union.[47] Even such language in the U.S. Constitution's supremacy clause has not precluded the Supreme Court from adopting the "later-in-time rule."[48] Thus, despite a constitutional text that was arguably less favorable to dispensing with the later-in-time rule, the CJEU reached an outcome more international law friendly than the U.S. Supreme Court, although perhaps unsurprisingly so given that it is an international court.

The earlier noted *Opinion 1/75* clearly indicated that the hierarchical status of EU agreements was infraconstitutional, and this was essentially confirmed by the previously considered ex post review case law. As concerns other treaties, confirmation of this infraconstitutional status came in the controversial *Kadi* litigation touched on further below.

Judicial Enforcement of Treaties Prior to 2000

The case law and academic commentary prior to the turn of the century was dominated by a narrow range of questions concerning the two core types of treaties being invoked before the Court: on the one hand, the mainly bilateral trade, cooperation, association, and partnership agreements, and on the other, GATT and World Trade Organization (WTO) Agreements.[49] It was the former types of agreements that arose in the seminal *Haegeman* and *Bresciani* rulings. The Court has taken a maximalist approach to their enforcement. This manifested itself especially in relation to direct effect and the substantive interpretation of provisions. Treaties and their provisions were held directly effective in the face of cogent arguments against this and substantial opposition by member states. The 1982 *Kupferberg* ruling was the clearest example.[50] Here, four member states protested vigorously against direct effect of a trade agreement with Portugal. Arguments were advanced against the direct effect of the fiscal discrimination prohibition at issue, but also against the capacity of that trade agreement, and a number of largely identical trade agreements, to be directly effective. They argued that the dispute resolution mechanisms in the agreements could not function properly if domestic judicial determinations of the obligations were permissible. These and other arguments were given short shrift. The Court concluded that neither the nature, nor the structure, of this trade agreement prevented traders from relying on its

[46] Though this expressly only answers the question as concerns EU-concluded agreements.

[47] *See* examples cited in MENDEZ, *supra* note 19, at 19.

[48] *See* BRADLEY, *supra* note 43, at 52–55.

[49] With the exception of the ECHR, which gave rise to a large body of literature, *see* CRAIG & DE BURCA, *supra* note 33.

[50] 104/81, *Kupferberg*, EU:C:1982:362.

provisions and that the specific provision at issue was an unconditional rule against fiscal discrimination which was directly effective. Direct effect findings followed in a range of significant instances in relation to provisions in agreements and their associated law, notwithstanding credible arguments against direct effect, not only by member states, but on occasion also by the Commission.[51]

Crucially, the Court did not shy away from taking bold approaches to the substantive interpretation of provisions in such agreements, often bearing parallels to the teleological approach taken with internal EU law, and brushing aside considerable member state opposition. To cite merely one example from this period, the Court transposed the internal EU law meaning of legal employment to the Turkey Association Agreement context in the face of opposition from the four intervening member states.[52]

As concerns the GATT, in the *International Fruit* ruling a twofold test for challenging EU action vis-à-vis international law was laid out: first, that the European Union must be bound and, second, that the relevant provision must confer rights on individuals.[53] The GATT failed to surmount this second hurdle. The Court in considering "the spirit, the general scheme and the terms of the General Agreement" concluded that it was "characterised by the great flexibility of its provisions, in particular those conferring the possibility of derogation, the measures to be taken when confronted with exceptional difficulties and the settlement of conflicts between the contracting parties." Accordingly, the provision invoked, Article XI, was not capable of conferring rights and thus could not affect the validity of the challenged EU regulations. The *International Fruit* reasoning was repeated in numerous cases between 1973 and 1995 involving challenges to either EU or member state action, and, most controversially, even when a member state sought the annulment of an EU regulation.[54]

The *International Fruit* reasoning was much criticized, with one distinguished international law scholar asserting that "[t]he Court's reasoning sinks below criticism."[55] The main strand of criticism was that a caricature of the GATT had been provided and that it was endowed with a much greater degree of legalism and much less flexibility.[56] However, critics often put forth revisionist accounts of the GATT system as being more legalistic and less flexible than was in fact the case.[57] The principled rejection of the GATT as a review criterion for EU and member state action

[51] For detailed discussion, *see* MENDEZ, *supra* note 19, ch. III.

[52] C-434/93, *Bozkurt*, EU:C:1995:168. [53] *See supra* note 38.

[54] *See* C-280/93, *Germany v. Council*, EU:C:1994:367. Many thought the *International Fruit* reasoning would not preclude a member state challenge to EU action. *See, e.g.*, Claus-Dieter Ehlermann, *Application of GATT Rules in the European Community*, *in* THE EUROPEAN COMMUNITY AND GATT 127 (Meinhard Hilf et al. eds., 1986).

[55] BENEDETTO CONFORTI, INTERNATIONAL LAW AND THE ROLE OF DOMESTIC LEGAL SYSTEMS 30 (1993). *See also* Ernst-Ulrich Petersmann, *Application of GATT by the Court of Justice of the European Communities*, 20 COMMON MKT. L. REV. 397 (1983).

[56] *See* KEES KUILWIJK, THE EUROPEAN COURT OF JUSTICE AND THE GATT DILEMMA (1996).

[57] *See, in particular*, the work of two leading GATT scholars JOHN JACKSON, WORLD TRADE AND THE LAW OF GATT (1969), and Robert Hudec, *The GATT Legal System: A Diplomat's Jurisprudence*, 4 J. WORLD TRADE L. (1970).

was, in this author's view, eminently defensible based as it was on the "rules" in practice not being sufficiently unconditional.[58]

There were exceptions to the nonjudicial applicability of the GATT. One is the previously noted consistent interpretation doctrine, whereby GATT norms could be employed as an aid to interpreting EU legislation.[59] Another was the so-called *Fediol* and *Nakajima* principles, judicial creations under which the Court would review EU measures vis-à-vis GATT rules where the EU measure referred expressly to precise GATT provisions, or where the European Union intended to implement a particular GATT obligation.[60] And, finally, judicial applicability via centralized infringement proceedings was essentially confirmed when Germany was found in non-compliance with an EU-concluded GATT-era agreement.[61]

With the entry into force of the WTO in 1995, many believed the *International Fruit* reasoning could no longer stand given the more legalized system with its bolstered dispute settlement mechanism and a strengthened safeguards regime.[62] These hopes were dashed by the *Portuguese Textiles* ruling, where the Court essentially concluded that review of EU action vis-à-vis WTO norms is only permissible where the previously noted *Fediol* and *Nakajima* principles apply.[63] The core reasoning was that the WTO's Dispute Settlement Understanding (DSU) permits, at least temporarily, alternatives other than full implementation of a ruling, including mutually agreed compensation and countermeasures, and judicial intervention would deprive the European Union of the DSU-sanctioned room for maneuver enjoyed by its trading partners.

Critics of the ruling frequently invoked Professor Jackson's view that there is an international law obligation to comply with adopted dispute settlement reports.[64] However, even if correct, this does not actually discredit the Court's reasoning, which faithfully recited DSU text that does expressly provide for negotiated compensation as at least a potential temporary alternative to full implementation of a Dispute Settlement Body (DSB) decision. On this basis, although one can certainly disagree with the rejection of judicial enforceability of WTO law within the European Union, it is difficult to contest the central premise of the Court's reasoning that EU judicial intervention would jeopardize the scope for maneuver that the DSU text provided.

[58] *See* for a detailed defense, MENDEZ, *supra* note 19, ch. IV.

[59] E.g., C-105/90, *Goldstar*, EU:C:1992:69; C-70/94, *Werner*, EU:C:1995:328; T-163/94 and T-165/94, *NTN and Koyo Seiko*, EU:T:1995:83.

[60] 70/87, *Fediol*, EU:C:1989:254; C-69/89 *Nakajima*, EU:C:1991:186.

[61] C-61/94, *Commission v. Germany*, EU:C:1996:313.

[62] *See*, e.g., Anne Peters, *The Position of International Law Within the European Community Legal Order*, 40 GERMAN Y.B. INT'L L. 9 (1997).

[63] C-149/96, *supra* note 26. On WTO review in Japan, *see* Matsuda, *supra* note 25.

[64] John Jackson, *The WTO Dispute Settlement Understanding—Misunderstandings on the Nature of the Legal Obligation*, 91 AM. J. INT'L L. 60 (1997), later developed in John Jackson, *International Law Status of WTO DS Reports: Obligation to Comply or Option to "Buy-Out"?*, 98 AM. J. INT'L L. 109 (2004). To cite just one prominent contribution relying on the Jackson argument, *see* Stefan Griller, *Judicial Enforceability of WTO Law in the European Union: Annotation to Case C-149/96, Portugal v. Council*, 3 J. INT'L ECON. L. 441 (2000).

Judicial Enforcement of Treaties Since 2000

The period since 2000 has seen the CJEU faced with a broader array of treaties, partly reflecting the growing remit of the European Union's treaty-making, but some post-2000 developments concerning the agreements that dominated the pre-2000 era will first be highlighted. In relation to the WTO, the dominant issue following the *Portuguese Textiles* case was how the Court would respond where a DSB decision had found EU legislation WTO-incompatible.[65] In the 2005 *Van Parys* ruling, it rejected review in such instances by reinforcing its *Portuguese Textiles* reasoning.[66] The Court now added that unresolved disputes remained on the DSB agenda and that possibilities other than compensation existed in the post-implementation period, notably suspension of concessions and mutually satisfactory solutions, and that WTO dispute settlement procedures were provided for where there was disagreement over the WTO compatibility of compliance measures. Again some criticism drew on Jackson's argument that there is an international law obligation to comply with DSB decisions.[67] But critics usually did not acknowledge Jackson's concession that the DSU afforded a measure of temporary additional time "during which compensation and suspension can fend off some of the pressures of full compliance."[68] Post-DSB decision review is ultimately about removing that additional time, which the CJEU has been unwilling to countenance. It was thus arguably unsurprising that the damages actions of exporters subjected to DSB authorized cross-sector retaliation due to EU noncompliance with a DSB ruling was rejected, as this would be another way to remove the European Union's scope for maneuver.[69]

Another major WTO issue concerned the application of the *Fediol* and *Nakajima* principles. But through to at least 2011, the only occasion in which *Fediol* type review appeared to have been conducted was in *Fediol* itself. And the impact of *Nakajima* is contestable in that the oft-cited example of its use in the WTO era, the 2003 *Petrotub* ruling,[70] is arguably but a particular species of consistent interpretation.[71] The consistent interpretation doctrine has become increasingly significant. A prominent example involved provisions of the EU Anti-Dumping and Anti-Subsidy Regulations being expressly interpreted in line with their counterparts in the WTO's Anti-Dumping

[65] Even some supporting the *Portuguese Textiles* ruling considered that a different outcome would be warranted where a litigant had a DSB decision in support. *See*, e.g., Piet Eeckhout, *Does Europe's Constitution Stop at the Water's Edge? Law and Policy of External Relations*, Fifth Walter van Gerven Lecture, 2005.

[66] C-377/02, *Van Parys*, EU:C:2005:121.

[67] E.g., Nikolaos Lavranos, *The Chiquita and Van Parys Judgments: An Exception to the Rule of Law*, 32 LEG. ISSUES ECON. INTEG. 449 (2005).

[68] Jackson, *International Law Status*, *supra* note 64, at 122.

[69] C-120 & 121/06 P, *FIAMM v. Council and Commission*, EU:C:2008:476. For critical analysis, *see* ANNE THIES, INTERNATIONAL TRADE DISPUTES AND EU LIABILITY (2013).

[70] C-76/00 P, *Petrotub*, EU:C:2003:4.

[71] *See* Pieter Jan Kuijper & Marco Bronckers, *WTO Law in the European Court of Justice*, 42 COMMON MKT. L. REV. 1313, 1326–1328 (2005). Recent attempts to invoke the *Nakajima* principle were unsuccessful. *See* C-306/13 *LVP*, EU:C:2014:2465, and C-21/14 P *Commission v. Rusal*, EU:C:2015:494.

Agreement and Subsidies and Countervailing Measures Agreement.[72] In addition, there is mounting evidence that the WTO is having a judicially determined, but unacknowledged, impact on the interpretation of EU norms.[73]

Since 2000 there has been much litigation on the primarily bilateral, trade, association, cooperation, and partnership agreements, including many more centralized infringement rulings against member states than prior to 2000.[74] Although there have been numerous new direct effect findings, it is primarily the substantive interpretation accorded particular provisions that has been controversial. The bold stance on the agreements with North African countries and Turkey has continued apace, but of perhaps even greater interest were certain cases concerning the Europe agreements with Central and Eastern European Countries. In particular, the Court transposed its *Bosman* ruling, interpreting EU law fundamental freedoms to interdict nationality restrictions on EU nationals by sporting federations, to provisions on non-discrimination as regards working conditions in Europe agreements.[75] This was then transposed to an agreement devoid of the accession-oriented dimension characterizing the Europe Agreements: the Russian Partnership and Cooperation Agreement.[76]

A final crucial point is that at least through 2011, no EU measure was annulled exclusively due to breaching of a trade, association, cooperation, or partnership agreement. Bold enforcement of such agreements has in practice been unleashed vis-à-vis the member states. And the vast bulk of this case law has involved a small number of different agreements, usually with states that the European Union has developed especially close relations, and sometimes they are a precursor to accession. Only a few different types of provisions have arisen that are mainly of the non-discrimination or standstill variety and often with similarly worded directly effective counterparts in EU law. Accordingly, this has been ripe terrain for a receptive judicial stance.

In the post-2000 period, different types of agreements arose and the Court initially appeared generous. The 2001 *Biotech* ruling seemed to reject a direct effect or rights conferral threshold for legality review.[77] The Netherlands sought the annulment of the Biotech Directive, alleging that it breached the EU-concluded Biodiversity Convention. It was held that even if the Convention contained provisions that did not have direct effect, in the sense that they did not create rights which individuals could rely on directly before the courts, that did not preclude reviewing compliance with the European Union's obligations under the Convention. This receptiveness to enforcing EU agreements even vis-à-vis EU legislative action was bolstered in the *IATA* case involving a challenge to an EU regulation that allegedly breached the Montreal Convention on the Unification of Certain Rules for International Carriage by Air.[78]

72 T-45/06, *Reliance Industries*, EU:T:2008:398.

73 *See* Marco Bronckers, *From "Direct Effect" to "Muted Dialogue": Recent Developments in the European Courts' Case Law on the WTO and Beyond*, 11 J. INT'L ECON. L. 885 (2008).

74 For detailed coverage of case law through 2011, *see* MENDEZ, *supra* note 19, ch. III.

75 C-438/00, *Kolpak*, EU:C:2003:255.

76 C-265/03, *Simutenkov*, EU:C:2005:213.

77 C-377/98, *Netherlands v. Parliament and Council*, EU:C:2001:523.

78 C-344/04, *IATA*, EU:C:2006:10.

The Court concluded in a single sentence that this EU agreement's provisions were among the rules in the light of which it reviewed EU Acts since neither the nature nor the broad logic of the Convention precluded this, and the invoked provisions appeared unconditional and sufficiently precise. This conclusion was not preceded by any actual analysis of the Convention and its provisions, and, crucially, the language of direct effect and individual rights was wholly absent. The case seemed based on a presumption of judicial enforceability of EU agreements, an interpretation bolstered via extra-judicial writings of one of the judges.[79]

The early 2000s also saw the Court faced with its first non-trade-related agreement, the Athens Protocol to the Convention for the Protection of the Mediterranean Sea against Pollution (the Barcelona Convention), in a challenge to member state level action.[80] The French *Cour de Cassation* asked whether a provision of that Protocol was directly effective and whether it prohibited certain discharges. In a mere two sentences of direct textual analysis of the provision, the Court held that it clearly, precisely, and unconditionally laid down a member state obligation to subject discharges to prior authorization and that this was in no way diminished by the domestic authority's discretion in issuing authorizations. This conclusion was bolstered by reference to the purpose and nature of the Protocol, with the Court also asserting that direct effect would only serve its purpose and reflect its nature, which is intended to prevent pollution resulting from public authorities failing to act.

The picture in early 2006 following the aforementioned rulings suggested that the Court had built a generous construct for enforcing treaties, the GATT and WTO justifiably treated differently. In 2008, a number of rulings challenged this reading, and case law since has made it even harder to sustain. The *Intertanko* ruling dealt with a challenge to the Ship Source Pollution Directive for allegedly breaching the MARPOL Convention, to which all the member states are party but not the European Union, and the EU-concluded UN Convention on the Law of the Sea (UNCLOS).[81] On the MARPOL Convention, it was held that there had not been a full transfer of member states' powers to the European Union and accordingly review vis-à-vis its provisions would not be possible.[82] The *Intertanko* ruling has been viewed as manifesting a restrictive interpretation of the functional succession doctrine.[83] As to UNCLOS, it was concluded that its nature and broad logic precluded its use for validity review. The Court reasoned that UNCLOS does not in principle grant independent rights and freedoms to individuals, but rather rights, freedoms, and obligations that attach to the flag state. To the extent that any UNCLOS provisions appeared to attach rights to ships,

[79] *See* Koen Lenaerts & Tim Corthaut, *Of Birds and Hedges: The Role of Primacy in Invoking Norms of EU Law*, 31 Eur. L. Rev. 287, 299 (2006).

[80] C-213/03, *Pêcheurs de l'Etang de Berre v. EDF*, EU:C:2004:464. In related infringement proceedings, France was found to have breached its obligations under the Barcelona Convention and the Mediterranean Sea Protocol. *See* C-239/03, *Commission v. France*, EU:C:2004:598.

[81] C-308/06, *Intertanko*, EU:C:2008:312.

[82] This was tempered by a consistent interpretation obligation.

[83] For criticism, *see* Piet Eeckhout, EU External Relations Law 398–400 (2d ed. 2011).

it did not follow that such rights were conferred on the individuals linked to those ships. The Court concluded, "UNCLOS does not establish rules intended to apply directly and immediately to individuals and to confer upon them rights or freedoms capable of being relied upon against States." The individual rights conceptualization suggested a more demanding threshold for review than in the earlier *Biotech* and *IATA* ruling, and the application of that conceptualization to the facts was an unconvincing attempt to paint a picture of an inter-state treaty far removed from the rights of the individual.

The seminal *Kadi* ruling annulling EU regulations implementing UN Security Council Resolutions under Chapter VII due to fundamental rights violations appeared only some months after *Intertanko*.[84] The European Union is not a party to the UN Charter, but the Charter itself expressly stipulates in Article 103 that it prevails over other international treaties. Although mainly praised for challenging the anticonstitutionalism apparent in the United Nations' terrorist listing system,[85] the ruling was also critiqued for representing a sharp departure from the European Union's traditional embrace of international law.[86] It can, however, also be read as upholding international law in the form of international human rights standards.[87]

The 2011 *Air Transport Association of America (ATAA)* case involved a challenge to the European Union's emissions trading scheme invoking both EU- and non-EU-concluded agreements.[88] The European Union was held not to have succeeded to the Chicago Convention obligations, a Convention to which all member states are parties, despite the European Union having legislative competence in the air transport field and having legislated extensively in the fields covered by this Convention. The ruling is viewed as further narrowing the remit of the functional succession doctrine and thus shielding the European Union from direct review vis-à-vis non-EU agreements.[89] As concerns the EU agreements, a Kyoto Protocol provision requiring the contracting parties to pursue limitations or reduction of certain emissions through the International Civil Aviation Organization was found not to be unconditional or sufficiently precise. An Air Transport Agreement with the United States was allowed to be invoked to challenge EU Acts, the Court seemingly persuaded by the presence of specific provisions designed to confer rights directly on airlines and other provisions designed to impose obligations on them. But, as in previous instances where agreements surmounted the invocability thresholds for challenging EU action, such as the *Biotech* and *IATA* cases, the EU measure emerged unscathed from review.

[84] C-402/05 P and C-415/05 P, *Kadi*, EU:C:2008:461.

[85] *See*, e.g., EECKHOUT, *supra* note 83, at 420–421.

[86] *See* Gráinne de Búrca, *The European Court of Justice and the International Legal Order after Kadi*, 51 HARV. INT'L L.J. 1 (2010).

[87] *See*, e.g., EECKHOUT, *supra* note 83.

[88] C-366/10, *ATAA*, EU:C:2011:864.

[89] *See* Jan Wouters et al., *Worlds Apart? Comparing the Approaches of the European Court of Justice and the EU Legislature to International Law*, *in* THE EUROPEAN COURT OF JUSTICE AND EXTERNAL RELATIONS LAW (Marise Cremona & Anne Thies eds., 2014).

Another striking ruling emerged in 2014 when the CJEU held that the EU-concluded UN Convention on the Rights of Persons with Disabilities could not be used to challenge EU action.[90] The Convention was considered "programmatic," as its provisions were subject in their implementation or effects to the adoption of subsequent measures by the Contracting Parties and thus not unconditional and sufficiently precise to be directly effective. The key Convention provision invoked to support this was the general implementation clause (Article 4(1)(a)), which numerous treaties contain a variant of, providing for the "States Parties . . . [t]o adopt all appropriate legislative, administrative and other measures for the implementation of the rights recognized in the . . . Convention." Thus, by 2014, another multilateral treaty had been held unable to form a validity review criterion for EU action, with arguably even thinner reasoning than in earlier cases, and surprisingly so given that the treaty pertains to human rights.

More recently, a 2015 ruling placed the European Union on a collision course with its obligations under a EU-concluded UN regional environmental treaty.[91] An EU regulation was successfully challenged before the General Court for noncompliance with the key access to justice provision of the Aarhus Convention (Article 9(3)). This was overturned by the Court, which relied on an earlier ruling rejecting the direct effect of the relevant provision.[92] The Court also rejected the applicability of the *Fediol* and *Nakajima* principles outside the WTO context.[93] The irony is that the access to justice provision of a treaty, a central pillar of which is precisely about access to justice, was held insufficiently unconditional and precise to allow for review of EU action. The clash with the Aarhus Convention Compliance Committee materialized when it adopted its findings in a complaint about the European Union's standing rules and found a failure to comply with Aarhus Convention obligations.[94]

IV. Customary International Law

In contrast to many other constitutional texts,[95] including those of founding member states such as Germany and Italy, the European Union's text was not born with any

[90] C-363/12, *Z*, EU:C:2014:159.

[91] C-401/12P to C-403/12 P, *Council v. Vereniging Milieudefensie and Stichting Stop Luchtverontreiniging Utrecht*, EU:C:2015:4.

[92] C-240/09, *Lesoochranárske zoskupenie VLK*, EU:C:2011:125.

[93] For detailed commentary, *see* Szilárd Gáspár-Szilágyi, *The Relationship Between EU Law and International Agreements: Restricting the Application of the Fediol and Nakajima Exceptions in Vereniging Milieudefensie*, 52(4) Common Mkt. L. Rev. 1059 (2015).

[94] Communication ACCC/C/2008/32. In contrast, the CJEU has been bold when member state level action is challenged. For example, in C-240/09, *supra* note 92, the court imposed a powerful obligation upon member state courts to interpret domestic law compatibly with Aarhus Convention obligations.

[95] *See generally* Ginsburg, *supra* note 4.

express references to customary international law.[96] The Court has nonetheless used customary international law in various ways. A well-known classification distinguished between four main (though potentially overlapping) usages.[97] First, to demarcate the limits of member state or EU jurisdiction and powers, this already being apparent in case law from the 1970s, but most famously so in the 1992 *Poulsen* ruling.[98] *Poulsen* concerned an EU regulation on fishery resources conservation and the ruling opened with the observation that the European Union "must respect international law in the exercise of its powers and that, consequently. . . . [the relevant provision in the Regulation] . . . must be interpreted, and its scope limited, in the light of the relevant rules of the international law of the sea." In interpreting the EU regulation, a range of treaties on the law of the sea were drawn upon insofar as they reflected customary international law.

Second, customary international law rules of treaty law are regularly used in the context of interpreting both EU and non-EU agreements. The 1969 VCLT applies only to states and the 1986 VCLT between states and international organizations or between international organizations has not entered into force (and the European Union is not a party), but the Court regularly relies on them insofar as they reflect customary international law.[99] The Court has been expressly invoking the VCLT since a 1991 ruling interpreting the Draft European Economic Area Agreement first invoked the general rules of interpretation in Article 31.[100] A controversial instance occurred when the Court proceeded to apply the *pacta tertiis* rule, as consolidated in Article 34 VCLT, to interpret the Israel Association Agreement such that products originating in the West Bank would not fall within its territorial scope.[101] It has been argued that the Court stretched "the scope of the *pacta tertiis* rule . . . to refrain from a politically more sensitive pronouncement on the limits of the notion of territory of Israel."[102]

Third, customary international law has been used in a gap-filling capacity as illustrated in *Factortame*, where it was held that in the absence of specific EU rules on vessel registration "it is for the Member States to determine, in accordance with the

[96] *See* Paul Gragl, *The Silence of the Treaties: General International Law and the European Union*, 57 GERMAN Y.B. INT'L L. (2014) (acknowledging the inclusion by the Lisbon Treaty of Arts. 3(5) and 21 TEU).

[97] *See* Jan Wouters & Dries van Eeckhoutte, *Enforcement of Customary International Law through European Community Law*, *in* DIRECT EFFECT: RETHINKING A CLASSIC OF EC LEGAL DOCTRINE 183 (Jolande Prinssen & Annette Schrauwen eds., 2002).

[98] C-286/90, *Poulsen*, EU:C:1992:453. *See*, more recently, C-364/10, *Hungary v. Slovakia*, EU:C:2012:630.

[99] *See* Pieter-Jan Kuijper, *The European Courts and the Law of Treaties: The Continuing Story*, *in* THE LAW OF TREATIES BEYOND THE VIENNA CONVENTION 256 (Enzo Cannizzaro ed., 2011).

[100] Opinion 1/91, EU:C:1991:490.

[101] C-386/08, *Brita*, EU:C:2010:91. *See also Front Polisario*, *supra* note 26.

[102] Helmut Philipp Aust, Alejandro Rodiles, & Peter Staubach, *Unity or Uniformity? Domestic Courts and Treaty Interpretation*, 27 LEIDEN J. INT'L L. 75, 103 (2014).

general rules of international law, the conditions which must be fulfilled in order for a vessel to be registered."[103]

Fourth, and most controversially, custom has been used to challenge EU action, including the conclusion of EU agreements.[104] Express judicial recognition of this possibility came in the 1998 *Racke* ruling addressing the validity of a regulation suspending trade concessions under a Cooperation Agreement with Yugoslavia in light of the *rebus sic stantibus* rule in Article 62 VCLT (the European Union having suspended the agreement due to the breakup of Yugoslavia).[105] The ruling opened with confirmation that Article 62 reflects customary international law, and that these rules concerning the termination and suspension of treaty relations by reason of a fundamental change of circumstances bind the European Union and form part of the EU legal order. The Court held, however, that because of the complexity of these particular customary international rules, and the imprecision of some of the concepts to which they refer, judicial review must be limited to whether "the Council made manifest errors of assessment concerning the conditions for applying those rules." No such manifest error of assessment was found as the maintenance of peace in Yugoslavia and institutions capable of ensuring implementation of the cooperation envisaged by the agreement throughout Yugoslavia's territory constituted an essential condition for that cooperation. International lawyers have criticized both the high threshold for review, a manifest error of assessment,[106] and the application of the *rebus sic stantibus* doctrine, it being viewed as a significant relaxation.[107]

That the threshold for review vis-à-vis customary international law would be set at the high level of "manifest errors of assessment" was confirmed in the aforementioned *ATAA* case where various customary international law rules were unsuccessfully invoked in challenging the allegedly extraterritorial application of the European Union's emissions trading scheme.[108] That case also added a twofold requirement for the Court to examine the validity of an EU act in light of customary international law principles relied upon by an individual: first, the principles must be capable of calling into question EU competence to adopt the act, and, second, the act must be liable to affect rights which the individual derives from EU law or create obligations under EU law in this regard. This additional tightening of the gateway to review vis-à-vis customary international law has generated criticism,[109] as did the actual review vis-à-vis the customary international law norms that surmounted these hurdles.[110]

[103] C-221/89, *Factortame*, EU:C:1991:320.

[104] *See*, recently, *Front Polisario*, *supra* note 26.

[105] C-162/96, *Racke*, EU:C:1998:293.

[106] *See* Wouters & van Eeckhoutte, *supra* note 97.

[107] *See* Jan Klabbers, *Re-inventing the Law of Treaties: The Contribution of the EC Courts*, 30 NETH. Y. B. INT'L L. 45, 57–59 (1999).

[108] *See supra* note 88.

[109] *See, e.g.*, Wouters et al., *supra* note 89, at 264–65, Theodore Konstadinides, *Customary International Law as a Source of EU Law: A Two-Way Fertilisation Route?*, 35 Y.B. EUR. L. 513 (2016).

[110] *See* Geert De Baere & Cedric Ryngaert, *The ECJ's Judgment in Air Transport Association of America and the International Legal Context of the EU's Climate Change Policy*, 18 EUR. FOREIGN AFF. REV. 389 (2013); Andrea Gattini, *Between Splendid Isolation and Tentative Imperialism: The EU's*

V. Conclusion

As concerns the relationship between the European Union and international law that the Court has constructed, the traditionally dominant narrative in EU law scholarship had been one of openness.[111] Frequently the language of monism, in the sense of the Court having developed a monistic construct vis-à-vis international law, has been used to characterize this relationship.[112] Ultimately, the main evidence for this lay in the mantra that EU agreements are an integral part of EU law and take primacy over the European Union's secondary legislation, combined with the practical manifestation of this integral status in the way principally that the Court treated a range of trade, association, cooperation, and partnership agreements, and an apparent openness to reviewability of EU action vis-à-vis EU agreements and customary international law.

Since 2008, however, a number of rulings can be cited where greater openness to international law seemed possible. Chief among these has been the treatment accorded to the UN Charter and UN Security Council Resolutions; the wholesale rejection of UNCLOS and the UN Disability Rights Convention, as well as certain Aarhus Convention provisions, in reviewing EU action; a restrictive approach to international dispute settlement precluding the European Union from adhering to certain treaties; a rigid functional succession doctrine that treaties, GATT aside, never meet; an exigent threshold for using customary international law to challenge EU action; an overly zealous approach to reviewing member state treaties; as well as international law being interpreted in a manner that jars with the views of international law scholars.

Most of these developments have come in the wake of more international law friendly language being added to the European Union's constitutional text by the Lisbon Treaty, in particular that "the Union . . . shall contribute to . . . the strict observance and the development of international law,"[113] thus bolstering the criticism. To be sure, the aforementioned rulings are contested, but it is hard to look at them collectively and nonetheless conclude with sweeping and unequivocal assertions as to the international law friendly, or international law receptive, or monistic, approach of the CJEU. The balance sheet concerning application of international law looks rather different in 2018 than it did a mere decade or so earlier. It is worth highlighting that even if the Court does not have a formal doctrine of deference to the executive branch in foreign affairs, as might be the case in other constitutional systems, the recent case

Extension of Its Emission Trading Scheme to International Aviation and the ECJ's Judgment in the ATA Case, 61 I.C.L.Q. 977 (2012).

[111] *See* Christiaan Timmermans, *The EU and Public International Law*, 4 Eur. Foreign Aff. Rev. 181 (1999).

[112] Including recently extrajudicially by a judge, now president, of the Court. *See* Koen Lenaerts, *Direct Applicability and Direct Effect of International Law in the EU Legal Order*, *in* The European Union in the World (Inge Govaere et al. eds., 2013).

[113] Art. 3(5) TEU.

law exhibiting less openness toward international law has often been consistent with the submissions of the European Union's political institutions.[114]

The previously dominant international law friendly narrative has now mainly given way to recognition of greater closure toward international law.[115] It would be a vast oversimplification, however, to suggest that the CJEU has now become closed to international law. The relationship is a much more complex and multifaceted one that could never be encapsulated by simply attaching the label of international law friendly or open, or unfriendly and closed, at a single point in time. However, recent developments have allowed one scholar, drawing on a comparative analysis of case law over a ten-year period, to argue that there are more commonalities between the approaches of the CJEU and the U.S. Supreme Court to the internalization of international law than the conventional depiction acknowledges.[116] In many quarters within Europe this is a most uncomfortable finding in light of the European Union being viewed as an international organization long professing a normative commitment to international law, and now constitutionally obliged to do so, and with a Court that internalizes international law. This can be contrasted with the United States, where more isolationist rhetoric has long proliferated and where its Supreme Court has often been viewed as shielding the domestic legal order from international norms.

[114] In recent years, the European Union's political institutions have also sought to exclude the direct effect of bilateral trade agreements either in the agreements themselves, or through EU law. *See* Federico Casolari, *The Acknowledgment of the Direct Effect of EU International Agreements: Does Legal Equality Still Matter?*, *in* THE PRINCIPLE OF EQUALITY IN EU LAW 83 (Lucia Serena Rossi & Federico Casolari eds., 2017).

[115] *See*, e.g., Katja Ziegler, *Autonomy: From Myth to Reality—Or Hubris on a Tightrope? EU Law, Human Rights and International Law*, *in* RESEARCH HANDBOOK ON EU HUMAN RIGHTS LAW 267 (Sionaidh Douglas-Scott & Nicholas Hatzis eds., 2017), and various chapters (e.g., Enzo Cannizzaro, Christina Eeckes, Jan Klabbers, and Ramses Wessel), *in* INTERNATIONAL LAW AS LAW OF THE EUROPEAN UNION (Enzo Cannizzaro et al. eds., 2012).

[116] Gráinne de Búrca, *Internalization of International Law by the CJEU and the US Supreme Court*, 13 INT'L J. CONST. L. 987 (2015).

PART VI

IMMUNITY, COMITY, AND RELATED ISSUES

CHAPTER 35

INTERNATIONAL IMMUNITIES IN U.S. LAW

DAVID P. STEWART

THIS chapter provides an overview of the immunities enjoyed by foreign states, governments, and officials, as well as international organizations, from the jurisdiction of domestic courts in the United States. Those immunities differ in several respects, both structurally and substantively, from those in other countries described in this volume.

From its earliest days, the United States embraced the principle that its courts should forgo the exercise of domestic jurisdiction over foreign sovereigns because of the inherent sensitivity of such cases from the perspective of international relations.[1] In practice, that meant "absolute" immunity. Such abstention was considered "a matter of grace and comity" rather than a legal restriction imposed by the U.S. Constitution, and courts often deferred to the decisions of the political branches on whether to exercise jurisdiction over claims against foreign sovereigns and their instrumentalities.[2]

Over time, the U.S. approach evolved significantly, not least by adopting the so-called "restrictive" theory in 1952.[3] The rules for sovereign (or state) immunity were codified (as is also now the case in a number of other common law systems) in the 1976 Foreign Sovereign Immunities Act (FSIA)[4] and are now applied directly by the courts

[1] *See*, e.g., The Schooner Exchange v. McFaddon, 11 U.S. 116, 137 (1812), referring to the "perfect equality and absolute independence of sovereigns" and a "common interest impelling them to mutual intercourse, and an interchange of good offices with each other, [which] have given rise to a class of cases in which every sovereign is understood to waive the exercise of a part of that complete exclusive territorial jurisdiction, which has been stated to be the attribute of every nation," thus endorsing the classic *par in parem non habet imperium* doctrine.

[2] Verlinden B.V. v. Central Bank of Nigeria, 461 U.S. 480, 486 (1983).

[3] *See* the so-called "Tate Letter" of May 19, 1952, *reprinted in* Dunhill v. Rep. of Cuba, 425 U.S. 682, 711–715 (1976).

[4] The Foreign Sovereign Immunities Act, codified at 28 U.S.C. § 1602 et seq. and 28 U.S.C. § 1330(a). It controls in state as well as federal courts. *See generally* DAVID P. STEWART, THE FOREIGN SOVEREIGN IMMUNITIES ACT: A GUIDE FOR JUDGES (Fed. Jud. Cntr. 2d ed. 2018).

rather than the executive.[5] Moreover, the FSIA itself was expressly understood to reflect and codify principles of international law.[6] Today, there can be little question that the rules of sovereign immunity as applied in the United States largely reflect principles of customary international law and are not based simply upon discretionary notions of "comity" or mutual respect.[7]

By contrast, the immunity of visiting heads of state and government (and other foreign) officials remains rooted in common law decision-making, rather than statute, although they are informed by the executive's views, which in turn reflect its appreciation of relevant principles of customary international law. The Vienna Conventions on Diplomatic and Consular Relations (to which the United States is a party) are directly applicable as binding federal law in all courts, supplemented by some statutory provisions. The law relating to the immunities of international organizations is a complicated amalgam of treaties, statutes, and judicial decisions, but also reflects the international obligations of the United States.

The result is a rich, if not simple, body of "international immunities" law that continues to evolve.

I. Sovereign (State) Immunity

The jurisdiction of U.S. courts in civil litigation against foreign states (including their agencies and instrumentalities) is governed by the Foreign Sovereign Immunities Act (FSIA), adopted in 1976 and subsequently amended several times. That statute provides the sole basis for obtaining jurisdiction over foreign states. It provides that, subject to the treaties in place at the time of the FSIA's enactment, foreign states are immune from the jurisdiction of all U.S. courts (federal and state) except where expressly permitted by the Act. Unless one of the enumerated exceptions applies, foreign states have immunity from trial and the attendant burdens of litigation (not a defense to liability on the merits).

The statute codified the so-called "restrictive" theory of sovereign immunity, so that the primary exception to immunity from adjudication encompasses the commercial

[5] *See* Republic of Argentina v. NML Capital, Ltd., 134 S. Ct. 2250, 2255 (2014) (in adopting the FSIA, Congress "replac[ed] the old executive-driven, factor-intensive, loosely common-law-based immunity regime with the Foreign Sovereign Immunities Act's 'comprehensive set of legal standards governing claims of immunity in every civil action against a foreign state'") (*citing Verlinden*, 461 U.S. at 488).

[6] *See* H.R. Rep. 94-1487, at 6606 (Sept. 9, 1976) (noting that "decisions on claims by foreign states to sovereign immunity are best made by the judiciary on the basis of a statutory regime which incorporates standards recognized under international law."). The Tate Letter was also premised on the U.S. understanding of evolving principles of customary international law.

[7] "The Act for the most part embodies basic principles of international law long followed both in the United States and elsewhere." Bolivarian Republic of Venezuela v. Helmerich & Payne Intern. Drilling Co., 137 S. Ct. 1312, 1319 (2017). *See also* Restatement (Fourth) of the Foreign Relations Law of the United States § 451 (American Law Institute 2018).

activities of foreign states in or directly affecting the United States.[8] Similarly, the main exception to immunity from execution of judgments concerns state property "used for a commercial activity in the United States." However, significant categories of property remain immune from postjudgment attachment and execution, including, for example, funds held in the name of a foreign central bank or monetary authority for its own account, property of a military character or used for a military activity, and diplomatic and consular properties.

Prior to the FSIA, sovereign immunity determinations were often made by the executive branch and communicated to the courts through "suggestions of interest." The courts routinely gave effect to those determinations. A primary purpose of the FSIA was to place these decisions squarely in the hands of the judiciary, insulated from political considerations. Courts today will nonetheless consider (and sometimes affirmatively seek) the executive branch's views in certain cases.[9]

Although this area of U.S. law is codified, it remains dynamic. Several significant developments in FSIA law have occurred over the past several years, both through statutory amendments and judicial interpretation. While the United States is not party to the 2004 UN Convention on the Jurisdictional Immunities of States and Their Properties,[10] the FSIA is largely consistent with its approach and (together with the many judicial interpretations of the statute) is generally reflective of, and helps to contribute to, the relevant rules of customary international law.

Scope of Application

The FSIA applies both to "foreign States" and their "agencies and instrumentalities."[11] It does not, however, cover foreign heads of state or government or other individual foreign officials.

Whether an entity qualifies as a "state" for FSIA purposes is a question of statutory interpretation, often informed by the views of the executive branch, taking into account criteria from international law. The term "state" includes components of the national government such as the armed forces and ministries of defense, foreign affairs, and treasury, as well as embassies, consulates, and permanent missions to international

[8] A number of other states have also adopted the restrictive theory. *See*, e.g., Hennie Strydom, *South African Law on Immunities*, ch. 37 in this volume.

[9] *See*, e.g., Schermerhorn v. Israel, 235 F. Supp. 3d 249 (D.D.C. 2017), *aff'd*, 876 F.3d 351 (D.C. Cir. 2017).

[10] United Nations Convention on Jurisdictional Immunities of States and Their Property (2004), UN Doc. A/59/508, *available at* https://treaties.un.org/. U.S. reluctance to sign or ratify this Convention may be ascribed to concerns that (1) it does not explicitly recognize exceptions to immunity for foreign expropriations or state-sponsored terrorism, and (2) implementation would require amending the FSIA, opening the door to potential efforts to include other exceptions, for example, covering widespread human rights abuses in other countries.

[11] *See* RESTATEMENT (FOURTH), FOREIGN RELATIONS LAW, *supra* note 7, § 452.

organizations. It also covers political subdivisions and other subnational units of government (e.g., states, provinces, cantons, counties, capital districts, and cities).

An "agency or instrumentality" is defined less clearly to cover entities that are (1) separate legal persons; (2) either "organs" of the foreign state or political subdivision, or majority-owned by a foreign state or political subdivision; and (3) neither citizens of the United States nor created under the laws of any third country.[12] U.S. law recognizes a "presumption of separateness," so that agencies and instrumentalities established as distinct juridical entities independent from the state should normally be treated as such (meaning the foreign sovereign is typically not liable for the acts of its instrumentalities).[13]

By including "agencies and instrumentalities," the FSIA applies more broadly than, for example, the statutory regimes of Canada or the United Kingdom. In contrast, by excluding individuals (whether heads of state or government, officials of lesser rank, or special envoys), it applies more narrowly.[14]

Exceptions to Immunity

Because the FSIA is jurisdictional and mandates a presumption of immunity for foreign states and their agencies and instrumentalities, U.S. courts must determine in all cases whether an exception applies, including in default circumstances when the defendant does not appear to defend the litigation.

The most significant exceptions to adjudicative immunity arise when a foreign state has: (1) waived its immunity; (2) engaged in commercial activity; (3) expropriated property in violation of international law; (4) committed certain torts within the United States; (5) agreed to arbitrate certain disputes; or (6) been designated a "State sponsor of terrorism" or is responsible for an act of terrorism within the United States and has engaged in certain specific acts resulting in injury or death.[15]

[12] 28 U.S.C. § 1603(b). For an example of what constitutes an "organ," *see* Janvey v. Libyan Investment Authority, 840 F.3d 248, 259 (5th Cir. 2016).

[13] First Nat'l City Bank v. Banco Para El Comercio Exterior de Cuba, 462 U.S. 611, 626–6227 (1983) ("Bancec"). There are limited exceptions, including when the state exercises extensive control over the separate agency or instrumentality, when recognizing the latter's separate status would work a fraud or injustice, and with respect to executing certain judgments under the state-sponsored terrorism exception against assets of an agency or instrumentality. *Cf.* Rubin v. Islamic Republic of Iran, 138 S. Ct. 816 (2018).

[14] *See* Philippa Webb, *International Immunities in English Law*, ch. 36 in this volume; *see also* Canada State Immunity Act, R.S.C. 1985, c. S-18.

[15] The FSIA also creates exceptions for cases related to rights in certain kinds of property in the United States, maritime liens and preferred mortgages, and counterclaims. No specific statutory exception exists for employment contracts; cases against foreign states arising from such contracts are considered under the "commercial activities" exception.

Waiver of Immunity

Under the FSIA, a foreign state is not immune from suit in any case in which it has waived its immunity either explicitly or by implication.[16] Explicit waivers are most commonly encountered in the relevant contract in dispute but can sometimes be found in treaties.[17] Implicit waivers are construed narrowly and require clear evidence of the foreign sovereign's intention to dispense with its immunity. Traditionally, they have been found only when the state has either agreed to arbitrate disputes in another country, specified that U.S. law will govern the relevant agreement,[18] or participated formally in the relevant judicial proceeding without raising a claim of immunity.[19]

Commercial Activity

The commercial activity exception lies at the heart of the "restrictive" theory of sovereign immunity. While it is the most often-invoked provision of the FSIA, it is hardly open-ended. U.S. courts have jurisdiction over suits against foreign sovereigns when the claim (1) is based upon commercial activity, and (2) has a sufficient jurisdictional connection with the United States.[20]

The term "commercial activity" is defined as "either a regular course of commercial conduct or a particular commercial transaction or act." Much like the South African rule, the Act specifies that whether a given activity is "commercial" must be determined by reference to its nature rather than its purpose.[21] Courts have distinguished between commercial and sovereign activity by limiting the latter to those acts which private parties would be unable to perform (essentially adopting the distinction between *acta jure imperii* and *acta jure gestionis*).

The U.S. Supreme Court has held that "[w]hen a foreign government acts, not as regulator of a market, but in the manner of a private player within it, the foreign sovereign's actions are 'commercial' within the meaning of the FSIA," so that the issue is "whether the particular actions that the foreign state performs (whatever the motive behind them) are the *type* of action by which a private party engages in 'trade and traffic or commerce'."[22]

[16] 28 U.S.C. § 1605(a)(1). *See* Restatement (Fourth), Foreign Relations Law, *supra* note 7, § 453.

[17] Blue Ridge Investments, L.L.C. v. Rep. of Argentina, 735 F.3d 72 (2d Cir. 2013).

[18] Farhang v. Indian Institute of Technology, 655 Fed. Appx. 569 (9th Cir. 2016).

[19] *See*, e.g., BAE Systems Technology Solution & Services, Inc. v. Republic of Korea's Defense Acquisition Program Administration, 884 F.3d 463 (4th Cir. 2018). The courts have declined to find implied waivers of FSIA immunity for *jus cogens* violations. *See*, e.g., Hwang Geum Joo v. Japan, 332 F.3d 679 (D.C. Cir. 2003), *aff'd on other grounds*, 413 F.3d 45 (D.C. Cir. 2005).

[20] *Cf.* Restatement (Fourth), Foreign Relations Law, *supra* note 7, § 454.

[21] 28 U.S.C. § 1603(d). *Cf.* Strydom, *supra* note 8.

[22] Republic of Argentina v. Weltover, Inc., 504 U.S. 607, 614 (1992).

Even if the relevant activity is found to be commercial, it must also have a sufficient jurisdictional connection to the United States. This "nexus" requirement can be satisfied when the suit involves (1) a commercial activity carried on in the United States; (2) an act performed in the United States in connection with a commercial activity carried on outside the United States; or (3) a commercial activity carried on outside the United States that has a "direct effect" in the United States.[23] The Supreme Court has ruled that a "direct effect" must follow "as an *immediate* consequence" of the defendant's activity.[24] Actions based on conduct abroad that is too "remote and attenuated" to have "direct effects" in the United States will be dismissed.[25]

Taking of Property in Violation of International Law

The FSIA also removes a foreign state's immunity where "rights in property" have been "taken in violation of international law." The aim of this provision is to provide a remedy to U.S. nationals whose property or investments in foreign countries had been nationalized or expropriated discriminatorily and without prompt, adequate, and effective compensation. Here, too, the statute requires a jurisdictional nexus: the relevant property (or any property exchanged for it) must be present in the United States in connection with a commercial activity carried on in the United States by the foreign state.[26]

Under this "expropriation" exception, the "cause of action" arises from the foreign state's violation of customary international law. In consequence, the exception does not encompass a sovereign state's taking of property from its own citizens.[27] The U.S. Supreme Court has stressed that the expropriation exception must be interpreted

[23] 28 U.S.C. § 1605(a)(2).

[24] *Weltover*, 504 U.S. at 618. Moreover, the plaintiff's claim must be "based upon" the relevant commercial activity, meaning that it must constitute the "gravamen" of the suit. OBB Personenverker AG v. Sachs, 136 S. Ct. 390, 396 (2015).

[25] *See*, e.g., Intercontinental Industries Corporation v. Wuhan State Owned Industrial Holdings Co., Ltd., 726 Fed. Appx. 619 (Mem) (9th Cir. 2018).

[26] 28 U.S.C. § 1605(a)(3). *See generally* Restatement (Fourth), Foreign Relations Law, *supra* note 7, § 455. In De Csepel v. Republic of Hungary, 859 F.3d 1094 (D.C. Cir. 2017), the appellate court held that a foreign state loses its immunity under this exception only if the expropriated property itself (or any property exchanged for such property) is present in the United States in connection with a commercial activity carried on by the foreign state in the United States. Alternatively, a suit may be brought against the relevant agency or instrumentality if the property (or any property exchanged for it) is owned or operated by that agency or instrumentality which is engaged in a commercial activity in the United States.

[27] Comparelli v. Republica Bolivariana De Venezuela, 891 F.3d 1311 (11th Cir. 2018); Arch Trading Corp. v. Republic of Ecuador, 2015 WL 3443906 (S.D.N.Y. May 28, 2015). Several courts have recently interpreted the exception to cover takings and expropriations that amounted to genocide during World War II. Simon v. Republic of Hungary, 812 F.3d 127 (D.C. Cir. 2016); Philipp v. Federal Republic of Germany, 894 F.3d 405, (D.C. Cir. 2018).

consistently with international law.[28] More broadly, it noted that the FSIA "for the most part embodies basic principles of international law long followed both in the United States and elsewhere . . . " and that "nothing in the history of the statute that suggests Congress intended a radical departure from these basic principles."[29]

Noncommercial Torts

The noncommercial tort exception[30] abrogates immunity for claims involving personal injury or death, or damage to or loss of property, occurring in the United States and caused by the tortious act or omission of a foreign sate or its official or employee while acting within the scope of his office or employment. The main purpose of the exception was to eliminate a foreign state's immunity for traffic accidents and other torts committed in the United States, for which liability is imposed under domestic tort law. It excludes claims based upon "the exercise or performance or the failure to exercise or perform a discretionary function" and "arising out of malicious prosecution, abuse of process, libel, slander, misrepresentation, deceit, or interference with contract rights."[31]

Although the text of the statute refers to "personal injury or death, or damage to or loss of property, occurring in the United States," U.S. courts have consistently held that the *entire* tort—including not only the injury but also the act precipitating that injury—must occur in the United States.[32] In contrast, foreign statutes cast a broader net, requiring only that the injury or damage occur within the territorial jurisdiction.[33]

Arbitration Agreements and Awards

While a state's agreement to arbitrate a given dispute had frequently been accepted as a "waiver" of immunity, the FSIA was amended in 1988 explicitly to remove immunity in actions (1) to compel foreign states to arbitrate pursuant to certain agreements to arbitrate, and (2) to enforce arbitral awards rendered pursuant to such agreements.[34] This provision applies only if (1) the arbitration takes place or is intended to take place

[28] Bolivarian Republic of Venezuela v. Helmerich & Payne Intern. Drilling Co., 137 S. Ct. 1312 (2017).

[29] *Id.* at 1319, 1320.

[30] 28 U.S.C. § 1605(a)(5). *See* Restatement (Fourth), Foreign Relations Law, *supra* note 7, at § 457.

[31] 28 U.S.C. § 1605(a)(5)(a) and (b).

[32] E.g., Doe v. Federal Democratic Republic of Ethiopia, 89 F. Supp. 3d 6 (D.D.C. 2016), *aff'd*, 851 F.3d 7 (D.C. Cir. 2017).

[33] *See,* e.g., Canadian State Immunity Act, *supra* at note 14.

[34] 28 U.S.C. § 1605(a)(6). Thus the question of "waiver" no longer arises in such cases. *See generally* Restatement (Fourth), Foreign Relations Law, *supra* note 7, § 458.

in the United States; (2) the agreement or award is or may be governed by a treaty in force for the United States for the recognition and enforcement of arbitral awards; (3) the underlying claim could have been brought under the FSIA in U.S. courts absent the agreement to arbitrate; or (4) the foreign state has otherwise waived its immunity.

Most frequently, courts are called upon to address issues related to enforcement of arbitral agreements and awards under the New York Convention.[35] Agreements governed by other treaties such as the Inter-American Convention on International Commercial Arbitration ("Panama Convention") and the International Convention for the Settlement of Investment Disputes (ICSID) are given similar respect.[36]

State-Sponsored Terrorism

Under what to date has surely been the most controversial FSIA provision, certain foreign states are not immune from the jurisdiction of U.S. courts in any case (not otherwise covered by the commercial activity exception) in which money damages are sought for personal injury or death that was caused by certain acts or the provision of material support for such acts by an official, employee, or agent of such foreign state while acting within the scope of his or her office, employment, or agency.[37]

This "state-sponsored terrorism" exception applies only to foreign states that have been formally designated by the U.S. Department of State as "state sponsors of terrorism."[38] It only permits claims by (or on behalf of) U.S. nationals, and only claims for personal injury or death caused by an act of torture, extrajudicial killing, aircraft sabotage, hostage-taking, or the provision of material support or resources for such an act.[39] Even those claims are precluded, however, if the foreign state where the act occurred was not first afforded a reasonable opportunity to arbitrate the claim in accordance with accepted international rules of arbitration.

In all cases, plaintiffs must establish their claims by evidence satisfactory to the court, and courts must ensure that the statutory requirements for jurisdiction are met, even when the foreign state fails to respond to the complaints or otherwise participate in the litigation (as typically occurs).

[35] UN Convention on the Recognition and Enforcement of Foreign Arbitral Awards, June 10, 1958, 21 U.S.T. 2517 ("New York Convention"), implemented in U.S. law by 9 U.S.C. §§ 201–208.

[36] Blue Ridge Investments LLC v. Rep. of Argentina, 735 F.3d 72 (D.C. Cir. 2013); Stati v. Republic of Kazakhstan, 199 F. Supp. 3d 179 (D.D.C. 2016).

[37] 28 U.S.C. § 1605A. *See* Restatement (Fourth), Foreign Relations Law, *supra* note 7, § 460.

[38] As of July 2018, the list includes Iran, Sudan, Syria, and North Korea (the latter was initially listed in 1998, removed in 2008, and redesignated in November 2017). *See* https://www.state.gov/j/ct/list/c14151.htm.

[39] It also permits actions if the claimant or the victim was, at the time the act, a member of the armed forces, or otherwise an employee of the U.S. government or of an individual performing a contract awarded by the U.S. government, acting within the scope of the employee's employment. 28 U.S.C. § 1605A(2)(A)(ii).

In addition, the "personal injury or death" in question must have been "caused" by the prohibited action of the foreign state or its official, employee, or agent. Several courts have concluded that claimants must demonstrate "some reasonable connection between the act or omission of the defendant and the damages which the plaintiff has suffered."[40] Suits may be dismissed when the link between that state's support and the acts in question was "unforeseeable." By contrast, the requirement can be satisfied when the evidence demonstrates that without the state's support, the terrorist acts at issue would "likely" not have been possible.[41]

JASTA

In September 2016, shortly after the fifteenth anniversary of the 9/11 attacks on the World Trade Towers and the Pentagon, the U.S. Congress enacted the Justice Against Sponsors of Terrorism Act (JASTA), which expanded jurisdiction over foreign states and their officials for aiding and abetting acts of international terrorism.[42]

JASTA made two major changes to existing federal law. First, it removed the immunity of foreign states and their agencies and instrumentalities for claims related to acts of international terrorism that occur in the United States, whether or not the states in question have been formally designated as "state sponsors." Second, it amended a related statute (the Anti-Terrorism Act (ATA)) to expose foreign states, their agencies and instrumentalities, and their officers and employees to civil liability for aiding and abetting and civilly conspiring acts of terrorism through the provision of material support.[43]

The first change permits suits against foreign states by U.S. nationals seeking money damages for claims arising from physical injury, death, and damage to property caused by (1) an act of international terrorism occurring in the United States, and (2) a tortious act of a foreign state or its officers, employees, or agents acting within the scope of their office, employment, or agency anywhere in the world. Importantly, the state in question need not have been designated as a state sponsor of terrorism.[44] The amendment did not modify the existing state sponsors of terrorism exception

[40] Roth v. Islamic Republic of Iran, 78 F. Supp. 3d 379 (D.D.C. 2015).

[41] Flanagan v. Islamic Republic of Iran, 190 F. Supp. 3d 138 (D.D.C. 2016); Foley v. Syrian Arab Republic, 249 F. Supp. 3d 186 (D.D.C. 2017).

[42] Justice Against Sponsors of Terrorism Act, Pub. L. 114-222, Sept. 28, 2016, 130 Stat. 854, codified at 28 U.S.C. § 1605B.

[43] Anti-Terrorism Act, 18 U.S.C. § 2333 et seq.

[44] New 28 U.S.C. § 1605B provides in relevant part: "A foreign state shall not be immune from the jurisdiction of the courts of the United States in any case in which money damages are sought against a foreign state for physical injury to person or property or death occurring in the United States and caused by (1) an act of international terrorism in the United States; and (2) a tortious act or acts of the foreign state, or of any official, employee, or agent of that foreign state while acting within the scope of his or her office, employment, or agency, regardless where the tortious act or acts of the foreign state occurred."

under § 1605A.[45] Instead, it in effect broadened the separate noncommercial tort rule under § 1605(a)(5) by eliminating the requirement (in relation to terrorism cases) that the "entire tort" must have taken place in the United States. Accordingly, *any* foreign state may now be subject to U.S. jurisdiction no matter where the alleged supporting tortious acts or omissions (the aiding and abetting) took place—but only when the act of terrorism itself occurred *in the United States.*

The second change addressed a perceived limitation on the civil provisions of the ATA, which had been interpreted not to permit suits against third parties (such as banks) based on claims of civil aiding and abetting through the provision of material support to those committing terrorist acts.[46] These entities of course were not entitled to immunity.

The primary motivation behind the amendments was understandable frustration that victims and survivors of the 9/11 attacks have been unable to recover any damages against alleged perpetrators despite having obtained some compensation under other provisions of law. In addition, repeated allegations of Saudi Arabian support for the perpetrators of the attacks provided a critical political impetus for the necessary congressional support. As enacted, the new law has potentially much broader application, and it has already proven controversial. Its implications are just beginning to be explored.

Art Exhibitions

A separate U.S. statute has long permitted the president to immunize state-owned works of art or other objects of cultural significance when on temporary exhibition in the United States.[47] The statute aimed at encouraging the exchange of artwork and objects that otherwise might not be made available for display. Several courts held, however, that such displays constituted commercial activity sufficient to establish jurisdiction under the expropriation exception.[48] The FSIA was amended in 2016 to overrule those decisions and remove the exhibited art from the scope of § 1605(a)(3).[49] Two exceptions apply: one for art allegedly taken by the German (or certain other affiliated) governments between 1933 and 1945, and the other for works taken by a foreign government "as part of a systematic campaign of coercive confiscation or misappropriation of works from members of a targeted and vulnerable group" after 1900.

[45] Under 28 U.S.C. § 1605A(a)(2), the foreign state must have been "designated as a state sponsor of terrorism at the time the act . . . occurred, or was so designated as a result of the act."

[46] E.g., Boim v. Holy Land Foundation for Relief and Development, 549 F.3d 685 (7th Cir. 2008).

[47] Immunity from Seizure Act, Pub. L. 89-259 (1965), codified at 22 U.S.C. § 2459.

[48] E.g., Malewicz v. City of Amsterdam, 517 F. Supp. 2d 322 (D.D.C. 2007); Cassirer v. Kingdom of Spain, 580 F.3d 1048 (9th Cir. 2009); *see also* De Csepel v. Rep. of Hungary, 169 F. Supp. 3d 143 (D.D.C. 2016), *aff'd in relevant part*, 859 F.3d 1094 (D.C. Cir. 2017).

[49] The Foreign Cultural Exchange Jurisdictional Immunity Clarification Act, Pub. L. No. 114-319 (2016), 130 Stat. 1618, to be codified at 28 U.S.C. § 1605(h).

Enforcement of Judgments

U.S. law, like some others, provides more extensive immunity from execution of judgments than it does from jurisdiction to adjudicate the underlying disputes. It is thus quite possible that courts may hear and decide a given claim but that the successful plaintiffs will be unable to enforce the resulting judgment.

Under the FSIA, a foreign state's property in the United States is immune from attachment, arrest, or execution unless a specific exception applies.[50] Prejudgment attachment[51] is not authorized without a specific waiver, and certain categories of property (including, for example, funds held in the name of a foreign central bank or monetary authority for its own account, or property of a military character or used for a military activity) are provided specific statutory immunity.[52]

The main exception for postjudgment execution is for state property used (1) for a commercial activity in the United States, *and* (2) for the commercial activity upon which the claim is based.[53] Under this exception, courts examine whether the actions the foreign state performed with respect to the property were those in which a private party engages in trade and traffic or commerce. The focus is not on how the state made or obtained the money, but on how it uses it.[54]

Special and complex rules govern the enforcement of judgments rendered against designated state sponsors of terrorism. Because successful plaintiffs have found it difficult to locate assets in the United States against which their judgments can be enforced, Congress has adopted a number of measures that have in turn raised complicated legal issues. The Terrorism Risk Insurance Act of 2002,[55] for instance, allows plaintiffs to execute their judgments against "blocked" or "frozen" assets of a terrorist party as well as the assets of an agency or instrumentality of that terrorist party.[56]

[50] 28 U.S.C. § 1609. *See* RESTATEMENT (FOURTH), FOREIGN RELATIONS LAW, *supra* note 7, § 464.

[51] This includes remedies that are the "functional equivalent" of attachment, arrest, and execution such as restraining notices, turnover proceedings, and injunctions against property. *See* Thai Lao Lignite (Thailand) Co., Ltd. v. Government of Lao People's Democratic Republic, 2013 WL 1703873 *3–4 (S.D.N.Y. 2013).

[52] 28 U.S.C. § 1611.

[53] 28 U.S.C. § 1610(a).

[54] Export-Import Bank of the Republic of China v. Grenada, Export-Import Bank of the Republic of China v. Grenada, 768 F.3d 75 (2d Cir. 2014); *cf.* Rubin v. Islamic Republic of Iran, 830 F.3d 470 (7th Cir. 2016), *aff'd*, 138 S. Ct. 812 (2018).

[55] The Terrorism Risk Insurance Act of 2002, Pub. L. No. 107-297, § 201, 116 Stat. 2322, 2337 (2002), *codified in part at* 28 U.S.C. § 1610.

[56] In the International Court of Justice, the Islamic Republic of Iran has challenged the validity of a separate statute (the Iran Threat Reduction and Syria Human Rights Act of 2012, *codified at* 22 U.S.C. § 8772) that permitted the execution of a specific U.S. judgment under § 1605A against certain frozen (blocked) assets held in a commercial bank in New York in which Bank Markazi (the Central Bank of Iran) claimed a beneficial interest. That statute was upheld by the U.S. Supreme Court in Bank Markazi v. Peterson, 136 S. Ct. 1310 (2016). Iran alleges, among other things, violations of the bilateral Treaty of Amity, Economic Relations, and Consular Rights. *See* Certain Iranian Assets (Islamic Rep. Iran v. United States), application filed June 12, 2016, *available at* http://www.icj-cij.org/en/case/164/institution-proceedings.

Postjudgment Discovery

Given the difficulty of finding state assets in the United States against which FSIA judgments can be executed, successful litigants increasingly look for such assets abroad. In 2014, the U.S. Supreme Court held that the FSIA itself does not restrict the discovery of a foreign state's extraterritorial assets in aid of postjudgment attachment.[57] Whether those assets would be accorded immunity (and whether such requests would be permissible) under the relevant foreign law are, of course, not covered by the U.S. statute.

II. Immunity of Foreign Officials

U.S. law addressing the immunity of individual foreign officials is separate from the Foreign Sovereign Immunities Act.

Diplomatic and Consular Immunity

Foreign diplomats and consular officials who are formally assigned and duly accredited to the United States enjoy, respectively, the privileges and immunities specified in the Vienna Convention on Diplomatic Relations (VCDR)[58] and the Vienna Convention on Consular Relations (VCCR).[59] The immunity provisions in both conventions are "self-executing" in the sense that they are directly applicable as federal law in all courts, without the need for implementing legislation. Federal district courts have original jurisdiction (exclusive of the state courts) over all civil actions and proceedings against members of a diplomatic mission or members of their families as well as those against consuls or vice consuls of foreign states.[60]

In addition, the VCDR has been implemented in some respects by the Diplomatic Relations Act (1978).[61] That statute provides among other things for the dismissal of "[a]ny action or proceeding brought against an individual who is entitled to immunity with respect to such action or proceeding under the Vienna Convention on Diplomatic Relations . . . or under any other laws extending diplomatic privileges and immunities . . . "

[57] Republic of Argentina v. NML Capital, Ltd., 134 S. Ct. 2250 (2014).

[58] Vienna Convention on Diplomatic Relations, Apr. 18, 1961, 23 U.S.T. 3227, 500 UNTS 95.

[59] Vienna Convention on Consular Relations, Apr. 24, 1963, 21 U.S.T. 77, 596 UNTS 261. In some circumstances, specialized bilateral agreements may modify or extend such immunities.

[60] 28 U.S.C. § 1351.

[61] Pub. L. 95-393, § 5, Sept. 30, 1978, 92 Stat. 809, *codified at* 22 U.S.C. § 254d; Brzak v. United Nations, 597 F.3d 107 (2d Cir. 2010).

Questions occasionally arise about the extent of the residual ("functional" or "official acts") immunity of former diplomats no longer accredited in the United States. In 2016, for example, a former financial attaché at a foreign embassy was denied residual immunity from criminal prosecution for conspiracy to launder money since the relevant acts had not been performed in the exercise of official functions.[62]

Similarly, U.S. courts respect the principles of diplomatic and consular immunity and inviolability. As might be expected, the typical questions arise in the consular area and concern the scope of official duties (consular functions).[63] In recent years courts have declined to dismiss allegations by household workers of abuse at the hands of their employers on the basis of immunity.[64]

Heads of State and Government

Visiting heads of foreign states and governments are accorded immunity from adjudicative and enforcement jurisdiction of U.S. courts.[65] This category of immunity does not fall under the FSIA (or any other statute) so that judicial decisions in specific cases are typically made on the basis of determinations made by the executive branch, communicated through formal "suggestions of immunity," which take into account principles of customary international law.[66]

Foreign Official Immunity

Other visiting officials (i.e., those who are not covered by head of state or government immunity and those not formally accredited as diplomats or consular officers) now fall within yet another category—for want of a more precise term, labeled "foreign official immunity."[67]

[62] United States v. Al-Sharaf, 183 F. Supp. 3d 45 (D.D.C. 2016).

[63] *See*, e.g., Sanchez-Ramirez v. Consulate General of Mexico in San Francisco, 603 Fed. Appx. 631 (9th Cir. 2015) (provision of notarial services and issuance of passports and visas); Morelo v. Columbia Consulate, 2015 WL 7749968 (W.D. Wash. Oct. 27, 2015) (determination of citizenship is an official function).

[64] Rana v. Islam, 305 F.R.D. 53 (S.D.N.Y. 2015); United States v. Khobragade, 15 F. Supp. 3d 383, 385 (S.D.N.Y. 2014).

[65] Wei Ye v. Zemin, 383 F.3d 620, 625 (7th Cir. 2004); Doe v. Roman Catholic Diocese of Galveston-Houston, 408 F. Supp. 2d 272 (S.D. Tex., 2005); Weixum v. Xilai, 568 F. Supp. 2d 35 (D.D.C. 2008); Habyarimana v. Kagame, 696 F.3d 1029, 1032 (10th Cir. 2012). In addition to the individual heads of state and government, this category encompasses those traveling with the principals in question (the "entourage") or traveling in their stead (such as foreign ministers).

[66] *Cf.* Yousuf v. Samantar, 699 F.3d 763, 772 (4th Cir. 2012) (State Department's pronouncements on head-of-state immunity are entitled to absolute deference).

[67] Although the United States is not a party to the 1969 UN Convention on Special Missions, 1400 UNTS 231, it has recognized such immunity under customary international law for official diplomatic

In 2010, the U.S. Supreme Court decided that the FSIA does not apply to individual government officials, even those present in the United States on official business.[68] Rather, such cases are properly governed by the common law. Depending on the specific circumstances (for example, whether the named defendant is a current or former official), he or she may be entitled to status-based immunity or conduct-based immunity. The precise scope of this form of immunity continues to evolve. The courts are not obligated to seek the government's views in specific cases, but foreign states can ask the Department of State for a "suggestion of immunity." If one is made, the question arises of how much deference the courts should give the government's views.

In *Samantar*, for instance, on remand from the Supreme Court's decision, the court of appeals distinguished cases involving sitting heads of state and government (in which the government's views are entitled to absolute deference) from those involving lower-level foreign officials and former officials (where the position of the executive branch is entitled only to "substantial weight").[69] It also held that conduct immunity does not extend to violations of *jus cogens* norms of international law. By contrast, a different court of appeals has ruled that "in the common-law context, we defer to the Executive's determination of the scope of immunity" and that "[a] claim premised on the violation of *jus cogens* does not withstand foreign sovereign immunity."[70] It therefore affirmed the lower court's finding of conduct-based foreign official immunity in accordance with the executive branch's statement of interest.

Clearly, the law on these issues remains in flux. It is possible that the U.S. Supreme Court will again address the issue.

III. International Organizations

The United States is host to the United Nations Headquarters as well as the headquarters and offices of many other international organizations. In consequence, questions of the immunities of those entities, their officials and staff, and representatives of member states arise with some frequency. While the details vary from organization to organization, the applicable principles are generally found in several interrelated instruments, including international agreements, domestic statutes, executive orders, and interpretive judicial decisions.

envoys traveling as part of a "special diplomatic mission." *See* Li Weixum v. Bo Xilai, 568 F. Supp. 2d 35, 37–38 (D.D.C. 2008).

[68] Samantar v. Yousuf, 560 U.S. 305, 315 (2010).

[69] Yousuf v. Samantar, 699 F.3d 763, 773 (4th Cir. 2012).

[70] Rosenberg v. Pasha, 577 Fed. Appx. 22 (2d Cir. 2014). *See* also Dogan v. Barak, 2016 WL 6024416 (C.D. Ca. 2016) (appeal pending); Mireskandari v. Mayne, 2016 WL 1165896 (C.D. Ca. 2016) (appeal pending).

International Organizations Immunities Act

The International Organizations Immunities Act (IOIA) permits the extension of various immunities to a "public international organization" (as well as its officers and employees) if (1) the United States participates in the organization pursuant to treaty or Act of Congress, and (2) the president has designated it by executive order as entitled to such immunity.[71] The list of designated organizations includes the United Nations, a number of its specialized agencies, the Organization of American States (OAS) and related entities, and various international financial and economic development organizations such as the World Bank and the International Financial Corporation. Other entities and organizations have been given equivalent rights by statute, even though the United States is not a member or participant.[72]

The IOIA provides that duly designated international organizations, together with their property and their assets, "shall enjoy the same immunity from suit and every form of judicial process as is enjoyed by foreign governments" except to the extent they may expressly waive that immunity.[73] This language has given rise to some questions. At the time of enactment, in 1945, it was understood to refer to the absolute immunity accorded to foreign states under then-prevailing principles of customary international law. Given the subsequent evolution of this area of the law and U.S. adoption of the "restrictive" theory (now codified in the FSIA), the question is whether the statute is properly read to incorporate the modified rules. Despite various challenges, most courts have to date declined to accept the "implicit amendment" theory, holding instead that such revisions fall to the president and/or the Congress.[74]

The issue has now been taken up by the Supreme Court, in a case that raises the question whether the statute permits U.S. courts to consider claims implicating the internal operations of designated international organizations, especially those arising out of "core operations."[75] The claims in question were brought against the International Finance Corporation, which is headquartered in Washington, D.C., and involved allegations of environmental and other damage and economic loss resulting from the IFC's allegedly inadequate supervision of construction projects in India funded under its loans. The case was dismissed by the trial court on the basis of the IOIA, and its decision was affirmed on appeal, although one judge noted the anomaly of granting international organizations broader immunity than foreign governments. Several relevant distinctions can be drawn, of course, among them that international organizations

[71] International Organizations Immunities Act, Dec. 29, 1945, c. 652, Title I, § 1, 59 Stat. 669, *codified at* 22 U.S.C. §§ 288 et seq., where the list of designated organizations can also be found.

[72] E.g., European Space Agency and the African Union, 22 U.S.C. §§ 288f-1 and f-2.

[73] 22 U.S.C. § 288a(b).

[74] *See*, e.g., Mendaro v. World Bank, 717 F.2d 610 (D.C. Cir. 1983); Atkinson v. Inter-American Development Bank, 156 F.3d 1335 (D.C. Cir. 1998). *But see* OSS Nokalva Inc. v. European Space Agency, 617 F.3d 756 (3d Cir. 2010).

[75] Jam v. International Finance Corp., 860 F.3d 703 (D.C. Cir. 2017), *cert. granted in part*, 138 S. Ct. 2026 (May 21, 2018).

are treaty-based entities, multilateral in nature, and engage in public rather than commercial endeavors. The situs of the headquarters alone does not justify giving that jurisdiction's domestic courts supervisory authority of the organization's worldwide activities. (As this chapter was going to press, the Supreme Court held that the IOIA affords international organizations only the same immunity from suit that foreign governments enjoy today under the FSIA.)

United Nations

Immunity issues involving international organizations also depend on the specific treaty and statutory arrangements pertaining to the particular organization in question. Because it generates the bulk of such cases, the United Nations serves to illustrate the multilayered structure of the issues.

The Charter of the United Nations[76] is the basic constitutive instrument of the organization and implicitly endows it with "legal personality" as well as "necessary" privileges and immunities for itself, its officials, and representatives of member states in the territory of all member states.[77] In addition, the UN Convention on the Privileges and Immunities of the United Nations (CPIUN)[78] (to which the United States is also a party) elaborates on the juridical status and immunities of the organization as well as the immunities of its officials, representatives and delegates of member states, and "experts on mission." As host to the UN Headquarters in New York, the United States entered into yet another treaty with the organization concerning its status within U.S. territory (the "Headquarters Agreement").[79] Through these instruments, a fourth treaty, the Vienna Convention on Diplomatic Relations, also applies to certain individuals in the Secretariat and accredited to the Missions of member states.[80]

As to the organization itself, these instruments extend absolute immunity. This principle was affirmed in litigation arising from a cholera epidemic in Haiti, allegedly caused by the negligence of the United Nations and its Stabilization Mission (MINUSTAH).[81] In that case, the court dismissed claims brought (on the basis of the UN Charter and the CPIUN) by U.S. and Haitian citizens claiming to have been harmed by

[76] Charter of the United Nations, June 26, 1945, 59 Stat. 1031.

[77] Charter Arts. 104 and 105; Reparation for Injuries Suffered in the Service of the United Nations (Advisory Opinion), [1949] ICJ Rep 174.

[78] UN Convention on the Privileges and Immunities of the United Nations, Feb. 13, 1946, 21 U.S. T. 1418, T.I.A.S. 6900, 1 U.N.T.S. 15. The Convention is a "self-executing" treaty, meaning that it applies directly, of its own force, in domestic litigation.

[79] Headquarters Agreement, Oct. 31, 1947, S.J. Res. 144, 61 Stat. 756, 12 Bevans 956, T.I.A.S. 1676.

[80] The United States is not a party to the 1947 Convention on the Privileges and Immunities of the Specialized Agencies.

[81] Georges v. United Nations, 84 F. Supp. 3d 246 (S.D.N.Y. 2015), *aff'd*, 834 F.3d 88 (2d Cir. 2016); *cf.* LaVenture v. United Nations, 279 F. Supp. 3d 394 (E.D.N.Y. 2017), appeal pending.

the epidemic, noting that such immunity was not conditional on any undertaking to provide for settlement of such disputes.

The UN Secretary-General and other senior UN officials are entitled to diplomatic immunities.[82] Lower-level officials in the Secretariat enjoy "functional immunity" from legal process in respect of words spoken or written and all acts performed by them in their official capacity.[83] Accredited representatives of member states, together with the members of their UN Missions, are accorded the same immunities as diplomats accredited to the United States.[84] Visiting heads of state or government, when attending official UN meetings at the Headquarters, are entitled to "head of state" immunity.[85]

Even though the permanent Missions of UN member states are entitled to inviolability and other immunities under the Vienna Convention on Diplomatic Relations, claims against them are often treated as claims against the state itself and thus covered by the FSIA,[86] including for purposes of disputes arising out of employment as well as personal injury.[87]

Other International Organizations

The headquarters of various other international organizations are located in Washington and elsewhere in the United States. Questions of their immunities are governed by their constitutive instruments and by the IOIA. The most common challenges to their immunity have involved employment disputes and other internal matters, and most have been unsuccessful.[88]

Such immunities can of course be waived and are generally considered unavailable with respect to commercial activities.[89] However, as illustrated by the *Jam* decision

[82] Koumoin v. Ban Ki-Moon, 2016 WL 7243551 (S.D.N.Y. 2016).

[83] *See* Brzak v. United Nations, 597 F.3d 107 (2d Cir. 2010); Georges v. United States, 834 F.3d 88 (2d Cir. 2016).

[84] Devi v. Silva, 861 F. Supp. 2d 135 (S.D.N.Y. 2012); Tachiona v. United States, 386 F.3d 205 (2004); Ahmed v. Hogue, 2002 WL 1964806 (S.D.N.Y. 2002).

[85] *Tachiona*, *supra* note 84.

[86] Permanent Mission of India to the United Nations v. City of New York, 551 U.S. 193 (2007) (real property taxes); USAA Cas. Ins. Co. v. Permanent Mission of Republic of Namibia, 681 F.3d 103, 107 (2d Cir. 2012) ("A foreign state's permanent mission to the United Nations is indisputably the 'embodiment' of that state.").

[87] Hijazi v. Permanent Mission of Saudi Arabia to United Nations, 403 Fed. Appx. 631 (2d Cir. 2010) (sexual harassment and discrimination based on gender and national origin); Weason v. Permanent Mission of Romania to UN and Romania, 43 Misc.3d 780, 984 N.Y.S.2d 800 (2013) (personal injury).

[88] *See* Sampaio v. Inter-Am. Dev. Bank, 468 Fed. Appx. 10 (D.C. Cir. 2012) (per curiam); Aguado v. Inter-Am. Dev. Bank, 85 Fed. Appx. 776 (D.C. Cir. 2004) (per curiam); Atkinson v. Inter-Am. Dev. Bank, 156 F.3d 1335 (D.C. Cir. 1998); Mendaro v. World Bank, 717 F.2d 610, 615–619 (D.C. Cir. 1983); Broadbent v. Org. of Am. States, 628 F.2d 27 (D.C. Cir. 1980).

[89] Price v. Unisea, Inc., 289 P.3d 914 (Sup. Ct. Alaska 2012) (waiver); Oss Nokalva, Inc. v. European Space Agency, 617 F.3d 756 (3d Cir. 2010) (commercial activity).

discussed above, efforts to obtain judicial review of the "core" functions or internal decision-making of these organizations, especially those involving the exercise of policy discretion, have been resisted.[90]

The immunities of the senior officials of these international organizations have similarly been recognized by U.S. courts.[91]

IV. Assessment

The FSIA was expressly intended both to displace the role of the executive in making sovereign immunity determinations by putting those issues in the hands of the courts, and to replace the "grace and comity" approach by codifying rules based on principles of international law.[92] As the Supreme Court recently observed, the statute "create[d] a doctrine that by and large continues to reflect basic principles of international law, in particular those principles embodied in what jurists refer to as the 'restrictive' theory of sovereign immunity."[93]

At least in most respects, the FSIA's provisions on immunity (as interpreted by the courts) are consistent with contemporary international practice and legal principles. Despite some definitional variations, the "commercial activities" exception reflects broadly accepted approaches, as do those regarding waivers, noncommercial torts, and arbitration agreements and awards.[94] The absence of exceptions for military activities or *jus cogens* violations is also unremarkable. By contrast, the expropriation exception finds few parallels in foreign or international practice, although it is expressly grounded in the United States' understanding of international principles regarding foreign takings in violation of international law.

Apart from a Canadian statute,[95] the U.S. terrorism exceptions (§§ 1605A and 1605B) are unique and remain controversial. They were adopted in response to attacks on U.S. citizens and installations, both abroad and at home. Since few of the judgments rendered under § 1605A have ever been satisfied, the effectiveness of that provision is clearly open to question; the record to date under § 1605B is inconclusive. Their

[90] Jam v. International Finance Corp., 860 F.3d 703 (D.C. Cir. 2017), *cert. granted in part*, 138 S. Ct. 2026 (May 21, 2018).

[91] Donald v. Orfila, 788 F.2d 36, 37 (D.C. Cir. 1986) (OAS Secretary General); Tuck v. Pan Am. Health Org., 668 F.2d 547 (D.C. Cir. 1981) (Director of PAHO).

[92] 28 U.S.C. § 1602.

[93] Bolivarian Republic of Venezuela v. Helmerich & Payne Intern. Drilling Co., 137 S. Ct. 1312, 1319 (2017). Justice Breyer cited inter alia to the Restatement (Third) of Foreign Relations Law § 451, the 2004 UN Convention on Jurisdictional Immunities of States and Their Property, and the related UNGA Report of the Ad Hoc Committee on Jurisdictional Immunities of States and Their Property, Supp. A/59/22 No. 1 (2004) (same). *Id.* at 1321.

[94] *Cf.* Strydom, *supra* note 8, and Webb, *supra* note 14.

[95] State Immunity Act, R.S.C., 1985, c. S-18. Iran and Cuba have adopted retaliatory statutes evidently aimed at offsetting judgments rendered against them under the FSIA's § 1605A provisions.

consistency with international law has also been challenged, particularly in light of the ICJ's judgment in the *Jurisdictional Immunities* case.[96]

Considering that the acts covered by the exceptions have been condemned as criminal by the international community, which has also emphasized the need to provide compensation to victims of terrorist acts, an argument can be made that states (and individual state officials) should no longer be shielded from civil suits arising from their actions in perpetrating (or materially supporting) acts of terrorism.[97] However, that proposition—at least in the form of unilateral assertions of domestic jurisdiction—has certainly not gained broad acceptance in the international community. Whether U.S. practice may presage an eventual evolution in customary international law (much as the adoption of the "restrictive approach" by various domestic systems did during the last century) remains to be seen.

In other uncodified areas, such as head of state/government and foreign official immunity, the relationship between the courts and the executive remains dynamic and the substantive rules (informed in significant part by customary international principles) continues to evolve.

[96] Jurisdictional Immunities of the State (Germany v. Italy: Greece intervening) (Judgment), [2012] I.C.J. Rep. 99 (Feb. 3).

[97] Granted, the ICJ did observe, at paragraph 61, that "States are generally entitled to immunity in respect of *acta jure imperii*" without regard to the illegality of those acts. To the extent that the Court was concerned that the Italian judiciary had misunderstood and misapplied customary international law, U.S. practice (based on statutory enactments) may be distinguished.

CHAPTER 36

INTERNATIONAL IMMUNITIES IN ENGLISH LAW

PHILIPPA WEBB

THE law on immunities is a salient example of an area of domestic law that governs how a state interacts with the rest of the world.[1] Resolving disputes concerning immunity has traditionally been the domain of national courts. It is before national courts that "definitionally, issues of immunity from local jurisdiction arise."[2] There is also, by definition, interaction with other states as it is their officials, property, acts, or omissions that are in issue. Moreover, national courts decide such cases by drawing on customary international law, international treaties, or domestic legislation enacted in accordance with international legal requirements.

This chapter sets out the approach of the courts of England and Wales (English courts)[3] to the immunities of states, foreign officials, and international organizations. It discusses similarities with and differences from other jurisdictions, with a focus on the United States as the other key influence in the development of the restrictive doctrine of state immunity.

I. STATE IMMUNITY

State immunity in the United Kingdom is regulated by the 1978 State Immunity Act (U.K. SIA), which was enacted two years after the 1976 U.S. Foreign Sovereign

[1] *See* Curtis A. Bradley, *What Is Foreign Relations Law?*, ch. 1 in this volume.

[2] ROSALYN HIGGINS, PROBLEMS AND PROCESS: INTERNATIONAL LAW AND HOW WE USE IT 81 (1995).

[3] The United Kingdom does not have a unified judicial system—the courts of the United Kingdom are separated into the courts of England and Wales, the courts of Scotland, and the courts of Northern Ireland. The greatest amount of judicial activity on the law of state immunity has taken place in the courts of England and Wales.

Immunities Act (U.S. FSIA). The U.S. FSIA was very much in the mind of the U.K. government during the drafting of its own legislation. There were constant reminders that the U.S. FSIA "renders foreign states amenable to the jurisdiction of US courts in respect of practically all non-sovereign activities and permits execution against their commercial assets."[4]

Although the U.K. SIA was based on the 1972 European Convention on State Immunity 1972 (ECSI),[5] it has proven to be the more successful instrument than ECSI. It has served as the model for many jurisdictions, including Singapore, Pakistan, and South Africa. The 2004 UN Convention on the Jurisdictional Immunities of States and their Property (UNCSI)[6] closely followed the SIA in its structure and formulation of exceptions, although the United Kingdom has signed but not ratified the Convention. English courts have referred to certain aspects of the UNCSI as evidence of customary international law, but they have also treated it with caution. In *Jones v. Saudi Arabia*, Lord Bingham observed that, "[d]espite its embryonic status, . . . [UNCSI is] the most authoritative statement available on the current international understanding of the limits of state immunity in civil cases," and went onto to find that the absence of a codified exception for torture or jus cogens violations was telling.[7] In *Belhaj v. Straw*, Lord Mance noted the specific context of Lord Bingham's statement regarding the *absence* of a provision that it would have been expected to cover had a customary rule existed. He warned that it would be taking Lord Bingham's words out of context to attach equivalent relevance to the use of ambiguous terms ("interests and activities") to adopt a broad view of indirect impleading of the state (see further the section on Indirect Impleading).[8]

Scope of Application and Definition of the State Separate Entity

Under Section 14(1) of the U.K. SIA, the definition of the "state" does not include reference to separate entities. Separate entities are generally not entitled to immunity from adjudicative jurisdiction and consequently do not enjoy immunity from execution. However, under Section 14(2), a separate entity may enjoy immunity "if the proceedings relate to anything done by it in the exercise of sovereign authority and the circumstances are such that a State would have been so immune."[9] If a separate entity (other than the central bank or other monetary authority) submits to the jurisdiction of

[4] UK Solicitor-General Peter Archer, House of Commons, Hansard, 3 May 1978, vol. 949, col. 412. *See* Hazel Fox, *The Restrictive Rule of State Immunity: The 1970s Enactment and its Status as a Treaty in 2017*, *in* THE CAMBRIDGE HANDBOOK ON IMMUNITIES AND INTERNATIONAL LAW (Tom Ruys & Nicolas Angelet eds., forthcoming 2019).

[5] CETS No. 074, opened for signature 16 May 1972, entered into force 11 June 1976.

[6] Opened for signature on 2 Dec. 2004, A/RES/59/38. It had twenty-two parties as of July 1, 2018.

[7] Jones v. Minister of Interior of Kingdom of Saudi Arabia, [2007] 1 AC 270, para. 26.

[8] Belhaj v. Straw, [2017] UKSC 3, para. 25.

[9] Kuwait Airways Corporation v. Iraqi Airways Co., [1995] 1 WLR 1147.

the English court in proceedings where it is entitled to such immunity under Section 14(2), it enjoys the same immunity as the state.[10]

In the U.S. FSIA, a "state" *includes* "an agency or instrumentality of a foreign state," which is broad enough to include a state trading corporation, mining enterprise, transport organization, steel company, central bank, export association, "governmental procurement agency or department or ministry which acts and is suable in its own name."[11] Subject to some qualifications, such an agency or instrumentality is entitled to immunity from jurisdiction on the same basis as the state itself.[12]

When it comes to immunity from enforcement, Section 13(2)(b) of the U.K. SIA provides that the property of the "state" enjoys immunity from the enforcement of a judgment or award. Under Section 14(3), this immunity extends to a separate entity only if it would have been entitled to immunity under Section 14(2) if it had not submitted to the jurisdiction of the English court. Otherwise, a separate entity (other than a central bank or monetary authority) does not enjoy immunity from enforcement.[13] Under the U.S. FSIA, the approach is more straightforward. The property in the United States of a foreign "state" includes the property of an agency or instrumentality, and it is immune, subject to certain exceptions that apply to foreign states in the FSIA.[14]

Constituent Units

Constituent units and political subdivisions are treated as separate entities under the U.K. SIA and only enjoy immunity when exercising sovereign powers in accordance with Section 14(2)(a) and (b). The SIA does not distinguish between constituent units and political subdivisions of a federal state. This differs from the U.S. FSIA, which expressly states that political subdivisions are included in Section 1603, which defines a "state" for the purposes of immunity.[15]

Central Banks

Many states provide a high level of protection to central bank assets and this approach is also reflected in UNCSI, which makes special provision for the immunity from

[10] Hazel Fox & Philippa Webb, The Law of State Immunity 218 (2015). Sec. 13(1)–(4) UK SIA would apply.

[11] *See* David P. Stewart, *International Immunities in U.S. Law*, ch. 35 in this volume; *see also* HR Rep. No. 94-1987, 6 at 16 (1976).

[12] Stewart, *supra* note 11 (e.g., takings exception).

[13] Botas v. Tepe, [2018] UKPC 31 at para. 10 per Lord Mance; Andrew Dickinson, *State Immunity and State-Owned Enterprises*, Report prepared for the Special Representative of the UN Secretary-General on business and human rights, at 16 (2008), *available at* https://www.business-humanrights.org/sites/default/files/media/bhr/files/Clifford-Chance-State-immunity-state-owned-enterprises-Dec-2008.PDF.

[14] Stewart, *supra* note 11. [15] *Id.*

enforcement of all central bank property in all circumstances. Other states accord immunity to central bank property used for sovereign purposes, removing immunity if the primary or sole purpose is commercial. And some make no provision for central bank property, treating it the same as any other state asset.

The U.K. SIA is in the first category of providing a high level of protection. It has special provisions regarding central banks in subsections 14(4) and 13(1)–(3). Consequently, accounts held by central banks are separately immune from enforcement even if the state has made a general waiver of its immunity. *Trendtex*[16] illustrated the importance of examining the status of a central bank on a case-by-case basis to determine whether it is an emanation, alter ego, or department of the foreign state. Recent cases have clarified that a third-party debt order will not be available against a central bank acting as a state entity, irrespective of whether assets are held for commercial purposes,[17] and a freezing order is similarly not available even where a state waives immunity.[18]

Section 1611(b)(1) of the U.S. FSIA extended immunity from attachment and execution only to property of a central bank "held for its own account"—a standard that was slightly lower than the blanket protection in the United Kingdom.[19]

Individuals

The U.K. SIA is largely silent as to the extent to which individuals are included in the definition of the "state." Section 14(1)(a) provides: "The immunities and privileges conferred by this Part of this Act apply to any foreign or commonwealth State other than the United Kingdom; and references to a State include references to (a) the sovereign or other head of that State in his public capacity." The *Propend Finance* decision in the late 1990s confirmed that an individual may fall within the definition of the "state" in the U.K. SIA. The English Court of Appeal held that the Commissioner of the Australian Federal Police was immune from suit in respect of contempt of court even though there was no express reference to individuals in the SIA. The protection available to states under the U.K. SIA would be undermined if employees and officers could be sued as individuals for matters of state conduct in respect of which the state

[16] Trendtex Trading Corporation v. Central Bank of Nigeria, [1977] 1 QB 529.

[17] AIG Capital Partners Inc. v. Republic of Kazakhstan (National Bank of Kazakhstan intervening), [2006] 1 All ER 284.

[18] Thai-Lao Lignite (Thailand) Co. Ltd. v. Lao People's Democratic Republic, [2013] All ER (Comm) 883.

[19] In relation to Iran, the Iran Threat Reduction and Syria Human Rights Act of 2012, codified at 22 U.S.C. § 8772, expanded the scope of assets that may be subject to execution or attachment in aid of execution in order to satisfy judgments against Iran (*see* subsection 502(a)(1)(C) and 502(d)(3) defining "financial asset of Iran" in sec. 502(a)(1)(C) as encompassing such assets owned by the State of Iran, by the central bank or monetary authority of that government and by any agency or instrumentality of that government). This statute was upheld in Bank Markazi v. Peterson, U.S. Supreme Court, 20 Apr. 2016, 578 U.S. 1 (2016).

enjoyed immunity. Section 14(1) had to be read as affording to individual employees or officers protection under the same cloak as protects the foreign state itself.[20] The rule in *Propend* was affirmed by the House of Lords in *Jones v. Saudi Arabia*, with the Lords holding that state immunity applied both to an organ (Ministry of the Interior) and to individuals acting in an official capacity. Lord Bingham declared, "A State can only act through its servants and agents; and their official acts are the acts of the state; and the state's immunity in respect of them is fundamental to the principle of state immunity."[21] This supports the earlier distinction made in *Rahimtoola v. Nizam of Hyderabad*[22] that immunity may be accorded to an individual either as state organ or as an individual acting as an officer or employee.[23]

In the United States, by contrast, the Supreme Court has held that "state" in the FSIA cannot be read to include officials.[24] Instead, individual official immunity is currently determined in the United States as a matter of judicially developed common law. As David Stewart observes, by excluding individuals from its scope, the U.S. FSIA applies more narrowly than the U.K. SIA.[25]

Indirect Impleading of the State

The plea of state immunity has long been recognized as a bar to impleading the state, both directly and indirectly. Section 1(2) of the SIA simply states, "A court shall give effect to the immunity conferred by this section even though the State does not appear in the proceedings in question." Article 6(2)(b) of the UNCSI, not yet in force, is more expansive:

> A proceeding before a court of a State shall be considered to have been instituted against another State if that other State . . . is not named as a party to the proceeding but the proceeding in effect seeks to affect the property, rights, interests or activities of that other State.

The leading recent decision in the English courts has interpreted the test for indirect impleading rather narrowly. In *Belhaj v. Straw*, Mr. Belhaj and his wife alleged that U.K. security services cooperated with U.S., Malaysian, Thai, and Libyan authorities in their unlawful rendition to, and detention in, Libya (six years in Mr. Belhaj's case and several months in his wife's case), where they were allegedly tortured.

[20] Fox & Webb, *supra* note 10, at 185.

[21] Jones v. Minister of Interior of Kingdom of Saudi Arabia, [2007] 1 AC 270, para. 30.

[22] [1958] AC 379.

[23] Fox & Webb, *supra* note 10, at 371. *See also* Philippa Webb, *British Contribution to the Law of State Immunity*, *in* British Influences on International Law, 1915–2015, at 145–166 (Robert McCorquodale & Jean-Pierre Gauci, eds., 2016).

[24] Stewart, *supra* note 11; Samantar v. Yousuf, 130 S. Ct. 2278 (2010).

[25] Stewart, *supra* note 11, at p.628.

The Foreign & Commonwealth Office (FCO) submitted that a state is to be treated as indirectly impleaded in any case where the issues would require the court to adjudicate on its legal rights or liabilities, albeit as between other parties. In its view, indirect impleading is wide enough to cover cases where it is integral to the claims made that foreign states or their officials must be proved to have acted contrary to their own law. Mr. Belhaj argued that nothing in the proceedings would involve any form of judgment against, or in any way affect any legal interests of, the relevant foreign states or their officials.

The U.K. Supreme Court found that there was no indirect impleading of foreign states. The case law did not carry the "concept of interests so far as to cover any reputational or like disadvantage that could result to foreign states or their officials" from findings in the case.[26] What mattered was whether the *legal* position of the foreign states would be affected by proceedings to which they are not party.[27] It would be easier to find an impact on the legal position of a state in a case that involved its property as compared to its abstract reputation,[28] but even then there would need to be some legal foundation for the impleading.

Exceptions to Immunity

The exceptions to immunity are where the differences between the U.K. and U.S. approaches are the most obvious, in particular with the U.S. exceptions for taking of property in violation of international law and for "state-sponsored terrorism."[29]

Waiver

Section 2 of the U.K. SIA provides for four ways in which a state may give or be deemed to give consent to proceedings: submission after the dispute, by prior written agreement, by institution of proceedings, or by intervening or "taking any step in the proceedings" other than to claim immunity or to assert an interest in property in certain cases.[30] Of these, the last is the most controversial. What constitutes "a step in the proceedings" is to be judged on ordinary principles of English law. These principles have for the most part evolved in the context of the Arbitration Acts.[31] The test advanced by Lord Denning MR has been adopted in the construction of Section 2:

[26] Belhaj v. Straw, [2017] UKSC 3, para. 29 per Lord Mance. *See* Eirik Bjorge & Cameron Miles, *Crown and Foreign Acts of State before British Courts:* Ramatullah, Belhaj, *and the Separation of Powers*, ch. 40 in this volume.

[27] *Belhaj*, *supra* note 26, para. 31 per Lord Mance.

[28] *Id.*, para. 196 per Lord Sumption.

[29] Stewart, *supra* note 11.

[30] Webb, *British Contribution*, *supra* note 23.

[31] Fox & Webb, *supra* note 10, at 190.

> a step by which the defendant evinces an election to abide by the Court proceedings and waives his right to arbitration. Like any election it must be an unequivocal act done with knowledge of the material circumstances. . . . to deprive a defendant of his recourse to arbitration a "step in the proceedings" must be one which impliedly affirms the correctness of the proceedings and the willingness of the defendant to go along with a determination by the courts of law instead of arbitration.[32]

The U.K. SIA is silent as to revocation of waiver. The irrevocability of waiver by submission to the jurisdiction was confirmed in *High Commissioner of Pakistan in UK v. National Westminster Bank*:

> [A] waiver of sovereign immunity by submission to the jurisdiction of the court must be irrevocable, and must extend to procedural steps properly taken, any orders of an interim nature made by the court, in the conduct of the proceedings, as well as to the final determination of the proceedings by the court and any appeal therefrom.[33]

The English position remains that any submission to the jurisdiction of the court under Section 2 of the U.K. SIA extends only to the *adjudicative* function of the court. Submission to enforcement jurisdiction of the English court must be express and made separately.[34]

Given the lack of detail in the U.K. SIA, the technical rules on waiver have emerged from case law, such as the two cases arising from the actions of the seventh Nizam of Hyderabad. The 2015 *High Commissioner of Pakistan in UK v. National Westminster Bank* case related to a fund today worth £35 million that amounted to £1 million in 1948 and has been "the subject of a celebrated legal stalemate."[35] On September 20, 1948, the money was transferred to the English bank by the first High Commissioner of the new state of Pakistan, Mr. Rahimtoola, ostensibly on behalf of the seventh Nizam of Hyderabad, apparently the absolute ruler of the largest and richest of the Indian princely states. Two days earlier Hyderabad had been annexed to India after the surrender of the Nizam's army. On September 27, 1948, the Nizam sought to reverse the transfer, claiming it had been made without his authority. Mr. Rahimtoola did not consent to the reversal and the matter remained unresolved. Mr. Rahimtoola applied, inter alia, to stay proceedings against the Bank on the ground of Pakistan's sovereign immunity, and the case made its way to the House of Lords, which accepted the immunity argument.[36] An indefinite period of deadlock ensued, as predicted by Lord Denning:

> The bank cannot safely pay either Rahimtoola or the State of Pakistan because, once it does so, there will clearly thenceforward be no immunity available to protect the

[32] Eagle Star Insurance Co. Ltd. v. Yuval Insurance Co. Ltd., [1978] 1 Lloyd's Rep. 357, 361.

[33] [2015] EWHC (Ch), para. 74, per Henderson J.

[34] Fox & Webb, *supra* note 10, at 191.

[35] The High Commissioner for Pakistan in the United Kingdom v. National Westminster Bank & Others, [2015] EWHC 55 (Ch), para. 1.

[36] Rahimtoola v. Nizam of Hyderabad, [1958] AC 379.

> bank. The bank must wait until it is sued by Rahimtoola or the State of Pakistan: and once that is done, the State automatically waives its immunity.[37]

From 1957 to 2013 the fund grew in value, but no agreement on its distribution could be reached. In the meantime, other potential claimants emerged in addition to Pakistan and India, including the eighth Nizam of Hyderabad, Prince Muffakham Jah, and various members of the family of the seventh Nizam, who is reputed to have had 49 concubines and 150 illegitimate children.[38] In 2015, the English High Court held that that where a state commences proceedings, it thereby waives its immunity from the Court's jurisdiction, and that waiver is irrevocable and extends to claims that it could have anticipated would be brought by nonparties that would apply to join.[39]

Commercial Transactions

Although most countries recognize a commercial or private law exception to state immunity, establishing a common understanding of the exception has proven difficult. National systems classify public and private acts in diverse ways.[40] Different criteria are used; some jurisdictions emphasize the nature of the activity, others the purpose. This diversity is acknowledged in UNCSI Article 2(2):

> In determining whether a contract or transaction is a "commercial transaction" under paragraph 1(c), reference should be made primarily to the nature of the contract or transaction, but its purpose should also be taken into account if the parties to the contract or transaction have so agreed, or if, in the practice of the State of the forum, that purpose is relevant to determining the non-commercial character of the contract or transaction.

The U.K. SIA uses plain words to define "commercial transaction" in Section 3(3) as "any contract of the supply of goods or services," "any loan or other transaction for the provision of finance...," and "any other transaction or activity... into which a State enters or in which it engages otherwise than in the exercise of sovereign authority." Lord Diplock has observed that the SIA does not "adopt the straightforward dichotomy between acts jure imperii and acts jure gestionis that had become familiar doctrine in public international law."[41] It adopts a list approach to identifying non-immune

[37] *Id.* at 421. [38] *High Commissioner of Pakistan*, *supra* note 35, para. 7.

[39] *High Commissioner of Pakistan*, *supra* note 35, para. 74.

[40] Fox & Webb, *supra* note 10, at 399. *See also* the seminal article by James Crawford, *International Law and Foreign Sovereigns: Distinguishing Immune Transactions*, 54 Brit. Y.B. Int'l L, 75 (1983).

[41] Alcom Ltd. v. Republic of Colombia, [1984] AC 580.

transactions, irrespective of their purpose.[42] While not fully aligned with the international law dichotomy, the U.K. approach has probably given rise to fewer difficulties of interpretation than the U.S. FSIA Section 1605(a)(2) definition of "commercial activity . . . of the foreign state," which has required a close reading of the legislative history and intense judicial interpretation.[43]

The application of the commercial exception in English courts does not require any territorial connection with the United Kingdom.[44] This is in striking contrast to the U.S. FSIA, where each exception, except for waiver, requires a jurisdictional nexus with the United States. In the United Kingdom, the jurisdictional requirement is left to regulation by procedural conditions for service of a writ rather than built into the statutory exceptions to immunity.[45]

Employment Contracts

The U.K. legislation is one of the strictest in the world when it comes to the scope for employees to sue a state under the employment contract exception; the U.K. approach is matched only by the legislation of South Africa, Pakistan, and Malawi.[46]

There have been cases concerning the alleged exploitation and trafficking of employees of foreign embassies and residences in the United Kingdom that have engaged the employment contract exception to state immunity. These cases involve the legality and enforceability of the terms of employment imposed by a foreign state (or its diplomats) in relation to international human rights requirements and/or the host state's labor regulations. They have exposed sharp differences between U.K. and international and regional requirements: in particular, U.K. SIA Sections 4(2) and 16(1)(a) as compared to European Convention on Human Rights (ECHR) Article 6 and the EU Charter of Fundamental Human Rights Articles 45 and 47.[47]

Under Section 4(1), a state is not immune in respect of proceedings relating to a contract of employment between a state and an individual where the contract was made in the United Kingdom or work is to be wholly or partly performed there. But this broad exception is narrowed by Section 4(2), which provides that an employee cannot bring suit if he or she is a national of a foreign state unless he or she was habitually resident in the United Kingdom at the time the contract was made. The remaining rights of embassy employees under the SIA are in effect removed by

[42] Fox & Webb, *supra* note 10, at 196.

[43] Stewart, *supra* note 11; Fox, *supra* note 4.

[44] UK SIA § 3(1)(a); NML Capital Limited v. Republic of Argentina, [2011] UKSC 31.

[45] Fox & Webb, *supra* note 10, at 618.

[46] *See*, for a multijursidictional analysis, Philippa Webb, *The Immunity of States, Diplomats and International Organizations in Employment Disputes: The New Human Rights Dilemma?*, 27 Eur. J. Int'l L. 745 (2016).

[47] Fox & Webb, *supra* note 10, at ix; Benkharbouche v. Secretary of State for Foreign and Commonwealth Affairs, [2017] UKSC 62.

Section 16(1)(a), which excludes from Section 4 claims regarding "employment of members of a mission," which includes low-level administrative and technical staff.

Arbitration

Under Section 9 of the U.K. SIA, where a state has agreed in writing to submit a dispute to arbitration, there is no immunity before English courts in respect of proceedings that relate to the arbitration. Arbitration agreements between states are excluded from the section. Whereas the U.S. FSIA was amended in 1998 to introduce a waiver to state immunity based on an arbitration agreement (Section 1605(a)(6)),[48] the U.K. SIA has remained untouched.

Unlike the U.S. approach, the U.K. SIA does not require a jurisdictional connection with the United Kingdom. The English court has held that there is "no basis for construing section 9 . . . (particularly when viewed in the context of the provisions of section 13 dealing with execution) as excluding proceedings relating to the enforcement of a foreign arbitral award."[49] Section 9 is intended to apply to *any* foreign arbitral award.[50]

Immunity from Enforcement

As with most jurisdictions, including South Africa and the United States, the U.K. SIA treats immunity from enforcement as a distinct regime, although the rules appear in both Parts I and II of the legislation (Sections 13, 14, 16, and 17). The general approach to immunity from enforcement is strict in that property of a state is immune unless the state has expressly waived immunity from enforcement measures, made an allocation of state property, or the property is proved to be in use or intended for use for commercial purposes.

Showing property is in use for commercial purposes is challenging, given the practice of many states, especially developing states, of depositing state assets in accounts held in the name of their diplomatic missions or of their central bank.[51] English courts have clarified that it does not matter how the state obtained the property—through a commercial transaction or the exercise of sovereign authority. The key question is what the state now uses or intends to use the property for.[52] Property will not be immune from enforcement if the use or intended use is *exclusively* commercial.[53]

48 *See* Stewart, *supra* note 11.

49 Svenska Petroleum Exploration AB v. Lithuania and Another, [2007] 2 WLR 876, para. 117.

50 Fox & Webb, *supra* note 10, at 397.

51 *Id.* at 212.

52 SerVaas Incorporated v. Rafidain Bank and Others, [2012] UKSC 40.

53 Alcom v. Republic of Colombia, [1984] AC 580; *cf.* Orascom Telecom v. Chad, [2008] EWHC 1841, where a London bank account for general use was treated as non-immune because the oil revenues of a foreign state were paid into separate accounts to (1) discharge loans owed to the World Bank; (2) for general use in the management of the economy and government revenues of Kazakhstan.

In a recent case, the arbitration exception (Section 9) and the question of immunity from injunctive relief (Section 13) coincided. The claimants sought to enforce a peremptory order against the Kurdistan Regional Government of Iraq (KRG) in a dispute concerning a concession given by the KRG to exploit gas fields.[54] The KRG claimed, inter alia, that it was entitled to immunity from injunctive relief under Section 13(2) of the U.K. SIA, which provides that "relief shall not be given against a State by way of injunction or order for specific performance or for the recovery of land or other property." Under Section 13(3), it states that Section 13(2) "does not prevent the giving of any relief or the issue of any process with the written consent of the State concerned."

The case raised a multitude of technical questions. In the event, the court held that the KRG was a "separate entity" that had been acting in the exercise of its *own* sovereign authority (not that of Iraq) and was therefore not entitled to immunity. However, if it had enjoyed state immunity, it would have been lost or waived. The peremptory order was not "injunctive relief" under Section 13(2)(a). And the express wording in its arbitration agreement would have been sufficient to amount to a waiver of immunity from suit, including an injunction.[55]

II. Immunity of Foreign Officials

Diplomatic Immunity

London, as a major international transport hub and capital city, has been the site of controversial cases involving diplomatic immunity.[56] In 1984, Policewoman Yvonne Fletcher was killed by shots fired from the Libyan Embassy in St. James Square. The U.K. authorities carefully complied with the requirements of the Vienna Convention on Diplomatic Relations (VCDR)[57] so far as any entry to the buildings and arrests were concerned, generating public outrage, even decades after the event. In 2012, facing extradition to Sweden following a decision of the U.K. Supreme Court,[58] Julian Assange sought refuge at the Ecuadorean Embassy in London and remains there until now, the U.K. police unable under the VCDR to enter the embassy to arrest him.

English courts have heard cases involving accusations of abuse, including human trafficking, made by domestic servants against diplomatic agents.[59] In a judgment in the era of mass surveillance and online leaks, the Court of Appeal held that a

[54] Pearl Petroleum Company Ltd. v. The Kurdistan Regional Government of Iraq, [2015] EWHC 3361. For separate entities, see Botas v. Tepe, [2018] UKPC 31.

[55] *Id.*, paras. 40–44.

[56] *See* Webb, *British Contribution*, *supra* note 23.

[57] 500 UNTS 95, opened for signature 18 Apr. 1961 and entered into force 24 Apr. 1964.

[58] Assange v. The Swedish Prosecution Authority, [2012] UKSC 22.

[59] Reyes v. Al-Malki, [2017] UKSC 61.

diplomatic cable released by WikiLeaks could be admitted and form the basis for a cross-examination.[60] It clarified that the "inviolability" of mission documents and correspondence in Articles 24 and 27(2) of the VCDR does not prevent such a cable being admitted as evidence in court:

> [Inviolability] involves the placing of a protective ring around the ambassador, the embassy and its archives and documents which neither the receiving state nor the courts of the receiving state may lawfully penetrate. If, however, a relevant document has found its way into the hands of a third party, even in consequence of a breach of inviolability, it is prima facie admissible in evidence. The concept of inviolability has no relevance where no attempt is being made to exercise compulsion against the embassy.

There were recently two conflicting English court decisions on judicial review of the qualifications of diplomats. This is an aspect of the law of diplomatic immunity that is rarely considered by the courts because it is unusual publicly to challenge the decision of who qualifies as a diplomat.[61] In the first case, *Al-Juffali*,[62] the respondent was a wealthy Saudi citizen who married the applicant, a former model. He had previously been married and divorced. They had one child together, who was thirteen years old at the time of the proceedings. After twelve years of marriage, the respondent married a younger woman, and she had a baby. He then filed for divorce from his second wife. His second and third marriages overlapped by one and a half years.[63]

Eight months after initiating divorce proceedings, the respondent was appointed Permanent Representative of St. Lucia to the International Maritime Organization (IMO),[64] a UN specialized agency responsible for the safety and security of shipping and the prevention of marine pollution by ships. It has its headquarters in London.

When his ex-wife brought a divorce claim for financial relief, the respondent applied to strike out the claim on the basis of his diplomatic immunity as St. Lucia's Permanent Representative to the IMO.[65] The judge pointed out that several facts indicated that this diplomatic appointment was solely intended to defeat the ex-wife's claims in the English court,[66] including the fact that since he was appointed Permanent Representative, the respondent had has not undertaken *any* duties of *any* kind related to his IMO role. The judge accordingly found that the diplomatic post was "a mere empty husk."[67]

However, in a similar case, a different judge rejected the functional test and took a "formal approach."[68] Under this approach, a person should be treated as a diplomatic agent if there is evidence that he or she has been appointed as such and that

[60] Bancoult v. Secretary of State for Foreign and Commonwealth Affairs, [2014] EWCA Civ 708, upheld on appeal in [2018] UKSC 3.

[61] Philippa Webb, *Judicial Review of Qualifications Made by Receiving States and Host States of International Organizations, in* CAMBRIDGE HANDBOOK ON IMMUNITIES, *supra* note 4.

[62] Estrada v. Al-Juffali [2016] EWHC 213 (Fam).

[63] *Id.*, paras. 6 and 7.

[64] *Id.*, para. 7.

[65] *Id.*

[66] *Id.*, para. 35.

[67] *Id.*, para. 40.

[68] Al Attiya v. Al Thani, [2016] EWHC 212 (QB), paras. 73–5 and 37(i).

appointment has been communicated to and accepted by the relevant ministry of the receiving state. In *Al Attiya*, the defendant was a member of a prominent Qatari family who served as minister of foreign affairs (1992–2013) and prime minister (2007–2013). He was one of the richest persons in the world, with his wealth estimated at £7.8 billion.[69] In June 2013 he resigned as foreign minister and prime minister, and on August 28, 2013, Qatar notified the FCO that the defendant was appointed as minister counsellor at the Embassy of Qatar in London. The claimant alleged, inter alia, that the defendant confiscated his land in 2003 and had him detained and tortured in Qatar from October 2009 to January 2011.[70]

Again, several facts suggested that the diplomatic appointment was to protect the defendant from litigation and that he was not actually performing diplomatic functions, including that he adduced no evidence of having performed diplomatic functions in the twenty-six months since he was appointed to the London Embassy.[71] The judge noted that the FCO had issued a certificate stating that the defendant's appointment as a member of the diplomatic staff had been notified to it.[72] The FCO had accepted his accreditation and that was to be regarded "as good evidence of the fact of membership of diplomatic staff."[73]

The conflict between the approaches was resolved by the English Court of Appeal in the *Al-Juffali* case, which ruled in favor of the formal approach, confirming that the prerogative power of conducting foreign relations is exercised by the executive through the FCO and not by the courts. It found that "there is no support in the relevant international instruments of the case law for a functional review by a court where there is a challenge to a claim to immunity by a diplomat or Permanent Representative."[74] The court pointed out that the sending state had a duty to waive immunity of the diplomat if their immunity impeded the course of justice. As noted above, St. Lucia had refused to consider such a waiver. The "correct response," according to the court, was not to "look behind the status of the representative," but to take the FCO certification of the defendant's diplomatic status at face value.[75]

Heads of State

The immunities of a foreign head of state in English law have required judicial interpretation due to the confusing treatment in the U.K. SIA. Section 14(1)(a) provides that "state" is defined to include "the sovereign or other head of that state in his *public capacity*."[76] Section 20(1) then sets out that the Diplomatic Privileges Act 1964 (largely implementing the Vienna Convention on Diplomatic Relations in domestic law) applies to a head of state as it applies to the head of a diplomatic

[69] *Id.*, para. 2. [70] *Id.*, paras. 4 and 5. [71] *Id.*, para. 70. [72] *Id.*, para. 9.
[73] *Id.*, para. 74. [74] Al-Juffali v. Estrada, [2016] EWCA Civ 176, para. 25.
[75] *Id.*, para. 26. [76] Emphasis added.

mission, "subject to any necessary modifications." The U.K. SIA thus splits the immunities of the head of state: Section 14 addresses his or her immunities when acting in a public capacity while Section 20 extends diplomatic immunity to his/her private acts subject to an unclear proviso about "necessary modifications."[77]

In *Harb v. Aziz*, an alleged wife of the late King of Saudi Arabia sued his estate to enforce the performance of a contract to pay her the sum of £12 million and give her the title to two London properties. The Court of Appeal interpreted Section 20(1) not to confer immunity from suit for the estate of a head of state who has died in office, when the estate is thereafter sued in respect of a private, as opposed to an official, act.[78] The Court observed that, "[t]o call the drafting of section 20(1) of the SIA clumsy would be an understatement," noting that "the section has all the hall-marks of being concocted in a hurry without much thought as to how it was intended to work in conjunction with the DPA and the [Vienna] Convention."[79] In interpreting the phrase "necessary modifications," the Court of Appeal followed the House of Lords in *Pinochet (No 3)* in holding that "Parliament cannot have intended to give heads of state, or former heads of state any greater rights than they already enjoyed under customary international law, so that the immunity granted to a head of state and a former head of state by section 20 must reflect customary international law."[80] There was no "necessary modification" that created an immunity from suit of the estate of a head of state for private acts.[81]

In the United States, such uncertainty as to the position of the head of state is generally avoided by judicial deference to the views of the State Department in such cases, especially those involving sitting heads of state.[82]

Immunity of State Officials and Individuals Acting on Behalf of the State

As regards immunity *ratione personae*, English courts have gone further than the holding of the International Court of Justice (ICJ) that such immunity is enjoyed by "holders of high-ranking office in a State, such as the Head of State, Head of Government and Minister for Foreign Affairs."[83] English courts have accorded immunity *ratione personae* to a minister of defense and a minister of commerce.[84] This expansion

[77] UK SIA § 20(5).

[78] HRH Prince Abdul Aziz Bin Fahd Bin Abdul Aziz v. Harb [2015] EWCA Civ 481, paras. 26 and 48. In reaching this result, the Court of Appeal relied in part on the House of Lords in *Regina v. Bow Street Magistrates ex p Pinochet (No 3)*, [2000] 1 AC 147, 202F-G in particular.

[79] *Aziz v. Harb*, *supra* note 78, para. 29. [80] *Id.*, para. 31. [81] *Id.*, para. 44.

[82] *See* Stewart, *supra* note 11, at p.637.

[83] Arrest Warrant of 11 April 2000 (Democratic Republic of the Congo v. Belgium), Judgment, I.C.J. Reports 2002, at 3, para. 51.

[84] *Re Mofaz*, Bow St. Magistrates' Court, 12 Feb. 2004, 128 ILR 709; *Re Bo Xilai*, Bow St. Magistrates' Court, 8 Nov. 2005, 128 ILR 713.

of the categories of officials entitled to immunity *ratione personae* beyond the "troika" has thus far not been followed by the International Law Commission in its ongoing work on the immunity of state officials from criminal jurisdiction.[85]

As for immunity *ratione materiae*, the judgment of the House of Lords in *Pinochet (No 3)* has become the "touchstone" case on the immunity of former senior officials and ordinary officials (whether incumbent or out of office). It stands for the proposition that immunity *ratione materiae* is enjoyed by state officials, regardless of their position in the hierarchy, in respect of their official acts. However, the extent to which *Pinochet (No 3)* has established a human rights exception to immunity *ratione materiae* is much less certain. Indeed, with hindsight, *Pinochet (No 3)* is beginning to look like the high-water mark for the setting aside of immunity in the face of allegations of grave human rights violations.[86]

English courts have also been at the cutting edge of interpreting the nature and scope of special missions immunity. In the *Khurts Bat* case, the English High Court held that the Head of the Executive Office of the Mongolian National Security Office was not a member of a special mission sent to the United Kingdom: "no invitation was issued, no meeting was arranged, no subjects of business were agreed or prepared."[87] He could therefore be extradited to Germany to face charges of abduction and serious bodily injury.

Special missions immunity was before the English courts again in the *Freedom and Justice Party* case. The Freedom and Justice Party and individual claimants brought a challenge to the decision of the Metropolitan Police not to arrest Lt. General Mahmoud Hegazy, the director of the Egyptian Military Intelligence Service, when he was visiting the United Kingdom as a member of a "special mission."[88] The police refused to arrest Hegazy because his membership in the special mission gave him immunity from criminal process. The FCO and Director of Public Prosecutions supported this position.[89]

The FCO had issued a certificate stating that Hegazy was a member of an Egyptian special mission to the United Kingdom. The United Kingdom has not ratified the 1969 UN Convention on Special Missions, and there is no applicable bilateral treaty on special missions. Therefore, the existence and extent of the immunity had to be determined under customary international law. In 2016, the English Divisional Court

[85] *See* draft art. 3, UN Doc. A/CN.4/L.814 (4 June 2013).

[86] Webb, *British Contribution*, *supra* note 23.

[87] Khurts Bat v. The Investigating Judge of the German Federal Court, [2011] EWHC 2029 (Admin), quote from Michael Wood, *The Immunity of Official Visitors*, 16 MAX PLANCK Y.B. U.N. L. 35, 93 n.176 (Armin von Bogdandy & Rüdiger Wolfrum eds., 2012).

[88] Freedom and Justice Party v. Secretary of State for Foreign and Commonwealth Affairs, [2016] EWHC 2010 (Admin).

[89] There were conflicting positions on who had ultimately taken the "decision" not to arrest, and on what advice.

concluded, after a survey of state practice, the work of the International Law Commission, and academic commentary, that:

> there has emerged a clear rule of customary international law which requires a State which has agreed to receive a special mission to secure the inviolability and immunity from criminal jurisdiction of the members of the mission during its currency. There is, in our view, ample evidence in judicial decisions and executive practice of widespread and representative State practice sufficient to meet the criteria of general practice. Furthermore, the requirements of *opinio juris* are satisfied here by State claims to immunity and the acknowledgment of States granting immunity that they do so pursuant to obligations imposed by international law. Moreover, we note the absence of judicial authority, executive practice or legislative provision to contrary effect.[90]

The decision was upheld on appeal, with the Court of Appeal observing:

> If an international court had to consider the question whether a member of a special mission enjoyed the core immunities as a matter of customary international law, it would have regard to the importance and long acceptance of the role of special missions. Special missions have performed the role of *ad hoc* diplomats across the world for generations. They are an essential part of the conduct of international relations: there can be few who have not heard, for instance, of special envoys and shuttle diplomacy. Special missions cannot be expected to perform their role without the functional protection afforded by the core immunities. No state has taken action or adopted a practice inconsistent with the recognition of such immunities. No state has asserted that they do not exist. We do not, therefore, doubt but that an international court would find that there is a rule of customary international law to that effect. We consider that the Divisional Court was right in their conclusion and that this Court should uphold it.[91]

III. Immunity of International Organizations

The United Kingdom is host state to several international organizations. Like for the United States, the applicable principles are contained in international agreements, domestic statutes, and case law. Unlike the U.S. International Organizations Immunities Act, however, the United Kingdom does not link the immunity of international organizations with that of the state.

[90] *Id.*, para. 163.

[91] Freedom and Justice Party v. Secretary of State for Foreign and Commonwealth Affairs, [2018] EWCA Civ 1719, para. 79.

The most famous English case on international organizations is the series of decisions concerning the winding up of the International Tin Council (ITC).[92] This litigation turned on a number of questions relating to the legal status of the ITC and the position of its member states in relation to its activities.[93] Findings by the English courts during the course of the litigation included: that the ITC enjoyed a personality separate from its member states; a contractual provision waiving immunity was a sufficient basis on which to found the jurisdiction of the court in relation to claims arising from an alleged breach of that contract; the scope of the inviolability of the archives of an international organization, in the context of disclosure to the court, in which it was found that inviolability did not extend to documents which had gone outside the organization; and the court's ability to order the ITC to disclose the whereabouts of its assets in the United Kingdom.[94]

IV. Assessment

The United Kingdom, along with the United States, has been a leader in the development and application of the restrictive doctrine of state immunity. The state immunity legislation of both states has proved influential, shaping the active litigation in domestic courts and providing a model for other jurisdictions. Interestingly, neither state has ratified the United Nations Convention on the Jurisdictional Immunities of States and their Property. This may be explained in part by the wealth of jurisprudence that has accrued under their own legislation since the late 1970s.

In the United Kingdom, we do not observe the same legislative involvement in foreign relations decision-making in the field of immunities as we can see in the United States. The U.S. Congress has used amendments to remedy deficiencies in the U.S. FSIA,[95] and also to incorporate new exceptions to immunity that reflect foreign policy choices, such as those directed at "state sponsors of terrorism."[96] The U.K. SIA, by contrast, has not been amended, but certain provisions have been both declared incompatible with the ECHR and disapplied under the Charter of Fundamental Rights of the European Union in relation to the employment contract exception.[97]

[92] *See* Webb, *British Contribution*, *supra* note 23.

[93] Chanaka Wickremasinghe, *The Immunity of International Organizations in the United Kingdom*, 10 Int'l Org. L. Rev. 434, 439 (2013).

[94] *Id.* at 439, 443; Standard Chartered Bank v. International Tin Council, [1987] 1 WLR 641; Shearson Lehman v. Maclaine Watson (No. 2), [1988] 1 WLR 16; Maclaine Watson v. International Tin Council (No. 2), [1987] 1 WLR 1711.

[95] Sec. 1605(a)(6) addresses the need for a sufficient U.S. nexus where implicit waiver arises due to an arbitration clause in an agreement. Fox & Webb, *supra* note 10, at 261.

[96] Sec. 1605A.

[97] Benkharbouche v. Secretary of State for Foreign and Commonwealth Affairs, [2017] UKSC 62 in relation to UK SIA §§ 4(2) and 16(1)(a).

An apparent difference with the United States is that English courts have firmly held that immunity is a rule of international law and not a matter of comity.[98] The U.S. Supreme Court, while not denying that immunity is a rule of international law, has stated that immunity merely provides "some *present* protection from the inconvenience of suit as a gesture of comity."[99] The ICJ has since confirmed in its *Jurisdictional Immunities* judgment that immunity is a rule of international law.[100]

As William Dodge explains, the notion of comity continues to flourish in U.S. jurisprudence.[101] This may explain the terrorism-related exceptions to immunity in the United States: "state sponsors of terrorism" do not deserve comity, so their immunity is abrogated. Similarly, the emphasis on comity may have made U.S. courts more deferential to the executive on matters of immunity as compared to the English courts.[102] Admittedly, Section 21(a) of the U.K. SIA gives statutory force to the previous executive practice pursuant to which a certificate from the foreign secretary is treated as conclusive evidence of whether a party is a state or a person is to be regarded as the head or government of a state. But apart from this provision and provisions regarding the notification of diplomatic appointments,[103] English courts have generally shown less deference than U.S. courts to the views of the executive on foreign relations.

As the English Court of Appeal has noted in the context of the act of state doctrine, although "deference to executive suggestion as to the likely consequences for foreign relations may well be suited to the very different constitutional arrangements in the United States, it has played no part in the development of the act of state doctrine in this jurisdiction."[104] The argument that English courts may be precluded from investigating acts of a foreign state when and if the FCO communicated the government view that such an investigation would be "embarrassing" to the United Kingdom in its

[98] For further analysis, *see* Christopher J. Greenwood, *Sovereignty and Sovereign Immunity*, Lauterpacht Lecture Series, Lecture 1, Jan. 2015; Trendtex Trading Corp. v. Central Bank of Nigeria, [1977] 1 QB 529, 552; *I Congreso del Partido*, [1983] 1 AC 244, 262, 265.

[99] 327 F.3d 1246 (2004), *citing* Dole Food Co v. Patrickson, 538 U.S. 468, 479 (2003) (emphasis added). *See* William S. Dodge, *International Comity in Comparative Perspective*, ch. 39 in this volume.

[100] Jurisdictional Immunities of the State (Germany v. Italy, Greece intervening), Judgment, I.C.J. Reports 2012, at 99, para. 57.

[101] *See* Dodge, *supra* note 99.

[102] Rosalyn Higgins, *International Law*, *in* THE JUDICIAL HOUSE OF LORDS 1876–2009, at 457 (Louis Blom-Cooper, Brice Dickson, & Gavin Drewry eds., 2009); Ingrid Wuerth, *Foreign Official Immunity Determinations in U.S. Courts: The Case Against the State Department*, 51 VA. J. INT'L L. 915 (2011). For state immunity, the United States stopped the practice of relying on executive suggestions when the FSIA was enacted in 1976.

[103] *See* sec. 4, Diplomatic Privileges Act; Al-Juffali v. Estrada, [2016] EWCA Civ 176. For its application by analogy with regard to a Protocol letter in a case about whether an individual came to the United Kingdom on a special mission, *see* Khurts Bat v. The Investigating Judge of the German Federal Court, [2011] EWHC 2029 (although Foskett J noted that it was "open" whether the letter was of conclusive effect because there could be a scenario where other evidence suggested to the court a contrary view, at para. 110).

[104] Belhaj v. Straw, [2014] EWCA Civ 1394.

international relations has been found unattractive by senior judges.[105] In the context of the act of state doctrine (but not immunity), the U.S. Supreme Court has drawn a distinction between cases where the court would have to do no more than make ancillary factual findings about the acts of a foreign states and those where the court would have to adjudicate upon the lawfulness of the foreign state's acts.[106] Only the latter fall within the act of state doctrine and cannot be considered by the court.

There are no regular filings of "suggestions of immunity" in English courts. Courts are not obliged to seek certificates from the executive and may choose to establish facts in another way. In the first phase of the *Pinochet* case, the House of Lords did not request a certificate from the FCO, and the case proceeded on the basis that the evidence showed that Pinochet had been the head of state of Chile in the relevant period.[107] In the second phase, counsel submitted questions to the FCO as to whether Pinochet had been recognized as head of state, and, if so, on what dates; the FCO replied by letter.[108] The FCO is not required to provide its view. When the High Court asked the FCO to confirm whether two Saudi princes involved in a commercial dispute could be regarded as members of the king's family within Section 20(1) of the U.K. SIA, the FCO declined because there was "no relevant fact within the particular knowledge of the FCO which can provide an answer to this question."[109]

Looked at in the round, the United Kingdom has engaged in incremental development of the law on immunity as compared to the more *sui generis* developments in the United States and Canada with respect to terrorism,[110] and the activist approach driven by domestic constitutional norms or universal jurisdiction legislation in Italy, Greece, Belgium, and Spain. The U.K. SIA, underpinned by four decades of interpretation and practice, can be said to represent a middle ground in the evolving landscape of immunity.

[105] Belhaj v. Straw, [2017] UKSC 3, para. 41 (Lord Mance: "I see little attraction in and no basis for giving the Government so blanket a power over court proceedings, although I accept and recognise that the consequences for foreign relations can well be an element feeding into the question of justiciability").

[106] W.S. Kirkpatrick Co. Inc. v. Environmental Tectonics Corp. International, 493 U.S. 400 (1989).

[107] R v. Bow Street Metropolitan Stipendiary Magistrate, ex parte Pinochet (No 1), (2000) 1 AC 61. Joanne Foakes, *Foreign Affairs in National Courts: The Role of the Executive Certificate*, Chatham House Briefing, at 3 (2015), *available at* https://www.chathamhouse.org/sites/default/files/field/field_document/20150916ForeignAffairsNationalCourtsFoakes.pdf.

[108] Foakes, *supra* note 107, at 3.

[109] *Id.* at 4; Apex Global Management Ltd. v. Fi Call Ltd. & Others, [2013] EWHC 587 (Ch).

[110] *See, e.g.*, the "State sponsors of terrorism" provision (Foreign Sovereign Immunity Act, § 1605(A)(7)) introduced by the Anti-Terrorism and Effective Death Penalty Act of 1996; State Immunity Act, 23 R.S.C. 1985, c. S-18 § 6.1 (Canada).

CHAPTER 37

SOUTH AFRICAN LAW ON IMMUNITIES

HENNIE STRYDOM

THE law governing immunities in South Africa is made up of a combination of customary international law, international treaty law, English law, parliamentary legislation and constitutional law. It is therefore necessary to first explain, by way of introduction, the place of international customary and treaty law in South Africa's legal system and the impact of the post-1994 constitutional order in this regard.

I. Domestic Status of International Law in South Africa

In several judgments prior to the 1970s, South African courts simply assumed that the principles of customary international law formed part of South African law and could be applied by the courts without being proved as a foreign legal system.[1] Its place in the domestic legal system of South Africa was expressly asserted only in 1971 in the *South Atlantic Islands* case, where it was stated that international law "forms part of our law" and the duty of a domestic court is "to ascertain and administer the appropriate rule of international law."[2] While in this matter, the Cape Provincial Division of the Supreme Court (as it then was) justified this proposition with reference to Anglo-American Law,

[1] *See*, e.g., Ex parte Belli, 1914 CPD 742, 745–746; Marburger v. Minister of Finance, 1918 CPD 183, 187; Crooks & Co. v. Agricultural Cooperative Union Ltd., 1922 AD 423; R v. Lionda, 1944 AD 348, 352; Ex parte Sulman, 1942 CPD 407; S v. Penrose, 1966(1) SA 5 (N), 10. *See also* JOHN DUGARD, INTERNATIONAL LAW: A SOUTH AFRICAN PERSPECTIVE 46 (4th ed. 2011).

[2] South Atlantic Islands Development Corporation Ltd. v. Buchan, 1971(1) SA 234 (C), 283 C-D.

seven years later the Appellate Division in the *Nduli* case asserted that the "fons et origo of this proposition must be found in Roman Dutch law,"[3] the common law of South Africa.

Following these developments, the Supreme Court in the *Inter-Science* case ruled that:

> International law is part of the law of South Africa, save in so far as it conflicts with South African legislation or common law. Our courts will take judicial cognizance of international law, and it is their duty in any particular case to ascertain and administer the appropriate rule of international law.[4]

This subordination of international law to legislation in particular was somewhat weakened by the statutory presumption in South African law that the legislature does not intend to violate international law.[5]

Breaking with past traditions, the 1996 Constitution, which followed the first democratic elections and the 1993 Interim Constitution, brought clarity to the position of international law in the country's domestic legal order. Section 232 constitutionally endorsed customary international law by determining that: "Customary international law is law in the Republic unless it is inconsistent with the Constitution or an Act of Parliament." This means that, hierarchically, customary international law is no longer subordinate to the common law since it is only the Constitution and national legislation that will prevail in the case of inconsistencies. The statutory presumption mentioned above was also retained. According to Section 233 of the 1996 Constitution, every court, when interpreting any legislation, "must prefer any reasonable interpretation of the legislation that is consistent with international law over any alternative interpretation that is inconsistent with international law." Although Section 232 clarifies the place of customary international law in the domestic legal order, the rules which will qualify as customary international law and how they are to be proven are still matters of judicial precedent that South African courts can take judicial notice of, when turning to the decisions of international tribunals and local or foreign domestic courts and scholarly works for an answer.[6]

As far as treaty law is concerned, South Africa used to follow a dualist approach to the incorporation of treaties into domestic law. The negotiation, signing, and ratification of treaties were treated as powers of the executive while parliament gave domestic effect to a treaty by legislative enactment. Generally, this state of affairs still prevails

[3] Nduli v. Minister of Justice, 1978(1) SA 893 (A), 906B.

[4] Inter-Science Research and Development Services (Pty) Ltd. v. Republica Popular de Moçambique, 1980 (2) SA 111 (T), at 124H. *See also* Kaffraria Property (Pty) Ltd. v. Government of the Republic of Zambia, 1980 (2) SA 709 (E), 712F, 715A.

[5] *See,* e.g., CC Maynard v. The Field Cornett of Pretoria, (1894) 1 SAR 214; Achterberg v. Glinister 1903 TS 326, 334; *Ex parte* Adair Properties (Pty) Ltd., 1967 (2) SA 622 (R), 627B-F.

[6] *See* DUGARD, *supra* note 1, at 51.

under the 1996 Constitution, with slight variations. In following the practice of the Vienna Convention on the Law of Treaties, Section 231 of the Constitution distinguishes between the negotiating and signing process and the ratification process. Negotiating and signing a treaty is the responsibility of the national executive,[7] while parliament is responsible for the ratification of the treaty by means of a resolution in both Houses of Parliament. Only after completion of this process will the treaty bind the Republic in its relations with the other party/parties to the treaty.[8] For the treaty to have domestic legal effect, parliamentary enactment is required.[9]

Excluded from this process are treaties of a technical, administrative, or executive nature, or a treaty that does not require ratification or accession and is entered into by the executive. Such treaties will bind the Republic without the approval of parliament, but they must at least be tabled in parliament.[10] This exception is aimed at less formal treaties responsible for regulating matters of a routine nature for which the executive signature will suffice.[11] Another exception is the so-called self-executing treaty. Such treaties automatically acquire domestic validity without parliamentary enactment under Section 231(4) of the Constitution, provided that they are not inconsistent with the Constitution or an Act of Parliament. The concept of self-executing treaties was taken over from U.S. law and has been criticized by some scholars as being unsuitable to the South African context.[12] Case law on the matter has also failed to bring clarity to the matter.[13]

Apart from the above constitutional provisions on the applicability of international customary and treaty law, international law, and in particular, international human rights law, may enter judicial decision-making through the Bill of Rights, which is partly modeled on international human rights conventions. Of specific relevance is Section 39(1)(b) of the Constitution, which directs that when interpreting the Bill of Rights, a court, tribunal, or forum must consider international law. In one of its earliest decisions, the Constitutional Court ruled that in the context of this provision (Section 35(1) of the Interim Constitution at the time) public international law must be understood as including nonbinding as well as binding law and that both may be used as tools of interpretation.[14]

Yet another avenue for international law to influence judicial decision-making is through the judicial review powers of the courts under Section 172 of the Constitution. This may take the form of a direct challenge, where, for instance, the ratification procedures under Section 231 are challenged on the basis that they were incorrectly

[7] Constitution of the Republic of South Africa, 1996, § 231(1) [hereinafter *Constitution*].

[8] *Id.* § 231(2). *See also* the Constitutional Court ruling in Glenister v. President of the Republic of South Africa, 2011 (3) SA 347 (CC), para. 92.

[9] *Constitution*, § 231(4). [10] *Id.*, § 231(3). [11] DUGARD, *supra* note 1, at 54, 55.

[12] *Id.* at 56, 57, and sources cited there.

[13] *See* Neville J. Botha, *Extradition, Self-execution and the South African Constitution: A Non-event?*, 33 S. AFR. Y.B. INT'L L. 253 (2008); Neville J. Botha, *Rewriting the Constitution: The "Strange Alchemy" of Justice Sachs, Indeed!*, 34 S. AFR. Y.B. INT'L L. 253 (2009); DUGARD, *supra* note 1, at 59.

[14] S v. Makwanyane, 1995 (3) SA 391 (CC), 413–414.

applied in a specific matter,[15] or indirectly, where international law is relied upon to challenge the constitutionality of a law or conduct.[16] Whatever the case in point, the constitutional entrenchment of the judiciary's power to review the validity of legislative and other measures is an unequivocal replacement of the pre-1994 system of parliamentary supremacy with a system of constitutional supremacy.

II. Immunity of Foreign States

Prior to the 1980s, the doctrine of absolute sovereign immunity found its way into South African law via English law by means of judicial precedent. In upholding this doctrine it was argued that "grave and weighty considerations of public policy, international law and comity" prevented the courts of a country from making "a foreign state a party to legal proceedings against its will."[17] Shortly after this judgment was handed down, court rulings and legislative enactments in the United States[18] and the United Kingdom[19] emerged that favored a restrictive approach to sovereign immunity as a result of a changing international sentiment toward distinguishing between the official acts of a state (*acta uire imperii*) and its commercial transactions (*acta uire gestionis*) and allowing for immunity to apply only in the case of the former.

In order to bring South African law in line with these developments, two judgments in 1980, *Inter-Science Research*[20] and *Kaffraria Property*,[21] did groundbreaking work in rejecting the absolute doctrine of immunity in favor of the restrictive doctrine. The legislature followed suit, and in 1981 the *Foreign States Immunities Act* was adopted, closely following the United Kingdom's State Immunity Act of 1978.

General Immunity from Jurisdiction

In terms of the Act, a foreign state enjoys immunity from the jurisdiction of the courts and a court is obliged to give effect to the immunity conferred by the Act even when the

[15] *See* Earthlife Africa and Another v. The Minister of Energy and Others Case, No 19529/2015, High Court, Western Cape Division (26 April 2017).

[16] *See* Dugard, *supra* note 1, at 64–68, for a more detailed discussion of these matters.

[17] *See* Leibowitz v. Schwartz, 1974 (2) SA 661 (T) at 662. *See also* Lendalease Finance Co. (Pty) Ltd. v. Corp. de Mercadeo Agricola, 1974 (4) SA 397 (C).

[18] *See*, e.g., Alfred Dunhill of London Inc. v Republic of Cuba 425 U.S. 682, 702 (1976), and the Foreign Sovereign Immunities Act of 1976.

[19] *See*, e.g., Trendtex Trading Corp. v. Central Bank of Nigeria, [1976] 3 All ER 437 (QB); Trendtex Trading Corp. v. Central Bank of Nigeria, [1977] 1 All ER 887 (CA); the State Immunity Act of 1978.

[20] Inter-Science Research and Development Services (Pty) Ltd. v. Republica Popular de Moçambique, 1980 (2) SA 111 (T) at 124H.

[21] Kaffraria Property (Pty) Ltd. v. Government of the Republic of Zambia, 1980 (2) SA 709 (E), 712F, 715A.

foreign state does not appear in the proceedings.[22] A reference to a foreign state includes a reference to the head of state, the government, and government department of the foreign state.[23]

Excluded are separate entities, which the Act defines as an entity that is distinct from the executive organs of government and capable of suing or being sued, or any territory that forms a constituent part of a federal foreign state.[24] However, a separate entity will be entitled to immunity if the proceedings relate to anything done by that entity in the exercise of sovereign authority and the circumstances were such that a foreign state would have enjoyed immunity.[25]

If a separate entity, not being the central bank or other monetary authority of a foreign state, waives the immunity it is entitled to, the following procedural privileges apply as if references to a foreign state were references to a separate entity:[26]

(a) relief against a foreign state will not be given by means of an interdict or order for specific performance or for the recovery of movable or immovable property;
(b) the property of a foreign state, other than property used or intended for use for commercial purposes,[27] will not be subject to any process for attachment *ad fundandam jurisdictionem*, the enforcement of a judgment or arbitration award, or an action *in rem* for attachment or sale.

The operation of these provisions does not prevent the giving of any relief or the issue of any process with the written consent of the foreign state concerned, provided that a mere waiver of immunity is not regarded as a form of consent.[28]

Waiver of Immunity

A foreign state may waive its immunity, in which case the South African courts will be entitled to exercise jurisdiction. A foreign state may expressly waive its immunity or may be deemed to have done so if it has instituted proceedings or has intervened or taken any step in the proceedings, except if it was done for the purpose of claiming immunity or for asserting an interest in property and circumstances were such that the foreign state would have been entitled to immunity if proceedings had been brought against it.[29]

A waiver may be notified after the dispute giving rise to the proceedings has arisen or by prior written agreement, but the mere fact that an agreement stipulates that a dispute shall be governed by the law of the Republic does not in and of itself constitute a waiver.[30]

[22] Foreign States Immunities Act 87 of 1981, § 2(1) &(2) [hereinafter *Foreign State Immunities Act*].
[23] *Id.*, § 1. [24] *Id.*, § 2, read with the definition of "separate entity" in § 1. [25] *Id.*, § 15(1).
[26] *Id.*, § 15(2), read with § 14.
[27] *Id.*, § 14(3). The property of a central bank or other monetary authority of a foreign state shall not be regarded as in use or intended for use for commercial purposes. *See also id.*, § 15(3).
[28] *Id.*, §14(2). [29] *Id.*, § 3(1), (3) & (4). [30] *Id.*, § 3(2).

The head of a foreign state's diplomatic mission and the person who has entered into a contract on behalf of and with the authority of a foreign state shall be deemed to have authority to waive immunity on behalf of the foreign state.[31]

When Immunity Does Not Apply

Under Section 4 of the Act, immunity from jurisdiction does not apply in proceedings relating to commercial transactions entered into by the foreign state, or a contractual obligation of a foreign state to be performed wholly or partly in the Republic.[32] However, where the parties to the dispute are foreign states or have agreed in writing that the courts of a foreign state will exercise jurisdiction over the dispute, immunity before the South African courts will still apply.[33] A commercial transaction means:[34]

(a) any contract for the supply of services or goods;
(b) any loan or other transaction for the provision of finance and any guarantee or indemnity in respect of any such loan or other transaction or of any other financial obligation; and
(c) any other transaction or activity of a commercial, industrial, financial, professional, or other similar character into which a foreign state enters or in which it engages otherwise than in the exercise of sovereign authority.

In applying Section 4, the test for what will constitute a commercial transaction is objective and based upon the nature of the transaction. Section 14(3),[35] on the other hand, introduces a subjective test that relates to the purpose for which the property was used or for which it was intended to be used. Thus, in the context of Section 14(3), property acquired by a state by means of a commercial transaction could be immune from attachment if the property was used or intended for use for noncommercial purposes.[36]

Excluded from the definition in Section 4 are contracts of employment between a foreign state and an individual, except if:

(a) the contract was entered into in the Republic or the work is to be performed wholly or partly in the Republic; and
(b) at the time when the contract was entered into the individual was a South African citizen or was ordinarily resident in the Republic; and
(c) at the time when the proceedings are brought the individual is not a citizen of the foreign state.[37]

[31] *Id.*, § 3(6). [32] *Id.*, § 4(1). [33] *Id.*, § 4(2). [34] *Id.*, § 4(3).

[35] *Id.*, § 14(3). The property of a central bank or other monetary authority of a foreign state shall not be regarded as in use or intended for use for commercial purposes. *See also id.*, § 15(3).

[36] *See also* The Akademik Fyodorov: Government of the Russian Federation v. Marine Expeditions Inc., 1996 (4) SA 422 (C) 447D-I; Portion 20 of Plot 15 Athol (Pty) Ltd. v. Rodriques, 2001 (1) SA 1285 (W) 1296A-D; KJ International v. MV Oscar Jupiter, [1977] 3 All SA 475 (D).

[37] *Foreign State Immunities Act* § 5(1).

But the exercise of jurisdiction by the South African courts in these instances will be interdicted if (1) the parties to the contract have agreed in writing that a dispute between them shall be heard in a foreign jurisdiction; or (2) the proceedings relate to the employment of the head of a diplomatic or consular post or a member of the diplomatic or consular staff.[38]

State immunity will also not apply in proceedings relating to the death or injury of a person, or damage to or loss of tangible property;[39] an interest of the foreign state in immovable property in the Republic;[40] patents or trademarks belonging to the foreign state;[41] or an action *in rem* against a ship belonging to the foreign state as well as an action *in personam* for enforcing a claim in connection with the ship, if at the time of the cause of action the ship was used or intended for use in commercial activities.[42]

III. Diplomatic Immunity

The international customary law position on diplomatic immunities was first codified in parliamentary legislation in 1951 with the adoption of the Diplomatic Privileges Act 71 of 1951. In 1989, South Africa acceded to the 1961 Vienna Convention on Diplomatic Relations and the 1963 Vienna Convention on Consular Relations, which led to the enactment of the Diplomatic Immunities and Privileges Act 74 of 1989. But since this Act was ambiguous about whether it incorporated the two Vienna Conventions, it was replaced by a new Diplomatic Immunities and Privileges Act 37 of 2001 to clarify the position. The 2001 Act states unequivocally that the two conventions have the force of law in the Republic and that they apply, respectively, to all diplomatic missions and members of such missions and to all consular posts and members of such posts in the Republic.[43] The two conventions are also appended to the Act in the form of schedules to the Act.

Apart from the applicability of the two conventions, heads of state, who are rendered immune from criminal and civil jurisdiction of the courts of the Republic by the Act, will also enjoy the privileges they may claim under customary international law, granted to them by agreement, or conferred on them by the minister of international relations if, in a particular case, it is not expedient to enter into an agreement and if it is in the interest of the Republic.[44] A similar position applies in the case of special envoys representing another state, government, or organization.[45]

In 2002, South Africa acceded to the 1946 Convention on the Privileges and Immunities of the United Nations and the 1947 Convention on the Privileges and Immunities of the Specialized Agencies of the United Nations. By virtue of Act 37 of 2001, these conventions apply to the United Nations and its officials in the Republic and to any specialized agency and its officials in the Republic.[46] The United

[38] *Id.*, § 5(2). [39] *Id.*, § 6. [40] *Id.*, § 7. [41] *Id.*, § 8. [42] *Id.*, § 11.
[43] Diplomatic Immunities and Privileges Act 37 of 2001, §§ 2, 3. [44] *Id.*, § 4(1) read with § 7(2).
[45] *Id.*, § 4(2). [46] *Id.*, § 5.

Nations and its agencies are also vested with the legal capacity of a body corporate in the Republic to the extent consistent with the organization's constitutive instrument.[47]

A sending state, the United Nations, or any specialized agency or organization may waive any immunity or privilege that a person is entitled to under the Act, provided that the waiver is express and in writing.[48]

IV. Regional Organizations

South Africa is a member of a number of regional organizations. This section considers the immunity arrangements that apply in relations between states and two of these organizations: the African Union (AU) and the Southern African Development Community (SADC).

The African Union (AU)

In the case of the AU, the 1965 General Convention on the Privileges and Immunities of the Organization of African Unity (OAU), the predecessor of the AU, provides the legal framework for the AU's immunities and privileges. The Convention has a twofold objective, namely, to ensure that (1) the AU enjoys in the territory of each of its member states such legal capacity that will enable it to perform its functions, and (2) members of the AU as well as officials of the organization will be entitled to claim such privileges and immunities that will enable them to perform their official functions on behalf of the organization. Consequently, the Convention bestows juridical personality on the AU with the capacity to enter into contracts and to institute legal proceedings,[49] and determines that representatives of member states to the AU, its subsidiary institutions, and conferences convened by the AU shall be entitled to immunities and privileges while exercising their functions and during their travel to and from the place of meetings.[50]

The immunities and privileges provided for in the Convention are typical and in the case of the organization they render the premises, buildings, archives, and assets of the AU inviolable and immune against legal process except in case of a waiver of immunity, which, in any case, may not extend to any measure of execution.[51]

The privileges and immunities accorded representatives include immunity from personal arrest and detention and from official interrogation as well as from inspection or seizure of their personal belongings; immunity from legal process of any kind in

[47] *Id.*, § 5(4). [48] *Id.*, § 8(3).

[49] General Convention on the Privileges and Immunities of the Organization of African Unity of 1965, art. I.

[50] *Id.*, art. V. [51] *Id.*, art. II.

respect of acts performed in the exercise of their functions; inviolability of their correspondence; exemption from immigration restrictions; and such other immunities and privileges accorded to diplomatic envoys that are not inconsistent with the aforementioned.[52] These immunities, with slight variations, are also accorded officials of the AU[53] and experts on AU missions.[54]

With regard to the enjoyment of these immunities and privileges, the Convention contains the important caveat that they are not for the personal benefit of the individuals themselves but are aimed at safeguarding the independent exercise by representative of their official functions with the result that an AU member has not only the right but also the duty to waive the immunity of a representative in the case where the immunity would impede the course of justice.[55]

The Southern African Development Community (SADC)

In the case of SADC, the SADC Treaty, by virtue of Article 31, establishes the basis for the immunities and privileges that the organization and its staff will enjoy in the territory of each member state for the proper performance of their functions and determines that the privileges and immunities will be prescribed in a separate protocol. This was given effect to in 1992 with the adoption of the SADC Protocol on Immunities and Privileges, which is substantially the same as the OAU Convention with regard to the nature and scope of the immunities and privileges as well as the duty to waive that will apply to SADC and the individuals representing it.

The privileges and immunities available under the OAU Convention became an issue of judicial scrutiny in 2015 as a result of South Africa's failure, in clear violation of a court order, to arrest Al Bashir, the president of Sudan, and surrender him to the International Criminal Court (ICC) to stand trial on charges of war crimes, crimes against humanity, and genocide. South Africa's obligation to cooperate with the ICC arose from the country's ratification of the Rome Statute and the subsequent enactment of the Implementation of the Rome Statute of the International Criminal Court Act 27 of 2002 to give domestic effect to the Rome Statute as required by Section 231(4) of the Constitution. The occasion for acting in accordance with its member state obligations under the Rome Statute and under domestic law arose when Al Bashir attended the AU Summit in South Africa in June 2015. This was seized upon by a nongovernmental organization, the South African Litigation Centre (SALC), to commence proceedings in the High Court seeking an order to prevent Al Bashir from leaving the country and to direct the South African government to arrest and surrender Al Bashir to the ICC.

In the ensuing proceedings, the government relied on the immunity provisions in the host country agreement with the AU Commission, which stipulated that South Africa "shall accord to the members of the commission and staff members, the

[52] *Id.*, art. V (1). [53] *Id.*, art. VI. [54] *Id.*, art. VII. [55] *Id.*, art. V(4).

delegates and other representatives of intergovernmental organizations attending the meetings, the privileges and immunities in sections C and D, articles V and VI of the General Convention on the Privileges and Immunities of the Organization of African Unity."[56] This part of the agreement was published in the Government Gazette, which caused it to become part of domestic law. The government sought to reinforce the immunity provisions in the agreement by invoking similarities between the relevant provisions in the OAU Convention, the Vienna Convention on Diplomatic Relations (1961), and South Africa's *Diplomatic Immunities and Privileges Act* referred to earlier on.[57]

In response, the High Court dismissed the government's reliance on the agreement with the AU in view of the fact that the immunity arrangement did not cover heads of state and government and was therefore not applicable to Al Bashir.[58] Moreover, the agreement, which finds its way into South African law in the form of a government notice pursuant to an executive decision, cannot, according to the Court, displace the Rome Statute or the Implementation Act, which was adopted by a parliamentary enactment process.[59] The Court further reasoned that the referral of the Al Bashir case to the ICC by the Security Council in Resolution 1593 (2005) had the effect of obligating UN members to assist in Al Bashir's apprehension and that this obligation prevailed in the event of a conflict with any other international agreement.[60] On appeal by the government, the Supreme Court of Appeal confirmed the position taken by the High Court with regard to the applicability of the agreement with the AU as regards the position of Al Bashir.[61]

These events led to the initiation of proceedings pursuant to Article 87(7) of the Rome Statute in terms of which South Africa was requested to submit to the ICC its views on the events surrounding Al Bashir's attendance of the AU Summit and the government's failure to arrest and surrender Al Bashir to the ICC. Following submissions in early 2017 before Pre-Trial Chamber II of the ICC, the Court, on July 6, 2017, rendered its decision on South Africa's noncompliance with the ICC's request for the arrest and surrender of Al Bashir.[62] Regarding the immunity issue under the host agreement with the AU, which was raised again by South Africa before the Pre-Trial Chamber, the Court came to the same conclusion as the domestic courts, namely, that the agreement does not apply to Al Bashir as head of state and that, consequently, the agreement could not confer immunity on him.[63]

[56] Southern African Litigation Centre v. Minister of Justice and Constitutional Development and Others, 2015 (5) SA (GP), at paras. 13–15.

[57] *Id.*, at paras. 16 and 17. [58] *Id.*, at para. 30. [59] *Id.*, at para. 31.

[60] *Southern African Litigation Centre, supra* note 56, at para. 32.

[61] Minister of Justice and Constitutional Development and Others v. Southern African Litigation Centre and Others, 2016 (3) SA 317 (SCA), at paras. 47 and 48.

[62] Decision under art. 87(7) of the Rome Statute on the noncompliance by South Africa with the request by the Court for the arrest and surrender of Omar Al Bashir, ICC-02/05-01/09 (6 July 2017).

[63] *Id.*, paras. 65–67.

In the Al Bashir appeal case referred to above, the South African government largely abandoned the host agreement argument as the basis for Al Bashir's immunity against arrest and surrender and relied instead on head of state immunity *ratione personae* under customary international law.[64] Given the fact that the position in customary international law as regards a serious crimes exception to the immunity of heads of state in a foreign national jurisdiction is still unclear, the Supreme Court of Appeal concluded that ordinarily Al Bashir could have been entitled to immunity at the time he was in South Africa for the AU Summit.[65] This turned the attention of the Court to the argument by the respondent (applicant in the High Court), namely, that the position is different in South Africa by virtue of the government's own Implementation Act.

According to its long title, the Act is intended to provide "for a framework to ensure the effective implementation of the Rome Statute ... to ensure that South Africa conforms with its obligations set out in the Statute ... [and] to provide for the arrest of persons accused of having committed the said crimes and their surrender to the said Court ... "[66] In the preamble to the Act, South Africa has unequivocally committed itself to bring perpetrators of the Rome Statute crimes to justice "either in a court of law of the Republic" or "pursuant to its international obligations to do so when the Republic became party to the Rome Statute ... " However, more directly relevant for the proceedings in question is the provision in Section 4(2) of the Act, which determines inter alia that the fact that a person is or was a head of state or government is not a defense to a crime despite "any other law to the contrary, including customary and conventional international law ... " At this juncture it may also be pointed out that under Section 232 of the Constitution, customary international law is law in the Republic unless it is inconsistent with the Constitution or an Act of Parliament. Furthermore, courts, when interpreting any legislation must, in terms of Section 233 of the Constitution, prefer any reasonable interpretation that is consistent with international law over one that is not. In the instance of the Implementation Act, the court is therefore constitutionally bound to follow an interpretation that would align the Act with South Africa's Rome Statute obligations notwithstanding a potential conflict with customary international law.

The focus on the domestic law situation also caused the relationship between the Implementation Act and the Diplomatic Immunities Act to assume relevance. Since the latter was adopted earlier in time and provided for head of state immunity, it became an issue whether the Implementation Act must be construed as having tacitly repealed or amended the Diplomatic Immunities Act. Aware of the legal complications that such a construction may cause, the court approached the matter from a different angle, namely, the application of the *generalia specialibus non derogant* rule. Here, the reasoning is that the Implementation Act is a specific law with the sole objective to ensure the effective implementation of the Rome Statute at the domestic level while the

[64] *Minister of Justice and Constitutional Development*, *supra* note 61, at para. 49.

[65] *Id.*, paras. 84 and 85.

[66] International Criminal Court Act 27 of 2002.

Diplomatic Immunities Act is a general law on diplomatic immunities and privileges. To reconcile them in the circumstances of the case, the extent of the general law's reach must be limited by the specific law in the sense that head of state immunity that ordinarily exists under the Diplomatic Immunities Act must be excluded when it comes to South Africa's obligations under the Rome Statute in relation to international crimes and their prosecution.[67]

This part of the judgment causes one to reflect on a rather puzzling aspect of the legislative history of the two Acts. When the Implementation Act was considered by parliament, the Diplomatic Immunities Act as well as the Foreign States Immunities Act were already in force. Thus, parliament should have been aware of the conflicting immunity provisions in the relevant laws and could have amended the conflicting law to align it with the Implementation Act. Instead, the cure parliament opted for is the unequivocal formulation in Section 4(2) of the Implementation Act to the effect that immunity as a defense is excluded in the case of Rome Statute crimes "[d]espite any other law to the contrary, including customary and conventional international law . . . " This proviso in itself constituted a virtually insurmountable obstacle for the government, which explains the rather artificial distinction by the government between prosecution and arrest, which, with the passing of time, appears more like a desperate attempt to find a way out of an impasse forced upon the South African government by the (not unexpected) presence of a sitting African head of state who, coincidentally, happens to be a fugitive of justice.

Before the Pre-Trial Chamber of the ICC, the government steered away from the domestic law position in an attempt to put forward a stronger case by relying on the customary international law position on head of state immunity. In this instance, the determination concerned the legal ramifications of Article 27(2) of the Rome Statute and its relationship with Article 98(1) of the Statute.[68] According to Article 27(2), "[i]mmunities or special procedural rules which may attach to the official capacity of a person, whether under national or international law, shall not bar the Court from exercising its jurisdiction over such person." South Africa's reading of this provision is that it does not affect the rights and obligations of states vis-à-vis the Court since it is only intended to uphold the jurisdiction of the Court when it is challenged on the basis of a person's immunity as a result of the person's official capacity.[69]

Here, as in the case with the interpretation of domestic law, the government was attempting to take arrest and surrender out of the reach of the immunity provision in Article 27(2), a restrictive interpretation that the Court rejected as incompatible with the language used and because it would create an insurmountable obstacle for the Court whose ability to exercise jurisdiction over Rome Statute crimes is dependent upon states parties' execution of warrants of arrests and other requests for assistance.[70] In concluding that Article 27(2) covers both horizontal and vertical relationships, the

[67] *Minister of Justice and Constitutional Development*, *supra* note 61, paras. 102, 103.

[68] *Decision under art. 87(7) of the Rome Statute*, *supra* note 62, para. 71.

[69] *Id.*, para. 73.

[70] *Id.*, paras. 74 and 75.

Court ruled that head of state immunity cannot be raised as justification for a refusal to arrest and surrender a person sought by the Court since the irrelevance of immunities based on official capacity "is incorporated in the Statute as a basic principle to which States Parties subscribe by having voluntarily ratified the Statute."[71] In addition, it is a necessary corollary of the general obligation of parties, the Court reasoned, to cooperate with the Court as provided for in Article 86 of the Statute.[72] As a result, the Article 98 obligation to first seek a waiver of immunity or consent from arrest from a third state has no effect within the scope of Article 27(2) in relations with states parties as well as states that have accepted the jurisdiction of the Court under Article 12(3) of the Statute. In the case of nonstate parties, since they have no obligation to cooperate with the Court, Article 27(2) leaves their rights under international law unaffected.[73]

But since the Court's jurisdiction was originally triggered by a Chapter VII Security Council referral in terms of Resolution 1593 (2005) and pursuant to Article 13(b) of the Statute, the position of nonstate parties does not remain unaffected by the legal framework of the Statute, since, as the Court explained, referral has the effect that the Court is enabled to act with regard to the referred situation and to do so, first and foremost, by applying the Statute.[74] Hence, the effect is that a nonstate party such as Sudan has, by virtue of the Security Council resolution, an obligation to cooperate fully with the Court for the purpose of the referral,[75] and immunity on the ground of official capacity is, as far as Sudan is concerned, equally inapplicable by virtue of Article 27(2) of the Statute[76] and can therefore also not be invoked by states parties, such as South Africa, when they are called upon to execute a request by the Court for arrest and surrender.[77]

Domestic Enforcement of the SADC Tribunal's Judgments

This issue is part of a series of legal challenges to the so-called agrarian reform in Zimbabwe introduced by a constitutional amendment in 2005. The amendment entitled the state to expropriate land identified for resettlement purposes without compensation (except for improvements on the land), barred an affected landowner from challenging the state's decision, and suspended the courts' jurisdiction to entertain a legal challenge.

Without a remedy at the domestic level, a number of landowners—mostly white farmers—who lost their land in this manner successfully challenged the state's action before the SADC Tribunal, entitling them to compensation for the expropriation of their land.[78] Zimbabwe refused to comply with the ruling, and this led to contempt

[71] *Id.*, para. 80. *See also id.*, paras. 76 and 77. [72] *Id.*, para. 78. [73] *Id.*, paras. 81 and 82.
[74] *Id.*, paras. 84–86. [75] *Id.*, paras. 87–89. [76] *Id.*, para. 91 and 92.
[77] *Id.*, paras. 93 and 94.
[78] Mike Campbell and Others v. Zimbabwe SADC (T), Case No 2/2007.

proceedings before the Tribunal and a cost order against the Zimbabwean government.[79] When this was also ignored, the applicants approached the High Court in South Africa to have the cost order enforced and obtained from the High Court a writ of execution authorizing the attachment and sale of certain properties in Cape Town owned by the Zimbabwean government.[80]

Zimbabwe challenged the ruling before the South African Supreme Court of Appeal, citing immunity against legal proceedings in South Africa's domestic courts, and also arguing that the High Court lacked jurisdiction because the SADC Treaty and the Tribunal's Protocol had not been enacted into law as required by Section 231(4) of the South African Constitution. The Zimbabwean government lost on both grounds, and the Supreme Court of Appeal held that South African common law on the enforcement of foreign judgments applied to international tribunals and that the cost order was, therefore, enforceable in South Africa.[81]

The Zimbabwean government then sought leave to appeal to the Constitutional Court against the order made by the Supreme Court of Appeal. On the basis that a constitutional matter was involved, namely, the question of access to courts, as well as the human rights and rule of law basis of the dispute between the parties, the majority granted leave to appeal.[82]

The Constitutional Court first dealt with the binding effect on South Africa of the amended SADC Treaty, which incorporated the Tribunal's Protocol. South Africa acceded to the SADC Treaty on August 29, 1994, and this accession was approved by parliament in 1995 in accordance with Section 231(2) of the South African Constitution. This had the effect that the treaty became binding on South Africa at the international level. For the treaty's domestic enforcement, parliamentary enactment is required under Section 231(4) of the Constitution. This did not happen. It is this issue that the Zimbabwean government seized upon in arguing that the Tribunal's cost order was not enforceable in a South African domestic court. The Constitutional Court rejected the argument that noncompliance with Section 231(4) rendered the Tribunal's order unenforceable at the domestic level, accepting instead that ratification by parliament alone is sufficient to make it obligatory for South Africa to take steps to give effect to the Tribunal's decisions in accordance with Article 32(2) of the Tribunal's Protocol.[83]

For its claim to immunity in proceedings before domestic courts in South Africa, Zimbabwe relied on Section 2(1) of the Foreign States Immunities Act 87 of 1981. However, under Section 3(1) of the Act, such immunity will be forfeited in proceedings in which the foreign state has *expressly* waived its immunity. Such a waiver, according

[79] Fick and Another v. Republic of Zimbabwe SADC (T), Case No 01/2010.

[80] Fick and Others v. Government of the Republic of Zimbabwe, Case No. 77881/2009, North Gauteng High Court 25 February 2010 (Case No. 77881/2009).

[81] Government of the Republic of Zimbabwe v. Fick and Others, [2012] ZASCA 122.

[82] Government of the Republic of Zimbabwe v. Fick & Others, 2013 (5) SA 325 (CC) [hereinafter *Fick*].

[83] *Id.*, paras. 29–31.

to the Constitutional Court, had indeed taken place when Zimbabwe decided to ratify the SADC Treaty and to adopt the Amending Agreement incorporating the Tribunal's Protocol, which provides in Article 32(3) that decisions of the Tribunal shall be binding upon the parties and enforceable within their territories. By accepting this obligation, Zimbabwe had, for all intents and purposes, relinquished its claim to sovereign immunity before South African courts in respect of the registration and enforcement of decisions made against it by the Tribunal.[84]

The remaining question then, was whether South African law provided for the enforcement of the decisions of an international Tribunal in the same manner as foreign civil orders under the Enforcement of Foreign Civil Judgements Act 32 of 1988. According to this Act, foreign judgments given in countries designated by the minster for purposes of enforcement in South Africa, become enforceable in South Africa. However, there has been no such designation regarding decisions of the SADC Tribunal. The second obstacle was that the Act only applied to enforcement by magistrates' courts. Thus, with the applicability of the Act rendered impossible, the matter had to be dealt with in terms of the common law.

With regard to the jurisdictional issue, it was pointed out that in the proceedings before the Tribunal, Zimbabwe did not object to the jurisdictional capacity of the Tribunal as such, but merely challenged the Tribunal's jurisdiction to rule on the alleged human rights violations and the land expropriation without compensation program. Zimbabwe's argument, in this instance, was that the SADC instruments did not contain any specific standards against which Zimbabwe's conduct could be measured, and that the Tribunal could therefore not invoke norms and standards of other international treaties.[85] This explains, according to the Court, why the Tribunal simply relied on Article 4(c) of the SADC Treaty, which obliges SADC states to act in accordance with human rights, democratic principles, and the rule of law. Moreover, by participating in the proceedings before the Tribunal, Zimbabwe had submitted to the jurisdiction of the Tribunal.[86]

With the jurisdictional question answered, the Court turned to the common law position in South Africa regarding the enforcement of foreign judgments. In pointing out that the common law only allows for enforcement of judgments or orders by foreign domestic courts, the question then was whether the common law should be developed by the court (as is required by Sections 8(3) and 39(2) of the Constitution) to include judgments and orders by international tribunals.[87]

In finding itself obliged to develop the common law to provide for such a solution, the Court took into consideration a number of reasons, including the need to ensure that lawful judgments are not evaded with impunity by any state or person.[88] But the reasons that weighed most heavily with the Court were those enunciated in the Constitution itself, namely the right of access to courts and to an effective remedy in Section 34 of the Constitution; the obligation in Section 8(3) to develop the common

[84] *Id.*, paras. 32–35. [85] *Id.*, paras. 41 and 42. [86] *Id.*, para. 42. [87] *Id.*, paras. 52.
[88] *Id.*, para. 54.

law to give effect to the bill of rights; the obligation in Section 39(1)(b) to consider international law when interpreting the bill of rights; and the provision in Section 233 under which the courts, when interpreting any legislation, must prefer any reasonable interpretation that is consistent with international law over any other interpretation that is inconsistent with international law.[89]

The Court read this constitutional framework together with the obligation in Article 32 of the Tribunal's Protocol, which places an obligation on member states to take the measures required for ensuring the execution of the Tribunal's decisions in their domestic legal systems. Consequently, "[S]ection 34 of the Constitution must therefore be interpreted, and the common law developed, so as to grant the right of access to our courts to facilitate the enforcement of the decisions of the Tribunal in this country."[90] This will be achieved, the Court concluded, by regarding the Tribunal as a foreign court, and to that end the "concept of a 'foreign court' will henceforth include the Tribunal."[91]

It must be pointed out that this ruling only affects the position of the SADC Tribunal and does not bring clarity with regard to the domestic enforcement of the judgments of other international tribunals. A legislative amendment to the Enforcement Act addressing this issue is perhaps preferable to ad hoc judicial interventions.

While it is admirable that the Constitutional Court's decision provided an opportunity in common law for the enforcement of an important SADC ruling against a member state (Zimbabwe),[92] which had not only denied the applicants a remedy under domestic law but also notoriously remained dismissive of the SADC Tribunal, the approach followed by the Court to arrive at this conclusion is not unproblematic[93] and needs further scrutiny. For current purposes two issues stand out, namely, the enforceability of the decisions of international tribunals in the domestic courts of third states, i.e., states that are not party to the dispute, and the waiver of immunity requirements under South African law.

As regards the first issue, the standard treaty practice is that decisions by international courts and tribunals are only binding on the parties to the dispute and if provision is made for the enforceability of a decision, it is a matter for the domestic law of the losing party to resolve.[94] In instances of noncompliance it is often the case

[89] *Id.*, paras. 54–69. [90] *Id.*, para. 69. [91] *Id.*, para. 70.

[92] *See also* Erika de Wet, *The Case of Government of the Republic of Zimbabwe v Louis Karel Fick: A First Step Towards Developing a Doctrine on the Status of International Judgments within the Domestic Legal Order*, 17 POTCHEFSTROOM ELECTRONIC L.J. 554 (2014).

[93] *See also* Hannah D. Woolaver, *Domestic Enforcement of International Judicial Decisions against Foreign States in South Africa: Government of the Republic of Zimbabwe v Fick*, 6 CONST. CT. REV. 217 (2015).

[94] *See* Statute of the International Court of Justice of 1946, art. 59; European Convention for the Protection of Human Rights and Fundamental Freedoms of 1956, art. 46(1); American Convention on Human Rights of 1969, art. 68; Protocol to the African Charter on Human and Peoples' Rights on the Establishment of an African Court on Human and Peoples' Rights of 1998, art. 30 [hereinafter Protocol to the African Charter]; Protocol on the Statute of the African Court of Justice and Human Rights of 2008, art. 46; Statute of the International Tribunal for the Law of the Sea of 1982, art. 33.

that the matter is then referred to another body with enforcement powers. For instance, in the case of the International Court of Justice (ICJ) it is the UN Security Council[95] and in the case of the African Human Rights Court it is the Council of Ministers that oversees the execution of judgments on behalf of the Assembly of Heads of State and Government.[96]

As far as enforcement and execution of judgments are concerned, this practice is seemingly followed by the SADC Tribunal. Of direct relevance is Article 32 of the Tribunal's Protocol, which provides as follows:

1. The law and rules of civil procedure for the registration and enforcement of foreign judgments in force in the territory of the State in which the judgment is to be enforced shall govern enforcement.
2. States and institutions of the Community shall take forthwith all measures necessary to ensure execution of decisions of the Tribunal.
3. Decisions of the Tribunal shall be binding upon the parties to the dispute in respect of that particular case and enforceable within the territories of the States concerned.
4. Any failure by a State to comply with a decision of the Tribunal may be referred to the Tribunal by any party concerned.
5. If the Tribunal established the existence of such failure, it shall report its finding to the Summit for the latter to take appropriate action.

While the wording in the first paragraph clearly follows the general trend, namely, that the enforceability of a judgment is a matter for the losing party to the dispute to give effect to in terms of its domestic laws, the wording of the second and third paragraphs may be open to a more extensive interpretation.[97] The second paragraph contains a general instruction to "States and institutions of the Community" to adopt the measures necessary for giving effect to the decisions of the Tribunal without any reference to the "parties to the dispute." Then, in the third paragraph the *binding nature* of the Tribunal's decisions is mentioned in relation to the "parties to the dispute" while the *enforcement* of such decisions may take place "within the states concerned." If the wording were "and enforceable within their territories," it would have been clear that Article 32(3) had in mind the "parties to the dispute."

In the *Fick* case, the Constitutional Court seems to have relied on an extensive interpretation of the wording of Articles 32(2) and (3)[98] of the Protocol to construe an international obligation on the part of South Africa, as a SADC member, and mindful

[95] United Nations Charter of 1945, art. 94(2).

[96] Protocol to the African Charter, arts. 29(2) and 31.

[97] *See* Woolaver, *supra* note 93, at 13, who is of the view that the text of art. 32 closely mirrors the general practice and that the enforceability of judgments under art. 32(3) is confined to the parties to the dispute. In addition, she argues that art. 32(2) has the effect that member states must see to it that they have the necessary measures in place to ensure the execution of the Tribunal's decisions to which they are party.

[98] De Wet, *supra* note 92, at 555, seems to be in agreement with such an interpretation.

of Article 231 of the South African Constitution, to give effect to the Tribunal's judgment.[99] This was despite the fact that it was not a party to the dispute and enforcement could only be achieved by developing the common law. That said, the argument that the Constitutional Court enforced an interpretation of the Protocol—allowing for third-party jurisdiction in providing a remedy—that is not supported by the wording in the Protocol's text,[100] is itself based on an interpretation that is not unequivocally borne out by the wording in question. Thus, by choosing the wording in question, the parties to the Protocol have exposed themselves to an interpretation by a judicial organ of a third state that operates under a set of rules that is diametrically opposed to what the losing state in the original dispute was accustomed to. In the contemporary world it is also doubtful whether issues of this kind, including the relationship between international and domestic law and between international and domestic courts, can be resolved with reference to the traditional dualist and monist distinction. What is more likely to occur is that international cooperation will be balanced with the preservation of the judicial forum's distinct character and normative judicial framework.

But even so, the waiver of immunity issue remains controversial. As indicated earlier on, the Zimbabwean government's claim to immunity under international law as well as South African domestic law was dismissed by the Constitutional Court on the basis that by consenting to the jurisdiction of the Tribunal, Zimbabwe had effectively waived the immunity it would have been ordinarily entitled to in proceedings before South African courts. It should be recalled at this point that South African law, as indicated earlier in this chapter, follows the restrictive theory of state immunity, which allows for immunity from jurisdiction only in the case of *acta iure imperii*. Since the act of expropriation, which was the subject matter in the dispute before the SADC Tribunal, was an official act of the Zimbabwean government and not a commercial transaction, the South African courts would, in principle, be barred from exercising jurisdiction over such conduct. But since we are in this matter dealing with the enforcement of a cost order against property of the Zimbabwean government rented for commercial purposes at the time[101] the relevance of Section 14(1)(b) of the Foreign States Immunities Act is of immediate importance. It states as follows:

> [T]he property of a foreign state shall not be subject to any process –
> (i) for its attachment in order to found jurisdiction;
> (ii) for the enforcement of a judgment or an arbitration award; or
> (iii) in an action in rem, for its attachment or sale.

By virtue of this provision a distinction is made between immunity from jurisdiction and immunity from enforcement. Moreover, this distinction is further emphasized in

[99] *See Fick*, *supra* note 82, paras. 54–70, and especially para. 59.
[100] *See* Woolaver, *supra* note 93, at 218.
[101] *See* Republic of Zimbabwe v. Sheriff Wynberg North, 2010 ZAGPJHC 118.

Section 14(2), which states that "a mere waiver of a foreign state's immunity from jurisdiction of the courts of the Republic shall not be regarded as a consent for the purposes of... subsection [1]." What Section 14(2) then requires is written consent by a foreign state for the granting of any relief sought against the property of that state.

In the *Fick* case, the Constitutional Court relied on Article 32 of the SADC Tribunal's Protocol for its argument that the Zimbabwean government had waived its immunity before South African courts,[102] without specifying which part of Article 32 supports the waiver in question. But even if Articles 32(2) and (3) were relied upon, it is highly questionable whether they can be construed to constitute a written and express waiver of immunity within the meaning of Section 14(1) and (2) of the Act. Even if the result could be reconciled with the text of Articles 32(2) and (3),[103] it would be problematic more generally from the perspective of what constitutes a waiver. The discretion to waive immunity in the Foreign States Immunities Act is case, time, and circumstance specific. Thus, if waiver is fixed to a once-off event such as the ratification of a multilateral treaty, it constitutes a waiver for all future incidents, which is irreconcilable with a foreign state's sovereign power to decide in each specific case what course of action to take.

V. Conclusion

Before World War II, the Union of South Africa was a respected member of the international community of states, which, at the time, was dominated by Western states.[104] After the war, the country's relationship with Western democracies became strained over time as a result of the South African government's racial policies, which were in stark contrast to the new human rights agenda in the United Nations. This source of discontent eventually also alienated South Africa from the British Commonwealth.[105]

Despite this estrangement, which became more acrimonious with the imposition of the United Nations' sanction regime against South Africa, the country has maintained its strategic and ideological links with the West. This orientation, coupled with the Western roots of its legal system, were compelling reasons in the early life of the new Republic for carrying out legislative changes in response to legal developments in Western countries with whom the South African government were strategically and economically closely connected, especially when foreign relations issues were involved. The Foreign States Immunities Act is a case in point. In other cases, such as the Diplomatic Immunities and Privileges Act, legislative renewal was prompted by South

[102] *Fick*, *supra* note 82, paras. 32–35. [103] *See also* Woolaver, *supra* note 93, at 239.

[104] South Africa only gained full independence from Britain in 1961.

[105] On these developments, *see* Deon Geldenhuys, *South Africa and the West*, *in* SOUTH AFRICA: PUBLIC POLICY PERSPECTIVES 299 (Robert A. Schrire ed., 1982).

Africa's accession to the relevant UN conventions, which required legislative enactment to have the force of law in the Republic.

With the advent of the new constitutional order in 1994, the interpretation and application of all laws became subject to an entirely new set of considerations informed by the concept of constitutional supremacy, the rule of law, fundamental rights guarantees, and the relevance of international law. The *Fick* and *Al Bashir* judgments, among others, are important illustrations of the new jurisprudence taking shape under the courts' engagement with the new dispensation, even in cases with foreign policy implications. These and other precedents illustrate that the judicial branch of government, armed with the constitution, is prepared to enter an area that was previously the exclusive domain of the executive. Whether this meets with the approval of government is a matter for debate. Government's dissatisfaction with the outcome of the *Al Bashir* litigation is part of the public record and the unfavorable result of the proceedings before the ICC did not lay to rest the dispute over whether Al Bashir was entitled to immunity.

CHAPTER 38

JURISDICTIONAL IMMUNITIES, CONSTITUTIONAL VALUES, AND SYSTEM CLOSURES

ANDREA BIANCHI

THIS chapter analyzes the invocation of constitutional norms and values to prevent the recognition of the effects of an international judgment in domestic law, against the background of the Italian Constitutional Court decision No. 238 of 2014. The chapter then explores more generally the significance and function of so-called "system closures" effectuated by judicial organs in domestic and international law. While less frequently resorted to by judicial organs than balancing or coordinating techniques in case of potential conflict between legal orders, system closures have become quite common. Although they perform important symbolic functions, domestic legal systems' closures are detrimental to the role that domestic courts may play in implementing international law. This is why international adjudicators such as the International Court of Justice (ICJ) should give more consideration to the impact of their decisions on domestic legal orders.

I. THE ICJ JUDGMENT IN *GERMANY V. ITALY* AND ITS IMPACT

When the International Court of Justice decided the Jurisdictional Immunities of the State (Germany v. Italy) case in 2012,[1] I wrote that the issue of how to solve the

[1] ICJ, Jurisdictional Immunities of the State (Germany v. Italy: Greece intervening), Judgment, 3 Feb. 2012.

clash between state immunity and human rights had been settled once and for all.[2] Paraphrasing Wittgenstein and not without irony, I emphasized that the ICJ provided us with a twofold certainty. On the one hand, it shed light on a highly controversial point, namely, that states cannot be sued before the domestic courts of another state for serious violations of human rights, as they enjoy jurisdictional immunity. On the other hand, the ICJ reassured us that—if need be—the Court is always there to tell international lawyers (and possibly the whole world) what the law is.[3]

As is well known, the ICJ held that states are immune under customary international law for their sovereign acts, and that such an immunity is required also "in proceedings for torts allegedly committed on the territory of another State by its armed forces."[4] Furthermore, under customary international law, a state could not be deprived of immunity "by reason of the fact that it is accused of serious violations of human rights law or the law of armed conflict."[5] As regards Italy's main contention, namely, that *jus cogens* norms should trump any rule with which they come into conflict, including those on foreign states' jurisdictional immunities, the ICJ quickly dismissed the gist of Italy's argument. It did so by denying the existence of a conflict between, on the one hand, the rules of the law of armed conflict that were relevant to the instant case (murder of civilians in occupied territories; deportation of civilian inhabitants to forced labour; and deportation of prisoners of war to slave labor), allegedly of a *jus cogens* character; and, on the other hand, the jurisdictional immunity of Germany before Italy's domestic courts.

The denial of the conflict is based on a well-known and often-rehearsed argument, namely, that "[t]he two sets of rules address different matters."[6] While the rules on jurisdictional immunities aim at establishing whether or not the domestic courts of one state may exercise jurisdiction over a foreign state, the rules of the law of armed conflict are geared toward establishing the illegality of a state's behavior. In other words, the procedural rules on jurisdictional immunity would never cross paths with the substantive rules of behavior that establish the lawfulness—or lack thereof—of state conduct. Against the backdrop of the distinction between procedure and substance, the Court also explains why the applicability of the contemporary law of state immunity to events occurring during World War II neither violates the principle that the law should not apply retrospectively to establish issues of legality and responsibility nor amounts to a recognition that a violation of a rule of *jus cogens* is lawful under Article 41 of the International Law Commission's Articles on State Responsibility.[7]

The ICJ based its conclusion that the *jus cogens* character of substantive rules of conduct does not affect or displace procedural rules bearing on jurisdiction on both its own case law as well as the case law of domestic courts. As regards its own precedents,

[2] Andrea Bianchi, *On Certainty*, *EJIL: Talk!*, Feb. 16, 2012, *available at* https://www.ejiltalk.org/on-certainty/ (accessed Jan. 15, 2018).

[3] *Id.* [4] *Jurisdictional Immunities of the State*, *supra* note 1, para. 78.

[5] *Id.*, para. 91. [6] *Id.*, para. 93. [7] *Id.*

the Court refers to both the *Armed Activities*[8] and *Arrest Warrant*[9] cases for the proposition that the status of a rule as *jus cogens* does not bear on the jurisdiction of the ICJ or on a state's right to invoke and rely on its own immunities under customary international law.[10] Furthermore, the fact that the argument based on the hierarchical superiority of *jus cogens* rules has not prevailed before domestic courts and that no national legislation on state immunity provides for an exception to the general rule of immunity for *jus cogens* violations[11] led the Court to conclude rather smoothly "that even on the assumption that the proceedings in the Italian courts involved violations of *jus cogens* rules, the applicability of the customary international law on State immunity was not affected."[12]

Given the almost unfettered reverence of international lawyers toward the judicial pronouncements of the International Court of Justice, it had to be expected that this was the final word on the matter. As Robert Jennings once put it, the ICJ's judgments are regarded as if they were a sort of "holy writ." Every single line is scrutinized and "gobbets" of the judgments are authoritatively relied upon, often regardless of context and facts, as if they were incontestable truths. I predicted that those sentences in the judgment dealing with "custom" and/or "customary law" would become particularly popular. International law textbooks and manuals would be revised to include in their latest edition the last chapter of the long saga of the clash between state immunity and human rights. Invariably the last paragraph of any such chapter would read "The ICJ conclusively held . . . " "The die is cast," I wrote.[13]

The subsequent developments hardly allowed a different speculation. Italy, while passing enabling legislation after the ratification of the 2001 UN Convention on the jurisdictional immunities of states and their property, included language that expressly

[8] Armed Activities on the Territory of the Congo (New Application: 2002) (Democratic Republic of the Congo v. Uganda), Judgment, ICJ Reports 2006, at 6, paras. 64 and 125.

[9] Arrest Warrant of 11 April 2000 (Democratic Republic of Congo v. Belgium), Judgment, ICJ Reports 2002, at 3, paras. 58 and 78.

[10] *Jurisdictional Immunities of the State*, *supra* note 1, para. 95. For criticism, *see* Kimberley N. Trapp & Alex Mills, *Smooth Runs the Water Where the Brook Is Deep: The Obscured Complexities of Germany v. Italy*, 1 CAMBRIDGE J. INT'L L. 153, 160 (2012): "Neither of these precedents is however, particularly apposite to the Court's conclusion in this case. The *Arrest Warrant* case dealt with the absolute immunity afforded to such high level officials as Heads of State and Foreign Ministers. For such immunity to satisfy its function (allowing such officials total freedom to travel and thus conduct diplomatic business) no exception can in any case be allowed. In *DRC v Rwanda*, the Court was considering an argument that the *ius cogens* status of the norm was effective to confer jurisdiction on the ICJ by invalidating a reservation against the compromissory clause in the Genocide Convention, which it rightly dismissed because of the consensual nature of the Court's jurisdiction. In *Germany v Italy*, the Court was faced with the very different question of whether the *ius cogens* status of the norms violated would provide an exception to state immunity, which is itself an exception to the usual jurisdiction which states enjoy within their territory."

[11] *Jurisdictional Immunities of the State*, *supra* note 1, para. 96.

[12] *Id.*, para. 97. For a critique of this line of argumentation, *see* Andrea Bianchi, *Gazing at the Crystal Ball (Again): State Immunity and Jus Cogens beyond Germany v Italy*, 4 J. INT'L DISP. SETT. 457, 459–462 (2013).

[13] Bianchi, *On Certainty*, *supra* note 2.

mandated that domestic courts comply with the ICJ's judgment and dismiss for lack of jurisdiction cases brought against foreign states on grounds of human rights violations.[14]

II. The Italian Constitutional Court Judgment No. 238

Nobody could reasonably have expected that the Italian Constitutional Court would dramatically break away from this order of things by refusing to recognize domestically the effects of such an interpretation of customary international law by the ICJ. In its judgment No. 238 of 10 October 2014,[15] the Constitutional Court held that a foreign state that commits war crimes, crimes against humanity, and other serious violations of human rights cannot shield itself behind the screen of immunity, as this would run counter Articles 2 and 24 of the Italian Constitution, which respectively concern the recognition and guarantee of inviolable rights as well as their judicial protection. The Court reasoned that those two provisions should be considered as the "supreme values" of the Italian Constitution and that they would be jeopardized if victims of crimes against humanity and other serious human rights violations were prevented from seeking redress before domestic courts by the rule on state immunity as interpreted by the ICJ.

The Constitutional Court conceded that the rule on state immunity could restrict the right to a judicial remedy, but held that immunity must be deemed to protect only legitimate manifestations of sovereign powers, and not conduct in violation of fundamental human rights. The Constitutional Court underscored that the ICJ itself acknowledged that other than the prospect of international negotiations with a view to achieving agreement to pay compensation to the victims of Nazi crimes, no remedy was available to the victims. By contrast, the ICJ had considered this argument about the lack of an alternative remedy, which underlies the long-standing debate on the clash between state immunity and human rights, to be irrelevant.

The case arose out of three distinct deferrals issued by the Tribunal of Florence concerning the alleged unconstitutionality of the enabling legislation, which would allow the implementation of the ICJ's judgment in the *Germany v. Italy* case in the

[14] *See* Legge 14 gennaio 2013, no. 5: Adesione della Repubblica italiana alla Convenzione delle Nazioni Unite sulle immunità giurisdizionali degli Stati e dei loro beni, fatta a New York il 2 dicembre 2004, nonchè norme di adeguamento all'ordinamento interno. (13G00023) (GU n. 24 del 29-1-2013), *reproduced at* http://www.normattiva.it/uri-res/N2Ls?urn:nir:stato:legge:2013;5 (accessed Jan. 18, 2018).

[15] *See* the Italian text of the judgment (Sentenza 238/2014) on the Italian Constitutional Court's website, *available* at http://www.cortecostituzionale.it/actionPronuncia.do. For an English translation of the judgment, *see* http://www.cortecostituzionale.it/documenti/download/doc/recent_judgments/S238_2013_en.pdf.

Italian domestic legal order. The Constitutional Court held that the domestic statute implementing the UN Charter—and in particular Article 94 of the Charter that requires UN member states to comply with the rulings of the ICJ—is unconstitutional in as much as it would allow enforcing the ICJ's judgment in Italy. By the same token, the statutory provisions enacted by the Italian Parliament to both ratify the 2004 UN Convention on the jurisdictional immunities of states and their property and to enforce the ICJ's *Germany v. Italy* judgment were also declared to be unconstitutional. Both findings of unconstitutionality were based on the infringement of Articles 2 and 24 of the Italian Constitution.[16]

As regards the automatic recognition and incorporation of customary international law rules via Article 10 of the Constitution,[17] the Constitutional Court found that Article 10 does not trigger the *renvoi* to the rule of state immunity to the extent that the rule, as interpreted by the ICJ, would allow a foreign state to shield itself from the jurisdiction of domestic courts in case of alleged serious violations of human rights. In other words, the rule of state immunity would not "enter" the Italian legal order and, consequently, would not display any legal effect.[18] There is thus no potential conflict between Article 10 on the one hand, and Articles 2 and 24 on the other hand, as the rule on state immunity cannot make its way within the domestic legal system through the ordinary constitutional mechanisms of incorporation.

III. System Closures

The decision of the Constitutional Court provides food for thought to anyone who is interested in the interplay between international law and domestic legal orders. In many ways, the judgment represents what I would term a "system closure," that is, the refusal by one system—the Italian legal system in the case at hand—to communicate with another, namely, the international legal system. To say that the Italian legal system will neither comply with an ICJ judgment nor allow introduction into the domestic legal order of an international law rule that would run counter to its fundamental values is tantamount to stating that such fundamental values cannot be compromised. Arguably, this is not the first time that the Italian Constitutional Court has sent such a message. In the *Venezia* case, the Constitutional Court sent a similar signal regarding the impossibility of extraditing an individual to a retentionist state where he could be

[16] Sentenza 238/2014, *supra* note 15, at 8–9.

[17] Article 10 of the Italian Constitution reads: "The Italian legal system conforms to the generally recognised principles of international law . . ." English translation provided at https://www.senato.it/documenti/repository/istituzione/costituzione_inglese.pdf.

[18] Sentenza 238/2014, *supra* note 15, at 7–8.

sentenced to death.[19] There, too, the Constitutional Court hinted at the intransgressible character of the constitutional provision prohibiting the death penalty.[20]

The *Venezia* case concerned a challenge brought before the Regional Administrative Tribunal regarding the constitutionality of Article 698 of the Italian Code of Criminal Procedure, as well as the domestic statute that incorporated the 1983 U.S.-Italy Extradition Treaty and gave effect to Article IX of the Treaty.[21] Both Article 698 of the Code of Criminal Procedure and Article IX of the Extradition Treaty, on which the extradition decree was based, provided that when the offense for which extradition is requested is punishable by death under the laws of the requesting party, extradition shall be refused, unless the requesting party provides such assurances as the requested party considers sufficient that the death penalty shall not be imposed, or, if imposed, shall not be executed. Mr. Venezia argued that the statutes violated several provisions of the Italian Constitution, including Article 2, which protects fundamental human rights, and Article 27(4), which prohibits the death penalty.[22]

The administrative tribunal suspended the operation of the extradition decree, stayed the proceedings, and referred the matter to the Constitutional Court. The Constitutional Court delivered its judgment on June 27, 1996. It held that Article 698 of the Code of Criminal Procedure and the act of incorporation of the U.S.-Italy Extradition Treaty, as far as the incorporation of Article IX is concerned, were unconstitutional. The extradition of a fugitive indicted for a crime for which capital punishment is provided by the law of the requesting state would violate Articles 2 and 27 of the Italian Constitution, the Court reasoned, regardless of the sufficiency of the assurances provided by the requesting state that the death penalty would not be imposed or, if imposed, would not be executed. In its judgment, the Court first addressed the issue of the preeminence of the values embodied in Articles 2 and 27 of the Italian Constitution. In particular, the Court stressed that the drafters of the Constitution had deemed the prohibition of the death penalty and inhuman forms of punishment laid down in Article 27 to be derived from the right to life, which is one of the fundamental human rights protected by Article 2. The absolute character of the protection granted by Article 2 to fundamental human rights affects the exercise of powers by all public authorities, including those in charge of international judicial cooperation.

[19] For my comment on the case, *see* Venezia c. Ministero di Grazia e Giustizia (Italian Constitutional Court, Judgment No. 223 of 27 June 1996), 88 Am. J. Int'l L. 727 (1997).

[20] *Id.* at 727–728.

[21] Extradition Treaty, Oct. 13, 1983, Italy-U.S., TIAS No. 10,837, 24 ILM 1525 (1985) (entered into force Sept. 24, 1984).

[22] Art. 2 reads: "The Republic recognizes and guarantees the inviolable rights of man, both as an individual and as a member of the social groups in which his personality finds expression and imposes the performance of unalterable duties of a political, economic and social nature." Art. 27, paragraph 4 states: "The death penalty is not admitted save in cases specified by military laws in time of war." Italian Constitution, arts. 2 and 27(4), *translated in* Constitutions in Countries of the World (Albert P. Blaustein & Gisbert H. Flanz eds., 1987). The death penalty was also abolished in military law by art. 1 of Act No. 589, Oct. 13, 1994.

The Court found that the relevant issue in the case at hand was to determine whether the assurances provided by the requesting state could be an appropriate means to protect the values enshrined in the Italian Constitution. The Court held that the very concept of "sufficient assurances" that the death penalty shall not be imposed or executed was constitutionally inadmissible. This is so because the prohibition of Article 27 and its underlying values such as the right to life require absolute protection. Such protection cannot be made to depend on the discretion of public authorities who, on a case-by-case basis, would have to decide whether the assurances given by the requesting state were effective and reliable.

Interestingly enough, the Constitutional Court avoided the international responsibility issues underlying both cases. In particular, it avoided addressing the issue of whether, and, if so, when, the principles and values enshrined in national constitutions are to prevail over international law in case of conflicting requirements. The issue, which hovers over the intersection of law, politics, and philosophy, is beyond the scope of this chapter. It must suffice here to mention that, notwithstanding the long-established principle that a state may not invoke its municipal law to justify a violation of international law,[23] some authors have argued that respect for the fundamental principles of a state's constitution may represent a circumstance precluding wrongfulness under international law.[24] This argument, yet to be tested in international practice, may be persuasive when applied to the protection of fundamental human rights as enshrined in national constitutions, especially when domestic constitutional values provide a higher standard of protection than the applicable international standard or can be grounded in some established trends of international practice.

The "system closure" attitude taken by the Italian Constitutional Court is not unprecedented. The European Court of Justice (ECJ) took a similar stance in *Kadi*, when it set aside any consideration concerning the alleged hierarchy of international law regimes by simply stating that according to the EU constitutional legal order it was empowered to exercise judicial review over any act of EU law.[25] The ECJ thus departed from the approach of the Court of First Instance, which had previously held that—although Article 103 of the UN Charter gives priority to the obligations stemming from the Charter over other conflicting treaty obligations—the Security Council is bound to

[23] *See* Polish Nationals in Danzig, 1931 PCIJ (ser. A/B) No. 44, at 24 ("a State cannot adduce as against another State its own Constitution with a view to evading obligations incumbent upon it under international law"); and Pinson v. United Mexican States, 5 R.I.A.A. 327, 393–394 (1932) (umpire of the France-Mexico Claims Commission rejected the view that a state's constitution could prevail over international law as "absolutely contrary to the very axioms of international law"). *See also* 1 OPPENHEIM'S INTERNATIONAL LAW 84 (Robert Jennings & Arthur Watts eds., 1992); Vienna Convention on the Law of Treaties, art. 27; and International Law Commission, Draft Articles on Responsibility of States for Internationally Wrongful Acts, November 2001, Supplement No. 10 (A/56/10), chp.IV.E.1, *available at* http://www.refworld.org/docid/3ddb8f804.html (accessed Jan. 5, 2018).

[24] BENEDETTO CONFORTI, DIRITTO INTERNAZIONALE 343–344 (4th ed. 1992).

[25] European Court of Justice, Joined Cases C-402/05 P and C-415/05 P, Kadi v. Council of the EU and Commission of the EC, (2008) ECR I-6351, judgment of Sept. 3, 2008.

respect *jus cogens*, i.e., peremptory rules of human rights law.[26] The Court maintained that, regardless of any alleged supremacy of UN law as a matter of international law, EU judicial organs must exercise full judicial review over any EU legal act against the background of the constitutive treaties, in particular Article 6 of the Treaty on European Union that provides that the European Union shall respect fundamental human rights. In the case at hand, the ECJ found that Mr. Kadi's rights of defense, effective judicial protection, and property had been infringed. The ECJ, unlike the Court of First Instance that had tried to articulate a vision of an integrated international legal order, in which EU law and UN law would be coordinated and subjected to the overarching principles of *jus cogens*, postulated the self-contained character of the European Union legal system. On this vision, the constitutional values of the EU legal system stand out as the only benchmarks against which the ECJ can exercise its judicial review. Once again, one is faced with an instance of system closure that "shuts off" a legal system and makes it impermeable to external normative considerations.

It is interesting to note that in the *Kadi* and *Venezia* cases as well as in the recent judgment No. 238 of the Italian Constitutional Court, what was at stake was the "internal" position of preeminence of human rights norms. The conflict, actual or potential, consisted of "external" international law rules calling into question values underlying the relevant norms, which were perceived by the social community to which the judicial organ belongs as *particularly* worthy of protection. Faced with a potential threat, the system shut down all the channels of communication and opted for a closure, rather than resorting to balancing techniques.

By no means should one believe that system closures are always prompted by the risk of jeopardizing human rights values. More generally, such system closures occur when the autonomy or cultural identity of a system is threatened or called into question. The U.S. Supreme Court's decision in *Medellín v. Texas* could be considered an apt example of such system closures.[27] In 2004 the ICJ had decided in the *Avena* case that the United States should review and reconsider the conviction of Mexican nationals on death row on the ground that the United States had violated their rights of consular notification under the 1963 Vienna Convention on consular relations.[28] The Supreme Court, however, held that the ICJ decision was not binding federal law and that, therefore, it was not enforceable against Texas in the federal courts. Thus the state's procedural bar to the Mexican nationals' habeas corpus claims could not be preempted.

A closure is often induced by a system's effort to protect itself from losing its distinct identity, be it legal or cultural or both. When this is expressed in terms of constitutional values and it is judicially sanctioned by a constitutional court or by a court of last instance, its symbolic value is even greater. In that respect, the U.S. Supreme Court's

[26] *See* the judgment of the Court of First Instance of September 21, 2005 in Kadi v. Council of the EU and the Commission of the EC, Case T-315/01, (2005) ECR II-3649.

[27] Medellín v. Texas, 552 U.S. 491 (2008).

[28] Case Concerning Avena and Other Mexican Nationals (Mexico v. U.S), Judgment of 31 March 2004, I.C.J. Rep., at 12.

decision does not have much to do with an alleged disrespect by the United States for international law. It is rather the reflex of an isolationist legal culture, which tends to frame international law within the general framework of the constitutional law discourse.[29] The primacy of constitutional law ensues not only from the fact that "[a] rule of international law or provisions of an international treaty of the United States will not be given effect as law in the United States if it is inconsistent with the United States Constitution,"[30] but more generally and quite understandably from the sense that courts, particularly the Supreme Court, are entrusted with the task of preserving the integrity of the constitutional text and upholding the values underlying it. In this respect, there is nothing peculiar to U.S. courts as compared to courts in other jurisdictions. However, the way in which the U.S. Constitution is interpreted and the priorities that are established among the values enshrined in it, including the consideration to be accorded to international law, varies over time and is strongly influenced by a number of extralegal variables.[31] This is all the more so given the "overtly political nature of American Constitutional law," as opposed to the European tradition.[32]

In a way, the posture taken by the ICJ in the *Jurisdictional Immunities of the State* case could also be seen as some kind of system closure. Somewhat paradigmatically, the ICJ judgment sanctioned the priority of a state-centered vision of international law, prioritizing states and their sovereign prerogatives, to the detriment of one based on the primacy of human rights. Sassoli[33] had already highlighted the tension between these two often-conflicting foundational layers of international law in the aftermath of the *Arrest Warrant* case.[34] In that case, too, rather than balancing human rights considerations and jurisdictional immunities concerns as desired by some judges,[35] the ICJ gave priority to immunities, thereby leaving little room for prosecuting high-ranking foreign state's officials before the domestic courts of another state even in case of alleged serious violations of human rights.[36] With the *Jurisdictional Immunities of the State* case, the ICJ reiterated its choice, by having jurisdictional immunities—this time state immunity—yet again prevail over human rights. One may take issue with the

[29] *See* Andrea Bianchi, *International Law and U.S. Courts: The Myth of Lohengrin Revisited*, 15 EUR. J. INT'L L. 751 (2004).

[30] *See* RESTATEMENT (THIRD) OF THE FOREIGN RELATIONS LAW OF THE UNITED STATES § 115 (3) (1987).

[31] *See* Bianchi, *The Myth of Lohengrin Revisited*, *supra* note 29, at 780.

[32] *See* Jed Rubenfeld, *The Two World Orders*, 27 WILSON Q. 22, 27 (Autumn 2003) ("[I]if the law is to be democratic, the law and courts that interpret it must retain strong connections to the nation's democratic political system.").

[33] Marco Sassoli, *L'arrêt Yerodia: quelques remarques sur une affaire au point de collision entre les deux couches du droit international*, 106 REVUE GÉNÉRALE DE DROIT INTERNATIONAL PUBLIC 791 (2002).

[34] Case Concerning the Arrest Warrant of 11 April 2000 (Democratic Republic of the Congo v. Belgium), Judgment, I.C.J. Reports, 2002, at 3.

[35] *See* the Separate Opinion by judges Higgins, Kooijmans, and Buergenthal, para. 75.

[36] Andrea Bianchi, *L'immunité des Etats et les violations graves des droits de l'homme: la fonction de l'interprète dans la détermination du droit international*, 108 REVUE GÉNÉRALE DE DROIT INTERNATIONAL PUBLIC 63 (2004).

ICJ's unfaltering support of states' sovereign prerogatives, as some dissenting judges vehemently did,[37] but the signal sent out is uncontroversial. In the inter-state system of international law, of which the ICJ considers itself the guarantor, there is no space for challenging the conduct of states before the municipal courts of another state. The supreme "quasi-constitutional" value of the sovereign equality of states, enshrined in the UN Charter and considered one of the fundamental principles of international law, would not allow it.

IV. Multiple Legal Orders Coordinating Doctrines

It should be kept in mind that "system closures" are by no means the only way to address potential conflicts between values and/or rules that belong to different legal orders.[38] A cursory look at judicial practice, both domestic and international, suffices to reveal that other techniques can be used to perform system coordination. Among them the well-known *Solange* doctrine, inaugurated by the German *Bundesverfassungsgericht* to challenge the legal order of the then European Community, stands out. The doctrine consists of reserving the right by the Court to exercise judicial scrutiny of European Community's acts against the background of the German Constitution's human rights provisions, as long as analogous human rights guarantees were not developed at the level of the European Community.[39]

A similar tool, developed at the international level, is the "equivalent protection" doctrine, elaborated by the European Court of Human Rights (ECtHR) to provide an incentive to international organizations to develop mechanisms of human rights control that can be comparable to those that are in place in the European Convention on Human Rights (ECHR) system. The doctrine has been developed by the European Court of Human Rights in a string of cases from *Waite & Kennedy v. Germany*[40] to

[37] *See*, for instance, Judge Yusuf's and Judge Cançado Trinidade's dissenting opinions in the *Jurisdictional Immunities* case.

[38] Also, at a "horizontal" level, national courts have refused to recognize foreign acts perceived by them to be in violation of international law, on the basis of such doctrines as act of state, political question, nonjusticiability, and *ordre public*. *See* Eyal Benvenisti, *Judicial Misgivings Regarding the Application of International Law: An Analysis of Attitudes of National Courts*, 4 Eur. J. Int'l L. 159, 172 (1993).

[39] *See* the *Solange* I (1974) and II (1986) decisions (unofficial English translations respectively *available at* http://www.utexas.edu/law/academics/centers/transnational/work_new/german/case.php?id=588, and at http://www.utexas.edu/law/academics/centers/transnational/work_new/german/case.php?id=572).

[40] ECtHR, Waite and Kennedy v. Germany (Application no. 26083/94), Judgment of 18 February 1999.

Bosphorus v. Ireland,[41] and it has been recently revamped in the context of UN Security Council sanctions in the *Al-Dulimi v. Switzerland* case.[42]

In *Waite & Kennedy* the Court was seized with the issue of whether the jurisdictional immunity granted to an international organization by the domestic courts of a contracting party can be compatible with Article 6, in particular with the right of access to a court. The Court recognized that the immunity granted to an international organization may lead to an infringement of an individual's right of access to court unless offset by the availability of adequate alternative means of redress. Relying on its previous case law with regard to the inherent limitations of Article 6(1) ECHR,[43] the Court held that, while states were permitted to regulate the right of access to court, any resulting limitations must not impair the essence of this right. According to the ECtHR, a limitation would not be compatible with Article 6 if (1) it did not pursue a legitimate aim, and (2) there was not a reasonable relationship of proportionality between the means employed and the aim sought to be achieved. With regard to the first part of this compatibility test, the Court accepted that the immunity of international organizations was "an essential means of ensuring the proper functioning of such organisations free from unilateral interference by individual governments"[44] and thus regarded the corresponding restriction of access to court as a legitimate objective. Concerning the second element, the required proportionality, the Court held that "a material factor in determining whether granting... immunity from... jurisdiction is permissible is whether the applicants had available to them reasonable alternative means to protect effectively their rights under the Convention."[45]

A manifestly deficient protection of human rights within an international organization has also been a reason for the Court to hold a contracting party accountable for having violated one of the rights enshrined in the Convention by implementing an international obligation. In the *Bosphorus* case,[46] the Court recalled that "a Contracting party is responsible under Article 1 of the Convention for all acts and omissions of its organs regardless of whether the act or omission in question was a consequence of domestic law or of the necessity to comply with an international obligation."[47] According to the ECtHR, "State action taken in compliance with such legal obligations is justified as long as the relevant organisation is considered to protect fundamental human rights, as regards both the substantive guarantees offered and the mechanisms controlling their observance, in a manner which can be considered at least equivalent to that for which the

[41] ECtHR (Grand Chamber), Bosphorus Hava Yollari Turizm Ve Ticaret Anonim Sirketi v. Ireland (Application no. 45036/98), Judgment of 30 June 2005.

[42] ECtHR (2nd Sec.), Al-Dulimi and Montana Management Inc. v. Switzerland (Application no. 5809/08), Judgment of 26 November 2013.

[43] ECtHR, Osman v. United Kingdom, Application No. 23452/94, Judgment of 28 October 1998, [1998] ECHR 101, para. 147; Fayed v. United Kingdom, Judgment of 21 September 1994, Series A No. 294, para. 65.

[44] *Waite and Kennedy*, *supra* note 40, para. 63.

[45] *Id.*, para. 68.

[46] *Bosphorus*, *supra* note 41.

[47] *Id.*, para. 153.

Convention provides."[48] If the organization concerned has "comparable" human rights protections,[49] this would create a presumption that a contracting party has not violated the European Convention when implementing "legal obligations flowing from its membership of the organization."[50] Any such presumption, however, would be rebutted by a finding, in the particular circumstances of any given case, that "the protection of Convention rights was manifestly deficient,"[51] for "[i]n such cases, the interest of international cooperation would be outweighed by the Convention's role as a 'constitutional instrument of European public order' in the field of human rights."[52]

Incidentally, the case law of the ECtHR is fully consistent with the attitude taken by the European Court of Justice in the *Kadi* case,[53] and later confirmed also by the General Court in the follow-up to the very same case.[54] Of particular note is that the judicial organs of the European Union have affirmed their duty (in the context of the adoption of fund-freezing measures implementing UN Security Council antiterror resolutions) to uphold the rights of the defense and the right to effective judicial protection of an individual "so long as" the Security Council Sanctions Committee "fails to offer guarantees of effective judicial protection."[55] The striking similarity of this approach to the *Waite & Kennedy* and *Bosphorus* doctrines, developed by the ECtHR, attests to a growing coordination and even convergence of the case law of international tribunals to the effect of requiring that international organizations provide adequate guarantees for securing fundamental human rights protections. This tendency is further confirmed by the case law of domestic courts.

While a high level of judicial scrutiny of the adequacy of available dispute settlement mechanisms is rare, national courts in a number of cases have pursued the *Waite & Kennedy* rationale by denying the immunity of international organizations where no alternative means of redress are available. For instance, in *Banque Africaine de Développement v. M.A. Degboe*,[56] the French Cour de Cassation held that the impossibility

[48] *Id.*, para. 155.

[49] *Id.* ("By 'equivalent' the Court means 'comparable'; any requirement that the organisation's protection be 'identical' could run counter to the interest of international cooperation pursued.... However, any such finding of equivalence could not be final and would be susceptible to review in the light of any relevant change in fundamental rights protection.").

[50] *Id.*, para. 156. [51] *Id.*

[52] *Id.*, *citing in support* Loizidou v. Turkey, Preliminary Objections, Judgment of 23 March 1995, Ser. A No. 310, at 27–28, para. 75.

[53] Yassin Abdullah Kadi and Al Barakaat International Foundation v. Council of the European Union and Commission of the European Communities, Joined Cases C-402/05 P and C-415/05 P, Judgment of the European Court of Justice (Grand Chamber) of 3 September 2008, ECR [2008] I-6351 (*Kadi II*), on appeal from Yassin Abdullah Kadi v. Council of the European Union and Commission of the European Communities, Case T-315/01, Judgment of the Court of First Instance (Second Chamber, Extended Composition) of 21 September 2005, ECR [2005] II-3649 (*Kadi I*).

[54] Yassin Abdullah Kadi v. European Commission, Case T-85/09, Judgment of the General Court (Seventh Chamber), 30 Sept. 2010 (*Kadi III*).

[55] *Kadi III*, para. 127, and *Kadi II*, para. 322.

[56] Banque Africaine de Développement v. M.A. Degboe, French Cour de Cassation (Chambre sociale), 25 January 2005, No. 04-41012, JDI, 2005, p. 1142ff.

of any access to justice would constitute a denial of justice. Thus, the defendant organization was not entitled to immunity from suit.[57] In a similar fashion, the Italian Corte di Cassazione in *Drago v. International Plant Genetic Resources Institute*[58] denied an international organization's immunity. It held that the jurisdictional immunity conferred upon the defendant organization in the headquarters agreement with Italy was incompatible with the fundamental right to institute proceedings to protect one's rights contained in Article 24 of the Italian Constitution because the organization had not fulfilled its obligation pursuant to the headquarters agreement to provide an independent and impartial judicial remedy for the resolution of employment-related disputes.[59] In fact, the International Plant Genetic Resources Institute did submit to the jurisdiction of the International Labour Organization Administrative Tribunal. However, since this submission took place after the dispute arose, the tribunal lacked jurisdiction and the plaintiff had in fact no alternative means of dispute settlement.

The equivalent protection doctrine had been recently revamped by the decision of the Second Section of the European Court of Human Rights in the *Al-Dulimi v. Switzerland* case. In *Al-Dulimi*, the Court held Switzerland responsible for the violation of Article 6 of the European Convention, in the context of the domestic implementation of assets freezing measures adopted by the Security Council.[60] By applying the equivalent protection doctrine, the Court found the UN Security Council Resolution 1483 sanctions regime to be "manifestly deficient" in terms of human rights protection, and as such apt to rebut the presumption of equivalent protection to the guarantees offered by the European Convention. The fact that Swiss courts had exercised no judicial scrutiny over the implementing measures of Resolution 1483 led the European Court to find that Switzerland had violated the right of access to court, protected by Article 6 of the European Convention. The Grand Chamber upheld the conclusion of the Second Section, although on slightly different grounds. In particular, the Grand Chamber thought that the issue of the equivalent protection doctrine was a "nugatory" one, given that there was no conflict between the provisions of the Security Council's

[57] *Id.* («Mais attendu que la Banque africaine de développement ne peut se prévaloir de l'immunité de juridiction dans le litige l'opposant au salarié qu'elle a licencié dès lors qu'à l'époque des faits elle n'avait pas institué en son sein un tribunal ayant compétence pour statuer sur des litiges de cette nature, l'impossibilité pour une partie d'accéder au juge chargé de se prononcer sur sa prétention et d'exercer un droit qui relève de l'ordre public international constituant un déni de justice fondant la compétence de la juridiction française lorsqu'il existe un rattachement avec la France . . . »).

[58] Alberto Drago v. International Plant Genetic Resources Institute, Corte di Cassazione (Sez. Unite civili), 19 Feb. 2007, No. 3718, ILDC 827 (IT 2007).

[59] *Id.*, para. 64 ("Occorre verificare la conformità di questa disposizione che riconosce univocamente l'immunità dell'ente dalla giurisdizione italiana estesa anche alle controversie relative ai rapporti di lavoro con i suoi dipendenti alla garanzia costituzionale della tutela giudiziaria, di cui all'art. 24 Cost., che rappresenta un principio cardine dell'ordinamento.")

[60] The relevant sanctions regime was the one laid down in Resolution 1483 of 23 May 2003, providing for the freezing of financial assets removed from Iraq, or acquired, by Saddam Hussein, or other senior officials of the Iraqi regime and their immediate family members, including entities owned or controlled, directly or indirectly, by them or by persons acting on their behalf or at their direction (§ 23).

resolution and the obligations stemming from the European Convention.[61] Incidentally, the presumption of consistency of Security Council resolutions with human rights standards, originally formulated by the European Court in *Al-Jedda*,[62] and reiterated in *Al-Dulimi*,[63] is in and of itself a coordinating device to avoid clashes between different legal orders.

V. The Significance and Function of System Closures

Arguably, the kind of rigid stance taken by the Italian Constitutional Court is the result of a deliberate choice, as the above techniques of balancing or coordination among different legal systems could have been used instead. I suspect that one may look at this in different ways depending on one's personal, professional, or institutional preferences. To the committed international law generalist, this would attest to the short-sighted character of domestic legal communities and to the vain attempt to resist the unifying force of international law. To the domestic constitutional lawyer or the foreign relations scholar, the judgment of the Italian Constitutional Court might provide evidence of the inherent hierarchy between the domestic and the international legal order. The latter should never interfere with domestic constituencies' fundamental values that most of the time are the expression of democratic decision-making processes. Finally, such instances of system closures may look to the pragmatist as just an illustration of what happens in a pluralistic society in which a plurality of legal orders coexists. Each and every order has their own logic and rationality, and the communication between them is episodic and not necessarily coherent and constant over time. Contingencies often determine normative outcomes and the degree of communication among them varies a great deal depending on a variety of different factors.

More generally, in a world that could be viewed as a network of different systems, it is interesting to wonder by what mechanisms communication and coordination take place among this plurality of systems.[64] Short of a unitary representation of the whole—which hardly seems suitable to account for the current realities of international law—the range of interactions between different systems is symptomatic of a wide array of postures not always amenable within clear-cut and straightforward

[61] ECtHR (Grand Chamber), Al-Dulimi and Montana Management Ltd. v. Switzerland (Application no. 5809/08), Judgment of 21 June 2016, para. 149.

[62] ECtHR (Grand Chamber), Al Jedda v. United Kingdom (Application no. 27021/08), Judgment of 7 July 2011, [2011] ECHR 1092, upholding "a presumption that the Security Council does not intend to impose any obligation on Members States to breach fundamental principles of human rights." (para. 102).

[63] *Al-Dulimi*, *supra* note 61, para. 140.

[64] On law as a communication process, *see* Gunther Teubner, *Global Bukowina: Legal Pluralism in Law and Society*, *in* Global Law Without a State (Gunther Teubner ed., 1997).

rationalities. What seems clear, however, is that a perceived threat to some fundamental constitutional values that provide societal identity and that are attuned to the societal culture of domestic constituencies are more likely to trigger system closures. The language used is that of constitutional law and the conflict is usually construed as resistance from intrusion of external values that are likely to jeopardize internal fundamental values. The hierarchy of rules implied by any such decision inevitably postulates the superiority of domestic constitutional values.

Arguably this is also the reason for international courts and tribunals to have shown a great deal of cautiousness in operationalizing the notion of *jus cogens* in a way that would trump conflicting rules, regardless of their nature and origin. To have *jus cogens* rules sweep away any other conflicting norms in a way similar to what domestic constitutional rules can do at the domestic level might have dire consequences for an international legal system, which is not homogeneous enough to afford imposing a hierarchy of values on domestic legal systems.[65] International tribunals have shied away from mechanically applying rules of *jus cogens* precisely because they know very well that the international legal system can hardly afford a system closure. Domestic legal orders can be inward-looking as their internal efficacy and credibility rarely depend on the external international legal system. International law, however, needs domestic legal systems to thrive. Rather than causing domestic legal systems to shut off, it would be wise for international courts to give more consideration to contemporary societal values in domestic legal systems. To hold that foreign states are immune from jurisdiction even when they commit serious violations of human rights is, in this author's view, hardly proof of any such consideration.[66]

[65] *See* Andrea Bianchi, *Human Rights and the Magic of Jus Cogens*, 19 EUR. J. INT'L L. 491 (2008).

[66] *See* Bianchi, *Crystal Ball*, *supra* note 12, at 474 ("[O]ne needs to notice that the blatant denial of any legal remedy to victims of serious human rights violations strikes a chord with transnational civil society that no technical reasoning or justification based on jurisdictional immunities can effectively counter. The idea that the privilege of immunity may shield a state just because of its status is unlikely to be well received by those who are unfamiliar with the law.").

CHAPTER 39

INTERNATIONAL COMITY IN COMPARATIVE PERSPECTIVE

WILLIAM S. DODGE

FOREIGN relations law may be defined in various ways, but for the purposes of this book the term encompasses "the domestic law of each nation that governs how that nation interacts with the rest of the world."[1] Foreign relations law thus includes not just domestic law allocating the authority to conduct foreign relations and to use military force but also domestic law mediating the relationships between one legal system and another. Domestic laws governing the jurisdiction of courts, the applicable law, and the enforcement of foreign judgments—traditional topics of the conflict of laws, or private international law—fall squarely within the definition of foreign relations law.[2] Indeed, the doctrines in this particular category of foreign relations law may be the most frequently used. They arise daily in litigation around the world.

[1] Curtis A. Bradley, *What Is Foreign Relations Law?*, ch. 1 in this volume; *see also* 1 RESTATEMENT (THIRD) OF THE FOREIGN RELATIONS LAW OF THE UNITED STATES § 101 (AM. LAW INST. 1987) (defining the foreign relations law of the United States to include "international law as it applies to the United States" and "domestic law that has substantial significance for the foreign relations of the United States or has other substantial international consequences").

[2] The American Law Institute's three Restatements of Foreign Relations Law cover these topics in considerable detail. *See* RESTATEMENT (FOURTH) OF THE FOREIGN RELATIONS LAW OF THE UNITED STATES, Part IV (AM. LAW INST. 2018) (covering jurisdiction and state immunity); 1 RESTATEMENT (THIRD) OF THE FOREIGN RELATIONS LAW OF THE UNITED STATES, Part IV (AM. LAW INST. 1987) (covering jurisdiction and foreign judgments); RESTATEMENT (SECOND) OF THE FOREIGN RELATIONS LAW OF THE UNITED STATES, Part I (AM. LAW INST. 1965) (covering jurisdiction). The American Law Institute restates rules on choice of law separately. *See* RESTATEMENT (SECOND) OF CONFLICT OF LAWS (AM. LAW INST. 1971); RESTATEMENT OF CONFLICT OF LAWS (AM. LAW INST. 1934). The conflicts restatements focus primarily on choice of law in interstate cases, but the same rules are generally applied in international cases too. *See* RESTATEMENT (SECOND) OF CONFLICT OF LAWS § 10 (AM. LAW INST. 1971) (stating that the Restatement's rules "are generally applicable to cases with elements in one or more foreign nations").

In the United States, the principle of international comity provides the basis for many different doctrines of foreign relations law that recognize foreign laws, foreign judgments, and foreign governments as plaintiffs, or that restrain the reach of U.S. laws, the jurisdiction of U.S. courts, and particularly the jurisdiction of U.S. courts over foreign states and their officials as defendants.[3] More specifically, U.S. doctrines of international comity include choice of law, the act of state doctrine, the presumption against extraterritoriality, the doctrine of foreign state compulsion, the recognition and enforcement of foreign judgments, limits on personal jurisdiction, the doctrine of *forum non conveniens*, limits on antisuit injunctions, the privilege of a foreign government to bring suit in U.S. courts, and the doctrine of foreign sovereign immunity.[4]

In continental Europe, one finds similar doctrines, or at least doctrines that serve similar functions. EU law governs some of these doctrines. Choice of law, for example, has been codified for contractual obligations, noncontractual obligations, and divorce in the European Union's Rome Regulations, whose rules apply regardless of whether the law to be applied is the law of an EU member state.[5] Personal jurisdiction, *lis pendens*, and the enforcement of foreign judgments are codified at the EU level with respect to other member states in the Brussels I Regulation (Recast).[6] But the domestic law of European states generally continues to govern these same doctrines with respect

[3] William S. Dodge, *International Comity in American Law*, 115 COLUM. L. REV. 2071 (2015); *see also* Thomas Schultz & Niccolò Ridi, *Comity: The American Development of a Transnational Concept*, 18 Y.B. PRIV. INT'L L. 211 (2016/2017).

[4] In some instances, doctrines of international comity overlap with rules of international law. For example, under customary international law, states are immune from the jurisdiction of the courts of other states with respect to certain activities. *See* Jurisdictional Immunities of the State (Ger. v. It.), Judgment, 2012 I.C.J. 99, ¶ 77 (Feb. 3) (finding that customary international law requires immunity for *acta jure imperii* committed by armed forces during armed conflict). But states may, as a matter of international comity, provide foreign states with greater immunity than international law requires. *See id.* ¶ 55 (noting that "States sometimes decide to accord an immunity more extensive than that required by international law" and that "the grant of immunity in such a case is not accompanied by the requisite *opinio juris* and therefore sheds no light upon" the content of customary international law). In other words, the doctrine of foreign sovereign immunity has a core of customary international law and a penumbra of international comity. For an overview foreign sovereign immunity in U.S. law, *see* David P. Stewart, *International Immunities in U.S. Law*, ch. 35 in this volume.

[5] Regulation (EC) No. 593/2008 on the Law Applicable to Contractual Obligations (Rome I) art. 2, 2008 O.J. (L 177) 6 (hereinafter "Rome I Regulation"); Regulation (EC) No. 864/2007 on the Law Applicable to Non-Contractual Obligations (Rome II) art. 3, 2007 O.J. (L 199) 40; Council Regulation (EU) No. 1259/2010 Implementing Enhanced Cooperation in the Area of the Law Applicable to Divorce and Legal Separation art. 4, 2010 O.J. (L 343) 10. For an overview of the Rome Regulations, *see* MICHAEL BOGDAN, CONCISE INTRODUCTION TO EU PRIVATE INTERNATIONAL LAW 114–147, 157–158 (3d ed. 2016).

[6] Regulation (EU) No. 1215/2012 of the European Parliament and of the Council of 12 December 2012 on Jurisdiction and the Recognition and Enforcement of Judgments in Civil and Commercial Matters (Recast), 2012 O.J. (L 351) 1 (hereinafter "Brussels I Regulation (Recast)"). The Brussels I Regulation (Recast) (or technically, its forerunners the Brussels Convention and the Brussels I Regulation) has also been interpreted to prohibit antisuit injunctions directed at other EU member states. *Allianz SpA* et al. *v. West Tankers Inc.*, [2009] ECR I-663; *Turner v. Grovit*, [2004] ECR I-3565.

to non-EU member states.[7] Other doctrines, like the act of state doctrine, have not been codified in EU law at all and, to the extent they have been recognized, are governed by national law.[8] But continental European states do not think of these doctrines as resting on international comity.[9]

This chapter examines the reasons for the difference in approach and asks whether the difference matters.[10] The chapter concludes that history largely explains the different approaches, with the United States showing the influence of Justice Joseph Story, who adopted comity as the basis for the conflict of laws, and continental Europe showing the influence of Friedrich Carl von Savigny, who decided to build a system of private international law on different foundations. This chapter further suggests that international comity has something to contribute to this area of foreign relations law even in continental European states, by highlighting the distinction between domestic law and international law, by emphasizing the freedom of each state to shape these doctrines of domestic law as it sees fit, and by making it easier to see interrelationships among different doctrines.

I. The United States

The principle of comity that lies at the foundation of so much U.S. foreign relations law originated in continental Europe with the seventeenth-century Dutch writer Ulrich Huber. Huber used comity to solve a problem created by territorial sovereignty. Since the laws of each state are binding only within its own territory, how could rights acquired in one state be enforced in another? Huber posited that "[s]overeigns will so act by way of comity that rights acquired within the limits of a government retain their

[7] *See* Brussels I Regulation (Recast), *supra* note 6, art. 6 (allowing EU member states to apply their national laws on jurisdiction to defendants domiciled in non-EU member states); Campbell McLachlan, Lis Pendens in International Litigation 91–102, 111–112 (2009) (discussing national laws on *lis pendens*).

[8] *See* Belhaj v. Straw, [2017] UKSC 3, ¶ 201 (Lord Sumption) (discussing French, German, and Dutch counterparts to the act of state doctrine).

[9] *See* Tim W. Dornis, *Comity*, *in* Encyclopedia of Private International Law 55, 57 (Jürgen Basedow et al. eds., 2017) (noting the "dismissive attitude of European doctrine towards an acknowledgment of international comity"); Ralf Michaels, *Public and Private International Law: German Views on Global Issues*, 4 J. Priv. Int'l L. 121, 126 (2008) ("In Germany, a public concept of comity plays hardly any role today, except perhaps to express a generally friendly attitude towards foreign law."). Within the European Union, some of these doctrines are considered to rest on "mutual trust." For a comparison of international comity and mutual trust, *see infra* notes 76–86 and accompanying text.

[10] Although the influence of international comity seems greatest in the United States, it underpins doctrines of foreign relations law in other common law countries too. *See* Thomas Schultz & Jason Mitchenson, *Navigating Sovereignty and Transnational Commercial Law: The Use of Comity by Australian Courts*, 12 J. Priv. Int'l L. 344 (2016) (discussing Australian law); Adrian Briggs, *The Principle of Comity in Private International Law*, 354 Receuil des Cours 67 (2012) (discussing English law). For reasons of space, I will focus on the United States and continental Europe.

force everywhere so far as they do not cause prejudice to the power or rights of such government or of its subjects."[11] Huber's principle of comity allowed one state to enforce the laws of another, while reserving to that state the right not to enforce foreign laws that it found harmful. English courts adopted this approach, and early American courts followed the English decisions.[12]

The key figure in the development of international comity in the United States was Justice Joseph Story, who made the principle the basis for his 1834 treatise on the conflict of laws. Like Huber, Story assumed that law was generally territorial, and he used comity to explain how the laws of one country could have effect outside its own territory. The "'comity of nations,'" Story wrote, "is the most appropriate phrase to express the true foundation and extent of the obligation of the laws of one nation within the territories of another."[13] For Story, "whatever force and obligation the laws of one country have in another, depend solely upon the laws and municipal regulations of the latter."[14] This meant that no nation would be required "to enforce doctrines which, in a moral or political view, are incompatible with its own safety or happiness, or conscientious regard to justice and duty."[15]

Both Huber and Story focused on choice of law and the enforcement of foreign judgments. But the principle of comity was used to explain other kinds of deference to foreign states too. Writing for the Supreme Court, Story explained that the doctrine of foreign sovereign immunity "stands upon principles of public comity and convenience."[16] The Court also used comity to explain the converse proposition that a foreign sovereign could bring suit in U.S. courts.[17] Comity provided a basis for the modern presumption against extraterritoriality.[18] And as the U.S. act of state doctrine developed into a doctrine distinct from foreign sovereign immunity, the Supreme Court explained it in terms of comity as well.[19]

Criticism of comity in the United States focused on its supposed indeterminacy. Story left comity open to this line of attack by endorsing the view that "comity is, and ever must be uncertain" and "must necessarily depend on a variety of circumstances,

[11] Ulrich Huber, *De Conflictu Legum Diversarum in Diversis Imperiis* (Ernest G. Lorenzen trans., 1919) (1689), *reprinted in* ERNEST G. LORENZEN, SELECTED ARTICLES ON THE CONFLICT OF LAWS 164 (1947).

[12] *See* Dodge, *supra* note 3, at 2086–2087.

[13] JOSEPH STORY, COMMENTARIES ON THE CONFLICT OF LAWS § 38, at 41 (2d ed. 1841) (1834).

[14] *Id.* § 23, at 30. [15] *Id.* § 25, at 31.

[16] The Santissima Trinidad, 20 U.S. (7 Wheat.) 283, 353 (1822).

[17] *See* The Sapphire, 78 U.S. (11 Wall.) 164, 167 (1870) ("To deny him this privilege would manifest a want of comity and friendly feeling.").

[18] *See* American Banana Co. v. United Fruit Co., 213 U.S. 347, 356 (1909) ("For another jurisdiction, if it should happen to lay hold of the actor, to treat him according to its own notions rather than those of the place where he did the acts, not only would be unjust, but would be an interference with the authority of another sovereign, contrary to the comity of nations, which the other state concerned justly might resent.").

[19] *See* Oetjen v. Central Leather Co., 246 U.S. 297, 303–304 (1918) (noting that the act of state doctrine "rests at last upon the highest considerations of international comity and expediency").

which cannot be reduced to any certain rule."[20] Judge Benjamin Cardozo subsequently complained that "[t]he misleading word 'comity'... has been fertile in suggesting a discretion unregulated by general principles."[21] And Professor Joseph Beale, who drafted the American Law Institute's first *Restatement of Conflicts*, wrote that "[t]he doctrine seems really to mean only that in certain cases the sovereign is not prevented by any principle of international law, but only by his own choice, from establishing any rule he pleases for the conflict of laws."[22]

In the United States, however, comity not only weathered such criticisms but continued to flourish. Comity is still the foundation for the conflict of laws[23] and the enforcement of foreign judgments in the United States.[24] The Supreme Court still refers to foreign sovereign immunity as "a gesture of comity between the United States and other sovereigns"[25] and discusses the privilege of foreign sovereigns to bring suit in U.S. courts in similar terms.[26] The Court has recently adopted the phrase "prescriptive comity" to describe limits on the extraterritorial application of U.S. law.[27] Even when the Justices of the Supreme Court disagree about how to restrain U.S. jurisdiction, they often phrase the debate in comity terms. Thus, in *RJR Nabisco Inc. v. European Community*, Justice Ginsburg argued in dissent that the Court should not have applied the presumption against extraterritoriality to limit the reach of the private right of action in the Racketeer Influenced and Corrupt Organizations Act (RICO) but should instead have addressed "comity concerns" through due process limits on general personal jurisdiction and the doctrine of *forum non conveniens*.[28] In short, courts in the United States continue to view a wide range of foreign-relations-law doctrines through an international comity lens.

[20] STORY, *supra* note 13, § 28, at 34 (*quoting* Saul v. His Creditors, 5 Mart. (n.s.) 665, 678 (La. 1827) (Porter, J.)).

[21] Loucks v. Standard Oil Co. of New York, 120 N.E. 198, 201–202 (N.Y. 1918).

[22] 3 JOSEPH H. BEALE, A TREATISE ON THE CONFLICT OF LAWS § 71, at 1965 (1935).

[23] U.S. conflicts decisions directly invoke comity only rarely today. *See*, e.g., Fu v. Fu, 733 A.2d 1133, 1140–1141 (N.J. 1999) (listing "the interests of interstate comity" among those reflected in the *Restatement (Second) of Conflicts*). But comity's influence is apparent, for example, in the widespread adoption of a public policy exception, *see* RESTATEMENT (SECOND) OF CONFLICT OF LAWS § 90 (AM. LAW INST. 1971), which is a direct descendant of Huber's maxim that governments should enforce foreign laws "so far as they do not cause prejudice to the power or rights of such government or of its subjects," Huber, *supra* note 11, at 164.

[24] *See* Sung Hwan Co. v. Rite Aid Corp., 850 N.E.2d 647, 650–651 (N.Y. 2006) (characterizing 1962 Uniform Foreign Money-Judgments Recognition Act as adoption of "well-settled comity principles").

[25] Dole Food Co. v. Patrickson, 538 U.S. 468, 479 (2003). It bears repeating that some foreign sovereign immunity is required by customary international law. *See supra* note 4.

[26] *See* Banco Nacional de Cuba v. Sabbatino, 376 U.S. 398, 408–409 (1964) ("Under principles of comity governing this country's relations with other nations, sovereign states are allowed to sue in the courts of the United States.").

[27] F. Hoffmann-La Roche Ltd. v. Empagran S.A., 542 U.S. 155, 169 (2004).

[28] RJR Nabisco, Inc. v. European Community, 136 S. Ct. 2090, 2115 (2016) (Ginsburg, J., concurring in part and dissenting in part). For further discussion of *RJR Nabisco*, *see infra* notes 72–74 and accompanying text.

II. Continental Europe

It is tempting to attribute the absence of international comity in continental European thinking about such questions to a civil-law preference for clear rules rather than open-ended standards. Mathias Reimann has observed that "European conflicts lawyers continue to look primarily for and to rules."[29] But this explanation fails on at least two grounds. First, continental European countries do not rely on comity to explain even those doctrines that do allow for discretion in their application.[30] Second, as we shall see in Section III, many U.S. comity doctrines take the form of rules rather than standards. Story's comments notwithstanding, there is no inherent inconsistency between international comity and a rules-based approach.

The answer seems to lie instead in the historical development of European private international law on a basis other than comity. The key figure in this development was Friedrich Carl von Savigny, whose treatise on conflicts appeared in 1849 as the eighth volume of his *System of Current Roman Law*.[31] Savigny began a "Copernican Revolution" in conflicts thinking by rephrasing the basic question.[32] Rather than beginning with a law and asking what legal relationships it governs, he began with the legal relationship and sought "*that legal territory to which, in its proper nature, it belongs or is subject (in which it has its seat).*"[33] Savigny's aim was what would come to be called "decisional harmony"—or, as he put it in his treatise, "that in cases of *conflict of laws*, the same legal relations (cases) have to expect the same decision, whether the judgment be pronounced in this state or in that."[34]

Savigny agreed with Huber and Story on a number of points. He agreed that "[e]very state is entitled to demand that its own laws only shall be recognized within its bounds" and that "[n]o state can require the recognition of its law beyond those bounds."[35] Citing Huber and Story, Savigny also acknowledged that the application of foreign law "may be designated a friendly concession among sovereign states."[36] But, Savigny

[29] Mathias Reimann, Conflict of Laws in Western Europe: A Guide Through the Jungle 9 (1995); *see also id.* at 84 (attributing rejection of *forum non conveniens* to "the general preference for clear-cut rules and predictable results").

[30] To take one example, although the Brussels I Regulation (Recast) adopts a strict "first seized" rule for parallel proceedings, it adopts a discretionary approach to related actions. *Compare* Brussels I Regulation (Recast), *supra* note 6, art. 29 (parallel proceedings), *with id.* art. 30 (related actions). Moreover, those EU member states that have adopted the "first seized" rule in their domestic laws with respect to nonmember states have generally made the rule discretionary. *See* McLachlan, *supra* note 7, at 115.

[31] 8 Friedrich Carl von Savigny, System des Heutigen Romischen Rechts (1849). The most commonly cited English translation is Friedrich Carl von Savigny, A Treatise on the Conflict of Laws (William Guthrie trans., 2d ed. 1880), which is the translation I shall use.

[32] O. Kahn-Freund, *General Problems of Private International Law*, 143 Recueil des Cours 139, 244 (1974).

[33] Savigny, *supra* note 31, § 360, at 133.

[34] *Id.* § 348, at 69–70.

[35] *Id.* § 348, at 68.

[36] *Id.* § 348, at 70.

continued, "this sufferance must not be regarded as the result of mere generosity or arbitrary will, which would imply that it was also uncertain and temporary."[37] The problem with comity as a foundation for choice of law, in other words, was that it depended on the will of each state. To achieve decisional harmony, Savigny aimed for a universalist approach: "We have always to ask ourselves whether such a rule would be well adopted for reception into that common statute law of all nations."[38]

Savigny's private-law perspective also seems to have influenced his exclusion of comity. Ralf Michaels has observed that "[b]ecause private law is, in Savigny's conception, distinct from the will of any legislator, private international law has little to do with the mutual respect between sovereigns."[39] But ultimately, it proved impossible for Savigny to exclude states from his system in at least two respects. First, Savigny's universalist approach could not become a reality unless states adopted it either by court decision or by statute.[40] Savigny needed states to implement his universalist approach.[41] Second, just like Huber and Story, Savigny left room for states to prefer their own laws when they had particularly strong reasons to do so. Specifically, he acknowledged exceptions to his rules for what we would today call public policy (*ordre public*)[42] and mandatory rules (*loi d'application immediate*).[43] Savigny hoped "that these exceptional cases will gradually be diminished with the natural legal development of nations."[44] But in the end, these exceptions and other difficulties combined to thwart Savigny's goal of decisional harmony.[45]

[37] *Id.* § 348, at 70–71. [38] *Id.* § 360, at 137.

[39] Michaels, *supra* note 9, at 127; *see also* REIMANN, *supra* note 29, at 113 ("At least since the days of Savigny, [European conflicts lawyers] have asked which law is most appropriate to determine the status or rights of litigants, not which law best promotes the policies of the state.").

[40] *See* SAVIGNY, *supra* note 31, § 360, at 137 (noting that "accord in the treatment of questions of collision in all states" might be brought about by "the practice of tribunals" or "by a positive law, agreed to and enacted by all states").

[41] *See* Dornis, *supra* note 9, at 57 ("Savigny's concept was still rooted in the law of nations and in an idea of comity insofar as he expected cooperation among sovereign nations to form the basis of a functioning and effective conflicts system.").

[42] *See* SAVIGNY, *supra* note 31, § 349, at 77 (referring to "[l]egal institutions of a foreign state, of which the existence is not at all recognized in ours, and which, therefore have no claim to the protection of our courts."). Savigny gave slavery as an example of an institution that would not be recognized on grounds of public policy. *Id.* § 349, at 79–80 ("So in a state which does not recognize slavery, a negro slave who is found there cannot be treated as property of his master, nor as under general legal incapacity.").

[43] *See id.* § 349, at 77 ("Laws of a strictly positive, imperative nature, which are consequently inconsistent with that freedom of application which pays no regard to the limits of particular states."). In a passage that is jarring today, Savigny gave laws forbidding Jews from acquiring property as an example of mandatory rules. *Id.* § 349, at 79 ("If our law forbids to Jews the acquisition of landed property, our judges must forbid such acquisition not only to native Jews, but also to those foreign Jews in whose state there is no such prohibition.").

[44] *Id.* § 349, at 80.

[45] *See* FREIDRICH K. JUENGER, CHOICE OF LAW AND MULTISTATE JUSTICE 86 (1993) ("The experience gathered over more than a century demonstrates that Savigny's approach is incapable of ever accomplishing its goal of decisional harmony.").

Despite its shortcomings, however, Savigny's "view has characterized European choice of law methodology ever since."[46] Tim Dornis has suggested that Savigny's influence "may explain much of the still dismissive attitude of European doctrine towards an acknowledgment of international comity."[47] Of course, Savigny dealt only with choice of law and, in fact, only with choice of private law. Dornis argues that there is a place for comity in European choice of law with respect to international economic law, which "is concerned with issues of economic regulation, and thus with conflicting national policies."[48]

There are also the other doctrines of foreign relations law that U.S. courts rest upon international comity, for which European legal systems must find another basis—like the recognition and enforcement of foreign judgments, limits on adjudicative jurisdiction, the privilege of foreign sovereigns to bring suits as plaintiffs, and (to the extent it goes beyond the requirements of customary international law) the immunity of foreign sovereigns from suit as defendants. At least in the areas of jurisdiction and judgments, the Court of Justice for the European Union has turned to the principle of "mutual trust" to guide its interpretation of the rules.[49] Whether "mutual trust" differs fundamentally from "international comity" will be considered below.[50]

III. What Does Comity Add?

Does it matter that courts in the United States tend to view the doctrines of foreign relations law through an international comity lens while courts in continental Europe do not? As I noted in the introduction, there is a strong correspondence between U.S. doctrines and their European counterparts. Is anything gained—or lost—by employing the principle of international comity to explain these doctrines and guide their development?[51]

It is best to begin by noting what international comity does *not* add. International comity does not require that doctrines take the form of open-ended standards rather than clear-cut rules. In the United States, a great number of international comity doctrines take the form of rules rather than standards. This is perhaps most apparent with what I have in other writings called sovereign-party comity, which includes

[46] Reimann, *supra* note 29, at 107; *see also* Michaels, *supra* note 9, at 138 ("[Savigny's] thinking still permeates German discussions on private international law.").

[47] Dornis, *supra* note 9, at 57.

[48] *Id. But see* Case 89/85, Åhlström Osakeyhtiö v. Comm'n (Wood Pulp), 1988 E.C.R. 5193, ¶ 22 (dismissing "international comity" as a limitation on the geographic scope of European competition law).

[49] *See,* e.g., Case C-116/02, Erich Gasser GmbH v. Misat Srl., [2003] ECR I-14693, ¶ 72; *see also* Matthias Weller, *Mutual Trust: In Search of the Future of European Union Private International Law*, 11 J. Priv. Int'l L. 64, 85–90 (2015) (discussing CJEU decisions).

[50] *See infra* notes 76–86 and accompanying text.

[51] While I have used the word "lens," one might instead approach the difference as one of "legal paradigms." *See* Ralf Michaels, *Two Paradigms of Jurisdiction*, 27 Mich. J. Int'l L. 1003, 1022–1027 (2006) (explaining the idea of legal paradigms).

foreign sovereign immunity and a foreign government's privilege of bringing suit.[52] In the area of prescriptive comity, the presumption against extraterritoriality limits the geographic scope of U.S. law in rule-like fashion.[53] The U.S. act of state doctrine also takes the form of a rule requiring the application of foreign law in limited circumstances,[54] while U.S. approaches to choice of law more generally reflect a mix of rules and standards.[55] In the area of adjudicative comity, the recognition of foreign judgments in the United States is governed in most states by two uniform acts that set forth relatively clear rules.[56] It is primarily when comity is used to restrain the exercise of adjudicative jurisdiction by U.S. courts that doctrines like *forum non conveniens* take the form of discretionary standards.[57] To the extent that the continental European rejection of international comity is based on its inherently discretionary character, that rejection is based on a misapprehension.[58]

It is also important to recognize that international comity does not exclude the possibility of a doctrine's codification in the form of a treaty, supranational regulation, or domestic statute. The rules governing foreign sovereign immunity and the enforcement of foreign judgments have both been codified in the United States.[59] Yet U.S. courts continue to recognize international comity as the basis of these rules.[60]

[52] In *Sabbatino*, the Supreme Court not only adopted a rule that any government recognized by and not at war with the United States could bring suit in U.S. courts but also rejected an alternative standard of "friendly relations." *See* Banco Nacional de Cuba v. Sabbatino, 376 U.S. 398, 410 (1964). The Foreign Sovereign Immunities Act similarly adopts a series of nondiscretionary rules governing when foreign states may be sued in U.S. courts. *See* 28 U.S.C. §§ 1605, 1605A, 1605B & 1607.

[53] *See* RJR Nabisco, Inc. v. European Community, 136 S. Ct. 2090, 2101 (2016) (adopting a two-step framework for applying the presumption); *see also* William S. Dodge, *The Presumption Against Extraterritoriality in Two Steps*, 110 AJIL UNBOUND 45 (2016).

[54] *See* W.S. Kirkpatrick & Co. v. Envtl. Tectonics Corp., Int'l, 493 U.S. 400, 409 (1990) ("The act of state doctrine does not establish an exception for cases and controversies that may embarrass foreign governments, but merely requires that, in the process of deciding, the acts of foreign sovereigns taken within their own jurisdictions shall be deemed valid."). For discussion of the act of state doctrine in English law, *see* Eirik Bjorge & Cameron Miles, *Crown and Foreign Acts of State before British Courts:* Rahmatullah, Belhaj, *and the Separation of Powers*, ch. 40 in this volume.

[55] *See* Adam I. Muchmore, *Jurisdictional Standards (and Rules)*, 46 VAND. J. TRANSNAT'L L. 171, 183–187 (2013) (discussing approaches).

[56] Uniform Foreign-Country Money Judgments Recognition Act (Nat'l Conference of Comm'rs on Unif. State Laws 2005) (uniform law on recognition and enforcement of foreign judgments adopted in twenty-one states and the District of Columbia); Uniform Foreign Money-Judgments Recognition Act (Nat'l Conference of Comm'rs on Unif. State Laws 1962) (uniform law on recognition and enforcement of foreign judgments adopted in fourteen states and the U.S. Virgin Islands).

[57] *See, e.g.*, Piper Aircraft Co. v. Reyno, 454 U.S. 235, 257 (1981) ("The *forum non conveniens* determination is committed to the sound discretion of the trial court.").

[58] For further discussion, *see* Dodge, *supra* note 3, at 2125–2132.

[59] *See* Foreign Sovereign Immunities Act, 28 U.S.C. §§ 1330, 1602–1611 (federal statute codifying rules of foreign sovereign immunity); Uniform Acts, *supra* note 56 (uniform state acts codifying rules recognition and enforcement of foreign judgments).

[60] *See, e.g.*, Dole Food Co. v. Patrickson, 538 U.S. 468, 479 (2003) (referring to foreign sovereign immunity, codified in the FSIA, "as a gesture of comity between the United States and other sovereigns"); Sung Hwan Co. v. Rite Aid Corp., 850 N.E.2d 647, 650–651 (N.Y. 2006) (characterizing 1962 Uniform Foreign Money-Judgments Recognition Act as adoption of "well-settled comity principles").

The role that comity plays with respect to these statutes is similar to the role that mutual trust plays under the Brussels I Regulation (Recast).[61] The codification reflects an underlying principle, which continues to guide interpretation of the text.

Looking at doctrines of foreign relations law through a comity lens does, however, sharpen the distinction between national law and international law.[62] The *Restatement (Fourth) of Foreign Relations Law* notes the distinction: "As a matter of international comity, states often limit the exercise of jurisdiction to a greater extent than international law requires. International comity reflects deference to foreign states that international law does not mandate."[63] Thus, "disregard of comity is not a wrongful act that entails liability under international law."[64] To recognize that choice of law, the enforcement of foreign judgments, limits on adjudicative jurisdiction, and a foreign government's privilege of bringing suit are questions of international comity is to recognize that they are not governed by international law.[65] It is, of course, possible for doctrines that originate in comity to evolve into rules of customary international law.[66] It is also possible for countries to elevate doctrines of national law to the international law level by writing them into treaties or supranational regulations, as the members of the European Union have done with respect to choice of law on the one hand[67] and with respect to jurisdiction and judgments on the other.[68]

[61] *See infra* notes 76–86 and accompanying text.

[62] To be sure, courts do not always distinguish as clearly as they should between doctrines of international comity and rules of international law. *See* CAMPBELL MCLACHLAN, FOREIGN RELATIONS LAW 217 (2014) (noting that Anglo-Commonwealth courts sometimes use "the label 'comity'" when they mean "principles of public international law"); *see also* Dodge, *supra* note 3, at 2120 (giving examples of confusion by U.S. judges). Peter Malanczuk has written that comity is "a wonderful word to use when one wants to blur the distinction between public and private international law." PETER MALANCZUK, AKEHURST'S MODERN INTRODUCTION TO INTERNATIONAL LAW 73 (2002). The fault, however, lies not with the word "comity" but rather with those who misuse it.

[63] RESTATEMENT (FOURTH) OF THE FOREIGN RELATIONS LAW OF THE UNITED STATES § 401 cmt. a (AM. LAW INST. 2018); *see also* Thomas Schultz & Niccolò Ridi, *Comity and International Courts and Tribunals*, 50 CORNELL INT'L L.J. 577, 581 (2017) ("In traditional public international law scholarship, the term 'comity' traditionally designates, first and foremost, those acts performed . . . for reasons other than the belief that there is a binding legal norm mandating them.").

[64] Jörn Axel Kämmerer, *Comity* ¶ 9, *in* MAX PLANCK ENCYCLOPEDIA OF PUBLIC INTERNATIONAL LAW (Rüdiger Wolfrum ed., 2006); *see also* Dodge, *supra* note 3, at 2121 ("International comity. . . . does *not* bind the United States on the international plane or give rise to international responsibility.").

[65] *See* Schultz & Ridi, *supra* note 63, at 581 (noting that comity "explain[s] what international law *is not*").

[66] *See* JAMES CRAWFORD, BROWNLIE'S PRINCIPLES OF PUBLIC INTERNATIONAL LAW 24 n.18 (8th ed. 2012) (giving example of tax exemptions for diplomats). It is also possible for customary international law to shrink, leaving gaps that are filled by doctrines of international comity, which is what happened with the presumption against extraterritoriality in American law. *See* Dodge, *supra* note 3, at 2092–2093.

[67] In 1980, the member states of the European Community concluded a Convention on the Law Applicable to Contractual Obligations, 1998 O.J. (C 27) 2 (consolidated version), commonly known as the Rome Convention. In 2009, the Rome Convention was superseded by the Rome I Regulation except with respect to Denmark. There is also a Rome II Regulation on noncontractual obligations and a Rome III Regulation on divorce and legal separation. *See supra* note 5.

[68] In 1968, the members of the European Economic Community concluded the Brussels Convention, 1990 O.J. (C 189) 1, governing jurisdiction and judgments in civil matters. This was superseded for all

By highlighting the distinction between national law and international law, the international comity lens also emphasizes that each nation is free to shape these doctrines as it thinks best. This discretion has long been part of the American conception of comity, as Justice Story indicated when he wrote that "[e]very nation must be the final judge for itself, not only of the nature and extent of the duty, but of the occasions on which its exercise may be justly demanded."[69] As we have already seen, such discretion need not be exercised on a case-by-case basis. Countries are free to adopt comity-based rules rather than comity-based standards. With respect to parallel proceedings, for example, the members of the European Union may adopt a strict doctrine of *lis pendens* requiring deference to the first court seized,[70] while the United States may address the same question through the flexible doctrine of *forum non conveniens*.[71] International comity expressly permits such differences in approach.

Viewing a broad range of doctrines as based on international comity also brings into focus the interrelationships among such doctrines. A recent example may clarify the point. As noted above, in *RJR Nabisco*, the U.S. Supreme Court applied the presumption against extraterritoriality—a U.S. doctrine partially based on international comity—to limit the geographic scope of RICO's private right of action by requiring injury in the United States.[72] Dissenting from this aspect of the Court's decision, Justice Ginsburg noted that there were comity interests on the other side of the case too, particularly since the plaintiffs seeking to invoke RICO's private right of action were the European Community and twenty-six of its member states.[73] She further observed that "[t]o the extent extraterritorial application of RICO could give rise to comity concerns not present in this case, those concerns can be met through doctrines that serve to block litigation in U.S. courts of cases more appropriately brought elsewhere" like *forum non conveniens* and due process constraints on the exercise of personal jurisdiction.[74]

EU member states but Denmark by the Brussels I Regulation and then by the Brussels I Regulation (Recast). *See supra* note 6. The rules of the Brussels Convention were extended to certain nonmember states under the Lugano Convention. *See* Convention of 16 September 1988 on Jurisdiction and the Recognition and Enforcement of Judgments in Civil and Commercial Matters, 2007 O.J. (L 339) 3.

[69] Story, *supra* note 13, § 33, at 38.

[70] *See* Brussels I Regulation (Recast), *supra* note 6, art. 29.

[71] In addition to the doctrine of *forum non conveniens*, some lower courts in the United States have adopted a doctrine of international comity abstention that applies in cases of parallel proceedings. *See* Dodge, *supra* note 3, at 2112–2114. While the elements of international comity abstention differ somewhat from those of *forum non conveniens*, it does not adopt a strict "first seized" approach.

[72] RJR Nabisco, Inc. v. European Community, 136 S. Ct. 2090, 2110 (2016).

[73] *See id.* at 2115 (Ginsburg, J., concurring in part and dissenting in part) ("Making such litigation available to domestic but not foreign plaintiffs is hardly solicitous of international comity or respectful of foreign interests.").

[74] *Id.* For a range of views on the *RJR* case, *see AGORA: Reflections on RJR Nabisco v. European Community*, 110 AJIL Unbound, *available at* https://www.cambridge.org/core/journals/american-journal-of-international-law/ajil-unbound-by-symposium/agora-reflections-on-rjr-nabisco-v-european-community (published online Aug. 9, 2016).

Justice Ginsburg saw that the *RJR* case raised questions of sovereign-party comity (a foreign government's privilege of bringing suit in U.S. courts), prescriptive comity (the geographic scope of RICO), and adjudicative comity (*forum non conveniens* and other limits on personal jurisdiction). She also understood that comity interests might pull in different directions in a particular case—in *RJR* the sovereign-party comity reflected in the European Community's suit, against the prescriptive comity limiting RICO's private right of action. Finally, Justice Ginsburg understood that different comity doctrines might be available to address different comity concerns—in this instance, that the availability of *forum non conveniens* might weaken the need to limit the geographic scope of RICO's private right of action. To note the relationships among different comity doctrines is not to suggest that the same comity analysis should be applied in every context. It is rather to suggest that courts should consider how one comity doctrine may impact another and that courts possess a range of tools to mediate the relationships between one legal system and another.

Of course, a legal system need not look at doctrines through a comity lens to see interrelationships. Campbell McLachlan has pointed to the close connection in the laws of continental European states between the doctrine of *lis pendens* and the recognition of foreign judgments.[75] Yet neither doctrine is understood in those states to be a manifestation of international comity. On the other hand, placing such doctrines on a common theoretical basis may help one to see connections and to shape the doctrines accordingly.

The Court of Justice of the European Union (CJEU) may be doing something similar in developing "mutual trust" as a foundational principle. In *Gasser*, the Court stated "that the Brussels Convention is necessarily based on the trust which the Contracting States accord to each other's legal systems and judicial institutions."[76] "It is that mutual trust," the Court continued, that makes possible "a system of compulsory jurisdiction" and "a simplified mechanism for the recognition and enforcement of foreign judgments."[77] The Court has applied the principle of mutual trust in developing doctrines under the Brussels regime, like *lis pendens*[78] and antisuit injunctions,[79] doctrines that

[75] *See* McLachlan, *supra* note 7, at 100.

[76] Case C-116/02, Erich Gasser GmbH v. Misat Srl., [2003] ECR I-14693, ¶ 72.

[77] *Id.* The Brussels I Regulation (Recast) has now explicitly embraced mutual trust as the basis for its rules. *See* Brussels I Regulation (Recast), *supra* note 6, recital 26. For other examples of regulations adopting mutual trust as a foundation, *see* Weller, *supra* note 49, at 82–84.

[78] The Brussels I Regulation (Recast) art. 29 establishes a doctrine of *lis pendens* under which parallel proceedings must be stayed in favor of the first court seized. In *Gasser*, the CJEU relied on mutual trust in rejecting an exception to this rule in cases where the length of proceedings in the first court seised is excessively long. *Gasser*, [2003] ECR I-14693, 70–73.

[79] In *Turner v. Grovit*, [2004] ECR I-3565, the CJEU relied on mutual trust in interpreting the Brussels Convention to prohibit antisuit injunctions against other EU member states. *Id.* 24–31. And in *Allianz SpA* et al. *v. West Tankers Inc.*, [2009] ECR I-663, the Court again relied on mutual trust in extending the prohibition on antisuit injunctions to actions filed in breach of an arbitration clause. *Id.* 30.

U.S. courts would consider manifestations of international comity. Like international comity, mutual trust also allows for a measure of national control.[80]

Adrian Briggs has gone so far as to suggest that mutual trust is really comity by another name:

> In the European context, the references made by the Court of Justice of the European Union to "mutual trust", as the underpinning explanation for answers which cannot be derived from the literal test of the Brussels I Regulation itself, for example, may be presented as a version of the comity which courts observe in relation to each other.[81]

But mutual trust is narrower than international comity. First, mutual trust has been applied primarily under the Brussels regime governing jurisdiction and judgments, though it has been extended related issues like antisuit injunctions.[82] International comity, at least in the U.S. view, covers a broader range of doctrines, including choice of law, the act of state doctrine, limits on prescriptive jurisdiction, foreign state compulsion, the privilege of a foreign government to bring suit in U.S. courts, and the doctrine of foreign sovereign immunity.[83] Second, mutual trust applies only with respect to other EU member states that are subject to the Brussels regime. The obligation to enforce foreign judgments, for example, applies only to "judgment[s] given in a Member State."[84] In fact, the closer analogue to mutual trust in the U.S. legal system is full faith and credit,[85] which does not extend to states outside the U.S. legal system.[86]

[80] *See, e.g.*, Brussels I Regulation (Recast), *supra* note 6, art. 45(1)(a) (allowing states to refuse recognition "if such recognition is manifestly contrary to public policy (ordre public) in the Member State addressed"); *see also* Weller, *supra* note 49, at 100 ("Both on the level of recognition of foreign judicial acts as well as of choice of law, trust is never granted unconditionally but is balanced against forms of residual control, in particular public policy clauses."); Xandra E. Kramer, *Cross-Border Enforcement and the Brussels I-bis Regulation: Towards a New Balance between Mutual Trust and National Control over Fundamental Rights*, 60 NETH. INT'L L. REV. 343, 365 (2013) ("Every member state has the right and the obligation to protect public policy.").

[81] Briggs, *supra* note 10, at 88.

[82] *See supra* note 79 and accompanying text.

[83] *See supra* note 4 and accompanying text. In other words, international comity covers not just doctrines of adjudicative comity, but doctrines of prescriptive comity and sovereign-party comity as well. For explanation of these categories, *see* Dodge, *supra* note 3, at 2099–2120.

[84] Brussels I Regulation (Recast), *supra* note 6, art. 36(1).

[85] U.S. CONST. art. IV, § 1 ("Full Faith and Credit shall be given in each State to the public Acts, Records, and judicial Proceedings of every other State."); *see also* 28 U.S.C. § 1738 (federal statute implementing constitutional provision). There are differences, of course. The mutual trust reflected in the Brussels I Regulation (Recast) allows EU member states to refuse recognition of a judgment on public policy grounds, Brussels I Regulation (Recast), *supra* note 6, art. 45(1)(a), while the Full Faith and Credit Clause of the U.S. Constitution does not, Baker v. General Motors Corp., 522 U.S. 222, 233–234 (1998).

[86] Aetna Life Ins. Co. v. Tremblay, 223 U.S. 185, 190 (1912). The U.S. Supreme Court has distinguished full faith and credit from comity. *See* Estin v. Estin, 334 U.S. 541, 546 (1948) ("The Full Faith and Credit Clause . . . substituted a command for the earlier principles of comity and thus basically altered the status of the States as independent sovereigns.").

The comparison of international comity to mutual trust is nevertheless appropriate in suggesting the usefulness of a principle on which to found those doctrines of domestic law that mediate relationships with other legal systems. Although the CJEU has found mutual trust to be of assistance in elaborating the Brussels regime, no similar principle seems to have emerged in continental European states to underpin the rules on jurisdiction and judgments with respect to states that lie outside that regime or to tie doctrines of jurisdiction and judgments (adjudicative comity) to doctrines governing applicable law (prescriptive comity) and foreign governments as litigants (sovereign-party comity). It is submitted that international comity might supply such a principle.

IV. Conclusion

In the United States, many doctrines of foreign relations law are understood to be based on international comity, largely because of the influence of Justice Joseph Story. This understanding does not preclude such doctrines from taking the form of rules or from being codified by statutes. But this understanding does emphasize that many of these questions are not governed by international law and that different countries are therefore free to adopt different solutions. It also helps to highlight the interrelationships among different comity doctrines.

Continental European states share many of the same doctrines but do not understand them to be based on international comity. This may partly be the result of misunderstanding what comity entails, but it clearly also shows the influence of Friedrich Carl von Savigny, who built a choice of law system on different foundations and with universalist aspirations. Universalism, however, has proved to be a mirage. Continental European legal systems, and even the law of the European Union itself, have recognized (just as Savigny did) the need to combine deference to foreign states with some measure of national control.

In recent years, the CJEU has started to tie together some of the doctrines that U.S. courts would label international comity under the heading of mutual trust. But mutual trust is currently limited, both in the doctrines it covers and in the states to which it applies. If continental European nations desire a broader principle, they might profitably look to the U.S. experience with international comity.

CHAPTER 40

CROWN AND FOREIGN ACTS OF STATE BEFORE BRITISH COURTS

Rahmatullah, Belhaj, *and the Separation of Powers*

EIRIK BJORGE AND CAMERON MILES

> [T]here exists a particular aspect of that wide topic which in this country, as opposed to the United States of America, has been somewhat neglected by those interested in first principles, viz. the relationship between the Law and the Executive in foreign affairs. In many respects that relationship has developed in a rather haphazard way, in a spirit of subconsciousness and inarticulateness.[1]

THUS wrote F. A. Mann in 1943, in one of his first writings on a topic related to international law. That piece, originating in a speech given to the Grotius Society and later published in its *Transactions*, formed the basis of Mann's lifelong interest in the related doctrines of Crown and foreign act of state. One wonders if he considered this interest particularly fruitful. Some five years before his death, he described the wider field of foreign affairs in English courts as displaying "much confusion of thought and lack of precision, about the reason for which one can only speculate."[2] With the benefit of a further quarter-century of jurisprudence and scholarly commentary, it is difficult today to detect more than marginal progress from this position.

In two significant judgments during its 2016–2017 judicial year—*Rahmatullah v. Ministry of Defence*[3] and *Belhaj v. Straw*[4]—the Supreme Court of the United Kingdom

[1] F. A. Mann, *Judiciary and Executive in Foreign Affairs*, 29 GROT. SOC. TRANS. 143 (1943), *reprinted in* F. A. MANN, STUDIES IN INTERNATIONAL LAW ch. XI (1973).

[2] F. A. MANN, FOREIGN AFFAIRS IN ENGLISH COURTS vi (1986).

[3] Rahmatullah v. Ministry of Defence, [2017] 2 WLR 287.

[4] Belhaj v. Straw, [2017] 2 WLR 458.

undertook to demarcate better the relationship between the judiciary and the executive with respect to Crown and foreign act of state. This chapter aims to unpack *Rahmatullah* and *Belhaj* for the reader and further, in the limited space available, to use these decisions to enquire into the constitutional underpinnings of the British act of state doctrines—particularly as they pertain to the separation of powers.

I. *Rahmatullah* and Crown Act of State

Rahmatullah concerned actions brought by individuals who claimed to have been wrongfully detained or mistreated by British or American troops during the course of the conflicts in the early 2000s in Iraq and Afghanistan. Rahmatullah was a Pakistani national who had been captured by British forces in Iraq in 2004 and then transported to an American detention facility on the same day and transferred to another American facility in Afghanistan, where he was kept until his release in 2014. He had brought proceedings against the Ministry of Defence and the Foreign and Commonwealth Office in respect both of his treatment at the hands of U.K. officials and the United Kingdom's alleged complicity in his detention and mistreatment while in American custody. In relation to the second aspect of that claim, the U.K. government raised the defenses of state immunity and foreign act of state. The arguments relating to these defenses were dealt with in *Belhaj*.

The *Rahmatullah* case also concerned Mohammed, an Afghan national captured in an International Security Assistance Force operation targeting a senior Taliban commander on April 7, 2010, and detained by British troops until July 25, 2010, when he was transferred into Afghan custody. He, too, had claimed that his detention was unlawful under both Afghan law of tort and the Human Rights Act 1998 (HRA 1998). The U.K. government argued that, in relation to the HRA 1998 claim, his detention was not in breach of Article 5 of the European Convention on Human Rights,[5] as Article 5 must be modified to take account of detention during armed conflict, which is permitted, either under resolutions of the UN Security Council or under international humanitarian law. The argument concerning Article 5 was heard together with a similar argument raised against the Ministry of Defence by Waheed, an Iraqi national detained in the course of the conflict in Iraq.[6] The claims of both Rahmatullah and Mohammed were accompanied by a third class of claims brought by certain Iraqi civilians who were detained in Iraq by British forces and, similar to Rahmattulah, were then transferred to U.S. custody in purported violation of Iraqi tort law.

The questions pertaining to Crown act of state arose only in connection with the tort claims: the human rights claims arising in the proceedings were not subject to the

[5] 4 November 1950, 213 UNTS 222.

[6] Al-Waheed v. Ministry of Defence, [2017] 2 WLR 327.

doctrine and fell to be determined according to the HRA 1998.[7] The Supreme Court thus proceeded on the basis that Crown act of state does not run against human rights claims. This is no doubt because, as Lord Bingham held in *Gentle*, in relation to the deployment of troops in Iraq, "if the [claimants] have a legal right it is justiciable in the courts."[8]

The majority judgment of the Supreme Court in *Rahmatullah* was given by Lady Hale, with whom Lord Wilson and Lord Hughes expressly agreed.[9] Her Ladyship began her analysis by asking, "what is this doctrine of Crown act of state?"[10] She cited the definition given in 1934 by ECS Wade, according to which, "[a]ct of state means an act of the Executive as a matter of policy performed in the course of its relations with another state, including its relations with the subjects of that state, unless they are temporarily within the allegiance of the Crown,"[11] a definition that, she observed, had also been cited, albeit not entirely approvingly, in the leading case of *Attorney-General v. Nissan*.[12] Lady Hale took from that decision the important point that, although it was a necessary component of the doctrine that the act at issue falls within some such definition, "that does not tell us what the doctrine is, or to what rule or rules of law it gives rise."[13]

Crown act of state is rarely pleaded, and authority for the doctrine is scant.[14] Lady Hale felt it necessary, therefore, to go back to the nineteenth century and beyond to set out the rationale of the doctrine.[15] In that regard, her Ladyship pointed to the fundamental rule of English law, dating to *Entick v. Carrington*,[16] that English law "does not recognize that there is an indefinite class of acts concerning matters of high policy or public security which may be left to the uncontrolled discretion of the Government and which are outside the jurisdiction of the courts."[17] She developed this point by reference to the words of Viscount Finlay in *Johnstone v. Pedlar*, according to which:

> [I]f a wrongful act has been committed against the person or the property of any person the wrongdoer cannot set up as a defence that the act was done by the command of the Crown. The Crown can do no wrong, and the Sovereign cannot be sued in tort, but the person who did the act is liable in damages, as any private person would be.[18]

[7] *Rahmatullah*, *supra* note 3, para. 17.

[8] R (Gentle) v. Prime Minister, [2008] 1 AC 1356, para. 8.

[9] Lord Neuberger gave a separate judgment that also agreed with Lady Hale's reasoning, giving her Ladyship a majority within the panel. *See Rahmatullah*, *supra* note 3, para. 106.

[10] *Id.*, para. 2.

[11] E. C. S. Wade, *Act of State in English Law: Its Relations with International Law*, 15 Brit. Y.B. Int'l L. 98, 103 (1934).

[12] A-G v. Nissan [1970] AC 179, 212 (Lord Reid), 218 (Lord Morris), 231 (Lord Wilberforce).

[13] *Rahmatullah*, *supra* note 3, para. 2.

[14] *Cf.* Johnstone v. Pedlar, [1921] 2 AC 262; A-G v. Nissan, [1970] AC 179; Al-Jedda v. Secretary of State for Defence (No 2), [2011] QB 773.

[15] *Rahmatullah*, *supra* note 3, para. 3.

[16] Entick v. Carrington, (1765) 19 St Tr 1029.

[17] H. Street, Government Liability: A Comparative Study 50 (1953).

[18] Johnstone v. Pedlar, [1921] 2 AC 262, 271.

Against this, the question for the Supreme Court was "whether there is indeed a qualification such as that expressed by Viscount Finlay and, if so, how far that qualification goes."[19] In drawing on the authorities predating *A-G v. Nissan*, said Lady Hale, it was necessary to keep in mind that those were decided "against a legal landscape which was very different from the legal landscape of today."[20] Lady Hale stressed that:

> The conduct of foreign affairs, making treaties, making peace and war, conquering or annexing territories, are all aspects of the Royal prerogative. Until the decision of the House of Lords in *Council of the Civil Service Unions v Minister for the Civil Service* [1985] AC 374 (the *GCHQ* case), the general position was that the courts would review whether what had been done fell within the scope of the Royal prerogative but would not review how that prerogative had been exercised. After that case, the exercise of executive power might be excluded from the scope of judicial review, not because of its *source*, whether statute or the prerogative, but because of its *subject matter*.[21]

She also made the point that the pre-*Nissan* cases were largely decided against the backdrop of the principle that "the King can do no wrong," it having been impossible at that time to sue the king in his own courts. The Crown Proceedings Act 1947 abolished the general immunity of the Crown from liability in tort, enabling litigants to sue government departments, and not only their servants, such as the defendants in *Rahmatullah*.[22]

In *A-G v. Nissan*, Lord Wilberforce had taken the view that the doctrine of Crown act of state encompassed two rules. The first was drawn from the case of *Buron v. Denman*,[23] and was:

> one which provides a defendant, normally a servant of the Crown, with a defence to an act otherwise tortious or criminal, committed abroad, provided that the act was authorized or subsequently ratified by the Crown. It is established that this defence may be pleaded against an alien, if done abroad, but not against a friendly alien if the act was done in Her Majesty's Dominions.

The second rule, Lord Wilberforce said, was:

> one of justiciability: it prevents British municipal courts from taking cognizance of certain acts. The class of acts so protected has not been accurately defined: one formulation is "those acts of the Crown which are done under the prerogative in the sphere of foreign affairs" (*Wade and Phillips's Constitutional Law*, 7th ed. (1956), p. 263). As regards such acts it is certainly the law that the injured person, if an alien, cannot sue in a British court and can only have resort to diplomatic protest.

[19] *Rahmatullah*, *supra* note 3, para. 7. [20] *Id.*, para. 15. [21] *Id.*, para. 15.
[22] *Id.*, para. 16. [23] Buron v. Denman, (1848) 2 Exch 167, 154 ER 450.

> How far this rule goes and how far it prevents resort to the courts by British subjects is not a matter on which clear authority exists. From the terms of the pleading it appears that it is this aspect of the rule upon which the Crown seeks to rely.[24]

Having reviewed the case law, Lady Hale found that the foundations of the rule in *Buron v. Denman* were "very shaky,"[25] and that authority for the core (and arguably antecedent) rule of nonjusticiability was on the whole far more certain.[26] Furthermore, her Ladyship said, there were conceptual advantages in confining the doctrine to a rule of nonjusticiability, and holding that the rule in *Buron v. Denman* was nothing more than a necessary corollary of the same.[27] Such confinement would, however, require a broad concept of nonjusticiability:

> It would have to encompass aspects of the conduct of military operations abroad as well as the high policy decision to engage in them, and perhaps also some other aspects of the conduct of foreign relations, even though their subject matter was entirely suitable for determination by the court. It is necessary that the courts continue to recognise that there are some acts of a governmental nature, committed, abroad, upon which the courts of England and Wales will not pass judgment. They may, of course, have to hear evidence and find facts in order to determine whether the acts in question fall into that category. It is also necessary to confine that category within very narrow bounds.[28]

As such, it appears that the division between the rule in *Buron v. Denman* and the wider rule of nonjusticiability identified by Lord Wilberforce in *A-G v. Nissan* remains intact post-*Rahmatullah*. The latter is, according to Lady Hale, confined to certain decisions of "high policy" in the conduct of foreign relations, e.g., the decision to participate in armed conflict. These decisions are deemed to be removed entirely from the court's adjudicative ambit. The former covers all consequential acts carried out by the departments or agents of the Crown in pursuit of that high policy.[29] These are not so removed, and may be subjected to the ordinary forensic processes of the court, which may then determine that the rule in *Buron v. Denman* applies as a defense to tort or crime.

But this left unresolved the central question of Crown act of state: the precise *character* of the acts that will attract the protection of the doctrine. Lady Hale refused to identify the relevant category with precision, noting that "[i]t would be unwise for this court to attempt a definitive statement of the circumstances in which [Crown act of state] might apply."[30] She did, however, provide some general guidance, by noting that the doctrine could be raised only in respect of:

> a very narrow class of acts: in their nature sovereign acts—the sorts of thing that governments properly do; committed abroad; in the conduct of the foreign policy of

[24] A-G v. Nissan, [1970] AC 179, 231.
[25] *Rahmatullah, supra* note 3, paras. 22 and 31.
[26] *Id.*, para. 31.
[27] *Cf. id.*, paras. 47, 65, and 69 (Lord Mance).
[28] *Id.*, para. 33.
[29] *Rahmatullah, supra* note 3, para. 31.
[30] *Id.*, para. 36.

> the state; so closely connected to that policy to be necessary in pursuing it; and at least extending to the conduct of military operations which are themselves lawful in international law (which is not the same as saying that the acts themselves are necessarily authorised in international law).[31]

This was further qualified in three significant ways: (1) the doctrine is not of general application "to all torts committed against foreigners abroad just because they have been authorised or ratified by the British government"; (2) by concession of the Ministry of Defence, it does not apply to acts of torture or to the mistreatment of prisoners or detainees; and (3) it does not apply to expropriation, which can always be the subject of compensation.[32] The idea of a broad-based public policy exception to the doctrine was rejected,[33] and the question of the doctrine's application to a British national left open.[34] Lady Hale held on this basis that the defense applied to all three claims at bar—the appeal was accordingly allowed and the matters dismissed.

Lady Hale's reasoning seems to have been based on the rule in *Buron v. Denman* alone, and sought overtly to limit the doctrine of Crown act of state to the narrowest ambit possible while still upholding its existence. The judgments of Lord Mance and Lord Sumption, however, reflect a more searching inquiry, investigating not only the defense to tort and crime provided by *Buron v. Denman* but also the antecedent question of nonjusticiability.[35] Lord Mance sought to merge the two rules into a single principle of nonjusticiability, arguing that the continued independence of the rule in *Buron v. Denman* created "unnecessary confusion"[36] and that the tort defense was nothing more than the logical corollary of the Court's unwillingness to take cognizance of certain Crown acts, reflecting (in particular) its prerogative over foreign affairs.[37] Lord Sumption held that the division between the two rules should be maintained,[38] and further investigated the precise character of a qualifying state act. Both concurring opinions pointed out that the doctrine of Crown act of state is rooted in the constitutional principle of the separation of powers, in particular the reservation of the "paradigm functions of the state," such as the conduct of warfare, to the Crown, so that it would be "incoherent and irrational" for the courts to acknowledge the Crown's power to conduct foreign relations of a certain kind, and at the same time treat as civil wrongs acts inherent in its exercise of that power.[39]

[31] *Id.*, para. 37. [32] *Id.*, para. 36. [33] *Id.*, paras. 34 and 35. [34] *Id.*, para. 37.

[35] For further analysis, *see* Ali Malek & Cameron Miles, *International Dimensions*, *in* The UK Supreme Court Yearbook, Volume 8: 2016–2017 Judicial Year 447 (Daniel Clarry ed., 2017).

[36] *Rahmatullah*, *supra* note 3, para. 47.

[37] *Id.*, paras. 65 and 69. *See* in this regard Jenny S. Martinez, *The Constitutional Allocation of Executive and Legislative Power over Foreign Relations: A Survey*, ch. 6 in this volume.

[38] *Rahmatullah*, *supra* note 3, para. 78.

[39] *Id.*, para. 88 (Lord Sumption). *See also id.*, paras. 50–54 (Lord Mance).

II. *Belhaj* and Foreign Act of State

The U.K. government had in *Belhaj* relied on the defense of foreign act of state in relation to various torts in a case in which Belhaj, a Libyan opponent of Colonel Gaddafi, contended that, together with his Moroccan wife, he had been detained at Kuala Lumpur, compulsorily rendered to a CIA black site in Thailand, subjected to inhumane treatment, and then transported to Libya, where he was tortured. Also involved in the case was Rahmatullah, whose claim for the accessorial liability of the Ministry of Defence for torts committed against him by American forces was joined to Belhaj and his wife's appeal. As in *Rahmatullah*, the act of state questions arose only in relation to the tort claims; what was at issue was the accessorial liability of certain government agents and the Ministry of Defence for torts committed against the claimants by the third states.[40]

Was the U.K. government entitled to rely on the defense of foreign act of state on the basis that Belhaj's claim could not be heard because Malaysia, Thailand, the United States, and Libya would be impleaded and their legal position affected, whether directly or indirectly? Although the primary actor was the United States, there was no basis for concluding that the issues would involve sovereign, international, or inter-state considerations of such a nature that a domestic court could not or should not appropriately adjudicate upon them.[41] The mere fact that an individual is handed over to a state under an agreement could not suffice to make the claims for alleged wrongful detention combined with severe mistreatment by the United States nonjusticiable in respect of either the United States' primary, or the United Kingdom's ancillary, involvement.[42] It was accepted that "detention overseas as a matter of considered policy during or in consequence of an armed conflict and to prevent further participation in an insurgency could in some circumstances constitute a foreign act of state, just as it may constitute Crown act of state when undertaken by the United Kingdom."[43] But it was pointed out that the court was concerned, in *Belhaj*, with allegations of arbitrary detention with a view to the individual being forcibly handed over to an arbitrary ruler:

> Even if one could say that such treatment reflects some policy of the various foreign states involved, or indeed of the United Kingdom, it goes far beyond any conduct previously recognised as requiring judicial abstention. There is certainly also no lack of judicial and manageable standards by which to judge it.[44]

[40] *Belhaj*, *supra* note 4, paras. 1 (Lord Mance), 113 (Lord Neuberger), 175 (Lord Sumption). *See also* Malek & Miles, *supra* note 35, at 448–453.
[41] *Belhaj*, *supra* note 4, para. 96. [42] *Id.*, para. 96. [43] *Id.*, para. 96. [44] *Id.*, para. 97.

In relation to indirect impleading, the Supreme Court rejected the government's argument based on the *Monetary Gold* doctrine,[45] that is, the international law doctrine according to which an international tribunal will declare inadmissible a claim the very subject matter of which requires a determination of the rights or interests of a state that is not before the court.[46] The argument was rejected on the grounds that "*Monetary Gold* is not about state immunity, and does not on its facts assist on the issue now before the court, even by way of analogy."[47] The Court did so in spite of the government[48] having adduced authorities to the effect that the *Monetary Gold* doctrine "is the nearest direct analogue in international law to the rule of State immunity,"[49] with the significant addition that, "although the international rule prohibiting adjudication against foreign States without their consent may not apply directly to municipal courts, it has much force as an analogy."[50] The Court's approach was clearly correct: notwithstanding certain theoretical parallels, in the final balance, the *Monetary Gold* doctrine considers the indirectly impleaded interests of a third state to be a question of admissibility arising from the consensual character of international jurisdiction (*ratione voluntatis*); the rule has nothing to do with the jurisdictional immunity of states (*ratione personae*) before domestic courts. As such, however inventive the argument, the Court gave it short shrift, pointing out that if correct it could be used to remove a court's jurisdiction (*ratione materiae*) in any case where state interests could be indirectly raised.[51]

As with Crown act of state, the parameters of foreign act of state can be uncertain.[52] Again, one of the more authoritative earlier statements of the doctrine was given by Lord Wilberforce, in *Buttes Gas v. Hammer*. Two limbs of the doctrine were identified. The first limb involves questions deriving from cases such as *Luther v. Sagor*,[53] which were:

> concerned with the applicability of foreign municipal legislation within its own territory, and with the examinability of such legislation—often, but not invariably arising in cases of confiscation of property. Mr Littman gave us a valuable analysis of [the relevant cases], suggesting that these are cases within the area of conflict of laws, concerned essentially with the choice of the proper law to be applied.[54]

[45] Monetary Gold Removed from Rome in 1943 (Italy v. France, UK and US), [1954] ICJ Rep 19, 32–33.

[46] *See* John Collier & Vaughan Lowe, The Settlement of Disputes in International Law 158–161 (1999).

[47] *Belhaj*, *supra* note 4, para. 27 (Lord Mance).

[48] Joint Case for the Appellants, 24 July 2015, paras. 39 and 40.

[49] James Crawford, *International Law and Foreign Sovereigns: Distinguishing Immune Transactions*, 54 Brit. Y.B. Int'l L. 75, 80 (1983).

[50] *Id.* at 80–81.

[51] *Belhaj*, *supra* note 4, paras. 30 (Lord Mance), 196 (Lord Neuberger).

[52] *See*, e.g., Campbell McLachlan, Foreign Relations Law 523–545 (2014).

[53] Aksionairnoye Obschestvo AM Luther v. James Sagor & Co., [1921] 3 KB 532.

[54] Buttes Gas and Oil Co. & Another v. Hammer & Another (No 3), [1982] AC 888, 931A.

The second limb involves the question of:

> whether . . . there exists in English law a more general principle that the courts will not adjudicate upon the transactions of foreign sovereign states. Though I would prefer to avoid argument on terminology, it seems desirable to consider the principle, if existing, not as a variety of "act of state," but one for judicial restraint or abstention . . . . This principle is not one of discretion, but is inherent in the very nature of the judicial process . . . I find the principle clearly stated that the courts in England will not adjudicate upon acts done abroad by virtue of sovereign authority.[55]

In developing the category of restraint, the House of Lords in *Buttes Gas* was drawing on influences from the courts of the United States,[56] especially *Baker v. Carr*[57] and *Goldwater v. Carter.*[58] Not mentioned by Lord Wilberforce in *Buttes Gas v. Hammer* in conjunction with the first rule was the closely allied notion that a British court will not question a foreign executive act—as distinct from legislation—on its own territory. This derived not from *Luther v. Sagor* but another case, *Princess Paley Olga.*[59]

Three fully reasoned judgments were delivered in *Belhaj*: by Lord Mance, Lord Sumption, and Lord Neuberger. Lord Mance gave the first judgment and set out the facts—an arrangement that traditionally identifies a judgment as that of the majority. Lord Mance's judgment was, however, a minority judgment, as none of the other Justices agreed with his reasoning in its entirety. Rather, Lord Wilson, Lady Hale, and Lord Clarke agreed with Lord Neuberger—whose judgment and reasoning accordingly speaks for the majority by dint of simple arithmetic.[60] To the extent that Lord Neuberger endorsed the reasoning of Lord Mance and Lord Sumption (with whom Lord Hughes agreed), that endorsement also formed part of the ratio.

Lord Neuberger disaggregated act of state into "four rules"—or, rather, four *potential* rules. The first two reflected the private international law rules of *Luther v. Sagor* and *Princess Paley Olga*, whereby a British court will not adjudicate on the validity of a foreign law or executive act on its own territory in connection with movable or immovable property.[61] The third rule was the second principle of nonjusticiability identified by Lord Wilberforce in *Buttes Gas v. Hammer*, whereby British courts will not interpret or question sovereign dealings of or between states.[62] The fourth rule (which, in fairness, was *not* the subject of argument before the Court and was in fact expressly *denounced* by both parties) was derived from a remark of Rix LJ in

[55] *Id.* at 931G–932A. [56] *See* Lord Mance, *Justiciability*, 67 Int'l & Comp. L.Q. 739 (2018).

[57] Baker v. Carr, 369 U.S. 186 (1962). [58] Goldwater v. Carter, 444 U.S. 996, 998 (1979).

[59] Princess Paley Olga v. Weisz, [1929] 1 KB 718.

[60] This understanding of *Belhaj* has since been adopted by the High Court of England and Wales, in AAA v. Unilever plc, [2017] EWHC 371 (QB), para. 36 (Laing J).

[61] *Belhaj*, *supra* note 4, paras. 121 and 122. For the American approach to similar rules, *see Banco Nacional de Cuba v. Sabbatino*, 376 U.S. 398, 428 (1964); *see also* William S. Dodge, *International Comity in Comparative Perspective*, ch. 39 in this volume.

[62] *Belhaj*, *supra* note 4, para. 123.

Yukos v. Rosneft, whereby "courts will not investigate acts of a foreign state where such an investigation would embarrass the government of our own country"[63]—though this could only arise upon a communication of the Foreign and Commonwealth Office.[64] Lord Neuberger explained that the fourth rule had no clear basis in any judicial decision from the United Kingdom, and that if a member of the executive was to say formally to a court that the judicial determination of an issue could embarrass the government's relation with another state, the court would not be bound to refuse to determine the issue: "[t]hat would involve the executive dictating to the judiciary, which would be quite unacceptable."[65] The end result was that only the first three of Lord Neuberger's rules were held to be part of the positive law.

As pointed out by Bill Dodge,[66] in American law the doctrine is by way of comparison limited to "the official act of a foreign sovereign performed within its own territory."[67] But the American version of the doctrine has no public policy exception: if it is found that the doctrine applies, then an American court is bound to accept its validity "[h]owever offensive to the public policy of this country" it may be.[68]

As with Crown act of state, this analysis left the substantive application of foreign act of state to be decided. Three questions were of relevance, namely: (1) the jurisprudential underpinnings of the doctrine, (2) the type of state acts rendered nonjusticiable by its operation, and (3) the scope and character of any public policy exception thereto.

With respect to (1), Lord Neuberger did not delve into the underpinning of foreign act of state in anything more than a transitory sense, but expressed some agreement with both Lords Mance and Sumption, who were more expansive on the point.[69] As to questions (2) and (3), Lord Neuberger said that "it would be unwise to be too prescriptive about [the doctrine's] ambit," although he made some reference to the fact that "in practice, it will almost always apply to actions involving more than one state" and "involve some sort of comparatively formal, relatively high level arrangement."[70] With respect to the scope of the public policy exception,[71] Lord Neuberger applied the same standard as in relation to the first (private international law) rule, noting that the exception depended "ultimately on domestic law considerations, although generally accepted norms of international law are plainly capable of playing

[63] Yukos Capital SARL v. OJSC Rosneft Oil Co (No 2), [2014] QB 458, [65].

[64] *Belhaj*, *supra* note 4, para. 124. [65] *Id.*, para. 149.

[66] William S. Dodge, *The UK Supreme Court's Landmark Judgment Belhaj v. Straw: A View from the United States*, JUST SECURITY (Jan. 19, 2017), *available at* https://www.justsecurity.org/36507/uk-supreme-courts-landmark-judgment-belhaj-v-straw-view-united-states/.

[67] W.S. Kirkpatrick & Co, Inc. v. Environmental Tectonics Corp., 493 U.S. 400, 405 (1990).

[68] Banco Nacional de Cuba v. Sabbatino, 376 U.S. 398, 436 (1964). *But cf.* Kadic v. Karadzic, 70 F.3d 232, 250 (2d Cir. 1995) (noting that it is doubtful that acts of a state official committed "in violation of a nation's fundamental law and wholly unratified by that nation's government, could properly be characterized as an act of state").

[69] *Belhaj*, *supra* note 4, para. 151. [70] *Id.*, para. 147.

[71] This was already well established as an exception to foreign act of state in English law. *See* Oppenheimer v. Cattermole (Inspector of Taxes), [1976] AC 249, 278B–C (Lord Cross).

a decisive role."[72] In the final balance, his Lordship held that the types of acts alleged by both claimants would not attract the doctrine's protection—and, even if they did, the public policy exception would apply.[73]

Rather more clarity was provided by the separate opinions of Lord Mance and Lord Sumption, although their Lordships seemed to differ with Lord Neuberger—and with each other—on several points of principle. Lord Sumption set out the clearest view of foreign act of state, holding that the rule was confined to acts *jure imperii* (with that term bearing the same meaning as it did in relation to questions of state immunity)[74] and was not solely concerned with armed conflict but are "altogether more general," concluding that "[o]nce the acts alleged are into the 'area of an international dispute' the act of state doctrine is engaged."[75] On this basis, both claims in *Belhaj* were prima facie precluded by foreign act of state.[76] He further held that the public policy exception, while remaining strictly domestic in character, was to be guided by reference to international law, and in particular whether the conduct alleged would violate *jus cogens* norms.[77] Citing the 2012 Report of United Nations Working Group on Arbitrary Detention on the matter,[78] Lord Sumption held that "the irreducible core of the international obligation . . . [is] that detention is unlawful it if is without any legal basis or recourse to the courts."[79] He then concluded that the acts alleged by the claimants in *Belhaj*—encompassing torture, unlawful detention, enforced disappearance and cruel, inhuman and degrading treatment—were subject to the exception as they violated peremptory norms of international law and fundamental principles of the administration of justice in England.[80]

In Lord Mance's view, the critical point was:

> the nature and seriousness of the misconduct alleged in both cases before the Supreme Court, at however high a level it may have been authorised. Act of state is and remains essentially a domestic law doctrine, and it is English law which sets its limits. English law recognises the existence of fundamental rights, some long-standing, others more recently developed.[81]

To that end, his Lordship cited *Abbasi*, where in the context of a claim judicially to review the Secretary of State for alleged inaction in respect of the plight of a British citizen detained at Guantanamo, the Court of Appeal observed that "where fundamental human rights are in play, the courts of this country will not abstain from reviewing

[72] *Belhaj*, paras. 153–157. [73] *Id.*, paras. 167 and 168. [74] *Id.*, para. 199.

[75] *Id.*, para. 234. [76] *Id.*, para. 238. [77] *Id.*, para. 257.

[78] UN Doc. No. A/HRC/22/44 (24 December 2012), paras. 38 and 39.

[79] *Belhaj*, *supra* note 4, paras. 270 and 271. [80] *Id.*, paras. 238–280.

[81] *Id.*, para. 98. Similarly, it has been argued in the American literature that the act of state doctrine is not a doctrine of international law but one of international comity, the latter describing "an internationally oriented body of domestic law that is distinct from international law and yet critical to legal relations with other countries." William S. Dodge, *International Comity in American Law*, 115 COLUM. L. REV. 2071, 2077 (2015).

the legitimacy of the actions of a foreign sovereign state."[82] On the whole, however, Lord Mance did not speak in terms of principles (i.e., the act of state) versus exceptions (i.e., public policy), but rather held that public policy might persuade or dissuade a court from declaring a matter nonjusticiable, and that there was no presumption that a court would abstain in respect of any particular state act.[83]

The appeals were upheld and the matters remitted to the High Court for trial.

III. Analysis

The cases of *Rahmatullah* and *Belhaj* presented the Supreme Court with a unique opportunity. The Court was confronted with doctrines that had been historically bedeviled with uncertainty and for which the most authoritative statements on both had been given comparatively long ago by Lord Wilberforce in *A-G v. Nissan* (1970) and *Buttes Gas v. Hammer* (1982). Furthermore, Lord Wilberforce was not so fortunate as to be able to deal with both aspects of act of state simultaneously and in the context of cases that shared considerable factual DNA. The Court was clearly aware of its good fortune and arranged itself accordingly. The same panel of seven Justices sat in each, and the decisions were clearly drafted and intended to be read together—indeed, they were handed down *seriatim* on the same day.

While the two judgments do provide clarity in certain vital respects, the upshot of *Rahmatullah* and *Belhaj* is that aspects of both doctrines and the relationship between them remain obscure. The obscurities concern both questions of the *internal* coherence of each doctrine, and also their *external* justification as a matter of constitutional principle.

Internal Coherence: Clarifying the Operation of the Act of State Doctrines

The difficulties identified by many commentators with respect to the act of state doctrines are summed up admirably by Lord Reid's aside in *A-G v. Nissan*: "a good deal of trouble has been caused by using the loose phrase 'act of state' without making clear what is meant."[84] This comment is almost as apt post-*Rahmatullah* and *Belhaj* as it was in 1970. In neither case was clear direction given as to precisely which acts of state would be protected from judicial scrutiny. At the highest level, both doctrines may be said to apply to "acts which are by their nature sovereign acts, acts which are

[82] R (Abbasi) v. Secretary of State for Foreign and Commonwealth Affairs, [2002] EWCA Civ 1598, [53].

[83] *Belhaj*, *supra* note 4, paras. 89 and 90.

[84] A-G v. Nissan, [1970] AC 179, 211G.

inherently governmental, committed to the conduct of the foreign relations [of the Crown or state in question]."[85] The scope of such acts have been delineated extensively in public international law by the rules on state immunity, which serve as a useful analogy.[86] Less certain is the outer limit of the doctrine. In *Rahmatullah*, Lady Hale held that the rule in *Buron v. Denman* protects acts "so closely connected to [the foreign policy of the state] as to be necessary in pursuing it"[87]—with no explanation given as to what might be considered "necessary" in that context.[88]

At the same time, useful clarification was provided with respect to other aspects of the act of state doctrines. The extraterritorial aspect of Crown act of state was confirmed, as was the dual territorial (in the cases of the principle of *Luther v. Sagor* and *Princess Paley Olga*) and extraterritorial (in the case of *Buttes Gas v. Hammer* nonjusticiability) of foreign act of state. Also confirmed as removed (or diminished) was the dictum of Lord Wilberforce in *Buttes Gas v. Hammer* that a further case for nonjusticiability when considering a foreign act of state is a lack of "judicial or manageable standards" on which to found a decision.[89] This abnegation of a British court's decision to apply international law—trenchantly criticized when handed down,[90] but in reality always blown somewhat out of proportion—was deemed to be irrelevant in *Belhaj*.[91] Given the relative development and wider acceptance of international law by British courts since *Buttes Gas v. Hammer* was decided, the utility of that dictum has likely been reduced to the vanishing point.

Nevertheless, areas of uncertainty remain in respect of both act of state doctrines that disrupt their internal coherence. This may well have been by design, the Supreme Court in both cases having seemed cognizant of the risk of overprecision in relation to the act of state doctrines. Lady Hale noted that "[i]t would be unwise for this court to attempt a definitive statement of the circumstances in which [Crown act of state] might apply."[92] Lord Neuberger urged a similar caution with respect to foreign act of state.[93] This political aspect serves as a neat link between questions pertaining to the internal coherence of the act of state doctrines and their wider (or external) justification from the perspective of constitutional principle.

[85] *Rahmatullah*, *supra* note 3, para. [36] (Lady Hale).

[86] *Belhaj*, *supra* note 4, para. 199 (Lord Sumption).

[87] *Rahmatullah*, *supra* note 3, para. 37. *See also id.*, paras. 56–58 (Lord Sumption), 64 (Lord Mance), 88–93 (Lord Sumption).

[88] *Cf. id.*, para. 92 (Lord Sumption) (referring to the principle of military necessity as a possible analogy).

[89] Buttes Gas v. Hammer, [1982] AC 888, 938B.

[90] *See*, e.g., James Crawford, *Public International Law*, 53 BRIT. Y.B. INT'L L. 253, 268 (1982); J. G. Collier, *Transactions Between States—Non-Justiciability—International Law and the House of Lords in a Judicial No-Man's Land*, 41 CAMBRIDGE L.J. 18, 18–21 (1982).

[91] *Belhaj*, *supra* note 4, para. 90.

[92] *Rahmatullah*, *supra* note 3, para. 36.

[93] *Belhaj*, *supra* note 4, para. 101.

External Coherence: Rooting the Act of State Doctrines in Constitutional Principle

The greatest principled advance in *Rahmatullah* and *Belhaj* was confirmation by the Supreme Court that the doctrines of Crown and foreign act of state arise from something approximating a common constitutional source.

The Court was at pains in both cases to stress the increasing importance of the principles of the constitutional division of power in the act of state analysis. Further and in addition, the relationship between the branches of power under the constitution goes some way in explaining the difference in outcome in *Belhaj* and *Rahmatullah.* In his judgment in *Rahmatullah*, Lord Mance observed that it would be wrong to suggest that the principle of abstention identified by Lord Wilberforce in *A-G v. Nissan* and *Buttes Gas v. Hammer* applies with the same force or by reference to the same considerations in relation to the two types of act of state:

> Both Crown act of state and the third type of foreign act of state are based on an underlying perception of the role of domestic courts. The constitutional relationship of a domestic court with its own State differs from its relationship with that of any foreign sovereign state. Crown act of state is reserved for situations of sovereign authority exercised overseas as a matter of state policy. In these circumstances, a straight-forward principle of consistency directly underpins Crown act of state.... In contrast, if and when the third type of foreign act of state applies, its underpinning is a more general conception of the role of a domestic court, and, more particularly, the incongruity of a domestic court adjudicating upon the conduct of a foreign sovereign state, even though the foreign state is neither directly or indirectly impleaded or affected in its rights.... [I]t must be easier to establish that a domestic court should abstain from adjudicating on the basis of Crown act of state than on the basis of the third type of foreign act of state. The relationship is closer and the threshold of sensitivity lower in the case of the former than the latter.[94]

Lord Mance's comments—echoed by Lord Sumption[95]—make it clear that although the doctrines may prima facie encompass the same class of acts, the different origins of each may compel a different result. Foreign act of state is based on a nebulous but elemental conception of how a domestic court operates, and contemplates that there are some substantive questions in respect of which the court is not incompetent to issue an opinion, but from which is should nevertheless refrain. Crown act of state, on the other hand, is animated by a more hard-edged rule drawn from the relationship of the judiciary to the executive in a constitutional democracy. This explains the additional degree of caution animating the Court in *Rahmatullah* and the absence from

[94] *Rahmatullah, supra* note 3, paras. 50–52. [95] *Id.*, para. 88.

Crown act of state of the defined public policy exception that was the subject of extended discussion in *Belhaj*.[96]

In other words, with respect to Crown act of state, it would be inconsistent for the common law to give, with the one hand, the function of deploying armed force in the conduct of international relations to the executive only to take away, with the other, by treating as civil wrongs the acts carried out by the executive in that connection. The argument is similar to that which was taken to be good law in relation to judicial review and the royal prerogative until the landmark *GCHQ* judgment in the mid-1980s, which confirmed the reviewability by the judiciary of the prerogative.[97] In addition to confirming that the exercise of the prerogative could be reviewed, the Appellate Committee of the House of Lords in *GCHQ* established that justiciability depended on the subject matter rather than on the source of the power; the fact that a case concerns the exercise of the prerogative would not automatically take the act or omission out of the scope of judicial review.[98] Lord Mance explicitly pointed out the connection with *GCHQ*.[99]

The old orthodoxy was that, as Sir William Wade put it, "the logical basis for 'act of state'" was geography: "the Crown enjoys no dispensation for acts done within the jurisdiction, whether the plaintiff be British or foreign; but foreign parts are beyond the pale (in Kipling's words, 'without the law')."[100] As will have been seen, the perspective has changed from one of geography—foreign parts having been considered beyond the pale—to one of constitutional competence as regards subject matter, some matters being "beyond the constitutional competence assigned to the courts under our conception of the separation of powers."

This is a welcome development. Lord Sales argued more than a decade ago that it would assist the rational development of the law in relation to the act of state doctrine for separation of powers type analysis to be brought more to the forefront of the courts' reasoning, so that the competing interests and policy considerations might be balanced more explicitly and coherently.[101] Viewing the act of state doctrine through the prism of separation of powers would lead to the suggestion that the doctrine should, as compared to its traditional version, be qualified to some extent.[102] This is indeed what is happening. Prefiguring this move, Lauterpacht observed that, already in the beginning of the twentieth century, one was seeing a gradual development where "the doctrine of separation of powers is being in practice reduced to its *proper proportions*."[103] Some decades later Lord Sumption, speaking extrajudicially, echoed this important point, referring to the developing framework as "the advance of the qualified

[96] Malek & Miles, *supra* note 35, at 462–463.

[97] Council of Civil Service Unions v. Minister for the Civil Service, [1985] AC 374.

[98] R (Abbasi and Juma) v. Foreign Secretary, (2002) 123 ILR 599, 605–606, para. 14 (Richards J).

[99] *Rahmatullah*, *supra* note 3, para. 56.

[100] HWR Wade, Administrative Law 230 (1961).

[101] Lord Sales, *Act of State and the Separation of Powers*, 11 Jud. Rev. 94, 97 (2006).

[102] *Id.* at 94.

[103] Hersch Lauterpacht, The Function of Law in the International Community 398 (1933) (emphasis added).

division of powers theory."[104] There is no doubt that, in the delimitation of executive power in foreign affairs before British courts, the development of the law is aided by the concept of the separation of powers, and that the principle of constitutional separation of powers is a qualified one as compared with the principle that operated in the twentieth century. The separation of powers is no longer only a byword for judicial abstention and the executive enjoying a free reign in foreign affairs.

This may be said to apply with respect to Crown act of state. Important questions still persist, however, in respect of its foreign counterpart. Historically, the jurisprudential underpinning of the doctrine—at least insofar as it reflected a principle of judicial abstention—was, as a matter of English law, unclear. When Mann came to the topic for the first time in 1943,[105] he asserted that it was based upon mere rhetoric, and was reflective of policy preferences that could not be justified as a matter of constitutional principle. As such, it carried little more weight than a legal maxim—a category of aphorism that he considered dangerous, and despised accordingly.[106]

In returning to foreign act of state some four decades later, Mann did not consider the situation to have improved. He drew an unfavorable comparison between the development that had occurred with respect to the equivalent doctrine in the United States, tracking a jurisprudential shift from an analysis that prioritized comity between states to one that prioritized comity between branches of government.[107] In this, he cited Judge Brieant's remarks in *Banco Nacional de Cuba v. Chemical Bank New York Trust*, that:

> Historically [courts under the foreign act of state doctrine] should respect the acts of foreign sovereigns conducted within their borders.... That has since been refined and the doctrine is now cited more as a means of maintaining the proper balance between the judicial and political branches of the government on matters bearing upon foreign affairs.[108]

Mann then went on to note that no such jurisprudential justification had been advanced in English law—indeed, it had been denied in other, related fields.[109] Lord Mance's principled justification of the division between Crown and foreign act of state may now be said to provide that underpinning. But it does so only up to a point. His Lordship's language, referring to "a more general conception of the role of a domestic court, and, more particularly, the incongruity of a domestic court adjudicating upon the conduct of a foreign sovereign state,"[110] is couched in terms broadly redolent of the separation of powers, it is true. But one may ask whether, beyond identifying the

[104] Lord Sumption, Foreign Affairs in the English Courts since 9/11, at 8 (Lecture given at the London School of Economics, 14 May 2012).

[105] Mann, Studies in International Law, *supra* note 1, at 455–465.

[106] *Id.* at 420–422.

[107] Mann, *supra* note 2, at 176.

[108] Banco Nacional de Cuba v. Chemical Bank New York Trust, 594 F. Supp. 1553, 1557 (S.D.N.Y. 1984).

[109] Mann, *supra* note 2, at 176.

[110] *Rahmatullah*, *supra* note 3, paras. 50–52.

constitutional space in which the rule is said to operate, Lord Mance has shed any light upon its basis in anything other than the most general of terms. From where does this "general conception" arise? Is it rooted in precedent? Is it of relevance elsewhere in English law? And why exactly is a domestic court sitting in judgment over a foreign state's acts—in circumstances where the hard rules of state immunity do not apply—so incongruous anyway? In this, his Lordship may be said to have done little more than coin yet another of Mann's dreaded maxims, in respect of which Lord Wright famously said:

> [T]hese general formulae are found in experience often to distract the court's mind from the actual exigencies of the case, and so to induce the court to quote them as offering a ready-made solution. It is not yet safe to act upon them, however, unless, and to the extent that, they received definition and limitation, from judicial determination.[111]

Given the vagueness with which Lord Mance expressed himself, the "definition and limitation" that Lord Wright required before he could deem a maxim safe to act upon is not yet present. As such, from a certain point of view, the opportunity presented to the Supreme Court by *Rahmatullah* and *Belhaj*—being the opportunity to articulate the place of these doctrines within the United Kingdom's constitutional framework—has been wasted. But perhaps not completely. In at least identifying the basic root of the doctrine and, to a degree, sketching out its relationship with Crown act of state, Lord Mance may be said to have wrestled the English conception of foreign act of state onto a recognized jurisprudential base. As Lord Sales noted, this is eminently desirable—and may now serve as a seed from which more articulated judicial thoughts may grow.[112] One hopes that the Supreme Court will not need to wait another thirty-five years to tackle the subject.

IV. Conclusion

This chapter has attempted to provide a synthesis and criticism of the U.K. Supreme Court's judgments in *Rahmatullah* and *Belhaj*, and to contextualize both within the wider doctrines of Crown and foreign act of state, as applied by British courts. In the final balance, many of the criticisms made by Mann in 1986 may be said to apply today: a general uncertainty regarding the scope of the doctrines, and a lack of jurisprudential development with respect to their constitutional underpinnings (an observation that rings particularly true with respect to foreign act of state). But it is

[111] Lissenden v. Bosch Ltd., [1940] AC 412, 435.

[112] Sales, *supra* note 101, at 97.

undeniable that progress, however minor, has been made in these decisions. While the act of state doctrines in English law are not yet as clear and hard-edged as their American counterparts, the scene has been set in *Rahmatullah* and *Belhaj* for further developments—even if litigants will still need to refer to the earlier case law (and particularly the remarks of Lord Wilberforce in *A-G v. Nissan* and *Buttes Gas v. Hammer*) in order to get the full picture.

PART VII

THE USE OF MILITARY FORCE

CHAPTER 41

TECHNIQUES FOR REGULATING MILITARY FORCE

MONICA HAKIMI

Decisions to use military force can be among the most consequential that a government makes. They can also be difficult to regulate. Even a preliminary survey reveals that there is considerable variation, both across countries and over time within particular countries, in how democratic societies regulate the use of force.[1] In this Chapter, I examine three regulatory techniques that states use: (1) establish substantive standards on when the government may or may not use armed force, (2) allocate among different branches of government the authority to deploy the country's armed forces, and (3) subject such decisions to oversight or review. After presenting this typology, I reflect on its implications for further comparative research on war powers regulation.

Three points at the outset help frame what follows. First, I am an American lawyer with limited exposure to the war powers regulations of other countries, so I draw heavily on the work of the other contributors to this volume. My approach has certain limits, including that the typology that I present does not purport to be exhaustive or representative. Other accounts of how specific countries regulate war powers would deepen our understanding of those countries and could bring to light additional techniques that are used. Yet building on the work of scholars who are themselves immersed in the relevant legal systems has real virtues. It allows me to capture the law

[1] Other studies have come to the same conclusion. *See*, e.g., Sandra Dieterich, Hartwig Hummel, & Stefan Marschall, *Parliamentary War Powers: A Survey of 25 European Parliaments*, Occasional Paper No. 21, Geneva Centre for the Democratic Control of Armed Forces, 9 (2010) (finding "a remarkable variance regarding the war powers of national parliaments in Europe"); Wolfgang Wagner, Dirk Peters, & Cosima Glahn, *Parliamentary War Powers Around the World, 1999–2004*, Occasional Paper No. 22, Geneva Centre for the Democratic Control of Armed Forces, 11 (2010) ("The powers of parliaments in this issue area vary widely among democracies around the world.").

not only as it appears on the books but also as it plays out in discrete institutional settings. It thus enriches the analysis.

Second, war powers regulation can have manifold functions and effects. In some contexts, it might constrain governmental actors and curb the use of force. But it need not serve those functions to be legally relevant or effective. For example, it might instead legitimize decisions to use force and thus empower the people who want to make those decisions. It might structure reasoned public debates. It might make apparent the considerations that are or ought to be at stake in the exercise of military power. It might provide the normative material for criticism or sanction. Or it might catalyze subsequent processes for accountability or reform. We should not assume that war powers regulation always does one thing or that any particular regulatory technique consistently does the same thing(s).

Third, this chapter is mostly descriptive and analytic, rather than normative. It is worth underscoring, however, that no single regulatory technique is inherently good or bad in the abstract. Some situations call for quick and decisive, rather than constrained or cautious, action. Some require secrecy, instead of transparency. Some warrant a serious military response, despite the uncertainties or risks of escalation. And in general, reasonable people can—and often do—disagree about whether, when, and subject to what constraints military operations are desirable. Normative assessments of war powers regulation should, in my view, account for that variance. This chapter's typology can enhance such assessments by expanding an appraiser's frame of reference and illuminating the different ways in which a country's legal architecture can shape behavior on war powers.

I. Substantive Standards

One technique for regulating war powers is to establish substantive standards on when the government may or may not use military force. This is a commitment device. It helps preserve a country's long-term military policies by limiting the discretion of governmental officials to deploy the armed forces in the heat of a moment. Yet the stickiness of any such commitment is likely to vary, depending on where the standards are established—for example, whether they are constitutionalized or just legislatively enacted—how easy they are to change, and how precisely they are defined.

Japan stands out for its particularly strict substantive standards on the use of force. As Tadashi Mori explains, any use of force by Japan must be consistent with both the international *jus ad bellum* and additional restrictions under Japanese law.[2] The precise content of the *jus ad bellum* is unsettled, but it generally is thought to prohibit cross-border force except: (1) in individual or collective self-defense, (2) pursuant to the

[2] Tadashi Mori, *Decisions in Japan to Use Military Force or to Participate in Multinational Peace-keeping Operations*, ch. 46 in this volume.

authorization of the UN Security Council, or (3) with the territorial state's consent.[3] Beyond that, Japan's Constitution provides that "the Japanese people forever renounce war as a sovereign right of the nation" and that "land, sea, and air forces, as well as other war potential, will never be maintained."[4] Historically, this language was thought to permit Japan to use force only in individual self-defense. Further, the Japanese government interpreted that authority narrowly—to mean that it could deploy the armed forces only if an armed attack on Japanese soil occurred, Japan's survival and the protection of its people were at stake, there was not a feasible alternative for repelling the attack, the minimum amount of force that was necessary for self-defense was used, and the force was otherwise consistent with the *jus ad bellum*'s requirements for self-defense.[5]

Over time, the government has interpreted the Constitution more permissively but still to allow the government to use force only in very limited circumstances. As Mori explains, the government now claims the authority to use force in *collective* self-defense, so long as such force is consistent with international law, the minimum necessary to repel an attack against a foreign country that is in a close relationship with Japan, and necessary to ensure Japan's survival and the protection of its people.[6] In addition, the Diet has occasionally enacted legislation to permit Japanese forces to operate outside theaters of hostility or to provide logistical or ancillary support for security operations.[7] For example, Japanese forces may now support operations in situations that the UN Security Council or General Assembly has determined are threats to international peace and security.[8] Japanese forces may also participate in international peacekeeping and humanitarian relief operations, subject to certain

[3] UN Charter, arts. 2(4), 39, and 51; *see also* Military and Paramilitary Activities in and Against Nicaragua (Nicar. v. U.S.), Judgment, 1986 I.C.J. Rep. 14, para. 246 (June 27) (recognizing that an outside state's intervention "is already allowable at the request of the government of a State"). I have recently argued that this formulation of the *jus ad bellum* is not altogether accurate. *See* Monica Hakimi, *The* Jus ad Bellum*'s Regulatory Form*, 112 AM. J. INT'L L. 151 (2018).

[4] NIHONKOKU KENPŌ [KENPŌ] [CONSTITUTION], art. 9 (Japan). Japan has considered revising this constitutional provision. As of March 15, 2018, there were seven competing draft amendments in circulation. *See* Reiji Yoshida, *LDP Panel Fails to Form Consensus over Revision of War-Renouncing art. 9*, JAPAN TIMES (Mar. 15, 2018), *available at* https://www.japantimes.co.jp/news/2018/03/15/national/politics-diplomacy/ldp-panel-fails-form-consensus-revision-war-renouncing-article-9/#.WrAJgoIpBTZ.

[5] Mori, *supra* note 2. [6] *Id.*

[7] E.g., Heisei Jusan-nen Ku-gatsu Juichi-nichi no Amerika Gasshukoku ni oite Hassei shita Terorisuto niyoru Kogeki to ni Taio shite Okonawareru Kokusairengokensho no Mokuteki-tassei no tameno Shogaikoku no Katsudo ni taishite Waga Kuni ga Jisshi suru Sochi oyobi Kanren suru Kokusairengo Ketsugi to ni Motozuku Jindoteki-sochi ni kansuru Tokubetsu-sochi Ho [Anti-Terrorism Special Measures Law], Law No. 113, 2001, *amended by* Law No. 147, 2003, *tentative English summary available at* http://japan.kantei.go.jp/policy/2001/anti-terrorism/1029terohougaiyou_e.html; Iraku ni okeru Jindofukko-Shienkatsudo oyobi Anzenkakuho-Shienkatsudo no Jisshi ni kansuru Tokubetsu-sochi Ho [Law Concerning the Special Measures on Humanitarian and Reconstruction Assistance in Iraq], Law No. 137, 2003, *translated in* Mika Hayashi, *The Japanese Law Concerning the Special Measures on Humanitarian and Reconstruction Assistance in Iraq*, 13 PAC. RIM L. & POL'Y J. 579, 587 (2004).

[8] Mori, *supra* note 2.

constraints that significantly reduce the risk that they will find themselves in situations where they will need to resort to the use of force.[9] All of these prescriptions limit a sitting leader's discretion over military policy; they are designed to preserve the country's strong constitutional norm against using force.

Germany's legal architecture similarly subjects use of force decisions to both the international *jus ad bellum* and other constitutional constraints. With respect to the *jus ad bellum*, Germany's Basic Law provides that "[t]he general rules of international law shall be an integral part of federal law."[10] The Constitutional Court has interpreted that language to mean that Germany must "compl[y] with the prohibition of the use of force under customary international law."[11] The Basic Law also declares that "[a]cts tending to and undertaken with intent to disturb the peaceful relations between nations, especially to prepare for a war of aggression, shall be unconstitutional . . . [and] made a criminal offence."[12]

On top of those prescriptions, the Basic Law limits the use of military force to circumstances that involve self-defense or are otherwise "expressly permitted by this Basic Law."[13] The Basic Law then recognizes that Germany may "enter into a system of mutual collective security" "[w]ith a view to maintaining peace."[14] Anne Peters explains that, in the past, some within Germany interpreted those provisions to permit deployments only in individual self-defense.[15] However, the German Constitutional Court adopted a different interpretation in 1994. It clarified that the collective security provision allows German armed forces to be deployed for peacekeeping and other operations that "occur within and pursuant to the rules" of an international organization, such as the United Nations or the North Atlantic Treaty Organization (NATO).[16] The outer bounds of this collective security authority remain unclear, but German forces may now participate in at least some operations that are not taken to defend the German state.

France has also established substantive standards on the use of military force, but these standards are very different from the ones in Japan and Germany. In France, the standards are crafted not as concrete directives but as broad policy principles, and they are not formally binding. They posit, for example, that the use of force should

[9] *Id.* (describing the 2015 International Peace Support Bill); *see also* Kokusairengo Heiwaiji-Katsudo to ni taisuru Kyoryoku ni kansuru Horitsu [Act on Cooperation for United Nations Peacekeeping Operations and Other Operations], Law No. 79, 1992, *amended by* Law No. 157, 2001 *and* Law No. 118, 2006, *translation at* http://www.pko.go.jp/pko_j/data/law/pdf/law_e.pdf.

[10] Grundgesetz für die Bundesrepublik Deutschland [GG] [Basic Law] [Constitution], art. 25, *translation at* http://www.gesetze-im-internet.de/englisch_gg/index.html.

[11] BVerfG, 2 BvE 2/07, July 3, 2007, para. 73, *translation at* https://www.bundesverfassungsgericht.de/SharedDocs/Entscheidungen/EN/2007/07/es20070703_2bve000207en.html.

[12] German Basic Law, *supra* note 10, art. 26(1). [13] *Id.* art. 87(a)(2). [14] *Id.* art. 24(2).

[15] Anne Peters, *Military Operations Abroad under the German Basic Law*, ch. 44 in this volume.

[16] BVerfG, 2 be 1/03, May 7, 2008, para. 62 (*citing* BVerfG 90, 2BvE 3/92, July 12, 1994, para. 255), *translation available at* https://www.bundesverfassungsgericht.de/SharedDocs/Entscheidungen/EN/2008/05/es20080507_2bve000103en.html. The 2008 judgment, which I quote in the main text, has been translated and uses the same language as the 1994 judgment. *See* Peters, *supra* note 15, at p.793.

generally be in response to a serious security threat; based on an assessment of the available alternatives and of the mission's goals, scope, and costs; subject to French political control; and consistent with international law.[17] These standards are not designed to constrain the government's authority or discretion to act. Instead, they articulate some of the policy considerations that should inform its decisions on whether to use military force.

Countries that incorporate the international *jus ad bellum* into their domestic legal systems might at some point have to address the question of how changes at the international level affect their domestic authorities. For example, international lawyers increasingly recognize that, over the past fifteen years, the right of self-defense has become more permissive. Although the contours of this right remain unclear and contested, a number of states now claim the authority to conduct operations that reflect very expansive interpretations—particularly, for operations against nonstate actors or in anticipation of attacks that are not temporally immediate. These states also routinely act on their expansive claims, with little or no repercussion.[18]

That dynamic within international law raises important questions for countries that define their domestic authorities by reference to it. For instance, does a change in the *jus ad bellum* automatically become part of domestic law and license a government to use force in ways that had previously been assumed to be prohibited? Or does the change lack domestic legal effect until it is in some way incorporated through a national process? Insofar as the *jus ad bellum* for a particular operation is unclear, who within a government may define its content for purposes of domestic law? And what steps, if any, should a country take to ensure that a government does not exploit the fluidity in the *jus ad bellum* and push it in a permissive direction in order to justify more easily operations under domestic law?

II. Allocation of Decisionmaking Authority

To the extent that force is not proscribed, a country must identify the governmental organ that may decide to use it. Many countries divide decisionmaking authority in this area between the executive and legislative branches of government. Because the executive ultimately implements the decision, the key questions are whether, and if so, when, how, and at what point in the process the legislature must participate.

[17] For the complete list of these standards, *see* Mathias Forteau, *Using Military Force and Engaging in Collective Security: The Case of France*, ch. 45 in this volume.

[18] For a fuller discussion of this trend within the *jus ad bellum*, *see* Monica Hakimi & Jacob Katz Cogan, *The Two Codes on the Use of Force*, 27 Eur. J. Int'l L. 257, 278–286 (2016).

Some studies suggest that the robustness of any requirement of legislative participation turns on whether the legislature must authorize or consent to an operation before it occurs.[19] That metric for assessment is too simplistic. If a campaign is sprawling or long-lasting, and the legislature participates only in the initial decision to use force, then its endorsement could become quite attenuated from the actual exercise of military force.

The U.S. experience with the 2001 Authorization for the Use of Military Force (AUMF) is a stark example. There, Congress authorized the president "to use all necessary and appropriate force against those nations, organizations, or persons he determines planned, authorized, committed, or aided the terrorist attacks that occurred on September 11, 2001, or harbored such organizations or persons."[20] All three branches of the U.S. government have said that the 2001 AUMF authorizes force not only against groups that, in some way, participated in the 9/11 attacks but also against the "associated forces"of those groups.[21] Further, the executive branch has interpreted the "associated forces" language broadly. For example, the Obama administration claimed that the 2001 AUMF authorized a massive military campaign against the so-called Islamic State in Iraq and Syria (ISIS). The administration's theory was that ISIS was an associated force of al Qaeda because, although the two groups were no longer formally affiliated, they once were, and the links between them had not dissolved.[22] In addition, the Trump administration has claimed that the 2001 AUMF authorized it to use force against states, like Syria and Iran, that put at serious risk the nonstate groups that collaborate with the United States to defeat ISIS.[23] Whatever one thinks of these particular applications of the AUMF, Congress's 2001 authorization is not good evidence of its robust participation in U.S. military decisions that were made more than fifteen years later.

Requiring the executive to obtain the legislature's approval for specific military operations can contribute to the interests of transparency and accountability. Open debate within the legislature helps air the reasons for and against an operation. It presses those who want to conduct the operation to defend it publicly. A requirement of legislative approval might also shape the content of the decision. Because a broader range of officials have to accept that using force in a given case is appropriate, legislative

[19] *See, e.g.*, Yasuo Hasebe, *War Powers, in* The Oxford Handbook of Comparative Constitutional Law 463, 464–465 (Michel Rosenfeld & András Sajó eds., 2012); Wolfgang Wagner, *Parliamentary Control of Military Missions: Accounting for Pluralism*, Occasional Paper No. 12, Geneva Centre for the Democratic Control of Armed Forces, 4 (Aug. 2006) (describing as countries with "a high level of parliamentary control" those in which "parliament must give its prior approval").

[20] Pub. L. No. 107–140, § 2(a), 115 Stat. 224 (2001).

[21] *See* U.S. White House, Report on the Legal and Policy Frameworks Guiding the United States' Use of Military Force and Related National Security Operations 4 (Dec. 2016) [hereinafter White House 2016 Report].

[22] *Id.* at 4–7.

[23] Letter from David J. Trachtenberg, Deputy Under Secretary of Defense (Policy), to Senator Tim Kaine (Jan. 29, 2018), *available at* https://www.documentcloud.org/documents/4383185-Kaine-Trump-ISIS-war-power-letters.html.

involvement often has a cooling effect, making use of force decisions more prudent, cautious, and constrained than they otherwise would be.[24] Yet the legislature's involvement does not necessarily have that effect. If the legislature defers heavily to an executive's security assessments or policy choices, then its endorsement might instead increase the government's willingness to pursue a risky or uncertain military strategy; it might diffuse responsibility for the decision and thus shield the executive from some of the fallout if the operation goes badly.[25]

Countries clearly weigh those eventualities differently. For countries that rely heavily on the military as an instrument of foreign policy, there are real downsides to creating impediments to military action. A recent debate in the United Kingdom is illustrative. U.K. decisions to use force are part of the royal prerogative and fall exclusively within the executive's domain, but the government recently considered changing that arrangement and requiring Parliament to participate in at least some use of force decisions. A 2013 report by the House of Lords Constitution Committee recommended against the change, in part because it could unduly constrain military action.[26] The committee worried that, if Parliament participated in use of force decisions, it might try to restrict how force is used, which "could harm military effectiveness and limit commanders' freedom of maneuver."[27] Further, a requirement of parliamentary participation might undercut the government's capacity to project its military might. The committee's explained:

> There may be instances where the UK's international obligations require the Government to commit to action—for example to achieve collective security with fellow NATO members. In such instances it would be detrimental to the Government's position to be in doubt as to whether they can secure the commitment of Her Majesty's armed forces.[28]

Here, a state's longstanding military policy depends in part on empowering the executive to resort, relatively easily, to the use of force.

Allocation Based on the Nature of the Operation

States have various options for dividing authority between the executive and legislative branches of government. One approach is to allocate such authority differently,

[24] E.g., Dieterich, Hummel, & Marschall, *supra* note 1, at 9 ("[European] states with very strong or strong parliamentary war powers tended to be significantly less involved in the 2003 Iraq war compared to states with weak parliaments.").

[25] *See* Jide Nzelibe, *Are Congressionally Authorized Wars Perverse?*, 59 STAN. L. REV. 907 (2007).

[26] CONSTITUTION COMMITTEE, CONSTITUTIONAL ARRANGEMENTS FOR THE USE OF ARMED FORCE, 2013–14, HL 46, para. 61 (U.K.), *available at* https://www.publications.parliament.uk/pa/ld201314/ldselect/ldconst/46/46.pdf.

[27] *Id.* at para. 57.

[28] *Id.* at para. 58.

depending on the nature of the operation. Most, if not all, states allow the executive branch to act unilaterally in at least certain kinds of cases—for example, during emergencies or in self-defense. These states might then distinguish those cases from others that require legislative participation.

Consider again Japan. Under the 2015 International Peace Support Act, the Japanese Prime Minister must seek prior Diet approval before deploying the country's armed forces outside Japan.[29] But as Tadashi Mori explains, prior approval is not required—and the prime minister may decide unilaterally to use force—if it is necessary to address a domestic emergency. In that event, the prime minister must expeditiously obtain the Diet's retroactive approval or cease the military operation.[30] This arrangement affords the prime minister limited room to make a unilateral decision only because and to the extent that the nature of the operation requires it.

The situation in Germany is similar. Under both constitutional and statutory law, the *Bundestag* must generally agree to the "deployment of German armed forces," meaning situations in which German soldiers are involved or are expected to be involved in armed undertakings.[31] However, German law recognizes an exception and entitles the executive branch to act unilaterally in cases of imminent danger. If the executive acts on its own, it must promptly end the operation or seek the *Bundestag*'s approval.[32] Separately, German law clarifies that the *Bundestag* need not authorize military operations that do not have the characteristics of a "deployment"—operations in which the military takes measures that are only preparatory, for planning purposes, or to provide humanitarian aid, without any concrete expectation of combat.[33] Again, the nature of the operation is what determines whether and when the *Bundestag* must participate.

The U.S. president has discretion to act unilaterally in a much broader range of cases, but that range is still defined partly by the nature of the operation. As Curtis Bradley explains, the bounds of executive authority in this area are unclear and contested. Most believe that, as a matter of original understanding, the Constitution entitles the president to decide unilaterally to use force only in cases of self-defense.[34] But that understanding has eroded over time, as the executive has claimed the authority to

[29] Kokusai Heiwa Kyōdōtaisho jittai ni saishite Waga Kuni ga jisshisuru Shogaikoku no Guntai nadoni taisuru Kyōryoku Shijikatsudō nado ni kansuru Hōritsu [Law Related to the Implementation of Japan's Cooperative Support for the Armed Forces of Foreign Countries in Circumstances of International Peace and Security Cooperation Activity] [International Peace Support Act], Law No. 77, 2015, arts. 4–6, *available at* http://www.cas.go.jp/jp/gaiyou/jimu/housei_seibi.html, *English language summary available in* JAPAN MINISTRY OF DEFENSE, 2015 DEFENSE OF JAPAN ANNUAL WHITE PAPER 147 fig. II-1-3-12, *available at* http://www.mod.go.jp/e/publ/w_paper/2015.html.

[30] Mori, *supra* note 2.

[31] Federal Law on Parliamentary Approval of International Deployment of Armed Forces [2005 Parliamentary Act], Mar. 18, 2005, BGBl. 2005 I, 775, § 1(2), *unofficially translated in* Katja S. Ziegler, *The Model of a "Parliamentary Army" Under the German Constitution*, HOUSE OF LORDS CONST. COMM. (Dec. 7, 2005), at Annex II, *available at* https://publications.parliament.uk/pa/ld200506/ldselect/ldconst/236/5120707.htm#n141.

[32] *Id.* at § 5.

[33] *Id.* at § 2(2).

[34] Curtis A. Bradley, *U.S. War Powers and the Potential Benefits of Comparativism*, ch. 42 in this volume.

use force without congressional participation in an increasingly expansive set of circumstances. Thus, when the executive articulated its legal justification for the 2011 Libya operation, it recognized only "one possible constitutionally-based limit on this presidential authority to employ military force in defense of important national interests."[35] It asserted that "a planned military engagement that constitutes a 'war' ... may require prior congressional authorization."[36] It then defined "war" in terms of the "'anticipated nature, scope, and duration' of the use of force," and contended that "this standard generally will be satisfied only by prolonged and substantial military engagements."[37] In short, the president now claims unilateral authority for all but the most extensive military operations, at least insofar as Congress has not expressed a contrary view.[38] The claim rests partly on the nature of the operation.

Allocation Based on the Duration of the Operation

Another approach for allocating decisionmaking authority is temporal—to permit the executive branch to use force only for a set period absent legislative approval. The Japanese and German examples show that this approach can be used concurrently with the first. In each of those countries, the executive may act unilaterally in certain kinds of cases for very limited periods. It must expeditiously obtain the legislature's consent in order to continue those operations. In other countries, the executive's unilateral authority is defined primarily in temporal terms. It has broad discretion to decide on its own to use military force, but it may do so only for a set period.

The temporal approach reflects a balance. The executive has discretion to conduct operations that it decides, based on its expertise, are in the national interest. But its discretion is limited to inhibit it from taxing the country for prolonged periods without buy-in from other domestic actors. This approach carries some risks. First, the costs of extricating the armed forces from a theater of combat might be very high or unpredictable. An executive that unilaterally takes the country into hostilities might box the legislature in, such that it feels compelled to acquiesce in an operation that it thinks is bad policy and would not have accepted ex ante. Second, if a country's enemies are well-attuned to its domestic situation, they might try to wait out the clock in the expectation or hope that the country will unilaterally withdraw its forces at a date certain.

The relevant time period varies by country. In the Czech Republic, parliamentary approval is required after sixty days.[39] In France, the period is four months.[40] In the

[35] Memorandum Opinion from Caroline D. Krass, Principal Deputy Assistant Attorney General, Office of Legal Counsel, to the Attorney General, "Authority to Use Military Force in Libya" (Apr. 11, 2011).

[36] *Id.* [37] *Id.* [38] *See also* Bradley, *supra* note 34 (analyzing U.S. executive claims).

[39] Ústava České Republiky [Constitution], 1/1993 Sb. (as amended), art. 43, *translated at* http://www.psp.cz/en/docs/laws/constitution.html.

[40] 1958 Const. art. 35, *translated at* http://www.conseil-constitutionnel.fr/conseil-constitutionnel/english/constitution/constitution-of-4-october-1958.25742.html.

United States, the situation is more complicated. As discussed, the U.S. president claims the authority to act unilaterally for the vast majority of operations. However, the War Powers Resolution (WPR) requires him to withdraw U.S. forces within sixty days from situations in which hostilities are occurring or are expected to occur unless: (1) Congress authorizes the operation or extends the sixty-day clock, (2) Congress is physically unable to meet due to an attack on the United States, or (3) the president decides that "unavoidable military necessity respecting the safety of the United States Armed Forces requires the continued use of such armed forces" for up to thirty additional days.[41] Congress may also cut short the sixty-day period, at least for operations involving hostilities outside the United States.[42]

The Obama administration softened the bite of the WPR clock in 2011, when it narrowly interpreted the circumstances that qualify as "hostilities." The administration asserted that its participation in a multilateral operation in Libya did not need to be approved or terminated within sixty days because the nature of the U.S. mission, the exposure of U.S. armed forces, the risk of escalation, and the military means employed by the United States were all sufficiently limited so as not to count as hostilities under the WPR.[43] The practical effect of this position is to narrow the range of cases that are subject to the sixty-day clock.

Allocation of Ancillary Authorities

Finally, a legislature might have ancillary authorities with which to influence use of force decisions. For example, although the Japanese Constitution does not assign to any branch of government the authority to decide to use military force, the Diet has repeatedly passed legislation to elaborate on the sparse constitutional text. Here, a legislature uses its interpretive and prescriptive authorities to define the circumstances in which the armed forces may be deployed and thus to delineate the scope of the executive's authority in this area.

In the United States, Congress controls the purse, and the Constitution provides that no appropriation "[t]o raise and support Armies . . . shall be for a longer Term than two Years."[44] Many consider this to be Congress's principal mechanism for participating in use of force decisions.[45] It requires Congress periodically to decide what military

[41] War Powers Resolution §§ 4(a)(1) & 5, Pub. L. No. 93–148, 87 Stat. 555 (1973), 50 U.S.C. §§ 1543–1544 [hereinafter WPR].

[42] *Id.*

[43] *Libya and War Powers: Hearing Before the S. Foreign Relations Comm.*, 112th Cong. 7–40 (June 28, 2011) (testimony of Harold Hongju Koh, Legal Adviser, U.S. Department of State), *available at* http://fas.org/irp/congress/2011_hr/libya.pdf.

[44] U.S. CONST., art. 1, sec. 8, cl. 12.

[45] *See,* e.g., Reid Skibell, *Separation-of-Powers and the Commander in Chief: Congress's Authority to Override Presidential Decisions in Crisis Situations*, 13 GEO. MASON L. REV. 183, 195 (2004) ("[T]he spending power has become Congress's primary tool in influencing military and, to a large degree,

capabilities the president will have and thus whether he will be equipped to implement his preferred military policies. It might also exert some control on his decisions. Congress has occasionally used its spending power to limit specific military operations. Moreover, even when it does not try to restrict the president's decisions, his dependence on it for funding gives him an incentive to obtain its support, both before initiating a major military operation and over the course of the campaign. Yet in the modern era, various factors—ranging from a lack of political will in Congress to the complexities of the appropriations process to the vast scale of the U.S. military—limit the extent to which the Congress uses its appropriations power to participate in specific use of force decisions.[46]

III. Oversight and Review

No matter whether the decision to use force is made unilaterally or with legislative participation, it might be subject to various mechanisms for oversight or review. These mechanisms again differ in their details, but most involve the sharing of information. They help bring to light the facts that triggered the use of force, whether alternatives to military force were considered or taken, the operation's objectives, its expected duration, or its likelihood of success. Such information can then be used to hold the government accountable for a decision. It might also shape the content of a decision. Officials might be disinclined to exceed their authorities or to act imprudently if they know that bad decisions will be publicly scrutinized or sanctioned.

Legislative Oversight

Legislatures have different tools for reviewing use of force decisions. They might summon executive branch officials for public hearings. They might interrogate these officials orally or in writing. They might demand access to certain documents. Or they might initiate processes of judicial review.[47]

A legislature's oversight authority can but need not be coextensive with its authority to participate in the decision to use force. The distinction was evident, for example, in

foreign policy decisions."); John Yoo, *The Continuation of Politics by Other Means: The Original Understanding of War Powers*, 84 Cal. L. Rev. 167, 295, 297 (1996) (arguing that "the Framers intended to participate in war-making by controlling appropriations" and that this framework perseveres in the modern era because "Congress fully understands that its appropriations may be used to check executive military decisions").

[46] *See generally* Bruce Ackerman & Oona Hathaway, *Limited War and the Constitution: Iraq and the Crisis of Presidential Legality*, 109 Mich. L. Rev. 447 (2011).

[47] *See* Dieterich, Hummel, & Marschall, *supra* note 1, at 11.

the 2015 German Constitutional Court judgment on a rescue operation in Libya.[48] The operation took place in 2011, after the Libyan civil war broke out but before the UN Security Council authorized the use of force. At the German chancellor's direction, German forces evacuated 132 people from an industrial base in Libya, without any combat action. Afterward, a parliamentary group filed a complaint before the Constitutional Court, arguing that the executive's unilateral decision to use force had to be submitted to the *Bundestag* for its retroactive approval. The court disagreed. It determined that the executive had unilateral authority to act because the situation presented an emergency. However, the court then said that the executive was obligated to inform the *Bundestag* of the details of the operation, so that it could meaningfully perform its oversight functions. Here, the executive was not required to obtain the *Bundestag*'s authorization for the use of force but was required to share with it information so that it could review the decision.

Other countries also require the executive branch to inform the legislature of decisions to use force. In France, the executive must, within three days of initiating a sustained operation in another country, inform Parliament of the operation and describe its objectives.[49] The French Parliament may then choose to debate, without taking a formal vote on, the decision. In the United States, the WPR requires the president to inform Congress within two days of a deployment.[50] U.S. presidents have routinely complied with this reporting obligation, even though they have resisted other aspects of the WPR.

The role of the U.K. Parliament in overseeing use of force decisions is more informal and, as Katja Ziegler explains, in flux.[51] The House of Lords does not have any legal authority to participate in use of force decisions, but the government has in recent years recognized a constitutional convention—an accepted practice—of consulting with Parliament and affording it the opportunity to debate and vote on decisions to use force before troops are committed.[52] This convention, which was initiated with the 2003 Iraq War, appears to have had some bite in a few cases. Perhaps most notably, the prime minister chose in 2013 to abide by Parliament's vote not to intervene in

[48] BVerfG, 2 BvE 6/11, Sept. 23, 2015, *available at* http://www.bverfg.de/e/es20150923_2bve000611en.html. For an excellent review of this decision, *see* Anne Peters, *The (Non-)Judicialisation of War: German Constitutional Court Judgment on Rescue Operation Pegasus in Libya of 23 September 2015 (Part I)*, EJIL Talk! (Oct. 21, 2015), http://www.ejiltalk.org/the-non-judicialisation-of-war-german-constitutional-court-judgment-on-rescue-operation-pegasus-in-libya-of-23-september-2015-part-1/.

[49] 1958 Const. art. 35; *see also* Forteau, *supra* note 17 (explaining that the executive need not inform Parliament of military operations, like those to rescue nationals abroad, that do not fall within the scope of art. 35 because they are so small in scale that they do not qualify as "interventions").

[50] WPR, *supra* note 41, § 4.

[51] Katja S. Ziegler, *The Use of Force by the United Kingdom: The Evolution of Accountability*, ch. 43 in this volume.

[52] For an argument that a constitutional convention on parliamentary oversight has also emerged in Canada, *see* Ryan Patrick Alford, *War with ISIL: Should Parliament Decide?*, 20 Rev. Const. Stud. 118 (2015). Alford argues that the Canadian convention requires a parliamentary debate before troops are deployed in combat operations.

Syria in response to that government's use of chemical weapons.[53] But in practice, the convention has not consistently been followed, and its scope of application remains unclear.[54] Indeed, when Syria was caught still using chemical weapons in 2018, the prime minister participated in military strikes without first taking the issue to Parliament.[55]

As discussed, the U.K. government has considered transforming this convention into a formal requirement of parliamentary participation. However, a 2013 report by the U.K. House of Lords Constitution Committee ultimately argued for preserving it in its current form, as a tool for political oversight and control.[56] The committee argued that one benefit of this arrangement is that formalization might invite courts to review more rigorously the government's use of force decisions.[57] "There was consensus amongst our witnesses that the appropriate forum for controlling and scrutinising deployment decisions is Parliament, not the courts."[58]

Judicial Oversight

The United Kingdom is not alone in limiting the availability of judicial review in this area. As Mathias Forteau explains, French courts regularly invoke the so-called "act of government theory" to find that they lack jurisdiction to rule on claims against the government concerning the use of force.[59] Similarly, Curtis Bradley explains that U.S. "courts in the modern era have invoked various 'justiciability' limitations to avoid addressing these issues."[60] In these countries, courts restrain themselves and decline to review specific use of force decisions. By contrast, German courts have actively overseen such decisions.[61] They have repeatedly assessed the legality of particular military operations.

Courts might be institutionally ill-equipped to oversee use of force decisions for any number of reasons. They might lack the expertise necessary to assess a government's national security claims. They might be incapable of checking the government's factual assertions. They might have to rely on secret information that they cannot then use to

[53] Prime Minister David Cameron, Statement to House of Commons, Sept. 9, 2013, *available at* https://publications.parliament.uk/pa/cm201314/cmhansrd/cm130909/debtext/130909-0001.htm ("I am clear that it was right to advocate a strong response to the indiscriminate gassing of men, women and children in Syria, and to make that case in this Chamber. At the same time I understand and respect what this House has said. So Britain will not be part of any military action. . . .").

[54] *See* Claire Mills, *Parliamentary Approval for Military Action*, Briefing Paper No. 7166, at 3, House of Commons Library (May 12, 2015), *available at* https://researchbriefings.parliament.uk/ResearchBriefing/Summary/CBP-7166.

[55] *See* House of Commons Library, *Parliamentary Approval for Military Action* (Apr. 17, 2018), *available at* https://researchbriefings.parliament.uk/ResearchBriefing/Summary/CBP-7166#fullreport.

[56] Constitutional Arrangements for the Use of Armed Force, *supra* note 25, paras. 61 and 64.

[57] *Id.* at para. 54. [58] *Id.* [59] Forteau, *supra* note 17.

[60] Bradley, *supra* note 34, at p.760. [61] Peters, *supra* note 15.

justify their decisions.[62] And if the country's laws do not define, in relatively specific terms, when force is or is not permissible, they might lack judicially manageable standards based on which to evaluate specific operations. It is not surprising that U.K., French, and U.S. courts refrain from assessing use of force decisions, given that the executive in each country has or claims to have so much discretion in this area; these courts lack concrete legal standards to apply. Inviting courts to review the legality of specific operations thus can put them in difficult positions. It might require them to make the kinds of judgments that are better suited for the other branches of government.

But judicial review can also be quite valuable. First, the possibility of courts evaluating specific decisions might check the officials who want to make those decisions and inhibit them from overstepping their legal authorities. In this way, judicial review can help preserve the basic structure of and allocation of authority within a government. Second, when courts apply the law in concrete cases, they elaborate on its content and flesh out the legal framework that governs future decisions. This lawmaking component of judicial decisions is especially useful if the constitutional and statutory texts that regulate the use of force are sparse, inconsistent, or disconnected from contemporary sensibilities or realities. For example, the 1994 decision of the German Constitutional Court on collective security operations in effect updated Germany's Basic Law for the modern era. Third, judicial review of governmental decisions prods those who exercise authority to justify their decisions publicly, in legal terms, and for external scrutiny. It thus contributes to basic rule of law values.[63]

Diffuse Oversight

Most democratic states also have other, more diffuse mechanisms for oversight or review. In the case of the United States, Jack Goldsmith has described a national security apparatus that is heavily scrutinized by an amalgam of actors, who are formally disconnected from one another and operate from both within and outside of government.[64] As Goldsmith describes it, dozens of executive branch officials, with diverse institutional perspectives and priorities, weigh in on national security decisions, especially as they relate to targeted killing and covert operations. These officials can shape the president's decisions before they are taken and through systematic assessments

[62] *Cf.* Mohamed v. Jeppesen Dataplan, Inc., 614 F.3d 1070 (9th Cir. 2010) (en banc).

[63] Here, I am relying on a conception of the rule of law that Jeremy Waldron has been especially influential in advancing. In this conception, the rule of law is not just about constraining the exercise of authority with relatively precise, transparent, and impartially administered standards. It is also about committing to "a certain method of arguing about the exercise of public power" and creating "opportunities for active engagement in the administration of public affairs." Jeremy Waldron, *The Rule of Law as a Theater of Debate*, *in* DWORKIN AND HIS CRITICS 319, 330 (Justine Burley ed., 2004); Jeremy Waldron, *The Concept and the Rule of Law*, 43 GA. L. REV. 1, 9 (2008).

[64] JACK GOLDSMITH, POWER AND CONSTRAINT: THE ACCOUNTABLE PRESIDENCY AFTER 9/11 (2012).

over time. In addition, executive branch officials routinely leak information about the government's security operations to the press. This allows the operations to be aired publicly and contested by civil society groups that oppose them. If enough constituents disagree with the government's military decisions, they can then try to change its policies by voting for different officials in the next election.

IV. Reflections on Comparative War Powers Work

Although the above typology is only preliminary, it raises fairly fundamental questions about comparative war powers work: to what extent and in what ways is such work valuable? How might it help lawyers and policymakers who make or analyze use of force decisions?

There are at least two reasons to be cautious. First, countries vary significantly in how strictly and through what techniques they regulate the use of force. Indeed, the relevance of a given technique might vary even within a single country. Take the division of authority, as between the U.S. president and Congress, on decisions to use force. Although the president's authority in this area has expanded considerably since World War II, there continues to be widespread support for the norm that requires the president to obtain Congress's approval before initiating at least some armed operations. Yet the salience of that norm is extremely variable. It depends on a host of case-specific factors, including the security problem that the president wants to address, the nature of the anticipated operation, and the politics that surround it, both within and outside of the United States. For example, President Obama sought congressional support when he was contemplating even a limited strike against Syria for its use of chemical weapons in 2013,[65] but he did not go to Congress for the fairly extended campaign against Libya in 2011.[66] Likewise, he invoked Congress's authorization in the 2001 AUMF to justify using defensive force against al-Shabaab militants in Somalia, but he relied on his own constitutional authority for very similar strikes against Houthi militants in Yemen.[67] The point is not that the norm on congressional authorization does not do any work but that the work that it does is highly contingent on the circumstances of a case.

A similar point might be made about other countries. Since the U.K. convention on parliamentary consultations emerged in 2003, its salience has varied considerably across cases. The differential treatment of the 2013 and 2018 Syria cases is illustrative.

[65] *See* Peter Baker & Jonathan Weisman, *Obama Seeks Approval by Congress for Strike in Syria*, N.Y. Times (Aug. 31, 2013), *available at* http://www.nytimes.com/2013/09/01/world/middleeast/syria.html.

[66] *See supra* notes 35–37 and accompanying text.

[67] White House 2016 Report, *supra* note 21, at 5, 7, 17, 18.

Likewise, the circumstances in which Germany may participate in multilateral operations under the Basic Law's collective security provision are unsettled and, in at least some respects, contingent on the facts.[68] Such variance within countries complicates efforts to extract general principles on how they regulate the use of force, let alone general principles that can then be translated for comparison and contrast with the entirely different institutional arrangements of a foreign country.

The second reason why comparative work on war powers is particularly challenging is that, relative to other areas of foreign affairs, this one seems more deeply connected to each country's national ethos—its sense of its own character as a country. Here, Philip Bobbitt's work on what he calls ethical reasoning in U.S. constitutional law is illuminating. As Bobbitt describes it, ethical reasoning invokes a country's ethos, either expressly or by implication, as a justification or source of authority for concrete legal positions. Ethical reasoning is not the same as moral reasoning. It does not "claim that a particular solution is right or wrong in any sense larger than that the solution comports with the sort of people we are and the norms we have chosen to solve political and customary constitutional problems."[69] To say that ethical reasoning is salient in war powers regulation is to say that the country's ethos is routinely at issue and part of what is at stake in concrete legal battles and decisions on the use of force.[70] War powers regulation would reflect, be a vehicle for arguing about, and help shape deeply held views about what the country stands for.

Of course, people within a country might disagree about its ethos. For example, most Americans seem to accept that the United States is and ought to be a military superpower. But they routinely disagree about when, where, and how it ought to project its military might. This means that the American ethos relating to the military is not entirely stable or shared. The "true" ethos might be hard to pin down, and arguments about it might not be reliable indicators of what it really is.[71] Ethical reasoning would still be prevalent in U.S. war powers regulation if Americans routinely tap into variants of the national ethos to argue about or make specific decisions on the use of force.

They seem to do quite a bit of that. As a concrete example, recall that the U.S. executive branch claims that the president has unilateral authority "to direct U.S. military forces in engagements necessary to advance American national interests

[68] *See* Peters, *supra* note 15.

[69] Philip Bobbitt, Constitutional Fate 94–95 (1982). In *Constitutional Fate*, Bobbitt described ethical argument as resting on "a characterization of American institutions and the role within them of the American people." *Id.* Bobbitt also advanced, as a particular vision of the U.S. constitutional ethos, the commitment to limited government. *Id.* at 230. He and others have since recognized that that vision is too narrow and not the only plausible way to characterize the American ethos. *See* Philip Bobbitt, *Reflections Inspired by My Critics*, 72 Tex. L. Rev. 1869, 1937 (1994); Richard Primus, Response, *The Functions of Ethical Originalism*, 88 Tex. L. Rev. See Also 79, 80–81 (2010).

[70] *See* Primus, *The Functions of Ethical Originalism*, *supra* note 69, at 82, 89.

[71] *See* Richard Primus, *Unbundling Constitutionality*, 80 U. Chi. L. Rev. 1079, 1133–1135 (2013); Jack M. Balkin, *The New Originalism and the Uses of History*, 82 Fordham L. Rev. 641, 678 (2013).

abroad," except perhaps when those engagements amount to full-scale "wars."[72] The executive branch has never publicly articulated the criteria for identifying the national interests that this claim covers. But it has invoked the claim to justify, on a case-by-case basis, forcible operations for a range of amorphous foreign policy goals. According to the executive branch, the national interests for which the president may unilaterally decide to use force include things like preserving stability in various parts of the world, bolstering the credibility of NATO or the United Nations, and deterring of the use and proliferation of chemical weapons.[73]

These executive branch justifications for the use of force are dripping with ethical reasoning. They invoke and rely on a particular view of the United States and its relationship with the rest of the world. In this view, virtually any security problem anywhere in the world affects U.S. interests, deploying the U.S. military is often the appropriate response, and the military is such a routine part of U.S. foreign policy that the president need not go through all that much trouble to sell particular operations to the U.S. Congress or, for that matter, to the American public; using the military to address global security issues is just part of what we do and who we are as Americans.

Ethical reasoning also seems to animate how other countries regulate war powers. Remember that one reason that the United Kingdom chose not to turn the convention on parliamentary consultations into a binding requirement is that any such requirement might be "detrimental" to U.K. foreign and military policy.[74] This reasoning again has ethical notes. It reflects a vision of the United Kingdom's standing in the world, defined partly through the projection of a strong and active military. Along similar lines, when Germany's Constitutional Court applies the Basic Law's collective security provision, its reasoning seems to be heavily ethical. It portrays Germany as a good global citizen that is committed to establishing peace and security by working through international institutions. It defines Germany's ethos in those terms.

If ethical reasoning drives a lot of war powers regulation, as it seems to do, then national officials are likely to be hesitant to use comparative methods to address specific use of force questions. Rather than look to other countries for guidance, these officials will probably tap into their own sense of the national ethos. This might be true even as between countries, like the United States and the United Kingdom, that share certain histories and traditions, and use many of the same regulatory techniques. The ethos is ultimately a national construct. Moreover, where ethical reasoning is prominent, comparative war powers work is unlikely to have much explanatory force. The questions of why specific countries adopt the regulatory techniques that they do or

[72] Memorandum Opinion for the Counsel to the President, Office of Legal Counsel, "April 2018 Airstrikes Against Syrian Chemical-Weapons Facilities" (May 31, 2018).

[73] For an excellent overview, *see* Curtis Bradley & Jack Goldsmith, *OLC's Meaningless "National Interests" Test for the Legality of Presidential Uses of Force*, LAWFARE (June 5, 2018), *available at* https://www.lawfareblog.com/olcs-meaningless-national-interests-test-legality-presidential-uses-force.

[74] CONSTITUTIONAL COMMITTEE, *supra* note 26, at para. 58.

how those techniques play out in concrete cases will best be answered by looking internally.

Yet this does not mean that comparative research on war powers regulation is fruitless. Quite the contrary. Because ethical reasoning seems so prominent in this area, such research can help crystallize and bring to the public consciousness aspects of a national ethos that otherwise go unnoticed. Learning how different countries regulate the use of force can deepen our understanding not only of those countries but also, and perhaps more critically, of our own. It can bring into sharp relief what a country is really about—how it defines itself as a polity and conceives of its relationship to the rest of the world.

CHAPTER 42

U.S. WAR POWERS AND THE POTENTIAL BENEFITS OF COMPARATIVISM

CURTIS A. BRADLEY

THERE may be no issue of foreign relations law more important than the allocation of authority over the use of military force. This issue is especially important for the United States given the frequency with which it is involved in military activities abroad. Yet there is significant uncertainty and debate in the United States over this issue—in particular, over whether and to what extent military actions must be authorized by Congress. Because U.S. courts in the modern era have generally declined to review the legality of military actions, disputes over this issue have had to be resolved, as a practical matter, through the political process. For those who believe that it is important to have legislative involvement in decisions to use force, the political process has not proven to be satisfactory: presidents have often used military force without obtaining congressional approval, and Congress generally has done little to resist such presidential unilateralism.

The United States is not the only country to struggle with regulating the domestic authority to use military force. This issue of foreign relations law is common to constitutional democracies, and nations vary substantially in how they have addressed it. Comparative study of such approaches should be of inherent interest to scholars and students, including those trying to better understand the U.S. approach. Whether and to what extent such study should also inform the interpretation or revision of U.S. law presents a more complicated set of questions that are affected in part by one's legal methodology and how the comparative materials are being invoked.

This chapter begins by describing the exercise of war powers authority in the United States, both before and after World War II, as well as some of the limitations on congressional and judicial checks on presidential uses of military force. It then considers the potential value of studying the war powers law and practice of other countries, as well as some of the reasons to be cautious about relying on such comparative materials.

I. Constitutional Text and Pre–World War II History

The law governing the distribution of war authority in the United States is complicated and, in many respects, uncertain. The U.S. Constitution makes the president the commander in chief of the armed forces.[1] But it assigns a variety of war-related powers to Congress, including the powers to appropriate and spend money, raise and support the military, and declare war.[2] Although Congress's authority to issue declarations of war might suggest that its approval is needed before the United States enters into a war, there is some question about this, given that undeclared wars were common at the time the Constitution was adopted and are now the norm. Indeed, the United States has been involved in hundreds of military conflicts in its history but has declared war in only five of them, and the last time that the United States declared war was during World War II. Even if Congress has the sole power to declare war for the United States, the text of the Constitution does not clearly say that Congress has the sole power to authorize uses of military force when war is not declared.[3] Moreover, it may be that not all uses of force qualify as acts of "war" for purposes of the Constitution.

Most scholars studying the issue have nevertheless concluded that the Constitution, as originally understood, requires the president to obtain congressional authorization before using military force against another state, except when acting in self-defense. This view appears to have been the understanding of early presidents. For example, the first U.S. president, George Washington, expressed the view that "[t]he Constitution vests the power of declaring war in Congress; therefore no offensive expedition of importance can be undertaken until they have deliberated on the subject, and authorized such a measure."[4]

Despite this early understanding, there were uncertainties in the nineteenth century about when congressional authorization was required. These uncertainties included: What constitutes self-defense, as opposed to offensive action? Does self-defense include, for example, the protection of American citizens (and perhaps also their property) abroad? Does it include counterattacks or reprisals, or just repelling attacks?

[1] U.S. Const., art. II, § 2. [2] U.S. Const., art. I, § 8.

[3] For an argument that "declare" would have originally been understood to include acts of war even without a verbal declaration, *see* Michael D. Ramsey, *Textualism and War Powers*, 69 U. Chi. L. Rev. 1543 (2002).

[4] Letter from George Washington to Governor William Moultrie (Aug. 28, 1793), *in* 10 The Writings of George Washington 366, 367 (Jared Sparks ed., New York, Harper & Bros. 1847).

To what extent must Congress authorize military action against nonstate actors, such as pirates or other nonstate entities? More generally, are there instances in which the use of force does not amount to "war," and, if so, must Congress authorize those lower-level uses of force?

Against a backdrop of such uncertainties, there were a number of instances during the nineteenth century in which the United States used military force without congressional authorization—for example, to protect Americans and their trade activities abroad. Most of these military actions were small in scale and did not involve protracted engagements. On occasion, they triggered domestic controversy. For example, in the mid-nineteenth century there was debate in Congress over whether the military had exceeded its constitutional authority in bombarding Greytown, Nicaragua, in retaliation for damage to American property and an injury to a U.S. official. In justifying the military's action, President Franklin Pierce likened Greytown to "a piratical resort of outlaws or a camp of savages" rather than to a nation and argued that the U.S. action was consistent with international practice.[5] A court later upheld the constitutionality of the bombardment, reasoning that the core "object and duty" of governments is to protect their citizens "whether abroad or at home" and that the president is the appropriate actor within the United States to whom "citizens abroad must look for protection of person and of property."[6]

The understanding of war powers described above, even with its many uncertainties, came under further strain during the early twentieth century. In 1900, President William McKinley sent over 5,000 U.S. troops to China during the Boxer Rebellion, as part of a multinational coalition, without congressional authorization. In doing so, he emphasized that the U.S. action "involved no war against the Chinese nation" and was justified in part by the need to "secur[e] wherever possible the safety of American life and property in China."[7] In addition, on numerous occasions during the early twentieth-century, presidents used military force to intervene in Latin American countries, without congressional authorization, ostensibly to restore order and protect American citizens and their property.[8] These interventions were justified as "police actions," on the theory that the countries involved were not capable of maintaining law and order on their own. As President William Howard Taft explained after he left the presidency, while using force to protect American citizens abroad was potentially an "act of war [as a matter of constitutional law] if committed in a country like England or

[5] President Franklin Pierce, Second Annual Message (Dec. 4, 1854), *in* 5 A Compilation of the Messages and Papers of the Presidents 1789–1897, at 273, 282, 284 (James D. Richardson ed., 1896).

[6] 8 F. Cas. 111, 112 (C.C.S.D.N.Y. 1860) (No. 4186).

[7] President William McKinley, Message to Congress (Dec. 3, 1900), *in* 34 Cong. Rec. 2, 4 (1901).

[8] *See* David Gartner, *Foreign Relations, Strategic Doctrine, and Presidential Power*, 63 Ala. L. Rev. 499, 503, 527 (2012); *see also* Max Boot, The Savage Wars of Peace: Small Wars and the Rise of American Power 129–156 (2002) (describing American military interventions in Latin America between 1898 and 1914).

Germany or France," this was not the case in countries where "law and order are not maintained, as in some Central and South American countries."[9]

Despite this practice, Congress expressly declared war for the two most significant conflicts that the United States was involved in during the first half of the twentieth century—World War I and World War II. But World War II was the last military conflict in which Congress formally declared war.

II. Post-World War II History

The establishment of the United Nations in 1945 added another complication to the legal analysis concerning U.S. war powers. Article 42 of the UN Charter gives the Security Council the power to authorize nations to use military force to address threats to the peace, breaches of the peace, and acts of aggression. This delegation of authority to the Council presents questions for the U.S. domestic law of war powers: In particular, given that the Senate approved the Charter, including the Charter's delegation of authority to the Council, does a Council authorization of force remove the need for congressional authorization of such force?[10] Additional questions are implicated by Article 43 of the Charter, which envisions that nations will enter into agreements to make military forces available for use by the Council. Neither the United States nor any other country has entered into an Article 43 agreement, but Congress contemplated that such an agreement might be made when it enacted the UN Participation Act in 1945, which specifically authorized the president to negotiate an Article 43 agreement. Although the Act specified that any such agreement would have to be approved by Congress, it also made clear that once this happened the forces could be used without further congressional approval.[11]

This new legal landscape was quickly tested in 1950 when President Harry Truman sent forces to defend South Korea in the Korean War. Although this was a substantial military campaign that lasted several years and involved tens of thousands of U.S. casualties, Truman never sought or obtained formal congressional authorization,

[9] William Howard Taft, *The Boundaries Between the Executive, the Legislative and the Judicial Branches of the Government*, 25 Yale L.J. 599, 610–611 (1916).

[10] For debate over this issue, *compare* Thomas M. Franck & Faiza Patel, *UN Police Action in Lieu of War: "The Old Order Changeth,"* 85 Am. J. Int'l L. 63, 72 (1991) ("When the President commits U.S. forces to a UN police action in accordance with art. 42 of the Charter, it is because the U.S. Government is obliged by international law to comply. Such compliance by the President with international law is not prohibited—indeed, it is required—by the Constitution."), *with* Michael J. Glennon, *The Constitution and Chapter VII of the United Nations Charter*, 85 Am. J. Int'l L. 74, 88 (1991) ("What the President constitutionally needs from the United States Congress, he cannot get from the United Nations Security Council."). Somewhat similar issues are raised by the self-defense treaties such as the North Atlantic Treaty, in which the Senate has consented to commitments whereby the United States has promised to use force to defend allies if they are attacked.

[11] *See* 22 U.S.C. § 287d.

let alone a declaration of war. In defending the president's actions, the State Department emphasized that the Security Council had authorized the use of force, and it argued that the "continued existence of the United Nations as an effective international organization is a paramount United States interest."[12] The Department also cited to past presidential uses of force that did not have express congressional authorization, such as in the Boxer Rebellion.

Although the Korean War is potentially an important precedent in favor of presidential unilateralism in using military force, its precedential weight has generally been thought to be limited, for several reasons: There has long been debate about whether Truman's action was constitutional; it occurred at a time when there was significant uncertainty about how the UN Charter framework interacted with the U.S. law of war powers; and most subsequent military actions that have involved substantial and protracted use of ground troops have been authorized by Congress (namely, the Vietnam War, both Iraq wars, and the war in Afghanistan).

Historical practice is often given significant weight by courts and other interpreters when ascertaining the distribution of constitutional authority between Congress and the president,[13] so the post-Korean War practice of congressional authorization for the largest ground campaigns may have constitutional significance. On the other hand, it is also the case that presidents have often used military force since World War II in smaller or shorter-term military operations without obtaining express congressional authorization.

III. The War Powers Resolution

The Vietnam War of the 1960s and 1970s, which was authorized at least to some extent by Congress, became highly controversial and led to Congress's most vigorous effort to regulate presidential war-making. In 1973, Congress enacted the War Powers Resolution over President Richard Nixon's veto, and the Resolution (which, despite its title, is a binding statute, to the extent that it is constitutional) continues in force today. The Resolution states that its purpose is to "insure that the collective judgment of both the Congress and the President will apply to the introduction of United States Armed Forces into hostilities, or into situations where imminent involvement in hostilities is clearly indicated by the circumstances, and to the continued use of such forces in hostilities or in such situations."[14]

[12] *Authority of the President to Repel the Attack in Korea*, Dep't St. Bull. (U.S. Dep't of State, Washington, D.C.), July 31, 1950, at 177.

[13] *See* Curtis A. Bradley & Trevor W. Morrison, *Historical Gloss and the Separation of Powers*, 126 Harv. L. Rev. 411 (2012).

[14] 50 U.S.C. § 1541(a).

In addition to provisions requiring that the president consult with and report to Congress about the introduction of U.S. forces into hostilities, the Resolution provides that if a president has introduced U.S. forces into hostilities, the president must terminate the use of these forces within sixty days unless Congress authorizes the operation.[15] Such authorization, the Resolution further states, is not to be inferred from any treaty unless Congress has implemented the treaty with legislation that specifically authorizes the use of U.S. armed forces.[16] Finally, the Resolution more generally expresses the view (in a provision that the executive branch contends is not legally binding) that:

> The constitutional powers of the President as Commander-in-Chief to introduce United States Armed Forces into hostilities, or into situations where imminent involvement in hostilities is clearly indicated by the circumstances, are exercised only pursuant to (1) a declaration of war, (2) specific statutory authorization, or (3) a national emergency created by attack upon the United States, its territories or possessions, or its armed forces.[17]

This provision does not mention a presidential power to use force to protect and rescue Americans threatened abroad, but it is generally assumed that there is some such power, and presidents have exercised such a power on a number of occasions since the enactment of the Resolution, often without controversy.[18]

Presidential administrations have varied in whether they have accepted the constitutionality of the sixty-day cutoff provision. But even with this uncertainty about whether the provision is constitutional, it appears to have had some effect on presidential action. Instead of openly disregarding the sixty-day provision, when presidents have acted without congressional authorization they have typically either (1) concluded the military campaigns quickly (such as in Grenada and Panama in the 1980s); (2) claimed (sometimes questionably) that they had statutory authority that satisfied the requirements of the Resolution (such as with the 1999 bombing campaign in Kosovo and the conflict against the Islamic State that began in 2014); or (3) interpreted the Resolution as inapplicable (such as the Barack Obama administration's claim in 2011 that continued U.S. participation in a bombing campaign against Libya did not amount to "hostilities" for purposes of the Resolution).

Even though the Resolution has not been entirely disregarded by presidents, most observers do not view it as a success.[19] Because courts to date have declined to play a

[15] *See* 50 U.S.C. § 1544(b). The sixty-day period can be extended for up to thirty days "if the President determines and certifies to the Congress in writing that unavoidable military necessity respecting the safety of United States Armed Forces requires the continued use of such armed forces in the course of bringing about a prompt removal of such forces."

[16] *See* 50 U.S.C. § 1547(a)(2). [17] 50 U.S.C. § 1541(c).

[18] Some of the key congressional supporters of the War Powers Resolution later conceded that such an authority should have been included. *See* John Hart Ely, War and Responsibility 117 (1995).

[19] *See*, e.g., John Hart Ely, *Suppose Congress Wanted a War Powers Resolution that Worked*, 88 Colum. L. Rev. 1379 (1988); Michael Glennon, *Too Far Apart: Repeal the War Powers Resolution*, 50 U. Miami L. Rev. 17 (1995).

role in enforcing it, its effectiveness depends on the extent to which the executive branch either voluntarily complies with it or is induced to do so by Congress. But Congress has shown little political will to enforce it, and the executive branch has interpreted it in a manner designed to preserve executive branch flexibility. For example, although probably not its intent, the Resolution's sixty-day cutoff provision has been interpreted by the executive branch as a congressional acceptance of presidential authority to use force for less than sixty days.[20] Moreover, although the Resolution expressly states that appropriations statutes are not to be construed as authorizations to use force, the executive branch has maintained that the Resolution—since it is merely a statute—cannot control how later statutes (including appropriations statutes) are construed.[21] Furthermore, the Resolution leaves undefined the key term "hostilities," and the executive branch has interpreted that term in a manner that allows it to bypass the Resolution for some uses of force.[22]

IV. Congressional and Judicial Checks on Presidential War-Making

Apart from its enactment of the War Powers Resolution, Congress generally has not done much to resist presidential unilateralism in the war powers area. Sometimes there has been widespread support in Congress for the presidential action, and therefore its members have seen no reason to insist on the formality of specific statutory authorization. This appears to have been true, for example, with the initiation of the Korean War and may also be true to some extent with the campaign against the Islamic State. On other occasions, Congress has been content to wait and see how a campaign unfolds without taking a vote on it, thereby avoiding accountability if the campaign does not turn out well.

Even when Congress has concerns about a military campaign, it is often reluctant to take actions that might appear unsupportive of U.S. troops or that might hurt the

[20] *See* Memorandum Opinion from Caroline D. Krass, Principal Deputy Assistant Attorney General, Office of Legal Counsel, to the Attorney General, "Authority to Use Military Force in Libya," at 8 (Apr. 1, 2011), *available at* https://fas.org/irp/agency/doj/olc/libya.pdf.

[21] *See* Memorandum Opinion for the Attorney General, *Authorization for Continuing Hostilities in Kosovo*, 24 Op. Off. Legal Counsel 327 (Dec. 19, 2000).

[22] *See, e.g.*, Testimony of Harold Hongju Koh, U.S. Department of State, on Libya and War Powers, Before Senate Foreign Relations Committee (June 28, 2011), *available at* https://www.foreign.senate.gov/imo/media/doc/062811_Transcript_Libya%20and%20War%20Powers.pdf (arguing that continued U.S. participation in the use of military force against Libya in 2011 did not constitute "hostilities" within the meaning of the War Powers Resolution, given the limited nature of the mission, the low risk to U.S. troops, the low risk of escalation, and the limited means of force being used).

chances of U.S. success. More generally, Congress as a collective body often has difficulty mobilizing opposition to the president, especially if one or both houses of Congress are controlled by the president's political party. At other times, partisan conflict may simply create gridlock, making it impossible to reach agreement on legislation. In early 2015, for example, President Obama proposed to Congress that it enact an authorization statute for the conflict against the Islamic State, but as of 2018 (with a new presidential administration) Congress still had not acted, even though it does not appear that Congress is opposed to the use of force in that conflict.[23]

None of this is to suggest that Congress's inaction should by itself be construed as providing legal authority for executive action. Moreover, if we look only at the times in which the executive has used force unilaterally, we are likely to understate congressional influence by overlooking instances in which the executive decided *not* to act because of congressional pressure. Nevertheless, many observers have concluded that in practice Congress does not impose a significant check on executive decision-making relating to the use of force.

The United States has a powerful court system, so in theory the judiciary could police executive violations of either the constitutional law of war powers or the War Powers Resolution. In practice, however, courts in the modern era have invoked various "justiciability" limitations to avoid addressing these issues. They have insisted that the plaintiffs meet the requirements for standing and have generally disallowed members of Congress from claiming standing.[24] They have also refused to consider cases that are not sufficiently "ripe," either because it is not clear whether or to what extent force will be used or because Congress has not yet attempted to use its own resources to resist a president's unilateral action.[25] And, most significantly, courts have tended to treat issues concerning the distribution of war authority as presenting a nonjusticiable "political question."[26] To be sure, the Supreme Court has signaled in recent years that the political question doctrine should have a narrow scope.[27] But very few cases ever get

[23] *See* Matthew C. Weed, *A New Authorization for Use of Military Force Against the Islamic State: Issues and Current Proposals* (Cong. Res. Serv., Feb. 21, 2017), *available at* https://fas.org/sgp/crs/natsec/R43760.pdf. There have been rare instances in which Congress has used its authority over funding to curtail or terminate U.S. military operations, such as near the end of the Vietnam War, and in connection with U.S. military operations in Somalia in the 1990s after a number of U.S. service personnel were killed there. *See* Richard F. Grimmett, *Congressional Use of Funding Cutoffs Since 1970 Involving U.S. Military Forces and Overseas Deployments* 1–3 (Cong. Res. Serv., Jan. 16, 2007), *available at* https://fas.org/sgp/crs/natsec/RS20775.pdf.

[24] *See,* e.g., Campbell v. Clinton, 203 F.3d 19 (D.C. Cir. 2000) (dismissing challenge by thirty-one members of Congress to President Clinton's use of force in Yugoslavia in 1999); Kucinich v. Obama, 821 F. Supp. 2d 110 (D.D.C. 2011) (dismissing challenge by members of Congress to President Obama's use of force against Libya in 2011).

[25] *See,* e.g., Doe v. Bush, 323 F.3d 133, 137–139 (1st Cir. 2003); Dellums v. Bush, 752 F. Supp. 1141, 1149–1152 (D.D.C. 1990).

[26] *See,* e.g., Smith v. Obama, 217 F. Supp. 3d 283 (D.D.C. 2016); Ange v. Bush, 752 F. Supp. 509 (D.D.C. 1990).

[27] *See* Zivotofsky v. Clinton, 132 S. Ct. 1421, 1427 (2012) (describing the political question doctrine as a "narrow exception" to the judiciary's "responsibility to decide cases properly before it").

reviewed by the Supreme Court, and the lower federal courts continue to apply the political question doctrine with some vigor in the foreign affairs area.[28]

In light of modern practice and the lack of significant judicial review, some academic observers have suggested that presidents now have the de facto authority to initiate at least short-term military campaigns that they deem to be in the national interest, especially if there is no significant use of ground troops.[29] Under this view, one would in effect need to distinguish between certain "big wars" that require congressional authorization and "small wars" that would not. But other scholars either read the historical practice differently or argue that it should not legitimize this degree of presidential unilateralism.[30] Still other scholars accept that the above account might describe the de facto war powers regime today, but they contest its legality and desirability.[31] These scholars maintain that Congress should be doing more to maintain an authorizing role, and that, outside of narrow self-defense and rescue situations, it is problematic to allow the executive branch unilateral authority to use force abroad. Various proposals have been made over the years to improve the situation, such as through increased judicial review or amendments to the War Powers Resolution, but so far little has been done.

V. Example: Syria in 2013 and in 2017–2018

The uncertain state of the constitutional law of U.S. war powers is illustrated by the deliberations in the Obama administration in 2013 about whether to use military force against Syria. The prior year, President Obama had announced that the use of chemical weapons by the Assad regime in Syria in its civil war would involve crossing a "red line"

[28] *See* Alex Loomis, *Why Are the Lower Courts (Mostly) Ignoring Zivotofsky I's Political Question Analysis?*, Lawfare (May 19, 2016), *available at* https://www.lawfareblog.com/why-are-lower-courts-mostly-ignoring-zivotofsky-political-question-analysis. *See also*, e.g., Jaber v. United States, 861 F.3d 241 (D.C. Cir. 2017) (applying political question doctrine to bar challenge, under domestic and international law, to drone strike by the U.S. military in Yemen).

[29] *See*, e.g., Harold Hongju Koh, *The War Powers and Humanitarian Intervention*, 53 Houston L. Rev. 971, 978 (2016); Peter J. Spiro, *War Powers and the Sirens of Formalism*, 68 N.Y.U. L. Rev. 1338, 1348 (1993) (reviewing Ely, *supra* note 18).

[30] *See*, e.g., Michael J. Glennon, *The Executive's Misplaced Reliance on War Powers "Custom,"* 109 Am. J. Int'l L. 551, 552 (2015); Jane E. Stromseth, *Understanding Constitutional War Powers Today: Why Methodology Matters*, 106 Yale L.J. 845, 882–886 (1996) (reviewing Louis Fisher, Presidential War Power (1995)).

[31] *See*, e.g., Ely, *supra* note 18; Louis Fisher, Presidential War Power 294–297 (3d ed. 2013); Jules Lobel, *"Little Wars" and the Constitution*, 50 U. Miami L. Rev. 61 (1995).

that would carry "enormous consequences."[32] When it appeared that the regime had crossed that line by using sarin gas against a rebel-held suburb of Damascus, Obama began preparing a military response. At that point, it appeared that he would act without seeking authorization from Congress. Abruptly, however, he changed course and said that he would first seek congressional approval.[33] This was a politically risky move, because it was far from clear that Congress would provide such authorization. The issue soon became moot, however, when Russia facilitated a diplomatic solution.[34]

Obama's change of heart occurred shortly after Britain's prime minister indicated that he would accept a vote by the House of Commons rejecting that country's participation in using force against Syria.[35] In Obama's public statement explaining his decision to seek authorization from Congress, he specifically referred to "what we saw happen in the United Kingdom this week when the Parliament of our closest ally failed to pass a resolution with a similar goal, even as the Prime Minister supported taking action."[36] Obama also noted that, while he thought that he had the authority to carry out this military action without congressional authorization, he was also "mindful that I'm the President of the world's oldest constitutional democracy."[37]

The decision to seek congressional authorization for the use of force against Syria was consistent with the views of presidential war powers that Obama had expressed while he was a candidate for the presidency in 2007. In a newspaper interview, Obama stated that "[t]he President does not have power under the Constitution to unilaterally authorize a military attack in a situation that does not involve stopping an actual or imminent threat to the nation."[38] In privately discussing with his aides his decision to seek congressional authorization for using force against Syria, Obama apparently referred back to that 2007 interview.[39]

The Obama administration's practice, however, was not always consistent with Obama's earlier views. Most notably, the administration used military force against the Qaddafi regime in Libya in 2011 without first obtaining congressional authorization, even though the United States did not face any actual or imminent threat. In defending the constitutionality of this action, the Justice Department's Office of Legal Counsel (OLC) expressed a view of presidential war powers that is substantially broader than the one that Obama had expressed while a candidate for the presidency. Quoting from prior executive branch legal opinions, the OLC observed that "the

[32] Remarks by the President to the White House Press Corps (Aug. 20, 2012), *available at* https://www.whitehouse.gov/the-press-office/2012/08/20/remarks-president-white-house-press-corps.

[33] *See* Peter Baker & Jonathan Weisman, *Obama Seeks Approval by Congress for Strike in Syria*, N.Y. Times, Aug. 31, 2013.

[34] *See* Mark Lander & Jonathan Weisman, *Obama Delays Syria Strike to Focus on a Russian Plan*, N.Y. Times, Sept. 10, 2013.

[35] For additional discussion of the vote in the United Kingdom, *see* Katja S. Ziegler, *The Use of Military Force by the United Kingdom: The Evolution of Accountability*, ch. 43 in this volume.

[36] Statement by the President on Syria (Aug. 31, 2013), *available at* https://www.whitehouse.gov/the-press-office/2013/08/31/statement-president-syria.

[37] *Id.*

[38] Charlie Savage, *Barack Obama's Q&A*, Boston Globe (Dec. 20, 2007).

[39] *See* Charlie Savage, Power Wars: Inside Obama's Post-9/11 Presidency 653 (2015).

President has the power to commit United States troops abroad, as well as to take military action, for the purpose of protecting important national interests, even without specific prior authorization from Congress."[40] The OLC did acknowledge that the president might be required to obtain congressional authorization for a use of force amounting to a "war," but it insisted that such a requirement would be triggered "only by prolonged and substantial military engagements, typically involving exposure of U.S. military personnel to significant risk over a substantial period," a standard that it argued was not met with respect to the use of force against Libya.[41] Even for the subsequent aborted action in Syria, executive branch lawyers had apparently advised the president that he had the authority take unilateral action,[42] and Obama himself claimed that although he was seeking congressional authorization, "I believe I have the authority to carry out this military action without specific congressional authorization."[43]

The story concerning the use of force against Syria does not end there. In both 2017 and 2018, Obama's successor, President Donald Trump, ordered missile strikes against the Syrian regime in response to that country's use of chemical weapons.[44] The Trump administration claimed that, "[a]s our commander in chief, the president has the authority under Article II of the Constitution to use military force overseas to defend important U.S. national interests."[45] Notably, the government of the United Kingdom also acted in Syria in 2018 without first seeking parliamentary approval.[46]

The Justice Department's Office of Legal Counsel subsequently published a legal opinion explaining why it had concluded that the Trump administration's missile strikes against Syria in April 2018 were constitutional.[47] As in its prior war powers

[40] Memorandum Opinion for the Attorney General, *Authority to Use Military Force in Libya*, at 6 (Apr. 1, 2011) (internal quotation marks omitted), *available at* https://www.justice.gov/sites/default/files/olc/opinions/2011/04/31/authority-military-use-in-libya.pdf.

[41] *Id.* at 8. [42] *See* SAVAGE, *supra* note 39, at 630.

[43] Statement, *supra* note 36.

[44] *See* Michael R. Gordon, Helene Cooper, & Michael D. Shear, *Dozens of U.S. Missiles Hit Air Base in Syria*, N.Y. TIMES (Apr. 6, 2017); Helene Cooper, Thomas Gibbons-Neff, & Ben Hubbard, *U.S., Britain and France Strike Syria over Suspected Chemical Weapons Attack*, N.Y. Times (Apr. 13, 2018).

[45] Statement by Secretary James N. Mattis on Syria, U.S. Dep't of Defense (Apr. 13, 2018), *available at* https://www.defense.gov/News/News-Releases/News-Release-View/Article/1493610/statement-by-secretary-james-n-mattis-on-syria/; *see also* Marty Lederman, *(Apparent) Administration Justifications for Legality of Strikes Against Syria*, JUST SECURITY (Apr. 8, 2017) (reporting that Trump administration talking points asserted that, "[a]s Commander in Chief, the President has the power under art. II of the Constitution to use this sort of military force overseas to defend important U.S. national interests."), *available at* https://www.justsecurity.org/39803/apparent-administration-justifications-legality-strikes-syria/. For the view that "[r]ecent uses of military force by American presidents are increasingly indicating that the exclusive congressional authority to declare war is moribund or perhaps already defunct," *see* Keith E. Whittington, *R.I.P. Congressional War Power*, LAWFARE (Apr. 20, 2018), *available at* https://www.lawfareblog.com/rip-congressional-war-power.

[46] *See* House of Commons Library, *Parliamentary Approval for Military Acton* (Apr. 17, 2018), *available at* http://researchbriefings.parliament.uk/ResearchBriefing/Summary/CBP-7166.

[47] *See* Memorandum Opinion for the Counsel to the President, *April 2018 Airstrikes Against Syrian Chemical-Weapons Facilities* (May 31, 2018), *available at* https://www.justice.gov/olc/opinion/file/1067551/download.

opinions, the OLC placed significant weight on historical practice, noting that, "[w]hile our Nation has sometimes debated the scope of the President's war powers under the Constitution, his authority to direct U.S. forces in hostilities without prior congressional authorization is supported by a 'long continued practice on the part of the Executive, acquiesced in by the Congress.'"[48] The OLC appeared to accept that the president would be constitutionally obligated to seek congressional authorization before committing the nation to a military operation that would rise to the level of a "war," but it found that the "nature, scope, and duration" of the operation in Syria did not rise to that level.[49]

VI. Potential Benefits of Comparativism

In considering whether to seek congressional authorization for the use of force against Syria in 2013, President Obama seemed to take into account the action by Britain's prime minister in seeking and respecting parliamentary input. This example is a reminder that other constitutional democracies may face similar issues in deciding how to regulate the use of military force.

There is substantial variation in how countries have approached the relationship between the legislative and executive branches with respect to war powers, so there is rich material for comparative evaluation.[50] For example, a 2010 study found that there was "a remarkable variance regarding the war powers of national parliaments in Europe, ranging from 'very strong' in Austria, Germany and Finland to 'very weak' in the cases of France, the UK and Greece."[51] Similarly, Professor Tom Ginsburg has found, based on data from the Comparative Constitutions Project (which is coding all

[48] *Id.* at 5 (citation omitted).

[49] For discussion of why OLC's approach entails very little legal constraint on modern uses of force by presidents, *see* Curtis Bradley & Jack Goldsmith, *OLC's Meaningless "National Interest" Test for the Legality of Presidential Uses of Force*, Lawfare (June 5, 2018), *available at* https://www.lawfareblog.com/olcs-meaningless-national-interests-test-legality-presidential-uses-force.

[50] *See*, e.g., Sandra Dieterich, Hartwig Hummel, & Stefan Marschall, *Parliamentary War Powers: A Survey of 25 European Parliaments*, Geneva Centre for the Democratic Control of Armed Forces, Occasional Paper No. 21 (2010) (describing range of parliamentary control among European countries over deployment of the military), *available at* https://www.dcaf.ch/sites/default/files/publications/documents/OP21_FINAL.pdf; Wolfgang Wagner, Dirk Peters, & Cosima Glahn, *Parliamentary War Powers Around the World, 1999–2004. A New Dataset* 11 (2010) ("The powers of parliaments in this issue area vary widely among democracies around the world."); Katja S. Ziegler, *Executive Powers in Foreign Policy: The Decision to Dispatch the Military*, *in* Constitutionalism and the Role of Parliaments 143 (Katja S. Ziegler et al. eds., 2007) ("[I]n an international comparison parliamentary involvement in decisions to deploy military forces is anything but uniform.").

[51] Dieterich et al., *supra* note 50, at 9. In 2008, France amended its constitution to require parliamentary approval for uses of force that last longer than four months. *See* Mathias Forteau, *Using Military Force and Engaging in Collective Security: The Case of France*, ch. 45 in this volume.

of the world's constitutions since 1789), that "there are a wide variety of approaches to the problem of declaring war."[52] Moreover, the distribution of war authority in other countries has not been static, and the trends and changes over time may themselves be instructive. For example, even though the initiation of war is considered a "royal prerogative" of the Crown in Great Britain, in recent years the executive branch in that country has sought legislative approval before using military force.[53] That said, it is not clear that the overall trend among constitutional democracies is in favor of legislative control over the use of force.[54]

Importantly, comparing the role of legislatures in decisions to use force is much more complicated than simply looking to see whether their ex ante legislative approval is required. As one comparative study that focused on ex ante approval acknowledged:

> *Ex ante* veto power is certainly not the only way in which parliaments could exert control over deployments. Even *ex ante* consultation, for example, could give parliament the opportunity to affect executive decisions somewhat. Parliaments, moreover, may become involved in other phases of a mission, not only before troops are deployed. Parliaments may, for example, be empowered to call the troops back home in the early phase of an operation. They may become involved at later stages of a deployment by retaining the right to monitor activities, thus acting as a watchdog whose presence may continue to affect executive decisions. Finally, parliament may become influential after a deployment has ended by performing an evaluation and exposing weaknesses in how government and the military leadership handled an operation.[55]

There is thus a wide range of variables relating to domestic control over war powers that could be compared.[56]

Despite such rich material, any comparative analysis of how nations regulate war powers should be approached with caution. Each country's laws and practices are embedded within that country's particular legal culture, political system, and historical tradition. Moreover, there may be limitations on how much one can translate the approach of a parliamentary system to the U.S. presidential system. There may also be particular pathologies that apply to the U.S. Congress (such as the extent of its partisanship, unpopularity, or vulnerability to lobbying interests) that do not apply to other legislatures. In addition, nations vary widely in the extent to which they can

[52] Tom Ginsburg, *Chaining the Dog of War: Comparative Data*, 15 Chi. J. Int'l L. 138, 147 (2014).

[53] *See* Claire Mills, *Briefing Paper: Parliamentary Approval for Military Action* (May 12, 2015), *available at* http://researchbriefings.parliament.uk/ResearchBriefing/Summary/CBP-7166; Zoe Bedell, *British Parliament (Unlike the U.S. Congress) Actually Votes on Use of Force in Syria*, Lawfare (Dec. 3, 2015), *available at* https://www.lawfareblog.com/british-parliament-unlike-us-congress-actually-votes-use-force-syria.

[54] *See* Wagner et al., *supra* note 50, at 25 ("[S]ince the 1990s this trend seems to be reversed, with the executive (re)gaining autonomous decision-making power over military deployments.").

[55] *Id.* at 19.

[56] For additional discussion of this point, *see* Monica Hakimi, *Techniques for Regulating Military Force*, ch. 41 in this volume.

and do project military power abroad—both unilaterally and as part of collective operations—and there are not many nations that are comparable to the United States in this regard.[57] More generally, there is a danger that comparative materials will be invoked selectively with a focus only on those most helpful to a particular position.

With appropriate caution, however, there are various ways in which a study of comparative war powers might be useful, including to those who seek to regulate war powers in the United States.[58] For example, knowledge of other nations' approaches can be useful for statutory drafting—for example, in considering how the War Powers Resolution might be improved. Consider, for example, Germany's 2005 Parliamentary Participation Act.[59] In requiring the consent of the *Bundestag* (the lower house of Germany's legislature) for military deployments, the Act does a number of things that are distinct from the U.S. War Powers Resolution. Instead of having the consent requirement hinge on the undefined term "hostilities," it uses "deployment" as the trigger and defines it to mean "when soldiers of the German Federal Armed Forces are involved in armed engagements, or their involvement in an armed engagement is to be anticipated." It also specifies in detail the information that the executive must provide to the *Bundestag* in its request for authorization. In addition, to make the scheme more workable, it sets forth a more simplified procedure for the approval of "deployments of minor scope and intensity," which it proceeds to define and illustrate. The Act further provides that advance legislative approval is not needed for "deployments in the event of imminent danger which allow no scope for delay" and for "operations whose purpose is to rescue persons from particularly dangerous situations, provided that the holding of a public debate in the Bundestag would endanger the lives of the persons in need of rescue," but it requires that the *Bundestag* "be informed appropriately prior to and during deployment."

Comparativism can also highlight alternatives to statutory regulation. For example, another form of regulation can occur through the development of "constitutional conventions" of expected political behavior. Constitutional conventions are "maxims, beliefs, and principles that guide officials in how they exercise political discretion."[60] The recent practice of Great Britain might be instructive. Even though it has a tradition

[57] Although beyond the scope of this chapter, there are theoretical debates within the field of comparative constitutional law that reflect differing views about the significance of historical and contextual differences like these. *See* Michel Rosenfield & András Sajó, *Introduction*, *in* THE OXFORD HANDBOOK OF COMPARATIVE CONSTITUTIONAL LAW 16–18 (Michel Rosenfeld & András Sajó, eds. 2012).

[58] Conversely, other countries may benefit from looking at the U.S. war powers experience, including at what has not worked well. *Cf.* Yasuo Hasebe, *War Powers*, *in* THE OXFORD HANDBOOK OF COMPARATIVE CONSTITUTIONAL LAW, *supra* note 57, at 479 ("While there are some moves towards the strengthening of parliamentary control in the United Kingdom and France, these efforts may encounter difficulties similar to those under the US War Powers Resolution.").

[59] For additional discussion of the German statute, *see* Anne Peters, *Military Operations Abroad under the German Basic Law*, ch. 44 in this volume.

[60] Keith E. Whittington, *The Status of Unwritten Constitutional Conventions in the United States*, 2013 U. ILL. L. REV. 1847, 1860.

of executive control over war as part of the prerogative powers of the Crown, in recent years the government appears to have accepted that a constitutional convention has emerged whereby, except in emergency situations, the House of Commons is to be given an advance opportunity to debate the issue.[61] Proposals to convert this convention into a more binding statute, along the lines of the U.S. and German approaches, have to date been rejected.[62]

Studying comparative practice might also allow for a reassessment of the proper role and capacity of U.S. courts in examining war powers questions. Again, Germany is an interesting model, given that its courts have been especially willing to address war powers issues, including in challenges brought by the legislative branch.[63] By contrast, courts in some countries like Japan and Great Britain seem to be closer to the U.S. practice of avoiding war powers adjudication, and their rationales also would be worth study.[64] In addition to general questions of judicial capacity, comparativism might be instructive in thinking about whether and to what extent courts (or the legislature) might draw upon international law in assessing executive war powers authority (something noticeably absent from the U.S. War Powers Resolution, for example).[65]

The most controversial use of comparativism, at least in the United States, would be in constitutional interpretation. Given how difficult it is to amend the U.S. Constitution (which would typically require supermajority votes in both houses of Congress and approval by three-fourths of the states), it is unlikely that comparative study would lead to a formal change in the constitutional text. As illustrated above, however, there is substantial room for interpretive disagreements over the meaning of the existing Constitution as it relates to war-making. Yet there has been robust debate in the United

[61] *See Parliamentary Approval for Military Action* (May 13, 2015), *available at* http://researchbriefings.parliament.uk/ResearchBriefing/Summary/CBP-7166. *See also* Ziegler, *supra* note 35.

[62] *See Ministers Drop Plan for War Powers Law*, THE GUARDIAN (Apr. 18, 2016).

[63] *See* Peters, *supra* note 59; *see also* Lori Fisler Damrosch, *Constitutional Control over War Powers: A Common Core of Accountability in Democratic Societies*, 50 MIAMI L. REV. 181, 196 (1995) (arguing that the German experience "shows, inter alia, that judicial organs can play a constructive role in giving contemporary meaning to constitutional war powers provisions"); THOMAS M. FRANCK, POLITICAL QUESTIONS, JUDICIAL ANSWERS ch. 7 (1992) (discussing and generally praising the "German model" of judicial review of foreign relations law cases); *see also* Jaber v. United States, 861 F.3d 241, 250 (D.C. Cir. 2017) (Brown, J., concurring) (observing, in a case in which the court applied the political question doctrine to bar consideration of the legality of a U.S. drone strike in Yemen, that "[i]n other liberal democracies, courts play (or seem to play) a significant supervisory role in policing exercises of executive power").

[64] *See, e.g.*, Damrosch, *supra* note 63, at 195 ("Using a version of the 'political question doctrine' and related techniques similar to those applied by U.S. courts, the Japanese Supreme Court (like its American counterpart) has refrained from articulating limits on the government's military powers."). In restricting the standing of federal legislators to challenge statutes or executive branch actions, the Supreme Court acknowledged that "[t]here would be nothing irrational about a system that granted standing in these cases; some European constitutional courts operate under one or another variant of such a regime." Raines v. Byrd, 521 U.S. 811, 828 (1997). But the Court contended that "[o]ur regime contemplates a more restricted role for Article III courts." *Id.*

[65] *See, e.g.*, Craig Martin, *Taking War Seriously: A Model for Constitutional Constraints on the Use of Force in Compliance with International Law*, 76 BROOKLYN L. REV. 611 (2011).

States over the propriety of looking to foreign and international materials to interpret the U.S. Constitution—for example, in determining the meaning of the Constitution's ban on "cruel and unusual punishments." One's position in this debate depends to some extent on one's general approach to constitutional interpretation.[66] Those who adhere to a strictly "originalist" approach to constitutional interpretation may dismiss modern comparative practice as irrelevant because it does not shed light on what the Constitution was understood to mean when it was adopted.[67] By contrast, interpreters who are willing to consider additional sources of constitutional meaning—such as the purposes of constitutional provisions, inferences from the constitutional structure, and the practical effects of adopting a particular interpretation—are more likely to view comparative materials as potentially relevant.[68]

Despite such debate, a majority of the Supreme Court has been willing at various times to consider comparative materials.[69] Moreover, some of the objections to considering those materials may have less force in the war powers context, which is inherently international, than in the context of issues that seem more domestic in nature (such as the death penalty). For example, if Congress's authority to control the use of military force turns on whether the use of force amounts to a "war," as some scholars (and, at least sometimes, the executive branch) contend, then it may be instructive to see how other countries have drawn such a distinction (or similar distinctions). This is especially so given that the Constitution does not define the term "war," and its meaning may have evolved over time as the result of international law and practice.

In any event, even if one rejects a "borrowing" of comparative practice as part of constitutional interpretation, there is a subtler way in which comparative materials might be relevant to constitutional analysis: they can provide a backdrop against which it is possible to gain a better understanding of one's own constitution. Knowing about

[66] *See* Roger P. Alford, *In Search of a Theory for Constitutional Comparativism*, 52 UCLA L. Rev. 639 (2005).

[67] Writing for a 5–4 majority of the Supreme Court in *Printz v. United States*, 521 U.S. 898, 921 n.11 (1997), Justice Scalia rejected looking to experiences abroad when considering the U.S. Constitution's requirements relating to federalism, contending that "such comparative analysis is inappropriate to the task of interpreting a constitution, though it was of course quite relevant to the task of writing one."

[68] *See, e.g.*, Justice Breyer's dissent in *Printz*, 521 U.S. at 977 ("Of course, we are interpreting our own Constitution, not those of other nations, and there may be relevant political and structural differences between their systems and our own. But their experience may nonetheless cast an empirical light on the consequences of different solutions to a common legal problem."); *see also* Mark Tushnet, *The Possibilities of Comparative Constitutional Law*, 108 Yale L.J. 1225, 1232 (1999) ("[I]f one believes that constitutional interpretation is the application of reason to problems of governance within a framework set out in the Constitution's words, experience elsewhere is relevant because it provides information that an interpreter committed to reason might find helpful.").

[69] *See, e.g.*, Roper v. Simmons, 543 U.S. 551 (2005); Graham v. Florida, 560 U.S. 48 (2010). *See also* Vicki C. Jackson, *Constitutions as "Living Trees": Comparative Constitutional Law and Interpretive Metaphors*, 75 Fordham L. Rev. 921, 922 (2006) ("The U.S. Supreme Court has a longstanding practice of (at least episodically) considering foreign legal experience in resolving American constitutional questions.").

alternative constitutional approaches can, for example, highlight the ways in which U.S. law reflects particular choices that could have been made differently. This is true even when (or perhaps especially when) the interpreter concludes that the constitutional analysis adopted by other countries is not well suited to the U.S. context.[70] For example, whereas the U.S. Constitution assigns the power to declare war to Congress, many modern constitutions assign that power to the executive, while also often subjecting the executive's military action to legislative approval.[71] Certainly such comparative information should at least be of interest to scholars of the U.S. Constitution. And, as a practical matter, judges and other officials are likely to take it into account once they are aware of it, even if they do not expressly rely on it in their decision-making.[72]

VII. Conclusion

The U.S. Constitution is more than two centuries years old and is relatively short compared to many modern constitutions. Since the Constitution was adopted, there have been fundamental changes in the size of the U.S. military, the U.S. role in the world, the general scope of presidential authority, and the international law governing the use of force. Moreover, at least in the post–World War II era, U.S. courts have generally stayed out of disputes over the Constitution's distribution of war authority. This judicial reticence has meant that substantial war powers practice has developed without any clear indication from the courts whether it is lawful. Furthermore, Congress's one effort to enact a general regulatory statute concerning the distribution of war authority—the War Powers Resolution—implicates its own set of interpretive

[70] *See, e.g.*, Sujit Choudhry, *Globalization in Search of Justification: Toward a Theory of Comparative Constitutional Interpretation*, 74 Ind. L.J. 819, 825 (1999) ("Through a process of interpretive self-reflection, courts may conclude that domestic and foreign assumptions are sufficiently similar to one another to warrant the use of comparative law. Conversely, courts may conclude that comparative jurisprudence has emerged from a fundamentally different constitutional order; this realization may sharpen an awareness of constitutional difference or distinctiveness."); Vicki C. Jackson, *Constitutional Comparisons: Convergence, Resistance, Engagement*, 119 Harv. L. Rev. 109, 114 (2005) ("[C]onstitutional law can be understood as a site of engagement between domestic law and international or foreign legal sources and practices" such that "[t]ransnational sources are seen as interlocutors, offering a way of testing understanding of one's own traditions and possibilities by examining them in the reflection of others'"); Tushnet, *supra* note 68, at 1236 ("The expressivist approach to comparative constitutional law takes as its premise that comparative inquiry may help us see our own practices in a new light and might lead courts using *non*-comparative methods to results they would not have reached had they not consulted the comparative material.").

[71] *See* Ginsburg, *supra* note 52, at 149–151. *See also* Jenny S. Martinez, *Inherent Executive Power: A Comparative Perspective*, 115 Yale L.J. 2480, 2494 (2006) (arguing that "comparative examples do not support the essentialist thesis that waging war is inherently an executive function").

[72] *Cf.* Jackson, *supra* note 70, at 119 ("Comparison today is inevitable. It is almost impossible to be a well-informed judge or lawyer now without having impressions of law and governance in countries other than one's own.").

and constitutional uncertainties. As the United States continues to think about how best to regulate the use of military force, and about the proper role of the judiciary in policing such regulation, it can potentially learn from the experiences of other countries that have grappled with similar questions. At a minimum, such comparative reflection can allow for a deeper understanding of the United States' particular approach to war powers.

CHAPTER 43

THE USE OF MILITARY FORCE BY THE UNITED KINGDOM

The Evolution of Accountability

KATJA S. ZIEGLER

ACCOUNTABILITY for decisions to go to war has evolved in the United Kingdom in recent years. Although historical practice reflects a varied picture of contestation and political bargaining between Parliament and the executive, the constitutional narrative has been consistently based on the constitutional orthodoxy of the executive's prerogative.[1] The Iraq War of 2003 served as trigger, or at least accelerator, for an *evolution* toward greater accountability. Legal responses to military actions against organized terrorist groups such as the Islamic State of Iraq and the Levant (ISIL) and al Qaeda have further contributed to the developing accountability framework. Two dimensions characterize the framework: democratic accountability through Parliament and accountability under the rule of law, particularly individual rights, implemented by courts.[2] This chapter focuses on the evolution of democratic accountability. It begins in Section I by outlining the emergence in the United Kingdom of a constitutional convention requiring parliamentary approval for uses of military force. It will then discuss in Section II some uncertainties about the threshold and scope of the approval requirement and its exceptions. Finally, it will reflect in Section III on the U.K. practice from a comparative perspective.

[1] ROSARA JOSEPH, THE WAR PREROGATIVE. HISTORY, REFORM, AND CONSTITUTIONAL DESIGN 15, 22 (2013).

[2] PETER ROWE, LEGAL ACCOUNTABILITY AND BRITAIN'S WARS 2000–2015 (2016); NIGEL D. WHITE, DEMOCRACY GOES TO WAR: BRITISH MILITARY DEPLOYMENTS UNDER INTERNATIONAL LAW (2009); Eirik Bjorge & Cameron Miles, *Crown and Foreign Acts of State before British Courts:* Rahmatullah, Belhaj, *and the Separation of Powers*, ch. 40 in this volume.

I. Emergence of a Constitutional Convention of Parliamentary Approval

The decision to deploy the military falls within the prerogative powers of the U.K. government in the area of foreign policy. Traditionally it was a decision of the government in an area of reserved powers, which were nonjusticiable. More recently, however, the scope of the prerogative has become more limited and is in a process of rebalancing.[3]

Vote on the Iraq War

Historically, the House of Commons did not vote on military deployments. Since the 1688 settlement between Parliament and the Crown, parliamentary consent was required only to maintain a standing army in peacetime, to introduce conscription to the army, and to introduce taxation. Parliament was informed about the government's decision to deploy the military, and debates occurred retrospectively.[4]

In the 1991 Gulf War, after retrospective debate, the House of Commons overwhelmingly supported the deployment by a *vote,* notably on a substantive motion.[5] This was a significant development, as debates about war had typically been held under a so-called "motion of adjournment," tabled by the government, even though it had no interest for the House to adjourn. The purpose of such a motion is to allow the Commons to debate a topic without the need for a clear division of votes at the end of the debate. That process was heavily criticized because it did not reflect the significance of a decision of military deployment, which "ought to require the dignity of a more meaningful procedure,"[6] and because it obscured the position of the Parliament as a whole. It also was not readily understood in the population, and, therefore, ill-suited as an instrument of accountability.[7]

A turning point occurred with the vote on the Iraq War in March 2003. Following public and media discussions on the possible participation of British troops in a war against the regime of Saddam Hussein's Iraq, the House of Commons voted in favor of

[3] For an overview, *see* Joseph, *supra* note 1; *see also* Paul Craig, *Engagement and Disengagement with International Institutions: The U.K. Perspective*, ch. 22 in this volume.

[4] In regard to World War I (1918–1918), World War II (1939–1945), the Korean War (1950–1953), Suez (1956), Falklands (1982), Kosovo (1999), Sierra Leone (2000), and Afghanistan (2001–2014).

[5] 563 to 34 votes, HC Deb. (Jan. 21, 1991), Vol. 184, cc23-109. A further substantive motion was debated Feb. 21, 1991.

[6] E.g., by the late former Foreign Secretary, Robin Cook, The Point of Departure 187–188 (2003).

[7] *See* Veronika Fikfak & Hayley J. Hooper, Parliament's Secret War 4–9 (2018).

a motion supporting government policy.[8] For the first time, parliamentary debate and vote occurred *prior* to the deployment,[9] even though a parliamentary vote was not considered to be a constitutional requirement at the time.

However, the vote turned out not to be such a high watermark of democratic control of the war powers as it seemed. The approval of the war in Iraq has haunted Parliament, governments, and the British public. As it was subsequently and successively revealed and finally authoritatively confirmed by the Chilcot Report in 2016,[10] the "case for war" had not only *not* been made out because the point of last resort had not been reached, but the government had actively misled Parliament about intelligence, the threat of chemical weapons, and the legal advice of the attorney general. In spite of the involvement of Parliament in the decision to go to war, the Chilcot Report also criticized the informal decision-making structures that eliminated challenge of government decisions ("ad hoc Cabinet committee," "sofa government") and motivating factors external to the decision of the then Labour Government of Tony Blair (e.g., the relationship with the United States), as well as the "strategic failure" in Iraq, due to a lack of planning and preparation in particular for the post-invasion phase. In other words, rather than unequivocally confirming the value of democratic participation in a decision so fundamental as to go to war, the Iraq vote also revealed a number of problems with involving Parliament in decisions about military deployment.

After the Iraq vote, practice was not consistent with regard to a parliamentary vote. Most notably, the deployment to Afghanistan 2001–2014 was not subject to a government-tabled debate or vote. Even when in 2006 there was a major extension of the engagement in Helmand province, Parliament was not involved.[11] Nevertheless, events from around 2011 onward consolidated a constitutional convention requiring a parliamentary vote.

Emergence of a Constitutional Convention

The emergence of a convention occurred in the context of an ongoing political and public debate about the executive's war powers, kept live by the Chilcot Inquiry. Until 2016, the specter of the Iraq war led to a spate of reform proposals to regulate war powers either by convention, resolution, or statute. These mechanisms of regulation differ in the degree of their legally binding character and the extent to which they might be subject to adjudication by courts. The ultimate arbiter of a constitutional convention is the executive. A parliamentary resolution would create a binding rule about the procedure under which Parliament would be involved in deployment decisions. This

[8] 412 to 149 votes.

[9] HC Deb. (Mar. 18, 2003), Vol. 419, c703; *see* adjournment debate, HC Deb. (Sept. 24, 2002), Vol. 410, cc24-25, in which the procedural question was raised.

[10] Report of the Iraq Inquiry (HC 264, July 6, 2016).

[11] The Backbench Business Committee scheduled a debate in 2010, which ended with a vote supporting continued presence. HC Deb. (Sept. 9, 2010), Vol. 515, c494.

would remove the procedure (and triggering criteria) from the executive's discretion and would be likely to create a stronger expectation of compliance. A statute would provide binding rules and the greatest potential for judicial involvement. How far this would materialize in practice would depend on the scope of the statute and the extent of judicial restraint.[12]

In its 2004 review of prerogative powers, the House of Commons Select Committee on Public Administration concluded that prerogative powers, including war powers, should be put on a statutory basis.[13] The House Lords Constitution Committee proposed a convention in 2006,[14] reiterated in 2013,[15] while the House of Commons Political and Constitutional Reform Committee strongly disagreed, calling for legislation in 2014,[16] after having suggested an incremental approach in 2011, progressing from a reference to the convention in the Cabinet Manual, to resolution, and statute.[17] It reiterated its call for a resolution and submitted a draft in 2014.[18]

Successive governments put the reform of war powers on their agenda.[19] The constitutional reform package of 2008 put forward a draft resolution,[20] an approach that the Joint Select Committee on the Draft Constitutional Renewal Bill endorsed.[21]

Although some of the steps toward a convention were taken, none of the proposals for formalization were implemented. In 2016, the government announced that it was not seeking further formalization of the convention "in order to retain the ability of this and future Governments and the armed forces to protect the security and interests of

[12] *See also* Monica Hakimi, *Techniques for Regulating Military Force*, ch. 41 in this volume.

[13] House of Commons Select Committee on Public Administration, *Taming the Prerogative: Strengthening Ministerial Accountability to Parliament*, HC 422 (Mar. 4, 2004), paras. 18ff. *See also* draft bill by the Specialist Adviser, Rodney Brazier, appendices to the report, and Government Response of July 2004.

[14] House of Lords Select Committee on the Constitution, *Waging War: Parliament's Role and Responsibility*, HL 236-I and 236-II (2006).

[15] House of Lords Constitution Committee, *Constitutional Arrangements for the Use of Armed Force*, HL 46 (2013).

[16] Political and Constitutional Reform Committee, *Parliament's Role in Conflict Decisions: The Way Forward*, HC 892 (2014), paras. 4 and 9.

[17] *Id.*, para. 21; Political and Constitutional Reform Committee, *Parliament's Role in Conflict Decisions*, HC 923 (2011), paras. 6 and 7.

[18] Political and Constitutional Reform Committee, *The Work of the Committee in the 2010 Parliament*, HC 1128, para. 24. For the text of the draft Resolution, *see supra* note 16 and HC Deb. (June 19, 2014) Vol. 582, c129WH.

[19] Governments of Blair, Brown, the Cameron coalition government of 2010, which expressed its intention to create a statute. *See* Foreign Secretary William Hague, HC Deb. (Mar. 21, 2011), Vol. 525, c799.

[20] Ministry of Justice, *The Governance of Britain—Constitutional Renewal* (White Paper) (Cm 7342-I, 2008), para. 210. *See* Annex A for a draft resolution that provided that no approval would be required in emergency situations, where it would affect the effectiveness of the operation, security, or safety of the armed forces, or where it concerned special forces.

[21] Joint Committee on the Draft Constitutional Renewal Bill, *Draft Constitutional Renewal Bill* (July 31, 2008), Vol. 1: Report, HC 551-I.

the U.K. in circumstances that we cannot predict, and to avoid such decisions becoming subject to legal action."[22]

The convention further crystallized during events in 2011, around the time of the U.K. intervention in Libya. Because of the specifics of the situation, the evidence supports the emerging constitutional convention only in hindsight from a post-2013 (Syria) perspective. Assessing it at the time, it had to be considered inconclusive,[23] with the Iraq vote of 2003 remaining the only precedent. In 2011, the government participated in the policing of the no-fly zones imposed over Libyan airspace without a prior debate or vote in Parliament. However, three days into the deployment, it put a motion in front of Parliament to "support" government action in Libya, which was passed by an overwhelming majority.[24] Similarly, the British support of the French intervention in Mali in 2013 was not put to a prior debate or vote.

However, the Coalition Government, and also the Leader of the House,[25] had accepted the existence of a constitutional convention on several occasions around that time, and a reference was included in the 2011 Cabinet Manual:

> A convention has developed in the House that before troops are committed, the House should have an opportunity to debate the matter. We propose to observe that convention except when there is an emergency and such action would not be appropriate. As with the Iraq war and other events, we propose to give the House the opportunity to debate the matter before troops are committed.[26]

The lack of prior parliamentary involvement in the interventions in Libya and Mali was explained under the terms of the convention, rather than by denying its existence. Both interventions were argued to fall under the emergency exception. In relation to Mali, it was also emphasized that troops were not involved in combat roles, which arguably would place the deployment outside the scope of the convention.[27]

Vote against Using Force against Syria in 2013

The constitutional convention was unequivocally affirmed by the parliamentary vote in 2013, rejecting intervention in Syria, following reports of the use of chemical weapons against civilians. The relevant part of the rejected motion was that the House:

> Agrees that a strong humanitarian response is required from the international community and that this may, if necessary, require military action that is legal,

[22] Written Statement by then Secretary of State for Defense Michael Fallon on Apr. 18, 2016, HCWS678.

[23] *See* Claire Mills, *Parliamentary Approval for Military Action*, HC Briefing Paper No. 7166 (May 8, 2018), at 26 for an overview of commentators doubtful about the existence of a convention.

[24] 557 to 13 votes.

[25] Sir George Young, HC Deb. (Mar. 10, 2011), Vol. 524 cc 1066.

[26] The Cabinet Manual, para. 5.38.

[27] HC Deb. (Jan. 14, 2013), Vol. 556, cc621–2.

> proportionate and focused on saving lives by preventing and deterring further use of Syria's chemical weapons.[28]

This was a constitutional "first." For the first time, Parliament defeated a government's motion to go to war, and, crucially for the affirmation of a convention, the government respected this decision. Prime Minister Cameron stated:

> It is very clear tonight that, while the House has not passed a motion, it is clear to me that the British parliament, reflecting the views of the British people, does not want to see British military action. I get that and the government will act accordingly.[29]

This statement, by a prime minister in Parliament, was a milestone in the attempts to restrict the royal prerogative to go to war and hence for a democratic foundation of a decision of far-reaching significance. With hindsight, this moment crystallized a constitutional convention that had been in the making for some time.

The votes approving two further deployments against ISIL in Iraq 2014 upon request of the Iraqi government,[30] and Syria after attacks on British tourists in Tunisia and the Paris attacks in 2015,[31] consolidated the existence of a constitutional convention. Notably, the motion upon which Parliament voted explicitly was limited to "taking military action, specifically airstrikes, exclusively against ISIL in Syria."[32]

However, when Theresa May's government launched airstrikes against Syria on April 14, 2018, following the use of chemical weapons by the Syrian government, there was no prior parliamentary debate or vote. This cast again some doubts on how solidly established the convention is and on its precise scope, and reignited the academic and political debate about the need for a statutory regime.[33] Commentators are divided over whether the action fell within the convention's emergency exception and whether ex post approval is dispensable in relation to emergency situations, as the government claims,[34] or whether it was a breach of the convention with the potential to erode it.

This debate about the convention demonstrates unresolved issues about its clarity and precise content. Although there have been only a limited number of military deployments since Iraq in which the issue of parliamentary approval has been discussed, the following section will demonstrate that the convention continues to lack clarity, in particular with respect to the threshold of the convention and the scope of exceptions.

[28] David Cameron, HC Deb. (Aug. 29, 2013), Vol. 566, c1425.

[29] *Id.* at cc1555–6 (emphasis added). [30] By 543 to 43 votes. [31] By 397 to 223 votes.

[32] HC Deb. (Dec. 2, 2015), Vol. 603, c323.

[33] Maya Oppenheim, *Syria bombing: Jeremy Corbyn calls for War Powers Act to limit government's ability to launch air strikes without asking MPs first*, The Independent (Apr. 15, 2018).

[34] HC Deb. (Apr. 17, 2018), Vol. 639, cc201, 203.

II. Threshold and Scope of a Parliamentary Approval Requirement

A House of Commons Briefing Paper, in attempting to sum up the present state of the convention, explains that it applies under the following conditions:[35]

- There is a possibility of premeditated military action.
- Deployment occurs in an offensive capacity (excluding training, humanitarian, or logistical assistance; escalation of noncombat to offensive operations—"mission creep"—requires approval).
- Retrospective debate is sufficient in emergency situations (to prevent a humanitarian catastrophe or where "critical British national interest" is at stake). After the Syria airstrikes of April 2018, it is unclear whether any, and if so, which, emergency situations require retrospective approval.[36]
- The government must call debate as soon as possible if the House is in recess at the time of deployment.

The Threshold Criterion

The core scenario requiring parliamentary approval may be described as *premeditated* military action in an *offensive* capacity. Beyond that, it is unclear how the threshold of a deployment requiring approval is defined. Descriptively, no approval was sought for humanitarian assistance and the mere provision of logistical support in Iraq.[37]

Early on in the debate over the scope of the convention, some proposals focused on the nature of the situation, e.g., whether it fell within the international law of armed conflict,[38] a criterion that did not seem practical given the more fluid nature of present-day military deployments.[39] In the context of the Libya intervention 2011, the government referred to requiring approval by the House of Commons "before

[35] Mills, *supra* note 23, at 5–6, 34–36. *See also infra* note 36.

[36] Mills, *supra* note 23, at 4, 32–33 (May 12, 2015, version) still states that retrospective *approval* would be required, but sufficient in emergency situations, but dropped the requirement from the May 8, 2018, version: "the Convention does not explicitly commit the Government to a vote in such [emergency] situations, merely the opportunity to debate the issue." (at 36). This change in the Parliamentary Briefing Paper was made after only one deployment, the April 2018 airstrikes in Syria where no retrospective vote was taken.

[37] This may be inferred from the fact that humanitarian operations in Iraq were not subject to parliamentary approval, but air strikes contemplated later in the autumn of 2014 were.

[38] *See* Clare Short's private members bill, *Armed Forces (Parliamentary Approval for Participation in Armed Conflict) Bill*, June 2005, and the draft resolution of the constitutional reform package (*supra*, note 20).

[39] *See also* Joseph, *supra* note 1, at 201–202.

troops are committed."[40] If this described the scope of the convention, it was potentially[41] narrowed in 2013 when referring to "before troops are committed *to conflict*."[42] This could be understood in two possible ways: as limiting the approval requirement to situations where troops are actually *committed to combat*[43] (in a premeditated, offensive capacity) or as referring to the nature of the operation in a *wider sense* of a deployment abroad with a possibility or degree of likelihood of armed activities. The former seems to have emerged as the government's position (though based on limited practice), in view of the deployment of the training and military advisory mission to Ukraine in 2015,[44] and a logistical assistance mission after the Ebola outbreak in Sierra Leone in 2014. In both cases no debate or approval was sought.[45] But a wider reading of what amounts to "conflict" arguably could still fall within the meaning of the word and cross the threshold of the convention.[46]

Scope of the Convention

There are a number of issues relating to the scope of the convention that have yet to be conclusively determined. They relate partly to more technical aspects of the approval requirement, such as the duration of the approval and repeat deployments, and the appropriate way of dealing with evolving situations ("mission creep"). In addition, there are ongoing debates relating to approval in situations of collective security, multilateral, or integrated units. The most significant "open" questions concern whether certain scenarios are a priori excluded from the convention because of the nature of the deployment, in the case of drones and missions of special forces; and the definition of "emergency" situations that might allow exceptions from the convention, and the rules applicable to emergency situations.

Duration of Approval

The question of the duration of the approval has not been raised in U.K. practice. Two principles can be drawn upon to define the scope of the convention: the principle that deployments require prior approval as a rule, and the fact that the scope of the

[40] Leader of the House, Sir George Young, MP, HC Deb. (Mar. 10, 2011), Vol. 524, c1066.

[41] As the debate in 2011 referred to the specific deployment to Libya, the omission of a reference committing troops "to conflict" does not necessarily imply that a wider scope of the convention was assumed.

[42] HC Deb. (Jan. 31, 2013) Vol. 557, cc1059–1060.

[43] In this sense, *see* ROWE, *supra* note 2, at 96.

[44] *See* statement by Michael Fallon, HC Deb. (Feb. 25, 2015), Vol. 593, c327.

[45] *See* answer of Development Secretary Justine to written question 212430—Sierra Leone (Nov. 5, 2014).

[46] For a wider reading ("any significant deployment of forces"), *see* Nigel White, Written Evidence to the Political and Constitutional Reform Committee Inquiry: *Parliament's Role in Conflict Decisions: A Way Forward* (PCD01, Oct. 10, 2013), para. 22.

authorization of a use of military force can be defined in the authorizing act. The authorization, which would depend on the government's motion, may specify a temporary limit in order to review the situation at a certain point in time. Likewise, repeat deployments, which meet the threshold criterion of the convention, ought to be considered as coming within the full scope of the convention if not authorized by an earlier approval.

Although a case of "mission creep" (a material change of an existing mission or escalation of conflict) has not yet arisen, the position of the government may be gleaned by then defense secretary Michael Fallon's statement that if a training mission to Ukraine were to become an offensive military operation, approval would be sought.[47] The logic of the convention would also require that a deployment, which crosses the convention threshold only at a later time because of subsequent developments, would require approval.

Collective Security and Integrated Multilateral Units

Whether deployments in a collective security or multilateral context (e.g., United Nations, NATO) fall within the scope of the convention has been debated in different contexts where British forces might be integrated into multilateral forces and command structures outside of the national context.

In relation to collective security, the U.K. government has suggested that the existence of a UN Security Council resolution authorizing the use of force means that no parliamentary approval is needed. The scenario arose with regard to the 2013 Mali deployment. However, the noncombat role of U.K. troops was considered to be the main argument against a parliamentary approval requirement, which makes the Mali deployment an inconclusive precedent.[48] It may be noted that parliamentary approval for the Libya intervention was obtained (retrospectively) even though a Security Council resolution existed.

While the mere deployment as part of other forces or integrated units (or command staff centers such as NATO) may not be sufficient to trigger the convention, the threshold should be considered crossed, and parliamentary consent required, when the U.K. troops actually participate in armed operations,[49] in whatever form of integration. The decisive factor is the crossing of the convention threshold by British military, not in which context it is crossed. The need for flexibility can be taken into account in the terms and scope of the authorization.

Embedding of Armed Forces

The bilateral integration of soldiers into another unit in individual short-term missions, such as the participation of U.K. troops in airstrikes in Syria flying in U.S. aircraft,

[47] HC Deb. (Feb. 25, 2015), Vol. 593, c327. Similarly also the Leader of the House regarding a potential escalation of the Mali deployment, Andrew Lansley, HC Deb. (Jan. 31, 2013), Vol. 557, cc1059–1060.

[48] *See* discussion *supra* in the text accompanying note 27.

[49] *Cf.* Rowe, *supra* note 2, at 75 n.45.

wearing U.S. uniforms,[50] also has raised the question of when parliamentary approval is required. Parliament had approved only action against ISIL in Iraq at the time (2014) and explicitly excluded air strikes in Syria.[51]

Then defense secretary Michael Fallon contended that personnel embedded in other forces fall outside the scope of the convention, because:

> they operate as if they were the host nation's personnel, under that nation's chain of command, while remaining subject to UK domestic, international and host nation law. This is in line with international practice. To do so otherwise would risk undermining the usefulness and viability of these exchanges.[52]

Contrary to this position, embedded personnel should be treated in the same way as collective security/integrated unit scenarios discussed above. It follows already from the fact that embedded personnel remain subject to U.K. law that it is subject to the parliamentary convention. To allow otherwise, and to make the approval requirement depend on whose weaponry and aircraft are used and whose operational orders are followed, would open the door to strategic avoidance of the approval requirement.

The Emergency Exception

The government invoked an emergency exception in the contexts of the intervention in Libya 2011, the assistance to France in Mali in 2013, for the targeted killing by drone of terrorist fighters, e.g., Mohammed Emwazi ("Jihadi John") in Syria in 2015, and for airstrikes in April 2018 in response to the use of chemical weapons in Syria by the Assad regime. The problem with the emergency exception is not so much its existence but its lack of clarity in two ways: first, the definition of its scope, and second, Parliament's role, in particular whether retrospective parliamentary approval is required, or merely a debate.[53]

The definition of "emergency" is not uniform and language varies. The Cabinet Manual of 2011 refers to an exception to the convention "when there is an emergency and such action would not be appropriate."[54] In other contexts, in addition to referring to an emergency, it has invoked a "humanitarian catastrophe," "national security," and, more broadly, the "national interest," "critical British national interest," or "national

[50] Loulla-Mae Eleftheriou-Smith, *SAS troops "dressed in US uniforms and joined special forces on Isis Abu Sayyaf overnight raid in Syria,"* The Independent (Aug. 10, 2015).

[51] HC Deb. (Sept. 26, 2014), Vol. 585, c1265. Air strikes in against ISIL in Syria were only authorized in December 2015. *See supra* note 32.

[52] HC Written Statement 678, Armed Forces Update (Apr. 18, 2016).

[53] The Cabinet Manual only refers to debate, but many ministerial statements refer to debate *and vote*. *See supra* text at note 26. The varied language is likely to be an attempt to keep flexibility for emergency situations and not a principled challenge to the parliamentary approval by vote.

[54] *See supra* note 26.

security interest" or "security and interests of the UK."[55] Theresa May justified the airstrikes in Syria in April 2018 by reference to both the humanitarian catastrophe and the national interest[56] in taking a stand against the use of chemical weapons and deterring their future use.[57] The vagueness and loose use of the terms give much latitude to the government.

The vagueness of the criteria is compounded by uncertainty about Parliament's role in emergencies. Before April 2018, it was probably thought that retrospective approval of emergency situations was required under the convention, as statements by David Cameron suggest.[58] But the Cameron government did not schedule a vote after the killing by drone of U.K. national Reyad Khan in Syria in 2015,[59] and neither did May's government after the airstrikes in April 2018. Her insistence that she had done what was required[60] cast doubts on the requirements and scope of the convention in emergency scenarios and the need for retrospective approval. The immediacy with which the convention is described as having changed[61] also demonstrates its volatility and potential for executive bias.

Not to require retrospective approval in concluded emergency situations seems at first sight a very narrow and sensible exception to the approval requirement. However, it could significantly undermine the convention. First, many present-day deployments

[55] Then defense secretary Michael Fallon referred to the need of the government to retain flexibility about "how best to protect the security and interests of the UK," *supra* note 22; then prime minister David Cameron in the 2014 Syria debate: "if there were a critical British national interest at stake or there were the need to act to prevent a humanitarian catastrophe," HC Deb. (Sept. 26, 2014) c1265; "to prevent an immediate humanitarian catastrophe or, indeed, secure a really important, unique British interest," HC Deb. (Sept. 8, 2014) c663.

[56] "It was necessary to strike with speed so we could allow our Armed Forces to act decisively, maintain the vital security of their operations, and protect the security and interests of the UK." Prime Minister's Office Press release *Syria action—background. Background to the military action taken by the UK along with France and the United States on 14 April 2018* (Apr. 15, 2018), *available at* https://www.gov.uk/government/news/syria-action-background?utm_source=2705c1e3-5ba2-49ed-8855-290ca2faca2a&utm_medium=email&utm_campaign=govuk-notifications&utm_content=immediate.

[57] Prime Minister's press conference statement on Syria, Apr. 14, 2018, *available at* https://www.gov.uk/government/speeches/pms-press-conference-statement-on-syria-14-april-2013?utm_source=a18d4dfb-d36f-41b9-9643-a1ea29afdae4&utm_medium=email&utm_campaign=govuk-notifications&utm_content=immediate.

[58] HC Deb. (Sept. 12, 2014), Vol. 585, c1193: "the Government, while wanting to put such a matter to Parliament, including for a vote, as rapidly as possible, will need the freedom to act in the case of an urgent threat to the security of the United Kingdom or of an impending humanitarian disaster, and to come to the House as soon as possible after such action."

[59] The government relied on self-defense of the U.K. territory as the international legal basis, and this may have influenced how it saw Parliament's role. For a critical review, questioning, among other things, the immediacy of the threat, *see* Intelligence and Security Committee, *UK Lethal Drone Strikes in Syria*, HC 1152 (Apr. 26, 2017), para. 30.

[60] Namely, to have a debate in Parliament (*see supra* note 57): "if it is the case that a decision is taken without that prior consideration by Parliament, the Prime Minister should come at the first possible opportunity to the House, which is what I have done."

[61] The Parliamentary Briefing Paper was changed immediately after the April 2018 events, dropping the vote requirement from the convention. *See supra* note 36.

will be, using Theresa May's words,[62] "limited, targeted . . . [strikes] with clear boundaries," and hence fall into this category. Second, the uncertainties about the definition of the emergency exception, especially the loose term "national interest," make the exception prone to wide interpretation. Third, the potential exclusion from the convention of two types of operations (drones and special forces) would bypass the convention further, although these operations should be framed in the context and by the standards of the emergency exception.

Drones

It has been speculated that the government might argue for excluding drones from the convention on the basis that no troops are physically deployed to a theater of conflict.[63] The government has not done so explicitly, but neither has it confirmed that the convention applies. The government's justifications of targeted killings seem to refer to the emergency exception—for example, Cameron, when justifying the policy.[64] As the parliamentary Joint Committee on Human Rights affirmed, the prime minister's statement must be seen in the context of the convention on parliamentary approval of military use of force abroad:[65] the deployment of drones is a type of military force that is not a priori excluded but must meet the conditions for an exception.

Special Forces

Special forces have been widely considered to be exempt from the convention.[66] The rationale for a blanket exclusion is not clearly articulated, but seems to relate to a confluence of a number of factors: the presumed situation of urgency and need for secrecy where special forces are deployed, and the fact that currently special forces are not subject to meaningful parliamentary scrutiny.[67] This leads to far-reaching

[62] *See supra* note 57.

[63] Veronika Fikfak, *The Convention as a Battlefield*, *in* PARLIAMENT'S SECRET WAR, *supra* note 7, at 67, 98–99.

[64] Statement by the Prime Minister, HC Deb. (Nov. 17, 2015), Vol. 602, c538 (emphasis added) in a debate about the parliamentary approval of military action in Syria: "I have always said very clearly at this Dispatch Box that, in the case of premeditated action—for instance, against ISIL in Syria—it is right that we have a debate and a vote, and I am happy to repeat that. However, when action *in the national interest* needs to be taken very quickly and rapidly, and when *confidentiality* is needed before taking it, I reserve the right to do so and am prepared to act. That is what I did in the case of Hussain and Khan with the UK drone strike and, obviously, in the case of Emwazi, where we worked hand in glove with the Americans. *I think it was right to take that action and to explain afterwards, but I will try to stick to that clear demarcation.* I think that is the right approach for our country."

[65] Joint Committee on Human Rights, *The Government's policy on the use of drones for targeted killing*, HC 574, HL Paper 141 (May 10, 2016) 6, 32–35.

[66] Both the 2008 White Paper, *supra* note 20, and the draft resolution of the House of Commons Political and Constitutional Reform Committee, *supra* note 16 at Annex 1, at 61, 67 (point 5), excluded special forces.

[67] Liam Walpole & Megan Karlshoej-Pedersen, *Britain's Shadow Army: Policy Options for External Oversight of UK Special Forces* (Report of the Oxford Research Group Remote Warfare Programme, April 2018).

limitations of access to intelligence by Parliament and its committees in governmental practice.[68] The lack of parliamentary scrutiny mechanisms for special forces in the United Kingdom must be considered in the light of a trend in recent years that saw both the numbers of and the budget for special forces significantly increased.[69] This reflects a shift in military strategy, which can lead to bypassing parliamentary scrutiny, and which has prompted calls to include special forces in the convention or a war powers act.[70] This would mean that special forces would not be exempt a priori from parliamentary approval and scrutiny, but only where the conditions of an emergency situation are met.

III. Comparative Assessment

Comparative analysis can help to identify alternatives and possible solutions, both as positive and negative examples. For example, the House of Lords Select Committee on the Constitution, in its 2005-2006 inquiry on *Waging War: Parliament's Role and Responsibility*, took extensive evidence on the legal regimes governing military deployment,[71] while also considering arguments challenging the usefulness of comparison.[72]

The significant differences with respect to constitutional law, government institutions, interbranch divisions of power, political and societal cultures, historic experiences, and propensity and power to deploy military force may limit the value of comparisons. But there is at least one general benefit. Comparative approaches, when applied in a considerate way, can function as a kind of laboratory. They allow reflection on variables and to make predictions of consequences that may "depoliticize" a subject matter, in particular one that is politically charged like the use of force. Comparisons may also reveal trends of restricting the use of force in other democratic constitutional states. Trends are important empirically and in order to evaluate normative claims against actual practice. From a normative perspective, it is important to consider why such trends may arise, what constitutional reasons and policy justifications exist, and whether they are supported by actual practice. It must be asked whether and how far

[68] *See*, e.g., the criticisms in the (highly redacted) report of the Intelligence and Security Committee, *UK Lethal Drone Strikes in Syria*, HC 1152 (Apr. 26, 2017).

[69] Walpole & Karlshoej-Pedersen, *supra* note 67.

[70] Ewen MacAskill, *Special forces need to face scrutiny from parliament, say MPs. SAS and other elite units operate without democratic oversight—unlike MI5, MI6 and GCHQ*, The Guardian (Apr. 24, 2018); Nadia Khomami, *Jeremy Corbyn calls for law to limit PM's powers to deploy special forces*, The Guardian (Aug. 1, 2016); Jon Moran, *Time to Move out of the Shadows? Special Operations Forces and Accountability in Counterterrorism and Counter-Insurgency Operations*, 39 UNSW Law Journal 1239 (2016).

[71] *See supra* note 14, at, for example, Vol. I, at 49 ff, Volume II: Evidence.

[72] *See, e.g.*, *id.*, Vol. I, para. 19 and Appendix: Note on international comparisons by Specialist Adviser Colin Warbrick, at 49 ff, para. 4.

normative conclusions are merely descriptive of facts or historical practice or based on theoretical frameworks and normative values (and what these are).

Comparatively, the overall trend[73] reflects increasing accountability in both the democratic and rule of law dimensions of accountability. In part this is because parallel legal responses are triggered by specific events where international or national law is considered to have failed. Since the Iraq War of 2003, France,[74] Spain,[75] and the United Kingdom have enhanced their parliamentary involvement in deployment decisions.[76] The genocides in Srebrenica and Rwanda have generated new accountability mechanisms or activated existing ones.[77]

A comparison with the chiseling out of the war powers regime in Germany is illuminating from a U.K. perspective. Although there are many differences that limit the value of such a comparison, in particular the involvement of a strong constitutional court in Germany in shaping the rules, there are a number of parallels with German experience in regard to the method of creation or emergence of a parliamentary approval requirement, the definition of criteria for its threshold, scope, and exceptions, and the identification of constitutional principles underpinning the war powers regime. Furthermore, conclusions may be drawn from the role of the courts, which are potentially relevant to the United Kingdom.

Emergence of the Approval Requirement and Constitutional Justification

There are similarities in the evolutionary nature of creating a parliamentary approval requirement. Contrary to what one might have expected, Germany did not have

[73] *See*, for a survey, Sandra Dietrich, Hartwig Hummel, & Stefan Marschall, *Parliamentary War Powers: A Survey of 25 European Parliaments*, Geneva Centre for the Democratic Control of Armed Forces (DCAF), Occasional Paper no. 21 (2010). The 2010 study maps criteria of parliamentary involvement in European states on a simplified scale from "very weak" to "very strong" parliamentary war powers. Since this classification, at least three European states included in the study (United Kingdom, France, Spain) have increased the involvement of their parliaments in deployment decisions. France must be considered to have moved up from "very weak" to "weak," Spain from weak to strong, and the United Kingdom probably from very weak to strong (with some uncertainty due to the evolving nature of the convention).

[74] Since the amendment of art. 35 of the constitution by the 2008 reform, Parliament must be informed and allowed debate and vote on extensions of missions beyond four months, *see* in more detail Mathias Forteau, *Using Military Force and Engaging in Collective Security: The Case of France*, ch. 45 in this volume, at p.815.

[75] Organic Law 5/2005 of Nov. 17, 2005 on National Defense (translation by John Bell in HL Constitution Committee Inquiry, *supra* note 14, at 52–53).

[76] Dietrich, Hummel, & Marschall, *supra* note 73.

[77] *See*, e.g., Cedrick Ryngaert & Nico Schijver, *Lessons Learned from the Srebrenica Masssacre: From UN Peacekeeping Reform to Legal Responsibility*, 62 NETH. INT'L L. REV. 219 (2015); Otto Spijkers, *Questions of Legal Responsibility before the Dutch Courts*, 14 J. OF INT'L CRIM. J. 819 (2014).

explicit constitutional rules on military deployment decisions.[78] Such rules were developed by interpretation in an ad hoc way when needed when Germany first started deploying armed forces outside of the United Nations in the former Yugoslavia and Somalia in the 1990s. They bear the characteristics of a political compromise.[79]

The initial constitutional justification was a specific one of a more technical nature, relying on rather specialized constitutional rules dealing with (other) aspects of oversight and accountability of the military.[80] Only over time was the constitutional rationale of deployment decisions clarified and related to broader fundamental constitutional principles as "normalization" of foreign policy became more accepted.[81] In later decisions, the Federal Constitutional Court has shifted toward a conceptually more convincing account, rooting the approval requirement in the constitutional significance of the decision and ultimately in the democratic principle and rights-based rationale for the requirement of parliamentary approval.[82] This anchoring in constitutional principle is important in that it guides the interpretation of the parliamentary approval requirement.

Defining the Threshold and Scope of the Approval Requirement

Even though the German Parliamentary Participation Act 2005 (PPA) codified the constitutional rules, there was still a significant need for interpretation of the parliamentary approval requirement. Details needed to be fleshed out by interpretation in an incremental fashion, not too dissimilar to the evolution of the convention in U.K. practice, the main difference being that the constitutional court acts as a final arbiter.

A comparative perspective on the experience with threshold criteria reveals that Germany also grappled with clarifying the threshold requirement in the light of the general wording of the statute. The consent requirement is triggered under the terms of the Act by the "deployment of armed forces," which is further defined as "involvement or anticipated involvement . . . in armed operations."[83] The risk of armed engagement is an indicator for when involvement may be anticipated.[84]

[78] As Germany was demilitarized and its international sovereignty limited when the Basic Law was drafted in 1948–1949.

[79] The compromise may be considered to read into the constitution a constitutional power of the government to deploy the armed forces beyond the scope of self-defense of the territory, but to limit that power at the same time by requiring parliamentary consent. Katja S. Ziegler, *AWACS I (Ger)*, *in* Max Planck Encyclopedia of Comparative Constitutional Law (Rainer Grote et al. eds., Oxford University Press, online database), para. 16.

[80] BVerfGE 90, 286, 382 ff (*AWACS I*); Ziegler, *supra* note 79, paras. 16, 29–32.

[81] Ziegler, *supra* note 79.

[82] BVerfGE 121, 135 (*AWACS II*), para. 70 f; *see also* BVerfGE 123, 267 (*Lisbon Treaty*), para. 254, both available in English translation at https://www.bverfg.de; Ziegler, *supra* note 79.

[83] Sec. 1 PPA.

[84] *Id.*, Sec. 2(1); BVerfGE 90, 286, 388 (*AWACS I*).

The threshold criterion is thus the action of the "deployment" and the possible involvement in armed activities, not the type of conflict per se, as was debated initially in the United Kingdom. Although not identical, and possibly using a slightly lower threshold than the United Kingdom at present,[85] it points in the same direction in that the *form of involvement* of the military is key, *not the situation in the abstract*. Such an approach was considered to be a "sensible solution" in the United Kingdom[86] and may serve as an example for the usefulness of a comparative approach in rule formation in the context of a convention (by analogy to statutory drafting) and reflection on possible regulatory choices.[87] Such a reflection is not a one-way street, but may also lead to rule-affirmation where a certain approach has been considered to be convincing.

The definition of the threshold criteria is squarely shared by the United Kingdom and Germany, with respect to humanitarian assistance or support operations that do not require parliamentary consent. Mere support missions where arms are carried only for self-defense purposes would also fall outside the scope of the PPA.[88] The Mali operation, for which the U.K. government did not seek parliamentary approval, may be used as an example. The United Kingdom supported France logistically with surveillance aircraft and troops to train forces in the African-led International Support Mission in Mali (AFISMA), but arms were carried only for self-defense.

In contrast, the integration of the military in collective security mechanisms or foreign or international units is not treated differently from other deployments under the PPA. Parliamentary consent is necessary if the intensity threshold of deployment is met. Although similar concerns have been raised to those in the United Kingdom about the "interoperability" with other troops and a greater need for flexibility, in particular in the context of the European rapid reaction force, these appear less widespread. A review of the PPA in 2015[89] concluded that no exception to the deployment threshold was necessary but recommended some soft measures aimed at raising awareness, both with international military partners about national procedures and with German parliamentarians about the alliance commitments. The Commission also concluded that the way government requests for consent were drafted could help to provide authorizations with flexibility, for example in the context of UN actions.[90]

The comparative perspective on the PPA reveals a narrower scope of the emergency exception, which is cast in language reminiscent of police powers. The Act requires an "imminent danger, which allows no scope for delay" or "operations whose purpose is to rescue persons from particularly dangerous situations, provided that

[85] Possibly the United Kingdom requires a greater immediacy to combat operations than the mere risk of involvement, but this cannot be said with certainty at present.

[86] E.g., JOSEPH, *supra* note 1, at 203; White, *supra* note 46, para. 21.

[87] *See also* Curtis A. Bradley, *U.S. War Powers and the Potential Benefits of Comparativism*, ch. 42 in this volume, at p.766.

[88] Sec. 2(2).

[89] By the *Rühe Commission*, named after its chair, former defense secretary Volker Rühe. For its report, *see* Deutscher Bundestag, Drucksache 18/5000 (June 16, 2015).

[90] Report, *supra* note 89, at 31–33.

the holding of a public debate in the Bundestag would endanger the lives of the persons in need of rescue."[91]

The PPA is also clear in requiring not just ex post information, but retrospective approval. Failing that, an ongoing deployment needs to be terminated. Nevertheless, not so dissimilar to the debate in the United Kingdom regarding targeted killings and the Syria strikes in April 2018, the German Federal Constitutional Court has distinguished ongoing from concluded emergency interventions. In its *Pegasus* judgment concerning a rescue mission in Libya in 2011,[92] it clarified that there is no need for retrospective approval where the deployment has already been concluded, although Parliament needs to be informed without delay in a detailed and meaningful way.[93]

Role of the Courts

There is a widespread concern in the United Kingdom that courts might review military deployment decisions. Some, therefore, reject the greater formalization of the convention to a resolution (with limited potential of judicial review[94]) or a statute (with somewhat greater "risk" of judicial involvement) outright. For others, the concern does not arise because of the solid track record of judicial restraint of U.K. courts in matters concerning foreign relations, especially the use of force.[95]

A comparative perspective might be useful in two respects. First, it demonstrates that a procedural review of the appropriate parliamentary involvement and a substantive review of the legality of the decision to deploy the military can be separated. The German Federal Constitutional Court has strictly confined its adjudicative competence to the procedural review of whether the Parliament's competence to approve a military deployment has been observed. Although the court has contributed to defining the boundaries of the approval requirement, it cannot be said that this has hindered the government to deploy the military or operational efficiency. In fact, the outcomes were not so dissimilar to those argued for by the U.K. government. However, the involvement of the court removed the executive bias from the rule formation/interpretation process, i.e., the judges "keep the Government and Parliament honest in the way they

[91] Sec. 5.

[92] BVerfGE 140, 160, paras. 95 ff., 99–101 (*Pegasus*). For critical analysis, *see* Dieter Wiefelspütz, Der Auslandseinsatz der Bundeswehr und das Parlamentsbeteiligungsgesetz 498 (2d ed. 2012). *See also* Anne Peters, *Military Operations Abroad under the German Basic Law*, ch. 44 in this volume.

[93] BVerfGE, *supra* note 92, paras. 70, 102–104.

[94] *See*, recently, R (Miller) v. Secretary of State for Exiting the European Union, [2017] UKSC 5, paras. 151, 145, in regard to the Sewel Convention: "judges . . . are neither the parents or guardians of political conventions; they are merely observers."

[95] R (on the application of the Campaign for Nuclear Disarmament) v. Prime Minister, [2002] EWHC 2777 (CND); R (Noor Kahn) v. Secretary of State for Foreign and Commonwealth Affairs, [2014] EWCA Civ 24. *See also* Bjorge & Miles, *supra* note 2.

interpret" the rules.[96] For the United Kingdom, this implies that a potential War Powers Act could be designed in a way, which could also limit how courts could get involved to procedural questions and "clear abuse of the process."[97]

Second, the comparative perspective also reveals that a procedural review does not necessarily lead to a substantive legality review of deployment decisions. Litigation resulting from military engagement of the United Kingdom based on individual rights are conceptually separate from the democratic dimension of parliamentary involvement in deployment decisions. The former concern accountability under the rule of law where soldiers or victims of U.K. state (military) power are bringing actions based on the alleged violation of subjective/individual rights.[98] In contrast, a possible adjudication of parliamentary involvement in the decision-making process would be about the competences of Parliament and the executive in terms of a procedural involvement.

Again, the example of the German Federal Constitutional Court might be considered to allay concerns: although rights-based review is part of the court's core business, it has not expanded its competence/procedural review in the context of military deployments into substantive review of the legality of a military deployment. Although parliamentary minorities have occasionally attempted such arguments,[99] the Constitutional Court has firmly rejected them in the context of the review of the competences of Parliament vis-à-vis the government. With the caveat of necessary caution when transplanting considerations from one legal order to another, this may at least give a general sense that the risk of spillover into a substantive legality review is perhaps somewhat overstated.

IV. Conclusion

While accountability is a central characteristic of a democratic constitutional state, many of the detailed rules about the democratic accountability of the government for deployment decisions in the United Kingdom are still in flux and contested. The evolutionary and fluid character of the subject matter is characteristic of a constitutional convention, which needs to form in a process over time.

The lack of definition and basic normative guidance of the present constitutional convention on core questions relating to war powers, however, raises the issue whether its subject matter is in fact suitable for mere regulation by convention,[100] as conventions create weak rules with the inherent problem of inferring normative claims from

[96] *Cf.* White, *supra* note 46, para. 19 (commenting on the potential role of U.K. courts).

[97] White, *supra* note 46, para. 17.

[98] E.g., Smith, Ellis and Allbutt and others v. Ministry of Defence, [2013] UKSC 41; Al-Skeini et al. v. United Kingdom, App. No. 55721/07 (GC), Reports 2011-IV.

[99] *See,* for details, Ziegler, *supra* note 79, paras. 33–35.

[100] On the difficulties of codifying conventions, *see* Andrew Blick, *The Cabinet Manual and the Codification of Conventions*, 67 Parliamentary Aff. 191 (2014).

practice. This creates an executive control over the rule formation process and substantive rules that is compounded in the United Kingdom by the greater malleability of interpretation-guiding substantive constitutional principles under an unwritten constitution and the absence of a formal mechanism of rule interpretation. Although a comparative perspective on the regime of the German Parliamentary Participation Act reveals largely parallel outcomes in Germany and the United Kingdom, the executive bias over war powers in the United Kingdom means that there are largely only political safeguards regarding the use of the war prerogative.

One of the main reasons for not going further and formalizing war powers in a statute are concerns about the courts' involvement.[101] These concerns may not be as powerful a counterargument as they have been considered to be in the debate about formalizing war powers in the United Kingdom.

[101] *See supra* note 14, Vol. I, para. 104; *supra* note 15, para. 54.

CHAPTER 44

MILITARY OPERATIONS ABROAD UNDER THE GERMAN BASIC LAW

ANNE PETERS

GERMAN history has produced a unique and complicated constitutional regime on the deployment of the German military abroad.[1] In acknowledgment of its responsibility for the wars of aggression initiated since 1939, and in line with the initial complete demilitarization of the country after its defeat in 1945, the state is constitutionally committed to world peace and to the renunciation on aggression.[2] At the same time, it has retained its right of national self-defense, and it is also an active participant in international institutions, including institutions that utilize military force. This chapter reviews the evolution and current state of German constitutional law, statutory law, and judicial decisions concerning the use of military force. This successful practice demonstrates that foreign relations law can be conducted in a democratic fashion and under judicial scrutiny, not categorically distinct from other areas of public law.

I. Constitutional and Statutory Framework

The German Constitution is referred to as the Basic Law. The most immediately relevant provisions in the Basic Law for military operations are Article 24(2) (dating

[1] For more detail, *see* Anne Peters, *Between Military Deployment and Democracy: Use of Force under the German Constitution*, 5 J. ON THE USE OF FORCE & INT'L L. 246 (2018).

[2] For the similar situation in Japan, *see* Tadashi Mori, *Decisions in Japan to Use Military Force or Participate in Multinational Peacekeeping Operations*, ch. 46 in this volume.

from 1949) and Article 87a GG on armed forces (in its current form dating from 1968). Further relevant constitutional provisions are Article 26 (the ban on a war of aggression) and Article 115a (declaration of state of defense). Article 24(2) GG provides: "With a view to maintaining peace, the Federation may enter into a system of mutual collective security; in doing so it shall consent to such limitations upon its sovereign powers as will bring about and secure a lasting peace in Europe and among the nations of the world." The relevant sections of Article 87a GG read: "(1) The Federation shall establish Armed Forces for purposes of defense. . . . (2) Apart from defense, the Armed Forces may be employed only to the extent expressly permitted by this Basic Law."

Article 87a(2) GG has so far always been considered as the second-best source of authority, as a residual constitutional basis for military operations abroad that cannot be called "collective" in the sense of Article 24(2) GG. And in fact, except for two evacuation operations (in Albania in 1997 and in Libya in 2011), Germany has so far never acted outside a multilateral scheme very broadly conceived (the United Nations and/or NATO, or at a minimum as part of a "coalition of the willing"). The government regularly cites Article 24(2) GG as the constitutional basis for the German participation in these operations. Before a seminal judgment by the Constitutional Court in 1994, however, scholarship struggled to bring in line the facially very restrictive Constitution, notably the seemingly clear wording of Article 87a GG, with the practice of military activity abroad (such as airborne monitoring and humanitarian aid) that emerged at the beginning of the 1990s.

Constitutional Court's Seminal 1994 Judgment

In its 1994 judgment,[3] the Constitutional Court clarified the key parameters both for the admissibility of military deployment (and the substantive requirements flowing from the choice of the legal basis), and the respective powers of government and Parliament when deciding on deployments.

This judgment was rendered in a dispute between constitutional organs[4] upon requests by two parliamentary factions and their members. It joined four proceedings concerning the German government's decisions to contribute to various military operations. All were authorized by the UN Security Council (partly mediated by implementation decisions of NATO and the Western European Union (WEU)), in two different settings: Yugoslavia and Somalia. Germany contributed planes, ships, and troops. For example, German soldiers participated in an integrated NATO unit in AWACS planes (Airborne Early Warning and Control System) to monitor the no-fly zone over Bosnia-Herzegovina, German ships patrolled the Mediterranean Sea to enforce an embargo against the then-Federation of Serbia and Montenegro, and

[3] BVerfGE 90, 286, judgment of July 12, 1994 - 2 BvE 3/92 -, - 2 BvE 5/93 -, - 2 BvE 7/93 -, - 2 BvE 8/93 -.

[4] *Organstreitverfahren*. For more detail on this type of proceeding, *see* sec. III *infra*.

German supply- and transport-battalions distributed humanitarian aid under UNOSOM II. Hence, the judgment dealt exclusively with military operations in the framework of international organizations proper (as opposed to unilateral action or coalitions of the willing).

As regards the constitutional admissibility of extraterritorial military activity and their legal basis, the Court made four points. First, NATO is a "system of mutual collective security" in the sense of Article 24(2) GG, even though the drafters had the United Nations in mind. Second, the parliamentary statute under Article 59(2) GG approving the German accession to NATO in 1955[5] also covers the incorporation of military staff into integrated units and their participation in military action conducted by NATO and under NATO command to the extent that such integration or participation has already been pitched in the founding treaty.[6] Third, in a kind of implied powers argumentation, the Court held that Article 24(2) GG, which expressly allows the German Federation to "enter" (*sich einordnen*) into such a system of mutual collective security, must implicitly likewise allow the country to assume those tasks that are typically connected to membership. This means—importantly—that Article 24(2) GG is also the constitutional basis for the use of the German armed forces in operations "insofar as these occur within and pursuant to the rules of such a system."[7] Fourth, Article 87a GG does not bar such operations.[8]

Having clarified that the German constitution allows extraterritorial military operations, the next set of findings by the Court concerns the constitutional powers of the executive and legislative branches in this matter. First, the out of area action under NATO's new strategy of 1991 did not require a parliamentary statute under Article 59(2) GG, because this new strategy did not constitute a treaty amendment.[9] However, the bench was split on this point. Four of the eight judges opined that the powers of Parliament were undermined by the purely executive development of NATO. In order to accommodate this concern, and to avoid allowing the executive branch to decide alone on military deployment, the Court ruled: "The Basic Law requires a constitutive parliamentary approval for any military deployment of armed forces."[10] This requirement corresponded to the constitutional tradition since 1918, the

[5] Art. 59(2) GG requires a parliamentary statute for the ratification of certain types of important international treaties, namely, those "that regulate the political relations of the Federation or relate to subjects of federal legislation." *See* Stefan Kadelbach, *International Treaties and the German Constitution*, ch. 10 in this volume.

[6] BVerfGE 90, 286, *supra* note 3, para. 238.

[7] This English translation is taken from BVerfGE 121, 135, judgment of May 7, 2008, - 2 BvE 1/03 -, *AWACS Turkey*, para. 62, which uses the identical German phrase as BVerfGE 90, 286, *supra* note 3, para. 255 (no official translation available of the 1994 judgment).

[8] *Id.*, paras. 253–256.

[9] BVerfGE 90, 286, *supra* note 3, paras. 257–295, especially para. 291. *See also* BVerfGE 104, 151, judgment of Nov. 22, 2001, - 2 BvE 6/99 -, *NATO new strategic concept of 1999*.

[10] BVerfGE 90, 286, *supra* note 3, para. 324 (my translation). On the parliamentary power, *see* paras. 319–350 of the judgment. "Constitutive" means that the approval by the *Bundestag* is a necessary basis of the constitutional legality of the deployment. If it is missing, deployment is unconstitutional.

Court said.[11] The Court then described in detail which types of military action demanded a parliamentary assent in each concrete case. It also asked the legislature to draw up a statute—which was finally adopted a decade later, in 2005. The creative reading adapted the constitution to totally new circumstances after 1990 that had not been foreseen in 1949. The requirement of parliamentary approval was not the only possible answer to the global change,[12] but it was an admissible progressive interpretation of the Basic Law (probably transgressing the blurry boundary to judicial law-making) in line with the constitutional spirit.

Parliamentary Participation Act of 2005

The case law has interpreted the Basic Law as creating a "combined power"[13] of the government and the Parliament's first chamber to decide on any military deployment abroad. The statute on parliamentary participation (*Parlamentsbeteiligungsgesetz*) of 2005[14] says that any "deployment of German armed forces outside the scope of the Basic Law requires approval of the Bundestag" (§ 1(2) *Parlamentsbeteiligungsgesetz*).[15] This requirement flows "directly from the constitution."[16] The statute only regulates the "form and extent of the *Bundestag*'s participation," as its opening paragraph puts it.[17]

The term around which the parliamentary approval turns is "deployment." Section 2(1) of the statute defines this term as follows: "A deployment of armed forces is present when soldiers of the German army are involved in armed undertakings or when the involvement in an armed undertaking is to be expected."[18] Section 2(2) defines which activities are *not* to be considered as a "deployment." These are, first, "preparatory measures and planning," and, second, "humanitarian aid service and auxiliary action," with arms carried only for self-defense "when it is not to be expected that soldiers will be involved in armed undertakings."

2008 AWACS II Judgment

In 2008, the Federal Court fleshed out in more detail the concept of deployment. It also established a legal presumption of the requirement of parliamentary approval.[19]

[11] *Id.*, paras. 325, 329.

[12] For a parallel trend toward intensification of parliamentary involvement in the United Kingdom, triggered by the Iraq war of 2003, *see* Katja S. Ziegler, *The Use of Military Force by the United Kingdom: The Evolution of Accountability*, ch. 43 in this volume.

[13] *Entscheidungsverbund* (BVerfGE 140, 160 of Sept. 23, 2015, *Pegasus*, - 2 BvE 6/11 -, *Organstreit-proceeding* - Fraktion BÜNDNIS 90/DIE GRÜNEN versus the Federal Government, para. 73, my translation). *See also* BVerfGE 121, 135, *supra* note 7, para. 71.

[14] *Parlamentsbeteiligungsgesetz* of Mar. 18, 2005 (BGBl. 2005 I, 775).

[15] My translation.

[16] BVerfGE 90, 286, *supra* note 3, para. 349.

[17] § 1(1) sentence 1, *Parlamentsbeteiligungsgesetz*, my translation.

[18] § 2(1), my translation.

[19] BVerfGE 121, 135, *supra* note 7, para. 72.

"Deployment" can be distinguished from law enforcement activities by looking at the "genuinely military" character of an operation and at the belligerent context.[20] The qualification as a "deployment" is independent of the constitutional and international legal basis of the military operation. This also means that putative illegality under national or international law is irrelevant for the requirement of the *Bundestag*'s approval.

The 2008 judgment of the Constitutional Court clarified that it is irrelevant whether an armed conflict or combat was already going on. The "concrete expectation that German soldiers will be involved" in armed conflicts (*bewaffnete Auseinandersetzungen*) suffices, says the Court.[21] The statute uses the term armed undertakings (*bewaffnete Unternehmungen*).[22] What is meant here is combat activity, not the existence of an armed conflict in terms of international humanitarian law. If combat is only a remote and abstract "mere possibility," then the action does not yet require approval by the *Bundestag*.[23] The expectation of combat must be "concrete" and "well-founded," with "sufficient tangible actual evidence that a deployment . . . may lead to the use of armed force" and a "particular proximity to the use of armed force."[24] Involvement in armed conflicts (in the sense of actually using arms) "must be expected immediately."[25] The assessment of probability must examine the "aggregation of factual circumstances."[26] In integrated NATO operations, the participation of German soldiers in, for example, the aerial surveillance of an adjacent country, can lead to their use of armed force, because once the soldiers are dispatched, Germany can no longer influence the course of events.[27] It does not matter whether combat actually takes place; what counts is the ex ante assessment of factual and temporal proximity.[28] It is neither necessary nor sufficient that the deployed personnel carry arms themselves. The threshold to deployment can be reached even if members of the military only supply combat-relevant information, perform reconnaissance, or give orders for the use of arms.[29]

For assessing when Parliament needs to be involved, the most difficult line to draw is probably between the "preparatory measures" and the point where deployment begins. Borderline activities are the movement of troops to the territory of an ally, the delivery of arms, training, surveillance, and furnishing information. In the aftermath of 9/11, logistic activity such as air transports of other nations' peacekeeping soldiers and of material and the transfer of AWACS airplanes in October 2001 to the United States were considered below the threshold. In contrast, the dispatch of German soldiers and transfer of AWACS aircraft from their home base in Germany to a Turkish base

[20] *Id.*, para. 81 (*militärisches Gepräge*); BVerfGE 140, 160, *supra* note 13, para. 109: *kriegerischer Gesamtkontext.*

[21] BVerfGE 121, 135, *supra* note 7, headnote (official translation).

[22] § 2(1) of the Statute, *supra* note 14.

[23] BVerfGE 121, 135, *supra* note 7, para. 77.

[24] *Id.*, paras. 76–79.

[25] *Id.*, para. 79.

[26] *Id.*, para. 79.

[27] *Id.*, para. 89. The structure of command and the importance of German troops' tasks is immaterial (*id.*).

[28] BVerfGE 140, 160, *supra* note 13, para. 108.

[29] BVerfGE 121, 135, *supra* note 7, para. 81.

with a view to monitoring the airspace over Turkey in 2003 was determined to be a deployment by the Court, because of the fear of a spillover from the war in Iraq.[30]

Pegasus Judgment of 2015 on Rescue Operations

A judgment of 2015 concerned the rescue operation "Pegasus" in which 22 German nationals and 110 citizens of other states had been evacuated from Nafurah in Libya from the civil war.[31] The question was whether the approval of the *Bundestag* is constitutionally required for urgent military actions once they are *completed.* Under the statute of 2005, the government is empowered to decide alone on a deployment in the case of "imminent danger" and "for the rescue of humans from specific danger when their lives would be endangered by the public involvement of the *Bundestag.*"[32] The statute says that the *Bundestag* must be informed before and in the course of action. It also says that the government must "immediately raise the request for approval. If the *Bundestag* rejects the request, deployment must be terminated."[33]

Most commentary had opined that the obligation to ask for approval would also govern deployments that are *completed.* But the Court found that in this scenario the Constitution does not oblige the government to seek an ex post approval, but only to furnish the *Bundestag* timely, complete, detailed, and written information.

The doctrinal explanation was that the government's lawful use of its emergency powers has the same legal effect as the exercise of the combined governmental and parliamentary power in normal situations. It is an "auxiliary" stand-alone power that "modifies" the principle of parliamentary co-decision in situations where—for purely factual reasons—Parliament cannot exercise its competence.[34] If an operation is still ongoing, the parliamentary approval or disapproval has only an *ex nunc* effect.

The rationale and effect of parliamentary involvement as identified by the Court points against the need for an ex post approval of operations that are already terminated. The purpose of the parliamentary prerogative normally is that Parliament decides jointly with the executive and influences the concrete shape of the operation. Once the operation is over, this function can no longer be fulfilled.[35] By contrast, the purpose of parliamentary approval is not to assess authoritatively (*verbindlich*) the legality of an operation; this is incumbent upon the Court.[36] *Political* control by Parliament can be exercised through other types of instruments, e.g., parliamentary resolutions or even a motion of censure against government.[37]

[30] *Id.*, paras. 83–92.

[31] BVerfGE 140, 160, *supra* note 13.

[32] § 5(1) *Parlamentsbeteiligungsgesetz, supra* note 14.

[33] *Id.*, § 5(3).

[34] BVerfGE 140, 160, *supra* note 13, para. 88 (the official English translation of the judgment says "subsidiary"). *See also id.*, para. 99.

[35] *Id.*, para. 99.

[36] *Id.*, para. 99.

[37] *Id.*, para. 101.

Importantly, the Court for the first time ruled that parliamentary approval is needed for *all* deployments of German armed military forces abroad. The executive branch does not enjoy a margin of purely military and political appreciation that would be beyond the reach of Parliament and of the Constitutional Court. Such a margin does not exist, even in situations of emergency.[38]

Applying these principles as a benchmark, the Court found that the rescue operation in Nafurah (Libya) was indeed a "deployment" in the sense of the Basic Law and the relevant statute of 2005, not the least because "at the time of the executive's decision on the deployment the likelihood of having to use armed force was particularly high."[39]

The core contribution of the judgment is the new constitution-based obligation to inform. In order to allow Parliament to exercise the various forms of political control, it is the duty of the government to inform it in detail about the military operation. Parliament enjoys an "entitlement to information":[40] the government "must inform the Bundestag promptly and in a qualified manner about the deployment of armed forces."[41] It must present the factual and legal considerations on which the government based its decision, details of the operation (with the level of detail depending on its political and military importance), and the outcome. This must happen as soon as possible, to the *Bundestag* as a whole, and normally in writing. The information must be "clear, complete," so that it "can be easily reproduced."[42]

II. Alignment between Constitutional and International Law on the Use of Force

The German Constitution is specifically connected to the international law of peace. It contains a "constitutional precept of peace,"[43] and a constitutional principle of "friendliness towards international law."[44] Moreover, Article 25 GG says that the "general rules of international law shall be an integral part of federal law." This clause thus transports the international law-based prohibition on the use of force into domestic law.[45] A breach of the ban on force as a "general rule" of international law

[38] *Id.*, para. 70. [39] *Id.*, para. 115.

[40] *Id.*, para. 104, my translation of *der parlamentarische Informationsanspruch*. Government has an "obligation of formal information" (para. 103; official translation).

[41] *Id.*, headnote 4. [42] *Id.*, paras. 103–104, quotes from para. 104.

[43] BVerfGE 104, 151, *supra* note 9, para. 159 (para. 30 of the English shortened translation). This "precept" is read out of numerous provisions that mention peace (notably the prohibition of aggression in art. 26, the preamble, art. 24(2), and art. 1(2) GG).

[44] Most recently, *see* BVerfGE 141, 1, judgment of Dec. 15, 2015, - 2 BvL 1/12 - *Treaty Override* paras. 65–72.

[45] BVerfGE 104, 151, *supra* note 9, para. 160 (para. 31 i of the shortened English translation).

will however not automatically also lead to a violation of the constitution, because the "general rules"—while taking precedence over federal laws—still rank below the Basic Law.

Finally, the constitutional prohibition of a war of aggression (Art. 26 GG) is "tied to that concept in international law."[46] The constitutional concept follows the definition of aggression as spelled out in the UN GA Resolution of 1974 and in Article 8*bis* of the ICC Statute after the amendments of Kampala.

The result of the combination of these constitutional provisions is that any manifest violation of the relevant rules of international law in the area of the use of force will normally also violate the German Constitution. This means that German constitutional law cannot—as a rule—be more permissive toward the use of force than international law.

The more difficult question is whether the Constitution sets a higher bar and is more "pacifist" than international law. As a historical matter, this assumption was and is widespread as a lesson to learn from Germany's past as an aggressor state. Because the Basic Law mentions only defense and collective security, there is no obvious constitutional basis for other types of military action.

"Collective Security" under Article 24(2) GG

The key contemporary constitutional question is whether military action that is only loosely linked to the United Nations or NATO still occurs "within and pursuant to the rules" of such "systems" (organizations), as the 1994 judgment demands. Examples of German actions that are not easy to describe as occurring within a system of collective security are the contribution to Operation Enduring Freedom (OEF) at various places on the globe, from October 2001 to 2010, the participation in the anti-Islamic State coalition in Syria and Iraq since 2014, which in 2018 was modified toward capacity building in Iraq,[47] and the involvement in the training mission in Mali (EUTM) (since 2013).

In all instances, the German government argued that—from a constitutional perspective—the German deployments pursuant to these resolutions do "occur within and pursuant to the rules" of a system of collective security and are therefore safely covered by Article 24(2) GG.[48] But this constitutional coverage has been doubted by critics.

[46] Federal Administrative Court, BVerwGE 127, 302 (2 WD 12.04), judgment of June 21, 2005, sec. 4.1.2.5 (para. 101, my translation).

[47] Germany started to contribute to the anti-IS action in the fall of 2015. Training of Peshmerga in Northern Iraq had already begun in 2014. The Peshmerga training mission was completed in the spring of 2018. The new mandate combining anti-IS action and capacity building in Iraq was approved by the *Bundestag* on March 22, 2018. *See also infra* note 54.

[48] For EUTM Mali, *see* Last Gov. Request of Apr. 11, 2018 (Deutscher Bundestag Drucksache BT-Drs. 19/1597; *Bundestag* approval of Apr. 26, 2018 (Plenarprotokoll 19/29), 2744 et seq.).

Qualms relate to the international legality of the operation and to the constitutionality of German participation, and both aspects are linked.

Consider, for example, the operation against the "Islamic State" (IS) in Syria. The UN Security Council's Resolution 2249 (2015) did not exactly "authorize" the operations, as the Constitutional Court wanted it in its lead judgment of 1994.[49] Another special feature is that the operation is directed against a terror group (IS), and not against an attacker state and therefore resembles collective defense as opposed to "collective security," which is the object of the constitutional provision of Article 24(2) GG.[50]

The nonactivation of Chapter VII of the UN Charter might taint the constitutionality of the deployment. Does it kick the SC resolution out of the "framework" of a "system of mutual collective security"? This is what the critics of German contributions to the anti–Islamic State operation had argued. They opined that the German deployment decision is not covered by the state's ratification of the UN Charter in 1973 and therefore lacks a constitutional basis (because it is not covered by Article 24(2) GG).

Against the critique, I submit that the anti–Islamic State operation fulfills the Federal Constitutional Court's legal requirements for coverage by Article 24(2) GG, even short of "authorization." In its lead judgment, the Constitutional Court had said that UN membership will be the constitutional basis for German participation in operations "when the competent organs of the UN assume tasks, competences, and powers that are laid out in the Charter."[51]

With Resolution 2249 (2015), the Security Council issued a binding decision,[52] albeit outside Chapter VII. The resolution was adopted unanimously. It characterized the Islamic State as "a global and unprecedented threat to international peace and security" (in the preamble). It used typical Chapter VII language, namely, to "take all necessary measures."[53] Operation Inherent Resolve, undertaken pursuant to this resolution, is multilateral. Germany never launched any unilateral strike. This satisfies the rationale of the constitutional provision of Article 24(2) GG, which is to make Germany a reliable ally, and which in turn requires that Germany not shy away from military contributions. The German contribution has therefore been given—I submit—"within and pursuant to the rules" of the United Nations and is thus covered by Article 24(2) GG. However, it is a borderline case that strains the Constitution, notably because the anti–Islamic State operation is "collective" only in a minimal sense (with two UN members, the United States and Russia, indirectly fighting *against* each other).

It does not and should not follow that Security Council resolutions simply condemning terrorism without suggesting any member state action would suffice to bring

[49] BVerfGE 90, 286, *supra* note 3, para. 240.

[50] The legal situation was similar with regard to Operation Enduring Freedom after 9/11 in 2001. The Security Council did not authorize the use of force under ch. VII but only mentioned self-defense (in the preambles of resolutions 1368 (2001) and 1373 (2001)).

[51] BVerfGE 90, 286, *supra* note 3, para. 240 (my translation).

[52] *See* UN Charter, art. 25.

[53] UN SC Res. 2249, para. 5.

military deployments under the umbrella of Article 24(2) GG. But such an extrapolation becomes a risk once the slippery slope of reliance on a rather soft Security Council resolution has been taken.

Article 24(2) GG had been stretched even more with the training mission in Northern Iraq to which Germany has contributed from summer 2014 to the spring of 2018,[54] and which was in 2018 transformed into a mandate on capacity building in Iraq.[55] The most solid international legal basis of this operation is a formal invitation by the government of Iraq of June 2014.[56] In its initial request for approval of the *Bundestag*,[57] the German government relied on that letter, and also mentioned UN Security Council Resolution 2178 (2014) against foreign terrorist fighters, a statement of the President of the Security Council of November 19, 2014,[58] and the conclusions of the EU Council of Foreign Ministers of October 20, 2014.

Again, the constitutional basis of the operation is to some extent linked to the international legal basis. The government relied only on Article 24(2) GG.[59] But the government's view that the Security Council's presidential statement suffices to bring a military operation "within and pursuant to the rules" of a system of collective security is far-fetched. Such presidential statements are not legally binding and are issued as a political pronouncement exactly because no agreement could be reached in the Security Council, and because the Council President is not empowered to determine a "threat to the peace" in terms of Chapter VII. It is therefore better to admit that the northern Iraqi training mission was during its initial eighteen months (before the adoption of UN Security Council Resolution 2249) not covered by Article 24(2) GG.[60] In contrast, it should and could rather have been based on Article 87a(2) GG—which would have entered "constitutional virgin territory," as the Parliament's academic service put it.[61]

It has rightly been criticized that the "key" of Article 24(2) GG risks to become a master key.[62] The breaking point of Article 24(2) GG might have been reached with the anti–Islamic State Operation Inherent Resolve. To avoid a further dilution of the constitutional concept of a "system of mutual collective security," and instead of using Article 24(2) GG as a mere facade, it might be better to "activate" Article 87a GG where possible as a legal basis. However, Article 87a—to which we now turn—is also fraught with problems and notably does not offer a clear solution for anti-terror operations.

[54] The government involved Parliament only five months after starting the training. Gov. Request of Dec. 17, 2014 (BT-Drs. 18/3561); *Bundestag* approval of Jan. 29, 2015, Plenarprotokoll 18/82, at 7814 et seq.; vote at 7823.

[55] Gov. Request of Mar. 7, 2018 (BT-Drs. 19/1093); *Bundestag* approval of Mar. 22, 2018, Plenarprotokoll 19/23, at 2062–2074.

[56] Letter by the Iraq of June 25, 2014 to the UN Secretary General (UN Doc. S/2014/440).

[57] *See* Request of Dec. 17, 2014, *supra* note 54.

[58] UN Doc. S/PRST/2014/23.

[59] Request of Dec. 17, 2014, *supra* note 54.

[60] *Wissenschaftliche Dienste des Bundestages*, WD 2–3000–239/14, legal opinion of Jan. 9, 2015, at 9.

[61] *Id. at* 12 (my translation).

[62] Bardo Fassbender, § 244, *Militärische Einsätze der Bundeswehr*, *in* HANDBUCH DES STAATSRECHTS DER BUNDESREPUBLIK DEUTSCHLAND 643 (Paul Kirchhof & Josef Isensee eds., Vol. XI, 3d ed. 2013), para. 69.

"Defense" under Article 87a GG

Article 87a GG only covers operations "for purposes of defense" (sec. 1). The interpretative question is what "defense" means here. The constitutional notion of "defense" is a concept of domestic law and as such is autonomous from international law. Facially, the constitutional principle of friendliness toward international law would seem to require that the interpretation of the constitutional term should follow the evolution of international law. Indeed, both the German Federal Administrative Court[63] and almost all commentary assume that the constitutional term "defense" in Article 87a GG is fully congruent with the international law of self-defense (and therefore would seem to obey the same yardstick of legality).

This discussion has involved two distinct questions: Who may be defended? And against whom? Both questions have emerged simultaneously and have become intertwined, because all controversial German contributions to collective action outside the framework of Article 5 of the NATO Treaty or Chapter VII of the UN Charter (after 2011 in Afghanistan and after 2014–2015 in Syria) took place far away from German soil and were directed against terrorist attacks.

The first question is whether defense in terms of Article 87a GG means only defense of German statehood. A conventional understanding had been that the Constitution only allows military action needed to defend against attacks that—even if remotely—threaten Germany as a state. This assumption had led a German minister of defense in 2002 to proclaim—with regard to German engagement in Afghanistan—that the security of Germany is also defended at the Hindu Kush.

Today, probably the prevailing scholarly view is that Article 87a GG covers actions to defend Germany as a state and collective self-defense—even if this requires operations outside and far away from the country. This would mean that collective self-defense, e.g., in favor of France (as an ally) and Iraq (asking for military support) in 2015, is permitted under Article 87a GG—as long as it is covered by the international law of self-defense.

"Defense" as a constitutional concept might be read to include defense against nonstate actors. Along that line, the constitutional concept would follow a putative evolution of the international legal concept of self-defense moving toward allowing self-defense against large-scale armed attacks by terrorists (with a tenuous link to a state, or even without any attribution to the territorial state in which defensive military action unfolds).

Proponents of relying on Article 87a GG as the basis for "defense" against terrorist threats argue that this constitutional construction would avoid the overuse of the constitutional concept of "collective security," bring the Constitution more in line with the two distinct tracks (Chapter VII action or self-defense) available under international law, and open the way for more military engagement. The preference

[63] BVerwGE 127, 302, *supra* note 46, para. 93.

of German political actors to always rely on Article 24(2) GG had the historical motive of signaling to the citizens and to the world that Germany was firmly integrated into multilateral structures and would not go it alone. Such a signal and reassurance is arguably no longer needed.

On the other hand, important arguments speak in favor of sticking to a narrow reading of the constitutional concept of "defense." The chief consideration is that the international law of self-defense is currently unclear and in flux. This counsels against schematically linking the constitutional concept to the (blurry) international one.

The problem appears in the anti–Islamic State operation in and over Syria and Iraq. The international legal basis suggested by the German government, namely, collective self-defense for Iraq and for France, is controversial.[64] In the *Bundestag*'s debate some days earlier, the German government and the parliamentary majority heavily relied on a legal opinion by the Parliamentary academic service in which that service opined that "obviously, last but not least against the background of the recent Paris attacks—an evolution of customary law is ongoing" in the direction of admitting self-defense against nonstate actors.[65] But this evolution is less obvious than the academic service claims. The international lawfulness of self-defense against armed attacks by nonstate actors without any imputation to the state on whose territory the defensive action strikes back is disputed.[66]

This uncertainty is mirrored in the controversial interpretation of Article 87a(2) GG. The literature is actually split on this point. Some authors allow defense against terrorist attacks without further conditions.[67] Others opine that military reactions against terrorist attacks counts as "defense" in the sense of Article 87a GG only if the threat resembles an inter-state armed attack.[68] Finally, a sizable number of commentators insist on the need of attributing the attack to a state.[69] However, they do not explain which criteria of attribution must be satisfied so as to trigger "defense" in terms of Article 87a GG.

Presuming that an evolution of the international law of self-defense is ongoing (which is controversial) and that a novel, broader reading of Article 51 of the UN Charter is gaining ground,[70] it is not clear that the *constitutional* concept of "defense" automatically follows. The parliamentary oppositional faction of the Left Party, in its

[64] Letter by Germany of Dec. 10, 2015, to the UN Security Council (UN Doc. S/2015/946).

[65] WD 2-3000-203/15, Part 2, updated version of Nov. 30, 2015, at 14 (my translation).

[66] On this controversy, *see* the contributions in *Self-Defence Against Non-State Actors: Impulses from the Max Planck Trialogues on the Law of Peace and War*, 77 Heidelberg J. Int'l. L. 1 (Anne Peters & Christian Marxsen eds., 2017).

[67] *See*, e.g., Volker Epping, *in* Grundgesetz—Kommentar art. 87a, para. 11–11.2. (Volker Epping & Christian Hillgruber eds., 2d ed. 2013).

[68] *See*, e.g., Juliane Kokott, *in* Grundgesetz: Kommentar art. 87a, para. 36 (Michael Sachs ed., 8th ed. 2018).

[69] *See*, e.g., Heike Krieger, *in* GG Kommentar zum Grundgesetz art. 87a, para. 13 (Hans Hofmann & Hans-Günter Henneke eds., 14th ed. 2018).

[70] I leave aside the additional problem of a putative evolution of underlying customary law and its interplay with the interpretation of the UN Charter.

pending complaint to the Constitutional Court, argues that—should the Constitutional Court follow the broad (and fairly novel) interpretation of Article 51 of the UN Charter in the direction of admitting self-defense against armed attacks by nonstate actors—this would be an inadmissible judge-driven evolution of the UN Charter. Then, so the argument runs, this judicial lawmaking would no longer be covered by the initial approval of Germany's accession to the UN Charter by the federal statute of 1973, but would require a fresh approval by the legislative branch or at least by the *Bundestag*.[71]

Against the fluid and uncertain state of international law, in order to be safely in conformity with the international law on the use of force (as the Basic Law prescribes[72]), German constitutional law needs to remain restrictive as long as the presumed evolution of international law toward extension is not yet firm. I would therefore argue that—for the time being—Article 87a GG covers only operations that respond to ongoing or imminent armed attacks by a state or are attributable to a state under the "classic" uncontroversial *Nicaragua* criteria.[73] In contrast, antiterrorist and antipiracy operations need to be based on Article 24(2) GG and may thus be conducted only within a collectivity, as a multilateral action broadly conceived.

III. Judicial Review of Deployment Decisions

Deployment decisions are subject to judicial review by the Federal Constitutional Court. Although judicial scrutiny is closely circumscribed, it is—from a comparative law perspective—a far-reaching involvement of the judicial branch in foreign and military affairs.

Organstreit Proceedings

The available proceeding is the *Organstreitverfahren* ("dispute between constitutional organs").[74] The prospect of an *Organstreit* proceeding—a weapon in the hand of the

[71] *Organstreit* proceeding, launched by the parliamentary faction *Die Linke* against the deployment decision (complaint lodged on May 31, 2016; proceeding is pending).

[72] *See* text *supra* accompanying notes 43–46.

[73] ICJ, Case Concerning Military and Paramilitary Activities in and against Nicaragua (Nicaragua v. USA), Merits, ICJ Reports 1986, 14, para. 195.

[74] Art. 93 (1) No. 1 GG; § 13 No. 5 and § 63 et seq. Federal Constitutional Court Act (BVerfGG) in the version of Aug. 11, 1993 (*Bundesgesetzblatt* (Federal Law Gazette) 1993 I, at 1473), last amended on July 18, 2017 (Federal Law Gazette 2017 I, at 2730). In contrast, the so-called "abstract" norm control proceeding does not fit and has so far never been tried out. Neither does a constitutional complaint by an individual, e.g., a soldier, seem admissible.

political opposition—looms over every government and motivates careful legal assessment both in the formal request by the executive and in the parliamentary debates. The double legal scrutiny performed by both branches of government is then often complemented or rectified by the third layer of *limited* legal scrutiny by the Court. This has so far happened in more than ten cases on foreign deployments since the early 1990s, sometimes accompanied by provisional measures.

The *Organstreit* proceeding inter alia allows a political group (faction) in the *Bundestag* to file a complaint.[75] So far, every complaint against a military deployment has been instituted by one or several factions. The purpose of the *Organstreit* proceeding is to protect the competences of constitutional organs. This means that plaintiffs cannot directly attack the substantive decision of the government to participate in military action. The only admissible complaint is that a constitution-based power ("right") of the *Bundestag* has been breached by the government.[76] The Court may thus only examine whether the constitutional competences of the organs have been respected and whether the procedure of parliamentary involvement was correct.

Historically, the first two cases arose because the government had failed to seek the parliamentary chamber's approval or had not sought approval as a matter of constitutional obligation. In both instances, one or several political factions complained that the *Bundestag*'s right to participation was violated by those decisions.[77] Since then, the government has been careful to seek approval of the *Bundestag*. The more difficult question is now under what conditions an *Organstreit* proceeding might be admissible and meritorious even after the *Bundestag* had approved a deployment.

Overstepping the Mandate of the *Bundestag*

It would seem admissible for a parliamentary faction to claim that the *Bundestag*'s right to participation is violated when a concrete operation oversteps the confines of the *Bundestag*'s prior approval in geographic, temporal, or substantive terms. So far, no judicial decision on a putative ultra vires operation has been rendered. The proceeding that comes closest to this scenario relates to Kosovo. The ongoing German deployment is based on Security Council Resolution 1244 (1999) and Article 24(2) GG. The Security Council authorization itself is not time limited. It is a constitutional practice to annually renew the mandate in the *Bundestag*.[78]

[75] Factions are parts of a constitutional organ equipped with their own rights under the rules of Parliament and therefore enjoy standing.

[76] § 64(1) BVerfGG.

[77] This was the scenario giving rise to the lead cases BVerfGE 90, 286, *supra* note 3, and BVerfGE 121, 135, *supra* note 7.

[78] For the beginning of this constitutional convention, *see* Plenarprotokoll 14/108, at 10155 (MP Lamers, CDU/CSU), Deutscher Bundestag, Stenografischer Bericht, 108. Sitzung, June 8, 2000, Plenarprotokoll 14/108.

When Kosovo declared its independence in 2008, the parliamentary faction of the Left Party instituted an *Organstreit* proceeding against the government, arguing that the government should have sought a new approval of the *Bundestag* for German participation in the Kosovo Force (KFOR), because the new circumstances (the state's independence) had led to an expiration of the *Bundestag*'s mandate. The Court ruled that only a manifest change of circumstances could lead to expiration of the parliamentary assent, and that the declaration of independence of Kosovo was no such case. It refused to examine the overall constitutionality or the international lawfulness of the deployment but only declared that the competences of the *Bundestag* had not been violated.[79]

No Overall Constitutional Control

A more difficult issue is presented when the faction claims that the deployment violated international law, and—by extension—the parallel constitutional law. In 1998, the German government had decided to contribute to air operations as part of the NATO operation against Serbia, undertaken without a UN Security Council authorization. The *Bundestag* had approved.[80] The faction PDS (Party of Democratic Socialism) that had been outvoted in Parliament then instituted a complaint with the argument that the "humanitarian" Kosovo intervention breached international law and thus also violated the constitutional ban on aggressive war (Arts. 25 and 26(1) GG). But the Federal Constitutional Court found this complaint inadmissible because the *Organstreit* proceeding does not permit an "overall constitutional review."[81] Constitutional law as a whole is no benchmark in the *Organstreit* proceeding, because the *Bundestag* has not been installed as the overseer of the executive branch's compliance with the Basic Law.[82]

The Logic and Review of "Excess"

In contrast, the 2007 *Tornados* judgment[83] introduced a specific type of constitutional scrutiny that even takes into account clear breaches of international law in individual

[79] BVerfGE 124, 267, order of Oct. 13, 2009 - 2 BvR 4/08 -, (inadmissibility decision by judicial order because the complaint was manifestly ill-founded; § 24 BVerfGG)—independence of *Kosovo*, esp. paras. 21–27.

[80] Gov. Request for the authorization of the deployment of around 14 aircraft and around 500 troops of Oct. 12, 1998 (BT-Drs. 13/11469). The *Bundestag* approved after an intensive debate on the extraordinary character of this mission. *See Deutscher Bundestag*, 248. Sitzung, Oct. 16, 1998, Plenarprotokoll 13/248, 23127–23161; vote at 23161.

[81] BVerfGE 100, 266, order finding inadmissibility, of Mar. 25, 1999, - 2 BvE 5/99 -, para. 13.

[82] *See also* BVerfGE 126, 55, order of May 4, 2010, - 2 BvE 5/07 -.

[83] BVerfGE 118, 244 of July 3, 2007, - 2 BvE 2/07 -. This was an *Organstreit* proceeding instituted by the parliamentary faction of *PDS/Die Linke* against the prolongation of ISAF, although the *Bundestag* had approved it on March 9, 2007.

deployments. The background to the *Tornados* judgment was that the UN Security Council had in 2003 geographically extended the International Security Assistance Force (ISAF) mission to Afghanistan as a whole, and NATO had agreed to continue carrying out the extended mission. This led to a territorial overlap with the U.S. Operation Enduring Freedom. In parallel, NATO had successively revised its overall strategy in the direction of global security and response to novel threats, notably in 2006 at the Riga summit.[84] On this basis, NATO furnished airborne intelligence and surveillance in Afghanistan, and German Tornados contributed to this. The *Bundestag* had approved the German participation in ISAF annually. The mandate allowed transfer of data gathered by German surveillance to Operation Enduring Freedom "only if necessary for the successful realization of the ISAF-operation or for the security of ISAF-forces."[85] The complaint of the suing factions PDS/*Die Linke* (as interpreted and partly reformulated by the Constitutional Court) was that the government's decision to participate in the extended ISAF mission overstepped the statutory approval of Germany's original accession to NATO (in 1955) and thus violated rights of the *Bundestag*.

The Court examined both the *regional* extension of NATO activity beyond the Euro-Atlantic area and its *substantive* orientation toward peace. An excess in either dimension would not be covered by the original NATO Treaty and thus not covered by the parliamentary statute approving of Germany's accession to the organization and would thus escape parliamentary co-responsibility. The Court first performed a "constitutional review as to whether essential structural decisions of the NATO Treaty—in this case a connection to NATO's regional purpose—have been exceeded."[86] Importantly, the Court did not review the actions of NATO in themselves but limited itself to a "review of the *connection* between the NATO actions and the regional framework."[87] On this point, the Court found that NATO had "not . . . departed in a general sense from its connection to a specific region."[88] Notably, "[t]hose responsible in connection with NATO were and are entitled to assume that the securing of the rebuilding of Afghanistan's civil society also contributes directly *to the Euro-Atlantic area's own* security; in view of present-day threats from globally acting terrorist networks, as 11 September 2001 showed, threats to the security of the NATO area cannot any longer be territorially restricted."[89]

Second, NATO's (putative) *turning away from peace* would constitute a substantive excess.[90] Such an excess would not only mean that NATO and its operations were no longer covered by the NATO Treaty (and the complementary federal statute) but also that they would violate the constitutional provision of Article 24(2) GG, which allows

[84] *See* the "Comprehensive Political Guidance" endorsed by NATO Heads of State and Government on Nov. 29, 2006.

[85] Gov. Request of Feb. 8, 2007, BT-Drs. 16/4298, at 3, my translation.

[86] BVerfGE 118, 244, *supra* note 83, para. 66. The alleged regional excess is discussed in paras. 51–71.

[87] *Id.*, para. 68 (emphasis added). [88] *Id.*, para. 71. [89] *Id.*, para. 67 (emphasis added).

[90] The Court reviewed the substantive excess in *id.*, paras. 72–90.

Germany to participate only in systems of collective security that are directed at maintaining peace. This would mean that Germany would have to leave NATO. If not, the powers of the *Bundestag* would be violated "because it [the excess] removes the treaty basis of the alliance from the responsibility of the German *Bundestag* and in doing so infringes the German *Bundestag*'s right under Article 59(2) sentence 1 of the Basic Law in conjunction with Article 24(2) of the Basic Law."[91]

Importantly, this review allowed for and required an incidental assessment of international law. The reason is that a breach of international law through individual NATO military operations, "in particular the violation of the prohibition of the use of military force, may be an indicator" that NATO has transformed itself and that it "is structurally departing from its constitutionally mandatory orientation towards the maintenance of peace."[92] On this point, the Court did not see any tendency of NATO to turn away from its objective of securing peace. Notably the cooperation of ISAF with the Operation Enduring Freedom did not change the character of the NATO Treaty, because the two operations remained distinct in legal and factual terms.[93] The Court therefore rejected the application as unfounded on the merits. However, the judgment marks some extension of judicial review whose exact scope and impact is not yet fully clear.

This extension will be tested in a pending proceeding launched by the faction *Die Linke* against the anti–Islamic State operation *with* the approval of the *Bundestag*. The complaint filed in 2016 is directed both against the federal government and against the *Bundestag*.[94] The applicant seeks the declaration that the respondents, with their joint deployment decision (of December 1 and 4, 2015), violated competences of the *Bundestag* flowing from Article 24(2) in conjunction with Article 59(2) GG. The faction argues that the deployment occurred outside a system of collective security[95] and would therefore have required a new statute (Article 24(2) in conjunction with Article 59(2) GG), and also that the deployment constituted an extensive reading of Article 51 of the UN Charter, which oversteps the parliamentary statute approving of Germany's accession to the United Nations in 1973.

It remains to be seen whether the logic of "excess" and departure from the original federal statutes approving the membership in the two organizations (NATO and UN)—which is the only window to constitutional review—will suffice to confer standing on the faction. Then, the related question is whether this logic will, on the merits, allow for a (however summary) assessment of the lawfulness of self-defense against nonstate actors (under the heading of an "excess" beyond the original meaning of Article 51 of the UN Charter and Article 5 of the NATO Treaty).

[91] *Id.*, para. 74.

[92] *Id.*, para. 74. So the *Organstreit* does not allow an international-law-based review *tout court. Id.*, and paras. 66 and 87.

[93] *Id.*, paras. 77–84.

[94] Application filed on May 31, 2016; a judicial decision is expected in the course of 2019. *See supra* note 67.

[95] For the relevant concerns, *see supra* section II.

IV. Conclusion

From a comparative law perspective, the German constitutional regime on the use of military force abroad is heavily legalized through case law and codification.[96] The dominant role of the Constitutional Court that created the regime stands out, but it corresponds to the overall strong position and eminent political function of this body in the German constitutional setup. It is the Court that insists on the strong role of Parliament, and on the combined decision-making power of the government and the first parliamentary chamber (*Bundestag*) on each single deployment.

In the German parliamentary system of government in which the government is elected by Parliament and accountable to it, the case for an *additional* parliamentary decision on the use of military force might seem less obvious than in a presidential system where the executive branch enjoys legitimacy independent from Parliament. But it finds its explanation in the idea of the "parliamentary army." Parliamentary involvement is not only superimposed onto a genuinely executive power, but co-constitutes every deployment decision. The consequence for timing is that approval of the *Bundestag* must be sought *at the outset*, not only after a certain lapse of time, such as after sixty days in the United States,[97] or after four months as in France.[98] Although parliamentary involvement does not necessarily lead to more consideration of foreign and global interests, it leads to *public* debate. Together with the need for official governmental explanations in their formal request to Parliament, these procedures contribute to the expression of an *opinio iuris* of the state on matters of the use of force.

The German experience is relevant for the debate on the exceptionalism of foreign and notably military affairs and their law.[99] The normative claim of exceptionalism is that governance decisions in this sphere are and need only be subjected to less demanding constitutional standards: perceived or assumed requirements of speed, uniformity, and flexibility would, according to the exceptionalist thesis, allow for less democracy, less transparency, less checks and balances, less rule of law, less judicial control, and less respect for human rights than other areas of law and governance. But this claim is weakened by the successful German practice, which shows that foreign affairs law need not follow a completely distinct logic of legitimacy than other areas of public law.

[96] For comparative analyses of war powers, *see* Jenny S. Martinez, *The Constitutional Allocation of Executive and Legislative Power over Foreign Relations: A Survey*, ch. 6 in this volume, and Monica Hakimi, *Techniques for Regulating Military Force*, ch. 41 in this volume.

[97] *See* Curtis A. Bradley, *U.S. War Powers and the Potential Benefits of Comparativism*, ch. 42 in this volume.

[98] *See* Mathias Forteau, *Using Military Force and Engaging in Collective Security: The Case of France*, ch. 45 in this volume.

[99] For a discussion in U.S. law, *see* Ganesh Sitaraman & Ingrid Wuerth, *The Normalization of Foreign Relations Law*, 128 Harv. L. Rev. 1897 (2015).

This ties back to global constitutionalism, which holds that, in a world characterized by global flows of information and digital hyperconnectivity, global supply chains, intense global trade, foreign investment, and migration, the starting point of any analysis should be that foreign affairs are not a categorically distinct type of politics but rather resemble "world internal politics." Therefore, prima facie, foreign relations measures and the law that governs them is and should be subject to the usual constitutional standards. The burden of explanation lies on those who advocate the exception and who seek to reduce the constitutional standards governing foreign relations law. German constitutional law and practice of deciding on military deployments abroad demonstrates that it is sufficient to lower the standards only slightly.

CHAPTER 45

USING MILITARY FORCE AND ENGAGING IN COLLECTIVE SECURITY

The Case of France

MATHIAS FORTEAU

As a permanent member of the UN Security Council, as a "nuclear-weapon state" under the 1968 Treaty on the Non-Proliferation of Nuclear Weapons, as a military power involved in many United Nation (UN) or other collective peacekeeping or antiterrorism operations, in particular in Africa, and as a state specially affected by international terrorism since the 2015–2016 Paris and Nice attacks, France is particularly interested in the identification and development of international rules related to the use of force and collective security. It is by the same token expected to have developed over time strong domestic rules governing activities of its military forces abroad as well as a clear doctrine on the use of force in the international sphere.[1]

This chapter will address both aspects, which can be considered as integral components of "Foreign Relations Law." It will first present domestic rules that are applicable in France to the use of force abroad. It will then concentrate on the identification of

[1] Conversely, France's practice and *opinio juris* need to be carefully addressed in order to identify applicable international law in that field since France, on the basis of the above elements, is, to quote the ILC Draft Conclusions on the identification of customary international law, "particularly involved in the relevant activity" or "most likely to be concerned with the alleged rule." *See* Text and commentaries of the draft conclusions adopted by the ILC on second reading on the identification of customary international law, *in* Report on the work of the seventieth session of the ILC (2018), A/73/10, p. 136, para. 4 of the commentary on draft conclusion 8. The ILC refers to the *dictum* of the ICJ in *North Continental Shelf* according to which, for state practice to create a rule of customary international law, "an indispensable requirement would be that within the period in question, short though it might be, State practice, *including that of States whose interests are specially affected*, should have been both extensive and virtually uniform." ICJ Reports 1969, at 43, para. 74 (emphasis added).

France's legal position (its *politique juridique extérieure*, to paraphrase Lacharrière)[2] as regards the permissible use of force under international law.

At the outset, it is important to stress that on both issues, the present chapter is intended to be mainly descriptive of France's current legal positions and practice in order to facilitate comparisons with the practice of other states in the same field.[3] In addition, it is based on a realistic approach to the regulation of the use of force in domestic law. Since the field of operation of the use of force is the international sphere, the decision to use it is likely not framed in the same terms as the adoption of common domestic legislation. The role of the legislative and the judicial branches can then hardly be presumed to be the same as the one characterizing purely domestic rules or activities. To that extent, it is indispensable to assess the foreign relations law of the use of force on its own, as a specific field, without any preconceived ideas and without assuming in particular that it should be as a matter of principle driven by classical domestic rules or principles.

I. Domestic Rules Applicable to the Use of Force Abroad

The decision to use force or to participate in collective security is, as a matter of principle, a decision that has to be taken in France by the executive branch. This being said, the Parliament has recently been granted some powers on the use of force, which vary depending on the nature of the operations concerned. On the other hand, there is no judicial control of the decision to use force.

The Decision to Resort to Force: The Province of the Executive Branch

The rules applicable to the use of force are fragmented in French law. Contrary to other countries where any kind of use of force (whether or not formally being labeled as a war) is submitted to the same legal regime, in France four distinct legal regimes can be distinguished.

[2] Guy de Lacharrière, La Politique Juridique Extérieure (1983).

[3] For a comparable assessment of the practice of Germany, Japan, the United Kingdom, and the United States, *see* in the present volume chs. 42–44 and 46. For the assessment of the practice of Australia, Canada, New Zealand, and the United Kingdom, *see* Campbell McLachlan, Foreign Relations Law 129–141 (2014). For a comparison of the perspectives of the United States and France on the law applicable to the use of force, *see* (even though it is somewhat outdated), *Symposium: French and American Perspectives towards International Law and International Institutions*, 58 Maine L. Rev. 508–587 (2006).

First, in some very specific circumstances, when the existence of the state is at stake, the president is entrusted with exceptional powers that he can use alone, without any real control. According to Article 16 of the Constitution:

> Where the institutions of the Republic, the independence of the Nation, the integrity of its territory or the fulfillment of its international commitments are under serious and immediate threat, and where the proper functioning of the constitutional public authorities is interrupted, the President of the Republic shall take measures required by these circumstances, after formally consulting the Prime Minister, the Presidents of the Houses of Parliament and the Constitutional Council.
>
> He shall address the Nation and inform it of such measures.
>
> The measures shall be designed to provide the constitutional public authorities as swiftly as possible, with the means to carry out their duties. The Constitutional Council shall be consulted with regard to such measures.
>
> Parliament shall sit as of right.
>
> The National Assembly shall not be dissolved during the exercise of such emergency powers.
>
> After thirty days of the exercise of such emergency powers, the matter may be referred to the Constitutional Council [i.e., France's Constitutional Court] by the President of the National Assembly, the President of the Senate, sixty Members of the National Assembly or sixty Senators, so as to decide if the conditions laid down in paragraph one still apply. It shall make its decision by public announcement as soon as possible. It shall, as of right, carry out such an examination and shall make its decision in the same manner after sixty days of the exercise of emergency powers or at any moment thereafter.[4]

France attaches a particular importance to this constitutional provision, even though it has been applied only once, from April to September 1961, to react to the failed coup attempt carried out by army generals in the French colony of Algeria. France accordingly made a reservation upon the ratification of the European Convention on Human Rights in May 1974 and the 1966 Covenant on Civil and Political Rights in November 1980, according to which the terms "to the extent strictly required by the exigencies of the situation" contained in Article 15 of the Convention and Article 14 of the Covenant "shall not restrict the power of the President of the Republic to take the measures required by the circumstances."[5]

[4] Translation from the website of the *Conseil constitutionnel* (France's constitutional court), *available at* http://www.conseil-constitutionnel.fr/conseil-constitutionnel/english/constitution/constitution-of-4-october-1958.25742.html.

[5] For the text of these two reservations, *see* http://www.coe.int/en/web/conventions/full-list/-/conventions/treaty/005/declarations?p_auth=WJ1bPUzU; and https://treaties.un.org/Pages/ViewDetails.aspx?src=TREATY&mtdsg_no=IV-4&chapter=4&clang=_en#EndDec.

Second, a specific regime applies to "war" in the strict meaning of the term, i.e., a decision to use force against another state without any authorization from the UN Security Council or in cases other than self-defense. According to Article 35 (1) of the Constitution, "A declaration of war shall be authorized by Parliament." This provision has however never been used, because it has been understood as referring only to inter-state use of force outside the context of UN operations. Since, according to the fourteenth paragraph of the preamble of the 1946 Constitution (which forms an integral part of the 1958 Constitution in force),[6] France "shall undertake no war aimed at conquest, nor shall it ever employ force against the freedom of any people," and since France ratified the UN Charter and thus cannot attack another state if there is no prior armed attack against France or no UN authorization to use force, it is difficult to see how this provision, interpreted so narrowly, could be triggered today.[7]

Admittedly, in 1991, France, together with other countries, launched a war against Iraq. But on that occasion, French authorities concluded that Article 35(1) did not apply because the use of force was authorized by the UN Security Council. The action was therefore to be considered, in legal terms, as an "international police operation" and not as a "war" in the classical meaning of the term. This decision not to apply Article 35 has been criticized, on the ground that it was based on a formalistic definition of "war" as referring only to inter-state conflicts outside the context of a UN mandate.[8] Article 35 was not applied either for the armed action against Serbia in 1999 or in Afghanistan in 2001, because, according to French executive authorities, there was no involvement of military personnel on the ground but only air operations.[9] This interpretation of Article 35 of the Constitution makes it largely obsolete, and thereby seems to neutralize the requirement of parliamentary consent for decisions to go to war. In addition, this narrow definition of "war" is at odds with some decisions of French courts that considered that the military operations in Iraq in 1991 qualified as "operations de guerre" ("war operations").[10]

Third, uses of force that do not amount to a "war" (i.e., in practice every instance of the use of force, since there is essentially no more war in the strict meaning of the term) under French law are qualified as *opérations extérieures* (OPEX) (which means

[6] *See Conseil constitutionnel*, Decision No. 71-44 DC, 16 July 1971.

[7] *See* Guy Carcassonne, La Constitution 182–184 (2013).

[8] *See in particular* Elisabeth Zoller, Droit des Relations Extérieures 86–88, 239–242, 247–248 (1992).

[9] *See* David Guillard, *Le Président, le Parlement et L'emploi de la Force*, 61 Défense Nationale et Sécurité Collective 135–136 (2005). This reasoning sounds similar to the reasoning of the executive branch in the United States in military actions such as against Libya and Syria. *See* Curtis A. Bradley, *U.S. War Powers and the Potential Benefits of Comparativism*, ch. 42 in this volume; *see also* Curtis Bradley & Jack Goldsmith, *OLC's Meaningless "National Interests" Test for the Presidential Uses of Force*, June 5, 2018, *available at* https://www.lawfareblog.com/olcs-meaningless-national-interests-test-legality-presidential-uses-force.

[10] *See*, e.g., Conseil d'Etat, 17 March 2004, No. 255460.

"operations abroad").[11] They include in particular military operations launched under a UN mandate. Before 2008, these operations were decided by the executive branch without any involvement of the Parliament. Following a revision of the Constitution in 2008,[12] Paragraphs 2–4 of Article 35 of the Constitution now provide that:

> The Government shall inform Parliament of its decision to have the armed forces intervene abroad, at the latest three days after the beginning of said intervention. It shall detail the objectives of the said intervention. This information may give rise to a debate, which shall not be followed by a vote.
>
> Where the said intervention shall exceed four months, the Government shall submit the extension to Parliament for authorization. It may ask the National Assembly to make the final decision.
>
> If Parliament is not sitting at the end of the four-month period, it shall express its decision at the opening of the following session.[13]

These provisions only provide for the provision of information to Parliament, and the need for its authorization for the extension of the intervention after four months. Moreover, the requirement to get an authorization applies only once; once the renewal of the intervention is authorized, there is no obligation to ask for a new authorization in the future. The duration of the intervention will be within the sole prerogative of the executive branch. In other words, despite the constitutional revision, the role of the Parliament remains very limited in France regarding the decision to use force.[14]

Paragraph 3 of Article 35 of the Constitution was applied just after its adoption, in 2008, to extend the military presence of France in Afghanistan. It was used again in 2009 for military operations in Chad, the Central African Republic (Operation Sangaris), the Ivory Coast, Lebanon, and Kosovo; in 2011 for Libya; in 2013 for Mali; in 2014 for Operation Barkhane in Chad; and in 2015 for Operation Chammal in Iraq and for the military airstrikes in Syria.[15]

[11] For a recent, very detailed, and comprehensive assessment of the legal basis, practice, and operational aspects of OPEX, *see* (from members of France's Senate) the *Rapport d'information no 794 (2015–2016) fait au nom de la commission des affaires étrangères, de la défense et des forces armées, Interventions extérieures de la France: renforcer l'efficacité militaire par une approche globale coordonnée*, July 13, 2016, *available at* https://www.senat.fr/rap/r15-794/r15-794.html.

[12] Resulting from the *Loi constitutionnelle No. 2008-724*. On the rules and practice before the 2008 revision of the Constitution, *see in particular* (from the French National Assembly) the *Rapport d'information no. 2237 de la Commission de la défense nationale et des forces armées sur le contrôle parlementaire des opérations extérieures*, Mar. 8, 2000, *available at* http://www.assemblee-nationale.fr/rap-info/i2237.asp.

[13] Translation from the website of the *Conseil constitutionnel*, *supra* note 4.

[14] For an overall appraisal, *see* Mihaela Ailincai, *Le contrôle parlementaire de l'intervention des forces armées à l'étranger. Le droit constitutionnel français à l'épreuve du droit comparé*, 127 REVUE DU DROIT PUBLIC 129–155 (2011).

[15] These authorizations are not published in the Official Journal. The information is available on the National Assembly website. *See* http://www2.assemblee-nationale.fr/decouvrir-l-assemblee/role-

Paragraph 3 of Article 35 of the French Constitution could be compared to what is set out by Section 5(b) of the U.S. War Powers Resolution, which requires Congress's authorization for the continuation of a military intervention after sixty days. However, whereas the French executive authorities always seek (and obtain) the Parliament's approval pursuant to Article 35(3) of the Constitution, the American executive branch almost never seeks an authorization of an extension of an operation under the War Powers Resolution. Instead, it either concludes operations within sixty days or relies on other purported statutory authority for an operation, such as the 2001 and 2002 Authorization for the Use of Military Force given by Congress after 9/11.[16] This relatively limited role of the legislature in France and in the United States contrasts with the German system, in which the German government cannot use force abroad without the consent of the *Bundestag*, the only limit being situations of imminent danger (*Gefahr im Verzug*).[17]

Even though there is in France limited control by the Parliament, there exist some guiding standards or general principles applicable to the sending abroad of military personnel. In the *Livre blanc sur la défense*, published in 2008, seven "guiding principles" on the engagement of military forces abroad, which are of a *soft law* nature, have been articulated as follows:

- There must be a grave and serious nature of the threat against national or international peace or security.
- There should be an assessment of other possible measures, before the use of force, without prejudice of the urgency related to self-defense or the responsibility to protect.
- International law should be respected.
- The military operation should be subject to the sovereign discretion of the French political authority, which should keep its ability to assess the situation at all times.
- There should be democratic legitimacy, involving transparency of the aims pursued and the support of the national community, expressed notably by the parliamentary representatives.
- There should be sufficient military capacity, full national control of the forces, and political strategy aimed at a sustainable settlement of the crisis.

et-pouvoirs-de-l-assemblee-nationale/les-fonctions-de-l-assemblee-nationale/les-fonctions-de-controle-et-l-information-des-deputes/la-declaration-de-guerre-et-les-interventions-armees-a-l-etranger. *See also* art. 4 of *Loi No. 2013-1168*, 18 December 2013; and Jeanne Valax, *Le contrôle parlementaire des interventions militaires françaises en Syrie*, Revue Générale de Droit International Public 599–615 (2018).

[16] *See*, e.g., *Report on the legal and policy frameworks guiding the United States' use of military force and related national security operations*, Dec. 2016, at 5, *available at* https://www.justsecurity.org/wp-content/uploads/2016/12/framework.Report_Final.pdf.

[17] On the practice of Germany, *see* Anne Peters, *Military Operations Abroad under the German Basic Law*, ch. 44 in this volume.

- The engagement should be defined in time and space, with a precise evaluation of the costs.[18]

The most interesting part of these guidelines is the reference to the "responsibility to protect" as an additional basis for using force, in addition to self-defense, in case of "urgency." On the other hand, the guidelines also stress the need to act in compliance with international law, which, presumably, should mean that even in case of mass crimes triggering the responsibility to protect, it is required that the use of force be authorized by the UN Security Council. Nonetheless, *Livres blancs sur la défense* are merely general guidelines. Their aim is mostly to define France's defense and national security strategy. They set up the principles, priorities, frameworks, and means to ensure France's security for the years to come. But the seven guiding principles listed above and the necessity for military interventions to respect international law were never formalized as "hard law." They are nonbinding, as the French Senate noted in a report, stating that *Livres blancs* have "no legal force, as the President's autonomy during the defence councils cannot be conditioned."[19]

Lastly, any other military operation is, presumably, not considered as coming within the ambit of Article 35 of the Constitution and, thus, is seen as being of the sole prerogative of the executive branch. In particular, uses of force to rescue nationals abroad have not been considered, as of today, as requiring any authorization by or information to the Parliament, presumably because of their lower scale or intensity, and because they are often undercover operations.

The Decision to Use Force: The Supremacy of the President

It is not entirely clear who exactly within the executive branch is in charge, under French law, of the conduct of military operations, once decided. According to Article 15 of the Constitution, "The President of the Republic shall be Commander-in-Chief of the Armed Forces. He shall preside over the higher national defense councils and committees."[20] This provision vests the president with the supreme power so far as the use of force is concerned. It does not mean, however, that the presidency benefits from an exclusive power. According to Article 20 of the Constitution, the government

[18] (My translation.) For more information, *see in particular* the *Rapport d'information no. 200 (2014–2015) de M. Jean-Pierre Raffarin, fait au nom de la commission des affaires étrangères, de la défense et des forces armées, déposé le 17 décembre 2014, en vue du débat sur l'autorisation de prolongation de l'opération Chammal en Irak, en application de l'article 35 de la Constitution, available at* http://www.senat.fr/rap/r14-200/r14-200.html.

[19] *Rapport d'information du Sénat no. 794 (2015–2016) de MM. Jacques Gautier, Daniel Reiner, Jean-Marie Bockel, Jeanny Lorgeoux, Cédric Perrin et Gilbert Roger, fait au nom de la commission des affaires étrangères, de la défense et des forces armées sur le bilan des opérations extérieures, le 13 juillet 2016, available at* https://www.senat.fr/rap/r15-794/r15-7941.pdf (my translation).

[20] Translation from the website of the *Conseil constitutionnel*, *supra* note 4.

(i.e., the prime minister and the ministers) "shall determine and conduct the policy of the Nation" and to that end it "shall have at its disposal the civil service and the armed forces."[21] In addition, Article 21 states that:

> The Prime Minister shall direct the actions of the Government. He shall be responsible for national defense. He shall ensure the implementation of legislation. Subject to article 13, he shall have power to make regulations and shall make appointments to civil and military posts.... He shall deputize, if the case arises, for the President of the Republic as chairman of the councils and committees referred to in article 15 ...[22]

In 2014 and 2015, France's Constitutional Court (*Conseil constitutionnel*) held that, as a result of the combination of Articles 15, 20, and 21, "*le Gouvernement décide, sous l'autorité du Président de la République, de l'emploi de la force armée*" (that is, the decision to use force is taken by the government, under the authority of the president).[23] Thus, in principle, the use of force is a shared power, but with the supreme authority vested in the president. In practice, the decision to use force has usually been considered as being primarily if not exclusively the prerogative of the president.[24]

To enforce these provisions, in particular Article 21 of the Constitution on the responsibility for national defense, the *Code de la défense* contains specific provisions on nuclear deterrence (*dissuasion nucléaire*) and more specifically on the procedures to be followed for the decision to use nuclear weapons, which can only be taken by the President of the Republic.[25]

The Absence of Any Judicial Control

French courts usually conclude that they cannot rule on claims against the French executive branch when the litigious act or conduct is "not separable from the conduct of France's international relations" (*non détachable de la conduite des relations internationales de la France*). In such a case, French courts reason that they do not have jurisdiction. As a result, no French court (either civil or administrative) can rule on these claims. This theory is generally labeled as the "act of government theory" (*théorie de l'acte de gouvernement*).

This well-established theory, which blocks any judicial review, has been applied to decisions to use force or participate in collective security. It has been applied in

[21] *Id.* [22] *Id.*

[23] *See Conseil constitutionnel*, Decision No. 2014-432 QPC, 28 November 2014, at para. 9. *See also* Decision No. 2014-450 QPC, 27 February 2015, at para. 6.

[24] *See* CARCASSONNE, *supra* note 7, at 110–111, 124; Justine Castillo Marois, *Controverse sur la suprématie du Président de la République en matière de défense nationale*, 110 REVUE FRANÇAISE DE DROIT CONSTITUTIONNEL 343–366 (2017).

[25] *See Code de la défense*, Articles R 1411-1 to R 1411-5. *See in particular* Article R 1411-5.

particular to the following decisions and actions[26]: the decision to launch nuclear tests before negotiating a treaty prohibiting such tests[27]; the decision taken by French authorities during the Kosovo crisis in 1999 to send military forces to Serbia and the subsequent decisions defining the military objectives[28]; the French military action in Chad and its compatibility with international law[29]; the decision to withdraw French troops from Afghanistan[30]; and the alleged illegality (based in particular on a breach of the UN Charter) of the decision taken by French authorities to authorize U.K. and U.S. military aircrafts to fly over French territory during the Iraq conflict in 2003.[31]

Interestingly, the rationale used by French courts is somewhat similar to the one used by British courts. Indeed, as Lord Hoffman wrote in *R v. Jones* (Margaret) in 2007, "The decision to go to war, whether one thinks it was right or wrong, fell squarely within the discretionary powers of the Crown to defend the realm and conduct its foreign affairs. To say that these matters are not justiciable may be simply another way of putting the same point."[32] The constitutional convention that emerged in the early 2000's in the United Kingdom, establishing the role of the Parliament in the decision-making process, is not enforceable by the courts either. Much like in the French system, decisions to use force thus remain completely unreviewable by the courts in the United Kingdom.

These schemes are slightly different from the United States' approach toward judicial review of such decisions. Although American courts do not attempt to control the conformity of decisions to use force with international law,[33] it is in theory possible for them to review the executive branch's domestic authority to use force, including its compliance with the War Powers Resolution in a specific case. In practice, however, U.S. courts have generally declined to review the legality of decisions to use force, usually invoking justiciability limitations such as the political question doctrine, lack of ripeness, mootness, or lack of congressional standing. Judicial review would be more likely, according to a decision of the U.S. District Court for the District of Columbia, were Congress to pass a resolution "to the effect that the forces should be withdrawn,

[26] *See also* Zoller, *supra* note 8, at 307–308.

[27] Conseil d'Etat, 29 September 1995, No. 171277.

[28] Conseil d'Etat, 5 July 2000, No. 206303 and No. 206965.

[29] Conseil d'Etat, 17 April 2006, No. 292539.

[30] Conseil d'Etat, 15 October 2008, No. 321470; *see* the commentary in Revue Générale de Droit International Public 948–950 (2009).

[31] Conseil d'Etat, 10 April 2003, No. 255905. *See also* 30 December 2003, No. 255904.

[32] Lord Hoffman, R v. Jones (Margaret), [2006] UKHL 16, on appeal from [2004] EWCA Crim 1981 and [2005] EWHC 684 (Admin), paras. 66 and 67. *See also* Lord Hope of Craighead, R (on the application of Gentle (FC) and another (FC)) (Appellants) v. The Prime Minister and others (Respondents), [2008] UKHL 20, on appeal from [2006] EWCA Civ 1689, paras. 24–26; Baroness Hale of Richmond, R (on the application of Gentle (FC) and another (FC)) (Appellants) v. The Prime Minister and others (Respondents), [2008] UKHL 20, on appeal from [2006] EWCA Civ 1689, paras. 57 and 58.

[33] Michael Stokes Paulsen, *The Constitutional Power to Interpret International Law*, 118 Yale L.J. 1762, 1823 (2009). *See also* Robert J. Delahunty & John Yoo, *Executive Power v. International Law*, 30 Harv. J. L. & Pub. Pol'y 90 (2006).

and the president disregarded it," because in that situation a "constitutional impasse appropriate for judicial resolution would be presented."[34]

The German system stands out when it comes to judicial review of decisions to use force. Not only did the German Constitutional Court establish the right for the German state to use force outside its territory in 1994,[35] but the Court has not hesitated to rule on matters concerning the distribution of powers between the executive and the German Parliament through the *Organstreit* proceedings, even in the sensitive case of military intervention decisions.[36] This is partly because there is no such thing as a "political question doctrine" in German law, but also because in the German legal system the organs have no supremacy over each other, and the *Organstreit* proceedings before the Constitutional Court make it possible for constitutional organs to judicially scrutinize each other's actions. Furthermore, the German Constitutional Court clearly affirmed that the German State has to comply with "the prohibition of the use of military force under customary international law . . . , the domestic application of which is laid down in Article 25 of the Basic Law."[37]

This being said, French criminal courts have jurisdiction over any military personnel who commit war crimes or crimes against humanity, or who use force for other purposes than or beyond what is authorized by domestic or international law. But this jurisdiction is limited to individual criminal liability. It does not encompass State responsibility.

So far as individual criminal responsibility is concerned, a new provision (Article L 4123-12-II) has been inserted in 2005 in the *Code de la défense*, stating that:

> There shall be no criminal liability for a member of the military who, in the respect of the rules of international law and within the framework of an operation mobilizing military capacities, taking place outside of the French territory or territorial waters, regardless its purpose, duration or scope, including cyber-actions, the release of hostages, the evacuation of French nationals or high seas police, undertakes coercive measures or uses the armed force, or gives the order to, when it is necessary to the exercise of his or her mission.[38]

[34] Crockett v. Reagan, 558 F. Supp. 893 (D.D.C. 1982).

[35] Judgment of the Second Senate of 12 July 1994—BverfGE 90, 286.

[36] *See*, e.g., Judgment of 23 September 2015-2 BvE 6/11, in which the Court ruled: "In cases of imminent danger, the Federal Government may, by way of exception, preliminarily order on its own that armed military forces be deployed. In such a case, it has to immediately bring the continuing deployment to the attention of the Bundestag, and, upon request by the Bundestag, withdraw the armed forces deployed." *See also* Judgment of 7 May 2008-2 BvE 1/03, in which the Court ruled: "There is a requirement of parliamentary approval under the provisions of the Basic Law which concern defence if the context of a specific deployment and the individual legal and factual circumstances indicate that there is a concrete expectation that German soldiers will be involved in armed conflicts. This precondition is subject to full judicial review."

[37] Judgment of 3 July 2007-2 BvE 2/07.

[38] (My translation.) "Cyber-actions" have been included in this provision by *Loi No. 2018-607 of 13 July 2018*.

This provision has been adopted to allow military personnel to use force beyond self-defense. The problem before the adoption of that provision was that "OPEX" actions do not qualify as "war" and therefore used to be subject to rules applicable in times of peace, which were not well-suited for this kind of operation and were creating considerable risks for the military personnel in terms of possible criminal responsibility for the use of force. Hence the need to have a specific provision, under French law, for the use of force for purposes other than war on the one hand and self-defense on the other hand.[39]

As a result, under French domestic law today, the legality of the use of force has to be ascertained not only on a "macro" state level, namely, with regard to the decision taken by the authorities competent for using force, but also on a "micro" individual level, each time that a soldier decides to use force on the ground. The legality of the individual decision to use force also depends in that context on the nature of the armed conflict (whether international or noninternational).[40] This may explain why France is quite hesitant to delegate the use of force to private contractors. In a recent report on delegations in the context of military operations abroad, it has been made clear that in principle, any mission involving the use of force cannot be assigned to private contractors and remains the sole prerogative of state authorities,[41] that is to say, the executive branch.

II. France's Legal Position as Regards the Permissible Use of Force under International Law

To a large extent, the decision to use military force or to participate in collective security remains in France a discretionary power of political (primarily executive) authorities. To that extent and provided that the core provisions of the UN Charter are complied with, such a decision is a matter of policy or strategy rather than a question of legality. Such a strategy can of course be formally articulated and made public. To take an important example, France made clear in 1995 before the International Court of Justice (ICJ) that its nuclear strategy consists in having nuclear weapons designed to serve as deterrent to prevent war, not to serve as aggressive weapons.[42]

[39] On this provision, *see* Catherine Bergeal, *Nouveau cadre juridique de l'emploi de la force en opérations extérieures*, 61 Défense Nationale et Sécurité Collective 91–99 (2005).

[40] *See* Claire Landais, Director of the Legal Service of the Ministry of Defense, La Revue des Droits de l'Homme 3 (2015).

[41] *See* Rapport du sénateur Krattinger sur les externalisations en opérations extérieures, 2013–2014, no. 673, 2 July 2014, *available at* http://www.senat.fr/rap/r13-673/r13-673.html, in particular at 31–32.

[42] *See* France's Written Statement in Legality of the Threat of Use of Nuclear Weapons, ICJ, 20 June 1995, at 2, *available at* https://www.icj-cij.org.

Such a statement is primarily aimed at establishing a policy rather than as expressing a legal position.

It does not mean, however, that no legal issues arise in practice when the decision to use force is planned or taken. To the contrary, recent developments and new forms of use of force tend to strengthen (albeit in a modest way) the role of law in the process of deciding whether or not or under what circumstances French authorities can have recourse to force or can participate in collective security. As a result, the legality of decisions by French authorities to use force depends nowadays on a variety of legal factors, which oblige domestic authorities to assess with great care and caution whether or not it is possible to take such a decision in any given concrete case, and thus to frame a clear doctrine on permissible use of force under international law.

Obviously, it is not an easy task as France needs to accommodate possible conflicting interests. In particular, France is usually seen (or at least portrays itself) as a strong advocate of multilateral solutions, under the umbrella of the UN Security Council when the use of force is at stake, as exemplified by the position France took in 2003 when the United States was planning to use force against Iraq and was seeking to that end to obtain the approval of the UN Security Council.[43] But since the Paris and Nice terror attacks and more broadly because of the threat resulting from the emergence and multiplication of foreign terrorist fighters,[44] France seems willing to benefit from more flexibility in order to be able to fight terrorism even in the absence of a clear Chapter VII mandate emanating from the UN Security Council. The rise of cyberattacks could also lead to some adjustment of France's legal policy in that field in a near future.

With regard to the legal basis for the use of force, a mere enforcement measure, even if implying the use of coercive force, is generally not seen as passing the threshold established by the UN Charter for grounding it in Article 51 or Chapter VII of the Charter. This is in particular true regarding enforcement measures at sea or in air space. Of course, it can be difficult in some instances to determine whether a coercive action is limited to an enforcement measure or qualifies as an instance of use of force under international law. But it does not seem that this kind of enforcement measure or distinction raises any specific difficulty so far as France is concerned. France's concerns have only been related to the compatibility of some of these measures (arrest and detention following the boarding of a foreign vessel) with human rights, in particular regarding anti-piracy enforcement measures at sea. That issue led France to recently modify its domestic legislation[45] in order to take into account in particular adverse rulings of the European Court of Human Rights.[46]

[43] On France's position at that time, *see* UNSC, S/PV.4707, 14 February 2003, at 11–13.

[44] On the foreign terrorist fighters threat, *see in particular* https://www.un.org/sc/ctc/focus-areas/foreign-terrorist-fighters/.

[45] The rules applicable in French law to coercive actions at sea are set forth in the *Code de la défense* at Articles L 1521–1521 *ff.* In 2011, France adopted the *Loi No. 2011-13 of 5 January 2011* on enforcement measures at sea.

[46] *See in particular* the judgment of the Grand Chamber of the European Court of Human Rights in *Medvedyev and other v. France*, No. 3394/03, 29 March 2010.

For the use of force as such, France needs to base its actions on the UN Charter, either by invoking an authorization to use force based on a Chapter VII mandate granted by the UN Security Council, or by relying on self-defense under Article 51 of the Charter.

As a permanent member of the UN Security Council, France has a privileged status, which grants it specific powers when the UN Security Council adopts, or refuses to adopt, an authorization to use force. This privilege is also a responsibility. In the last years, France has been willing to strengthen that responsibility by proposing in particular in 2013 that the permanent members of the UN Security Council should undertake not to use the veto in cases of international crimes amounting to "mass atrocities."[47] A comparable proposal of a code of conduct was made in September 2015 by the group ACT (Accountability, Coherence, Transparency).[48] In 2015, France and Mexico presented a political statement on their initiative on framing the use of the veto in case of mass atrocities, according to which, in particular:

> We underscore that the veto is not a privilege, but an international responsibility. In that respect, we welcome and support the initiative by France, jointly presented with Mexico, to propose a collective and voluntary agreement among the permanent members of the Security Council to the effect that the permanent members would refrain from using the veto in case of mass atrocities.[49]

According to France, as of October 21, 2015 (last update available on France's relevant website), the initiative was supported by eighty countries.[50] So far, however, this proposal has not been endorsed by other permanent members, and there is no prospect that it will be adopted in the near future.

On a more general level, practice shows that France does not really have a coherent position regarding the conditions under which the use of force is seen as compatible with the UN Charter. In 2003, France followed a legalistic approach regarding the use of force against Iraq, warning against the dramatic consequences it could have on peace and security in the region and on the development of terrorism, asking "how do we ensure that the considerable risks of such an intervention can actually be kept under control?"[51] On the other hand, it adopted a more liberal interpretation of the same applicable rules in the Libya situation in 2011, insisting on that occasion on values rather than risks, notably by asserting that "we must not abandon civilian populations, the victims of brutal repression, to their fate; we must not allow the rule of law and international morality to be trampled underfoot," and by stating that the UN Security

[47] On this proposal, *see* https://onu.delegfrance.org/France-and-UN-Reform.

[48] *See* http://www.centerforunreform.org/sites/default/files/Final%202015-09-01%20SC%20Code%20of%20Conduct%20Atrocity.pdf.

[49] *See* https://onu.delegfrance.org/IMG/pdf/2015_08_07_veto_political_declaration_en.pdf.

[50] *See* https://onu.delegfrance.org/France-and-UN-Reform.

[51] *See* UNSC, S/PV.4707, 14 February 2003, at 11–13.

Council has to ensure "that Libya law prevails over force, democracy over dictatorship and freedom over oppression."[52]

France's legal position regarding the circumstances under which the use of force can be resorted to beyond the authorization of the UN Security Council under Chapter VII of the UN Charter or self-defense in case of aggression by another state is even more uncertain since the 2015 Paris attacks. In 2014, France announced that it would launch Operation Chammal in Iraq on the basis of Iraq's consent, following the request of assistance expressed by Iraq in two letters sent to the UN Security Council in June and September 2014.[53] But after the first Paris attacks, in January 2015, France's position evolved. First, France decided in September 2015 to extend its military operations to Syria, in order to fight against Da'esh/the Islamic State of Iraq and the Levant (ISIL) operating from Syria.[54] Second, it decided to justify its intervention in Syria on a quite broad interpretation of the right of self-defense.[55] The official position of France was expressed as follows in a letter from the Permanent Representative of France to the United Nations addressed to the Secretary-General and the President of the Security Council on September 8, 2015:

> By resolutions 2170 (2014), 2178 (2014) and 2199 (2015) in particular, the Security Council has described the terrorist acts of Islamic State in Iraq and the Levant (ISIL), including abuses committed against the civilian populations of the Syrian Arab Republic and Iraq, as a threat to international peace and security. Those acts are also a direct and extraordinary threat to the security of France. In a letter dated 20 September 2014 addressed to the President of the Security Council (S/2014/691), the Iraqi authorities requested the assistance of the international community in order to counter the attacks perpetrated by ISIL. In accordance with Article 51 of the Charter of the United Nations, France has taken actions involving the participation of military aircraft in response to attacks carried out by ISIL from the territory of the Syrian Arab Republic.[56]

France's position was expressed in that letter in a quite ambiguous way. On the one hand, France invoked self-defense, even though there had been no *state* armed attack against France. In light of the advisory opinion of the ICJ in the *Wall* case in 2004, according to which self-defense only applies to inter-state use of force,[57] France's

[52] *See* UNSC, S/PV.6498, 17 March 2011, at 2–3.

[53] *See* S/2014/440, 25 June 2014, and S/2014/691, 22 September 2014. On the articulation of France's position as regards its intervention in Iraq, *see* Frédérique Coulée, *Pratique française du droit international*, ANNUAIRE FRANÇAIS DE DROIT INTERNATIONAL 965–966 (2015).

[54] According to a very extensive reporting of the French daily newspaper *Le Monde*, dated Jan. 5, 2017, France (under the authority of the President of the Republic, relying on French Special Services) had recourse, since 2015, not only to airstrikes but also to a wide practice of targeted killings in order to neutralize terrorists in Iraq and Syria, and also in Mali (*see* LE MONDE, Jan. 5, 2017, at 10, 11, 13, and 22).

[55] *See* Coulée, *supra* note 53, at 966–969, with the relevant declarations of French authorities.

[56] S/2015/745, 9 September 2015.

[57] ICJ, Advisory Opinion, 9 July 2004, ICJ Reports 2004, at 194, para. 139.

invocation of self-defense can be seen as stretching the scope of Article 51 of the UN Charter. On the other hand, France did not indicate whether it was acting under individual or collective self-defense. The insistence in the letter quoted above on Iraq authorities' request for assistance indicates, however, that France in fact was availing itself of collective self-defense.[58]

The November 2015 Paris attacks resulted in an explicit invocation of the right to *individual* self-defense, based on the assertion that the said attacks constituted an armed attack ("aggression," as the President of the Republic put it on November 16, 2015).[59] Before the UN Security Council, the Permanent Representative of France stated without any ambiguity that:

> The events of 13 November were an armed aggression against France. Our military action, of which we informed the Security Council from the outset and which was justified as legitimate collective self-defence, can now also be characterized as individual self-defence, in accordance with Article 51 of the Charter of the United Nations.[60]

Such a broad interpretation of self-defense departs from France's traditional position according to which only states can commit armed attacks under Article 51 of the UN Charter, causing France to join those states advocating the possibility of resorting to force against nonstate entities such as Da'esh under Article 51, such as the United States, the United Kingdom, Russia, Belgium, and Germany. France's position in November 2015 was that very exceptional circumstances justify the use of force in Syria even in the absence of a state armed attack or a UN mandate.[61]

At the same time, France strongly advocated for the adoption of a resolution by the UN Security Council authorizing, or at least legitimatizing, the use of force against ISIL. On November 20, 2015, Resolution 2249 (2015) was adopted. The resolution does not explicitly authorize the use of force and does not expressly invoke Chapter VII of the Charter. But it characterizes ISIL terrorist acts as a "threat to international peace and security" and, in operative Paragraph 5:

> calls upon Member States that have the capacity to do so to take all necessary measures, in compliance with international law, in particular with the United Nations Charter, as well as international human rights, refugee and humanitarian law, on the territory under the control of ISIL also known as Da'esh, in Syria and Iraq, to redouble and coordinate their efforts to prevent and suppress terrorist

[58] *See* François Alabrune, *Fondements juridiques de l'intervention militaire française contre Daech en Irak et en Syrie*, Revue Générale de Droit International Public 45 (2016). *See also* François Alabrune, *Le cadre juridique des actions militaires menées par la France en Syrie le 14 avril 2018*, Revue Générale de Droit International Public 545–548 (2018).

[59] *See* Coulée, *supra* note 53, at 968–969.

[60] S/PV.7565, 20 November 2015, at 2. *See also*, for other statements, Coulée, *supra* note 53, at 969–970.

[61] *See* Alabrune, *supra* note 58, at 45–47.

> acts committed specifically by ISIL also known as Da'esh as well as ANF, and all other individuals, groups, undertakings, and entities associated with Al Qaeda, and other terrorist groups . . . and to eradicate the safe haven they have established over significant parts of Iraq and Syria.

Since then, France considers that its military action in Syria is covered by a UN Security Council resolution in the sense that the Council "supports" French military actions.[62] France's position with regard to both self-defense and the legal effect of Resolution 2249 has been challenged by French scholars on the ground that it is hardly in conformity with the UN Charter and state practice, which limit the use of force to self-defense in case of *state* armed attacks and operations based on an *explicit* Security Council's authorization.[63]

So far as the use of force based on consent is concerned, it can be grounded in bilateral treaties expressing the consent of the host state to see French forces deployed in its territory and using force. It remains to be seen whether recourse to the provisions of these treaties (which are applicable in French legal order), or any other instance of the use of force based on the foreign government's consent,[64] is fully compatible with the prohibition on assisting one party in the case of a noninternational armed conflict and whether these authorizations can be relied on without any authorization by the UN Security Council under Article 53 of the Charter. The current position of France is that when a foreign state asks for the military assistance from France, and in particular when this request is based on a bilateral treaty that provides for this assistance, no additional authorization or basis under international law is needed. Such treaties have been concluded, for instance, with the Ivory Coast, the Central African Republic, and Senegal. They contain a provision according to which both parties agree to engage in a defense partnership aimed at sustainable peace and security on their territories and in their respective regional environment and another provision according to which cooperation with regard to defense matters can cover any activity agreed upon by the parties taking into account their common interests.[65]

Finally, the possibility of using force for rescuing nationals abroad (or other similar interventions) is still disputed. France considers that it is a valid exception to the

[62] *Id.* at 48–49.

[63] *See in particular* Franck Latty, *Le brouillage des repères du jus contra bellum. A propos de l'usage de la force par la France contre Daech*, REVUE GÉNÉRALE DE DROIT INTERNATIONAL PUBLIC 19–39 (2016); Nabil Hajjami, *De la légalité de l'engagement militaire de la France en Syrie*, REVUE DU DROIT PUBLIC 156–164, 168–174 (2017).

[64] *See*, for instance, France's intervention in Mali. Karine Bannelier & Theodore Christakis, *Under the UN Security Council's Watchful Eyes: Intervention by Invitation in the Malian Conflict*, 26 LEIDEN J. INT'L L. 855–874 (2013).

[65] For the text of the agreements with Ivory Coast, *see* the Decree 2014-1764; with Central African Republic, the Decree 2011-1109; and with Senegal, the Decree 2014-1152. By contrast, other agreements only provide for cooperation to improve defense capacities, without any provision on the possibility to use force. *See*, for instance, the 2011 agreement with Serbia, published by the Decree 2011-1835.

prohibition on the use of force and has availed itself of this exception on various occasions.[66]

III. Conclusion

To conclude, it is fair to say that France's law and practice on the use of force is not very original. As in many other countries, the decision to use force largely remains the province of the executive branch, despite some recent evolutions in constitutional law aimed at enhancing the role of the Parliament. In addition, domestic courts continue to practice self-restraint in that field. So far as policies are concerned, France seeks to combine the need to comply with the relevant international rules with its security concerns, in particular in relation to the fight against terrorism. To put it in a nutshell, although (or perhaps because) the use of force is a grave decision that may have dramatic consequences, it is still largely considered as requiring a low level of legal review or democratic supervision. It remains to be seen whether recourse to comparative foreign relations law will legitimate and strengthen a trend towards greater parliamentary involvement, or, to the contrary, make the case for executive control more compelling.

[66] *See* Zoller, *supra* note 8, at 247; Mathias Forteau, *Rescuing Nationals Abroad*, *in* The Oxford Handbook of the Use of Force in International Law ch. 44, 947–961 (Marc Weller ed., 2015).

CHAPTER 46

DECISIONS IN JAPAN TO USE MILITARY FORCE OR PARTICIPATE IN MULTINATIONAL PEACEKEEPING OPERATIONS

TADASHI MORI

THIS chapter describes the law in Japan governing the country's use of military force and participation in multinational peacekeeping operations. Although Article 9 of Japan's post-World War II constitution[1] seems to disallow the development of armed forces, the country has long maintained limited armed forces for purposes of self-defense. According to the Japanese government's traditional constitutional interpretation, these forces can only be used when necessary to repel an armed attack on Japan. Under this interpretation, Japan can use armed force only for individual self-defense, not for collective self-defense or collective security. In addition, although Japanese law since the 1990s has allowed for some participation of Japanese forces in multinational peacekeeping operations, this allowance has been very limited.

In 2015, however, Japan enacted two important statutes that broaden the government's ability to use the country's armed forces. One statute allows the country for the first time to exercise a right of collective self-defense, although the legislation only permits Japan to exercise this right for the purpose of ensuring its survival and protecting its people in situations that are called "existential crisis situations." The other statute broadens the ability of Japanese forces to engage in various support

[1] Nihonkoku Kenpō [Constitution], art. 9 (*in Japanese*), translated in *Japanese Law Translation* [JLT DS], *available at* http://www.japaneselawtranslation.go.jp.

activities in multinational peacekeeping operations. Because of Article 9 of the Constitution, however, Japan's ability to use its military is still substantially more limited than for many other countries. As a result, there has been some discussion in recent years about whether Article 9 should be amended to relax the constraints on the use of the military. There are sharply differing views in Japan on this issue.

As the Supreme Court of Japan has not yet dealt with the constitutionality of the Self-Defense Forces (SDF), the Japanese courts do not play a significant role regarding Japan's use of military force and participation in multinational peacekeeping operations.[2] Thus, the following examination will be focused on the interpretation of the Japanese Constitution by the Japanese government and on legislation.

I. Article 9 of the Constitution and the Self-Defense Forces Act

After Japan was defeated in the Second World War, the Allied powers ordered the country to disarm. The Japanese Constitution was drafted in 1946 and enacted on May 3, 1947, when Japan was under Allied occupation. Article 9 of the Japanese Constitution provides:

> *Paragraph 1:* Aspiring sincerely to an international peace based on justice and order, the Japanese people forever renounce war as a sovereign right of the nation and the threat or use of force as a means of settling international disputes.
>
> *Paragraph 2:* In order to accomplish the aim of the preceding paragraph, land, sea, and air forces, as well as other war potential, will never be maintained. The right of belligerency of the state will not be recognized.[3]

In 1950, in the wake of the outbreak of the Korean War, the National Police Reserve of Japan was established. While its primary purpose was to maintain the nation's public order, the police reserves gradually became more heavily armed. In 1952, the reserves were reorganized as the National Safety Forces, and in 1954, they were again reorganized as the SDF. This period marked the end of the Allied

[2] Yasuo Hasebe, *War Powers, in* The Oxford Handbook of Comparative Constitutional Law 463, 478 (Michael Rosenfeld & Andreás Sajó eds., 2012).

[3] By contrast, the German Basic Law of 1949 does not contain an explicit prohibition against the establishment of armed forces. By the time of its enactment, the Cold War had begun. The Japanese Constitution was drafted in 1946 when the Cold War had not gone into full swing. *See id.* at 475; Georg Nolte, *Germany: Ensuring Political Legitimacy for the use of Military Forces by Requiring Constitutional Accountability, in* Democratic Accountability and the Use of Force in International Law 231, 231–232 (Charlotte Ku & Harold K. Jacobson eds., 2003).

occupation of Japan, which officially ceased with the entry into force of the Treaty of Peace with Japan of 1952.[4]

The creation of the SDF sparked a major debate over whether the SDF constituted the "war potential" that Japan was prohibited from maintaining under Paragraph 2 of Article 9. The government outlined its official view on the matter in December 1954,[5] reasoning that: (1) the Constitution did not deny the right of self-defense; (2) Japan renounced war, but did not renounce the right to defend itself; and (3) establishment of the SDF was not contrary to the Constitution because the SDF's mission was self-defense and its ability was limited to necessary and adequate levels of self-defense.[6]

The government has also argued for the constitutionality of the SDF's use of military force by citing the preamble and Article 13 of the Constitution.[7] In 2004, the government explained:[8]

> the provisions of Article 9 of the Constitution seem to prohibit Japan completely from using force in international relations, but in light of the preamble of the Constitution that confirms the right of the Japanese people to live in peace and of Article 13 of the Constitution that states that people's right to life, liberty, and the pursuit of happiness shall be the supreme consideration in legislation and in other governmental affairs, the government interprets that Article 9 of the Constitution does not prohibit Japan from using minimum and necessary force to remove the risk caused to the people's lives and persons by an armed attack from the outside.

Thus, the government has consistently asserted the constitutionality of the SDF. Today, the Japanese people by and large accept the government's case.[9] On the other hand, it is commonly understood that the use of force by the SDF should be limited to the minimum extent necessary for self-defense.

The allocation of domestic authority concerning the use of military force is not provided for by the Constitution. Article 9 is the only constitutional provision

[4] Akiho Shibata, *Japan: Moderate Commitment within Legal Structures*, *in* DEMOCRATIC ACCOUNTABILITY AND THE USE OF FORCE IN INTERNATIONAL LAW, *supra* note 3, at 207, 211–212.

[5] SEIFU NO KENPŌ KAISHAKU [HOW THE GOVERNMENT INTERPRETS THE CONSTITUTION] 9–10 (Masahiro Sakata ed., 2013) (*in Japanese*).

[6] 2 Dai 21kai Kokkai Shūgiin Yosan Iinkaigiroku [Official Record of the Proceedings of the House of Representatives Budget Committee of the 21st Diet] 1 (Dec. 22, 1954) (statement of Seiichi Ōmura, Director General of the Defense Agency) (*in Japanese*).

[7] The preamble provides that "[w]e recognize that all peoples of the world have the right to live in peace, free from fear and want." Article 13 provides that "[a]ll of the people shall be respected as individuals. Their right to life, liberty, and the pursuit of happiness shall, to the extent that it does not interfere with the public welfare, be the supreme consideration in legislation and in other governmental affairs."

[8] Shūgiin Giin Shima Satoshi-kun Teishutsu Seifu no Kenpō Kaishaku Henkō ni kansuru Shitsumon ni taisuru Tōbensho [Cabinet Reply to the Question Submitted by Mr. Satoshi Shima, Member of the House of Representatives, concerning an Alteration of Interpretation of Constitution by the Government (Reply No. 114, at the 159th Diet)] (June 18, 2004), *available at* http://www.shugiin.go.jp/internet/itdb_shitsumon_pdf_t.nsf/html/shitsumon/pdfT/b159114.pdf/$File/b159114.pdf (*in Japanese*).

[9] Hasebe, *supra* note 2, at 478.

regarding the use of force. This matter is thus addressed in separate legislation, principally the SDF Act,[10] which was enacted in 1954.[11]

Under the SDF Act before the amendment of 2015, in order for the government to use force, the following conditions must be met: there must be an armed attack against Japan[12]; there must be no other appropriate means available to repel the attack to ensure Japan's survival and to protect its people[13]; the use of force must be limited to the minimum extent necessary for individual self-defense[14]; measures taken must be reported to the UN Security Council[15]; and the measures are to be taken only "until the Security Council has taken the measures necessary to maintain international peace and security."[16] With regard to the allocation of authority, the prime minister has the authority to mobilize the SDF subject to the approval of the Diet.[17] Prior Diet approval is required in principle. It is not required in case of an emergency, but the prime minister must order the SDF to stand down immediately if he or she does not obtain ex post facto approval.[18]

II. Collective Self-Defense

Amid the increasingly severe security environment surrounding Japan,[19] the Cabinet, in July 2014, decided on a basic policy for developing a new legislative framework to

[10] Jieitaihō [SDF Act], Law No. 165 of 1954 (*in Japanese*).

[11] Hasebe, *supra* note 2, at 478.

[12] SDF Act, art. 76, para. 1, no. 1 & art. 88, para. 1; Buryoku Kōgeki Jitai tō oyobi Sonritsu Kiki Jitai ni okeru Wagakuni no Heiwa to Dokuritsu narabini Kuni oyobi Kokumin no Anzen no Kakuho ni kansuru Hōritsu [the Act on the Peace and Independence of Japan and Maintenance of the Nation and the People's Security in Armed Attack Situations etc.], Law No. 79 of 2003 [Armed Attack Security Act], art. 9, para. 4 (*in Japanese*).

[13] SDF Act, art. 88, para. 2; Armed Attack Security Act, art. 3, para. 4.

[14] SDF Act, art. 88, para. 2; Armed Attack Security Act, art. 3, para. 4.

[15] Armed Attack Security Act, art. 18.

[16] This condition is not provided for in legislation but is accepted by the government.

[17] SDF Act, art. 76, para. 1, before the amendment of 2015 provided:

> The Prime Minister may, in responses to a situation where an armed attack against Japan from the outside occurs, or a situation where imminent danger of an armed attack against Japan from the outside occurring is clearly perceived, give the whole or part of the Self-Defense Forces the Defense Operations Order when necessary to defend Japan. In this case, the approval of the Diet must be obtained pursuant to the provisions of Article 9 of the Act on the Peace and Independence of Japan and Maintenance of the Nation and the People's Security in Armed Attack Situations etc.

[18] Armed Attack Security Act, art. 9. For the comparison of Japan's law with that of other states, *see* Hasebe, *supra* note 2, at 466–479; Curtis A. Bradley, *U.S. War Powers and the Potential Benefits of Comparativism*, ch. 42 in this volume; Mathias Forteau, *Using Military Force and Engaging in Collective Security: The Case of France*, ch. 45 in this volume; Monica Hakimi, *Techniques for Regulating Military Force*, ch. 41 in this volume; and Katja S. Ziegler, *The Use of Military Force by the United Kingdom: The Evolution of Accountability*, ch. 43 in this volume.

[19] *See* Shunji Yanai, *New Japanese Legislation for Peace and Security—Its Background and Salient Points*, 60 Japanese Y.B. Int'l L. 136, 136–138 (2017).

deal with these challenges.[20] In accordance with this basic policy, two new statutes were enacted: the Act for Partial Amendments to the Self-Defense Forces Law and other Existing Laws for Ensuring Peace and Security of Japan and the International Community (Act for the Development of Legislation for Peace and Security)[21]; and the Act Concerning Japan's Cooperation and Support Activities for Foreign Military Forces and other Personnel in Situations that the International Community is Collectively Addressing for Peace and Security (International Peace Support Act).[22] These statutes, collectively referred to as "the New Legislation for Peace and Security," were passed on September 19, 2015, and took effect on March 29, 2016. The New Legislation constitutes an especially significant revision of the existing legislation in that it includes a provision expanding the scope of the use of military force by the SDF.

Regarding the government's ability to exercise collective self-defense, the Japanese government has long maintained the following position: Japan, as a sovereign nation, has an inherent right to collective defense under international law, but the restrictions imposed by Article 9 of the Constitution are such that the government cannot constitutionally exercise this right.[23] However, in the above-mentioned Cabinet Decision of July 1, 2014, the government expressed the following view:[24]

> [T]he Government has reached a conclusion that not only when an armed attack against Japan occurs but also when an armed attack against a foreign country that is in a close relationship with Japan occurs and as a result threatens Japan's survival and poses a clear danger to fundamentally overturn people's right to life, liberty and pursuit of happiness, and when there is no other appropriate means available to repel the attack and ensure Japan's survival and protect its people, use of force to the minimum extent necessary should be interpreted to be permitted under the Constitution as measures for self-defense in accordance with the basic logic of the Government's view to date.

While the term "collective self-defense" is not mentioned in the above statement, a sentence in the next paragraph reads: "In certain situations, the aforementioned 'use of force' permitted under the Constitution is, under international law, based on the right

[20] Kuni no Sonritsu o Mattōshi Kokumin o Mamoru tame no Kireme no nai Anzen Hoshō Taisei no Seibi ni tsuite (Kakugi Kettei) [Cabinet Decision on Development of Seamless Security Legislation to Ensure Japan's Survival and Protect its People] (July 1, 2014), *available at* http://www.cas.go.jp/jp/gaiyou/jimu/pdf/anpohosei.pdf (*in Japanese*), and https://www.cas.go.jp/jp/gaiyou/jimu/pdf/anpohosei_eng.pdf (*Provisional Translation*).

[21] Wagakuni oyobi Kokusai Shakai no Heiwa oyobi Anzen no Kakuho ni Shisuru tame no Jieitaihō tō no Ichibu o Kaiseisuru Hōritsu [Act for the Development of Legislation for Peace and Security], Law No. 76 of 2015 (*in Japanese*). This act, as its title suggests, is an amendment of ten existing statutes, including the SDF Act and the Armed Attack Security Act.

[22] Kokusai Shakai Kyōdō Taisho Jitai ni saishite Wagakuni ga Jisshisuru Shogaikoku no Guntai tō ni taisuru Kyōryoku Shien Katsudō tō ni kansuru Hōritsu [International Peace Support Act], Law No. 77 of 2015 (*in Japanese*).

[23] Seifu no Kenpō Kaishaku, *supra* note 5, at 64.

[24] Cabinet Decision of July 1, 2014, *supra* note 20, at 3(3).

of collective self-defense." This understanding was subsequently incorporated into the New Legislation for Peace and Security of 2015.

The requirements for the use of force in collective self-defense under the new Japanese legislation are as follows[25]: there must be an armed attack against a foreign country that is in a close relationship with Japan; as a result, there must be a threat to Japan's survival, i.e., occurrence of an incident that as a result threatens Japan's survival and poses a clear danger to fundamentally overturn people's right to life, liberty, and pursuit of happiness, which is a situation called an "existential crisis situation"[26]; there must be no other appropriate means available to repel the attack and ensure Japan's survival and protect its people[27]; the use of force must be limited to the minimum extent necessary[28]; there must be a request for, or at least consent to, assistance by a foreign country subjected to armed attack[29]; measures taken must be reported to the UN Security Council[30]; and measures are to be taken only "until the Security Council has taken the measures necessary to maintain international peace and security."[31]

The most important condition in the new legislation is that there must be a threat to Japan's survival, i.e., the occurrence of an existential crisis situation. As shown by the Cabinet Decision of July 1, 2014, this restriction was thought to be imposed by the Japanese Constitution.[32] According to Article 76, Paragraph 1 of the SDF Act of 2015, an existential crisis situation is defined as "[a] situation in which an armed attack against a foreign country that is in a close relationship with Japan occurs and as a result threatens Japan's survival and poses a clear danger to fundamentally overturn people's right to life, liberty, and pursuit of happiness." The nature of this requirement was fiercely debated in the Diet, but it has not been clarified through the debate.[33]

With regard to the requirement that the use of force must be limited to the minimum extent necessary, in the Diet deliberations over the proposed new peace and security legislation, the government clearly acknowledged that international law provides two conditions for the exercise of the right of collective self-defense: necessity

[25] *See* Tadashi Mori, *Collective Self-Defence in International Law and in the New Japanese Legislation for Peace and Security (2015)*, 60 JAPANESE Y.B. INT'L L. 158, 166–167 (2017).

[26] SDF Act, art. 76, para. 1, no. 2.

[27] Although, according to the statement by the Japanese government, this condition is provided for in SDF Act, art. 88, para. 2, Armed Attack Security Act, art. 3, para. 4, there are no explicit provisions for such.

[28] SDF Act, art. 88, para. 2; Armed Attack Security Act, art. 3, para. 4.

[29] This condition is not provided for in legislation but is admitted by the government. *See* text *infra* accompanying note 37.

[30] Armed Attack Security Act, art. 18.

[31] This condition is not provided for in legislation but is admitted by the government.

[32] Cabinet Decision of July 1, 2014, *supra* note 20.

[33] *See* MASAHIRO SAKATA, KENPŌ 9JŌ TO ANPOHŌSEI [ARTICLE 9 OF THE JAPANESE CONSTITUTION AND THE NEW LEGISLATION FOR PEACE AND SECURITY] 21–29 (2016) (*in Japanese*). Regarding the existential crisis situation, *see* Akira Mayama, *The Constitutional Limitation on the Exercise of the Right of Collective Self-Defense: Minesweeping in Foreign Territorial Waters and Close-In Logistical Support for Belligerents*, 60 JAPANESE Y.B. INT'L L. 171–185 (2017).

and proportionality.[34] According to the government's view, these requirements mean that, in the case of Japan, the force must be of "the minimum extent necessary to repel an armed attack against a foreign country that is in a close relationship with Japan, which would consequently threaten Japan's survival and pose a clear danger to fundamentally overturn people's right to life, liberty, and pursuit of happiness, and to ensure Japan's survival and protect its people."[35] It is notable that the force would need, on the one hand, to be of "the minimum extent necessary to repel an armed attack against a foreign country . . . " and, on the other hand, be of "the minimum extent necessary to ensure Japan's survival and protect its people." Thus, the use of force would have to fulfill two conditions: the requirements of international law and those of Japanese law.[36] It was aptly pointed out that these sets of conditions are to be applied cumulatively; moreover, it was made abundantly clear that the requirements of international law for collective self-defense are such that, unlike in the case of individual self-defense, the force must be of "the minimum extent necessary to repel an armed attack against a foreign country [that has been attacked] . . . " The government takes the position that the requirements of necessity and proportionality are stipulated in Article 88, Paragraph 2 of the SDF Act and Article 3, Paragraph 4 of the Act concerning the Measures for Protection of the People in Armed Attack Situations (Armed Attack Security Act).

On the condition that there must be a request for, or at least consent to, assistance to a foreign country subjected to armed attack, the above legislation does not provide any explicit stipulations. However, the government maintains that these requirements are implied in the provisions of Article 88, Paragraph 2 of the SDF Act.[37] The provisions

[34] 6 Dai 189kai Kokkai Shūgiin Wagakuni oyobi Kokusai Shakai no Heiwa Anzen Hōsei ni kansuru Tokubetsu Iinkaigiroku [Official Record of the Proceedings of the House of Representatives Security Bills Special Committee of the 189th Diet] 19 (June 1, 2015) (statement of Fumio Kishida, Minister for Foreign Affairs) (*in Japanese*).

[35] 28 Dai 189kai Kokkai Shūgiin Kaigiroku [Official Record of the Proceedings of the House of Representatives Plenary Sittings of the 189th Diet] 10 (May 26, 2015) (statement of Fumio Kishida, Minister for Foreign Affairs) (*in Japanese*).

[36] 20 Dai 189kai Kokkai Shūgiin Wagakuni oyobi Kokusai Shakai no Heiwa Anzen Hōsei ni kansuru Tokubetsu Iinkaigiroku [Official Record of the Proceedings of the House of Representatives Security Bills Special Committee of the 189th Diet] 10 (July 13, 2015) (statement of Fumio Kishida, Minister for Foreign Affairs) (*in Japanese*).

[37] In the Diet deliberations over the proposed New Peace and Security Legislation, Defense Minister Gen Nakatani made the following remarks:

> Under international law, the use of collective self-defense is naturally premised on a scenario where a country under armed attack has requested and consented to such intervention. As was made clear in a cabinet decision in July last year, in using military force, Japan would observe international law as a matter of course; moreover, Article 88, Paragraph 2 of the SDF Act provides that, in mobilizing the SDF, Japan must adhere to international statutes and customs, when so required.

12 Dai 189kai Kokkai Shūgiin Wagakuni oyobi Kokusai Shakai no Heiwa Anzen Hōsei ni kansuru Tokubetsu Iinkaigiroku [Official Record of Proceedings of the House of Representatives Security Bills Special Committee of the 189th Diet] 39 (Aug. 25, 2015) (statement of Gen Nakatani, Minister of Defense) (*in Japanese*). Nakatani made the same remarks in 5 Dai 189kai Kokkai Shūgiin Wagakuni

stipulate that in using force when the SDF are ordered to be in an operation, "international statutes and/or customs will be adhered to, when so required, and the limit as legitimately adjudged necessary for meeting the prevailing situation will not be exceeded."

With regard to the allocation of authority, the prime minister has the authority to mobilize the SDF subject to the approval of the Diet.[38] As with uses of force in individual self-defense, prior Diet approval is required in principle; it is not required in the case of an emergency, but if the prime minister does not obtain ex post facto approval, he or she must order the SDF to stand down immediately.[39] However, the second paragraph of supplementary resolutions, added just before the above revised legislation was approved in the House of Councilors, provides that prior Diet approval must be sought without exception.[40]

III. Participation in Multinational Peacekeeping Operations

Multinational Forces

The Japanese government has stated that, as there are potentially many different types of multinational forces, it cannot make blanket statements on the permissibility of the SDF's participation in multinational forces, and that the SDF's participation would be

oyobi Kokusai Shakai no Heiwa Anzen Hōsei ni kansuru Tokubetsu Iinkaigiroku [Official Record of Proceedings of the House of Representatives Security Bills Special Committee of the 189th Diet] 41 (July 30, 2015) (statement of Gen Nakatani, Minister of Defense) (*in Japanese*).

[38] SDF Act, art. 76, para. 1 of 2015 provides:

> The Prime Minister may, in responses to the situations listed below, give the whole or part of the Self-Defense Forces the Defense Operations Order when necessary to defend Japan. In this case, the approval of the Diet must be obtained pursuant to the provisions of Article 9 of the Act on the Peace and Independence of Japan and Maintenance of the Nation and the People's Security in Armed Attack Situations etc. and Situations where an Armed Attack against a Foreign Country Consequently Threatens Japan's Survival.
>
> (i) A situation where an armed attack against Japan from the outside occurs, or a situation where imminent danger of an armed attack against Japan from the outside occurring is clearly perceived.
> (ii) A situation in which an armed attack against a foreign country that is in a close relationship with Japan occurs and as a result threatens Japan's survival and poses a clear danger to fundamentally overturn people's right to life, liberty, and pursuit of happiness.

[39] Armed Attack Security Act, art. 9.

[40] Wagakuni oyobi Kokusai Shakai no Heiwa oyobi Anzen no Kakuho ni Shisuru tame no Jieitaihō tō no Ichibu o Kaiseisuru Hōritsuan oyobi Kokusai Shakai Kyōdō Taisho Jitai ni saishite Wagakuni ga Jisshisuru Shogaikoku no Guntai tō ni taisuru Kyōryoku Shien Katsudō tō ni kansuru Hōritsuan ni taisuru Futai Ketsugi (Sangiin Wagakuni oyobi Kokusai Shakai no Heiwa Anzen Hōsei ni kansuru Tokubetsu Iinkai) [House of Councillors Security Bills Special Committee Resolution on the Bill for the Development of Legislation for Peace and Security and the International Peace Support Bill] (Sept. 17, 2015), *available at* http://www.sangiin.go.jp/japanese/gianjoho/ketsugi/189/f429_091701.pdf (*in Japanese*).

contingent on it refraining from using constitutionally impermissible military force and on its activities not forming an "integral part" of the use of force by other countries.[41] In order to avoid integration with the use of foreign military force, the government has restricted the SDF's deployment to noncombat areas.[42]

The SDF has participated in a multinational force that was assisting the reconstruction of Iraq. This force operated under UN Security Council Resolution 1483, which was adopted on May 22, 2003, to resolve matters resulting from the 2003 Iraq War. However, since there was no general legislation that could serve as the basis for dispatching the SDF overseas in order to aid the activities of a multinational force, the government has resorted to special measures legislation, which was the Act on Special Measures concerning Humanitarian Relief and Reconstruction Work and Security Assistance in Iraq (Iraq Special Measures Act).[43] This led to the establishment of a general statute on this issue in 2015.

In order to have general legislation that would provide for the appropriate and speedy implementation of support activities, including supplies and logistical support, to a foreign military engaged in a mission to secure peace and security for the international community, the government drafted the International Peace Support Bill, which was passed in September 2015. Before drafting the bill, at a press conference following the Cabinet Decision of July 2014, Prime Minister Shinzō Abe stated: "It still remains the case that the SDF will never participate in such warfare as the Gulf War or the Iraq War in the past."[44] Thus, the activities in which the SDF is allowed to take part are still limited.

The International Peace Support Act was enacted with the aim of contributing to the peace and security of the international community through support activities for foreign military forces and other personnel in "situations that the international community is collectively addressing for peace and security." Such situations are defined as situations that threaten the peace and security of the international community so that it becomes necessary for the international community to take collective action to repel the threat in accordance with the purposes of the Charter of the United Nations, and for Japan to contribute to such efforts proactively as a member of the international community (Article 1). For a situation to qualify as a "situation that the

[41] Shūgiin Giin Nagatsuma Akira-kun Teishutsu Jieitai no Takokusekigun Sanka ni kansuru Shitsumon ni taisuru Tōbensho [Cabinet Reply to the Question Submitted by Mr. Akira Nagatsuma, Member of the House of Representatives, concerning the SDF's Participation in the Multinational Forces (Reply No. 184, at the 159th Diet)] (June 22, 2004), *available at* http://www.shugiin.go.jp/internet/itdb_shitsumon_pdf_t.nsf/html/shitsumon/pdfT/b159184.pdf/$File/b159184.pdf (*in Japanese*).

[42] Noncombat area was defined as an area wherein combat activities are not conducted at the time when the decision to dispatch the SDF is to be made and an area in which, it is to be regarded, such activities will not be conducted during the dispatch of the SDF.

[43] Iraku ni okeru Jindō Fukkō Shien Katsudō oyobi Anzen Kakuho Shien Katsudō no Jisshi ni kansuru Tokubetsu Sochihō [Iraq Special Measures Act], Law No. 137 of 2003 (*in Japanese*).

[44] Press Conference by Prime Minister Abe (July 1, 2014), *available at* http://www.kantei.go.jp/jp/96_abe/statement/2014/0701kaiken.html (*in Japanese*), and https://japan.kantei.go.jp/96_abe/statement/201407/0701kaiken.html (*Provisional Translation*).

international community is collectively addressing for peace and security," there must be a resolution of the UN Security Council or General Assembly to the effect that this situation poses a threat to the peace and security of the international community.[45]

The SDF is allowed to do support activities that qualify as logistical support (Article 3, Paragraph 2[46]) and do not include the provision of weapons, and it is also permitted to do search and rescue operations (Article 3, Paragraph 3). To ensure that the activities do not constitute a use of force, they are not to be conducted at a scene where combat activities are taking place at the time.[47]

The International Peace Support Act includes clear provisions on ensuring the safety of SDF units (Article 9). Support activities are to be immediately suspended if the place where they are being conducted or a place nearby has become or is likely to become the scene of combat activities, or if such a suspension is deemed necessary to ensure the safety of the units (Article 2, Paragraph 3, Article 7, Paragraphs 3–5). In addition, in order for the SDF to conduct activities in territories outside Japan, Japan must first obtain consent for the undertaking of such activities from the host countries. If the territory concerned lacks a government that can give consent, Japan must obtain permission from the organ that administers the territory, if such an organ exists under a resolution of the UNSC or General Assembly (Article 2, Paragraph 4). With regard to the domestic allocation of authority, the prime minister has the authority to mobilize the SDF subject to the prior approval of the Diet (Articles 4–6, International Peace Support Act).

As mentioned above, the Japanese government has taken the stance that participation in multinational forces is not permissible in situations that involve the use of military force. Deliberations regarding the New Legislation for Peace and Security focused on either the exercise of the right to collective self-defense, or the establishment of general legislation regarding the provision of logistical support for multinational forces. Little attention was paid to the use of military force as a participant in a multinational force. Indeed, this point was barely discussed. However, the establishment of the New Legislation for Peace and Security made participation in a multinational force that involves the use of military force possible in an extremely limited set of circumstances called existential crisis situations.

[45] Such a resolution can come in two forms: (1) a resolution (of the UNSC or General Assembly) that decides, calls upon, recommends, or authorizes actions by member states (art. 3, para. 1, no. 1, i); and (2) a resolution (of the UNSC or General Assembly) that recognizes that the situation amounts to threats to the peace or breaches of the peace, and requests member states to take certain measures in relation to the situation (art. 3, para. 1, no. 1, ii). Multinational forces' actions would fall under the first type of resolution.

[46] Such activities include the provision of goods and services to foreign military forces and other personnel, including supply, transportation, repair and maintenance, medical activities, communications, airport and sea services, and base services. The provision of weapons is not included.

[47] Art. 2, para. 3. This provision substitutes the "noncombat area" concept that was specified in the Iraq Special Measures Act, which was designed to ensure that the SDF's activities did not become an "integral part" of the use of force by other countries. *See supra* note 42. The area wherein the support activities can be conducted under the new act is defined more flexibly.

The logical basis of the New Legislation for Peace and Security on this point is as follows. As the Cabinet decision of July 1, 2014, shows, according to the government's interpretation, the following three requirements must be fulfilled for the use of military force to be permitted under Article 9 of the Japanese Constitution: (1) the occurrence of an armed attack against Japan, or the occurrence of an armed attack against a foreign country being in a close relationship with Japan that as a result threatens Japan's survival and poses a clear danger to fundamentally overturn people's right to life, liberty, and pursuit of happiness; (2) there is no other appropriate means available to repel the attack and ensure Japan's survival and protect its people; and (3) use of force is limited to the minimum extent necessary. These are the requirements for the use of military force to be constitutionally permitted, and "the basis in international law of [such use of force] are the exercise of a right to individual self-defense, that to collective self-defense, and the collective security measures enumerated in UN Security Council Resolutions that authorize the exercise of use of force."[48] Furthermore, it has been pointed out that "when Japan 'uses armed force' that meets Japan's three requirements for the use of military force and that is justified as the exercise of a right to individual or collective defense under international law, even if the basis of this justification under international law changes from self-defense to a UN Security Council Resolution, [Japan's government] is under no constitutional obligation to cease any 'use of military force' that meets the three requirements for the use of military force."[49]

As Article 76, Paragraph 1 of the SDF Act indicates, the circumstances necessary to allow the prime minister to dispatch the SDF are "1 The occurrence of an external military attack against Japan or a situation in which the imminent danger of an external military attack against Japan is recognized," or "2 A situation involving an armed attack against a foreign country that is in a close relationship with Japan, which would consequently threaten Japan's survival and pose a clear danger to the rights of the Japanese people to life, liberty and the pursuit of happiness." However, as the Cabinet Legislation Bureau has pointed out, even if a UN Security Council Resolution were adopted and a multinational force was organized, so long as a condition such as the one described above continued, the use of military force by the SDF would also be permitted. Hence, in such a scenario, the participation of the SDF in a multinational force is permitted.

With regard to the allocation of authority, the prime minister has the authority to mobilize the SDF subject to the approval of the Diet.[50] As with the other uses of the military discussed above, prior Diet approval is required in principle; it is not required in the case of an emergency, but if the prime minister does not obtain ex post facto

[48] Naikaku Hōseikyoku [Cabinet Legislation Bureau], Kenpō Kankei Tōbenreishū (Dai 9jō, Kenpō Kaishaku Kankei) [A Casebook for Constitutional Law (Concerning Article 9 and Its Interpretations)] 219 (2016), *cited in* Seifu no Kenpō 9jō Kaishaku [Interpretation of Article 9 of the Japanese Constitution by the Japanese Government] (Ichirō Urata ed., 2d ed. 2017) (*in Japanese*).

[49] *Id.* [50] SDF Act, art. 76, para. 1.

approval, he or she must order the SDF to stand down immediately.[51] Furthermore, the second paragraph of the above-mentioned supplementary resolutions provides that, in case of the existential crisis situations, prior Diet approval must be sought without exception.[52]

UN Peacekeeping Operations

It was in 1988 when Japan dispatched personnel to participate in peacekeeping operation activities for the first time. Before 1992, the personnel that Japan could dispatch to foreign territories were limited to those who could be treated as members of the Ministry of Foreign Affairs. This limitation meant that Japan only dispatched administrators and small teams of election monitoring personnel.[53]

In 1992, Japan enacted the Act on Cooperation with United Nations Peacekeeping Operations and Other Operations (International Peace Cooperation Act).[54] This law permitted Japan to dispatch large-scale teams of personnel, including the SDF, to participate in peacekeeping operations (PKOs) and international humanitarian relief operations.[55]

To govern the use of weapons and ensure the constitutionality of the operations, the government established five principles of PKO participation. These five principles must be met before Japan can participate in a PKO. These five principles correspond to the (internationally recognized) traditional principles on PKOs established during the Cold War: the principles of consent, impartiality, and the use of weapons only for self-defense.

The five principles in the International Peace Cooperation Act of 1992 are as follows: (1) agreement on a ceasefire shall have been reached among the parties to armed conflicts; (2) consent for the undertaking of UN peacekeeping operations as well as Japan's participation in such operations shall have been obtained from the host countries as well as the parties to armed conflicts; (3) the operations shall strictly maintain impartiality, not favoring any of the parties to armed conflicts; (4) should any

[51] Armed Attack Security Act, art. 9.

[52] House of Councillors Security Bills Special Committee Resolution of September 17, 2015, *supra* note 40.

[53] Examples of the personnel dispatched before 1992 include an election monitoring team that participated in the UN Transition Assistance Group (deployed in Namibia), administrators who participated in the UN Good Offices Mission in Afghanistan and Pakistan, and administrators who participated in the UN Iran-Iraq Military Observer Group. Fumio Iwai, *Nihon no Kokusai Heiwa Kyōryoku Seido [Japanese System for International Peace Cooperation]*, *in* KOKUSAI HEIWA KYŌRYOKU NYŪMON [INTRODUCTION TO INTERNATIONAL PEACE COOPERATION] 175, 177–178 (Takahiro Shin'yo ed., 1995) (*in Japanese*).

[54] Kokusai Rengō Heiwa Iji Katsudō tō ni taisuru Kyōryoku ni kansuru Hōritsu [International Peace Cooperation Act], Law No. 79 of 1992 (*in Japanese*), translated in JLT DS, *available at* http://www.japaneselawtranslation.go.jp.

[55] Shibata, *supra* note 4, at 207–208, 213–216.

of the requirements in the above-mentioned guidelines cease to be satisfied, the government of Japan may terminate the dispatch of the personnel engaged in International Peace Cooperation Assignments; and (5) the use of weapons shall be limited to the minimum necessary extent to protect the lives of personnel.

The International Peace Cooperation Act was subsequently amended several times to reflect the diversification of and qualitative changes in international peace cooperation operations. An amendment approved in 1998 dropped the requirement for a ceasefire for missions involving cooperation in the provision of goods for international humanitarian support activities organized by certain international bodies, including the UN High Commission for Refugees. In addition, the amendment permitted the use of weapons for the legitimate self-defense of SDF personnel participating in SDF units under the order of senior officers.

Under an amendment in 2001, the core peacekeeping roles that had hitherto been "frozen" were unfrozen. These roles are: monitoring the observance of cessation of armed conflicts or the implementation of relocation, withdrawal, or demobilization of armed forces agreed upon among the parties to armed conflict; stationing in and patrol of buffer zones and other areas demarcated to prevent the occurrence of armed conflicts; and collection, storage, or disposal of abandoned weapons and their parts. However, the unfrozen roles do not include protection of civilians of the areas where the SDF is dispatched. The revisions expanded the range of individuals whom the SDF could protect using weapons, including individuals who have come under their control during the performance of their duties.

Under the International Peace Cooperation Act, the SDF has participated in thirteen missions, including the UN Angola Verification Mission II (UNAVEM II), the UN Transitional Authority in Cambodia (UNTAC), and the UN Mission in the Republic of South Sudan (UNMISS). However, insofar as the SDF has been operating under the International Peace Cooperation Act and the five principles of PKO participation, it could not participate in "robust" operations, and this situation has exposed gaps between the legal principles and the reality on the ground. To rectify this situation, the International Peace Cooperation Act was amended in 2015.

The key provisions of the Revised International Peace Cooperation Act of 2015 are as follows: the SDF is allowed to take on additional roles[56]; the authority on the use of weapons has been broadened[57]; and there has been a revision of the five principles of PKO participation to permit the use of weapons in the performance of protection of

[56] International Peace Cooperation Act, art. 3, no. 5. In addition to ceasefire monitoring and disaster relief, the SDF is permitted to engage in protection of civilians of the areas where the SDF is dispatched, coming to the aid of geographically distant units or personnel under attack (the so-called kaketsuke keigo [coming-to-aid] operation), headquarters-related operations, and operations related to the building of governmental structures and restoration assistance. For a kaketsuke keigo [coming-to-aid] operation, *see* Masahiro Kurosaki, *The Legal Framework of "Coming-to-Aid" Duty—The Pluralism of the Concept of Self-Defense and Its Multi-Layered Legal Grounds*, 60 JAPANESE Y.B. INT'L L. 194 (2017).

[57] International Peace Cooperation Act, art. 26. Use of weapons becomes permitted for the performance of duties during protection of civilians or coming-to-aid operations.

civilians or rushed escort operations in a form that goes beyond the level of self-defense or protection of weapons or other equipment. With regard to the allocation of authority, the prime minister has the authority to mobilize the SDF subject to the prior approval of the Diet.[58]

IV. Conclusion

As we have seen, the scope of Japan's use of military force and its participation in collective security have gradually expanded. The enactment of the New Legislation for Peace and Security in 2015 is a particularly unprecedented example of this expansion. However, this scope is still more restricted than in many other countries, and the current Japanese government has expressed the view that—as a result of Article 9 of the Constitution—further expansion will be difficult. There is increasing consideration, therefore, of the possibility of revising Article 9. Any such revision would likely be controversial. It remains to be seen whether Article 9 will be changed and, if so, what impact such a change will have on the scope of Japan's use of military force and its participation in collective security.

[58] International Peace Cooperation Act, art. 6.

Index

F

G

J

N

P

T

U

V

W

Z